THE ROUGH GUIDE TO

New Zealand

written and researched by

Laura Harper, Catherine Le Nevez,
Tony Mudd and Paul Whitfield

ROUGH
GUIDES

roughguides.com

Contents

INTRODUCTION   4

Author picks   9   Things not to miss   14

Where to go   10   Itineraries   24

When to go   13

BASICS   26

Getting there   27   Spectator sports   55

Getting around   29   Culture and etiquette   56

Accommodation   36   Shopping   57

Food and drink   41   Travelling with children   57

The media   45   Living in New Zealand   58

Festivals and public holidays   46   Travel essentials   59

Outdoor activities   48

THE GUIDE   68

1 Auckland and around   68   8   Marlborough, Nelson and Kaikoura 442

2 Northland   138   9   Christchurch and south to Otago   506

3 Western North Island   200   10 Central South Island   548

4 Central North Island   260   11 Dunedin to Stewart Island   584

5 The Coromandel, Bay of Plenty and   12 The West Coast   634
   the East Cape   310
                                          13 Central Otago   682
6 Poverty Bay, Hawke's Bay and
   the Wairarapa   368   14 Fiordland   748

7 Wellington and around   410

CONTEXTS   784

History   785   Books   818

Maoritanga   799   Language   822

Landscapes and wildlife   806   Glossary   825

Film and music   815

SMALL PRINT & INDEX   828

Introduction to
New Zealand

Kiwis – the people, not the emblematic flightless bird – can't believe their luck at being born in what they call "Godzone" (God's own country). Year after year, travellers list New Zealand in the top ten of places they'd like to visit – and you never meet anyone who has been and didn't love the place. And what's not to like? With craggy coastlines, sweeping beaches, primeval forests, snowcapped mountains and impressive geysers, the scenery is truly majestic. The forests come inhabited by strange birds that have evolved to fill evolutionary niches normally occupied by mammals, while penguins, whales and seals ring the coast. Maori have only been here for 800 years but retain distinct and fascinating customs overlaid by colonial European and increasingly Asian cultures that together create a vibrant, if understated, urban life.

Given this stunning backdrop it's not surprising that there are boundless diversions, ranging from strolls along moody windswept beaches and multi-day tramps over alpine passes to adrenaline-charged adventure activities such as bungy jumping, skiing, sea kayaking and whitewater rafting. Some visitors treat the country as a large-scale adventure playground, aiming to tackle as many challenges as possible in the time available.

Much of the scenic drama comes from tectonic or volcanic forces, as the people of Canterbury know only too well following the **Christchurch earthquakes** of September 4, 2010 and February 22, 2011. The quakes, along with several thousand aftershocks, collectively devastated the city, which is slowly recovering.

Thousands of residents have left Christchurch, but it remains the second-largest city after **Auckland,** just pushing the capital, **Wellington**, into third place. Elsewhere, you can travel many kilometres through stunning countryside without seeing a soul: there are spots so remote that, it's reliably contended, no human has yet visited them.

Geologically, New Zealand split away from the super-continent of Gondwana early, developing a unique **ecosystem** in which birds adapted to fill the role of mammals, many becoming flightless because they had no predators. That all changed about

ABOVE SHEEP GRAZING IN THE CATLINS **OPPOSITE** HIKING IN THE FOX GLACIER AREA

800 years ago, with the arrival of Polynesian navigators, when the land they called **Aotearoa** – "the land of the long white cloud" – became the last major landmass to be settled by humans. On disembarking from their canoes, these **Maori** proceeded to unbalance the fragile ecosystem, dispatching forever the giant ostrich-sized moa, which formed a major part of their diet. The country once again settled into a fragile balance before the arrival of **Pakeha** – white Europeans, predominantly of British origin – who swarmed off their square-rigged ships full of colonial zeal in the mid-nineteenth century and altered the land forever.

An uneasy coexistence between **Maori** and **European** societies informs the current wrangles over cultural identity, land and resource rights. The British didn't invade as such, and were to some degree reluctant to enter into the 1840 **Treaty of Waitangi**, New Zealand's founding document, which effectively ceded New Zealand to the British Crown while guaranteeing Maori hegemony over their land and traditional gathering and fishing rights. As time wore on and increasing numbers of settlers demanded ever larger parcels of land from Maori, antipathy surfaced and escalated into hostility. Once Maori were subdued, a policy of partial integration all but destroyed **Maoritanga** – the Maori way of doing things. Maori, however, were left well outside the new European order, where difference was perceived as tantamount to a betrayal of the emergent sense of nationhood. Although elements of this still exist and Presbyterian and Anglican values have proved hard to shake off, the Kiwi psyche has become infused with Maori generosity and hospitality, coupled with a colonial mateyness and the unerring belief that whatever happens, "she'll be right".

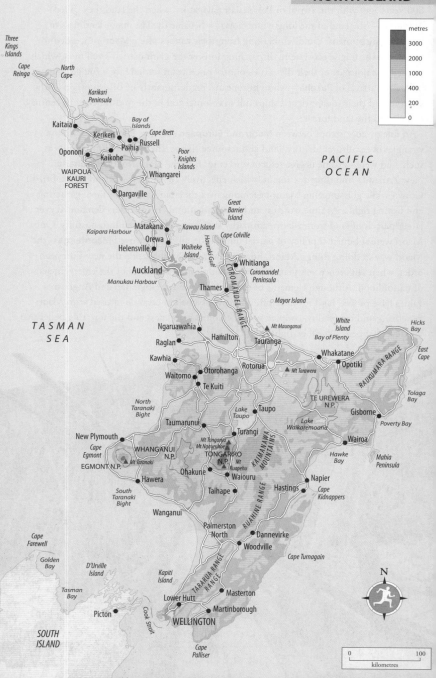

metres
3000
2000
1000
400
200
0

Three Kings Islands
Cape Reinga
North Cape
Karikari Peninsula
Kaitaia
Kerikeri
Bay of Islands
Cape Brett
Paihia
Russell
Opononi
Kaikohe
Poor Knights Islands
WAIPOUA KAURI FOREST
Whangarei
Dargaville
Matakana
Kaipara Harbour
Kawau Island
Great Barrier Island
Orewa
Helensville
Waiheke Island
Cape Colville
Whitianga
Auckland
Manukau Harbour
Hauraki Gulf
Coromandel Peninsula
Thames
Mayor Island

PACIFIC OCEAN

TASMAN SEA

Ngaruawahia
Hamilton
▲ Mt Maunganui
White Island
Hicks Bay
Raglan
Tauranga
Bay of Plenty
Kawhia
Rotorua
Whakatane
East Cape
Otorohanga
Opotiki
Waitomo
▲ Mt Tarawera
Tolaga Bay
Te Kuiti
TE UREWERA N.P.
Gisborne
Taupo
Lake Taupo
Poverty Bay
Taumarunui
Turangi
Lake Waikaremoana
Wairoa
New Plymouth
Mt Tongariro
Mt Ngauruhoe
Mahia Peninsula
Cape Egmont
WHANGANUI N.P.
TONGARIRO N.P.
Mt Ruapehu
Hawke Bay
▲ Mt Taranaki
EGMONT N.P.
Ohakune
Waiouru
Napier
Hawera
Taihape
Hastings
Cape Kidnappers
South Taranaki Bight
North Taranaki Bight
Wanganui
KAIMANAWA MOUNTAINS
RUAHINE RANGE
Palmerston North
Dannevirke
Cape Farewell
Woodville
Cape Turnagain
Golden Bay
D'Urville Island
Kapiti Island
Tasman Bay
TARARUA RANGE
Masterton
Lower Hutt
Martinborough
Picton
Cook Strait
WELLINGTON
SOUTH ISLAND
Cape Palliser

COROMANDEL RANGE
RAUKUMARA RANGE

N

0   100
kilometres

SOUTH ISLAND

NORTH ISLAND

metres
3000
2000
1000
400
200
0

Cape Farewell
Farewell Spit
Collingwood
Golden Bay
Takaka
ABEL TASMAN N.P.
Tasman Bay
D'Urville Island
Marlborough Sounds
Kapiti Island
WELLINGTON
Cook Strait
Cape Palliser

KAHURANGI N.P.
Karamea Bight
Karamea

Nelson
Picton
Blenheim

St Arnaud
KAIKOURA RANGES

Westport
Cape Foulwind
Murchison
PAPAROA N.P.
Reefton
NELSON LAKES N.P.
Kaikoura

Punakaiki
Hanmer Springs

TASMAN SEA

Lewis Pass
Greymouth
Lake Brunner

Hokitika
Arthur's Pass
ARTHUR'S PASS N.P.

Ross
Arthur's Pass Village

Pegasus Bay
Christchurch
Banks Peninsula
Lyttelton
Akaroa

Whataroa
Franz Josef Glacier
Fox Glacier
Methven

SOUTHERN ALPS
Aoraki/Mount Cook
WESTLAND N.P.
AORAKI/MOUNT COOK N.P.
Aoraki/Mount Cook Village
Lake Tekapo

Ashburton

Canterbury Bight

Haast
Twizel
Lake Pukaki
Timaru

Jackson Bay
Haast Pass
Lake Ohau

MOUNT ASPIRING N.P.
Mount Aspiring
Lake Howea

Lake Wanaka
Wanaka
Oamaru

PACIFIC OCEAN

Milford Sound
Mount Tutoko
Arrowtown
Cromwell
Ranfurly

George Sound
Glenorchy
Queenstown
Alexandra
Palmerston

Lake Te Anau
Lake Wakatipu
Otago Peninsula

Secretary Island
Doubtful Sound
FIORDLAND N.P.
Manapouri
Te Anau
Dunedin

Lake Manapouri
Lumsden

Resolution Island
Dusky Sound
Ohai
Gore
Balclutha

Lake Hauroko
Tuatapere
Invercargill

Puyseger Point
Riverton
Bluff

Foveaux Strait

Oban (Halfmoon Bay)

RAKIURA N.P.

Stewart Island

N

0   kilometres   100

FACT FILE

• At latitude 41° south, Wellington is the world's southernmost capital city and shares the honour of being the most remote with Canberra, over 2000km away.

• Possums are the national pest. When seen on the road, these introduced marsupials turn normally mild-mannered folk into killers. Flattened examples are everywhere.

• Kiwis love foreign affirmation: *Flight of the Conchords* were turned down by domestic television and only became a local success after their HBO hit series.

• Maori ex-prostitute Georgina Beyer became the world's first transsexual MP in 1999.

• There are no snakes in New Zealand, and only a few venomous spiders, rarely seen.

• The numerous Maori words that have crept into everyday conversation easily confound visitors: *aroha* is love; *kia kaha* means be strong; *kia ora* can be hi or might signify agreement; and *koha* is a donation or offering.

• New Zealand's eels live to 80 years and only breed once, at the end of their life – and they swim all the way to Tonga to do it.

Only in the last forty years has New Zealand come of age and developed a true national self-confidence, something partly forced on it by Britain severing the colonial apron strings, and by the resurgence of Maori identity. Maori demands have been nurtured by a willingness on the part of most Pakeha to redress the wrongs perpetrated over the last 170 years, as long as it doesn't impinge on their high standard of living or overall feeling of control. More recently, integration has been replaced with a policy of **biculturalism** – the somewhat fraught notion of promoting two cultures alongside each other, but with maximum interaction. This policy has been somewhat weakened by relatively recent and extensive **immigration** from China, Korea and South Asia.

Despite having and achieving much to give them confidence, Kiwis (unlike their Australian neighbours) retain an underlying shyness that borders on an inferiority complex: you may well find yourself interrogated about your opinions on the country almost before you've even left the airport. Balancing this is an extraordinary enthusiasm for **sports** and **culture**, which

Author picks

Our authors have bussed, walked, rafted and ridden the length and breadth of New Zealand. These are some of their own favourite travel experiences.

Superb natural hot pool Kerosene Creek has no changing rooms, no café, no gift store – just a naturally heated stream which tumbles over a short waterfall into a bath-like pool. Bliss. p.280

The kleptomaniac kea It's hard not to love these trickster alpine parrots, even if one has just shredded your windscreen wipers. p.560

DIY caving There's something raw and thrilling about an un-aided exploration of Cave Stream, a 600m-long tunnel carved by an alpine stream. p.558

Most entertaining stroll For a diverse slice of Kiwi life, take a late evening wander along Auckland's Karangahape Road, a grungy yet vibrant strip of cafés and shops where boozy suits, gay couples, dining suburbanites and preening transvestites all mix to kaleidoscopic effect. p.80

Seafood restaurant heaven At Fleur's Place, a quirky shed restaurant, you know the fish is fresh as you can see Fleur's fishing boat bobbing in the bay outside. p.547

Best coastal drive Savour the Picton–Kaikoura route, with Sauvignon Blanc vineyards heralding a craggy coastal ribbon of crashing azure waves backed by the magnificent Kaikoura Ranges. p.498

Bush baths Light a fire under an old metal bath then get a friend to join you watching the southern skies as you soak your bones. p.533, p.646 & p.650

Trout fishing in the Tongariro River New Zealand's fishing rules dictate that trout can't be sold, so if you've got a taste for them you'll need to catch them yourself, best done in the Tongariro River near Turangi. p.295

Our author recommendations don't end here. We've flagged up our favourite places – a perfectly sited hotel, an atmospheric café, a special restaurant – throughout the guide, highlighted with the ★ symbol.

LEFT QUEENSTOWN **FROM TOP** A KEA GETS CURIOUS; RELAXING IN KEROSENE CREEK; A PLATTER OF SEAFOOD

THE MAORI

Tribal costume is only worn on special occasions, facial tattoos are fairly rare and you'll probably only see a *haka* performed at a rugby match or cultural show. In fact, Maori live very much in the modern world. But peel back the veneer of the song-dance-and-*hangi* performance and you'll discover a parallel world that non-Maori are only dimly aware of.

Knowledge of **whakapapa** (tribal lineage) is central to Maori identity. **Spirituality** connects Maori to their traditional local mountain or river, while **oratory**, and the ability to produce a song at a moment's notice, are both highly valued. All New Zealanders understand **mana**, a synthesis of prestige, charisma and influence, which is enhanced through brave or compassionate actions.

Sadly, the Maori community is riven by social problems: average incomes are lower than those of Pakeha; almost half of all prison inmates are Maori; and health statistics make appalling reading.

Hope for redress comes through a **bicultural** approach stressing equality and integration while allowing for parallel identities.

For more on what it means to be Maori, and how visitors are likely to tap into it, see p.799.

generate a swelling pride in New Zealanders when they witness plucky Kiwis taking on and sometimes beating the world.

Where to go

New Zealand packs a lot into a limited space, meaning you can visit many of the main sights in a couple of weeks, but allow at least a month (or preferably two) for a proper look around. The scenery is the big draw, and most people only pop into the big cities on arrival and departure (easily done with open-jaw air tickets, allowing you to fly into Auckland and out of Christchurch) or when travelling to Wellington from the South Island across the **Cook Strait**.

Sprawled around the sparkling Waitemata Harbour, go-ahead **Auckland** looks out over the island-studded Hauraki Gulf. Most people head south from here, missing out on **Northland**, the cradle of both Maori and Pakeha colonization, cloaked in wonderful subtropical forest that harbours New Zealand's largest kauri trees. East of Auckland the coast follows the isolated greenery and long, golden beaches of the **Coromandel Peninsula**, before running down to the beach towns of the **Bay of Plenty**. Immediately south your senses are assailed by the ever-present sulphurous whiff of **Rotorua**, with its spurting geysers and bubbling pools of mud, and the volcanic plateau centred on the trout-filled waters of **Lake Taupo**, overshadowed by three snowcapped volcanoes. Cave fans will want to head west of Taupo for the eerie limestone caverns of **Waitomo**; alternatively it's just a short hop from Taupo to the delights of canoeing the **Whanganui River**, a broad, emerald-green waterway banked by virtually impenetrable bush thrown into relief by the cone of **Mount Taranaki**, whose summit is

LEFT MAORI WOOD CARVING

HOT POOLS, GEYSERS AND BOILING MUD

One of New Zealand's most sensual pleasures is lying back in a **natural hot pool** surrounded by bush and gazing up at the stars. The country lies on the Pacific Ring of Fire, and earthquakes and volcanic activity are common. Superheated steam escapes as **geysers** (around Rotorua), **boiling mud pools** (Rotorua and Taupo) and **hot springs** – around eighty of them across the northern two-thirds of the North Island and another fifteen along a thin thread down the western side of the Southern Alps.

Over thirty are commercial **resorts** offering tepid swimming pools, near-scalding baths, mineral mud and hydrothermal pampering. The remainder are **natural pools** – in the bush, beside a stream or welling up from below a sandy beach – which require a little sleuthing; locals like to keep the best spots to themselves. Check out ⓦ**nzhotpools.co.nz**, read the notes on **amoebic meningitis** (see p.63) and sample the following (listed north to south).

Polynesian Spa Commercial resort in Rotorua with something for everyone: mineral pools, family spa, adult-only open-air complex and all manner of body treatments. See p.268

Hot Water Beach Come at low tide, rent a spade and dig a hot pool beside the cool surf. See p.336

Maruia Springs Small resort in the hills 200km north of Christchurch. Particularly magical in winter. See p.556

Welcome Flat Hot Springs Four natural pools sited amid mountain scenery just south of Fox Glacier. It is a six- to seven-hour walk in and you can stay at the adjacent DOC hut. See p.677

accessible in a day. East of Taupo lie ranges that form the North Island's backbone, and beyond them the **Hawke's Bay wine country**, centred on the Art Deco city of Napier. Further south, the wine region of Martinborough is just an hour or so from the capital, **Wellington**, its centre squeezed onto reclaimed harbourside, the suburbs slung across steep hills overlooking glistening bays. Politicians and bureaucrats give it a well-scrubbed and urbane sophistication, enlivened by an established café society and after-dark scene.

ABOVE HOT WATER BEACH

The **South Island** kicks off with the world-renowned wineries of **Marlborough** and appealing **Nelson**, a pretty and compact spot surrounded by lovely beaches and within easy reach of the hill country around the **Nelson Lakes National Park** and the fabulous sea kayaking of the **Abel Tasman National Park**. From the top of the South Island you've a choice of nipping behind the 3000m summits of the Southern Alps and following the West Coast to the fabulous **glaciers** at Fox and Franz Josef, or sticking to the east, passing the whale-watching territory of **Kaikoura** en route to the South Island's largest centre, **Christchurch**. Its English architectural heritage may have been ravaged by earthquakes – and its people still reeling from the upheaval – but signs of normality are returning, and, as the rebuilding process picks up pace, the city looks set to become the country's most exciting.

From here you can head across country to the West Coast via Arthur's Pass on one of the country's most scenic train trips, or shoot southwest across the patchwork Canterbury Plains to the foothills of the **Southern Alps** and **Aoraki/Mount Cook** with its distinctive drooping-tent summit.

The patchwork-quilt fields of Canterbury run, via the grand architecture of **Oamaru**, to the unmistakably Scottish-influenced city of **Dunedin**, a base for exploring the wildlife of the **Otago Peninsula**, with its albatross, seal, sea lion and penguin colonies. In the middle of the nineteenth century, prospectors arrived here and rushed inland to gold strikes throughout central Otago and around stunningly set **Queenstown**, now a commercialized activity centre where bungy jumping, rafting, jetboating and skiing hold sway. Just up the road is Glenorchy, a tramping heartland, from which

LOCATION, LOCATION, LOCATION...

When Peter Jackson filmed his *Lord of the Rings* trilogy in New Zealand the country rejoiced, even appointing a special minister for the project. However, few could have anticipated how completely it would take over the country. For thousands of visitors, no stay in Aotearoa is complete without a hobbit hole visit to Hobbiton, a pilgrimage to Wellington's *Weta Workshop*, where the prosthetics and miniatures were done, and a tour of film locations around Queenstown.

The next wave of scene-seeking tourists took Disney's *The Chronicles of Narnia: The Lion, the Witch and the Wardrobe* as their inspiration, and now there is the prospect of a tsunami of tourists eager to stand where the hobbits of Peter Jackson's new two-part epic (based on J.R.R Tolkien's *The Hobbit*) planted their feet. Trips to location sites undoubtedly visit some magnificent scenery, but don't expect scenes to look as they did in the films. Digital enhancement works wonders, but the landscape stands up just fine without CGI trickery.

the **Routeburn Track** sets out to rain-sodden **Fiordland**; its neighbour, Te Anau, is the start of many of New Zealand's most famous treks, including the Milford Track. Further south you'll feel the bite of the Antarctic winds, which reach their peak on New Zealand's third landmass, isolated **Stewart Island**, covered mostly by dense coastal rainforest that offers a great chance of spotting a kiwi in the wild.

When to go

With ocean in every direction it is no surprise that New Zealand has a maritime climate, warm in the summer months, December to March, and never truly cold, even in winter. **Weather** patterns are strongly affected by prevailing westerlies, which suck up moisture from the Tasman Sea and dump it on the western side of both islands. The South Island gets the lion's share, with the West Coast and Fiordland ranking among the world's wettest places. Mountain ranges running the length of both islands cast long rain shadows eastward, making those locations considerably drier. The south is a few degrees cooler than elsewhere, and subtropical Auckland and Northland are appreciably more humid. In the North Island, warm, damp summers fade imperceptibly into cool, wet winters, while the further south you travel the more the weather divides the year into four distinct seasons.

Most people visit New Zealand in the summer, but it is a viable destination at any time provided you pick your destinations. From December to March you'll find everything open, though often busy with holidaying Kiwis from Christmas to mid-January. In general, you're better off joining the bulk of foreign visitors during the **shoulder seasons** – October, November and April – when sights and attractions are quieter, and accommodation easier to come by. **Winter** (May–Sept) is the wettest, coldest and consequently least popular time, unless you are enamoured of winter sports, in which case it's fabulous. The switch to prevailing southerly winds tends to bring periods of crisp, dry and cloudless weather to the West Coast and heavy snowfalls to the Southern Alps and Central North Island, allowing for some of the most varied and least-populated **skiing and snowboarding** in the world.

LEFT CLINTON VALLEY AT DAWN, MILFORD TRACK

29

things not to miss

It's not possible to see everything that New Zealand has to offer in one trip – so don't try. What follows, in no particular order, is a selective taste of the islands' highlights, including outstanding national parks, natural wonders, adventure activities and exotic wildlife. All highlights have a page reference to take you straight into the guide, where you can find out more. Coloured numbers refer to chapters in the Guide.

1

1 MILFORD SOUND
Page 765

Experience the grandeur and beauty of Fiordland on the area's most accessible fiord, great in bright sunshine and wonderfully atmospheric in the mist with the waterfalls at their most impressive.

2 TREE FERNS
Page 810

Sometimes reaching up to 10m, these outsize specimens provide shade for some of the more delicate species in New Zealand's unique ecosystem.

3 JETBOATING
Page 53

Charging up rapids perilously close to rocks is a countrywide obsession, with some superb trips around Queenstown, in Fiordland and just north of Taupo.

4 TAIERI GORGE RAILWAY
Page 601

Ride the stately old train through otherwise inaccessible mountain landscapes on this dramatic journey along a line established back in 1859.

5

6

7

5 WHALE WATCHING
Page 502

An impressive range of cetaceans populates the deep canyons off the Kaikoura Peninsula, visited on a cruise or spied from a plane or helicopter.

6 OTAGO CENTRAL RAIL TRAIL
Page 743

Taking three leisurely days on a bike is the best way to tackle this 150km trail, which follows the route of a former rail line through some ruggedly barren country.

7 WHITE ISLAND
Page 356

Take an appealing boat trip out to New Zealand's most active volcano, and stroll through the sulphurous lunar landscape to peer into the steaming crater.

8 NINETY MILE BEACH
Page 186

This seemingly endless wave-lashed golden strand is a designated highway, plied by tour buses that regularly stop to let passengers toboggan down the steep dunes.

9 MOERAKI BOULDERS
Page 546

Stroll along the beach to visit these large, perfectly round, natural spheres with a honeycomb centre, just sitting in the surf.

10 THE GLACIERS
Page 670

The steep and dramatic Fox and Franz Josef glaciers can be explored by glacier hike, ice climbing and helicopter flights landing on the snowfields above.

11 FAREWELL SPIT
Page 486

This slender 25km arc of sand dunes and beaches is a nature reserve protecting a host of bird species including black swans, wrybills, curlews and dotterels.

12 MUSEUM OF NEW ZEALAND (TE PAPA)
Page 418

A celebration of the people, culture and art of New Zealand that's as appealing to kids as it is to adults, with an impressive use of state-of-the-art technology.

13 THE CATLINS
Page 509

Seals and dolphins and a laidback approach to life make this rugged coast a great place to unwind for a few days.

14 DIVING AT THE POOR KNIGHTS ISLANDS
Page 157

Two-dive day-trips visit any of several dozen sites at one of the world's best diving destinations. A couple of scuttled navy boats nearby add to the possibilities.

15 HOKIANGA HARBOUR
Page 190

As a low-key antidote to the commercialization of the Bay of Islands, the sand dunes, quiet retreats and crafts culture of this vast inlet are hard to beat.

14

15

16 RE:START CHRISTCHURCH
Page 523

This new take on the earthquake-shattered Cashel Mall is symbolic of the city's fight to re-invent itself.

17 WHANGANUI RIVER JOURNEY
Page 242

This relaxing three-day canoe trip along a historic waterway takes you through some of the North Island's loveliest scenery.

18 SURFING AT RAGLAN
Page 213

One of the world's longest left-hand breaks, reliable swells and a chilled-out vibe make this New Zealand's prime surfing destination.

19 ZEALANDIA: THE KARORI SANCTUARY EXPERIENCE
Page 425

On the edge of Wellington, this beautiful fenced-in nature reserve is being restocked with purely native flora and fauna.

20 WAI-O-TAPU
Page 280

The best of Rotorua's geothermal sites offers beautiful, mineral-coloured lakes, a geyser that erupts on cue each morning and pools of plopping mud.

21 ABEL TASMAN NATIONAL PARK
Page 473

Visitors flock to this accessible coastal park, to hike its Coast Track and kayak its magnificent coastline.

22 WINE
Page 44

Spend a day or two sampling fine wines and dining overlooking the vines in Hawke's Bay, Martinborough, Marlborough, Central Otago or any of half-a-dozen other major wine regions.

23 EAST CAPE
Page 364

A varied coastline, tiny, predominantly Maori communities and the slow pace of life make this isolated region a place to linger.

24 THE ROUTEBURN TRACK
Page 718

One of the country's finest walks, showcasing forested valleys, rich birdlife, thundering waterfalls, river flats, lakes and wonderful mountain scenery.

25 BUNGY JUMPING
Page 53

New Zealand's trademark adventure sport can be tried at Kawarau Bridge, the original commercial jump site, the super-high Nevis site nearby, and several other spots around the country.

26 HANGI
Page 41

Sample fall-off-the-bone pork and chicken along with sweet potatoes and pumpkin, disinterred after several hours' steaming in a Maori earth oven.

27 TONGARIRO ALPINE CROSSING
Page 300

A superb one-day hike through the volcanic badlands of the Tongariro National Park, passing the cinder cone of Mount Ngauruhoe.

28 ART DECO, NAPIER
Page 387

The world's most homogeneous collection of small-scale Art Deco architecture owes its genesis to the devastating 1931 earthquake that flattened this lovely provincial city.

29 THE PENGUIN PLACE
Page 606

Watch yellow-eyed penguins waddle up the beach to their nests each night from hides here and from viewing platforms all along the southwestern coast of the South Island.

Itineraries

The following itineraries pick out New Zealand's best, from a quick overview combining beaches, Maori culture, cool cities and majestic scenery, to something more specific – either the strange birdlife, soaking in hot pools and stargazing, or going for the giant adventure playground experience. Complete one list or mix and match to gain a wonderful insight into Aotearoa's stunning diversity.

THE GRAND TOUR

New Zealand may be small but it really packs in the sights, so allow at least 3 weeks to see it all.

❶ **Northland** Drive sweeping beaches, slide down vast sand dunes and visit the quaint harbours of the winterless north. **See p.138**

❷ **Rotorua** Don't let the bad-egg smell put you off this geothermal wonderland of geysers and boiling mud pools where *haka*, dance and an earth-steamed *hangi* dinner showcase Maori culture. **See p.266**

❸ **Napier** The small-scale Art Deco architecture provides the backdrop to Hawke's Bay's fine food and some of New Zealand's best red wines. **See p.385**

❹ **Wellington** The capital is New Zealand's most beguiling city, with a walkable heart of museums, cafés and lively bars elegantly strung around a picturesque harbour. **See p.412**

❺ **Nelson and Golden Bay** Golden beaches, hippy markets and the coastal pleasures of the Abel Tasman National Park make this the most blissed-out corner of the country. **See p.458**

❻ **The West Coast** Native bush and precipitous glacier plunge steeply to the crashing surf along this wild and fabulously scenic coast. **See p.634**

❼ **Aoraki/Mount Cook** New Zealand's highest peak stands as snowy sentinel over the impossibly blue lakes and golden grasses of the Mackenzie Country. **See p.574**

❽ **Queenstown** Don't miss the fabulous mountain scenery, incredible concentration of adventure activities, great hikes and some of the South Island's best restaurants and bars. **See p.689**

❾ **Fiordland** Cruise, kayak or even dive the waters of Milford and Doubtful Sounds in between multi-day tramps along the Kepler Track or the exalted Milford Track. **See p.748**

NATURAL NEW ZEALAND

Geysers, fiords, alpine parrots, cute penguins, whales and several species of dolphin supplement New Zealand's clear skies and stunning scenery.

❶ **Kiwi spotting in the kauri forest** Move quietly among the kauri forest night as kiwi call plaintively and maybe – just maybe – show themselves. **See p.196**

❷ **Hot Water Beach** Dig a hole in the beach and ease into a shallow pool of hot water occasionally cooled by the surf. **See p.336**

❸ **Birds on Kapiti Island** Explore this island sanctuary full of intriguing birds – bush parrots, parakeets, fantails, little spotted kiwis and even a few of the 250 takahe left in the world. **See p.256**

ABOVE VIEW OF AORAKI/MOUNT COOK

❹ **Swimming with seals** Give the dolphins a break: seals are often more playful, particularly in the clear waters of Abel Tasman National Park. **See p.476**

❺ **Otago Peninsula wildlife** Dunedin's doorstep harbours a fabulous concentration of wildlife with two species of penguin, seals and an accessible colony of albatrosses. **See p.603**

❻ **Night sky viewing** The wonderful stargazing is helping Tekapo get itself declared as the country's first Starlight Reserve. **See p.572**

❼ **Stewart Island** After being welcomed by flocks of parrots, visit saddlebacks, red-crowned parakeets and bellbirds on Ulva Island then spot kiwi at Mason Bay. **See p.626**

ADVENTURE NEW ZEALAND

Nowhere in the world has as many adrenaline-fuelled and low-key adventures as New Zealand.

❶ **Raft the Kaituna** Short and sweet, the Kaituna packs in a gorgeous verdant gorge, plunging rapids and a massive 7m waterfall. **See p.272**

❷ **Lost World caving** The ground below Waitomo is riddled with limestone caverns, best explored by a massive abseil followed by several hours of squeezes, scrambles and floating. **See p.221**

❸ **Hiking the Tongariro Alpine Crossing** Take on New Zealand's finest one-day tramp across the barren volcanic wastes of the Tongariro National Park. **See p.300**

❹ **Kayaking Abel Tasman National Park** Opt for an overnight paddle on the sheltered, warm waters then camp beside a golden beach. **See p.476**

❺ **Glacier hike Franz Josef** Get choppered up onto the glacier and left for a couple of hours of guided hiking across snowfields and through ice caves. **See p.672**

❻ **Canyon the Niger Stream** Jump into deep pools and abseil down waterfalls in Wanaka's beautiful canyons. **See p.732**

❼ **Bungy the Nevis** Go for the big one, a 134m monster from a gondola eight freefall seconds above a tiny stream. **See p.694**

❽ **Bike the Wakatipu Basin** Easy lakeside jaunts, great cross-country rides, and the country's only cable-car-assisted downhill mountain bike tracks make Queenstown the perfect biking destination. **See p.699**

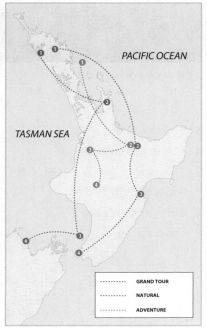

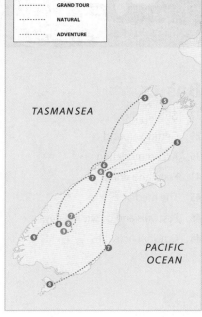

AORAKI/MOUNT COOK NATIONAL PARK

Basics

27 Getting there

29 Getting around

36 Accommodation

41 Food and drink

45 The media

46 Festivals and public holidays

48 Outdoor activities

55 Spectator sports

56 Culture and etiquette

57 Shopping

57 Travelling with children

58 Living in New Zealand

59 Travel essentials

Getting there

The quickest, easiest and cheapest way to get to New Zealand is to fly. It is possible to arrive by sea, but there are no international passenger ferries, so unless you own a boat this means joining a cruise, crewing on a private yacht, or paying for your passage on a cargo ship (a rewarding experience for those who like sea journeys – find out more at ⓦfreightertravel.co.nz.

Air **fares** depend on the season, with the highest during the New Zealand summer (Dec–Feb); prices drop during the shoulder seasons (Sept–Nov & March–May) and you'll get the cheapest rates during the low (ski) season (June–Aug).

Arriving in New Zealand, your only real choice, unless you're coming from Australia, is between the international airports at **Auckland** and **Christchurch**. Christchurch receives fewer direct flights but many scheduled airlines have a codeshare shuttle from Auckland at no extra cost. The most desirable option, an **open-jaw** ticket (flying into one and out of the other), usually costs no more than an ordinary return. For **internal flights** within NZ, see box, p.29.

Tourists and those on short-term working visas (see p.51) are generally required by New Zealand immigration to arrive with an **outward bound ticket**, so one-way tickets are really only viable for Australian and NZ residents.

If you've purchased a return ticket and find you want to stay longer or head off on a totally different route, it's possible to **change** the dates and, more rarely, route with the airline or travel agent, depending on the conditions of your ticket, though there is often a fee.

Flights from the UK and Ireland

Over a dozen airlines compete to fly you **from Britain** to New Zealand for as little as £757, including British Airways (ⓦba.com), but prices depend upon the time of year, and can be double

that amount at Christmas. Going for the **cheapest flight** typically means sacrificing some comfort (multiple stops, longer layovers), which you may regret, given that even the shortest journey will last at least 24 hours including an obligatory refuelling stop. There are no direct flights to New Zealand **from Ireland**, and prices are proportionally higher, since the short hop to London (around £100 return, cheaper with internet deals) has to be added to the fare.

Most **scheduled flights** allow multiple **stopovers** either in North America and the Pacific, or Asia and Australia. The vast majority of direct scheduled flights depart from London Heathrow, though some services operate from London Gatwick, Manchester and Newcastle.

Flights from the US and Canada

Direct trans-Pacific flights to Auckland operate from Los Angeles with Air New Zealand (ⓦairnewzealand.com), Qantas (ⓦqantas.com), Virgin (ⓦvirgin.com/airlines), Singapore Airlines (ⓦsingaporeair.com) and various US airlines including American (ⓦaa.com). Air New Zealand and Virgin fly from San Francisco, while your best option from Vancouver is with Air New Zealand, a flight of 12–16 hours. Assorted codeshare partners – Air Canada, American Airlines, British Airways – sell tickets to New Zealand, usually offering several connections a day to Wellington and Christchurch.

From the US a direct LA–Auckland or San Francisco–Auckland round-trip **fare** goes for around US$1400 during the southern winter, rising to around US$1800 or more in peak southern summer season. Flights from all other US cities are routed via California. Off-peak you might expect to pay US$1800–2000 from New York or Chicago, but shopping around could save you money.

From Canada, Air New Zealand runs direct Vancouver–Auckland flights three days per week, and codeshares with Air Canada for links to provincial capitals. Depending on the season, fares from Vancouver are around Can$1600; from Toronto, around Can$2100; and from Montréal,

---

A BETTER KIND OF TRAVEL

At Rough Guides we are passionately committed to travel. We believe it helps us understand the world we live in and the people we share it with – and of course tourism is vital to many developing economies. But the scale of modern tourism has also damaged some places irreparably, and climate change is accelerated by most forms of transport, especially flying. All Rough Guides' flights are carbon-offset, and every year we donate money to a variety of environmental charities.

around Can$2300; substantial savings can often be made through discount travel companies and websites.

Apart from a **RTW** ticket (see below), an alternative approach from North America is to fly **via Asia**, which may work out cheaper. Korean Air, for example, has flights from Atlanta, Chicago, Dallas, Las Vegas, Los Angeles, New York, San Francisco, Seattle, Toronto, Vancouver and Washington DC, all changing at Seoul (Incheon) before continuing to Auckland. An equally exotic option is to stop off at a **Pacific island** or two along the way. Air New Zealand visits half a dozen islands and often charges less than US$100 per stopover.

Flights from Australia and South Africa

Qantas (Ⓦqantas.com), Jetstar (Ⓦjetstar.com), Air New Zealand (Ⓦairnewzealand.com) and Virgin (Ⓦvirginaustralia.com) all fly between **Australia** and New Zealand, as do Thai (Ⓦthaiairways.com), Emirates (Ⓦemirates.com), Aerolineas Argentinas (Ⓦaerolineas.ar) and LanChile (Ⓦlan.com). Prices vary enormously depending on demand (book well in advance in summer), but the level of competition generally keeps them reasonable – as low as Aus$300 return from Australia's east coast (including a basic baggage allowance) if you're prepared to go for non-refundable tickets. Return flights from Perth start at around Aus$760.

Flying time from Sydney or Melbourne to New Zealand is around three hours. Auckland, Christchurch, Dunedin, Hamilton, Rotorua, Queenstown and Wellington international airports all have direct flights to/from Australia.

From Australia, there's a huge variety of **package holidays** to New Zealand. Air New Zealand's holiday subsidiary offers short **city-breaks** (flight and accommodation), winter skiing packages and **fly-drive** deals for little more than the cost of the regular air fare.

Travelling to New Zealand from **South Africa** invariably involves flying via Australia. Qantas (Ⓦqantas.com) flies Johannesburg–Sydney then on to New Zealand. South African Airways (Ⓦflysaa .com) operates the same route as a codeshare with Qantas and Air New Zealand. Expect to pay around Zar16,000–27,000 depending on the season.

Round-the-world flights

If New Zealand is only one stop on a longer journey, you might consider buying a **Round-the-World (RTW)** ticket. An "off-the-shelf" RTW ticket will have you touching down in about half a dozen cities (Auckland is on many itineraries), or you can assemble one tailored to your needs, though this is liable to be more expensive.

Agents and operators

If time is limited and you have a clear idea of what you want to do, numerous companies offer **organized tours**, from backpacker excursions to no-expense-spared extravaganzas. Full "see-it-all" packages, with most meals and transport included, can be good value, considering what you'd be spending anyway. Some companies offer tours specifically for those aged 18–35, such as Contiki (UK Ⓦcontiki.co.uk; US Ⓦcontiki.com); or seniors, such as Road Scholar (Ⓦroadscholar.org); while others are adventure specialists, such as UK-based The Adventure Company (Ⓦprimeadventures.co .uk) or US-based Adventures Abroad (Ⓦadventures -abroad.com). You can also find tours to suit your interest (such as hiking or kayaking). For details of **NZ-based tour operators**, see box, p.52.

A number of companies operate **flexible bus tours**, which you can hop off whenever you like and rejoin a day or two later when the next bus comes through (see box, p.30).

Pretty much all the major tour operators can also book you onto **tramping trips**, including some of the guided Great Walks (see p.49); you'll still need to book way in advance, though. For **skiing trips**, the cheapest option is usually to contact ski clubs at the fields directly: check out contact details at Ⓦsnow.co.nz.

Even if an all-in package doesn't appeal, it still may be worth investigating potential savings by pre-booking some accommodation, tours or a rental vehicle.

AGENTS AND OPERATORS

Backpackers World Travel Australia ☎ 1800 676 763, Ⓦbackpackersworld.com.au.

North South Travel UK ☎ 01245 608 291, Ⓦnorthsouthtravel .co.uk. Competitive travel agency, offering discounted fares worldwide. Profits are used to support projects in the developing world, especially the promotion of sustainable tourism.

Quest Worldwide UK ☎ 01483 427 031, Ⓦquest-worldwide .com. Specialist in RTW and Australasian discount fares.

STA Travel UK ☎ 0871 2300 040, US ☎ 1-800 781 4040, Australia ☎ 134 782, NZ ☎ 0800 474 400, South Africa ☎ 0861 781 781; Ⓦstatravel.co.uk. Worldwide specialists in independent travel; also student IDs, travel insurance, car rental, rail passes and more. Good discounts for students and under-26s. Experts on NZ travel with branches in major Kiwi cities.

Trailfinders UK ☎ 0207 368 1200, Ireland ☎ 01 677 7888, Australia ☎ 1300 780 212; ⓦ trailfinders.com. One of the best-informed and most efficient agents for independent travellers.
Travel Cuts Canada ☎ 1 866 246-9762, US ☎ 1 800 667-2887; ⓦ travelcuts.com. Canadian student-travel organization.
USIT Ireland ☎ 01 602 1906; Northern Ireland ☎ 028 9032 7111; ⓦ usit.ie. Ireland's main student and youth travel specialists.

Getting around

New Zealand is a relatively small country and getting around is easy, with some form of public transport going to many destinations, though sometimes limited to one service per day. There are still some places that are hard to access, yet all of these can be reached with will, flexibility and a little ingenuity.

Internal **flights** are reasonably priced if booked well in advance, but you'll appreciate the scenery better by travelling at ground level. The cheapest and easiest, though slowest, way to get around is by **bus** (coaches or shuttle buses). The **rail service**, by contrast, is limited and expensive.

Rental **cars** and campervans, particularly the little ones (see p.34), can be remarkably good value for two or more people, but if you are staying in the country for more than a couple of months, it's more economical to buy a vehicle. New Zealand's green countryside encourages **cyclists**, but even the keenest vary their transport options.

Competition on the **ferries** connecting the North and South islands means passenger fares are good value, though transporting vehicles is pricey. Planes and boats give limited access to offshore islands and the parts of the mainland that remain stubbornly impenetrable by road, though more specialist **tours** make getting into the wilds easier.

The frequency of long-distance bus, train and plane services is listed, where relevant, in each chapter in "Arrival and Departure", while local buses and trains, again where relevant, appear in "Getting Around".

By plane

Many visitors fly into Auckland at the beginning of their trip and out from Christchurch at the end, so don't touch **domestic flights**, but those with a tight timetable wanting to hit a few key sights in a short time might be tempted by reasonable-value internal fares.

The biggest domestic operator is Air New Zealand (ⓦ airnewzealand.com), serving all the

INTERNAL FLIGHTS

If you decide to use **internal flights**, booking tickets online and well in advance can save you up to fifty percent. It's also worth looking at **air passes** offered by Air New Zealand (ⓦ airnewzealand.co.nz), including a variety of cheap one-way flights from Auckland and Christchurch to various destinations, if booked at the same time as an international flight. Alternatively, within the "Domestic Booking" section of its website, you can buy one-way tickets to various destinations at Smart Saver or Flexi Plus rates, and create a multi-stop itinerary within New Zealand. Jetstar (ⓦ qantas.com.au) runs similar multi-destination tickets at less favourable rates.

main centres and numerous minor ones (25 destinations in all). The main competition is from Jetstar (ⓦ jetstar.com), which serves Auckland, Wellington, Christchurch, Dunedin, Rotorua and Queenstown. Air New Zealand runs single-class planes with **fares** that come in three levels, offering lower fares for decreased flexibility: there are fewer low-cost fares at popular times. Jetstar has a similar system. For example, a one-way standard flight between Auckland and Christchurch is about $399, a Flexi Plus around $289, a Smart Saver as little as $139 and a seat only (no hold baggage) $89. Other flights you might take are scenic jaunts from Auckland to Great Barrier Island, the hop over Cook Strait, or the short trip from Invercargill to Stewart Island.

AIRLINES

Air New Zealand ☎ 0800 737 000, ⓦ airnewzealand.co.nz.
Great Barrier Airlines & Air Coromandel ☎ 0800 900 600, ⓦ greatbarrierairlines.co.nz. Flights between Auckland, Coromandel and Great Barrier Island.
Fly My Sky ☎ 0800 222 123, ⓦ flymysky.co.nz. Flights between Auckland and Great Barrier Island.
Jetstar ☎ 0800 800 995, ⓦ jetstar.com/nz.
Soundsair ☎ 0800 505 005, ⓦ soundsair.com. Small planes across Cook Strait.
Stewart Island Flights ☎ 03 218 9129, ⓦ stewartislandflights .com. Scheduled services between Invercargill and Stewart Island.

By bus

You can get most places on long-distance **buses** ("coaches") and smaller **shuttle buses**, which essentially offer the same service but are more likely to drop you off and pick up at hotels, hostels and the like. Services are generally reliable and reasonably comfortable, and competition keeps prices competitive. The larger buses are usually air-conditioned, and some have toilets, though all services stop every couple of hours, at wayside tearooms and points of interest along the way. Most of your fellow passengers are likely to be visitors to New Zealand so drivers often give a commentary, the quality of which varies.

InterCity and Newmans

The biggest operator, **InterCity**, runs high-quality full-size buses all over the country. They operate closely with **Newmans**, who pitch themselves as slightly more luxurious and target sightseeing excursions. In practice, the two companies share a timetable and InterCity passes can often be used on Newmans buses: when we refer to InterCity we are generally referring to services run collectively by InterCity and Newmans.

BACKPACKER BUSES

One of the cheapest ways to cover a lot of ground is on a **backpacker bus**, which combines some of the flexibility of independent travel with the convenience of a tour. You typically purchase a ticket for a fixed route (usually valid for 12 months), and then take it at your own pace. You can either stick with the one bus for the entire journey with nights spent at various towns along the route, or stop off longer in places and hop on a later bus. During peak times some buses may be full, so you'll need to plan onward travel several days in advance. Most companies operate year-round, though services are reduced in winter.

The emphasis is on **experiencing the country** rather than travelling from one town to the next, so you'll be stopping off to bungy jump, hike or somesuch. Being part of a group of forty rowdy backpackers arriving at some idyllic spot isn't everyone's idea of a good time and, by using assorted public transport, it is often just as cheap to make your own way around New Zealand. But if you want almost everything organized for you, and a ready-made bunch of like-minded fellow travellers, this sort of travel might appeal.

It can be 5–10 percent cheaper to book before you arrive, as some deals are not available once you step off the plane: check the websites or with your travel agent. You might also save a few dollars by being a YHA, VIP, BBH or ISIC cardholder. Tickets don't generally cover accommodation, activities (although these are often discounted), side trips, food or travel between the North and South islands.

Operators are listed below. For those interested in multi-day tours and adventure activities check out "Outdoor activities" (see box, p.52), where more intimate and specialized excursions are listed.

Flying Kiwi Wilderness Expeditions

(⚑flyingkiwi.com). Operator specializing in tours that get off the beaten track and eschew city hostels in favour of camping. Converted buses are equipped with bikes, canoes, windsurfers, kitchen, awning, fridge, beds, tents and hot shower, and everyone mucks in with domestic chores. Trips operate all year and once on board you stick with the same group. Options range from the Northern Express from Wellington to Auckland via Taupo (2 days; $268) to a full NZ tour (27 days; $3740 including food and camping fees).

Kiwi Experience (⚑kiwiexperience.com).

With a deserved reputation for attracting high-spirited party animals, Kiwi Experience offers a huge array of passes, from a trip to Cape Reinga starting in Auckland (min 3 days; $199) to the Full Monty (minimum 32 days; $2125).

Magic Travellers Network (⚑magicbus

.co.nz). Offering a comprehensive selection of trips with guaranteed seats, if you book at least 24hrs in advance, these guys are kings of the backpacker buses. Working with the YHA, they offer substantial discounts to YHA cardholders and target independent-minded travellers. The Spirit of New Zealand pass is valid for a year and covers the whole country in 22 travel days ($1395), while the Northern Discovery heads from Auckland to Rotorua, Taupo, Napier, Wellington and Waitomo, returning to Auckland, over a minimum of six days ($485).

Stray (⚑straytravel.com). Stray have

attempted to take the mantle of ultimate party bus away from Kiwi Experience. Trips include a Round South Island (RON) circuit (minimum 16 days; $940) and a North Island circuit (minimum 9 days; $535).

As an example, a standard one-way fare on the North Island, Auckland to Rotorua, is $50, while on the South Island, Christchurch to Queenstown, it's $85.

Prices often plummet during off-peak periods and a range of **discounted fares** is available, with an advance-purchase Saver fare yielding a 25-percent **discount** and a Super Saver 50 percent. Extreme Saver and Web Saver fares are also available: book early for the best prices. YHA, VIP and BBH cardholders get fifteen-percent discounts off Standard rates but you'll find cheaper deals by chasing down the various Saver fares.

InterCity also offers numerous fixed-route **passes** such as the Auckland, Bay of Islands Pass, including Cape Reinga ($209; backpacker $179); Auckland, Rotorua, Napier via Taupo, Wellington and back (Maui's Catch: $215; backpacker $195); Nelson to Queenstown via the west coast ($159; backpacker $145); and various all-New Zealand experiences (from Kia Ora: $645; backpacker $579), with ever increasing fares.

Other buses

A host of **bus** and **shuttle bus** companies compete directly with InterCity/Newmans on the main routes and fill in the gaps around the country, often linking with the major operators, to take you off the beaten track. Generally they cost less (sometimes appreciably) and can be more obliging when it comes to drop-offs and pick-ups, though seldom as comfortable over distance. We've listed a number of the operators below, but there are many more mentioned in the appropriate sections of this guide.

Official (i-SITE) visitor centres carry **timetables** of bus and shuttle companies operating in their area, so you can compare frequencies and prices. **Fare structures** are generally straightforward, with fixed prices and no complicated discounts. Auckland to Rotorua, on the North Island, costs about $34, while on the South Island, Christchurch to Queenstown will be roughly $45.

BUS COMPANIES

Atomic Shuttles ☎ 03 349 0697, ⓦ atomictravel.co.nz. Major long-distance bus operator in the South Island.

InterCity & Newmans Auckland call centre ☎ 09 583 5780, ⓦ intercitycoach.co.nz & ⓦ newmanscoach.co.nz. Long-distance buses nationwide.

NakedBus ☎ 0900 62533 (premium rate), ⓦ nakedbus.com. Cheap, frill-free trips on both islands.

Northliner Express ☎ 09 583 5780, ⓦ northliner.co.nz. Bus travel around Northland, owned by InterCity.

Southern Link ☎ 0508 458 835, ⓦ southernlinkcoaches.co.nz. Routes all over the South Island.

By train

Not much is left of New Zealand's passenger train service besides **commuter** services in Wellington and Auckland and a few inter-city trains. The **long-distance services** that exist are scenic runs, primarily used by tourists; trains are so slow that they have ceased to be practical transport for New Zealanders. Minimal investment in infrastructure and rolling stock is beginning to have an effect on standards, but railway travel remains a pleasant experience.

Trains have reclining seats, buffet cars with reasonable food, beer, panoramic windows, and occasionally a glass-backed observation carriage. Tickets guarantee a seat: passengers check in on the platform before boarding and bags are carried in a luggage van.

Long-distance trains are all run by **Tranz Scenic** (☎ 04 495 0775 & ☎ 0800 872 467, ⓦ tranzscenic .co.nz), which operates three passenger routes. The longest is the *Overlander* **between Auckland and Wellington**, past the volcanic peaks of the Tongariro National Park. Interesting stops along the way include Te Awamutu, Te Kuiti (where the train is met by a shuttle bus to Waitomo Caves) and National Park (with access to Mount Ruapehu and the Tongariro Alpine Crossing). The service leaves both Auckland and Wellington daily around 7.35am and reaches its destination around 7.20pm.

In the South Island, the *TranzCoastal* runs **between Christchurch and Picton**, a pretty run sometimes hugging the coast. It leaves Christchurch at 7am for the run up through Kaikoura (9.54am) and Blenheim (11.33pm) to Picton (12.13pm). It then returns from Picton (1pm) through Blenheim (1.33pm) and Kaikoura (3.28pm) to Christchurch (6.21pm).

The finest rail journey in New Zealand is the *TranzAlpine* **between Christchurch and Greymouth** on the West Coast – it is covered in detail on p.517.

Fares are higher than the comparable bus tickets, but with discounts and the use of a travel pass (see box, p.32), travelling is still reasonably good value. Most people get the standard or **Flexi fare**, which gives a discount in return for advance

TRAVEL PASSES

If you're doing a lot of travelling by bus and train, there are savings to be made with travel passes. Tranz Scenic's **Scenic Rail Pass** (Ⓦtranszscenic.co.nz) gives unlimited travel on Tranz Scenic trains for a week ($307).

InterCity/Newmans offer their own **Flexi-Pass**, allowing you to buy bus travel by the hour – the more hours you buy the better the savings. You would typically need 45 hours ($349) to cover one of the main islands, 60 hours upwards ($449) for a full tour, and if that's not enough you can top-up your pass with, say, 15 hours ($117). The Flexi-Pass is valid for 12 months and journeys can be booked online or by free-calling Ⓣ0800 222 146. Travellers wanting to move around pretty quickly might be better off with one of the **New Zealand Travel Passes** (Ⓦtravelpass.co.nz) which make extensive use of InterCity and throw in a ferry journey and a few extras (the cheapest option is $695; backpacker $625); other options and more money get you a train journey and/or a domestic flight.

The backpacker tour buses (see box, p.30) offer lower prices in return for older buses and – often – a more boisterous time.

---

booking, limited availability and only a fifty-percent refund if cancelled after the departure time. As an example, a standard, one-way ticket from Auckland to Wellington is about $129, from Christchurch to Greymouth around $185. Seniors (60-plus) can get a thirty-percent discount on standard fares, though most folk do better by going for a Scenic Rail Pass (see box above). Blind and some disabled travellers (see p.67) are entitled to a forty-percent discount on the standard fare.

Apart from a couple of short-run steam trains, the only other passenger trains are along the **Taieri Gorge Railway** (see box, p.548) between Dunedin and Middlemarch, again run almost entirely for the benefit of tourists and an extremely beautiful scenic route.

By car

For maximum flexibility, it's hard to beat **driving** around New Zealand: you'll be able to get to places beyond the reach of public transport and to set your own timetable. With the freedom to camp or stay in cheaper places away from town centres this can be a very economical option for two or more people.

In order to drive in New Zealand you need a valid **licence** from your home country or an International Driver's Licence valid for up to a year in New Zealand and you must always carry the licence when driving.

In New Zealand you **drive on the left** and will find **road rules** similar to those in the UK, Australia and the US. All occupants must wear **seatbelts** and drivers must park in the same direction as that in which they are travelling.

The **speed limit** for the open road is 100kmph, reduced to 70kmph or 50kmph in built-up areas. Speeding fines start at $30 and rapidly increase as the degree of transgression increases. Some drivers flash their headlights at oncoming cars to warn of lurking police patrols, but there are also hidden cameras on the roads. **Drink driving** has traditionally been a problem in New Zealand: as part of a campaign to cut the death toll, random breath tests exist and offenders are dealt with severely.

Road conditions are generally good and traffic is relatively light except around Auckland and Wellington in the rush hour. Most roads are sealed (paved), although a few have a metalled surface, composed of an aggregate of loose chippings. Clearly marked on most maps, these are slower to drive along, prone to washouts and landslides after heavy rain, and demand considerably more care and attention from the driver. Some rental companies prohibit the use of their cars on the worst metalled roads – typically those at Skippers Canyon and around the northern tip of Coromandel Peninsula. Always check conditions locally before setting off on these routes.

Other **hazards** include one-lane bridges: a sign before the bridge will indicate who has right of way, and on longer examples there'll be a passing place halfway across.

Unleaded and super unleaded **petrol** and diesel are available in New Zealand, and in larger towns petrol stations are open 24hr. In smaller towns, they may close after 8pm, so be sure to fill up for long evening or night journeys.

If you're driving your own vehicle, check if the **New Zealand Automobile Association** (Ⓦnzaa .co.nz) has reciprocal rights with motoring organizations from your country to see if you qualify for their cover; otherwise, you can join as an overseas visitor. Apart from a free 24hr **emergency breakdown** service (☎0800 500 222) – excluding vehicles bogged on beaches – membership entitles you to free maps, accommodation guides and legal assistance, discounts on some rental cars and accommodation, plus access to insurance and pre-purchase vehicle inspection services.

Car rental

Visitors driving in New Zealand typically pick up a car in Auckland, tour the North Island to Wellington where they leave the first vehicle, cross Cook Strait, pick up a second car in Picton, then drive around the South Island dropping off the car in Christchurch. The whole thing can be done in reverse, and may work out cheaper, or you can stick with the same car across Cook Strait, which with domestic companies doesn't entail a big price hike.

You'll see rental deals for under $37 a day, though only for older, small cars rented for over a month in winter (June–Aug). Demand is high over the main summer season and prices rise accordingly.

Most of the major **international companies** are represented and offer good deals for virtually new cars. **Domestic** firms offer cheaper rates partly by minimizing overheads and offering older (but perfectly serviceable) vehicles. You may find even cheaper deals with cut-rate local companies, which are fine for short stints, though for general touring domestic nationwide companies are the best bet. Their infrastructure helps when it comes to crossing between the North and South islands (see p.431) and they typically offer free breakdown assistance.

In peak season it usually pays to have a car **booked in advance**. At quieter times you can often pick up something cheaper once you arrive; and in winter (except in ski areas) you can almost name your price. Provided your rental period is four days or more the deal will be for **unlimited kilometres**. The rates quoted below are for summer season assuming a two-week rental period, but don't be afraid to haggle at any time.

As a general rule, Ace, Apex, Omega and Pegasus offer reasonably new cars at moderate prices, while the rest of the companies listed below try desperately to undercut each other and offer **low prices**.

Based on a two-week rental in summer, for two people, a **small car** (1.3–1.8 litre) might cost $45–70 a day from the majors and $37–60 from domestic national firms. A **medium-sized car** (2–3 litre) might cost $65–90 from the majors and $35–80 from domestic national companies. Unless you're here in winter and want to get up to the ski-fields without tyre chains you don't really need a **4WD**, which generally cost $70–130 a day; you'll be better off renting one for short trips in specific areas.

If you are renting for several weeks, there is often no **drop-off fee** for leaving the vehicle somewhere other than where you picked it up. For shorter rental periods you may be charged $170–300, though if you're travelling south to north, you may be able to sweet-talk your way out of drop-off charges. At different times in the season Wellington, Picton, Christchurch and Queenstown have a glut of cars that are needed elsewhere, and companies will offer **relocation deals**. Look at hostel notice boards or call the firms listed below. Some companies want quick delivery, while others will allow you to spend a few more days en route for a reduced rental rate.

You must have a full, clean **driver's licence** and be over 21; drivers under 25 often pay more for insurance. In most cases insurance is included in the quoted cost but you are liable for any windscreen damage and the first $1000 of any damage. With some of the cheaper companies this excess can be as much as $3000 if the accident is your fault. This can usually be reduced to $250 or zero by paying an additional $10–20 a day Collision Damage Waiver. Usually before giving you a car rental companies take a credit-card imprint or a cash bond from you for $1500. If you have an accident, the bond is used to pay for any damage: in some cases you can pay anything up to the value of the bond; in others you pay the entire bond no matter how slight the damage. Read the small print, look around the car for any visible **defects**, so you won't end up being charged for someone else's mistakes, and check whether there are any restrictions on driving along certain roads.

DOMESTIC CAR-RENTAL AGENCIES

A2B Rentals ☎0800 545 000, ⓦ a2brentals.co.nz.
Ace Rental Cars ☎0800 502 277, ⓦ acerentalcars.co.nz.
Apex ☎0800 939 597, ⓦ apexrentals.co.nz.
Bargain Rental Cars ☎0800 001 122, ⓦ bargainrentals.co.nz.
Jucy ☎0800 399 736, ⓦ jucy.co.nz.
Omega ☎0800 112 2333, ⓦ omegarentalcars.com.
Pegasus ☎0800 803 580, ⓦ rentalcars.co.nz.

Campervan rental

Throughout the summer, roads are clogged with **campervans**, almost all driven by foreign visitors who rent them for a few weeks and drive around the country staying in campsites and freedom camping (see p.40). A small campervan is generally suitable for two adults and a couple of kids and comes with a fold-down bed and compact kitchen. Larger models sleep four or more and often have a shower and toilet.

Medium **campervan rentals** (based on a 3-week rental) average about $200–330 a day during the high season (Dec–Feb), dropping a little for a couple of months either side and plummeting to around $160 in winter with the two biggest rental firms, Maui and Britz (effectively the same company). A few smaller firms (listed below) offer cheaper rates, saving 20–30 percent.

Small vans are often cramped and aimed at backpackers prepared to sacrifice comfort to save money. These typically cost $80–95 a day during summer, $75–85 in the shoulder season and $60–70 in the depths of winter. The current trend is for wildly painted vans, often with arcane, quirky or downright offensive comments graffitied on them: witness Escape Rentals and Wicked Campers. Other good bets are the distinctive orange Spaceships that have been imaginatively converted to suit two adults. For an affordable and slightly offbeat experience go for a restored, classic VW campervan (possibly with a pop-top), from Auckland-based Kiwi Kombis, who charge $140–210 a day, depending on dates and van.

For all campervans there's usually a minimum rental period of 5–7 days, but you get unlimited kilometres, a kitchen kit and perhaps airport transfer. Insurance is often included but you may be liable for the first $2000–7500 and you should seriously consider paying extra fees to get this liability reduced. Most companies have a supply of tents, camping kits, outdoor chairs and tables that can be rented for a few dollars.

No special **licence** is required to drive a campervan, but some caution is needed, especially in high winds and when climbing hills and going around tight corners.

For information on freedom camping.

CAMPERVAN RENTALS: MEDIUM TO LARGE

Adventure ☎ 0800 123 555, Ⓦ nzmotorhomes.co.nz.
Backpacker Campervans ☎ 800 422 267, Ⓦ backpacker campervans.com.
Britz ☎ 0800 831 900, Ⓦ britz.com.
Eurocampers ☎ 0800 489 226, Ⓦ breakaway.co.nz.
Freedom Campers ☎ 0800 325 939, Ⓦ freedomcampers.co.nz.
Jucy ☎ 0800 399 736, Ⓦ jucy.co.nz.

Kea Campers ☎ 0800 520 052, Ⓦ keacampers.com.
Maui ☎ 0800 651 080, Ⓦ maui.co.nz.

SMALL VANS AND CONVERSIONS

Backpackers Transport ☎ 0800 226 769, Ⓦ backpackernz.co.nz.
Escape ☎ 0800 216 171, Ⓦ escaperentals.co.nz.
Jucy ☎ 0800 399 736, Ⓦ jucy.co.nz.
Kiwi Kombis ☎ 09 533 9335, Ⓦ kiwikombis.com.
Spaceships ☎ 0800 772 237, Ⓦ spaceshipsrentals.co.nz.
Wicked Campers ☎ 0800 246 870, Ⓦ wicked-campers.co.nz.

Buying a used vehicle

Buying a **used vehicle** can be cost-effective if you are staying in the country for more than a couple of months. Reselling can recoup enough of the price to make it cheaper than using public transport or renting. If you buy cheap there's also a greater risk of breakdowns and expensive repairs. The majority of people buy cars in Auckland and then try to sell them in Christchurch, so there's something to be said for buying in Christchurch where you'll often have more choice and a better bargaining position.

Some of the best deals are found on backpacker **hostel notice boards** where older cars and vans are typically offered for $500–5000. Realistically you can expect to pay upwards of $3000 for something half-decent. It may not look pretty and with a **private sale** there's no guarantee the vehicle will make yet another trip around the country, but you might get an added bonus like camping gear thrown in with the car (or offered at a snip).

For a little more peace of mind, buy from a **dealership**. There are plenty all over the country, especially in Auckland, Christchurch and Wellington. Prices begin at around $5000 and some yards offer a **buy-back service**, usually paying about fifty percent of the purchase price. If you're confident of your ability to spot a lemon, you can try to pick up a cheap car at an **auction**; they're held weekly in Auckland (see p.97) and Christchurch and are advertised in the local press. Be aware that you'll usually be liable for the **buyer's premium** of ten percent over your bid.

Before you commit yourself, consult the vehicle ownership section of the NZ Transport Agency website (Ⓦ nzta.govt.nz), which has good advice on buying and the pitfalls. The *Buying a used car* factsheet is particularly helpful.

Unless you really know your big end from your steering column you'll want to arrange a mobile **vehicle inspection**, either from the AA (☎0800 500 333, Ⓦ aa.co.nz; members $147; non-members $169) or the Car Inspection Services (☎0800 500

800 in Auckland and Wellington, W carinspections .co.nz). The inspection may give you enough ammunition to negotiate a price reduction. Finally, before you close a private sale, call AA LemonCheck (T 0800 536 662, W aalemoncheck.co.nz) – its staff will fill you in on registration history, possible odometer tampering and any debts on the vehicle ($20 members; $30 non-members).

Before they're allowed on the road, all vehicles must have a **Warrant of Fitness** (WOF), which is a test of its mechanical worthiness and safety. WOFs are carried out and issued by specified garages and testing stations and last for a year if the vehicle is less than six years old, or six months if older. Check the expiry date, as the test must have been carried out no more than one month before sale. The vehicle should also have current **vehicle registration**, which must be renewed before it expires (6 months, starting at $299.90; 12 months $431.06 for petrol-driven, private vehicles – 1300–2600cc): post offices and AA offices are the most convenient for this, though you can also do it online at W nzta.govt.nz.

You **transfer ownership** with a form (filled in by buyer and seller) at a post office: the licence plates stay with the vehicle. Next you'll need **insurance**: Comprehensive (which covers your vehicle and any other damaged vehicles), or Third Party, Fire & Theft (which covers your own vehicle against fire and theft, but only pays out on damage to other vehicles in case of an accident). Shop around as prices vary widely, but expect to pay a minimum of $350 for six months' Third Party, Fire & Theft cover.

By motorcycle

Visitors from most countries can ride in New Zealand with their normal licence, though it (or your international licence) must specify motorbikes. Helmets are compulsory, and you'll need to be prepared to ride on gravel roads from time to time.

Few people bring their own bike but **bike rental** is available from the companies running guided bike tours (see below). It isn't cheap, and for a 650cc machine in summer you can expect to pay $190–280 a day. Bike Adventure New Zealand (T 0800 498 600, W bikeadventure.co.nz) offers 600cc enduro machines for $95 per day for short periods, dropping to $55 per day for ten weeks. Alternatively, try the same channels as for "Buying a used vehicle" opposite.

MOTORBIKE TOURS

The obvious alternative is an organized tour, self-guided or guided, usually incorporating top-of-the-range accommodation, restaurants and bikes.

Adventure New Zealand Motorcycle Tours & Rentals W gotournz.com. Nelson-based company providing upmarket, small-group guided or self-guided tours around the South Island, with itineraries tweaked to suit and a luxury coach in your wake. Rates start at $9000 for a standard 10-day trip on a relatively modest bike.

New Zealand Motorcycle Rentals & Tours W nzbike.com. Another specialist top-end company, offering guided all-inclusive tours staying in quality accommodation, semi-guided tours and bike rental. A fully guided 21-day tour round both islands will set you back about $8300, staying in hotels and riding a modest bike.

Te Waipounamu Motorcycle Hire & Tours W motorcycle-hire .co.nz. These folk do upscale tours round the bottom of the South Island and bike rentals including Beamers at $230/day in the high season.

By bike

If you have time, **cycling** is an excellent way of getting around. Distances aren't enormous, the weather is generally benign, traffic is light, and the countryside is gorgeous. Most everywhere you go you'll find hostels and campsites well set up for campers, but also equipped with rooms and cabins for when the weather really sucks.

But there are downsides. New Zealand's road network is skeletal, so in many places you'll find yourself riding on main roads or unsealed minor

---

NGA HAERENGA – THE NEW ZEALAND CYCLE TRAIL

With quiet roads, brilliant scenery and superb camping, New Zealand has long been on the cycle touring map and now looks set to become a major off-road cycle touring destination.

As a recession-busting project, the government has funded a series of **18 Great Rides**, stand-alone, mostly off-road routes that comprise **Nga Haerenga** (W nzcycletrail.com). The rides (from a few hours to several days) should all be complete by early 2013 and boosters hope that they will emulate the successful Otago Central Rail Trail (see box, p.743), providing superb riding while boosting the local economy. Eventually these may be linked together in an end-to-end network along the lines of Te Araroa (see box, p.48).

Rent a bike locally and just tackle rides such as "From the Mountains to the Sea" in the north and "The Old Ghost Road" in the south, or come for a month or so and collect the set.

roads. You'll also experience a fair bit of rain and have to climb quite a lot of hills.

Cycling the **South Island** is an easier proposition than the **North Island**. The South Island's alpine backbone presents virtually the only geographical barrier, while the eastern two-thirds of the island comprise a flat plain. In the North Island you can barely go 10km without encountering significant hills – and you have to contend with a great deal more traffic, including intimidating logging trucks.

New Zealand law requires all cyclists to wear a **helmet**. Some **fitness** is important, but distances don't have to be great and you can take things at your own pace. If you'd rather go with a **guided group**, see box, p.52.

For more **information** get the *Pedallers' Paradise* guides (**W** paradise-press.co.nz) or Bruce Ringer's *New Zealand by Bike* (see p.821).

The bike

Since the vast majority of riding will be on sealed roads with only relatively short sections of gravel, it is perfectly reasonable (and more efficient) to get around New Zealand on a touring bike. But fashion dictates most people use a **mountain bike** fitted with fat but relatively smooth tyres.

On long trips it's cheaper to **bring your own bike**, set up to your liking before you leave home. Most international airlines simply count bikes as a piece of luggage and don't incur any extra cost as long as you don't exceed your baggage limit. However, they do require you to use a **bike bag** or box, or at the very least remove pedals and handlebars and wrap the chain. Some airlines will sell you a cardboard bike box at the airport. Soft bags are probably the most convenient (they're easy to carry on the bike once you arrive), but if you are flying out from the same city you arrive in you can often store hardshell containers (free or for a small fee) at the backpacker hostel where you spend your first and last nights: call around.

Renting bikes for more than the odd day can be an expensive option, costing anything from $30–55 a day, depending on whether you want a bike with little more than pedals and brakes, a tourer or state-of-the-art mountain bike. Specialist cycle shops do more economical monthly rentals for around $200–250 for a tourer and $300 or more for a full-suspension superbike.

For long-distance cycle touring, it's generally cheaper to **buy a bike**. It will cost at least $1500 to get fully kitted out with new equipment, but it's worth checking hostel notice boards for **second-hand bikes** (under $500 is a reasonable deal), often accompanied by extras such as wet-weather gear, lights, a helmet and a pump. Some cycle shops offer **buy-back deals**, guaranteeing to refund about fifty percent of the purchase price at the end of your trip – contact Adventure Cycles, 9 Premier Ave, Western Springs, in Auckland (**T** 09 940 2453, **W** adventure-auckland.co.nz/adventurecycles.html). If you're bringing your own bike, the same folk will let you store the bike box you transported your machine in, help organize an emergency package of spare parts and extra clothing to be forwarded at your request, and give your bike a once-over before you set off, all for around $50.

Transporting bikes

Lethargy, boredom, breakdowns or simply a need to shift your bike between islands mean you'll use **public transport** at some point. You can usually get your bike onto a bus (generally $15–20) or train ($15–20/journey), though space is often limited so book well in advance. Crossing Cook Strait, the Interislander and Blue Bridge ferries charge $15–20.

Bikes usually travel free on buses, trains and ferries if packed in a bike bag and treated as ordinary luggage. Air New Zealand will fly your bike free, if it is within your baggage allowance; Jetstar will charge you at its normal excess baggage rate, though that doesn't cut into your free allowance.

By ferry

The **ferries** you're most likely to use are vehicle-carrying services plying Cook Strait between Wellington on the North Island and Picton on the South Island. Details are given on p.431.

Passenger ferries link Bluff, in the south of the South Island, to Stewart Island, and both vehicle and passenger ferries connect Auckland with the Hauraki Gulf islands, principally Waiheke, Rangitoto and Great Barrier. Information about these short trips is included in the accounts of Invercargill and Auckland. Most visitors spend more boat time on cruises – whale watching, dolphin swimming, sightseeing – or **water taxis**.

Accommodation

Accommodation will take up a fair chunk of your money while in New Zealand, but the good news is that standards across all categories are excellent. Almost every town has a motel or hostel of some description, so finding accommodation

is seldom a problem – though it's essential to book in advance during the peak summer season from Christmas through to the end of March.

Kiwis travel widely at home, most choosing to self-cater at the country's huge number of well-equipped **campsites** (a.k.a. holiday parks) and **motels**, shunning **hotels**, which cater mainly to package holiday-makers and the business community. The range of **B&Bs**, **homestays**, **farmstays** and **lodges** forms an appealing alternative, covering the whole spectrum from a room in someone's suburban home to pampered luxury in a country mansion.

Since the mid-1980s, New Zealand has pioneered the **backpacker hostel**, a less regimented alternative to traditional YHAs, which have transformed themselves dramatically to compete. Found all over the country, hostels offer superb value to budget travellers.

Wherever you stay, you can expect unstinting hospitality and a truckload of valuable advice on local activities and onward travel. We've included a wide selection of New Zealand's best accommodation throughout the book, and more detail can be gleaned from specialist accommodation guides.

Many places are now accredited using the nationwide **Qualmark** system (W qualmark.co.nz), which grades different types of accommodation – exclusive, hotel, self-contained, guest and hosted, holiday parks and backpackers – from one to five stars. Most fall between three stars (very good) and four plus (at the top end of excellent), but there is no way of knowing whether, for example, a four-star backpacker is superior to rooms at a five-star holiday park. Many places choose not to join the system, but may be just as good or better.

ACCOMMODATION GUIDES AND WEBSITES

AA Accommodation Guide W aatravel.co.nz. Annual advertising-based guide for the whole country; concentrates mostly on motels and holiday parks. Also a B&B guide and various regional variants. Available free from most motels and i-SITE offices.

BookABach W bookabach.co.nz. Many Kiwis own a holiday home (a.k.a. *bach* or *crib*), which they rent out when they're not using them. Some are in superb locations next to beaches or lakes. Some have a two- or three-night minimum stay, rising to a week from Christmas to late February when rates rise dramatically and availability reduced. There are real bargains in winter. Holiday houses (W holidayhouses.co.nz) has a similar range of places.

Charming Bed & Breakfast W bnbnz.com. Glossy B&B guide concentrating on mid-range places but also country and farmstays. View online, download as one massive PDF, get the book for the price of postage, or pick up (often free) at B&Bs. Nominally $20.

Hotels, motels and pubs

In New Zealand, **hotel** is a term frequently used to describe old-style **pubs**, once legally obliged to provide rooms for drinkers to recuperate. Many no longer provide accommodation, but some have transformed themselves into backpacker hostels, while others are dedicated to preserving the tradition. At their best, such hotels offer comfortable rooms in historic buildings (for $100–140/night), though just as often lodgings are rudimentary. Hotel bars are frequently at the centre of small-town life and at weekends in particular can be pretty raucous, so you may find a budget room at a hostel a better bet.

In the cities and major resorts, you'll also come across **hotels** in the conventional sense ($180–$350), predominantly business- or tour-bus-oriented places. Rack rates are generally high but many places vary their rates according to demand and bargains can definitely be had, particularly at weekends.

Most Kiwi families on the move prefer the astonishingly well-equipped **motels** ($100–200) which congregate along the roads running into town, making them more convenient for drivers than for those using trains or buses. They usually come with Sky TV, bathroom, some sort of kitchen and tea and coffee, but are often fairly functional concrete-block places with little to distinguish one from another. Rooms range from all-in-one **studios**,

---

BOOKING ACCOMMODATION

You should **book accommodation** at major towns and popular tourist locales at least a few days in advance from December to March. Reserving several weeks ahead is a good idea if you're particular about where you stay. Most Kiwis take two to three weeks off from Christmas onwards, so from **December 26 to mid-January** anywhere near a nice beach or lake is likely to be packed, particularly holiday parks (campsites) and motels, which usually rack up their prices considerably during this period. Places that don't attract Kiwi holiday-makers can be relatively peaceful at this time. Towns near **ski resorts** are typically busiest between July and September, particularly on weekends and during school holidays.

with beds, kettle, toaster and a microwave, through **one-bedroom units**, usually with a full and separate kitchen, to two- and **three-bedroom suites**, sleeping six or eight. Suites generally go for the same basic price as a one-bedroom unit, with each additional adult paying $20–25, making them an economical choice for groups travelling together. Anything calling itself a **motor inn** ($140–240) or similar will be quite luxurious, with a bar, restaurant, swimming pool and sauna but no cooking facilities.

B&Bs, lodges and boutique hotels

While families might prefer the freedom and adaptability of a motel, couples are often better served by a **bed and breakfast** (B&B; $100–250). This might be a simple room with a bathroom down the hall and a modest continental breakfast included in the price. But the term also encompasses luxurious colonial homes with well-furnished en-suite rooms and sumptuous home-cooked breakfasts. Those at the top end fashion themselves as lodges, boutique hotels and "**exclusive retreats**" ($300–2000), where standards of service and comfort reach extraordinary levels, with prices to match.

Rates drop in the low season, when these places can often be good value. If you're travelling alone and don't fancy hostels, B&Bs can also be a viable alternative, usually charging **lone travellers** 60–80 percent of the double room rate, though some only ask fifty percent.

Homestays and farmstays

Homestays ($120–200) usually offer a guest room or two in an ordinary house where you muck in with the owners and join them for breakfast the following morning. Staying in such places can be an excellent way to meet ordinary New Zealanders; you'll be well looked after, sometimes to the point of being overwhelmed by your hosts' generosity. It

is courteous to **call in advance**, and bear in mind you'll usually have to **pay in cash**. Rural versions often operate as **farmstays** ($120–200), where you're encouraged to stay a couple of nights and are welcome to spend the intervening day trying your hand at farm tasks: rounding up sheep, milking cows, fencing, whatever might need doing. Both homestays and farmstays charge for a double room, including breakfast; some cook dinner on request for $25–75 per person, and you may pay a small fee for lunch if you spend the day at the farm or for a packed lunch.

Hostels, backpackers and YHAs

New Zealand has over 350 budget and self-catering places, pretty much interchangeably known as **hostels** or **backpackers** and offering a dorm bed or bunk for around $23–32. They're often in superb locations – bang in the centre of town, beside the beach, close to a ski-field or amid magnificent scenery in a national or forest park – and are great places to meet other travellers and pick up local information. Backpacker hostels range in size from as few as four beds up to huge premises accommodating several hundred. Beds are generally fully made up (places discourage or ban sleeping bags to prevent the spread of bed bugs); you should bring your own towel, though you can rent one for a few dollars. **Internet access** (and increasingly wi-fi) is pretty standard, though a few rural places intentionally eschew such mod cons. Depending on the area, there may be a pool, barbecue, bike and/or canoe rental and information on local work opportunities. Many places offer cupboards for your gear, though you'll usually need your own lock. Almost all hostels are affiliated with local and international organizations that offer **accommodation discounts** to members, along with an array of other travel- and activity-related savings.

Some hostels allow you to pitch a tent in the grounds and use the facilities for around $17 per person, but generally the most basic and cheapest

For advice on backcountry camping and trampers' huts, see the "Outdoor activities" section (see p.50).

accommodation is in a six- to twelve-bunk **dorm** ($23–28), with three- and four-bed rooms (also known as three-shares and four-shares) usually priced a couple of dollars higher. Most hostels also have **double**, **twin** and **family rooms** ($50–80 for two), the more expensive ones with en-suite bathrooms. Lone travellers who don't fancy a dorm can sometimes get a **single room** ($30–50), and many larger places (especially YHAs and Base backpackers) also offer **women-only dorms**.

YHA

Around 25 places are classified as **YHA hostels** (ⓦyha.co.nz), which have abandoned lock-outs, curfews and arcane opening hours, but maintain a predominance of single-sex dorms. Newer hostels have been purpose-built to reflect the YHA's environmental concerns, promoting recycling and energy conservation. Non-members pay the price we've quoted but you can save 10 percent by joining and obtaining a **Hostelling International Card**, preferably in your home country before travelling. Alternatively you can buy a $42 annual membership in New Zealand, which includes one free dorm night.

Another 26 hostels are affiliated **associate YHA hostels**, where there is often a discount of a dollar or so for YHA members. You can book ahead either from another hostel or through the YHA National Reservations Centre and through Hostelling International offices in your home country.

YHA and associate YHA hostels are listed on the annual *YHA Backpacker Map*.

BBH

YHAs are vastly outnumbered by other **backpacker hostels**, where the atmosphere is more variable; some are friendly and relaxed, others more party-oriented. Many are aligned with the NZ-based **Budget Backpacker Hostels** (ⓦbbh.co.nz), and are listed (along with current prices) in the *BBH Accommodation* booklet, widely available from hostels and visitor centres. The entries are written by the hostels and don't pretend to be impartial but each hostel is given a customer **percentage rating** which is determined by an annual customer survey and by online voting. These are a reliable quality indicator, though city hostels tend not to rate as well as similarly appointed places next to nice

beaches. Anything above 80 percent will be excellent: the few places rating below 60 percent should be treated with suspicion.

Anyone can stay at BBH hostels, but savings can be made by buying a BBH Club Card ($45), which generally saves the holder $3–4 on each night's stay in either a dorm or a room. Cards are available from BBH and all participating hostels, and each card doubles as a rechargeable phonecard loaded with $20 worth of calling time.

Base and Nomads

Two Australasian hostel chains, **Base** (ⓦstayatbase .com) and **Nomads** (ⓦnomadshostels.com), each run half a dozen or so hostels across the country, in major tourist hangouts. Both offer discounts if you sign up to a card or accommodation package.

Holiday parks, cabins and camping

New Zealand has some of the world's best **camping** facilities, and even if you've never camped before, you may well find yourself using **holiday parks** (also known as **motor camps**), which come with space to pitch tents, numerous powered sites (or hook-ups) for campervans and usually a broad range of dorms, cabins and motel units. You'll find more down-to-earth camping at wonderfully located DOC sites.

Camping is largely a summer activity (Nov–May), especially in the South Island. At worst, New Zealand can be very wet, windy and plagued by voracious winged **insects**, so the first priority for tent campers is good-quality gear with a fly sheet which will repel the worst that the elements can dish out, and an inner tent with bug-proof ventilation for hot mornings.

Busy times at motor camps fall into line with the school holidays, making Easter and the summer period from Christmas to the end of January the most hectic. Make **reservations** as far in advance as possible at this time, and a day or two before you arrive through February and March. DOC sites are not generally bookable, and while this is no problem through most of the year, Christmas can be a mad free-for-all.

See p.40 for information about responsible overnight stops outside official areas.

Holiday parks

Holiday parks are typically located on the outskirts of towns and are invariably well equipped, with a communal kitchen, TV lounge, games area, laundry and sometimes a swimming pool. You should bring your own pans, plates and cutlery, though some places have limited supplies and full sets can be rented for a few dollars a night. Non-residents can often get **showers** for around $2–5. **Campers** usually get the quietest and most sylvan corner of the site and are charged around $13–20 per person; camping prices throughout the guide are per person unless followed or preceded by "per site". There is often no distinction between tent pitches and the **powered sites** set aside for campervans, but the latter usually cost an extra $2–3 per person for the use of power hook-ups and dump stations.

Most holiday parks also have some form of on-site accommodation (see below). **Sheets** and **towels** are rarely included at the cheaper end, so bring a sleeping bag or be prepared to pay to rent bed linen (typically $5–10/stay).

Holiday parks are independently run but some have now aligned themselves with nationwide organizations that set minimum standards. Look out for **Top 10** sites (Ⓦ top10.co.nz), which maintain a reliably high standard in return for slightly higher prices and a degree of identikit sameness. By purchasing a membership card ($40) you save ten percent on each night's stay and get local discounts; the card (valid 2 years) is transferable to Australia.

HOLIDAY PARK ACCOMMODATION OPTIONS

Tent site ($13–20/person). Usually a patch of grass with a tap nearby.

Powered site ($15–23/person). Patch of grass or concrete with electrical hook-up and a dump station nearby. Fancier places charge a minimum of two people per site.

Lodge ($20–25/person). Dorm accommodation, often 8–12 bunks.

Standard cabin ($50–85 for two, plus $10–15 for each extra person). Often little more than a shed with bunks and perhaps a table. They sleep 2–4 and bedding is usually extra.

Kitchen cabin ($70–110 for two, plus $10–20 for each extra person). Like a standard cabin but with cooking facilities, table and chairs, and pans and plates provided. Often sleeps four and bedding is extra.

Tourist cabin/flat ($80–130 for two, plus $15–25 for each extra person). A kitchen cabin but with your own shower, toilet and maybe TV. Sometimes known as a self-contained unit, it typically sleeps four, and bedding is sometimes included.

Motel unit ($100–195 for two, plus $15–30 for each extra person). Larger than cabins and probably with one or more separate bedrooms and TV/DVD. Bedding and towels included.

DOC campsites

Few holiday parks can match the idyllic locations of the 250-plus **campsites** operated by the **Department of Conservation** (DOC; Ⓦ doc.govt.nz) in national parks, reserves, maritime and forest parks, the majority beautifully set by sweeping beaches or deep in the bush. This is back-to-nature camping, low-cost and with simple **facilities**, though sites almost always have running water and toilets of some sort. Listed in DOC's free North Island and South Island *Conservation Campsites* booklets (available from DOC offices), the sites fall into one of four categories: **Basic** (free), often with nothing but a long-drop toilet and water nearby; **Backcountry** ($1.50–6), with perhaps a cooking shelter and/or fireplace; the more common **Standard** ($5–16, typically $6), all with vehicular access and many with barbecues, fireplaces, picnic tables and refuse collection; and the rare **Serviced** ($7–19), which are similar in scope to the regular holiday parks. Children aged 5–17 are charged 25–50 percent off the adult price, and only the Serviced sites can be booked in advance.

Freedom camping

One of the pleasures of driving a campervan around New Zealand is the ability to sneak the odd free night in wayside rest areas or in car parks beside beaches. This **freedom camping** has never been strictly legal, but when numbers were small nobody worried too much. However, the sheer popularity of the privilege and indiscriminate littering took its toll and a new law now gives councils the power to hand out **instant fines** (minimum $200) to people found camping where they are instructed not to. No Camping signs have sprung up in likely spots all over the country, forcing freedom campers to quieter places between towns.

Freedom camping is definitely getting tougher but the approach varies throughout the country. Almost everyone takes a dim view of freedom camping in vehicles without a plumbed-in toilet. **Full self-contained campers** (marked with a green diamond sticker) have more options. Some councils impose a blanket ban on freedom camping within 10km of town, other places designate specific spots for freedom campers. DOC have responded to the changes by opening up more Conservation Campsites (some free, but mostly $5/person), usually in pretty areas close to towns. There's also **Native Parks** (Ⓦ nativeparks.co.nz), a scheme where travellers in fully self-contained motorhomes can stay free on hosts' property. When you join ($75) you get a guidebook outlining around 90 member properties spread all over the country.

We've listed many of the best and most convenient camping areas throughout the guide but there's lots more information out there. Consult

ⓦcamping.org.nz for guidelines on freedom camping and a link to a site marking all camping areas throughout the country. There are also useful **apps**; try the free one from **ⓦcampermate.co.nz** showing camping spots, toilets, budget accommodation and wi-fi hotspots all over the country, and the paid app from **ⓦrankers.co.nz/respect**, which focuses on the camping but has deeper coverage.

Food and drink

New Zealand's food scene is brilliant all round, from the quality of the ingredients, its cooking, presentation and the places where it's served.

Kiwi **gastronomy** has its roots in the British culinary tradition, an unfortunate heritage that still informs cooking patterns for older New Zealanders. Indeed, it is only in the last 25 years or so that New Zealand's chefs have really woken up to the possibilities presented by a fabulous larder of super-fresh, top-quality ingredients. Along with tender lamb, succulent beef and venison and superb shellfish you'll find some of the world's best dairy products and stone and pip-fruit which, at harvest time, can be bought for next to nothing from roadside stalls.

All this has been combined into what might be termed **Modern Kiwi** cuisine, drawing on Californian and contemporary Australian cooking, and combining it with flavours drawn from the **Mediterranean**, **Asia** and the **Pacific Rim**: sun-dried tomatoes, lemongrass, basil, ginger, coconut, and many more. Restaurants and cafés throughout the country feel duty-bound to fill their menus with as broad a spectrum as possible, lining up seafood linguini, couscous, sushi, Thai food, venison meatballs and chicken korma alongside the rack of lamb and gourmet pizza. Sometimes this causes gastronomic overload, but often it is simply mouthwatering.

Meat and fish

New Zealanders have a taste for **meat**, the quality of which is superb, with New Zealand lamb often at the head of the menu but matched in flavour by venison and beef.

With the country's extensive coastline, it's no surprise that **fish** and seafood loom large. The white, flaky flesh of the **snapper** is the most common saltwater fish, but you'll also come across tuna, John Dory, groper (often known by its Maori name of **hapuku**), flounder, gurnard, blue cod and the firm, delicately flavoured **terakihi**. Salmon is common, but not trout, which cannot be bought or sold, though most hotels and restaurants will cook one if you've caught it. This archaic law was originally intended to protect sport fishing when trout were introduced to New Zealand in the nineteenth century. All these fish are very tasty smoked, though *terakihi*, *hapuku*, blue cod, marlin and smoked eel take some beating.

One much-loved delicacy is **whitebait**, a collective name for five species of tiny, silvery, native fish mostly caught on the West Coast and eaten whole in fritters during the August to November season.

Shellfish are a real New Zealand speciality. You'll occasionally come across **tuatua**, dug from

---

THE HANGI

To sample traditional cooking methods go to a **hangi** (pronounced nasally as "hungi"), where meat and vegetables are steamed for hours in an earth oven then served to the assembled masses. The ideal way to experience a *hangi* is as a guest at a private gathering of extended families, but most people have to settle for one of the commercial affairs in Rotorua or Christchurch. There you'll be a paying customer rather than a guest but the *hangi* flavours will be authentic, though sometimes the operators may have been creative in the more modern methods they've used to achieve them.

At a traditional *hangi*, first the men light a fire and place river stones in the embers. While these are heating, they dig a suitably large pit, then place the hot stones in the bottom and cover them with wet sacking. Meanwhile the women prepare lamb, pork, chicken, fish, shellfish and vegetables (particularly *kumara*), wrapping the morsels in leaves then arranging them in baskets (originally of flax, but now most often of steel mesh). The baskets are lowered into the cooking pit and covered with earth so that the steam and the flavours are sealed in. A couple of hours later, the baskets are disinterred, revealing fabulously tender steam-smoked meat and vegetables with a faintly earthy flavour. A suitably reverential silence, broken only by munching and appreciative murmurs, usually descends.

THE EDMONDS COOKERY BOOK AND KIWI DESSERTS

Almost every Kiwi household has a battered copy of the **Edmonds Cookery Book**, first produced in 1908 and still selling over 20,000 copies a year. Parents often give the kids a copy when they first leave home. The recipes are wide-ranging but the focus is on the baking, usually using Edmond's baking powder which is still prominent on supermarket shelves. This is the first place people turn for making the sort of cakes and desserts that have always filled the shelves of rural tearooms. Fancier modern cafés following a retro tip are now re-inventing these Kiwi classics.

Afghans The origin of the name is lost, but these chocolate-and-cornflake-dough biscuits topped with cocoa icing are an eternal favourite.

Anzac biscuit Textured cookie made with oats and coconut.

Carrot cake A Kiwi favourite still found in cafés and tearooms all over.

Lamington A light sponge slice slathered in pink icing and desiccated coconut.

Pavlova No more than a giant, soft meringue covered in cream and fruit, this is the apotheosis of Kiwi desserts.

Northland beaches, on menus, but you're more likely to come across the fabulous **Bluff oysters** (see box, p.626), scallops and sensational **green-lipped mussels**, which have a flavour and texture that's hard to beat and are farmed in the cool clear waters of the Marlborough Sounds, especially around Havelock. Live green-lipped mussels can be bought from any decent supermarket.

Wonderfully rich and delicate **crayfish** is also available round the coast and should be sought out, particularly when touring Kaikoura and the East Cape.

Maori and ethnic food

In New Zealand restaurants you'll find few examples of Polynesian or **Maori cuisine**, though the cooking style does now have a foothold in forward-looking establishments where you might find a fern frond salad, or steak rubbed with peppery *horopito* leaves. To sample Maori food you'll really need to get along to a *hangi* (see box, p.41), most likely in Rotorua. One Pacific staple you'll certainly come across is *kumara* (sweet potato), which features in *hangi* and is often deep-fried as *kumara* chips.

A major influx of immigrants from south and east Asia has really changed the Kiwi restaurant scene over the last couple of decades. There's barely a town in the land without an **Indian** restaurant and **Chinese** restaurants are almost equally widely distributed. **Thai** is also common though you'll need to go to larger towns to find **Malaysian**, **Singaporean**, **Japanese** and **Korean** places. In the bigger cities there has recently been a resurgence of **Mexican** places after being out of favour for a couple of decades.

Vegetarian food

Self-catering **vegetarians** can eat well, though in restaurants they are less well served. Outside the major centres you'll find hardly any dedicated vegetarian restaurants and will have to rely on the token meat-free dishes served in most cafés. **Vegans** may develop an unhealthy reliance on nachos and the ubiquitous veggieburger, though these days many new "organic" outlets offer home-made vegan and vegetarian pies.

If you are taking a multi-day expedition on which food is provided, give them plenty of notice of your dietary needs.

Eating out

The quality of **cafés** and **restaurants** in New Zealand is typically superb, portions are respectable, and many are good value for money. In most restaurants you can expect to pay upwards of $25 for a main course, perhaps $55 for three courses without wine. There is no expectation of a tip, though a reward for exceptional service is welcomed. On **public holidays** you'll normally be expected to pay a surcharge (typically 15 percent) to ensure staff get financially compensated for their giving up their statutory holiday.

The traditional staple of the Kiwi dining scene is the **tearoom**, a self-service cafeteria-style establishment with no atmosphere but cheap pre-packaged sandwiches, unsavoury savouries, sticky cakes and other crimes against the tastebuds. The coffee is middling at best. You'll still find such places in rural towns: long-distance buses sometimes made their comfort stops at such places.

In more urbane areas, tearooms have largely been replaced by **cafés** selling everything from often excellent espresso and muffins to full breakfasts and lunch with a range of wines. Many close around 4pm, but others stay open and transform themselves into **restaurants**. There is minimal distinction between the two so you may find yourself eating a full meal while elbow to elbow with folk just out for a beer or coffee. At a café you normally order and pay at the front counter and then are brought your food. In restaurants full table service is the norm.

Restaurants, and many cafés, have alcohol licences, but some still maintain the old **BYO** tradition. Corkage fees are typically $5–15 per bottle, though some places charge per person.

Most bars serve **pub meals**, often the best-value budget eating around, with straightforward steak and chips, lasagne, pizza or burritos all served with salad for under $20. The country's ever-burgeoning wine industry has also spawned a number of moderate-to-expensive **vineyard restaurants**, particularly in the growing areas of Hawke's Bay and Marlborough. The food is almost invariably excellent, with many of the dishes matched to that vineyard's wines.

Snacks and takeaways

In the cities you'll come across **food courts**, usually in shopping malls with a dozen or so stalls selling bargain plates of all manner of ethnic dishes. Traditional **burger bars** continue to serve constructions far removed from the limp international-franchise offerings: weighty buns with juicy patties, thick ketchup, a stack of lettuce and tomato and the ever-present Kiwi favourite, slices of beetroot. **Meat pies** are another stalwart of snacking; sold in

---

TOP 5 FOR FISH & CHIPS

The Fishmonger Auckland. See p.105
Kaiaua Fisheries Kaiaua. See p.120
Original Smokehouse Mapua. See p.472
Shippey's Paihia. See p.168
Wellington Trawling Sea Market Wellington. See p.438

---

bakeries and from warming cabinets in pubs everywhere, the traditional steak and mince varieties are now supplemented by bacon and egg, venison, steak and cheese, steak and oyster, smoked fish and *kumara* and, increasingly, vegetarian versions.

Fish and chips (or "greasies") are also rightly popular – the fish is often shark (euphemistically called lemon fish or flake), though tastier species are always available for slightly more. Look out too for **paua fritters** – battered slabs of minced abalone that are something of an acquired taste.

Self-catering and farmers' markets

If you're **self-catering**, your best bet for cheap supplies is the local supermarket: *Pak 'n Save* is usually the cheapest; *New World* usually has the widest variety of quality foods. In emergencies you can top up with supplies from the plethora of convenience corner shops (known as "dairies") stocking bog-standard essentials. These, along with shops at campsites and those in isolated areas with a captive market, tend to have inflated prices.

Gourmet foodstuffs are best sought at the wide range of small independent outlets, offering predominantly local and/or organic supplies. These

---

QUALITY FOOD AND DRINK TO LOOK OUT FOR

Ice Cream Firm, scooped ice cream in a cone is a Kiwi institution and is sold all over, but to taste some of the best head for a good supermarket and buy Kapiti and Kohu Road, both in numerous delicious flavours including the indulgent hokey pokey – vanilla ice cream riddled with chunks of honeycomb toffee.
Jams and preserves Artisans sell preserves at various farmers' markets but supermarket brands Anathoth and Te Horo are amazingly flavoursome at modest prices.
Cheese Bland cheddar is the de facto

national standard, but New Zealand now makes a wide range of delicious cheeses, with the Kapiti brand widely available. Their super-rich Kikorangi blue is particularly good. Look out, too, for smaller producers such as Whitestone, Meyer and Puhoi Valley.
Beer Shun the mainstream stuff and zero in on small-batch craft brews such as: Auckland's Epic; Croucher from Rotorua; McCashin's, from Stoke, near Nelson; Emerson's from Dunedin; and the deep south's Invercargill Brewery. Most are available in bottle stores and good supermarkets.

can be supplemented with visit to farmers' markets: every town of any size now seems to have one, usually on Saturday or Sunday morning – we've mentioned several throughout the guide.

Drinking

Licensed cafés and restaurants all over the land make a point of stocking a wide range of New Zealand wines and beers, but for the lowest prices and a genuine Kiwi atmosphere you can't beat the **pub**. It's a place where folk stop off on their way home from work, its emphasis on consumption and back-slapping camaraderie rather than ambience and decor. In the cities, where competition from cafés is strong, pubs tend to be more comfortable and relaxing, but in the sticks little has changed. Rural pubs can initially be daunting for strangers, but once you get chatting, barriers soon drop. Drinking hours are barely limited at all; theoretically you can drink in most bars until at least midnight on weeknights and until 4am or later at weekends though places often close much earlier if there are few customers. The **drinking age** is 18. Smokers are banished to the open air, often in small, purpose-built shelters.

Beer

Beer is drunk everywhere and often. Nearly all of it is produced by two huge conglomerates – New Zealand Breweries and DB – who market countless variations on the lager and Pilsener theme, as well as insipid, deep-brown fizzy liquid dispensed from taps and in bottles as "draught" – a distant and altogether feebler relation of British-style bitter. One eternal favourite is Steinlager, now marketed in a "no-additive" version Pure. There really isn't a lot to choose between the beers except for alcohol content, normally around four percent, though five percent is common for premium beers usually described as "export".

Beer consumption generally is on a decline, but there is a boom in small breweries making **craft beers** (see box, p.43). Tap into the craft beer scene at ⓦ realbeer.co.nz and ⓦ beertourist.co.nz.

Draught beer is usually sold in **pints** (just over half a litre). Keep in mind that a half-pint will always be served as a ten fluid ounce glass and therefore will be a little over half the price of a pint. In rural areas, traditions die hard and you can buy a one-litre **jug**, which is then decanted into the required number of glasses, usually a **seven** (originally seven fluid ounces, or 200ml), a **ten**, or even an elegantly fluted **twelve**.

Prices vary enormously, but you can expect to pay $6–9 for a pint. It is much cheaper to buy in bulk from a **bottle shop** (off-licence or liquor store) which will stock a fair range of mainstream and boutique beers, usually in a six-pack of 330ml bottles (around $12–15) or multiple thereof.

Wine

Kiwis are justifiably loyal to New Zealand winemakers, who now produce **wines** that are among the best in the world, especially **white wines**. New Zealand is rapidly encroaching on the Loire's standing as the world benchmark for Sauvignon Blanc, while the bold fruitiness of its Chardonnay and apricot and citrus palate of its Rieslings attract many fans. Restaurant menus are packed with New Zealand whites, but **red wines** have traditionally been of the broad-shouldered Aussie variety. This has largely changed as improved canopy management and better site selection have brought Kiwi reds up alongside their Australian cousins, though sometimes at a higher price. There

---

MAJOR WINE AREAS

The following wine areas are listed from north to south:

Henderson and Kumeu. Most of these wineries, 15km west of Auckland, source their grapes elsewhere, making this a good place to sample wines from around the country.

Hawke's Bay. Premium wine area around Napier and Hastings with about thirty vineyards open to the public, some with tours and winery restaurants. Some of the country's best Chardonnay, Cabernet Sauvignon blends and Syrahs.

Martinborough The most accessible cluster of vineyards, many within walking distance of the town. Fine Pinot Noirs and Cabernet Sauvignon blends.

Marlborough Sixty percent of New Zealand's grapes are grown around Blenheim and Renwick, with a huge range of fantastic vineyards, several with restaurants. Famous for its Sauvignon Blanc, though strong on Pinot Noir and most whites.

Central Otago. Cool-climate wine growing at the limit of practicability, mostly around Bannockburn near Queenstown. Excellent Pinot Noir in particular.

are certainly some superb wines based on Cabernet Sauvignon and Merlot (particularly from Waiheke Island and Hawke's Bay), but the reds garnering the most praise are Pinot Noirs from Central Otago, Marlborough and Martinborough, and Hawke's Bay Syrah – essentially a Shiraz but made in a subtler fashion than the Aussie style.

A liking for **champagne** no longer implies "champagne tastes" in New Zealand: you can still buy the wildly overpriced French stuff, but good Kiwi Méthode Traditionelle (fermented in the bottle in the time-honoured way) starts at around $13 a bottle. Montana's Lindauer Brut is widely available, and justly popular. Many people round out their restaurant meal with **dessert wines** (or "sticky"), typically made from grapes withered on the vine by the **botrytis** fungus, the so-called "noble rot".

Most bars and licensed restaurants have a tempting range of wines, many sold by the glass ($7–12; $8 and up for dessert wine), while in shops the racks groan under bottles starting from $11 ($15–25 for good quality).

If you want to try before you buy, visit a few wineries, where it is usually free to sample half a dozen different wines. There is sometimes a small fee, especially to try the reserve wines, but it is always redeemable if you buy a bottle or two. A good starting point for information on the Kiwi wine scene is ⓦnzwine.com.

Spirits

The big success story for New Zealand spirits is **42 Below vodka** (ⓦ42below.com). It's pretty good, and comes in numerous infused flavours including kiwifruit, passionfruit, and Kiwi favourites such as feijoa and manuka honey. They also make delicious South Gin (ⓦsouthgin.com).

The commercial success of these tipples has spawned Kiwi pretenders such as Stolen Rum (ⓦstolenrum.com), Smoke & Oakum's rum (ⓦgunpowderrum.com), Broken Shed vodka (ⓦbrikenshed.com) and others.

A few places, mostly in the south of the South Island, produce a little single malt **whisky**, the best being Oamaru's New Zealand Malt Whisky Co. (ⓦthenzwhisky.com). Minor players dabble in fruit **liqueurs**; some are delicious, though few visitors develop an enduring taste for the sickly sweet kiwifruit or feijoa varieties, which are mostly sold through souvenir shops.

Tea and coffee

Tea is usually a down-to-earth Indian blend (sometimes jocularly known as "gumboot"), though you may also have a choice of a dozen or so flavoured, scented and herbal varieties. **Coffee** drinking has been elevated to an art form with a specialized terminology: an Italian-style espresso is known as a **short black** (sometimes served with a jug of hot water so you can dilute it to taste); a weaker and larger version is a **long black**, which, with the addition of hot milk, becomes a **flat white**. Better places will serve all these decaffeinated, skinny or made with soya milk. Flavoured syrups are available but are not common.

The media

For a country of only some 4.3 million inhabitants, New Zealand has a vibrant media scene. Auckland claims to have more radio stations per capita than any other city in the world, and magazine racks are crammed with Kiwi-produced weeklies and monthlies. The standard of media coverage sometimes leaves a little to be desired, but for the most part this is a well-informed country with sophisticated tastes. Online, a good starting point is ⓦpublicaddress.net, the leading Kiwi blog site.

TV

New Zealanders receive five main free-to-air **broadcast channels**, a handful of local channels and Sky TV (which you'll find in most motels).

The biggest broadcaster is the state-owned **TVNZ**, which operates two advertising-heavy channels. TV ONE has slightly older and more information-based programming while TV2 is younger and more entertainment-oriented. Both channels present a diet of local news, current affairs, sport, drama and entertainment, plus a slew of US, British and Australian programmes: you'll find most of your favourites, often three to six months behind. Visitors may already be acquainted with long-running, home-grown Kiwi soap opera, Shortland Street, set in the fictional suburb of Ferndale in Auckland.

The main opposition comes from **TV3**, which pitches itself roughly between TV ONE and TV2, and **Prime**, backed by Sky TV, which often has quirkier programming.

Maori TV launched in 2004 with substantial government support (though it also has ads). Broadcasting in Maori and English, it promotes the language and culture but is far from a stuffy educational channel. Along with good movies and engaging Maori language lessons, you might catch Maori cooking shows, lifestyle makeovers, sitcoms and Maori angles on news, current affairs and sport.

Radio

New Zealand has few countrywide radio stations, but syndication means that some commercial stations can be heard in many parts of the country, with local commercials. All websites listed stream the channel over the **internet**.

For news, current affairs and a thoughtful look at the arts and music, tune into the government-funded **Radio New Zealand National** (101.0–101.6 FM; Ⓦ radionz.co.nz), which is the nearest New Zealand gets to, say, NPR or BBC Radio 4. You'll pick it up most places, though there are blank spots. Its sister station, **Radio New Zealand Concert** (89–100 FM), concentrates on classical music.

Though often amateurish, **student radio stations** provide excellent and varied "alternative" listening in their home cities. In Auckland tune to bFM (95.0; Ⓦ 95bfm.co.nz); in Wellington to Active (89.0; Ⓦ wradioactive.co.nz); in Christchurch to RDU (98.5; Ⓦ rdu.org.nz); and in Dunedin to Radio One (91.0; Ⓦ r1.co.nz).

The rest of the airwaves are clogged by **commercial stations**: keep an ear out for **KiwiFM** (102.1–102.5; Ⓦ www.kiwifm.co.nz), predominantly Kiwi music to Auckland, Wellington and Canterbury.

Newspapers and magazines

New Zealand has no national **daily newspaper**, but rather four major regional papers (all published Mon–Sat mornings) as well as a plethora of minor rags of mostly local interest. All are politically fairly neutral. The North Island is shared between the Auckland-based *New Zealand Herald* (Ⓦ nzherald .co.nz) and Wellington's *Dominion Post* (Ⓦ dom post.co.nz), while *The Press* (Ⓦ stuff.co.nz) covers Christchurch and its environs, and the *Otago Daily Times* (Ⓦ odt.co.nz) serves the far south of the country. All offer a pretty decent selection of national and international news, sport and reviews, often relying heavily on wire services and syndication deals with major British and American newspapers. On **Sunday**, check out the tabloid-style *Sunday News*; the superior, broadsheet *Sunday Star-Times*; or Auckland's *Herald on Sunday*.

Kiwi newspaper journalists get little scope for imaginative or investigative journalism, though the broad-ranging and slightly left-leaning **weekly magazine** the *Listener* (Ⓦ listener.co.nz) does it best. With coverage of politics, art, music, TV, radio, books, science, travel, architecture and much more, it's perhaps the best overall insight into what makes New Zealand tick.

Topics are covered in greater depth in the nationwide **monthly** *North and South*, though for an insight into the aspirations of Aucklanders you might be better off with the snappier glossy, *Metro*.

Specialist magazines cover the range: *Wilderness* (Ⓦ wildernessmag.co.nz) has a good spread of tramping, kayaking, climbing and mountain biking, and *Real Groove* is the best of the general music mags.

The bi-monthly *Mana* (Ⓦ manaonline.co.nz) pitches itself as "the Maori news magazine for all New Zealanders", and gives an insight into what sometimes seems like a parallel world barely acknowledged by the mainstream media. It is in English, but comes peppered with Maori words and concepts, with a convenient glossary.

Festivals and public holidays

In the southern hemisphere, Christmas falls near the start of the school summer holidays, which run from mid-December until early February. From Boxing Day through to the middle of January Kiwis hit the beaches en masse and during this time you'll find a lot more people about. Motels and campsites can be difficult to book and often raise their prices, though B&Bs and hostels rarely up their rates. To help you chart a path through the chaos, i-SITE visitor centres are open longer hours, as are many other tourist attractions. Other school holidays last for two weeks in mid- to late April, a fortnight in early to mid-July and the first two weeks of October, though these have a less pronounced effect.

Public holidays are big news in New Zealand and it can feel like the entire country has taken to the roads, so it's worth staying put rather than trying to travel on these days. Each region also takes one day a year to celebrate its **Anniversary Day**, remembering the founding of the original provinces that made up New Zealand, and generally celebrated with an agricultural show, horse-jumping, sheepshearing, cake-baking and best-vegetable contests and novelty events (such as gumboot throwing). We've listed official dates below, but days are usually observed on the nearest Monday (or occasionally Friday) to make a long weekend.

PUBLIC HOLIDAYS AND FESTIVAL CALENDAR

Many of the festivals listed below are covered in more detail in the relevant section of the guide. **PH** indicates a public holiday.

January 1 New Year's Day (PH) Whaleboat Racing Regatta, Kawhia (Ⓦ kawhiaharbour.co.nz); Highland Games, Waipu (Ⓦ highlandgames.co.nz).

January 2 (PH)

First Saturday in January Glenorchy Races (Ⓦ glenorchy-nz.co.nz).

January 17 Anniversary Day (PH in Southland).

January 22 Anniversary Day (PH in Wellington).

January 29 Anniversary Day (PH in Auckland, Northland, Waikato, Coromandel, Taupo and the Bay of Plenty), celebrated with a massive regatta on Auckland's Waitemata Harbour.

February 1 Anniversary Day (PH in Nelson).

February 6 Waitangi Day (PH); formal events at Waitangi.

First Saturday in February (in even-numbered years) Rippon Open Air Festival, Wanaka (see box, p.736).

First Saturday in February Martinborough Fair, Martinborough Ⓦ martinboroughfair.org.nz.

Second Saturday in February Wine Marlborough Festival, Blenheim (Ⓦ wine-marlborough-festival.co.nz).

Second weekend in February Coast-to-Coast multisport race, South Island (Ⓦ coasttocoast.co.nz).

Third weekend in February Art Deco Weekend, Napier (Ⓦ artdeconapier.com); Devonport Food, Wine & Music Festival (Ⓦ devonportwinefestival.co.nz).

Mid-February to early March Wellington Fringe Festival (Ⓦ fringe.org.nz).

Mid-February to mid-March Burst: The Festival of Flowers, Christchurch (Ⓦ festivalofflowers.co.nz).

Late February to late March NZ International Arts Festival, Wellington (even-numbered years only; Ⓦ nzfestival.co.nz).

First week in March Golden Shears sheepshearing competition in Masterton (Ⓦ goldenshears.co.nz).

First Saturday in March Martinborough Fair, Martinborough Ⓦ martinboroughfair.org.nz.

Second Saturday in March Pasifika Festival, Auckland (Ⓦ aucklandcouncil.govt.nz); Wildfoods Festival, Hokitika (Ⓦ wildfoods.co.nz).

Mid-March WOMAD world music festival, New Plymouth (see box, p.231); Sounds of Aotearoa, New Plymouth, featuring NZ's finest musicians (Ⓦ http://soundsaotearoa.com).

Mid-March Ellerslie International Flower Show, Christchurch (Ⓦ ellerslieflowershow.co.nz). NZ's largest, running for 5 days.

Mid-March Round-the-Bays Sunday fun run, Auckland (Ⓦ roundthebays.co.nz).

Third weekend in March Te Houtaewa Challenge and Te Houtaewa Surf Challenge, Ahipara (see box, p.184).

Closest Saturday to March 17 Ngaruawahia Maori Regatta, near Hamilton (see p.209).

March 23 Anniversary Day (PH in Otago).

March 31 Anniversary Day (PH in Taranaki).

Late March to late April Good Friday (PH) and Easter Sunday (PH).

Easter week Royal Easter Show, Auckland (Ⓦ royaleastershow .co.nz); Warbirds Over Wanaka airshow (even-numbered years only; see box, p.109); National Jazz Festival, Tauranga (Ⓦ jazz.org.nz).

April 25 ANZAC Day (PH). Dawn services at cenotaphs around the country.

Late April Five-day Festival of Colour, Wanaka (odd-numbered years only; see box, p.736).

Mid-April to late April Arrowtown Autumn Festival (Ⓦ arrowtownautumnfestival.org.nz).

First Monday in June Queen's Birthday (PH).

Middle weekend in June Fieldays, the southern hemisphere's largest agricultural show, Hamilton (Ⓦ fieldays.co.nz).

Mid- to late June Matariki, Maori New Year festivities (Ⓦ matarikievents.co.nz).

Late June to early July Queenstown Winter Festival (Ⓦ winterfestival.co.nz).

Early July to late November New Zealand International Film Festival, held for two weeks each in the nation's 14 largest cities (Ⓦ nzff.co.nz).

Third weekend in June Deco Decanted Jazz Festival, Napier (Ⓦ artdeconapier.com).

Early August Taranaki International Festival of the Arts (odd-numbered years only; see box, p.231).

Late September to early October Alexandra Blossom Festival (Ⓦ blossom.co.nz).

Late September to early October World of Wearable Art Awards (WOW), Wellington (Ⓦ worldofwearableart.com).

Fourth Monday in October Labour Day (PH).

October 31 Halloween.

Late October to early November Taranaki Garden Spectacular, New Plymouth (see box, p.231).

November 1 Anniversary Day (PH in Hawke's Bay and Marlborough).

November 5 Guy Fawkes' Night fireworks.

Second week in November New Zealand Cup & Show Week, Canterbury (Ⓦ nzcupandshow.co.nz).

Third Friday in November Anniversary Day (PH in Canterbury).

Third Sunday in November Toast Martinborough Wine, Food & Music Festival (Ⓦ toastmartinborough.co.nz).

December 1 Anniversary Day (PH in Westland).

Mid-December to January Festival of Lights, New Plymouth. See box, p.231.

December 25 Christmas Day (PH).

December 26 Boxing Day (PH).

Late Dec Rhythm and Vines three-day music festival, culminating on New Year's Eve, Gisborne (Ⓦ rhythmandvines.co.nz).

Outdoor activities

Life in New Zealand is tied to the Great Outdoors, and no visit to the country would be complete without spending a fair chunk of your time in intimate contact with nature.

Kiwis have long taken it for granted that within a few minutes' drive of their home they can find a deserted beach or piece of "bush" and wander freely through it, an attitude enshrined in a fabulous collection of national, forest and maritime parks. They are all administered by the **Department of Conservation** (DOC; ⓦdoc.govt.nz), which seeks to balance the maintenance of a fragile environment with the demands of tourism. For the most part it manages remarkably well, providing a superb network of signposted paths studded with trampers' huts, and operating visitor centres that present highly informative material about the local history, flora and fauna. They also publish excellent leaflets (downloadable online) for major walking tracks.

The lofty peaks of the Southern Alps offer challenging **mountaineering** and great **skiing**, while the lower slopes are ideal for multi-day **tramps** which cross low passes between valleys choked with subtropical and temperate rainforests. Along the coasts there are sheltered lagoons and calm harbours for gentle **swimming** and **boating**, but also sweeping strands battered by some top-class **surf**.

The country also promotes itself as the **adventure tourism** capital of the world. All over New Zealand you'll find places to bungy jump, whitewater or cave raft, jetboat, tandem skydive, mountain bike, scuba dive and much more – if you name it someone somewhere organizes it. While thousands of people participate in these activities every day without incident, standards of instructor training vary. It seems to be a point of honour for operators, instructors and guides to put the wind up you as much as possible. Such bravado shouldn't be interpreted as a genuine disregard for safety, but the fact remains that there have been a few well-publicized injuries and deaths – a tragic situation that's addressed by industry-regulated codes of practice, an independent system of accreditation and home-grown organizations that insist upon high levels of professionalism and safety instruction.

Before engaging in any adventure activities, check your insurance cover (see p.64).

Tramping

Tramping, trekking, bushwalking, hiking – call it what you will, it is one of the most compelling reasons to visit New Zealand, and for many the sole objective.

Hikes typically last three to five days, following well-worn trails through relatively untouched wilderness, often in one of the country's national parks. Along the way you'll be either camping out or staying in trampers' huts, and will consequently be lugging a pack over some rugged terrain, so a moderate level of fitness is required. If this sounds daunting, you can sign up with one of the guided tramping companies that maintain more salubrious huts or luxury lodges, provide meals and carry much of your gear. Details are given throughout the guide.

The main tramping season is in summer, from October to May, although the most popular tramps – the Milford, Routeburn and Kepler – are in the cooler southern half of the South Island, where the season is shorter by a few weeks at either end.

The tramps

Rugged terrain and a history of track-bashing by explorers and deer hunters has left New Zealand with a web of tramps following river valleys and linking up over passes, high above the bushline. As far as possible, we've indicated the degree of

---

TE ARAROA – THE LONG PATHWAY

Since the mid-1970s it has been a Kiwi dream to have a continuous path from one end of the country to the other. In recent years, **Te Araroa – The Long Pathway** (ⓦteararoa.org.nz) has been championed by the Te Araroa Trust, a private group that aspired to compete the whole 2900km route, from Cape Reinga to Bluff, which opened in December 2011. Short trails, built with the trust's involvement, link the fragmented network of existing tracks into a continuous whole. A provisional, impressively varied, route exists, much of it running through fairly remote country, although it intentionally visits small communities so that trampers can re-supply.

A few hardy souls have already tramped the whole route but it's envisaged that most people will tackle short sections.

difficulty of all tramps covered in the guide, broadly following DOC's classification system: a **path** is level, well graded and often wheelchair-accessible; **walking tracks** and **tramping tracks** (usually way-marked with red and white or orange flashes on trees) are respectively more arduous affairs requiring some fitness and proper walking equipment; and a **route** requires considerable tramping experience to cope with an ill-defined trail, frequently above the bushline. DOC's estimated **walking times** can trip you up: along paths likely to be used by families, for example, you can easily find yourself finishing in under half the time specified, but on serious routes aimed at fit trampers you might struggle to keep pace. We've given estimates for moderately fit individuals and, where possible, included the distance and amount of climbing involved, aiding route planning.

Invaluable information on walking directions, details of access, huts and an adequate map are contained in the excellent DOC tramp **leaflets** (usually $1 apiece). The title of each leaflet relating to an area is included in the appropriate places throughout this book, though we only include the price if it is $2 or over. Many are also available free online at ⓦ doc.govt.nz.

The maps in each DOC leaflet should be sufficient for trampers sticking to the designated route, but experienced walkers planning independent routes and folk after a more detailed vision of the terrain should fork out for specialized **maps** that identify all the features along the way. Most trampers' huts have a copy of the local area map pinned to the wall or laminated into the table. In describing tramps we have used "**true directions**" in relation to rivers and streams, whereby the left bank (the "true left") is the left-hand side of the river looking downstream.

Eight of New Zealand's finest, most popular tramps, plus one river journey, have been classified by DOC as **Great Walks** and are covered in detail in the guide. Great Walks get the lion's share of DOC track spending, resulting in relatively smooth, broad walkways, with boardwalks over muddy sections and bridges over almost every stream – a sanitized side of New Zealand tramping.

Access to tracks is seldom a problem in the most popular tramping regions, though it does require planning. Most finish some distance from their start, so taking your own vehicle is not much use; besides, cars parked at trailheads are an open invitation to thieves. Great Walks always have transport from the nearest town, but there are often equally stunning and barely used tramps close by which require a little more patience and tenacity to get to – we've included some of the best of the rest in the guide, listed under "Tramps" in the index.

TREMENDOUS TRAMPS

New Zealand is crisscrossed by thousands of kilometres of walking tracks. Eight of New Zealand's finest tramps, and one river journey, have been classified as Great Walks; even the most well-trodden of these reveal magnificent natural wonders in the raw.

NORTH ISLAND

The Tongariro Northern Circuit (3–4 days; see p.301) Takes in magnificent volcanic and semi-desert scenery.

Waikaremoana Track (3–4 days; see p.381) A gentle circumnavigation of one of the country's most beautiful lakes.

The Whanganui River Journey (2–4 days; see p.244) Best explored by canoe and a series of highly atmospheric short walks.

SOUTH ISLAND

The Abel Tasman Coast Track (2–4 days; see p.475) Skirts beaches and crystal-clear bays, ideally explored by sea kayak.

The Heaphy Track (4–5 days; see p.488) Passes through the Kahurangi National Park, balancing subalpine tops and surf-pounded beaches.

The Kepler Track (4 days; see p.759) Renowned for ridge walks and virgin beech forest.

Milford Track (4 days; see p.771) The world-famous track accesses stunning glaciated alpine scenery and stupendous waterfalls.

The Rakiura Track (3 days; see p.630) Follows the rainforest-bordered coast of Stewart Island and provides opportunities to see kiwi in the wild.

The Routeburn Track (3 days; see p.718) One of the country's finest walks, with quality time spent above the bushline.

Backcountry accommodation: huts and camping

New Zealand's backcountry is strung with a network of almost nine hundred **trampers' huts**, sited less than a day's walk apart, frequently in beautiful surroundings. All are simple, communal affairs that fall into five distinct categories as defined by DOC.

Basic Huts (free) are often crude and rarely encountered on the major tramps. Next up is the **Standard Hut** ($5.10/person/night): basic, weatherproof, usually equipped with individual bunks or sleeping platforms accommodating a dozen or so, an external long-drop toilet and a water supply. There is seldom any heating and there are no cooking facilities. **Serviced Huts** ($15.30) tend to be larger, sleeping twenty or more on bunks with mattresses. Water is piped indoors to a sink, and flush toilets are occasionally encountered. Again, you'll need to bring your own stove and cooking gear, but heating is provided; if the fire is a woodburning one, you should replace any firewood you use. More sophisticated still are the **Great Walk Huts**, found along the Great Walks. They tend to have separate bunkrooms, gas rings for cooking (but no utensils), stoves for heating, a drying room and occasionally solar-powered lighting. Great Walks huts cost $15–52 per adult per night. Children of school age generally pay half the adult fee and, thanks to a DOC initiative, under-18s can now use Great Walk huts and campsites for free – though you must still book in advance.

Hut fees are best paid in advance online, at the local DOC office, visitor centre or other outlet close to the start of the track. If you're planning to tramp any of the Great Walks you **must** buy a **Great Walks Hut Pass**, covering the cost of your accommodation for the walk you intend to complete, and carry the confirmation with you, otherwise the wardens will charge you for each hut again. The pass and reservation, made simultaneously, guarantee trekkers a bed on the Kepler, Milford, Routeburn, Abel Tasman and Heaphy. No similar reservation is made with a hut pass bought for the remaining Great Walks, primarily because it's considered very unlikely that each hut will fill up.

To get more information about the Great Walks and other tramps, check Ⓦtramper.co.nz.

In winter (May–Sept) the huts on Great Walks are often stripped of heating and cooking facilities and downgraded to Standard status, so if you have a Hut Pass you can use them, though possessing the pass or a ticket doesn't guarantee you a bunk; beds go on a first-come-first-served basis.

Should you wish to do a lot of tramping outside the Great Walks system, or on the Great Walks out of season, it's worth buying a **Backcountry Hut Pass** ($122.60 for 12 months; $92 for 6 months), which allows you to stay in all Standard and Serviced huts.

Camping is allowed on all tracks except the Milford. Rules vary, but in most cases you're required to minimize environmental impact by camping close to the huts, whose facilities (toilets, water and gas rings where available) you can use.

Equipment

Tramping in New Zealand can be a dangerous and/or dispiriting experience if you're not equipped for both hot, sunny days and wet, cold and windy weather, as conditions can change rapidly. The best tramps pass through some of the world's wettest regions, with parts of the Milford Track receiving over 6m of rain a year. It's essential to carry a good waterproof jacket. Keeping your lower half dry is less crucial and many Kiwis tramp in shorts. Early starts often involve wading through long, sodden grass, so a pair of knee-length gaiters can be useful. Comfortable boots with good ankle support are a must; take suitably broken-in leather boots or lightweight walking boots, and some comfortable footwear for the day's end. You'll also need a warm jacket or jumper, plus a good sleeping bag; even the heated huts are cold at night and a warm hat never goes amiss. All this, along with lighter clothing for sunny days, should be kept inside a robust backpack, preferably lined with a strong waterproof liner such as those sold at DOC offices.

Once on the tramp, you need to be totally self-sufficient. On Great Walks, you should carry **cooking** gear; on other tramps you also need a cooking stove and fuel. **Food** can be your heaviest burden; freeze-dried meals are light and reasonably tasty but expensive; many cost-conscious trampers prefer pasta or rice, dried soups for sauces, a handful of fresh vegetables, muesli, milk powder and bread or crackers for lunch. Consider taking biscuits, trail mix (known as "scroggin"), tea, coffee and powdered fruit drinks (the Raro brand is good), and energy-boosting spreads. All huts have drinking **water** but DOC advise treating water taken from lakes and rivers to protect yourself from giardia; see p.63 for more on this and water-purification methods.

You should also carry basic supplies: a first aid kit, blister kit, sunscreen, insect repellent; a torch (flashlight) with spare battery and bulb, candles, matches or a lighter; and a compass (though few bother on the better-marked tracks).

In the most popular tramping areas you will be able to **rent equipment**. Most important of all, remember that you'll have to carry all this stuff for hours each day. Hotels and hostels in nearby towns will generally let you leave your surplus gear either free or for a small fee.

Safety

Most people spend days or weeks tramping in New Zealand with nothing worse than stiff legs and a few sandfly bites, but **safety** is nonetheless a serious issue and deaths occur every year. The culprit is usually New Zealand's fickle **weather**. It cannot be stressed too strongly that within an hour (even in high summer) a warm, cloudless day can turn bitterly cold, with high winds driving in thick banks of track-obscuring cloud. Heeding the weather forecast (posted in DOC offices) is crucial, as is carrying warm, windproof and water-proof clothing.

Failed **river crossings** are also a common cause of tramping fatalities. If you are confronted with something that looks too dangerous to cross, then it is, and you should wait until the level falls or backtrack. If the worst happens and you get swept away while crossing, don't try to stand up; you may trap your leg between rocks and drown. Instead, lie on your back and float feet first until you reach a place where swimming to the bank is feasible.

If you do get lost or injured, your chances of being found are better if you've left word of your intentions with a **friend** or with a **trusted person** at your next port of call, who will realize you are overdue. DOC make no attempt to track hikers so make your intentions clear to friends by using Ⓦ adventuresmart.org .nz., but by the time they're checked you could have been missing too long for it to matter. While on the tramp, fill in the hut logs as you go, so that your movements can be traced, and check in with the folk you told about the trip on your return.

Animals are not a problem in the bush, the biggest irritants being sandflies whose bites itch (often insufferably), or kea, alpine parrots that delight in pinching anything they can get their beaks into and tearing it apart to fulfil their curiosity.

Swimming, surfing and windsurfing

Kiwi life is inextricably linked with the beach, and from Christmas to the end of March (longer in warmer northern climes), a weekend isn't complete without a dip or a waterside barbecue – though you should never underestimate the ferocity of the southern **sun** (see p.63 for precautions). Some of the most picturesque beaches stretch away into salt spray from the pounding Tasman surf or Pacific rollers. **Swimming** here can be very hazardous, so only venture into the water at beaches patrolled by surf lifesaving clubs and always swim between the flags, see box, p.63. Spotter planes patrol the most popular beaches and warn of the occasional **shark**, so if you notice everyone heading for the safety of the beach, get out of the water.

New Zealand's coastline offers near-perfect conditions for **surfing** and windsurfing. At major beach resorts there is often an outlet renting dinghies, catamarans, canoes and windsurfers; in regions where there is reliably good surf you might also come across boogie boards and surfboards, and seaside hostels often have a couple for guests' use. For more information, see Ⓦ surf.co.nz and Ⓦ surf2surf.co.nz.

Sailing

New Zealand's numerous harbours, studded with small islands and ringed with deserted bays, make **sailing** a favourite pursuit, which explains why New Zealand and Kiwi sailors have been so influential in the fate of the America's Cup. People sail year-round, but the summer months from December to March are busiest. Unless you befriend a yachtie you'll probably be limited to commercial yacht **charters** (expensive and with a skipper), more reasonably priced and often excellent **day-sailing trips**, or renting a dinghy for some inshore antics.

Scuba diving and snorkelling

The waters around New Zealand offer wonderful opportunities to scuba **dive** and **snorkel**. What they lack in long-distance visibility, tropical warmth and colourful fish they make up for with the range of diving environments. Pretty much anywhere along the more sheltered eastern side of both islands you'll find somewhere with rewarding snorkelling, but much the best and most accessible spot is the **Goat Island Marine Reserve**, in Northland, where there's a superb range of habitats close to the shore. Northland also has world-class scuba diving at the **Poor Knights Islands Marine Reserve**, reached by boat from Tutukaka, and wreck diving on the *Rainbow Warrior*, from Matauri Bay, plus a stack of good sites around Great Barrier Island. On the South Island, there are wrecks worth exploring off **Picton** and fabulous growths of **black and red corals** relatively close to the surface, in the southwestern fiords near Milford.

MULTI-DAY TOURS

Tours included in this box involve taking part in one or other or, in extreme cases, all of the activities featured in this section. Although New Zealand is an easy place to explore independently, tours offer specialist insight, logistical help and company along the way.

HIKING AND WILDLIFE

Active Earth ⓦactiveearthnewzealand .com. Suitable for anyone who is reasonably fit and wants to see things few other tourists will. Good-humoured and informative guides take small groups tramping, climbing and wilderness camping in virtually untouched country from $920 for four nights.

Hiking New Zealand ⓦhikingnewzealand .com. Conservation-minded company offering everything from hiking trips around the far north of Northland (6 days; $995) to boat trips to NZ's sub-Antarctic islands (9 days; $4082, plus US$250 landing fees).

Kiwi Wildlife Tours ⓦkiwi-wildlife.co.nz. Upmarket small-group birding tours starting at around $300/person/day.

Kiwi Wildlife Walks ⓦnzwalk.com. Expertly run guided walks including Stewart Island, where they go kiwi spotting (4 days; $1995).

Real Journeys ⓦrealjourneys.co.nz. Professionally run trips include an overnight cruise on the *Fiordland Navigator*, taking in Doubtful Sound (quad-share/double from $263/473), with on-board kayaks.

Ruggedy Range ⓦruggedyrange.com. Stewart Island-based company offering enthusiastic and entertaining trips visiting the unique wildlife (from 1 day, 1 night; $470).

CYCLING, HORSE RIDING AND KAYAKING

Adventure South ⓦadvsouth.co.nz. This environmentally conscious company runs guided cycling and multi-activity tours around the South Island, with accommodation in characterful lodges or track huts – for example, 21 days cycling (and walking) on the South Island ($9659). All tours carry a single supplement.

Alpine Horse Safaris, Waitohi Downs ⓦalpinehorse.co.nz. Treks intended for serious riders, including food and accommodation, that follow old mining tracks well away from civilization, or at least roads (4 days; $1340).

Cycle Touring Company ⓦcycletours .co.nz. Tailored self-led or guided tours of Northland, with several routes of 2–21 days, and the option to have your gear carried for you. Accommodation is in lodges and homestays (or a cheaper backpacker option). Prices start around $1607 for seven

nights if you carry your gear.

New Zealand Sea Kayak Adventures ⓦnzkayaktours.com. Fully catered Northland- and Bay of Islands-based guided sea kayak camping tours catering to a wide range of abilities, including a popular seven-day trip ($1225).

Pacific Cycle Tours ⓦbike-nz.com. Mountain-bike, road-bike and hiking tours round both islands with varying degrees of adventurousness, including a five-day cycling and wine-tasting trip (from $835).

Pakiri Beach Horse riding ⓦhorseride-nz .co.nz. Highly professional multi-day tours through native bush and along clifftops including an epic coast-to-coast trip (7 days; $3999).

Pedaltours ⓦpedaltours.co.nz. Guided road- and mountain-biking tours of both islands, including a week-long ride around the Nelson Lakes ($3150).

For the inexperienced, the easiest way to get a taste of what's under the surface is to take a **resort dive** with an instructor. If you want to dive independently, you need to be PADI-qualified. For more information consult ⓦdivenewzealand.com.

Rafting

The combination of challenging rapids and gorgeous scenery makes **whitewater rafting** one of New Zealand's most thrilling adventure activities. Visitor numbers and weather restrict the main **rafting season** to October to May, and most companies set an **age limit** at 12. You'll usually be supplied with everything except a swimming costume and an old pair of trainers and, after safety instruction, spend a couple of hours or so on the water.

Thrilling though it is, rafting is also one of the most **dangerous** of the adventure activities, claiming a number of lives in recent years. Operators have a self-imposed code of practice, but there are still cowboys out there. It might be stating the obvious but fatalities happen when people fall out of rafts: heed the guide's instructions about how best to stay on board and how to protect yourself if you do get a dunking.

Canoeing and kayaking

New Zealand is a paddler's paradise, and pretty much anywhere with water nearby has somewhere you can rent either canoes or kayaks. Sometimes this is simply an opportunity to muck around in boats but often there are guided trips available, with the emphasis being on soaking up the scenery. The scenic **Whanganui River** is a perennial favourite.

Jetboating

The shallow, braided rivers of the high Canterbury sheep country posed access difficulties for run-owner Bill Hamilton, who got around the problem by inventing the **Hamilton Jetboat** in the early 1960s. His inspired invention could plane in as little as 100mm of water, reach prodigious speeds (up to 80km/hr) and negotiate rapids while maintaining astonishing, turn-on-a-sixpence manoeuvrability.

The jetboat carried its first fare-paying passengers on a deep and glassy section of the Shotover River, which is still used by the pioneering Shotover Jet. **Rides** last around thirty eye-streaming minutes, time enough for hot dogging and as many 360-degree spins as anyone needs. **Wilderness trips** can last two hours or longer.

Bungy jumping and bridge swinging

For maximum adrenaline, minimum risk and greatest expense, bungy jumping is difficult to beat. Commercial bungy jumping was pioneered by Kiwi speed skiers A.J. Hackett and Henry Van Asch. They began pushing the bungy boundaries, culminating in Hackett's jump from the Eiffel Tower in 1987. He was promptly arrested, but the publicity sparked worldwide interest that continues to draw bungy aspirants to New Zealand's sites – some of the world's best, with bridges over deep canyons and platforms cantilevered out over rivers. The first commercial operation was set up just outside Queenstown on the 43m Kawerau Suspension

Bridge. Its accessible location and the chance to be dunked in the river make this the most popular jump of many on both islands. For a bit of variety you could try a close relative of the bungy, **bridge swinging**, which provides a similar gut-wrenching fall accompanied by a super-fast swing along a gorge while harnessed to a cable.

Canyoning

The easiest way to get your hands on New Zealand rock is to go **canyoning** (or its near relative by the sea, **coasteering**), which involves following steep and confined river gorges or streambeds down chutes and over waterfalls for a few hours, sliding, jumping and abseiling all the way. Guided trips are available in a handful of places, the most accessible being in Auckland, Queenstown, Turangi and Wanaka.

Mountaineering

In the main, New Zealand is better suited to **mountaineering** than rock climbing, though most of what is available is fairly serious stuff, suitable only for well-equipped parties with a good deal of experience. For most people the only way to get above the snowline is to tackle the easy summit of Mount Ruapehu, the North Island's highest point, the summit of Mount Taranaki, near New Plymouth, or pay for a guided ascent of one of the country's classic peaks. Prime candidates are New Zealand's highest mountain, Aoraki/Mount Cook (3754m), accessed from the climbers' heartland of Aoraki/ Mount Cook Village, and the nation's most beautiful peak, the pyramidal Mount Aspiring (3030m), approached from Wanaka. In both cases networks of climbers' huts are used as bases for what are typically twenty-hour attempts on the summit.

Flying, skydiving and paragliding

Almost every town in New Zealand seems to harbour an airstrip or a helipad, and there's inevitably someone happy to get you airborne for half an hour's **flightseeing**. Helicopters cost around fifty percent more than planes and can't cover the same distances but score on manoeuvrability and the chance to land. If money is tight take a regular flight somewhere you want to go anyway. First choice here would have to be the journey from either Wanaka or Queenstown to Milford Sound, which overflies the very best of Fiordland.

In **tandem skydiving**, a double harness links you to an instructor, who has control of the parachute. The plane circles up to around 2500m and after you leap out together, you experience around 45 seconds of eerie freefall before the instructor pulls the ripcord.

Tandem paragliding involves you and an instructor jointly launching off a hilltop, slung below a manoeuvrable parachute, for perhaps ten to twenty minutes of graceful gliding and stomach-churning banked turns. Alternatively **tandem hang-gliding** or **parasailing** are usually available.

Skiing and snowboarding

New Zealand's **ski season** (roughly June–Oct) starts as snows on northern hemisphere slopes melt away, which, combined with the South Island's backbone of 3000m peaks, the North Island's equally lofty volcanoes and the relative cheapness of the skiing, means New Zealand is an increasingly popular inter-national ski destination. Most fields are geared to the domestic downhill market, and the eastern side of the Southern Alps is littered with **club fields** sporting a handful of rope tows, simple lifts and a motley collection of private ski lodges. They're open to all-comers, but some are only accessible by 4WD vehicles, others have a long walk in, and ski schools are almost unheard of. Throughout the country there are, however, a dozen exceptions to this norm: **commercial resorts**, with high-speed chairs, ski schools, gear rental and groomed wide-open slopes. What you won't find are massive on-site resorts of the scale found in North America and Europe; skiers commute daily to the slopes from nearby après-ski towns and **gear rental** is either from shops in these or on the field.

The main **North Island ski-fields** include the country's two largest and most popular skiing destinations, Turoa and Whakapapa, both on the volcanic Mount Ruapehu.

On the **South Island**, the west coast of the Southern Alps offers a variety of glacier-climbing experiences on the Franz Josef and Fox glaciers. On the other side of the Alps you can shoot up to Mount Cook and take a boat or a kayak to the foot of a glacier and watch the ice crumble. Mix all this in with the party atmosphere and uncrowded runs on the commercial ski-fields – Coronet Peak and The Remarkables by Queenstown; Treble Cone, Cardrona and the Waiorau Snow Farm near Wanaka; and Porter Heights and Mount Hutt, both within two hours' drive of Christchurch – and you're guaranteed a memorable time, as well as some of the most spectacular snow-dusted scenery you'll ever see.

The best up-to-date source of skiing information is the annual **Ski & Snowboard Guide** published by Brown Bear Publications (W brownbear.co.nz). It is freely downloadable from the website, and the printed guide can be picked up from visitor centres ($5). For each field it gives a detailed rundown of facilities, season length, lift ticket prices and an indication of suitability for beginners, intermediates and advanced skiers. Heli-skiing is also dealt with and there's coverage of the main ski towns. Another **website** for all things skiing in New Zealand is W snow.co.nz.

Fishing

All around the coast there are low-key canoe, yacht and launch trips on which there is always time for a little **casual fishing**, but you'll also find plenty of trips aimed at more dedicated anglers. From December to May these scout the seas off the northern half of the North Island for marlin, shark and tuna. Regulations and bag limits are covered on the Ministry of Fisheries website, W fish.govt.nz.

Inland, the **rivers** and **lakes** are choked with rainbow and brown trout, quinnat and Atlantic salmon, all introduced for sport at the end of the nineteenth century. Certain areas have gained enviable reputations: Lake Taupo is world-renowned for its rainbow trout; South Island rivers, particularly around Gore, boast the finest brown trout; and the braided gravel-bed rivers draining the eastern slopes of the Southern Alps bear superb salmon.

A national **fishing licence** ($113 for the year from Oct 1–Sept 30, $22.50/24hr) covers all New Zealand's lakes and rivers except for those in the Taupo catchment area, where a local licensing arrangement applies. They're available from sports shops everywhere and directly from Fish and Game New Zealand (W fishandgame.org.nz), the agency responsible for managing freshwater sports fisheries. The website also lists bag limits and local regulations.

Wherever you fish, **regulations** are taken seriously and are rigidly enforced. If you're found with an undersize catch or an over-full bag, heavy fines may be imposed and equipment confiscated. Other fishy websites include W fishinginnew zealand.com and W fishing.net.nz.

Horse trekking

New Zealand's highly urbanized population leaves a huge amount of countryside available for horse **trekking**, occasionally along beaches, often through patches of native bush and tracts of farmland. There are schools everywhere and all levels of experience are catered for, but more experienced riders might prefer the greater scope of full-day or even week-long wilderness treks (see box, p.52). We've highlighted some noteworthy places and operators throughout the guide, and there's a smattering of others listed at Ⓦtruenz.co .nz/horsetrekking.

Mountain biking

You'll find a stack of places renting **mountain bikes**. The main trail-biking areas around Rotorua, Queenstown, Mount Cook and Hanmer Springs will often have a couple of companies willing to take you out on **guided rides**. For information about Kiwi **off-road biking** consult Ⓦmountainbike.co.nz.

Spectator sports

If God were a rugby coach almost every New Zealander would be a religious fundamentalist. News coverage often gives headline prominence to sport, particularly the All Blacks, and entire radio stations are devoted to sports talkback, usually dwelling on occasions when Kiwi underdogs overcome better-funded teams from more populous nations.

Most major sports events are televised. Increasingly these are on subscription-only Sky TV, which encourages a devoted following in pubs.

Anyone with a keen interest in sport or just Kiwi culture should attend a rugby game. Local papers advertise games along with ticket booking details. **Bookings** for many of the bigger events can be made through Ticketek (Ⓦticketek.co.nz), although, except for the over-subscribed internationals and season finals, you can usually just buy a ticket at the gate.

Rugby

Opponents quake in their boots at the sight of fifteen strapping **All Blacks**, the national **rugby** team, performing their pre-match *haka*, and few spectators remain unmoved. Kiwi hearts swell at the sight, secure in the knowledge that their national team is always among the world's best, and anything less than a resounding victory is considered a case for national mourning in the leader columns of the newspapers. The All Blacks made up for their recent relative failure in the **Rugby World Cup** by winning the 2011 competition on home soil, defeating France.

Rugby is played through the winter, the season kicking off with the **Super 15 series** (mid-Feb to May) in which regional southern hemisphere teams (five apiece from New Zealand, South Africa and Australia) play each other with the top four teams going on to contest the finals series. Super 15 players make up the All Blacks team which, through the middle of winter, hosts an international test series or two, including the annual **tri-nations series** (mid-July to Aug) against South Africa and Australia. Games between the All Blacks and Australia also contest the **Bledisloe Cup**, which creates much desired bragging rights for one or other nation for a year.

The international season often runs over into the **National Provincial Championship** (NPC), played from the middle of August until the end of October. Each province has a team, the bigger competing in the first division with the minor provinces generally filling up the second division. Throughout the season of the **Ranfurly Shield** (Ⓦscrum.co.nz), affectionately known as the "log of wood", the holders accept challenges at their home ground, and the winner takes all. Occasionally minor teams will wrest the shield, and in the smaller provinces this is a huge source of pride, subsequent defences prompting a huge swelling of community spirit.

Domestic rugby ticket prices vary, depending on where you are in the ground, but start at around $15, while a similar seat for an international will start at $45. To find out more, visit the New Zealand Rugby Union's official **website** Ⓦnzrugby.co.nz.

Rugby league (Ⓦrugbyleague.co.nz and Ⓦnzrl .co.nz) has always been regarded as rugby's poor cousin, though success at international level has raised its profile. New Zealand's only significant provincial team are the Auckland-based **Warriors**, who play in Australia's NRL during the March to early September season, with home games played at Mount Smart Stadium, where you can buy tickets at the gate. The top eight teams in the league go through to the finals series in September.

Cricket

Most visitors spend their time in New Zealand from October to March, when the stadiums are turned over to the country's traditional summer sport, **cricket** (Ⓦnzcricket.co.nz). The national team – the

Black Caps – hover around mid-table in international test and one-day rankings but periodic flashes of brilliance – and the odd unexpected victory over Australia – keep fans interested. You can usually just turn up at a ground and buy a **ticket**, though games held around Christmas and New Year fill up fast and internationals "sell out" in advance. **Tickets** start at around $25–30 for an international, less for a domestic match.

Other sports

Other team sports lag far behind rugby and cricket, though women's **netball** (@netballnz.co.nz) has an enthusiastic following and live TV coverage of the Silver Ferns' international fixtures gets good audiences.

Although more youngsters play **soccer** than rugby, it was the New Zealand All Whites' participation in the 2010 World Cup (the only team not to lose a game, with three draws in the group stage) that boosted the game's profile nationally. For domestic fixtures, see @nzfootball.co.nz. New Zealand's only representative in the Australian A-League (@a-league.com.au) is the Wellington Phoenix (@wellingtonphoenix.com). The season runs from October to early April and home games are played at Westpac Stadium in Wellington; **tickets** (from around $40 for a domestic match) can be bought at the gate or on the team's website.

Auckland is a frequent midway point for round-the-world **yacht** races and has twice hosted the **America's Cup**. New Zealand's **Olympic** heritage is patchy, with occasional clutches of medals from rowing and yachting and a long pedigree of **middle-distance runners**. These days, however, multi-event championships and endurance events like triathlons and Iron Man races seem to dominate.

Culture and etiquette

Ever since Maori arrived in the land they named Aotearoa, New Zealand has been a nation of immigrants. The majority of residents trace their roots back to Britain and Ireland, and northern European culture prevails with a strong Maori and Polynesian influence. New Zealand's policy of bi-culturalism gives Maori and Pakeha (white European) values equal status, at least nominally. In practice, the operation of Parliament and the legal system is rooted in the old country, the Queen continues as head of state and beams out from all coins and the $20 note, and, along with "God Defend New Zealand", "God Save the Queen" remains one of the country's two official national anthems.

That said, **Maori** are very much part of mainstream contemporary NZ society (see p.799). The racial tension that does exist mostly stays below the surface (aside from some issue-specific protests), and as a visitor you'll experience little and probably come away from New Zealand with the impression of a relatively tolerant society.

In the last couple of decades **Asian immigration** (principally from China and Korea, as well as the Indian subcontinent) has seen Asians make up around seven percent of the population (around half that of Maori) nationwide. In the Auckland region, though, this figure rises to over eighteen percent, making some form of tri-culturalism a possibility in the future.

Notwithstanding this mix, the archetypal **Kiwi personality** is rooted in the desire to make a better life in a unique and sometimes unaccommodating land. New Zealanders are inordinately fond of stories of plucky little Kiwis overcoming great odds and succeeding, perceiving the NZ persona to be rooted in self-reliance, inventiveness and bravery, tempered by a certain self-deprecating humour. Over-achieving "tall poppies" are routinely cut down.

Sport is a huge passion; the country has consistently punched above its weight in international competition, especially on the rugby field. Despite a reputation for a rugby-playing, beer-swilling, male-dominated culture, Kiwis like to point out that they run an open-minded and egalitarian society, in everything from women's suffrage to nuclear-free waters (see p.796), and broadly liberal social attitudes prevail, with Japanese whaling and genetic modification hot topics.

New Zealand's relationship with its larger neighbour, Australia, is a cause for endless entertainment on both sides of "the ditch" (the Tasman Sea). Kiwis and **Aussies** are like siblings: there are lots of scraps (mostly just good-natured ribbing), especially when it comes to sport, but they're the first to jump to each other's defence in everything from military conflict to pub brawls.

Etiquette

New Zealanders are refreshingly relaxed, low-key and free of pretension, and you're likely to be greeted with an informal "gidday!", "Kia ora!" (Hi) or "Kia ora, bro!" (Hi, mate). **Dress standards** are as informal as the greetings, and unless you're on business or have a diplomatic function to attend you can leave your suit and tie at home; even the finest restaurants only require smart attire.

The legal **drinking age** is 18, but by law you may be asked to prove your age by showing ID, which must be either a New Zealand driver's licence or a passport (foreign driver's licences aren't accepted).

Smoking is increasingly outlawed. It's banned on all public transport and in public buildings and some outdoor areas – see ⓦsmokefreecouncils .org.nz.

The Kiwi attitude to **tipping** is pleasingly uncomplicated. No tip is expected, though reward for excellent service in restaurants and cafés is appreciated.

Shopping

One of the most popular souvenirs from NZ is a curvaceous greenstone (jade) pendant, probably based on a Maori design. They're available all over the country, though it makes sense to buy close to the main source of raw material around Greymouth and Hokitika on the West Coast of the South Island. Most of the cheaper goods are manufactured from Chinese jade, which is regarded as inferior: for the genuine article, insist on NZ *pounamu* carved locally (see box, p.664).

A variation on this theme is the **bone pendant**. Several places around the country give you a chance to work a piece of cattle bone into your own design or something based on classic Maori iconography. With a little talent and application you should be able to whip up something to be proud of in a few hours. Something similar can be made of iridescent paua shell, or you can simply buy ready-made pieces fashioned into anything from buttons to detailed picture frames.

Sheepskin and **wool** products are also big, as are garments – socks, sweaters etc – at least partly made from **possum fur**. New Zealanders hate these pests and will thank you for supporting any industry which hastens their demise. A quality possum-fur throw will set you back over $1000 but cushion covers come much cheaper. Sheepskins go for around $100.

There's plenty of outdoor clothing around, but look out for the Icebreaker (ⓦicebreaker.com), Untouched World (ⓦuntouchedworld.co.nz) and Glowing Sky (ⓦglowingsky.co.nz) brands of stylish Merino-wool garments, which are fairly pricey but feel great, keep you warm and don't harbour nasty odours.

Some of New Zealand's top fashion designers are world-class. Garments by Karen Walker, Kate Sylvester, Trelise Cooper, Alexandra Owen, Zambesi and World are expensive but coveted and unique.

Travelling with children

New Zealand is a child-friendly place, and while other people's kids aren't revered in the way they are in Mediterranean Europe, if you're travelling with children you'll find broad acceptance.

Accommodation is well geared for families: family rooms are almost always available at motels and hostels, and holiday parks (campsites) typically offer self-contained units where the whole family can be together. The better holiday parks also have kids' play areas and often a swimming pool. To be more self-sufficient, consider renting a medium-sized **campervan** with its own shower and toilet, though the downside is that you'll have no escape.

Travelling around you'll find **public toilets** in most towns and anywhere tourists congregate – cleanliness standards are usually good.

Older kids can often join in adult **adventure activities**, though restrictions may apply. Bungy operators usually require a **minimum age** of 10, though this might rise to 12 or 13 for the bigger jumps. Whitewater rafting is typically limited to those 13 and over, though there are a few easier family-oriented trips. Similar restrictions apply to other activities – ask when you book. **Family tickets** are often available and usually cost about the same as two adults and one child.

Children are welcomed in most cafés and **restaurants**, and most will make a reasonable effort to accommodate you.

Living in New Zealand

New Zealand is the sort of place people come for a short visit and end up wanting to stay (at least for a few months). Unless you have substantial financial backing, this will probably mean finding some work. And while your earning potential in New Zealand isn't necessarily going to be great, you can at least supplement your budget for multiple bungy jumps, skydiving lessons and the like. Paid casual work is typically in tourism-linked service industries, or in orchard work.

For the last few years unemployment has remained relatively low and, providing you have the necessary paperwork, finding casual work shouldn't be too difficult, while better-paid, short-term **professional jobs** are quite possible if you have the skills. Employment agencies are a good bet for this sort of work, or simply look at general job-search websites such as ⓦsearch4jobs.co.nz and the jobs section of ⓦtrademe.co.nz. The **minimum wage** for all legally employed folk over the age of 16 (other than 16- and 17-year-old new entrants or trainees) is $13 an hour. If you'd rather not tackle the red tape you can simply reduce your travelling costs by **working for your board** (though technically the Immigration Department still considers this to be work).

Working for board and lodging

A popular way of getting around the country cheaply is to **work for your board and lodging**, typically toiling for 4–6 hours a day. **FHiNZ** (Farm Helpers in New Zealand; ⓦfhinz.co.nz) organizes stays on farms, orchards and horticultural holdings for singles, couples and families; no experience is needed. Almost two hundred places are listed in its booklet ($25; sold online) and accommodation ranges from basic to quite luxurious. The international **WWOOF** (Willing Workers on Organic Farms; ⓦwwoof.co.nz) coordinates over a thousand properties (membership, for one or a couple, with online access $40 or printed booklet $50), mostly farms but also orchards, market gardens and self-sufficiency-orientated smallholdings, all using organic methods to a greater or lesser degree. They'll expect a stay of around five nights, though much longer periods are common; you **book direct** (preferably a week or more in advance).

There have been occasional reports of taskmasters; make sure you discuss what's expected before you commit yourself. Property managers are vetted but **solo women** may prefer placements with couples or families. Other organizations have fewer guarantees, though many are perfectly reputable.

A similar organization is the online **Help Exchange** (ⓦhelpx.net), which supplies a regularly updated list of hosts on farms as well as at homestays, B&Bs, hostels and lodges, who need extra help in return for meals and accommodation; you register online and book direct.

Visas, permits and red tape

Australians can work legally in New Zealand without any paperwork. Otherwise, if you're aged 18–30, the easiest way to work legally is through the **Working Holiday Scheme** (WHS), which gives you a temporary work permit valid for twelve months. An unlimited number of Brits, Irish, Americans, Canadians, Japanese, Belgian, Danish, Finnish, French, German, Italian, Dutch, Norwegian and Swedish people in this age bracket are eligible each year, plus various annual quotas of Argentinians, Brazilians, Chilean, Chinese, Czech, Estonians, Hong Kong citizens, Koreans, Latvians, Polish, Singaporeans, Spanish, Malaysians, Maltese, Mexicans, Peruvians, Taiwanese, Thai, Turkish and Uruguayans on a first-come-first-served basis; apply as far in advance as you can. You'll need a passport, NZ$140 for the application, evidence of an onward ticket out of New Zealand (or the funds to pay for it), and a minimum of NZ$350 per month of your intended stay (or, depending on your country of origin, NZ$4200 in total) to show you can support yourself. Some nationals can (and in some instances must) apply online (using a Visa or MasterCard). Brits can apply for a 23-month stay, the last 11 months of which can be applied for in New Zealand as an extension. Working holiday-makers who can show they've worked in the horticulture or viticulture industries for at least three months may be eligible to obtain an extra three-month stay in New Zealand with a **Working Holidaymaker Extension** (WHE) permit. Applications are made through **Immigration New Zealand** (☏09 914 4100, ⓦimmigration.govt.nz), which has details and downloadable forms on its website.

Some visitors are tempted to **work illegally**, something for which you could be fined or deported. However, there is a variety of other visa options, including the new Silver Fern visa for 20–35-year-olds, and visas for seasonal horticulture and viticulture seasonal work – contact the **Immigration Service** for details. The only other legal option is trying to gain resident status – not something to be tackled lightly.

Anyone working legally in New Zealand needs to obtain a **tax number** from the local Inland Revenue Department office (⓪ird.govt.nz); without this your employer will have trouble paying you. The process can take up to ten working days, though you can still work while the wheels of bureaucracy turn. Depending on your level of income, the tax department rakes in from 10.50 to 47.04 percent of your earnings and you probably won't be able to reclaim any of it. Many companies will also only pay wages into a New Zealand **bank account** – opening one is easy (see p.65).

Casual work

One of the main sources of casual work is **fruit-picking** or related **orchard work** such as packing or pruning and thinning. The main areas are Kerikeri in the Bay of Islands for citrus and kiwifruit, Hastings in Hawke's Bay for apples, pears and peaches, Tauranga and Te Puke for kiwifruit, and Alexandra and Cromwell in Central Otago for stone fruit. Most work is available during the autumn **picking season**, which runs roughly from January to May, but you can often find something just as easily in the off season. In popular working areas, some hostels cater to short-term workers, and these are usually the best places to find out what's going.

Picking can be hard-going, physical work and **payment** is usually by the quantity gathered, rather than by the hour. When you're starting off, the poor returns can be frustrating, but with persistence and application you can soon find yourself grossing $100 or more in an eight-hour day. Rates vary considerably so it's worth asking around, factoring in any transport, meals and accommodation, which are sometimes included. Indoor packing work tends to be paid hourly.

Particularly in popular tourist areas – Rotorua, Nelson, Queenstown – **cafés**, **bars** and **hostels** often need extra staff during peak periods. If you have no luck, try more out-of-the-way locales, where there'll be fewer travellers clamouring for work. Bar and restaurant work pays minimum wage and upwards, depending on your level of experience, but tips are negligible. Generally you'll need to commit to at least three months. **Ski resorts** occasionally employ people during the June to October season, usually in catering roles. Hourly wages may be supplemented by a lift pass

and subsidized food and drink, though finding affordable accommodation can be difficult and may offset a lot of what you gain. Hiring clinics for ski and snowboard instructors are usually held at the beginning of the season at a small cost, though if you're experienced it's better to apply directly to the resort beforehand.

In addition to local hostels and backpackers, handy **resources** include ⓦjob.co.nz; for fruit picking and the like, check out sites such as ⓦseasonalwork.co.nz, ⓦpickapicker.net and ⓦpicknz.co.nz.

Volunteering

A useful starting point is the online service from the UK-based **The Gapyear Company** (ⓦgapyear .com), which offers free membership plus heaps of information on volunteering, travel, contacts and living abroad. The Department of Conservation's **Conservation Volunteer Programme** (search at ⓦdoc.govt.nz) provides an excellent way to spend time out in the New Zealand bush while putting something back into the environment. Often you'll get into areas most visitors never see, and learn some skills while you're at it. Projects include bat surveys, kiwi monitoring and nest protection, as well as more rugged tasks like track maintenance, tree planting and hut repair. You can muck in for just a day or up to a couple of weeks, and sometimes there is a fee (of around $50–200) to cover food and transport. Application forms are available on the website. Programmes are in high demand and often book up well in advance, so it's worth applying before you reach New Zealand.

Travel essentials

Climate

The sunny summer months (October to April) are the most popular time for travellers visiting New Zealand, but winter offers great skiing and snowboarding and the days are often clear and bright, if chilly. The far north of the country is often dubbed the "winterless north", although even in this subtropical area, winters can be nippy. The far south is the coldest part of the country – if you're surfing you'll need a wetsuit year-round.

Costs

The relatively strong Kiwi dollar and effects of the global financial crisis means that New Zealand is no bargain, but with high standards of quality and service the country is still decent value for money.

Daily costs vary enormously, and the following estimates are per person for two people travelling together. (With the prevalence of good hostels, **single travellers** can live almost as cheaply as couples, though you'll pay around thirty percent more if you want a room to yourself.)

If you're on a tight budget, using public transport, camping or staying in hostels, and cooking most of your own meals, you could scrape by on $60 a day. Renting a car, staying in budget motels, and eating out a fair bit, you're looking at more like $160 a day. Step up to comfortable B&Bs and nicer restaurants, throw in a few trips, and you can easily find yourself spending over $350 a day. Also, you can completely blow your budget on **adventure trips** such as a bungy jump or tandem parachuting, so it pays to think carefully about how to get the maximum bang for your buck.

The price quoted is what you pay. With the exception of some business hotels, the 15-percent Goods and Service Tax (**GST**) is always included in the listed price. GST refunds are available on more expensive items bought then taken out of the

country – keep your receipts and carry the items as hand luggage.

Student **discounts** are few and far between, but you can make substantial savings on accommodation and travel by buying one of the backpacker or YHA cards (see p.38). **Kids** (see p.57) enjoy reductions of around fifty percent on most trains, buses and entry to many sights.

Crime and personal safety

New Zealand's rates of violent crime are in line with those in other developed countries and you'll almost certainly come across some grisly stories in the media. Still, as long as you use your common sense, you're unlikely to run into any trouble. Some caution is needed in the **seedier quarters** of the larger cities where it's unwise to walk alone late at night. One major safety issue is "**boy racers**" using city and town streets as racetracks for customized cars, leading to bystander fatalities. Although the police do take action, their presence is relatively thin on the ground so be careful when out late in city suburbs.

Always take precautions against petty theft, particularly from cars and campervans. When

AVERAGE MONTHLY TEMPERATURES AND RAINFALL

	Jan	Feb	Mar	Apr	May	Jun	July	Aug	Sep	Oct	Nov	Dec
AUCKLAND												
max/min (°C)	23/16	23/16	22/15	19/13	17/11	14/9	13/8	14/8	16/9	17/11	19/12	21/14
max/min (°F)	73/61	73/61	72/59	66/55	63/52	57/48	55/46	57/46	61/48	63/52	66/54	70/57
rainfall (mm)	79	94	81	97	112	137	145	117	102	102	89	79
WELLINGTON												
max/min (°C)	21/13	21/13	19/12	17/11	14/8	13/7	12/6	12/6	14/8	16/9	17/10	19/12
max/min (°F)	70/55	70/55	66/54	63/52	57/46	55/45	54/43	54/43	57/46	61/48	63/50	66/54
rainfall (mm)	81	81	81	97	117	117	137	117	97	102	89	89
CHRISTCHURCH												
max/min (°C)	21/12	21/12	19/10	17/7	13/4	11/2	10/2	11/2	14/4	17/7	19/8	21/11
max/min (°F)	70/54	70/54	66/50	63/45	55/39	52/36	50/36	52/36	57/39	63/45	66/46	70/52
rainfall (mm)	56	43	48	48	66	66	69	48	46	43	48	56
HOKITIKA												
max/min (°C)	19/12	19/12	18/11	16/8	14/6	12/3	12/3	12/3	13/6	15/8	16/9	18/11
max/min (°F)	66/54	66/54	64/52	61/46	57/43	54/37	54/37	54/37	55/43	59/46	61/48	64/52
rainfall (mm)	262	191	239	236	244	231	218	239	226	292	267	262
QUEENSTOWN												
max/min (°C)	21/10	21/10	20/9	15/7	11/3	9/1	9/0	11/1	14/3	18/5	19/7	20/10
max/min (°F)	70/50	70/50	68/48	59/45	52/37	48/34	48/32	52/34	57/37	64/41	66/45	68/50
rainfall (mm)	79	72	74	72	64	58	59	63	66	77	64	62

staying in cities you should move valuables into your lodging. Thieves also prey on visitors' vehicles left at trailheads and car parks. Campervans containing all your possessions make obvious and easy pickings. Take your valuables with you, put packs and bags out of sight and get good insurance. When setting out on long walks use a secure car park if possible, where your vehicle will be kept safe for a small sum.

Police and the law

If you do get arrested, you will be allowed one phone call; a solicitor will be appointed if you can't afford one and you may be able to claim legal aid. It's unlikely that your consulate will take more than a passing interest unless there is something strange or unusual about the case against you.

The laws regarding **alcohol consumption** have traditionally been pretty lenient, though persistent rowdy behaviour has encouraged some towns to ban drinking in public spaces. Still, most of the time nobody's going to bother you if you fancy a beer on the beach or glass of wine at some wayside picnic area. The same does not apply to drink driving (see p.32), which is taken very seriously.

Marijuana has a reputation for being very potent and relatively easily available. It is, however, illegal, and although a certain amount of tolerance is sometimes shown towards personal use, the police and courts take a dim view of larger quantities and hard drugs, handing out long custodial sentences.

Prejudice

New Zealanders like to think of themselves as a tolerant and open-minded people, and foreign visitors are generally welcomed with open arms. Racism is far from unknown, but you're unlikely to experience overt **discrimination** or be refused service because of your race, colour or gender. In out-of-the-way rural pubs, women, foreigners – and just about anyone who doesn't live within a 10km radius – may get a frosty reception, though this soon breaks down once you get talking.

Despite constant efforts to maintain good relations between Maori and Pakeha, tensions do exist. Ever since colonization, **Maori** have achieved lower educational standards, earned less and maintained

disproportionately high rates of unemployment and imprisonment. Slowly Maori are getting some restitution for the wrongs perpetrated on their race, which of course plays into the hands of those who feel that such positive discrimination is unfair.

Recent high levels of immigration from East Asia – Hong Kong, China and Taiwan in particular – have rapidly changed the demographics in Auckland, where most have settled. Central Auckland also has several English-language schools that are mostly full of Asian students. The combined effect means that in parts of Auckland, especially downtown, longer-established New Zealanders are in the minority. It is a sensation that some Maori and Pakeha find faintly disturbing. There's little overt racism, but neither is there much mixing.

Electricity

New Zealand operates a 230/240-volt, 50Hz **AC power supply**, and sockets take a three-prong, flat-pin type of plug. Suitable socket adaptors are widely available in New Zealand and at most international airports; and for phone chargers and laptops that's all you'll need. In most cases, North American appliances require both a transformer and an adaptor, British and Irish equipment needs only an adaptor and Australian appliances need no alteration.

Entry requirements

All visitors to New Zealand need a passport, which must be valid for at least three months beyond the time you intend to stay. When flying to New Zealand you'll probably need to show you have an **onward or return ticket** before they'll let you board the plane.

On arrival, British citizens are automatically issued with a permit to stay for up to six months, and a three-month permit is granted to citizens of most other European countries, Southeast Asian nations, Japan, South Africa, the US and Canada, and several other countries. Australian citizens can stay indefinitely.

Other nationalities need to obtain a visitor visa in advance from a New Zealand embassy, costing the local equivalent of NZ$140 and usually valid for three months. Visas are issued by Immigration New Zealand (Ⓦ immigration.govt.nz). See p.58 for advice on working visas.

Websites and contact details for all NZ embassies and consulates **abroad** can be found at Ⓦ nzembassy.com.

Quarantine and customs

In a country all too familiar with the damage that can be caused by introduced plants and animals, New Zealand's Ministry of Agriculture and Forestry (MAF; ⓦ maf.govt.nz/quarantine) takes a hard line. On arrival you'll be asked to **declare any food**, plants or parts of plants, animals (dead or alive), equipment used with animals, wooden products (including musical instruments), camping gear, golf clubs, bicycles, biological specimens and hiking boots. Outdoor equipment and walking boots will be taken away, inspected and perhaps cleaned then returned shortly thereafter. After a long flight it can seem a bit of a pain, but such precautions are important and there are huge fines for non-compliance. Be sure to dispose of any fresh fruit, vegetables and meat in the bins provided or you're liable for an instant $400 fine (even for that orange you forgot about in the bottom of your bag). Processed foods are usually allowed through, but must be declared.

Visitors aged 18 and over are entitled to a **duty-free allowance** (ⓦ customs.govt.nz) of 200 cigarettes (or 250 grams of tobacco, or 50 cigars), 4.5 litres of wine or beer, three 1125ml bottles of spirits, and up to $700 worth of goods. There are **export restrictions** on wildlife, plants, antiquities and works of art.

Gay and lesbian travellers

Homosexuality was decriminalized in New Zealand in 1986 and the **age of consent** was set at 16 (the same as for heterosexuals). It is illegal to discriminate against gays and people with HIV or AIDS, and New Zealand makes no limitation on people with HIV or AIDS entering the country.

Though there remains an undercurrent of redneck intolerance, particularly in rural areas, it generally stays well below the surface, and New Zealand is a broadly gay-friendly place. The mainstream acceptance is such that the New Zealand Symphony Orchestra and Auckland Philharmonia composer, Gareth Farr, also performs as drag queen Lilith LaCroix. This tolerant attitude has conspired to de-ghettoize the gay community; even in **Auckland** and **Wellington**, the only cities with genuinely vibrant gay scenes, there aren't any predominantly gay areas and most venues have a mixed clientele. Auckland's scene is generally the largest and most lively, but the intimate nature of Wellington makes it more accessible and welcoming. Christchurch, Nelson and Queenstown also have small gay scenes.

Major **events** on the gay calendar include the **Vinegar Hill Summer Camp** (ⓦ vinegarhill.co.nz), held 5km north of the small town of Hunterville, in the middle of the North Island, from Boxing Day to just after New Year. It's a very laidback affair, with a couple of hundred gay men and women camping out, mixing and partying. There's no charge (except around $5 for camping) and no hot water, but a large river runs through the grounds and everyone has a great time.

The best source of on-the-ground information is the fortnightly gay newspaper *Express* (ⓦ express today.co.nz), available free in gay-friendly cafés and venues and almost any decent bookshop.

GAY TRAVEL WEBSITES

ⓦ **gaynewzealand.com** A virtual tour of the country with a gay and lesbian slant.

ⓦ **gaynz.net.nz** Useful site with direct access to gay, lesbian, bisexual and transgender information including the Pink Pages, covering what's on in the gay community and a calendar of events all over the country.

ⓦ **gaytravel.net.nz** A gay online accommodation and travel reservation service.

ⓦ **rainbowtourism.com** An excellent resource for gay and lesbian travellers in both NZ and Oz, listing accommodation, events, clubs and tours.

ⓦ **samesextravel.com** Lists gay and lesbian owned and operated accommodation throughout NZ and Oz.

ⓦ **purpleroofs.com** Comprehensive listing for gay-owned and gay-friendly accommodation in NZ and beyond.

Health

New Zealand is relatively free of serious health hazards and the most common pitfall is simply underestimating the power of nature. **No vaccinations** are required to enter the country, but you should make sure you have adequate health cover in your travel insurance, especially if you plan to take on the great outdoors (see p.51 for advice on tramping health and safety).

New Zealand has a good health service that's reasonably cheap by world standards. All visitors are covered by the accident compensation scheme, under which you can claim some medical and hospital expenses in the event of an accident, but without full cover in your travel insurance you could still face a hefty bill. For more minor ailments, you can visit a doctor for a consultation (from around $60) and, armed with a prescription, buy any required medication at a pharmacy at a reasonable price.

Sun, surf and earthquakes

Visitors to New Zealand frequently get caught out by the intensity of the **sun**, its damaging ultraviolet rays easily penetrating the thin ozone layer and reducing burn times to as little as ten minutes in spring and summer. Stay out of the sun (or keep covered up) as much as possible between 11am and 3pm, and always slap on plenty of sunblock. Re-apply every few hours as well as after swimming, and keep a check on any moles on your body: if you notice any changes, during or after your trip, see a doctor right away.

The sea is a more immediate killer and even strong swimmers should read our **surf** warning (see box below).

New Zealand is regularly shaken by **earthquakes** (see p.806), but, although Christchurch experienced major quakes in 2010 and 2011, most are minor and it is generally not something to worry about. If the worst happens, the best advice is to stand in a doorway or crouch under a table. If caught in the open, try to get inside; failing that, keep your distance from trees and rocky outcrops to reduce the chances of being injured by falling branches or debris.

Wildlife hazards

New Zealand's wildlife is amazingly benign. There are no snakes, scorpions or other nasties, and only a few venomous **spiders**, all rarely seen. No one has died from an encounter with a spider for many years, but if you get a serious reaction from a bite be sure to see a doctor or head to the nearest hospital, where antivenin will be available.

Shark attacks are also rare; you're more likely to be carried away by a strong tide than a great white, though it still pays to be sensible and obey any local warnings when swimming.

A far bigger problem is the country's **mosquitoes** and **sandflies**, although they're generally free of life-threatening diseases. The West Coast of the South Island in the summer is the worst place for these irritating insects, though they appear to a lesser degree in many other places across the country. A liberal application of repellent helps keep them at bay; for a natural deterrent, try lavender oil.

At the microscopic level, **giardia** inhabits many rivers and lakes, and infection results from drinking contaminated water, with symptoms appearing several weeks later: a bloated stomach, cramps, explosive diarrhoea and wind. The Department of Conservation advises you to purify drinking water by using iodine-based solutions or tablets (regular chlorine-based tablets aren't effective against giardia), by fast-boiling water for at least seven minutes or by using a giardia-rated filter (obtainable from any outdoors or camping shop).

The relatively rare **amoebic meningitis** is another waterborne hazard, this time contracted from hot pools. Commercial pools are almost

---

SWIM BETWEEN THE FLAGS

The New Zealand coast is frequently pounded by ferocious surf and even strong swimmers can find themselves in difficulty in what may seem benign conditions. Every day throughout the peak holiday weeks (Christmas–Jan), and at weekends through the rest of the summer (Nov–Easter), the most popular surf beaches are monitored daily from around 10am to 5pm. Lifeguards stake out a section of beach between two red and yellow flags and continually monitor that area: **always swim between the flags**.

Before entering the water, watch other swimmers to see if they are being dragged along the beach by a strong along-shore **current** or **rip**. Often the rip will turn out to sea, leaving a "river" of disturbed but relatively calm water between the pattern of curling breakers. On entering the water, feel the strength of the waves and current before committing yourself too deeply, then keep glancing back to where you left your towel to judge your drift along the shore. Look out too for **sand bars**, a common feature of surf beaches at certain tides: wading out to sea, you may well be neck deep and then suddenly be only up to your knees. The corollary is moments after being comfortably within your depth you'll be floundering around in a **hole**, reaching for the bottom. Note that **boogie boards**, while providing flotation, can make you vulnerable to rips, and riders should always wear fins (flippers).

If you do find yourself in **trouble**, try not to panic, raise one hand in the air and yell to attract the attention of other swimmers and surf rescue folk. Most of all, don't struggle against the current; either swim across the rip or let it drag you out. Around 100–200m offshore the current will often subside and you can swim away from the rip and bodysurf the breakers back to shore. If you have to be rescued (or are just feeling generous), a large donation is in order. Surf lifeguards are dedicated volunteers, always strapped for cash and in need of new rescue equipment.

always safe, but in natural pools surrounded by earth you should avoid contamination by keeping your head above water. The amoeba enters the body via the nose or ears, lodges in the brain, and weeks later causes severe headaches, stiffness of the neck, hypersensitivity to light, and eventually coma. If you experience any of these symptoms, seek medical attention immediately.

Insurance

New Zealand's Accident Compensation Commission (Ⓦacc.co.nz) provides limited medical treatment for visitors injured while in New Zealand, but is no substitute for having comprehensive **travel insurance** to cover against theft, loss and illness or injury.

Before paying for a new policy, it's worth checking whether you are already covered: some home insurance policies may cover your possessions when overseas, and many private medical schemes include cover when abroad. Students will often find that their student health coverage extends during the vacations and for one term beyond the date of last enrolment.

After exhausting the possibilities above, you might want to contact a specialist travel insurance company, or consider the travel insurance deal we offer (see box below). Most of them exclude so-called **dangerous activities** unless an extra premium is paid. In New Zealand this can mean scuba diving, bungy jumping, whitewater rafting, windsurfing, surfing, skiing and snowboarding, and even tramping under some policies.

Many policies can exclude coverage you don't need. If you do take medical coverage, ascertain whether benefits will be paid as treatment proceeds or only after return home, and if there's a 24-hour medical emergency number. When securing **baggage cover**, make sure that the per-article limit will cover your most valuable possession. If you need to make a claim, you'll need to keep receipts for medicines and medical treatment, and

in the event you have anything stolen, you must obtain an official statement from the police.

Internet

Internet access is abundant and fairly cheap though seldom blindingly fast. You'll find coin-operated machines at most **visitor centres**, backpacker hostels, motels and campsites, generally charging around $6 an hour. Most are set up with card readers, headsets and webcams, and often loaded with Skype and iTunes. At more expensive accommodation there'll often be a free-use computer, and laptop connections may be available.

There's often better functionality and lower prices at the abundant **internet cafés** lining city streets, which typically charge $3–6 per hour. **Libraries** typically have internet access – some offer this service free, while others charge.

Wi-fi access is increasingly widespread. In addition to internet **cafés**, many holiday parks, hostels, motels and hotels have hotspots accessible using your credit card or by buying access from reception. Rates vary considerably: an hour might cost $10 but you can often get a full 24-hour day for under $25. Swankier B&Bs and lodges will usually have free wi-fi in all rooms. Organizations such as Zenbu (Ⓦzenbu.net.nz) allow you to store your purchased time for future use. Note that in New Zealand, there's often a kilobyte cap, so make sure your device isn't using up your kilobytes in automatic updates.

Mail

Stamps, postcards, envelopes, packing materials and a lot more can be bought at **post offices** (a.k.a. **PostShops**), which are open Monday to Friday 8.30am to 5pm, plus Saturday 9 or 10am to noon or 1pm in some large towns and cities. Red and silver **post boxes** are found outside post offices and on street corners, and mail is collected daily.

ROUGH GUIDES TRAVEL INSURANCE

Rough Guides has teamed up with WorldNomads.com to offer great **travel insurance** deals. Policies are available to residents of over 150 countries, with cover for a wide range of **adventure sports**, 24hr emergency assistance, high levels of medical and evacuation cover and a stream of **travel safety information**. Roughguides.com users can take advantage of their policies online 24/7, from anywhere in the world – even if you're already travelling. And since plans often change when you're on the road, you can extend your policy and even claim online. Roughguides.com users who buy travel insurance with WorldNomads.com can also leave a positive footprint and donate to a community development project. For more information, go to Ⓦroughguides.com/shop.

Parcels are quite expensive to send overseas as everything goes by air and the economy service only saves fifteen percent for a considerably delayed delivery.

One post office in each major town operates a **Poste Restante** (or **General Delivery**) service where you can receive mail; we've listed the major ones in town accounts. Most hostels and hotels will keep mail for you, preferably marked with your expected date of arrival.

Maps and GPS

Specialist outlets should have a reasonable stock of **maps** of New Zealand. **Road atlases** are widely available in bookshops and service stations; the most detailed are those produced by Kiwi Pathfinder, which indicate numerous points of interest and the type of road surface. Also look out for *A Driving Guide to Scenic New Zealand* ($40) with handy angled projections giving a real sense of the lay of the land. Many car- and van-rental places have **GPS navigation systems**, usually for an additional $5–15 a day.

With a road atlas and our city plans you can't go far wrong on the roads, but more detailed maps may be required for tramping. All the major walks are covered by the **Park Map** series, complete with photos (around $19 from DOC offices and bookshops in NZ), while the larger-scale 1:50,000 Topo50 and 1:250,000 Topo250 (downloadable at ⓦlinz.govt.nz and sold in i-SITEs, book and outdoors shops and DOC offices) cover the whole country.

Money

The **Kiwi dollar** is divided into 100 cents. There are $100, $50, $20, $10 and $5 notes made of a sturdy plastic material, and coins in denominations of $2, $1 (both gold in colour), 50¢, 20¢ and 10¢. Grocery prices are given to the nearest cent, but the final bill is rounded up or down to the nearest ten cents. All prices quoted in the guide are in New Zealand dollars.

Cards, cheques and ATMs

For purchases, visitors generally rely on **credit cards**, particularly Visa and MasterCard, which are widely accepted, though many hostels, campsites and homestays will only accept cash. American Express and Diners Club are far less useful. You'll also find credit cards handy for advance booking

of accommodation and trips, and with the appropriate PIN you can obtain **cash advances** through 24-hour ATMs found almost everywhere. **Debit cards** are also useful for purchases and ATM cash withdrawals.

Banks

The major **banks** – ASB, ANZ, BNZ, Kiwibank (found in post offices), National Bank and Westpac – have branches in towns of any size and are open Monday to Friday from 9.30am to 4.30pm, with some city branches opening on Saturday mornings (until around 12.30pm). The big cities and tourist centres also have **bureaux de change**, which are typically open from 8am to 8pm daily.

Especially if you are working in New Zealand you may want to open a **bank account**. A New Zealand EFTPOS (debit) card can be used just about anywhere for purchases or obtaining cash. An account can usually be set up within a day; remember to take your passport.

Opening hours

New Zealand's larger cities and tourist centres are increasingly open all hours, with cafés, bars and supermarkets open till very late, and shops open long hours every day. Once you get into rural areas, things change rapidly, and core **shopping hours** (Mon–Fri 9am–5.30pm, Sat 9am–noon) apply, though tourist-orientated shops stay open daily until 8pm.

An ever-increasing number of **supermarkets** open 24/7 and small "dairies" (corner shops or convenience stores) also keep long hours and open on Sundays. **Museums** and sights usually open around 9am, although small-town museums often open only in the afternoons and/or only on specific days.

Public holidays and festivals are listed on p.46.

Phones

Given the near-ubiquity of mobile phones, and the prominence of Skype (or similar services) for international calling, most people don't have much need of **public payphones**, though they are still fairly widespread across New Zealand. Coin-operated phones are now rare, but all payphones accept major credit cards, account-based phone-cards and slot-in disposable PhoneCards sold at post offices, newsagents, dairies, petrol stations, i-SITEs and supermarkets.

Phone numbers

New Zealand **landline numbers** have only five area codes. The North Island is divided into four codes, while the South Island makes do with just one (☎03); all numbers in the guide are given with their code. Even within the same area, you may have to dial the code if you're calling another town some distance away. **Mobile numbers** start with ☎021, ☎022, ☎027 or ☎029, and you'll all come across **freephone** numbers which are all ☎0800 or ☎0508. Numbers prefixed ☎0900 are **premium-rated** and cannot be called from payphones.

IMPORTANT PHONE NUMBERS

National directory assistance ☎018
International directory assistance ☎0172
Emergency services Police, ambulance and fire brigade (no charge) ☎111

International dialling codes

To call New Zealand from overseas, dial the international access code (☎00 from the UK, ☎011 from the US and Canada, ☎0011 from Australia, ☎09 from South Africa), followed by ☎64, the area code minus its initial zero, and then the number.

To dial out of New Zealand, it's ☎00, followed by the country code (see box below), then the area code (without the initial zero if there is one) and the number.

Phonecards and calling cards

For **long-distance and international calling** you are best off with pre-paid account-based **phonecards** that can be used on any phone. There are numerous such cards around offering highly competitive rates, but be wary of the very cheap ones: they are often internet-based and the voice quality can be poor and delayed. Be warned, though, that public payphones have an additional per-minute charge for account-based phonecards, so try to use them from private phones whenever possible.

Mobile phones

New Zealand has three **mobile** providers: Telecom (ⓦtelecom.co.nz), Vodafone (ⓦvodafone.co.nz) and 2degrees (ⓦ2degreesmobile.co.nz). All have excellent reception in populated areas but sporadic coverage in remoter spots.

If you're thinking of bringing your phone from home, check with your service to see if your phone will roam in New Zealand and check roaming costs, which can be excessive. Providing your phone is unlocked, you can also buy a New Zealand SIM card and pre-pay.

Time and seasons

New Zealand Standard Time (NZST) is twelve hours ahead of Greenwich Mean Time, but, from the last Sunday in September to the first Sunday in April, Daylight Saving puts the clocks one hour further forward. Throughout the summer, when it is 8pm in New Zealand, it's 6pm in Sydney, 7am in London, 2am in New York, and 11pm the day before in Los Angeles.

New Zealand follows Britain's lead with **dates**, and 1/4/2013 means April 1 not January 4.

Don't forget that the southern hemisphere **seasons** are reversed: summer is officially December 1 to February 28 (or 29), and winter is June 1 to August 31.

Tourist information

New Zealand promotes itself enthusiastically abroad through **Tourism New Zealand**, and its extensive website ⓦnewzealand.com.

Many information centres, as well as some cafés, bars and hostels, keep a supply of **free newspapers** and **magazines** oriented towards backpackers – they're usually filled with promotional copy, but are informative nonetheless. *TNT* (ⓦtntdownunder .com) is about the best.

Visitor centres

Every town of any size has an official **i-SITE visitor centre**, staffed by helpful and knowledgeable personnel and sometimes offering some form of video presentation on the area. Apart from dishing out local maps and leaflets, they offer a **free booking service** for accommodation, trips and activities, and onward travel, but only for businesses registered with them. Some (usually small) businesses choose not to register and may still be worth seeking out; we've mentioned them where relevant. In the more popular tourist areas, you'll also come across places representing themselves as **independent information centres**

CALLING HOME

Note that the initial zero is omitted from the area code when dialling the UK, Ireland and Australia.
Australia 00 + 61 + area code.
Republic of Ireland 00 + 353 + area code.
South Africa 00 + 27 + area code.
UK 00 + 44 + area code.
US and Canada 00 + 1 + area code.

that usually follow a hidden agenda (ie commission), typically promoting a number of allied adventure companies. While these can be excellent, it's worth remembering that their advice may not be impartial.

Other useful resources are **Department of Conservation** (DOC; W doc.govt.nz) offices and field centres, usually sited close to wilderness areas and popular tramping tracks, and sometimes serving as the local visitor centre as well. These are highly informative and well geared to trampers' needs, with local weather forecasts, intentions forms and maps as well as historic and environmental displays and audiovisual exhibitions. The website contains loads of detail on the environment and the latest conservation issues plus details of national parks and Great Walks.

Travellers with disabilities

Overall, New Zealand is disabled-traveller friendly. Many public buildings, galleries and museums are **accessible**, and many tour operators will make a special effort to help you participate in all manner of activities, such as swimming with dolphins or seals. However, restaurants and local public transport generally make few concessions.

Planning a trip

A good starting point is Tourism New Zealand's W newzealand.com which has a "People with Special Needs" section containing several useful links. There are also organized **tours** and **holidays** specifically for people with disabilities.

Independent travellers should advise travel agencies, insurance companies and travel companions of limitations. Reading your travel **insurance** small print carefully to make sure that people with a pre-existing medical condition aren't excluded could save you a fortune. Your travel agent can help make your journey simpler: airline or bus companies can better cater to your needs if they are expecting you. A **medical certificate** of your fitness to travel, provided by your doctor, is also extremely useful; some airlines or insurance companies may insist on it.

Accommodation

New accommodation must have at least one room designed for disabled access, and many pre-existing places have converted rooms, including most YHA hostels, some motels, campsites and larger hotels. Older buildings, homestays and B&Bs are the least likely to lend themselves to such conversions.

For listings, visit W accomobility.co.nz, which has a searchable database of places that have signed up for the service.

Travelling

Few airlines, trains, ferries and buses allow complete independence. Air New Zealand provides aisle wheelchairs on international (but not domestic) flights, and the rear toilet cubicles are wider than the others to facilitate access; for more details search for "Special Assistance" on its website. Other **domestic airlines** have poorer facilities. Interislander Cook Strait **ferries** have reasonable access for disabled travellers, including help while boarding, if needed, and adapted toilets. If given advance warning, trains will provide attendants to get passengers in wheelchairs or sight-impaired travellers on board, but moving around the train in a standard wheelchair is impossible and there are no specially adapted toilets; the problems with **long-distance buses** are much the same.

In cities there are some **taxis** specifically adapted for wheelchairs, but these must be pre-booked; otherwise taxi drivers obligingly hoist wheelchairs into the boot and their occupant onto a seat.

CONTACTS IN NEW ZEALAND

Access Tourism NZ W accesstourismnz.org.nz. Informative advocacy site.
Disability Resource Centre 14 Erson Ave, Royal Oak, Auckland T 09 625 8069, W disabilityresource.org.nz. General resource centre.
DPA Level 4/173–175 Victoria St, Wellington, NZ T 04 801 9100, W dpa.org.nz. Disability advocacy organization with useful links.
Enable New Zealand T 0800 362 253, W enable.co.nz. Organization assisting people with disabilities, though not specifically focused on travellers.

Women travellers

Kiwi men have fairly progressive attitudes towards women, and travelling in New Zealand doesn't present any particular problems.

In the unlikely event of trouble, contact W rape crisis.org.nz. For support, Women's Centres around the country are listed on the Ministry of Women's Affairs website at W mwa.govt.nz/directory. You might also consider partly organizing your holiday through **Women Travel New Zealand** (W women travel.co.nz), which offers information, links to retreats, women-oriented tour operators and its newsletter. Auckland's Women's Bookshop (p.87; W womensbookshop.co.nz) is a handy resource and hosts literary events.

Auckland and around

70 Auckland

110 West of Auckland

116 North of Auckland

119 Southeast of Auckland

120 Islands of the Hauraki Gulf

AUCKLAND'S SKYLINE AS SEEN FROM MOUNT EDEN

1

Auckland and around

Auckland is New Zealand's largest city and, as the site of the major international airport, most visitors' first view of the country. Planes bank over the island-studded Hauraki Gulf and yachts with bright spinnakers tack through the glistening waters of the Waitemata Harbour towards the "City of Sails". The downtown sprouts skyscrapers and is surrounded by the grassy humps of some fifty-odd extinct volcanoes, and a low-rise suburban sprawl of prim wooden villas surrounded by substantial gardens. Look beyond the glitzy shopfronts and Auckland has a modest small-town feel and measured pace, though this can seem frenetic in comparison with the rest of the country.

Auckland is one of the least densely populated cities in the world, occupying twice the area of London and yet home to only 1.5 million inhabitants. It is also the **world's largest Polynesian city**. Around eleven percent of the population claim Maori descent while fourteen percent are families of migrants who arrived from Tonga, Samoa, the Cook Islands and other South Pacific islands during the 1960s and 1970s. Nevertheless, the Polynesian profile has traditionally been confined to small pockets, and it is only now, as the second generation matures, that Polynesia is making its presence felt in mainstream Auckland life, especially in the arts.

Many visitors only stay in the city long enough for a quick zip around the smattering of key sights, principally the **Auckland Museum**, with its matchless collection of Maori and Pacific Island carving and artefacts. A better taste of the city is gleaned by ambling around the fashionable **inner-city suburbs** of Ponsonby, Parnell, Newmarket and Devonport, and using the city as a base for exploring the wild and desolate West Coast **surf beaches** and the **wineries**, all less than an hour from the city centre. With more time, head out to the **Hauraki Gulf islands**: craggy, volcanic Rangitoto, sophisticated Waiheke, bird-rich Tiritiri Matangi and chilled-out Great Barrier.

Auckland's **climate** is temperate and muggy, though never scorching hot, and the humidity is always tempered by a sea breeze. Winters are generally mild but rainy.

Auckland

AUCKLAND's urban sprawl smothers the North Island's wasp waist, a narrow isthmus where the island is all but severed by river estuaries probing inland from the city's two harbours. To the west, the shallow and silted **Manukau Harbour** opens out onto the

Auckland's volcanic cones p.75
Guided and self-guided walks in
   Auckland p.81
Les Harvey: Parnell's saviour p.84
One Tree Hill p.92
Auckland harbour activities p.94
Auckland transport information and
   passes p.96
First-night camping p.98
Festivals p.109

West Coast tours p.111
The Hillary Trail p.113
West Coast beaches tours and
   activities p.114
Northern Gateway Toll Road p.116
Rangitoto summit walk p.122
Waiheke Island tours and
   activities p.127
Great Barrier Island walks and
   activities p.134

NORTH HEAD, DEVONPORT

Highlights

❶ **Auckland Art Gallery** With an impressive $90 million refit, Auckland's Art Gallery now ranks as the best showcase for Kiwi art in the country. **See p.79**

❷ **Auckland Museum** The exemplary Maori and Pacific Island collection is the highlight of this popular museum. **See p.81**

❸ **Devonport** Stroll the streets of this refined waterside suburb where North Head provides wonderful harbour views. **See p.88**

❹ **Otara Market** Island print fabrics, veg stalls and a lot of life make this New Zealand's finest multicultural market. **See p.93**

❺ **Karekare and Piha** Swim, surf or simply laze on the black-and-gold sands of these wild, bush-backed beaches less than an hour from the city. **See p.113**

❻ **Rangitoto Island** Make a day-trip to this gnarled lava landscape draped in pohutukawa forest with great views back to the city. **See p.121**

❼ **Great Barrier Island** Step back in time to this compact, laidback land of golden beaches, mountain bushwalks, indented harbours and hot springs. **See p.129**

❽ **Tiritiri Matangi** Enjoy close encounters with some of New Zealand's rarest birds amid regenerating bush on one of the Hauraki Gulf's prettiest islands. **See p.136**

HIGHLIGHTS ARE MARKED ON THE MAP ON P.72

Tasman Sea at a rare break in the long string of black-sand beaches continually pounded by heavy surf. Maori named the eastern anchorage the **Waitemata Harbour** for its "sparkling waters", which constitute Auckland's deep-water port and a focus for the heart of the city. Every summer weekend the harbour and adjoining Hauraki Gulf explode into a riot of brightly coloured sails.

Auckland is increasingly focusing on its **waterfront**, with former docks and fishing wharves now dotted with bobbing yachts and the rejuvenated surrounds converted to flashy restaurants and swanky apartments. This is very much the place to hang out, sucking life from **downtown Auckland**, which is fighting back with the superbly renovated Auckland Art Gallery.

At the top of Queen Street lies **Karangahape Road**, an altogether groovier strip of cheaper shops, ethnic restaurants and more down-and-dirty clubs. To the east lies **The Domain**, an extensive swathe of semi-formal parkland centred on the city's most-visited attraction, the **Auckland Museum**, exhibiting stunning Maori and Pacific Island artefacts.

Neighbouring **Parnell** forms the ecclesiastical heart of the city, with one of Auckland's oldest churches and a couple of historical houses. At the foot of the hill, **Tamaki Drive**

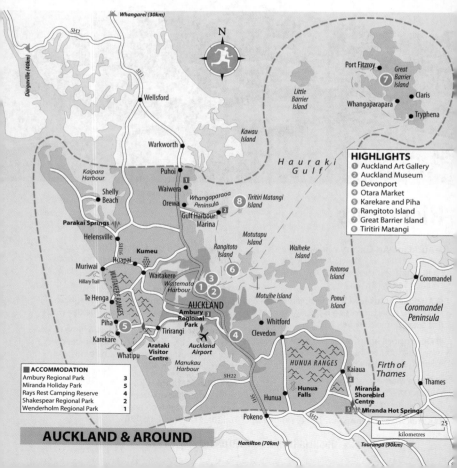

HIGHLIGHTS
1. Auckland Art Gallery
2. Auckland Museum
3. Devonport
4. Otara Market
5. Karekare and Piha
6. Rangitoto Island
7. Great Barrier Island
8. Tiritiri Matangi

ACCOMMODATION	
Ambury Regional Park	3
Miranda Holiday Park	5
Rays Rest Camping Reserve	4
Shakespear Regional Park	2
Wenderholm Regional Park	1

AUCKLAND & AROUND

follows the eastern waterfront past the watery attractions of Kelly Tarlton's to the city beaches of Mission Bay and St Heliers.

West of the centre, the cafés, shops and bars of **Ponsonby Road** and up-and-coming **Kingsland** give way to Western Springs, home of the **MOTAT** transport museum and the excellent **zoo**.

Across the Waitemata Harbour the seemingly endless suburbs of the **North Shore** stretch into the distance, though you're only likely to want to spend much time in the old waterside suburb of **Devonport** and perhaps the long golden beach at **Takapuna**.

Immediately south of the centre, two of Auckland's highest points, **Mount Eden** and **One Tree Hill** with its encircling **Cornwall Park**, provide wonderful vantage points for views of the city. **Pah Homestead** presents more great art, but the main reason for heading further south is to visit Saturday's **Otara Market**.

Brief history

The earth's crust between the Waitemata and Manukau harbours is so thin that, every few thousand years, magma finds a fissure and bursts onto the surface, producing yet another volcano. The most recent eruption, some six hundred years ago, formed Rangitoto Island.

The Maori arrive

The Rangitoto eruption was witnessed by some of the region's earliest Maori inhabitants, settled on adjacent Motutapu Island. Legend records their ancestors' arrival on the Tamaki Isthmus, the narrowest neck of land. With plentiful catches from two harbours and rich volcanic soils on a wealth of highly defensible volcano-top sites, the land, which they came to know as **Tamaki Makaurau** ("the maiden sought by a hundred lovers"), became the prize of numerous battles over the years. By the middle of the eighteenth century it had fallen to **Kiwi Tamaki**, who established a three-thousand-strong *pa* (fortified village) on Maungakiekie ("One Tree Hill"), and a satellite *pa* on just about every volcano in the district, but who was eventually overwhelmed by rival *hapu* (sub-tribes) from Kaipara Harbour to the north.

The Europeans arrive

With the arrival of musket-trading **Europeans** in the Bay of Islands around the beginning of the nineteenth century, Northland Ngapuhi were able to launch successful raids on the Tamaki Maori, which, combined with smallpox epidemics, left the region almost uninhabited, a significant factor in its choice as the new capital after the signing of the Treaty of Waitangi in 1840. Scottish medic **John Logan Campbell** was one of the few European residents when this fertile land, with easy access to major river and seaborne trading routes, was purchased for £55 and some blankets. The capital was roughly laid out and Campbell took advantage of his early start, wheeling and dealing to achieve control of half the city, eventually becoming mayor and "the father of Auckland". After 1840, immigrants boosted the population to the extent that more land was needed, a demand which partly precipitated the **New Zealand Wars** of the 1860s (see p.790).

Loss of capital status

During the depression that followed, many sought their fortunes in the Otago goldfields, and, as the balance of European population shifted south, so did the centre of government. Auckland lost its **capital status** to Wellington in 1865 and the city slumped further. Since then, Auckland has never looked back, repeatedly ranking as New Zealand's fastest-growing city and absorbing waves of migrants, initially from Britain, then, in the 1960s and 1970s, from the Polynesian Islands of the South Pacific. A steady stream of rural Maori has been arriving on Auckland's doorstep for over half a century, now joined by an influx of East Asians whose tastes have radically altered the city centre.

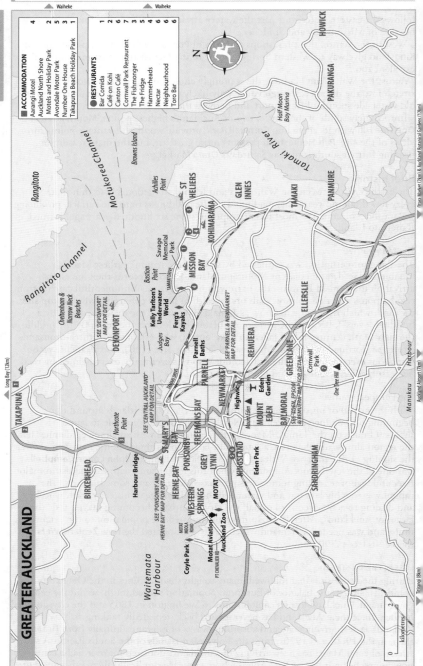

GREATER AUCKLAND

■ ACCOMMODATION

Aarangi Motel	4
Auckland North Shore Motels and Holiday Park	2
Avondale Motor Park	5
Number One House	3
Takapuna Beach Holiday Park	1

● RESTAURANTS

Bar Comida	1
Café on Kohi	2
Canton Café	6
Cornwall Park Restaurant	7
The Fishmonger	3
The Fridge	5
Hammerheads	4
Nectar	6
Neighbourhood	6
Toro Bar	6

AUCKLAND'S VOLCANIC CONES

Within 20km of the centre of Auckland there are **fifty small volcanoes**, but on the whole the city hasn't been very respectful of its geological heritage. Even the exact number is hard to pin down, not least because several cones have disappeared over the last 150 years, mostly chewed away by scoria and basalt quarrying.

That might sound a Herculean feat, but Auckland's largest volcano, Rangitoto Island out in the Hauraki Gulf (see p.121), is only 260m tall, and in the city itself none is taller than Mount Eden, just under 200m. Many are pimples barely 100m high that only just poke above the surrounding housing. Early on, **Maori** recognized the fertility of the volcanic soils, and set up *kumara* gardens on the lower slopes, usually protected by fortified *pa* sites around the summit. Europeans valued the elevated positions for water storage – most of the main volcanoes have **reservoirs** in the craters.

It is only in the last few decades that volcanic features have been protected from development, often by turning their environs into parks – all or part of 37 of them have some form of protection. City ordnances dictate that some summits can't be obscured from certain angles, and yet recently the edge of one volcano was only just saved from removal for a motorway extension. Some see UNESCO World Heritage Site status as the best means of protection, but it is unlikely anything will happen soon.

In the meantime, the volcanoes make wonderful **viewpoints** dotted all over the city, notably from Mount Eden, One Tree Hill, Devonport's North Head and the top of Rangitoto Island where you can also explore lava caves.

The oldest volcanoes erupted 250,000 years ago, though it is only 600 years since the last eruption, and the volcanic field remains active. No one knows when the next eruption will be, but it is unlikely to be through one of the existing volcanoes – meaning one day a new peak will emerge.

Asians now comprise almost twenty percent of Greater Auckland's population, many of them inhabiting the high-rise apartments that pepper the city centre, and Korean, Thai, Malaysian, Chinese and Japanese restaurants are everywhere. Over 35 percent of Aucklanders were born overseas compared to a national average of 23 percent.

The waterfront

Through much of the twentieth century, Auckland's city centre was cut off from its harbour frontage by working docks. As business gradually moved to the container port, the **waterfront** (ⓦwaterfrontauckland.co.nz) is finally getting a chance to shine.

The **Ferry Building** remains the nexus of the harbour ferries, whose history and social importance are covered at the nearby **Voyager** maritime museum. **Viaduct Harbour** and **Princes Wharf** were smartened up around the millennium, though the torch has now moved a little west to the newly revitalised **Wynyard Quarter**.

The Ferry Building

The waterfront meets the central business district at the northern end of Queen Street by the dockside **Ferry Building**, a neoclassical 1912 brick structure that is still the hub of the Waitemata Harbour ferry services. The chaotic bustle of the days before the harbour bridge is now a distant memory, but the ebb and flow remains, as commuters and sightseers board speedy catamarans to Devonport and Rangitoto, Waiheke and Great Barrier islands.

Voyager: New Zealand Maritime Museum

Corner of Quay and Hobson sts • Daily 9am–5pm; guided tours Mon–Fri 10.30am & 1pm; cruises on the *Ted Ashby* Wed & Fri 11.30am & 1.30pm, Sat & Sun noon & 1pm • $17; tour free; audioguide $5; cruises $12 • ☎ 09 373 0800, ⓦ maritimemuseum.co.nz

Anyone with the slightest interest in sailing and the sea should make straight for **Voyager: New Zealand Maritime Museum**, which pays homage to the maritime history

1

of an island nation reliant on the sea for colonization, trade and sport. The short *Te Waka* video shows an imagined Maori migration voyage, setting the scene for a display of South Pacific outrigger and double-hulled canoes. Designs for fishing, lagoon sailing and ocean voyaging include the massive 21m-long *Taratai*, which carried New Zealand film-maker and writer James Siers and a crew of thirteen over 2400km from Kiribati to Fiji in 1976. The creaking and rolling innards of a migrant ship and displays on New Zealand's coastal traders and whalers lead on to *Blue Water Black Magic*,

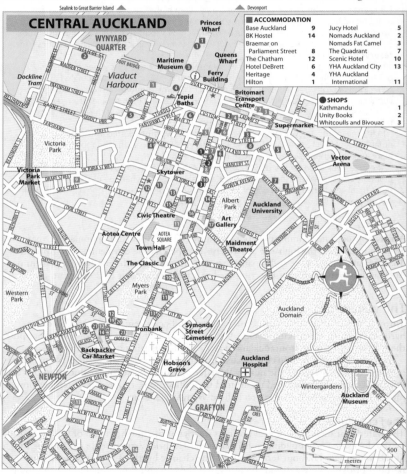

CENTRAL AUCKLAND

■ ACCOMMODATION			
Base Auckland	9	Jucy Hotel	5
BK Hostel	14	Nomads Auckland	2
Braemar on		Nomads Fat Camel	3
Parliament Street	8	The Quadrant	7
The Chatham	12	Scenic Hotel	10
Hotel DeBrett	6	YHA Auckland City	13
Heritage	4	YHA Auckland	
Hilton	1	International	11

● SHOPS	
Kathmandu	1
Unity Books	2
Whitcoulls and Bivouac	3

● CAFÉS & RESTAURANTS					
Alleluya	20	Imperial Lane	7	The Roxy	7
Art Gallery Café	17	Market Seafood		Soul	4
Atrium Food Gallery	13	Brasserie	2	Sri Pinang	23
Bellota	12	Mezze Bar	10	Tanuki's Cave	18
Coco's Cantina	22	Middle East Café	15	Theatre	21
The Depot	11	Mister Morning	22	Wildfire	3
Euro	1	No. 1 Pancake	16		
Food Alley	6	Pho Saigon	14		
Grand Harbour	5	Rasoi	19		
Ima	8	Raw Power	9		

■ PUBS, BARS & CLUBS			
Cowboy	1	Sale St	9
Family Bar	12	Smith	4
Flight Lounge	6	Stark's	11
Galbraith's Alehouse	14	Tabac	5
Globe	10	Tyler St Garage	3
Kings Arms	13		
The Occidental	7		
O'Hagan's	1		
Northern Steamship Co	2		
Rakino's	8		

a tribute to New Zealand's most celebrated sailor, **Peter Blake**, who was killed on the Amazon while conducting environmental work in 2001. Wins in the 1990 Whitbread Round the World Race and two America's Cups (1995 and 2000) are celebrated along with high-tech boat construction and an opportunity to work as a team at the helm and grinders of an interactive America's Cup yacht. Other highlights include an early example of the Hamilton Jetboat, which was designed for shallow, braided Canterbury rivers, and a fine collection of boat figureheads and maritime art.

There are interesting guided tours and one-hour **cruises** on the *Ted Ashby*, a 1990s replica of one of the traditional flat-bottomed, ketch-rigged scows that once worked the North Island tidal waterways.

Viaduct Harbour and Princes Wharf
Viaduct Harbour was a scruffy fishing port until it was smartened up for New Zealand's successful defence of the **America's Cup** in 2000. Bobbing yachts still dominate a waterfront lined with exclusive apartments, flash restaurants, themed bars and the maritime museum. More restaurants and bars flank **Princes Wharf**, which spears out into the harbour to the dramatically sited *Hilton* hotel.

Wynyard Quarter
Cross Wynyard Crossing pedestrian bridge from Viaduct Harbour or get the City Link bus from Queen St (50¢); every second bus goes to Wynyard Quarter • Dockline Tram daily: Nov–March 9am–6pm; April–Oct 10am–5pm; every 10min • Adults $5 all day, under-16s $1 • Ⓦ aucklandtram.co.nz

The latest section of waterfront to get the makeover treatment is the **Wynyard Quarter**, which successfully blends the still-operational fish market and Great Barrier Island ferry terminal with parks and a handful of middle-of-the-road restaurants. A "six pack" of old industrial silos has been retained and provides a backdrop for the Friday-evening movies, playgrounds make use of imported sand, there's a piano brought out when the weather's fine, and long-hidden sculptures have been dusted off and put on display. It is all best seen from a 12m-high gantry, randomly stretching along the north side.

Aucklanders have embraced the area, flocking to the restaurants that occupy a 1930s shed and a couple of shiny new buildings along North Wharf. Catch it on a fine day and the whole area can be a delight.

The quarter is prettified by the somewhat pointless **Dockline Tram**, using restored 1920s trams to make a 1.5km loop which goes around Jellicoe, Halsey, Gaunt and Daldy streets. It doesn't take you anywhere you couldn't easily walk, but makes a pleasant enough way to see the area.

Downtown
Downtown Auckland spreads south from the waterfront along downbeat **Queen Street**, the main drag, largely sustained by banks and insurance companies. Once the beating heart of the city, it has now largely been supplanted by dining and shopping areas both along the waterfront and in central suburbs such as Parnell, Newmarket and Ponsonby. That said, there is still useful **shopping** along Queen Street, notably for books at Whitcoulls at no. 210 and, at the same address but in the basement, outdoor gear at Bivouac, which competes with the more budget-oriented Kathmandu at no. 151.

Either side is a grid of streets commemorating prime movers in New Zealand's early European history: the country's first governor-general, William Hobson; Willoughby Shortland, New Zealand's first colonial secretary; and William Symonds, who chivvied along local Maori chiefs reluctant to sign the Treaty of Waitangi.

Immediately east of Queen Street, restored old warehouses and a couple of new office blocks form the lively **Britomart Precinct**, new home of many of the city's top fashion shops, but at its best in the evening when the restaurants and bars are packed.

1

Further south, specific interest comes in the form of more **designer shopping** around High Street and O'Connell Street, the kitsch beauty of the **Civic Theatre**, the **casino** and **Skytower**, and the superbly revamped and expanded **Auckland Art Gallery**. Wedged between the Art Gallery and the University, **Albert Park** makes a nice break from the concrete jungle.

Britomart Precinct

At the foot of Queen Street the neoclassical 1910 former post office has been transformed into the striking **Britomart Transport Centre** by imaginatively grafting an elegant glass box onto the back. It goes some way to recapturing the majesty of train travel, though useful services are limited to the daily train to Wellington and a couple of suburban services.

The glass box opens out onto a broad lane running down to **Takutai Square** with its fountain, lawns and scattered beanbag chairs. This forms the heart of the **Britomart Precinct** where heritage buildings are rapidly being populated by restaurants, bars and some of the city's top fashion boutiques.

Fort Street, High Street and Vulcan Lane

The waterfront once lapped at **Fort Street** (originally Fore Street), but progressive reclamation shifted the shoreline 300m to the north. Something of a backpacker ghetto (with three hostels and several bars catering to them), it is also Auckland's (admittedly tame) red-light district, with a few raunchy clubs. Britomart's rejuvenation is now spreading south and the area is gradually getting a makeover.

Moving south, head up **High Street** or **O'Connell Street**, one of the liveliest sections of the central city energized by trendy clothes stores and the excellent Unity Books, 19 High St. Just off High Street, **Vulcan Lane** was originally a street of blacksmiths, now replaced by bars and restaurants.

Civic Theatre

One of Queen Street's few buildings of distinction is the Art Nouveau **Civic Theatre**, on the corner of Wellesley Street. The talk of the town when it opened in 1929, the management went so far as to import a small Indian boy from Fiji to complement the ornate Moghul-style decor, all elephants, Hindu gods, a proscenium arch with flanking red-eyed panthers and star-strewn artificial sky. You may be able to stick your head in for a glimpse, but, sadly, the only way to see inside properly is to attend a performance (see p.109).

Aotea Square

The city centre's premier open space is **Aotea Square**, flanked by the Town Hall, a chunky postmodern multiplex cinema and the **Aotea Centre**, the city's foremost concert hall where Kiri Te Kanawa performed on the opening night in 1990. Aotea Square is at its best for public events such as the Auckland Festival when performance tents and bars take over.

Skytower

Corner of Victoria and Federal sts • Mon–Thurs & Sun 8.30am–10.30pm, Fri & Sat 8.30am–11.30pm • $25; upper viewing extra $3 • ☎ 0800 759 2489, ⍟ skycityauckland.co.nz/attractions

Since the mid-1990s, the city centre has been dominated by the concrete **Skytower**, which sprouts from the **Skycity Casino**. At 328m, the Skytower is New Zealand's tallest structure and just pips the Eiffel Tower and Sydney's Centrepoint. You can admire the stupendous views over the city and Hauraki Gulf either from one of two observation decks (186m and 220m) or from outside on the Skywalk. There's also a revolving restaurant and the chance to throw yourself off, via the SkyJump.

Skywalk

Daily 10am–6pm • $145; backpacker $125 • ☎ 0800 759 586, ⓦ skywalk.co.nz

The views from inside the Skytower are even better from the **Skywalk** – if you dare to look around. At the 192m level you tentatively make a twenty-minute circumnavigation of the Skytower exterior on a narrow, handrail-free walkway with just a rope tether to steady the nerves. At first it is petrifying, but the guide will soon have you hanging over the edge trusting that tether with your life.

SkyJump

Daily 10am–6pm • $225; backpacker $195 • ☎ 0800 759 586, ⓦ skyjump.co.nz

The **SkyJump** – claimed as the world's highest tower-based jump – is a close relation of bungy jumping. You plummet 192m towards the ground in a kind of ten-second arrested freefall at 80km/h, with a cable attached to your back. You approach the ground frighteningly fast, but miraculously touch gently down onto the target platform.

Auckland Art Gallery

Corner of Kitchener and Wellesley sts • Daily 10am–5pm; free tours 11.30am, 12.30pm & 1.30pm • Free • ☎ 09 379 1349, ⓦ aucklandartgallery.com

A recent $120 million expansion of the **Auckland Art Gallery** has made the country's best art gallery a whole lot better. The elaborate old mock-chateau galleries have been gutted and, though elegantly integrated, now play second fiddle to a superb new glass-cube atrium supported by kauri-wood columns that fan out to form an organic, forest-like canopy. The gallery feels open to the street and integrated with Albert Park behind, allowing everyone to see the atrium's keynote sculpture, which changes annually.

There is a significant international collection, but the emphasis is on the world's **finest collection of New Zealand art**. Works on display are frequently changed, but might include anything from original drawings by artists on Cook's expeditions and overwrought oils depicting Maori migrations through to site-specific installations.

Europeans depicting Maori

Romantic and idealized images of Maori life seen through European explorers' eyes frequently show composite scenes that could never have happened, contributing to a mythical view that persisted for decades. Two works show contrasting but equally misleading views: Kennett Watkins' 1912 *The Legend of the Voyage to New Zealand*, with its plump, happy natives on a still lagoon; and Charles Goldie's 1898 *The Arrival of the Maoris in New Zealand*, modelled on Géricault's *Raft of the Medusa* and showing starving, frightened voyagers battling tempestuous seas.

Much of the early collection is devoted to works by two of the country's most loved artists – both highly respected by Maori as among the few to accurately portray their ancestors. **Gottfried Lindauer** emigrated to New Zealand in 1873 and spent his later years painting lifelike, almost documentary, portraits of *rangatira* (chiefs) and high-born Maori men and women, in the mistaken belief that the Maori people were about to become extinct. In the early part of the twentieth century, **Charles F. Goldie** became New Zealand's resident "old master" and earned international recognition for his more emotional portraits of elderly Maori regally showing off their traditional tattoos, or *moko*, though they were in fact often painted from photographs (sometimes after the subject's death).

Pakeha depicting New Zealand

It took half a century for European artists to grasp how to paint the harsh Kiwi light, an evolutionary process that continued into the 1960s and 1970s, when many works betrayed an almost cartoon-like quality, with heavily delineated spaces daubed in shocking colours.

1

Look out for oils by **Rita Angus**, renowned for her landscapes of Canterbury and Otago in the 1940s; **Colin McCahon**, whose fascination with the power and beauty of New Zealand landscape informs much late twentieth-century Kiwi art; and **Gordon Walters**, who drew inspiration from Maori iconography, controversially appropriating vibrant, graphic representations of traditional Maori symbols.

You may well see one of the gallery's most expensive works, **Tony Fomison**'s 1973 painting *Study of Holbein's "Dead Christ"*. It's typical of his later, more obsessive, period, combining the artist's passion for art history and his preoccupation with mortality.

Maori artists

More recent acquisitions are strong on art by Maori artists. You'll usually find some of the excellent contemporary work by painter **Shane Cotton**, dark pieces by New Zealand's most lauded living artist, **Ralph Hotere**, and sculptor **Michael Parekowhai**, whose bull-on-a-grand-piano entry for the 2011 Venice Biennale turned more than a few heads.

Albert Park

East of Queen Street, the formal Victorian-style gardens of **Albert Park** were originally the site of a Maori *pa*. The land was successively conscripted into service as Albert Barracks in the 1840s and 50s, and then as a labyrinthine network of air-raid shelters during World War II, before relaxing into its current incarnation as parkland filled with oaks and Morton Bay figs, and thronged with sunbathing students and office workers.

Karangahape Road

The southern end of Queen Street climbs to vibrant and grungy **Karangahape Road**, universally known as **K' Road**. Originally home to prosperous nineteenth-century merchants, it became the heart of Auckland's Polynesian community in the 1970s, and was subsequently notorious for its massage parlours, strip joints and gay cruising clubs. For twenty years K' Road has been slated for a mainstream shopping renaissance, and while most of the strip joints and sex shops are gone, K' Road remains determinedly niche. Groovy cafés, bars and vinyl music shops rub shoulders with colourful Indian- and Chinese-run stores, and a handful of intriguing boutiques, particularly Cherry Bishop, at no. 500, and Hailwood, at no. 516.

There are few specific sights, but architecture buffs won't miss the stunning **Ironbank**, 150 K' Rd, an eight-storey office block that looks like five stacks of rusty steel boxes. Having caught a glimpse of it, you can then easily pass a few hours browsing the shops and eating in ethnic restaurants. In the evening, particularly at weekends, the pavement becomes an entertaining kaleidoscope of preening transvestites, boozed-up office workers, gay couples, spaced-out street people and the upwardly mobile in from the suburbs.

Symonds Street Cemetery

At its eastern end, K' Road crosses Symonds Street by the somewhat neglected **Symonds Street Cemetery**, one of Auckland's earliest burial grounds, partly destroyed by the motorway which was cut through Grafton Gully in the 1960s. A patch of deciduous woodland shades the grave of New Zealand's first governor, **William Hobson**, tucked away almost under the vast concrete span of Grafton Bridge.

The Domain

Grafton Gully separates the city centre and K' Road from **The Domain**, a swathe of semi-formal gardens draped over the low profile of an extinct volcano known as Pukekawa or "hill of bitter memories", a reference to the bloodshed of ancient inter-tribal fighting. Set aside in the 1840s, it is the city's finest park, furnished with mid-nineteenth-century accoutrements: a band rotunda, phoenix palms, formal

GUIDED AND SELF-GUIDED WALKS IN AUCKLAND

The most ambitious walking normally attempted by visitors to Auckland is a stroll through The Domain or a short hike up to one of the volcano-top viewpoints. More ambitious hikers can head to Rangitoto Island (see p.121) or pick off sections of the **Hillary Trail** (see p.113) out west in the hills of the Waitakere Ranges. Most of the West Coast tours (see p.111) also include some gentle walking.

SELF-GUIDED WALKS

Coast to Coast Walkway (16km one-way; 4hr) The best of the city's sights are threaded together on this fine walk which straddles the isthmus. All is revealed in the free *Beyond your Backyard – Discovering Auckland City by Foot or Bike* leaflet available from the tourist offices, and a route map can be found at ⓦ aucklandcity.govt.nz. The northern section is the most interesting: stop after One Tree Hill (12km; 3hr) and get the #328, #334 or #348 bus back to the city from Manukau Road.

North Shore Coastal Walk (23km one-way) Free leaflet from visitor centres. The Devonport ferry wharf marks the southern end of the North Shore Coastal Walk (part of the tip-to-toe Te Araroa; see box, p.48) which follows the waterfront past the Navy Museum, close to North Head then up the coast past several pretty beaches with views of Rangitoto. If you've come over by ferry, consider following the walk as far as Takapuna (10km; 2–3hr) then getting the bus back to the city from there.

GUIDED WALKS

Auckland Walks ⓣ 0800 300 100, ⓦ aucklandwalks .co.nz. Learn more about the city centre on these informative guided walks (daily 10am; 2hr; $30; booking essential) leaving the Harbour information Centre at the Ferry Building, 99 Quay St.

Tamaki Hikoi ⓣ 0800 282 552, ⓦ tamakihikoi.co .nz. Maori-led walks giving a Ngati Whatua perspective on Tamaki Makaurau. Choose from a tour of Pukewaka (Auckland Domain; 1hr 30min; $40), and interpretation of the Maori galleries at the Auckland Museum complete with the cultural performance (3hr; $95), and a guided walk around Maungawhau (Mount Eden; 3hr; $95). All come with lots of stories and give a completely different perspective on Auckland and colonization.

TIME Unlimited ⓣ 0800 868 463, ⓦ newzealand tours.travel. Maori-led city tour explaining the significance to Maori of locations around the city (full day; $245). Their "Extra" package ($295) includes a visit to a *marae* that's far more intimate and authentic than the mass-market extravaganzas around Rotorua, and they'll even organize *marae* stays and host Maori dinners on request.

flowerbeds and spacious lawns. In summer, the rugby pitches metamorphose into cricket ovals, and stages are erected in the crater's shallow amphitheatre for outdoor musical extravaganzas.

Auckland Museum

Auckland Domain • Daily 10am–5pm; Maori cultural performance daily 11am, noon & 1.30pm, also Jan–April 2.30pm; Maori galleries tour daily 11.30am & 2pm • $10; Maori cultural performances $25; Maori galleries tour $10 • ⓣ 09 309 0443, ⓦ aucklandmuseum.com • The museum is on the route of the Coast to Coast Walkway and city tour buses; the Inner Link bus stops on Parnell Rd, five minutes' walk away

The imposing Greco-Roman-style **Auckland Museum** sits at the highest point of the Auckland Domain, and contains the world's finest collections of Maori and Pacific art and craft. Traditional in its approach yet contemporary in its execution, the museum was built as a World War I memorial in 1929 and has been progressively expanded, most recently in 2006 with the capping of a courtyard with an undulating copper dome. Below the dome, a striking slatted Fijian kauri structure hanging from the ceiling like some upturned beehive dominates the new **Auckland Atrium** entrance.

At the opposite end of the building, the original colonnaded Grand Foyer entrance is the place to head for the thirty-minute **Maori Cultural Performance** of frightening eye-rolling challenges, gentle songs and a downright scary *haka*, all heralded by a conch-blast that echoes through the building.

1

Maori Court

As traditional Maori villages started to disappear towards the end of the nineteenth century, some of the best examples of carved panels, meeting houses and food stores were rescued and brought here. The central **Maori Court** is dominated by **Hotunui**, a large and wonderfully carved meeting house built in 1878, late enough to have a corrugated-iron rather than rush roof. The craftsmanship is superb; the house's exterior bristles with grotesque faces, lolling tongues and glistening paua-shell eyes, while the interior is lined with wonderful geometric *tukutuku* panels. Outside is the intricately carved prow and stern-piece of **Te Toki a Tapiri**, a 25m-long *waka taua* (war canoe) designed to seat a hundred warriors, the only surviving specimen from the pre-European era.

The transition from purely Polynesian motifs to an identifiably Maori style is exemplified by the fourteenth- or fifteenth-century **Kaitaia Carving**, a 2.5m-wide totara carving thought to have been designed for a ceremonial gateway, guarded by the central goblin-like figure with sweeping arms that stretch out to become lizard forms: Polynesian in style but Maori in concept.

Pacific Masterpieces

The **Pacific Masterpieces** room is filled with exquisite Polynesian, Melanesian and Micronesian works. Look out for the shell-inlaid ceremonial food bowl from the Solomon Islands, ceremonial clubs and a wonderfully resonant slit-drum from Vanuatu. The textiles are fabulous too, with designs far more varied than you'd expect considering the limited raw materials: the Hawaiian red feather cloak is especially fine.

Pacific Lifeways

Daily life of Maori and the wider Pacific peoples is covered in the **Pacific Lifeways** room, which is dominated by a simple yet majestic breadfruit-wood statue from the Caroline Islands depicting **Kave**, Polynesia's malevolent and highest-ranked female deity, whose menace is barely hinted at in this serene form.

Middle floor

The middle floor of the museum comprises the **natural history galleries**, an unusual combination of modern thematic displays and stuffed birds in cases. Displays such as the 3m-high giant moa (an ostrich-like bird) and an 800kg ammonite shouldn't be missed, but there's also material on dinosaurs, volcanoes and a **Maori Natural History** display, which attempts to explain the unique Maori perspective unencumbered by Western scientific thinking. The middle floor is also where you'll find hands-on and "discovery" areas for **kids**.

Upper floor

Scars on the Heart occupies the entire upper floor and explores how New Zealanders' involvement in war has helped shape national identity. The New Zealand Wars of the 1860s are interpreted from both Maori and Pakeha perspectives and World War I gets extensive coverage, particularly the Gallipoli campaign in Turkey, when botched leadership led to a massacre of ANZAC – Australian and New Zealand Army Corps – troops in the trenches. Powerful visuals and rousing martial music accompany newsreel footage of the Pacific campaigns of World War II and Vietnam, with personal accounts of the troops' experiences and the responses of those back home.

The Wintergardens and the Fernz Fernery

Auckland Domain • Nov–March Mon–Sat 9am–5.30pm, Sun 9am–7.30pm; April–Oct daily 9am–4.30pm • Free

The Domain's volcanic spring was one of Auckland's original water sources and was used by the Auckland Acclimatization Society to grow European plants, thereby promoting the rapid Europeanization of the New Zealand countryside. The spirit of this enterprise lingers on in the **Wintergardens**, a formal fishpond flanked by two barrel-roofed glasshouses – one temperate, the other heated to mimic tropical climes. Next door, a former scoria quarry has been transformed into the **Fernz Fernery**, a green dell with over a hundred types of fern in dry, intermediate and wet habitats.

The inner east: Parnell and Newmarket

The Auckland Domain separates the city from the established, moneyed inner suburb of **Parnell**, once the city's ecclesiastical heart, which retains a modest line in churches and historical houses along with a street of restaurants, boutiques and dealer galleries.

Parnell Road leads south past the **cathedral** becoming Broadway, the main drag of **Newmarket**, on the eastern flanks of Mount Eden. In recent years this has become one of the city's top fashion-conscious shopping districts, complete with good places to eat. Just south of the shops, Great South Road is lined with motels (see p.100).

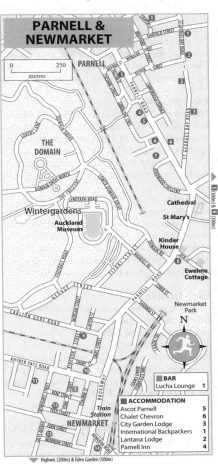

St Mary's and the Holy Trinity Cathedral

Corner of Parnell Rd and St Stephens Ave • St Mary's Mon–Sat 10am–4pm, Sun 11am–4pm; Holy Trinity Cathedral Mon–Sat 10am–4pm, Sun 12.30am–4pm • Free • ☎ 09 303 9500, ⓦ holy-trinity.co.nz

At the southern end of Parnell Road stands one of the world's largest wooden churches, **St Mary's**, built from native timbers in 1886 and almost 50m long. Inside, check out the series of photos taken on the dramatic day in 1982 when the church was rolled in one piece from its original site across Parnell Road to join its more modern kin.

The original Gothic chancel of the **Holy Trinity Cathedral** was started in 1959 then left half-finished until the early 1990s, when an incongruous, airy nave with a Swiss chalet-style roof was grafted on, supposedly in imitation of the older church alongside. Pop in to admire the modern stained-glass windows at the back; the bold and bright side panels symbolize Maori and Pakeha contributions to society. The most recent additions are the eighteen glass panels lining the nave, several by Maori artist Shane Cotton, who has used a unifying palette of muted reds, browns and greens to create an effect very different from most stained glass.

PARNELL & NEWMARKET

PARNELL

0 — 250
metres

THE DOMAIN

Wintergardens

Auckland Museum

Cathedral
St Mary's

Kinder House

Ewelme Cottage

Newmarket Park

N

KHYBER PASS ROAD

Train Station

NEWMARKET

▼ Highwic (200m) & Eden Garden (500m)

BAR

Lucha Lounge	1

ACCOMMODATION

Ascot Parnell	5
Chalet Chevron	6
City Garden Lodge	3
International Backpackers	1
Lantana Lodge	2
Parnell Inn	4

RESTAURANTS, CAFÉS & MARKETS

Basque Kitchen Bar	10	Little & Friday	11
Cibo	1	Newmarket Plaza Food Hall	12
Di Mare	4	Non Solo Pizza	5
Domain Ayr	8	Oh Calcutta!	3
Dunk Espresso	6	Otto Woo	14
Java Room	7	Urban Café	9
La Cigale French Market	2	Zarbo	13

1

> **LES HARVEY: PARNELL'S SAVIOUR**
>
> In the mid-1960s, **Parnell** narrowly escaped a high-rise-concrete fate when eccentric dreamer **Les Harvey** raised enough money to whisk the quaint but dilapidated shops and wooden villas from under the developers' noses. He then campaigned against New Zealand's strict trading laws, with the result that during the 1970s and much of the 1980s Parnell was the only place in Auckland where you could shop on a Saturday. Parnell Road soon established a reputation for chic clothes shops, swanky restaurants and dealer art galleries that it retains today.

Kinder House

2 Ayr St, Parnell • Wed–Sun noon–3pm • Free • ☎ 09 379 4008, ⊛ kinder.org.nz

The Gothic flourishes of nearby St Mary's church show the influence of New Zealand's prominent ecclesiastical architect, Frederick Thatcher, who designed **Kinder House** for the headmaster of the new grammar school – a post filled by John Kinder, an accomplished watercolourist and documentary photographer. Built of rough-hewn Mount Eden volcanic rock, the house contains some interesting photos and reproductions of Kinder's paintings of nineteenth-century New Zealand.

Ewelme Cottage

14 Ayr St, Parnell • Sun 10.30am–4.30pm • $8.50 • ☎ 09 379 0202, ⊛ historicplaces.org.nz

For a glimpse of pioneer life in New Zealand, visit **Ewelme Cottage**, a kauri house built as a family home in 1864 for the wonderfully named clergyman Vicesimus Lush. The appeal of the place lies not so much in the house but in its furniture and possessions, left just as they were when Lush's descendants finally moved out in 1968, the family heirlooms betraying a desire to replicate the home comforts of their native Oxfordshire.

Highwic

40 Gillies Ave, Newmarket • Wed–Sun 10.30am–4.30pm • $8.50 • ☎ 09 524 5729, ⊛ historicplaces.org.nz

The Gothic timber mansion of **Highwic** was built as a "city" property by a wealthy rural auctioneer and landowner in 1862. Its vertical battening and gingerbread barge-boards make it quite unlike most New Zealand architecture of the time. Though hardly *Downton Abbey*, the estate, complete with outbuildings and servants' quarters, gives a fair indication of the contrasting lives of the time.

Eden Garden

24 Omana Ave, Newmarket • Daily: Oct–April 9am–4.30pm; May–Sept 9am–4pm; Bloom Café daily 9.30am–3.30pm • $8 • ☎ 09 638 8385, ⊛ edengarden.co.nz

Occupying a small former quarry hewn into the eastern flank of Mount Eden, **Eden Garden** is a remarkably manageable varied place with year-round interest in the form of ferns, tulips, roses, proteas, a small waterfall and Australasia's largest and widest collection of camellias, in bloom from April to October. Everywhere you look there are peaceful dells where you can sit awhile and listen to the birdlife, sustained by visits to the very good Bloom Café.

The waterfront: along Tamaki Drive

The waterfront immediately east of the city centre contains some of Auckland's prime real estate, traced by **Tamaki Drive**, a twisting thoroughfare that skirts 8km of Auckland's most popular city beaches – **Mission Bay**, **Kohimarama** and **St Heliers**. During the summer, the waterfront is the favoured hangout of joggers and cyclists. The undersea world of **Kelly Tarlton's** is the only specific sight, but the harbour views out to Rangitoto and the Hauraki Gulf are excellent both from shore level and from a couple of headland viewpoints. The gentle hills behind are dotted with the secluded mansions of leafy Remuera, Auckland's patrician suburb.

Kelly Tarlton's Antarctic Encounter & Underwater World

23 Tamaki Drive, Okahu Bay, 6km west of the city • Daily 9.30am–5.30pm • $34 valid all day; booking online saves 10 percent • Shark dive $129 including Kelly Tarlton's entry, certified divers only; Shark Cage snorkel $79 including entry • ☎ 0800 805 050, ⓦ kellytarltons.co.nz • Explorer Bus and city buses #745, #757, #767 and #769 stop outside; Tarlton's free shuttle runs on the hour (9am–4pm) from opposite the Ferry Building, 172 Quay St

Kelly Tarlton's Antarctic Encounter & Underwater World was opened in 1985 by Kiwi diver, treasure hunter and salvage expert Kelly Tarlton in some huge converted sewage tanks that, from 1910 until 1961, flushed the city's effluent into the Waitemata Harbour on the outgoing tides. Its pioneering walk-through acrylic tunnels have become commonplace, but it is still a pleasure to stand on the moving walkway and glide through two tanks: one dominated by flowing kelp beds, colourful reef fish and twisting eels; the other with smallish sharks, all appearing alarmingly close in the crystal-clear water. If you want to get in among them, join one of the dives. Tanks in the **Stingray Bay** section feature specimens with a 2m wingspan.

Some of the remaining sewage tanks have become **Antarctic Encounter**, which includes a convincing replica of the capacious hut Robert Falcon Scott and his team used on their ill-starred 1911–12 attempt to be the first to reach the South Pole. It contains expedition artefacts, including a printing press from which the *South Polar Times* rolled every few months, and contemporary footage and tales of their exploits add to the haunting atmosphere. This leads to a penguinarium visited on a naff Disneyesque **Snowcat** ride made bearable by the close-up views of king and gentoo penguins shooting through the water and hopping around on fake icebergs.

Bastion Point

Grassy **Bastion Point** has great views of the Hauraki Gulf and makes a wonderful picnic spot. It's topped by the **M.J. Savage Memorial Park**, the nation's austere Art Deco homage to its first Labour prime minister, who ushered in the welfare state in the late 1930s. More recently, Bastion Point was the site of a seventeen-month standoff between police and its traditional owners, the Ngati Whatua, over the subdivision of land for housing. The occupiers were removed in 1977, but the stand galvanized the land-rights movement, and paved the way for a significant change in government attitude. Within a decade, the Waitangi Tribunal recommended that the land be returned.

Mission Bay, Kohimarama and St Heliers

Tamaki Drive, 7km east of the city

Swimming conditions are best at half-tide and above at three pohutukawa-backed beach suburbs strung along Tamaki Drive. Just past the kayak and bike rental place, Fergs (see p.97), you reach **Mission Bay**, the closest of the truly worthwhile city **beaches**, where a grassy waterside reserve is backed by a lively row of cafés and restaurants. Below half-tide, when the sea is shallow, kids make good use of the Sicilian marble **fountain** complete with its three bronze ornamental sea monsters gushing water and an after-dark light show.

The bay is named after the **Melanesian Mission**, a college for the Anglican education of Melanesian boys. The 1859 former dining hall, built from scoria quarried on Rangitoto Island (visible across the harbour), still stands and operates as a café.

Beyond Mission Bay there are similar but usually quieter café-backed beaches at **Kohimarama** (1km on) and **St Heliers** (1km beyond that).

West of the city centre

The suburbs of West Auckland developed later than their eastern counterparts, mainly because of their distance from the sea in the days when almost all travel was by ferry. The exceptions were the inner suburbs of **Ponsonby** and newly fashionable **Kingsland**.

1

Sights are scarce until you get out to **Western Springs**, which, in the late nineteenth century, was the major water source for the burgeoning city of Auckland. The area is now home to a pleasant park flanked by the classy **Auckland Zoo** and the transport and technology museum known as **MOTAT**.

Freeman's Bay

Victoria Park Market daily 9am–6pm • ⓦ victoria-park-market.co.nz

Victoria Street runs west from Queen Street to **Freeman's Bay**, which was long ago reclaimed to accommodate early sawmilling operations. The land is now given over to the sports fields of Victoria Park, all overshadowed by the 38m-high chimney of **Victoria Park Market**, a recently rejuvenated cluster of shops and restaurants which occupies Auckland's former refuse incinerator. The **Link bus** passes on its way to Ponsonby, and city tour buses also stop here.

Ponsonby and Herne Bay

The once fashionable suburb of **Ponsonby** had fallen on hard times by the 1960s when large numbers of immigrant Pacific Islanders made the area their home. Ponsonby took

PONSONBY & HERNE BAY

● RESTAURANTS & CAFÉS	
Café Cézanne	3
Dida's	1
Dizengoff	4
Il Forno	9
Moo Chow Chow	8
Ponsonby Road Bistro	6
Renkon Express	5
Satya	10
Soto	2
SPQR	7

■ BARS	
The Long Room	3
Mea Culpa	2
The Whiskey	1

● SHOP	
The Women's Bookshop	1

■ ACCOMMODATION	
23 Hepburn	6
Abaco on Jervois	1
Brown Kiwi	2
Freemans Lodge	5
Great Ponsonby Art Hotel	3
Uenuku Lodge	4
Verandahs	7

a bohemian turn in the 1970s and before long young professionals were moving in, restoring old houses and spending fistfuls of dollars.

For the last twenty-odd years **Ponsonby Road** has been a byword for designer clothing, cafés and see-and-be-seen lunching for long-term residents and the overspill from the adjacent media suburb of Grey Lynn. The street itself may not be beautiful, but the people sure are; musicians, actors and media folk congregate to lunch, schmooze and be seen in the latest fashionable haunt here. The cutting edge is now fragmented around the central city, but Ponsonby retains a great vibe and is a prime target for some of the city's classiest clothes shopping, a good meal and some people-watching. While in the area you might want to check out The Women's Bookshop at 105 Ponsonby Rd, which has plenty for men too, and knowledgeable staff.

To the north of Ponsonby, the waterside suburb of **Herne Bay** also has a cluster of excellent spots to eat, mostly along Jervois Road.

Kingsland

Along New North Rd, 1km south of Ponsonby • Kingsland train station can be reached from the downtown Britomart station and from Newmarket. Buses #210, #211, #212, #223, #224 and others go to Kingsland from stop M4 at 19 Victoria St

There's not a great deal to go-ahead **Kingsland**, with no real sights unless you count **Eden Park**, where the All Blacks finally lifted the Rugby World Cup in 2011, after a 24-year drought. But it's a fun place to hang out for a few hours, with some lively cafés (see p.106), a couple of good bars (see p.108) and a handful of funky shops. Check out the industrial furniture at The Boiler Room, at no. 486, and the beautiful, contemporary jewellery at Royal, at no. 486.

MOTAT

805 Great North Rd, Western Springs, 5km southwest of the city centre • Daily 10am–5pm • $14 • ☎ 0800 668 286, ⓦ motat.org.nz • Numerous buses from downtown including #020, #030, #080, #113, #135 or #163

The **Museum of Transport & Technology** (MOTAT) offers an entertaining trawl through New Zealand's vehicular and industrial past, nicely balancing preserving the nation's machinery while keeping the kids entertained. The jumble of sheds and halls is centred on the restored Western Springs' **pumphouse** where the massive 1877 beam engine and associated boiler room mostly sit grandly immobile, except when fired up (generally Thurs noon–1pm & 2–3pm).

Appropriately for an agricultural nation there's an impressive array of tractors through the ages, with pride of place given to the one Edmund Hillary used to reach the South Pole in 1958, the first overland party there since Scott and Amundsen 46 years earlier.

Elsewhere there's an entertaining, science-oriented, hands-on section, a Victorian village built around the original pumphouse engineer's cottage, and a shed full of trams that plied the city's streets from 1902–56.

An ancient, rattling Melbourne **tram** (every 10–30min; included in admission price) takes you 1km to MOTAT's **Meola Road** site, with its impressive new **Aviation Display Hall**, a hangar eco-designed with vast laminated wood beams. Star attractions are one of the few surviving World War II Lancaster bombers, early crop-dusting planes and fragile-looking things that took early tourists to the Fox and Franz Josef glaciers in the days before decent roads. Imminent completion of restoration should see centre stage occupied by a double-decker Solent flying boat, decked out for dining in a more gracious age and used on Air New Zealand's South Pacific "Coral Route" until the early 1960s.

Auckland Zoo

Motions Rd, Western Springs, 5km southwest of the city centre • Daily: Sept–April 9.30am–5.30pm; May–Aug 9.30am–5pm; check the website for Animal Encounters times • Adults $22, kids $11; Animal Encounters free • ☎ 09 360 3805, ⓦ aucklandzoo.co.nz • Western Springs is on city tour bus routes; reach it on the #093, #113 and #163 buses from 17 Albert St, near Customs St in the city; there's also a zoo stop on the tramline between the two MOTAT sites

1

The **Auckland Zoo** is the best in the country. There are still a few tigers in cages but the zoo is strong on spacious, naturalistic habitats and captive breeding programmes. The "rainforest walk" threads its way among artificial islands inhabited by colonies of monkeys, you can walk through the wallaby and emu enclosure unhindered, and the trailblazing Pridelands development has lions, hippos, rhinos, giraffes, zebras and gazelles all roaming across mock savannah behind enclosing moats.

Te Wao Nui

The zoo's New Zealand environments are grouped as the brand-new **Te Wao Nui**, a major development divided into six environments – coast, islands, wetlands, forest, high country and a nocturnal section. It's beautifully designed with loads of sculptures, water features and clever deceits such as entering a free-flight aviary through what appears to be a high-country hut. It is great to see the animals in something approaching their natural setting – kiwi are kept with ruru (native owls) and nocturnal flax snails; reptilian tuatara share island space with skinks, geckos and luminous green kakariki (parakeets); and penguins are found next to the fur seals.

There's plenty on the desperate attempt to save various species from extinction, and you can even watch animals being operated on in the treatment room at the nearby **Conservation Medicine Centre**.

The North Shore

The completion of the harbour bridge in 1959 provided the catalyst for the development of the **North Shore**, previously a handful of scattered communities linked by a web of ferries crisscrossing the harbour. By the early 1970s, the volume of traffic to the suburbs log-jammed the bridge – until a Japanese company attached a two-lane extension (affectionately dubbed "the Nippon Clip-ons") to each side. The bridge and its additional lanes can now be seen at close quarters on the Auckland Bridge Climb (see p.94).

The vast urban sprawl marches inexorably towards the Hibiscus Coast (see p.116), with most interest to be found in the maritime village of **Devonport**, at the southern end of a long string of calm swimming **beaches**. Further north, try the more open and busier **Takapuna**, a short stroll from dozens of good cafés and reached by a host of buses mostly in the #800s and #900s.

Devonport

Devonport is one of Auckland's oldest suburbs, founded in 1840 and still linked to the city by a ten-minute ferry journey. The naval station was an early tenant, soon followed by wealthy merchants, who built fine kauri villas. Some of these are graced with little turrets ("widows' watches") that served as lookouts where the traders could scan the seas for their precious cargoes and wives watch hopefully (or warily) for their returning husbands. Wandering along the peaceful streets and the tree-fringed waterfront past grand houses is the essence of Devonport's appeal and there's no shortage of tempting bookshops, small galleries, cafés and even an aged cinema (see p.110) along the main street to punctuate your amblings. Walkers should consider the **North Shore Coastal Walk** (see box, p.81).

Navy Museum

64 King Edward Parade • Daily 10am–5pm; free guided tours Sat & Sun 10.30am & 1pm • Free • ☎ 09 445 5186, ⓦ navymuseum.mil.nz

It is a pleasant waterfront stroll from central Devonport to the **Navy Museum**, a former submarine mining station beside Torpedo Bay, at the base of North Head. There are plenty of the expected guns, medals and naval uniforms, supplemented with coverage of New Zealand's military involvement in the battle of River Plate in World War II to the HMNZS *Otago*'s visit to Mururoa Atoll in 1973 to protest against French nuclear

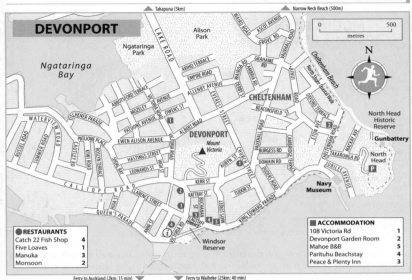

DEVONPORT

Takapuna (5km)   Narrow Neck Beach (500m)

Alison Park

Ngataringa Park

Ngataringa Bay

CHELTENHAM

DEVONPORT
Mount Victoria

North Head Historic Reserve

Gunbattery

North Head

Navy Museum

Windsor Reserve

● RESTAURANTS

Catch 22 Fish Shop	4
Five Loaves	1
Manuka	3
Monsoon	2

■ ACCOMMODATION

108 Victoria Rd	1
Devonport Garden Room	2
Mahoe B&B	5
Parituhu Beachstay	4
Peace & Plenty Inn	3

Ferry to Auckland (2km; 15 min)   Ferry to Waiheke (25km; 40 min)

testing. Try your hand at sending morse code, kids can try on uniforms, and don't miss the World War II Japanese map of New Zealand with a detail of Auckland.

The on-site *Torpedo Bay Café* has great views across the harbour to the city.

Mount Victoria

Unrestricted access for pedestrians • Closed to vehicles from dusk on Thurs, Fri & Sat

On a fine day, take a stiff walk up one of the two ancient volcanoes that back Devonport. The closest, about fifteen minutes' walk away, is **Mount Victoria** (Taka-a-ranga), from where you get fabulous gulf views. The hill was once the site of a Maori *pa*, and the remains of terraces and *kumara* pits can still be detected on the northern and eastern slopes.

North Head Historic Reserve

Daily 6am–10pm; vehicles 6am–8pm • Free

The grass- and flax-covered volcanic plug of **North Head** (Maungauika) guards the entrance to the inner harbour and makes a wonderful vantage point during yachting events or on any sunny afternoon. A strategic site for pre-colonial Maori, it was later co-opted to form part of the young nation's coastal defences. In the wake of the "Russian Scares" of 1884–86, which were precipitated by the opening of the port of Vladivostok, North Head became Fort Cautley. It is now operated by DOC as the **North Head Historic Reserve** and you can amble around the peripheral remains – pillboxes, concrete tunnels linking gun emplacements and even a restored eight-inch "disappearing gun", which recoiled underground for easy reloading. The hilltop former kitchen now has a twelve-minute video (daily 8.30am–4pm; free) on the site's history.

South of the city centre

Southern Auckland, arching around the eastern end of Manukau Harbour, is neglected by most visitors, though the airport at Mangere is where most arrive. The city's most lofty volcano, **Mount Eden**, offers superb views, and its near-identical twin, **One Tree Hill**, has some of the best surviving examples of the terracing

MOUNT EDEN, EPSOM & REMUERA

● RESTAURANT
Molten 1

■ ACCOMMODATION
Bamber House	1	Off Broadway	2
Bavaria	3	Omahu Lodge	11
Eden Park B&B	5	Pentlands	6
Hansens	7	Siesta	4
Oak Tree	8	Tudor Court	9
Oaklands Lodge	10		

undertaken by early Maori inhabitants. The surrounding Cornwall Park is one of the city's best, while the nearby art gallery at **Pah Homestead** complements downtown's Auckland Art Gallery beautifully.

Beyond Cornwall Park and Pah Homestead is **South Auckland**, the city's poorest sector and the less-than-flatteringly-depicted gangland setting of Lee Tamahori's film *Once Were Warriors*. It isn't a no-go zone, and is certainly worth a look on Saturday morning when Auckland's Polynesian community (along with many other immigrant communities) plies its wares at **Otara Market**.

Yet further south, the **Auckland Botanic Gardens** are a relaxing place to spend an hour before continuing out of town.

Mount Eden
2km south of the city centre

At just 196m, **Mount Eden** (Maungawhau) is Auckland city's highest volcano. It is only a few metres higher then several other cones, and doesn't poke far above the surrounding suburban housing, but the summit car park affords extensive views all around. Unfortunately it is on just about every tour bus itinerary, so once at the summit take a walk around the cone rim for a more peaceful viewpoint. Alternatively, walk here on the Coast to Coast Walkway (see p.81).

One Tree Hill Domain
7km south of the city centre • Daily 7am–11pm • Free • Accessible off Manukau Rd, which can be reached on buses #328, #334, #347, #348 & #354 from 55 Customs St East in central Auckland

Mount Eden may be slightly loftier, but Auckland's most distinctive peak is **One Tree Hill** (Maungakiekie; 183m), topped by a 33m-tall granite obelisk – but no tree. The hilltop views are equally good and the surrounding **One Tree Hill Domain** makes this a more rewarding overall destination.

For a century, until just before the arrival of Europeans, Maungakiekie ("mountain of the kiekie plant") was one of the largest *pa* sites in the country; an estimated 4000 people were drawn here by the proximity to abundant seafood from both harbours and the rich soils of the volcanic cone, which still bears the scars of extensive earthworks including the remains of dwellings and *kumara* pits. The site was abandoned and then bought by the Scottish medic and "father of Auckland", Sir John Logan Campbell, one of only two European residents when the city was granted capital status in 1840.

1

ONE TREE HILL

Sir John Logan Campbell is buried at the summit where a single totara tree originally gave One Tree Hill its name. Settlers cut it down in 1852, and Campbell planted several pines as a windbreak, a single specimen surviving until the millennium. Already ailing from a 1994 chainsaw attack by a Maori activist avenging the loss of the totara, the pine's fate was sealed by a similar attack in 1999 and the tree was removed the next year. Immediate demands for a replacement have gone quiet in recent years though it seems likely that in mid-2012 a grove of six pohutukawa and three totara will be planted in the hope that a single dominant tree will flourish. Then again, many people seem happy enough with, as it were, None Tree Hill.

Stardome Observatory

670 Manukau Rd • Wed–Sun 7pm & 8pm, plus Sat & Sun 9pm • $10; Zeiss telescope additional $8 • ☎ 09 624 1246, ⓦ stardome.org.nz

If you fancy learning something about the southern night sky or astronomy generally, head to one of the evening shows at the **Stardome Observatory**. You'll typically get a topical introduction to a 45-minute show in the planetarium followed by twenty minutes looking through a modest-sized telescope. If actual star viewing is more your thing, go to the 8pm session on Thursday, Friday and Saturday; weather permitting, they'll open up the dome for a chance to look through the half-metre-diameter Zeiss telescope.

Cornwall Park

Off Green Lane West, 7km south of the city centre • Daily 7am–dusk • Free • ⓦ cornwallpark.co.nz

One Tree Hill Domain is almost entirely encircled by **Cornwall Park**, which "father of Auckland" Sir John Logan Campbell created from his One Tree Hill Estate and gifted to the people of New Zealand to commemorate the 1901 visit of Britain's Duke and Duchess of Cornwall. There are attractive formal areas, but large sections of the park are farmed, the grazing sheep and cattle making for an odd sight in the midst of a large modern city. Cornwall Park puts on its best display around Christmas, when avenues of pohutukawa trees erupt in a riot of red blossom.

Huia Lodge and Acacia Cottage

Green Lane Rd entrance • Huia Lodge daily 10am–4pm; Acacia Cottage daily 7am–dusk • Free • Huia Lodge ☎ 09 630 8485

Most of Cornwall Park's amenities are clustered on the northern flank of One Tree Hill around **Huia Lodge**, built by Campbell as the park caretaker's cottage and now containing displays on the park and the man. It also contains a **visitor centre**, which has free leaflets outlining the archeological and volcanic sites of the hill. Call at the adjacent *Cornwall Park Restaurant* (see p.105) for sustenance.

Immediately opposite Huia Lodge is the pit-sawn kauri **Acacia Cottage**, Campbell's original home and the city's oldest surviving building, built in 1841 and re-sited from central Auckland in 1920. Inside, the four simple rooms are furnished as they might have been in the 1840s.

Pah Homestead and Monte Cecilia Park

72 Hillsborough Rd, 9km south of the city centre • Tues–Fri 10am–3pm, Sat & Sun 10am–5pm; free tours Tues–Sun 1.30pm • Free • ☎ 09 639 2010, ⓦ tsbbankwallaceartscentre.org.nz • Bus #304 or #305 takes 1hr from Wellesley St East in the city

One of the best reasons to stray south from the city centre is to visit **Pah Homestead**, an Italianate residence perched on top of a small volcanic cone. When completed in 1879, it was the largest house in the Auckland region and an ideal place for its owner, businessman James Williamson, to throw lavish parties. Much of its wood panelling and elaborate ceiling bosses are original, despite spending much of its life as a novitiate home for the Sisters of Mercy, a boarding house and emergency housing.

The homestead overlooks the graceful, mature cedars and Moreton Bay fig trees of the surrounding **Monte Cecilia Park** and has great views of One Tree Hill.

Wallace Arts Centre

Though impressive by New Zealand standards, and extensively restored in 2010, Pah Homestead alone wouldn't warrant a special trip. What does is what's within: an array of pieces from the five thousand-work **Wallace Arts Trust collection**, created by Kiwi meat-processing magnate, James Wallace. In the mid-1960s Wallace began collecting works by emerging New Zealand artists and has continued to buy their best stuff (and commission more) as they've risen to become some of the country's most eminent. The result is a wide-ranging collection particularly strong on artists such as Toss Woollaston, Philip Trusttum and Michael Parakowhai. What's on show is constantly changing but always superb. The equally excellent on-site *Pah Café* spills out onto the veranda, overlooking the sculpture garden.

Otara Market

Otara Town Centre, 18km southeast of the city centre • Sat 6am–noon • Take East Tamaki Rd (Exit 444) off the southern motorway or catch the Waka Pacific bus (#487 or #497) for the 50min journey from 55 Customs St East downtown

On Saturday morning, **Otara Market** sprawls across the car park of the Otara Town Centre. Though often promoted as the largest Maori and Polynesian market in the world, these days it is far more diverse than that, reflecting the racial makeup of modern South Auckland. Certainly there is still a strong Polynesian influence. Reggae beats and Pasifika rhythms ring out across the market, and the adjacent Community Hall is full of *kete* (woven baskets), tapa cloth and island-style floral print fabrics. Reasonably priced Maori greenstone carvings and Maori sovereignty shirts (look for tees emblazoned with the words "*Tino Rangatiratanga*") can be found next to Sikhs flogging gold bracelets, Koreans selling Korean-language DVDs and Chinese (lots of Chinese) selling truckloads of cheap fruit and veg.

There's plenty of low-cost **eating** from coffee and pastries to wieners, goat curry, pork buns, whitebait fritters and even a classic Maori boil-up of pork bones, watercress, pumpkin and fry bread ($10). The market is liveliest from 8–11am.

Auckland Botanic Gardens

102 Hill Rd, Manurewa, 24km southeast of the city centre • Daily: mid-Oct to mid-March 8am–8pm; mid-March to mid-Oct 8am–6pm • Free • ☎ 09 267 1457, ⒲ aucklandbotanicgardens.co.nz

Southbound drivers might want to spend an hour or two just off the motorway at the large and youthful **Auckland Botanic Gardens**, which only opened in 1982. What was once farmland has a long way to grow, but already there's a beautiful rock garden, a children's garden, a great section of African plants, an instructive section on threatened New Zealand native species and, at the far northern end, bushwalks through native bush that form part of the Te Araroa pathway. There are great picnic spots, or visit *Café Miko* (daily 8am–4pm).

ARRIVAL AND DEPARTURE   AUCKLAND

As New Zealand's major gateway city, Auckland receives the bulk of **international arrivals**, a few disembarking from cruise ships at the dock by the Ferry Building downtown, but the vast majority arriving by air.

BY PLANE

Auckland International Airport The airport (⒲ auckland -airport.co.nz) is 20km south of the city centre in the suburb of Mangere. There is no train service, but buses, collective minibuses and taxis run into the city.

Destinations Bay of Islands (4–5 daily; 40min); Blenheim (4–6 daily; 1hr 20min); Christchurch (17–20 daily; 1hr 20min); Dunedin (3 daily; 1hr 50min); Gisborne (6 daily; 1hr); Great Barrier Island (6–8 daily; 40min); Hamilton (3 daily; 30min); Kaitaia (2 daily; 45min); Napier/Hastings (7–9 daily; 1hr); Nelson (8 daily; 1hr 20min); New Plymouth (5–6 daily; 45min); Palmerston North (5 daily; 1hr); Queenstown (5–6 daily; 1hr 50min); Rotorua (2–3 daily; 40min); Taupo (3 daily; 45min); Tauranga (5 daily; 35min); Wanganui (4 daily; 1hr); Wellington (5 daily; 1hr); Whakatane (4 daily; 45min); Whangarei (4–5 daily; 35min).

AIRPORT INFORMATION

i-SITE There's a well-stocked international terminal office (daily 24hr; ☎ 09 275 6467) with a free accommodation

1

AUCKLAND HARBOUR ACTIVITIES

Though most visitors head out into the "real" New Zealand for a little adventure, Auckland has plenty on its doorstep. The city is so water-focused that it would be a shame not to get out on the harbour at some point, either on a ferry to one of the outlying islands (see p.120), a **cruise**, a **dolphin and whale safari** or a **sea-kayaking** trip. You can also do a bridge climb and a bungy jump off the Harbour Bridge. For more activities nearby, check out the boxes on p.111 and p.114.

CRUISES AND SAILING

America's Cup Sailing ☎ 0800 724 569, ⊛ explorenz .co.nz. Head around to Viaduct Harbour to crew on America's Cup racing yachts NZL41 (raced by Japan in the 1995 cup) and NZL68 (used as a trial boat by New Zealand in 2007). There's a chance to grind the winches or take the helm as you get a real sense of power and speed. $160 for a two-hour sail or $210 as part of a team in a three-hour match race between the two boats.

Auckland Harbour Cruise ☎ 09 367 9111, ⊛ fullers.co.nz. Fullers offer a two-hour cruise (daily 10.30am & 1.30pm; $36) that leaves the Ferry Building, briefly visiting the Harbour Bridge and Rangitoto Island. You can stay on Rangitoto and return on a later cruise, and the ticket gives you a free return ferry ride to Devonport.

Pride of Auckland ☎ 0800 724 569, ⊛ explorenz .co.nz. Leisurely sailing trips (1pm & 3.15pm; 1hr 30min; $75), a lunch cruise (1pm; 1hr 30min; $90), a dinner cruise (6pm; 2hr 30min; $120) and a sail to Waiheke Island with a ferry trip back (9am; 3hr; $85).

DOLPHIN AND WHALE WATCHING

Whale & Dolphin Safari Viaduct Harbour ☎ 0800 397 567, ⊛ explorenz.co.nz. There are stacks of common and bottlenose dolphins out in the Hauraki Gulf year-round, often forming huge pods in winter and spring when Bryde's whale and orca sightings increase. Educational and entertaining trips (daily: 4hr30min; $160) head out on a fast, 20m ctamaran which also undertakes marine mammal reserach. Dolphins (which are seen on ninety percent of trips) are often located by the cluster of gannets spectacularly dive-bombing schools of fish. If you don't see any marine mammals you can go again, free, either here on in the Bay of Islands.

KAYAKING AND KAYAK FISHING

Auckland Sea Kayaks ☎ 0800 999 089, ⊛ auckland seakayaks.co.nz. Great guided kayak tours including an easy paddle over to Browns Island (7hr; $165), a longer trip to Rangitoto with a summit hike (10hr; $185), a Rangitoto evening/night trip with sunset from the summit and excellent food along the way (7hr; $195), and a range of overnight trips including camping on Motuihe Island, where there are Little Spotted kiwi ($385).

Fergs Kayaks 12 Tamaki Drive, Okahu Bay ☎ 09 529 2230, ⊛ fergskayaks.co.nz. Offers guided trips 7km across the Waitemata Harbour to Rangitoto Island, hiking to the summit, then paddling back (departures 9.30am plus Mon–Fri 5.30pm, Sat & Sun 4pm; 6hr; $120). Alternatively, opt for their 3km paddle to Devonport (same times; 3hr; $95) with a hike up North Head. In both cases, the later departure gives you a chance to paddle by moon or torchlight. Single sea kayaks ($20/hr, $35/half-day), doubles ($40/hr, $70/half-day), or slightly cheaper sit-on-tops are also available to rent; trips to Rangitoto and Devonport are not generally allowed for rentals.

TIME Unlimited ☎ 0800 868 463, ⊛ newzealand tours.travel. Gorgeous bays and islands are the focus of these trips (half-day $145, full day $245). Groups are generally limited to six and (unusually for kayak operators) single kayaks are available. They even run an overnight trip ($490) with lots of fishing and camping out. Fishing takes precedence with full-day kayak-fishing tours ($295) on which you might expect to catch snapper, kingfish and John Dory, and swim after lunch on a gorgeous beach.

AUCKLAND BRIDGE CLIMB AND BUNGY

Auckland Bridge Climb ☎ 0800 462 5462, ⊛ aucklandbridgeclimb.co.nz. Take in the excellent city views from the highest point on the city's harbour, crossing some 65m above the Waitemata Harbour (3 climbs daily; $120). There's no actual climbing involved, just 90min strolling along steel walkways while harnessed to a cable as guides relate detail on the bridge's fulcrums, pivots and cantilevers. Reservations are essential and anyone over seven can go. Cameras are not allowed but there'll be someone on hand to take a snap and sell it to you later. Free transport from Viaduct Harbour.

Auckland Bridge Bungy ☎ 0800 462 5462, ⊛ bungy.co.nz. The place to go for an adrenalin rush, a 40m leap and a water touch (5 times daily; $150). There's free transport from Viaduct Harbour and you get the free bragging T-shirt.

booking service, courtesy hotel-booking phones, left luggage ($15/day for suitcase or pack) and showers (free; $5 for soap and use of a towel). There's also a domestic terminal office (daily 7am–9pm; ☎ 09 256 8480).

Services There are several ATMs at both terminals, as well as numerous foreign exchange offices at the international terminal that are open whenever flights arrive.

AIRPORT TRANSPORT

Between terminals The international terminal is connected to the domestic terminal by a shuttle bus (5am–10.20pm; every 15min), or you can walk in around ten minutes – follow the blue and white lines.

Taxis Taxis wait outside both terminals. Expect to pay $70 into the central city, Ponsonby or Parnell; $90–100 to Northcote or Devonport.

Bus The Airbus Express (daily: 6am–7.15pm every 15min; 7.15pm–6am every 30min; $16 one-way, $26 return; ⓦ airbus.co.nz) follows a fixed route from both terminals into the city (roughly 45min). Good value for solo travellers.

Collective minibus Most travellers catch one of the door-to-door minibuses that wait outside the terminals. Ask at the first in line and if they're not going to the part of town where you're staying they'll point you to one that is: you'll seldom have to wait more than 15min. Fares are $30 to downtown and $55 to Devonport; groups travelling to the same location get a significant reduction, adding only $8–10 per additional person.

To the airport For pick-up on departure call Super Shuttle (☎ 0800 748 885) or phone a taxi (see p.97).

BY TRAIN

The Overlander ☎ 0800 872 467, ⓦ tranzscenic.co.nz. The train to Hamilton, National Park and Wellington arrives at the Britomart Transport Centre, at the harbour end of Queen St. It operates daily in summer but only Fri, Sat & Sun from May to Aug.

Destinations Hamilton (3–7 weekly; 2hr 30min); National Park (3–7 weekly; 5hr 30min); Ohakune (3–7 weekly; 6hr 30min); Otorohanga (3–7 weekly; 3hr); Palmerston North (3–7 weekly; 9hr 30min); Taihape (3–7 weekly; 7hr 30min); Wellington (3–7 weekly; 12hr).

BY BUS

InterCity/Newmans, Great Sights and Northliner long-distance bus services arrive at the Sky City Coach Terminal.

All other operators stop outside 172 Quay St, opposite the Downtown Ferry Terminal.

BUS COMPANIES

Go Kiwi ☎ 07 866 0336, ⓦ go-kiwi.co.nz. Daily to the Coromandel Peninsula with en route pick-ups at Auckland Airport – ideal if you want to head straight to Whitianga.

InterCity, Newmans, Northliner, Great Sights ☎ 09 583 5780, ⓦ intercity.co.nz. National coverage.

Main Coachline ☎ 09 278 8070, ⓦ maincoachline .co.nz. Almost daily to Dargaville and Warkworth.

NakedBus ☎ 0900 62 533 (calls cost $2/min, more from mobiles), ⓦ nakedbus.com. National coverage.

The 'Naki Bus ☎ 0508 465 622, ⓦ nakibus.co.nz. Auckland–Hamilton–New Plymouth–Hawera daily.

Destinations Dargaville (1 daily, not Sat; 3hr); Gisborne (1 daily; 9hr 15min); Hamilton (16–19 daily; 2hr); Hastings (2 daily; 7hr 30min); Helensville (Mon–Fri 6 daily; 1hr 15min); Kerikeri (2–3 daily; 4hr 30min); Kumeu (6 daily; 35min); Napier (2 daily; 7hr); National Park (1 daily; 6hr); New Plymouth (3 daily; 6hr–6hr 30min); Ohakune (1 daily; 6hr 30min); Orewa (5–7 daily; 30min); Paihia (6–8 daily; 4hr); Palmerston North (3 daily; 9–10hr); Rotorua (9–12 daily; 4hr); Taihape (4–5 daily; 7hr); Taupo (7–9 daily; 5hr); Tauranga (4–5 daily; 4hr); Thames (5 daily; 1hr 45min); Waipu (5–7 daily; 2hr); Waitomo Caves (1 daily; 3hr); Warkworth (6–8 daily; 1hr); Wellington (4–5 daily; 11–12hr); Whangarei (5–7 daily; 2hr 40min); Whitianga (1 daily; 3hr).

BY CAR

Car rental For information on car rental, see p.97.

Departing When it comes time to leave, northbound drivers can take either SH1 directly over the harbour bridge, or go west around the head of the Waitemata Harbour past the wineries, West Coast beaches and Waitakere Ranges to meet SH1 at Wellsford. Southbound, either head straight down SH1 to Hamilton, branch east to the Coromandel Peninsula, or take the slow road down the Seabird Coast.

BY BIKE

Northbound Cyclists must use the Devonport Ferry rather than the harbour bridge if heading north but will do well to take the western route, possibly riding a suburban train to Waitakere ($1 for the bike; travel outside peak hours).

Southbound Cyclists heading south are better off following the Seabird Coast, avoiding the Southern Motorway, the main route south out of the city.

GETTING AROUND

You can get to many of the most interesting parts of Auckland on foot, notably along the Coast to Coast Walkway. Auckland's poor but improving public transport system is centred on the Britomart Transport Centre at the harbour end of Queen St – suburban trains pull in here while buses have various stops nearby. Out on the harbour, ferries connect the city to the inner suburb of Devonport and the islands. Taxis are best contacted by phone (see p.97). Parking isn't a major headache, but drivers aren't courteous and you may be better off renting a car just before you leave the city.

1

AUCKLAND TRANSPORT INFORMATION AND PASSES

For integrated information on Auckland's buses, trains and ferries consult **Maxx** (☎0800 103 080, ⓦmaxx.co.nz), which includes a timetable helpline and comprehensive journey planner. Alternatively, pick up the five free *Maxx Guide* transport maps from Britomart: the Central and Eastern regions are the most useful.

For short-stay visitors, the best deal is the one-day **Discovery Pass** ($15 from bus drivers, ferry ticket offices and Britomart and Newmarket train stations), which covers all the areas you're likely to want to explore and includes the Inner Link, suburban trains and all ferries to the north shore (including Devonport), though not those to Rangitoto or Waiheke.

Those staying longer should get a stored-value **Hop card** (ⓦmyhop.co.nz), saving you fiddling with change and earning a ten to fifteen percent discount on bus, rail and ferry fares. Buy the card ($10) from Britomart or numerous retailers around town.

BY TRAIN

Suburban trains Few visitors will find much use for the services which start from the Britomart Transport Centre and call at places that are mostly of little interest to tourists. The main exceptions are the suburbs of Newmarket (every 10–30min; 7min) and Kingsland (every 15–30min; 16min). Tickets ($1.70 to both) can be bought at Britomart or on board.

BY BUS

Departures Most buses don't depart from the Britomart Transport Centre (see p.95) but from any of a couple of dozen stops along city streets within a 10min walk of there. It is confusing, so ask at Britomart or get the exact stop location from ⓦmaxx.co.nz. The Link buses listed below are the most useful services.

Fares For buses other than the Link, fares are zoned: the inner city is $0.50, Parnell, Newmarket, Mount Eden and Ponsonby are all $1.80, Epsom is $3.40 and so on.

LINK SERVICES

City Link (Mon–Sat 6.30am–11.30pm every 7–8min; Sun 7am–11pm every 20min; 50¢; free to Hop card users). The red buses of this central city service travel the length of Queen St from K' Rd to Britomart Transport Centre. Every second bus continues to the Wynyard Quarter.

Inner Link (Mon–Sat 6.30am–11pm, Sun 7am–11pm; every 10–15min; $1.80). The single most useful route, with green buses continuously looping through the city, Parnell, Auckland Museum, Newmarket, K' Rd and Ponsonby; buy tickets on the bus.

Outer Link (Mon–Sat 6.30am–11pm, Sun 7am–11pm; every 15min; $1.80–3.40). Orange bus making a larger loop than the Inner Link and visiting Mt Eden, MOTAT and Herne Bay. Connects with the Inner Link in Parnell, the Auckland Museum, Newmarket and Three Lamps in Ponsonby.

OTHER BUS SERVICES

NightRider Journey planner at ⓦmaxx.co.nz. A secure service designed to get you home after a night out (Sat & Sun 1–3am; $4.50).

Explorer Bus ☎0800 439 756, ⓦexplorerbus.co.nz. Get around the main sights on this hop-on-hop-off bus (mid-Oct to mid-April every 30min 9am–4pm; mid-April to mid-Oct hourly 10am–3pm; 1-day pass $40, 2-day pass $65, pay cash to the driver) that comes with commentary. The circuit starts from the Ferry Building on Quay St, goes along Tamaki Drive to Bastion Point and Kelly Tarlton's, up to Parnell and the Auckland Museum, and back via Viaduct Harbour. In summer (mid-Oct to mid-April), a second loop from the Auckland Museum takes in Mount Eden, MOTAT and the zoo.

BY FERRY

The Waitemata Harbour was once a seething mass of ferries bringing commuters in from the suburbs, and ferries remain a fast, pleasurable and scenic way to get around. The main destinations are the Hauraki Gulf islands and Devonport; several Rangitoto-bound and Waiheke-bound ferries also stop at Devonport.

FERRY OPERATORS

Fullers ☎09 367 9111, ⓦfullers.co.nz. Auckland's principal ferry company runs ferries to Devonport (Mon–Sat 6.15am–11.15pm, Sun 7.15am–10pm; $11 return, bikes free), the cheapest ferry in town, which is included in the Discovery Pass (see box above). It also operates ferries to Rangitoto, Waiheke and Great Barrier Island.

360 Discovery ☎0800 360 3472, ⓦ360discovery .co.nz. Passenger ferry services to Tiritiri Matangi, Rotoroa Island and a regular service across the Hauraki Gulf to Coromandel Town ($55 one-way): for non-drivers it's a pleasant alternative to taking the bus via Thames.

Destinations Coromandel (5–7 weekly; 2hr); Devonport (every 30min; 10min); Great Barrier (4–9 weekly; 2–5hr); Gulf Harbour Marina (1–3 daily; 50min); Rangitoto (3–4 daily; 40min); Rotoroa Island (5–7 weekly in summer; 1hr 15min); Tiritiri Matangi Island (4 weekly; 1hr 30min); Waiheke (roughly hourly; 35min).

BY CAR

With many of the Auckland region's sights conveniently accessible on foot or by public transport, there isn't an advantage in having a car while in the city centre, though you'll need one to explore the Kumeu wineries and surf beaches of the West Coast. If you've just flown in you may want to wait and rent a car when you're ready to leave the city.

Car rental The international and major national companies all have depots close to the airport and free shuttle buses to pick you up; smaller companies are mostly based in the city or inner suburbs. In the central city, you'll find several close together along Beach Rd. The main international and local operators are listed in Basics (see p.33).

Buying a car If you're planning on some serious touring, you may be interested in buying a car. For general advice, consult Basics (see p.34), then peruse the notice boards in hostels, or visit ⓦ trademe.co.nz and ⓦ autotrader.co.nz. One of the best bets is the Backpackers Car Market, 20 East St (daily 9.30am–5pm; ☎ 09 377 7761, ⓦ backpackerscarmarket.co.nz), just off K' Rd, where backpackers buy and sell directly to each other. Alternatively, head to the Auckland Carfair, Ellerslie Racecourse, Greenlane (every Sun 9am–noon; ☎ 09 529 2233, ⓦ carfair.co.nz), which is well organized, with qualified folk on hand to check roadworthiness.

Driving Getting around Auckland by car isn't especially taxing, though it is worth avoiding the rush hours (7–9am & 4–6.30pm). On first acquaintance, Auckland's urban freeways are unnerving, with frequent junctions, lane changing at whim and vehicles overtaking aggressively on all sides. Inner-city streets are metered, which means that parking is best done in the multistorey car parks dotted round the city; some are not open 24hr, so check the latest exit time.

BY TAXI

Taxi ranks are scattered around the city including along Queen St, at Viaduct Harbour and along K' Rd. Alternatively, call Discount (☎ 09 529 1000) which is

cheap, or sustainability-oriented Green Cabs (☎ 0508 447 336, ⓦ greencabs.co.nz) who use hybrids and are only a little pricier. From the city centre to Ponsonby should be $12–14.

BY BIKE

Routes Cycling around Auckland's hills can be a tiring and dispiriting exercise, compounded by motorists' lack of bike-awareness. However, a few areas lend themselves to exploration, most notably the delightful harbourside Tamaki Drive east of the city centre, which forms part of a signposted 50km cycle route around the city and its isthmus.

BIKE RENTAL

Adventure Capital 23 Commerce St ☎ 09 337 0633, ⓦ adventurecapital.co.nz. Handy downtown location for low-grade mountain bikes ($15 4hr; $20/day; $60/5 days) that are ideal for knocking about town, through parks and along the waterfront.

Cycle Auckland Devonport Wharf ☎ 09 445 1189, ⓦ cycleauckland.co.nz. A great selection (from $28/day; $115/week), including road, touring, tandem, hybrid and kids' bikes, plus self-guided and guided tours. The people to talk to if you fancy more than just a meander around town.

Fergs Kayaks 12 Tamaki Drive, Okahu Bay ☎ 09 529 2230, ⓦ fergskayaks.co.nz. Rents cruisers ($20/2hr; $30/day) perfect for a spin along the waterfront. Mon–Fri 10am–5pm, Sat & Sun 9am–5pm.

Adventure Cycles 9 Premier Ave, Western Springs ☎ 0800 245 38687, ⓦ adventure-auckland.co.nz. Somewhat inconveniently sited west of the zoo, but a great resource for short-term bike rental (city bikes $20/day; mountain bikes $25/day) and touring bikes ($90/week; $200/month; panniers $40/week). They also do repairs, have lots of great information and operate buy-back schemes for those who are staying longer. Call ahead to make sure they're about and have what you want, then catch bus #042, #043 or #045 from stand D8 at Britomart. Thurs–Mon 7.30am–7pm.

INFORMATION AND TOURS

i-SITE Auckland has two central visitor centres: 137 Quay St (daily: Nov–April 8.30am–6.30pm; May–Oct 9am–5pm; ☎ 0800 282 552, ⓦ aucklandnz.com); and the more cramped branch inside the Sky City Casino (daily 8.30am–6pm; same contact details), on the corner of Victoria and Federal streets. Both stock leaflets from around the country including a number of advertisement-heavy free publications such as Auckland A–Z (ⓦ aucklandtourism .co.nz). The Devonport branch at 3 Victoria Rd (daily 8.30am–5pm; ☎ 09 446 0677, ⓦ devonport.co.nz) stocks maps and the free *Old Devonport Walk* leaflet outlining points of historic and architectural interest.

DOC office Inside the Quay St i-SITE (Nov–April Mon–Fri 9am–5pm, Sat & Sun 10am–4pm; May–Oct Mon–Fri 9am–5pm; ☎ 09 379 6476, ✉ aucklandvc@doc.govt.nz). Great for hiking information, stocks DOC leaflets and does track bookings for the whole country although it specializes in the Auckland and Hauraki Gulf region.

Maps This guide's maps and those in Auckland A–Z are adequate for most purposes, though you might want to splash out on the *KiwiMap Auckland Pathfinder Directory* ($29), which includes 26 regional town maps.

Backpacker information Check the notice boards in hostels, where the adverts cover rides, vehicle sales and

1

job opportunities. Some hostels offer an extensive booking service for onward travel; try *Base Auckland*, both *Nomads* hostels and the *YHA International*.

Devonport Explorer Tours (daily, roughly every hour;

📞 09 357 6366, 🌐 devonporttours.co.nz). Operates hour-long mini-bus tours ($35) of the main sights, including both volcanoes. You can get off at North Head and catch the next tour as it comes around.

ACCOMMODATION

With several efficient door-to-door shuttle services into central Auckland there's hardly any reason to stay in any of the hotels at, or near, the **airport**, though Auckland is a place where you might choose to stay **outside the city centre**. Most sightseeing can be done as easily from the suburbs, particularly Ponsonby, less than 2km west of the centre, Mount Eden, 2km south of the centre, Devonport, a short ferry journey across the harbour, and Parnell, 2km east of the centre. All are generally more peaceful than the city centre but still well supplied with places to eat and drink, and access is good on the Inner Link and Outer Link buses (see p.96). Note that airport shuttle buses will drop you in these suburbs for a similar price to downtown, and Devonport only costs a few dollars extra. Predictably, **camping** involves staying further out and it's not really worth the hassle unless you've rented a campervan.

ESSENTIALS

Seasons With a broad range of accommodation, Auckland meets the needs of most budgets, but that doesn't stop everywhere filling up between December and March, when you should book ahead. At other times, it's less critical, and through the quiet winter months (June–Sept) you'll be spoiled for choice and significant discounts on room rates can be had; it's worth asking.

Costs Room rates in Auckland are across the board a touch higher than in the rest of the country, though not unreasonably so. Check 🌐 aucklandnz.com for deals.

CENTRAL AUCKLAND

Central Auckland is the place to find international four- and five-star hotels, mostly geared towards business travellers and tour groups; walk-in rates are usually high, though there are often good weekend deals. There's also a stack of backpacker hostels, most set up to assist new arrivals to plan onward travel, to the extent of having fully staffed on-site travel services – sometimes pushing favoured trips and activities, but generally offering impartial advice. With the exception of the YHAs, most downtown hostels cram in the beds and, with bars and clubs only a short stagger away, cater to a party crowd. Wherever you stay, you'll probably have to pay for parking.

Base Auckland 229 Queen St 📞 0800 227 369, 🌐 stay atbase.com; map p.76. Enormous, well-run hostel in a ten-storey converted office building. Despite the inevitable impersonality of housing over five hundred, everything

runs smoothly and it seldom feels too crowded. They've thought of everything, including a downstairs bar, separate terrace bar, massive internet centre, helpful travel office, jobs centre, laundry, gear storage and electronic key access to each floor and public areas. Mixed dorms sleep up to eight but it's worth the extra for a mixed four-bed dorm supplied with sheets or a further dollar for the separate women-only "sanctuary" with extra pampering. All sorts of evening activities, and parking nearby ($10/overnight, $20/24hr). Big dorms $29, small dorms $31, double $75, en suites with TV $93

BK Hostel 3 Mercury Lane 📞 09 307 0052, 🌐 bkhostel .co.nz; map p.76. Well-kept, pastel-painted hostel in the heart of the lively K' Rd district, so outside rooms can be noisy. No dorms as such, just three-bed shares, doubles and twins with cheaper rates for those without windows. Common areas are spacious and security is good. Shares $26, doubles $76

Braemar on Parliament Street 7 Parliament St 📞 09 377 5463, 🌐 parliamentstreet.co.nz; map p.76. This very welcoming 1901 townhouse B&B in the heart of the city has retained its late Victorian feel. There's a large suite, a smaller en-suite room and two rooms that share a bathroom (all baths are clawfoot), and breakfast is a major affair with dishes cooked to order. There's free internet, guest parking and a strong sustainability ethic. Shared bath $225, room $250, suite $350

The Chatham 70–76 Pitt St 📞 09 303 0309, 🌐 chatham auckland.co.nz; map p.76. Predominantly two-bedroom

---

FIRST-NIGHT CAMPING

If you're picking up a car or campervan near the airport after a long flight you may not fancy tangling with central city traffic. The closest appealing **campsite** is *Ambury Regional Park* (see p.102). There are also numerous tempting **beachside spots** only an hour or two from the airport, including: *Miranda Holiday Park* (see p.120); *Rays Rest Camping Reserve* (see p.120); *Muriwai Beach Motor Camp* (see p.115); *Orewa Beach Top 10 Holiday Park* (see p.117); *Wenderholm Regional Park* (see p.117); *Piha Domain Motor Camp* (see p.115); and *Shakespear Regional Park* (see p.117).

serviced apartments in a seven-storey block with views over the rooftops to the distant harbour. The fit-out isn't particularly high quality but each apartment has a full kitchen with dishwasher, washing machine and Sky TV. Great value. One-bedroom $140, two-bedroom $165

Heritage 35 Hobson St ⓣ 0800 368 888, ⓦ heritagehotels.co.nz; map p.76. Top-class hotel partly fashioned from the original Farmers department store. Occasional bits of aged planking and wooden supports crop up in public areas, but it is fitted out to a very high standard and many rooms have views across the harbour or into the glassed-in atrium. The outside pool has views over the city. $200

★ **Hilton** Princes Wharf, 147 Quay St ⓣ 09 978 2000, ⓦ hilton.com; map p.76. Fabulously sited on a wharf jutting into the harbour, this majestic hotel comes with a classy restaurant and the *Bellini* cocktail bar – a taste of the high life. The beautifully decorated rooms all have a terrace or balcony but it is worth paying the extra $80 for a good view. $350

★ **Hotel DeBrett** 2 High St ⓣ 09 925 9000, ⓦ hoteldebrett.com; map p.76. The height of Auckland chic, this classy 25-room boutique hotel references its Art Deco origins while adding bold colours and mismatched but complementary furniture. Bathrooms are gorgeous, continental breakfast and wi-fi are included and guests have access to a lovely lounge with honesty bar. There's also the *Kitchen* restaurant and a couple of excellent bars open to the public. Rooms $300, suites $400

Jucy Hotel 62 Emily Place ⓣ 09 379 6633, ⓦ jucyhotel.com; map p.76. It's backpacker standards without the dorms – or much of the spirit – in this compact and central hotel brought to you by the same people who rent budget cars and campers. Rooms aren't big, and some have little natural light, but they're brightly painted in signature green and purple, decent value and surprisingly quiet. The en suites are considerably nicer. There's a basic communal kitchen, TV lounge, an espresso bar on site and a cheap breakfast deal with a local café. Secure parking is available for $12.50/day. Singles $49, doubles $69, en suites with TV $99

Nomads Auckland 16–20 Fort St ⓣ 0508 666 237, ⓦ nomadshostels.com; map p.76. Classy conversion of a city office building into an upscale hostel on seven floors, complete with a women-only floor, rooftop kitchen and outdoor barbecue area. There's also a spa pool, sauna, good travel desk and the lively Fort Street Union bar, which offers very cheap meals to guests. Accommodation is in a range of mixed and female dorms (6–12 beds), and en-suite doubles and twins (the cheaper ones without windows). Dorms $24, en-suite 4-shares $36, en-suite doubles $91

Nomads Fat Camel 38 Fort St ⓣ 09 307 0181, ⓦ nomadshostels.com; map p.76. Solid downtown hostel with six- and eight-bed mixed and female dorms (windowless ones are the cheapest in town), twins and doubles all arranged in small apartments, each group having its own kitchen, lounge and showers. There's a bar with very cheap meals for guests, and a travel desk. Windowless dorms $19, other dorms $26, doubles $65

★ **The Quadrant** 10 Waterloo Quadrant ⓣ 0800 666 611, ⓦ thequadrant.com; map p.76. Designer hotel chic without the high prices, this four-star place has a fresh appearance and great city and harbour views from the balcony of most of its 250 rooms. Most come with kitchenette and some have a washing machine and dishwasher. There's also a compact and intimate bar, a breakfast and lunch café, spa, sauna, a small gym and 10Gb of free wi-fi daily. Studio $130, one-bed apartment $155

Scenic Hotel 380 Queen St ⓣ 09 374 1741, ⓦ scenichotelgroup.co.nz; map p.76. Good mid-range hotel with lobby areas restored to their Art Deco glory. Many of the hundred rooms have city views and/or full kitchens and there's a small fitness room. $180

YHA Auckland City Corner of City Rd & Liverpool St ⓣ 09 309 2802, ⓦ yha.co.nz; map p.76. Large and central YHA with seven floors of mostly twin and double rooms – the upper ones with fine city views – plus well-equipped common areas. No dedicated parking. Single-sex and mixed dorms $26, four-shares $30, doubles $80

★ **YHA Auckland International** 5 Turner St ⓣ 09 302 8200, ⓦ yha.co.nz; map p.76. The pick of the two YHAs, this purpose-built 168-bed establishment comes with excellent cooking facilities, spacious rooms, separate TV and quiet lounges, a travel centre and wi-fi throughout. There are even a few free parking spaces; book early. Single-sex dorms $28, single-sex and mixed four-shares $32, doubles $85, en suites $98

TOP 5 ROOMS WITH A VIEW

Hilton p.99
The Quadrant p.99
Number One House p.101
Peace and Plenty Inn p.101
Takapuna Beach Holiday Park p.102

PARNELL

Parnell is strong on B&Bs and hostels, is close to the Auckland Museum, has plenty of places to eat and drink and has good Inner Link bus connections.

Ascot Parnell 32 St Stephens Ave ⓣ 09 309 9012, ⓦ ascotparnell.com; map p.83. Tranquil, comfortable Belgian-run B&B in a small, modern apartment block, with two mini-suites and a huge harbour suite. An enormous guest lounge with balcony overlooks the city and harbour, and there's a 12m pool, secure parking, free wi-fi and computer, and airport pick-up (for a small fee). Try the signature savoury Flemish toast for breakfast. Rooms $225, harbour suite $265

1

Chalet Chevron 14 Brighton Rd ☎09 309 0290, ⓦchaletchevron.co.nz; map p.83. Comfortable twelve-room B&B with a range of en-suite rooms, some with distant sea views, two with baths and several well geared for singles. An all-you-can-eat breakfast is served and there's free wi-fi throughout plus a guest computer. Singles $125, doubles $250

★ **City Garden Lodge** 25 St George's Bay Rd ☎09 302 0880, ⓦcitygardenlodge.co.nz; map p.83. Friendly backpackers in a large, well-organized villa originally built for the Queen of Tonga, and surrounded by expansive lawns. Along with spacious dorms and some lovely doubles/twins there are little touches such as hot water bottles in winter and even a yoga/meditation room (classes available). Dorms $30, shares $32, doubles $70

International Backpackers 2 Churton St ☎09 358 4584, ⓦaucklandinternationalbp.com; map p.83. One-time home for wayward girls but now a friendly, spacious hostel in a quiet area with street parking and rejuvenated rooms. Dorm $23, doubles $56, en-suite room $68

Lantana Lodge 60 St George's Bay Rd ☎09 373 4546, ⓦlantanalodge.co.nz; map p.83. Clean and friendly hostel with a maximum of 25 guests, free wi-fi, free local calls and a homely feel. Dorms $28, doubles $75

Parnell Inn 320 Parnell Rd ☎0800 472 763, ⓦparnellinn.co.nz; map p.83. Compact and simple hotel right in the heart of Parnell. Rooms are fairly small but there are some good views and kitchenettes are available. Off-street parking. $105

PONSONBY

Ponsonby isn't especially close to the main sights, but its B&Bs and hostels are well sited for the Ponsonby Rd café, bar and shopping strip. The Inner Link bus runs right along Ponsonby Rd.

★ **23 Hepburn** 23 Hepburn St ☎0800 283 000, ⓦ23hepburn.co.nz; map p.86. Whites and creams are the dominant tones in this lovely three-room B&B on a quiet, leafy street a 2min walk from Ponsonby Rd. Continental breakfast ingredients are supplied in your room and are best eaten out on the sunny porch (if the weather behaves). Book ahead to secure one of the larger rooms at the front ($230). $210

Abaco on Jervois 59 Jervois Rd ☎0800 220 066, ⓦabaco .co.nz; map p.86. Attractive motel close to the Ponsonby cafés, with a range of rooms and plenty of off-street parking. Spacious rooms come with cooking facilities, and deluxe suites ($185) add spa baths and distant harbour views. $125

Brown Kiwi 7 Prosford St ☎09 378 0191, ⓦbrownkiwi .co.nz; map p.86. Compact, cosy little hostel in a restored Victorian villa on a quiet street close to the Ponsonby cafés. A patio and tiny garden at the back adds to the relaxing atmosphere. Daytime parking is poor but there are good bus connections. Dorms $27, share $30, doubles $72

Freemans Lodge 65 Wellington St ☎09 376 5046 ⓦfreemansbandb.co.nz; map p.86. There's a relaxed no-shoes-inside feel to this very central hostel in a pair of houses that are aging but well looked after and clean. One spacious dorm has beds rather than bunks, doubles come with TV, there's a small garden and free internet and wi-fi. Dorms $30, doubles $80

★ **Great Ponsonby Art Hotel** 30 Ponsonby Terrace ☎09 376 5989, ⓦgreatpons.co.nz; map p.86. This welcoming boutique hotel, in a restored 1898 villa a 3min walk from Ponsonby Rd, is boldly decorated in ocean tones using native timbers and Pacific artworks. Guests can make use of the sunny lounge and shaded garden and the breakfasts are a delight. The luxurious en-suite rooms come with Sky TV, iPod docks and free wi-fi; there are also self-catering studio units ($260). Rooms $245

Uenuku Lodge 217 Ponsonby Rd ☎09 378 8990, ⓦuenukulodge.co.nz; map p.86. Comfortable, good-value hostel worked into a warren of an old boarding house just steps from the action on Ponsonby Rd and on the Inner Link bus route. It's bright, clean and there's parking. Dorms $27, shares $30, doubles $69

★ **Verandahs** 6 Hopetoun St ☎09 360 4180, ⓦverandahs.co.nz; map p.86. Welcoming and beautifully appointed backpackers in a pair of grand 1905 villas overlooking a leafy park close to the Ponsonby Rd and K' Rd nightlife. The hostel has a selection of spacious rooms, limited off-street parking and intentionally lacks TV. Dorms $27, shares $30, doubles $72, en suites $92

NEWMARKET AND EPSOM

The widest selection of motels is in Newmarket and Epsom where at least a dozen nestle in one kilometre. They're close to Newmarket's shopping but relatively far from most sights and beaches.

Hansens 96 Great South Rd ☎0800 898 797, ⓦhansensmotel.co.nz; map p.90. It's old but well kept, and is the best-value budget motel along this strip. All units (except for two budget rooms) come with full cooking facilities. There's a small pool and spa, and free internet in the office. Budget $81, units $95

Oak Tree 104 Great South Rd ☎0800 625 8733, ⓦoaktree.co.nz; map p.90. Considerably more swish than most of the motels along Great South Rd, the Oak Tree has nicely modernized studios with a basic kitchen, and one-bedroom apartments. Some of both have a/c. Studios $120, apartments $195

Off Broadway 11 Alpers Ave ☎0800 427 623, ⓦoff broadway.co.nz; map p.90. Business-oriented hotel with a/c, soundproofed en-suite studios (go for the larger ones with bathtub and balcony), and several one-bedroom suites with spa bath. There's undercover parking, a small gym, and breakfast can be served in your room. Studios $120, suites $195

Siesta 70 Great South Rd ☎0800 743 782, ☜siesta motel.co.nz; map p.90. Ageing but decent motel with studios and self-catering units, some recently remodelled, and all with free wi-fi. Communal barbecue area. Studios **$100**, kitchen units **$120**

Tudor Court 108 Great South Rd ☎0800 826 878, ☜tudor.co.nz; map p.90. Compact motel with small hotel-style rooms and slightly larger ones with kitchenettes. Free wi-fi and HDTVs in most rooms. Rooms **$100**, rooms with kitchenettes **$115**

MOUNT EDEN

Suburban Mount Eden is strong on hostels and B&Bs. The Outer Link bus runs close to all the places listed below.

★ **Bamber House** 22 View Rd ☎09 623 4267, ☜hostelbackpacker.com; map p.90. Spacious, well-managed hostel spread across two houses – a lovely old villa and a swish modern house – in expansive grounds, plus several en-suite cabins that come with a kettle and fridge. There's a large lawn out front and a host of other facilities including wi-fi. Dorms **$28**, shares **$30**, doubles **$70**, en-suite cabins **$90**

Bavaria 83 Valley Rd ☎09 638 9641, ☜bavaria bandbhotel.co.nz; map p.90. Modest eleven-room B&B in a comfortable suburban villa. It's popular with German-speakers and there are Teutonic touches to the buffet continental breakfast. Rooms come with renovated bathrooms, some have a deck, and there's free internet and wi-fi. **$160**

Eden Park B&B 20 Bellwood Ave ☎09 630 5721, ☜bedandbreakfastnz.com; map p.90. Welcoming B&B in renovated grand villa in a suburb that's very peaceful – except when there's a game on at nearby Eden Park. With a chandelier, fresh flowers, home-made biscuits, a three-course breakfast and heated everything you can't go far wrong. Three en suites, plus one room with a private bath and its own deep tub. Good single rates ($135). **$235**

Oaklands Lodge 5a Oaklands Rd ☎09 638 6545, ☜oaklands.co.nz; map p.90. Large two-storey Victorian house right by Mount Eden shops, mostly comprising dorms with beds rather than bunks, and an abundance of separate lounge areas. Dorms **$25**, shares **$27**, doubles **$64**

Pentlands 22 Pentlands Ave ☎09 638 7031, ☜pentlands.co.nz; map p.90. Appealing, renovated hostel on a quiet suburban street a 10min walk from Mount Eden shops and cafés. There's a big lounge (with piano), plenty of DVDs and loads of parking. Dorms **$24**, shares **$27**, doubles **$66**

REMUERA

Omahu Lodge 33 Omahu Rd ☎09 524 5648, ☜omahulodge.co.nz; map p.90. The spa and deep, solar-heated swimming pool are central to this four-room B&B, housed partly in a 1940s bungalow in a refined suburb.

Robes, bed turndowns, complimentary sherry and free wi-fi and internet are all part of the service. There's also a separate TV lounge and a sauna. **$230**

KOHIMARAMA

Aarangi Motel 1 Melanesia Rd ☎09 521 2649, ☜aarangimotel.co.nz; map p.74. Proximity to a good beach, just a block away, is the main selling point for this ageing but neat and tidy hacienda-style motel in a quiet neighbourhood. Several units have separate bedroom and kitchenette, and some have a balcony overlooking the little, manicured garden. **$175**

DEVONPORT

Devonport has Auckland's densest cluster of fine B&Bs, all close to the Devonport ferry and some reasonable cafés (though none of the city's really good restaurants).

108 Victoria Rd 108 Victoria Rd ☎09 445 7565, ✉smj@ihug.co.nz; map p.89. A B&B with two rooms overlooking a saltwater swimming pool and a cottage in lush gardens. Breakfast costs extra, there's a late checkout and both rooms can be rented as one. **$120**

Devonport Garden Room 23 Cheltenham Rd ☎09 445 2472, ☜devonportgardenroom.co.nz; map p.89. You get your own entrance to this lovely modernized studio in an 1870s villa opening out onto a brick courtyard and leafy garden with BBQ area and spa pool. Sumptuous breakfasts can be served under an arbour or in your room. **$180**

Mahoe B&B 15b King Edward Parade ☎09 445 1515, ☜mahoe.co.nz; map p.89. Lovely property in the heart of Devonport, set back from the waterfront, tastefully furnished and offering either B&B accommodation in the house or a separate, self-contained apartment. Breakfast is $15/person extra. Rooms **$170**, apartment **$220**

Parituhu Beachstay 3 King Edward Parade ☎09 445 6559, ☜parituhu.co.nz; map p.89. A gay-friendly budget B&B homestay in the heart of Devonport that overlooks the harbour. There's just the one room, a private bath, access to a secluded garden and self-service breakfast. **$185**

★ **Peace & Plenty Inn** 6 Flagstaff Terrace ☎09 445 2925, ☜peaceandplenty.co.nz; map p.89. This is one of New Zealand's finest B&Bs, but it's relaxed, well priced and has an ethical emphasis on using local produce and services. Elegantly restored kauri floorboards lead through to a lovely veranda, past exquisite rooms filled with fresh flowers and equipped with sherry and port. Venture outside the bounds of the inn and you're right in the heart of Devonport. **$265**

BIRKENHEAD AND NORTHCOTE

Number One House 1 Princes St, Northcote Point ☎09 480 7659, ☜nz-homestay.co.nz; map p.74. Hospitable B&B with views across Waitemata Harbour to the city and Rangitoto Island. It has a small beach, city access by ferry

1

(frequent weekdays, sparse at weekends), two rooms, a self-contained apartment and a quirky garden with a little hobbit house. Breakfasts are great, plus there's the opportunity to go out on the owner's yacht ($295/person/day including lunch). **$240**

CAMPSITES AND HOLIDAY PARKS

There are several well-equipped motor camps within the city limits that are fine for campervans and offer bargain cabins, though without your own vehicle you'll end up spending a lot of money on buses. Ambury is the nicest spot to pitch a tent.

Ambury Regional Park Mangere, 6km north of the airport ☎09 366 2000; map p.74. Basic, flat sites (no power) in a sheep field overlooking the Manukau Harbour – a great location for those wanting to rest up after flying in to NZ. It's sometimes closed to campervans in winter, so call ahead. The adjacent farm park (with pigs, sheep, rabbits etc) has toilets and free showers. Camping **$10**

Auckland North Shore Motels and Holiday Park 52 Northcote Rd, Northcote ☎0508 909 090, ⓦnsmotels .co.nz; map p.74. Well-appointed site with an indoor swimming pool and extensive BBQ areas, on the North Shore just off the northern motorway and only a 15min drive from the city centre. Bus #921 from lower Albert St, City (and others) stop nearby. Tents and vans **$40**, cabins **$85**, tourist flats **$110**, motel units **$145**

Avondale Motor Park 46 Bollard Ave, Avondale ☎0800 100 542, ⓦaucklandmotorpark.co.nz; map p.74. Restful site 6km southwest of the city centre and accessible by bus #210 or #211 from Victoria St in the city. Camping **$16**, on-site vans **$50**, cabins **$60**, tourist cabin **$70**, motel unit **$90**

★ **Takapuna Beach Holiday Park** 22 The Promenade, Takapuna ☎09 489 7909, ⓦtakapunabeachholidaypark .co.nz; map p.74. Small beachside caravan park on the North Shore overlooking Rangitoto, and a 5min walk from Takapuna shops and restaurants. It's neither very well equipped nor particularly spacious but you can't beat the setting. Frequent buses (#822, #839, #858, #879 etc) from lower Albert St in central Auckland. Camping **$40**, on-site caravans **$72**, kitchen cabins **$72**, tourist flats **$125**

EATING

Aucklanders take their eating seriously and, as befits a city of this size, there's a huge range of places – and standards are generally very high. Daytime cafés often morph into full-blown restaurants, with alcohol consumption becoming an increasingly significant activity as the night wears on. A couple of culinary highlights reside in the shopping district of Newmarket, nearby suburban Mount Eden and up-and-coming Kingsland. If you find yourself peckish while visiting Kelly Tarlton's or swimming at Mission Bay, try one of the selection of places along Tamaki Drive. Sadly, Devonport doesn't have the culinary heft you'd expect of a wealthy suburb with several pricey B&Bs.

THE WATERFRONT

Fine summer days are a perfect time to venture down to the cafés, restaurants and bars along the waterfront, specifically Princes Wharf, Viaduct Harbour and the new cluster of places in the Wynyard Quarter. Some places are ostentatious and soulless, though the best (listed below) have great food and luscious vistas of super-yachts.

Euro Princes Wharf ☎09 309 9866, ⓦeurobar.co.nz; map p.76. Classy, waterside à la carte dining helmed by local celebrity chef Simon Gault. The service is always spot on and the food imaginative and tasty. Most mains are over $40, but the signature rotisserie chicken served with mash and peanut slaw is a modest $32. Mon–Fri noon–11pm or later, Sat & Sun 10am–11pm or later.

Grand Harbour 18 Customs St West ☎09 357 6889, ⓦgrandharbour.co.nz; map p.76. More opulent than

most of the city's Chinese places and heavily patronized by the Chinese community, this bustling modern restaurant is popular for business lunches and serves great *yum cha* (daily 11am–3pm). Daily 11am–3pm & 5.30–10pm.

Market Seafood Brasserie Auckland Fish Market, 22 Jellicoe St, Wynyard Quarter ☎09 303 0262, ⓦafm .co.nz; map p.76. Take a step back from the glitzy waterfront places and dine among the counters of wet fish at this casual, order-at-the-counter spot that's perfect for 6 tempura scallops ($19), seafood risotto ($18, large $25) or quality fish and chips ($16). Also coffee at the attached café. Licensed. Daily 7am–7pm.

Soul Viaduct Harbour ☎09 356 7249, ⓦsoulbar.co.nz; map p.76. An icon of Auckland's waterfront dining scene, *Soul* is perfect for slick, modern bistro meals on the terrace, with fish and seafood a speciality. Go for their classic salt and pepper squid ($20) followed perhaps by roasted hapuku with clams, white beans and gremolata ($39). Alternatively, just nip in for a cocktail or a beer overlooking the yachts. Daily 11am–10pm or much later.

Wildfire Princes Wharf ☎09 353 7595, ⓦwildfire restaurant.co.nz; map p.76. Flashy and popular Brazilian barbecue restaurant with some tables overlooking the water. The churrasco experience ($55) involves assorted

TOP 5 PLACES TO DINE IN STYLE

The Roxy p.103
Bellota p.103
SPQR p.106
Urban Café p.105
Dida's p.106

tapas-style appetizers followed by a vast selection of meats and seafood marinated in herbs, roasted over manuka coals then carved off skewers at the table. Come early (noon–3pm & 5–7pm) and you can drop the tapas for their *churrasco special* ($40). If you can't face that much meat, call in for one of the fabulous *caipirinha* cocktails. Daily noon–1am.

CITY CENTRE AND BRITOMART

Watery views are traded for urban chic around the lively Britomart Precinct, which borders on the central city and is where numerous cafés, low-cost Asian restaurants and a few handy food halls meet the needs of office workers. In the evening, Britomart hums while parts of the city centre feel pretty dead.

Art Gallery Café Kitchener St ☎09 379 1349; map p.76. No reservations. Classy licensed café with a small terrace and great views of the gallery's atrium. Go for the lambs fry and bacon at breakfast ($17.50) or perhaps a twice-baked blue cheese soufflé with pear, walnut and fennel salad ($16). Mon–Fri 7.30am–4.30pm, Sat & Sun 10am–4.30pm.

Atrium Food Gallery Elliot St; map p.76. Daytime food hall that's slightly more salubrious than others, with a wide range of counters – Vietnamese, sushi, Korean, pizza, kebabs, Taiwanese – plus a bakery and decent coffee. Mon–Wed 7am–6pm, Thurs & Fri 7am–7pm, Sat 8am–7pm, Sun 9am–5pm.

★ **Bellota** 91 Federal St ☎09 363 6301, ⓦskycity .co.nz/bellota; map p.76. Fans of celebrated Kiwi chef Peter Gordon flock to the booths in this retro 1970s cave for his fusion take on Spanish tapas (mostly $12), such as lamb chilli and feta spring rolls with tamarind aioli. The name means "acorn", a reference to the bellota-fed pigs that feature on the menu (though there are plenty of veggie options). Mon–Sat 4–11pm or later, Fri from noon.

★ **The Depot** 86 Federal St ☎09 363 7048, ⓦeatat depot.co.nz; map p.76. Bustling, hip industrially styled bar and restaurant that's the Auckland outpost of Wellington celebrity chef Al Brown. Waiters carrying plates of fresh oysters weave around stools clustered at high tables, quality wine comes by the carafe and the menu offers small plates of kingfish sashimi ($17) and large dishes of wood-roasted lemon chicken with white bean ragout ($29). They don't take bookings, so add your name to the list and pop across to Bellota while you wait. Daily 7am–around 11pm.

★ **Food Alley** 9 Albert St ☎09 373 4917; map p.76. Auckland's best food hall is spartan and inexpensive, with twenty kitchens over two levels exhibiting a strong East Asian bias. Daily 10am–10pm.

Ima 57 Fort St ☎09 300 7252, ⓦimacuisine.co.nz; map p.76. A relaxed Mediterranean and Middle Eastern café, where everything they make is super-fresh, including egg breakfasts with spinach and sumac ($15.50) and the best falafel in town ($14). The Moroccan chicken dinner ($28) is also excellent. Mon–Fri 7am–2pm, Tues–Fri 7am–2pm & 6–10pm, Sat 6–10pm.

★ **Imperial Lane** 7 Fort Lane ☎09 929 2703, ⓦtheimperiallane.co.nz; map p.76. Industrial chic café and bar with metal tables flanking a broad service ramp that links through to Queen St. Come for coffee and superb sandwiches and pastries during the day, and return for drinks and tapas such as duck fat chips, smoked octopus and chorizo, and chicory, pear and blue cheese salad (all $10–14). Mon–Sat 7.30am–10pm or much later.

★ **Mezze Bar** 9 Durham Lane East ☎09 307 2029, ⓦmezzebar.co.nz; map p.76. Spanish, Moroccan and Middle Eastern dishes predominate at this relaxed café, restaurant and bar that offers respite from the buzz of Queen St. Great for coffee and a slice of orange almond cake, tapas and meze ($9–17) with sherry or Spanish wine, or dishes such as lamb tajine ($30) or chargrilled salmon Niçoise ($27), all washed down with a broad selection of beers and wines. Daily 7am–11pm.

★ **Middle East Café** 23a Wellesley St West ☎09 379 4843, ⓦmiddleeastcafe.co.nz; map p.76. Tiny, simple, camel-themed eat-in or takeaway unlicensed café that's an Auckland institution, deservedly celebrated for its shawarma and falafel ($9–11), both cloaked in creamy garlic, spicy tomato sauce or hot chilli sauce. Mon–Fri 11am–3pm & 5–10pm, Sat 5–10pm, Sun 5–9pm.

No. 1 Pancake 10 Wellesley St, at Lorne St; map p.76. Bargain hole-in-the-wall serving Korean pancakes with delectable fillings such as pork, red bean, chicken and cheese, or sugar and cinnamon for $3–4 each. Mon–Fri 10.30am–7.30pm, Sat 11am–6.30pm.

Pho Saigon 6–8 Lorne St ☎09 377 3288; map p.76. Budget but high-standard Vietnamese and Malaysian quickie serving beef *rendang* ($12), rare steak *pho* ($12), pork ball Vietnamese spring rolls ($13) and *sambal* chicken ($20) with a smile. Mon–Sat 10am–9pm.

Raw Power 10 Vulcan Lane ☎09 303 3624; map p.76. Great little upstairs juice bar with heaps of veggie and vegan offerings – salads, tofu burgers, falafel, curried corn fritters etc (mostly $12–20) – plus excellent fresh juices and smoothies. Mon–Fri 7am–4pm, Sat 11am–4pm.

The Roxy 7 Fort Lane ☎09 929 2701, ⓦroxy.co.nz; map p.76. Stylish fine dining in a newly converted former theatre that had been abandoned for 40 years. Petite portions packed with exquisite flavours are served in a setting that combines patches of rough brick with sumptuous furnishings. Expect the like of Razorback pig with caramelized celeriac, quince and crumbs of ginger bread ($42), either à la carte or as part of a tasting menu ($100, with wine matches $155; 10 courses $140/235). Tues–Sat 6–11pm, plus Fri noon–3pm.

1

Tanuki's Cave 319b Queen St ☎ 09 379 5353, ⓦ sakebars.co.nz; map p.76. Excellent *yakitori* and sake bar in a cave-like basement setting, with a more formal restaurant above. You can tuck into various delicacies, from octopus balls to teriyaki chicken (most dishes around $8), and wash it all down with sake or Japanese beer. Often busy; no bookings. Daily 5.30–11.30pm or later.

KARANGAHAPE ROAD AND AROUND

There's a relaxed vibe along Karangahape Road with laidback cafés, an abundance of low-cost ethnic restaurants and a couple of smarter places moving in.

★ **Alleluya** St Kevin's Arcade, 179 K' Rd ☎ 09 377 8482; map p.76. Soak up the city views at this no-nonsense café among the potted kentia palms in a pretty 1920s arcade. Try the smoked fish and kumara hash ($19). Licensed. Mon–Sat 8am–5pm, Sun 8am–3pm.

★ **Coco's Cantina** 376 K' Rd ☎ 09 300 7582, ⓦ cocos cantina.co.nz; map p.76. A funky and very popular restaurant with a strong gay following. Its short, Italian-style menu might include *arancini* risotto balls ($10) followed by steak with anchovy butter and home fries ($28) or its signature spaghetti and meatballs ($28). The outside tables are great for watching the characters along K' Rd, especially on Friday and Saturday nights. No bookings, so grab a glass of wine at the bar and wait your turn. Tues–Sat 5pm–midnight.

Mister Morning 374 K' Rd ☎ 09 307 0076; map p.76. Delightful new café with fabulous strong coffee, wall menus on butcher's paper and airmailed copies of the *New York Times*. Try the short-rib and cheese pies ($7.50), or the walnut, avocado and celery sandwich ($7.50). They even do sausage rolls and bottomless filter coffee. Mon–Fri 7am–3pm.

Rasoi 211 K' Rd ☎ 09 377 7780; map p.76. It feels almost like you're in South India at this budget vegetarian café that dishes up *dosas*, *uttapams* and *thalis* for $11–18; there's also an all-you-can-eat maharajah *thali* for $25. Great Indian sweets, too. Mon–Sat 11am–9pm.

Sri Pinang 356 K' Rd ☎ 09 358 3886; map p.76. A simple Malaysian restaurant where you can start with half a dozen satay chicken skewers and follow with dishes such as *sambal* okra, beef *rendang* or clay-pot chicken rice scooped up with excellent roti. Most dishes $15–23. BYO only but you can buy wine and beer from the shop across the road. Mon 6–10pm, Tues–Fri 11am–2.30pm & 6–10pm, Sat 6–11pm.

Theatre 256 K' Rd ☎ 09 303 0501; map p.76. Elegant and super-slender restoration of the 1920s former entranceway to the old Mercury Theatre, complete with original mosaic floor and couches at the back, where sun streams through the stained-glass barrel-vaulted roof. Operates as a café during the day (New York lox bagel for $8.50 and Greek breakfast with spicy lamb sausage and butter beans for $18.50) and a bar at night. Mon–Fri 7am–3am, Sat 9am–3am, Sun 10am–3am.

PARNELL

Parnell is one of the main urban-fringe eating areas with everything from budget cafés and ethnic restaurants to some of the finest restaurants in Auckland.

Cibo 91 St George's Bay Rd ☎ 09 303 9660; map p.83. Fine dining a little off the main drag, worth seeking out. Reliable favourites such as steak and duck leg are available but there's always something unexpected on the menu. Popular for business lunches so best left for evening dining on the likes of roasted hapuku and lobster in a coconut Indian broth with a *dosai* pancake ($38). Mon–Fri noon–10pm, Sat 6–11pm.

Di Mare Shop 9, 251 Parnell Rd ☎ 09 300 3260, ⓦ dimare.co.nz; map p.83. Family-run surf-and-turf restaurant, serving delicious traditional and innovative dishes in an intimate back-alley courtyard. Try the ocean platter for two ($60) or the lamb Siciliana ($34). Lunch specials $12.50. Licensed & BYO. Daily 11.30am–3pm & 5–10pm.

★ **Domain Ayr** 492 Parnell Rd ☎ 09 379 2868; map p.83. Join the communal table or tuck yourself away with a magazine at this modern organic and free-range café serving Fair Trade organic coffee (including decaf), all made with organic milk. The growers are namechecked on the recycled-paper menus, which include the likes of creamy mushrooms on corn bread ($16), salmon orzo ($17.50) and great salads. Mon–Fri 7am–3pm, Sat & Sun 8am–3pm.

Dunk Espresso 297 Parnell Rd ☎ 09 377 2414; map p.83. A reliable, airy modern café with a good range of breakfasts and lunches, such as salmon hash with poached egg ($16), fresh salads and good coffee. Mon–Fri 7am–4pm, Sat & Sun 8am–4pm.

Java Room 317 Parnell Rd ☎ 09 366 1606, ⓦ javaroom .co.nz; map p.83. Intimate Indonesian-ish restaurant serving dishes with Malaysian, Vietnamese and Indian influences but also prawn and pork dim sum starters ($10), chicken laksa ($13) and Siamese snapper ($27). Mon–Sat 6–10pm.

La Cigale French Market 69 St George's Bay Rd; map p.83. Not especially French but a great excuse to sample delicious morsels and perhaps pick up some picnic ingredients. It's always alive with folk sampling savouries such as raclette, delicious dips, paella, Cornish pasties and whitebait fritters, or just sitting around over a coffee and great baking. Sat 8am–1pm, Sun 9am–2pm.

Non Solo Pizza 259 Parnell Rd ☎ 09 379 535, ⓦ nonsolopizza.co.nz; map p.83. As the name says, not just pizza, but they do create wonderfully thin-crust concoctions with classic Italian toppings. Pasta and assorted *secondi piatti*, such as confit of duck with beans and chorizo ($35), is served inside or on the intimate patio. Daily noon–10pm or later.

★ **Oh Calcutta!** 151 Parnell Rd ✆ 09 377 9090, ⓦ ohcalcutta.co.nz; map p.83. Bronzed statues of Shiva and Ganesh look down on diners from Moghul alcoves in this classy curry restaurant that picks the best dishes from across the subcontinent and imbues them with wonderfully distinct flavours. A range of lunchtime tiffin menus lets you sample three curries, rice, naan and poppadoms for $25. For dinner try the prawn cutlets marinated in yogurt and saffron ($23). Lunch Wed–Fri noon–2pm, dinner nightly 5.30–10pm.

NEWMARKET, MOUNT EDEN AND ONE TREE HILL

There's a dense concentration of restaurants of all stripes in Newmarket with a smattering of notable places in the suburbs nearby.

Basque Kitchen Bar 61 Davis Crescent ✆ 09 523 1057 ⓦ basque.co.nz; map p.83. All the wines are Spanish (ask for recommendations) at this fun concrete-floored tapas bar where you might tuck into saffron-fried cauliflower ($9) and whole sardines in sherry vinegar & smoked paprika ($13.50), perhaps washed down with a flight of 3 sherries ($18). Mon–Sat 4.30–10pm or later.

Cornwall Park Restaurant Cornwall Park ✆ 09 630 2888, ⓦ cornwallparkrestaurant.co.nz; map p.74. If you're visiting One Tree Hill, set time aside for lunch, an ice cream or a high tea (9–11.30am & 2–4pm; $24) of savouries, dainty sandwiches and sweets on a three-tier tray with tea or coffee. Daily 9am–4pm.

★ **Little & Friday** 12 Melrose St, Newmarket ✆ 09 524 8742; map p.83. Don't expect meals – just exquisite savouries, pastries and cakes, and excellent coffee at this bakery/café tucked in the corner of a fabric warehouse. The industrial feel goes nicely with the delicate old-fashioned plates, recycled cutlery and old milk bottles used for drinking water. Try a beetroot, spinach and blue cheese tart ($7.50) or a raspberry and coconut friand ($4.50). Mon–Fri 8am–3pm, Sat & Sun 9am–3pm.

★ **Molten** 422 Mt Eden Rd ✆ 09 638 7236, ⓦ molten .co.nz; map p.90. All the best qualities of a top suburban bistro: comfortable and relaxed with efficient, friendly service, great food and a well-thought-out wine list. It's good value, too, with generously portioned mains, such as tuna steak on rimu-smoked bacon risotto (around $33). Pop next door for a drink at *Liquid Molten*. Licensed. Mon 6–11pm, Tues–Sat noon–3pm & 6–11pm.

Newmarket Plaza Food Hall Teed St, next to the fish market ✆ 09 529 1868; map p.90. A little slice of East Asia in Auckland with Malaysian, Thai, Korean and a couple of Chinese places all serving national staples for $10–15. Daily 10.30am–9pm.

Otto Woo 21 Remuera Rd ✆ 09 522 2272, ⓦ otto-woo

.com; map p.83. Excellent unlicensed noodle bar, primarily for takeaways, but with a few stools at stark white tables. Choose from freshly prepared tempura prawns, chicken laksa, satay vegetable noodles and a dozen other dishes (all $12–15), and finish off with some sweet rice balls and a fresh juice. Mon–Sat 11.30am–3pm & 4.45–9pm, Sun 4.45–9pm.

★ **Urban Café** 139 Carlton Gore Rd ✆ 09 966 6977, ⓦ urbancafenewmarket.co.nz; map p.83. Sharp, modern café where efficient service and superb coffee complement a counter full of delicious stuffed *pide* ($10), imaginative salads and a short menu of breakfast and lunch dishes (mostly $13–17) such as Baghdad eggs with spiced lentils. Heaps of current magazines, too, and free wi-fi. Mon–Fri 7am–3pm, Sat & Sun 8am–2pm.

Zarbo 24 Morrow St ✆ 09 520 2721, ⓦ zarbo.co.nz; map p.83. Great deli/café with a fabulous range of products from around the world put to good use in a delicious range of salads, frittatas and the like (mostly $10–13), plus lunches such as pork medallions with kumara and pumpkin rosti ($20; served until 3pm). They also serve high tea (Mon–Fri 2.30–4.30pm; $20). Mon–Fri 6.30am–6pm, Sat 8am–5pm, Sun 8am–4pm.

TAMAKI DRIVE: OKAHU BAY AND MISSION BAY

Dining along Auckland's beach strip can be a hit-and-miss affair, but these spots are reliably good.

Bar Comida 81 Tamaki Drive ✆ 09 521 7000; map p.74. Mediterranean-type place that's perhaps the best of a middling bunch of café/restaurants in Mission Bay, serving quality wood-fired gourmet pizza (including Rangitoto-shaped spinach pizza for $25), a strong line in tapas ($13–17), Persian flatbreads, grilled vegetables with hummus, plus coffee and desserts such as tarte tatin ($13). Mon–Fri 9am–11pm, Sat & Sun 7.30am–11pm.

Café on Kohi 237 Tamaki Drive, Kohimarama ✆ 09 528 8335; map p.74. A touch more formal than other Tamaki Drive cafés, and a dollar or two more expensive, but worth it for the best café food in these parts and great views across the beach to Rangitoto. The associated The Store on Kohi, around the corner in the same building, does superb pastries, savouries, gelati and coffee all to take away and eat on the beach. Daily 7am–4pm.

The Fishmonger 16 Polygon Rd, St Heliers ✆ 09 575 0537, ⓦ thefishmonger.co.nz; map p.74. Head one street back from the waterfront to find this top-quality chippy where several species of fish ($4–7 each) come battered, Panko-crumbed, blackened or grilled with lemon. Perfect eaten on the beach. Mon–Sat 10.30am–9pm, Sun noon–9pm.

Hammerheads 19 Tamaki Drive, Okahu Bay, by Kelly Tarlton's ✆ 09 521 4400, ⓦ hammerheads.co.nz; map p.74. The perfect spot for an upmarket lunch on a sunny

1

day, or dinner, preceded by a cocktail while you admire the tremendous views over the water to the city skyline. The fish and seafood mains, such as snapper with lemon gnocchi and caperberries ($37), are excellent. Daily noon–3pm & 5–10pm or later.

PONSONBY

Fashion-conscious foodies should make for Ponsonby, where devotion to style is as important as culinary prowess. But don't be intimidated; the food is excellent and competition keeps prices reasonable.

Café Cézanne 296 Ponsonby Rd ⚐09 367 3338; map p.86. This casual, ramshackle place is a welcome retreat from the glitz of the rest of Ponsonby Rd; great for reading the papers over hearty breakfasts, excellent quiches or huge wedges of cake. Licensed & BYO. Mon–Fri 7.30am–10pm, Sat & Sun 8.30am–10pm.

★ **Dida's** 54 Jervois Rd ⚐09 376 2813, ⓦdidas.co.nz; map p.86. The smart set flocks to this classy tapas bar and wine lounge, sinking into the leather sofas to choose from a fantastic wine selection and an array of delectable small plates such as pork albóndigas in sherry tomato sauce ($9) or tuna and artichoke skewers ($10). Mon–Wed & Sun 11.30am–midnight, Thurs–Sat 11.30am–1am.

Dizengoff 256 Ponsonby Rd ⚐09 360 0108; map p.86. Buzzy breakfast and lunch café specializing in wonderful bagels, eggs with fried pastrami and other Jewish deli favourites, plus luscious char-grilled vegetables, all at reasonable prices. No alcohol. Mon–Fri 6.30am–5pm, Sat & Sun 7am–5pm.

★ **Il Forno** 55 Mackelvie St; map p.86. Great daytime bakery and café, especially notable for its delectable made-on-the-premises cakes, pastries and coffee, but also doing fine sandwiches, rolls and cannelloni, lasagne and chicken schnitzel lunches (10.30am–1.30pm; $10). Daily 7am–4pm.

Moo Chow Chow 23 Ponsonby Rd ⚐09 360 0262, ⓦmoochowchow.co.nz; map p.86. A modern take on Thai cuisine, particularly good for a small group so that you can sample as many of the small plates as possible. You might try the green papaya salad with bird's-eye chillies ($14), the soy and ginger dressed smoked salmon ($22) or even a full plate of goat massaman curry ($30). Tues–Fri noon–3pm & 4–10pm or later, Sat 4–11pm.

★ **Ponsonby Road Bistro** 165 Ponsonby Rd ⚐09 360 1611, ⓦponsonbyroadbistro.co.nz; map p.86. Blackboard specials lend a relaxed ambience to this consistently good, casually sophisticated restaurant where dishes such as lamb chump with parsnip purée or Mediterranean fish stew come flexibly served as both appetizer and main. Prices are modest for the quality (most mains around $30), and there are $18 quick lunch specials. Mon–Fri noon–midnight, Sat 4pm–midnight.

Renkon Express 211 Ponsonby Rd ⚐09 307 8008;

map p.86. This is essentially a Japanese takeaway, but there are a few small tables where you can dig into delicious donburi and noodle dishes such as grilled eel with dry udon for $11. It's not licensed but you can take your food and go sit next door over a glass of wine at Mea Culpa (see p.108). Daily 11.30am–3pm & 5–9.30pm.

★ **Satya** 17 Great North Rd ⚐09 361 3612, ⓦsatya .co.nz; map p.86. This excellent South Indian place steps outside the usual range of curries with the likes of bhel puri ($8) followed by murg badami with almonds and marinated chicken ($22). Licensed & BYO. Lunch deals from $8. Mon–Sat 11.30am–2.30pm & 5.30–10pm, Sun noon–10pm.

Soto 13 St Mary's Bay Rd ⚐09 360 0021, ⓦsoto.co.nz; map p.86. Delicate screens and a Zen garden have transformed this former fire station into a beautiful modern Japanese restaurant that's probably the finest in town. Choose from Western or Oriental low tables and select from a menu of wonderfully flavoursome dishes, all immaculately presented. Try the sashimi platter ($37), or just drop in to sample the range of sake. Tues–Fri noon–2pm & 6–10pm, Sat 6–10pm.

★ **SPQR** 150 Ponsonby Rd ⚐09 360 1710, ⓦspqrnz .co.nz; map p.86. Dimly lit and eternally groovy restaurant/bar with a strong gay following that's always popular for its quality Italian-influenced food. The crispy pizzas ($26) are superb and there's nothing the slightest bit shabby about the likes of cockle linguini ($28) or veal scallopine ($31). Many treat it more as a bar and venue for spotting actors and rock stars. Excellent cocktails and a wide range of wines (sold by the glass). Daily noon–11pm or much later.

KINGSLAND

Canton Café 477 New North Rd ⚐09 846 7888; map p.74. The staff are brusque (especially if you've eaten and they have people waiting) and the decor is plain, but portions are large and wonderfully flavoursome at this eternal budget favourite. Try the lemon chicken ($24) or beef ginger fried noodles ($21) and share. BYO ($2/person corkage). Daily noon–11pm.

★ **The Fridge** 507 New North Rd ⚐09 845 5321; map p.74. The brick-lined main room and an airy outdoor deck downstairs are both great spaces to enjoy a superb range of sandwiches, wraps (chicken enchilada; $10.50), gourmet pies (Moroccan lamb; $8.50) and breakfast dishes (eggs Benedict on hash cakes; $17.50), all washed down with great coffee. Always packed at weekends. Mon–Fri 7.30am–4pm, Sat & Sun 8am–4pm.

DEVONPORT

Catch 22 Fish Shop 19 Victoria Rd ⚐09 445 2225; map p.89. On a nice evening it's hard to beat fish and chips or a straightforward burger ($6) across the road in the park or on the beach. Tues–Sun 11.30am–8pm.

★ **Five Loaves** 29 Church St ☎ 09 445 8954; map p.89. Casual neighbourhood café a few blocks from central Devonport, with great coffee, mandarin and chocolate muffins and heartier dishes such as huevos rancheros ($17.50) or a South-by-Southwest burger ($18.50) with fried onion and jalapeño cheddar. Mon–Sat 7.30am–5pm, Sun 8am–4pm.

Manuka 49 Victoria Rd ☎ 09 445 7732, ⒲ manuka restaurant.co.nz; map p.89. Quality restaurant specializing in pasta, wood-fired pizza (around $24) and the likes of squid salad ($19) or pumpkin and feta ravioli ($21), but good at any time of the day for light snacks and salads or just for coffee and cake. Mon–Fri 9am–10pm, Sat & Sun 8.30am–10pm or later.

Monsoon 71 Victoria Rd ☎ 09 445 4263, ⒲ monsoonthai .co.nz; map p.89. Value-for-money Thai/Malaysian place with tasty dishes such as fish and tiger prawns in a red curry sauce ($21). Licensed & BYO. Daily 5–10pm or 11pm.

DRINKING, NIGHTLIFE AND ENTERTAINMENT

With a million plus people to entertain, there's always something going on in Auckland. One of the best ways to see local acts is to attend one of the free summer concerts held in The Domain and elsewhere under the *Music in Parks* banner (Jan–March; ⒲ musicinparks.co.nz), mostly on Friday, Saturday and Sunday afternoons.

ESSENTIALS

Listings and tickets The best way to find out what's on is to look at the *New Zealand Herald*, pick up the free *Groove Guide*, or visit ⒲ eventfinder.co.nz. For more specialist gig information, buy the monthly *Rip It Up* magazine (⒲ ripitup.co.nz) or go to the entertainment guide section of the bFM radio station website ⒲ 95bfm.co.nz or GeorgeFM (⒲ georgefm.co .nz). Concert and smaller gig tickets can be booked through ⒲ ticketek.co.nz, ⒲ ticketmaster.co.nz or ⒲ iticket.co.nz.

Gay and lesbian Auckland Auckland has a fairly small but progressive and proactive gay scene largely woven into the café/bar mainstream of Ponsonby and the western end of K' Road, where strip clubs mingle freely with gay bars and cruise clubs. The best way to link into the scene is to pick up the free, fortnightly *Express* magazine (⒲ gayexpress.co.nz), found in gay-friendly shops, cafés and bars and at the more raunchy Out! Bookshop, 39 Anzac Ave (☎ 09 377 7770). Alternatively, pick up a copy of the free Gaynz.com gig guide, which covers gay hotspots around the country.

PUBS, BARS, CLUBS AND LIVE MUSIC

As elsewhere in the country, the distinction between eating and drinking places is frequently blurred. The places listed below concentrate on the drinking, though even old-style booze barns have been dramatically smartened up and do a sideline in inexpensive counter meals. Closing times are relaxed, with rowdier places staying open until 3am or later at weekends.

The clubbing torch currently burns brightest around Britomart and Viaduct Harbour, where you can join the nightly flow of young things meandering between the bars and clubs. Unless someone special is on the decks or a band is playing, most clubs are free early in the week, charge $5–10 on Thursday and something over $10 on Friday and Saturday. Lots of pubs and bars double as venues for live acts, employ DJs or put on some form of entertainment.

Many of the clubs have one area set up as a stage, and on any night of the week you might find top Kiwi acts and even overseas bands blazing away in the corner; a few pubs may also put on a band from time to time. Big acts from North America and Europe visit sporadically and tend to play only in Auckland, usually in the larger venues.

THE WATERFRONT

Cowboy 95 Customs St West ☎ 09 377 7778; map p.76. Small faux-Western bar where the trick is to knock back a few bourbons, tequilas or whatever, help yourself to a cowboy hat and dance around to 1980s music. It might sound cheesy but everyone has a great time. Daily noon–midnight or later.

O'Hagan's 103 Customs St West ☎ 09 363 2106, ⒲ ohagans.co.nz; map p.76. Classy Irish-themed pub spilling out onto the Market Square. Guinness, Kilkenny and English ales on tap, a good range of meals (roast chicken with caramelized onion tart $27) and big-screen sports. Daily 8am–10pm or later.

CITY CENTRE AND BRITOMART

Flight Lounge 1 Fort Lane ☎ 09 309 6569; map p.76. Basement joint with a white glass bar and penchant for funky house, electro, disco funk and hip-hop. Really only gets going late on Friday and Saturday. Wed–Sat 9pm–4am.

Globe 229 Queen St, under Base Auckland hostel, ☎ 09 357 3980, ⒲ globebar.co.nz; map p.76. Long, thin, noisy backpackers-get-drunk bar that's full most nights of the week. Nightly 6pm–late.

Northern Steamship Co 122 Quay St ☎ 09 374 3952, ⒲ northernsteamship.co.nz; map p.76. Large, brick-walled, eclectically furnished brewbar. Early on you can settle by the fireplace for a quiet beer or quality pub meal (mostly $20–30), but things get rowdy after dark, particularly on weekends when top local DJs hold the fort. Free wi-fi. Daily 11.30am–10pm or much later.

The Occidental 8 Vulcan Lane; map p.76. Belgian bar serving bargain pots of mussels (half-kilo $18; kilo $23) dressed with lobster bisque and brandy, mustard and cream, or coconut cream and lemongrass. Every item on

1

the menu comes with a suggested libation and the beer pouring is conducted with ritualistic zeal. Mon–Fri 7pm–late, Sat & Sun 8pm–late.

Rakino's First floor, 35 High St ☎09 358 3535, ⓦrakinos.com; map p.76. Daytime café with tables shaped like Hauraki Gulf islands. Later, it transforms into a compact venue serving up anything from acoustic and live jazz to DJs. Mon–Fri 7am–10pm or later, Sat 9am–late, Sun 3pm–late.

Sale St 7 Sale St, Freeman's Bay ☎09 307 8148, ⓦsale-st.co.nz; map p.76. Big, open semi-industrial space with something for everyone. Wingback chairs for a tête-à-tête, fairly formal dining, a small selection of beers brewed on site and a big sunny deck. Attracts the after-work crowd but gets progressively more glam later on. Daily 10am–10pm or much later.

Smith Corner of Galway & Commerce sts ☎09 309 5529, ⓦsmith-bar.co.nz; map p.76. Lush and classy but unpretentious bar that's so small it is almost always full, mainly with pretty things lolling on a velvet chaise and sipping retro cocktails. Mon–Sat 3pm–late.

Stark's 269 Queen St, City ☎09 377 0277; map p.76. Cool, relaxing and stylish little cocktail bar offering the best gin and tonics in town, people-watching and highly polished professional service. Mon–Fri 7.30am–late, Sat & Sun noon–late.

Tabac 6 Mills Lane ☎09 366 6067, ⓦtabac.co.nz; map p.76. Cool backstreet bar that takes a bit of finding. You're rewarded with a casual vibe, great cocktails and cutting-edge DJs. Occasional live bands (especially Thurs) and record launches as well. Tues–Fri 4pm–late, Sat 8pm–late.

Tyler St Garage 120 Quay St ☎09 300 5279, ⓦtyler streetgarage.co.nz; map p.76. Stylish and bustling semi-industrial bar topped by a great roof terrace for sipping cocktails with views across the docks. There's half-price pizza on Tues and live music and DJs at weekends. Daily 11.30am–11pm or much later.

KARANGAHAPE ROAD AND NEWTON

Family Bar 270 K' Rd ☎09 309 0213, ⓦfamilybar .co.nz; map p.76. Lively, predominantly gay and lesbian bar that welcomes all comers for drinks during the day and plenty of action at night – karaoke on Wed, DJs Thurs–Sat and drag shows from 1am on Fri and Sat nights. Mon–Thurs 9.30am–4am, Fri–Sun 9.30am–5am.

Galbraith's Alehouse 2 Mount Eden Rd, Newton ☎09 379 3557, ⓦalehouse.co.nz; map p.76. The closest Auckland gets to an English pub, with some of NZ's finest English-style ales brewed on site plus guest beers by other craft brewers and fifty-odd bottled varieties. A limited range of quality bar meals includes kaffir lime roasted chicken ($18) and fish and chips ($20). Mon–Sat noon–11pm, Sun noon–10pm.

Kings Arms 59 France St, Newton ☎09 373 3240, ⓦkingsarms.co.nz; map p.76. Popular pub and second-string venue hosting local and touring acts who can't quite fill the bigger venues. There's something on most nights (typically $10–20) and Sunday afternoons. Daily noon–11pm or later.

PONSONBY

Long Room 114 Ponsonby Rd, Ponsonby ☎09 360 8803, ⓦlongroom.co.nz; map p.86. Cocktails are just the thing early in the evening but DJ-led dancing and occasionally live bands take over as the night wears on, when the place is usually packed. There's a big open courtyard if it all gets a bit sweaty inside. Daily 11am until late (or very late).

Mea Culpa 175 Ponsonby Rd, Ponsonby ☎09 376 4460; map p.86. There's a cosy feel to this tiny bar where you can sit outside on wrought-iron chairs on the Turkish rug. Mon–Wed 5pm–1am, Thurs & Fri 5pm–3am, Sat 6pm–3am.

The Whiskey 210 Ponsonby Rd, Ponsonby ☎09 361 2666, ⓦwhiskeybars.com; map p.86. Stylish bar with something of the feel of a groovy gentleman's club, all chocolate leather sofas and white brick walls hung with superb photos of Little Richard, the New York Dolls, Jimi Hendrix and more. Great cocktails ($17–20). Daily 5pm–3am.

NEWMARKET

Lucha Lounge 1 York St ☎09 524 6001, ⓦluchalounge .co.nz; map p.83. Tiny bar – and an equally minuscule courtyard – with a 1960s suburban look, except for the images of lucha libre wrestlers on the tables and Mexican drinks such as Tecate and Bohemia beers and passionfruit chilli margarita ($14). Rowdy bands play at weekends. Arrive late and stay later. Tues–Fri 5pm–late, Sat 6pm–late.

KINGSLAND

Nectar 472 New North Rd ☎09 849 5777, ⓦfacebook .com/BarNectar; map p.74. Sophisticated roof bar with a great terrace centred on a fireplace, lounge seating and a vibe that's relaxed early on and increasingly lively. Salsa on Wed, jazz on Thurs and funk DJs on Fri. Tues & Wed 6–10pm, Thurs–Sat 4pm–1am or later, Sun 4pm–11pm.

Neighbourhood 498 New North Rd ☎09 846 3773, ⓦneighbourhood.co.nz; map p.74. A stylish, modern take on a local pub with lots of sunny outdoor seating, a full range of Mac's beers on tap and big windows overlooking the north stand of Eden Park. DJs Wed–Sun. Free wi-fi. Daily 11.30am–11pm or later.

Toro Bar 484 New North Rd ☎09 845 6990; map p.74. Cool little Mexican-themed bar that's great for a Bohemia or a margarita, plus enchiladas, *albóndigas* and daily specials ($10–20). Wed–Fri 5–10pm or later, Sat & Sun 4–10pm or later.

CLASSICAL MUSIC, THEATRE AND COMEDY

Auckland's theatre, classical music and comedy scene seldom sets the world alight, though it is reasonably lively, and you'll usually have a choice of a couple of plays, comedy and dance or opera.

Aotea Centre Aotea Square, Queen St ☎09 309 2677, ⓦthe-edge.co.nz. New Zealand's first purpose-built opera house and the home stage for the New Zealand Symphony Orchestra and the New Zealand Ballet. The sometimes edgy Silo Theatre Company performs in its Herald Theatre.

Civic Theatre Corner of Queen & Wellesley sts ☎09 357 3355, ⓦthe-edge.co.nz. A lovely theatre that's worth visiting if there's anything at all on; options range from dance and theatre to classic movies.

The Classic 321 Queen St ☎09 373 4321, ⓦcomedy .co.nz. Bar and comedy venue hosting top local names and touring acts. Shows are Mon–Sat but the best line-ups are at weekends. $20–25 for the main acts, $15 for the regular 10.30pm improv sessions.

Maidment Theatre Corner of Princess & Alfred sts ☎09 308 2383, ⓦmaidment.auckland.ac.nz. Two university theatres, with mainstream works in the larger venue and more daring stuff in the studio. The Auckland Theatre Company (ⓦatc.co.nz) mainly performs here.

Q 305 Queen St ☎09 309 8325, ⓦqtheatre.co.nz. Auckland's newest theatre space, flexible enough to handle everything from Maori contemporary dance to cutting-edge plays and burlesque. Friday is improv night.

FESTIVALS

As befits a city of its size, Auckland has numerous festivals and annual events. These are some of the best.

JANUARY

Anniversary Day Massive sailing regatta on Auckland's Waitemata Harbour. Last Monday in January.

International Buskers Festival ⓦauckland buskersfestival.co.nz. Buskers from around the world take over the city streets. Free. Late January.

FEBRUARY

Big Gay Out ⓦbiggayout.co.nz. An extravaganza of comedy, music, drag and community events that takes place in Coyle Park, Point Chevalier, just west of the zoo. Usually held the second Sunday in February.

Devonport Food, Wine and Music Festival ⓦdevonportwinefestival.co.nz. Windsor Reserve is the venue for top chefs, local musicians and plenty of wine. It's a great occasion, particularly if the weather's good. Tickets $40. Third weekend in February.

Mission Bay Jazz and Blues Streetfest ⓦjazzandbluesstreetfest.com. Beachside evening bash with a stack of bands and food stalls. Tickets $20. Last Saturday in February.

MARCH

Auckland Festival ⓦaucklandfestival.co .nz. Major international arts and culture festival at venues all over the city with everything from street performances to ballet. Held during two middle weeks in March, every odd-numbered year.

Pasifika Twenty thousand people enjoy this free, all-day celebration of Polynesian and Pacific Island culture – music, culture, food and crafts – at Western Springs Park. Free. Second Saturday in March.

Round the Bays Fun Run ⓦroundthebays .co.nz. Up to 70,000 people jog 9km along the Tamaki Drive waterfront. Second or third Sunday in March.

Royal Easter Show ⓦroyaleastershow .co.nz. Family entertainment, Kiwi-style, with equestrian events, lumberjack show, wine tasting and arts and crafts, all held at the ASB showgrounds along Greenlane. $20. Easter weekend (moveable feast; check website for dates).

MAY

International Comedy Festival ⓦcomedyfestival.co.nz. Three weeks of performances by the best from New Zealand and around the world; recent acts have included Danny Bhoy and Arj Barker. Early May.

JULY

Auckland International Film Festival ⓦnzff.co.nz. The nationwide film tour usually kicks off in the city where it all started back in 1969. Tickets $16. Mid- to late July.

1

CINEMAS

Multiplexes rule Auckland, but the following boutique cinemas run more interesting programmes. Admission (normally $16–17) is often reduced before 5pm and all day Tues; ⓦ flicks.co.nz has listings.

Academy 44 Lorne St ⓣ 09 373 2761, ⓦ iconiccinemas .co.nz. Dedicated art-house cinema with two screens tucked underneath the main library.

Bridgeway 122 Queen St, Birkenhead ⓣ 09 481 0040, ⓦ bridgeway.co.nz. Intimate North Shore cinema with good foyer food and coffee and luxurious seating. Screens the smarter end of mainstream movies.

Lido 427 Manukau Rd, Epsom ⓣ 09 630 1500, ⓦ lido .co.nz. Grab a beer or wine, sink into wide seats, and enjoy mainstream and classic movies with digital sound.

Rialto 167 Broadway, Newmarket ⓣ 09 369 2417, ⓦ rialto.co.nz. One of the handiest of the fringe cinemas, showing mainstream and slightly left-field fare.

Victoria Picture Palace 48 Victoria Rd, Devonport ⓣ 09 446 0100, ⓦ iconiccinemas.co.nz. New Zealand's oldest cinema (built in 1912) has been revived with three screens and an imaginative programme of arty movies, classics and special mini-seasons. Worth an evening out in Devonport.

DIRECTORY

Automobile Association 99 Albert St ⓣ 09 966 8919, ⓦ aa.co.nz.

Consulates Australia Level 7, PWC Tower, 186–194 Quay St ⓣ 09 921 8800, ⓦ australia.org.nz; Canada ⓣ 09 309 8516, ⓦ international.gc.ca/newzealand; Ireland Level 7, Citigroup Building, 23 Customs St East ⓣ 09 977 2252, ⓦ ireland.co.nz; UK Level 17, 151 Queen St ⓣ 09 303 2973, ⓦ ukinnewzealand .fco.gov.uk; US Level 3, Citigroup Building, 23 Customs St East, ⓣ 09 303 2724, ⓦ newzealand.usembassy.gov.

Emergencies Police, fire and ambulance ⓣ 111; Auckland Central police station ⓣ 09 302 6400.

Gay and lesbian helpline ⓣ 0800 688 5463, ⓦ outline nz.com. Operates Mon–Fri 10am–9pm, Sat & Sun 6–9pm.

Internet The library has free-use computers and wi-fi (max 100Mb/day). Numerous internet cafés (many marked on this guide's maps) have access for around $3/hr.

Laundry Travellers Laundromat, 458 K' Rd ⓣ 09 376 6062. Daily 5am–9.30pm.

Left luggage Sky City Bus Terminal, 102 Hobson St, has lockers (daily 7am–8.15pm; $6 all day; ⓣ 09 623 1503), and most of the larger hostels also have long-term storage for one-time guests at minimal or no charge.

Library Central City Library, 44–46 Lorne St ⓣ 09 377 0209, ⓦ aucklandlibraries.govt.nz. Mon–Fri 9am–8pm, Sat & Sun 10am–4pm.

Medical treatment For emergencies go to Auckland City Hospital, Park Rd, Grafton ⓣ 09 367 0000. The Travel Doctor, Level 1, 170 Queen St (Mon–Fri 9am–5pm; ⓣ 09 373 3531), offers vaccinations and travel health advice. CityMed, 8 Albert St (Mon–Fri 8am–6pm; ⓣ 09 377 5525, ⓦ citymed.co.nz), has doctors and a pharmacy.

Pharmacy Newmarket Night & Day Pharmacy, 160 Broadway, Newmarket (Mon–Fri 8am–11.30pm, Sat & Sun 9am–11.30pm; ⓣ 09 520 6634, ⓦ dayandnightpharmacy .co.nz), is the most convenient late-closing pharmacy. Emergency departments of hospitals (see above) have 24hr pharmacies.

Post office The central city branch at 24 Wellesley St (Mon–Fri 8.30am–5.30pm; ⓣ 0800 501 501) has poste restante facilities.

Swimming Central pools include the indoor Edwardian Tepid Baths at 100 Customs St West (ⓣ 09 379 4745), which will reopen after a major revamp in June 2012, and the lovely open-air saltwater Parnell Baths on Judges Bay Rd (late Nov–Easter Mon–Fri 6am–8pm, Sat & Sun 8am–8pm; ⓣ 09 373 3561, ⓦ clmnz.co.nz/parnellbaths). Otherwise, simply head for one of the beaches (see p.84 & p.88).

Women's centre Auckland Women's Centre, 4 Warnock St, Grey Lynn (Mon–Fri 9am–4pm; ⓣ 09 376 3227, ⓦ womenz .org.nz), offers counselling and health advice and has a library.

West of Auckland

Real New Zealand begins, for many, in **West Auckland**, where verdant hills and magnificent beaches replace tower blocks, suburbs and sanitized wharves. The suburban sprawl peters out some 20km west of the centre among the enveloping folds of the **Waitakere Ranges**. Here, some of Auckland's finest scenery and best adventures can be had little more than thirty minutes' drive from downtown.

Despite being the most accessible expanse of greenery for 1.5 million people, the hills remain largely unspoilt, with plenty of trails through native bush. On hot summer days, thousands head over the hills to one of half a dozen thundering **West Coast surf beaches**, largely undeveloped but for a few holiday homes (known to most Kiwis as *baches*), the odd shop and New Zealand's densest concentration of surf-lifesaving patrols.

The soils around the eastern fringes of the Waitakeres nurture long-established **vineyards**, mainly around Kumeu, just short of the Kaipara Harbour town of **Helensville** and the **hot pools** at Parakai.

GETTING AROUND

By train Auckland's suburban trains make it to the outlying communities of Henderson and Waitakere but don't get you to the wineries or beaches.
By car The easiest access to the majority of the walks and

beaches is via the Waitakere Scenic Drive (Route 24), which winds through the ranges from the dormitory suburb of Titirangi, in the foothills past the informative Arataki Visitor Centre.

Kumeu and Huapai

Once a viticultural powerhouse, West Auckland has been eclipsed by bigger enterprises elsewhere. There is still some production, centred on the contiguous and characterless villages of **KUMEU** and **HUAPAI**, though much of the grape juice comes from Marlborough, Gisborne and Hawke's Bay.

As early as 1819 the Reverend Samuel Marsden planted grapes, ostensibly to produce sacramental wine, in Kerikeri in the Bay of Islands, but commercial winemaking didn't get under way until Dalmatians turned their hand to growing grapes after the kauri gum they came to dig ceased to be profitable. Many of today's businesses owe their existence to immigrant families, a legacy evident in winery names such as Babich, Nobilo, Selak and Soljan. The region's vines still produce Pinot Noir, Pinot Gris and superb Chardonnay. If you plan some serious tasting, designate a non-drinking driver or join Fine Wine Tours (see box below).

ARRIVAL AND INFORMATION | KUMEU AND HUAPAI

By bus Richies buses #060 and #080 run through Henderson to Kumeu and Huapai; check ⓦmaxx.co.nz for schedules.
Kumeu Visitor Centre 49 Main Rd (SH16), Kumeu (daily

9am–5pm; ☏09 412 9886, ⓦkumeuinfo.co.nz). Pick up the free *Kumeu Wine Country* booklet detailing the dozen wineries that can be visited.

WEST COAST TOURS

You'll need your own transport to do justice to the beaches and most of the ranges, unless you join one of the West Coast tours, or perhaps join a canyoning trip (see p.114). All trips pick up around central Auckland.

Bush & Beach ☏0800 423 224, ⓦbushandbeach .co.nz. Afternoon trips ($140) include a short bushwalk to waterfalls and kauri trees, and a visit to Piha beach. The more satisfying full-day tour ($225) has longer walks and more bushcraft.
Fine Wine Tours ☏0800 023 111, ⓦinsidertouring .co.nz. Phil Parker personally leads small-group, half-day tours ($175; $195 with additional cheese tasting) including three Kumeu wineries, lunch and a visit to Muriwai. Also full-day wine tours to Kumeu ($245) with five wineries and honey tasting, plus tours to Waiheke Island ($399 including ferry, classy lunch and premium tasting) and Matakana ($245).
Potiki Adventures ☏0800 692 3836, ⓦpotiki adventures.com. Run by a couple of passionate Ngapuhi women who bring a Maori world-view to

their full-day, small-group Urban Maori Experience trips (daily 10am–6pm; $195), which include morning and afternoon tea. Tours visit Maungakiekie (One Tree Hill) before heading west to the Waitakere Ranges and Whatipu beach to learn creation stories and medicinal plant usage. Saturday trips include a visit to Otara Market.
TIME Unlimited ☏0800 868 463, ⓦnewzealand tours.travel. Personal service and a willingness to go the extra mile characterize these small-group tours focusing on Titirangi and Whatipu beach with an excellent bushwalk and pounding surf. Go for the half-day ($145) or include it as part of a full-day city and coast tour ($245). More hiking-focused trips through the Waitakeres are available at similar prices.

EATING AND DRINKING

Dante's 316 Main Rd (SH16), Huapai ☎09 412 8644, ⓦdantespizza.co.nz. Real wood-fired takeaway pizza ($20–24) done the Neapolitan way – they've even got special certification from Naples – using only the freshest ingredients. Wed–Sun 3–10pm.

★**Hallertau Brewbar & Restaurant** 1171 Coatsville Riverhead Hwy, off SH16 ☎09 412 5555, ⓦhallertau .co.nz. An airy bar and a casual restaurant makes this a refreshing alternative to all the wine hereabouts. Sink a pint or two of their superb brewed-on-thee-premises kolsch, pale ale, red ale, schwartzbier and cider, or try a tasting tray of five ($14), then tuck into light snacks ($11–15) or full meals such as pumpkin risotto, duck confit pasta or steak ($23–36). Daily 11am–midnight.

★**The Riverhead** 68 Queen St, Riverhead ☎09 412 8902, ⓦtheriverhead.co.nz. It's all about the location at one of New Zealand's oldest taverns, which has occupied this site on a high bank above one of the uppermost tentacles of the Waitemata Harbour since 1857, and now has extensive terraces with views down to the mangroves. You can grab a beer and play pool in the public bar or head for the lounge bar for smoked fish soft tacos ($12), rib eye fillet and mushroom ravioli ($36) or pizza ($15–18) under the oaks. Daily 11am–10pm or later.

THE WINERIES

Kumeu River 550 SH16, Kumeu ☎09 412 8415, ⓦkumeuriver.co.nz. The Brajkovich family produces several of New Zealand's finest Chardonnays, all grown hereabouts. Generous tastings, including three single-vineyard varieties, make this an essential stop. Mon–Fri 9am–5pm, Sat 11am–5pm.

Soljans 366 SH16, Kumeu ☎09 412 5858, ⓦsoljans .co.nz. Quality winery making locally grown Pinot Gris and a fun sparkling Muscat. There are free tastings and a smart but casual café serving the likes of vine-smoked salmon on dill hashcakes ($20). Daily 9am–5pm.

Waitakere Ranges and the West Coast beaches

Auckland's western limit is defined by the bush-clad **Waitakere Ranges**, rising up to 500m. The hills are a perennially popular weekend destination for Aucklanders intent on a picnic or a stroll and the western slopes roll down to the wild, black-sand **West Coast beaches**. Pounded by heavy surf and punctuated by precipitous headlands, these tempestuous shores provide a counterpoint to the calm, gently shelved beaches of the Hauraki Gulf.

The Kawerau a Maki people knew the region as Te Wao Nui a Tiriwa or "the Great Forest of Tiriwa", aptly describing the kauri groves that swathed the hills before the arrival of Europeans. By the turn of the twentieth century, diggers had pretty much cleaned out the kauri gum, but logging continued until the 1940s, leaving the land spent. The Auckland Regional Council bought the land, built reservoirs and designated a vast tract as the Centennial Memorial Park, with 200km of walking tracks leading to fine vistas and numerous waterfalls that cascade off the escarpment.

Call by the Arataki Visitor Centre, then follow Scenic Drive which swings north along the range, passing side roads to the **beaches**, noted for their foot-scorching gold-and-black sands and demanding swimming conditions. Before entering the water, read the box on p.63, and heed all warning signs.

Arataki Visitor Centre

300 Scenic Drive • Sept–April daily 9am–5pm; May–Aug Mon–Fri 10am–4pm, Sat & Sun 9am–5pm • ☎09 817 0077

The best introduction to the area is the **Arataki Visitor Centre**, which shows an excellent twelve-minute DVD about the area on demand (free). A felled kauri has been transformed by Kawerau a Maki carvers into a striking *pou*, or guardian post, which marks the entrance and sets the tone for several smaller carvings within. Outside, walkways forge into the second-growth forest: the ten-minute plant identification loop trail identifies a dozen or so significant forest trees and ferns; a longer trail (1hr 15min) visits one of the few mature kauri stands to survive the loggers. Arataki is also the place to pick up the *Waitakere Ranges Recreation and Track Guide* map ($8), excellent for the numerous **short walks** in the ranges.

THE HILLARY TRAIL

In honour of the 2008 passing of New Zealand's mountaineering hero, Sir Edmund Hillary, Auckland has linked a series of existing walking tracks through the Waitakere Ranges into the **Hillary Trail** (70km; 3–4 days; ⊕ arc.govt.nz). Running from the Arataki Visitor Centre via Whatipu, Karekare, Piha and Te Henga to Muriwai, it gives a great sense of the region – regenerating rainforest, stands of kauri, rocky shores, black-sand beaches and historic remains. The highest point is only 390m but it is an undulating track and moderate to good fitness is required. Occasionally slippery, steep paths and unbridged streams can make it a good deal harder in winter, and in any season the last 27km day takes most people at least 10hr.

Nights are generally spent in primitive campsites ($5; book on ☎ 09 366 2000), though you can stay under a roof in Whatipu, Piha and Te Henga. The best source of on-the-ground information is the Arataki Visitor Centre (see p.112).

Whatipu

45km southwest of the city centre, at the north head of Manukau Harbour

Whatipu is the southernmost of the West Coast surf beaches and located by the sand bar entrance to Manukau Harbour, the watery grave of many a ship. The wharf at Whatipu was briefly the terminus of the precarious coastal **Parahara Railway**, which hauled kauri from the mill at Karekare across the beach and headlands during the 1870s. The tracks were continually pounded by surf, but a second tramway from Piha covered the same treacherous expanse in the early twentieth century. Scant remains are visible, including an old tunnel that proved too tight a squeeze for a large steam engine whose boiler still litters the shore.

Over the last few decades, the sea has receded more than half a kilometre, leaving a broad beach backed by wetlands colonized by cabbage trees, tall toetoe grasses and waterfowl. It's a great, wild place to explore, particularly along the base of the cliffs to the north where, in half an hour, you can walk to the **Ballroom Cave**, fitted with a sprung dancefloor in the 1920s that apparently still survives, buried by 5m of sand that drifted into the cave in the intervening years.

ACCOMMODATION   WHATIPU

Whatipu Lodge ☎ 09 811 8860, ⊕ whatipulodge .co.nz. This 1870 former mill manager's house is the only habitation at Whatipu and a great base to experience a wild area of New Zealand, just an hour's drive from Auckland. Think camping without the tent: there's no mains electricity (it generates its own for limited hours) and no mobile phone coverage but there are communal cooking facilities and hot showers. Bring a sleeping bag or sheets and duvets. Booking is essential. Rooms are charged at $35 per person, but $45 for one-night stays. Camping __$15__, double __$90__

Karekare

Perhaps the most intimate and immediately appealing of the West Coast settlements is **KAREKARE**, 17km west of the Arataki Visitor Centre and accessed along Piha Road, with manuka, pohutukawa and cabbage trees running down to a broad beach and only a smattering of houses. In one hectic year, this dramatic spot was jolted out of its relative obscurity, providing the setting for beach scenes in Jane Campion's 1993 film *The Piano* and the inspiration for Crowded House's *Together Alone* album. The Karekare Surf Club patrols a relatively safe swimming area on summer weekends, or there is a pool below **Karekare Falls**, a five-minute walk on a track just inland from the road. There is nowhere to stay here, and no facilities.

Piha

For decades **PIHA**, 20km west of the Arataki Visitor Centre and accessed along Piha Road, has been an icon for Aucklanders. A quintessential West Coast beach

1

with a string of low-key weekend cottages and crashing surf, it lures a wide spectrum of day-trippers and the party set, whose New Year's Eve antics hastened in a dusk-till-dawn alcohol ban on holiday weekends. Despite the gradual gentrification of the old *baches* and the opening of the modern *Piha Café*, it is hanging onto its rustic charm.

The 3km sweep of gold-and-black sand is hemmed in by bush-clad hills and split by Piha's defining feature, 101m-long **Lion Rock**. With some imagination, this former *pa* site resembles a seated lion staring out to sea. The rock was traditionally known as Te Piha, referring to the wave patterns around it that resemble the bow wave of a canoe.

Most **swimmers** flock to South Piha, where the more prestigious of two surf-lifesaving clubs hogs the best **surf**. Piha Surf Shop (see opposite) sells and rents gear. If battling raging surf isn't your thing, head for **Kitikite Falls** (see below).

ARRIVAL AND DEPARTURE
PIHA

By shuttle The Piha Surf Shuttle (Dec–Feb daily; March–Nov on demand; $40 each way; ☏0800 952 526, ⓦsurfshuttle.co.nz) picks up at lodgings around Auckland around 9.30am and leaves Piha for the city at 4pm.

WEST COAST BEACHES TOURS AND ACTIVITIES

The West Coast's bush-clad hills, steep gullies and wild, open beaches are the setting for a bunch of activities including walks to waterfalls and lookouts, horse riding in the dunes, sand yachting and a couple of the best canyoning trips around.

PIHA WALKS

Kitikite Falls (1hr 30min loop) Starting 1km up Glen Esk Rd, which runs inland opposite Piha's central Domain, this fairly easy track passes the three-stage plunge of Kitikite Falls, below which is a cool pool.
Lion Rock (20–30min return) An energetic climb to a shoulder two-thirds of the way up Lion Rock, best done as the day cools. The summit is out of bounds.
Tasman Lookout Track (30–40min return) From the south end of the beach this track climbs up to a lookout over the tiny cove of The Gap, where a spectacular blowhole performs in heavy surf.

HORSE RIDING

Muriwai Beach Riding Centre 290 Oaia Rd ☏09 411 8480, ⓦaucklandhorsehire.org.nz. Offers the chance to explore the beach, dunes and pine forests to the north ($70/2hr). Treks leave daily at 10am & 1.30pm, but call ahead.

SURFING AND SAND YACHTING

Muriwai Surf School By the beach ☏021 478 734, ⓦmuriwaisurfschool.co.nz. Rents surf gear (board and wetsuit $40/3hr), sand yachts ($60/hr) and mountain bikes ($10/hr), and conducts surf lessons (introductory $60, advanced $100).

CANYONING

AWOL Adventures ☏0800 462 965, ⓦawol adventures.co.nz. About the most fun you can have in a wetsuit around Auckland is canyoning, a combination of swimming, abseiling, jumping into deep pools and sliding down rock chutes. AWOL run an excellent trip near Piha, with pick-ups at accommodation around Auckland. The emphasis is on abseiling, particularly on their full-day trip ($175). The lower section is host to the half-day trip ($145) and night canyoning ($165; mostly in winter) with just a headtorch and glowworms for illumination. The trip finishes with a visit to one of the West Coast surf beaches.
Canyonz ☏0800 422 696, ⓦcanyonz.co.nz. Offers full-day trips in Blue Canyon, near Karekare, with pick-ups around Auckland accommodation. Trips include an 8m waterfall-jump or abseil, and a visit to a surf beach ($195). Canyonz also offers day-trips down the magnificent Sleeping God canyon near Thames (Oct–May only; $290). In this wonderfully scenic spot you descend 300m in a series of twelve drops using slides, and abseils as long as 70m (some through the waterfall), with the opportunity to leap 13m from a rock ledge into a deep pool. It's tough enough that you'll need to be water-confident and fairly fit.

ACCOMMODATION

Black Sands Lodge 54 Beach Rd ☎021 969 924, ⓦpihabeach.co.nz. A beach-chic style runs through these three stylishly decorated *baches*: a beach cabin and two suites with big decks, French doors and quality furnishings and bedding. The hosts will also prepare romantic four-course dinners, served in your suite (around $140 a head, excluding wine). Cabin $130, suites $180

Jandal Palace 38 Glenesk Rd ☎09 812 8381, ⓦjandal palace.co.nz. Excellent and very peaceful modern back-packers tucked away from the beach in a verdant valley. There's free wi-fi, late checkout and rooms that open onto

sunny decks. Dorm $33, doubles $86, en suite $120

Piha Domain Motor Camp 21 Seaview Rd ☎09 812 8815, ⓦpihabeach.co.nz. Close to the beach with flat camping, fairly simple facilities and a few on-site caravans and cabins. Camping $13, on-site vans $50, cabins $60

Piha Surf Shop 122 Seaview Rd ☎09 812 8723, ⓦpihasurf.co.nz. Located a couple of kilometres before the beach on the road in to Piha, this place has a range of rustic self-contained caravans, plus cabins with long-drop toilets and a shared single shower. There are great distant views over the beach. Caravans and cabins, per person $30

EATING AND DRINKING

Piha Bowling Club Near the Piha Domain Motor Camp ☎09 812 8845. This casual spot has the best of the evening dining. Just sign yourself in then tuck into good pub meals ($20–25) and cheap drinks. Wed–Sun 6–10pm.

★ **The Piha Café** 20 Seaview Rd ☎09 812 8808, ⓦthepihacafe.co.nz. Piha's only real café, a casual but stylish rough-hewn timber place with plenty of seating inside and out and dishes such as crepes with fresh fruit ($14), char-grilled veg polenta cakes ($16.50), beef burger

with caramelized onions and rocket ($17), lots of fresh baking and great coffee. Wed & Thurs (plus Mon & Tues in Jan & Feb) 9am–4pm, Fri, Sat & Sun 9am–7pm.

Piha Surf Lifesaving Club 23 Marine Parade South, overlooking South Piha beach ☎022 424 7442. You can eat here, but it's really more of a spot to watch the sunset over the sea with a beer in hand. Sign yourself in. Summer Mon–Fri 5–10pm, Sat & Sun noon–10pm; winter Fri 4–10pm, Sat & Sun noon–10pm.

Te Henga

TE HENGA (also known as Bethell's Beach), 27km northwest of the Arataki Visitor Centre, is similar to but less dramatic than Karekare, Piha or Muriwai, and is correspondingly less visited, making it good for escaping the crowds in the summer. There are no shops, but there is a surf club.

ACCOMMODATION

TE HENGA

Bethells Beach Cottages ☎09 810 9581, ⓦbethells beach.com. Located on a hill just behind the dunes, these three casually bohemian self-contained cottages

have great sea views and a wonderfully relaxing tenor. Hot tub and holistic health treatments available. Bring everything you need to cook. $290

Muriwai

MURIWAI, 15km north of Piha and 15km southwest of Huapai, is the most populous of the West Coast beach settlements and has wonderful surf, and a long beach stretching 45km north to the heads of Kaipara Harbour.

Muriwai Gannet Colony

Muriwai's main attraction is at the southern end of the beach where a **gannet colony** (best seen late Oct to mid-Feb) occupies Motutara Island and Otakamiro Point, the headland between the main beach and the surfers' cove of Maori Bay. The gannets breed here before migrating to sunnier climes, a few staying behind with the fur seals that inhabit the rocks below. Gannets normally prefer the protection of islands, but this is one of the few places where they nest on the mainland, just below viewing platforms from where you get a bird's-eye view. Short paths lead up here from near the surf club and off the road to Maori Bay.

ACCOMMODATION AND EATING

MURIWAI

Muriwai Beach Motor Camp 451 Motutara Rd ☎09 411 9262, ⓦmuriwaimotorcamp.co.nz. Pines shade this spacious campsite behind the dunes. There are power sites, hot showers (50¢ coins), kitchen, laundry and a small

lounge. Camping $14

Sand Dunz Café 455 Motutara Rd ☎09 411 8558. Good café with sandwiches and salads from the counter, a standard range of breakfasts and lunches (mostly $12–18;

served until 4pm or 5pm) and takeaway burgers and chips.   Oct–March 7.30am–7.30pm.
Daily: April–Sept 7.30am–4pm (takeaways to 5pm);

Helensville and around

Helensville Pioneer Museum, 98 Mill Rd • Wed, Sat & Sun 1–3.30pm • $5 • ☎ 09 420 7881, ⦿ helensvillemuseum.org.nz

Venture beyond the vineyards of Kumeu and you'll soon find yourself in uninspiring **HELENSVILLE**, 45km northwest of Auckland but more closely associated with the massive Kaipara Harbour. Kauri logs were floated here in huge rafts then loaded onto rail wagons bound for Auckland. Dairying has replaced the timber trade, but photos and displays on the town's halcyon days can be seen at the **Helensville Pioneer Museum** as you enter town from Muriwai.

Parakai Springs

Daily 10am–9pm • $18, private spa $8 extra/hr • ☎ 09 420 8998, ⦿ parakaisprings.co.nz

PARAKAI, 3km north of Helensville, is chiefly noted for its family-oriented aquatic park, where pools are filled by natural hot springs to around 34°C. Private pools are a more sybaritic 40°C. Entry includes free use of a couple of buffeting water chutes, and there's an adjacent campsite.

ACCOMMODATION AND EATING	HELENSVILLE
The Art Stop Café 5 Commercial Rd ☎ 09 420 8580. The place to go for coffee and excellent light lunches such as smoked chicken salad ($15) and Cajun chicken burger ($12), plus secondhand books. Daily 7.30am–4.30pm.	**Malolo House** 110 Commercial Rd (SH16) ☎ 09 420 7262, ⦿ malolohouse.co.nz. Attractively decorated B&B in a kauri villa with 7 rooms, mostly sharing bathrooms and a communal kitchen, though there are two en suites, one with deep bath. Doubles $75, en suites $120

North of Auckland

The straggling suburbs of north Auckland merge into the **Hibiscus Coast**, which starts 40km north of the city and is increasingly favoured by retirees and long-distance commuters. The region centres on the suburban **Whangaparaoa Peninsula** and the anodyne beachside community of **Orewa**, now mostly bypassed by the northern motorway. Immediately to the north, the hot springs at **Waiwera** herald the beach-and-BBQ scene of **Wenderholm Regional Park** and the classic old village of **Puhoi**.

Passing beyond Puhoi puts you into **Northland**; coverage of that region begins with Warkworth (see p.143).

Orewa and the Whangaparaoa Peninsula

The most striking of the Hibiscus Coast beaches is the 3km strand backed by **OREWA**, predominantly a retirement and dormitory town dominated by the

---

NORTHERN GATEWAY TOLL ROAD

Just inland from Orewa the main Northern Motorway becomes a toll road for the final 5km before Puhoi. To avoid paying the **$2.20 toll**, come off the motorway at Silverdale and follow the coast road through Orewa – it'll only add ten minutes to your journey.

The toll road has no staffed booths and is monitored by cameras that read licence plates. It is cheapest to pay online (⦿ tollroad.govt.nz) either before or up to five days after your journey, but you can also use the roadside pay kiosk (northbound at a BP service station; southbound in a small lay-by; extra 40c) or by phone (☎ 0800 402 020; Mon–Fri 8am–6pm; extra $3.70). You'll need to know your vehicle plate number.

twelve-storey Nautilus apartment block. It's a relaxing spot with plenty of good spots for swimming, sunbathing and kitesurfing (for those with their own gear), and occasionally someone on the beach rents stand-up paddleboards. As home to the bulk of the region's accommodation and restaurants Orewa works as a base for exploring the area.

South of Orewa, the **Whangaparaoa Peninsula** juts out 12km into the Hauraki Gulf to Gulf Harbour Marina, launching point for trips to the delightful bird sanctuary of **Tiritiri Matangi** (see p.136).

Shakespear Regional Park

20km southeast of Orewa • Daily: Oct–March 6am–9pm; April–Sept 6am–7pm

You can spend a few pleasant hours swimming, camping and birdwatching at **Shakespear Regional Park**, which envelops the tip of the Whangaparaoa Peninsula. This open sanctuary is protected by a predator-proof fence and, after extensive pest poisoning and trapping in 2011, bird numbers should be on the up. Easy walks wander through regenerating bush where you might see red-crowned parakeets, bellbirds and tui.

ARRIVAL AND INFORMATION

OREWA

By bus Auckland bus routes #893–896 (all under the North Star brand), from 13 Albert St in central Auckland, stop at numerous places. The pricier Northland-bound InterCity and Northliner buses stop on the corner of Hibiscus Coast Hwy and Riverside Rd in central Orewa. Destinations Auckland (11 daily; 1hr).

i-SITE 214a Hibiscus Coast Hwy (Mon–Fri 9am–5pm, Sat & Sun 10am–4pm; ☎ 09 426 0076, ⓦ orewabeach.co.nz).

ACCOMMODATION

Orewa Backpackers Lodge 2d Hammond Ave, Hatfields Beach, 2km north ☎ 09 26 8455, ⓦ orewa backpackers.co.nz. Small and attractive hostel with doubles, twins, quads and an eight-bunk dorm ranged around a central garden overhung with banana and fig trees. Good facilities and lots of local discounts. Dorms $30, doubles $60

Orewa Beach Top 10 Holiday Park 265 Hibiscus Coast Hwy ☎ 09 426 5832, ⓦ orewabeachtop10.co.nz. High-standard campsite in a lovely beachside location shaded by pohutukawas. Camping $19, beachfront camping $22, cabins $57, kitchen cabins $74, tourist cabins $96

Pillows Travellers Lodge 412 Hibiscus Coast Hwy ☎ 09 426 6338, ⓦ pillows.co.nz. Comfortable and conveniently central hostel that's ranged around a central courtyard with a piano in the lounge. Dorms $25, doubles $50, en suite $65

Shakespear Regional Park Whangaparaoa Rd ☎ 09 366 2000, ⓦ aucklandcouncil.govt.nz. Large, grassy camping area amid an open wildlife sanctuary and close to a great swimming beach. There's tap water, flush toilets, and campervans are permitted. Booking essential. $10

Villa Orewa 264 Hibiscus Coast Hwy ☎ 09 426 3073, ⓦ villaorewa.co.nz. Classy, whitewashed Greek-island-style B&B offering airy rooms with bold-coloured furnishings, beach-view balconies and delicious breakfasts. It's close to restaurants and dinner is available on request. $210

Waves 1 Kohu Rd, off Hibiscus Coast Hwy ☎ 0800 426 6889, ⓦ waves.co.nz. The town's fanciest motel is just steps from the beach, has underfloor heating and stylish decor. The premium rooms have the best views. $180, premium $210

EATING

Kippers Takeaway 292 Hibiscus Coast Hwy ☎ 09 426 3969. The best chippy around. Grab some chips, a couple of pieces of fish ($4–6 each) or perhaps their steak-and-mushroom Lusty Burger ($10) and head for the beach. Mon–Wed & Sun 11.30am–7.30pm, Thurs–Sat 11.30am–8pm.

Oliver's 340 Hibiscus Coast Hwy ☎ 09 421 1156. Catch the morning sun roadside at this relaxed café with a tempting array of counter food (including sweet and savoury muffins) and the likes of sautéed mushrooms and scrambled eggs on focaccia ($14) and beef burger with caramelized onions ($17). Free wi-fi. Daily 7am–5pm.

The Pioneer 9 Tamariki Ave, in the base of The Nautilus ☎ 09 421 1053. The most reliable evening dining is at this upscale pub with Monteith's beers on tap, dishes such as excellent salt-and-pepper squid ($17) and loads of regular daily specials – check out the blackboard. Daily noon–10pm or later.

1

Waiwera

The coastal highway runs through the cluster of holiday and retirement homes that make up Hatfields Beach to **WAIWERA**, 6km north of Orewa, where Maori once dug holes in the sands to take advantage of the natural hot springs.

Waiwera Thermal Resort

21 Waiwera Rd • Mon–Thurs & Sun 9am–9pm, Fri & Sat 9am–10pm; movies daily 4pm & 7pm • $26; children $15; adult residents $10.50; child residents $6.50 • ☎ 09 427 8800, ⓦ waiwera.co.nz

To hurtle down suicidal waterslides, drift along the fairly functional Lazy River or soak your bones while watching a PG-rated movie, head to the family-oriented **Waiwera Thermal Resort**, a cluster of indoor and outdoor pools naturally heated to between 24°C and 40°C. You can enjoy all manner of spa treatments and massages and tuck into some wood-fired pizza, gourmet burgers and ice cream. If you're staying in the area ask your accommodation about the temporary resident discount.

Wenderholm Regional Park

SH1, 2km north of Waiwera • Daily: Oct–March 6am–9pm; April–Sept 6am–7pm; kayak rental: Christmas to mid-Jan daily; mid-Jan–Feb Sat & Sun only • Free; kayak rental $25/hr

Wenderholm Regional Park is bordered by the Puhoi river estuary and a sweeping golden beach backed by pohutukawa-shaded swathes of grass that's often packed with picnicking families on summer weekends. There are coin-op barbecues, cold showers and, three hours either side of high tide, the chance to rent sit-on-top kayaks and muck about on the estuary. Walking tracks (20min–2hr) wind up to a headland viewpoint through nikau palm groves alive with birds that have repopulated the area from Tiritiri Matangi (see p.136).

Couldrey House Museum

Christmas–Easter daily 1–4pm; Easter–Christmas Sat & Sun 1–4pm • $3 • ☎ 09 528 3713, ⓦ historiccouldreyhouse.co.nz

Take a peek inside Couldrey House, an 1860s beach house that was built as a winter home and hence gave the park its name. Though added to numerous times and often poorly treated, it has been restored and decorated in period fashion (except for the classic pink and Formica 1950s bathroom). Check out the beautiful 1884 map of Greenwood Estate, a proposed resort and housing development that would have seen all of Wenderholm covered by a housing subdivision.

ACCOMMODATION AND EATING   **WAIWERA**

Wenderholm Regional Park SH1, 1km north of Waiwera ☎ 09 366 2000. Campers pitch in the 20-person estuary-side tent-only site with water, toilets and 24hr access. Self-contained campervans can stay one night in the main car park (access only when park gates are open) where there are toilets; book in arrival using the car park phone or call ☎ 09 301 0101. Camping $̲1̲0̲, vans, per person $̲5̲

Puhoi

A pale blue wayside crucifix marks the entrance to tiny **PUHOI**, 6km north of Waiwera, a bucolic place, settled by staunchly Catholic Bohemian migrants who arrived in 1863 from Egerland, in what was then the Austro-Hungarian Empire (now the Czech Republic). The land was poor, and settlers were forced to eke out a living by cutting the bush for timber. They stuck with it, though, and Mass is still held in the 1881 weatherboard Saints Peter and Paul **church**, which was heavily restored in 2011.

Opposite, Puhoi River Canoe Hire (Sept–May daily; 2hr; $50, including pick-up; booking essential ☎ 09 422 0891, ⓦ puhoirivercanoes.co.nz) rents **kayaks** for gentle, unguided trips downriver to Wenderholm.

Puhoi Bohemian Museum
Christmas–Easter daily 1–4pm; Easter–Christmas Sat, Sun & school holidays 1–4pm • $3 • ☎ 027 211 0316, ⓦ puhoihistoricalsociety.org.nz

Most visitors to Puhoi get no further than the pub, but try to look in at the **Puhoi Bohemian Museum**, in the former Convent School. The model of the village as it was in 1900 is a gem and really comes alive if you engage the interest of one of the volunteers on duty.

EATING AND DRINKING   PUHOI

Puhoi Pub Puhoi Rd ☎ 09 422 0812, ⓦ puhoi pub.co.nz. Iconic Kiwi pub dating back to 1879 with a single-roomed bar festooned with pioneering paraphernalia and photos including the horns of famed bullock teams that once helped clear the dense bush hereabouts. It's less about the average beer or meals – fish and chips ($18) or beef nachos ($15) – than it is chilling in the beer garden as locals, tourists, motorbike groups and Auckland weekenders come and go. Holds occasional events, such as wood chopping on the lawn. Daily 10am–10pm or later.

★ **Puhoi Valley Café & Cheese Store** 275 Ahuroa Rd, 3km north ☎ 09 422 0671, ⓦ puhoivalley.co.nz. Pop in for free samples of the delicious cheeses, super-rich gelati (the Puhoi hokey is locally famous) and sorbets such as forest berry, all made on the premises, but plan to stick around for something from the café. Many of the dishes incorporate the house cheeses, including aged cheddar Welsh rarebit and bacon ($12), or beef, brie and red wine pie with mash and salad ($20). It's all elegantly served inside or on the terrace overlooking lawns with bush-clad hills behind. Daily 9am–5pm.

Southeast of Auckland

Most southbound travellers hurry along Auckland's southern motorway to Hamilton or turn off to Thames and the Coromandel Peninsula at Pokeno – either way missing out on the modest attractions of the **Hunua Ranges** and the **Seabird Coast** on its eastern shore.

Even for Auckland day-trippers the older and more rounded Hunuas play second fiddle to the more ecologically rich Waitakeres, but there are some decent walks around the **Hunua Falls** and greater rewards further south with excellent migratory seabird viewing and hot pools at **Miranda**.

GETTING AROUND

By bike Cyclists will find that the coast road to the southeast is an excellent way into and out of Auckland, following Tamaki Drive from the city centre through Panmure and Howick to Clevedon and the coast.

Hunua Falls
50km southeast of Auckland

A considerable amount of rain is dumped on the 700m-high **Hunua Ranges**, flowing down into a series of four dams that jointly supply over half the city's water. The bush surrounding the reservoirs was once logged for kauri but has largely regenerated, providing a habitat for birds rarely seen in the city. The main attraction is **Hunua Falls**, a 30m waterfall located 20km southeast of central Auckland, where the Wairoa River carves its way through the crater of an ancient volcano. There's good swimming here, or you could take the **Cossey/Massey loop** walk (3hr; 5km) which follows the Massey Track to Cosseys Dam and back down the Cosseys Gorge Track to the falls.

Miranda Seabird Coast

The Firth of Thames, a sheltered arm of the Hauraki Gulf separating South Auckland from the Coromandel Peninsula, borders the Hunua Ranges to the east. Its frequently windswept western littoral comprises land built up from successive deposits of shell banks; much has been converted to farmland but newer shell banks in the making can be seen along what is known as the **Seabird Coast**. Almost a quarter of all known species of migrating shore birds visit the region, and 30,000-strong flocks of wrybill plover avoid the northern winter by spending it at this internationally significant site. During the southern summer (Sept–March) you'll see arctic migrants – notably bar-tailed godwits and lesser knots – who fly 15,000km from Alaska and Siberia.

Kaiaua

The tiny village of Kaiaua comprises little more than a pub, a fish and chip shop and a tiny marina where half a dozen boats squeeze in between the mangroves. It is like much of New Zealand was half a century ago.

Miranda Shorebird Centre

283 East Coast Rd, 7km south of Kaiaua • Daily 9am–5pm, and often later in the summer • Free • ☎ 09 232 2781, ⓦ miranda-shorebird.org.nz

The excellent **Miranda Shorebird Centre** is typically awash with twitchers reluctant to leave. They'll fill you in on the current hot sightings and point you in the direction of the best viewing spots, generally along the walk to the hide (1hr return). There's also a good stock of natural history books and a sunny deck.

Miranda Hot Springs

Front Miranda Rd, 13km south of Miranda • Daily 9am–9.30pm • General entry $13, private spa $15/person for 30min, combo $23 each • ☎ 07 867 3187, ⓦ mirandahotsprings.co.nz

Just twenty minutes' drive short of Thames, the slightly alkaline **Miranda Hot Springs** is an open-air affair with an Olympic-size warm pool kept at 36–38°C, a cooler children's pool and private kauri spa tubs (40–41°C).

ACCOMMODATION AND EATING   MIRANDA SEABIRD COAST

Kaiaua Fisheries 939 East Coast Rd, Kaiaua ☎ 09 232 2776. You can sit in at the small fish restaurant, but the real pleasure here is to order fish and chips to go (around $7), buy a couple of takeaway beers from the pub and sit by the water watching the world go by. Daily 9am–8.30pm.

Miranda Holiday Park Miranda Hot Springs ☎ 0800 833 144, ⓦ mirandaholidaypark.co.nz. Very high-quality campsite with separate tent area, a wide range of cabins, a tennis court and delightful landscaped mineral pools. Camping $22, tourist cabins $145, motel units $195

Miranda Shorebird Centre 283 East Coast Rd, 7km

south of Kaiaua ☎ 09 232 2781, ⓔ miranda-shorebird .org.nz. Keen birders can stay here in 4–6-person bunk rooms or self-contained units. There's a good kitchen and a sunny veranda. Bring food and bedding (or rent for $5). Dorms $25, units $85

Rays Rest Camping Reserve 5km south of Kaiaua. A line of campervans is normally parked on the shoreline where self-contained vans can stay for up to two nights. When it is full, some people camp outside the designated area (though you shouldn't). Public toilets are available in Kaiaua. Free.

Islands of the Hauraki Gulf

Auckland's greatest asset is the island-studded **Hauraki Gulf**, a 70km-square patch of ocean to the northeast of the city. In Maori, Hauraki means "wind from the north" – though the gulf is somewhat sheltered from the prevailing winds and ocean swells by Great Barrier Island, creating benign conditions for Auckland's legions of yachties. Most just sail or fish, but those who wish to strike land can visit some of the 47 islands, administered by the Department of Conservation, designated either for recreational use with full access, or as sanctuaries for endangered wildlife, requiring permits.

Auckland's nearest island neighbour is **Rangitoto**, a flat cone of gnarled and twisted lava that dominates the harbourscape. The most populous of the gulf islands is **Waiheke**, increasingly a commuter suburb of Auckland, with sandy beaches and some quality wineries. Wine was definitely verboten at nearby **Rotoroa Island**, once a Salvation Army de-tox centre and now open for day visits.

Waiheke's sophistication is a far cry from laidback **Great Barrier Island**, the largest hereabouts, with its sandy surf beaches, hilly tramping tracks and exceptional fishing. The Department of Conservation's policy of allowing access to wildlife sanctuaries is wonderfully demonstrated at **Tiritiri Matangi**, where a day-trip gives visitors an unsurpassed opportunity to see some of the world's rarest birds.

Rangitoto and Motutapu islands

The low, conical shape of **Rangitoto**, 10km northeast of the city centre, is a familiar sight to every Aucklander. Yet few set foot on the island, missing out on a freakish land of fractured black lava with the world's largest pohutukawa forest clinging precariously to its crevices. Alongside lies the older, and geologically quite distinct, island of **Motutapu** or "sacred island", linked to Rangitoto by a narrow causeway.

A **day-trip** is enough to get a feel for Rangitoto, make the obligatory hike to the summit (from where there are magnificent views of the city and Hauraki Gulf) and tackle a few trails, but **longer stays** are possible if you pitch your tent at the primitive campsite at Home Bay on Motutapu.

Brief history

Rangitoto is Auckland's youngest and largest **volcano**. Molten magma probably pushed its way through the bed of the Hauraki Gulf around six hundred years ago – watched by Motutapu Maori, who apparently called the island "blood red sky" after the spectacle that accompanied its creation.

The government purchased Rangitoto for £15 in 1854, putting it to use as a military lookout point and a work camp for **prisoners**. From the 1890s, areas were leased for camping and unauthorized **baches** were cobbled together on the sites. Over 100 *baches* had sprouted by the late 1930s when legislation stopped any new construction. In recent years, the cultural value of this unique set of 1920s and 1930s

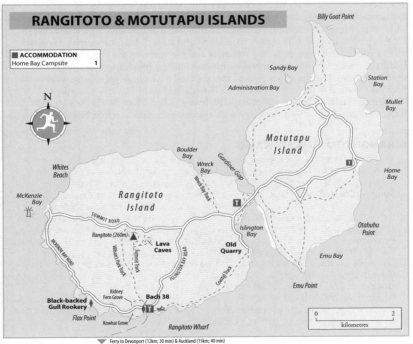

RANGITOTO & MOTUTAPU ISLANDS

ACCOMMODATION
Home Bay Campsite   1

N

Billy Goat Point

Sandy Bay

Administration Bay

Station Bay

Mullet Bay

Motutapu Island

Boulder Bay

Whites Beach

Wreck Bay

Gardiner Gap

Wreck Bay Track

Home Bay

McKenzie Bay

Rangitoto Island

SUMMIT ROAD

Rangitoto (260m)

MCKENZIE BAY ROAD

Wilsons Park Track

Summit Track

Lava Caves

ISLINGTON BAY ROAD

Islington Bay

Old Quarry

Gossip Track

Otahuhu Point

Emu Bay

Kidney Fern Grove

Bach 38

Black-backed Gull Rookery

Flax Point

Kowhai Grove

Rangitoto Wharf

Emu Point

0   2
kilometres

▼ Ferry to Devonport (12km; 30 min) & Auckland (15km; 40 min)

houses has been appreciated and the finest examples of the remaining 34 are being preserved for posterity, their corrugated-iron chimneys and cast-off veranda-railing fenceposts capturing the Kiwi make-do spirit.

Flora and fauna

Rangitoto's youth, lack of soil and porous rock have created unusual conditions for **plant life**, though the meagre supply of insects attracts few birds, making it eerily quiet. Pohutukawa trees seeded first, given a head start by their roots, which are able to tap underground reservoirs of fresh water up to 20m below the surface. Smaller and fleshier plants then established themselves under the protective canopy. Harsh conditions have led to some strange **botanical anomalies**: both epiphytes and mud-loving mangroves are found growing directly on the lava, an alpine moss is found at sea level, and the pohutukawa has hybridized with its close relative, the northern rata, to produce a spectrum of blossoms ranging from pink to crimson. Successful possum and wallaby clearing programmes in the 1990s allowed the pohutukawa to rebound with vigour, and the 2009 eradication of other mammal pests will allow DOC to introduce more native bird species – native parakeets (*kakariki*) recently bred on Motutapu for the first time in a century.

Bach 38

Near Rangitoto Wharf • Usually open summer weekends 10am–4pm • Free • ☎ 09 445 1894, ⦿ rangitoto.org

Bach 38 has been restored to its 1930s condition and you're free to look around the outside. If you're lucky you might strike one of the days when the Rangitoto Island Historic Conservation Trust opens it up for inspection. Several more *baches* are being preserved by the trust, though it is slow work.

Motutapu

The moment you step across the **causeway** onto **Motutapu** the landscape changes dramatically; suddenly, you are back in rural New Zealand, with its characteristic grassy paddocks, ridge-top fencelines, corrugated-iron barns and macrocarpa windbreaks. DOC's plan is to gradually restore its cultural and natural landscape, replanting the valleys with native trees, restoring wetlands and interpreting the numerous Maori sites. Until the trees grow, Motutapu will continue to have a much more open, pastoral feel than Rangitoto, but the views of the Hauraki Gulf make time spent here worthwhile. Around Home Bay there are World War II relics and some beautiful coastline. Numerous tracks include the **Motutapu Walkway** (12km loop; 3–4hr) which links the Rangitoto causeway at Islington Bay with the campsite and beach at Home Bay.

RANGITOTO SUMMIT WALK

The best way to appreciate Rangitoto Island is on foot, but bear in mind that, though not especially steep, the terrain is rough and it can get very hot on the black lava. Consequently the best walks are those that follow shady paths to the summit. A favourite is the clockwise **Summit/Coastal Loop Track** (12km; 5–6hr; 260m ascent) around the southeast of the island. Turn left just past the toilets at Rangitoto Wharf and follow signs for the **Kowhai Grove**, a typical Rangitoto bush area with an abundance of the yellow-flowering kowhai that blossoms in September. Turn right onto the coastal road from Rangitoto Wharf then left into **Kidney Fern Grove**, which is packed with unusual miniature ferns that unfurl after rain. The well-worn **Summit Track** winds through patches of pohutukawa forest. Around three-quarters of the way to the summit, a side track leads to the **lava caves** (20min return) that probe deep into the side of the volcano. Further along the main track a former military observation post on the **summit** provides views out across Auckland city and the Hauraki Gulf.

Continue northwards to the east–west road across the island and follow it towards Islington Bay; from there, pick up the **coastal track** south, initially following the bay then cutting inland through some little-frequented forests back to Rangitoto Wharf.

ARRIVAL AND DEPARTURE

RANGITOTO AND MOTUTAPU

By ferry Fullers (3–4 daily; $27 return) takes 25min to reach Rangitoto Wharf. Most crossings also call at Devonport. Catch the 7.30am ferry on Sat or Sun and the round-trip is just $15.

INFORMATION AND TOURS

Bio-security Pests have been eradicated from Rangitoto and Motutapu. Check your shoes for seeds and your bags for stray mice – it does happen.

What to bring Apart from a couple of toilets and a sun-warmed saltwater swimming pool (filled naturally by the high tide; great for kids) there are no facilities on Rangitoto, so bring everything you need – including strong shoes to protect you from the sharp rocks, a sun hat and a raincoat. If you're planning a walk, carry plenty of water and a torch for exploring the lava caves.

Volunteering The Motutapu Restoration Trust

(⌨ motutapu.org.nz) runs volunteer day-trips (usually first, third and fifth Sundays of each month), typically involving 4–5 hours' weed busting and sapling planting. A ferry ($21 return) takes you direct to Home Bay.

Fullers Volcanic Explorer Tour This tour ($58 including cost of ferry) saves you the trouble of walking to the top of Rangitoto by using a kind of tractor-drawn buggy that operates a sometimes-dusty two-hour summit round-trip with a full and informative commentary; the final 900m is on foot along a boardwalk.

ACCOMMODATION

Home Bay Campsite Eastern side of Motutapu, 3hr walk from Rangitoto Wharf ⌨ doc.govt.nz. The only place to stay on the twin islands is this primitive but pleasant and spacious beachside DOC campsite, with toilets and water. Booking essential Christmas to Jan. $\underline{\overline{\$5}}$

Waiheke Island

Pastoral **WAIHEKE**, 20km east of Auckland, is the second largest of the gulf islands and easily the most populous, particularly on summer weekends when day-trippers and weekenders quadruple its population of around 8000. The traffic isn't all one way, though, as the fast and frequent ferry service makes it feasible for a growing proportion of the islanders to commute daily for work (or school) in the city – a trend that has turned the western end of Waiheke into a suburb. But, with its chain of sandy beaches along the north coast, a climate that's less humid than Auckland's and some great wineries, Waiheke is popular with international visitors in search of a peaceful spot to recover from jet lag or to idle away a day or two before flying home.

The bulk of Waiheke's population lives around **Oneroa**, which also has the densest concentration of cafés and restaurants. You can swim here, but most head elsewhere: to the almost circular **Enclosure Bay** for snorkelling, **Palm Beach** for swimming, and the more surf-oriented **Onetangi**. All over the island, the bays and headlands lend themselves to short, often steep, walks, wineries tempt, and if you're still restless, there's kayaking or sailing.

Waiheke is busy on **summer weekends** and throughout January, when Aucklanders come to relax, taste wine, and dine at restaurants and bars where there's often live music. Midweek is more peaceful but fewer wineries will be open, artists occasionally close their studios and trips requiring minimum numbers are harder to organize.

Brief history

The **earliest settlers** on Waiheke trace their lineage back to the Tainui canoe that landed at Onetangi and gave the island its first name, Te Motu-arai-Roa, "the long sheltering island". Waiheke, or "cascading waters", originally referred to a particular creek but was assumed by **Europeans** to refer to the island. Among the first **settlers** to set foot on Waiheke was Samuel Marsden, who preached here in 1818 and established a mission near Matiatia. The island then went through the familiar cycle of kauri logging, gum digging and clearance for farming. Gradually, the magnificent coastal scenery gained

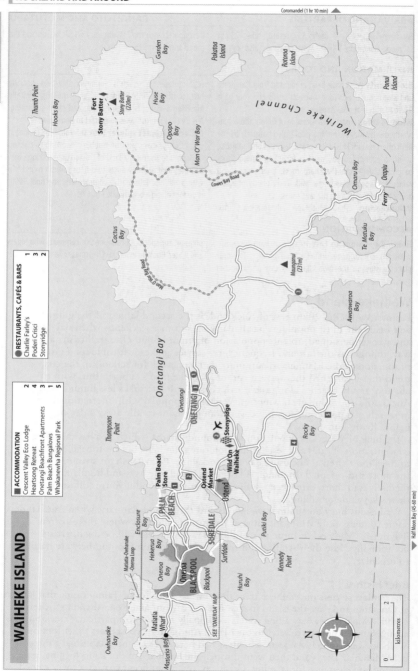

WAIHEKE ISLAND

■ ACCOMMODATION	
Crescent Valley Eco Lodge	2
Heartsong Retreat	4
Onetangi Beachfront Apartments	3
Palm Beach Bungalows	1
Whakanewha Regional Park	5

● RESTAURANTS, CAFÉS & BARS	
Charlie Farley's	1
Poderi Crisci	3
Stonyridge	2

Coromandel (1 hr 10 min)

Waiheke Channel

Fort Stony Batter

Stony Batter (220m)

Thumb Point

Hooks Bay

Garden Bay

Huse Bay

Pakatoa Island

Rotoroa Island

Ponui Island

Opopo Bay

Man O' War Bay

Cowes Bay Road

Cactus Bay

Man O' War Bay Road

Omanu Bay

Orapiu

Ferry

Te Matuku Bay

Maunganui (231m)

Awaawaroa Bay

Onetangi Bay

Onetangi

ONETANGI

Stonyridge

Wild On Waiheke

Ostend Market

Ostend

Thompsons Point

Palm Beach Store

PALM BEACH

Enclosure Bay

SURFDALE

Rocky Bay

Putiki Bay

Kennedy Point

Hekerua Bay

Oneroa Bay

Matiatia–Owhanake –Oneroa Loop

Oneroa

BLACKPOOL

Blackpool

Surfdale

Huruhi Bay

SEE 'ONEROA' MAP

Owhanake Bay

Matiatia Wharf

Matiatia Bay

Auckland (35 min)

Auckland (50 min)

Half Moon Bay (45–60 min)

N

0   2
kilometres

popularity as a setting for grand picnics, and hamper-encumbered Victorians, attired in formal dress, arrived in boatloads.

Development was initially sluggish, but the availability of cheap land amid dramatic landscapes drew painters and **craftspeople**; others followed as access from Auckland became easier and faster.

Oneroa

The main settlement of **ONEROA** is draped across a narrow isthmus between the sandy sweep of Oneroa Bay and shallow, silty Blackpool Beach. The ridge-top main street runs past the main points of interest: the i-SITE, several cafés and restaurants, the library and the cinema.

One of the island's finest **walks** is the Matiatia–Owhanake–Oneroa loop (2–3hr; undulating) which visits secluded beaches and windswept headlands, both peppered with some of New Zealand's finest modern mansions, many with sculptures visible in the grounds.

Whittaker's Music Museum

2 Korora St • Daily: 1–4pm; performances Sat 1.30pm • Free; performances $12.50 • ☎ 09 372 5573, ⓦ musicalmuseum.org

Oneroa's only site is this slightly eccentric museum full of flageolets, piano accordions, player pianos, xylophones and more, some dating back two hundred years. You're allowed to play most of them, and all are ably demonstrated during the occasional musical performances.

Ostend Market

Ostend Hall, corner of Ostend Rd and Belgium St • Sat 8am–noon

What passes for a main road on Waiheke winds east from Oneroa through the contiguous settlements of Little Oneroa, Blackpool and Surfdale to **Ostend**. The island's light-industrial heart, far from any appealing beaches, Ostend is best ignored except for its **market** when the island's neo-hippies come out to offer organic produce, arts and crafts, food stalls, massage, iridology readings and entertainment.

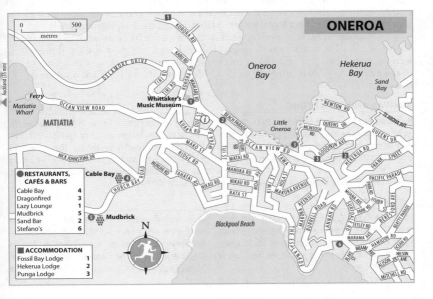

1

Stonyridge Winery
80 Onetangi Rd · Daily: 11.30am–5pm; tour and tasting Sat & Sun 11.30am · $10 · ☎ 09 372 8822, ⓦ stonyridge.co.nz

Waiheke is packed with highly regarded wineries, but none more so than *Stonyridge*, where organic, hand-tended vines produce the world-class Larose, one of New Zealand's top Bordeaux-style reds. Most vintages are sold out (at around $220 a go) before they're even bottled so there are often limited cellar-door sales. On weekends there's an entertaining **tour and tasting**, while at the restaurant (see p.128), wines are on offer by the glass (including Larose at $46 a pop).

Wild on Waiheke
82 Onetangi Rd · Nov–April daily 11am–4pm; May–Oct Thurs–Sun 11am–4pm · Tastings $2 each · ☎ 09 372 3434, ⓦ wildonwaiheke.co.nz

Skip the archery, clay-bird shooting and other team-building-oriented activities in favour of the flavour – Waiheke Island Brewery flavour that is. Try their *Baroona* original or their malt, wheat beer, dark ale and a lot more.

Palm Beach and Onetangi
Palm Beach is 4km east of Oneroa · Onetangi is 9km east of Oneroa

Palm Beach takes a neat bite out of the north coast, with houses tumbling down to a small sandy beach separated by a handful of rocks from the nude bathing zone at its western end.

Waiheke's longest and most exposed beach is **ONETANGI**, popular in summer with surfers, board riders and swimmers, and an occasional venue for beach horse races, usually in mid-March.

Stony Batter Historic Reserve and Fort Stony Batter
Stony Batter Historic Reserve Open 24hr · Free · Fort Stony Batter generally daily 10am–3pm but call ahead · Entry $8, guided tours $15; cash only · ☎ 027 305 2772

There's very little habitation east of Onetangi, just tracts of open farmland, vineyards and **Stony Batter Historic Reserve**, a mass of abandoned World War II defences at the northeastern tip of the island, 23km from Matiatia wharf. It is a twenty-minute walk from the car park to the site where you can wander around topside, or head into **Fort Stony Batter**, a labyrinth of dank concrete tunnels and gun emplacements built to protect Auckland from a feared Japanese attack during World War II. The attack never came and after the war the guns and equipment were removed. Bring or rent ($5) a torch to explore on your own, or join one of the guided tours that bring the place to life. Stony Batter is visited on several island tours.

ARRIVAL AND DEPARTURE   WAIHEKE ISLAND

By passenger ferry Fullers (☎ 09 367 9111, ⓦ fullers .co.nz; roughly hourly; 35min; $35 return, bikes free) operate from the Ferry Building in Auckland to Matiatia Wharf, just over 1km from the main settlement of Oneroa.

By car ferry If you're staying for a couple of days or more, it becomes cost-effective to bring your vehicle over using the Sealink car ferry (☎ 0800 732 546, ⓦ sealink.co.nz; roughly hourly; 45–60min; car only $142 return, each person $34 return) from Half Moon Bay in Auckland's eastern suburbs to Kennedy Point, 4km south of Oneroa.

INFORMATION

i-SITE 118 Ocean View Rd, Oneroa (daily 9am–5pm; ☎ 09 372 1234, ⓦ waiheke.aucklandnz.com). Efficient visitor centre where bags can be stored for $5 apiece (office hours only). Be sure to pick up the free *Island of Wine* map and guide.

Newspaper The weekly *Gulf News* ($2; ⓦ waihekegulf news.co.nz) is published on Thurs and has details of what's on, as well as a rundown of arts and crafts outlets.

Services Internet access is available for free at the library, 2 Korora Rd (Mon–Fri 9am–5.30pm, Sat 10am–4pm). There are a couple of banks on the main street.

GETTING AROUND

By bus Ferry arrivals connect with Fullers buses, which run to Onetangi via Oneroa, Surfdale and Ostend, and to Rocky Bay via Oneroa, Little Oneroa and Palm Beach. Tickets ($1.50—4.20/ride, $8.20 all day) are available on the bus. **By car** Waiheke Auto Rentals, Matiatia Wharf (☎09 372 8635, ⓦ waihekerentalcars.co.nz), have fairly new cars from $59/day and 4WDs for $79.

By bike Waiheke Bike Hire (☎09 372 7937, ⓦ waiheke bikehire.co.nz) rents low-speed mountain bikes for $35/day. Waiheke is undulating, so you'll need to be pretty fit.

By taxi Waiheke Independent Taxis (☎0800 300 372, ⓦ waihekeindependenttaxis.co.nz).

ACCOMMODATION

Accommodation is generally plentiful except for the three weeks after Christmas and all summer weekends. While Oneroa is convenient for buses, restaurants and shops, many prefer the more relaxing **beaches** such as Palm Beach and Onetangi. Lots of accommodation will demand a two-night minimum for Friday and Saturday, or will charge an additional fee.

ONEROA AND LITTLE ONEROA

Fossil Bay Lodge 58 Korora Rd, Oneroa ☎09 372 8371, ⓦ fossilbay.webs.com; map p.125. A relaxed collection of two-person huts a 5min walk from an all-but-private beach 1km from town on an organic farm. Single $40, double $75

Hekerua Lodge 11 Hekerua Rd, Little Oneroa ☎09 372 8990, ⓦ hekerualodge.co.nz; map p.125. Peaceful, pool-equipped backpackers set in the bush 10min walk from Oneroa. Has some private rooms and a self-contained unit. Camping $18, dorms $30, shares $36, doubles $86, unit sleeping seven $270

★ **Punga Lodge** 223 Ocean View Rd, Little Oneroa ☎09 372 6675, ⓦ pungalodge.co.nz; map p.125. Delightful and hospitable B&B, well located in the bush close to Oneroa beach, with tea and muffins available from the helpful hosts. Accommodation consists of a range of comfortable and spacious en-suite doubles with verandas, and four self-catering apartments of different sizes. There's a spa pool, and good-value off-season deals. They also run the nearby *Tawa Lodge*, which has a well-priced shared-bathroom B&B and a very comfortable apartment with wonderful sea views. Ferry transfers available. Shared bath $120, B&B rooms $145, garden rooms $165, apartments $200

ONETANGI

Onetangi Beachfront Apartments 27 The Strand ☎0800 663 826, ⓦ onetangi.co.nz; map p.124. Only a road separates these upscale motel apartments from Onetangi beach. All are self-contained, with Sky TV and DVD players, access to a free sauna and spa pools, plus kayaks for rent. Apartments $170, "beachfront" $210

PALM BEACH AND AROUND

Crescent Valley Eco Lodge 50 Crescent Rd ☎09 372 4321, ⓦ waihekeecolodge.co.nz; map p.124. Lovely lodge in a bush setting and a 20min walk from Palm Beach. Each of the two large rooms has its own kitchen, bathroom and indoor and outdoor dining areas, and you can relax in the hot tub under the stars. Excellent meals are available and delicious breakfasts are served in your room ($15/person). There's also free use of kayaks and bikes. $145

WAIHEKE ISLAND TOURS AND ACTIVITIES

Unless you've got your own (or rented) transport, tours can be the most effective way to see something of the island, particularly the wineries.

TOURS

Ananda Tours ☎09 372 7530, ⓦ ananda.co.nz. Island-based operator running personalized wine, eco, art and scenic tours around the island from around $105/person (minimum numbers apply). Trips are timed to ferry arrivals; try the *Gourmet Food and Wine Tour*, particularly on Saturday, when they take in the Ostend Market.

Fullers ☎09 367 9111, ⓦ fullers.co.nz. The ferry company runs a bunch of tours, all timed with boat arrivals. The Explorer Tour (daily year-round departing Auckland 10am, 11am & noon; $49) includes an open-dated return ferry trip from Auckland, an hour-and-a-half island tour, plus an all-day bus pass so you can explore further on your own. Their Wine on Waiheke tour (daily, departing Auckland 1pm; $115, without lunch $85) has the same benefits but spends four hours visiting three top vineyards.

KAYAKING

Ross Adventures ☎09 372 5550, ⓦ kayakwaiheke .co.nz. Guided paddling trips from Matiatia including half-day trips ($85), full-day trips with the wind behind you plus a shuttle back to your starting point ($145), and overnight trips ($425 for three days). They also rent sea kayaks (from $35/half-day).

1

Palm Beach Bungalows 9 Palm Rd, Palm Beach ☎ 09 372 5146, ⓦ palmbeachbungalows.com; map p.124. Hippyish collection of self-contained wood and mud-brick cottages deeply set in the bush but well equipped with small kitchens and Sky TV. Romantic sojourns are a focus and the luxury bungalow comes with a double spa bath. Cottages **$160**, luxury bungalow **$280**

ROCKY BAY

Heartsong Retreat 8 Omiha Rd ☎ 09 372 2039, ⓦ heartsongretreat.co.nz; map p.124. Tranquil B&B delightfully sited amid bush with sea views. You've a choice of two elegantly appointed rooms in the house (both with breakfast included), a self-contained cabana and a separate cottage (both with breakfast ingredients provided), and everyone has access to a large bush-girt hot pool and a boathouse. Massage and assorted holistic treatments are available. Rooms **$250**, cabana **$260**, cottage **$400**

Whakanewha Regional Park ☎ 09 366 2000; map p.124. The island's only official campsite is simple but attractively sited on a tidal bay. It has flush toilets, potable water and free gas barbecues but no showers. The nearest bus stop is 3km away. Reserve in Jan & Feb. **$10**

EATING AND ENTERTAINMENT

The bulk of the restaurants are in Oneroa, with additional spots at the various beaches and at a bunch of excellent wineries. Live music mostly happens at weekends, with *Sand Bar* in Ostend being a worthy bet.

ONEROA AND SURFDALE

★ **Cable Bay** 12 Nick Johnstone Drive, 1km west ☎ 09 372 5889, ⓦ cablebayvineyards.co.nz; map p.125. This starkly modern winery comes with magnificent views across sculpture-dotted lawns back to Auckland. The wines are excellent and the vineyard restaurant is one of New Zealand's finest, serving dishes such as pan-roasted fish with globe artichoke cream and roasted fennel ($45). There's also an exquisite seven-course tasting menu (evenings only; $120, $205 with matched wines). Wine tasting daily 11am–5pm; restaurant open in summer daily noon–3pm & 6–10pm; some winter closures.

Dragonfired Little Oneroa Beach ☎ 027 296 1655; map p.125. Very Waiheke, this beachside caravan contains a wood-fired oven that's perfect for creating thin-base margherita pizza ($13) and polenta squares with salad ($12). Grab a beer from the nearby shop and head for the beach. Summer only, daily 11am–8pm.

★ **Lazy Lounge** 139 Ocean View Rd ☎ 09 372 5132, ⓦ thelazylounge.com; map p.125. A chilled place to hang out and watch an endless parade of local characters call in for coffee, wine, beer or food options such as Thai chicken salad ($16), pizza, full veggie breakfast ($18) or a hearty slice of cake. Free wi-fi. Daily 8.30am–5pm, plus some Fri & Sat evenings.

Mudbrick Church Bay Rd, 2km west of Oneroa ☎ 09 372 9050, ⓦ mudbrick.co.nz; map p.125. Delightful vineyard that feels more traditional than Cable Bay, and concentrates on its classy restaurant that's all white linen, polished stemware and views over the lavender beds. Start with an entrée such as king scallops with salted watermelon ($26), followed by Waiheke lamb with celeriac purée ($45). Tasting daily 11am–5pm; restaurant daily 11.30am–3pm & 6–10pm.

Sand Bar 153 Ocean View Rd ☎ 09 372 9458, ⓦ sandbar .co.nz; map p.125. Chic little bar, great for a cocktail as the sun goes down and frequently hosting DJs at the weekend.

Daily noon–10pm or later, closed Mon & Tues in winter.

Stefano's 18 Hamilton Rd, Surfdale ☎ 09 372 5309, ⓦ stef.co.nz; map p.125. Cosy little pizzeria with plenty of outdoor seating and a strong line in simply topped thin-crust pizzas (mostly $23–26) plus a few pasta dishes and great tiramisu. BYO and licensed. Daily 5.30–10pm, plus Fri–Sun in summer noon–2.30pm; closed Mon in winter.

Waiheke Island Community Centre 2 Koroka Rd ☎ 09 372 4240, ⓦ wicc.co.nz; map p.125. Runs nightly screenings of recent movies.

OSTEND AND AROUND

Stonyridge 80 Onetangi Rd ☎ 09 372 8822, ⓦ stonyridge .co.nz; map p.124. Lunch alfresco, overlooking the vines, at this excellent vineyard café. Expect assorted bruschetta, tasting platters and a handful of beef, fish and duck mains ($30), plus a great wine list. You can also sample olive oil sourced from the winery's own orchard, which dates back to the 1980s, making it one of the country's oldest. There's often acoustic music on the deck at weekends. Daily 11.30am–5pm.

ONETANGI AND BEYOND

Charlie Farley's 21 The Strand ☎ 09 372 4106, ⓦ charliefarleys.co.nz; map p.124. Casual licensed café with a decent range of dishes (around $20) and a deck with sea views across to Little Barrier Island – perfect for a sundowner. Tues–Sun 9am–10pm or later.

Poderi Crisci 205 Awaawaroa Rd, Awaawaroa Bay, 7km southeast of Onetangi ☎ 09 372 2148, ⓦ poderi crisci.co.nz; map p.124. Stylish vineyard restaurant that's out of the way but worth getting to for the traditional Italian lunches and dinners in a great setting. Produce from the garden is used in dishes such as octopus carpaccio with broad beans and chilli citrus salsa ($21) and skewer of lamb with sautéed artichokes ($34). Also does wine tasting. Dinner bookings are essential. Tues–Sun noon–sundown.

Rotoroa Island

Cruise a fair bit of the Hauraki Gulf, swim off a gorgeous beach and experience something of Auckland's social history all in one compact day out. For over a hundred years **Rotoroa Island** (ⓦ rotoroa.org.nz), off the eastern tip of Waiheke Island, was a Salvation Army alcohol and drug rehab centre, off-limits except to detoxing residents.

Still mostly grassland, the island has been planted with native saplings that are gradually taking over. You can walk around the island in an hour or so, stopping off at beaches, headland viewpoints graced with sculptures and several buildings left from its working days. Visit the chapel, the diminutive jail and an 1860s-era schoolhouse.

There's no food for sale but there are free barbecues, so take picnic supplies.

ARRIVAL AND INFORMATION   ROTOROA ISLAND

By ferry 360 Discovery (ⓣ 0800 360 3472, ⓥ 360discovery .co.nz) ferries call in to Rotoroa (5–7 weekly in summer; bookings essential; $55 return) on the way to Coromandel. The journey takes 1hr 15min and you get just over 4hr on the island.

Information The island's story is told in the superb Exhibition Centre (generally daily 9am–5pm).

Amenities Open daily 10am–5pm.

Great Barrier Island

Rugged and sparsely populated, **Great Barrier Island** (Aotea) lies 90km northeast of Auckland on the outer fringes of the Hauraki Gulf and, though only 30km long and 15km wide, packs in a mountainous heart which drops away to deep indented harbours in the west and eases gently to golden surf beaches in the east. It's only a half-hour flight from the city but exudes a tranquillity and detachment that makes it seem a world apart. There is no mains electricity or water, no industry, no towns to speak of and limited public transport.

Much of the pleasure here is in lazing on the **beaches**, ambling to the **hot springs** and striking out on foot into the **Great Barrier Forest**, a rugged chunk of bush and kauri-logging relics between Port Fitzroy and Whangaparapara that takes up about a third of the island. The forest is New Zealand's largest stand of deer- and possum-free bush, offering a unique walking environment. Because the area is so compact, in no time at all you can find yourself climbing in and out of little subtropical gullies luxuriant with nikau palms, tree ferns, regenerating rimu and kauri, and onto scrubby manuka ridges with stunning coastal and mountain views. Many of the tracks follow the routes of mining tramways past old kauri dams. Tracks in the centre of the island converge on 621m **Hirakimata** (Mount Hobson), which is surrounded by boardwalks and wooden steps designed to keep trampers on the path and prevent the disturbance of nesting **black petrels**. If you're looking for more structure to your day, a few small-time tour and activity operators can keep you entertained (see p.132).

The vast majority of visitors arrive from Auckland **between Boxing Day and the middle of January**, many piling in for the New Year's Eve party at the sports club at Crossroads. The rest of the year is pretty quiet.

Brief history

Great Barrier is formed from the same line of extinct **volcanoes** as the Coromandel Peninsula and shares a common geological and human past. Aotea was one of the places first populated by **Maori**, and the Ngatiwai and Ngatimaru people occupied numerous *pa* sites when Cook sailed by in 1769. Recognizing the calming influence of Aotea on the waters of the Hauraki Gulf, Cook renamed it Great Barrier Island. From 1791, the island's vast stands of kauri were seized for ships' timbers, and kauri **logging** didn't cease until 1942, outliving some early copper mining at Miners Head and sporadic attempts to extract gold and silver. Kauri logging and gum digging were replaced by a short-lived whale-oil extraction industry at Whangaparapara in the

1

1950s, but the Barrier soon fell back on tilling the poor clay soils and its peak population of over 5000 dropped to around 1000.

Back to the land

Alternative lifestylers arrived in the 1960s and 1970s, and while 1970s idealism has largely been supplanted by modern pragmatism, **self-sufficiency** remains, more out of necessity than lifestyle choice. People grow their own vegetables, everyone has their

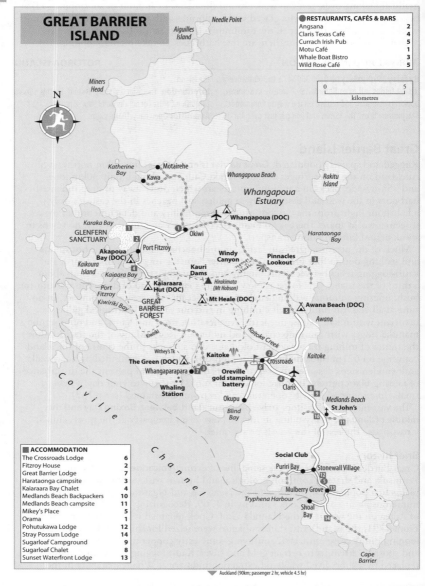

GREAT BARRIER ISLAND

Needle Point
Aiguilles Island

● **RESTAURANTS, CAFÉS & BARS**
Angsana	2
Claris Texas Café	4
Currach Irish Pub	5
Motu Café	1
Whale Boat Bistro	3
Wild Rose Café	5

0   5
kilometres

Miners Head

N

Katherine Bay
Kawa • Motairehe

Whangapoua Beach

Rakitu Island

Whangapoua Estuary

✈ ⛺ **Whangapoua (DOC)**

Karaka Bay
GLENFERN SANCTUARY ▣**1**
Akapoua Bay (DOC) ⛺ ▣**2**
Port Fitzroy
①
Okiwi

Harataonga Bay

Kaikoura Island
Kaiaara Bay

Windy Canyon

Pinnacles Lookout
▣**3**

Port Fitzroy
Kiwiriki Bay

Kauri Dams

✕ ⛺ **Kaiaaraa Hut (DOC)**
▲ Hirakimata (Mt Hobson)

✕ **Mt Heale (DOC)**

✕ ⛺ **Awana Beach (DOC)**
▣**5**
Awana

GREAT BARRIER FOREST

Kiwiriki

Kaitoke Creek

Kaitoke

Withey's Tk
The Green (DOC) ⛺
Whangaparapara ⛺▣**7**

Kaitoke ♨
②
Crossroads 🅿
▣**6**
Oreville gold stamping battery
✈ ▣**4**
Claris
▣**8**
▣**9**

Whaling Station

Okupu

Blind Bay

Medlands Beach
St John's
▣**10**
▣**11**

Social Club

Puriri Bay **Stonewall Village**
▣**12**
Mulberry Grove ▣**13**
Tryphena Harbour

Shoal Bay
▣**14**

Cape Barrier

C o l v i l l e   C h a n n e l

■ **ACCOMMODATION**
The Crossroads Lodge	6
Fitzroy House	2
Great Barrier Lodge	7
Harataonga campsite	3
Kaiaraara Bay Chalet	4
Medlands Beach Backpackers	10
Medlands Beach campsite	11
Mikey's Place	5
Orama	1
Pohutukawa Lodge	12
Stray Possum Lodge	14
Sugarloaf Campground	9
Sugarloaf Chalet	8
Sunset Waterfront Lodge	13

▼ Auckland (90km; passenger 2 hr, vehicle 4.5 hr)

own water supply and wind-driven turbines and solar panels reduce the strain on diesel generators. **Agriculture** takes a back seat to **tourism**, however, and wealthy second-home owners are moving in. Islanders have resisted this trend but as land prices rocket, some on low incomes are forced to leave, while others head out when their kids reach high-school age. Indeed, a dropping population and the need to cater for visitors means there's often **casual work** available in the summer.

Tryphena

Pretty Tryphena is the southernmost harbour and Great Barrier's main settlement spread over four bays: Shoal Bay (where ferries arrive), Mulberry Grove, Stonewall Village (the largest settlement) and Puriri Bay (a short walk along the coast from Stonewall Village). Tryphena has good accommodation and places to eat, but there's not much to do except hang out, swim or rent a kayak.

Medlands Beach

Most people head straight for **Medlands Beach**, a long sweep of golden sand broken by a sheltering island and often endowed with some of the Barrier's best (un-patrolled) surf. The pretty blue and white **St John's Church** looks suitably out of place, having only been moved here from the mainland by barge in 1986 before being dragged over the dunes.

Claris

Most flights arrive at **Claris**, just north of Medlands, where the post office claims to be the world's first place to have run an airmail service. The story goes that when the SS *Wairarapa* was wrecked on the northwest coast of Great Barrier in 1898, the news took a sobering three days to get to Auckland. In response the island set up a **pigeon-mail** service that was used until 1908, when a telephone was installed.

Milk, Honey and Grain Museum

47 Hector Sanderson Rd • Open most days • Donation • ☏ 09 429 0227

The **Milk, Honey and Grain Museum** does what it says on the box, thanks to a neatly organized collection of memorabilia, but also ranges far wider, covering odd aspects of the island's development. It's a worthwhile stop if the weather's bad.

Crossroads, Whangaparapara and the road north

Crossroads, 2km north of Claris, is just that – the junction of roads to Okupu, Port Fitzroy and Whangaparapara. The Whangaparapara road runs past the scant roadside remains of the **Oreville gold stamping battery** (unrestricted entry) and the start of a path to **Kaitoke Hot Springs** (see box, p.134). At **Whangaparapara**, a short stroll around the bay brings you to the foundations of a whaling station built here in the 1950s.

North of Crossroads, the Port Fitzroy road passes the lovely surf and swimming beach of **Awana Bay** and the roadside **Pinnacles Lookout** before reaching the start of a track to **Windy Canyon** (see p.134). The tiny settlement of **Okiwi** offers little but the appealing *Motu Café*.

Port Fitzroy

The harbour at **PORT FITZROY** remains remarkably calm under most wind conditions, a quality not lost on yachties who flock here in summer. It also makes an ideal jumping-off point for tramps in the Great Barrier Forest. You'll find a shop, burger bar, a sporadically staffed information kiosk and a few places to stay.

Glenfern Sanctuary

Glenfern Rd • Self-guided walk $20; guided tour by appointment $40 • ☏ 09 429 0091, ⊚ glenfern.org.nz

The northern shore of Port Fitzroy's harbour is formed by the Kotuku Peninsula, which since 2008 has been separated from the rest of the island by a 2km-long predator-proof fence forming the 2.3-square-kilometre **Glenfern Sanctuary**. Rats have been eliminated and birdlife is slowly returning, with reintroductions of North Island robins and kokako planned. You can hike up to a tree canopy walkway, or learn a good deal more on a guided tour.

Kaiaraara kauri dam

Port Fitzroy makes the best base for **tramping** or shorter day-walks (see box, p.134) to the impressive **Kaiaraara kauri dam** – about the largest and best preserved you'll find. For three years from 1926, the Kauri Timber Company hacked trees out of the relatively inaccessible Kaiaraara Valley, then built dams which, when the water was released, sluiced the cut logs down to Kaiaraara Bay, where they were lashed together in rafts and floated to Auckland.

Karaka Bay

At **Karaka Bay**, 4km north of Port Fitzroy, Orama (see p.136) is home to OPC (☎09 429 0762, ⓦopc.org.nz), an outdoor education school that's a great spot for renting aquatic gear (double sea kayak $65/day, dinghy $40/half-day, snorkelling gear $15) and exploring the area.

ARRIVAL AND DEPARTURE   GREAT BARRIER ISLAND

With a pair of airlines and two ferry services, getting to Great Barrier is easy, and you can often save money by going for a pre-paid travel, accommodation and transport package (see "Tour Agencies" below).

BY FERRY

Fullers ☎09 367 9111, ⓦfullers.co.nz. Runs fast passenger ferries (2–5 trips daily; 2hr journey; $75 one-way; $139 return; bikes $15) from Auckland to Tryphena and on to Port Fitzroy from Christmas to early Feb, plus Easter weekend.

SeaLink ☎0800 732 546, ⓦsealink.co.nz. Sedate year-round car ferry, which also carries passengers. Leaves Brigham Street in Auckland's Wynyard Quarter for Tryphena (3–7 weekly; 4hr 30min), with one service a week (Tues) to Port Fitzroy. Return fares: passengers $85 ($120 in Dec & Jan); bikes $20; cars $370.

BY PLANE

Claris Airport Most flights arrive from Auckland International Airport in the east at Claris, the island's administrative centre and convenient for the best beaches at Medlands and Awana Bay. Companies do fly/ferry combos, and Great Barrier Airlines also flies to Whangarei and Whitianga, allowing you to use Great Barrier as a stepping stone.

AIRLINES

FlyMySky ☎0800 222 123, ⓦflymysky.co.nz. Flights from Auckland ($119 each way, with assorted discounts).
Great Barrier Airlines ☎0800 900 600, ⓦgreatbarrierairlines.co.nz. Flights from Auckland ($124 each way, with assorted discounts).
Destinations Auckland (6–8 daily; 40min).

INFORMATION AND TOURS

Tourist information There is no visitor centre on the island, but GBI Shuttle Buses run an unstaffed kiosk (daily 7am–7pm) opposite the airport in Claris and there's lots of information on ⓦgreatbarriernz.com.
DOC information This is best sought in Auckland, though there is a sporadically staffed field station 1km west of the Port Fitzroy wharf (Mon–Fri 8am–4.30pm; ☎09 429 0044) and sometimes a summer ranger in Tryphena.
Services There are no banks or ATMs on the island. Most places accept credit and debit cards, but bring some cash. Mobile coverage is patchy at best; Tryphena and the hilltops offer some coverage. Internet access is limited and expensive, although Tryphena's *Curragh Irish Pub* has free

wi-fi for customers; the store in Claris has paid wi-fi ($8/day) and the *Claris Texas Café* has a computer ($3/15min).

TOUR AGENCIES

Bush & Beach ☎09 837 4130, ⓦbushandbeach.co.nz. Auckland-based company offering a fly-in day-tour ($695) which includes a visit to the hot springs.
Great Barrier Island Tourism ☎0800 997 222, ⓦgreatbarrierislandtourism.co.nz. Engaging a local company to put together a tailor-made itinerary can often work out cheaper than doing it yourself as they can get transport and accommodation discounts, and this operator really knows its stuff.

MEDLANDS BEACH, GREAT BARRIER ISLAND (P.131) >

1

GREAT BARRIER ISLAND WALKS AND ACTIVITIES

The Aotea brochure (available from DOC in Auckland) has an adequate map and covers all the **walks**: some of the best are listed below. Many of these can be combined to provide 2–3 days of rewarding tramping, making use of the campsites at the Kaiaraara Hut and the lovely new Mount Heale Hut (see p.136). If you've come specifically to tramp, it is best to catch one of the infrequent ferries direct to Port Fitzroy. Alternatively, call one of the shuttle operators in advance to organize transport from the airport or Tryphena.

There are **kayaks** for guests at Great Barrier Lodge, rentals at OPC up north at Karaka Bay and guided trips from Aotea. Great Barrier also has an enviable reputation for the quality of its **fishing** and several operators vie for your business. Alternatively, opt for something altogether more sedate – **golf**.

WALKS AND TRAMPS

Harataonga/Okiwi Coastal Track (12km one-way; 5hr; undulating) Superb coastal views and easy walking along an old coast road that passes through some private property. Get one of the shuttle companies to pick you up at the far end, or just walk partway and back.

Hirakimata via Windy Canyon (6km return; 3hr; 400m ascent) The easiest way to get to the highest point on the island is via Windy Canyon (see below). Beyond, you follow a broad ridge with long coastal views, then hike boardwalks and climb stairs up through lovely, mature kauri and rimu forest to the summit.

Kaiaraara Kauri Dam (10km return; 3hr; 250m ascent) Lovely forest road and track bushwalk to New Zealand's best example of a kauri dam (see p.132). The hike starts at a locked gate around 2km south of the Port Fitzroy DOC office, altogether around a 40min walk from the wharf. Along the way you pass the Kaiaraara Hut (see p.136),

around a 15min walk from the locked gate. From the kauri dam you can continue steeply uphill to a second, far less impressive, dam (50min on) then ascend steps to the summit of Hirakimata (a further 30–40min).

Kaitoke Hot Springs (6km return; 1hr 30min; flat) Gentle, wheelchair-accessible path that skirts the attractive wetlands of Kaitoke Swamp en route to the Kaitoke Hot Springs, where a couple of dammed pools in a stream make a great place for a soak. The best spot is 50m upstream (follow the path) where a pool is tucked into a small chasm.

Windy Canyon (1km return; 20–30min; 50m ascent) An easy walk to a narrow passage that gets its name from the eerie sounds produced by certain wind conditions. The narrow path winds through nikau palms and tree ferns to a viewpoint that gives a sense of the island's interior, as well as coastal views. Starts 4km northwest of Awana Bay.

KAYAKING

Aotea Kayak Adventures Tryphena ☏ 09 429 0664. Explore the sheltered harbours of the island's west coast on guided trips, including a full-day kayak and snorkelling trip ($65).

FISHING AND SCUBA DIVING

Freedom Fishing Charters Medlands ☏ 09 429 0861, ⓦ freedomfishingcharters.co.nz. Ivan "Skilly" McManaway has been fishing the island for approaching fifty years and will take you out for $120 a head for half a day (minimum 2 people). He's also equipped for scuba diving, with gathering crayfish the main goal.

GOLF

Claris Golf Club Whangaparapara Rd, Claris ☏ 09 429 0420. Odd-ball nine-hole par-three course surrounded by bush with pukeko strutting across the fairways. Green fees are $20, club rental is $5 and there's a lively bar with cheap drinks and decent meals (Thurs & Sun 10am–6pm).

GETTING AROUND

Great Barrier has no scheduled public transport but there are several shuttle buses; they generally meet all ferries and flights, but it's better to book in advance. It is often more convenient to rent a car, or even a bike, though the hills are steep and the roads dusty and hot in summer.

By shuttle bus GBI Shuttle Buses (☏ 09 429 0062, ⊛ great barrierisland.co.nz) and Great Barrier Travel (☏ 0800 426 832, ⊛ greatbarriertravel.co.nz) both operate ferry and flight transfers for similar prices. From Tryphena, fares are around $15 to Medlands, $20 to Claris and $30 to Whangaparapara.

By rental car Aotea Rentals (☏ 0800 426 832, ⊛ aoteacar rentals.co.nz) in Tryphena has cars from $60/day and scooters for $49/day. GBI Rent A Car (☏ 09 429 0062, ⊛ greatbarrierisland.co.nz) in Claris has basic cars from $40/day.

By mountain bike Paradise Cycles (☏ 09 429 0700, ✉ paradisecycles@xtra.co.nz) in Tryphena rent bikes from $25. Off-road mountain biking is only allowed on the Forest Rd between Whangaparapara and Port Fitzroy.

ACCOMMODATION

Accommodation on Great Barrier ranges from camping and hostels to plush lodges. Some of the best of the island's **self-catering cottages** are mentioned below, though many more excellent places are listed on sites such as ⊛ greatbarriernz .com and ⊛ greatbarrierislandtourism.co.nz. The owners often live close by and can arrange breakfast and sometimes dinner. Some places **pick up** from ferries and flights, though those in Tryphena and Medlands will expect you to catch the shuttles that meet each boat or plane. Accommodation is generally more **expensive** than on the mainland, particularly from Christmas to mid-January when the island is packed – and you'll need to **book well ahead** to stand any chance of finding a place. There are numerous, simple DOC **campsites** (all marked on this guide's map and costing $8–9), the best of them listed below, along with one of the better-located private sites. DOC sites all have toilets, water and cold showers (except *The Green*) and fires are not allowed. Book online during peak periods (⊛ doc.govt.nz).

TRYPHENA AND AROUND

★ **Pohutukawa Lodge** Stonewall, Tryphena ☏ 09 429 0211, ⊛ currachirishpub.co.nz. The pick of the places around Tryphena – homely, small and welcoming, with a great pub and restaurant spilling out onto the veranda, all conveniently close to the shop. There are attractive rooms plus a single four-bed backpacker room (linen supplied) that can be noisy with pub patrons leaving. There's also a self-catering kitchen. Good-value flight, transport and accommodation packages available. Backpacker rooms $25, doubles $135

Stray Possum Lodge 64 Cape Barrier Rd ☏ 0800 767 786, ⊛ straypossum.co.nz. A little out on a limb, this bush-girt hostel has six-bed dorms, doubles, cabins and lovely self-contained chalets ideal for groups of up to six. There's also a licensed pizza restaurant (nightly in Jan, plus summer weekends). Linen $5 for your stay, or bring a sleeping bag. Camping $15, dorms $27, rooms $79, chalets $155

Sunset Waterfront Lodge Mulberry Grove, Tryphena ☏ 09 429 0051, ⊛ sunsetlodge.co.nz. Motel-style accommodation in grassy grounds that aren't really water-front but have close sea views. Choose from A-frames sleeping four and several smaller studios. Studio $195, A-frames $245

MEDLANDS

Medlands Beach Backpackers 9 Mason Rd ☏ 09 429 0320, ⊛ medlandsbeach.com. Basic, low-key backpackers with four-bed dorms, a secluded chalet and a couple of villas on a small farm a 10min walk from Medlands Beach – making it popular with surfers. There are bodyboards for guests' use, but there are no meals and no shops nearby, so bring your own food. Dorms $35, room $70, chalet $80, villa $120

CLARIS, CROSSROADS AND AROUND

The Crossroads Lodge 1 Blind Bay Rd, Crossroads ☏ 09 429 0889, ⊛ www.xroadslodge.com. Comfortable hostel well sited within walking distance of the airport, hot springs and island tramps. Accommodation is in doubles and dorms with a central lounge and kitchen. Dorm $30, doubles $75

★ **Sugarloaf Chalet** Sugarloaf Rd, Kaitoke ☏ 09 429 0229. A gorgeous, rustic-chic self-catering cottage with barbecue area, fire pit and solar power, just steps from a lovely beach and with a real outdoors flavour (complete with external shower and toilet). $150

WHANGAPARAPARA

Great Barrier Lodge Whangaparapara Harbour ☏ 09 429 0488, ⊛ greatbarrierlodge.com. This harbour-side lodge is pretty much all there is at Whangaparapara, and also serves as the local grocery and dive shop. Accommodation is in cottages and studio units, the main building houses a bar/restaurant and there are free kayaks and a dinghy for guests. Bunkroom per person $55, studios & cottages $205

PORT FITZROY

Fitzroy House Glenfern Rd, Port Fitzroy ☏ 09 429 0091, ⊛ fitzroyhouse.co.nz. Stay inside Glenfern Sanctuary at the owner's wood-floored self-contained cottage sleeping six, with views over the harbour and free access to canoes and a dinghy. Sea kayaks are $45/24hr. Check out the multi-night discounts and excellent, four-day tramping and sailing packages. Closed June–Sept. $200

Kaiaraara Bay Chalet Kaiaraara Bay Rd, Port Fitzroy ☏ 09 429 0040. Modern one-bedroom self-catering unit that's just a 30min walk from the Port Fitzroy wharf, with

1

long sea views and room for four. Well sited for the kauri dam walk. $170

Orama Karaka Bay ☎ 09 429 0063, ⌨ orama.co.nz. A Christian centre also operating as both a waterfront holiday park and home to the OPC outdoor centre (see p.132). There's a swimming pool, shop and access to magnificent bushwalks, fishing and diving. Camping $25, bunkrooms $33, cabins $90, self-contained houses and cottages $195

CAMPSITES AND HUTS

Harataonga Campsite Harataonga. Excellent, shady DOC site 300m back from the beach and very popular with families in the fortnight after Christmas. $9.20

Kaiaraara Hut Near Port Fitzroy ⌨ doc.govt.nz. Less well sited than the new Mount Heale Hut, this longstanding 28-bunker huddles in the bush and has water and a wood stove for heating. Book through DOC and take pots, utensils

and all food. $15

Medlands Beach Campsite Medlands Beach. Attractive DOC site beside an estuary and just over the dunes from an excellent beach. Very crowded for most of Jan but at other times you'll have it to yourselves. $9.20

Mount Heale Hut Superb new 20-bunk hut set in a saddle below Mt Heale with great views across the Hauraki Gulf to Little Barrier Island. There's a gas cooking stove but take pots, utensils and food. No bookings. $15

Mikey's Place Awana ☎ 09 429 0140. Hospitable but primitive campsite 25km north of Tryphena that's less well located than the nearby DOC site but has hot showers, toilets and a basic cookhouse. $7

Sugarloaf Campground Sugarloaf Rd, Kaitoke ☎ 09 429 0229. A great private campsite overlooking the southern end of Kaitoke Beach. It has water, toilets and showers. Ask about exploring the Mermaid Pool at low tide. $8

EATING AND DRINKING

The limited number of stand-alone **restaurants** encourages lots of accommodation operators to offer meals, and those that don't will almost certainly have self-catering facilities. Restaurants often close early if business is slow, so **book ahead**. There are also **shops** in Tryphena, Claris, Whangaparapara and Port Fitzroy, where you can pick up picnic provisions. **Drinking** tends to happen in bars attached to accommodation establishments or in the social clubs at Tryphena and Claris.

★ **Angsana** 63 Grays Rd, just north of Crossroads ☎ 09 429 0272. A quality Thai restaurant seems incongruous for the Barrier, but the island is a better place for it. The menu features all the Thai favourites (mains around $30) with friendly service. Summer daily 6–9pm; winter Thurs–Sat 6–8pm.

Claris Texas Café 129 Hector Sanderson Rd, Claris ☎ 09 429 0811. Reliable café with a sunny courtyard and a grassy patch for the kids. Visit for a full range of breakfasts, fish burger and chips ($13), soups and great desserts. Daily 8am–4pm.

★ **Currach Irish Pub** Stonewall, Tryphena ☎ 09 429 0211, ⌨ currachirishpub.com. An Irish pub that's about as traditional as you can get on a South Pacific island – a lot of the paraphernalia came from the owner's grandmother's pub in County Kerry, which closed in 1950. There's Guinness and Kilkenny on tap and great hot bar meals served in the evening (crumbed scallops and chips $26). There's also often live acoustic music, especially on Thurs when anyone

is welcome to jam.

Motu Café Okiwi ☎ 09 429 0002. The best spot for daytime eating in the north of the island. The range of food is limited but the coffee's good and you can while away an hour reading magazines or discussing the island's ecology with the owners. Wed (movie at 7.30pm, preceded by dinner), Sat & Sun 9am–4pm.

Whale Boat Bistro Great Barrier Lodge, Whangaparapara ☎ 09 429 0488, ⌨ greatbarrierlodge .com. Bar and restaurant serving meals indoors or on the spacious deck with harbour views. For the 2–3 weeks after Boxing Day they do great gourmet barbecue dinners. Daily 8am–8pm or later.

Wild Rose Café Stonewall, Tryphena ☎ 09 429 0905. Sit on the veranda or in the garden at this daytime café specializing in organic products, fine teas and juices. Also does a good range of breakfasts, burgers ($12) and nachos. Summer daily 9am–3pm.

Tiritiri Matangi

A visit to **Tiritiri Matangi** is the high point of many a stay in Auckland. About 4km off the tip of the Whangaparaoa Peninsula and 30km north of Auckland, Tiritiri Matangi is an "open sanctuary", and visitors are free to roam through the predator-free bush where, within a couple of hours, it's possible to see rarities such as takahe, saddlebacks, whiteheads, red-crowned parakeets, North Island robins, kokako and brown teals. To stand a chance of seeing the little-spotted kiwi and tuatara, you'll have to stay overnight.

Four of the species released here are among the rarest in the world, with total populations of around a couple of hundred. The most visible are the flightless **takahe**, lumbering blue-green turkey-sized birds long thought to be extinct (see p.755); the birds were moved here from Fiordland, have bred well and are easily spotted as they are unafraid of humans and very inquisitive. **Saddlebacks**, **kokako** and **stitchbirds** stick to the bush and its margins, but often pop out if you sit quietly for a few moments on some of the bush boardwalks and paths near feeding stations. **Northern blue penguins** also frequent Tiritiri and can be seen all year round but are most in evidence in March, when they come ashore to moult, and from September to December, when they nest in specially constructed viewing boxes located along the seashore path west of the main wharf.

The standard loop along the east coast then back via the central Ridge Track passes **Hobbs Beach**, where you might want to indulge in a little swimming from the only sandy strand around.

Brief history

Evidence from *pa* sites on the island indicates that Tiritiri Matangi was first populated by the Kawerau-A-Maki **Maori** and later by Ngati Paoa, both of whom are now recognized as the land's traditional owners. They partly **cleared the island** of bush, a process continued by Europeans who arrived in the mid-nineteenth century to graze sheep and cattle. Fortunately, **predators** such as possums, stoats, weasels, deer, cats, wallabies and the like failed to get a foothold, so after farming became uneconomic in the early 1970s Tiritiri was singled out as a prime site for helping to restore bird populations. The cacophony of birdsong in the bush is stark evidence of just how catastrophic the impact of these predators has been elsewhere.

Since 1984, a **reforestation** programme has seen the planting of over 300,000 saplings, and though the rapidly regenerating bush is far from mature, the **birds** seem to like it. Most are thriving with the aid of feeding stations to supplement diets in the leaner months, with nesting boxes standing in for decaying trees.

ARRIVAL AND DEPARTURE
TIRITIRI MATANGI

By ferry Tiritiri Matangi is typically visited as a day-trip, giving five hours on the island. 360 Discovery Ferries (Christmas to mid-Jan daily 9am; rest of year Wed–Sun and public holidays 9am; $66 return; Gulf Harbour return $49; **☎**0800 360 3472, **◍**360discovery.co.nz) depart from Pier 4 at Auckland's Downtown Ferry Terminal, call at Gulf Harbour (see p.117) 50min later and arrive at Tiritiri around 10.10am. Boats arrive back in Auckland around 5pm.

INFORMATION AND TOURS

Tourist information There's lots of fascinating information about the island on the Supporters of Tiritiri Matangi website, **◍** tiritirimatangi.org.nz.
Food There is no food on the island – make sure you bring your own lunch.

Guided walks Ferry passengers can join a guided walk (1–2hr; $5) from the wharf, led by volunteers steeped in bird-lore. They typically finish near the lighthouse at the modern interpretation centre.

ACCOMMODATION

Tiritiri Island Bunkhouse **◍**doc.govt.nz/tiritiribunk house. The island's only accommodation is this self-contained bunkhouse near the lighthouse. Book as far in advance as you can (months ahead for weekends), and bring a sleeping bag and food in sealed rodent-proof containers. <u>$24.50</u>

Northland

143 The Matakana Coast to Bream Bay

151 Whangarei

156 Around Whangarei

160 North of Whangarei to the Bay of Islands

162 The Bay of Islands

179 Matauri Bay to the Karikari Peninsula

184 Kaitaia and around

186 Ninety Mile Beach and Cape Reinga

190 Hokianga Harbour

194 The kauri forests and around

197 The northern Kaipara Harbour

CAPE REINGA

Northland

Thrusting 350km from Auckland into the subtropical north, Northland separates the Pacific Ocean from the Tasman Sea. The two oceans swirl together off Cape Reinga, New Zealand's most northerly road-accessible point, which tourists often approach via the sands of Ninety Mile Beach. Kiwis regularly describe this staunchly Maori province as the "Winterless North", a phrase that evokes the citrus trees, avocado plantations, vineyards, warm aquamarine waters and beaches of white silica or golden sand. These attractions have increasingly made the upper reaches of the region a magnet for discerning tourists and holidaying Kiwis, keen to escape the hullabaloo of Auckland traffic. Increased tourism has, in turn, slowly brought back some prosperity and a more positive and welcoming attitude to a region once noted for its ambivalence to visitors.

Scenically, Northland splits down the middle. The **east coast** is a labyrinth of coves hidden between plunging headlands. Beaches tend to be calm and safe, with the force of occasional Pacific storms broken by clusters of protective barrier islands. There could hardly be a greater contrast than the long, virtually straight, **west coast** pounded by powerful Tasman breakers and broken only by occasional harbours. Tidal rips and holes make swimming dangerous, and there are no lifeguard patrols. Some beaches are even designated as roads but are full of hazards for the unwary – and rental cars aren't insured for beach driving. Exploration of the undulating **interior** involves long forays down twisting side roads.

Beyond Auckland's extended suburbs, on the east shore, is the rural **Matakana Coast**, popular with yachties circumnavigating Kawau Island and snorkellers exploring the underwater world of the **Goat Island Marine Reserve**. The broad sweep of **Bream Bay** runs to the dramatic crags of Whangarei Heads at the entrance to Northland's major port and town, **Whangarei**. Off the coast here lie the **Poor Knights Islands**, one of the world's premier dive spots with a multitude of unique dives around the islands. Tourists in a hurry tend to make straight for the **Bay of Islands**, a jagged bite out of the coastline steeped in New Zealand history and dotted with islands suitable for cruising, diving and swimming (some of the time) with dolphins. Everything north of here is loosely referred to as **The Far North**, a region characterized by the quiet remoteness of the **Whangaroa Harbour, Doubtless Bay**, and the **Aupori Peninsula**, which backs **Ninety Mile Beach** and leads to **Cape Reinga**.

The west coast is clearly discernable from the east, marked by the struggle out of economic neglect caused by the cessation of kauri logging and establishment of farming

Goat Island tours and activities p.145
Whangarei tours and activities p.154
Activities at the Poor Knights p.158
The Cape Brett Track p.161
The Treaty of Waitangi p.166
Bay of Islands tours and activities pp.170–171
French nuclear testing in the Pacific p.179
Whangaroa Harbour and Doubtless Bay tours and activities p.181

Kaitaia festivals and events p.184
Ahipara tours and activities p.185
Going it alone on Ninety Mile Beach p.187
Cape Reinga Walks p.189
Opononi the dolphin p.192
Opononi and Omapere tours and activities p.193
The kauri and its uses p.195

WAIPOUA KAURI FOREST

Highlights

❶ The Arts Factory, Te Hana Offers the chance to see the work of a Kiwi icon and his team sculpting beautiful and enormous jewellery-like pieces out of massive lumps of swamp kauri that are thousands of years old. **See p.146**

❷ Poor Knights Islands World-class scuba diving and snorkelling in caves, along walls and under rock arches, all abundant with beautiful and unusual sea life. **See p.157**

❸ Bay of Islands Sail, kayak and soak up the history and scenery of Northland's tourism hot spot and – if you're lucky – swim with dolphins. **See p.162**

❹ Ninety Mile Beach and Cape Reinga Journey the length of one of the country's best-known beaches, stopping to sandboard giant dunes along the way, before taking in views of the Pacific Ocean and Tasman Sea meeting in a swirling mass. **See p.186**

❺ Hokianga Harbour Settle in to watch the sun set in a fiery rainbow of orange, fuchsia and indigo, or explore the wind-sculpted dunes that overlook this scenic, laidback harbour. **See p.190**

❻ Kauri forests Marvel at New Zealand's largest tree, the majestic 2000-year-old Tane Mahuta, and the other ancient kauri in the same stand. **See p.196**

HIGHLIGHTS ARE MARKED ON THE MAP ON P.142

and tourism in its stead, both of which are finally beginning to alter the landscape and create a more positive atmosphere. First stop on the way back south from Ninety Mile Beach is the fragmented but alluring **Hokianga Harbour**, one of New Zealand's largest, with spectacular sand dunes gracing the north head. South of here you're into the **Waipoua Forest**, which is all that remains after the depredations of the kauri loggers – a story best told at the excellent Kauri Museum at Matakohe.

GETTING AROUND

By car With no trains and few airports, you'll be hitting Northland's roads. Driving is the only sensible option as there is little public transport and only Magic buses (see opposite) seem to encourage stopping and exploring from their designated routes. Road choices are limited to the state highways running up each side of the peninsula.

These form a logical loop formalized as the Twin Coast Discovery Highway: there's no need to follow it slavishly, but the brown signs emblazoned with a dolphin and curling wave make a good starting framework.

By bus The main bus line is InterCity (☎ 09 583 5780, ⊛ intercity.co.nz), which also runs Northliner services,

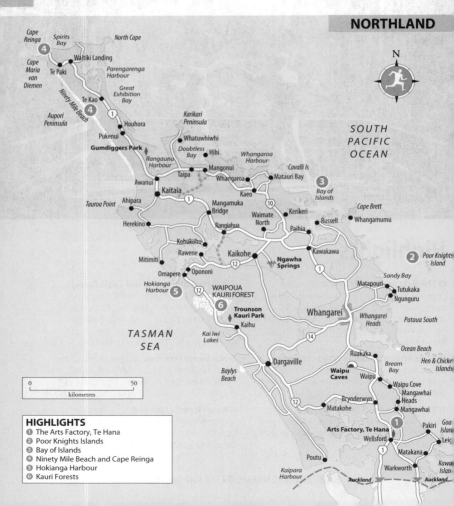

NORTHLAND

HIGHLIGHTS
1. The Arts Factory, Te Hana
2. Poor Knights Islands
3. Bay of Islands
4. Ninety Mile Beach and Cape Reinga
5. Hokianga Harbour
6. Kauri Forests

sometimes using the same bus, and Nakedbus (premium charged ☎ 0900 62533, ⓦ nakedbus.com). Magic Bus (☎ 09 358 5600, ⓦ magicbus.co.nz) and Main Coachline (☎ 09 278 8070, ⓦ maincoachline.co.nz) run more limited services.

By plane Northland has a limited number of flights and since distances are relatively short you're unlikely to need them, except perhaps for flights from Whangarei to Great Barrier Island with Great Barrier Airlines (ⓦ greatbarrier airlines.co.nz) or a flightseeing trip from Paihia to Cape Reinga via the Bay of Islands.

INFORMATION

Websites The Northland website is ⓦ northlandnz.com. The Far North region of Northland has regional i-SITE offices in Paihia, Kaitaia and Opononi; see ⓦ visitfarnorthnz .com for more information.

Brief history

Northland was the site of most of the early contact between Maori and European settlers, and the birthplace of New Zealand's most important document, the **Treaty of Waitangi**. Maori legend tells of how the great Polynesian explorer Kupe discovered the Hokianga Harbour and, finding the climate and abundance of food to his liking, encouraged his people to return and settle there. It was their descendants in the Bay of Islands who had the dubious honour of making the first contact with white men, as European whalers plundered the seas and missionaries sought converts. Eventually, the northern chiefs signed away their sovereignty in return for assurances on land and traditional rights, which were seldom respected. There is still a perception among some Maori in the rest of the country that the five northern *iwi* gave Aotearoa away to the Pakeha.

As more fertile farmlands were found in newly settled regions further south, rapacious **kauri loggers** and **gum diggers** cleared the bush, and later, as extractive industries died away, pioneers moved in, turning much of the land to **dairy country**. Local dairy factories closed as larger semi-industrial complexes centralized processing, leaving small towns all but destitute, though the planting of fast-growing exotic trees and sporadic horticulture keep local economies ticking over.

The Matakana Coast to Bream Bay

Around 50km north of central Auckland the city's influence begins to wane, heralding the **Matakana Coast** (ⓦ matakanacoast.com), a 30km stretch of shallow harbours, beach-strung peninsulas and small islands. Its individual character becomes apparent once you pass pretty **Warkworth** and head out either to **Kawau Island**, or up the coast to the village of **Matakana** and the snorkelling and diving nirvana of **Goat Island**.

The journey from Auckland to Warkworth has been made quicker, though less scenic, by the introduction of a 7km stretch of toll road ($2.20/car). Sadly, confusing signage means people miss toll pay areas (see box, p.116) on the way north and south, as well as the great views on the alternative route, via Orewa on the Hibiscus Coast Highway.

Other than the excellent wood carving on display at **Te Hana**, there's little to detain you on SH1 between Warkworth and Waipu as it passes the road junction at **Brynderwyn**, where SH12 loops off to Dargaville, the Waipoua kauri forest and the Hokianga Harbour. If you're heading north and want a scenic route, it's better to stay on the coast and follow **Bream Bay**, named by Cook when he visited in 1770 and his crew hauled in tarakihi, which they mistook for bream. There are no sizeable towns here, only the small beach communities of **Mangawhai Heads** and **Waipu Cove**, looking out to the **Hen and Chicken Islands**, refuges for rare birds such as the wattled saddleback.

Warkworth

The peaceful and slow-paced rural town of **WARKWORTH** only really comes to life in high summer when thousands of yachties moor their boats in the numerous estuaries and coves nearby. From the late 1820s for about a century, the languid stretch of river behind the town seethed with boats shipping out kauri: a boardwalk now traces its shores past the *Jane Gifford* (⊚janegifford.org.nz), a rebuilt scow which once worked the tidal waterways and now runs occasional trips (1hr; $15).

Warkworth and Districts Museum

Tudor Collins Drive, 3km south of Warkworth off the SH1 • Daily 9am–3pm • $8 • ⊚ wwmuseum.orconhosting.net.nz

Spend a few minutes at the **Warkworth and Districts Museum**, which explores the region's history through re-created rooms, and a 5m-long, 130-link chain carved from a single piece of kauri. The two ancient kauri outside mark the start of two well-presented twenty-minute boardwalk nature trails through the preserved bush of the **Parry Kauri Park** (9am–dusk; donation). A free leaflet at the museum's entrance explains the trees in detail.

Brick Bay Sculpture Trail

Arabella Lane, 6km east of Warkworth off SH1 • Daily 10am–5pm • $12; wine tastings $5; olive oil tastings $8 • ☎ 09 425 4690, ⊚ brickbaysculpture.co.nz

For a combination of outdoor sculpture and striking architecture, try the **Brick Bay Sculpture Trail**. An hour wandering the 2km-long bush, vines and parkland trail past the art – fifty plus sculptures mostly by New Zealand artists and all for sale (and likely to remain so) – gets you back to the predominantly glass café, where wine tastings, olive oil tastings and platters (for two) of local-ish produce ($27) may slow you down further.

Kawau Island

With a resident population of around seventy (plus lots of weekenders), **KAWAU ISLAND** is chiefly given over to holiday homes, each with its own wharf. For information on how to get to the island, see p.147.

Mansion House

Mid-Dec to Feb daily noon–3.30pm; March to mid-Dec Mon–Fri noon–2pm, Sat & Sun noon–3.30pm • $4

The only sight of note on Kawau Island is the grand, kauri-panelled **Mansion House**, the former private home of George Grey – then doing his second stint as New Zealand's governor – and furnished much as it would have been in the late 1880s, including with Grey's writing desk.

Grey's pursuit of the Victorian fashion for all things exotic resulted in **grounds** stocked with flora and fauna from all over the world, such as Chilean wine palms and coral trees. He also brought in four species of **wallaby**, which have overtaken the island and have to be regularly culled. You might even see Australian kookaburras and a white peacock.

A path runs through the gardens to the tiny beach at **Lady's Bay** and on to a network of short tracks that weave through pine forest and kanuka scrub. The most popular destination is the ruins of the island's old **copper mine** (40min each way). The on-site café (see p.149) provides sustenance.

Matakana and around

Over the last decade or so, **MATAKANA**, 9km northeast of Warkworth, has transformed itself from an inconsequential crossroads to the heart of an aspiring **wine** region, and minor Slow Food centre. It is close enough to Auckland to attract weekenders who arrive for the farmers' market (Sat 8am–1pm) and stick around to visit the local boutique cinema (2 Matakana Valley Rd; ☎09 422 9833, ⊚matakanacinemas.co.nz), browse the shops – which include a heritage butchers, a quality bookshop and an excellent deli (see p.150) – and stop in at the wineries (see p.150).

Morris & James Pottery & Tileworks

2km west of Matakana at Tongue Farm Rd • Daily 9am–5pm; café/bar 9am–4pm; free tour daily 11.30am • Free

The catalyst for the region's development was the **Morris & James Pottery & Tileworks**, which has been producing vibrant, handmade terracotta tiles and bright, large garden pots from local clay since the late 1970s. You can catch a free thirty-minute tour of the pottery and visit the café/bar.

Tawharanui Regional Park

10km southeast of Matakana, along Takatu Rd • Gates open daily 6am–dusk • Free

Tawharanui Regional Park has great beaches and swathes of regenerating bush, and makes for a pleasant spot to visit before leaving the Matakana area. Predators have been eradicated and native birds are returning to this designated **open sanctuary**: come to swim, snorkel, picnic and walk or bike the easy trails, but you'll have to bring everything with you. You can camp here ($10; book ahead on ☏09 366 2000, ☻arc.govt.nz/parks).

Leigh and Goat Island

The village of **LEIGH**, 13km northeast of Matakana, holds a picturesque harbour with bobbing wooden fishing boats. Heading a further 4km northeast brings you to the **Cape Rodney–Okakari Marine Reserve**, usually known simply as **Goat Island** for the bush-clad islet 300m offshore. In 1975, this became New Zealand's first marine reserve, with no-take areas stretching 5km along the shoreline and 800m off the coast. Some 35 years on, the undersea life is thriving, with large rock lobster, huge snapper and rays. Feeding has been discouraged since blue maomaos developed a taste for frozen peas and began to mob swimmers and divers. Easy beach access (from the road-end parking area), clear water, rock pools on wave-cut platforms, a variety of undersea terrains and relatively benign currents combine to make this an enormously popular year-round diving spot, as well as a favourite summer destination for families: aim to come midweek if you value tranquillity.

GOAT ISLAND TOURS AND ACTIVITIES

The waters surrounding Goat Island have good visibility, making them perfect for snorkellers and scuba divers who can enjoy a lush world populated by kelp forest and numerous multi-coloured fish, while deeper still are more exposed seascapes with an abundance of sponges. Because of the clarity of the water this is also an excellent spot for the less adventurous who want to observe from glass-bottomed boats or kayaks.

Glass Bottom Boat ☏09 422 6334, ☻glass bottomboat.co.nz. Tours on the *Aquador* depart from the beach (3 trips daily in winter, more in the summer; $25), last about 45min and are best in fine, calm weather. Phone ahead to check conditions and make bookings.

Goat Island Dive 142a Pakiri Rd, Leigh ☏0800 348 369, ☻goatislanddive.co.nz. A highly professional outfit that rents mask, snorkel and fins ($30), plus offers a 2hr snorkel dive course ($55). They also run scuba courses and trips either to Goat Island Marine Reserve or beyond and will rent scuba gear if you want to go independently, assuming you have the relevant qualification. Open daily in summer, and on weekends in winter.

Kayak Experience Goat Island On the beach, opposite the island ☏021 460 121, ☻goatisland @xtra.co.nz. Rents glass-bottomed ($40/hr) and traditional kayaks (double; $30/hr), mask, snorkel, fins and wetsuit ($30), and offers an all-day kayak-snorkel combination ($150), during which you're encouraged to try to spot a massive hair-lipped snapper called Charlie Lip.

Seafriends 25m along Goat Island Road, at the beach ☏09 422 6212, ☻seafriends.org.nz. Rents snorkelling gear (mask, snorkel, fins and wetsuit; $30) in summer only. They also have a marine education centre with an array of aquarium tanks re-creating different Goat Island ecosystems, plus a small café. Daily 9am–7pm.

Pakiri

There's not much to **PAKIRI**, 10km north of Leigh, except for a beautiful long deserted white surf beach, backed by farmland, dunes and stands of mature pohutukawa trees that bloom with vibrant red flowers in December (hence their nickname: Christmas trees). This is a perfect setting for leisurely beachcombing, birdwatching, sunset gazing and **horseriding** (see p.148).

Te Hana

Spread out along either side of SH1 is the small roadside settlement of **TE HANA**, 4km north of Wellsford. It's your next chance to turn off towards the coast and a settlement that until recently most people have passed through without pause. This does Te Hana an injustice, as it is home to one of New Zealand's most adventurous and spectacular wood carvers.

The Arts Factory

Behind the Te Hana Café · Summer daily 9am–5pm; winter Mon–Fri 9am–5pm, Sat & Sun by appointment · ☎ 09 423 8069, ⓦ artprimitiveandmodern.com

Te Hana is home to the ★ **The Arts Factory**, where unique and iconic artist Kerry Strongman and his team carve breathtaking "jewellery for giants" – massive pieces of swamp kauri that are thousands of years old. The pieces are innovatively and experimentally carved (sometimes as interpretations of traditional Maori and/or other ancient peoples' designs) and all are supersized to fill and enhance large spaces. Most of the pieces go to galleries and commissioners in New Zealand and abroad, but other, smaller pieces are on sale in the gallery shop. Best of all, you get to wander round the expansive studio, inside and out, and watch the works being created.

Te Hana Cultural Experience

317 SH1 · Guided tour daily on the hour 10am–3pm; multicultural package daily 11.30am (booking essential); starlight tour daily 7.30pm (booking essential) · Guided tour $25; multicultural package $65; starlight tour $100 · ☎ 09 423 8701, ⓦ tehana.co.nz

On the opposite side of SH1 is the newly constructed *pa* and Maori village, all part of the ★ Te Hana cultural experience. The originally flat site needed 250 lorry-loads of mud to create a hill for the *pa*, and the money and effort that went into building this authentic and thoughtful Maori experience is clear to see. Currently, they offer a 45-minute guided tour; a multicultural package that includes a tour, concert and light lunch; and a starlight tour that includes a traditional performance and *hangi*-style dinner. As they progress, more tours and options will be added.

Mangawhai

Tiny **Mangawhai**, 20km northeast of Te Hana, is a commercial farm supply settlement that has transmogrified into a weekend village for holidaying Aucklanders. It has a few restaurants, retail outlets such as the Smashed Pipi gallery, 40 Moir St (daily 9am–5.30pm), which is crammed with colourful glass, jewellery, woven flax and ceramics, a chic farmers' market at the weekends and access to the infinitely more scenic Mangawhai Heads.

Mangawhai Heads

On the coast 3km north of Mangawhai sits **Mangawhai Heads**, at the mouth of the Mangawhai Harbour, marked by holiday homes straggling over the hillsides behind a fine surf beach. Long a Kiwi summer-holiday favourite, Mangawhai Heads is relaxed outside the peak summer blitz and is chiefly of interest for the extraordinary views on the scenic **Mangawhai Cliffs Walkway** (2–3hr; year-round). Walk north along the beach for fifteen minutes then follow the orange markers up through bush-backed farmland along the top of the sea cliffs until the path winds back down to the beach. Provided the tide is below half, you can return along the beach through a small rock arch.

Mangawhai Museum

Molesworth Drive • $10 • ☎ 09 431 4663, ⓦ mangawhai-museum.org.nz

At the time of writing, the new **Mangawhai Museum** was still under construction, although was expected to be open by December 2012. It will contain exhibitions that chart human habitation of the area from Maori settlement to the present day and, if the interior is as impressive as the exterior's stingray-shaped design (the area was once famous for large rays), then it will be well worth paying a visit. The building is on the left as you approach Mangawhai Heads, before you reach the roadside information centre.

Lang's Beach and Waipu Cove

Surfing and swimming are both reliable and can be spectacular at **Lang's Beach**, 12km north of Mangawhai heads, and **WAIPU COVE**, a further 4km north. However, apart from a cluster of houses, a dairy/takeaway and a few places to stay (see p.149) beside a sweeping stretch of Bream Bay, there is little else to detain you.

Waipu and around

An Aberdeen granite monument topped by a Scottish lion rampant dominates the quirky village of **WAIPU**, 11km north of Lang's Beach. It's a nod to the nine hundred Scottish settlers who followed charismatic preacher, the Reverend Norman McLeod, here in the mid-1800s. On New Year's Day, Waipu hosts its **Highland Games** (ⓦhighlandgames.co.nz), in which competitors heft large stones and toss cabers and sheaves in Caledonian Park.

Waipu Museum

36 The Centre • Tues–Sat 9.30am–4.30pm, Sun & Mon 10am–4pm • $8 • ☎ 09 432 0746, ⓦ waipumuseum.com

The excellent **Waipu Museum** tells the tale of Scottish settlers and their journey via Nova Scotia where famine and a series of harsh winters drove them on to form a strict, self-contained Calvinist community. All is admirably illustrated, with everything from McLeod's old pocket watch to genealogical records that are regularly consulted by Kiwi Scots tracing their ancestry. Also worth a look are the various Caledonian-themed rotating exhibitions.

Waipu Caves

Just past the Waipu Caves Estate gate, about 16km away from town (signposted) via Shoemaker and Waipu Caves roads

Waipu Caves is a popular local excursion, and in among its many limestone formations is one of the longest stalagmites in New Zealand, in a 200m glowworm-filled passage. Obtain a free map from the visitor centre in the Waipu Museum, wear old clothes and good footwear, and take a couple of reliable torches. The cave is impenetrable after heavy rain; even when it's dry you'll get muddy, so use the cold shower, located on the wall away from the road, of the public toilets on the site.

ARRIVAL AND DEPARTURE	MATAKANA COAST TO BREAM BAY

WARKWORTH

By bus Intercity, Northliner, Main Coachlines and NakedBus buses stop outside the i-SITE on Baxter St.
Destinations Auckland (4–6 daily; 1hr); Dargaville (4–6 daily; 2hr); Whangarei (4–6 daily; 1hr 45min).

KAWAU ISLAND

By boat All boats to Kawau Island leave from the wharf (parking $10/24hr) at Sandspit, a small road-end community on the Matakana Estuary, 8km east of Warkworth. Reubens (☎ 0800 111 616, ⓦ kawaucruises .co.nz) run one or two trips direct to Mansion House Bay daily ($50), which allow for roughly twice the time ashore as the Royal Mail Run tour (see below), which also takes you to the island.

LEIGH AND GOAT ISLAND
By taxi Without your own vehicle, the only way to get to Leigh is via taxi from Matakana. Matakabs (☎ 0800 522 743) cost around $38 one-way.

INFORMATION AND TOURS

WARKWORTH
i-SITE 1 Baxter St (Nov–Easter Mon–Fri 8.30am–5pm, Sat & Sun 9am–4pm; Easter–Oct Mon–Fri 8am–5pm, Sat & Sun 9am–3pm; ☎ 09 425 9081, ⓦ warkworthnz.com). The office can help with travel bookings and has free internet access.

KAWAU ISLAND
Royal Mail Run ☎ 0800 111 616, ⓦ kawaucruises .co.nz. Reubens (see p.147) operates the mail run service (daily 10.30am; 4hr; $68 return; $90 with BBQ lunch), delivering mail, papers and groceries to all the wharves on the island and giving you around an hour and a half ashore at Mansion House Bay – plenty of time to enjoy the native bush and beach, take a swim or have a look around the house before meeting the boat for the return. Lunch is served on board on the outward leg of the trip.

WAIPU
By bus InterCity/Northliner and NakedBus drop off and pick up on request outside the Pear Tree gift shop (☎ 09 432 0046), 13 The Centre, which also acts as a ticket agent.
Destinations Auckland (4–7 daily; 2hr 20min); Whangarei (4–6 daily; 30min).

Blue Adventures Sandspit Wharf ☎ 022 630 5705, ⓦ blueadventures.co.nz. Offers jetboat tours ($75/person/ hr; minimum four people), plus rentals and lessons for stand-up paddleboarding ($45/person/hr), wakeboarding ($60/person/hr; minimum four people) and kitesurfing (2hr private lesson $75).

MATAKANA
Winery information The widely available *Matakana Wine Trail* leaflet details eighteen wineries and wine-related sites that offer tastings, mostly for a small charge.

WAIPU
Visitor information 36 The Centre (daily 9.30am–4.30pm; ☎ 09 432 0746). Located in the museum, and run by volunteers. Internet access is available for a small charge.

ACCOMMODATION

WARKWORTH
Cedarhouse 450 Matakana Rd, 3km northeast of Warkworth ☎ 09 425 0952, ⓦ cedarhouse-bb.co.nz. A spacious and airy studio loft overlooking the vines with access to seven acres of native bush, the Ascension and Matakana Estate wineries and a restaurant, as well as offering a conti-nental breakfast to get you started in the morning. $140
★ **Sandspit Holiday Park** 1334 Sandspit Rd ☎ 09 425 8610, ⓦ sandspitholidaypark.co.nz. Set among mature trees and situated next to the ferry landing for Kawau Island, the camp offers free use of canoes and paddle boats, safe swimming, proximity to surf beaches and an internet kiosk. Camping $16, cabins $60
Warkworth Country House 18 Wilson Rd, 300m north of Warkworth and Districts Museum (see p.144) ☎ 09 422 2485, ⓦ warkworthcountryhouse.co.nz. Two cosy en suites with their own private patio entrances that overlook an acre of well-tended garden, with a further acre of native bush full of birds nearby – all run efficiently by a friendly ex-school teacher. $120

LEIGH AND GOAT ISLAND
The *Leigh Sawmill Café* (see p.150) is largely known for its food, drink and entertainment, but also has rooms.
Goat Island Camping & Backpackers 123 Goat Island Rd ☎ 09 422 6185, ⓦ goatislandcamping.co.nz.

A welcoming site about 500m back from the reserve on the way to Goat Island, with four simple cabins and nine basic caravans nestled among the trees. The bay views are great, plus there's snorkel gear rental. Cash only. Camping $18, cabins $60, on-site caravans $60

PAKIRI
Pakiri Beach Holiday Park Pakiri River Rd ☎ 09 422 6199, ⓦ pakiriholidaypark.co.nz. Well sited by a river estuary and overlooking the golden sands of the beach, this flatland campsite offers camping pitches, simple cabins, en-suite cabins and more luxurious studios and beachfront cottages, as well as a luxury beachfront lodge sleeping four ($30/extra adult). Camping $16, cabins $50, en-suite cabins $70, studios $160, cottages $250, lodge $350
Pakiri Beach Horse Rides Rahuikiri Rd ☎ 09 422 6275, ⓦ horseride-nz.co.nz. Has a range of wonderfully atmospheric accommodation: riverside backpacker rooms; self-contained, beachside *baches* for two with a bed, stove and loo; a family cabin for seven; and a luxurious four-bedroom beach house sleeping up to eight. The café, at the stables, is a one-room supply store and eatery serving basic food at basic prices from around 9am until 5pm. The horse-riding part of the operation runs year-round and offers some stunning trips. Rides ($65/hr; $120/2hr, $165/half day, $290/full day) go along the beach, among

the dunes, across streams and through a pohutukawa glade. Cabins $70, beachside cabins $150, family cabin per couple $155, beach house per day $500

MANGAWHAI

Coastal Cow Backpackers 299 Molesworth Drive ☎09 431 5246. Hostel accommodation in a pleasant, modern house with all the usual facilities, run by a helpful and informative host. Choose from either dorms or rooms, and be sure to make use of the deck and BBQ area. Dorms $25, rooms $65

★ **Milestone Cottages by the Sea** 27 Moir Point Rd ☎09 431 4018, ⓦmilestonecottages.co.nz. This cluster of six lovingly constructed timber and mud-brick cottages is divided into studio and family units, all luxurious but still extremely good value. Two of the cottages overlook the sea, while the other four sit amid sumptuous organic gardens and coastal bush. A short walk down a private track leads to a secluded estuary beach where kayaks are available (free) to transport you along the river or over to the bird reserve on a sand dune, for a glimpse of dotterels and fairy terns. All units are self-catering and include a BBQ deck, plus there's a saltwater lap pool for guests' use. Studio $125, cottages $230

LANG'S BEACH AND WAIPU COVE

Camp Waipu 869 Cove Rd, Waipu Cove ☎09 432 0410, ⓦcampwaipucove.com. Beachside accommodation is extensive at the southern end of Bream Bay north of Lang's Beach, but packed in January. Most cabins are pretty basic but there are a few high-end self-contained units. Camp facilities are clean and there's access to the beach on foot. Camping $34, cabins $60, self-contained units $120

★ **Stone House** ☎09 432 0432, ⓦstonehousewaipu .co.nz. Halfway between Lang's Beach and Waipu, this is the pick of the options hereabouts. It's a quiet, restful and delightful spot with solicitous hosts and a variety of accommodation, including a cabin with bunks, a self-contained cabin and cottage, plus spare rooms in the house. The grounds extend to the estuary, which you can explore – including by paddling over to the bird reserve – with the free dinghies and kayaks. There's also free wi-fi, and great breakfasts for $10–15, including a full Swiss (muesli, juice, meat, cheese, eggs and bread). Cabin $80, self-contained cabin $120, self-contained cottage $160, house rooms $120

★ **Waipu Cove Cottages and Camping** 685 Cove Rd, Waipu Cove ☎09 432 0851, ⓦwaipucovecottages .co.nz. Adjacent to *Camp Waipu*, this is a smaller establishment with a more exclusive feel and modern cottages. The grounds contain well-spaced camping sites, plus there's free use of dinghies. Camping $36, rooms $50, cottages $115

WAIPU

Uretiti Beach campsite 6km north of Waipu, signposted on SH1. The wonderful long white beach at Uretiti is backed by a basic DOC camping area with running water, toilets, cold showers and an adjacent (and unofficial) naturist beach. $8

Waipu Wanderers 25 St Mary's Rd ☎09 432 0532, ⓔwaipu.wanderers@xtra.co.nz. Offers cosy, homey, welcoming budget accommodation in a separate house with its own kitchen and bathroom, as well as one double, a twin and a three-share. About a 2min walk from the town centre. Dorms $29, room $66

EATING AND DRINKING

WARKWORTH

You can eat well enough in town – there are New World and Four Square supermarkets in town for those wanting to stock up – or at a price in the surrounding vineyards, such as Ascension and Ransoms; check the *Matakana Wine Trail* leaflet (see opposite).

Ginger 21 Queen St ☎09 422 2298. Has good coffee and bakes their own bagels and bread (which they stuff with lots of goodies), as well as offering an impressive breakfast menu and veggie meals (mains around $20). Mon–Fri 6am–4pm, Sat & Sun 7.30am–4pm.

★ **Quince** Corner of Matakana and Falls rds in the centre of town ☎09 442 2555. A local favourite, serving up dishes such as lamb shanks with pea and lentil gravy and mint jelly pistachio mash (mains around $26). It's licensed, but you can also bring your own booze. Wed–Sun 9am–late.

Tahi 1 Neville St ⓦtahibar.com. Located in an alley opposite the i-SITE, this tapas bar stocks a good range of

boutique beers and dishes up a number of booze-soaking platters as well as some decent fish and chips ($10–20). Tues–Thurs 3.30pm–late, Fri & Sat noon–midnight, Sun 11am–9pm.

WINERIES

Ransom Wines 46 Valerie Close, 1.5km off SH1, south of Warkworth ☎09 425 8862, ⓦransomwines.co.nz. At both the cellar door and wine bar, elegance of taste and high-quality products, as well as tasty lunches, are on offer during the summer. Tues–Sun 10am–5pm.

KAWAU ISLAND

Mansion House Bay Café ☎09 422 8903. Licensed café open for lunches as well as snacks and light meals ($10–30), including the likes of all-day breakfast, seared beef on noodles, or seared salmon. Most people visit as part of one of the guided trips so lunch is your most likely option, but a water taxi from Reubens (see p.147) will get you there

2

and back for dinner. Open weekends and most days in summer; call ahead for exact hours.

The Sandspit The wharf at Sandspit, 8km east of Warkworth. A pleasant, licensed café in a wooden shed offering passable nosh, specializing in seafood, such as chowder ($13), fish and chips ($17) and burgers ($14.50), and serving up post-cruise liquid restoratives. Mon–Thurs 9am–4pm, Fri–Sun 9am–late.

MATAKANA

Black Dog Café Corner of Torea and Market Valley rds. A local favourite for coffee, chocolate cake, breakfasts, big juicy burgers ($12.50) with beetroot, and bagels with a variety of good-quality fillings. Mon–Fri 7.30am–3.30pm, Sat 7am–4pm, Sun 8am–4pm.

★ **Blue** 2 Matakana Valley Rd ☎ 09 422 7797, ⊚ blue .co.nz. Traditional parlour serving organic ice creams ($6), sorbets and great smoothies ($7), using blueberry flavours from their renowned orchard. If you're after something more substantial they also have good sandwiches and coffee. Daily 10am–6pm.

Matakana Market Kitchen 2 Matakana Valley Rd ☎ 09 423 0383, ⊚ matakanamarketkitchen.com. Expect classy and expensive dining at this designer restaurant with schist walls, wooden furniture and a big shiny bar. Savoury dishes include avocado on toast ($10.50), brunch with free-range eggs ($19.50), salads ($18) and assorted dinner mains ($34). Daily 9am–late.

★ **Nosh** 2 Matakana Valley Rd ☎ 09 422 9534. Great nosh for less dosh in the form of a substantial deli that has something to tempt everyone, including local meats and cheeses and some stunning imports from Italy and France. Mon–Fri 9am–7pm, Sat & Sun 7.30am–7pm.

Plume 49a Sharp Rd ☎ 09 422 7915, ⊚ plume restaurant.co.nz. A stylish, expensive vineyard restaurant with an open kitchen, serving bagels and lox ($20), crispy rabbit with mandarin pancakes, Asian slaw, roasted peanuts and hoisin sauce ($26) and dinners of ribeye steak ($38) or lamb loin with soft herb crust, yoghurt and harissa sauce ($39). Tues–Sun 11am–3.30pm, Fri & Sat 6pm–late.

WINERIES

Heron's Flight 49 Sharp Rd ☎ 09 950 6643, ⊚ herons flight.co.nz. Italian Sangiovese and Dolcetto have been planted at this Tuscan-influenced vineyard and olive grove with considerable success. It's a slick operation, but tastings are by appointment only.

Hyperion 188 Tongue Farm Rd, off Leigh Rd ☎ 09 422 9375, ⊚ hyperion-wines.co.nz. Compared with Heron's Flight, this is more in the Kiwi tradition of a passionate personal quest, with the only decent Cabernet Sauvignon north of Auckland, as well as other delicious wines, all

sampled in a small shed surrounded by moss-covered trees and fences. Tastings are free, but call before arriving.

LEIGH AND GOAT ISLAND

Leigh Fish and Chip Shop 18 Cumberland St ☎ 09 422 6035. Legendary, locally, for tasty fish and chips, mussel fritters and gourmet burgers, this is a traditional takeaway serving fresh fish, mostly cooked to order with nothing on the menu over $15. April–Dec Thurs–Sun 11am–7pm, until 8pm Fri & Sat; Dec–Easter weekend daily 11am–8pm, until 9pm Fri & Sat.

★ **The Leigh Sawmill Café** 142 Pakiri Rd ☎ 09 422 6019, ⊚ sawmillcafe.co.nz. Largely known for food and entertainment, this sensitively converted former sawmill also has five spacious en-suite doubles, a self-contained cottage, two dorms and a communal kitchen. The smart café/bar has an abundance of historic milling paraphernalia (closed Mon–Wed in winter) and is the premier gig venue in these parts. Food is mostly clever tapas ($9–28) or gourmet pizzas ($22.50) – you'll need to book in the summer for weekend lunches – and there is a good wine list, plus tasty beers from the excellent micro-brewery next door, which does takeaway sales. Live music is usually at weekends in the massive-beamed area in front of the bar. En-suite doubles $125, self-contained cottage $300, dorms without bedding $25, dorms with bedding $40

MANGAWHAI AND MANGAWHAI HEADS

Bennetts Café 52 Moir St, Mangawhai ☎ 09 431 5500. Specializes in imaginative, if expensive, breakfasts and lunches ($15–20) using quality ingredients in a pseudo-Tuscan setting – but it's best visited for the very passable hot chocolate and the wonderful chocolatier just across the courtyard. Daily 9am–5pm.

★ **Frog and Kiwi** The Hub, 6 Molesworth Drive, Mangawhai ☎ 09 431 4439. As the name suggests, the food here is of the Franco-New Zealand fusion variety. Particular treats include a bowl of coffee, snails and sauté de lapin (rabbit with Dijon mustard, gherkins and olives), and a six-course dégustation tasting menu with drinks ($116). Most dishes cost $10–31. Licensed. Daily 9am–2.30pm & 6pm–late.

Harvest Café 5 Molesworth Drive, Mangawhai Heads. Lively, ultra-friendly little café, much loved by locals, serving home-made pies and cakes before switching to a tapas evening menu ($8–13). Daily 8am–5pm and on Thurs–Sat reopens 6pm–late.

Mangawhai Tavern 2 Moir St, Mangawhai ☎ 09 431 4505. This traditional Kiwi pub serving traditional Kiwi grub would have little to recommend it except a beautiful location were it not a world-famous (in Northland, at least) venue for live music. Every weekend, summer and winter, Kiwi favourites and touring international acts strut their stuff in front of up to 1,200 whooping drinkers. Daily 11am–late.

★ **Sail Rock Café** 12a Wood St, Mangawhai Heads ☎ 09 431 4051, ⊛ sailrockcafe.co.nz. This fabulous bistro-bar-restaurant serves fresh seafood, Angus steaks, salt and pepper squid and carrot cake that would make a saint kick a hole in a stained-glass window (mains $21.50–39). Check out the live music on Saturdays, including solo piano and guitar workshops, and say hi to the landlady, one of the friendliest this side of the dateline. Licensed. Daily 8.30am–11pm or later.

LANG'S BEACH AND WAIPU COVE
Beach House 891 Cove Rd, behind the Waipu Cove Resort, Lang's Beach ☎ 09 432 0877. Menus (mains around $30) are printed on paper bags and the succulent,

"retro" fish and chips ($26) come elegantly wrapped in newspaper and are the order of the day. The restaurant opens onto a deck in warm weather. There's an upstairs sports bar, too. Daily 5.30pm–late; closed Mon & Tues in winter.

WAIPU
Pizza Barn 2 Cove Rd ☎ 09 432 1011. The tastiest fare is traditional pub food or pizza in Waipu's former post office. Well-priced lunches and dinners (mains $15–25) vie with pizzas sporting elaborate toppings. You can either eat in the cosy corrugated iron, timber and McLeod tartan bar, or the garden room, which is filled with surfboards and a massive stuffed fish. Take a minute to peek at the toilets, a veritable art installation of 1950s kitsch. Dec–March daily 11.30am–late; April–Nov Wed–Sun same hours; closed in June.

Whangarei

Despite its prime gateway location to Whangarei Heads' sweeping beaches and world-class diving around the Poor Knights Islands, Northland's capital, **WHANGAREI** (pronounced Fahn-ga-ray), has never had the wherewithal to slow down tourists on their mad dash to the Bay of Islands. But things are changing. The newly developed Town Basin, a shopping and restaurant complex, provides a focal point for visitors and overlooks sleek yachts dotted along the river. Now home to an art museum in the new i-SITE visitor centre, which itself is a welcome extension of the i-SITE on the way into town (see p.155), the complex is to be enhanced further, over the next two years, by the addition of a Hundertwasser Arts Centre, based on designs Hundertwasser (see p.160) offered the local council before his untimely demise. Married with the area's rewarding arts trail, the scenic track to Whangarei Falls and a handful of new tours and activities, Whangarei should finally be able to persuade tourists to stick around, for a day or so at least.

Whangarei's most appealing features currently are its state-of-the-art Kiwi House, the peaceful parks, and the easy walks within a few minutes of the town, the best of which are outlined in the free *Whangarei Walks* leaflet.

The Town Basin

Centred on an 1880s villa that's now a restaurant, the redeveloped **Town Basin**, a primarily pedestrian area between Lower Dent Street and the Hatea River, is an attractive, sometimes bustling hub of retail outlets and restaurants beside an arts trail along the riverside. Check out the **Burning Issues Gallery** (daily 10am–5pm; free), a glass and ceramics studio where you can watch glass-blowing, or **Clapham's Clocks** (daily 9am–5pm; $8, tours free), a museum of some 1300 clocks ranging from mechanisms taken out of church towers to cuckoo clocks. On the regular guided tours you'll learn why the mouse ran up the clock in *Hickory, Dickory Dock* and see clock mechanisms put through their paces.

Whangarei Art Museum
The Hub, adjacent to the new i-Site, Dent St • Daily 10am–4pm • Donation • ☎ 09 430 4240, ⊛ whangareiartmuseum.co.nz
The art museum's new galleries host travelling exhibitions and a small percentage of the museum's own excellent collection. Worth seeking out are paintings by E. Kate Mair,

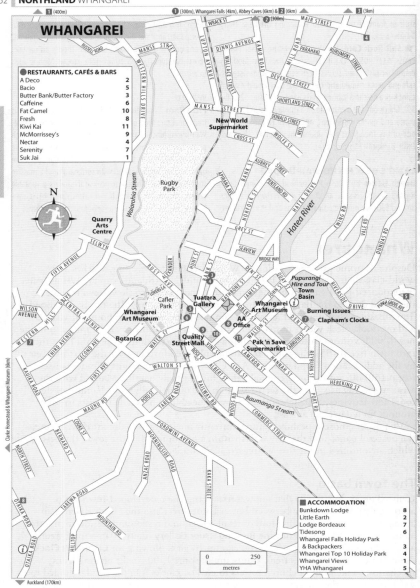

① (300m), Whangarei Falls (4km), Abbey Caves (6km) & ② (6km)

WHANGAREI

● RESTAURANTS, CAFÉS & BARS

A Deco	2
Bacio	5
Butter Bank/Butter Factory	3
Caffeine	6
Fat Camel	10
Fresh	8
Kiwi Kai	11
McMorrissey's	9
Nectar	4
Serenity	7
Suk Jai	1

■ ACCOMMODATION

Bunkdown Lodge	8
Little Earth	2
Lodge Bordeaux	7
Tidesong	6
Whangarei Falls Holiday Park & Backpackers	3
Whangarei Top 10 Holiday Park	4
Whangarei Views	1
YHA Whangarei	5

Auckland (170km)

one of the first Pakeha artists to paint Maori sympathetically despite being married to Captain Gilbert Mair, who spent a part of his career fighting them; sadly, of the two works held, neither is a Maori portrait. Also worth a look is the more familiar portrait of Harataori Harota Tarapata, painted by Goldie (see p.79) and presented to the gallery by former prime minister Helen Clarke, and a couple of Lindauer's (see p.79) skilfully executed portraits.

Botanica

Entrance from First Ave or Cafler Park • Daily 10am–4pm • Free

Should a rainy day threaten your equilibrium, cross the footbridge over the stream that runs through Cafler Park to the cool, restful **Botanica**, where the purpose-built Filmy Fernhouse contains the country's largest public collection of native ferns – there are over 80 different types. If you don't mind ratcheting up the temperature a notch or two, check out the garish glories of the Snow Conservatory, a sweaty subtropical oasis for orchids, cyclamen and begonias.

2

Kiwi North

SH14, 6km southwest of Whangarei • **Kiwi North** Daily 10am–4pm; steam locomotive rides third Sunday of every month, plus school and bank holidays • $15 combined ticket for kiwi house and museum; steam locomotive $2.50 **Whangarei Native Bird Recovery Centre** • Mon 1.30–4.30pm, Tues–Fri 10.30am–4.30pm • Donation • ☎ 09 438 9630, ⓦ kiwinorth.co.nz

Kiwi North consists of a fabulous new kiwi house, which sits at the centre of the rejuvenated **Whangarei Museum** and **Heritage Park compound**, beside the **Whangarei Native Bird Recovery Centre**, all in the same walled area, although the recovery centre is an independent entity.

Undoubted pride of place – and alone worthy of the entry fee – goes to the specially designed and spacious kiwi enclosure, where you'll be transfixed by the glorious, long-beaked curmudgeons and a couple of morepork, as well as several Duvaucel's gecko, some skink and a couple of tuatara.

A few paces up the hill, the museum has an intriguing selection of objects including a 200-year-old waka, a fine assortment of Maori cloaks, Hone Heke's (see p.169) musket, some revealing information on Ruapekapeka Pa – including some of the cannon balls from the battle (see p.160) – and photographic collections that include images of Maori and early settlers.

Surrounding these two attractions is the **Heritage Park**, the centrepiece of which is the **Clarke Homestead**, a rare example of an original un-restored homestead, built in 1886 for Scottish doctor Alexander Clarke. Also of note are the restored **steam locomotives** running through the compound.

A must-see for all twitchers is the **Native Bird Recovery Centre**, which attempts to rehabilitate injured birds. This collection of walking and hopping wounded is a mixture of temporary and permanent residents, among which you are almost certain to find a talking tui.

Mount Parihaka

1.5km northeast of the town centre

Extensive views over the harbour and town are the reward for climbing to the sheet-metal war memorial atop **Mount Parihaka**, which can be approached by car along Memorial Drive and then by clambering up the steps or by negotiating the steep Ross Track (40min ascent). Pick up the track from the end of Dundas Road, head through Mair Park past its selection of native and imported trees, the views improving as you climb, and ascend to the memorial, an ugly metallic obelisk to World War I and World War II – more rewarding are the *pa* remnants and interpretive boards.

Whangarei Falls

5km northeast of the town centre

A broad curtain of water cascades over a 26m-high basalt ridge into a popular swimming hole at **Whangarei Falls**. The nicest way to get here is to walk along a bushland trail, which winds up at a bridge overlooking the falls after following the

Hatea River (90min one-way) from the Parihaka Scenic Reserve on the opposite shore from the Town Basin; the i-SITE has a route map.

A.H. Reed Memorial Kauri Park

Northeast of the town centre, 1.5km down Whareora Rd

The **A.H. Reed Memorial Kauri Park** holds shady paths that weave through native bush, passing 500-year-old kauri trees; look out for the ten-minute Alexander Walk, which links with a short, sinuous **canopy boardwalk** high across a creek before reaching some fine kauri. From the lower car park, it's possible to take the Elizabeth track and link up with the trail along the Hatea River to Whangarei Falls (30min one-way).

Abbey Caves

6km east of the town centre on Abbey Caves Rd, accessed via Whareora Rd

The fluted and weather-worn limestone formations of **Abbey Caves** have stalactites and stalagmites in abundance, as well as glowworms. Armed with a torch plus a moderate level of fitness you can explore them at leisure. A little scrambling is required to get into the first, Organ Cave, where you can walk a couple of hundred metres along an underground stream, although it's best avoided after heavy rain. Middle Cave and Ivy Cave are badly signposted but, once found, are worth exploring.

ARRIVAL AND DEPARTURE   WHANGAREI

By bus InterCity/Northliner and NakedBus pull up on Bank St.
Destinations Auckland (4–7 daily; 3hr); Paihia (4–6 daily; 1hr 15min); Warkworth (4–6 daily; 1hr 45min).
By plane Several daily flights from Auckland arrive at Onerahi Airport, 5km east of town. Get into town on the #2 bus or with Kiwi Cabs (☎09 438 4444; around $25).
Destinations Auckland (7–9 daily; 35min); Great Barrier Island (1–2 weekly; 30min); Wellington (1 Mon–Fri; 1hr 30min).

GETTING AROUND

By bus Bank St is the hub of the skeletal local town bus service that runs frequently on weekdays, slightly less so on Saturday, and not at all on Sunday.

WHANGAREI TOURS AND ACTIVITIES

In and around Whangarei there are a number of tours taking in the various parks, riverside walks and areas of interest, including Whangarei Heads and the Abbey Caves. Most sights can be managed as well and more cheaply independently, but the two tour companies listed here will introduce you to experiences and places that you would be unlikely find for yourself.

Ballistic Blondes ☎0800 695 867, ⓦskydive ballisticblondes.co.nz. Great panoramic views of Whangarei Heads, via a tandem skydive (from $245) with this Paihia-based outfit – the only skydiving business to currently offer beach landing at Paihia. They'll pick you up from accommodation around Whangarei.

Pupurangi Hire and Tour Jetty One, opposite side of the sail bridge from Town Basin ☎09 438 8117, ⓦhirentour.co.nz. Runs more formal and better-informed tours than Tiki Escape but minimum numbers apply, so call to make a booking. All the trips are steeped in Maori history, nature and stories, including a basic walking *pa* tour (75min; $55) and a flora and fauna tour (45min; $35). They also offer river trips in an outrigger canoe with the same level of cultural input ($35; maximum five people). You can also rent paddlebikes and kayaks (double kayaks $22/hr; paddlebikes $12/30min).

Tiki Escape Tours Town Basin ☎09 437 2955. If you have no transport, no desire to walk and want to see the memorial atop Mount Parihaka (see p.153) and Whangarei Falls, join one of these informal mini-bus meanders about the town (half-day; $35; pre-book). Trips include a semi-traditional *hangi* meal from Kiwi Kai (see p.156), which you consume in the atmospheric *Tikipunga Tavern*, a typical suburban Kiwi pub that is an experience in itself.

INFORMATION

i-SITE There are two i-SITE offices in Whangarei: 92 Otaika Rd, 2km south of town (Nov–Easter Mon–Fri 8.30am–5.30pm, Sat & Sun 9am–5pm; Easter–Oct Mon–Fri 8.30am–5pm, Sat & Sun 9am–4.30pm; ☎ 09 438 1079, ⓦ whangareinz.com); and the new satellite branch in The Hub, within the Town Basin complex (daily 9am–5pm; ☎ 09 430 1188). Both have internet access.

ACCOMMODATION

Bunkdown Lodge 23 Otaika Rd ☎ 09 438 8886, ⓦ bunkdownlodge.co.nz. Aging, low-key, small hostel with dorms and rooms in and around a pretty 1903 villa. There are two kitchens, a bath, piano, heaps of DVDs, and the owners go out of their way to help with local information. Linen rental for dorms $2. Dorms $26, rooms $62

★ **Little Earth Lodge** 85 Abbey Caves Rd ☎ 09 430 6562, ⓦ littleearthlodge.co.nz. Tucked into a pastoral valley 7km northeast of Whangarei beside Abbey Caves, this hostel has one three-bed share and four double/twins, a DVD lounge, wi-fi, gear to explore the caves, and free-range eggs – but be quick, as the latter get snapped up fast. Dorms $32, rooms $72

Lodge Bordeaux 361 Western Hills Drive ☎ 09 438 0404, ⓦ lodgebordeaux.co.nz. Elegant modern motel with a summer-only heated outdoor pool. All rooms come with a/c, heated tile floors, spa bath and DVD players, and some have dishwashers. Studios $195, suites $230

★ **Whangarei Falls Holiday Park & Backpackers** Ngunguru Rd at Tikipunga, 5km from town near Whangarei Falls ☎ 0800 227 222, ⓦ whangareifalls.co .nz. On the edge of the countryside with a pool, spa and wi-fi, these dated units provide good value for money. Camping $18, dorms $25, cabins $60

Whangarei Top 10 Holiday Park 24 Mair St ☎ 0800 455 488, ⓦ whangareitop10.co.nz. Small, tranquil and friendly site in a pretty setting 2km north of town with a range of accommodation. Camping $19, cabins $62, en-suite cabins & self-contained units $113, motel units $115

Whangarei Views 5 Kensington Heights Rise ☎ 09 437 6238, ⓦ whangareiviews.co.nz. Great views over the town from modern accommodation kept tidy by a well-travelled Swiss–British couple who share their passion for the area and offer guided tours. Choose from a comfortable en-suite room with deep bath or a self-contained two-bedroom apartment with a deck and BBQ. Breakfast can be served in your room. Apartment $169, room $120

★ **YHA Whangarei** 52 Punga Grove Ave ☎ 09 438 8954, ⓦ yha.co.nz. Intimate, sociable hostel, a steep 15min walk from the centre of Whangarei with expansive views over town from the BBQ and deck area and glowworms illuminating the bush just a short walk away (torches available). Accommodation is in rooms or four- and six-bed dorms, all in a glass-fronted lodge below the house. Reception is manned by friendly, helpful and knowledgeable staff, but is closed 1–5pm. Free wi-fi. Dorms $26, rooms $60

EATING AND DRINKING

Cafés, **bars** and **restaurants** are spread through the town and the Pak 'n Save supermarket is on the corner of Robert and Carruth sts. Also in town is a vibrant **Farmers Market** (6–10.30am) every Saturday, in Water St, opposite the Shell station.

★ **À Deco** 70 Kamo Rd ☎ 09 459 4957, ⓦ adeco.co.nz. Probably Northland's finest restaurant, set in an elegant Art Deco home 2km north of the centre. Exquisite evening meals full of complex flavours and textures include the like of grilled hapuku with seared king prawn tails and crisp shallots (mains $37–40; full *degustation* with wine $145). Fri lunch, Tues–Sat dinner.

Bacio 31 Bank St ☎ 09 430 0446. A relative newcomer, this lively bar/café is listed mainly for its end-of-the-week music and drinking and is popular with locals in the know. They do serve passable pizza; try the chicken or lamb toppings (around $22). Daily 11.30am–11pm, later at weekends.

Butter Bank/Butter Factory 84 Bank St ☎ 09 438 0010, ⓦ butterfactory.co.nz. Whangarei's liveliest bar/restaurant caters to a slightly older crowd and serves the likes of tapas and stone-baked pizza ($8–20). There are often DJs and live acts, as well as more relaxed jazz evenings. Under the *Butter Bank* is the *Butter Factory*, an intimate wine bar (open Wed–Sat) with exposed rock walls, heavy beams and leather sofas for the late-night crowd. Wed–Sat 4pm–late.

Caffeine 4 Water St. Relaxed café with wi-fi, tasty muffins and wraps, including the "vego" ($15.50), seasonal lunch mains such as spiced kumara and lamb salad (around $12–18) in hearty portions, plus good strong coffee. Mon–Fri 7am–2pm, Sat & Sun 7am–1.30pm.

Fat Camel 12 Quality St Mall ☎ 09 438 0831. Tel Aviv-style café with bargain falafel, *borekas*, dolmades, shawarma and *shishlik* (all $15–25), which is worth a visit just to find out what they are and to try the truly hideous Israeli coffee. Mon–Sat 9am–9pm, Sun 9am–4pm.

Fresh 12 James St. Airy, licensed, daytime café with a great range of panini, pasta, frittata and salads – roasted vegetable and quinoa, for example – with lunch specials from $15–20. Mon–Fri 8am–4pm, Sat 8am–2pm.

Kiwi Kai 68a Cameron St ☎09 430 2931. Cheap takeaway for all things Kiwi. Expect big portions of *hangi*, roast meat, Maori bread, burgers, fritters and seafood, all of it rib-sticking stuff (under $15). Mon–Fri 9am–6pm, Sat 8am–3pm.

McMorrissey's 7 Vine St ☎09 430 8081. Irish bar that's primarily for drinking but also serves simple and hearty meals such as fish and chips, bangers and mash or stew (all around $20) to soak up the beer. Live music at weekends. Daily 11am–11pm or later.

Nectar 88 Bank St ☎09 438 8084. Contemporary café/ restaurant with big windows overlooking the town's rooftops, serving up classy breakfasts ($15–19) and dishes such as tea-smoked chicken fettucini ($18) or mussels in a Thai green sauce ($18). Mon–Fri 7.30am–3.30pm, Sat 8am–3.30pm.

★ **Serenity** Shop 6, 45 Quay St, Town Basin ☎09 430 0841. Pick of the Town Basin cafés, this local favourite serves excellent and generous breakfasts ($9–25), including a monster steak breakfast that would stop an All Black forward, and dishes such as delicious mussel chowder with garlic bread ($12). Mon–Sat 7am–3pm, Sun 8am–3pm.

★ **Suk Jai** 93 Kamo Rd ☎09 437 7287. Authentic Thai restaurant where attention to detail and good service complement tasty Thai favourites such as fish cakes ($7), *gang massaman* (red curry; $15.50) and pad thai ($14.50). Mon–Sat 11am–2.30pm & 5–10pm.

SHOPPING

Tuatara 29 Bank St ☎09 430 0121, ⊛tuataradesign store.co.nz. Small design store and gallery near the centre of town focusing on works by emerging Maori artists. The inventive shop stocks Maori-designed goods from contemporary clothing to fine jewellery and greenstone carving. Mon–Fri 9.30am–5pm, Sat 9am–2.30pm, plus Dec & Jan Sun 10am–4pm.

Around Whangarei

It's worth hanging around Whangarei to explore the surrounding area, particularly to the east and north of the town where craggy, weathered remains of ancient volcanoes abut the sea. Southeast of the town, **Whangarei Heads** is the district's volcanic heartland where dramatic walks follow the coast to calm harbour beaches and windswept coastal strands; a kayak trip is a great way to get the best views of a landscape built from often-violent activity. To the northeast, **Tutukaka** acts as the base for dive trips to the undersea wonderland around the **Poor Knights Islands**.

Whangarei Heads

Whangarei Heads, 35km southeast of Whangarei, is a series of small, residential beach communities scattered around jagged volcanic outcrops that terminate at Bream Head, the northern limit of Bream Bay. About the best way to see the area is from the sea, more specifically from the quiet, low viewpoint of a kayak, and one of the most accessible trips is a paddle over to, or around, Limestone Island.

Limestone Island

Just off the coast of Onerahi, a waterside suburb, Limestone Island (Matakohe) is a microcosm of New Zealand history. Now managed by DOC, it was originally home to part of the Ngaitahuhu iwi, and various tribes vied for control before European settlers established a flax pressing plant. Thereafter, settlers fleeing Hone Heke (see p.169) used the island as a refuge, before it became a farm and then a lime works until 1918. In 1989 it was gifted to the Whangarei District for ecological restoration. These days the process is well under way and fifty kiwi chicks have been raised on the island before being released on the mainland; there are interpretive boards at various sites across the island. Visiting the island (see opposite) – you can land on or circumnavigate it – is best done on an organized trip or with a DOC ranger.

Mount Manaia and around

For safe swimming stop at **McLeod Bay**, or continue until the road leaves the harbour and climbs to a saddle at the start of an excellent, signposted **walk** (3km return; 2hr–2hr

30min; 200m ascent) up the 403m **Mount Manaia**, crowned with five eroded pinnacles shrouded in Maori legend – the rocks are said to be Chief Manaia, his children and the last, facing away, his unfaithful wife. The pinnacles remain *tapu*, but you can climb to their base through native bush, passing fine viewpoints.

Beyond Mount Manaia, the road runs for 5km to **Urquharts Bay**, where a short walk (20min each way) leads to the white-sand **Smugglers Cove**. These and other walks are described in DOC's *Whangarei District Walks* leaflet, available from the i-SITE in Whangarei.

Pataua South and Pataua North

Pataua South is 30km east of Whangarei

There's a gorgeous surf beach at the holiday community of **Pataua South**, backed by the simple *Treasure Island Motor Camp* (see below). A footbridge over the estuary leads to another sweeping surf beach at Pataua North. *Tidesong* B&B (see below) is 6km to the southeast and serves tea, coffee and cakes to passers-by.

ARRIVAL AND DEPARTURE WHANGAREI HEADS

By bus City Link buses run (Mon–Sat; every hour) as far as Onerahi, a beachside community on the way to the Heads. If you want to get further on to the Heads you'll need a car.

GETTING AROUND

By boat ★ Pacific Coast Kayaks (☎ 09 436 1947, ⓦ nzseakayaking.co.nz) run trips to Limestone Island ($80/half day; $120/full day), leaving from the Onerahi Yacht Club. The DOC ranger (☎ 09 436 0923) operates a barge to the island ($60 return); call ahead.

ACCOMMODATION

★ **Tidesong** Beasley Rd, Onerahi ☎ 09 436 1959, ⓦ tidesong.co.nz; map p.152. Very welcoming B&B set in a peaceful spot on the mangrove-filled Taiharuru Estuary, a twitcher's paradise with 25 species on view in the extensive bush and gardens surrounding the property. On offer are a great-value self-contained apartment or smaller room, free kayaks, a putting course round the gardens and the chance to take a guided ride in the estuary on a small sailing boat. Home-cooked meals are available (lunch $20; dinner $30–35) and there's an outdoor pizza oven, which is also used for baking. Look out for a bit of family history in the hall – a picture of former prime minister Thomas McKenzie. Apartment __$145__, room __$145__

Treasure Island Motor Camp ☎ 09 436 2390, ⓦ treasureislandnz.co.nz. Treasured by in-the-know Kiwis as a secluded and picturesque spot with access to some even prettier areas and good fishing. There's also an on-site general takeaway and bakery (Dec–Feb) serving coffee and croissants. Camping __$18__

Tutukaka and the Poor Knights Islands

Boats set out from tiny **TUTUKAKA** – set on a beautiful, deeply incised harbour 30km northeast of Whangarei – for one of the world's premier dive locations, the **Poor Knights Islands Marine Reserve**, 25km offshore.

Poor Knights Islands Marine Reserve

The warm East Auckland current and the lack of run-off from the land combine to create visibility approaching 30m most of the year, though in spring (roughly Oct–Dec) plankton can reduce it to 10–15m. The clear waters are home to New Zealand's most diverse and plentiful range of sea life, including a few subtropical species found nowhere else, as well as a striking underwater landscape of near-vertical **rock faces** and arches that drop almost 100m. One dive at the Poor Knights, the Blue Mao Mao Cave, was rated by Jacques Cousteau as one of the top ten dive sights in the world. The Poor Knights lie along the migratory routes of a number of **whale** species, so blue, humpback, Bryde's, sei and minke whales, as well as dolphins, are not uncommon sights on the way to the islands. The waters north and south of Tutukaka

2

ACTIVITIES AT THE POOR KNIGHTS

The Poor Knights is a big draw for scuba divers (novices and experts), snorkellers and, outside the Marine Reserve, fishermen, primarily because of great visibility, the broad range of wildlife and the spectacular nature of the underwater environment. You'll get the most out of the area by scuba diving, as you'll be able to inspect the wildlife and scenery more closely.

Dive Tutukaka Marina Rd, Tutukaka ☎ 0800 288 882, ⓦ diving.co.nz. The largest, best and most flexible operator leaves from Tutukaka (with pick-ups from Whangarei at no extra charge) several times a day from Nov–April, and usually offers at least one trip a day for the rest of the year. It has several boats, so you are typically with similarly skilled divers. Two-dive trips ($199; including gear $249) also carry snorkellers and sightseers ($149) and everyone can use the on-board kayaks. Those with significant dive experience and the right qualifications can explore the two wrecks, nearby and deeper, on two-dive trips ($175 for tanks and weights), while first-timers can try a Discover Scuba dive ($299 with full gear and one-to-one instruction). A

five-day PADI open-water dive qualification costs $799. The company also runs a cruise boat on the Perfect Day trip (5hr; $149), taking you around the Poor Knights Islands then deep into Rikoriko Cave, the world's largest known sea cave, which penetrates 130m into the island. There's also time for snorkelling and kayaking.

Whangarei Deep Sea Anglers Club Marina Rd, Tutukaka ☎ 09 434 3818, ⓦ sportfishing.co.nz. Fishing for marlin, shark and tuna outside the Poor Knights Reserve (Dec–April) can be done by taking a quarter-share of a charter game-fishing boat for the day, which will coast around $250–350. The club (daily 8am–6pm during fishing season) can provide a list of operators who run fishing charters.

are home to two navy **wrecks**. The survey ship HMNZS *Tui* was sunk in 1999 to form an artificial reef, and it was so popular with divers and marine life that the obsolete frigate *Waikato* followed two years later.

ARRIVAL AND DEPARTURE

TUTUKAKA

By shuttle bus The only public transport from Whangarei to Tutukaka is with Tutukaka Shuttle ($15 each way if you're

not diving; ☎ 021 901 408), whose services are coordinated with dive trip departure and return times.

ACCOMMODATION AND EATING

★ **Sands Motel** Tutukaka Block Rd, Whangaumu Bay ☎ 09 434 3747, ⓦ sandsmotel.co.nz. There's a retro feel to this establishment, with comfortable, well-equipped and spacious two-bedroom units beautifully set beside a nice beach 4km off the highway. It's quiet (but within the sound of the crashing waves) and well run with friendly hosts. Units **$180**

Schnappa Rock Café Marina Rd ☎ 09 434 3774, ⓦ schnapparock.co.nz. The most notable of the restaurants around the harbour, this groovy bar-restaurant turns out a tempting range of meat and vegetarian dishes such as lamb rump ($27.50) and potato gnocchi ($27), as well as bar snacks. It's buzzing with divers and

serves good coffee. Book ahead for dinner in summer. Daily 8am–late.

★ **Tutukaka Holiday Park** Matapouri Rd ☎ 09 434 3938, ⓦ tutukaka-holidaypark.co.nz. An ever-expanding and improving site a 2min walk from the harbour that is very busy in Jan and Feb. It's also simply awash with pukeko (see p.811), who are not averse to panhandling. The self-contained cabins are spacious and the standard cabins adequate, while the en suites are great value. The camp kitchen and laundry are clean and well equipped. Camping **$17**, dorms **$25**, standard cabins **$70**, en-suite cabins **$95**, studio cabins **$120**, self-contained cabins **$140**

Matapouri and Whale Bay

MATAPOURI, 6km north of Tutukaka, is a lovely holiday settlement which backs onto a curving white-sand bay bounded by bushy headlands which separate it from the pristine **Whale Bay**, signposted off Matapouri Road 1km further north and reached by a twenty-minute bushwalk. There are virtually no facilities along this stretch, apart from a shop and takeaway at Matapouri.

North of Whangarei to the Bay of Islands

The roads that access the coast around Tutukaka and Matapouri rejoin SH1 at **Hikurangi** 16km north of Whangarei. About 6km further north you have a choice of routes: both go to the Bay of Islands but approach from different directions: carry straight on and you go direct to Paihia with opportunities for side trips to the Maori redoubt of Ruapekapeka Pa, and the **Hundertwasser toilets** at Kawakawa; turn right along Old Russell Road and you twist towards the coast on the tar-sealed but narrow and winding back road to Russell. The latter route is the most scenic way to approach the Bay of Islands, along a 70km narrow, winding road that takes about two hours. You can spin the drive out by admiring the wonderful coastline around the **Whangaruru Harbour**, stopping for swims in numerous gorgeous bays, and perhaps a short walk in the mixed kauri forest of the **Ngaiotonga Scenic Reserve**.

Ruapekapeka Pa

17km north of Hikurangi on SH1 then 5km east on a signposted road • Free

Ruapekapeka Pa is the site of the final battle in the War of the North in 1846, a grassy hilltop with a few earthworks, a commemorative wooden pole, one of the original cannons and stunning views of the surrounding countryside. Hone Heke's repeated flagpole felling in Russell (see p.169) precipitated nine months of fighting during which Maori learnt to adapt their *pa* defences to cope with British firepower. The apotheosis of this development is Ruapekapeka, the "Bat's Nest". Its hilltop setting, double row of totara palisades and labyrinth of trenches and interconnecting tunnels helped Hone Heke and his warriors defend the site, despite being heavily outgunned and outnumbered three to one. Signs explain the full story and trench lines and bunkers are clearly visible.

Kawakawa

The small town of **KAWAKAWA**, 15km north of Ruapekapeka, would be otherwise unremarkable if it wasn't known for being the home of the celebrated **Hundertwasser toilets** on the town's main drag, Gillies Street. These works of art were created in 1997 by the reclusive Austrian painter, architect, ecologist and philosopher, **Friedrich Hundertwasser**, who made Kawakawa his home from 1975 until his death in 2000, aged 71. The ceramic columns supporting the entrance hint at the interior's complex use of broken tiles, coloured bottles and found objects such as the old hinges on the wrought-iron doors. A steady trickle of visitors takes a peek in both the Gents and the Ladies after suitable warning. The local council is planning a Hundertwasser Visitor Centre, spurred on, no doubt, by the planned Whangarei tribute (see p.151). To learn more, meanwhile, pop along to the **Kawakawa Museum**, 3 Wynyard St (daily 10am–5pm; $3; ☎09 404 0406), where two DVDs on Hundertwasser run on request.

Vintage Railway

Fri, Sat & Sun 11am, noon, 1.15pm & 2.30pm, plus extra services during school holidays • $12 • ☎09 404 0684, ⓦ bayofislandsvintagerailway.org.nz

Kawakawa is New Zealand's only town with a rail track running down its main street, something exploited by the Bay of Islands **Vintage Railway** with steam- and diesel-hauled 1930s carriages trundled 5km north then back. The line is meant to eventually extend further north to Opua (30km return) but the work is progressing at an agricultural Northland pace.

Waka Huia Treasure Trove & Studio

68 Gillies St • Half-day carving course $85 • ☎ 09 404 0381, ⓦ newzealandmaoriart.co.nz

Talented young Maori carver Wiremu teaches **greenstone carving** in half a day (2hr 30min), starting with a pre-prepared stone and working towards making a simple shape by the end. The appeal is not so much the finished article as it is the journey through history, spirituality and gaining an understanding of the material, tools and method. You can check out his amazing work at the front of the Bay of Island Bookstore next door to the *Trainspotters Café* (see p.162).

2

Oakura

Leaving SH1, you travel through 14km of farmland along Old Russell Road before reaching Helena Bay, where's there's a gallery-café (see p.162), which is a good spot to stop for a bite (there's not much between it and Russell) before continuing north to **OAKURA**. Oakura itself is not much more than an island-studded bay backed by a gently curving beach and a cluster of holiday homes. Its primary appeal is that not a great deal ever happens, though there are plenty of places to swim and walk, and one decent place to stay (see p.162).

Whangaruru North Head Scenic Reserve

10km from Ngaiotonga

At Ngaiotonga, a sealed side road runs through hilly farmland to the broad sweep of **Bland Bay** with great beaches on both sides of an isthmus. Continue beyond Bland Bay to reach **Whangaruru North Head Scenic Reserve**, with yet more lovely beaches, fine walks around the end of the peninsula and a DOC campsite (see p.162).

Rawhiti

Back on the coast road it is 7km north to a junction where you turn left for Russell (25km further) and continue straight on for the scattered and predominantly Maori village of **Rawhiti**, the start of the Cape Brett Track (see box below). Just 1km along the Rawhiti road there's shorter, easier walking in the form of the **Whangamumu Track** (4km each way; 1hr; 150m ascent), a forest path that crosses the base of the Cape Brett Peninsula to a lovely beach. Here you can see the remains of a whaling station, which closed in 1940.

Following the Manawaroa Road back to the Russell Road and on toward Russell for 11km you'll come across a signposted side road to some fine stands of kauri. These can be visited on the **Twin Bole Track** (around 200m; 5min) and the **Kauri Grove Walk** (1km; 20min).

THE CAPE BRETT TRACK

Northland's best overnight tramp is the challenging but rewarding **Cape Brett Track** (20km each way; 6–8hr) which follows the hilly ridge along the centre of the peninsula with sea occasionally visible on both sides: a route outlined in DOC's *Cape Brett* leaflet. The former lighthouse keeper's house at the tip of the peninsula is now a DOC **hut** (23 beds; $12.20; backcountry hut pass not valid) and the only place to **stay** on the track itself, in a fabulous location surrounded by sea and views out to the Hole in the Rock. There are gas cooking stoves but no utensils, and camping is not allowed.

The track starts in Rawhiti (see above) and crosses private land, so all walkers must pay a **track fee** ($30; day walkers $10). The Russell Booking & Information Centre is the place to pay your track fee, book the DOC hut and ask about secure parking in Rawhiti. You might also enquire about a **water taxi** from Russell to Rawhiti (around $170 for up to six people), Deep Water Cove, three-quarters of the way along the track ($190), or Cape Brett ($230; conditions permitting). Secure parking is available at *Hartwells* in Kaimarama Bay, at the end of Rawhiti Road, for a small fee.

2

ACCOMMODATION   **NORTH OF WHANGAREI TO THE BAY OF ISLANDS**

Coast Road Farm Russell Rd, 12km north of Oakura ☎ 09 433 6894, ⊛ thefarm.co.nz. Along the Russell Road you can get involved with dairy farm life, ride horses ($45/hr) or motorbikes (lesson $60/hr/90min), go kayaking ($20/person/day) and much more, while staying in the dorm room, one of three doubles (one en suite), one of four cabins, or camping. Meals (breakfast $5; lunch $8; dinner $15) are by arrangement. Camping $̲1̲3̲, dorms $̲2̲0̲, doubles $̲5̲0̲, en suite $̲7̲0̲, cabins $̲7̲0̲

Puriri Bay campsite Whangaruru North Rd, Whangaruru North Head Scenic Reserve ✉ whangareiao@doc.govt.nz. DOC site overlooking Puriri Bay and Whangaruru Harbour, with 93 sites, running water, toilets and cold showers. The camp office is open 7.30am–8pm, and bookings are essential in the summer. $̲8̲

EATING AND DRINKING

The Gallery & Café Helena Bay Hill Old Russell Rd, Helena Bay ☎ 09 433 9616, ⊛ galleryhelenabay.co.nz. An imaginative gallery coupled with a great German-run daytime café with views across bush-clad hills down to Helena Bay. Stop for a coffee or a snack: schnitzel and strudel alongside more traditional Kiwi fare. Mon–Fri 10am–4pm, Sat & Sun 10am–5pm; Easter–Sept closed Mon–Wed. Gallery: daily 10am–5pm.

Trainspotters Café 39 Gillies St, Kawakawa ☎ 09 404 0361, ⊛ trainspottercafe.co.nz. You can watch the trains from the comfort of the café or the outdoor seating, which serves light meals, including eggs Benedict ($16), Greek salad ($11) and steak and eggs ($16) as well as good coffee. Mon–Fri 7.30am–5pm, Sat 9.30am–4pm, Sun 9.30am–noon.

The Bay of Islands

THE BAY OF ISLANDS, 240km north of Auckland, lures visitors to its beautiful coastal scenery, scattered islands and clear blue waters. There are other equally stunning spots along the Northland coast, such as the Whangaroa and Hokianga harbours, but what sets the bay apart is the ease with which you can get out among the islands, and its pivotal history. This was the cradle of European settlement in New Zealand, a fact abundantly testified to by the bay's churches, mission stations and orchards. It's also a focal point for Maori because of the **Treaty of Waitangi** (see box, p.166), still New Zealand's most important legal document.

Perhaps surprisingly, much of your time in the Bay of Islands will be spent on the mainland, as there are no settlements on the islands. Most visitors base themselves in beachside **Paihia**, which is set up to deal with the hordes who come here for the various cruises and excursions, as well as being the closest town to the Treaty House at **Waitangi**. The compact town of **Russell**, a couple of kilometres across the bay by passenger ferry, is prettier and almost equally convenient for cruises. To the northwest, away from the bay itself, **Kerikeri** is intimately entwined with the area's early missionary history, while **Waimate North**, inland to the west, was another important mission site and Mission House.

In 1927 American Western writer **Zane Grey** came here to fish for striped and black marlin, making the area famous with his book *The Angler's El Dorado*. Every summer since, the bay has seen game-fishing tournaments and glistening catches strung up on the jetties.

Brief history

A warm climate, abundant seafood and deep, sheltered harbours contributed to dense pre-European **Maori settlement** in the Bay of Islands, with many a headland supporting a *pa*. The bay also appealed to **Captain Cook**, who anchored here in 1769. Cook landed on Motuarohia Island at what became known as Cook's Cove, where he forged generally good relations with the inhabitants. Three years later the French sailor **Marion du Fresne**, en route from Mauritius to Tahiti, became the first European to have sustained contact with Maori, though he fared less well when a misunderstanding, probably over *tapu*, led to his death, along with 26 of his crew. The French retaliated, destroying a *pa* and killing hundreds of Maori.

2

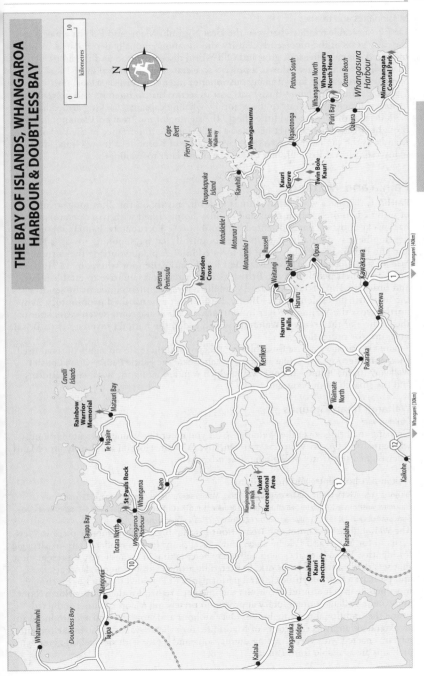

THE BAY OF ISLANDS, WHANGAROA HARBOUR & DOUBTLESS BAY

0   10
kilometres

N

Doubtless Bay

Whatuwhiwhi

Taupo Bay

Covalli Islands

Rainbow Warrior Memorial

Matauri Bay

Te Ngaire

St Paul's Rock

Whangaroa

Totara North

Whangaroa Harbour

Kaeo

Mangonui

Taipa

Manganangina Kauri Walk

Puketi Recreational Area

Kerikeri

10

Omahuta Kauri Sanctuary

Rangiahua

Mangamuka Bridge

Kaitaia

Kaikohe

12

1

Waimate North

Pakaraka

Moerewa

Kawakawa

1

Whangarei (30km)

Whangarei (40km)

Purerua Peninsula

Marsden Cross

Russell

Waitangi

Paihia

Haruru

Haruru Falls

Opua

Motuarohia I

Moturua I

Motukiekie I

Unupukapuka Island

Rawhiti

Cape Brett Walkway

Piercy I

Cape Brett

Whangamumu

Kauri Grove

Twin Bole Kauri

Ngaiotonga

Whangaruru North

Whangaruru North Head

Ocean Beach

Pataua South

Puriri Bay

Oakura

Whangasura Harbour

Mimiwhangata Coastal Park

2

Missionaries and treaties

Despite amicable relations between the local Ngapuhi Maori and Pakeha whalers in the early years of the nineteenth century, the situation gradually deteriorated. With increased contact, firearms, grog and Old World diseases spread and the fabric of Maori life began to break down, a process accelerated by the arrival in 1814 of Samuel Marsden, the first of many **missionaries** intent on turning Maori into Christians. In 1833, James Busby was sent to secure British interests and prevent the brutal treatment meted out to the Maori by whaling captains. Lacking armed backup or judicial authority, he had little effect. The signing of the **Treaty of Waitangi** in 1840 brought effective policing yet heralded a decline in the importance of the Bay of Islands, as the capital moved from its original site of Kororareka (now Opua, although many claim it was Russell), first to Auckland and later to Wellington.

Paihia and Waitangi

PAIHIA is the place where most things kick off, mostly on the 2km-long string of waterside motels, restaurants and holiday homes lined with trip operators, backpacker hostels, party-oriented bars and hotels. Fortunately, Paihia's low-rise development is sympathetic to its three beautiful, flat bays looking towards Russell and the Bay of Islands, encircled by forested hills. A plaque outside the current St Paul's Anglican Church on Marsden Road marks the spot where, in 1831, the northern chiefs petitioned the British Crown for a representative to establish law and order. In 1833 King William IV finally addressed their concerns by sending the first British resident, James Busby. Busby built a house on a promontory 2km north across the Waitangi River in **WAITANGI** – the scene some seven years later of the signing of the **Treaty of Waitangi**, which ceded the nation's sovereignty to Britain in return for protection.

Paihia is primarily a base for exploring the bay, and there are no sights in town itself. Fans of mangroves and estuarine scenery can tackle the gentle **Paihia–Opua Coastal Walkway** (6km; 90min–2hr one-way), which wanders along the wave-cut platforms and the small bays in between.

Waitangi Treaty Grounds
Tau Henare Drive

Crossing the bridge over the Waitangi River you enter the Waitangi Treaty Grounds, where in 1840 Queen Victoria's representative William Hobson and nearly fifty Maori chiefs signed the Treaty of Waitangi (see box, p.166).

Waitangi Visitor Centre and Treaty House
Tau Henare Drive • **Visitor Centre and Treaty House** Daily: Oct–March 9am–7pm; April–Sept 9am–5pm • $25 (valid for two consecutive days); free for NZ citizens; cultural performance or guided tour $18 • **Culture North Night Show** 4–6 nights/week • $60 • Book ahead on ☎ 09 402 5990, ⦿ culturenorth.co.nz • ☎ 09 402 7437, ⦿ waitangi.net.nz

The **Waitangi Visitor Centre and Treaty House** is the single most symbolic place in New Zealand for Maori and Pakeha alike, and a focal point for the modern nation's struggle for identity. You can easily spend half a day here, taking in an audiovisual presentation that sets the historical framework, bolstered by a small exhibition of Maori artefacts, and perhaps a short daytime cultural performance or a guided tour (all $18), though most people give it around two hours then perhaps return for the **Culture North Night Show**, an excellent contemporary approach to presenting Maori culture conducted inside the traditional meeting house. Over an hour and a quarter you're introduced to an extended family as the stories of Maori life from the arrival of Kupe to the present day are enacted with verve, mixing drama, song and dance with storytelling. Free pick-ups are available from Paihia.

2

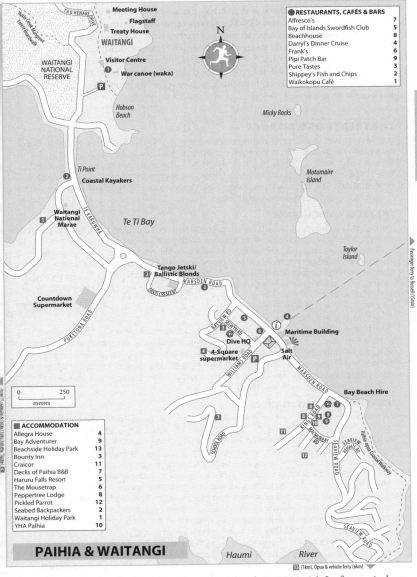

● RESTAURANTS, CAFÉS & BARS

Alfresco's	7
Bay of Islands Swordfish Club	5
Beachhouse	8
Darryl's Dinner Cruise	4
Frank's	6
Pipi Patch Bar	9
Pure Tastes	3
Shippey's Fish and Chips	2
Waikokopu Café	1

■ ACCOMMODATION

Allegra House	4
Bay Adventurer	9
Beachside Holiday Park	13
Bounty Inn	3
Craicor	11
Decks of Paihia B&B	7
Haruru Falls Resort	5
The Mousetrap	6
Peppertree Lodge	8
Pickled Parrot	12
Seabed Backpackers	2
Waitangi Holiday Park	1
YHA Paihia	10

PAIHIA & WAITANGI

The **Treaty House** was built in Georgian colonial style in 1833–34. Its front windows look towards Russell over sweeping lawns, where marquees were erected on three significant occasions: in 1834, when Maori chiefs chose the Confederation of Tribes flag, which now flies on one yardarm of the central flagpole; the meeting a year later at which northern Maori leaders signed the Declaration of Independence of New Zealand; and, in 1840, the signing of the Treaty of Waitangi itself.

The northern side of the lawn is flanked by the *whare runanga*, or **Maori meeting house**, built between 1934 and 1940 as a cooperative effort between all Maori. The interior richly carved panels represent all *iwi* (rather than the usual single tribe).

Housed in a specially built shelter in the Treaty House grounds is the world's largest **war canoe** (*waka*), the 35m-long *Ngatoki Matawhaorua*, named after the vessel navigated by Kupe when he discovered Aotearoa, and built from two huge kauri. It has traditionally been launched each year on Waitangi Day, propelled by eighty warriors.

2

THE TREATY OF WAITANGI

The Treaty of Waitangi is the **founding document** of modern New Zealand, a touchstone for both Pakeha and Maori, and its implications permeate New Zealand society. Signed in 1840 between what were ostensibly two sovereign states – the United Kingdom and the United Tribes of New Zealand, plus other Maori leaders – the treaty remains central to New Zealand's **race relations**. The Maori rights guaranteed by it have seldom been upheld, however, and the constant struggle for recognition continues.

THE TREATY AT WAITANGI

Motivated by a desire to staunch French expansion in the Pacific, and a moral obligation on the Crown to protect Maori from rapacious land-grabbing by settlers, the British instructed naval captain William Hobson to negotiate the transfer of sovereignty with "the free and intelligent consent of the natives", and to deal fairly with the Maori. Hobson, with the help of James Busby and others, drew up both the English Treaty and a Maori "translation". On the face of it, the treaty is a straightforward document, but the complications of having two versions (see p.789) and the implications of striking a deal between two peoples with widely differing views on land and resource ownership have reverberated down the years.

The treaty was unveiled on February 5, 1840, to a gathering of some 400 representatives of the five northern tribes in front of Busby's residence in Waitangi. Presented as a contract between the chiefs and Queen Victoria – someone whose role was comprehensible in chiefly terms – the benefits were amplified and the costs downplayed. As most chiefs didn't understand English, they signed the Maori version of the treaty, which still has *mana* (authority or status) among Maori today.

THE TREATY AFTER WAITANGI

The pattern set at Waitangi was repeated up and down the country, as seven copies of the treaty were dispatched to garner signatures and extend Crown authority over parts of the North Island that had not yet been covered, and the South Island. On May 21, before signed treaty copies had been returned, Hobson claimed New Zealand for Britain: the North Island on the grounds of cession by Maori, and the South Island by right of Cook's "discovery", as it was considered to be without owners, despite a significant Maori population.

Maori fears were alerted from the start, and as the settler population grew and demand for land increased, successive governments passed laws that gradually stripped Maori of control over their affairs – actions which led to the New Zealand Wars of the 1860s (see p.790). Over the decades, small concessions were made, but nothing significant changed until 1973, when **Waitangi Day** (February 6) became an official national holiday. Around the same time, Maori groups, supported by a small band of Pakeha, began a campaign of direct action, increasingly disrupting commemorations, thereby alienating many Pakeha and splitting Maori allegiances between angry young urban Maori and the *kaumatua* (elders), who saw the actions as disrespectful to the ancestors and an affront to tradition. Many strands of Maori society were unified by the *hikoi* (march) to Waitangi to protest against the celebrations in 1985, a watershed year in which Paul Reeves was appointed New Zealand's first Maori Governor General and the **Waitangi Tribunal** for land reform was given some teeth.

Protests have continued since as successive governments have vacillated over whether to attend the commemorations at Waitangi.

Haruru Falls

4km west of Waitangi, accessed from the main road

At **Haruru Falls**, the Waitangi River drops over a basalt lava flow, and though they're not that impressive by New Zealand standards, there's good swimming at their base. Haruru Falls are also reached from the Treaty House grounds via the very gentle **Hutia Creek Mangrove Forest Boardwalk** (2hr return) or on a guided **kayak** trip up the estuary and among the mangroves (see p.171).

ARRIVAL AND DEPARTURE

PAIHIA AND WAITANGI

2

By bus InterCity/Northliner and NakedBus arrive on the Marsden Rd, outside the Bay of Islands' main i-SITE.

Destinations Auckland (5–6 daily; 4hr 20min); Kaitaia (1 daily; 2hr); Kerikeri (3 daily; 20min); Mangonui (1 daily; 1hr 20min); Whangarei (4–6 daily; 1hr 15min).

By plane Flights from Auckland arrive at the Bay of Islands airport (☎09 407 6133, ⓦbayofislandsairport .co.nz), 22km northwest, near Kerikeri, and are met by a shuttle bus ($60 to Paihia).

Destinations Auckland (5–6 daily; 40min).

By vehicle ferry A small vehicle ferry runs between Paihia and Russell (daily 6.50am–10pm; every 20min; car & driver $11 each way, foot passengers $1; buy ticket on board; 20min), crossing the Veronica Channel at Opua, 6km south of Paihia. Taking the ferry shortens the 100km drive between Paihia and Russell to 15km.

By passenger ferry Foot passengers can use one of the three frequent passenger ferries (Oct–May 7am–10pm; June–Sept 7am–7pm; $7 one-way, $12 return; 15min) between Paihia and Russell.

GETTING AROUND

By car Paihia isn't big, and everywhere is within walking distance, but if you do have a car, note that parking is tight in the high season; your best bet is the pay-and-display car park opposite the 4-Square supermarket on Williams Rd.

By shuttle bus Paihia Tuk Tuk Shuttle Service (☎027 486 6071), based outside the i-SITE, will pick up and drop

off two to six people pretty much anywhere in town for around $5 each, run joy rides for $7, or run up to Haruru Falls for a bit more.

By bike Rent good-quality mountain bikes from Bay Beach Hire (☎09 402 6078; $20/half-day, $25/day, $30/ overnight) at the south end of Paihia Beach.

INFORMATION

i-SITE The Wharf, Marsden Rd (daily 8am–5pm, extended hours Nov–April; ☎09 402 7345, ⓦvisitfarnorthnz.com).

The office here – one of three for the Far North region of Northland – has internet access and books tours.

ACCOMMODATION

Paihia abounds in accommodation for all budgets, though rates can be stratospheric during the couple of weeks after Christmas. B&Bs and homestays vary their prices less than motels, and hostels mostly maintain the same prices year-round. Kings Road is a veritable backpackers' village with a selection of generally good places, noisy in the height of summer.

★ **Allegra House** 39 Bayview Rd ☎09 402 7932, ⓦallegra.co.nz. A choice of luxury B&B or self-contained apartment in a big, light and modern house at the top of a hill, and all with stupendous views right out over the Bay of Islands. All are a/c, sport their own balconies and have access to a hot tub in native bush. B&B $245, apartment $265

Bay Adventurer 28 Kings Rd ☎0800 112 127, ⓦbay adventurer.co.nz. Upmarket backpackers resort with apartments, an attractive pool, free bikes, kayaks and access to the nearby tennis courts (free in winter). It's particularly good for its rooms and fully self-contained studio apartments. Dorms $26, rooms $85, apartments $135

Bounty Inn Corner of Bayview and Selwyn rds ☎0800 472 444, ⓦbountyinn.co.nz. Pleasant central yet quiet motel, 100m from the beach and with ample off-street parking. Rooms without cooking facilities, and fully equipped motel units all come lined in timber with a sundeck or balcony.

Studios $159, studios with kitchen $199

Craicor 49 Kings Rd ☎09 402 7882, ⓦcraicor-accom .co.nz. A couple of excellent-value self-catering apartments, both spacious, well kept and with limited sea views, plus an attractive double room. Continental breakfast can be supplied for $10. Apartments $165, double room $165

Decks of Paihia B&B 69 School Rd ☎09 1402 6146, ⓦdecksofpaihia.co.nz. Welcoming three-room B&B in a comfortable, tastefully decorated modern house with swimming pool set into a large, sunny deck high on the hill above Paihia. $245

The Mousetrap 11 Kings Rd ☎0800 402 8182, ⓦmousetrap.co.nz. Welcoming, nautically themed, wood-panelled hostel that sets itself apart from the other backpackers on this lively street. Rooms are scattered all over the site, there are three small kitchens, a BBQ area, free bike use and a decent sea view. Dorms $25, rooms $67

2

Peppertree Lodge 15 Kings Rd ☎ 09 402 6122, ⓦ peppertree.co.nz. Very clean, central hostel with spacious eight-bunk dorms, four-bunk en-suite dorms, great en-suite doubles and a self-contained flat. Guests can make use of a tennis court, free good-quality bikes and kayaks, and there's an excellent DVD library. Be sure to book ahead Oct–April. Dorms $\overline{\$25}$, rooms $\overline{\$72}$, en suites $\overline{\$86}$, flat $\overline{\$110}$

Pickled Parrot Grey's Lane, off MacMurray Rd ☎ 0508 727 7682, ⓦ pickledparrot.co.nz. One of Paihia's smaller, more relaxed hostels, tucked away in a peaceful spot with a lovely courtyard. Secluded tent sites; four- and six-bed dorms as well as singles, doubles and twins, all with free continental breakfast, plus free pick-ups, bikes and tennis racquets. Camping $\overline{\$19}$, dorms $\overline{\$26}$, double and twin rooms $\overline{\$33}$

★ **Seabed Backpackers** 46 Davis Crescent ☎ 09 402 5567, ⓦ seabeds.co.nz. Pound for pound the best backpackers in town: grown-up accommodation with proper facilities in a one-time motel, with extremely good-value rates, run by a friendly professional who knows the area like John Cleese knows the Parrot Sketch. Dorms $\overline{\$26}$, singles $\overline{\$60}$, en-suite doubles $\overline{\$85}$

YHA Paihia Corner of Kings and MacMurray rds ☎ 09 402 7487, ⊖ yha.paihia@yha.co.nz. Well-maintained and run hostel with well-informed staff and a good kitchen, attracting a friendly mix of travellers and families. Most rooms and dorms are en-suite. Dorms $\overline{\$26}$, rooms $\overline{\$60}$, en suite $\overline{\$78}$, cabin $\overline{\$64}$

CAMPSITES

Beachside Holiday Park SH11, 3km south of Paihia ☎ 09 402 7678, ⓦ beachsideholiday.co.nz. Small and peaceful beautifully situated waterside site with a range of cabins and units, good kitchen and laundry, as well as dinghies and kayaks for rent. Camping $\overline{\$20}$, cabins $\overline{\$80}$, en-suite cabins $\overline{\$135}$

★ **Haruru Falls Resort** Puketona Rd, 4km north of Paihia ☎ 0800 757 525, ⓦ harurufalls.co.nz. Fabulous location by the river with commanding views of Haruru Falls, offering riverside tent sites and motel units around a pool. The resort has outdoor games such as pétanque and volleyball, a BBQ, and its own restaurant bar, plus kayaks and paddle bikes for rent. Camping $\overline{\$22}$, cabins $\overline{\$70}$, rooms $\overline{\$120}$, motel units $\overline{\$130}$

Waitangi Holiday Park 21 Tahuna Rd, Waitangi ☎ 09 402 7866, ⓦ waitangiholidaypark.co.nz. The closest campsite to both Waitangi and Paihia (a 20min walk), this simple site has pitches overlooking the Waitangi River and four spacious kitchen cabins. Camping $\overline{\$20}$, cabins $\overline{\$75}$

EATING, DRINKING AND ENTERTAINMENT

Paihia's range of places to eat is plentiful but, with a few notable exceptions, all are sort of similar; competition keeps prices reasonable and many spots specialize in seafood. The restaurants also tend to be good places to stick around for postprandial drinking in the summer and there are several raucous bars along Kings Road.

★ **Alfresco's** 6 Marsden Rd ☎ 09 402 6797. Relaxed café and bar that's excellent for a coffee, breakfasts (including great corn fritters), lunchtime burger-and-drink meal deals ($12–17) and some fine dining in the evening (mains $25–35). Daily 8am–late.

★ **Bay of Islands Swordfish Club** Marsden Rd ☎ 09 403 7857. Private club, overlooking the bay and welcoming visitors outside the peak summer season: just get the bar staff to sign you in. The great views are accompanied by ample, good-value food such as fish and chips and steak and chips (mains $18–25). "Swordy's" also has some of the cheapest drinks in town. Daily from 6pm.

Beachhouse 16 Kings Rd ☎ 09 402 6063. All-day café and juice bar better known for its *Sand Pit* bar with pool tables round the back, where live music clashes with the next-door *Pipi Patch Bar* (run by *Base Backpackers*) most nights in the summer. Daily 10am–late.

Darryl's Dinner Cruise Paihia Wharf ☎ 0800 334 6637, ⓦ dinnercruise.co.nz. Convivial and leisurely cruise (2hr 30min; $95) leaving from the wharf around 6.30pm and heading up the Waitangi River to Haruru Falls, where you tuck into prawns and mussels followed by T-bone steak, lamb and fish. There's a cash bar on board or BYO wine. If you catch it during a good sunset it's a great way to spend the evening. Trips are subject to minimum numbers.

Frank's Marsden Rd ☎ 09 402 7590. Chilled café-bar serving breakfasts such as eggs Benedict ($16) and decent coffee, plus pizzas ($19). There's occasional live music on Wednesdays and at the weekends in the summer. Service varies. Daily 8am–late.

Pure Tastes 116 Marsden Rd ☎ 09 402 0003. Fine-dining restaurant at the *Paihia Beach Resort*. Breakfasts will see you through to intricately prepared lunches (poolside in summer; mains around $25), but the dinners are more memorable, including lamb rump ($34), caramelized pork belly ($32) and a tasting menu of six courses with wine to match for $150. Daily 8am–late.

★ **Shippey's Fish and Chips** On the old Sugar Boat next to the Waitangi Bridge ⓦ shippeys.com. Sit-in fish and chip shop on the deck of the boat where you order at the bar, which also boasts a good range of beer and wine. The fish ($5) and chips ($3) are cooked fresh and it has a curious rough-hewn charm. Daily noon–late.

Waikokopu Café Treaty House Grounds, Waitangi ☎ 09 402 6275. Great daytime café accessed by a track through the rainforest and surrounded by picnic-table-strewn lawns.

Perfect for tucking into well-prepared breakfasts and lunches such as Cajun chicken or smoked BBQ pork ribs (mains $16–21), plus a range of cakes and great coffee. Licensed. Daily 9am–10pm.

The islands

The Bay is aptly named, with six large, and around 140 small, islands. Many are subject to the DOC-led **Project Island Song**, which aims to rid many islands of introduced predators and turn them into wildlife havens. Assorted birds have been reintroduced to many islands, notably **Urupukapuka Island**, which can be explored in a few hours using DOC's *Urupukapuka Island Archeological Walk* leaflet highlighting Maori *pa* and terrace sites.

Of the other large islands, by far the most popular is **Motuarohia** (**Roberton Island**), where DOC manages the most dramatic central section, an isthmus almost severed by a pair of perfectly circular blue lagoons. Snorkellers can explore an undersea nature trail waymarked by inscribed stainless-steel plaques.

Other sights that often feature on cruise itineraries include the **Black Rocks**, bare islets formed from columnar-jointed basalt – these rise only 10m out of the water but plummet a sheer 30m beneath. At the outer limit of the bay is the craggy peninsula of **Cape Brett**, named by Cook in 1769 after the then Lord of the Admiralty, Lord Piercy Brett. Cruises also regularly pass through the **Hole in the Rock**, a natural tunnel through Piercy Island, which is even more exciting when there's a swell running.

ACCOMMODATION	THE ISLANDS

Urupukapuka Island ⓦ doc.govt.nz. This is the only island in the Bay of Islands that accommodates overnight guests, with DOC managing three basic sites: Cable Bay, with running water, showers and toilets, and Sunset Bay, with running water and toilets, are both on the south shore; Urupukapuka Bay, with running water, toilets and showers, is the island's easternmost campsite. Book your site well in advance. **$8.10**

Russell

The isolated location of **RUSSELL** – on a narrow peninsula with poor road but good sea access – gives this small hillside settlement an island ambience. In summer, however, the place is often full of day-trippers who pile off passenger ferries from Paihia and vehicle ferries from nearby Opua to explore the village's historic buildings and stroll along its quaint waterfront.

Brief history

Modern-day Russell is a far cry from the 1830s when **Kororareka**, as it was then known, was a swashbuckling town full of whalers and sealers with a reputation as the "Hell Hole of the Pacific". Savage and drunken behaviour served as an open invitation to **missionaries**, who gradually won over a sizeable congregation and left behind Russell's two oldest buildings, the church and a printing works that produced religious tracts.

After the Treaty of Waitangi

By 1840, Kororareka was the largest settlement in the country, but after the signing of the Treaty of Waitangi, Governor William Hobson fell out with both Maori and local settlers and moved his capital progressively further south.

Meanwhile, initial Maori enthusiasm for the Treaty of Waitangi had faded: financial benefits had failed to materialize and the Confederation of Tribes flag that flew from Flagstaff Hill between 1834 and 1840 had been replaced by the Union Jack. This came to be seen as a symbol of British betrayal, and as resentment crystallized it found a leader in **Hone Heke Pokai**, Ngapuhi chief and son-in-law of Kerikeri's Hongi Hika. Between July 1844 and March 1845, Heke and his followers cut down the flagstaff no fewer than four times, the last occasion sparking the first **New Zealand War**, which

BAY OF ISLANDS TOURS AND ACTIVITIES

Unless you get out onto the water you're missing the essence of the Bay of Islands. The majority of yachting, scuba diving, dolphin-watching, kayaking and fishing trips start in Paihia, but all the major **cruises** and bay **excursions** also pick up in Russell. From December to March everything should be booked a couple of days in advance. Hotels and motels can book for you; hostels can usually arrange a discount of around ten percent for backpackers.

The two main operators are Fullers Great Sights and Explore NZ/Dolphin Discoveries, both offering sightseeing, sailing and dolphin trips. There are also numerous **yachts** that usually take fewer than a dozen passengers and go out for around six hours: competition is tight and standards vary. Most operators give you a chance to **snorkel**, **kayak** and **fish**.

The Bay of Islands is excellent for **dolphin watching**; there's an eighty percent chance of seeing bottlenose and common dolphins in almost any season, as well as orca from May to October and minke and Bryde's **whales** from August to January.

Your chances of **swimming with dolphins** are about 35–40 percent. Swimming is forbidden when there are juveniles in the pod, and only 18 people are allowed in the water with dolphins at any time. There's usually a money-back offer if you miss out (check when you book); your best chance is on a cruise with companies licensed to search for and swim with dolphins.

CRUISES, SAILING AND DOLPHIN ENCOUNTERS

Ecocruz ☎0800 432 627, ⊛ecocruz.co.nz. A three-day sail (Oct–April; dorm bunk $595, double cabin $1500) on the *Manawanui*, which takes up to ten people around the bay, with the emphasis on appreciation of the natural environment. Excellent meals are included, along with use of kayaks, snorkel gear, fishing tackle and a good deal of local knowledge and enthusiasm. Book early.

Explore NZ/Dolphin Discoveries ☎0800 365 744, ⊛explorenz.co.nz. The pioneers of dolphin swimming in this area operate a range of trips. The Dolphin/Sail Adventure Combo (Oct–May daily; 8hr; $160; $30 extra if you get the chance to swim with dolphins) involves cruising in the morning and watching dolphins, followed by a transfer to the *Lion New Zealand* yacht for a barbecue lunch, with optional kayaking and snorkelling.

Fullers Great Sights ☎0800 653 339, ⊛dolphin cruises.co.nz. The Cream Trip (a.k.a. "Day in the Bay"; Oct–April daily; 6hr 45min; $109) is the best all-round option, with a visit to the Hole in the Rock, an island stop, a chance to get wet boom-netting and a look around as the boat delivers groceries and mail (Mon, Wed & Sat only). You'll probably see dolphins and may have the chance to swim with them. There's also a dedicated dolphin-swimming cruise (2 daily; 4hr; $105) on the bay's smallest dolphin boat (35 passengers). The *Ipipiri* is Fuller's overnight cruise option (⊛overnight cruise.co.nz) and includes an en-suite king or twin room, afternoon tea, buffet dinner, cooked breakfast, free use of kayaks and snorkelling gear, guided walks and a twenty-four-hour cruise anchoring overnight in a sheltered bay ($375).

Phantom ☎0800 224 421, ⊛yachtphantom.com. Only ten can board this excellent, Russell-based ocean-racing sloop for six glorious hours around the bay ($110), relaxing on deck or taking the helm. Lunch included. Oct–April only.

R. Tucker Thompson ☎0800 882 537, ⊛tucker.co.nz. Day-trips to the islands on a beautiful Northland-built schooner (daily late Oct–April; 6hr; $145) with morning tea and freshly baked scones and cream before anchoring for a swim and BBQ lunch. Two-hour late-afternoon sails (Nov–March Wed, Fri & Sun; $69) including an antipasto platter and glass of wine are also available.

★**The Rock** ☎0800 762 527, ⊛rocktheboat.co.nz. Backpacker-style accommodation and group activities aboard a converted former car ferry, with a great range of ages and a real sense of kicking back.

raged for nearly a year, during which Kororareka was destroyed. The settlement rose from the ashes under a new name, Russell, and grew slowly around its beachfront into the tranquil village of today.

Pompallier

The Strand • Daily: Nov–April 10am–5pm; May–Oct 10am–4pm • $10 • ☎09 403 9015, ⊛historicplaces.org.nz

Russell's most striking building is the fascinating **Pompallier**, the last survivor of Russell's Catholic mission, and once the headquarters of Catholicism in the western Pacific.

Board in the late afternoon and chug out to some gorgeous bays for fishing, swimming, snorkelling and night kayaking – which usually includes the chance to experience phosphorescence – and then feast on a big BBQ before a walk on an island the next day and 3pm arrival back at Paihia. Six-berth dorms ($178) and private cabins ($396) all have sea views. Dinner and breakfast included, but not drinks. ~~Take a sleeping bag.~~

KAYAKING

Coastal Kayakers ☏ 09 402 8105, ⓦ coastalkayakers .co.nz. Operates from the Paihia wharf and runs a variety of trips, from half-day paddles in the bay or upstream to Haruru Falls ($75) to three-day guided camping excursions (Nov–May; $685).

Pacific Coast Kayaks ☏ 09 436 1947, ⓦ nzsea kayaking.co.nz. Runs a number of wonderful multi-day guided trips in the outer reaches of the Bay of Islands and slightly further afield.

FLIGHTS AND PARASAILING

Flying Kiwi Paihia Wharf ☏ 0800 359 691. Offers ten- to fifteen-minute mostly tandem flights from the back of a speedboat to a height of around 245m ($99).
Salt Air Marsden Rd, near the Maritime Building

☏ 0800 472 582, ⓦ saltair.co.nz. Runs chopper flights ($220/20min to the Hole in the Rock; $305/30min up the coast) along with awesome fixed-wing flights to Cape Reinga (see p.189).

JET SKI AND SKYDIVE

★ **Tango Jetski Adventure** 1 Davis Cresent ☏ 0800 253 8754, ⓦ tangojetskitours.co.nz. The self-drive, speed-lover's way to see the seascape can cover a lot of ground in a relatively short period of time. Try the one-hour Island Blaster ($160).
★ **Ballistic Blondes** 1 Davis Cresent ☏ 0800 695

867, ⓦ skydiveballisticblondes.co.nz. Offers tandem jumps of 4877m ($420) and all manner of other deals (see Whangarei, p.151) as well as the opportunity, unique in New Zealand, of landing on the beach after getting an eye full of the Bay of Islands.

SCUBA DIVING

Dive HQ Williams Rd ☏ 0800 107 551, ⓦ divenz.com. Will take you out in the Bay of Islands or to the wrecks of the *Rainbow Warrior* (see p.179) and the scuttled navy frigate *Canterbury*. Two-tank dives including gear cost $229 ($279 for the wrecks if you don't have Advanced

Open Water certification).
Dive North ☏ 09 402 5369, ⓦ divenorth.co.nz. Does a great job, with dive options including a trip to two wrecks ($299 without AOW certification) and dives off the Cavalli Islands.

TRIPS FROM THE BAY OF ISLANDS

As the main tourist centre in Northland, the Bay of Islands acts as a staging post for forays further north, in particular for day-long bus tours to **Cape Reinga** and **Ninety Mile Beach** (see p.189) – arduous affairs lasting eleven hours, most of them spent stuck inside the vehicle. You're better off making your way up to Mangonui, Kaitaia or Ahipara and taking a trip from there, or saving your dollars and taking Salt Air's fixed-wing Cape Reinga Flight (see above), which takes in the beach, Bay of Islands and includes a field landing and short run to the cape itself.

Fullers Great Sights (see opposite) also runs Discover Hokianga (daily; 7hr 30min; $102), another epic tour visiting the **Hokianga Harbour**, taking a Footprints Waipoua tour to the giant **kauri trees**, and taking a look at the **Wairere Boulders**. Again you are better off getting closer and spending more time at the actual attractions.

Pompallier was built in 1842 as a printing works for the French Roman Catholic bishop Jean Baptiste François Pompallier. He had arrived three years earlier to find the Catholic word of God under siege from Anglican and Wesleyan tracts, translated into Maori. The missionaries built an elegant rammed-earth structure in a style typical of Pompallier's native Lyon. The press and paper were imported, and a tannery installed to make leather bookbindings. During the next eight years over a dozen titles of Catholic teachings were printed, comprising almost forty thousand volumes, which were some of the first books printed in Maori.

2

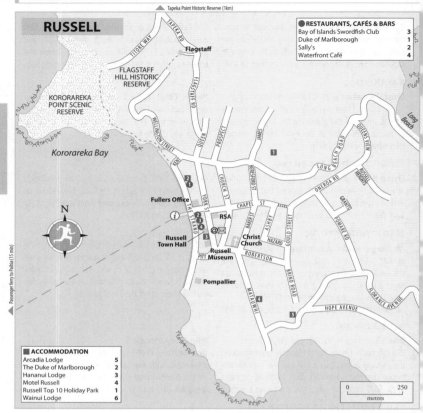

RUSSELL

Tapeka Point Historic Reserve (1km)

● **RESTAURANTS, CAFÉS & BARS**

Bay of Islands Swordfish Club	3
Duke of Marlborough	1
Sally's	2
Waterfront Café	4

Flagstaff

FLAGSTAFF HILL HISTORIC RESERVE

KORORAREKA POINT SCENIC RESERVE

Kororareka Bay

TITORE WAY · TAPEKA RD · FLAGSTAFF RD · WELLINGTON STREET · QUEEN · PROSPECT · JAMES · BERESFORD ST · CHURCH ST · YORK ST · CHAPEL ST · BAKER ST · ASHBY · HAZARD · GOULD STREET · ROBERTSON · BRIND ROAD · MATAUWHI · HOPE AVENUE · FLORANCE AVENUE · ONEROA RD · GRANT'S · POMARE RD · QUEENS VIEW · RUSSELL HEIGHTS · LONG BEACH ROAD · Long Beach

THE STRAND · KING

Fullers Office

ⓘ

RSA

Russell Town Hall

@

Christ Church

Russell Museum

Pompallier

N

Passenger ferry to Paihia (15 min)

■ **ACCOMMODATION**

Arcadia Lodge	5
The Duke of Marlborough	2
Hananui Lodge	3
Motel Russell	4
Russell Top 10 Holiday Park	1
Wainui Lodge	6

0 ———— 250
metres

In a building now restored to its 1842 state, artisans again produce handmade books, all best understood on the **free tours**, which explain the production processes in each room. You can even get your hands dirty in what is New Zealand's only surviving colonial tannery.

Christ Church
Robertson Rd

New Zealand's oldest church, the cream, weatherboard **Christ Church** was built in 1836 by local settlers – unlike most churches of similar vintage, which were mission churches. In the mid-nineteenth century the church was besieged during skirmishes between Hone Heke's warriors and the British, leaving several still-visible bullet holes.

Russell Museum
2 York St · Daily: Christmas–Jan 10am–5pm; Feb–Christmas 10am–4pm · $7.50 · ☎ 09 403 7701, ⑩ russellmuseum.org.nz

The small **Russell Museum** shows a video telling the town's history and contains great exhibits, including an impressive one-fifth scale model of Cook's *Endeavour*, which called in here in 1769. From the museum, a stroll along The Strand passes the prestigious *Bay of Islands Swordfish Club*, which was founded in 1924, and the *Duke of Marlborough Hotel* – the original building on this site held New Zealand's first liquor licence.

Flagstaff Hill and Tapeka Point Historic Reserve

30–40min return

At the end of The Strand, a short track climbs steeply to **Flagstaff Hill** (Maiki). The current flagpole was erected in 1857, some twelve years after the destruction of the fourth flagpole by Hone Heke, as a conciliatory gesture by a son of one of the chiefs who had ordered the original felling. The Confederation of Tribes flag, abandoned after the signing of the Treaty of Waitangi, is flown on twelve significant days of the year, including the anniversary of Hone Heke's death and the final day of the first New Zealand War. From Flagstaff Hill it's a further kilometre to the **Tapeka Point Historic Reserve**, a former *pa* site at the end of the peninsula – a wonderfully defensible position with great views and abundant evidence of terracing.

2

ARRIVAL AND DEPARTURE
RUSSELL

By ferry and car Most visitors reach Russell by ferry, but it's also accessible along the back road described on p.160. Foot passengers can take one of the three frequent passenger ferries (Oct–May 7am–10pm; June–Sept 7am–7pm; $7 one way, $12 return) between the main wharves in Paihia and Russell, a fifteen-minute journey.

INFORMATION AND TOURS

Russell Booking & Information Centre Located at the end of the wharf (daily: Sept–May 7.30am–8pm; June–Aug 8.30am–4pm; ☎ 0800 633 255, ⓦ russellinfo .co.nz). Makes bookings for local trips and accommodation. Also stocks the *Russell Heritage Trail* and *Bay of Islands Walks* leaflets.

Services There's daytime internet access at Enterprise Russell on York St.

Tour information Most of the bay's cruises and dolphin trips are based in Paihia but also pick up at Russell wharf (with prior reservation) around 15min later. Occasionally there are no pick-ups available, but you can catch the frequent, inexpensive passenger ferry between Paihia and Russell.

Fullers Russell Mini Tour ☎ 0800 646 486, ⓦ russell minitours.com. Offers a locals' view on the area's history and the town (six daily in the summer; $29).

ACCOMMODATION

Accommodation in Russell is much more limited than in Paihia and tends to be more upmarket, mostly B&Bs and lodges.

Arcadia Lodge 10 Florance Ave ☎ 09 403 7756, ⓦ arcadialodge.co.nz. Stylish B&B in an historic wooden house encircled by decks on a quiet hill overlooking cottage gardens and the bay. Five of the wooden-floored suites and rooms (one not en-suite) enjoy sea views and much of the produce is organic and grown in the garden, or locally. Free wi-fi. No under-15s. Two-night minimum in summer. Rooms $195, suites $340

★ **The Duke of Marlborough** 35 The Strand ☎ 09 403 7829, ⓦ theduke.co.nz. New owners have renovated and modernized to create a beating heart in the centre of the town. The ambience is of an old colonial hotel until you get into your room, at which point it becomes modern with a hint of romance. Some rooms have sea views, others sundecks, and there are a few cosy options with neither. Rooms $190, rooms with sundecks $290, rooms with sea views $360

Hananui Lodge 4 York St ☎ 09 403 7875, ⓦ hananui .co.nz. Well-run, modernized motel-style place by the water. The waterfront suites have the best views but even the standard units are comfortable, with sea glimpses, and all get spa access. There are also new apartments across the road with big-screen TV and a/c. Units $190, apartments $220, suites $320

Motel Russell 16 Matauwhi Rd ☎ 0800 240 011, ⓦ motelrussell.co.nz. Choose one of the comfortable, recently modernized units in an acre of well-tended subtropical garden full of birds surrounding this simple motel with an attractive pool. Studios $120, one-bedroom units $180

Russell Top 10 Holiday Park Long Beach Rd ☎ 09 403 7826, ⓦ russelltop10.co.nz. Central, well-ordered and spotless campsite with tent and campervan sites and an extensive range of high-standard cabins and motel units. Rates rise appreciably from Dec 20–late Jan. Camping $20, campervans $49, cabins $80, kitchen cabins $110, open-plan units $170, motel units $180

Wainui Lodge 92d Wahapu Rd, 7km south of Russell ☎ 09 403 8278, ⓦ bay-of-islands.pelnet.org. Excellent, tiny five-room backpackers with morning birdsong and kayaking from its own mangrove-lined beach. Closed June, July & Aug. Dorm $25, room $64

2

EATING AND DRINKING

Russell has a limited range of restaurants and prices are fairly high, but quality is good. For drinking the best bets are often the cheap private clubs – the *RSA* on Cass Street and the *Bay of Islands Swordfish Club* – which both welcome visitors, or the popular bar at *The Duke of Marlborough*.

Bay of Islands Swordfish Club 25 The Strand ☎09 402 7773. Technically a private club, much the same as the one in Paihia (see p.168), so you just sign yourself in or get the bartender to do it. Always a winner for cheap beer, fish and chips, simple bar meals (mains around $24) in big portions, and great sunset views from the veranda. Daily 4pm–late.

★ **Duke of Marlborough** 35 The Strand ☎09 403 7829, ⓦ theduke.co.nz. Waterside bar seating, a pub bar at the back and a restaurant all serving a broad range of wine and beer. Best of all is the food, stunningly presented in imaginative combinations and generous portions.

King on the menu is the 8hr cooked shoulder of lamb on the bone ($49 for two), which melts in the mouth and could feed a coach party. Daily 7.30am–late.

★ **Sally's** 25 The Strand ☎09 403 7652. Convivial, unpretentious and always busy licensed restaurant that's strong on seafood (mains around $32), and especially seafood chowder ($13). It's worth booking ahead in peak season. Mains around $32. Daily 10.30am–9pm.

Waterfront Café 23 The Strand. Simple café with waterfront seating, and great coffee, home-made muffins, cakes, pies and scones ($4–15), as well as all-day breakfasts and hearty lunches. Daily 8am–5pm; closed Mon in winter.

Kerikeri

KERIKERI, 25km north of Paihia, is central to the history of the Bay of Islands and yet geographically removed from it, strung out along the main road and surrounded by the orchards that form Kerikeri's economic mainstay. Two kilometres to the east of town, the thin ribbon of the Kerikeri Inlet forces its way from the sea to its tidal limit at **Kerikeri Basin**, the site chosen by Samuel Marsden for the Church Missionary Society's second mission in New Zealand.

For most of the year it's possible to get **seasonal work** weeding, thinning or picking in the subtropical orchards among citrus, tamarillos, feijoas, melons, courgettes, peppers and kiwifruit. Work is most abundant from January to July. The best contacts are the managers of the hostels and campsites, many of which also offer good weekly rates. In recent years Kerikeri has earned itself a reputation for its high-quality **craft shops** dotted among the orchards.

Kerikeri's past importance is evident at peaceful Kerikeri Basin, nearly 2km northeast of the current town where a few buildings have stood the test of time.

Kerikeri Mission House

246 Kerikeri Rd • Daily: Nov–April 10am–5pm; May–Oct 10am–4pm; entry by guided tour only; call ahead for tour times and prices • ☎ 09 407 9326, ⓦ historicplaces.org.nz

It was here, in 1821, that mission carpenters started work on what is now New Zealand's oldest European-style building, **Kerikeri Mission House** (access by guided tour when four or more accumulate; $10), a restrained two-storey Georgian colonial affair. The first occupants, missionary John Butler and family, soon moved on, and by 1832 the house was in the hands of lay missionary and blacksmith James Kemp, who extended the design. Since the last of the Kemps moved out in 1974 it has been restored, furnished in mid-nineteenth-century style, and surrounded by colonial-style gardens.

Old Stone Store

246 Kerikeri Rd • Daily: Nov–April 10am–5pm; May–Oct 10am–4pm • Free; upper floors $10 • ☎ 09 407 9326, ⓦ historicplaces.org.nz

Mission House guided tours start next door at the **Old Stone Store**, the only other extant building from the mission station and the country's oldest stone building, constructed mostly of local stone, with keystones and quoins of Sydney sandstone. Completed in 1836 as a central provision store for the Church Missionary Society, it successively served as a munitions store for troops garrisoned here to fight Hone Heke, then a kauri-trading store and a shop, before being opened to the public in 1975.

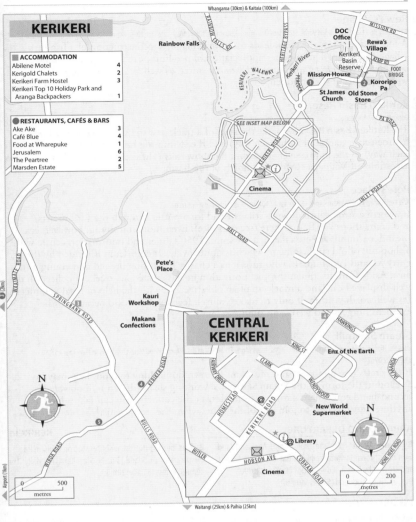

KERIKERI

ACCOMMODATION
Abilene Motel	4
Kerigold Chalets	2
Kerikeri Farm Hostel	3
Kerikeri Top 10 Holiday Park and Aranga Backpackers	1

RESTAURANTS, CAFÉS & BARS
Ake Ake	3
Café Blue	4
Food at Wharepuke	1
Jerusalem	6
The Peartree	2
Marsden Estate	5

CENTRAL KERIKERI

Waitangi (25km) & Paihia (25km)

The ground-floor **store** (free) sells some goods almost identical to those on offer almost 180 years ago, most sourced from the original manufacturers. You can still buy the once-prized Hudson Bay trading blankets, plus copper and cast-iron pots, jute sacks, gunpowder tea, old-fashioned sweets, and preserves made from fruit grown in the mission garden next door. The two **upper floors** admirably outline the history of Maori and European contact and the relevance of Kerikeri Basin, aided by old implements, including a hand-operated flour mill from around 1820, thought to be the oldest piece of machinery in the country.

From opposite the Old Stone Store, a path along the river leads to **Kororipo Pa**, which commands a hill on a prominent bend in the river from where local chief Hongi Hika launched attacks on other tribes using newly acquired firearms.

Rewa's Village

1 Landing Rd • Daily: Dec & Jan 9am–5pm; late Oct–April 9.30am–4.30pm; May–late Oct 10am–4pm • $5

A footbridge across the creek leads to **Rewa's Village**, a reconstruction of a fishing village where you'll get a better appreciation of pre-European Maori life. It comes complete with *marae*, weapons and *kumara* stores, as well as an authentic *hangi* site with an adjacent shell midden.

Kerikeri Basin Reserve

Opposite Rewa's Village

The **Kerikeri Basin Reserve** marks the start of a track past the site of Kerikeri's first hydroelectric station (15min each way) and the swimming holes at Fairy Pools (35min each way) to the impressively undercut **Rainbow Falls** (1hr each way). The latter are also accessible off Waipapa Road, 3km north of the Basin.

Pete's Place

460 Kerikeri Rd • Daily 10am–4pm • $10 • ☎ 09 407 7618, ⊛ petesmuseum.co.nz

It's worth a stroll south down Kerikeri Road for a potter through the various arts and crafts shops you'll find there (see opposite). Even more intriguing, however, is a meander around ★ **Pete's Place**, a museum, 1950's diner and information centre with a shop full of old stuff, some of which is quite lovely. The museum is funded by the entry fee and Pete himself, who runs it as a charity benefiting the old and young of the area. Aside from his philanthropic motivation he has created an excellent collection of well-displayed cars and a mock-up of an old street, all with the help of local volunteers. It's well worth visiting, if only to make yourself feel good and also because of the excellent burgers and ice-cream sundaes.

Steam Sawmill

Inlet Rd, 4km east of town • Mon–Fri 9am–4pm; tours Mon–Fri 10.30am & 1.30pm; closed from Christmas to New Year • $7.50 • ☎ 09 407 9707

If the crafts (see opposite) and museums in town do nothing for you, help may be at hand in the form of the **Steam Sawmill**, a working steam-driven mill powered by second-hand equipment garnered from all over the country. You can take a look anytime, but it is best to join one of the tours when the steam whistle is blown.

ARRIVAL AND DEPARTURE   KERIKERI

By plane Air New Zealand flights from Auckland land 5km out of town towards Paihia at Bay of Islands Airport and are met by Dial-A-Ride shuttles (☎ 021 498 790). Destinations Auckland (5 daily: 40min).

By bus InterCity/Northliner buses stop on Cobham Rd. Destinations Auckland (3 daily; 5hr); Kaitaia (1 daily; 1hr 40min); Paihia (3 daily; 20min).

INFORMATION

Tourist information There's no official visitor centre, but you can pick up leaflets inside the foyer of the library on Cobham Rd (Mon–Fri 8am–5pm, Sat 9am–2pm, Sun 9am–1pm), which also has internet access ($2/20min).

DOC 34 Landing Rd (Mon–Fri 8am–4.30pm; ☎ 09 407 0300). Advises on local walks and more ambitious treks into the Puketi Forest (see p.178).

ACCOMMODATION

Kerikeri has a good selection of accommodation in all categories, particularly budget places – a consequence of the area's popularity with long-stay casual workers. Seasonal price fluctuations are nowhere near as marked as in Paihia, though it's still difficult to find accommodation in January.

Abilene Motel 136 Kerikeri Rd ☎ 0800 224 536, ⊛ abilenemotel.co.nz. Centrally located, older-style, ten-unit motel (some of which are for families) in a garden setting with a solar-heated pool, spa and Sky TV and run by a couple of country and western fans. **$130**

Kerigold Chalets 326 Kerikeri Rd ☎ 0800 537 446,

ⓦkerigoldchalets.co.nz. Modern, spacious and spotless one-bedroom stand-alone wooden chalets with kitchens and access to a communal pool and barbecue area. Breakfast available on request. **$215**

★ **Kerikeri Farm Hostel** SH10, 5km west of Kerikeri ☏09 407 6989, ⓦkkfarmhostel.blogspot.com. Top-class bunk-free hostel on an organic citrus orchard, with comfortable dorms and rooms in a lovely wooden house. The owners speak German, there's free internet and wi-fi, an outdoor pool and free-range eggs are available. Dorm

$27, rooms $56, en suites $80

★ **Kerikeri Top 10 Holiday Park and Aranga Backpackers** Kerikeri Rd ☏0800 272 642, ⓦaranga .co.nz. Large, beautiful streamside site on the edge of town with a spacious camping area, well-equipped standard cabins with good weekly rates, comfortable self-contained units and a separate backpackers section (prices vary depending on length of stay). There's the occasional sound of kiwi in the night, and free kayaks to paddle up the river. Camping $18, dorms $30, cabins $80, units $145

EATING, DRINKING AND ENTERTAINMENT

★ **Café Blue** Kerikeri Rd, 3km west of town ☏09 407 5150, ⓦcafeblue.co.nz. Excellent licensed café for breakfast and lunch in a pretty garden setting. Dishes ($7–20) include a fine range of wraps, grills, pasta dishes and lighter choices, all prepared with care. Great coffee and cakes served outside or in the airy interior. Mon–Fri 8am–3pm, Sat & Sun 9am–3pm.

★ **Food at Wharepuke** 190 Kerikeri Rd ☏09 407 8936, ⓦfoodatwharepuke.co.nz. Stunning Thai-European fusion garden café serving high-quality nosh ($14–28) including Toulouse sausages, roast pork and tom yum with tiger prawns, to name but a few. Also plays some lounge-like live music to entertain diners. Tues–Sun 9am–late.

Jerusalem Cobblestone Mall ☏09 407 1001, ⓦcafe jerusalem.co.nz;. Small, friendly, licensed Israeli café beloved by Northlanders for its authentic, low-cost and wonderfully aromatic Middle Eastern dishes to eat in or take away, including falafel, *levivot* and *metuvlum* ($4–18). Closed Sun.

The Peartree 215 Kerikeri Rd ☏09 407 8479, ⓦthepeartree.co.nz. With a fabulous setting by Kerikeri Basin this spot is best used for midday tipples or sundowners, but if you're too lazy to get lunch or dinner elsewhere you can eat here in a semi-formal atmosphere, inside or on the veranda. Typical menu items are twice-baked kumara soufflé and tempura-battered fish and chips (mains around $32). Daily 10am–10pm.

WINERIES

Ake Ake Vineyard 165 Waimate North Rd ☏09 407 8230, ⓦakeakevineyard.co.nz. Vineyard producing intriguing wines (including Chambourcin, which has become a favourite with Northland grape growers) that's open for tastings ($5), vineyard tours ($5, refunded with any purchase) and for lunch or dinner (mains $26–36), including the likes of Denver leg of venison with parsnip, kumara and horopito dauphinoise. Tastings 10am–5pm; vineyard tours daily in summer 11.30am. Closed Mon & Tues.

Marsden Estate Wiroa Rd ☏09 407 9398, ⓦmarsdenestate.co.nz. A medium-sized winery producing a broad variety of excellent reds and whites sampled through free tastings, or in larger quantities in the moderately priced lunch restaurant. Well worth a taste are the French onion tart, the Basque seafood stew and the marinated Vietnamese beef salad (mains $15–27). Daily 10am–5pm.

CINEMA

Cathay Cinemas Hobson Avenue ☏09 407 4428. Entertainment is thin on the ground in Kerikeri, so thank goodness for this lovingly restored cinema showing mainstream and more off-beat movies, with three screens and a licensed café.

SHOPPING

You could easily spend a couple of hours pottering around the **craft outlets** that dominate the Kerikeri hinterland, guided by the free and widely available *Kerikeri Art & Craft Trail* leaflet: most places are open daily from 9am–5pm.

The Kauri Workshop 500 Kerikeri Rd ☏09 407 9196. Stocks anything you might hope to make from kauri, including spoons, bowls and carvings. Open daily.

Makana Confections 504 Kerikeri Rd ☏09 407 6800.

Boutique shop produces handmade chocolates, which you can see being made and then, of course, sample. It's hard not to leave with your wallet a little lighter. Daily 9am–5.30pm.

Around Kerikeri

At first glance the area around Kerikeri isn't the most inspiring part of Northland, but it is characterized by a few historic locations, some good walks and one magical tour that reveals bubbling mud beneath the otherwise peaceful surface of the earth.

2

Te Waimate Mission House

15km southwest of Kerikeri • Nov–April daily 10am–5pm; May–Oct Mon, Wed, Sat & Sun 10am–4pm • $10 • ☎ 09 405 9734,
Ⓦ tewaimatemission.co.nz

WAIMATE NORTH is home to the colonial Regency-style **Te Waimate Mission House**,
New Zealand's second-oldest European building. Now virtually in the middle of
nowhere, in the 1830s this was the centre of a vigorous **Anglican mission**. Missionaries
were keen to add European agricultural techniques to the literacy and religion they
were teaching the Maori, and by 1834 locally grown wheat was milled at the river,
orchards were flourishing and crops were sprouting – all impressing Charles Darwin,
who visited the following year. The house, built by converts from local kauri in 1832,
has been restored as accurately as possible to its original design. Guided tours highlight
prize possessions.

Kaikohe and the Hidden Walk

Kaikohe is on SH12, southwest of Waimate North • Hidden Walk by appointment only; phone or stop in at Kaikohe Photographic Centre,
89 Broadway • $28 • ☎ 021 277 7301, Ⓦ hiddenwalks.com

The primary reason to stop in **KAIKOHE**, almost equidistant from both coasts, is the
magical Hidden Walk, a guided tour through a section of the Ngawha Valley. The
tour begins inauspiciously with a meeting in the car park of the local golf club, but
after that it just gets better and better. Situated on private land is a large thermally
active area of bubbling mud and springs, where ancient kauri lay scattered by the
extraordinary natural forces unleashed over thousands of years. Among the various
bubbling pools are examples of everything you will see in Rotorua (see p.265),
just on a smaller scale and in a situation that enables you to get closer and lacks the
commercialism of New Zealand's most famous thermal town. The trip then moves
on to the remaining bones of a mercury extraction plant, some intermingled in
native regrowth, the remainder in ghostly clearings full of rusty, calcified and broken
remnants of human occupation. Trying to unravel how the various ruins fit together
and how the workers went about their tasks is an archeological puzzle that will have
you scratching your head for days after the tour.

Ngawha Springs

7km southeast of Kaikohe • Daily 9am–9pm • $9

If you have time and the need of some relaxation, soak your bones at **Ngawha Springs**
(pronounced "Naf-fa"), where eight individual pools (all with different mineral
contents and at different temperatures) are enclosed by native timber, but otherwise
uncluttered by tourist trappings or, for the most part, other people.

Puketi Kauri Forest

20km north of Kaikohe

The **Puketi Kauri Forest** comprises one of the largest continuous tracts of kauri forest
in the north. Signposted routes from Kaikohe and Kerikeri lead to the **Manginangina
Kauri Walk** where a five-minute boardwalk through lush forest brings you to a stand of
good-sized kauri.

ACCOMMODATION AND TOURS   AROUND KERIKERI

Puketi Recreation Area Campsite 2km south of Puketi
Kauri Forest Ⓦ doc.govt.nz. A wee, bog-standard DOC campsite in the Puketi Forest about 20km north of Kerikeri, with
running water, long-drop toilets, cold showers, BBQs and
picnic tables. No bookings; leave the fee in the honesty box. $8

Adventure Puketi 476 Puketi Rd ☎ 09 401 9095,
Ⓦ forestwalks.com. Runs a number of walks, one of which
takes place at night (2hr; $75), along the Manginangina
Kauri Walk (see above), with the hope of encountering
kiwi, morepork and other night owls.

Matauri Bay to the Karikari Peninsula

North of the Bay of Islands everything gets a lot quieter. There are few towns of any consequence along the coast and it is the peace and slow pace that attract visitors to an array of glorious beaches and the lovely Whangaroa Harbour. The first stop north of Kerikeri is tiny **Matauri Bay**, where a hilltop memorial commemorates the Greenpeace flagship, *Rainbow Warrior*, which now lies off the coast. A sealed but winding back road continues north, offering fabulous sea views and passing gorgeous headlands and beaches before delivering you to **Whangaroa Harbour**, one of the most beautiful in Northland, and an excellent place to go sailing or kayaking. Further north is the idyllic surfing and fishing hideaway of **Taupo Bay**.

Continuing north brings you to the huge bite out of the coast called **Doubtless Bay**, which had two celebrated discoverers: Kupe, said to have first set foot on Aotearoa in **Taipa**; and Cook, who sailed past in 1769 and pronounced it "doubtless, a bay". Bounded on the west and north by the sheltering **Karikari Peninsula**, the bay offers safe boating and is popular with Kiwi vacationers. In January you can barely move here and you'll struggle to find accommodation, but the shoulder seasons can be surprisingly quiet, and outside December, January and February room prices drop considerably. Most of the bay's facilities cluster along the southern shore of the peninsula in a string of beachside settlements – **Coopers Beach**, **Cable Bay** and **Taipa Bay** – running west from picturesque **Mangonui**.

Matauri Bay

A high inland ridge provides a dramatic first glimpse of the long, Norfolk-pine-backed **MATAURI BAY**, 20km north of Kerikeri, and the **Cavalli Islands** just offshore. At the northern end of the main bay a well-worn path (20min return; 70m ascent) climbs to

---

FRENCH NUCLEAR TESTING IN THE PACIFIC

Claiming that nuclear testing was completely safe, the French government for decades conducted tests on the tiny Pacific atolls of **Mururoa** and **Fangataufa**, a comfortable 15,000km from Paris, but only 4000km northeast of New Zealand.

In 1966 France turned its back on the 1963 Partial Test Ban Treaty, which outlawed atmospheric testing, and relocated Pacific islanders away from their ancestral villages to make way for a barrage of tests over the next eight years. The French authorities claimed that "Not a single particle of radioactive fallout will ever reach an inhabited island" – and yet radiation was routinely detected as far away as Samoa, Fiji and even New Zealand. Increasingly antagonistic public opinion forced the French to conduct their tests underground in deep shafts, where another 200 detonations took place, threatening the geological stability of these fragile coral atolls.

In 1985, Greenpeace coordinated a New Zealand-based protest flotilla, headed by its flagship, the **Rainbow Warrior**, but before the fleet could set sail from Auckland, the French secret service sabotaged the *Rainbow Warrior*, detonating two bombs below the waterline. As rescuers recovered the body of Greenpeace photographer Fernando Pereira, two French secret service agents posing as tourists were arrested. Flatly denying all knowledge at first, the French government was finally forced to admit to what then Prime Minister David Lange described as "a sordid act of international state-backed terrorism". The two captured agents were sentenced to ten years in jail, but France used all its international muscle to have them serve their sentences on a French Pacific island; they both served less than two years before being honoured and returning to France.

In 1995, to worldwide opprobrium, France announced a further series of tests. Greenpeace duly dispatched *Rainbow Warrior II*, which was impounded by the French navy on the tenth anniversary of the sinking of the original *Rainbow Warrior*. In early 1996 the French finally agreed to stop nuclear testing in the Pacific.

Chris Booth's distinctive **Rainbow Warrior Memorial**, which remembers the Greenpeace flagship (see box, p.179), now scuttled off the Cavalli Islands. The memorial comprises a stone arch (symbolizing a rainbow) and the vessel's salvaged bronze propeller. Paihia-based dive operators (see p.171) run trips out to the wreck, 10 minutes offshore from Matauri Bay. The best visibility is in April; from September to November plankton sometimes obscure the view but it's still pretty good.

Samuel Marsden Memorial Church
Matauri Bay Rd, just before the beach

Missionary Samuel Marsden first set foot in Aotearoa in 1814 at Matauri Bay, where he mediated between the Ngati Kura people – who still own the bay – and some Bay of Islands Maori, a process commemorated by the quaint wooden **Samuel Marsden Memorial Church**. The Ngati Kura tell of their ancestral *waka*, *Mataatua*, which lies in waters nearby. It was the resonance of this legendary canoe that partly led the Ngati Kura to offer a final resting place to the wreck of the *Rainbow Warrior*.

Whangaroa Harbour
West of Matauri Bay, the virtually landlocked and sheltered **Whangaroa Harbour** is the perfect antidote to Bay of Islands' commercialism. The scenery, albeit on a smaller scale, is easily a match for its southern cousin and, despite the limited facilities, you can still get out on a cruise or to join the big-game fishers. Narrow inlets forge between cliffs and steep hills, most notably the two bald volcanic plugs, **St Paul and St Peter**, which rise behind the harbour's two settlements, **WHANGAROA** on the south side, and **TOTARA NORTH** opposite.

Brief history
Whangaroa Harbour was among the first areas in New Zealand to be visited by European pioneers, most famously those aboard the *Boyd*, which called here in 1809 to load kauri spars for shipping to Britain. A couple of days after its arrival, all 66 crew were killed and the ship burned by local Maori in retribution for the crew's mistreatment of Tara, a high-born Maori sailor who had apparently transgressed the ship's rules. A British whaler avenged the incident by burning the entire Maori village, sparking off a series of skirmishes that spread over the north for five years. Later the vast stands of kauri were hacked down and milled, some at Totara North. Even if you're just passing through, it's worth driving the 4km along the northern shore of the harbour to Totara North, passing the remains of this historic community's last sawmills, which ceased operation a few years back.

Taupo Bay
A sealed 13km road from SH10 brings you to **TAUPO BAY**, a blissfully undeveloped holiday community with a smattering of beach shacks, and some of the best surfing and rock and beach fishing in Northland.

Mangonui and around
With its lively fishing wharf and a traditional grocery perched on stilts over the water there's an antiquated air to **MANGONUI**, strung along the sheltered Mangonui Harbour off Doubtless Bay. A handful of two-storey buildings with wooden verandas have been preserved, some operating as craft shops or cafés, but this is still very much a working village. To get a feel for the layout of Mangonui Harbour, take in the views at **Rangikapiti Pa Historic Reserve**, off Rangikapiti Road, between Mangonui and Coopers Beach.

WHANGAROA HARBOUR AND DOUBTLESS BAY TOURS AND ACTIVITIES

If you can't afford to charter a boat to take you to the rugged, uninhabited and beautiful **Cavalli Islands**, ask at the wharf or the local dairy (☎09 405 0230). In Whangaroa Harbour, you will find a limited number of distractions – unless you are an angler, fancy a solitary hike or a peaceful kayak paddle.

WALKS

St Paul hike (30min return; 140m ascent). One of the most immediately rewarding walks is the hike up the volcanic dome of St Paul from the top of Old Hospital Rd in Whangaroa. The final few metres involve an easy scramble with fixed chains to assist.

Wairakau Steam Track (6km each way; 90min–2hr). Located on the harbour's north side, this DOC track runs from Totara North, past freshwater pools, mangroves and viewpoints to Pekapeka Bay.

FISHING

Whangaroa Big Gamefish Club ☎09 405 0399, ⓦ whangaroasportfishingclub.co.nz. The people you want to see if you want to go game fishing are listed on the website, or you can phone them, but don't just rock up to the bar and expect to go out that day. Charter rates typically kick off at $990/day, with bait and ice costing extra. Expect mostly marlin off the Cavalli Islands and more modest edible domestic fish closer to shore.

KAYAKING, SURFING AND DIVING

Northland Sea Kayaking ☎09 405 0381, ⓦ northlandseakayaking.co.nz. Located on the north-eastern flank of Whangaroa Harbour, this knowledgeable operator arranges local kayak trips in the summer ($75 half-day; no credit cards).

Isobar Surf 43 Mako St, Taupo Bay ☎09 406 0719, ⓦ isobarsurf.co.nz. Surfers of all levels can take lessons starting from $75 for 2hr. There are also overnight options, staying at the school's surf lodge (one night $210; five nights $199/night).

A to Z Diving Whatuwhiwhi ☎09 408 7077, ⓦ atoz diving.co.nz. Offers diving off the Karikari Peninsula (two-tank dive $185), plus trips to the *Rainbow Warrior* wreck, including gear.

Mangonui also makes a good base for organized trips to **Cape Reinga and Ninety Mile Beach** (see p.189).

Brief history

Mangonui means "big shark", recalling the legendary chief Moehuri's *waka* which was supposedly led into Mangonui Harbour by such a fish. But it was whales and the business of provisioning **whaling** ships that made the town: one story tells of a harbour so packed with ships that folk could leap between the boats to cross from Mangonui to the diminutive settlement of Hihi on the far shore. As whaling diminished, the kauri trade took its place, chiefly around Mill Bay, the cove five minutes' walk to the west of Mangonui.

Coopers Beach

While ships were repaired and restocked at Mangonui, barrels were mended a couple of kilometres west at **COOPERS BEACH**, a glorious and well-shaded sweep of sand backed by a string of motels. The beach is popular in January and at weekends, but at other times you may find you have it pretty much to yourself.

Cable Bay

About 3km west of Coopers Beach, the smaller swimming and surfing settlement of **CABLE BAY** is separated by the Taipa River from the beachside village of **TAIPA**, now the haunt of sunbathers and swimmers, but historically significant as the spot where Kupe, the discoverer of Aotearoa in Maori legend, first set foot on land. There's a concrete memorial to him near the Shell station by the Taipa River.

The Karikari Peninsula

Doubtless Bay to the east and Rangaunu Harbour to the west are bounded by the crooked arm of the **Karikari Peninsula**, which strikes north swathed in unspoiled golden- and white-sand beaches. Outside Christmas to mid-February, they have barely a soul on them. Apart from the large and modern **Karikari Estate** golf resort, vineyard and winery, facilities remain limited. There's no public transport, and without diving or fishing gear, you'll have to resign yourself to lazing on the beaches and swimming from them.

Puheke Scenic Reserve

About 15km from SH10 via Inland Rd

The initial approach across a low and scrubby isthmus is less than inspiring, but 10km on, a side road leads to the peninsula's west coast and the **Puheke Scenic Reserve**, a gorgeous, dune-backed beach that's usually deserted. Another fine white strand spans the nearby hamlet of **RANGIPUTA**.

The peninsula's main road continues past the Rangiputa junction to the community of **TOKERAU BEACH**, a cluster of houses and shops at the northern end of the grand sweep of Doubtless Bay.

Karikari Estate winery

1km north of Tokerau Beach · Daily from 11am · $15 for five tastings · ☎ 09 408 7222, ⓦ karikariestate.co.nz

Passing between an international-standard golf course and a hillside swathed in vines you soon reach **Karikari Estate winery**, situated in a monstrous resort estate, the northernmost in New Zealand. The winery produced its first vintage in 2003, has lovely views and you can, of course, sample the wares.

Maitai Bay

6km north of of Karikari Estate winery

The Karikari Peninsula saves its best until last: **Maitai Bay**, a matchless double arc of golden sand split by a rocky knoll, encompassed by a campsite (see opposite). Much of the site is *tapu* to local Maori, and you are encouraged to respect the sacred areas.

ARRIVAL AND INFORMATION

By bus There is little public transport in the form of local buses but the area is a stopping point for InterCity buses, which drop off and pick up daily on their way toward Auckland. InterCity/Northliner buses serve the Mangonui waterfront, reached on a 2km loop road of the SH10; they run once a day in each direction between Paihia and Kaitaia.

Destinations Paihia (1 daily; 1hr 20min).

Tourist information Waterfront Drive, opposite 4-Square grocery, Mangonui (Nov–Easter daily 10am–4pm; Easter–Oct Tues–Sat 10am–3pm; ☎ 09 406 2046). The volunteer-staffed visitor centre can point you to accommodation, both here and along the coast, and has internet access.

ACCOMMODATION

WHANGAROA HARBOUR

Kahoe Farms Hostel SH10, 1.5km north of the Totara North turn-off ☎ 09 405 1804, ⓦ kahoefarms.co.nz. A small and extremely hospitable backpackers on a working cattle farm with a dorm and rooms in a house with polished wood floors and more rooms (some en-suite) in a separate villa on the hill behind. The owner whips up superb home-made pizza, pasta and farm steak dinners, generous breakfasts and a fine espresso, plus there's kayak rental and hiking trails to some lovely swimming holes.

The daily InterCity/Northliner bus passes the farm. Dorm $30, rooms $70, en suites 80

TAUPO BAY

Taupo Bay Holiday Park 1070 Taupo Bay Rd ☎ 09 406 0315, ⓦ taupobayholidaypark.co.nz. One of the few places worth staying at in the area, much beloved by Kiwi holidaymakers for its ample camping, good communal facilities and no frills but modern cabins. Camping $17, cabins $59, self-contained cabins $140

MANGONUI

★ **Beach Lodge** 121 SH10, Coopers Beach ☎ 09 409 0068, ⓦ beachlodge.co.nz. Five breezy yet elegant water-view apartments, on the beachfront at Coopers Beach and within the sound of the waves, each with its own deck, full kitchen and free wi-fi. No under-8s. Summer rates start at $400

Carneval 360 SH10, Cable Bay ☎ 09 406 1012, ⓦ carneval.co.nz. Perched high on a hill overlooking the sea is this relaxed, Swiss-run house with comfortable spacious rooms and a stunning view of the coastline, plus a full Swiss breakfast if you can handle it. Rooms $190

★ **Driftwood Lodge** SH10, Cable Bay ☎ 09 406 0418, ⓦ driftwoodlodge.co.nz. Great lodge right beside the beach with views of the Karikari peninsula from the broad deck where everyone gathers for sundowners and perhaps a BBQ. Accommodation is in fully self-contained units and there's free access to dinghies, kayaks and boogie boards. It's popular, so book well ahead. Studios $125, apartments $145

Macrocarpa Cottage 2 Bush Point Rd, Taipa ☎ 09 406 1245, ✉ maccottage@xtra.co.nz. An open-plan, self-catering cottage at the water's edge with one queen room, and two singles on a mezzanine. It comes with a full kitchen and cable TV and offers fabulous views across the Taipa Estuary. Great choice for couples. $150

Mangonui Hotel Waterfront Drive/Beach Rd, Mangonui ☎ 09 406 0003, ⓦ mangonuihotel.co.nz. Century-old, traditional hotel opposite the harbour with an upstairs veranda. Dorms, singles and en-suite doubles are cheerfully decorated in bright colours and those with harbour views go quickly, so book ahead or arrive early. Dorms $30, singles $40, doubles $100

Puketiti Lodge 10 Puketiti Drive, 7km south of Mangonui ☎ 09 406 0369, ⓦ puketitilodge.co.nz. There's a rural feel to this modern lodge with three en-suite rooms and a deluxe dorm all with long views to the coast. Everyone has access to the huge deck and well-equipped kitchen and lounge. Rooms $150

KARIKARI PENINSULA

Maitai Bay Campground Maitai Bay Rd ⓦ doc.govt .co.nz. Northland's largest DOC campsite has cold showers, toilets and drinking water, as well as campervan access. DOC rangers service the site daily in the high season. Ideal for birdlife and wildlife watching. Camping $8

Whatuwhiwhi Top 10 Holiday Park Whatuwhiwhi Rd, 18km off SH10 ☎ 0800 142 444, ⓦ whatuwhiwhi top10.co.nz. Within easy walking distance of a picturesque bay and beach, this is a quiet, basic and traditional Kiwi campsite with a spa pool and good communal facilities. It gets very busy in the summer. Camping $20, cabins & kitchen cabins $62, units $93, deluxe units $135

EATING AND DRINKING

MATAURI BAY

Matauri Top Shop Top of Matauri Bay Rd ☎ 09 405 1040. A combined store and good-value café, this is the only place to stop for a bite in town, serving sandwiches, rolls and ice cream (nothing over $12), as well as offering a few supplies for you to make up a picnic, which might be preferable. Daily from 8am until it's not busy.

WHANGAROA HARBOUR

Whangaroa Big Gamefish Club ☎ 09 405 0399, ⓦ whangaroasportfishingclub.co.nz. Overlooking the yacht harbour, the café here serves snacks and lunches ($5–24) when the club bar upstairs opens. Both are pleasant enough, only ever crowded at the height of the summer or on Friday nights or Saturdays. The food is adequate but there's no other option. Daily 10.30am–4pm.

MANGONUI

Committed drinking mostly happens at the *Mangonui Hotel* (see above), which often has bands at weekends.

The Bakerman 118 Waterfront Rd ☎ 09 406 1233.

A cheap and cheerful café offering breakfasts and lunches, burgers and fresh baked bread, with none of it costing over $18. Daily 7am–4pm.

Fresh & Tasty Inside the Mangonui Hotel, Waterfront Drive ☎ 09 406 0082. Rival chippy to neighbouring *Mangonui Fish Shop*, and much frequented by locals happy to trade location for lower prices (under $15), less waiting time and equally good tucker, plus roast dinners if you can't stand fish. Open daily 11am–8pm.

Mangonui Fish Shop 137 Waterfront Drive ☎ 09 406 0478. Famed fish and chip restaurant idyllically set on stilts over the water, and a regular afternoon stop for returning Cape Reinga buses. Expect fresh-cooked fish, buckets of chips and some more healthy seafood-oriented salads and seafood chowder (all under £21). Licensed and BYO. Daily 8.30am–late.

★ **Waterfront Café** Waterfront Drive ☎ 09 406 0850. Decent café/bar with harbour views, good coffee, breakfasts, light lunches, a wide range of dinner mains including fine pizzas, seared scallops and fresh oysters (mains $28–36). Occasional live music. Daily 8am–late.

NIGHTLIFE, ENTERTAINMENT AND SHOPPING

Bush Fairy Dairy 1195 Oruru Rd, Peria, 12km south of Taipa ☎ 09 408 5508. An authentic hippie-style commune

that hosts Sunday bazaars every few weeks throughout the summer, complete with poetry readings and acoustic jam sessions around a bonfire. It's also brimming with art, crafts, clothing, organic produce, plus standard dairy items. Call ahead for dates and times.

Far North Wine Centre 60 Waterfront Drive, Mangonui ☎09 406 2485. You can sample – and purchase – wines from throughout Northland at this shop, which has a good selection and a knowledgeable staff. Daily 11am–4pm, closed Sundays in the winter.

Flax Bush 50 Waterfront Drive, Mangonui ☎09 406 1510, ⓦflaxbush.co.nz. Carries reasonably priced woven flax items and other locally made crafts; the deals on woven baskets (kete) are worth it. Mon–Sat 9.30am–4.30pm.

Swamp Palace Oruru Rd, 7km south of Taipa ☎09 408 7040. A quirky cinema located in the Oruru Community Hall. It caters to an eclectic mix of tastes – cult and classic movies, as well as the very latest releases. Call ahead for show times.

Kaitaia and around

KAITAIA, 40km west of Mangonui, is the Far North's largest commercial centre, situated near the junction of the two main routes north. It makes a convenient base for some of the best trips to Cape Reinga and Ninety Mile Beach (see p.189), far preferable to the longer trips from the Bay of Islands. As a farming service town you'd expect there'd be little to detain you, but these days Kaitaia boasts a rather fine museum, built in 2011. If you have your own transport, however, you might want to base yourself at the magnificent beach in nearby **Ahipara** (see opposite), to sand-toboggan the giant dunes, surf or explore the old gumfields.

Brief history

A Maori village already flourished at Kaitaia when the first missionary, Joseph Matthews, came looking for a site in 1832. The protection of the mission encouraged European pastoralists to establish themselves here, but by the 1880s they found themselves swamped by the gum diggers who had come to plunder the underground deposits around Lake Ohia and Ahipara. Many early arrivals were young Croats fleeing tough conditions in what was then part of the Austro-Hungarian Empire, though the only evidence of this is a Serbo-Croat welcome sign at the entrance to town, and a cultural society that holds a traditional dance each year.

Te Ahu Far North Regional Museum

Corner of Matthews Ave and South Rd • Mon–Fri 10am–4pm, Sat 10am–3pm • $4 • ☎0800 920 029, ⓦteahuheritage.org.nz

The best place to gain a sense of the area will be the new **Te Ahu Far North Regional Museum**, which was not complete at the time of writing but is expected to open some time in 2012. Expect arresting displays on local life and history, including the Ahipara gumfields. Other exhibits include the massive anchor from the *De Surville*, wrecked in 1769, and a copy of the twelfth- or thirteenth-century Kaitaia Carving (the original is in the Auckland Museum), a fine example of the transitional period during which Polynesian art began to take on Maori elements. The museum will also house a cinema and the local i-SITE.

KAITAIA FESTIVALS AND EVENTS

If you're in the area around the third weekend of March, you can catch competitors from around the world taking part in a series of running events on Ninety Mile Beach, including the **Te Houtaewa Challenge** (ⓦtehoutaewachallenge.com), named after the tale of a great Maori athlete. The races are preceded by the **Te Houtaewa Waka Ama Surf Challenge**, a series of six-man outrigger *waka* races at Ahipara, and the five-day **Kai Maori Food Festival** and **Te Houtaewa Arts & Crafts Festival**, both held in Kaitaia. Around the same time, the **Snapper Classic** (ⓦsnapperclassic.co.nz) is among the world's biggest **surfcasting** competitions, with a $30,000 prize for the largest snapper.

Ahipara

The southern end of Ninety Mile Beach finishes with a flourish at **AHIPARA**, 15km west of Kaitaia, a secluded scattered village that grew up around the Ahipara gumfields. A hundred kilometres of sand recede into sea spray to the north, while to the south the high flatlands of the Ahipara Plateau tumble to the sea in a cascade of golden dunes. Beach and plateau meet at **Shipwreck Bay**, a surf and swimming beach with an underground following with surfers for its long tubes (sometimes 400m or more). The bay is named after the 1870 wreck of the *Favourite*, its paddle-shaft still protruding from the sand. At low tide you can pick mussels off the volcanic rocks and follow the wave-cut platform around a series of bays for about 5km to the dunes – about an hour's walk – although most do it by quad bike or mountain bike.

Ahipara is a more appealing place to stay than Kaitaia, though there is no useful public transport, supermarket or bank.

The gumfields

On a sandy dune plateau to the south of town

At their peak in the early twentieth century, the now barren **gumfields** supported three hotels and two thousand people. Unlike most gumfields, where experimental probing and digging was the norm, here the soil was methodically excavated, washed and sieved to extract the valuable kauri gum (see box, p.195). None of the dwellings remains on the plateau, and the gumfields are an eerie, desolately beautiful spot.

ARRIVAL AND DEPARTURE

KAITAIA AND AROUND

By bus The daily InterCity/Northliner joint bus service pulls up just down the street from the Kaitaia i-SITE. Destinations Kerikeri (1 daily; 1hr 40min); Paihia (1 daily; 2hr).

By plane Kaitaia's airport is 9km north of town, near Awanui, and is serviced by taxi shuttle ☏ 09 408 0116. Destinations Auckland (1–2 daily; 45min).

AHIPARA TOURS AND ACTIVITIES

Ahipara offers good chances to explore the nearby **beach**, either on foot, by horse or on a quad bike. The **dunes** and **gumfields** are best approached on foot or via a guided quad bike tour. There have been access problems of late across Shipwreck Beach, due to disagreements between operators and the local *iwi*; check with the tour guides listed below for the latest information.

WALKS

Foreshore Road Walk (500m; 10min return) A short but worthwhile walk on a track that begins at the end of Foreshore Road. It takes you to the western end of the beach to a lookout giving spectacular views all the way to Cape Reinga.

Gumfields Walk (12km loop; free maps and tide times from the Ahipara Adventure Centre and Kaitaia i-SITE) Keen hikers might fancy tackling a 6hr section of this tide-dependent walk, which begins at the bridge at Shipwreck Bay and takes you into an eerie and desolate landscape of wind-sculpted dunes before heading back along the beach. Let someone know where you're going and take plenty of water.

TOUR OPERATORS

Tua Tua Tours ☏ 0800 494 288, ☒ ahipara.co.nz /tuatuatours. Runs a variety of tours, one of which is a three-hour quad bike safari tour (single $185; double $200) north of the settlement along the beach because of access restrictions (see above) to the south. Sand-boarding is included.

Ahipara Adventure Centre 15 Takahe St ☏ 09 409 2055, ☒ ahiparaadventure.co.nz. Rents single-rider quad bikes ($88/hr; $145/2hr) heading north of the settlement along the beach; neither company is currently allowed into Shipwreck Bay. They also rent surfboards, kayaks and mountain bikes (all $30/half-day), and blo-karts for use on the beach ($45/30min).

Ahipara Horse Treks Foreshore Rd ☏ 09 409 4122 or ☏ 027 333 8645. Saddle up for two-hour rides ($60) along the beaches and across some of the local farmland.

INFORMATION

i-SITE Corner of Matthews Ave and South Rd, in the Te Ahu Centre, Kaitaia (daily 8.30am–5pm; ☎09 408 9450, ⓦvisit farnorthnz.com). The office – one of three for the Far North region of Northland – stocks DOC leaflets such as *Kaitaia Area Walks* and *Cape Reinga and Te Paki Walks*, sells bus tickets, rents sand toboggans ($10/day), and has internet access.

ACCOMMODATION

KAITAIA

Outside the post-Christmas peak, rooms are plentiful and prices are generally lower than at the coastal resorts to the east.

Loredo 25 North Rd ☎0800 456 733, ⓦloredomotel .co.nz. Clean, well-maintained and ever-popular motel 1km north of the town centre with a pool, spa and barbecue area, run by an aging biker couple and boasting some simple but comfortable units. $140

★ **Mainstreet Lodge** 235 Commerce St ☎09 408 1275, ⓦmainstreetlodge.co.nz. A welcoming, well-equipped and deceptively large hostel that's alive with folk headed for the Cape (tours pick up from the hostel). The doubles are spacious and there are a number of dorm rooms. You can also do half-day bone-carving sessions here. Dorms $27, rooms $68, en suites $78

Waters Edge 25b Kitchener St ☎09 408 0870, ⓦwaters edgebandbkaitaia.co.nz. An attractive B&B – owned by the last lighthouse keeper at Cape Reinga – in a modern suburban house with lush gardens, a pool and cosy rooms. You can have dinner, too, by prior arrangement. $120

AHIPARA

Ahipara Bay Motel 22 Reef View Rd ☎09 408 2010, ⓦahiparabaymotel.co.nz. A choice of pleasant older motel units, or six excellent luxury versions with tremendous sea and beach views. There's a decent on-site restaurant – useful if you arrive late or on Sunday. Units $100, luxury units $200

★ **Ahipara Holiday Park** 164 Takahe St ☎0800 888 988, ⓦahiparaholidaypark.co.nz. The area's best camping option, just 300m from the sea, offering YHA discounts across the accommodation range, which includes good-value cabins, en-suite doubles and well-equipped self-contained cabins. Camping $17, basic cabins $65, en-suite doubles $75, self-contained cabins $95

Beach Abode 11 Korora St ☎09 409 4070, ⓦbeach abode.co.nz. The three well-appointed (and serviced) beachfront apartments here each come with free wi-fi, full kitchen, BBQ, deck, great sea views and a private path to the sand. No under-12s. Apartments $175

★ **Endless Summer Lodge** 245 Foreshore Rd ☎09 409 4181, ⓦendlessummer.co.nz. Well-managed hostel in an atmospheric 1880 timber homestead with kauri floors, right across the road from the beach; choose from comfortable doubles, twins or two four-bed dorms. There's also a BBQ, free boogie boards, and surfboard rental; surfing instruction can be arranged. Bookings by phone only. Dorms $28, rooms $75

EATING AND DRINKING

KAITAIA

★ **Beachcomber** 222 Commerce St ☎09 408 2010, ⓦbeachcomber.net.nz. Probably Kaitaia's best restaurant, serving a fairly standard range of meat and fish dishes (lunches $17; dinner mains $28–35), which all come with a visit to the salad bar. Try the prawn, chilli and lemon pasta or the lamb rump with roasted garlic and herbs. Mon–Sat 11am–5pm, closed Sun.

★ **Birdie's** 14 Commerce St ☎09 408 4935. Fantastic old-school café with inventive modern touches, which is open for breakfast until 3.30pm and serves up huge portions of hearty Kiwi food at modest prices (mains $15–25), including some rib-sticking chilli beef nachos and good eggs Benedict. Daily 8am–3.30pm & from 6pm–late in the summer.

AHIPARA

Bayview Restaurant and Bar Ahipara Bay Motel, 22 Reef View Rd ☎09 408 2010, ⓦahipara.co.nz /baymotel. Decent (for these parts) licensed restaurant that benefits from sea views and serves traditional dishes (mains $25–35), including seafood chowder ($10.50), lamb steaks with mint sauce ($25) and pork filet with apple ($25). Daily 11.30am–11pm.

Gumdiggers Café Takahe Rd ☎09 409 2012. Café and takeaway, serving good coffee, cakes and snacks, as well as some truly mammoth breakfasts. All the food is under $20. Daily 7am–2pm; opens in the evening from Christmas–Feb.

Ninety Mile Beach and Cape Reinga

Northland's exclamation mark is the **Aupori Peninsula**, a narrow, 100km-long finger of consolidated and grassed-over dunes ending in a lumpy knot of 60-million-year-old marine volcanoes. To Maori it's known as Te Hika o te Ika ("The tail of the fish"),

2

GOING IT ALONE ON NINETY MILE BEACH

Rental cars and private vehicles are not insured to drive on Ninety Mile Beach and for good reason. Vehicles frequently get bogged in the sand and abandoned by their occupants. As there are no rescue facilities near enough to get you out before the tide comes in, and mobile phone coverage is almost nil, you could end up with a long walk. Even in your own vehicle, **two-wheel-drives** aren't recommended, regardless of weather conditions, which can change rapidly.

If you are determined to take your own vehicle for the 70km spin along the beach, seek local advice and prepare your car by spraying some form of water repellent on the ignition system – CRC is a common brand. Schedule your trip to coincide with a receding tide, starting two hours after high water and preferably going in the same direction as the bus traffic that day; drive on dry but firm sand, avoiding any soft patches, and slow down to cross streams running over the beach – they often have deceptively steep banks. If you do get stuck in soft sand, lowering the tyre pressure will improve traction. There are several access points along the beach, but the only ones realistically available to ordinary vehicles are the two used by the tour buses: the southern access point at **Waipapakauri Ramp**, 6km north of Awanui, and the more dangerous northern one along **Te Paki Stream**, which involves negotiating the quicksands of a river – start in low gear and don't stop, no matter how tempting it might be to ponder the dunes.

recalling the legend of Maui hauling up the North Island ("the fish") from the sea while in his canoe (the South Island).

The most northerly accessible point is **Cape Reinga**, where the spirits of Maori dead depart this world. Beginning their journey by sliding down the roots of an 800-year-old pohutukawa into the ocean, they climb out again on Ohaua, the highest of the Three Kings Islands, to bid a final farewell before returning to their ancestors in Hawaiiki. The spirits reach Cape Reinga along **Ninety Mile Beach** (actually 64 miles long), which runs straight along the western side of the peninsula. Most visitors follow the spirits, though they do so in modern buses specifically designed for belting along the hard-packed sand at the edge of the surf – officially part of the state highway system – then negotiating the quicksands of Te Paki Stream to return to the road; for many, the highlight is **sandboarding** on a boogie board (or in a safer but less speedy toboggan) down the huge dunes that flank the stream. The main road runs more or less down the centre of the peninsula, while the western ocean is kept tantalizingly out of sight by the thin pine ribbon of the **Aupori Forest**. The forests, and the **cattle farms** that cover most of the rest of the peninsula, were once the preserve of gum diggers, who worked the area intensively early last century.

Awanui

The eastern and western roads around Northland meet at **AWANUI**, 8km north of Kaitaia, Maori for "Big River" – though all you'll find is a bend in a narrow tidal creek that makes a relaxing setting for the daytime *Big River Café*, serving a range of light meals.

Ancient Kauri Kingdom

229 SH 1F, 1km north of Awanui • Daily 8.30am–5.30pm; later in summer • Free • ☎ 09 406 7172, ⓦ ancientkauri.co.nz

Almost all buses to Cape Reinga stop at the **Ancient Kauri Kingdom**, a defunct dairy factory now operating as a sawmill, cutting and shaping huge peat-preserved kauri logs hauled out of swamps where they have lain for around 45,000 years. You can watch slabs of wood being fashioned into bowls, sculptures and breadboards but the emphasis is on the shop. Be sure to climb up to the mezzanine on the spiral staircase hewn out of the centre of the largest piece of swamp kauri trunk ever unearthed, a monster 3.5m in diameter.

Gumdiggers Park Ancient Buried Kauri Forest

171 Heath Rd, 3km off SH1 • Daily summer 9am–5pm • $12 • ☎ 09 406 7166, ⓦ gumdiggerspark.co.nz

The delightfully low-key **Gumdiggers Park Ancient Buried Kauri Forest** is the pick of the local attractions. It features an easy thirty-minute nature trail through shady manuka forest and includes a gum diggers' camp, holes that have been excavated to show the methods used for gum digging, huts illustrating the living conditions and a small kauri gum collection. There's a longer trail through the bush with information boards speculating on what knocked over the two giant Kauri forests thousands of years ago: tidal wave, meteor or earthquake. Be sure to check out the monstrous section of a kauri dating back 100,000 years. The main southern entrance to Ninety Mile Beach, the **Waipapakauri Ramp**, is just south of the park's turn-off.

Houhora and Pukenui

The Aupori Peninsula's two largest settlements, 30km north of Awanui, are scattered **HOUHORA** and the working fishing village of **PUKENUI**, 2km to the south, where good catches are to be had off the wharf. At Houhora, a 3km side road turns east to **Houhora Heads**. A further 10km north is the turn-off for Rarawa Beach, home to a great DOC campsite (see p.190).

Te Kao

The Maori Ngati Kuri people own much of the land and comprise the bulk of the population in these parts, particularly around **TE KAO**, 20km north of Houhora. Beside SH1, you'll spot the twin-towered Ratana Temple – one of the few remaining houses of the Ratana religion, which combines Christian teachings with elements of Maori culture and spiritual belief.

Parengarenga Harbour

12km north of Te Kao on SH1, then follow the Paua Rd

Straggling **Parengarenga Harbour** was the drop-off point for the limpet mines (delivered by yacht from New Caledonia) that were used in the 1985 sabotage of the *Rainbow Warrior*. Bends in the road occasionally reveal glimpses of the harbour's southern headland. In late February and early March, hundreds of thousands of bar-tailed godwits turn the silica sands black as they gather for their 12,000km journey to Siberia. Insect repellent is a must here.

Waitiki Landing to Spirits Bay

The last place of any consequence before the land sinks into the ocean is **WAITIKI LANDING**, 21km from Cape Reinga. If you are heading to Spirits Bay this is your last chance to buy petrol and milk. From Waitiki Landing a dirt road twists 15km to the gorgeous and usually deserted 7km sweep of **Spirits Bay** (Kapowairua), where you'll find a DOC campsite (see p.190).

Te Paki

The main road (SH1) continues towards Cape Reinga. After 4km you pass a turn-off to the **Te Paki Stream entrance** to Ninety Mile Beach, where there's a small picnic area and parking, plus a twenty-minute **hike** to huge sand dunes ideal for **sandboarding** or **tobogganing**. Equipment can be rented at several places from Kaitaia northwards; and also by calling ahead to Ahikaa Adventures (☎09 409 8228), who often rent boards from the Te Paki road end, right by the dunes.

Cape Reinga

The last leg to **Cape Reinga** (Te Rerenga Wairua: the "leaping place of the spirits") runs high through the hills before revealing magnificent views of the Tasman Sea and the huge dunes that foreshadow it. At road-end there's just a car park with toilets and a 800m-long interpretive trail to the Cape Reinga **lighthouse**, dramatically perched on a headland 165m above Colombia Bank, where the waves of the Tasman Sea meet the swirling currents of the Pacific Ocean in a boiling cauldron of surf. On clear days the **view** from here is stunning: east to the Surville Cliffs of North Cape, west to Cape Maria van Diemen, and north to the rocky **Three Kings Islands**, 57km offshore, which were named by Abel Tasman, who first came upon them on the eve of Epiphany 1643.

2

GETTING AROUND   NINETY MILE BEACH AND CAPE REINGA

You can explore **Ninety Mile Beach** and **Cape Reinga** independently if you have your own vehicle. If you don't, then the best way to see the region is on one of the many tours listed below.

By plane The best way to experience the phenomenal length of Ninety Mile Beach and the wild beauty of Cape Reinga is to take the Salt Air plane trip (see p.171).
By bus Bus tours all make a loop up the Aupori Peninsula, travelling SH1 in one direction and Ninety Mile Beach in the other, the order being dictated by the tide. Trips start from Kaitaia, Mangonui and Paihia in the Bay of Islands. Those from Paihia are the most numerous but far too long (11hr), most leaving daily at around 7.30am. They go via Kerikeri, Mangonui and Awanui in one direction and pass

Kaitaia and the kauri trees of the Puketi Forest in the other, with pick-ups along the way, but there is little time for sightseeing. Tours starting further north give you less time in the bus and more for exploring.
By 4WD A few operators offer a somewhat more personalized experience than bus trips, via tours in 4WD vehicles, usually for anywhere from two to six people.
By car You can drive yourself along Ninety Mile Beach, although doing so is fraught with potential difficulties (see box, p.187).

TOURS

FROM KAITAIA AND AHIPARA
Far North Outback Adventures Kaitaia ✆09 408 0927, ⊛farnorthtours.co.nz. Exclusive 4WD custom tours (8hr; $650 for up to two passengers; $700 for three to six passengers) that include morning tea and

lunch. They go off the beaten track, taking in the white sands of Great Exhibition Bay to explore flora, fauna and archeological sites.
Harrisons Cape Runner Kaitaia ✆0800 227 373, ⊛ahipara.co.nz/caperunner. Bargain, basic coach tour

---

CAPE REINGA WALKS

A couple of worthwhile short **walks** radiate from the Cape Reinga car park: both form part of the much longer Cape Reinga Coastal Walkway. All are described in the DOC leaflet *Cape Reinga and Te Paki Walks*, containing a useful map of the area, and are available at Kaitaia and elsewhere. Beware of **rip tides** on all the beaches hereabouts and bear in mind the wild and unpredictable nature of the region's weather. Arrange with one of the more local bus tours (see above) for pick-up.

Cape Reinga Coastal Walkway (38km one-way; 2 days; constantly undulating). This spectacular and increasingly popular coastal hike starts at Kapowairua (Spirits Bay), heads west to Cape Reinga, continues to Cape Maria van Diemen, swings southeast to the northernmost stretch of Ninety Mile Beach, and then finally past the impressive dunes of Te Paki Stream. You need to be fit and self-sufficient: the only facilities are a couple of DOC campsites, and some ad hoc camping spots with no guaranteed water. Fresh water

from streams is limited and you'll need mosquito repellent.
Sandy Bay (3km return; 200m ascent on the way back; 50–90min). Eastbound walk through scrub and young cabbage trees to a pretty cove. You can continue to the lovely Tapotupotu Bay (a further 3km one-way; 1–2hr).
Te Werahi Beach (2.5km return; 200m ascent on the way back; 40min–1hr). A gradually descending westbound walk that keeps Cape Maria van Diemen in your sights as you go.

(8hr; $50) including the Cape, beach, Kaitaia pick-up and a light lunch.

Sand Safaris Kaitaia ☎ 0800 869 090, ⓦ sandsafaris .co.nz. Good-value tour (8hr; $60) that's similar to Harrisons but with Ahipara pick-ups and a Maori welcome. A light lunch is included.

FROM MANGONUI

Paradise 4X4 Tours ☎ 0800 494 392, ⓦ paradisenz .co.nz. The standard bus tour (including pick-up from your accommodation) is $75, and there are 4WD customized tours for two to four people ($800 for the vehicle) with a gourmet lunch.

FROM PAIHIA

Awesome NZ ☎ 0800 653 339, ⓦ awesomenz.com. Cape bus trip ($115) aimed at those with an adventurous spirit, with maximum sandboarding time. The cost of a lunch stop at Mangonui for fish and chips comes out of your own pocket.

Dune Rider ☎ 09 402 8681, ⓦ explorenz.co.nz. Upscale cape and beach trips ($145) in a comfortable high-clearance bus with reclining seats. Included in the cost are a stop at and guided tour of Gumdiggers Park, plus a lunch.

Salt Air ☎ 0800 475 582, ⓦ saltair.co.nz. Fly to the cape, landing at Waitiki, then cover the last section to Cape Reinga by 4WD ($425). Includes refreshments at Tapotupotu Bay and sandboarding, as well as a flight across the Bay of Islands.

INFORMATION

i-SITE The Far North region offices in Paihia (see p.167), Kaitaia (see p.186) and, if you're coming via Hokianga, in Opononi (see p.193), should be able to answer all your questions, including those pertaining to Ninety Mile Beach and Cape Reinga.

Services As with the rest of rural Northland, there is a paucity of facilities here. You can refuel at Houhora; petrol isn't always available in Waitiki.

ACCOMMODATION

There's sporadic accommodation along the Aupori Peninsula, ranging from some beautifully sited DOC campsites to motels, lodges and hostels. Most are reasonably priced, reflecting the fact that many visitors pass through without stopping; however, all are very busy immediately after Christmas.

PUKENUI

Rarawa Beach Campsite 10km north of Pukenui, down a signposted side road. The pure white silica sand at this shady, streamside DOC campsite is beautiful, and a great place for birdwatching and swimming in the lagoon – although abundant mosquitoes temper its paradisiacal appeal. Amenities include running water, toilets and cold showers. $7

★ **Wagener Holiday Park** 3km south of Pukenui, off SH1 ☎ 09 409 8511, ⓦ wagenerholidaypark.co.nz. A beautifully located, traditional, council-run campsite with great-value accommodation under canvas or in cabins, all nestled among tall trees with great views of the sea and just 500m from the Houhora Wharf. Camping $14, cabin $46, self-contained cabin $50

SPIRITS BAY

Kapowairua (Spirits Bay) campsite Spirits Bay Rd, 16km from Waitiki Landing. A simple DOC site with pitches in manuka woods, and campervan access. It has cold showers, running water and toilets, and is also ideal for fishing, swimming and walking. $7

CAPE REINGA

Tapotupotu Bay campsite Tapotupotu Rd, 3km south of Cape Reinga. A serene DOC site with toilets, cold showers, running water and lots of mosquitoes in the summer. It's beautifully sited where the beach meets the estuary and is a popular lunchtime picnic stop for tour buses. $7

EATING

Houhora Tavern Saleyard Ave, just off SH1, Pukenui ☎ 09 409 8805, ⓦ houhoratavern.co.nz. New Zealand's northernmost pub, dating from the 1800s, with lawns beside the harbour and great views, as well as one room with stuffed fish beside a saltwater aquarium. Basic meals that come with chips for the most part, fish and-, burger and-, as well as home-made pies and sausage rolls and decent coffee, all for under $25. Daily 9am–11pm.

★ **Pukenui Pacific Bar and Cafe** 816 Far North Rd (SH1), Pukenui ☎ 09 409 8816. Diners are often defeated by the huge burger known as PukuNui (Maori for "big stomach") at this good-value café-bar, the only takeaway north of Kaitaia (mains $10–25). Daily 11am–11pm in the summer.

Hokianga Harbour

South of Kaitaia, the narrow, mangrove-flanked fissures of the **Hokianga Harbour** snake deep inland past tiny and almost moribund communities. For a few days' relaxation, the tranquillity and easy pace of this rural backwater are hard to beat. From the southern shores, the harbour's incredible, deep-blue waters beautifully set off the mountainous **sand dunes** of North Head. The dunes are best seen from the rocky promontory of South Head, high above the treacherous Hokianga Bar, or can be reached by boat for sandboarding or the fantastic Sandtrails Hokianga tours (see p.193). The high forest ranges immediately to the south make excellent hiking territory, and the giant kauri of the Waipoua Forest are within easy striking distance.

Note that there are **no banks** between Kaitaia and Dargaville, 170km away to the south. The ATMs in Rawene and Omapere accept a limited range of cards so bring cash.

2

Brief history

According to legend, it was from here that the great Polynesian explorer **Kupe** left Aotearoa to go back to his homeland in Hawaiiki during the tenth century, and the harbour thus became known as Hokianganui-a-Kupe, "the place of Kupe's great return". Cook saw the Hokianga Heads from the *Endeavour* in 1770 but didn't realize what lay beyond, and it wasn't until a missionary crossed the hill from the Bay of Islands in 1819 that Europeans became aware of the harbour's existence. Catholics, Anglicans and Wesleyans soon followed, converting the local Ngapuhi, gaining their trust, intermarrying with them and establishing the well-integrated Maori and European communities that exist today. The Hokianga area soon rivalled the Bay of Islands in importance and notched up several firsts: European boat building began here in 1826; the first signal station opened two years later; and the first Catholic Mass was celebrated in the same year.

With the demise of kauri felling and milling (see p.195), Hokianga became an economic backwater, but over the last couple of decades, city dwellers, artists and craftspeople have started creeping in, settling in **Kohukohu** on the north shore, **Rawene**, a short ferry ride away to the south, and the two larger but still small-time settlements of **Opononi** and **Omapere**, opposite the dunes near the harbour entrance.

Kohukohu

Heading south from Kaitaia, the hilly SH1 twists its way through the forested Mangamuka Ranges for 40km to reach **Mangamuka Bridge** from where an equally tortuous road heads to **KOHUKOHU**, a waterside cluster of century-old wooden houses on the northernmost arm of Hokianga Harbour. Kohukohu was once the hub of Hokianga's kauri industry, but the subsequent years of decline have only partly been arrested by the recent influx of rat-race refugees.

Village Arts Gallery

1376 Kohukohu Rd • Summer daily 10am–3pm; winter Wed–Sun 10am–3pm • Free • ☎ 09 405 5827, ⓦ villagearts.co.nz

Check out the new, community-run **Village Arts Gallery**, which has already made a splash promoting Hokianga's artistic community, with exhibitions of sculpture, painting, photography, steampunk models and textiles at a much higher standard than you might expect for such a backwater.

Four kilometres further east, Narrows Landing is the northern terminus of the **Hokianga Vehicle Ferry** (see p.193).

Rawene and around

Delightful **RAWENE** occupies the tip of Herd's Point, a peninsula roughly halfway up the harbour. Though almost isolated by the mud flats at low tide, Rawene's strategic position made it an obvious choice for the location of a timber mill, which contributed material for the town's attractive wooden buildings, some perched on stilts out over the water.

Clendon House

Clendon Esplanade • Nov–April Sat & Sun 10am–4pm; May–Oct Sun 10am–4pm • $5

Clendon House is Rawene's only significant distraction, and was the last residence of British-born US Consul James Clendon, a pivotal figure in the early life of the colony. The house itself is mostly pit-sawn kauri construction. Downstairs, one room beside the veranda has been retained as the post office it once was.

Clendon Esplanade leads to the **Mangrove Walkway**, a pleasant fifteen-minute return boardwalk through the coastal shallows with boards telling of intertidal life and the sawmill, which once operated here.

Wairere Boulders

70 McDonnell Rd, signposted 14km north off SH12; 40km northeast of Rawene • Daily during daylight hours • $10 • ☏ 09 401 9935, ⓦ wairereboulders.co.nz

Wairere Boulders is a privately run park encompassing huge 2.8-million-year-old basalt rocks with natural fluting that makes them appear like carved corrugated iron. The main self-guided loop (40min) follows a narrow path weaving among boulders and across a stream turning it into a kind of nature trail. There are several additional loops plus a spur trail leading through the rainforested valley and up to a good viewpoint. Wairere is a bit out of the way, so bring supplies and make an afternoon of it.

Opononi and Omapere

The two small villages of **OPONONI** and **OMAPERE**, 20km west of Rawene, comprise little more than a roadside string of houses running seamlessly for 4km along the southern shore of the Hokianga Harbour, with great views across to the massive sand dunes on the north side. If you decide to break your journey in this area it will be because you want to explore the dunes, either on foot or by beach buggy (see opposite), or by viewing them from afar; the Arai te Uru Reserve is a wonderful viewpoint reached along Signal Station Road, 1km south of Omapere. The only other reason to stop in either settlement is to hook up with a guided tour of the Kauri forests to the south (see opposite).

Waiotemarama Bush Walk

647 Waiotemarama Gorge Rd, 8km southeast of Opononi • 2km loop

Labyrinth (see p.194) marks the start of the **Waiotemarama Bush Walk**, the best and most popular of the short walks in the district, running through a lovely fern-, palm- and kauri-filled valley. A ten-minute walk leads you to a waterfall with a small swimming hole, and after a further ten minutes you reach the first kauri.

GETTING AROUND   **HOKIANGA HARBOUR**

By bus Getting around the Hokianga and Waipoua region is difficult without your own vehicle, though Magic Bus loops past Rawene and Omapere en route from Paihia to Auckland several days a week in summer.

OPONONI THE DOLPHIN

If you didn't know about Opononi's moment of fame in the summer of 1955–56 when a wild bottlenose dolphin, dubbed "Opo", started playing with the kids in the shallows and performing tricks with beach balls, you will by the time you leave.

Christmas holidaymakers jammed the narrow dirt roads; film crews were dispatched; protective laws drafted; and Auckland musicians wrote and recorded the novelty song *Opo The Crazy Dolphin* in a day. Their tape arrived at the radio station for its first airing just as news came in that Opo had been shot under mysterious circumstances. The i-SITE shows a short video in classic 1950s-documentary style, which gives a sense of the frenzied enthusiasm for Opo.

OPONONI AND OMAPERE TOURS AND ACTIVITIES

Motoring over the magnificent sand dunes in a beach buggy on a cultural, historic and adventure tour is one way to spend time hereabouts, but you may also find yourself hurtling down the dunes on a plastic tray, trying desperately to stop before you hit the water. Alternatively, try your hand at Maori-style bone carving or visit the nearby kauri trees.

2

CRAFTS

Hokianga Bone Carving Studio 15 Ahika St, between Opononi and Omapere, off SH12 ☎021 298 8968, ⊜hokiangabonecarvingstudio@gmail .com. Spend an entertaining and fruitful day making a Maori bone carving with Maori carver, James Taranaki. Book ahead, have a design in mind and be prepared to spend as much of the day as you need to complete your carving: you'll be well fed while you're at it.

TOUR OPERATORS

Hokianga Express ☎09 405 8872 or ☎021 405 872, ⓦhokiangaexpress.webs.com. Operating from 10am daily, this charter service ($25) leaves from Opononi wharf and will drop you off at the dunes with sandboards (after a modicum of instruction) and pick you up a couple of hours later. Their cruise option ($75) involves a trip out to the harbour mouth and beyond (weather permitting), and a bit of local history.

Footprints Waipoua 334 SH12, Omapere ☎09 405 8207, ⓦfootprintswaipoua.co.nz. Runs excellent guided walks to the kauri trees in Waipoua Forest (see p.196). The pick of the tours is the Twilight Encounter ($85) through the forest to the two largest trees. You might see giant kauri snails, eels and ruru (native owl), but the emphasis is more on listening to and sensing the forest under the cover of darkness leavened with a strong Maori spiritual component – story, song and music. They pick up from accommodation in Opononi and Omapere.

Sandtrails Hokianga 32 Paparangi Drive, Mitimiti ☎09 409 5035, ⓦsandtrailshokianga.co.nz. Runs dune buggy tours ($95/hr; $135/90min; $185/3hr; maximum three people) using fat tyres with very little air, taking in the heights, local Maori history and stories, and visiting an area of wind-sculpted sand not unlike a mini Grand Canyon. Has overnight options in Mitimiti, too – whatever you plump for, you won't be disappointed.

By ferry Apart from a lengthy drive around the head of the harbour, the only way around the Hokianga is on the Hokianga Vehicle Ferry (car and driver $16 one-way; $24 return; campervan and driver $30; car passengers and pedestrians $2 each way), which shuttles from Narrows Landing, 4km east of Kohukohu on the northern shores, to Rawene in the south, a journey of 15min. Departures (around 7.30am–8pm) are on the hour southbound and on the half-hour northbound (7.30am–7.30pm).

INFORMATION

i-SITE 29 SH12, just outside Opononi (daily: Nov–April 8.30am–5pm; May–Oct 9am–5pm; ☎09 405 8869, ⓦhokianga.co.nz or ⓦvisitfarnorthnz.com). The office – one of three for the Far North region of Northland – has information for the Hokianga area and Waipoua Forest (see p.196), can book accommodation, and has internet access.

ACCOMMODATION

KOHUKOHU

★ **The Tree House** 168 West Coast Rd, 2km west of the car ferry terminus ☎09 405 5855, ⓦtreehouse .co.nz. Accommodation is scattered among the trees in two spacious dorms, double and twin cabins with sundecks and a well-equipped house bus in a macadamia orchard. There's also a self-contained cottage in Kohukohu itself, sleeping five. You get $4 off the price of dorms and doubles if you bring your own bedding. Camping $19, dorms $32, double cabin $82, twin cabin $82, house bus $82, cottage $160

RAWENE

Rawene Holiday Park 1 Marmon St, 1.5km from the ferry landing ☎09 405 7720, ⓦraweneholidaypark .co.nz. A low-key site with hilltop harbour views, sheltered areas for tents and good-value, spacious, well-kept cabins in bush enclaves. Camping $15, dorms $20, kitchenette cabins $60, full-kitchen cabins $70, en suites $90

OPONONI AND OMAPERE

Copthorne Hotel & Resort SH12, Omapere ☎09 405 8737, ⓦomapere.com. The best of the hotels in town, set opposite the dunes, with a solar-heated pool, nice bar and licensed restaurant and a range of accommodation including some beautifully appointed waterside rooms with all the usual big hotel touchs. $240

★ **Globetrekkers Lodge** SH12, Omapere ☎09 405 8183, ⊛globetrekkerslodge.com. Relaxing and very well-kept hostel with some harbour views. The five- and six-bed dorms and doubles are all spacious and airy, and there are a couple of nice cabins in the grounds. TV is intentionally absent and the evening BBQ usually brings everyone together. Camping $15, dorms $29, rooms $65

★ **Hokianga Haven** 226 SH12, Omapere ☎09 405 8285, ⊛hokiangahaven.co.nz. The owner only takes single-party bookings for her two attractively furnished beachside B&B rooms with private bathrooms, opposite the harbour entrance with fabulous views of the dunes and the sea. Two-night minimum. $180

McKenzie's Accommodation 4 Pioneers Walk, Omapere ☎09 405 8068, ⊛mckenziesaccommodation .co.nz. Excellent beachside options in either a spacious room rented as a B&B double or a twin, with a separate bathroom and private entrance, or the self-contained two-bedroom cottage rented as accommodation only. Room $110, cottage $120

Opononi Beach Holiday Park SH12, Opononi ☎09 405 8791, ⊛opononiholidaypark.co.nz. Spacious, very basic harbour-side campsite with facilities for laundry and a camp kitchen. You're better off with the self-contained cabins unless you're in a campervan. Camping $16, cabins $65, self-contained cabins $85

EATING AND DRINKING

KOHUKOHU

★ **The Koke Pub** 1372 Kohukohu Rd ☎09 405 5808. The best place to eat in town serves up a friendly welcome, not to mention tasty breakfasts, snacks and lunches. It also has great coffee, pork loin roast dinners, local seafood and the best chicken, leek and bacon pies in Northland. Live music every Thursday. Food served Sun–Wed 8am–8pm, Thurs–Sat 8am–late. Pub open daily 11am–late.

RAWENE

Boatshed Café 8 Clendon Esplanade ☎09 405 7728. A daytime and licensed establishment built out over the water, offering magazines to read on the sunny deck as you tuck into gourmet pizza slices or home-made muffins and soups, and espresso ($5–25). Daily 8.30am–4.30pm.

OPONONI AND OMAPERE

★ **Copthorne Hotel & Resort** SH12, Omapere ☎09 405 8737, ⊛omapere.com. The best dining hereabouts,

in both the elegant restaurant (mains around $35) and the *Sands* bar (mains around $28). Both have great views over the lawns and harbour to the sand dunes. Look out for dishes with a Maori influence, such as local seafood or *rawena* bread and butter pudding with *titoki* liqueur ($11.50). Daily 8am–late.

★ **Opononi Hotel** SH12, Opononi ☎09 405 8827, ⊛opononihotel.com. Lively pub offering the district's best-value eating, both bar food and à la carte; try out the surf and turf ($29.50); othr mains are $19–33. Regular Kiwi touring bands stop by in summer when 1200-odd people can crowd in. Daily 11am–11pm.

Opo Takeaways SH12, Opononi. Known locally as the best fish and chip takeaway, it also serves generous, well-stuffed burgers, mussel and paua fritters, battered sausages and other deep-fried delights. Fish is usually $3–6 a piece, depending on type. Daily 10am–7pm, until 9pm in summer.

SHOPPING

Hoki Smoki Signposted on SH12 1km south of Omapere. An excellent fish and seafood smokery – drop in and buy some to take on the road with you or for a picnic. It's only open for business if the sign is out.

Labyrinth Woodworks 647 Waiotemarama Gorge Rd, 8km southeast of Opononi ☎09 405 4581, ⊛nzanity

.co.nz. One of the region's better craft shops, with wares including carved kauri pieces and excellent woodblock prints. Pride of place, however, goes to the mind-bending puzzles in the puzzle museum, which include the smallest puzzles in the world, and a maturing hedge maze with an anagram problem that stumps many a visitor – it's great fun.

The kauri forests and around

Northland, Auckland and the Coromandel Peninsula were once covered in mixed forest dominated by the mighty kauri (see box opposite), the world's second-largest tree. By the early twentieth century, rapacious Europeans had nearly felled the lot, the only extensive pockets remaining in the **Waipoua and Trounson kauri forests** south of the Hokianga Harbour. Though small stands of kauri can be found all over Northland, three-quarters of all the surviving mature trees grow in these two small forests, which between them cover barely 100 square kilometres. Walks provide access to the more celebrated examples, which dwarf the surrounding tataire, kohekohe and towai trees.

Just south of the Trounson forest are the **Kai Iwi Lakes**, a trio of popular dune lakes that get busy in the summer season.

Brief history

This area is home to the Te Roroa people who traditionally used the kauri sparingly. Simple tools made felling and working these huge trees a difficult task, and one reserved for major projects such as large war canoes. Once the Europeans arrived with metal tools, bullock trains, wheels and winches, clear felling became easier, and most of the trees had gone by the end of the nineteenth century. The efforts of several

2

THE KAURI AND ITS USES

The **kauri** (*agathis australis*) ranks alongside the sequoias of California as one of the largest trees in existence. Unlike the sequoias, which are useless as furniture timber, kauri produce beautiful wood, a fact that hastened its demise and spawned the industries that dominated New Zealand's economy in the latter half of the nineteenth century.

The kauri is a type of pine that now grows only in New Zealand, though it once also grew in Australia and Southeast Asia, where it still has close relations. Identifiable remains of kauri forests are found all over New Zealand, but by the time humans arrived on the scene its range had contracted to Northland, Auckland, the Coromandel Peninsula and northern Waikato. Individual trees can live over 2000 years, reaching 50m in height and 20m in girth, finally toppling over as the rotting core becomes too weak to support its immense weight.

KAURI LOGGERS

Maori have long used mature kauri for dugout canoes, but it was the "rickers" (young trees) that first drew the attention of **European loggers** since they formed perfect spars for sailing ships. The bigger trees soon earned an unmatched reputation for their durable, easy-to-work and blemish-free wood, with its straight, fine grain. Loggers' ingenuity was taxed to the limit by the difficulty of getting such huge logs out of the bush. On easier terrain, bullock wagons with up to twelve teams lashed together to haul the logs onto primitive roads or tramways. Horse-turned winches were used on steeper ground and, where water could be deployed to transport the timber, dams were constructed from hewn logs. In narrow valleys and gullies all over Northland and the Coromandel, loggers constructed kauri dams up to 20m high and 60m across, with trapdoors at the base. Trees along the sides of the valley were felled while the dam was filling, then the dam was opened to flush the floating trunks down the valley to inlets where the logs were rafted up and towed to the mills.

GUM DIGGERS

Once an area had been logged, the **gum diggers** typically moved in. Like most pines, kauri exudes a thick resin to cover any scars inflicted on it, and huge accretions form on the sides of trunks and in globules around the base. Maori chewed the gum, made torches from it to attract fish at night and burned the powdered resin to form a pigment used for *moko* (traditional tattoos). Once Pakeha got in on the act, it was exported as a raw material for furniture varnishes, linoleum, denture moulds and the "gilt" edging on books. When it could no longer be found on the ground, diggers – mostly Dalmatian, but also Maori, Chinese and Malaysian – thrust long poles into the earth and hooked out pieces with bent rods; elsewhere, the ground was dug up and sluiced to recover the gum. Almost all New Zealand gum was exported, but by the early twentieth century synthetic resins had captured the gum market. Kauri gum is still considered one of the finest varnishes for musical instruments, and occasional accidental finds supply such specialist needs.

THE FUTURE

In recent years the kauri have been further threatened by a new disease known as PTA or **kauri dieback** (W kauridieback.co.nz) with symptoms including yellowed leaves, dead branches and resinous lesions close to the ground, eventually leading to the tree's death. The disease is transmitted through soil and water, so always keep to the tracks and boardwalks and clean your footwear after visiting a kauri forest.

campaigning organizations eventually bore fruit in 1952, when much of the remaining forest was designated the Waipoua Sanctuary. It's now illegal to fell a kauri except in specified circumstances, such as culling a diseased or dying tree, or when constructing a new ceremonial canoe.

Waipoua Kauri Forest

SH12, 15km south of Omapere

Heading south from the Hokianga Harbour area, you pass through farmland and arrive at Waimamaku, home to the daytime-only *Morrell's Café* (see opposite).

The highway then twists and turns through nearly 20km of mature kauri in the **WAIPOUA KAURI FOREST**. Eight kilometres south of Waimamaku you reach a small car park, from where it's a three-minute walk to New Zealand's mightiest tree, the 2000-year-old **Tane Mahuta**, "God of the Forest". A vast wall of bark 6m wide rises nearly 18m to the lowest branches, covered in epiphytes. A kilometre or so further south on SH12, a ten-minute track leads to a clearing where three paths split off to notable trees: the shortest (5min return) runs to the **Four Sisters**, relatively slender kauri all growing close together; a second path (30min return) winds among numerous big trees to **Te Matua Ngahere**, the "Father of the Forest", the second-largest tree in New Zealand – shorter than Tane Mahuta but fatter and in some ways more impressive. The third path, the **Yakas Track** (3km return; 1hr), leads to Cathedral Grove, a dense conglomeration of trees, the largest being the **Yakas Kauri**, named after veteran bushman Nicholas Yakas.

Trounson Kauri Park

Signposted off SH12, 7km down a side road

Trounson Kauri Park is a small but superb stand of kauri where the **Trounson Kauri Walk** (40min loop) weaves though lovely rainforest. In 1997, Trounson was turned into a "mainland island" in order to foster North Island brown kiwi survival. Numbers are up significantly, and you've a good chance of seeing them – along with weta and glowworms – if you stay over. A **tour** of the kauri stands is easy enough to do on your own, but Kauri Coast Top 10 Holiday Park (see opposite) offers a guided night walk (non-guests $25).

Kai Iwi Lakes

11km west off SH12, 20km south of Trounson

The **Kai Iwi Lakes** are a real change, with pine woods running down to fresh, crystal-blue waters fringed by silica-white sand. All three are dune lakes fed by rainwater and with no visible outlet. Though the largest, **Taharoa**, is less than 1km across, and **Waikere** and **Kai Iwi** are barely 100m long, they constitute the deepest and some of the largest dune lakes in the country. People flock here in the summer to swim, fish and waterski, but outside the first weeks in January you can usually find a quiet spot. Shallow and consequently warmer than the sea, they're good for an early-season dip.

INFORMATION
THE KAURI FORESTS AND AROUND

Te Roroa Waipoua Visitor Centre SH12, 9km south of Tane Mahuta (daily 8.30am–4.30pm. Has displays and information on the Waipoua Kauri Forest and its past.

ACCOMMODATION AND EATING

WAIPOUA KAURI FOREST

⭐ **Kaihu Farm Hostel** 3344 SH12, Kaihu, 23km south of the visitor centre ☎ 09 439 4004, ✆ kaihufarm.co.nz.

The budget accommodation here – in clean, homey and cosy rooms – is appealingly rural, and really more of a farm stay than a hostel. There are glowworms in the surrounding bush, and it's also just an atmospheric 7km tree-lined walk from the magnificent Trounson kauris (see opposite) or a 10min drive from the beach. Dinners available at $20 each, plus fresh eggs and home-made bread available on request. Dorms $33, singles $56, rooms $88, rooms with breakfast $110

★ **Morrell's Café** 7237 SH12, Waimamaku ☎ 09 405 4545. The best café in the area cooks up all-day breakfasts (under $25), light meals such as gourmet burgers, wraps and salads (all under $12), the best mussel chowder in the north ($10) and excellent coffee. Daily 9am–4pm.

TROUNSON KAURI PARK

★ **Kauri Coast Top 10 Holiday Park** Trounson Park Rd, off SH12 ☎ 0800 807 200, ⊛ kauricoasttop10.co.nz. A traditional Kiwi campsite with tidy communal areas, clean toilets and showers and well-tended campsites. There are also small but adequate basic cabins and roomy

motel units. You can join the site's two-hour guided night walk ($20) that explores the kauri forest. Camping $20, standard cabins $75, kitchen cabins $90, motel units $120
Trounson Kauri Park Campground Signposted off SH12, 17km south of Waipoua Forest. A simple but popular DOC campsite with sites by a small stand of kauri, and equipped with kitchen, toilets, tap water and hot showers. $10

KAI IWI LAKES

Kai Iwi Lakes ☎ 09 439 4757. Comprised of two locally run sites: the Pine Beach site on the gently shelving shores of Taharoa Lake, with running water, toilets and cold showers; and the intimate but primitive Promenade Point site, with just long-drop toilets. An attendant shows up once a day in the summer. Pay your fee to the honesty box. Camping $12, campervans $20

SHOPPING

Katui Kauri Gum Store SH12, 9km south of the Te Roroa Waipoua Visitor Centre ☎ 09 439 4733. This charmingly eccentric shop provides a little welcome relief

from the rigours of the road, offering cheap bits of kauri gum, carved kauri gum, polished gum and wood with gum inlays, all at rather reasonable prices. Daily 8.30am–late.

The northern Kaipara Harbour

South of the kauri forests are the muddy, mangrove-choked shores of the **Kaipara Harbour**, New Zealand's largest. The harbour once unified this quarter of Northland, with sailboats plying its waters and linking the dairy farming and logging towns on its shores. Kauri was shipped out from the largest northern town, **Dargaville**, though the fragile boats all too often foundered on the unpredictable Kaipara Bar. Many eventually washed up on **Ripiro Beach**, which just pips Ninety Mile Beach to the title of New Zealand's longest, running for 108km.

Dargaville and around

SH12, 30km south of Kai Iwi Lakes

The sleepy dairying and *kumara*-growing town of **DARGAVILLE**, 30km south of Kai Iwi Lakes, was founded as a port in 1872, on the strongly tidal but navigable Northern Wairoa River, by Australian Joseph McMullen Dargaville. Ships came to load kauri logs and transport gum (see box, p.195) extracted by Dalmatian settlers who, by the early part of the twentieth century, formed a sizeable portion of the community.

Dargaville Museum

Harding Park, 2km west of town • Daily: Oct–March 9am–5pm; April–Sept 9am–4pm • $12 • ☎ 09 439 7555, ⊛ dargavillemuseum.co.nz

Two masts rescued from the *Rainbow Warrior* (see box, p.179) mark the surprisingly good **Dargaville Museum**. It contains extensive displays of artefacts recovered from the shifting dunes, which occasionally reveal old shipwrecks. The only pre-European artefact is the Ngati Whatua *waka*, which lay buried under the sands of the North Head of the Kaipara Harbour from 1809 until 1972, and is a rare example of a canoe hewn entirely with stone tools. A fine collection of kauri gum gives pride of place to an 84kg piece – reputedly the largest ever found – and there is an ancient heated oil Blackstone engine-powered gum washer that they occasionally run to the delight of visitors.

Woodturners Kauri Gallery & Working Studio

4 Murdoch St (SH12) • Daily 9am–dark • ☎ 09 439 4975, ⓦ thewoodturnersstudio.co.nz

At the western end of town, at the **Woodturners Kauri Gallery & Working Studio**, leading woodturner Rick Taylor demonstrates what can be done with the extraordinarily varied grains and colours of kauri, sells all manner of kauri products, and runs courses for those prepared to dedicate a day or more.

Baylys Beach and Ripiro Beach

14km west of Dargaville, along a minor road

BAYLYS BEACH is a conglomeration of mostly holiday homes on a central section of 100km-long **RIPIRO BEACH**, a strand renowned for its mobility, with several metres of beach often being shifted by a single tide, and huge areas being reclaimed over the centuries; the anchors or prows of long-lost wrecks periodically reappear through the sand. As elsewhere on the West Coast, tidal rips and holes make swimming dangerous and there are no beach patrols. Beach driving is no less fraught with danger and shouldn't be undertaken without prior local consultation; vehicles frequently get stranded. Nevertheless, it's a fine place for long walks, and spotting seals and penguins in winter. When easterlies are blowing the coastline is adorned with kites, flown out from the shore and drawing fishing lines for anything up to 1km. They're left for twenty minutes or so then hauled in, often heavy with fish.

ARRIVAL AND DEPARTURE   DARGAVILLE AND AROUND

By bus Dargaville is served by Magic, InterCity and Main Coachline buses. The latter arrives once a day, via Warkworth.

Destinations Auckland (6 weekly; 3hr).

INFORMATION AND TOURS

Tourist information There is no official tourist office in Dargaville, but stop in at Woodturners Kauri Gallery & Working Studio (see above) for advice.

The Kumara Box 503 Pouto Rd, just south of Dargaville ☎ 09 439 7108, ⓦ kumarabox.co.nz. Low-key tours of a kumara farm, in the heart of kumara-growing country, would seem like a bit of a spud, but these are so full of charm, enthusiasm and ingenuity that you cannot fail to

be captivated. A kumara train takes you past the smallest church in Northland, and through a variety of minor hazards before depositing you in a barn where you see the home-made video about kumara and the area. It's all great fun and you won't be reaching for the kumara vodka, though you might get home-made kumara soup or a kumara muffin before you leave.

ACCOMMODATION

★ **Baylys Beach Holiday Park** 22 Seaview Rd, Baylys Beach ☎ 09 439 6349, ⓦ baylysbeach.co.nz. A well-run and tidy park with charming *bach*-style cabins just a short walk from the beach, good camping, clean cabins and some spacious units. You can rent quad bikes for a gentle putter up the beach to see the wind-crafted sand sculptures, and lines of burned kauri captured in sand banks. Camping $16, cabins $65, units $130, cottages $130

★ **Commercial Hotel** 75 River Rd, Dargaville ☎ 09 439 0878. The owners were renovating at the time of writing, turning this former colonial-style hotel into more of a very comfortable homestay in an historic building, which happens to overlook the river and provide very relaxing, spacious but as yet basic accommodation. They whip up good breakfasts ($15 extra/room) and have lots of local knowledge. Rooms with shared bathroom $100, en-suite rooms $135

Dargaville Holiday Park 10 Onslow St, Dargaville ☎ 0800 114 441, ⓦ kauriparks.co.nz. A traditional Kiwi campsite set in park-like grounds a 10min walk from town with well-kept but simple doubles and comfortable units. There's lots to keep the kids happy, too. Camping $14, cabins $50, units $100

Greenhouse Hostel 15 Gordon St, Dargaville ☎ 09 439 6342, ⓔ greenhousebackpackers@ihug.co.nz. Centrally located in a 1920s former school, this hostel is old-fashioned but clean and well run, with simple rooms, great-value doubles, bedding and a communal kitchen. Closed May–Aug. Dorms $23, rooms $70

★ **Kauri House Lodge** 60 Bowen St, Dargaville ☎ 09 439 8082, ⓦ kaurihouselodge.co.nz. Dargaville's grandest accommodation option is contained within an engagingly low-key yet vast and magnificent kauri villa. The large rooms are all en-suite, and there's a billiard room, library and swimming pool. $250

EATING AND DRINKING

★ **Blah Blah Blah** 101 Victoria St, Dargaville ☎ 09 439 6300. A licensed café specializing in dishes featuring Dargaville's famed kumara; try the kumara and mussel chowder ($13), or opt for a lamb shank pie ($26). They also serve tasty coffee and a selection of home-made cakes fit to tempt a nun. Tues–Sat 9am–late; kitchen closes at 9pm.

Shiraz 17 Hokianga Rd, Dargaville ☎ 09 439 0024. Restaurant and takeaway specializing in north Indian dishes, seafood and pizza – not a combination forged in heaven but there isn't much in the way of competition in town so it can get quite busy. The curries are pretty fair and there is nothing on the menu more than $22. Try the tandoori or the Amritsari fish, but give the pizza a miss. Mon–Sat 8am–3pm.

★ **The Funky Fish** 34 Seaview Rd, Baylys Beach ☎ 09 439 8883, ⓦ funkyfish.co.nz. Groovy, modern café and bar where you'll find great fish and chips, a speciality beer-battered dory with char-grilled lemon and salad, plus a range of burgers, baguettes and a varied à la carte evening menu. The great garden bar is the icing on the cake. Reserve for dinner in summer and for Sun lunch year-round. Prices range from $10–35. Summer Tues–Sun 11am–late; Winter Tues & Wed 5pm–late, Thurs–Sun 11am–late.

SHOPPING

Pounamu Greenstone Jade Jewelry Dargaville ☎ 09 439 5819, ⓦ jade-jewelry.co.nz. In a caravan attached next to the woodturner (see opposite) is Paul Graham, a licensed Ngai Tahu carver of greenstone who makes some intricate pounamu pendants ranging from $40 (for a simple carving) to whatever you are prepared to pay. Wed–Sun 10am–6pm.

Tokatoka Peak

SH12, 17km southwest of Dargaville

SH12 zips through flat farmland before reaching the knobby 180m **Tokatoka Peak**. Panoramic views unfold from the summit of this extinct volcanic plug, reached in ten breathless minutes from a trailhead 1km off SH12 near the *Tokatoka* pub.

Matakohe and the Kauri Museum

Matakohe is 30km south of Tokatoka Peak, on SH12 • Kauri Museum • Church Rd • Daily 9am–5pm • $25 • ☎ 09 431 7417, ⓦ kaurimuseum.com

If there's one museum you must see in the north it's the **Kauri Museum** at tiny **MATAKOHE**, 30km south of Tokatoka Peak. One of the best museums in the country, and deserving at least three hours, it explains the way the kauri's timber and its valuable gum shaped the lives of pioneers in Northland. The displays focus on the makeshift settlements around logging camps, the gumfields, and the lives of merchants who were among the few who could afford to buy the fine kauri furniture or beautifully carved gum on show. Diagrams show how even Tane Mahuta is a midget compared to the giants of yore, and the smell of the freshly sawn timber lures you to the replica steam sawmill. There is also a stunning collection of Kauri furniture, boats and gum (in the basement), and plenty more to keep you occupied for an afternoon.

If you're travelling by bus, visiting the museum will mean staying overnight.

ACCOMMODATION AND EATING

MATAKOHE

Gumdiggers Café Church Rd, opposite the museum ☎ 09 431 7075. Owned by the museum, the café makes a welcoming spot to rest before, during and after your meanderings round the galleries. Daytime food includes gumdiggers' pasties, excellent wraps, pies, burgers, sandwiches, chips and cakes, all fresh made or cooked to order, with nothing over $20. Daily 8.30am–5pm.

Matakohe Holiday Park ☎ 0800 431 6431, ⓦ matakoheholidaypark.co.nz. A well-kept small hillside campsite 500m beyond the museum offering great harbour views and a broad range of accommodation including decent well-spaced camping, cabins and comfortable motel units. Camping $17, cabins $65, motel units $120.

★ **Petite Provence** 703c Tinopai Rd, 9km south of Matakohe ☎ 09 431 7552, ⓦ petiteprovence.co.nz. A lovely Kiwi-French-run B&B amid rolling farmland with views of the Kaipara Harbour. Rooms are tastefully decorated and comfortable, and wonderfully tasty evening meals ($45) are available. The host also makes beautiful, handcrafted metal and wood furniture, featured in some rooms, which is stunningly comfortable and quite captivating. Rooms $150

Western North Island

205 Hamilton

208 Around Hamilton

212 Raglan

215 Kawhia

216 The King Country

224 The Taranaki Peninsula

238 Taumarunui

239 The Forgotten World Highway

240 Whanganui National Park

246 Wanganui

251 Palmerston North and around

254 Foxton and around

255 The Kapiti Coast

MOUNT EGMONT

Western North Island

The Western North Island is wetter than the east, the prevailing westerlies dropping rain on a lush land that's dense with bush in more remote areas and put to work raising dairy cattle on flatter country. Moisture seeps into cracks in limestone to dissolve out gorgeous caverns around Waitomo, falls as snow on the high peak of Taranaki, and works its way to the sea through the roadless tracts along the Whanganui River. The region's rivers spill out into the Tasman Sea where huge rollers create magical surf breaks and have gradually carved a coastline of rugged headlands and sea stacks.

3

Much of the region's appeal is tied to its extraordinary **history** of pre-European settlement and post-European conflict. It was on the west coast, at **Kawhia**, that the Tainui people first landed in New Zealand; the Tainui canoe in which they arrived is buried here, and the waterside tree it was moored to lives on. Kawhia was also the birthplace of **Te Rauparaha**, the great Maori chief who led his people from here down the coast to Kapiti Island and on to the South Island, to escape the better-armed tribes of the Waikato.

Approaching the region from the north, the farming country of the **Waikato** centres on the workaday provincial capital, **Hamilton**, which won't detain you long, but has enough to soak up a couple of days' exploration in the immediate vicinity. The nearby surfers' paradise of **Raglan** has world-class surf as well as some great places to stay, eat or just unwind. Southeast of Hamilton on SH1, there's a genteel English charm to **Cambridge**, while at Matamata, **Hobbiton** tours are an essential stop for *Lord of the Rings* and *The Hobbit* film fans.

South of the Waikato, the highlight is **Waitomo**, where fabulous adventure trips explore otherwordly glowworm-filled limestone caverns. The adjacent **King Country** took its name from the King Movement (see p.216), and was the last significant area in New Zealand to succumb to European colonization. Further south, the giant thumbprint peninsula of **Taranaki** is dominated by the symmetrical cone of **Mount Taranaki**, within the **Egmont National Park**. At its foot, **New Plymouth** warrants a visit for its excellent contemporary art gallery and access to a multitude of **surf beaches**.

Inland from Egmont National Park, the farming town of **Taumarunui** is one of the main jumping-off points for multi-day canoe trips along the **Whanganui River**, through the heart of the verdant **Whanganui National Park**. The river bisects **Wanganui**, a small, gracious and creative city whose river-port past can be relived on a restored paddle steamer. Some 60km to the southeast, the university city of

Raglan tours and activities p.213	Around the Mountain Circuit p.234
The King Movement p.216	Hiking and biking the Mangapurua
Glowworms p.219	Track p.245
Waitomo walks p.220	Whanganui River Road Mail Run p.246
Adventure caving p.221	Wanganui or Whanganui? p.248
Len Lye p.228	Glass-blowing and photography In
New Plymouth festivals p.231	Wanganui p.249
Safety on the Mount Taranaki summit	Walking around Kapiti p.256
route p.233	

SURFER AT RAGLAN

Highlights

❶ Raglan Surf New Zealand's finest waves, kayak around the harbour or just soak up the laidback atmosphere of this hypnotic harbourside town. **See p.212**

❷ Waitomo Abseil, squeeze or blackwater raft into labyrinthine caves on some of the world's best adventure caving trips, often illuminated by a glittering canopy of glowworms. **See p.217**

❸ Egmont National Park Scale the conical summit of the North Island's second-highest peak, Mount Taranaki, or get great views of the mountain from the less committing Pouakai Circuit. **See p.232**

❹ Forgotten World Highway Take the slow road through pristine countryside and get your passport stamped at the self-declared village republic of Whangamomona. **See p.239**

❺ Whanganui River Spend three chilled days far from roads canoeing through verdant canyons and tackling the gentle rapids of the country's longest navigable river. **See p.242**

❻ Kapiti Island Marvel at what birdsong in the Aotearoa bush used to be like on this pest-free island full of rare native birds. Go for the day or stay overnight to go kiwi spotting. **See p.256**

HIGHLIGHTS ARE MARKED ON THE MAP ON P.204

Palmerston North lies at the centre of the rich farming region of **Manawatu**. A cluster of rural communities lines the highway south to the **Kapiti Coast**, where laidback beachside **Paraparaumu** is the launch point for boat trips to the paradisiacal bird sanctuary of **Kapiti Island**.

GETTING AROUND

By train The main Auckland–Wellington rail line runs partly through the region, with a single service in each direction (Oct–April daily, May–Sept Fri, Sat & Sun only). Frequent commuter rail services also run between Wellington and Waikanae.

By bus Most long-haul bus services are run by InterCity/Newmans/Great Sights and NakedBus (who use a number of local operators). The main additional service is The Naki Bus (☎ 0508 465 622, ⓦ nakibus.co.nz), running Auckland–Hamilton–Otorohanga–Te Kuiti–New Plymouth–Hawera.

Hamilton

On the banks of the languid green Waikato River, New Zealand's fourth-largest city, **HAMILTON**, functions as a regional hub rather than a major tourist destination, but it's within striking distance of some of the North Island's top spots, such as the surf beaches of Raglan and Waitomo Caves, as well as Auckland, 127km north. It's worth devoting some time to the excellent **Waikato Museum** and the tranquil **Hamilton Gardens**.

Everything of interest in Hamilton is either along or just off the main drag, **Victoria Street**, which parallels the west bank of the tree-lined Waikato River. One of more striking buildings is the 1924 **Wesley Chambers** (now *Le Grand* hotel) on the corner of Collingwood Street, influenced by the buildings of boomtime Chicago. Diagonally opposite, a small open space is graced by a statue of the English-born *Rocky Horror Show* creator, **Richard O'Brien** – decked out as Riff Raff, the role he played in the film of the show – who spent his teens and early twenties in Hamilton visiting science fiction double features.

In mid-June, the annual four-day **Fieldays festival** (ⓦ fieldays.co.nz) is held at Mystery Creek Events Centre just outside the city. The largest agricultural field day in the southern hemisphere, it's a quintessentially Kiwi event with everything from sheep shearing to ploughing contests plus lots of entertainment, mostly with a rural tenor.

Waikato Museum

1 Grantham St · Daily 10am–4.30pm · Free · ☎ 07 838 6606, ⓦ waikatomuseum.co.nz

Set in a modern building that steps down to the river, the excellent **Waikato Museum** takes an imaginative approach to local history but really excels with its section devoted to **Tainui culture**, much of it curated by the local Maori community. Of course there are tools, ritual artefacts, woven flax and carvings, but the displays give a real sense of the living culture of the four main Tainui sub-tribes along with insights into tribal leaders, and there's frequently changing art. The magnificent *Te Winika* war canoe is housed beside a window where you can look out over the river at the mouldering hulk of the paddle steamer *Rangiriri*, which worked the river in early colonial times.

Hamilton Gardens

Cobham Drive (SH1), 4km southeast of the city centre · Gardens daily 7.30am–dusk; visitor centre daily 9am–5pm · Free · ☎ 07 838 6782, ⓦ hamiltongardens.co.nz · Bus #10 (#17 on Sat & Sun) from the Transport Centre

From Memorial Park, a riverside path follows the bends in the river to the huge, unfenced **Hamilton Gardens**, with extensive displays of roses, tropical plants, rhododendrons, magnolias and cacti.

Pick up a free map from the gardens' visitor centre then duck next door to the inner sanctum of the **Paradise Gardens Collection**, six beautiful enclosures each planted in a

3

different style from around the world. Here you can sit and enjoy the raked-stone Zen stillness of the Japanese Garden, stop and smell the flowers in the English Garden, visit the idealized Chinese Scholar's Garden, and catch a view of the Waikato from the terrace in the Italian Renaissance Garden. A surprise highlight is the American Modernist Garden, with aloe and grass mass plantings around a shallow pool, ringed with bright yellow loungers and a huge Marilyn Monroe screenprint.

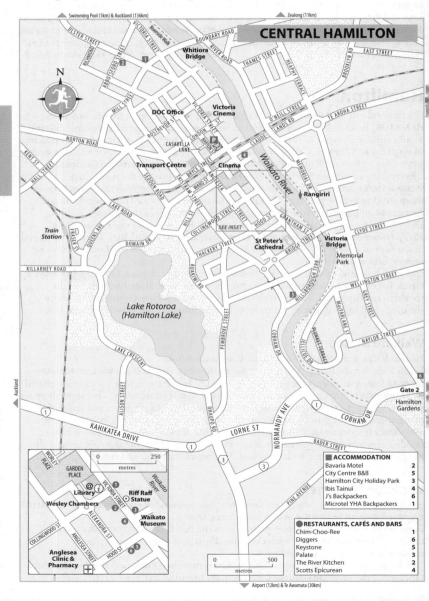

CENTRAL HAMILTON

■ **ACCOMMODATION**

Bavaria Motel	2
City Centre B&B	5
Hamilton City Holiday Park	3
Ibis Tainui	4
J's Backpackers	6
Microtel YHA Backpackers	1

● **RESTAURANTS, CAFÉS AND BARS**

Chim-Choo-Ree	1
Diggers	6
Keystone	5
Palate	3
The River Kitchen	2
Scotts Epicurean	4

Zealong

495 Gordonton Rd, 13km north of the city centre • Tours Tues–Sun 10.30am & 2.30pm; Camellia Teahouse Tues–Sun 10am–5pm • Tours $18 (bookings essential); tea with as many infusions as you wish $8; high tea $30 for one; high tea for two $48 • Tours ☎ 0800 932 566, ⓦ zealong.co.nz; teahouse ☎ 07 853 3018

The flat, low-lying sheep and cattle country of the northern Waikato seems an unlikely place to find rows of neatly tended *Camellia sinensis*, but in the late 1990s Taiwanese immigrant Vincent Chen pioneered growing tea in New Zealand – and very fine it is, too. They concentrate on **oolong tea** (partly fermented, somewhere between green and black tea), best experienced as part of the **fifty-minute guided tour**, which involves a couple of films explaining the history and process, a walk among the tea plants and an elaborate tea ceremony where you try several infusions of the three different roasts they produce.

Alternatively, just drop in to the Camellia Teahouse for a leisurely tea or the high tea with delicious savouries and exquisite cakes. They also serve lunch ($30), including an Asian-accented main, cakes and, of course, tea.

ARRIVAL AND DEPARTURE   HAMILTON

3

By plane Hamilton's airport is 15km south of town. Super Shuttle (☎ 0800 748 885) does the run to and from there for $23 each way.

Destinations Auckland (3 daily; 30min); Christchurch (2 daily; 1hr 45min).

By train The station is on Fraser St in the suburb of Frankton, almost 2km southwest of the city centre. Bus #3 runs to the Transport Centre in town, where you can also buy train tickets.

Destinations Auckland (3–7 weekly; 2hr 30min); Wellington (3–7 weekly; 9hr 30min).

By bus The Transport Centre, 373 Anglesey St (Mon–Thurs 7am–6pm, Fri 7am–7pm, Sat 9am–4.30pm, Sun 9am–4pm), is the hub for local and long-haul buses and has left luggage lockers ($4). An office here sells tickets for Intercity, NakedBus and The Naki Bus buses.

Destinations Auckland (16–19 daily; 2hr); Cambridge 12 daily; 30min); Matamata (4 daily; 1hr); New Plymouth (4 daily; 4hr); Ngaruawahia (14–16 daily; 15min); Otorohanga (5 daily; 1hr); Paeroa (2 daily; 1hr 30min); Raglan (2–3 daily; 1hr); Rotorua (8 daily; 1hr 45min); Taupo (6 daily; 2–3hr); Tauranga (4 daily; 1hr 45min); Te Aroha (3 daily; 1hr); Te Awamutu (8 daily; 30min); Te Kuiti (4 daily; 1hr–1hr 50min); Thames (2 daily; 1hr 45min); Tirau (11 daily; 35–55mins); Wanganui (2 daily; 6–8hr); Wellington (7 daily; 9hr).

GETTING AROUND

By bus Busit (☎ 0800 428 75463, ⓦ busit.co.nz) run services around town and to Cambridge, Te Awamutu, Raglan and Paeroa from the Transport Centre. Pick up the free timetable there or at the i-SITE. One-way fares within the city limits are $3.10 including free transfers for two hours.

By taxi There's a taxi rank at the Transport Centre, or call Hamilton Taxis on ☎ 0800 477 477.

INFORMATION

i-SITE 5 Garden Place (Mon–Fri 9am–5pm, Sat & Sun 9.30am–3.30pm; ☎ 07 958 5960, ⓦ visithamilton.co.nz). **DOC** Level 5, 73 Rostrevor St (Mon–Fri 8.30am–4.30pm; ☎ 07 858 1000). Come here for hiking information and hut passes.

Services Free wi-fi around Garden Place and free computers (and wi-fi) in the Central Library, 9 Garden Place (Mon–Fri 9am–8.30pm, Sat 9am–4pm, Sun noon–3.30pm; ☎ 07 838 6826).

ACCOMMODATION

Hamilton specializes in business accommodation for farm company reps in motels, mostly lining Ulster St, but there are also several B&Bs and hostels.

Bavaria Motel 203 Ulster St ☎ 07 839 2520, ⓦ bavaria motel.co.nz. Aging, but well cared for self-contained units, some of which have been substantially upgraded. There are DVD players with a decent library of discs, and they do a backpacker deal where you take your own bedding, towels and toiletries and save $10. **$90**

City Centre B&B 3 Anglesea St ☎ 07 838 1671, ⓦ city centrebnb.co.nz. There's a relaxed homey feel to the two spacious and good-value rooms with kitchenettes, both opening out to a courtyard garden with swimming pool. Generous breakfast ingredients are supplied, and extra nights are cheaper. **$130**

Hamilton City Holiday Park 14 Ruakura Rd ☏07 855 8255, ⓦhamiltoncityholidaypark.co.nz. Well-tended grassy campsite amid mature trees 2km east of the centre with a full range of cabins and units. Bedding extra. Camping $16, cabins $45, units $100

Ibis Tainui 18 Alma St ☏07 859 9200, ⓦibishotel.com /hamilton. Smart eight-storey hotel with river views from many rooms and the restaurant terrace. Rooms are fairly high standard considering the rates, which are modest, especially at weekends. $100

J's Backpackers 8 Grey St ☏07 856 8934, ⓦjs backpackers.co.nz. Relaxed and low-key hostel in a suburban house around 3km southeast of the centre. There's a small garden with a barbecue, and even a yurt, which works as a quiet lounge. Dorms $28, doubles $60

Microtel YHA Backpackers 140 Ulster St ☏07 957 1848, ⓦmicrotel.co.nz. Compact and contemporary urban associate YHA with Sky TV in its private rooms (some of which are en-suite) and plenty of singles. Mixed dorms $28, doubles $61, en suites $75

EATING AND DRINKING

The city's food and drink scene is concentrated along the southern end of Victoria Street and around the corner on Hood Street, where places start off as cafés and become restaurants/bars as the day wears on.

★ **Chim-Choo-Ree** 224 Victoria St ☏07 839 4329, ⓦchimchooree.co.nz. A bare concrete floor and a cluster of 1930s and 1940s lampshades greet you at this bustling bistro where bentwood chairs hang on the walls until needed. Nip in for a glass or two of wine or tuck into small-ish portions of the likes of roast hapuku on smoked prawn risotto with preserved lemon ($34) or kalamata olive gnocchi with seasonal vegetables ($32). Alternatively, settle in for the five-course tasting menu ($85; $115 with wine). Tues–Sat 4.30–11pm.

Keystone 150 Victoria St ☏07 839 4294, ⓦkeystone bar.co.nz. One of the best of a bunch of similarly good-value restaurant/bars clustered around the junction of Victoria and Hood sts. Expect hearty bistro meals around $25–30, and if you don't fancy this one try next door or across the street.

Palate 170 Victoria St ☏07 834 2921, ⓦpalate restaurant.co.nz. Hamilton's finest dining, done in a relaxed but professional style by people who really know what they're doing. Try the pork belly, seared scallop and apple salad ($19), followed by wagyu ravioli with beetroot purée on dauphinoise potatoes ($35). Mon–Sat 6–11pm.

★ **The River Kitchen** 237 Victoria St ☏07 839 2906. Sit in the window that opens out onto the street and try the breakfast of Spanish beans with ham hock, black pudding and poached eggs ($17.50) or some of the superb sandwiches and salads from the cabinet. They make a fine coffee, too. Mon–Fri 7am–4pm, Sat & Sun 8am–3pm.

Scotts Epicurean 181 Victoria St ☏07 839 6680. Bustling daytime café/restaurant with stacks of inviting sandwiches, cakes and muffins in the cabinet, great coffee and beautifully presented breakfasts and lunches such as scrambled eggs with black pudding ($17). Mon–Fri 7am–4pm, Sat & Sun 8.30am–4pm.

NIGHTLIFE AND ENTERTAINMENT

Hamilton's sizeable student population ensures lively term-time nightlife, both in establishments such as the one listed below and in the city's restaurants later on.

Diggers 17 Hood St ☏07 834 2228 ⓦdiggersbar.co.nz. Down-to-earth drinkers' den (that also serves pizzas) with a long kauri bar and live music most nights, though it is liveliest at weekends when there's a great atmosphere. Tues–Sun 3–10pm or later.

Victoria Cinema 690 Victoria St ☏07 838 3036, ⓦvictoriacinema.co.nz. Screens the latest and best in art-house films.

Around Hamilton

As the hub for the region, Hamilton makes a good base for exploring the Waikato region and its cluster of modest sights. Heading south from Auckland, the first place of real interest is the important Maori town of **Ngaruawahia**, though if you are headed for Raglan you may skip Ngaruawahia and follow the back roads past **Waingaro Hot Springs**. Art-lovers will want to nip east to the **Wallace Gallery** while Hobbit fans shouldn't miss **Hobbiton**, on the outskirts of Matamata. Southeast of Hamilton, Cambridge and Tirau are really just waystations on the route to Taupo, while to the south, **Te Awamutu** celebrates its Maori, Pakeha and Finn brothers heritage.

Waingaro Hot Springs

Waingaro Rd, 40km northwest of Hamilton • Daily 9am–9.30pm • $11; hot-water slide extra $6 for all day • ☎ 07 825 4761,
Ⓦ waingarohotsprings.co.nz

If you're working your way on the back roads between Auckland and Raglan consider stopping off at the old-fashioned (some might say dated) **Waingaro Hot Springs**, which offer a real slice of Kiwi family life with three hot-water pools and New Zealand's longest hot-water slide.

Ngaruawahia

The Waikato and Waipa rivers meet at the historically and culturally significant farming town of **NGARUAWAHIA**, 18km northwest of Hamilton on SH1. Both rivers were important Maori canoe routes and the **King Movement** (see p.216) has its roots here. Home to the Maori king, the town was the scene of the signing of the Raupatu Land Settlement (1995), whereby the government agreed to compensate Tainui for land confiscated in the 1860s.

The Maori heritage is most evident on **Regatta Day** (the closest Saturday to March 17). Watched by the Maori king, a parade of great war canoes takes place along the two rivers, with events such as hurdle races at the **Turangawaewae Marae** on River Road, off SH1 just north of the river bridge. The *marae* is only open to the public on Regatta Day; the rest of the year you can view it through the perimeter fence made of the dead trunks of tree ferns interspersed with robustly sculpted red posts and a couple of finely carved entranceways.

3

Wallace Gallery

167 Thames St, Morrinsville, 33km northeast of Hamilton • Tues–Sun 10am–4pm • Free • ☎ 07 889 7791, Ⓦ morrinsvillegallery.org.nz

The nondescript farming service town of Morrinsville seems an unlikely location for this small but classy gallery that's a rural offshoot of Auckland's Wallace Arts Centre (see p.93). It is housed in the town's mid-century former post office building where the old radiators have been put to imaginative use as doors and gallery seating. Changing exhibitions draw from the wider Wallace collection of contemporary New Zealand art.

Matamata

The dairy-farming and racehorse-breeding town of **Matamata**, 63km east of Hamilton, shot to prominence just after the millennium as the location of **Hobbiton** from the *Lord of the Rings* trilogy. Lifelike *Lord of the Rings* character **statues** have since been installed in the town centre but the only way to visit the Hobbiton location (on a working sheep farm 15km southwest of town) is on a tour.

Hobbiton Movie Set and Farm Tours

501 Buckland Rd, 16km southeast of Matamata • Daily 9.30am, 10.45am, noon, 1.15pm, 2.30pm, 3.45pm, plus 5pm and perhaps more in high season • $66 • ☎ 07 888 9913, Ⓦ hobbitontours.com • Drive straight there, get the free shuttle from Matamata i-SITE, or do the tour from Rotorua (2 daily; $99)

Between the filming of Peter Jackson's three *Lord of the Rings* films in the early 2000s and the master's return a decade later to shoot the two films of *The Hobbit* (due for release in December 2012 and December 2013), there really wasn't much to see at Hobbiton. The set was mostly dismantled and early visitors just got to see a handful of hobbit-hole facades amid the rolling hills of a working sheep farm. Interiors for all films were done in Wellington.

Since the shooting of *The Hobbit* in late 2011, however, almost all sets have been left intact. You can wander over a hillside of 42 hobbit-hole facades, some small, some large (to help give the sense of perspective when filming) and all superbly rendered to look old and hobbit-like. Chimneys appear to have soot on them, the fake lichen on fences looks totally authentic and there's an orchard of apple and pear trees (one of which was turned into a plum tree for the filming to satisfy a single line in the book). Across the lake the film-makers have created two of New Zealand's very few thatched buildings, a water mill connected by a "stone" bridge to *The Green Dragon* inn. Die-hard fans will revel in the tour guides' unexpurgated tales of the filming, but at ninety minutes the tour is a long one for the less ardent. The *Shire's Rest Café* sustains.

ARRIVAL AND INFORMATION — MATAMATA

By bus Intercity and NakedBus Auckland–Rotorua runs stop outside the i-SITE.
Destinations Auckland (1 daily; 3hr); Hamilton (4 daily; 1hr); Rotorua (1 daily; 50min); Tauranga (3 daily; 1hr).

i-SITE 45 Broadway (Mon–Fri 9am–5pm, Sat & Sun 9am–2.30pm; ☎ 07 888 7260, ⍫ matamatanz.co.nz). Useful for Hobbit-related information and has internet access.

EATING

★ **Workman's Café & Bar** 52 Broadway ☎ 07 888 5498. Funky, licensed café with more of a free spirit than you would expect to find in a place such as Matamata.

Great for coffee, cakes and snacks but also full meals such as beef salad with baby beets ($22). Tues 4–9pm, Wed–Sun 7am–9pm or later.

Cambridge

CAMBRIDGE, 24km southeast of Hamilton, was founded as a militia settlement at the navigable limit of the Waikato River in 1864, and today is surrounded by stud farms. Mosaics of Cambridge-bred winners are embedded in the pavements along the town's **Equine Stars Walk of Fame**. Contact the i-SITE if you fancy a ninety-minute stud farm tour ($110 for up to 3 people).

The town's collection of elegant **nineteenth- and twentieth-century buildings** is mapped on a heritage trail brochure (free from the i-SITE), making for a pleasant hour-long stroll.

ARRIVAL AND INFORMATION — CAMBRIDGE

By bus InterCity and NakedBus stop on Lake St, 50m from the i-SITE, on their Auckland–Wellington routes. Buslt (☎ 0800 287 5463) runs a local service from Hamilton that stops outside 36 Victoria St.
Destinations Hamilton (12 daily; 30min); Matamata (1–2 daily; 30min); Tauranga (1–2 daily; 1hr 30min).
i-SITE Corner of Queen and Victoria sts (Mon–Fri 9am–5pm, Sat & Sun 10am–4pm; ☎ 07 823 3456, ⍫ cambridge.co.nz). Located in the gracious former library building and has internet access.

EATING

The Deli on the Corner 48 Victoria St ☎ 07 827 5370. The pick of Cambridge's cafés is located in the airy 1920s Triangle Building, with a nice little corner seat for two in the apex. The sandwiches, pies and wraps are excellent, as are brunch dishes such as creamy mushrooms on toast

($14), which are served until 2pm. Or just stop in for great coffee, a pear and ginger muffin, bread and butter berry pudding ($6) or an ice cream. Mon–Fri 8am–5pm, Sat 8am–4pm, Sun 9am–3pm.

Tirau

Almost everyone seems to stop for a coffee in the farming settlement of **TIRAU**, 55km southeast of Hamilton, its highwayside strip completely taken over by corrugated iron. It kicked off with a corrugated-iron sheep housing a woolshop and followed with a sheepdog containing the **i-SITE**. The corrugated-iron constructions have attained iconic status and spawned a rash of sheet-metal structures and signs, including a biblical shepherd in the grounds of a church.

INFORMATION

i-SITE SH1 (daily 9am–5pm; ☎ 07 883 1202, ⍫ tirauinfo.co.nz).

EATING

Beanz & Machines 1 Hillcrest St ☎ 07 883 1146. The range of food is pretty limited so focus on the coffee at this small roastery where you can buy all sorts of coffee-making paraphernalia and drink top-class espresso. Daily 7am–4pm.

Te Awamutu

TE AWAMUTU, 30km south of Hamilton, is renowned for its musical and military history. The birthplace of fraternal Kiwi music icons Tim and Neil Finn, of **Split Enz** and **Crowded House** fame, "TA", as it's dubbed by locals, is surrounded by rolling hills and dairy pasture, and overlooked by Mount Pirongia. During the 1863 **New Zealand Wars**, Te Awamutu was a garrison for government forces and site of one of the most famous battles of the conflict, fought at the hastily constructed Orakau *pa*, where three hundred Maori held off two thousand soldiers for three days.

Immediately across the road from the i-SITE you'll find Te Awamutu's extensive **rose gardens** (open access; free), at their best between November and May. The i-SITE also holds the key to the 1854 garrison church, **St John's**, just across Arawata Street. Inside is a tribute from the British regiment, written in Maori, honouring Maori who crawled, under fire, onto the battlefield to give water to wounded British soldiers.

Te Awamutu Museum

135 Roche St • Mon–Fri 10am–4pm, Sat 10am–1pm, Sun 1–4pm • Free • ☎ 07 872 0085, ⚲ tamuseum.org.nz

The **Te Awamutu Museum** punches above its (admittedly modest) weight with interesting displays about European settlers and the New Zealand Wars, and a "*True Colours*" exhibit devoted to the Finn brothers, complete with home movies, newspaper clippings from the early days, an interview with the boys and assorted artefacts. The room of Maori artefacts is notable chiefly for **Uenuku**, a 2.7m-high wooden representation of an important Maori god. It looks quite unlike almost any other Maori carving you'll see, something that supports the contention that it was made before 1500 AD. No one really knows why it spent decades (perhaps centuries) in a lake near Te Awamutu where it was found in 1906. Uenuku currently forms part of a major Tainui exhibit at Te Papa in Wellington: until he returns in early 2014 you'll have to make do with recordings of Maori talking about what Uenuku means to them.

ARRIVAL AND DEPARTURE
TE AWAMUTU

Buses InterCity, NakedBus and The Naki Bus stop at the i-SITE. Bus!t runs to Hamilton.

Destinations Hamilton (8 daily; 30min); Otorohanga (5 daily; 20min).

INFORMATION AND TOURS

i-SITE 1 Gorst Ave (Mon–Fri 9am–5pm, Sat & Sun 10am–4pm; ☎ 07 871 3259, ⚲ teawamutuinfo.com). All the information you need, plus free hot showers.

Finn Tour Fans of the brothers Finn can take a self-guided jaunt around (the frankly fairly dull) places of significance from the brothers' formative years by buying the "Finn Tour" booklet ($5) from the i-SITE.

EATING AND DRINKING

Empire Espresso Bar 65 Sloane St ☎ 07 871 2095, ⚲ empireespresso.co.nz. Smart little café in the entrance to a 1915 former cinema with great counter food (roast vegetable filo), a light breakfast of German rye with honeycomb and lemon crème ($5.50), and lunches such as Cajun chicken with hummus and salad ($16). Try their passionfruit and macadamia macaroon with a long black.

Mon–Fri 6am–3.30pm, Sat 6am–2.30pm.

Fahrenheit 13 Roche St ☎ 07 871 5429. Find a sunny afternoon seat on the terrace overlooking the main street for a beer, a Caesar salad ($17) or tapas ($12) such as confit duck arancini balls or salt and pepper calamari. Tues–Sun 10am–10pm or later.

3

Raglan

Visitors often linger far longer than they intended to in **RAGLAN**, 48km west of Hamilton, which hugs the south side of the large and picturesque Whaingaroa Harbour. They're lured by the town's bohemian arts and crafts tenor and the laidback spirit of the **surfing** community – the waters here feature some of the best left-handed breaks in the world.

Cafés, banks and pubs line palm-shaded **Bow Street**, whose western end butts against the harbour, spanned by a slender footbridge where kids are always egging each other to jump off. Apart from wandering the foreshore, there are few sights as such, so you'll soon want to head 8km south of town to the surf beaches.

There's good **hiking** and **horse riding** both here and further south at **Bridal Veil Falls**. Sweeping views of Raglan Harbour and along the coast unfurl from the **summit** of **Mount Karioi** (755m), reached on a winding gravel-road loop around the Karioi Mountain.

Brief history

The horizon to the south is dominated by **Mount Karioi**, which according to Maori legend was the ultimate goal of the great migratory canoe Tainui. On reaching the mouth of the harbour a bar blocked the way, hence the name Whaingaroa ("long pursuit"). The shortened epithet, Whangaroa, was the name used for the harbour until 1855, when it was renamed Raglan after the officer who led the Charge of the Light Brigade.

Raglan Museum

15 Wainui Rd • Nov–March Mon–Thurs 9.30am–4pm, Fri 9.30am–5pm, Sat & Sun 10am–5pm; April–Oct Mon–Thurs 10am–4pm, Fri 10am–5pm, Sat 10am–4pm, Sun 10am–3pm • $2 • ☎ 07 825 0556, ⓦ raglanmuseum.co.nz

The i-SITE provides access to this small museum with modest displays on the area's history including the original telephone exchange and an apothecary chest. Surf fans should check out the short film on 1970s attempts to use early computers to predict ocean wave patterns and hence the best day to head to the coast at a time when high petrol prices limited the transport options of impecunious surfers.

Old School Arts Centre

Stewart St • ☎ 07 825 0023, ⓦ raglanartscentre.co.nz

Raglan is home to dozens of **artists** and a handful of **galleries** including the Old School Arts Centre, housed in a heritage building and run by the town's creative community. It hosts a funky **market** (second Sun of each month 10am–2pm; ⓦ raglanmarket.com) with everything locally produced. They also publish the free *Raglan Arts Trail* leaflet.

Te Kopua and Ocean beaches

The safest **swimming beach** is **Te Kopua**, in the heart of town, reached via the footbridge from lower Bow Street or by car along Wainui Road and Marine Parade. **Ocean Beach**, just outside the town off Wainui Road on the way to Whale Bay, gives great views of the bar of rock and sand that stretches across the mouth of the harbour and is a fine picnic spot, but strong undertows make swimming unsafe. For Raglan's renowned **surf beaches**, see box opposite.

Te Toto and Mount Karioi tracks

Both start 12km south of Raglan along Whaanga Rd • Te Toto 2km return; 1hr; 200m ascent on way back • Karioi 8km return; 5–6hr; 650m ascent; not to be attempted in bad weather

For a short walk head to **Te Toto Track** which heads down steeply from an obvious car park through coastal forest to the grassy margins of Te Toto Stream. From there it is easy enough to access the stony beach.

RAGLAN TOURS AND ACTIVITIES

There are great waves all around the country but Raglan is New Zealand's finest **surfing** destination – the lines of perfect breakers appear like blue corduroy southwest of town. The best place for inexperienced surfers is the rock-free **Ngarunui Beach**, 5km south of Raglan. For the experienced, the main breaks, both around 8km south of town, are **Whale Bay** and **Manu Bay** (Waireki), which featured in the cult 1960s surf film *Endless Summer*.

For non-surfers, Raglan is mostly about doing not much at all, but there is plenty to keep you occupied. You really should spend some time on the harbour, particularly exploring the horizontally jointed **Pancake Rocks** forming low cliffs just across Raglan's Whaingaroa Harbour. Kayaking is a perfect way to see them at their best.

Inland, saddles are the way to go, either on horseback or mountain bike.

SURFING AND BOARD SPORTS

GAgRAglan Volcom Lane ☎07 825 8702, ⓦgagraglan.com. A great range of rental surfboards (from $35/4hr) and loads of gear for sale.

Raglan Kitesurfing Lost Lane ☎07 825 8402, ⓦraglankitesurfing.com. Beginners can take one-on-one intro sessions (on demand; weather dependent) starting at $60 and building up to $95 when you're on the water. Experienced riders can rent kitesurfing gear ($80/day), while stand-up paddle boarding ($25/2hr, including a 10 or 20min lesson) is also an option.

Raglan Surfing School Whale Bay ☎07 825 7873, ⓦraglansurfingschool.co.nz. The main surf school with rentals (half-day from $35, including wetsuit) and assorted packages including starter lessons (3hr; group $89; private $129) using soft boards.

EXPLORING THE HARBOUR

Raglan Backpackers ☎07 825 0515, ⓦraglan backpackers.co.nz. Rent sit-on-tops (singles $35/3hr; doubles $45/4hr) then launch them from right next to the hostel and explore the harbour, particularly the Pancake Rocks over the far side, easily reached in 15–20min. $5 discounts for hostel guests.

Raglan Kayak ☎07 825 8862, ⓦraglaneco.co.nz. Join their guided "Kayak 'n' Coffee" tour (3hr; $75) across the harbour to Pancake Rocks, rent a kayak (singles: $40/half-day; $60/full day) or go stand-up paddle boarding ($20/hour, $40/half-day). Operates Nov–May.

Wahine Moe Raglan Wharf ☎07 825 7873, ⓦraglanboatcharters.co.nz. Delightful 2hr sunset cruises ($49) on Raglan Harbour aboard a powerful cruiser. A barbecue sandwich is included and there's a bar on board. Operated Nov–April daily on demand.

HORSE RIDING

Extreme Horse Adventures Ruapuke, 20km southwest of Raglan ☎07 825 0059, ⓦwildcoast .co.nz. Get almost 3hr of horse riding on this farm, through native bush and on to Ruapuke Beach for ($90/person). They'll provide low-cost transport out there if you get a group of four or more together.

Magic Mountain Horse Treks 334 Houchen Rd, 15km south of Raglan ☎07 825 6892, ⓦmagicmountain .co.nz. Ride an hour across farmland ($40) or take a two-hour trek to Bridal Veil Falls ($80; advance bookings essential). To get there, head 8km east of Raglan on SH23, then 6km up Te Mata Rd, and 3km up Houchen Rd.

CYCLING

Bike2Bay 24b Stewart St ☎07 825 0309, ⓦbike2bay .com. There's great riding in the countryside all around Raglan (some of it quite challenging) and these guys know it best. They specialize in self-guided tours including bike rental and plenty of local knowledge.

Go for the Round Mt Karioi (45km; $30), a sunset descent known as Ruapuke Thunder ($40 including car transfer), or a two-day tour to some limestone caves with B&B in a nearby cabin ($165).

The same car park is the start of the much more arduous **Mount Karioi Track**, which follows a ridge through manuka with rapidly improving views along the coast. A walk through dense forest and a short descent using a ladder brings you to the final hand-over-hand ascent using fixed chains.

Bridal Veil Falls

20km southeast of Raglan

Bridal Veil Falls hides in dense native bush just off the Kawhia Road. Water plummets 55m down a sheer rock face into a green pool where rainbows appear in the spray in the sunshine. From the car park it's a ten-minute walk down to the bottom of the falls; allow twice that for the walk back up.

ARRIVAL AND INFORMATION RAGLAN

By bus The #23 Hamilton city Busit bus arrives outside the i-SITE.

Destinations Hamilton (2–3 daily; 1hr).

i-SITE 15 Wainui Rd (Nov–March Mon–Thurs 9.30am–4pm, Fri 9.30am–5pm, Sat & Sun 10am–5pm; April–Oct Mon–Thurs 10am–4pm, Fri 10am–5pm, Sat 10am–4pm,

Sun 10am–3pm; ☎ 07 825 0556, ⓦ raglan.org.nz). Can help with booking accommodation, including holiday cottages and apartments.

Services There's wired and wi-fi internet access at the library, 7 Bow St (Mon–Fri 9.30am–5pm, Sat 9.30am–12.30pm).

ACCOMMODATION

Bow Street Studios 1 Bow St ☎ 07 825 0551, ⓦ bowstreet.co.nz All seven one-bedroom units have harbour views from the upstairs bedroom and a subtropical terrace accessed from the kitchen/lounge. Everything is well thought out, including New Zealand art and good magazines. There's also a pretty two-bedroom cottage. Units & cottage $\underline{\$230}$

Harbourview Hotel 14 Bow St ☎ 07 825 8010, ⓔ harbourviewhotel@vodafone.co.nz. A stay at Raglan's centrepiece old hotel comes with verandas overlooking the main street, pleasant rooms and an on-site sports bar and à la carte restaurant. $\underline{\$95}$

Karioi Lodge 5 Whaanga Rd, Whale Bay ☎ 07 825 7873, ⓦ karioilodge.co.nz. Pleasant hostel in native bush 8km southwest of Raglan, with four-bed dorms and doubles and hillside campervan sites. Amenities include a communal kitchen, sauna, cheap bike rental, mountain tracks to explore and free pick-up from Raglan. Also runs Raglan Surfing School. Van sites $\underline{\$15}$, dorms $\underline{\$30}$, doubles $\underline{\$75}$

★ **Raglan Backpackers** 6 Nero St ☎ 07 825 0515, ⓦ raglanbackpackers.co.nz. Wonderfully relaxed hammock-strewn backpackers in the town centre, laid out around a courtyard that backs onto the estuary. There's free use of kayaks, bikes, golf clubs, fishing gear, spa and sauna, plus nice touches such as free sunscreen. Also offers cheap surfboard rental ($25/half-day including wetsuit)

and lessons. Dorms $\underline{\$27}$, doubles $\underline{\$72}$

Raglan Kopua Holiday Park Marine Parade ☎ 07 825 8283, ⓦ raglanholidaypark.co.nz. Central campsite with a wide range of cabins, 1km by road from town and also accessible by a short footbridge. It is well sited next to Te Kopua, the harbour's safest swimming beach. Camping $\underline{\$17}$, dorms $\underline{\$25}$, cabins $\underline{\$85}$, motel units $\underline{\$130}$

Sleeping Lady Lodgings 5 Whaanga Rd, Whale Bay ☎ 07 825 7873, ⓦ sleepinglady.co.nz. *Karioi Lodge* (see above) also has half a dozen delightful self-contained holiday homes scattered through coastal bush 8km southwest of Raglan, sleeping from two to twelve (minimum two-night stay in peak season); prices can range as high as $290/night for two, and it's $35 for each additional person. $\underline{\$100}$

★ **Solscape Eco Retreat** Wainui Rd, Manu Bay, 6km south of Raglan ☎ 07 825 8268, ⓦ solscape .co.nz. Wonderfully idiosyncratic accommodation (and associate YHA) in imaginatively converted train carriages and cottages set on top of a hill with panoramic views. Eco-friendly initiatives include a home-made solar water heating system, solar LED lights, tipi-style accommodation and individual earth-wood units (timber frames and roofs with mud walls). There are also free pick-ups from Raglan, and surf lessons. Camping $\underline{\$16}$, dorms $\underline{\$27}$, tipis per person $\underline{\$34}$, double cabooses $\underline{\$115}$, eco self-contained studios $\underline{\$180}$

EATING AND DRINKING

One of Raglan's charms is the relaxed café-style places that make for a great post-surf breakfast or laidback meal. Most places are around the intersection of Bow Street and Wainui Road, and generally run considerably shorter hours in winter and close when they feel like it.

Harbourview Hotel 14 Bow St ☎ 07 825 8010. This reliable hotel/pub has good-value meals (mains $23–30), a bar menu of burgers, nachos and seafood chowder (all around $15) and draught beer and wine by the glass. Mon–Sat 10am–midnight, Sun 10am–10pm.

★ **Orca Restaurant & Bar** 2 Wallis St ☎ 07 825 6543, ⓦ orcarestaurant.co.nz. Raglan's best restaurant, serving casual brunches and standout modern Kiwi evening meals along the lines of artichoke and potato salad with truffle mayo, followed by pork belly with mustard mash or braised beef cheek (most mains $20–30). The attached bar opens to a deck overlooking the estuary, and has regular live bands (Fri free, Sat $5–10). Mon–Fri 10am–10pm, Sat & Sun 9am–10pm. Bar stays open until 1am when busy.

★ **Raglan Roast** Volcom Lane. Tucked down a laneway next to GAgRAglan surf shop, this tiny, daytime hole-in-the-wall spills out to a clutch of tables and roasts its knockout coffee on site. There's no food except a cookie jar, but you're welcome to bring your own. Mon–Sat 7.30am–5pm, Sun 8am–5pm.

The Shack 19 Bow St ☎ 07 825 0027. Newly refurbished café/bar with a laidback vibe, a steady flow of interesting locals and an extensive range of imaginative food such as creamy balsamic mushrooms with thyme on sourdough ($13). Free wi-fi with purchase. Mon–Thurs, Sat & Sun 8.30am–5pm, Fri 8.30am–10pm or later.

Kawhia

Far-flung **KAWHIA**, 55km south of Raglan and a similar distance northwest of Otorohanga, slumbers on the northern side of Kawhia Harbour but wakes up when its population of around five hundred people is joined by over four thousand holidaying Kiwis flocking to **Ocean Beach**, where **Te Puia Hot Springs** bubble from beneath the black sand. At peak time, many come to witness the annual **whaleboat races** (Jan 1), when 11m-long, five-crew whaling boats dash across the bay. The only other site of note is the modest **Kawhia Museum**, Kaora St (Oct–March daily 11am–4pm; April–Nov Wed–Sun noon–3pm; free), covering the region's rich Maori heritage with some good carved pieces, a fine modern flax and feather cloak and an 1880s-era kauri whaleboat.

The village centre is strung along Jervois Street, where there's a petrol station and a handful of combined shop/cafés.

Brief history

Legends tell of the arrival of the **Tainui** in 1350, in their ancestral **waka** (canoe), and of how they found Kawhia Harbour so bountiful that they lived on its shores for three hundred years. Tribal battles over the rich fishing grounds eventually forced them inland, and in 1821, after constant attacks by the better-armed Waikato Maori, the Tainui chief, Te Rauparaha, finally led his people to the relative safety of Kapiti Island.

When the original *waka* arrived in Kawhia, it was tied to a pohutukawa tree, Tangi te Korowhiti, still growing on the shore on Kaora Street, near the junction with Moke Street, 800m west of the museum, and reached along the waterside footpath. The Tainui canoe is buried on a grassy knoll above the beautifully carved and painted **meeting house** of the **Maketu Marae**, further along Kaora Street at Karewa Beach, with Hani and Puna stones marking its stern and prow. The arrival of **European** settlers and missionaries in the 1830s made Kawhia prosperous as a gateway to the fertile King Country, though its fortunes declined in the early years of the twentieth century, owing to its unsuitability for deep-draught ships.

Te Puia Hot Springs

Accessed 4km along the Tainui-Kawhia Forest Rd

It isn't easy to find **Te Puia Hot Springs**, and they're at their best an hour either side of low tide: check times and ask for detailed directions at the museum or any of the local stores. Park at the road-end car park and follow a track over the dunes to where you may find others have already dug shallow holes in the sand. Be warned: the black sand can scorch bare feet and dangerous rip tides make swimming unsafe.

ARRIVAL AND INFORMATION

KAWHIA

By car There is no public transport of any kind to Kawhia, so you'll have to use your own wheels to get here.

Tourist information There's a small visitor centre located inside the museum (Oct–March daily 11am–4pm; April–Nov Wed–Sun noon–3pm; ⊕ kawhiaharbour.co.nz). This is the best place to enquire about harbour cruises that usually run through the summer months.

ACCOMMODATION AND EATING

Quintessential eating Kawhia-style is fish and chips from one of the town takeaways, eaten on the wharf overlooking the harbour, followed with a beer in the very traditional *Kawhia Hotel* on Jervois St.

Annie's 146 Jervois St ☎07 871 0198. The best of Kawhia's limited selection of cafés, with seating on the back lawn and on the front deck with its distant harbour views. Expect espresso, milkshakes, toasted sandwiches and the likes of fish, chips and salad ($18). Internet available. Daily 9am–4pm or later.

Kawhia Camping Ground 73 Moke St ☎07 871 0863, ⓦkawhiacampingground.co.nz. Shady and fairly basic family campsite one block back from the beach with simple but adequate facilities. Camping $16.50, cabins $46, caravans with awnings $66

Kawhia Beachside S-cape 225 Pouewe St (SH31) ☎07 871 0727, ⓦkawhiabeachsidescape.co.nz. Waterside campsite where, a couple of hours either side of high tide, you can launch kayaks ($11/hr). The cabins are a bit scruffy but the cottages are modern. Camping sites $42, cabins $65, cottages $155

The King Country

The rural landscape inland from Kawhia and south of Hamilton is known as the **King Country**, because it was the refuge of **King Tawhiao** and members of the **King Movement** (see below), after they were driven south during the New Zealand Wars. The area soon gained a reputation among Pakeha as a Maori stronghold renowned for difficult terrain and a welcome that meant few, if any, Europeans entered. However, the forest's respite was short-lived: when peace was declared in 1881, loggers descended in droves.

Tourist interest focuses on **Waitomo**, a tiny village at the heart of a unique and dramatic landscape, honeycombed by limestone caves ethereally illuminated by

---

THE KING MOVEMENT

Before Europeans arrived, Maori loyalty was solely to their immediate family and tribe, but wrangles with acquisitive European settlers led many tribes to discard age-old feuds in favour of a common crusade against the Pakeha. **Maori nationalism** hardened in the face of blatantly unjust treatment and increasing pressure to "sell" land.

In 1856, the influential Otaki Maori sought a chief who might unite the disparate tribes against the Europeans, and in 1858 the Waikato, Taupo and other tribes, largely originating from the Tainui canoe (see p.215), chose **Te Wherowhero**. Taking the title of **Potatau I**, the newly elected king established himself at Ngaruawahia – to this day the seat of the **King Movement**. The principal tenet of the movement was to resist the appropriation of Maori land and provide a basis for a degree of self-government. Whether out of a genuine misunderstanding of these aims or for reasons of economic expediency, the settlers interpreted the formation of the movement as an act of rebellion – despite the fact that Queen Victoria was included in the movement's prayers – and tension heightened. The situation escalated into armed conflict later in 1858 when the Waitara Block near New Plymouth was confiscated from its Maori owners. The fighting spread throughout the central North Island: the King Movement won a notable victory at Gate Pa, in the Bay of Plenty, but was eventually overwhelmed at Te Ranga.

Seeing the wars as an opportunity to settle old scores, some Maori tribes sided with the British and, in a series of battles along the Waikato, forced the kingites further south, until a crushing blow was struck at Orakau in 1864. The king and his followers fled south of the Puniu River into an area that, by virtue of their presence, became known as the **King Country**.

There they remained, with barely any European contact, until 1881, when **King Tawhiao**, who had succeeded to the throne in 1860, made peace. Gradually the followers of the King Movement drifted back to Ngaruawahia. Although by no means supported by all Maori, the loose coalition of the contemporary King Movement plays an important role in the current reassessment of Maori–Pakeha relations, and the reigning Maori King is the recipient of state and royal visits.

glowworms, and overlaid by a geological wonderland of karst. North of Waitomo is the small dairy town of **Otorohanga**, with a kiwi house and Kiwiana displays. To the south of Waitomo, **Te Kuiti** provided sanctuary in the 1860s for Maori rebel Te Kooti, who reciprocated with a beautifully carved meeting house.

From Te Kuiti, SH4 runs south to **Taumarunui**, with access to the Whanganui River and the start of the **Forgotten World Highway** (see p.239).

Otorohanga

Surrounded by sheep and cattle country some 30km south of Te Awamutu, **Otorohanga** celebrates all things archetypally Kiwi with street signs bearing kiwi-bird icons and a series of glassed-in shrines to **Kiwiana icons** along the **Ed Hillary Walkway**, off Maniapoto Street next to the ANZ bank. Exhibits include Marmite, pavlova, the farm dog and Hillary himself. A few more displays spill over onto Maniapoto Street, where John Haddad Menswear Store, at #65, sells classic Kiwi menswear such as hats and oilskins.

Otorohanga Kiwi House & Native Bird Park

20 Alex Telfer Drive, off Kakamutu Rd • Daily: Sept–May 9am–4.30pm; June–Aug 9am–4pm; kiwi feeding daily 1.30pm; twilight tours daily around 6.30pm • $20; tours $50 • ☎ 07 873 7391, ⓦ kiwihouse.org.nz

Otorohanga prides itself on having one of the best kiwi houses in the country. The grumpy little bird's lifestyle is explained in the well-laid-out nocturnal enclosure where you really feel close to the birds. Outdoor enclosures contain the lizard-like tuatara and most species of the New Zealand native bird, many in a walk-through aviary. You can catch a kiwi feeding and there are also guided twilight tours with plenty of explanation and a chance to see the birds at their most active.

ARRIVAL AND INFORMATION

By train The station is centrally located on Wahanui Crescent.
Destinations National Park (3–7 weekly; 2hr 20min); Wellington (3–7 weekly; 9hr).
By bus InterCity, NakedBus and The Naki Bus all stop on SH3 in the middle of town.

Destinations Hamilton (5 daily; 1hr); Te Kuiti (5 daily; 15–50min); Waitomo (5 daily; 15min).
i-SITE 27 Turongo St (Mon–Fri 9am–5pm, Sat & Sun 10am–2pm; ☎ 07 873 8951, ⓦ otorohanga.co.nz).
Services You can pick up free wi-fi from the library, adjacent to the i-SITE.

ACCOMMODATION AND EATING

Otorohanga Holiday Park 20 Huiputea Drive ☎ 07 873 7253, ⓦ kiwiholidaypark.co.nz. Well-equipped central campsite in the centre of town with modern facilities and an Xbox 360 in the TV lounge. Camping $̲1̲6̲, cabin $̲6̲5̲, motel units $̲1̲0̲5̲
The Thirsty Weta 57 Maniapoto St ☎ 07 873 6699, ⓦ theweta.co.nz. This is your best bet for a beer in the sun – or try one of their hearty meals, such as a pot of mussels in chilli and coconut ($15). There's live music on

Friday nights and free wi-fi. Daily 10am–1am.
Origin Coffee Station 7 Wahanui St ☎ 07 873 8550, ⓦ origincoffee.co.nz. The old Otorohanga Railway Station is the venue for the best coffee in town, directly imported from Malawi, where the owner, Roger, once grew the stuff. It is roasted on the premises to produce mild but complex flavours. If you want to eat you'll need to BYO food. Mon–Fri 8.30am–4.30pm.

Waitomo

Some 16km southwest of Otorohanga (8km west of SH3), **WAITOMO** is a diminutive village of under fifty inhabitants with an outsize reputation for incredible **cave trips** and magnificent **karst features** – streams that disappear down funnel-shaped sinkholes (Waitomo means "water entering shaft" in Maori), craggy limestone outcrops, fluted rocks, potholes and natural bridges caused by cave ceiling collapses. Below ground, seeping water has sculpted the rock into eerie and extraordinary shapes. The ongoing process of **cave creation** involves the interaction of rainwater and carbon dioxide from the air, which together form a weak acid. As more carbon dioxide is absorbed from the soil the acid grows stronger, dissolving the limestone and enlarging cracks and joints, eventually forming the varied caves you see today. Each year a further seventy cubic metres of limestone (about the size of a double-decker bus) is dissolved. Many of the caves are dazzlingly illuminated by **glowworms**.

The bulk of the caves are in (or visited from) Waitomo: for DIY limestone scenery sightseeing in any weather, head west to **Mangapohue Natural Bridge** and **Piripiri Caves** (see p.222).

Brief history

Local chief **Tane Tinorau** introduced Waitomo's underground passages to English surveyor **Fred Mace**, in 1887. The pair explored further, building a raft of flax stems and drifting along an underground stream, with candles their only source of light. Within a year, the enterprising Tane was guiding tourists to see the spectacle. The government took over in 1906 and it wasn't until 1989 that the caves were returned to their Maori owners, who receive a percentage of all revenue generated and participate in the site's management.

Visiting the Waitomo caves

Only a fraction of the 45km of cave passages under Waitomo can be visited on **guided tours**. Operators lease access from farmers, so each offers the chance to explore different caves. The get-wet active caving trips are listed in the Adventure Caving box (see p.221).

In all cases, **heavy rain** can lead to cancellations if water levels rise too high. This happens perhaps ten days a year, so it pays to check weather forecasts and plan accordingly.

Waitomo Caves Discovery Centre

At the i-SITE, 21 Waitomo Caves Rd • Daily: Dec 26–Feb 8.15am–7pm; March–Dec 24 8.45am–5pm or 5.30pm • $5, though free or discounted with many caving trips • ☎ 07 878 7640, ⓦ waitomodiscovery.org

Your underground experience will be enhanced by a prior visit to this small museum with informative exhibits on the geology and history of the caves, interactive displays

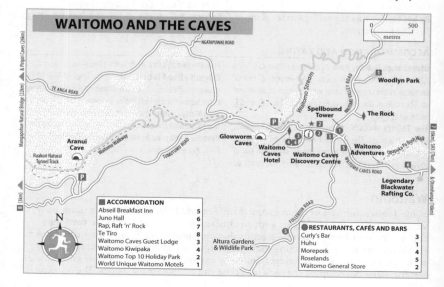

WAITOMO AND THE CAVES

0 — 500 metres

NGATAPUWAE ROAD
TE ANGA ROAD
Waitomo Stream
WAITOMO VALLEY ROAD
Woodlyn Park
Spellbound Tower
The Rock
Glowworm Caves
Aranui Cave
Waitomo Walkway
TUMUTUMU ROAD
Ruakuri Natural Tunnel Track
Waitomo Caves Hotel
Waitomo Caves Discovery Centre
Waitomo Adventures
Opapaka Pa Bush Walk
WAITOMO CAVES ROAD
Legendary Blackwater Rafting Co.
FULLERTON ROAD
Altura Gardens & Wildlife Park
& Piripiri Caves (26km)
Mangapohue Natural Bridge (22km)
(3km)
SH3 (7km)
Otorohanga (16km)

N

■ ACCOMMODATION	
Abseil Breakfast Inn	5
Juno Hall	6
Rap, Raft 'n' Rock	7
Te Tiro	8
Waitomo Caves Guest Lodge	3
Waitomo Kiwipaka	4
Waitomo Top 10 Holiday Park	2
World Unique Waitomo Motels	1

● RESTAURANTS, CAFÉS AND BARS	
Curly's Bar	3
Huhu	1
Morepork	4
Roselands	5
Waitomo General Store	2

GLOWWORMS

Glowworms (*Arachnocampa luminosa*) are found all over New Zealand, mostly in caves but also on overhanging banks in the bush where in dark and damp conditions you'll often see the telltale bluey-green glow. A glowworm isn't a worm at all, but the matchstick-sized larval stage of the fungus gnat (a relative of the mosquito), which attaches itself to the cave roof and produces around twenty or thirty mucus-and-silk threads or "fishing lines", which hang down a few centimetres. Drawn by the highly efficient chemical light, midges and flying insects get ensnared in the threads and the glowworm draws in the line to eat them.

The six- to nine-month larval stage is the only time in the glowworm **life cycle** that it can eat, so it needs to store energy for the two-week pupal stage when it transforms into the adult gnat that has no mouthparts. The gnat only lives a couple of days, during which time the female has to frantically find a mate in the dark caves (the glow is a big help here) and lay her batch of a hundred or so eggs. After a two- to three-week incubation, they hatch into glowworms and the process begins anew.

3

on the life cycle of glowworms and cave wetas (prehistoric grasshopper-like creepy crawlies) and a free eighteen-minute multimedia show, screened on request. If you're worried about tight underground passages, test out your nerve (and girth) on the cave crawl.

Waitomo Glowworm Caves

39 Waitomo Caves Rd • Daily 9am–5pm plus additional summer twilight tours; 45min tours depart every 30min • $48; combination ticket available: with Aranui cave $65; with Ruakuri cave $79; all 3 caves $89 • ☎ 0800 456 922, ⓦ waitomo.com

Bus tours all stop at Waitomo's original cave experience, **Waitomo Glowworm Caves**, 500m west of the i-SITE. Paved walkways and lighting pick out the best of the stalactites and stalagmites and there's a boat ride through the grotto, where glowworms form a heavenly canopy of ghostly pale-green pinpricks of light.

The fairly steep price is offset by combos with Ruakuri and Aranui caves (see below), and a 10 percent online discount when booked 48 hours in advance. To avoid the crowds and have the best experience, try and get on with either the first or last tour of the day.

Ruakuri and Aranui caves

Ruakuri Scenic Reserve, 3.5km west of the i-SITE **Ruakuri** Tours daily 9am, 10am, 11.30am, 12.30pm, 1.30pm, 2.30pm & 3.30pm; 2hr with 90min underground • $67 **Aranui** Tours daily 10am, 11am, 1pm, 2pm & 3pm; 45min • $46 • ☎ 0800 782 587, ⓦ waitomo.com

You descend into a vast theatrically lit void to access the "The Den of the Dogs" as **Ruakuri Cave**'s name translates. Waitomo's longest guided underground walking tour follows suspended walkways linking spectacular, subtly-lit cavern passages as guides thread the practicalities of cave creation and the glowworm life cycle with Maori stories. The whole trip is wheelchair accessible.

The Glowworm Caves office also sells tickets for tours around the **Aranui Cave**, which, although only 250m long, is geologically spectacular, with high-ceilinged chambers and magnificent stalactites and stalagmites. You'll see cave wetas but no glowworms.

Spellbound

10 Waitomo Caves Rd • Tours July–May 2–6 daily • 3hr • $75 • ☎ 0800 773 552, ⓦ glowworm.co.nz

For a gentle but impressive underground experience it is hard to beat this two-cave combo starting off with a peaceful drift along a subterranean stream under a canopy of magnificent glowworms. The second cave has the pick of the limestone formations, a moa skeleton and expert explanation of the processes that create the weird forms and force the passages to cross a natural faultline.

Woodlyn Park

1177 Waitomo Valley Rd, 1km north of Waitomo • Show daily at 1.30pm • $26 • ☎ 07 878 6666, ⓦ woodlynpark.co.nz

If the rain hits and caving is a washout head for **Woodlyn Park**, where a rustic barn hosts the entertaining hour-long **Billy Black's Kiwi Culture Show**, an offbeat look at the history of logging and farming, with loads of audience participation such as helping shear sheep or chop wood, always with a dollop of rural Kiwi humour. Even if this is normally the sort of thing you'd run a mile from, take a chance on this – it's good fun.

Altura Park

477 Fullerton Rd, 4km south of Waitomo • Daily 9am–5pm • $12; 1hr horse-riding treks $65 including park entry (book in advance) • ☎ 07 878 5278, ⓦ alturapark.co.nz

If you've got kids in tow, or just love farm animals, head for this working farm where you can wander through the award-winning gardens, visit (and sometimes feed) its emus, goats, rabbits and miniature horses, or go **horse trekking**, with trips customized for riders of all abilities including beginners. Bring a picnic.

ARRIVAL AND DEPARTURE   WAITOMO

By train and bus The nearest trains, InterCity and Naked buses stop 15km away in Otorohanga, from where the Waitomo Shuttle ($12 one-way; bookings essential; ☎ 0800 808 279) ferries people to Waitomo. Great Sights buses (run by InterCity) run daily to Waitomo on their Auckland–Rotorua run. The Waitomo Wanderer (☎ 0800 000 4321, ⓦ travelheadfirst.com) runs daily from Rotorua (and Taupo by prior booking). Tickets for trains and buses are available at the i-SITE.

Bus destinations Auckland (1 most days; 4hr 20min); Otorohanga (5 daily; 15min); Rotorua (2 daily; 2hr–2hr 30min).

INFORMATION

i-SITE 21 Waitomo Caves Rd, inside the Waitomo Caves Discovery Centre (daily: Dec 26–Feb 8.15am–7pm; March–Dec 24 8.45am–5pm or 5.30pm; ☎ 07 878 7640, ⓦ waitomoinfo.co.nz). This mine of information acts as a booking agent for cave trips; pick up the free *Waitomo Caves* map, which shows local walks.

Services Though there is an ATM, there is no bank, petrol or supermarket at Waitomo; the nearest are 15km away at Otorohanga and Te Kuiti. The i-SITE has a post office and internet access.

ACCOMMODATION

Backpackers are well provided for but other **accommodation** is fairly limited so **book in advance**, particularly between November and January.

Abseil Breakfast Inn 709 Waitomo Caves Rd, 400m east of the museum ☎ 07 878 7815, ⓦ abseilinn.co.nz. Charge up the very steep drive to this relaxing and stylish B&B on top of a hill with great views from the four individually styled rooms and the lovely BBQ deck. Your enthusiastic host will keep you entertained, or there's free

---

WAITOMO WALKS

Ruakuri Bushwalk (2km return; 45min). Tumutumu Road takes you 3.5km west to this wonderful track, one of the most impressive short walks in the country. Starting from the car park for the Aranui Cave, the track follows the Waitomo Stream on boardwalks and walkways past cave entrances. Ducking and weaving through short tunnel sections, you eventually reach a huge cave where the stream temporarily threads underground. The walk is especially magical at night when lit by glowworms in the bush, so head out there around dusk for the best of both worlds.

Waitomo Walkway (4km each way; 1hr). Waitomo village and the Ruakuri Bushwalk are linked by this pleasant track that starts opposite the i-SITE, disappears into the bush then follows the Waitomo Stream to the Aranui Cave car park. They make a great 3hr combo.

ADVENTURE CAVING

Waitomo excels at adrenaline-fuelled **adventure-caving trips**, which should be booked in advance, especially for the November to January period. Most trips involve getting kitted out in a wetsuit, rubber boots and a caver's helmet with lamp, and combine two or more adventure elements. Kids under 12 (or under a minimum weight) are not usually allowed on adventure trips, and the wilder trips are for those 16 and over.

Access to some caves is by **abseiling**. Some trips feature **cave tubing** (also known as blackwater rafting), generally involving wedging your derrière inside the inner tube of a truck tyre for a (usually) gentle float through a pitch-black section of cave gazing at a galaxy of glowworm light overhead.

OPERATORS

The Legendary Black Water Rafting Co 585 Waitomo Caves Rd ☎0800 228 464, ⦿waitomo.com. Two wetsuit-clad trips in Ruakuri Cave, the easiest being the Black Labyrinth (3hr; 1hr underground; $119), which is mostly spent on an idyllic float through a glowworm cave with the additional excitement of a short jump from an underground waterfall. The more adventurous Black Abyss (5hr; 2–3hr underground; $220) kicks off with a 35m abseil down a narrow *tomo* followed by an eerie flying-fox ride into darkness, some floating among glowworms and an exciting scramble back to the surface up two short waterfalls.

Rap, Raft 'n' Rock 95 Waitomo Caves Rd/SH37, 8km east of the i-SITE, 1km from the junction with SH3 ☎0800 228 372, ⦿caveraft.com. Budget, do-everything-in-one, small-group trips starting with a 27m abseil into a glowworm-filled cave explored partly on foot and partly floating on a tube, and ending with a rock climb out to the starting point (5hr; $160).

Waitomo Adventures Waitomo Valley Rd (moving to "The Rock" on Waitomo Valley Rd by early 2013) ☎0800 924 866, ⦿waitomo.co.nz. Professional outfit offering five trips, including its signature Lost World (4hr; $310) – a glorious, spine-tingling 100m abseil into the gaping fern-draped mouth of a spectacular pothole, followed by a relatively dry cave walk before climbing out on a seemingly endless ladder. Cave junkies should go for the Lost World Epic (7hr; $445, including lunch underground and BBQ dinner above), where an abseil is followed by several "wet" hours, navigating upstream through squeezes, behind a small waterfall and into a glittering glowworm grotto. There's also an abseil-free cave tubing trip (4hr; $165), the active abseil-heavy Haggas Honking Holes (4hr; $240) and St Benedict's Cavern (3hr 30min; $165), a dry trip with abseils and a flying fox. Save twenty percent on either trip if you book more than a day ahead.

wi-fi. Excellent breakfasts. **$140**

Juno Hall 600 Waitomo Caves Rd, 1km east of Waitomo ☎07 878 7649, ⦿junowaitomo.co.nz. Cosy, well-equipped associate YHA hostel in a timber-lined building set on a low hill by a pool, BBQ deck and a tennis court, with the chance to hand-feed baby animals. Some powered sites. Camping **$16**, dorms **$28**, doubles **$68**, en suites **$78**

Rap, Raft 'n' Rock 95 Waitomo Caves Rd/SH37, 8km east of the i-SITE, 1km from the junction with SH3 ☎0800 228 372, ⦿caveraft.com. Homey backpacker digs attached to an adventure-caving operator with brightly painted dorms sleeping ten, a cosy lounge, kitchen and sunny courtyard. Dorms **$30**, doubles **$70**

Te Tiro 9km west of Waitomo ☎07 878 6328, ⦿waitomocavesnz.com. Cosy self-contained cottages with fabulous views and a glowworm grotto. Breakfast goodies are included, but if you're cooking, bring food or something for the BBQ. **$120**

Waitomo Caves Guest Lodge 7 Te Anga Rd, 100m east of the museum ☎07 878 7641, ⦿waitomocaves guestlodge.co.nz. Eight comfortable, good-value rooms (some in cabins with good views) perched on a hillside in a lovely garden. Continental breakfast included. **$105**

Waitomo Kiwipaka School Rd ☎07 878 3395, ⦿kiwipaka.co.nz. Purpose-built and slightly soulless 120-guest hostel in the heart of Waitomo with beds and rooms in a lodge, separate chalets with private bathrooms, and an on-site café (see p.222). Dorms **$30**, rooms **$70**, chalets **$100**

Waitomo Top 10 Holiday Park 12 Waitomo Caves Rd ☎07 878 7639, ⦿waitomopark.co.nz. Well-equipped campsite in the heart of town, with lots of new cabins and a swimming pool and spa for soaking after your underground adventure. Camping **$21**, cabins **$70**, en-suite cabins **$120**, motel units **$140**

★ **World Unique Waitomo Motels** 1177 Waitomo Valley Rd, 1km north ☎07 878 6666, ⦿woodlynpark.co.nz. Ingenious motel-style accommodation on the site of Billy Black's Kiwi Culture Show (see p.220). Sleep in a Bristol freighter aircraft converted into two comfortable self-contained units; a 1914 railway carriage containing a three-room unit; two hobbit holes with circular entrances sunk into a hillside; and a converted World War II patrol boat. Book at least a month ahead for Dec–Feb. Self-contained campervans can park here for free. Doubles $175

EATING AND DRINKING

Curly's Bar 39 Waitomo Caves Rd ☎07 878 8448. Almost everyone eventually ends up at this unreconstructed Kiwi pub, either for convivial boozing or good-value meals in the steak, seafood and burger tradition (mains mostly $15–25). Occasional live music. Daily 11am–2am.

★ **Huhu** 10 Waitomo Caves Rd ☎07 878 6674, ⍵huhucafe.co.nz. Classy restaurant dining with a short lunch menu including soup with soft, chewy *rewana* (Maori bread) with herb butter. Dinner dishes include twice-baked three-cheese soufflé ($14) and slow-roasted duck with *kumara* mash ($35), all with suggested wine matches. Mike's Organic beer is on tap. Book in the evening. Daily 4–9pm or later.

Morepork School Rd ☎07 878 3395. Licensed café open from breakfast, serving made-to-order breakfasts, lunches and evening meals such as fettucini, Thai curry and pizzas ($18–22). Daily 8am–10pm.

Roselands 579 Fullerton Rd, 3km south of the i-SITE ☎07 878 7611, ⍵roselands-restaurant.co.nz. Fish or meat (or vegetarian options by prior arrangement) sizzles on the barbecue on the deck of this garden-set restaurant in a beautiful hillside location. Fixed-priced menu $30. Daily 11am–2pm.

★ **Waitomo General Store** 15 Waitomo Caves Rd ☎07 878 8613. A modern take on the classic general store with groceries, organic meat and cone ice cream, plus excellent espresso, great pies and a range of breakfasts, including eggs benny ($15). 30min free wi-fi. Daily 7.30am–6pm or later.

Mangapohue Natural Bridge

Te Anga Rd, 24km west of Waitomo

The finest free limestone sight hereabouts is the **Mangapohue Natural Bridge**, an easy fifteen-minute loop trail through forest to a riverside boardwalk leading into a narrow limestone gorge topped by a double bridge formed by the remains of a collapsed cave roof. It's especially dazzling at night when the undersides glimmer with constellations of glowworms. In daylight, don't miss the rest of the walk, through farmland past fossilized examples of giant oysters, 35 million years old.

Piripiri Caves and Marakopa Falls

Te Anga Rd, 4km west of Mangapohue Natural Bridge

A five-minute walk through a forested landscape full of weathered limestone outcrops brings you to **Piripiri Caves**. Inside the cavern you'll need a decent torch (and an emergency spare) to explore the Oyster Room, which contains giant fossil oysters, though there are no glowworms.

A kilometre or so on, a track (15min return) accesses one of the area's most dramatic waterfalls, the multi-tiered 30m **Marakopa Falls**, through a jungle-like rainforest of tawa, pukatea and kohekohe trees.

Te Kuiti

The "Shearing Capital of the World", **TE KUITI**, 19km south of Waitomo, greets visitors with a 7m-high statue of a man shearing a sheep at the southern end of Rora Street, and hosts the annual New Zealand **Shearing and Wool Handling Championships** in late March or early April; get details from the **i-SITE**.

At the south end of Rora Street on Awakino Road is a magnificently carved **meeting house**, Te Tokanganui-a-noho, left by Maori rebel Te Kooti in the nineteenth century in thanks for sanctuary.

MARAKOPA FALLS (P.222) >

3

i-SITE Rora St (Mon–Fri 9am–5pm, Sat 10am–2pm, Sun noon–4pm; ☎07 878 8077, ✉tkisite@waitomo.govt .nz). Can arrange accommodation, and has information on activities and transport requirements within the Waitomo region and beyond.

EATING AND DRINKING

★ **Bosco Café** 57 Te Kumi Rd (SH3), 1km north of town ☎07 878 3633. Hip daytime café in an airy pine-and-plywood building serving sensational Fairtrade coffee, cranberry smoothies, home-made muffins, pie and quiche slices and a lunch menu that spans mushroom and chicken penne ($15), and burgers ($14). Daily 8am–5pm.

SH3 towards the Taranaki Peninsula

Southwest of Te Kuiti, **SH3** makes a beeline for the Tasman Sea and the small coastal town of **Mokau**, noted for its run of whitebait from mid-August to November, when there are plenty of opportunities to sample it in the local cafés. The highway then twists its way through tiny communities, sandwiched between spectacular black beaches and steep inland ranges. Opportunities for exploration focus on the wonderful Whitecliffs Walkway (see below). Eventually the scenery opens out onto the Taranaki Plains just north of New Plymouth.

Whitecliffs Walkway

Starts on Pukearuhe Rd, off SH3, 11km northwest of Mimi, itself 47km south of Mokau • 5km return; 4–7hr; flat

Though billed as a 4–7hr loop walk over the hills and back along the beach, it is the beach section that really makes this special, and that's the walk described here. If you want to do the whole thing, start 2hr before low tide, but it is worth coming down for a short walk at any time. Start by the steep Pukearuhe boat ramp then simply follow the beach north with the Tasman breakers sweeping up the beach towards high, off-white sandstone cliffs. Calm pools, boulder fields and the odd stream crossing keep it interesting until you reach the **Te Horo Stock Tunnel**, a 80m-long passage bored through the cliff in the 1870s to allow stock to be driven along the beach, on up to the clifftops and then beyond to market. The tunnel itself is crumbling and is officially closed, though repairs are planned. Return along the beach or follow the Walkway signs back across the bush-clad hills following the route of a buried gas pipeline.

EATING AND DRINKING   **SH3 TOWARDS TARANAKI**

Mike's Organic Brewery 487 Mokau Rd (SH3), 48km south of Mokau ☎06 752 3676, ⊕organicbeer.co .nz. Stop by this craft brewery of international standing which produces eight organic brews using rainwater – including Strawberry Blonde, made from whole organic strawberries. Buy to take away or sit in the garden over a beer flight (4 small glasses for $12), a gourmet pie and chips ($14) or a pizza. Daily 10am–6pm.

The Taranaki Peninsula

The province of **Taranaki** (nicknamed "The 'naki") juts out west from the rest of the North Island forming a thumbprint peninsula centred on **Maunga Taranaki** (a.k.a. **Mount Egmont**), an elegant conical volcano rising 2500m from the subtropical coast to its icy summit. Taranaki means "peak clear of vegetation", an appropriate description of the upper half of "the mountain", as locals simply refer to it.

The mountain remains a constant presence as you tour the region, though much of the time it is obscured by cloud. The summit is usually visible in the early morning and just before sunset, with cloud forming through the middle of the day – the bane of summit aspirants who slog for no view.

Taranaki's vibrant provincial capital and largest city, **New Plymouth**, makes a good base for day-trips into the **Egmont National Park**, surrounding the mountain. It is also very convenient for short forays to the surfing and windsurfing hotspot of **Oakura**.

Rural Taranaki's attractions, including the **Surf Highway**, are best sampled on a one- or two-day loop around the mountain.

3

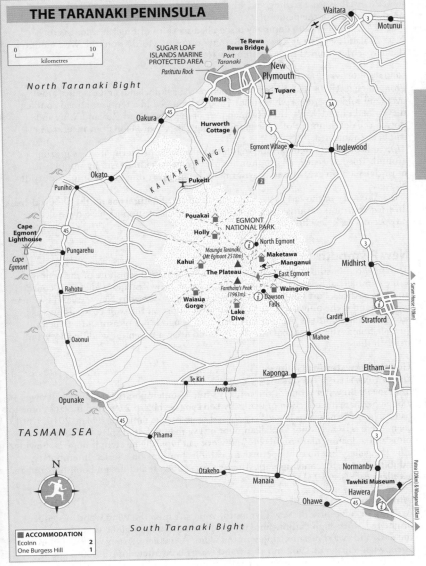

THE TARANAKI PENINSULA

0 — 10 kilometres

North Taranaki Bight

Waitara
Motunui
SUGAR LOAF ISLANDS MARINE PROTECTED AREA
Te Rewa Rewa Bridge
Port Taranaki
Paritutu Rock
New Plymouth
Omata
Tupare
3A
Oakura
45
Hurworth Cottage
Egmont Village
Inglewood
KAITAKE RANGE
Okato
Pukeiti
Puniho
Pouakai
EGMONT NATIONAL PARK
Holly
North Egmont
Cape Egmont Lighthouse
45
Cape Egmont
Pungarehu
Maunga Taranaki (Mt Egmont 2518m)
Kahui
Maketawa
Manganui
Midhirst
3
The Plateau
East Egmont
Rahotu
Fantham's Peak (1963m)
Waingoro
Dawson Falls
Waiaua Gorge
Lake Dive
Cardiff
Stratford
Oaonui
Mahoe
Eltham
Te Kiri
Kaponga
Awatuna
Opunake
45
TASMAN SEA
Pihama
3
N
Otakeho
Manaia
Normanby
Tawhiti Museum
Hawera
45
Ohawe
South Taranaki Bight
Sarjen House (10km)
Patea (20km) & Wanganui (85km)

ACCOMMODATION
EcoInn 2
One Burgess Hill 1

Brief history

According to Maori, the mountain-demigod Taranaki fled here from the company of the other mountains in the central North Island. He was firmly in place when spotted by the first European in the area, **Cook**, who named the peak Egmont after the first Lord of the Admiralty. In the early nineteenth century few **Maori** were living in the area as annual raids by northern tribes had forced many to migrate with Te Rauparaha to Kapiti Island. This played into the hands of John Lowe and Richard Barrett who, in 1828, established a trading and whaling station on the Ngamotu Beach on the northern shores of the peninsula.

In 1841, the **Plymouth Company** dispatched six ships of English colonists to New Zealand, settling at Lowe and Barrett's outpost. Mostly from the West Country, the new settlers named their community **New Plymouth**.

Land disputes, wars, and the modern era

From the late 1840s many Maori returned to their homeland, and disputes arose over land sold to settlers, which from 1860 culminated in a ten-year armed conflict, the Taranaki Land Wars. These formed part of the wider New Zealand Wars and slowed the development of the region, leaving a legacy of **Maori grievances**, some still being addressed.

Once hostilities were over, the rich farmlands were primarily used as grazing grounds for dairy cattle. As economies of scale became increasingly important, most dairy complexes closed down, finally leaving just one huge complex outside Hawera.

The discovery in the early 1970s of large deposits of **natural gas** off the Taranaki coast diverted attention towards petrochemical industries, but supplies have dwindled as prospectors seek new finds.

New Plymouth

The small but bustling city of **New Plymouth**, on the northern shore of the peninsula, is the commercial heart of Taranaki and renowned New Zealand-wide for its concerts and arts festivals. **Port Taranaki**, at the edge of the city, serves as New Zealand's western gateway and is the only deep-water international port on the west coast. There's a strong **arts** and **gardens** bias to its attractions, though it is a pleasure just to be in. Just offshore is the **Sugar Loaf Islands Protected Area**, a haven for wildlife above and beneath the sea.

Govett-Brewster Art Gallery

42 Queen St • Daily 10am–5pm • Free • ☎ 06 759 6060, ⓦ govettbrewster.com

The **Govett-Brewster** is one of the country's finest contemporary art galleries. It owns a huge permanent collection of works by **Len Lye** (see box, p.228), and if plans come to fruition a smart new Len Lye gallery should open on the same site by late 2014. Until then, there is usually only a small amount of Lye material on display but some of his films and a documentary on his life and work can typically be seen; if none is showing, ask. The gallery has no other permanent exhibits but puts on a series of temporary exhibitions, mostly contemporary. There's also a good art and design bookshop and an excellent café (see p.231).

Wind Wand

Arriving in the centre of New Plymouth, you can't miss the **Wind Wand**, a slender, bright-red, 45m-high carbon-fibre tube topped with a light globe that glows red in the dark and sways mesmerizingly in the wind. A smaller version was erected in Greenwich Village in 1962 but this wand wasn't constructed until 2000, taking advantage of advances in polymer engineering. Lye would probably have been

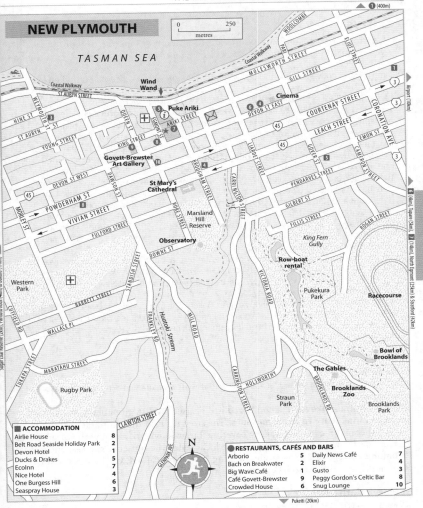

NEW PLYMOUTH

TASMAN SEA

ACCOMMODATION

Airlie House	8
Belt Road Seaside Holiday Park	2
Devon Hotel	1
Ducks & Drakes	5
EcoInn	7
Nice Hotel	4
One Burgess Hill	6
Seaspray House	3

RESTAURANTS, CAFÉS AND BARS

Arborio	5	Daily News Café	7
Bach on Breakwater	2	Elixir	4
Big Wave Café	1	Gusto	3
Café Govett-Brewster	9	Peggy Gordon's Celtic Bar	8
Crowded House	6	Snug Lounge	10

disappointed with this single example: his vision was for a forest of 125 wind wands swaying together in the breeze.

Coastal Walkway

Landscaping and pathways stretch a couple of hundred metres either side of the *Wind Wand*, making a **waterfront park** that's pleasant for an evening stroll. More ambitious walkers and cyclists can follow the **Coastal Walkway** that stretches 3km west to the port and 7km east to Bell Block.

The best bet is to head 2km east to East End Reserve where there is bike rental (see p.230) and the *Big Wave Café* (see p.231). Explore 2km further east as far as the Waiwhakaiho rivermouth, spanned by the stunning, 83m-long, white steel **Te Rewa Rewa Bridge**, said to be modelled on a curling wave but often likened to a whale's skeleton. In fine weather there's usually a coffee cart nearby.

LEN LYE

All of a sudden it hit me – if there was such a thing as composing music, there could be such a thing as composing motion. After all, there are melodic figures, why can't there be figures of motion?   Len Lye

Until fairly recently, New Zealand-born sculptor, film-maker and conceptual artist **Len Lye** (1901–80) was little known outside the art world, but his work is now earning well-deserved recognition. Born in Christchurch, Lye developed a fascination with movement, which expressed itself in his late teens in early experiments in **kinetic sculpture**. His interest in Maori art encouraged him to travel more widely, studying both Australian Aboriginal and Samoan dance. Adapting indigenous art to the precepts of the Futurist and Surrealist movements coming out of Europe, he experimented with sculpture, batik, painting, photography and animated **"cameraless" films** (he painstakingly stencilled, scratched and drew on the actual film). Lye spent time working on his films in London, but towards the end of World War II he joined the European artistic exodus and ended up in New York. Here he returned to sculpture, finding that he could exploit the flexibility of stainless-steel rods, loops and strips to create abstract "tangible motion sculptures" designed to "make movement real". The erratic movements of these motor-driven sculptures give them an air of anarchy, which is most evident in his best-known work, 1977's *Trilogy* (more commonly referred to as Flip and Two Twisters), three motorized metal sheets that wildly shake and contort until winding down to a final convulsion.

Lye envisaged his works as being monumental and set outdoors, but was always aware of the technical limitations of his era and considered his projects to be works of the twenty-first century. Just before his death in New York in 1980, friend, patron and New Plymouth resident, John Matthews, helped set up the Len Lye Foundation, which brought most of Lye's scattered work to New Plymouth's Govett-Brewster Art Gallery. The foundation has been instrumental in furthering Lye's work. The *Wind Wand* is the most visible and largest product of their work though the foundation has also been instrumental in creating Lye's *Water Whirler* on the Wellington waterfront (see p.422).

Puke Ariki

1 Ariki St • Mon–Fri 9am–6pm, till 9pm Wed, Sat & Sun 9am–5pm; Richmond Cottage Sat & Sun 11am–3.30pm • Free • ☎ 06 759 6060, ⓦ pukeariki.com

The city's hub is **Puke Ariki**, a combined i-SITE (see p.230), city **library**, **exhibition space** and interactive **regional museum**. The strength is in the temporary exhibitions, though there is an extensive gallery covering Taranaki Maori, along with volcanic rock carvings and woodcarvings in the unique local style. The museum site also encompasses **Richmond Cottage**, an 1854 stone dwelling built for local MP Christopher William Richmond, and moved to its current site in 1962.

St Mary's Cathedral

37 Vivian St • Free • ☎ 06 758 3111, ⓦ taranakicathedral.org.nz

The Frederick Thatcher-designed **St Mary's Church** is the oldest stone church in New Zealand. Built in 1845 along austere lines with an imposing gabled dark-wood interior, it finally became Taranaki's cathedral in 2010. The church contains a striking 1972 Maori memorial with carvings and *tukutuku* panels.

Pukekura Park and Brooklands Park

Main entrances on Liardet St and Brooklands Park Drive • Daily dawn–dusk • Free **Gables** Sat & Sun 1–4pm • Free **Rowboats** Dec–Feb daily 11am–4pm & 7–10pm • $10 for 30min • ⓦ pukekura.org.nz

Pukekura Park and Brooklands Park are effectively two sections of one large park – one of New Zealand's finest city parks and setting for both the Festival of Lights and WOMAD (see box, p.231). Pukekura is mostly semi-formal, with glasshouses, a boating lake and a cricket pitch. The more freely laid out Brooklands occupies the grounds of a long-gone homestead and includes the **Bowl of Brooklands** outdoor amphitheatre, attracting big-name artists, as well as numerous mature trees, among them a 2000-year-old puriri and a big ginkgo. Nearby, a former colonial hospital from 1847 is now the **Gables**, containing an art gallery and small medical museum. Near the renovated Pukekura Teahouse you can rent **rowboats**.

Paritutu Rock

4km west of the city centre

New Plymouth's port sprawls out from the foot of the 200m-high **Paritutu Rock**, a feature of great cultural significance to Maori and a near-perfect natural fortress that still marks the boundary between Taranaki and Te Atiawa territories. You can ascend it from a car park on Centennial Drive, signposted off Vivian Street. It's a steep scramble (20–50min return) with a steel rope providing support, but the reward is a great view along the coast.

Sugar Loaf Islands Marine Protected Area

1hr boat trips • 2–3 daily, weather permitting • $35 • ☎ 06 758 9133, ⓦ chaddyscharters.co.nz

A few hundred metres off the north Taranaki coast, a cluster of rocky islands is the eroded remnant of ancient volcanoes, a sanctuary for rare plants, little blue penguins, petrels and sooty shearwaters. The surrounding waters form the DOC-administered Sugar Loaf Marine Reserve, which harbours some 89 species of fish and a wealth of multicoloured anemones, sponges and seaweeds in undersea canyons. Humpback whales (Aug & Sept) and dolphins (Oct–Dec) migrate past, and the tidal rocks are populated by New Zealand's northernmost breeding colony of fur seals. Although the islands themselves are off-limits, Chaddy's Charters run entertaining **trips** around them.

Tupare

487 Mangorei Rd, 6km southeast of the city centre • Daily: Oct–March 9am–8pm; April–Sept 9am–5pm; house tours Oct–March Fri–Mon 11am • Free • ☎ 0800 736 222, ⓦ tupare.info

Taranaki's fertile volcanic soils and moist climate make for some great gardens, and there are few better than **Tupare**, developed since the1930s. There's pleasure in just wandering round the maples, azaleas and rhododendrons, and learning a little of the history in the pretty **Gardener's Cottage**, but it all makes more sense when combined with a tour of the quirky **Arts & Crafts house** designed by prominent Kiwi architect James Chapman-Taylor.

Hurworth Cottage

906 Carrington Rd, 9km south of the city centre • Sat & Sun 11am–3pm and by appointment • $5 • ☎ 06 753 3593, ⓦ historicplaces.org.nz

The charming and historic **Hurworth Cottage** was built in 1856 for Harry Atkinson, four times prime minister of New Zealand and famous for advocating women's suffrage and introducing welfare benefits. The plain two-room cottage is the only one to have survived the New Zealand Wars of the 1860s and is now furnished as it would have been in the mid-nineteenth century. Check out the ancient charcoal graffiti, one section depicting a Maori warrior with full-face *moko*.

Pukeiti

2290 Carrington Rd, 23km southwest of the city centre • Daily 9am–5pm; café daily 10am–4pm • Free • ☎ 0800 736 222, ⓦ pukeiti.org.nz

Carved out of the bush 370m up on the northern slopes of the Pouakai Range, **Pukeiti** are Taranaki's finest public gardens. They were established in 1951 by Douglas Cook, founder of Gisborne's Eastwoodhill Arboretum (see p.377), who needed a cooler, damper climate to grow New Zealand's largest collection of rhododendrons and azaleas. The result is a wild array of superb blooms, with bush paths linking up grassy avenues lined with fine specimens. The on-site *Founders Café* provides sustenance.

ARRIVAL AND DEPARTURE

By plane From the airport, 12km northeast of town, Scott's Airport Shuttle Service can drop you anywhere in the city ($22; $3/extra person in group; ☎06 769 5974 or ☎0800 373 001, ⌨npairportshuttle.co.nz). Shuttles meet all flights, but reserve ahead to guarantee a seat. Destinations Auckland (5–8 daily; 45min); Nelson (1 daily; 1hr); Wellington (4–5 daily; 55min).

By bus InterCity/Newmans, NakedBus and The Naki Bus (☎0508 465 622, ⌨nakibus.co.nz) stop at the bus station at 19 Ariki St, just along from the i-SITE.
Destinations Auckland (3 daily; 6hr–6hr 30min); Hamilton (4 daily; 4hr); Hawera (3 daily; 50min–1hr 15min); Te Kuiti (4 daily; 2hr 30min); Wanganui (2 daily; 2hr 30min); Wellington (2 daily; 7hr).

GETTING AROUND

By bus CityLink (☎0800 872 287, ⌨visittaranakibus.info) run local services. The limited routes may be useful for Tupare and Oakura, but services are infrequent.

By bike Cycle Inn, 133 Devon St East (☎06 758 7418; Mon–Fri 8.30am–5pm, Sat 9am–3pm, Sun

10.30am–1pm) rent city bikes for $15/day. Wind Wanders, East End Reserve (☎027 358 1182, ⌨windwanderers .co.nz) rent cruiser bikes ($20/hr) and 4-wheeled, pedal-powered buggies ($15/20min) for exploring the Coastal Walkway.

INFORMATION AND TOURS

i-SITE 65 St Aubyn St, in the foyer of Puke Ariki (Mon–Fri 9am–6pm, Wed till 9pm, Sat & Sun 9am–5pm; ☎06 759 6060, ⌨taranaki.co.nz). Excellent visitor centre with touch screens to access local info, and plenty on Egmont National Park, including hut tickets.

Services The library, 1 Ariki St, has free internet access (Mon–Fri 9am–6pm, Wed till 9pm, Sat & Sun 9am–5pm).
Wind Wanders East End Reserve ☎027 358 1182, ⌨windwanderers.co.nz. In addition to renting bikes (see above), this outfit runs guided walkway cycle tours ($90/3hr).

ACCOMMODATION

New Plymouth has a range of modestly priced accommodation, as well as options close to the city at the surf beach town of Oakura (see p.236), or on the flanks of the mountain (see p.234). Motels are strung along the approach roads into the city centre.

Airlie House 161 Powderham St ☎06 757 8866, ⌨airliehouse.co.nz; map p.227. Gracious B&B in a large villa dating from the turn of the last century, with crisp modern decor. The "drawing room", with a bay-window seat, and studio apartment (with kitchen) are both en-suite, while the "garden room", overlooking the flowering front garden, has a private bathroom with a claw-foot bath. There are hundreds of DVDs and excellent breakfasts. **$165**

Belt Road Seaside Holiday Park 2 Belt Rd ☎0800 804 204, ⌨beltroad.co.nz; map p.227. A scenic, seaside site that's a 25min walk along the coastal path from the city centre, with camping and cabins (some en-suite) in a tidy area mostly sheltered from the otherwise exposed clifftop location. Camping **$18**, cabins **$65**, motel units **$125**

Devon Hotel 390 Devon St East ☎0800 843 338, ⌨devonhotel.co.nz; map p.227. A smart business hotel with a heated pool and spa, room service, buffet restaurant, free bikes and a range of rooms, including some spacious suites. Rooms **$115**, suites **$240**

Ducks & Drakes 48 Lemon St ☎06 758 0403, ⌨ducks anddrakes.co.nz; map p.227. Choose to stay in the charming 1920s house, with a roomy kitchen and book-filled lounge, or the bright, airy bargain-priced motel units next door, opening onto a communal lawn. There's also a sauna ($5/person). Camping **$18**, dorms **$30**, rooms **$78**, units **$125**

EcoInn 671 Kent Rd, off SH3, 17km south of New Plymouth ☎06 752 2765, ⌨ecoinnovation.co.nz; map p.225. Accommodation on an eco-farm, 3km from the Egmont National Park boundary, with wind turbines, a water wheel and the solar panels supplying energy. There's also a wood-fired hot tub and good hiking. Good multi-night discounts. Dorms **$30**, doubles **$60**

★ **Nice Hotel** 71 Brougham St ☎06 758 6423, ⌨nice hotel.co.nz; map p.227. Book in advance to ensure you get one of the seven unique rooms in this intimate *pied-à-terre*, with designer bathrooms, contemporary artworks and luxurious fittings. Its on-site restaurant, *Table* (dinner only; mains $35), is renowned for its French-accented cuisine. **$230**

★ **One Burgess Hill** 1 Burgess Hill Rd, 5km south of the city centre ☎06 757 2056, ⌨oneburgesshill .co.nz; map p.225. Rurally set on a high promontory with great views across the cascading Waiwhakaiho River to a giant vertical garden of bush and tree ferns, these fifteen apartments (many with log fires) have state-of-the-art decor and furnishings including sleek self-catering kitchens and decadent bathrooms. Breakfast ingredients available ($10–12). Studio **$135**, one-bedroom **$175**

★ **Seaspray House** 13 Weymouth St ☎06 759 8934, ⌨seasprayhouse.co.nz; map p.227. With no bunks, no TV and shoes off inside, you soon relax at this central hostel that sleeps just 14, excluding the cat and the dog. Closed June & July. Dorms **$30**, doubles **$74**

EATING AND DRINKING

The majority of the cafés, restaurants, bars and clubs are on the so-called "**Devon Mile**", along Devon St between Dawson and Eliot sts. In recent times a second culinary hotspot has sprung up at Port Taranaki overlooking the water.

★ **Arborio** St Aubyn St, inside Puke Ariki ☎ 06 759 1241, ⓦ arborio.co.nz; map p.227. A brilliant, licensed, modern café overlooking the *Wind Wand*, with toothsome brunches and dishes such as smoked-spice calamari ($17) followed by chicken on saffron mash with shiraz peppercorn sauce ($30). Or just come for one of their thin-crust pizzas, served evenings only ($23). Daily 9am–10pm or later.

Bach on Breakwater Ocean View Parade, Port Taranaki ☎ 06 769 6967, ⓦ bachonbreakwater.co.nz; map p.227. Rustic *bach*-style licensed café opening to a timber deck overlooking the port, dishing up moderately priced daytime favourites such as nachos ($16) and contemporary evening meals including free-range smoked pork belly on red cabbage and mash (mains $27–37). Wed–Sun 9.30am–10pm.

★ **Big Wave Café** East End Reserve ☎ 027 305 7035; map p.227. Sit on old lounge chairs ranged along the waterfront overlooking the river mouth outside this caravan shaped like a curling wave. Lick an ice cream, sip a superb coffee or try pizzas ($20), stuffed bagels ($10) or upscale toasted sandwiches ($7–8). The menu is scrawled on old surfboards and everything is named after a surfing term or a break. Daily 9am–5pm unless the weather is awful.

★ **Café Govett-Brewster** Queen St ☎ 06 759 6060; map p.227. This airy café attached to the art gallery is a work of art in itself – specifically in the form of Sara Hughes' *The Golden Grain*, an installation piece that includes everything from the white banquettes and pie chart discs on the ceiling to the tables and crockery. None of it distracts from the excellent food and coffee, either, whether you opt for the great muffins, a breakfast of Baghdad eggs with cumin and flatbread ($15), or salads of roast beetroot, mint, almonds and grilled haloumi. Mon–Fri 8am–2.30pm, Sat & Sun 9am–2.30pm.

Crowded House 93 Devon St East ☎ 06 759 4921, ⓦ crowdedhouse.co.nz; map p.227. Fairly formulaic downtown bar that's often busy, particularly if there's a big game on TV. Monteith's beers are on tap and you can eat well on a chicken and bacon burger and chips or Thai beef salad (both $19). Daily 10am–10pm or later.

Daily News Café Level 1 in the library, 1 Ariki St; map p.227. Small, tranquil café, stocked with newspapers from across the country and around the world, serving coffee and snacks. Daily 9.30am–3pm.

Elixir 117 Devon St East ☎ 06 769 9902, ⓦ elixircafe .co.nz; map p.227. Chilled café plastered with posters of upcoming festivals and gigs, serving freshly baked muffins, panini, bagels and wraps, as well as delicious mains ($16–25) such as pecan-crumbed chicken or maple roast veggies. Licensed. Mon 7am–4.30pm, Tues–Thurs 7am–9.30pm, Fri & Sat 7.30am–10pm, Sun 8am–4pm.

Gusto Ocean View Parade, Port Taranaki ☎ 06 759 8133, ⓦ gustotaranaki.co.nz; map p.227. This minimalist-chic harbour-view fine-diner, hidden away in a semi-industrial marina area, is a winner for its classy, contemporary fare such as five-spice lamb shanks on mash with mushroom ragout ($35). Mon–Fri 10am–10pm, Sat 9am–10pm, Sun 9am–3pm.

Peggy Gordon's Celtic Bar 58 Egmont St ☎ 06 758 8561, ⓦ peggygordons.com; map p.227. With an extensive range of whiskies, twelve beers on tap, inexpensive meals – BBQ Guinness ribs ($16), Kilkenny battered blue cod ($18) – and regular live Irish music, it's no surprise that this is a popular haunt for both locals and travellers. The *Basement Bar* showcases alternative bands. Daily 10am–10pm or later.

Snug Lounge 134 Devon St West ☎ 06 757 9130, ⓦ snuglounge.co.nz; map p.227. Stylish reinvention of the corner bar at the classic *White Hart Hotel*, all plush seating, deer antler cushions and walls of ancient wallpaper stripped partly back to reveal the changing tastes over the decades. Come for the delectable cocktails and the ambience, though they also serve decent *yakitori*. Daily 3pm– late.

NEW PLYMOUTH FESTIVALS

Festival of Lights (mid-Dec to Jan nightly dusk–10.45pm; free; ⓦ festivaloflights.co.nz). On summer evenings, stroll the gorgeously lit pathways of Pukekura Park between illuminated trees, then rent a rowboat festooned with lights. There's live music most nights.

Taranaki Garden Spectacular (late Oct to early Nov; ⓦ taft.co.nz). Ten-day celebration of the region's fine gardens, timed to when the rhododendrons are at their best.

Taranaki International Festival of the Arts (two weeks in early Aug; ⓦ taft.co.nz) This biennial festival (odd-numbered years) features a wide range of music, films and plays in venues all over town.

WOMAD (mid-March; ⓦ taft.co.nz) Superb annual three-day festival of world music that takes place in Brooklands Park. Hundreds of international artists performing on six stages, workshops and a "global village" market.

ENTERTAINMENT

Arthouse Cinema 73 Devon St West ☎ 06 757 3650, ⓦ arthousecinema.co.nz. Grown-up films with a glass of wine.

Event Cinema 119–125 Devon St East ☎ 06 759 9077, ⓦ eventcinemas.co.nz. Screens mainstream films.

New Plymouth Observatory Robe St, Marsland Hill Reserve. Members of the Astronomical Society volunteer to point out highlights in the night sky for visitors ($5). Tues summer 8–10pm; winter 7.30–9.30pm.

Egmont National Park

Taranaki (Mount Egmont), a dormant volcano that last erupted in 1755, dominates the entire western third of the North Island. Often likened to Japan's Mount Fuji, its profile is a cone rising to 2518m, though from east or west the profile is disturbed by the satellite **Fantham's Peak** (1692m). In winter, snow blankets the mountain, but as summer progresses only the crater rim remains white. The mountain is the focal point for **EGMONT NATIONAL PARK**, the boundary forming an arc with a 10km radius around the mountain, interrupted only on its north side where it encompasses the **Pouakai Range** and **Kaitake Range**, older, more weathered cousins of Taranaki.

Surrounded by farmland, the mountain's lower slopes are cloaked in native bush that gradually changes to stunted flag-form trees shaped by the constant buffeting of the wind. Higher still, vegetation gives way to slopes of loose scoria (a kind of jagged volcanic gravel) – hard work if you're hiking.

Three sealed roads climb Taranaki's eastern flanks, each ending at a separate car park a little under halfway up the mountain from where the park's 140km of walking tracks spread out. **North Egmont** is the most easily accessible from New Plymouth but you can get higher up the mountain at **East Egmont**, and there are particularly good short walks around **Dawson Falls**. The i-SITE in New Plymouth has extensive **information** on the park.

All three trailheads are under an hour's drive from New Plymouth, but with accommodation close to all of them, avid hikers may choose to base themselves inside the park. Gung-ho hikers go for the summit (not a trivial ascent by any means:; deaths do occur). If you want to spend longer than a day on the mountain, the varied **Pouakai Circuit** or the testing **Around the Mountain Circuit** might fit the bill.

North Egmont

From New Plymouth, the easiest access point to the park is tiny **Egmont Village**, 13km to the southeast on SH3. From here, the 16km sealed Egmont Road runs up the mountain to **North Egmont** (936m), the starting point for the Pouakai Circuit, summit ascents and several easier walks.

The Taranaki summit route

10km return; 7–10hr; 1560m ascent

Poled all the way, the route to the summit of Taranaki begins at North Egmont and initially follows the gravel Translator Road (the appropriately dubbed "Puffer") to *Tahurangi Lodge*, a private hut run by the Taranaki Alpine Club. A wooden stairway leads to North Ridge, and after that you're onto slopes of scoria up the Lizard Ridge leading to the crater. Crossing the crater ice and a short scoria slope brings you to the summit and, hopefully, magical views over the western third of the North Island.

Pouakai Circuit

Year-round, but expect snow from May–Sept; get advice from DOC before embarking • 24km loop; 2–3 days; track varies in altitude from 700–1300m

For exposed wetlands, subalpine tussock, steep fern-draped gullies, cliffs of columnar basalt and superb views of Taranaki make straight for this delightful loop tramp. Much of it is above the bushline, giving long views over the flatlands and the coast. It is steep

SAFETY ON THE MOUNT TARANAKI SUMMIT ROUTE

The hike to the **summit** is possible in a day for anyone reasonably fit, but shouldn't be underestimated; expect to take a full day (setting off before 7.30am). The hiking season normally runs from Jan to mid-April.

The upper mountain is off-limits to ordinary hikers in winter, but even during the hiking season **bad weather**, including occasional snow, sweeps in frighteningly quickly, and hikers starting off on a fine morning frequently find themselves groping through low cloud before the day is through. Deaths occur far too often: consult the **hiking advice** in Basics (see p.51), get an up-to-date **weather forecast** (🌐 metservice.com/mountain/egmont-national-park) and obtain further information from the nearest DOC office or visitor centre in New Plymouth or North Egmont. Climb with at least one companion or a mountain guide, and leave a **record of your intentions** with your accommodation or at 🌐 adventuresmart.org.nz.

Take **warm clothing** at any time of year and, except for Jan and Feb, you should carry (and know how to use) an **ice axe and crampons**; if you don't have your own, rent equipment (from \$55) at Kiwi Outdoors, 18 Ariki St, in New Plymouth (📞 06 758 4152, 🌐 outdoorgurus .co.nz; Mon–Fri 8.30am–5pm, Sat 9.30am–2.30pm, Sun in summer 10am–2pm).

3

in places and the tracks are never as groomed as the Great Walks, making the rewards well earned. There are two huts with camping outside (see p.235).

Veronica Loop Track

2.5km loop; 2hr; 200m ascent

A fairly stiff walk which initially climbs steps along a ridge through mountain forest and scrub past a monument to Arthur Ambury, a climber who died trying to save another man. Continue uphill (go past the sign that points you back downhill to the car park) to a great lookout with fine views of the ancient lava flows known as Humphries Castle, and beyond to New Plymouth and the coast.

East Egmont

East Egmont is accessed through Stratford (see p.235), from where Pembroke Road runs 14km west to the *Stratford Mountain House* hotel then a further 3km to a rugged and windswept spot known as **The Plateau**. At 1172m this is the highest road-accessible point on Taranaki's flanks. As well as being on the upper route of the Around the Mountain Circuit (p.234), this acts as the wintertime parking area for the tiny **Manganui Ski Area** (🌐 skitaranaki.co.nz).

Curtis Falls Track

3.5km return; 2–3hr; 120m ascent

A fairly tough, short walk from the *Mountain House* hotel, crossing numerous deep gorges via steps and ladders, to the Manganui River Gorge, where you can follow the riverbed (no track or signs) to the base of a waterfall. This is part of the lower Around the Mountain Circuit (see p.234).

Enchanted Track

3km one-way; 3hr return; 300m ascent

Park at the *Mountain House* hotel then hike up the road to The Plateau before heading south and cutting down onto the Enchanted Track, named for the fabulous views to the east. Note how the vegetation gradually changes as you descend to the *Mountain House*.

Dawson Falls

Visitor centre Thurs–Sun & public holidays 8am–4.30pm

The most southerly access up Taranaki follows Manaia Road to **Dawson Falls** (900m), roughly 23km west of Stratford. Here you'll find the **Dawson Falls visitor centre** outside of which stands an impressive 8m-high *pou whenua* (carved pole) depicting famous Maori associated with the area. The *Dawson Falls Hotel* and restaurant, opposite the visitor centre, closed in August 2011 but there are hopes that it will reopen some day.

Kapuni Loop Track

2km loop; 1hr; 100m ascent

A delightful walk through the twisted and stunted kamahi trees of the so-called "Goblin Forest", gnarled trunks hung with ferns and mosses. You soon reach Dawson Falls, where the Kapuni Stream plummets 17m over the end of an ancient lava flow. On the way back, call at the shed that houses the tiny **Dawson Falls Power Station**, a historic hydro plant built in 1935 to provide power for the **Dawson Falls Hotel**.

Wilkies Pool Loop Track

2.3km loop; 1hr; 100m ascent

This walk from the Dawson Falls visitor centre heads uphill through more "Goblin Forest" to a series of pretty pools carved out by the Kapuni Stream. Take your time on the wet rocks and pause occasionally to appreciate the lush bush all around.

ARRIVAL AND DEPARTURE — EGMONT NATIONAL PARK

By shuttle bus Cruise New Zealand (☎0800 688 687, ✉kirkstall@xtra.co.nz) run shuttles that pick up at accommodation around New Plymouth around 7am, dropping you off at North Egmont before 8am; the pick-up at North Egmont for the return journey to New Plymouth accommodation is around 4pm and they charge $50 return.

INFORMATION AND GUIDES

North Egmont Visitor Centre End of Egmont Rd (daily 8am–4.30pm; ☎06 756 0990, ✉egmontvc@doc.govt.nz). This is the park's main information source, and has displays about the mountain, maps of all the tracks, good viewing windows, weather updates and a decent café.

Mountain guides Several guides offer bushwalking, guided summit treks and a range of more technical stuff. They generally take up to ten clients for summer hiking and summit attempts but perhaps only two for winter expeditions, rock climbing or instruction. Guiding rates are around $300 a day, plus around $50 for each extra person. Try Top Guides (☎0800 448 433, ⊕topguides.co.nz); Adventure Dynamics (☎06 751 3589, ⊕adventuredynamics.co.nz); or Mac Alpine (☎0800 866 484, ⊕macalpineguides.com).

ACCOMMODATION AND EATING

NORTH EGMONT

The Camphouse North Egmont ☎06 278 6523 or ☎06 756 9093, ⊕mttaranaki.co.nz This large mountain hut, built in 1891, now operates as a basic but comfy backpackers, with a heated communal lounge, full kitchen and hot showers. Check-in is at the Mountain Café. Dorms $35, double $80

The Pouakai Circuit Hikers on the Pouakai Circuit have

AROUND THE MOUNTAIN CIRCUIT

Dedicated hikers might consider tackling the testing Around the Mountain Circuit (44km; 3–5 days), an irregular loop around Taranaki varying in altitude from 500m to 1500m. The track is not fully maintained, so check conditions with DOC and obtain a detailed Topomap. From December through to February, the snow melts enough for hikers to occasionally loop off the main track onto the more strenuous **high-level route**, essentially making a few short cuts by heading higher up the slopes, shaving a day off the lower circuit.

ACCOMMODATION

DOC huts There are six well-spaced huts along the way. Backcountry hut passes (see p.50) are valid, or buy tickets from DOC visitor centres. Camping is only allowed alongside the huts, and is free outside Kahui hut. Huts $15, Kahui hut $5, camping $5

access to two huts: the 32-bunk Holly Hut, which can get very busy; and the less popular 16-bunk Pouakai Hut. Backcountry hut passes are valid and camping is allowed outside. Camping ~~$5~~, huts ~~$15~~

Mountain Café North Egmont, inside the visitor centre. Warm café with good views that's perfect for all-day breakfast ($12–18), soup ($11), burgers ($16) or just a post-hike coffee. Daily 10am–3pm.

EAST EGMONT

Alpine Lodge Pembroke Rd, 9km west of Stratford ☏ 06 765 6620, ⓦ andersonsalpinelodge.co.nz. The four pine-panelled rooms at this romantic chalet are spacious and comfortable and come with breakfast served in a cosy lounge with fabulous mountain views. There is one shared-bath double and the suite even has its own lounge. Shared bath ~~$100~~, en suite ~~$140~~, suite ~~$180~~

Stratford Mountain House Pembroke Rd, 14km west of Stratford ☏ 06 765 6100, ⓦ stratfordmountain house.co.nz. Beautifully sited and revamped lodge 4km inside the national park boundary and 850m above sea level. Birds chirp in the bush outside the windows of the ten very comfortable rooms, all with spa bath. Alongside the spacious lounge there's a café and restaurant with fine views of the tip of Taranaki. Typical lunch dishes include chicken salad ($17) while the quality dinner menu features items including pork belly on Asian greens ($31) or steak frites ($32). Restaurant daily 9am–9pm or later. Room-only ~~$155~~

DAWSON FALLS

Konini Lodge ☏ 06 756 0990, ⓦ doc.govt.nz. Essentially a DOC-run oversized hikers' hut sleeping 38, with three- and eight-bed bunkrooms, hot showers and a kitchen equipped with stoves and fridges. Bring your own sleeping bag, towel, food, pans and eating utensils. ~~$20.40~~

Stratford

Just over halfway between New Plymouth and Hawera, **STRATFORD** celebrates its name with a its kitsch mock-Elizabethan **clock tower** (built in 1996 to hide the 1920s version), from which a life-size Romeo and Juliet emerge to mark the hour (at 10am, 1pm, 3pm and 7pm), accompanied by recordings of Shakespearean quotes. Every street name is a character from the bard's plays.

If you're bound for the central North Island, Stratford marks the start of the scenic **Forgotten World Highway** (p.239).

ARRIVAL AND INFORMATION   STRATFORD

By bus Stratford provides direct access to the slopes of Mount Taranaki, particularly East Egmont and Dawson Falls. Eastern Taranaki Experience (☏ 06 765 7482, ⓦ eastern-taranaki.co.nz) operates a 4WD mountain transport to The Plateau ($20; minimum two people).

i-SITE Miranda St (Mon–Fri 8.30am–5pm, Sat & Sun 10am–3pm; ☏ 0800 765 670, ⓦ stratford.govt.nz). The office is in an alley opposite the clock tower.

The Surf Highway

The best route around Taranaki is the **Surf Highway** (SH45) from New Plymouth to Hawera, mostly travelling about 3km inland, with roads leading down to tiny uninhabited bays. It runs for only about 100km, but its beachy charms can consume half a day, longer if you want to surf its consistent glassy, even breaks. **Windsurfing** and **kiteboarding** are good too, with near constant onshore winds. Surf beaches are everywhere, but facilities are concentrated in the towns of **Oakura** and the quieter **Opunake**. Between the two towns is **Cape Egmont**, with its picturesque lighthouse.

Oakura

Seventeen kilometres west of New Plymouth, **OAKURA** is basically a commuter suburb for New Plymouth, wedged between the highway and the surf beach. It has managed to retain a hint of counter-cultural spirit thanks to its board-rider residents and a handful of funky **craft shops** and **cafés** that cluster along SH45.

Cape Egmont

At Pungarehu, about 25km southwest of Oakura, Cape Road cuts 5km west to the cast-iron tower of **Cape Egmont Lighthouse**, moved here in 1877 from Mana Island, north of Wellington. It perches on a rise on the westernmost point of the cape overlooking Taranaki's windswept coast, a great spot around sunset with the mountain glowing behind.

Opunake

Opunake, 20km south of Cape Egmont, is a large village with a golden beach and little to do but swim, surf and cast a line. The beach is patrolled in summer (Jan daily 10am–5pm, Feb & March Sat & Sun 10am–5pm). The Opunake Surf Co (Dreamtime), at the corner of Havelock and Tasman streets, arranges **surfboard rental**.

INFORMATION AND ACTIVITIES

Oakura Library 16 Donnelly St, Oakura ☎ 06 759 6060 (Mon, Wed & Fri noon–6pm; Tues, Thurs & Sat 9am–1pm). In the absence of a visitor centre, the library has the best local information.

THE SURF HIGHWAY

Vertigo 605 Main St, Oakura ☎ 06 752 7363, ⓦvertigosurf.com. Rents surfboards ($50/24hr) and stand-up paddle boards ($70/day), and offers stand-up paddle-board lessons ($80/hr).

ACCOMMODATION AND EATING

OAKURA

Ahu Ahu Beach Villas 321 Ahu Ahu Rd ☎ 06 752 7370, ⓦahu.co.nz. The four gorgeous and luxurious, self-contained villas here are fashioned from wharf piles, French clay tiles and all manner of salvaged architectural pieces. Each sleeps four and overlooks the ocean. $250

Butlers Reef 1133 South Rd (SH45) ☎ 06 752 7765, ⓦbutlersreef.co.nz. This lively pub is the centre of Oakura action, with hearty meals such as beer-battered fish and chips ($19), regular events and loads of concerts through the summer. Daily 11am–10pm or later

Oakura Beach Holiday Park 2 Jans Terrace ☎ 06 752 7861, ⓦoakurabeach.com. Perfectly sited campsite with aging but good facilities. Some tent sites are just two steps from the black-sand beach and there are cabins on a rise with awesome bay views. Camping $18, cabins $70, en-suite cabins $120

OPUNAKE

Opunake Beach Holiday Park Beach Rd ☎ 0800 758 009, ⓦopunakebeachnz.co.nz. A golden beach with good surf pretty much right on your doorstep is the main lure of this welcoming campsite. Camping $18, cabins $68, units $98

Sugar Juice Café 42 Tasman St ☎ 06 761 7062. Considerable care goes into everything at this brightly decorated, licensed café serving up huge breakfasts such as field mushroom, spinach, bacon and egg ($17), an old school counter selection of quiches, sausage rolls, filo wraps and carrot cake, and large pizzas ($26). Tues 9am–3pm, Wed–Sun 9am–9pm or later.

Hawera

Surrounded by gently undulating dairy country, **HAWERA** is the meeting point of the eastern and western routes around Taranaki. A service and administration centre for the district's farmers, Hawera is also home to the world's largest **dairy complex**, just south of town, which handles twenty percent of the country's milk production, mostly gathered from the rich volcanic soils of Taranaki but also brought by rail from other parts of the North Island. The town's dominant feature is the concrete former **Hawera Water Tower** (55 High St; Mon–Fri 8.30am–5.15pm, Sat & Sun 10am–3pm; $2.50), which was built in 1914 and soars 54m above town, offering fabulous views over South Taranaki; ask at the i-SITE for the key.

Morrieson's Café and Bar

58 Victoria St • Daily 11am–9pm or later

A working bar is an appropriate location for the town's ad hoc memorial to one of New Zealand's most celebrated authors, **Ronald Hugh Morrieson** (see p.820). He spent his entire life in Hawera and wrote well-observed and amusing Gothic novels about small-town life and loved jazz (and a drink or three). The house where he once lived was demolished to make way for a KFC, but his fireplace and staircase were relocated here, the bar's tabletops are made of timbers salvaged from the house, a few of his books lie stacked on the mantelpiece, and there's a short biography of the man himself on the bar.

Elvis Presley Museum

51 Argyle St • Visits by appointment • Donation • ☎ 06 278 7624, ⓦ elvismuseum.co.nz

Kevin Wasley loves Elvis Presley and, wanting to share that love around, opens up his garage-shrine to the King. Call ahead and walk the ten minutes from the i-SITE to see thousands of rare recordings, photographs and memorabilia amassed since his boyhood spent trading goods with his Memphis-based pen pal. Much is from the 1950s era Kevin so admires – ask him and you'll hear a tale or two.

Tawhiti Museum and Bush Railway

401 Ohangai Rd, 4km northeast of Hawera • **Museum** Jan daily 10am–4pm • Sept–Dec & Feb–May Mon & Fri–Sun 10am–4pm; June–Aug Sun 10am–4pm • $10 • **Bush railway** First Sun of the month, plus public holidays; daily during school holidays • $5 • ☎ 06 278 6837, ⓦ tawhitimuseum.co.nz

Unique and ever-expanding exhibits at the absorbing **Tawhiti Museum and Bush Railway** explore the social and technological heritage of both Maori and Pakeha using a multitude of life-size figurines modelled on local people. Other highlights include a diorama of 800 miniatures depicting the 1820s musket wars; an extraordinary account of the 1860s New Zealand Wars, seen through the eyes of a deserter from the British Army who lived out his days with the Ngati Ruanui tribe; and a small-scale **bush railway** that trundles 1km through displays recounting Taranaki's logging history; as well as a good on-site **café**.

ARRIVAL AND DEPARTURE

HAWERA

By bus InterCity, NakedBus and The Naki Bus all stop outside the i-SITE.

Destinations New Plymouth (3 daily; 50min–1hr 15min); Wanganui (2 daily; 1hr 15min).

INFORMATION AND ACTIVITIES

i-SITE 55 High St, at the base of the water tower (Mon–Fri 8.30am–5.15pm, Sat & Sun 10am–3pm; ☎ 06 278 8599, ⓦ southtaranaki.com).

Kaitiaki Adventures ☎ 06 752 8242, ⓦ damdrop.com. For an adrenalin rush with a difference go dam dropping, a variation on whitewater sledging. You're equipped with

a buoyant plastic sled, wetsuit, helmet and fins to slide 6–9m down the face of a dam. This is more fun – and less scary – than it sounds and you can do it as many times as you like before the gentle, guided, scenic float down the Wainongoro River. Most trips ($100) run Dec–March.

ACCOMMODATION AND EATING

Il Chefs 47 High St ☎ 06 278 4444, ⓦ twochefs.co.nz. Hawera's top restaurant places the emphasis on locally sourced ingredients and freshly prepared dishes. Lunch might be lamb salad with rocket, feta and roasted *kumara* ($24), while steak lovers shouldn't pass up a dinner of ribeye fillet on herbed rosti with salsa verde ($39). Mon 5–10pm, Tues–Sat 11am–2pm & 5–10pm or later, Sun 11am–2pm & 5–10pm.

Marracbo Down the alley at 172 High St ☎ 06 278 5334. The pick of Hawera's cafés has a wide range of breakfasts, counter food and more substantial mains (around $20). Mon–Thurs 8.30am–4pm, Fri & Sat 8.30am–10pm or later, Sun 9am–4pm.

Tairoa Lodge 3 Pouawai St ☎ 06 278 8603, ⓦ tairoa -lodge.co.nz. B&B in a gorgeous 1875 two-storey house set by a swimming pool in mature grounds on the edge of town. There are three tastefully appointed en suites in the main house, a self-catering cottage sleeping six and the more modern three-bedroom Gatehouse. B&B $180, cottage & gatehouse $220

Wheatly Downs Farmstay 484 Ararata St, 5km past the Tawhiti Museum ☎ 06 278 6523, ⓦ mttaranaki .co.nz. A great opportunity to stay out of town in a backpacker-style place on a peaceful and charming sheep and cattle farm with views of Mount Taranaki. Camping $18, dorms $33, doubles $76, en-suite rooms $125

Patea

Cutting through heavily cultivated farmland, SH3 splits **PATEA**, the only major community between Hawera and Wanganui. The township has a model of the Aotea canoe at the western end of the main street, commemorating the settlement of the area by Turi and his *hapu*; a good **surfing beach** at the mouth of the Patea River (unsafe for swimming); and a safe freshwater **swimming hole**, overlooked by the Manawapou Redoubt and *pa* site.

Museum of South Taranaki

127 Egmont St · Daily 10am–4pm · Donation · ☎ 06 273 8354

For an insight into the town, visit the **Museum of South Taranaki**, known as Aotea Utangunui in Maori. It features displays on the town and its freezing works (abattoir) that closed in 1982, spawning the creation of the Patea Maori club whose 1984 hit single *Poi-E* was imaginatively re-purposed in Taika Waititi's 2010 film *Boy*. The original *Poi-E* video was shot around the town's Aotea canoe.

Check out the **Waitore artefacts**, early fifteenth-century wooden tools and carvings found in a local swamp between 1968 and 1978; the canoe prow, bow cover and bailer are the oldest wooden pieces found in New Zealand, their patterns showing clear Polynesian stylings, predating the later specifically Maori patterns.

Bushy Park

791 Rangitatau East Rd, 47km southeast of Patea, 16km northwest of Wanganui · Daily 10am–5pm · $6 · ☎ 03 342 9879, Ⓦ bushypark.co.nz

A well-signposted side road runs 8km northeast off SH3 to **Bushy Park**, a charming historic homestead in native bush threaded by tracks. Encircled by a 5km fence, it's now a protected **bird sanctuary** with native birds including North Island robins, moreporks, saddlebacks, flocks of kereru and North Island brown kiwi.

ACCOMMODATION
BUSHY PARK

Bushy Park 791 Rangitatau East Rd, Kai Iwi ☎ 03 342 9879, Ⓦ bushypark.co.nz. Choose from antique-styled B&B doubles and twins in the main homestead or the simple self-catering bunkhouse accommodation in the grounds. Bunks $25, double $125

Taumarunui

At the confluence of the Ongarue and Whanganui rivers, **TAUMARUNUI**, 83km south of Te Kuiti, is a little down on its luck. Still, it is well located at the northern end of the Forgotten World Highway (with its associated cycle trail) and is a base for canoe trips on the Whanganui River (see p.242).

Taumarunui was one of the last towns in New Zealand to be settled by Europeans, who arrived in large numbers in 1908, when the railway came to town.

Raurimu Spiral

Visible from a signposted viewpoint 37km south of Taumarunui on SH4 · Departures daily in summer at noon · $48 one-way; $96 return

Finding a suitable route for the railroad on its steep descent north towards Taumarunui from the area around the Tongariro National Park proved problematic, but surveyor R.W. Holmes' ingenious solution, the **Raurimu Spiral**, is a remarkable feat of engineering combining bridges and tunnels to loop the track over and under itself. The cost may make riding the spiral from Taumarunui to National Park unappealing, especially if you've got to come back again.

ARRIVAL AND DEPARTURE

By train and bus The train station is on Hakiaha St; buses stop outside the train station.

Train destinations Auckland (3–7 weekly; 5hr); National Park (3–7 weekly; 50min); Wanganui (1 daily; 2hr 40min);

Wellington (3–7 weekly; 7hr 30min).

Bus destinations Hamilton (1 daily; 2hr 20min); National Park (1 daily; 30min); Te Kuiti (1 daily; 1hr); Wanganui (1 daily; 2hr 40min).

INFORMATION

i-SITE 116 Hakiaha St (daily 9am–5pm; ☎ 07 895 7494, ⓦ visitruapehu.com). Located at the train station, it has a model train replica of the Raurimu Spiral, internet access,

books accommodation and sells Whanganui National Park Hut and Camp passes.

ACCOMMODATION AND EATING

Jasmine's 43 Hakiaha St (SH4) ☎ 07 895 5822. Slightly odd synthesis of a traditional Thai restaurant and a standard Kiwi café. Come for decent coffee and cakes, bacon and egg breakfasts, a seafood pad cha lunch ($12.50) or a hot jungle curry dinner ($16). BYO wine. Daily 7am–9pm.

Kelly's Motel 10 River Rd ☎ 07 895 8175, ⓦ www .kellysmotel.co.nz. A modest and aging – but still comfortable – motel off the highway at the western end of

town with studios, two-bedroom units and breakfast on request. $80

Taumarunui Holiday Park SH4 3km east ☎ 0800 473 281, ⓦ taumarunuiholidaypark.co.nz. Small, well-run site wedged between the Whanganui River and a grove of native bush at the start of the riverside Mananui Walkway (3km). There are simple but attractive wood-lined cabins, a self-contained cottage sleeping seven and a nice kids' play area. Camping $17, cabins $60, cottage $85

The Forgotten World Highway

For a taste of genuinely rural New Zealand, follow the **Forgotten World Highway** between Taumarunui and Stratford (SH43), a rugged 155m road that twists through the hills west of Taumarunui. All but a 12km stretch through the Tangarakau Gorge is sealed, but allow at least three hours for the journey, and be sure to fuel up beforehand as there's **no petrol** along the route. Much of the route is covered on the Whanganui National Park map (see p.241).

Tangarakau Gorge

58km west of Taumarunui

Leaving behind the farmland around Taumarunui, SH43 snakes through the sedimentary limestone of the **Tangarakau Gorge**, possibly the highlight of the trip, with steep bush-draped cliffs rising up above the river. At the entrance to the gorge, a small sign directs you along a short trail to the picturesque site of **Joshua Morgan's grave**, the final resting place of an early surveyor. At the crest of a ridge you pass through the dark, narrow **Moki Tunnel** before reaching Whangamomona.

Whangamomona

A steady descent brings you alongside a little-used rail line that runs parallel to the road as far as tiny **WHANGAMOMONA**, 90km southwest of Taumarunui, with just ten residents. The population is boosted in late January of every odd-numbered year during celebrations of the village's independence, declared on October 28, 1989 after the government altered the provincial boundaries, removing it from Taranaki. The **republic** swears in a president and in full party mood hosts whip-cracking and gumboot-throwing competitions, amid much drinking, eating and merriment. Celebrations revolve around the 1911 *Whangamomona Hotel*, where year-round you can get your passport stamped or buy a Whangamomonian version ($1).

Leaving Whangamomona, SH43 climbs beside steep bluffs and passes a couple of saddles with views down the valley and across the **Taranaki Plains**. It then descends to flat dairy pasture, eventually rolling into **Stratford** as the permanently snowcapped Mount Taranaki looms into view, if the weather allows.

ACCOMMODATION AND EATING

THE FORGOTTEN WORLD HIGHWAY

Ohinepane campsite 21km west of Taumarunui. For a peaceful night beside the Whanganui River, stop at this grassy DOC campsite with water and long-drop toilets and possibly the company of canoeists stopping for their first night downstream from Taumarunui. $10

Whangamomona Domain Camp Whangamomona Rd ☎ 06 762 5822, ⓦ whangamomonacamp.webs .com. Simple campsite in a peaceful setting with campervan hookups, basic cabins and showers, all an easy wander from the *Whangamomona Hotel*. Camping $10, cabins for two $20

Whangamomona Hotel Ohura Rd ☎ 06 762 5823, ⓦ whangamomonahotel.co.nz. Classic country pub/ hotel that has been refurbished without losing any of its character. Airy guest rooms share bathrooms and a continental breakfast is included. The hotel serves basic pub meals (mains $10–20). $130

Whanganui National Park

The emerald-green Whanganui River tumbles from the northern slopes of Mount Tongariro to the Tasman Sea at Wanganui, passing through the **WHANGANUI NATIONAL PARK**, a vast swathe of barely inhabited and virtually trackless bush country east of Taranaki. The park contains one of the largest remaining tracts of lowland forest in the North Island, growing on a bed of soft sandstone and mudstone (*papa*) that has been eroded to form deep gorges, sharp ridges, sheer cliffs and waterfalls. Beneath the canopy of broad-leaved podocarps and mountain beech, an understorey of tree ferns and clinging plants extends down to the riverbanks, while abundant and vociferous **birdlife** includes the kereru (native pigeon), fantail, tui, robin, grey warbler, tomtit and brown kiwi.

The best way to explore the Whanganui National Park is on a multi-day **canoe trip** into the wilderness mostly stopping at riverside campsites. The most popular exit point for canoe trips is the small settlement of **Pipiriki**, where jetboat operators run trips upstream to the **Bridge to Nowhere**.

If you're not taking a river trip, you can explore the **roads** that nibble at the fringes of the park: the Forgotten World Highway (SH43) provides limited access to the northwest, but only the slow and winding **Whanganui River Road** stays near the river for any length of time.

Brief history

At 329km, the Whanganui is New Zealand's longest navigable river. It plays an intrinsic part in the lives of local **Maori**, who hold that each river bend had a *kaitiaki* (guardian) who controlled the *mauri* (life force). The *mana* of the old riverside settlements depended upon the maintenance of the food supplies and living areas: sheltered terraces on the riverbanks were cultivated and elaborate weirs constructed to trap eels and lamprey.

European missionaries arrived in the 1840s, traders followed, and by 1891 a regular boat service carried passengers and cargo to settlers at Pipiriki and Taumarunui. In the early twentieth century **tourist-carrying** paddle steamers plied the waters to reach elegant hotels en route to the central North Island.

Failed settlements

European attempts to stamp their mark on this wild landscape have been ill-fated, however. In 1917 the **Mangapurua Valley**, in the middle of the park, was opened up for settlement by returned World War I servicemen, but, plagued by economic

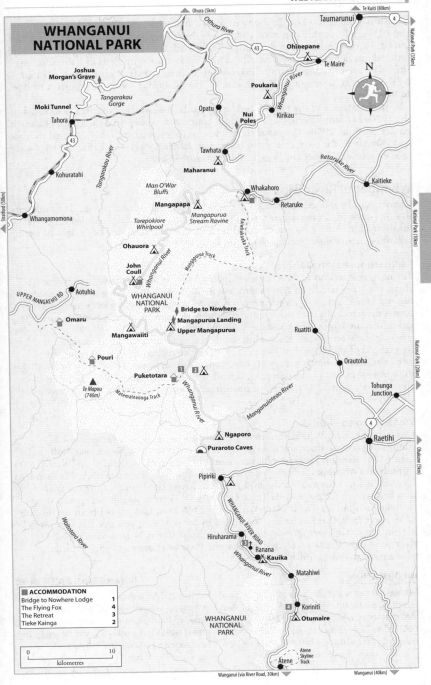

WHANGANUI NATIONAL PARK

ACCOMMODATION

Bridge to Nowhere Lodge	1
The Flying Fox	4
The Retreat	3
Tieke Kainga	2

hardship, remoteness and difficulty of access, many had abandoned their farms by the 1930s. Although a concrete bridge over the Mangapurua Valley opened in 1936, after a major flood in 1942 the bridge was cut off, the three remaining families were ordered out, and the valley officially closed. Today, the only signs of habitation in the valley are the disappearing road, old fence lines, stands of exotic trees planted by the farmers, occasional brick chimneys and the bridge, now the poignant **Bridge to Nowhere**.

With the coming of the railway and better roads, the riverboat tourist trade ceased in the 1920s but farms along the Whanganui continued to support a cargo and passenger service until the 1950s; thereafter the wilderness reclaimed land. This attracted recluses and visionaries, the most celebrated being poet **James K. Baxter** (p.245). The river was used extensively in Vincent Ward's 2005 film *River Queen*.

Whanganui River trips

Canoes, kayaks and jetboats work the river, tailoring trips to your needs. The rapids are mostly Grade I with the occasional Grade II, making this an excellent paddling river for those with little or no experience. That said, the river shouldn't be underestimated: talk to operators about variations in river flows before embarking.

Taumarunui to Whakahoro

The navigable section of river starts at Cherry Grove in **Taumarunui**, from where it's about two days' paddle to **Whakahoro**, essentially just a DOC hut and a boat ramp at the end of a 45km road (mostly gravel) running west from SH4. Between these two points the river runs partly through farmland with roads nearby, and throws up a few rapids that are larger than those downstream.

Beside the river, several kilometres southwest of Cherry Grove, a former stronghold of the Hau Hau (see p.357) is the site of a couple of **nui poles**. In 1862 the Hau Hau erected a war pole, **Rongo-nui**, here, with four arms indicating the cardinal points of the compass, intended to call warriors to their cause from all over the country. At the end of hostilities, a peace pole, **Rerekore**, was erected close by.

Whakahoro to Pipiriki

Downstream from Whakahoro most people take three days to get to Pipiriki. Along the way you'll see the Mangapapa Stream Ravine, the **Man-o-war Bluff** (named for its supposed resemblance to an old iron-clad battleship) and the **Tarepokiore Whirlpool**, which once completely spun a river steamer. At Mangapurua Landing it's an easy walk to the **Bridge to Nowhere** (1hr 15min return), a trail that becomes the Mangapurua Track (see p.245). Further downstream you come to **Tieke Kainga** (aka Tieke Marae), a former DOC hut (see p.244) built on the site of an ancient *pa* that has been re-occupied by local Maori; you can stay or camp here or across the river at *Bridge to Nowhere Lodge* (see p.244), a terrific base for river activities. The last stretch runs past the **Puraroto Caves** and into Pipiriki, where most paddlers finish.

INFORMATION

WHANGANUI RIVER TRIPS

Seasons The river is accessible year-round but paddling season is generally Oct–April, when all overnight river users must buy a Great Walk Ticket (see p.244).

DOC leaflets The free *Whanganui Journey* leaflet and map is the best source of practical information for river trips.

Pick it up at visitor centres and DOC offices in Taumarunui or Wanganui, or download it from ⓦ doc.govt.nz.

Supplies There are no shops along the river, so you need to take all your supplies with you: the nearest large supermarkets are in Taumarunui and Wanganui.

TOURS

CANOE AND JETBOAT OPERATORS

Most tour operators and accommodation options operating on the river can be accessed through ⓦ whanganuiriver .co.nz.

Awa Tours ⓣ 06 385 8012, ⓦ wakatours.com. Excellent three-day guided canoe tours ($670) from Whakahoro on the scenic middle reaches, during which you learn about the river environment from a Maori perspective in an effort to engender a true cultural exchange, take bushwalks and stay at *marae*.

Blazing Paddles 1033 SH4, 10km south of Taumarunui ⓣ 0800 252 946, ⓦ blazingpaddles.co.nz. Good-value gear rental for self-guided trips, with prices including drop-off, pick-up and the DOC Great Walk Ticket, with options ranging from one hour to five days.

Bridge to Nowhere ⓣ 0800 480 308, ⓦ bridgeto nowhere.co.nz. Popular and frequent jetboat tours from Pipiriki, principally to the Bridge to Nowhere (4hr; $125 return; 10.30am departures). They have an excellent option allowing you to canoe the last 10km downstream to Pipiriki ($145) taking an hour or two. Also has Mangapurua mountain bike options (see opposite).

Spirit of the River Jet ⓣ 0800 538 8687, ⓦ spiritof theriverjet.co.nz. A variety of trips upriver from the Pungarehu Marae. Their Bridge to Nowhere tours (from $160) take 6hr, giving more time on the river than other operators and plenty of stops.

Wades Landing Outdoors ⓣ 0800 226 631, ⓦ whanganui.co.nz. Whakahoro-based operator offering jetboat trips (1hr; $95) some visiting the Bridge to Nowhere (5hr; $150), as well as three-day self-guided canoe and kayak trips from Whakahoro to Pipiriki ($160). You can also kayak for a day downstream and catch a jetboat back ($125).

Whanganui Scenic Experience ⓣ 0800 945 335, ⓦ whanganuiscenicjet.com. Mainly jetboat (1hr; $80) and canoe trips on the lower reaches of the river, and best used for day-trips from Wanganui.

Yeti Tours ⓣ 0800 322 388, ⓦ yetitours.co.nz. Ohakune-based guided trips on the river from two ($420) to five days ($850), including transport to launch points or for the tracks, a plethora of rental gear for self-guided trips (canoes/kayaks from $160 for two days, camping equipment packages from $60 for two for 3 days) and lots of help and advice.

ACCOMMODATION

Great Walks Ticket Whanganui River canoeists stay at huts and campsites dotted along the riverbank. In summer (Oct–April) you must obtain a Great Walk Ticket, available online (where you can check hut and campsite availability and adjust your plans accordingly) or at DOC offices and i-SITEs for a small fee. The price depends on the number of places you book, and under-18s go free at both. Backcountry hut passes are valid in winter. Many operators offer canoe rental, transport and accommodation packages that include the Great Walks Ticket. Summer: huts $31, campsites $15. Winter: huts $15, campsites $5

Bridge to Nowhere Lodge 20km upstream from Pipiriki ⓣ 0800 480 308, ⓦ bridgetonowhere.co.nz; map p.241. The only comfortable accommodation beside the river is this boat-accessed lodge offering shared-bathroom doubles, twins and simple bunkrooms (bring a

sleeping bag), all with great bush or river views, and a bar. Either self-cater (bring all your food) or go for the home-cooked dinner, bed and buffet breakfast deal ($125/ person). Non-canoeists can get a package that includes a return jetboat (30min each way) transfer from Pipiriki, plus a Bridge to Nowhere tour, as well as accommodation and meals ($245). People taking packages get precedence for double rooms. Dorms $45, doubles $90

Tieke Kainga 20km upstream from Pipiriki; map p.241. Relaxing former DOC hut where you can stay in big sleeping huts for a small donation, or camp on terraces by the river (no alcohol allowed); if any of the Maori care-takers are about, you'll be treated to an informal cultural experience. You can just turn up, or pre-arrange through the *Bridge to Nowhere Lodge*.

The Whanganui River Road

The outlying sections of the park to the south can be accessed along the **Whanganui River Road**, from either **Raetihi**, a small town on SH4 near Ohakune, or Wanganui (see p.246). The River Road hugs the river's left bank from the riverside hamlet of **Pipiriki** 79km downstream to **Upokongaro**, just outside Wanganui. It's a winding road, prone to floods and landslips (though by early 2013 the final 13km of gravel should have been sealed). Still, even in the best conditions the route will take a minimum of two hours.

Opened in 1934, the road is wedged between river, farmland and heavily forested outlying patches of the Whanganui National Park, and forms the supply route for the

HIKING AND BIKING THE MANGAPURUA TRACK

One of the few tracks that investigates the deep, rugged valleys and bush-clad slopes is the wonderful **Mangapurua Track** (40km one-way; 3 days; 660m ascent), passing through semi-open former farmland. It can certainly be hiked but works better as a superb and moderately tough **mountain bike trip**. Contact Bridge to Nowhere (☎0800 480 308, ⓦbridgetonowhere.co.nz) whose Mangapurua Trail Package ($325) includes road transport, jetboat pick-up at Mangapurua Landing, a night at their riverside lodge and then canoeing back downstream. Bike rental costs an additional $50 for a hardtail, $95 for a fully sprung model. Conditions are best from October to April.

four hundred people or so who live along it. **Facilities** along the way are almost non-existent: there are no shops, pubs or petrol stations, and only a handful of places to stay. If you don't fancy the drive, consider joining one of the Wanganui-based bus tours (see box, p.246).

The road is detailed in the free *Whanganui River Road* leaflet (readily available from i-SITE and DOC offices and downloadable from ⓦwanganui.com), which highlights points of interest and lists their **distance from Wanganui.**

Pipiriki

The southern reaches of the Whanganui National Park are accessed from Raetihi along the winding 27km Pipiriki–Raetihi Road, meeting the river at **PIPIRIKI**, 76km north of Wanganui. It is little more than a bend in the road, the finishing point for canoe journeys and the start of jetboat trips upstream. A couple of operators run snack bars that are open whenever there's enough business.

Hiruharama

HIRUHARAMA (Maori for Jerusalem), 13km south of Pipiriki and 64km north of Wanganui, was originally a Maori village and Catholic mission but is now best known as the site of the **James K. Baxter commune** that briefly flourished in the early 1970s. Baxter, one of New Zealand's most (in)famous poets, attracted hundreds of followers to the area. A devout Roman Catholic convert, but also firm believer in free love in his search for a "New Jerusalem", he became father to a flock of his own, the *nga moki* (fatherless ones), who soon dispersed after his death in 1972. The main commune house is situated high on a hill to the northeast of the church, and Baxter is buried just below. Ask for directions from the remaining Sisters of Compassion, who still live beside the 1892 **church** (from the north head up the first driveway, with a mailbox marked "The Sisters"), which features a Maori-designed and carved altar.

Moutoa Island and Ranana

Moutoa Island, 59km north of Wanganui, was the scene of a vicious battle in 1864 when the lower-river Maori defeated the rebellious Hau Hau warriors, thus protecting the *mana* of the river and saving the lives of European settlers downstream at Wanganui. A cluster of houses 1km on marks **RANANA** (London), where there's a Roman Catholic mission church that's still in use today.

Koriniti

The only real settlement of note in these parts is **KORINITI** (Corinth), 45km north of Wanganui, home to a lovely small church and a trio of traditional Maori buildings, the best being a 1920s **meeting house**, all down a side road. It's a private community, so while you can enter the church, the rest you should view from the road, unless you're invited into the compound. A *koha* of a couple of dollars is appropriate.

Atene and the Oyster Shell Cliffs

Atene 35km north of Wanganui • Oyster Shell Cliffs 8km south of Atene

The **Atene Viewpoint Walk** (5km return; 2hr; 100m ascent) affords great views of Puketapu, a hill that was once on a peninsula almost entirely encircled by the river. Riverboat owner Alexander Hatrick saw an opportunity to shave some time off his trips and blasted through the isthmus to leave the hill surrounded by a dried-out oxbow. The Viewpoint Walk comprises the first few kilometres of the **Atene Skyline Track** (18km loop; 6–8hr), making a wide loop following a gently ascending ridgeline that ends with a 2km walk along the road back to the start.

Further downriver are the **Oyster Shell Cliffs**, roadside bluffs with oyster-shell deposits embedded in them.

Aramoana Summit

17km northwest of Wanganui

Soon the winding climb begins to the summit lookout of **Aramoana**, giving a last look at the river below. On a clear day you can enjoy views of the northeast horizon, dominated by Mount Ruapehu. From the junction of the River Road and SH4, it's 14km to Wanganui.

ACCOMMODATION	WHANGANUI RIVER ROAD

★ **The Flying Fox** Koriniti ☎ 06 342 8160, ⓦ the flyingfox.co.nz; map p.241. At this wonderfully remote and romantic hideaway, accessible only by boat or aerial cableway (prior booking essential), an eclectic range of found objects and scavenged pieces of old buildings have been imaginatively combined to create three separate self-contained buildings which encourage outdoor living amid the organic gardens and bush. Wood-fired bush baths, solar-heated showers, odourless composting toilets and a few spiders keeping the mosquitoes at bay add to the appeal. Browse through a fascinating range of books, old vinyl and CDs in the James K (self-catering, sleeping

five), the Brewers Cottage (self-catering, sleeping three), or the Glory Cart (modelled on a gypsy caravan), or camp. You can self-cater or pre-arrange predominantly organic breakfasts, and book canoeing trips (from $85/3hr). Camping one night $20, camping second night $10, Glory Cart $100, Brewers Cottage & James K $200

The Retreat Hiruharama ☎ 06 342 8190, ⓦ compassion .org.nz; map p.241. Basic dorm accommodation for up to twenty people at a renovated original wooden convent. There's a full kitchen but you'll need to bring all food and your own sleeping bag. $25

Wanganui

There's an old-fashioned charm to **WANGANUI**, the slow pace mirroring the speed of the river that bisects it. Founded on the banks of the **Whanganui River**, New Zealand's longest navigable watercourse, Wanganui is one of New Zealand's oldest cities and was the hub of early European commerce because of its access to the interior, and coastal links with the ports of Wellington and New Plymouth. The river traffic has long gone and the port is a shadow of what it was, leaving a city that feels too big for its

---

WHANGANUI RIVER ROAD MAIL RUN

If you have neither the time nor inclination to spend a few days canoeing in the Whanganui National Park, consider taking the **Whanganui River Road Mail Tour** (daily; $63; ☎ 06 345 3475, ⓦ whanganuitours.co.nz), a genuine mail-delivery service stopping frequently at houses along the way as well as points of interest. The trip starts early (accommodation pick-up can be arranged from Wanganui city) and doesn't return until mid- to late afternoon, so bring your own food or take up the $12 home-made lunch option, as there's nowhere to buy refreshments en route. Canoeing from Pipiriki, trampers' transport and jetboating can also be arranged.

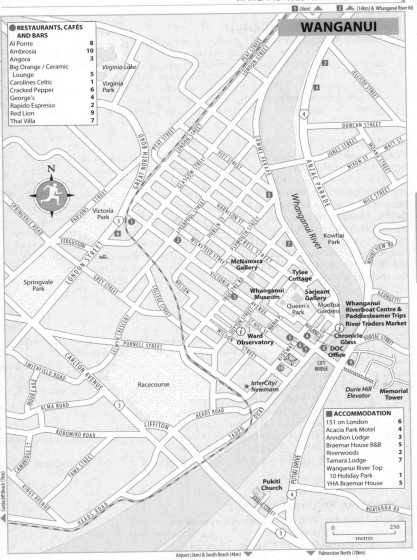

WANGANUI

RESTAURANTS, CAFÉS AND BARS

Al Ponte	8
Ambrosia	10
Angora	3
Big Orange / Ceramic Lounge	5
Carolines Celtic	1
Cracked Pepper	6
George's	4
Rapido Espresso	2
Red Lion	9
Thai Villa	7

ACCOMMODATION

151 on London	6
Acacia Park Motel	4
Anndion Lodge	3
Braemar House B&B	5
Riverwoods	2
Tamara Lodge	7
Wanganui River Top 10 Holiday Park	1
YHA Braemar House	5

42,000 people – it even has a small opera house. Still, it's a manageable place that exudes civic pride, both for its quality museums and well-tended streetscape.

The cultural heart of Wanganui beats around Pukenamu, a grassy hill that marks the site of Wanganui's last tribal war in 1832. Now known as **Queens Park**, it contains three of the city's most significant buildings.

The low cost of living has seen a thriving **arts community** spring up here, and it's a pleasant place to idle away some time in the renowned **art gallery**, watch a **glass-blowing** demonstration or take a class, and to ride on a restored **river steamer**.

WANGANUI OR WHANGANUI?

Unlike the Whanganui National Park and Whanganui River, the city of Wanganui has long been spelt without an "h". The pronunciation of both is the same, deriving from the local Maori dialect, pronouncing the "wh" prefix phonetically (as opposed to elsewhere in the country, where the "wh" is pronounced "f"). The spelling quirk results from a direct transcription of the Maori name (*whanga nui* translates as "big harbour"). Most locals opposed any streamlining of the spelling, but in 2009 authorities ruled that the "h" is optional. For consistency with the majority of current usage, the city spelling "Wanganui" has been retained in this guide.

Brief history

When **Europeans** arrived in the 1830s, land rights quickly became a bone of contention with the local Maori population. Transactions that Maori perceived as a ritual exchange of gifts were taken by the New Zealand Company to be a successful negotiation for the purchase of Wanganui and a large amount of surrounding land. Settlement went ahead regardless of the misunderstanding, and it was not until the **Gilfillan Massacre** of 1847 that trouble erupted – when a Maori was accidentally injured, his tribesmen massacred four members of the Gilfillan family. Further violent incidents culminated in a full-scale but inconclusive **battle** at St John's Hill. The next year the problems were apparently resolved by a payment of £1000 to the Maori. In the 1990s, the central Moutoa Gardens became the focus of renewed tensions, while the **spelling** of the city's name also creates divisions – see box above.

Sarjeant Gallery

Queens Park • Daily 10.30am–4.30pm • Free • ☎ 06 349 0506, ⓦ sarjeant.org.nz

The gleaming hilltop **Sarjeant Gallery** is housed in one of Wanganui's most impressive buildings, a 1919 Oamaru stone structure boasting a magnificent dome that filters natural light into the exhibition space. Rotating quarterly exhibitions partly draw on the highly regarded permanent collection that is strong on both colonial and contemporary New Zealand art and photography. One artist to look out for is the under-rated Edith Collier, a local painter whose career was overshadowed by that of her contemporary, Frances Hodgkins. All this is augmented by various strong touring exhibitions.

Much of the contemporary collection is the product of regular artist residencies at one of Wanganui's oldest buildings, the 1853 weatherboard **Tylee Cottage**, immediately to the north at the corner of Cameron and Bell streets.

The Quay Gallery, an offshoot of the Sarjeant, is upstairs at the i-SITE, and has quality exhibitions.

Whanganui Regional Museum

Watt St • Daily 10am–4.30pm • $8.50 • ☎ 06 349 1110, ⓦ wanganui-museum.org.nz

Southwest of the Sarjeant Gallery, the Veteran Steps lead towards the centre of the city past the **Whanganui Regional Museum**. Founded in 1892, it contains an outstanding collection of Maori artefacts and three impressive canoes, all displayed in the central court. In smaller galleries hang portraits of Maori in full ceremonial dress and *moko* (traditional tattoos) by Gottfried Lindauer. Look out too for the photos of Whanganui river life, and models of ancient Maori methods of trapping eels and lampreys.

Moutoa Gardens

Moutoa Gardens, where the river kinks around the central city on Somme Parade, is little more than a small patch of grass imbued with history. Traditionally Maori lived at Moutoa during the fishing season, until it was co-opted by Pakeha settlers, who renamed the area

Market Square. It was here that Maori signed the document agreeing to the "sale" of Wanganui, an issue revisited on Waitangi Day 1995, when simmering old grievances and one or two more recent ones reached boiling point. Maori occupied Moutoa Gardens, claiming it as Maori land, for 83 days. This ended peacefully in the High Court, but created much bitterness on both sides. By 2001 a more conciliatory atmosphere prevailed, and the government, city council and local *iwi* agreed to share management of the gardens.

Waimarie paddle steamer

1A Taupo Quay • Tues–Sun 1.30pm • $39 • ☎ 0800 783 2637, ⓦ riverboat.co.nz

Wanganui's history is inextricably tied with the Whanganui River, and though commercial river traffic has virtually stopped, you can still ride the *Waimarie* **paddle steamer**. New Zealand's last surviving paddle-steamer, it makes a two-hour run up a tidal stretch of the river. The huffing of the coal-fired steam engine and the slosh of the paddles make for a soothing background to an afternoon's sunning on deck, or you can retire to the wood-panelled saloon for scones and tea (or a glass of wine).

Yarrow and Company of London built the *Waimarie* in 1899 to a shallow-draught design with a tough hull, making it suitable for river work. It was transported to New Zealand in kit form, then put to work on the Whanganui River, where it saw service during the pre-Great War boom in tourism, when thousands from all over the world came to travel up the Whanganui River and stay at the hotel at Pipiriki. In 1949 the *Waimarie* made her last voyage and three years later sank at her moorings. It wasn't until 1993 that the boat was salvaged and it returned to the river in 1999.

Whanganui Riverboat Museum

1A Taupo Quay • Mon–Sat 9am–4pm, Sun 10am–2pm • Free

The restoration of the *Waimarie* took place at the **Whanganui Riverboat Museum**, adjacent to the cruise departure docks and flanked by old warehouses and stores. Housed in an 1881 two-storey timber-framed building, the museum concentrates on the river and its history in relation to the town and includes the partly restored MV *Ongarue*, which worked the river from 1900 to 1957.

Durie Hill Elevator and Memorial Tower

Elevator Mon–Fri 8am–6pm, Sat & Sun 10am–5pm • $2 each way Tower Daily 8am–dusk • Free

City Bridge takes you from downtown to the east bank of the river and the **Durie Hill Elevator**. A Maori carved gateway here marks the entrance to a 213m tunnel, at the

---

GLASS-BLOWING AND PHOTOGRAPHY IN WANGANUI

New Zealand's only **glass-blowing** school is based in Wanganui, and the city is home to around three dozen glass-blowing artists brought together as the Wanganui Glass Group (ⓦwanganuiglass .com). Many work out of private studios, which open their doors to the public during March as part of the Whanganui Artists Open Studios programme – dates and trails are listed at ⓦopenstudio .co.nz. The annual Wanganui **Festival of Glass** takes place from late September to early October. Wanganui also has one of New Zealand's very few galleries totally dedicated to **photography**.

Chronicle Glass Studio 2 Rutland St ☎ 06 347 1921, ⓦchronicleglass.co.nz. You can see glass-blowing demonstrations – and some superb pieces – year-round here, the workshop/gallery of acclaimed glass-blowers Katie Brown and Lyndsay Patterson. You can also make your own paperweight during a forty-minute course ($100, by appointment), or book in for

a weekend-long glass-blowing course ($375).
McNamara Gallery 190 Wickstead St ☎ 06 348 7320, ⓦmcnamara.co.nz. Paul McNamara's gallery is New Zealand's only dedicated photographic gallery, really just a couple of rooms in a house, though always with something challenging on show. Generally open Tues–Sat 11am–3pm.

end of which a historic 1919 elevator carries passengers 66m up through the hill to the summit. At the top of the hill two excellent vantage points grant extensive views of the city, beaches and inland. The viewpoint atop the elevator's machinery room is the easy option, but the best views are 176 steps up at the top of the 33.5m-high **Memorial Tower**. Head back to town using the 191 steps to the river – it only takes about ten minutes, and provides more satisfying views.

Putiki church

Anaua St • Often locked; contact the i-SITE for access • $2 donation

It's about 2km south along Putiki Drive to the small, whitewashed **St Paul's Memorial Church**, which contains magnificent Maori carvings adorned with paua, a painted rib ceiling (as in Maori meeting houses), two beautiful etched-glass windows and some intricate *tukutuku* panels.

ARRIVAL AND DEPARTURE WANGANUI

By plane Flights from Auckland and Wellington arrive at the airport, 5km southwest of the city; a taxi into town costs around $20–25.
Destinations Auckland (4 daily; 1hr); Wellington (5 weekly; 35min).
By bus InterCity buses drop off at the Wanganui Travel

Centre, 156 Ridgway St (☎06 345 4433). NakedBus stop outside the i-SITE.
Destinations Hamilton (2 daily; 6–8hr); New Plymouth (2 daily; 2hr 30min); Palmerston North (3 daily; 1hr–1hr 45min); Taumarunui (1 daily; 2hr 40min).

GETTING AROUND

By bus Tranzit buses (☎06 345 4433, ☻horizons.govt.nz) run a limited Mon–Sat bus service round the city (flat fare $2).

By taxi Wanganui Taxis (☎0800 343 5555).

INFORMATION

i-SITE 31 Taupo Quay (Mon–Fri 8.30am–5pm, Sat & Sun 9am–3pm; ☎06 349 0508, ☻wanganui.com). Has free internet access and wi-fi, timetables for the local buses and sells Whanganui National Park hut and camping passes.

Useful website For a list of gigs and events in town, check out ☻eventswanganui.com.
DOC 74 Ingestre St (Mon–Fri 8am–5pm; ☎06 349 2100). Sells Whanganui National Park hut and camping passes.

ACCOMMODATION

151 on London 151 London St ☎0800 151 566, ☻151onlondon.co.nz. The newest motel in town, with a range of studios and suites, sleek TVs, broadband, a/c, a small gym and even an on-site café. **$135**
Acacia Park Motel 140 Anzac Parade (SH4) ☎0800 800 225, ☻acacia-park-motel.co.nz. Budget, cabin-style rooms set in big grounds overlooking the river with a kids' play area. Fittings are from the 1960s but everything is well maintained and clean. **$95**
Anndion Lodge 143 Anzac Parade ☎0800 343 056, ☻anndionlodge.co.nz. Very professional combination of an upmarket backpackers and a very comfortable lodge all spread over three suburban houses. There are no dorms, just luxurious shared-bath rooms, en-suite rooms and one- and two-bedroom suites, all done out in slightly tacky black-and-crimson colour schemes. There is a communal kitchen complete with bread maker and dishwasher, plus a lovely BBQ area, swimming pool, spa and sauna, free wi-fi, courtesy city transport and even a restaurant. Double **$88**, en-suite double **$130**, suites **$140**

Braemar House B&B 2 Plymouth St ☎06 348 2301, ☻braemarhouse.co.nz. Bathrooms are shared in this excellent-value budget B&B situated in a lovely 1895 homestead surrounded by lawns. Some rooms front onto a sun-drenched veranda and there's a YHA hostel out back (see opposite). Add $15 a head for continental breakfast. **$100**
Riverwoods 234 Kaiwhaiki Rd, 14km northeast of Wanganui ☎06 342 5501, ☻riverwoods.co.nz. B&B accommodation in a restored Victorian villa relocated from Wanganui to this rural site beside the river. There's even a guest kitchen if you don't fancy driving back into town for dinner. **$235**
Tamara Lodge 24 Somme Parade ☎06 347 6300, ☻tamaralodge.com. A large and well-kept historic building with pretty gardens and a sociable vibe that makes it popular with younger backpackers. Offers free bikes, musical instruments, neat comfortable four-bed dorms, doubles and twins (some en-suite), plus a balcony with a river view, and a trampoline in the large garden. Dorms **$26**, rooms **$72**, en suites **$86**

Wanganui River Top 10 Holiday Park 460 Somme Parade ☎ 0800 272 664, ⓦ wrivertop10.co.nz. Well-tended site 6km northeast of the city centre, beside the river in the shade of giant trees. There's kayak and jetski rental too. Camping site <u>$42</u>, cabins <u>$72</u>, kitchen cabins <u>$84</u>, motel units <u>$135</u>

YHA Braemar House 2 Plymouth St ☎ 06 348 2301, ⓦ braemarhouse.co.nz. Welcoming backpackers attached to *Braemar House B&B* with separate male and female dorms, private rooms out back, a kitchen and cosy lounge and a peaceful atmosphere. Dorms <u>$29</u>, hostel rooms <u>$70</u>

EATING AND DRINKING

Al Ponte 49 Taupo Quay ☎ 06 345 5559, ⓦ alponte .co.nz. Cheap and cheerful Italian bistro in an airy converted warehouse that backs onto the river. Good value for its thin-crust pizzas with traditional toppings ($16), pasta dishes (entrée $11–18) and *secondi piatti* such as veal medallions with prawns and asparagus spears ($27). Locals flock for the $20 Wednesday-night pizza-and-wine specials. Tues–Sun 6–10pm or later.

★ **Ambrosia** 63a Ridgeway St ☎ 06 348 5528, ⓦ nzdeli.co.nz. Great little deli stocking all manner of gourmet and artisan goodies from New Zealand and around the world, including organic meats, cheeses and Wanganui olive oil, plus top-notch bagels, pastries, friands and excellent coffee to go. Mon 8.30am–4pm Tues–Fri 8.30am–5pm, Sat 9am–2pm.

Angora 199 Victoria Ave ☎ 06 348 8334, ⓦ angora restaurant.co.nz. Solid and reliable Turkish and wider Mediterranean restaurant where you might start off with haloumi served with sweet roasted peppers on Turkish bread ($13) and follow with stuffed aubergine ($18) or slow-cooked lamb cutlets ($29). Mon–Sat 11am–10pm or later, Sun 5–10pm.

Carolines Celtic 432 Victoria Ave ☎ 06 347 7037. Lively pub that's always good for a convivial beer or a straight-forward and very filling bar meal such as fish and chips ($18) or steak ($25–30). Daily 11am–11pm.

Cracked Pepper 21 Victoria Ave ☎ 06 345 0444. Licensed café serving gourmet twists on old favourites, including lamb's fry and bacon, calamari risotto, and good chicken caesar salad, all under $18. Mon–Sat 7.30am–4.30pm.

Big Orange/Ceramic Lounge 51 Victoria Ave ☎ 06 348 4449. Two names, same place: this buzzing café (*Big Orange*) transforms into the hip restaurant/cocktail bar *Ceramic Lounge*, where you might expect roast pork medallion on gnocchi ($27) followed by piña colada sago ($13). Mon & Tues 7am–5pm, Wed–Fri 7.30am–9pm or later, Sat 9am–9pm or later, Sun 9am–5pm.

George's 40 Victoria Ave ☎ 06 345 7937. A local institution, this old-fashioned fish and chip shop has an attached dining room and also sells good-value wet fish. Mon–Sat 8.30am–7.30pm, Fri to 8.30pm.

★ **Rapido Espresso** 71 Liverpool St ☎ 06 347 9475. Sink into a sofa in this chilled villa café that focuses on its superb organic coffee, though they sell a few muffins, cake slices and lunchtime veggie and meaty sandwiches ($5–6.50). Mon–Fri 7.30am–6pm, Sat 9am–3pm.

Red Lion 45 Anzac Parade ☎ 06 348 4080, ⓦ redlioninn .co.nz. Atmospheric pulse-of-the-town pub overlooking the river with meal deals and a lively atmosphere as the weekend approaches. Daily 11am–10pm or later.

River Traders Market On Taupo Quay, behind the i-SITE ⓦ therivertraders.co.nz. Come the weekend, get yourself along to this hugely popular market where local artisans and growers set up their stalls. Sat 9am–1pm.

Thai Villa 7 Victoria Ave ☎ 06 348 9089, ⓦ thaivilla .co.nz. Quality Thai place with all your favourite curries and stir-fries ($18–21) along with hot plate options such as Weeping Tiger, a dish of marinated beef and vegetables. ($23). Licensed and BYO. Tues–Sat 11am–2pm & 6–10.30pm.

ENTERTAINMENT

Embassy 3 Cinema 34 Victoria Ave ☎ 06 345 7958, ⓦ embassy3.co.nz. Mainstream films at Wanganui's only cinema, an Art Deco affair from the early 1950s.

Ward Observatory Hill St. Every clear Friday evening you can look through the 24cm refractor at this wonderful 1901 observatory ($2 donation). To arrange a viewing outside of the hours listed here, contact the i-SITE. Oct–March Fri 8.30pm, April–Sept Fri 8pm.

Palmerston North and around

One of New Zealand's largest landlocked cities, **PALMERSTON NORTH** (as opposed to Palmerston near Dunedin, and known as "Palmy") is the thriving capital of the province of Manawatu, with around 80,000 residents, including a lively student population attending **Massey University**. After the arrival of the rail line in 1886, Palmerston North flourished, thanks to its pivotal position at the junction of road and rail routes, reflected today by some fine civic buildings, notably an excellent museum and **gallery** and a stunning **library**. Nonetheless, an unimpressed John Cleese famously claimed, "If you want to kill yourself but lack the courage, I think a visit to Palmerston North will do the trick." The town responded by naming the local rubbish dump after him.

The city's main cultural event, the Festival of Cultures (⊛foc.co.nz), takes place around The Square in March (22nd & 23rd in 2013) with a Friday-night lantern festival and a Saturday craft, food and music fair. Artists who recently played at WOMAD in New Plymouth often turn up on the bill.

The Square

Library • Mon, Tues & Thurs 10am–6pm, Wed & Fri 10am–8pm, Sat 10am–4pm & Sun 1–4pm

Palmerston North centres on **The Square**, a smart, grassy expanse with an elegant clocktower. The adjacent **Te Marae o Hine**, or the Courtyard of the Daughter of Peace, is graced by a couple of 5m-high Maori figures carved by renowned artist **John Bevan Ford**. The Maori name is the one suggested for the settlement's central square by the chief of the Ngati Raukawa in 1878, in the hope that love and peace would become enduring features in the relationship between the Manawatu Maori and incoming Pakeha.

The most striking of the surrounding buildings is the **City Library**, a postmodern reworking of the original 1927 department store by Kiwi star architect, Ian Athfield.

Te Manawa

326 Main St • Daily 10am–5pm • Free • ☎ 06 355 5000, ⊛ temanawa.co.nz

The city's main cultural focus is **Te Manawa**, with well laid-out galleries covering Maori heritage and life in the Manawatu once Europeans arrived. Some of the best material is in the Te Awa section, covering all aspects of the Manawatu River from geology and ecology to bug life (there's a weta cave) and a tank of native fish (effectively grown-up whitebait). The stunning carpet is an aerial view of the entire region. Throughout the galleries there's masses of hands-on stuff for kids.

The adjacent **Art Gallery** displays Pakeha and Maori art from its permanent collection, alongside touring exhibitions.

New Zealand Rugby Museum

Upstairs at Te Manawa • Daily 10am–5pm • $12.50 • ☎ 06 358 6947, ⊛ rugbymuseum.co.nz

Knock down a tackle bag, try to move a scrum machine or kick goals better than Piri Weepu at the **New Zealand Rugby Museum**, where the interactive area is surrounded by an excellent decade-by-decade social history of rugby in New Zealand including games played by soldiers in Egypt during World War II. There's everything from old leather shoulder pads and footage of the 1905. All Black "originals" tour to cartoons lampooning rugby selectors and the coin tossed at the start of each Rugby World Cup final.

Manawatu Gorge

15km northeast of Palmerston North

Heading northeast from Palmerston North the skyline above the semi-rural town of **Ashhurst** is broken by the southern hemisphere's largest **wind farms**, draped across the Ruahine and Tararua ranges. These hills are separated by the Manawatu Gorge (Te Apiti in Maori), a narrow 10km-long defile through which a rail line, SH3 and the Manawatu River squeeze. The road has been closed by a massive slip since August 2011 but should reopen by late 2012. The gorge can be explored on foot along the **Manawatu Gorge Track** (3–4hr one-way; contact the i-SITE for gorge transport options), or you can see it on a jetboat tour (see opposite).

ARRIVAL AND DEPARTURE

By train The train station is on Matthews Ave, about 1500m northwest of the city centre.

Destinations Auckland (3–7 weekly; 9hr 30min); Hamilton (3–7 weekly; 7hr); Wellington (3–7 weekly; 2hr 30min).

By bus InterCity buses stop at the Palmerston North Travel Centre, at the corner of Pitt and Main sts, while NakedBus stops outside the i-SITE.

Destinations Auckland (3 daily; 9–10hr); Hastings (3 daily; 2hr 45min); Masterton (2 Mon–Fri; 2hr); Napier (3 daily;

PALMERSTON NORTH AND AROUND

3hr); Paraparaumu (10 daily; 1hr 30min); Rotorua (2 daily; 5hr); Taupo (4–5 daily; 4hr); Wanganui (3 daily; 1hr–1hr 45min); Wellington (10 daily; 2hr).

By plane The airport is 3km northeast of the city. SuperShuttle (☎ 0800 748 885) runs into town ($16 for one, $20 for two).

Destinations Auckland (5 daily; 1hr); Christchurch (4 daily; 1hr 15min); Wellington (2 daily; 30min).

GETTING AROUND

By bus A series of loop services ($2.50 single) runs from Main St, near the i-SITE, where you can pick up timetables.

By taxi Palmerston North Taxis (☎ 0800 355 5333).

INFORMATION AND TOURS

i-SITE The Square (Mon–Fri 9am–5pm, Sat & Sun 10am–2pm; ☎ 06 350 1922, ⓦ manawatunz.co.nz). Good for DOC leaflets and hut tickets plus showers ($2; $4 with towel).

Services Downtown Palmerston North has free wi-fi

(limited to 100Mb per month).

Manawatu Gorge Jet ☎ 0800 945 335, ⓦ manawatu gorgejet.com. Take a hair-raising 25min jetboat ride through Manawatu Gorge ($65).

ACCOMMODATION

Acacia Court Motel 374 Tremaine Ave ☎ 0800 685 586, ⓦ acaciacourtmotel.co.nz. Friendly, older-style motel with good prices for spotlessly clean if slightly dowdy self-contained units (some sleeping up to five) with Sky TV and off-street parking. $95

Arena Lodge 74 Pascal St ☎ 0800 881 255, ⓦ arena lodge.co.nz. Smart, modern motel in a quiet location 1km west of the Square with a range of deluxe rooms, some with barbecue area and spa bath. $155

Palmerston North Holiday Park 133 Dittmer Drive ☎ 06 358 0349, ⓦ palmerstonnorthholidaypark.co.nz. Quiet, spacious and shady campsite with excellent facilities, 2km south of the city centre and close to the Manawatu

River. Camping per site $32, cabins $45, kitchen cabins $65, tourist flats $80

Pepper Tree 121 Grey St ☎ 06 355 4054, ⓦ pepper treehostel.co.nz. The best of the city's limited range of hostels, located in a welcoming and comfortable villa within easy walking distance of the central square. Dorms $28, doubles $70

⭐ **Plum Trees Lodge** 97 Russell St ☎ 06 358 7813, ⓦ plumtreeslodge.co.nz. Lovely and tastefully decorated self-catering loft in a quiet suburban street, with a leafy deck where you can pick your own plums. An extensive breakfast hamper is supplied. $165

EATING AND DRINKING

Thanks to its term-time student population, Palmerston North supports a vibrant restaurant scene, with almost everything close to the Square.

Barista 59 George St ☎ 06 357 2614, ⓦ barista.co.nz. Minimalist espresso bar in a stripped industrial space of exposed pipes and concrete where they grind their own coffee and serve great cakes, snacks and full meals (most mains $20–28) such as pan-fried scallop salad, along with an excellent range of New Zealand wines. There's a Sunday high tea (3–5pm; $22), and Saturday-night live jazz and standards. Daily 8am–10pm or much later.

Brewers Apprentice 334 Church St ☎ 06 358 8888, ⓦ brewersapprentice.co.nz. Lively, modern Monteith's pub with plenty of open-air drinking space, and a good range of quality pub meals including pan-fried flounder and chips ($23). Mon–Fri 11am–10pm or later, Sat & Sun 10am–10pm or later.

⭐ **Café Cuba** 236 Cuba St ☎ 06 356 5750. Funky day/night café that's a local institution for breakfast, all-day brunch and lunch (under $20) and dinners such as fish on a lemon and prawn risotto (under $25). Lots of vegetarian fare, hip staff and usually live music on Friday or Saturday nights. Licensed & BYO. Mon, Tues & Sun 7am–10pm, Wed–Sat 7am–1am.

The Fish Regent Arcade, 57 Broadway Ave ☎ 06 357 9845. Cool little cocktail and wine bar that's particularly popular on Thursday when it is half price for ladies. Wed 4–11pm, Thurs 4pm–1am, Fri & Sat 4pm–3am.

High Flyers Corner of Main St and The Square ☎ 06 357 5155, ⓦ highflyers.net.nz. Studenty bar/club with a terrace overlooking the Square with good-value meals (around $20) and vast low-cost pizzas. Attracts a young crowd at night, especially on DJ dance nights. Wed 11am–late, Thurs–Sat 11am–3am.

Tomato 72 George St ☎ 6 357 6663. Faded Kiwi landscapes and a paua-shell counter give this relaxed café a retro vibe. Tuck into a breakfast of cannellini beans and Italian pork sausage ($16), or mains such as pan-fried flounder ($17) or pizza ($15). And don't miss the bathroom decor of 1970s women's magazine advertising. Mon, Tues & Sun 7.30am–4pm, Wed–Sat 7.30am–11pm-ish.

Yeda 78 Broadway Ave ☎ 06 358 3978, ⓦ yeda.co.nz. New pan-Asian restaurant and cocktail bar with a good line in the likes of steamed fish with ginger and soy ($18), chicken katsu ($18) and barbecue pork buns ($5). Daily 11am–9pm.

NIGHTLIFE AND ENTERTAINMENT

Centrepoint 280 Church St ☎ 06 354 5740, ⓦ centrepoint.co.nz. New Zealand's only professional provincial theatre is a 135-seater with shows from April to Christmas. $15 entry for under-30s.

Downtown Cinemas 70 Broadway Ave ☎ 06 355 5655, ⓦ dtcinemas.co.nz. Screens both mainstream and art-house films.

Foxton and around

Horowhenua's most interesting town is **FOXTON**, 38km southwest of Palmerston North, where the old-style shop facades line the broad main street bypassed by SH1.

Archeological evidence suggests that there was a semi-nomadic **moa-hunter** culture in this area between 1400 and 1650, predating larger tribal settlements. **Europeans** arrived in the early 1800s and settled at the mouth of the Manawatu River, subsequently founding Foxton on a tributary. It quickly became the **flax-milling** capital of New Zealand, the industry only finally dying in 1985. A **historic walk** tells the tale through 28 plaques around town.

By early 2013, look out for the proposed new cultural precinct next to the windmill. Known as **Te Awahou–Nieuwe Stroom**, it's designed to celebrate local Maori and the strong New Zealand–Dutch heritage, along with a visitor centre and library.

The long, sandy **Foxton Beach** is 5km away on the coast, where there's good surfing, safe swimming areas and abundant birdlife around the Manawatu river estuary.

De Molen

Main St · Daily 10am–4pm · Tours $5 · ☎ 06 363 5601

Low-rise Foxton is dominated by **de Molen**, a modern, full-scale **replica of a classic** seventeenth-century **Dutch windmill**. Self-guided tours visit the inner workings, and on three to four days a month you'll see it producing stoneground wholemeal flour. On the ground floor, you can buy Dutch groceries and the town's local soft drink, **Foxton Fizz**, in old-fashioned flavours such as creaming soda.

At the time of writing, de Molen was finalizing plans for its "bladerider", whereby you're strapped to the mill's blades and whirled through the air, fairground-style.

Flax Stripper Museum

Main St · Daily 1–3pm · $5 · ☎ 06 363 6846

A broad history of Foxton's flax industry is recounted in the **Flax Stripper Museum**, which shows examples of the handmade flax (*harakeke*) baskets and cloaks perfected by local Maori. But the real emphasis is on European operations, cultivating flax near swamps and on riverbanks in Manawatu and Horowhenua then exporting flax fibre around the country and abroad for binder twine, fibrous plaster and carpet. Subsequently, woolpacks were made in Foxton. The staff put the loud mechanical flax stripper through its paces, explain the history in fascinating detail and point out the benefits of various flax varieties planted outside.

Papaitonga Scenic Reserve

Off SH1, 23km south of Foxton

The main southbound road routes converge at the workaday town of **LEVIN**, the administrative centre of the Horowhenua region. Just south of town at the **Papaitonga Scenic Reserve**, a boardwalk leads to the Papaitonga Lookout (20min return) and great **views** of Lake Papaitonga. The surrounding wetlands provide a refuge for many **rare birds**, including the spotless crake, Australasian bittern and New Zealand dabchick.

The Kapiti Coast

The narrow plain between the rugged and inhospitable **Tararua Range** and the Tasman breakers is known as the **Kapiti Coast**, effectively part of Wellington's commuter belt, peppered with dormitory suburbs and golf courses. Still, it has sweeping beaches, a few minor points of interest and provides access to **Kapiti Island**, 5km offshore, a magnificent bush-covered sanctuary where birdlife thrives.

3

Otaki

OTAKI, 20km south of Levin, sits beside a broad, braided section of the Otaki River, surrounded by market gardens. For most of the year, this is a quiet place with strong Maori heritage (it was the first town in New Zealand to have bilingual road signs), but, like other towns along this coast, it swells to bursting point for the month or so after Christmas when Kiwi holidaymakers descend en masse.

Otaki comes in three parts: the train station and i-SITE on SH1; Otaki township 2km towards the sea along Mill Road; and the **beach**, a further 3km along Mill Road, safe to swim at in summer thanks to a surf patrol. Self-contained campervans can freedom camp here on the north bank of the river.

Along SH1 are around twenty **designer outlet stores**, mostly women's clothing but also outdoors shops such as Kathmandu and Icebreaker.

Rangiatea Church

33 Te Rauparaha St, 200m west of SH1 • Casual visits Mon–Fri 9.30am–1.30pm; guided tours Mon–Sat 10am & 2pm • Free; guided tours $35 • ☎ 06 364 6838, ⓦ rangiatea.maori.nz

Rangiatea Church is an exact replica of the 1849 original that was widely regarded as the finest Maori church in New Zealand. The church was consecrated in 2003, eight years after the original was razed in an arson attack. Inside, the building is simple, with *tukutuku* panels on the walls, the pattern representing both the stars and the departed.

The rafters are painted in Maori designs representing hammerhead sharks (symbols of power and privilege), and the exquisite model of the Tainui *waka*, which escaped the blaze. Outside, the simple, grey-slate headstone of the Maori chief Te Rauparaha can be found in a row of three by a decapitated Norfolk pine. Opposite the church is a memorial to the great chief.

Waikanae

WAIKANAE, 14km south of Otaki, is divided between the highwayside settlement and a beach community, 4km away along Te Moana Road, where the broad, dune-backed **beach** has safe swimming.

Nga Manu Nature Reserve

Ngarara Rd • Daily 10am–5pm • $15 • ☎ 04 293 4131, ⓦ ngamanu.co.nz

To see native wildlife in its more-or-less natural habitat, stop at the **Nga Manu Nature Reserve**, a large man-made bird sanctuary with easy walking tracks and some picnic spots. A circular track (1500m) cuts through a variety of habitats, from ponds and scrubland to swamp and coastal forest, which attract all manner of birds. There is also a nocturnal house containing kiwi, morepork and tuatara, plus eels, fed at 2pm daily, and some walk-in aviaries where kea and kaka strut their stuff. To get here, follow Te Moana Road off SH1 for just over 1km and turn right at Ngarara Road; the sanctuary is a further 3km.

Southward Car Museum

Otaihanga Rd, 3km south of Waikanae • Daily: Nov–April 9am–5pm; May–Oct 9am–4.30pm • $10 • ☎ 04 297 1221, ⓦ southward.org.nz

With over 250 vehicles in a specially built showroom, the **Southward Car Museum** contains one of the largest collections of cars, fire engines and motorbikes in Australasia. Well-kept examples of mundane models from the 1960s, 1970s and 1980s might strike older readers as barely museum-worthy, but there's no shortage of exotica, all in mint condition. Gems include Marlene Dietrich's Rolls-Royce, a 1915 Stutz Racer, and a 1955 gull-winged Mercedes Benz. Look out, too, for one of the futuristic white cars used in Woody Allen's 1973 film *Sleeper*, and half a dozen hand-built models that were the product of assorted Kiwi back sheds.

Paraparaumu

The burgeoning dormitory community of **PARAPARAUMU** (aka "Paraparam"), 7km south of Waikanae and 45km from Wellington, is the Kapiti Coast's largest settlement. It is primarily of interest as the only jumping-off point to Kapiti Island, which faces the long and sandy **Paraparaumu Beach**, 3km to the west along Kapiti Road. With safe swimming, accommodation and a few restaurants, this is the place to hang out.

Kapiti Island

Kapiti Island is one of the best and most easily accessible island **nature reserves** in New Zealand, a 15min boat ride offshore from Paraparaumu Beach. This magical spot, just 10km by 2km, was once cleared for farmland but is again cloaked in bush and home to birdlife that has become rare or extinct on the mainland. Much of New Zealand's bush is now virtually silent but here it trills to the sound of chirping birds – much as it did before the arrival of humans.

In 1824, famed Maori chief **Te Rauparaha** (original composer of the *haka*) captured the island from its first known Maori inhabitants and, with his people the Ngati Toa, used it as a base until his death in 1849. The island is considered extremely spiritual by Maori, and was designated a reserve in 1897.

Late January and February are the best months to visit, when the **birdlife** is at its most active, but at any time of the year you're likely to see kaka (bush parrots that may alight on your head or shoulder), weka, kakariki (parakeets), whiteheads (bush canaries), tui, bellbirds, fantails, wood pigeons, robins and a handful of the 300 takahe that exist in the world.

The **North End** of the island (about a tenth of its total area) is also part of the Kapiti Nature Reserve, though it's managed and accessed separately. The **Okupe Lagoon** has a colony of royal spoonbills, and there are plenty of rare forest birds and kiwi.

WALKING AROUND KAPITI

The island can be explored on two fairly steep **walking tracks**, the **Trig Track** and the **Wilkinson Track**, which effectively form a loop by meeting near the island's highest point, Tuteremoana (521m). There are spectacular views from the summit, though the widest variety of birdlife is found along the lower parts of the tracks – take your time, keep quiet and stop frequently (allow about 3hr for the round-trip).

A wedge of sea between Kapiti Island and Paraparaumu has been designated a **marine reserve**, and its exceptionally clear waters make for great **snorkelling** around the rocks (bring your own gear, or rent it from the *Kapiti Nature Lodge*). You'll need your own gear for **scuba diving**, which is particularly good to the west and north of the island.

Paekakariki and around

At the southern extent of the Kapiti Coast, the village of **Paekakariki** has a tiny but vibrant beach community. Families should make straight for the 6.5-square-kilometre **Queen Elizabeth Park** (daily 8am–8pm), which has entrances at MacKays Crossings on SH1, and off the Esplanade in Raumati. At the former entrance is the **Tramway Museum** (Sat & Sun 11am–4.30pm; daily in Jan; tram rides $8; ☎04 292 8361, ⊛wellingtontrams.org.nz), which runs restored Wellington trams along 2km of track to the beach. The adjacent **Stables on the Park** (Sat & Sun 10.30am–3.30pm; horse treks and pony rides from $20; ☎04 298 4609, ⊛stablesonthepark.co.nz) offers horse treks and pony rides for kids.

Pataka Museum of Arts and Cultures

22km south of Paekakariki, corner of Norrie and Parumoana sts • Mon–Sat 10am–4.30pm, Sun 11am–4.30pm • Free • ☎04 237 1511, ⊛pataka.org.nz

Just 20km north of Wellington, the expanding satellite city of **Porirua** is worth a brief stop for the excellent **Pataka Museum of Arts and Cultures**, which hosts local and touring exhibitions by leading contemporary New Zealand artists, plus regular Maori dance performances.

ARRIVAL AND DEPARTURE

THE KAPITI COAST

PARAPARAUMU

By train The *Overlander* and Wellington's TranzMetro commuter trains stop opposite the Coastlands shopping centre.

Destinations Paekakariki (every 30min; 8min); Plimmerton (every 30min; 25min); Porirua (every 30min; 35min); Wellington (every 30min; 1hr).

By bus InterCity and NakedBus stop at the train station.

Destinations Wellington (10 daily; 50min).

By plane Paraparaumu's airport (⊛kapiticoastairport.co.nz), midway between SH1 and the beach, is served by

Air New Zealand and Air2There (⊛air2there.com).

Destinations Auckland (2–3 daily; 1hr 10min); Blenheim (1–3 daily; 40min); Nelson (1–3 daily; 45min).

KAPITI ISLAND

By boat Kapiti Marine Charter (☎0800 433 779, ⊛kapitimarinecharter.co.nz) and Kapiti Tours (☎0800 527 484, ⊛kapititours.co.nz) both run boat trips to the island for $60. Boats generally leave from the beach beside Kapiti Boating Club around 9am and return around 3.30pm, with the option of a transfer to the North End (extra $5).

GETTING AROUND

By train The Auckland–Wellington rail line serves the coastal towns; services are much more frequent in the commuter belt from Waikanae south.

By bus The main bus companies serve the coastal towns, but off SH1 options are severely limited.

INFORMATION AND TOURS

OTAKI

i-SITE 239 SH1 (Mon–Fri 9am–5pm, Sat 10am–3pm, Sun 10am–2pm; ☎06 364 7620, ⊛naturecoast.co.nz). This twice-relocated 1891-built wooden courthouse is the place to come for hut passes for tracks in the Tararua Forest Park and the picturesque gorge of the Otaki River to the east.

PARAPARAUMU

i-SITE Coastlands shopping centre car park, Rimu Rd (Mon–Fri 9am–5pm, Sat 10am–3pm, Sun 10am–2pm;

☎04 298 8195, ⊛naturecoast.co.nz). Has local and DOC information and can help with permits for Kapiti Island.

KAPITI ISLAND

Permits DOC allows just fifty visitors a day to the main nature reserve, and a further eighteen to the North End. Obligatory landing permits ($11/person; valid for six months in case weather prevents a crossing) must be booked through DOC in Wellington (see p.434), though they can forward them to the Paraparaumu visitor centre

3

3

for pick-up. Book as far in advance as you can: a few days is generally OK, but on summer weekends the main reserve is often filled three months ahead. If you're visiting both ends of the island, get two permits.

Bio-security DOC is understandably wary about the reintroduction of pests, so your bags are checked for any stray mammals.

Facilities On the island you'll find toilets and a shelter at the landing point: take your own food and water, and bring back all rubbish.

Tours At the main reserve, an excellent half-hour introduction by one of the island rangers, along with the *Kapiti Island Nature Reserve* brochure, sets you up for a few hours' exploration, though there are optional hour-long guided tours ($20; run in conjunction with Kapiti Island Nature Tours), including tours focusing on Maori culture, and paua gathering.

ACCOMMODATION

PARAPARAUMU

There's an adequate range of accommodation, and freedom campers in self-contained vans can park up opposite 54, 62 & 69 Marine Parade beside Paraparaumu Beach.

Barnacles Seaside Inn 3 Marine Parade, Paraparaumu Beach ☎ 0800 555 856, ⓦ seasideyha.co.nz. This associate YHA in a rambling 1923 wooden hotel across the road from the beach has comfortable antique-furnished, shared-bath rooms and dorms. Dorms $29, doubles $72, sea view $82

Earthbush 197 Main North Rd, 3km north of town ☎ 04 298 7224, ⓦ earthbushbedandbreakfast.co.nz. The owners built this eco-friendly, modern rammed-earth home with very comfortable rooms, both opening out onto delightful gardens. There is a strong emphasis on organics, and free-range eggs get turned into delicious breakfasts. $150

Kapiti Court Motel 341 Kapiti Rd ☎ 0800 526 683, ⓦ kapiticourtmotel.co.nz. Beside the shops and a 2min walk from the beach, quiet with outdoor pool and pleasant rooms. $115

KAPITI ISLAND

Kapiti Nature Lodge Waiorua Bay ☎ 06 362 6606, ⓦ kapitiislandnaturetours.co.nz. At the northern reserve, private land owned by the descendants of Te Rauparaha is the setting for the island's only accommodation and the most rewarding way to experience Kapiti. There's a simple, comfortable lodge and an intimate communal feel running through to the family-style meals (which might include fresh seafood) and after-dark kiwi-spotting trips in the surrounding bush. Rates are per person and dependent on the type of accommodation, which is made up of singles, twin shares and triples/quads. All meals are provided, there are two excellent independent daytime walks (one beach, including spoonbills at certain

times of the year, and one bush) and the kiwi-spotting walks have a high success rate – there are an estimated 1200 to 1500 on the island. There are also 4hr sea-kayak trips ($40/person) and boat trips to the 120-strong seal colony at Arapawaiti Point (from $40). Alternatively, the day tour ($155) includes the ferry, DOC permit, lunch and hour-long guided walk. Transfers can be arranged from Wellington. Single $280, single en suite $320, twin share $265, twin share en suite $315, triple/quad $250, triple/quad en suite $300

PAEKAKARIKI AND AROUND

Hilltop Hideaway 11 Wellington Rd, Paekakariki ☎ 04 902 5967, ⓦ wellingtonbeachbackpackers.co.nz. Former backpackers close to the train station now offering just two budget en-suite doubles. Both have a kitchenette and a small terrace, one with great sunset views to the ocean. $80

★ **Moana Lodge** 49 Moana Rd, Plimmerton ☎ 04 233 2010, ⓦ moanalodge.co.nz. Superb bunk-free hostel that consistently ranks as one of New Zealand's best, set in a beautifully sited Edwardian villa with sea views from many rooms and dorms with three or four beds. There's free wi-fi and kayaks and a very friendly atmosphere. Dorms $33, doubles $84

Paekakariki Beachfront B&B 136 The Parade, Paekakariki ☎ 04 905 8595, ⓦ paekakaribnb.co.nz. Just one large self-contained studio (containing a queen and a single bed) with great sea views and mere steps from the beach. Free pick-up from the train station. $150

Paekakariki Holiday Park 180 Wellington Rd, Paekakariki ☎ 04 292 8292, ⓦ paekakarikiholidaypark .co.nz. Very popular and well-appointed family holiday park on the southern fringe of QE Park with good access to a safe swimming beach. Camping $15, kitchen cabins $65, units $85

EATING AND DRINKING

OTAKI

Brown Sugar SH1, 1km south ☎ 06 364 6359. Drop into this relaxed roadside stop with plenty of cottage

garden seating for coffee and cake, a pesto-filled cheese Danish or a pumpkin, spinach and olive pizza ($16). Daily 8.30am–4pm.

PARAPARAUMU

Fed Up Fast Foods 40 Marine Parade ☎04 902 6686. Simple but stylish fresh fare including the area's best fish and chips and Kapiti ice cream, to eat in or take away. Daily blackboard combos under $10. Daily 11am–8.30pm.

Kapiti Cheeses & Ice Cream Lindale Centre, SH1, 2km north of town ☎04 298 1352, ⓦ kapiticollection.co.nz. Sample ice cream (in rich flavours such as gingernut, and fig-and-honey) or some of the fine cheeses – among New Zealand's finest – at this shop in the Lindale shopping centre. Daily 9am–5pm.

Muang Thai 22 Maclean St ☎04 902 9699. Small, reliable spot serving quality Thai favourites such as pad thai and curries (all around $13). Mon–Thurs 5–10pm, Fri & Sat 5–11pm.

PAEKAKARIKI AND AROUND

The Beach Store 104 The Parade, Paekakariki ☎04 292 8330, ⓦ thebeachstore.wordpress.com. Essentially a cool design store with a kind of eclectic, *bach*-like, surf-shack feel, looking out across the water to Kapiti Island. Stop in for a coffee or a juice as you browse their goodies. Thurs–Sat 9.30am–5pm, Sun 10am–5pm.

3

Central North Island

265 Rotorua

276 Around Rotorua

282 Taupo

290 Around Taupo

292 The Napier–Taupo Road

292 Tongariro National Park and around

BLUE LAKE, TONGARIRO ALPINE CROSSING

Central North Island

The Central North Island contains some of New Zealand's star attractions, many the result of its explosive geological past. It's dominated by three heavyweight features: Lake Taupo, the country's largest; Tongariro National Park, with its trio of volcanoes; and the volcanic field that feeds colourful and fiercely active thermal areas, principally around Rotorua, where boiling mud pools plop next to spouting geysers fuelled by super-heated water, drawn off to fill hot pools around town. Accessible Maori cultural experiences abound here, with highly regarded Arawa carvings and groups who perform traditional dances and *haka* before a feast of fall-off-the-bone meat and succulent vegetables cooked in a *hangi* underground steam oven.

The dramatic volcanic scenery of Rotorua is striking for its contrast with the encroaching pines of the **Kaingaroa Forest**, one of the world's largest plantation forests, with serried ranks of fast-growing radiata (Monterey) relishing the free-draining pumice soils. In recent years, high international milk-powder prices have fuelled a large-scale conversion to dairying, but silviculture remains the area's chief earner.

The rest of the region is loosely referred to as the **Volcanic Plateau**, high country overlaid with a layer of rock and ash expelled two thousand years ago, when a huge volcano blew itself apart, the resultant crater and surrounds filled by expansive **Lake Taupo**. This serene lake, and the streams and rivers feeding it, have long lured anglers keen to snag brown and rainbow trout, while visitors flock to diverse sights and activities located near the thundering rapids on the Waikato River, which drains the lake. South of Lake Taupo rise three majestic volcanoes in **Tongariro National Park**, created in 1887 – a winter playground for North Island skiers and a summer destination for trampers drawn by spectacular walking trails.

The altitude of the Volcanic Plateau lends Taupo, the Tongariro National Park and environs a crisp **climate**, even in high summer. Spring and autumn are tolerably warm and have the added advantage of freedom from the summer hordes, though the freezing winter months from May to October are mainly the preserve of winter-sports enthusiasts. Rotorua is generally balmier but still cool in winter, making the thermal areas steamier and hot baths even more inviting.

Rotorua safety p.267
The love story of Hinemoa and Tutanekai p.268
Lake Rotorua and Mokoia Island tours and activities p.269
Rafting, kayaking and sledging around Rotorua p.272
Walks in and around Rotorua p.276
Rotorua scenic flights p.278
The Mount Tarawera eruption p.279
Lake Taupo: giant spirit p.285

Taupo tours and activities pp.288–289
The Maori mountain legends p.293
Fishing and watersports in Turangi p.295
The Tongariro power scheme p.297
Mount Ruapehu ski-fields p.298
Tramping in winter p.300
The 42 Traverse p.303
Ohakune outdoor activities p.305
Rafting the Rangitikei River p.308

HUKA FALLS, TAUPO

Highlights

❶ **Kaituna River** Raft this excellent short river and shoot its spectacular 7m Tutea's Falls. **See p.272**

❷ **Maori cultural performance** A delectable *hangi* feast wraps up an evening of chants, dance, songs, stories and insight into the Maori world-view. **See p.275**

❸ **Wai-O-Tapu** Luminous pools, bubbling mud and a spurting geyser make this the best of Rotorua's thermal areas. **See p.280**

❹ **Lake Taupo** Cruise, windsurf or kayak on New Zealand's largest lake, haul trout out of it,

or approach at dizzying speed while skydiving. **See p.282**

❺ **Huka Falls** For volume and power alone – some three hundred tonnes of water per second plunging into a maelstrom of eddies and whirlpools – this is the country's finest waterfall. **See p.290**

❻ **Tongariro Alpine Crossing** Quite simply the best and most popular one-day hike in New Zealand, climbing over lava flows, crossing a crater floor, skirting active geothermal areas, and passing emerald and blue lakes. **See p.300**

HIGHLIGHTS ARE MARKED ON THE MAP ON P.264

GETTING AROUND

By bus Public transport around the Central North Island is limited to buses, mostly run by InterCity and NakedBus who ply routes from Rotorua through Taupo and on south to Turangi, Waiouru and Taihape. A bunch of minor companies service the small towns and trailheads around the Tongariro National Park (see p.292).

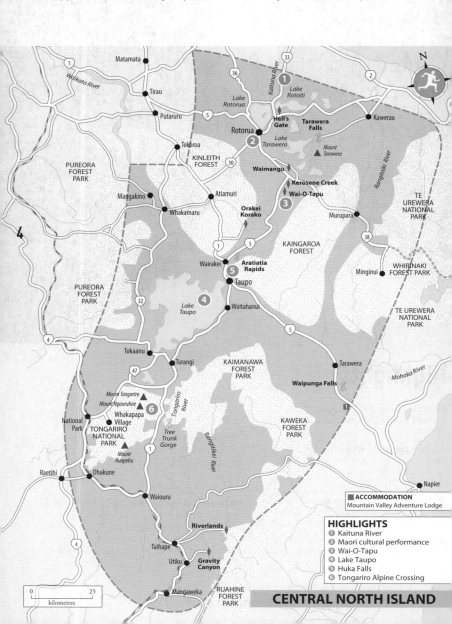

■ ACCOMMODATION
Mountain Valley Adventure Lodge

HIGHLIGHTS
❶ Kaituna River
❷ Maori cultural performance
❸ Wai-O-Tapu
❹ Lake Taupo
❺ Huka Falls
❻ Tongariro Alpine Crossing

CENTRAL NORTH ISLAND

Rotorua

You smell **Rotorua** long before you see it. Hydrogen sulphide drifting up from natural vents in the region's thin crust means that a whiff of rotten eggs lingers in the air, but after a few hours you barely notice it. The odour certainly doesn't stop any one from visiting this small city on the southern shores of **Lake Rotorua**. Indeed, this is the North Island's tourist destination *par excellence* – so much so that locals refer to the place (only half-jokingly) as Roto-Vegas.

A big part of the appeal is that Rotorua is one of the world's most concentrated and accessible geothermal areas, where 15m geysers spout among kaleidoscopic mineral pools, steam wafts over cauldrons of boiling mud and terraces of encrusted silicates drip like stalactites. Everywhere you look there's evidence of volcanism: birds on the lakeshore are relieved of the chore of nest-sitting by the warmth of the ground; in churchyards tombs are built topside as digging graves is likely to unearth a hot spring; and hotels are equipped with geothermally fed hot tubs, perfect after a hard day's sightseeing. Throughout the region, sulphur and heat combine to form barren landscapes where only hardy plants brave the trickling hot streams, sputtering vents and seething fumaroles. There's no shortage of colour, however, from iridescent mineral deposits lining the pools: bright oranges juxtaposed with emerald greens and rust reds. The underworld looms large in Rotorua's lexicon: there's no end of "The Devil's" this and "Hell's" that, prompting George Bernard Shaw to quip that the Hell's Gate thermal area "reminds me too vividly of the fate theologians have promised me".

But constant hydrothermal activity is only part of the area's appeal. The naturally hot water lured **Maori** to settle here, using the hottest pools for cooking and bathing, and building their *whare* (houses) on warm ground to drive away the winter chill. Despite the inevitably diluting effects of tourism, there's no better place to get an introduction to Maori values, traditions, dance and song than at a concert and *hangi* evening.

The lake's northern and southern boundaries are marked by two ancient villages of the Arawa sub-tribe, Ngati Whakaue: lakeshore **Ohinemutu** and inland **Whakarewarewa**. The original **Bath House** is now part of **Rotorua Museum**, set in the grounds of the oh-so-English **Government Gardens**, which successfully and entertainingly puts these early enterprises into context. Half a day is well spent on foot visiting the museum's fine collection of Maori artefacts and bathhouse relics, and strolling around the lakeshores to Ohinemutu, the city's original Maori village with its neatly carved church. Afterwards, you can ease your bones with a soak in the hot pools set in a native bird sanctuary by catching a boat out to **Mokoia Island**.

At the southern end of town, Maori residents still go about their daily lives amid the steam and boiling pools at **Whakarewarewa Thermal Village**, while the adjacent **Te Puia** offers the region's only natural geysers, plopping mud and a nationally renowned Maori carving school.

Where Rotorua's northwestern suburbs peter out, Mount Ngongotaha rises up, providing the necessary slope for a number of gravity-driven activities at the **Skyline Skyrides**. In its shadow, **Rainbow Springs Kiwi Wildlife Park**, provides a window into the life cycle of trout, and an excellent **Kiwi Encounter**, while the nearby **Agrodome** fills the prescription for adrenaline junkies.

Some of the region's finest geothermal areas lie outside the city – see p.276.

Brief history

The Rotorua region is the traditional home of the **Arawa** people. According to Maori history, one of the first parties to explore the interior was led by the *tohunga* (priest), **Ngatoroirangi**, who made it as far as the freezing summit of Mount Tongariro, where he feared he might die from cold. His prayers to the gods of Hawaiki were answered with fire that journeyed underground, surfacing at White Island in the Bay of Plenty, then at several more points in a line between there and the three central North Island volcanoes. Ngatoroirangi was saved, and he and his followers established themselves around Lake Rotoiti ("small lake") and Lake Rotorua ("second lake").

Battles and bloodshed

In revenge for an earlier raid, the Northland Ngapuhi chief, **Hongi Hika**, led a war party here in 1823, complete with muskets traded with Europeans in the Bay of Islands. The Arawa retreated to Mokoia Island, in the middle of Lake Rotorua; undaunted, Hongi Hika and his warriors carried their canoes overland between lakes (the track between

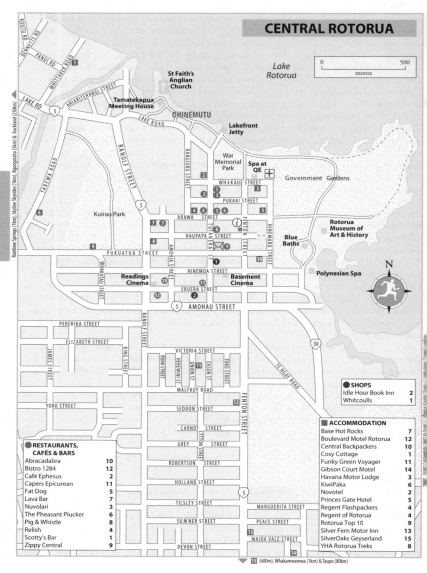

CENTRAL ROTORUA

Lake Rotorua

0 — 500 metres

SHOPS

Idle Hour Book Inn	2
Whitcoulls	1

ACCOMMODATION

Base Hot Rocks	7
Boulevard Motel Rotorua	12
Central Backpackers	10
Cosy Cottage	1
Funky Green Voyager	11
Gibson Court Motel	14
Havana Motor Lodge	6
KiwiPaka	6
Novotel	2
Princes Gate Hotel	5
Regent Flashpackers	4
Regent of Rotorua	4
Rotorua Top 10	9
Silver Fern Motor Inn	13
SilverOaks Geyserland	15
YHA Rotorua Treks	8

RESTAURANTS, CAFÉS & BARS

Abracadabra	10
Bistro 1284	12
Café Ephesus	2
Capers Epicurean	11
Fat Dog	5
Lava Bar	7
Nuvolari	3
The Pheasant Plucker	6
Pig & Whistle	8
Relish	4
Scotty's Bar	1
Zippy Central	9

ROTORUA SAFETY

A continuing problem in and around Rotorua is **theft from cars**, with thieves targeting those parked near hostels, as well as cars left at trailheads, tourist attractions and other unguarded areas (Kerosene Creek is a particular hotspot for break-ins). Take any valuables into your room or ask to use a safe. The general rate of crime in Rotorua is also higher than the national average; keep your wits about you. On the upside, the local police (p.275) are friendly and efficient at assisting visitors.

Lake Rotoiti and Lake Rotoehu still bears the name Hongi's Track) and defeated the traditionally armed Arawa. In the New Zealand Wars of the 1860s the Arawa supported the government. In return, colonial troops helped repulse **Te Kooti** (see box, p.383) and his people a decade later.

The birth of tourism

A few **Europeans** had already lived for some years in the Maori villages of Ohinemutu and Whakarewarewa, but it wasn't until Te Kooti had been driven off that Rotorua came into existence. **Tourists** began to arrive in the district to view the Pink and White Terraces, and the Arawa, who up to this point had been relatively isolated from European influence, quickly grasped the possibilities of tourism, helping make Rotorua what it is today. Set up as a **spa town** on land leased from the Ngati Whakaue, by 1885 the fledgling city boasted the Government Sanatorium Complex, a spa designed to administer the rigorous treatments deemed beneficial to the "invalids" who came to take the waters.

4

Government Gardens

With their juxtaposition of the staid and the exotic, **Government Gardens**, east of the town centre, are a bizarre vision of an antipodean little England. White-clad croquet players totter round sulphurous steam vents and palm trees loom over rose gardens centred on the Elizabethan-style **Bath House**, built in 1908. Heralded as the greatest spa in the South Seas, it was designed to treat patients suffering from just about any disorder – arthritis, alcoholism, nervousness – and offered ghoulish treatments involving electrical currents and colonic irrigation as well as the geothermal baths. The bathhouse limped along until 1963, although the era of the grand spas had come to a close long before. For a contemporary, altogether more luxurious version of the experience head to the nearby **Polynesian Spa** or the **Spa at QE**.

The Rotorua Museum

Queens Drive, Government Gardens • Daily: Oct to mid-March 9am–8pm; mid-March to Sept 9am–5pm; free guided tours on the hour • $12.50 • ⓦrotoruamuseum.co.nz

The old bathhouse is now home to the wonderful **Rotorua Museum of Art and History**, which was reopened after extensions, in part to the original plans of 1908. The spa's history is told through the "Taking the Cure" exhibit, set around the old baths themselves, complete with gloomy green and white tiling and exposed pipes. Several rooms have been preserved in a state of arrested decay while an entertaining film re-creates some of the history of both the area and baths. To see more of the inner workings of the building, head for the basement – all old pipes, foundations and mud baths – which gets hotter as you walk further south, closer to the geothermal source. The remains of the original ventilation system (which quickly proved inadequate for dealing with the high humidity and hydrogen sulphide gas in the bathhouse) are on show in the roofspace, on the way up to a great rooftop viewing platform. Apart from the displays listed below, make sure to catch the small but moving section on the **Maori battalion**, an infantry battalion of the New Zealand Army that served during World War II, with an evocative half-hour video.

THE LOVE STORY OF HINEMOA AND TUTANEKAI

The Maori love story of **Hinemoa and Tutanekai** has been told around the shores of Lake Rotorua for centuries. It tells of the illegitimate young chief Tutanekai of Mokoia Island and his high-born paramour, Hinemoa, whose family forbade her from marrying him. To prevent her from meeting him they beached their *waka* (canoe), but the strains of his lamenting flute wafted across the lake nightly and the smitten Hinemoa resolved to swim to him. One night, buoyed by gourds, she set off towards Mokoia, but by the time she got there Tutanekai had retired to his *whare* (house) to sleep. Hinemoa arrived at the island but without clothes was unable to enter the village, so she immersed herself in a hot pool. Presently Tutanekai's slave came to collect water and Hinemoa lured him over, smashed his gourd and sent him back to his master. An enraged Tutanekai came to investigate, only to fall into Hinemoa's embrace.

The Te Arawa display

Don't miss the small but internationally significant **Te Arawa** display showcasing the long-respected talents of Arawa carvers who made this area a bastion of pre-European carving tradition. Many pieces have been returned from European collections, and the magnificent carved figures, dog-skin cloaks, *pounamu* (greenstone) weapons and intricate bargeboards are all powerfully presented. Prized pieces include the flute played by the legendary lover Tutanekai (see box above), an unusually fine pumice goddess, and rare eighteenth-century carvings executed with stone tools.

The Tarawera eruption display

Extensive displays covering the dramatic events surrounding the **Tarawera eruption** include an informative relief map of the region, eyewitness accounts and reminiscences, an audiovisual presentation and photos of the ash-covered hotels at Te Wairoa and Rotomahana, both now demolished.

The Polynesian Spa

Hinemoa St, lake end • Daily 8am–11pm; spa therapies daily 9am–8pm • Adult pools $21.50; private pools $18.50 each/30min, lake view $26.50/30min; lake spa $43; family spa $36 for up to two adults and four kids; spa therapies from $85/30min available daily in Lake Spa and include Lake Spa entry • ☎ 07 348 1328, ⓦ polynesianspa.co.nz

A mostly open-air complex landscaped for lake views, the **Polynesian Spa** comprises four separate areas. Most people head straight for the **Adult Pools**, a collection of seven pools (36–42°C) ranged around the historic Radium and Priest pools. These are off-limits, but the Priest water (claimed to ease arthritis and rheumatism) is fed into three of the pools. If you only want half an hour in the water, you're probably better served by the **Private Pools** where two or three of you can soak in a shallow rock-lined pool. For a little exclusivity opt for the adjacent **Lake Spa**, with landscaped rock pools along with private relaxation lounge and bar; book ahead for massages, mud wraps and general pampering. Kids are catered for in the **Family Spa**, with one chlorinated 33°C pool, a couple of mineral pools and a waterslide.

The Blue Baths

Queens Drive, Government Gardens • Daily: Nov–March 10am–6pm; April–Oct noon–6pm • $11 • ⓦ historic-venues.co.nz

While the main bathhouse promoted health, the adjacent **Blue Baths** promised only pleasure when it opened in 1933. Designed in the Californian Spanish Mission style, this was one of the first public swimming pools in the world to allow mixed bathing. It closed in 1982, but has since partly reopened to allow swimming in an outdoor pool (29–33°C) and soaking in two smaller pools (38–40°C). Most of the building is given over to private functions so it's often closed at weekends.

4

The Spa at QE

1043 Whakaue St • Mon–Fri 8am–9pm, Sat 10.30am–4.30pm • Public pool $6; private pool $12; treatments from $20–150 •
☎ 07 348 0189, ⊛ qehealth.co.nz

The spirit of the original bathhouse lives on at the **Spa at QE**, where the emphasis is on cures and therapeutic treatments. It has a clinical, slightly scruffy feel but there's increasing sophistication in the areas devoted to pampering. Soak in a private pool filled with alkaline water from the Rachel Spring or book in for treatments such as a soak in a soothing mud bath or an Aix massage, like being rubbed down while under a horizontal hot shower.

Ohinemutu

On the lakeshore, 500m north of Rotorua • $2 donation • ☎ 07 348 0189 or ☎ 0800 527 8767

Before Rotorua the principal Maori settlement in the area was at **Ohinemutu**. Ohinemutu remains a Maori village centred on its hot springs and the small half-timbered neo-Tudor **St Faith's Anglican Church** built in 1914 to replace its 1885 predecessor. Within, there's barely a patch of wall that hasn't been carved or covered with *tukutuku* (ornamental latticework) panels. The main attraction is the window featuring the figure of Christ, swathed in a Maori cloak and feathers, positioned so that he appears to be walking on the lake. Outside is the grave of Gilbert Mair, a captain in the colonial army who twice saved Ohinemutu from attacks by rival Maori, becoming the only Pakeha to earn full Arawa chieftainship.

At the opposite end of the small square in front of the church stands the **Tamatekapua Meeting House**, again beautifully carved, though the best work, some dating back almost two hundred years, is inside and inaccessible. Call for details of guided tours.

4

LAKE ROTORUA AND MOKOIA ISLAND TOURS AND ACTIVITIES

Rotorua meets the water at the Lakefront Jetty, at the northern end of Tutaneka Street, where you can rent kayaks, pedalboats and the like. This is the starting point for trips to **Mokoia Island**, 7km north of the jetty, a predator-free bird sanctuary where a breeding programme supports populations of saddlebacks and North Island robins (often spotted at the feeder stations) and kokako. The island is better known, however, for the story of **Hinemoa and Tutanekai** (see box opposite); the site of Tutanekai's *whare* and Hinemoa's Pool can still be seen on guided island visits.

All sixteen lakes around Rotorua, but especially Lake Rotorua, given its proximity to the city, have a reputation for **trout fishing**. The angling is both scenic and rewarding, with waters stocked with strong-fighting rainbow trout.

CRUISES

Lakeland Queen ☎ 0800 572 784, ⊛ lakeland queen.com. For a leisurely cruise on the lake, try the *Lakeland Queen*, a replica paddle steamer that runs a series of trips including meals (breakfast $42; lunch 1–2hr $50/60; coffee $22; dinner $65).

FISHING

O'Keefe's 1113 Eruera St ☎ 07 346 0178, ⊛ okeefes fishing.co.nz. Has up-to-date information on lake and river conditions, and stocks the free *Lake Rotorua & Tributaries* leaflet published by Fish & Game New Zealand, explaining the rules of the fishery, and will provide contacts for fly-fishing guides, generally around

$500 for a day. For information on fishing licences, see p.54.

JETBOATING

Kawarau Jet ☎ 07 343 7600, ⊛ nzjetboat.co.nz. Runs high-octane spins around the lake ($69/30min) and trips across the lake to the Ohau Channel and Lake Rotoiti ($120/2hr 30min), giving an hour at Manupirua Hot Springs, which can only be accessed by boat.

TOURS

Mokoia Island WaiOra ☎ 07 345 7456, ⊛ mokoia island.co.nz. Offers guided visits ($69/2hr 30min) of Mokoia Island, with the emphasis on Maori cultural interpretation and conservation.

Whakarewarewa Thermal Reserve

17 Tryon St, 3km south of the centre • Daily: Nov–March 9am–5pm; April–Oct 9am–4pm; free hour-long guided tours on the hour • $43; daytime cultural show with hangi $54; evening show with hangi $138 • ☎ 07 348 9047, ⓦ tepuia.com

Rotorua's closest geothermal attractions, Te Puia and the Whakarewarewa Thermal Village, share the **Whakarewarewa Thermal Reserve**. Around two-thirds of the active thermal zone is occupied by **Te Puia**, a series of walkways past glooping pools of boiling mud, sulphurous springs and New Zealand's most spectacular geysers, the 7m **Prince of Wales' Feathers** and the granddaddy of them all, the 15m **Pohutu** ("big splash"). The latter performed several times a day until 2000, when it surprised everyone by spouting continuously for an unprecedented 329 days. It has since settled back to jetting water into the air two to three times an hour, immediately preceded by the Prince of Wales' Feathers.

The geothermal wonders are certainly impressive, but Te Puia is also home to a **nocturnal kiwi house**, a replica of a traditional **Maori village** that's used on ceremonial occasions, and an **Arts and Crafts Institute** where skilled artisans produce flax skirts and some enormous carvings. More portable (though expensive) examples can be bought in the gift shop.

Whakarewarewa Thermal Village

9a Tukiterangi St • Daily 8.30am–5pm • Guided tours hourly: $29; with hangi (served noon–2pm) $59; free cultural performance at 2pm, more frequently in the summer • ☎ 07 349 3463, ⓦ whakarewarewa.com

The rest of the thermal area falls under the auspices of **Whakarewarewa: The Thermal Village**, a living village founded in pre-European times and undergoing continual, though sympathetic, modernization. The focus here is not on geysers but on how Maori interact with this unique environment. You can stroll at leisure around the village, attend the free **cultural performance**, and partake in a **hangi**. You can even buy corn cobs boiled in one of the natural cauldrons.

Northwest Rotorua

Aside from visits to the thermal areas, much of Rotorua's daytime activity takes place around the flanks of **Mount Ngongotaha**, 5–10km northwest of the centre, which is increasingly being overtaken by the city's suburbs.

Skyline Skyrides

185 Fairy Springs Rd, 4km northwest of the centre • Daily 9am–late • Gondola $25; gondola and luge packages $35–46; gondola, luge and Sky Swing packages $52–62 • ☎ 07 347 0027, ⓦ skylineskyrides.co.nz/rotorua

At **Skyline Skyrides**, gondolas whisk you 200m up to the station on the mountain for views across the lake and town. It's only really worth the journey if you tie it in with adventure activities such as the **luge** and the adjacent **Sky Swing** ride, which drops semi-brave daredevils from 50m. The best of the various combo deals is the gondola, Sky Swing and two luge rides for $52.

Rainbow Springs Kiwi Wildlife Park

Fairy Springs Rd, 4km from the centre • **Wildlife Park** Daily 8am–9.30pm; to 10.30pm in summer • $30 • **Kiwi Encounter** Daily 10am–4pm; guided tour on the hour from 10am • Combo ticket with Rainbow Springs $35 • ☎ 07 350 0440, ⓦ rainbowsprings.co.nz

At the foot of Mount Ngongotaha lies **Rainbow Springs Kiwi Wildlife Park**, a series of pools where you can view massive rainbow, brown and North American brook trout. These are linked by nature trails which visit several free-flight bird enclosures, a tuatara, a talkative kea and a nocturnal kiwi house. Your ticket gives you access for 24 hours, so come back after dark when the trees and pools are colourfully lit and kiwi are out and about in a naturalistic enclosure with little separating you from the birds.

Also here is the excellent **Kiwi Encounter**, giving visitors an insight into the conservation work supporting the country's icon in the battle against extinction.

A heart-warming 30-minute guided tour demonstrates egg incubation and ends with a kiwi viewing.

Paradise Valley Springs

467 Paradise Valley Rd, 11km west of the centre • Daily 8am–5pm • $29 • ☎ 07 348 9667, ⓦ paradisev.co.nz

Trout share billing with lions at **Paradise Valley Springs**, a patch of mature bush where manicured pathways weave between pools of trout, an attractive wetland area, a walk-in aviary with kea, and paddocks containing tahr, wallabies and wild pigs. An elevated boardwalk nature trail gives a great introduction to New Zealand's trees, but the big draw is the breeding pride of lions which are fed daily at 2.30pm. At times they have lion cubs which, between the ages of four weeks and one year, can be petted.

The Agrodome

Western Rd, Ngongotaha, 10km north of the centre • Shows at 9.30am, 11am & 2.30pm • Show $27; organic farm tour and show $52 • ☎ 07 357 1050, ⓦ agrodome.co.nz

Just about every bus touring the North Island stops at the **Agrodome**, where the star attraction is an hour-long **sheep show**. Though undoubtedly corny, this popular spectacle is always entertaining: rams representing the nineteen major breeds farmed in New Zealand are enticed onto the podium, a sheep is shorn, lambs are bottle-fed and there's a sheepdog display. Afterwards, the dogs are put through their paces outside and you can watch a 1906 industrial carding machine turn fleece into usable wool. There's also a one-hour farm tour complete with honey tasting, a visit to an organic orchard, deer viewing and, between April and June, kiwifruit picking.

Agroventures

1335 Paradise Valley Rd, 10km from the centre • Daily 9am–5pm • Bungy jump $95; Swoop swing $49; Agrojet $49; Freefall Extreme $49/90sec, $85/3min; Shweeb $39 • ☎ 0800 949 888, ⓦ agroventures.co.nz

Adrenaline junkies can get a hit at **Agroventures**, where attractions include a 43m **bungy jump**, the **Swoop** swing ride, and the **Agrojet** where you're piloted around a short course at breakneck speed in a three-seater jetboat (purportedly New Zealand's fastest). The **Freefall Extreme** simulates a freefall skydive using a powerful vertical fan above which you hover (or at least try to). The **Shweeb** offers a chance to race recumbent bicycles encased in clear plastic fairings and slung from an overhead monorail. Either race the clock or your mates around the undulating track. It's nowhere near as geeky as it sounds, particularly if you can get two teams together. Assorted Agroventures combo deals get you more bang for your buck.

Zorb

SH5, at Western Rd, 10km from the centre • Daily 9am–5pm • $45/ride • ☎ 0800 227 474, ⓦ zorb.com

Another Kiwi-pioneered nutter ride is the **Zorb**. You dive into the centre of a huge clear plastic ball and roll down a 200m hill or the slower but wilder zigzag course; you can choose from wet and dry rides, the former being the more fun.

ARRIVAL AND DEPARTURE   **ROTORUA**

By plane Rotorua's lakeside airport is 8km northeast of town on SH30 (ⓦ rotorua-airport.co.nz). In addition to domestic flights, there are also direct services to/from Sydney, Australia.

Destinations Auckland (2–3 daily; 40min); Christchurch (4 daily; 1hr 40min); Queenstown (1 daily; 3hr 15min); Wellington (3–4 daily; 1hr 10min).

Getting to/from town Rotorua Taxi (☎ 07 348 1111) charges around $35 to the city centre. The #3 Cityride bus (Mon–Sat every 30min; Sun hourly; none on public

holidays) costs $2.30. Grumpy's Tours & Transfers (see p.272) is $10 for one adult.

By bus InterCity and NakedBus long-distance buses stop outside the i-SITE on Fenton St.

Destinations Auckland (8–9 daily; 4hr); Gisborne (2 daily; 4hr 30min); Hamilton (8–9 daily; 1hr 30min); Opotiki (2 daily; 2hr 10min); Palmerston North (3–4 daily; 5hr 15min); Taupo (7–8 daily; 1hr); Tauranga (6 daily; 1hr 30min); Waitomo (1–2 daily; 2hr 30min–3hr); Whakatane (2 daily; 1hr 30min).

4

RAFTING, KAYAKING AND SLEDGING AROUND ROTORUA

Rotorua has a considerable reputation for its nearby **whitewater rivers**, which you can tackle aboard rafts, kayaks (usually tandems) or, more in-your-face, by "sledging" – floating down rapids clinging to a buoyant plastic sledge (really only for good swimmers). There's no shortage of operators willing to take you out (usually from September to May); the most popular rivers are listed below, along with recommended outfitters.

Other options include renting kayaks or undertaking kayaking courses and guided trips on several of the larger lakes in the region, with the emphasis on scenic appreciation, soaking in hot pools and a little fishing. With more time and money, it's worth considering a multi-day wilderness rafting trip on the East Cape's Motu River (see box, p.359).

RIVERS

Kaituna River Much of the hype is reserved for this Grade IV river, or at least the 2km section after it leaves Lake Rotoiti 20km north of Rotorua, which includes the spectacular 7m Tutea's Falls (sledgers walk around the falls).

Wairoa River If you can get the timing right, this Grade IV+ river, 80km by road from Rotorua, on the outskirts of Tauranga, is the one to go for. It relies on dam-releases for raftable quantities of white water

(Dec–March every Sun; Sept–Nov & April–May every second Sun). This is one of the finest short trips available in New Zealand, negotiating a hazardous but immensely satisfying stretch of water.

Rangitaiki River If your tastes lean more towards appreciation of the natural surroundings with a bit of a bumpy ride thrown in, opt for this Grade III river, which also shoots Jeff's Joy, a Grade IV drop that's the highlight of the trip.

OUTFITTERS

Kaitiaki Adventures ☎ 0800 338 736, ⊛ kaitiaki .co.nz. Rafting and sledging trips with a cultural dimension – explaining the significance of the river to Maori. Along with trips down the Kaituna (rafting $89; sledging $109) they do summer Sunday trips down the Wairoa (rafting $99; sledging $299) with sledgers getting one-on-one guiding down this tricky river. They also do trips on the gentler Rangitaiki River ($125 including hot pools).

Kaituna Kayaks ☎ 07 362 4486, ⊛ kaitunakayaks .com. Tandem kayaking on the Kaituna River, including Tutea's Falls ($149) plus whitewater kayak courses.

Raftabout/Sledgeabout ☎ 0800 723 822, ⊛ raftabout.co.nz. Mostly trips down the Kaituna either on rafts ($99) or sledges ($115), plus summer Sunday rafting trips down the Wairoa ($115 including lunch), some trips down the Rangitaiki ($125) and a variety of combo deals with other adventure activities.

GETTING AROUND

By bike Lady Jane's Ice Cream Parlour (☎ 07 347 9340), centrally located at 1092 Tutanekai St, rents bikes for $30/day.

By bus Cityride (☎ 0800 442 928, ⊛ baybus.co.nz) is an urban bus system centred on Pukuatua St between Tutanekai and Amohia streets; its most useful services are #1 (to Skyline Skyrides, Rainbow Springs and the Agrodome) and #2 (to Te Puia); both run daily every 30min (hourly on Sun, none on public holidays). Timetables are available at the i-SITE. Tickets are $2.30 each way, or $7.20 for a day pass.

By car Most of the majors are represented but the best deals and service are with Pegasus (☎ 07 345 8455, ⊛ rentalcars.co.nz), 247 Te Ngae Rd, which delivers and

charges from $35/day. Shorter and one-way rentals can cost significantly more.

By shuttle Geyser Link (☎ 0800 004 321, ⊛ geyserlink .co.nz) provides transport to Waimangu and Wai-O-Tapu (each $25 one-way) as well as Paradise Valley (return $26). Grumpy's Tours & Transfers (☎ 07 348 2229, ⊛ grumpys limo.co.nz; cash only) has services to numerous attractions (central city one-way/all-day pass $5/25, outer city return $15–25) and the airport (see p.271), plus various entertaining tours. Tim's Thermal Shuttle (☎ 0274 945 508) runs to Waimangu, Wai-O-Tapu and the Buried Village (each $60 including entry).

INFORMATION AND TOURS

i-SITE 1167 Fenton St (daily: Nov to Easter 8am–6pm; Easter to Oct 8am–5.30pm; ☎ 07 348 5179, ⊛ rotoruanz.com). Handles local, DOC and New Zealand-wide travel enquiries, and offers copies of the free weekly visitor's guide.

Hot Deal Tickets These get you regular discounts on many attractions in the area or throws in useful extras. Deals vary seasonally. Available at the i-SITE.

ACCOMMODATION

There's a wide range of accommodation in Rotorua, and almost everywhere, no matter how low-budget, has a **hot pool**, though genuine mineral-water pools are less common. **Hostels** are all within walking distance of the city centre, while **motels** mostly line Fenton Street, which runs south towards Whakarewarewa. Competition is fierce and off-peak prices plummet. **B&Bs** and **guesthouses** are thinner on the ground, and the **hotels**, while plentiful, generally cater to bus-tour groups and have high "walk-in" rates.

CENTRAL ROTORUA

Base Hot Rocks 1286 Arawa St ☎0800 227 396, ⓦstayatbase.com. Large, lively hostel that's a perennial favourite of the backpacker tour buses, with heated outdoor spa and swimming pool and the *Lava Bar* next door. Accommodation is mostly eight-bunk en-suite dorms; girls can check into the female-only Sanctuary dorm ($28). Dorms $\underline{23}$, en-suite twins & doubles $\underline{52}$

Boulevard Motel Rotorua 265 Fenton St ☎07 346 1763, ⓦboulevardrotorua.co.nz. Smartly appointed, well-run motel with a range of room sizes and some of the best on-site mineral pools in town, as well as a heated swimming pool, spa and free wi-fi. $\underline{128}$

Central Backpackers 1076 Pukuatua St ☎07 349 3285, ⓦbbh.co.nz. Small, homely hostel, with beds rather than bunks in the four- and six-bed dorm rooms, plus a spa pool. Dorms $\underline{25}$, twins & doubles $\underline{60}$

★ **Cosy Cottage** 67 Whittaker Rd ☎07 348 3793, ⓦcosycottage.co.nz. Friendly holiday park 2km from town with an extensive range of comfortable cabins, self-contained cottages, powered and tent sites, some geothermally heated – great in winter. There's a swimming pool, a couple of pleasant mineral pools, naturally fed steam boxes for *hangi*-style cooking, city bikes ($28/day) and direct access to a lake beach where you can dig your own hot pool. Camping $\underline{38}$, cabins $\underline{65}$, cottages $\underline{133}$

Funky Green Voyager 4 Union St ☎07 346 1754, ⓦbbh.co.nz. Relaxed, eco-conscious hostel in a pair of suburban houses a 10min walk from the centre, with an easy-going communal atmosphere. Cooking facilities in particular are excellent and there's a cosy TV-less lounge. Dorms $\underline{24}$, doubles $\underline{58}$, en-suite doubles $\underline{66}$

★ **Gibson Court Motel** 10 Gibson St ☎07 346 2822, ⓦgibsoncourtmotel.co.nz. Welcoming motel in a quiet area with ten one-bedroom units that are showing their age but are great value, particularly since they each come with a private mineral-water pool in a secluded, leafy courtyard and free wi-fi. $\underline{90}$

Havana Motor Lodge 1078 Whakaue St ☎0800 333 799, ⓦhavanarotorua.co.nz. Quiet motel, close to the lakefront with spacious grounds, a heated pool and two small mineral pools. $\underline{105}$

KiwiPaka 60 Tarewa Rd ☎07 347 0931, ⓦkiwipaka. co.nz. This well-organized complex is only a 10min walk from the town centre (on the far side of Kuirau Park), yet it's far enough away to avoid late-night party noise. There's also an excellent low-cost, licensed café/restaurant and

small hot pool. Camping $\underline{10}$, dorms $\underline{28}$, rooms $\underline{62}$, chalets $\underline{85}$

Novotel Lake end Tutanekai St ☎0800 776 677, ⓦnovotel.com. Although it's part of a world-wide chain, and lacks unique character, this top-line hotel has a great location close to the lakeshore and restaurants, as well as a pool, gym and business centre. Rates vary wildly; check the website for deals. $\underline{129}$

Princes Gate Hotel 1057 Arawa St ☎07 348 1179, ⓦprincesgate.co.nz. Historic 1897-built wooden wide-verandahed hotel that's the sole survivor from the days when all of Hinemaru St was lined with places catering to folk taking the waters at the bathhouse. Lounges and bar are delightfully creaky (serving high tea) while the rooms have been modernized. Choose from rooms in the main building or larger apartments next door. Rooms $\underline{145}$, apartments $\underline{400}$

Regent Flashpackers 1181 Pukaki St ☎07 348 3338, ⓦregentflashpackers.co.nz. New, upscale backpackers with 1960s-style decor including a snazzy lounge room with comfy leather sofas, groovy artworks, a well-equipped stainless-steel kitchen and a couple of small mineral pools, as well as an in-house bar and a garden and BBQ area. Dorms $\underline{23}$, rooms $\underline{60}$

★ **Regent of Rotorua** 1191 Pukaki St ☎0508 734 368, ⓦregentrotorua.co.nz. Accommodation at this revamped 1950s motel is in immaculate all-white studio suites that come with a pristine bathroom, stylish wallpaper and furnishings straight out of the style mags. Naturally, wi-fi and iPod docking stations are standard and you can lounge next to the heated outdoor pool. There's also a mineral pool and small gym, and a stylish restaurant and bar. $\underline{199}$

Silver Fern Motor Inn 326 Fenton St ☎0800 118 808, ⓦsilverfernmotorinn.co.nz. Knockout modern motel with spacious, refurbished studios and one-bedroom units, all with spa pools, Sky TV, sunny balconies, oodles of space and helpful staff. Free city bikes and wi-fi. Studios $\underline{140}$, one-bedroom $\underline{180}$

SilverOaks Geyserland 424 Fenton St ☎0800 881 882, ⓦsilveroaks.co.nz. Comfortable-enough business hotel where you should book early to get a third- or fourth-floor room with unsurpassed views of the Whakarewarewa thermal area. $\underline{94}$

YHA Rotorua Treks 1278 Haupapa St ☎07 349 4088, ⓦyha.co.nz. This sparkling, purpose-built, 180-bed hostel comes with spacious communal areas including a big

4

timber deck plus a well-equipped kitchen and exemplary enviro credentials. Most dorms shun bunks; a female-only dorm is available. Dorms $29, rooms $68, en suites $81

CAMPING

Rotorua Top 10 1495 Pukuatua St ☎ 07 348 1886, ⓦ rotoruatop10.co.nz. This is the closest campsite to the city, with an outdoor pool and indoor hot tub. Camping $40, basic cabins $80, motel units $125

AROUND ROTORUA

Ariki Lodge 2 Manuariki Ave, Ngongotaha, 8km northwest of central Rotorua ☎ 07 357 5532, ⓦ ariki lodge.co.nz. Lawns studded with palm trees roll down to the lake from this welcoming B&B, with New Zealand art, fresh flowers in the guest rooms and a large lounge room where you can curl up with a book from the B&B's library. Room $160, lake view $210, suite $280

Aroden 2 Hilton Rd, just off the Tarawera Rd 4km from Rotorua ☎ 07 345 6303, ⓦ babs.co.nz/aroden. Comfortable suburban homestay B&B in a rambling timber house, with two nicely appointed, flower-filled queen-size rooms, books and games in the guest lounge, lush gardens and tasty cooked-to-order breakfasts, plus complimentary New Zealand wine on arrival. $145

Blue Lake Top 10 723 Tarawera Rd, Blue Lake, 9km southeast of Rotorua ☎ 0800 808 292, ⓦ bluelaketop10.co.nz. A well-organized rural site, just across the road from Blue Lake, featuring a games room and spa pool. Camping $18, cabins $52, kitchen cabins $66, self-contained units $89, motels $106

Koura Lodge 209 Kawaha Point Rd, 5km north of central Rotorua ☎ 07 348 5868, ⓦ kouralodge.co.nz. Go for a lakeside room in the main building at this stylish lodge equipped with secluded sauna and hot tub right on the water's edge, kayaks, tennis court and even a jetty for direct access to floatplane sightseeing. Understated rooms are tastefully furnished and well equipped, and there's a comfy guest lounge where a buffet breakfast is served. $345

The Lake House 6 Cooper Ave, Holdens Bay, 7km northeast of town ☎ 07 345 3313, ⓦ thelakehouse .co.nz. This luxurious but understated house filled with fresh flowers opens out on a sunny veranda with only lawns separating you from the lake. There's a big spa pool and free use of sit-on-top kayaks. Kids can be accommodated in the built-in bunks of the Ship's Cabin ($50) providing no other guests are booked in. Minimum stay is two nights. $225

EATING, DRINKING AND NIGHTLIFE

Head to the short strip at the lake end of Tutanekai Street (known as "Eat Street") for the greatest concentration of international cuisine – from Korean to Tunisian – and a few quality restaurants. Lots of great cafés enliven the town centre. There are several good bars in Rotorua, but otherwise nightlife is limited. Most visitors spend one evening of their stay at a combined *hangi* and **Maori concert** in either a tourist hotel or, preferably, one of the outlying Maori *maraes*. Rotorua's night market takes place on Thursday from 5pm on Tutanekai Street, with lots of food stalls plus arts and crafts.

RESTAURANTS AND CAFÉS

Abracadabra 1263 Amohia St ☎ 07 348 3883, ⓦ abracadabracafe.com. Maghrebi music provides a suitable accompaniment in this loosely Moroccan café and restaurant strung with filigree lamps and divided into intimate rooms. Come for coffee and almond cake, a falafel burger, tapas ($5–10) or dinner dishes such as chicken b'stilla or seafood tagine (mains $19.50–29.50). Tues–Sat 8.30am–11pm, Sun 9am–3pm.

Bistro 1284 1284 Eruera St ☎ 07 346 1284, ⓦ bistro1284.co.nz. Rotorua's best fine-dining restaurant has a relatively relaxed atmosphere despite the white-linen tablecloths. Classy mains ($34–39) include its classic crispy roast chicken with artichoke risotto and caramelised onion sausages. Tues–Sat 5pm–late.

Café Ephesus 1107 Tutanekai St ☎ 07 349 1735. Unassuming and cheap, dishing up generous portions of Turkish, Mediterranean and Middle Eastern fare. Traditional delights include pastas, *dolmades*, *guvec* and wood-fired pizza (mains $13–21.90). Tues–Sun

lunch & dinner.

Capers Epicurean 1181 Eruera St ☎ 07 348 8818, ⓦ capers.co.nz. Large, airy, licensed café/deli serving up wonderful breakfasts, healthy salads, overstuffed panini and a great range of dinner mains such as twice-cooked pork belly on Asian greens or garlic chilli-crusted salmon (mains $23.70–27.90). Daily 7.30am–9pm.

★ **Fat Dog** 1161 Arawa St ☎ 07 347 7586, ⓦ fatdogcafe.co.nz. Heaping portions of robust food are served at mismatched tables at this relaxed café/bar. The Fat Dog Works breakfast should sort out hangovers; lunches span salads and panini and huge burgers ($11.10– 22.60), while more substantial evening mains ($27.20– 31.40) include teriyaki salmon fillet and Cajun chicken. Daily 7am–9pm.

Nuvolari 1122 Tutanekai St ☎ 07 348 1122, ⓦ nuvolari .co.nz. Lunch specials ($9.20) span the globe – from Australia to the Netherlands, Malaysia and Qatar – but evening pizzas, antipasti platters and pastas and mains such as pan-seared scallops on pumpkin risotto

($15.90–29.90) are in keeping with its "Italiano Ristorante Bar" tagline, and the sleek bare-boards decor and candlelit tables could hold their own in Milan. Daily 11.30am–late.

⭐ **Okere Falls Store** 757A SH33, 15km northeast of town ☎07 348 1122, ⓦokerefallsstore.co.nz. A rambling beer garden (which hosts winter bonfire nights from 5–9pm on Friday, Saturday and Sunday) surrounds this fabulous gourmet and general store and café, while the big timber deck out front is also a choice spot for tucking into roast veggie frittata, ricotta-stuffed baked potatoes or beef lasagne (dishes $4.50–9). Daily 7am–7pm.

Relish 1149 Tutanekai St ☎07 343 9195, ⓦrelishcafe .co.nz. Excellent licensed café covering the bases from quality counter food, delicious cakes and coffee to dinners (mains $15.50–29.50) including porcini ravioli or salt and pepper squid plus a changing roster of tapas and a short menu of wood-fired pizza. Mon–Tues 7am–4pm, Wed–Fri 7am–9pm, Sat 8am–9pm, Sun 8am–4pm.

Zippy Central 1153 Pukuatua St ☎07 348 8288. Groovy licensed restaurant with haphazard retro 1950s and 1960s pop decor. Serves great coffee and imaginative and well-prepared food, from salads and bagels to smoothies (mains $14.40–22.50). Daily 7am–6pm.

BARS AND CLUBS

Lava Bar Base Hot Rocks hostel (see p.273). A pool table, discount drinks, budget meal deals and theme nights (Sunday pyjama party, Thursday ladies' night etc), are sure-fire winners with assorted backpackers, rafting guides and locals. Daily 5.30pm–3am.

The Pheasant Plucker 1153 Arawa St ☎07 343 7071. Convivial bar chiefly notable for its nightly live music – open mic on Tues, covers bands Fri & Sat. Tues–Sat 5pm–3am.

Pig & Whistle Corner of Haupapa and Tutanekai sts ☎07 347 3025, ⓦpigandwhistle.co.nz. Lively pub in a red-brick former police station with a garden bar, and live bands Thurs–Sat. There's also a wide range of large bar meals (mains $14.70–28.70). Daily 11.30am–late.

Scotty's Bar 1104 Tutanekai St ☎07 348 1810. There are just a few leaners and the bar itself in this intimate cocktail and wine bar among the restaurants. Daily noon–3am.

HANGI AND MAORI CONCERTS

Rotorua provides more opportunities than anywhere else to sample food steamed to perfection in the Maori earth oven or *hangi* and watch a Maori concert, typically an hour-long performance of traditional dance, song and chants. The bigger hotels all put on somewhat forced extravaganzas, so go for the "Maori experiences" below (daily, by reservation). All have buses picking up at hotels and hostels ready for a start around 6pm, then run for three to four hours. They follow largely the same format, giving instruction on *marae* customs and protocol (see the "Experiencing Maori Culture" box in Contexts, p.804) followed by a formal welcome, concert and *hangi*.

Mitai ☎07 343 9132, ⓦmitai.co.nz. All the standard elements are very well done, the excellent *hangi* is cooked in the ground, plus the events are conveniently sited beside Rainbow Springs, giving a chance of a night-time walk through the bush past a beautiful clear spring which feeds a stream where a fully manned *waka* arrives in flaming torchlight. $122.

Tamaki Maori Village ☎07 349 2999, ⓦmaoriculture .co.nz. You, and several busloads, are driven out to a specially built "Maori village" south of town for a spine-chilling welcome and tales of early Maori–European interaction. Everything is so professionally done that it is hard to quibble, but its popularity has become its biggest downfall and sightlines can be restricted. The *hangi* is good, though, and the overall experience memorable. $105.

Te Po ☎07 348 9047, ⓦtepuia.com. Wear clean socks as it is shoes off (and men to the front) for the thoroughly professional performance in a traditional meeting house at Te Puia (p.270). The *hangi* is top-class, and the night is rounded off with a night tour of the geothermal valley, and hopefully a sight of a floodlit geyser performing. $106; $138 combined with daytime entry to Te Puia.

CINEMAS

Basement Cinema 1140 Hinemoa St ☎07 350 1400, ⓦbasementcinema.co.nz. Intimate, two-screen art-house theatre with a licensed café, located under *Crank Backpackers*.

Readings Cinema 1263 Eruera St ☎07 349 0061, ⓦreadingcinemas.co.nz. The local multiplex showing the latest mainstream releases.

DIRECTORY

Internet At the i-SITE ($3/30min) and several places including Cybershed, 1176 Pukuatua St. Coin-op internet access available at the library (see below).

Left luggage i-SITE has storage lockers ($2/24hr).

Library 1127 Haupapa St (Mon–Fri 9.30am–8pm, Sat 9.30am–4pm; ☎07 348 4177).

Medical treatment For emergencies and urgent health care go to Lakes Care, at Arawa and Tutanekai sts (daily 8am–10pm; ☎07 348 1000).

Pharmacy Lakes Care Pharmacy is at 1155 Tutanekai St (daily 8.30am–9.30pm; ☎07 48 4385).

Police 64 Fenton St ☎07 348 0099.

Post office The main post office, with poste restante facilities, is at Pukuatua and Tutanekai sts.

Around Rotorua

Many of the best attractions in the area lie outside the city itself but shuttles and tours (see p.272) mean that just about every combination of sights can be packed into a day, as well as all manner of **adventure activities** – from rafting to skydiving.

Travellers can quickly dispatch minor sights along the eastern shore of Lake Rotorua, leaving time for the seldom-crowded **Hell's Gate** thermal area and the opportunity to watch terrified rafters plunging over **Tutea's Falls**. Rewards are more plentiful to the east and south especially around the shattered 5km-long massif of **Mount Tarawera**. During one cataclysmic night of eruptions in 1886 this chain split in two, destroying the region's first tourist attraction (the beautiful Pink and White Terraces), entombing the nearest settlement, Te Wairoa, now known as the **Buried Village**, and creating the **Waimangu Volcanic Valley**. It now ranks as one of the finest collections of geothermal features in the region alongside kaleidoscopic **Wai-O-Tapu**, with its daily triggered **Lady Knox Geyser**, boiling mud, and brilliantly coloured pools. Other magnificent geothermal areas around Rotorua include **Kerosene Creek**, which has the best free hot pools hereabouts, and **Orakei Korako**, which offers a peaceful geothermal experience. Meanwhile, the **Whirinaki Forest Park** presents great hiking and biking opportunities on the road to Lake Waikaremoana (p.381).

Te Ngae 3D Maze

On SH30, 10km northeast of the centre • Daily 9am–5pm • $9 • ☎ 07 345 5275, ⊛ 3dmaze.co.nz

Scenery aside, there isn't a great deal to stop for along the shoreline, apart from this huge wooden maze, in a cleared section of beautiful bushland (bring a picnic; snacks and drinks are also available on site). Bridges link separate sections that complicate things immeasurably: set an hour aside to navigate the maze's 1.7km of pathways.

WALKS IN AND AROUND ROTORUA

Rotorua isn't especially well endowed with serious tramps, though there are several good day-walks and Rotorua works well as a staging post for forays into the Whirinaki Forest and further afield to Waikaremoana. Rotorua's i-SITE and DOC visitor centres have details of the following:

Blue Lake (5.5km loop; 2hr; 500m ascent) This moderate loop around the Blue Lake starts by the Blue Lake Holiday Park, 9km southeast of Rotorua, and heads through regenerating bush, Douglas firs and past some sandy beaches perfect for a dip. The single major climb takes you away from the lake to a viewpoint.

Hamurana Springs Recreation Reserve (1.5km loop; 45min; mostly flat) On the shores of Lake Rotorua, 24km north of town, an easy trail meanders through a redwood grove to the North Island's largest spring. Almost 5 million litres an hour flow out, creating a crystal-clear stream with a faint tinge that's like looking through a bottle of Sapphire gin.

Lake Okareka Walkway (5km return; 1hr plus; mostly level) Located 12km southeast of Rotorua, this lakeside interpretive trail mostly borders farmland, leavened with patches of regenerating bush and a nice boardwalk through wetlands to a bird hide.

Okere Falls Scenic Reserve (2.5km return; 40min–1hr) An easy stroll starting 18km north of Rotorua, with river views and spectacular angles on rafters shooting Tutea's Falls.

Whakarewarewa State Forest Park Several easy trails meander through an experimental forest on the edge of Rotorua. The impressive Redwood Grove contains trees that grow three times as fast as in their native California. The i-SITE (see p.272) has maps. The park is also renowned for its mountain-biking trails (see p.278).

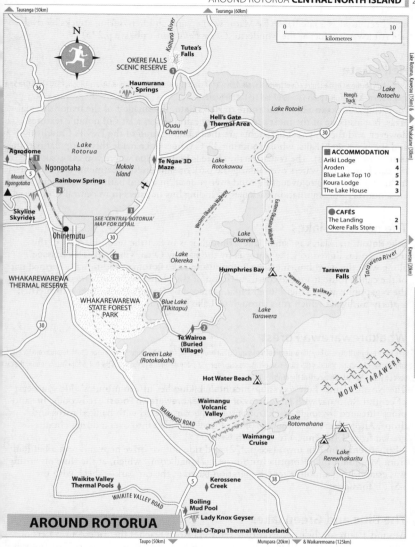

▲ Tauranga (50km)　　　　　　　▲ Tauranga (60km)

N

0　　　　　　　　　10
kilometres

Kaituna River

Tutea's Falls

OKERE FALLS SCENIC RESERVE

Haumurana Springs

Lake Rotoiti

Hongi's Track

Lake Rotoehu

Lake Rotorua, Kawerau (15km) &

Whakatane (36km)

Ouau Channel

Hell's Gate Thermal Area

Agrodome

Lake Rotorua

Ngongotaha

Mount Ngongotaha

Rainbow Springs

Skyline Skyrides

Ohinemutu

Mokoia Island

Te Ngae 3D Maze

Lake Rotokawau

SEE 'CENTRAL ROTORUA' MAP FOR DETAIL

Western Okataina Walkway

Eastern Okataina Walkway

Lake Okareka

ACCOMMODATION

Ariki Lodge	1
Aroden	4
Blue Lake Top 10	5
Koura Lodge	2
The Lake House	3

CAFÉS

| The Landing | 2 |
| Okere Falls Store | 1 |

WHAKAREWAREWA THERMAL RESERVE

WHAKAREWAREWA STATE FOREST PARK

Lake Okereka

Blue Lake (Tikitapu)

Humphries Bay

Tarawera Falls Walkway

Tarawera Falls

Tarawera River

Kawerau (20km)

Lake Tarawera

Te Wairoa (Buried Village)

Green Lake (Rotokakahi)

Hot Water Beach

MOUNT TARAWERA

Waimangu Volcanic Valley

WAIMANGU ROAD

Lake Rotomahana

Waimangu Cruise

Lake Rerewhakaritu

Waikite Valley Thermal Pools

WAIKITE VALLEY ROAD

Kerossene Creek

Boiling Mud Pool

Lady Knox Geyser

Wai-O-Tapu Thermal Wonderland

38

AROUND ROTORUA

▼ Taupo (50km)　　　　　　▼ Murupara (20km)　　▼ & Waikaremoana (125km)

4

Okere Falls Scenic Reserve

Trout Pool Rd, off SH33, 21km from central Rotorua

SH33 continues north towards Tauranga. Signs 6km north point down Trout Pool Road to **Okere Falls Scenic Reserve**, which surrounds the popular rafting destination of the Kaituna River. From the first car park, 400m along Trout Pool Road, a broad, well-maintained track follows the river to a second car park (2.5km return; 40min–1hr) passing glimpses of the churning river below, and a viewing platform that's perfect for observing rafters plummet over the 7m **Tutea's Falls**. From here, steps descend through short tunnels in the steep rock walls beside the waterfall to **Tutea's Caves**, thought to have been used as a safe haven by Maori women and children during attacks by rival *iwi*. Afterwards refuel at the wonderful *Okere Falls Store* café (see p.275).

Hell's Gate

SH30, 14km northeast of the centre · **Geothermal walk** daily: Oct–April 8.30am–5pm; May–Sept 8.30am–4.30pm · $30 · **Wai Ora Spa** daily: 8.30am–8.30pm · Hot pools $20 · ☎ 07 345 3151, ⓦ hellsgate.co.nz

Most traffic sticks to SH30, the route to **Hell's Gate**, the smallest of the major thermal areas, but also one of the most active. Its fury camouflages a lack of notable features, however, and the only real highlights are the bubbling mud of the Devil's Cauldron and the hot **Kakahi Falls**, whose soothing 38°C waters once made this a popular bathing spot (now off-limits). The real attraction here is **Wai Ora Spa** where you can soak in the sulphurous hot waters overlooking the park or sign up for treatments ($85–135), including slathering rejuvenating mud over yourself in a mud bath, and massages. There are a number of combination packages including bus transfers from central Rotorua.

The northern lakes

Lake Rotoiti translates as "small lake", though it is in fact the second largest in the region, and is linked to Lake Rotorua by the narrow Ohau Channel. This passage, along with the neighbouring **Lake Rotoehu** and **Lake Rotoma**, traditionally formed part of the canoe route from the coast. A section of this route, apparently used on a raid by the Ngapuhi warrior chief Hongi Hika, is traced by **Hongi's Track** (3km return; 1hr), a pretty bushwalk which runs through to Lake Rotoehu.

Whakarewarewa Forest

Free entry but you'll need to buy the waterproof trail map ($5) or book ($6.50) from bike shops in town · See ⓦ riderotorua.com for more information · Southstar Shuttles (ⓦ southstaradventures.com) operate a shuttle service to the top of the hill ($10) · Access is from the car park on Waipa Mill Rd, 5km south of the centre, off SH38

The North Island's best accessible **mountain biking** lies fifteen minutes' ride southeast of central Rotorua, with large areas of the **Whakarewarewa Forest**'s redwoods, firs and pines threaded by single-track trails especially constructed with banked turns and drops. Altogether there's round 70km of track, divided into over a dozen circuits graded from 1 (beginner) to 6 (death wish).

Either rent a bike in town (see p.272) and ride out, or drive here and rent a hardtail from Mountain Bike Rotorua (mtbrotorua@gmail.com), which, at the time of writing, was establishing a mobile rental operation based at the car park – check with the i-SITE for updates.

The Blue and Green lakes

Around 10km southeast of Rotorua, Tarawera Road reaches the iridescent waters of **Blue Lake** (Tikitapu) with its campsite, easy circuit walk (see p.274 & p.276) and safe

---

ROTORUA SCENIC FLIGHTS

The scenery around Rotorua is breathtaking from the air, particularly the region's volcanic spine centred on Mount Tarawera.

Volcanic Air Safaris ☎ 0800 800 848, ⓦ volcanicair .co.nz. Offers both float plane flights over Tarawera ($195/30min) and helicopter flights with a landing at Hell's Gate ($335/hr).

HeliPro ☎ 07 357 2512, ⓦ helipro.co.nz. Offers similar deals, with a short flight over Mount Tarawera and the local lakes at $195 (minimum 2) and a volcano landing flight for $340.

swimming beach with a waterslide for kids. A little further on, a ridge-top viewpoint overlooks both Blue Lake and **Green Lake** (Rotokakahi), whose name means "freshwater mussel lake", although because it's privately owned, no fishing or boating activity is allowed here. Tarawera Road then reaches the shores of Lake Tarawera 15km southeast of Rotorua.

The Buried Village and Lake Tarawera

Buried Village 1180 Tarawera Rd • Daily: Nov–March 9am–5pm; April–Oct 9am–4.30pm • $31 • ☎ 07 362 8287, ⓦ buriedvillage.co.nz

Just before the Tarawera lakeshore, the **Buried Village** kicks off with a **museum** that captures the spirit of the village in its heyday and the aftermath of its destruction, through photos, fine aquatints of the Pink and White Terraces and ash-encrusted knick-knacks. The Maori and European settlement here was larger than contemporary Rotorua until the Tarawera eruption when numerous houses collapsed under the weight of the ash; others were saved by virtue of their inhabitants hefting ash off the roof to lighten the load. From the museum, either opt for a free **guided tour** (available throughout the day; call for seasonal hours) with period-costumed guides or make your own way through the grounds.

What you see today is the result of 1930s and 1940s excavations plus some substantial reconstructions. The village itself is less an archeological dig than a manicured orchard: half-buried *whare* and the foundations for the Rotomahana Hotel sit primly on mown lawns among European fruit trees gone to seed, marauding hawthorn and a perfect row of full-grown poplars fostered from a line of fenceposts. Many of the *whare* house collections of implements and ash-encrusted household goods, and contrast starkly with the simplicity of other dwellings such as **Tohunga's Whare**, where the ill-fated priest lay buried alive for four days (see box below). Look out too for the extremely rare,

4

THE MOUNT TARAWERA ERUPTION

Volcanic activity provides the main theme for attractions southeast of Rotorua, most having some association with **Lake Tarawera** and the jagged line of volcanic peaks and craters along the southeastern shore, collectively known as **Mount Tarawera**, which erupted in 1886.

Prior to that eruption Tarawera was New Zealand's premier tourist destination, with thousands of visitors every year crossing lakes Tarawera and Rotomahana in whaleboats and *waka*, frequently guided by the renowned Maori guide Sophia, to the **Pink and White Terraces**, two separate fans of silica that cascaded down the hillside to the edge of Lake Rotomahana. Boiling cauldrons bubbled at the top of each formation, spilling mineral-rich water down into a series of staggered cup-shaped pools, the outflow of one filling the one below. Most visitors favoured the Pink Terraces, which were prettier and better suited to sitting and soaking. All this came to an abrupt end on the night of June 10, 1886, when the long-dormant Mount Tarawera erupted, creating 22 craters along a 17km rift, and covering over 15,000 square kilometres in mud and scoria. The Pink and White Terraces were shattered by the buckling earth, covered by ash and lava, then submerged deep under the waters of Lake Rotomahana.

The cataclysm had been foreshadowed eleven days earlier, when two separate canoe-loads of Pakeha tourists and their Maori guides saw an ancient *waka* glide out of the mist, with a dozen warriors paddling furiously, then vanish just as suddenly; the ancient *tohunga* (priest) Tuhoto Ariki interpreted this as a sign of imminent disaster. The fallout from the eruption buried five villages, including the staging post for the Pink and White Terrace trips, **Te Wairoa**, where the *tohunga*, lived. In a classic case of blaming the messenger, the inhabitants refused to rescue the *tohunga* and it wasn't until four days later that they allowed a group of Pakeha to dig him out. Miraculously he lived, for a week.

In 2011, scientists discovered that rather than being completely destroyed, parts of the Pink Terraces appear to have survived the 1886 eruption (the White Terraces are thought to have been more likely to have been affected). The gas and hot water vents discovered on the lake floor indicate rare active underwater geothermal systems, which scientists are continuing to research.

carved-stone *pataka* (storehouse) and the bow section of a *waka* once used to ferry tourists on the lake and allegedly brought to the district by Hongi Hika, when he invaded in 1823. Beyond the formal grounds a steep staircase and slippery boardwalk dive into the hill alongside **Te Wairoa Falls**, then climb up through dripping, fern-draped bush on the far side. If that's worked up an appetite, stop by the on-site café.

Tarawera Road ends 2km further on at the shore of **Lake Tarawera** with the mountain rising beyond. Contact staff at *The Landing* café if you fancy getting out on the water; in the warmer months you can paddle sit-on-top kayaks ($25/hr).

EATING AND DRINKING   **LAKE TARAWERA**

The Landing Lakeshore end of Tarawera Rd ☎ 07 362 8590, ⊛ thelandinglaketarawera.co.nz. There's no sense of culinary adventure at this café, but it's superbly situated right by the lakeshore and offers standards such as steak sandwiches, Caesar salad and a fish of the day (mains $14.50–25). Wed–Sun lunch & dinner.

Waimangu Volcanic Valley

587 Waimangu Rd, 5km east off SH5 • Daily: Jan 8.30am–6pm; Feb–Dec 8.30am–5pm • Walking and hiking $34.50; 45min lake cruises $42.50; combo package $77 • ☎ 07 366 6137, ⊛ waimangu.co.nz

Head 19km south of Rotorua on SH5 towards Taupo and you'll soon reach the southern limit of the volcanic rift blown out by Mount Tarawera, the **Waimangu Volcanic Valley**. This is one of the world's youngest geothermal areas, created in 1886 when a chain of eruptions racked the Mount Tarawera fault line. Pick up the comprehensive self-guided walking tour leaflet at the visitor centre then head downhill along a streamside path, which cuts through a valley choked with scrub and native bush that has regenerated since 1886. This process has been periodically interrupted by smaller eruptions, including one in 1917 that created the magnificent 100m-diameter **Frying Pan Lake**, the world's largest hot spring. Massive quantities of hot water well up from the depths of the **Inferno Crater**, an inverted cone where mesmerizing steam patterns partly obscure the powder-blue water and are stirred and swirled by breezes across the lake. The water level rises and falls according to a rigid 38-day cycle – filling to the rim for 21 days, overflowing for two then gradually falling to 8m below the rim over the next fifteen. Steaming pools and hissing vents line the path, which passes the muddy depression where, from 1900 to 1904, the **Waimangu Geyser** regularly spouted water to 250m (and occasionally to an astonishing height of 400m), carrying rocks and black mud with it.

The path through the valley ends at the wharf on the shores of Lake Rotomahana, where the rust-red sides of Mount Tarawera dominate the far horizon. From here, free buses run back up the road to the visitor centre and **cruises** chug around the lake past steaming cliffs, fumaroles and over the site of the Pink and White Terraces.

Kerosene Creek

1km south of SH38 junction turn east from SH5 along Old Waiotapu Rd and follow the gravel 2km to the parking area

If you're looking for free, hot soaking in natural surroundings, make straight for **Kerosene Creek**, 27km south of Rotorua, a stream that's usually the temperature of a warm bath and plunges over a metre-high waterfall into a nice big pool. It's always open and sometimes attracts a party crowd at weekends. Camping in the area is banned and there have been thefts from vehicles in the car park – see box, p.267.

Wai-O-Tapu

201 Waiotapu Loop Rd, just off SH5 • Daily 8.30am–5pm; last entry 3.45pm • $32.50 • ☎ 07 366 6333, ⊛ geyserland.co.nz

Wai-O-Tapu Thermal Wonderland, 10km south of Waimangu, is the area's most colourful and varied geothermal site. At 10.15am daily, the 10m **Lady Knox Geyser** is ignominiously induced to perform by a staff member who pours a soapy surfactant into the vent. If you miss the geyser your ticket allows you to come back next morning.

Everyone then drives 1km to the main site where an hour-long walking loop wends its way through a series of small lakes which have taken on the tints of the minerals dissolved in them – yellow from sulphur, purple from manganese, green from arsenic and so on. The gurgling and growling black mud of the **Devil's Ink-Pots** and a series of hissing and rumbling craters pale beside the ever-changing rainbow colours of the **Artist's Palette** pools and the gorgeous, effervescent **Champagne Pool**, a circular bottle-green cauldron wreathed in swirling steam and fringed by a burnt-orange shelf. The waters of the Champagne Pool froth over **The Terraces**, a rippled accretion of lime silicate that glistens in the sunlight.

As you drive back to the main road, follow a short detour to a huge and active **boiling mud pool** which plops away merrily, forming lovely concentric patterns.

Orakei Korako

494 Orakei Korako Rd • Daily: Oct–March 8am–5pm; April– Sept 8am–4.30pm • $36, shuttle boat journey included • ☎ 07 378 3131, ⓦ orakeikorako.co.nz

Diverting from either SH1 (14km) or SH5 (21km) and about 60km south of Rotorua is the atmospheric thermal area of **Orakei Korako**, characterized by its belching fumaroles, gin-clear boiling pools and paucity of tourists. A short shuttle-boat journey across the Waikato River (on demand throughout the day) accesses an hour-long trail which visits Ruatapu Cave, once used by Maori women to prepare themselves for ceremonies – hence Orakei Korako, "a place of adorning".

Orakei Korako can also be reached by **jetboat** along the Waikato River with NZ Riverjet (☎0800 748 375, ⓦriverjet.co.nz), based beside SH5, at Tutukau Road, 44km south of Rotorua and almost 20km south of Wai-O-Tapu. Its Riverjet Thermal Safari (3hr; $145) includes a jetboat ride and entry.

Te Urewera National Park

Midway between Waimangu and Wai-O-Tapu, 25km south of Rotorua, SH38 spurs southeast through the regimented pines of the Kaingaroa Forest towards the jagged peaks of **Te Urewera National Park** (see p.380), a vast tract of untouched wilderness separating the Rotorua lakes from Poverty Bay and the East Cape. The Kaingaroa Forest finally relents 40km on, as the road crosses the Rangitaiki River by the predominantly Maori timber town of **MURUPARA**.

INFORMATION   TE UREWERA NATIONAL PARK

Te Urewera Area DOC 1km southeast of Murupara, on SH38 (Nov–April Mon–Fri 8am–5pm, Sat & Sun 9am–3pm; May–Oct Mon–Fri 8am–5pm; ☎07 366 1080). Has stacks of information on the park and Lake Waikaremoana (see p.381).

Website ⓦ teurewera.co.nz has a wealth of information, including details of walking guides.

Whirinaki Forest Park

Adjoining Te Urewera National Park to the southeast is the wonderful but little-visited **Whirinaki Forest Park**, around 30km south of Murupara, which harbours some of the densest and most impressive stands of bush on the North Island: podocarps on the river flats, and native beech on the steep volcanic uplands between them, support a wonderfully rich birdlife with tui, bellbirds, kereru and kaka. The forest is now protected, after one of the country's most celebrated environmental battles, and is a wilderness paradise for hikers and mountain bikers.

You can sample some of the best of the forest on a stretch of the well-formed **Whirinaki Track** (4hr return) which passes magnificent podocarps, the Whaiti-nui-a-tio Canyon where the river cascades over an old lava flow, and Whirinaki Falls. Go as far as you like and turn back, but the track system continues, allowing tramps of up to five days.

INFORMATION AND TOURS

Tourist information DOC offices (the closest is at Murupara) in the region carry the *Ride Whirinaki* leaflet ($2), which details a couple of great mountain-bike rides in the area (2hr–2 days), but you'll need to have your own bike or rent one in Rotorua (see p.272).

WHIRINAKI FOREST PARK

Whirinaki Rainforest Experiences ☎ 0800 869 255, ⓦ whirinaki.com. Explore Whirinaki Forest Park on a friendly and involving day-long guided tour ($155) that offers a Maori perspective on the forest and its history.

ACCOMMODATION

Huts If you're planning a multi-day tramp through Whirinaki you can either camp or stay in the basic, standard or serviced DOC huts that pepper the park. Basic

campsites are free. Standard campsite $\overline{\$6}$, basic huts $\overline{\text{free}}$, standard huts $\overline{\$5}$, serviced huts $\overline{\$15}$

Taupo

The burgeoning resort town of **TAUPO**, 80km south of Rotorua and slap in the centre of the North Island, is strung around the northern shores of Lake Taupo, the country's largest lake, which is the size of Singapore. Views stretch 30km southwest towards the three snowcapped volcanoes of the Tongariro National Park, the reflected light from the lake's glassy surface combining with the 360m altitude to create an almost alpine radiance. Here, the impossibly deep-blue waters of the Waikato River ("flowing water" in Maori) begin their long journey to the Tasman Sea, and both lake and river frontages are lined with parks.

For decades, Kiwi families have been descending en masse for a couple of weeks' holiday, bathing in the crisp waters of the lake, and lounging around holiday homes that fringe the lakeshore. But there's no shortage of things to see and do, from the spectacular rapids and geothermal badlands north of town to **skydiving** – this is New Zealand's freefall capital – and **fishing**. The Taupo area is a most fecund trout fishery, extending south to Turangi and along the Tongariro River, with an enviable reputation for the quality of its fish. Year-round, you'll see boats drifting across the lake with lines trailing and, particularly in the evenings, rivermouths choked with fly-casters in waist-high waders.

Nowhere in **Taupo**'s compact low-rise core is more than five minutes' walk from the waters of the Waikato River or Lake Taupo, which jointly hem in three sides. The fourth side rises up through the gentle slopes of Taupo's suburbs. Most of the commercial activity happens along Tongariro Street and the aptly named Lake Terrace.

Taupo also makes a great base for exploring the surrounding area (see p.290), where highlights include Huka Falls, Aratiatia Rapids, Wairakei Terraces and the Craters of the Moon geothermal area.

Brief history

The Tuwharetoa people had lived in the area for centuries, but it wasn't until the New Zealand Wars that Europeans took an interest with the Armed Constabulary trying to track down **Te Kooti** (see p.383). They set up camp one night in June 1869 at Opepe, 17km southeast of Taupo (beside what is now SH5), and were ambushed by Te Kooti's men, who killed nine soldiers. Garrisons were subsequently established at Opepe and Taupo, but only Taupo flourished, enjoying a more strategic situation and being blessed

FROM TOP LAKE TAUPO; WAI-O-TAPU (P.280) >

with hot springs for washing and bathing. By 1877, Te Kooti had been contained, but the Armed Constabulary wasn't disbanded until 1886, after which several soldiers and their families stayed on, forming the nucleus of European settlement.

Taupo didn't really take off as a domestic resort until the prosperous 1950s, when the North Island's roads had improved to the point where Kiwi families could easily drive here from Auckland, Wellington or Hawke's Bay.

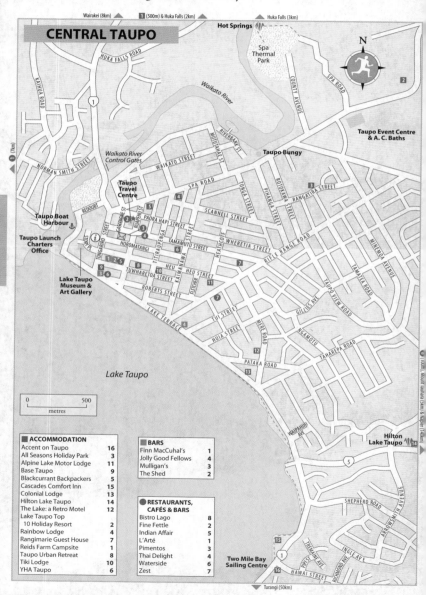

CENTRAL TAUPO

■ ACCOMMODATION	
Accent on Taupo	16
All Seasons Holiday Park	3
Alpine Lake Motor Lodge	11
Base Taupo	9
Blackcurrant Backpackers	5
Cascades Comfort Inn	15
Colonial Lodge	13
Hilton Lake Taupo	14
The Lake: a Retro Motel	12
Lake Taupo Top	
10 Holiday Resort	2
Rainbow Lodge	4
Rangimarie Guest House	7
Reids Farm Campsite	1
Taupo Urban Retreat	8
Tiki Lodge	10
YHA Taupo	6

■ BARS	
Finn MacCuhal's	1
Jolly Good Fellows	4
Mulligan's	3
The Shed	2

● RESTAURANTS, CAFÉS & BARS	
Bistro Lago	8
Fine Fettle	2
Indian Affair	5
L'Arté	1
Pimentos	3
Thai Delight	4
Waterside	6
Zest	7

LAKE TAUPO: GIANT SPIRIT

Lake Taupo (616 sq km, 185m deep) is itself a geological infant largely created in 186 AD when the Taupo Volcano spewed out 24 cubic kilometres of rock, debris and ash – at least ten times more than was produced by the eruptions of Krakatoa and Mount St Helens combined – and covered much of the North Island in a thick layer of pumice. Ash from the eruption was carried around the world – the Chinese noted a blackening of the sky and Romans recorded that the heavens turned blood-red. As the underground magma chamber emptied, the roof slumped, leaving a huge steep-sided **crater**, since filled by Lake Taupo. It's hard to reconcile this placid and beautiful lake with such colossal violence, though the evidence is all around: entire beaches are composed of feather-light pumice which, when caught by the wind, floats off across the lake. Volcanologists continue to study the Taupo Volcano (currently considered dormant) and treat the lake as a kind of giant spirit-level, in which any tilting could indicate a build-up of magma below the surface that might trigger another eruption.

The local Tuwharetoa people ascribe the lake's formation to their ancestor, Ngatoroirangi, who cast a tree from the summit of Mount Tauhara, on the edge of Taupo, and where it struck the ground water welled up and formed the lake. The lake's full name is Taupo-Nui-A-Tia, "the great shoulder mat of Tia" or "great sleep of Tia", which refers to an explorer from the Arawa canoe said to have slept by the lake.

Lake Taupo Museum and Art Gallery

Story Place, Tongariro Park, off SH1 • Daily 10am–4.30pm • $5 • ⓦ taupomuseum.co.nz

Set aside at least half an hour for the **Lake Taupo Museum and Art Gallery**, if only for the beautiful Reid Carvings, created in 1927–28 by the famous master carver Tene Waitere and exhibited in the form of a meeting house. They're as fine as you'll see anywhere and are supplemented with modern *tukutuku* panels and a lovely flax rain cape probably from the 1870s or earlier. Interesting displays on the geology of the area, fly-fishing and the logging industry line the way to the Tuwharetoa Gallery ranged around the decayed hull of a 150-year-old 14.5m *waka*, found in the bush in 1967. Paintings around the room include two of Ngati Tuwharetoa chiefs by local polymath Thomas Ryan, who was also a lake steamer captain and an All Black. The watercolours show the unmistakable influence of the artist's great friend Charles Goldie. Outside, the stunning **Ora Garden**, a 2004 Chelsea Flower Show winner, has been re-created in all its geothermal glory.

Taupo DeBrett Spa Resort

3km southeast on SH5 • Daily 7.30am–9.30pm• $20 • ⓣ 07 377 6502, ⓦ taupohotsprings.com

Geothermal bathing is best at the family-oriented **Taupo DeBrett Spa Resort**, which has a couple of large outdoor pools filled with natural mineral water plus private mineral pools in a range of temperatures; an additional $5 buys as many descents as you like on the hot-water hydroslide.

A.C. Baths and Taupo Events Centre

A.C. Baths Ave • **Baths** Daily 6am–9pm • Swimming $7; private hot pools $10/person/45min; combo $15 • **Climbing wall** Timetable varies monthly • Harness and shoes $8, plus $10 entry • A.C. Baths ⓣ 07 376 0350, Events Centre ⓣ 07 376 0350, ⓦ taupovenues.co.nz

Even without your own vehicle it's easy to reach the **A.C. Baths and Taupo Events Centre**, a sparkling new sports hall and 12m climbing wall, alongside the longstanding **A.C. Baths**, a well-maintained complex of thermally heated swimming and hot pools.

Spa Thermal Park and Hot Stream

County Ave • 24hr • Free

A small hot creek cascades through a series of wonderful soaking pools then mixes with the cool waters of the Waikato River at the **Spa Thermal Park and Hot Stream**. The stream is around 400m along the riverside walkway which continues downstream (2.8km one-way; 45min) to Huka Falls (see p.290).

ARRIVAL AND DEPARTURE

By plane Taupo's little airport, 10km south of the centre, has Air New Zealand flights to Auckland and Wellington.
Destinations Auckland (4 daily; 45min); Wellington (3 daily; 1hr).

By bus InterCity and Newmans buses stop at the Taupo Travel Centre bus station, 16 Gascoigne St (☎0800 222 145), in the middle of town. NakedBus stops outside the i-SITE on Tongariro St.
Destinations Auckland (6–7 daily; 4–5hr); Hamilton (5–6 daily; 2hr 30min); Hastings (5–6 daily; 2hr 30min); Napier (5–6 daily; 2hr); Palmerston North (3–4 daily; 4hr); Rotorua (7–8 daily; 1hr); Taihape (5–6 daily; 2hr); Tauranga (4 daily; 2hr 45min); Turangi (4–5 daily; 45min); Wellington (4–5 daily; 6hr).

GETTING AROUND

By shuttle For visiting the surrounding sights (and airport transfers), Shuttle 2U (daily 9am–9pm; ☎07 376 7638, ⍟shuttle2u.co.nz) does a hop-on-hop-off circuit of all the main attractions and charges just $4–10 per hop or $16 for a day pass, and will even pick up from your accommodation.
By car Pegasus Rental Cars (☎0800 803 580, ⍟rentalcars .co.nz) have the best deals, from $35/day, but check the fine-print, as shorter and one-way rentals can cost significantly more.

By bike Most hostels have basic bikes for guests' use. Pack & Pedal, 5 Tamamutu St (☎07 377 4346), rents MTBs from $35/half-day, $55 overnight. Rapid Sensations, 413 Huka Falls Rd (☎0800 35 34 35), run guided bike tours in Wairakei Forest (see box, pp.288–289), but also rent mountain bikes from $40/2hr or $55/day.
By taxi Call Top Cabs (☎07 378 9250) or Taupo Taxis (☎07 378 5100).

INFORMATION

i-SITE 30 Tongariro St (daily 8.30am–5pm; ☎07 376 0027, ⍟greatlaketaupo.com).
Experience Taupo 29 Tongariro St (daily: Oct–April 9am–7pm; May–Sept 9am–6pm; ☎0800 368 775, ⍟experiencetaupo.com). Provides good information and promotes its sponsor adventure companies.

ACCOMMODATION

Taupo maintains a high standard of accommodation for all budgets, but given its proximity to Tongariro National Park and host of events, it's worth booking ahead any time of year. Much of the lakefront is taken up with **motels**, and grassy spots on the fringes of town are given over to **campsites**, while **hostels** are abundant in the town centre.

Accent on Taupo 310 Lake Terrace ☎0800 222 368, ⍟accentontaupo.com; map p.284. Stylishly appointed motel with super-king-size beds, timber decks, a spa, trampoline and BBQ and attractive taupe-toned decor (right down to the fan-folded flannels). Fantastic value for money. $105
All Seasons Holiday Park 16 Rangatira St ☎0800 777 272, ⍟taupoallseasons.co.nz; map p.284. Situated 1.5km east of town, with thermal mineral pool, hedged tent sites scattered among cabins, some with kitchens, and a range of self-contained units ($5 for linen) plus budget rooms in a lodge. Camping $28, lodge $55, cabins $80, units $103
Alpine Lake Motor Lodge 141 Heu Heu St ☎0800 400 141, ⍟alpinelake.co.nz; map p.284. One of Taupo's newest motels, the luxurious *Alpine Lake* comes with underfloor heating, DVD players, free broadband and spa baths in most units. Most units also have cooking hobs, and some have their own BBQs in private courtyards. $129
Base Taupo 7 Tuwharetoa St ☎07 377 4464, ⍟stayatbase.com; map p.284. Secure 120-bed hostel in the heart of Taupo's bar zone and with a good lake-view deck, all the expected facilities (including wi-fi in the lobby), the women-only Sanctuary section ($30) and a lively bar, *Element*. Dorms $19, en-suite dorms $27, en-suite rooms $70
Blackcurrant Backpackers 20 Taniwha St ☎07 378 9292, ⍟blackcurrantbp.co.nz; map p.284. Bright, contemporary hostel in a former motel, now with new bathroom and kitchen, great beds, a 24-hour DVD lounge popular with guests watching their skydiving videos, and always a friendly welcome. Close to bus station. Dorms $27, female-only dorm $29, en-suite double $78

Cascades Comfort Inn 303 Lake Terrace, SH1, Two Mile Bay ☎0800 996 997, ⊛cascades.co.nz; map p.284. Ideally sited with direct access to an attractive heated pool and the lake. Units are spacious with a full kitchen, a mezzanine sleeping area, a patio and a spa bath. **$89**

Colonial Lodge 134 Lake Terrace ☎0800 353 636, ⊛colonial.co.nz; map p.284. Double spas in the bathrooms, kitchenettes, huge TVs and fast, free wi-fi are among the highlights of this efficient motel. Go for the upstairs rooms, opening to a sunny balcony. **$165**

Hilton Lake Taupo 80 Napier–Taupo Hwy ☎07 378 7080, ⊛hilton.com/laketaupo; map p.284. This Hilton hotel combines the beautifully restored 1889 original hotel with heritage rooms and distant lake views, and a modern wing with suites and apartments. With the classy *Bistro Lago* (below) and Taupo Hot Springs on site you've got all you need for a relaxed stay. **$255**

★ **The Lake: a Retro Motel** 63 Mere Rd ☎07 378 4222, ⊛thelakeonline.co.nz; map p.284. Taupo's first ever motel has gone back to its roots, from its striking black exterior to rooms fitted out with funky 1960s and 70s decor (with touches like shag-pile rugs, red-leather and moulded white-plastic chairs and Noddy and Big Ears egg cups), most opening to black-and-white-furnished gardens. Studio **$135**, one-bedroom units **$155**

Lake Taupo Top 10 Holiday Resort 28 Centennial Drive, 2km northeast of town ☎0800 322 121, ⊛taupotop10.co.nz; map p.284. Large, super-organized site with free activities including swimming pool, volleyball, tennis, games room, kids' playground, giant chess board and New Zealand's largest jumping pillow. The bathrooms even have heated floors. Camping **$25**, cabins **$123**, kitchen cabins **$151**, en-suite rooms **$203**, motel units **$232**

Rainbow Lodge 99 Titiraupenga St ☎07 378 5754, ⊛rainbowlodge.co.nz; map p.284. Spacious, relaxed backpackers spread over three buildings with a comfortable lounge, sauna, safe parking and bike rental ($20/day). A stack of local information and little touches create a homely atmosphere. Dorms have six to nine beds (female-only available on request) and there are some particularly good-value en-suite doubles and twins with TV and patio. Free pick-ups from the bus station. Dorms **$23**, en-suite dorms **$26**, rooms **$58**, en-suite rooms **$64**

Rangimarie Guest House 165 Tamamutu St ☎07 377 0329, ⊛rangimarie-bnb-taupo.co.nz; map p.284. Tranquil B&B (its name means "peaceful place" in Maori) with just two rooms, a large lounge, heated pool and hot tub, and free espresso. Wi-fi available. **$140**

Reids Farm Campsite 3km north of Taupo on Huka Falls Rd; map p.291. Spacious free campsite right by the Waikato River just 1km upstream of the exclusive *Huka Lodge*, left to the world by a previous owner who liked backpackers. The makeshift slalom course makes it a popular spot with kayakers. Maximum stay of 14 consecutive nights; closed April to late Oct. **Free**

Taupo Urban Retreat 65 Heu Heu St ☎0800 872 261, ⊛tur.co.nz; map p.284. A 96-bed oasis in the heart of town, this hostel comes with its own house bar, small garden, 1hr free internet, discounted gym passes, bike rental ($20/day) and off-street parking. Popular with the backpacker bus crowd, it has great four-bunk dorms with lake views, though others are windowless. Dorms **$24**, en-suite dorms **$28**, en-suite doubles **$69**

Tiki Lodge 104 Tuwharetoa St ☎0800 845 456, ⊛tikilodge.co.nz; map p.284. The best of the flashpacker-style hostels, purpose-built with a spacious kitchen and 24-hour lounge area plus a great balcony with lake views, and a spa. Dorms **$26**, en-suite doubles with kitchenettes **$80**

YHA Taupo 56 Kaimanawa St ☎07 378 3311, ⊛yha .co.nz; map p.284. Welcoming modern YHA hostel, close to town and with good lake and mountain views from the kitchen and BBQ balcony. There's a spa pool, volleyball court and a garden with hammocks. Dorms either have eight bunks or four beds. Camping **$18**, dorms **$26**, rooms and en suites **$72**

EATING, DRINKING AND NIGHTLIFE

Taupo is loaded with good **cafés** and restaurants, including plenty of Asian restaurants. **Nightlife** almost all happens along the westernmost block of Tuwharetoa Street through to the wee hours. Alternatively head out to Wairakei Terraces for a **Maori cultural experience** (p.291).

CAFÉS AND RESTAURANTS

Bistro Lago *Hilton Lake Taupo* (see above) ☎07 377 1400; map p.284. Taupo's finest dining in the beautifully modernized old wing of the hotel. Great service, immaculate presentation and delectable food that's similarly priced (mains $28–33) to far inferior places. Daily 9am–late.

Fine Fettle 39 Paora Hapi St; map p.284. Taupo's wholefood central – an excellent café specializing in gluten-free dishes such as tasty buckwheat pancakes, along with mussel chowder, panini and salads (many served with organic bread which is also available by the loaf), plus invigorating fruit smoothies (dishes $7–15.50). Daily 9am–4pm.

Indian Affair 34 Ruapehu St ☎07 378 2295; map p.284. Smart, modern surroundings and the best curries in town. There's a great vegetarian selection, including a rich malai kofta, a sublime paneer makhani (home-made cottage cheese in creamy tomato sauce), and a renowned Goan fish curry. Mains $14.90–29. Daily 11.30am–2pm & 5pm–late.

4

4

TAUPO TOURS AND ACTIVITIES

Taupo offers a huge range of air-, land- and water-based activities to relieve you of your holiday money. There's great **mountain biking** around Taupo, much of it maintained by Bike Taupo (ⓦbiketaupo.org.nz). With great scenery and very competitive prices, Taupo is claimed to be the busiest tandem **skydiving** drop zone in the world; all operators offer jumps from 12,000ft (45sec freefall; $250) and 15,000ft (60sec freefall; $340). **Cruises** visit striking, modern, Maori **rock carvings** that can only be seen from the water at Mine Bay, 8km southwest of town. The 10m-high carvings date from the late 1970s and depict a stylized image of a man's face heavy with *moko*, together with *tuatara* (lizard-like reptiles) and female forms draped over nearby rocks. All cruise trips operate two or three times daily, weather permitting; they can be booked through the Taupo Charters Office (ⓣ07 378 3444) at the boat harbour. Several **kayaking** trips also visit the carvings. New Zealand's **fishing** rules dictate that trout can't be sold, so if you've got a taste for them you'll need to catch them yourself. The easiest way is to fish the lake from a charter boat. Rivers flowing into Lake Taupo are the preserve of fly-fishers. The Taupo Launch Charters Office, by the boat harbour (ⓣ07 378 3444), can hook you up with something suitable. Although minimum numbers don't apply, the more on the boat the cheaper it is – book in advance from mid-December to February. Boat operators supply tackle and will organize the mandatory Taupo District Fishing Licence ($17). The charters office also has a list of fishing guides (about $300 for half a day).

MOUNTAIN BIKING

Huka Falls Walkway A scenic ride best reached by heading north from Spa Thermal park to Huka Falls (4km one-way) and on to Aratiatia Dam (additional 8km one-way).

W2K This challenging single-track route (16km one-way, with an additional 10km loop) starts at Whakaipo Bay, 20km west of Taupo, and finishes at Kinloch. Either plan to ride it both ways or arrange transport – it's around 40km by road.

Wairakei Forest Excellent loop riding: start by the Helistar Helicopter, 3km north of Taupo. Rapid Sensations (see opposite) does guided rides of the forest ($108/2hr). For bike rental, see p.286.

SKYDIVING

Taupo Tandem Skydiving ⓣ0800 826 336, ⓦtts.net.nz. Has the widest array of photo and video options.

Skydive Taupo ⓣ0800 586 766, ⓦskydivetaupo .co.nz. A smaller operator than Taupo Tandem, but offers a stretch-limo pick-up service.

BUNGY JUMPING

Taupo Bungy 202 Spa Rd ⓣ0800 888 408, ⓦtaupo bungy.co.nz. The river swirls right past one of New Zealand's finest bungy sites, cantilevered 20m out from the bank with a 47m drop and an optional dunking. Bungy $149, swing solo/tandem $99/120, swing/bungy combo $218. Daily 9am–5pm, until 7pm in summer if busy.

★ **L'Arté** 255 Mapara Rd, Acacia Bay ⓣ07 378 2962, ⓦlarte.co.nz; map p.284. A pretty 8km drive around the head of Lake Taupo to this rural sculpture gallery and garden of quirky mosaics, including some arranged as an outdoor living room. Great food, such as corn fritter stacks layered with home-made potato cakes and hollandaise (dishes $6.50–24), and drinks including a wonderful hot lemon, honey and ginger, are served inside or on a shady deck. Daily 9am–4pm in Jan, otherwise closed Mon & Tues.

Pimentos 17 Tamamutu St ⓣ07 377 4549; map p.284. Fairly casual, central restaurant specializing in modern takes on classic dishes, such as coconut-coated fresh fish

on Asian-dressed green vegetables, or marinated pork loin on roasted kumara. Mains $30–34. Daily noon–3pm & 6–11pm.

Thai Delight 19 Tamamutu St ⓣ07 378 9554; map p.284. Delights at this spacious Thai restaurant include curries, beef, pork, duck and seafood dishes; try the crisp taro cone filled with chicken, vegetables and Thai-style sweet and sour sauce. Mains $16.50–24. Tues–Sun lunch & dinner.

Waterside 3 Tongariro St ⓣ07 378 6894; map p.284. Big cooked breakfasts, beer-battered fish and chips and seafood chowder for lunch and evening meals such as duck confit, grilled New Zealand lamb salad and a house

SCENIC FLIGHTS AND HELICOPTER TRIPS

Taupo's Float Plane ☎ 07 378 7500, ✆ tauposfloat plane.co.nz. Scenic flights over the lake and its surrounds ($80/10min; Mount Ruapehu $310).
Helistar Helicopters ☎ 0800 435 478, ✆ helistar .co.nz. Runs the best helicopter trips, from $99/10min – from a 10-minute flight over Huka Falls to a two-hour voyage over the Tongariro World Heritage Park.

LAKE CRUISES

The Barbary Entertaining cruises (2hr 30min; $40), aboard a 1926 ketch once owned by Eroll Flynn (who, it's claimed, won it in a card game).
Cruise Cat ☎ 0800 252 628 Offers a touch of gin-palace style (1hr 30min; $44).

Ernest Kemp A replica 1920s steamboat that chugs to the carvings and back (2hr; $40).
Fearless Operated by Sail Lake Taupo, a trip on the *Fearless* (2hr; $40) includes a swimming stop in summer at the Maori rock carvings.

KAYAKING AND WATERSPORTS

Rapid Sensations ☎ 0800 353 435, ✆ rapids.co.nz. Runs a kayaking trip to the carvings ($98/3hr on the water), and offers rafting trips (from $88) on the Tongariro River.
Wilderness Escapes ☎ 07 378 3413, ✆ wilderness escapes.co.nz. Does half-day kayak trips to the carvings ($90) and various other trips on request.
Kiwi River Safaris ☎ 0800 723 857, ✆ krs.co.nz.

Kayak trips on the Waikato River ($45) and rafting trips on the Tongariro ($115) and Rangitaiki ($120) rivers.
2MileBay Watersports Centre Two Mile Bay ☎ 07 378 3299, ✆ sailingcentre.co.nz. Rents catamarans ($60/hr), windsurfing boards ($30/hr) and other sailboats (from $50/hr). Daily 9am–5pm in summer, otherwise sporadically.

JETBOATING

Huka Falls Jet ☎ 0800 485 2538, ✆ hukafallsjet .com. The peace at Huka Prawn Park (see p.291) is periodically shattered by one of this company's jetboats ($105/30min) roaring along the river and doing 360-degree spins on the way to the base of Huka Falls.
Rapids Jet Rapids Rd, 3km beyond Aratiatia Dam ☎ 0800 727 437, ✆ rapidsjet.com. The North Island's only true whitewater jetboating run gives you plenty of bang for your buck ($90), taking you down and up Nga Awapura rapids, during which the entire boat gets airborne. Listen closely to the safety spiel, hang on and prepare to get wet.

FISHING

White Striker ☎ 07 378 2736, ✆ troutcatching .com. Has a good strike rate and a wealth of local knowledge. Their smallest charter holds up to six ($220/2hr).

Taupo Rod & Tackle 7 Tongariro St ☎ 07 378 5337. You can rent all manner of tackle here and pick your own spot to cast from – but average catches are much larger if you engage the services of a fishing guide.

HORSE RIDING

Taupo Horse Treks Karapiti Rd ☎ 0800 244 3987, ✆ taupohorsetreks.co.nz. Offers one-hour ($65) and two-hour ($130) jaunts through the pine forests around the Craters of the Moon.

speciality coq au vin (mains $20–29), topped off with a "cheese of the week" with fresh honeycomb, satiate appetites from morning to night. Daily 9am–late.
Zest 65 Rifle Range Rd; map p.284. Stylish little navy-blue painted café out in the suburbs serving delicious dishes from BLTs and Caesar salads to wraps, crêpes, pumpkin, filo and feta pies, as well as excellent coffee (dishes $4–10.50). Mon–Fri 8.30am–3.30pm, Sat & Sun 8.30am–2pm.

BARS AND PUBS

Finn MacCuhal's Corner of Tongariro and Tuwharetoa sts ☎ 07 378 6165; map p.284. Large Irish bar popular with both backpackers and locals; most come for the Guinness, but they also do good-value steaks and fish and chips (mains $16.20–28.90). Daily 5pm–late.
Jolly Good Fellows 76–80 Lake Terrace ☎ 07 378 0457; map p.284. The nearest Taupo gets to a British pub, not in style but for its excellent range of draught ales (most of which have travelled well) and lively community feel. Pub meals are also in the English tradition, with all-day breakfast served including bacon butties and mains ($15–28.50) including toad-in-the-hole and steak and lambs fry. Lots of diners early on followed by revellers for the late shift. Daily 10am–late.

4

Mulligan's 15 Tongariro St ☎ 07 376 9100; map p.284. Dimly lit, Irish-style spot with stout on tap, mischievous Kiwi bar staff, live music, pool table, quiz nights and massive plates of bar food (mains $18–25) including Irish stew and steak and stout pie. Popular with both locals and tour buses. Daily 4pm–late.

The Shed 15 Tongariro St ☎ 07 376 5393; map p.284. Next door to *Finn MacCuhal's*, this chain pub is one of the liveliest in town, not least for its pub grub including beef nachos and BBQ spare ribs (mains $17.50–29). Daily 10am–late.

DIRECTORY

Internet Cybergate, 12 Gascoigne St, $1/10min (daily: summer 10am–11pm, winter 10am–10pm); Cybershed, 115 Tongariro St, $2.50/15min (Mon–Sat 9am–7.30pm).

Left luggage Lockers are available at the Superloo, Tongariro St, opposite the i-SITE ($2/day; daily 7.30am–5pm, until 8pm in summer).

Medical treatment Taupo Health Centre, 113 Heu Heu St

(Mon–Fri 8am–5.30pm; ☎ 07 378 7060).

Pharmacy Mainstreet Pharmacy, at Tongariro & Heuheu sts (daily 8.30am–8.30pm; ☎ 07 378 2636).

Police 21 Story Place, by the museum and art gallery (☎ 07 378 6060).

Post office At Horomatangi & Ruapehu sts, with poste restante facilities (☎ 07 378 9090).

Around Taupo

On the town's outskirts is a concentration of natural wonders, all within a few minutes of one another. Here you'll find boiling mud, hissing steam harnessed by the Wairakei power station, and the clear-blue Waikato River, which cuts a deep swirling course north over rapids and through deep-sided gorges.

The majority of sights and activities are within 10km of Taupo, flanking the Waikato River as it wends its way north, and are accessible through Taupo's tour companies. **Huka Falls Road** loops off SH1 a couple of kilometres north of Taupo and passes the *Reids Farm* (see p.287) free campsite and *Huka Lodge* (one of New Zealand's most exclusive luxury retreats) en route to the first port of call, the magnificent **Huka Falls** (*hukanui*, or "great body of spray"). Here the Waikato, one of New Zealand's most voluminous rivers, funnels into a narrow chasm before plunging over a 9m shelf into a seething maelstrom of eddies and whirlpools; the sheer power of some three hundred tonnes of water per second makes it a far more awesome sight than the short drop would suggest. A footbridge spans the channel, providing a perfect vantage point for watching the occasional mad kayaker making the descent, usually on weekend evenings. The car park is only open until 6pm but you can park outside and walk in at any time.

Honey Hive

65 Karetoto Rd, off Huka Falls Rd · Daily 9am–5pm · Free · ☎ 07 374 8553, ⓦ hukahoneyhive.com

Continuing along Huka Falls Road, a large Russian helicopter marks the launch pad for Helistar flights (see p.289) en route to the cutaway hives and educational video at the **Honey Hive**, 1km further north, where you can buy products from jars of the sweet stuff through to skin-care products and meads and wines.

Volcanic Activity Centre

Corner of Karetoto Rd and Huka Falls Rd · Mon–Fri 9am–5pm, Sat & Sun 10am–4pm · $10 · ☎ 07 374 8375, ⓦ volcanoes.co.nz

The **Volcanic Activity Centre** is a highly instructional museum where the dense text is alleviated by striking photos and interactive computer displays on all things tectonic. Watch one of several films run continuously then check out the seismograph linked to sensors on Mount Ruapehu, an earthquake simulator and a large relief map of Taupo Volcanic Zone, which extends from Mount Ruapehu to White Island.

Huka Prawn Park

Karetoto Rd • Daily: Dec & Jan 9am–5pm; Feb–Nov 9am–3.30pm • Prawn fishing $20; with nature walk $24 • ☎ 07 374 8474,
Ⓦ hukaprawnpark.co.nz

The new Taupo bypass road separates you from the Wairakei geothermal power station from where excess heat is channelled into the family-oriented **Huka Prawn Park**, large open ponds where tropical prawns are raised. Stroll around the ponds and nature walk, spend as long as you like fishing for prawns or combine the two. If learning about a day in the life of "Shawn the Prawn" doesn't fire your imagination, dine on some of Shawn's delicious little friends in the adjacent riverside restaurant.

Craters of the Moon

Karapiti Rd, off SH1 • Daily 8.30am–5.30pm • $6 •
Ⓦ cratersofthemoon.co.nz

The Huka Falls loop road rejoins SH1 near Karapiti Road which runs west to **Craters of the Moon**, a lively geothermal area that sprang to life in the 1950s, after the construction of the Wairakei geothermal power station drastically altered the underground hydrodynamics. While it lacks geysers and colourful lakes, the area is so vigorous that you must wear closed footwear to walk the 3km of trails among roaring fumaroles and rumbling pits belching out a pungent rotten-egg stench.

The Wairakei Terraces

SH1, 3km north of Craters of the Moon • Daily: Oct–March 9am–5pm; April–Sept 9am–4.30pm • $18; Maori cultural experience from 6pm, with reservation, $95 • ☎ 07 378 0913, Ⓦ wairakeiterraces.co.nz

The Wairakei power station is supplied by shiny high-pressure steam pipes that cross under SH1, twisting and bending like a giant ball-bearing racetrack. The power of mineral-laden steam is harnessed nearby at **Wairakei Terraces**, where a vigorously boiling cauldron feeds an artificial cascade of silica terraces and pools. It mimics the process that created Rotorua's Pink and White Terraces, and has grown since the late 1990s. Paths lead through the surrounding model Maori village that comes alive for a **Maori cultural experience**, where you can see weaving, tattooing, and stick games in action. The evening is an engagingly low-key affair (a world away from Rotorua's extravaganzas) with a good introduction to Maori culture and a *hangi* meal followed by the *haka* and dance performance.

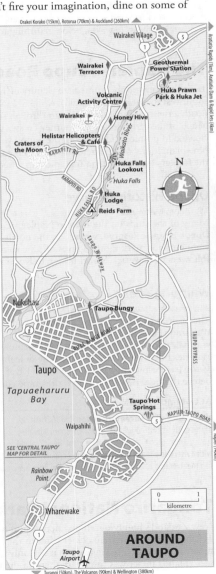

AROUND TAUPO

4

Aratiatia Rapids

2km downstream from Wairakei power station · Best seen Oct–March 10am, noon, 2pm & 4pm; April–Sept 10am, noon & 2pm

The Aratiatia Dam holds back the Waikato River immediately above the **Aratiatia Rapids**, a long series of cataracts that were one of Taupo's earliest attractions. In the 1950s, plans to divert the waters around the rapids were amended by public pressure, thus preserving the rapids, though it's something of a hollow victory since they are dry most of the time, only seen in their full glory during three or four thirty-minute periods each day. Stand on the dam itself or at one of two downstream viewpoints, and wait for the siren that heralds the spectacle of a parched watercourse being transformed into a foaming torrent of waterfalls and surging pressure waves, before returning to a trickle. For jetboat rides, see p.289.

The Napier–Taupo Road

Travelling beyond the immediate vicinity of Taupo, SH1 hugs the lake as it heads southwest to Turangi (see p.294), while SH5 veers southeast along the **Napier–Taupo Road**, a twisting ninety-minute run through some of the North Island's remotest country. Much of the early part of the journey crosses the Kaingaroa Plains, impoverished land cloaked in pumice and ash from the Taupo volcanic eruption and of little use save for the pine plantations which stretch 100km to the north. The history of this route is traced by the **Napier–Taupo Heritage Trail**; pick up a free booklet from either town's i-SITE.

Opepe Historic Reserve

SH5, 17km southeast of Taupo

Many of the stops on the road to Napier are of limited interest, but be sure to call in at **Opepe Historic Reserve**, where, on the north side of the road, a cemetery contains white wooden slabs marking the graves of nine soldiers of the Bay of Plenty cavalry, killed by followers of maverick Maori leader Te Kooti in 1869.

Waipunga Falls

SH5, 35km southeast of Opepe Historic Reserve

The Waipunga River, a tributary of the Mohaka, plummets 30m over the picturesque **Waipunga Falls**, and continues beside SH5 through the lovely Waipunga Gorge, packed with tall native trees and dotted with picnic sites which double as **campsites** with no facilities but river water. The highway descends to the Mohaka River and *Mountain Valley* (see below).Beyond the Mohaka River, the highway climbs the Titiokura Saddle before the final descent through the grape country of the **Esk Valley** into Napier.

ACCOMMODATION   **WAIPUNGA FALLS**

Mountain Valley Adventure Lodge 408 McVicar Rd, 5km south of SH5 ☎ 06 834 9756, ⓦ mountainvalley .co.nz; map p.264. A little slice of rural New Zealand with a riverside bar and restaurant and the opportunity to fish the river (rod hire from $15), mountain bike (bike hire from $35/half-day), go on a farm and forest horse trek (from $60/hr), or do some scenic rafting and kayaking on Grade I–II stretches of the Mohaka River (from $60). Camping $15, dorms $22, lodge rooms $32, cottages and self-contained chalets $100

Tongariro National Park and around

New Zealand's highly developed network of national parks owes much to Te Heu Heu Tukino IV, the Tuwharetoa chief who, in the Pakeha land-grabbing climate of the late nineteenth century, recognized that the only chance his people had of keeping their sacred lands intact was to donate them to the nation – on condition that they could

THE MAORI MOUNTAIN LEGENDS

When Te Heu Heu Tukino donated Tongariro's central volcanoes to the Crown (see opposite), he was motivated by a deep spiritual need for their protection. According to Maori, the mountains at the heart of the park have distinct personalities that symbolize the links between the community and its environment. This significance was recognized in 1991 when the park became the first UNESCO World Heritage Site included as a **cultural landscape**.

Legends tell of a number of smaller mountains clustered around the dominating **Ruapehu**, **Tongariro**, **Ngauruhoe** and **Taranaki**. Among these was the beautiful **Pihanga** in the northern section of the park, whose favours were widely sought. Pihanga loved only Tongariro, the victor of numerous battles with her other suitors, including one that had brought him to his knees, striking off the top of his head, giving him his present shape. Taranaki, meantime, defeated Ngauruhoe, but when he came to face Ruapehu, he was exhausted and badly wounded. He fled, carving out the Whanganui River as he made for the west coast of the North Island. Meanwhile the smaller **Putauaki** got as far north as Kawerau; but **Tauhara** was reluctant to leave and continually glanced back, so that by dawn, when the mountains could no longer move, he had only reached the northern shores of Lake Taupo, where he remains to this day, "the lonely mountain".

To the local Tuwharetoa people these mountains were so sacred that they averted their eyes while passing and wouldn't eat or build fires in the vicinity. The *tapu* stretches back to legendary times when their ancestor **Ngatoroirangi** came to claim the centre of the island. After declaring Tongariro *tapu*, he set off up the mountain, but his followers broke their vow to fast while he was away and the angry gods sent a snowstorm in which Ngatoroirangi almost perished before more benevolent gods in Hawaiki saved him by sending fire to revive his frozen limbs.

4

not be settled or spoiled. His 1887 gift formed the core of the country's first major public reserve, **Tongariro National Park**, which became a UNESCO **World Heritage Site** in 1991 due to its unique landscape and cultural significance (see box above). In the north a small, outlying section of the park centres on **Mount Pihanga** and the tiny **Lake Rotopounamu**, but most visitors head straight for the main body of the park, dominated by the three great volcanoes which rise starkly from the desolate plateau: the broad-shouldered ski mountain, Ruapehu (2797m); its squatter sibling, **Tongariro** (1968m); and, wedged between them, the conical **Ngauruhoe** (2287m).

Within the boundaries of the park is some of the North Island's most striking scenery – a beautiful mixture of semi-arid plains, steaming fumaroles, crystal-clear lakes and streams, virgin rainforest and an abundance of ice and snow. The more forbidding volcanic areas were used as locations for Mordor and Mount Doom in the *Lord of the Rings* trilogy. All of this forms the backdrop to two supremely rewarding tramps, the one-day **Tongariro Alpine Crossing** and the three- to four-day **Tongariro Northern Circuit**, one of New Zealand's Great Walks. The undulating plateau to the west of the volcanoes is vegetated by bushland and golden tussock, while on the eastern side the rain shadow of the mountains produces the **Rangipo Desert**. Although this is not a true desert, it is still an impressively bleak and barren landscape, smothered by a thick layer of volcanic ash from the 186 AD Taupo eruption. **Mount Ruapehu** frequently bursts into life (most recently 1995, 1996 and 2007), occasionally emptying its crater lake down the side of the mountain in muddy deluges known as lahars. In 2011 Mount Ruapehu's Volcanic Alert Level was elevated to level 1 (signs of volcanic unrest), but at the time of writing it was not affecting visitors. Keep tabs on its status with DOC and the local i-SITE office.

The northern approach to the region is through **Turangi**, which – though it lacks the mountain feel of the service town of **National Park** and the alpine **Whakapapa Village**, 1200m up on the flanks of Ruapehu – makes a good base both for the Tongariro tramps and for rafting and fishing the Tongariro River. The southern gateway is **Ohakune**, a more aesthetically pleasing place than National Park but distinctly comatose outside the

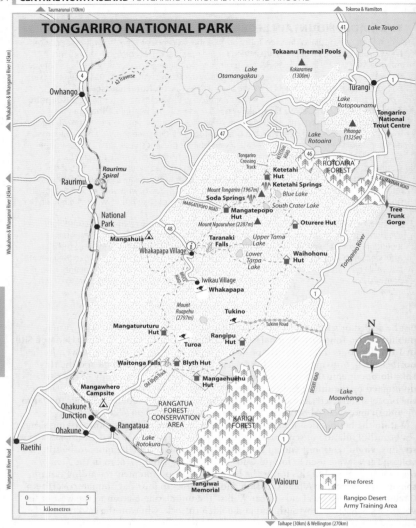

ski season. Heading south, the Army Museum at **Waiouru** marks the southern limit of the Volcanic Plateau, which tails off into the pastoral lower half of the region set around the agricultural town of **Taihape**, home to the North Island's highest bungy jump.

Pretty much everyone comes to the park either to **ski** or to **tramp**, staying in one of the small towns dotted around the base of the mountains. Note that this region is over 600m above sea level, so even in the height of summer you'll need **warm clothing**.

Turangi

The small town of **Turangi**, 50km south of Taupo, was planned in the mid-1960s and built almost overnight for workers toiling away at the tunnels and concrete channels of

FISHING AND WATERSPORTS IN TURANGI

Turangi is famed internationally for the quality of its **trout fishing**, both on the lake and in the Tongariro River. If you're keen to haul a trout from Lake Taupo or one of the local rivers, the i-SITE will help pair you with a **fishing** guide to match your experience and aspirations as well as a licence ($17/day); expect to pay around $280–300 for a half-day with gear and guiding. Alternatively, Sporting Life, The Mall (☎ 07 386 8996, ⓦ sportinglife-turangi.co.nz), sells and rents gear and has a huge amount of info on its website.

Rotorua and Taihape offer wilder **rafting** rivers, but for beautiful gorge scenery, the chance to see the endangered blue duck (*whio*) and fun rapids without the white knuckles, **rafting** the Tongariro River is unbeatable. Young families should opt for the Grade II lower section but most will want to try the Grade III Access 10 section upstream.

Rafting New Zealand 41 Ngawaka Place ☎ 0800 865 226, ⓦ raftingnewzealand.com. Local operators throw in a waterfall jump on their White Water tour, and have plenty of cultural interpretation ($119/4hr). Book ahead for the excellent, daylight-saving-only overnight ($350) that departs in late afternoon and spends the night camped beside the river with a barbecue dinner before finishing the next morning.

Tongariro River Rafting Atirau Rd, near Firestone Tires ☎ 0800 101 024, ⓦ trr.co.nz. Runs an equally good Grade III trip ($115), a family float down the Grade II section (1hr 15min on the water; $75), and raft fishing (Dec–May) only, which involves rafting the Tongariro and stopping off at the otherwise inaccessible pools to cast a fly. Rates are $750/day for two – little more than you'd pay for a fishing guide alone. The company also rents mountain bikes ($40/day).

the ambitious Tongariro Power Scheme (see box, p.297). It's legendary among trout fishers but otherwise is relatively quiet and a non-touristy alternative to Taupo, with Lake Taupo just 4km to the north.

Many people also stay in Turangi to hike the Tongariro Alpine Crossing (see p.300), 40km to the southwest, but there are less daunting alternatives (see below); the i-SITE (see p.296) has details of these and other walks in the area.

Tongariro National Trout Centre

SH1, 4km south of Turangi • Daily: Dec–April 10am–4pm; May–Nov 10am–3pm • $10 • ☎ 07 386 8085, ⓦ troutcentre.com

The massive amount of trout fishing around Turangi makes it essential that rivers are continually restocked from hatcheries such as the **Tongariro National Trout Centre**, set amid native bush between the Tongariro River and one of its tributaries, the Waihukahuka Stream. With an **aquarium** filled with native species such as eels, a chance to see fingerlings being raised and lots of material on water conservation, biodiversity protection and how to fish, it's a great place to spend an hour, especially if you've got kids in tow.

Tokaanu Thermal Pools

Mangaroa Rd, 5km west of Turangi • Pools Daily 10am–9pm • $6; private pools $9/20min, including public pool access • **Kayaks** Daily 10am–5pm • $40/person/half-day • ☎ 07 386 8575

If you want to wallow in hot water, head for **Tokaanu Thermal Pools** in tiny **Tokaanu**, which was the main settlement hereabouts in pre-European times. There's an open-air public pool and hotter, partly enclosed and chlorine-free private pools. Nearby, you can spend a pleasurable hour or two gently paddling along a narrow, lush, bush-fringed channel, past the hot tubs and back gardens of the locals in **kayaks** rented from Wai Maori, located by the hot pools.

Tongariro River Loop Track

Starts at end of Koura St • 4km

The pleasant **Tongariro River Loop Track** is well worth the hour it takes to complete, starting from the Major Jones footbridge at the end of Koura Street on the edge of town. It follows the true right bank of the river north past a couple of viewpoints and over a bluff then crosses the river and returns along the opposite side.

Lake Rotopounamu Circuit

Off SH47, 10km south of Turangi • 5km

A local favourite, the **Lake Rotopounamu Circuit** (90min) encircles the pristine "Greenstone Lake" surrounded by bush alive with native birds such as the kaka, robin, fantail, kakariki, whitehead, long-tailed cuckoo, kereru, grey warbler, bellbird and tui. The easy path is well graded and suitable for prams.

ARRIVAL AND DEPARTURE
TURANGI

By bus InterCity buses drop off at the i-SITE visitor centre, Ngawaka Place. Tongariro Expeditions (see p.302) also stop when taking Taupo hikers to the Tongariro Alpine

Crossing, although not if the weather is bad.
Destinations *The Chateau*, Whakapapa (on demand; 1hr); Auckland (4 daily; 2hr 15min); Wellington (5 daily; 6hr).

GETTING AROUND

By car and shuttle While a car makes life easier, there's a reasonable network of shuttles plying the more useful

routes and providing trailhead transport for trampers (see p.302).

INFORMATION

i-SITE Ngawaka Place (daily 8.30am–5pm; ☎0800 288 726, ⓦlaketauponz.com). Offers a more personalized service than the busy offices in Taupo and Rotorua and sells

bus tickets, Taupo fishing licences, maps, DOC tramping brochures and hut tickets. It also books accommodation for free and has wired and wi-fi internet access.

ACCOMMODATION

Turangi has a pretty good spread of **accommodation**; the budget places are congregated in the town centre, while plusher lodges and B&Bs line the Tongariro River to the east.

Club Habitat 25 Ohuanga Rd ☎07 386 7492, ⓦclub habitat.co.nz. Vast complex over 9.5 acres fashioned from a former workers' camp that's cheap and fairly faded with the exception of the refurbished "executive" units. There's also a spacious games bar, dining complex, spa and sauna. Camping $15, dorms $25, units $125

Creel Lodge 183 Taupahi Rd ☎07 386 8081, ⓦcreel.co.nz. A simple and well-run fishing-oriented motel comprising a cluster of self-contained one- and two-bedroom units in grounds running down to the river edge with barbecuing facilities. $125

Extreme Backpackers 26 Ngawaka Place ☎07 386 8949, ⓦextremebackpackers.co.nz. Amenable hosts take good care of guests at this purpose-built backpackers with simply decorated rooms set around a central court-yard. There's also a climbing wall ($15; $10 for guests) and an amiable café. Dorms $25, rooms $62, en suites $72

Ika Lodge 155 Taupahi Rd ☎07 386 5538, ⓦika.co.nz. Set in flowering gardens, this superior lodge by the Tongariro River has two rooms – a loft suite, with beamed ceilings, adjacent to the mezzanine guest lounge, and a

ground-floor garden suite – and a two-bedroom apartment accessed off the courtyard. Prices include breakfast. Double $160, apartment $170

Parklands Corner of SH1 and Arahori St ☎0800 456 284, ⓦparklandsmotorlodge.co.nz. Extensive motor lodge with pine-lined studios and spacious modernized units plus an outdoor pool, games room and a small restaurant serving home-style dinners. Studios $110, units $140

Riverstone Backpackers 222 Tautahanga Rd ☎07 386 7004, ⓦriverstonebackpackers.co.nz. Lovely purpose-built boutique backpackers in a converted house with lots of communal living space, both inside and out, a well-equipped modern kitchen, herbs from the garden, bike and walking-pole rentals. Dorms $27, rooms $68, en suites $78

★ **Tongariro River Motel** Corner of SH1 and Link Rd ☎0800 187 688, ⓦtongariporivermotel.co.nz. Homely, comfortable motel that is hugely popular with anglers, partly for its rod racks and smoker, but mainly because of its "manager", a lovable boxer named Boof. The friendly owner runs a lively website on everything to do with Turangi, and trout fishing in particular. $95

EATING AND DRINKING

Eating options in Turangi have improved considerably in recent years, with some smart cafés and restaurants serving modern New Zealand cuisine providing visitors with plenty of choice. The well-stocked New World supermarket is a help for self-caterers.

Mustard Seed Café 91 Ohuanga Rd ☎07 386 7377. Casual, modern licensed café with primary-coloured decor and a decent range of breakfasts, panini, salads and cakes, plus good espresso (dishes $7–13). Thurs–Mon 8.30am–3.30pm.

Oreti 88 Pukawa Rd, Pukawa ☎07 386 7070, ⓦoreti village.co.nz. Angus ribeye fillet with mushroom sauce, almond and sesame-crumbed pork fillet, and hot smoked Marlborough salmon (mains $29.50–34) star on the dinner menu of this romantic spot 8km northwest of Turangi on the shores of Lake Taupo. Sat and Sun breakfast from 9am, Thurs–Sun noon–3pm, Tues–Sun 6pm–late.

River Vineyard Restaurant 134 Grace Rd ☎07 386 6704. Fuel up for mountain treks with brunches featuring items such as muesli with yoghurt or brioche French toast; snack on caramelized onion and blue cheese filo tarts or burgers with honey-cured bacon; or relax over a dinner of braised white beans with red slaw and garlic, or apple-glazed lamb shank on beetroot and parsnip purée (mains $30–34) at this riverside winery a 4km drive north of town off SH1. Wed–

Sun 10am–3pm, bar menu 3–6pm, dinner 6–10pm.

Rod n' Gun Restaurant Bridge Fishing Lodge, SH1, 800m north of Turangi ☎07 386 8804, ⓦbridgefishing lodge.co.nz. Take a seat in front of the big fireplace for heart-warming meals such as double roasted pork belly with caramelized pears or wild mushroom risotto (mains $18–28). Mon–Sat 6–9pm.

Tongariro Lodge 83 Grace Rd ☎07 386 7946, ⓦtongarirolodge.co.nz. Mushroom and tofu dumplings, a duo of Hawke's Bay lamb and rack of venison with seasonal vegetables are among the inventive mains ($20–42) at the restaurant of the *Tongariro Lodge*, which also has pricey but luxurious chalets and villas (from $392/person). Daily 6–10pm.

Valentinos Ohuanga Rd ☎07 386 8821. A classic Kiwi Italian place that seems like it's barely changed since the tunnellers first came to town. Pastas include spaghetti with gorgonzola and cream; steaks, such as marinated venison glazed with red currant and port, are a speciality. Mains $23.50–33. Wed–Mon 6pm–late.

Whakapapa

Tiny **Whakapapa**, 45km south of Turangi on SH48, is the only settlement set firmly within the boundaries of Tongariro National Park and hugs the lower slopes of Mount Ruapehu. Approaching from the north, an open expanse of tussock gives distant views of the imposing *Chateau Tongariro* hotel, framed by the snowy slopes of the volcano behind and overlooked by the arterial network of tows on the Whakapapa ski-field.

Swarms of trampers use Whakapapa as a base for short walks or long tramps. The Tongariro Northern Circuit and the Round the Mountain track (see p.302) can both be tackled from here, but there are also easier strolls covered by DOC's *Walks in and around Tongariro National Park* leaflet ($3). Three of the best of these are the **Whakapapa Nature Walk** (1km; 20–30min), highlighting the unique flora of the park; the **Taranaki Falls Walk** (6km; 2hr), which heads through open tussock and bushland to where the Wairere Stream plunges 20m over the end of an old lava flow; and the **Silica Rapids Walk** (7km; 2hr 30min), which follows a stream through beech forests to creamy-coloured geothermal terraces.

THE TONGARIRO POWER SCHEME

The **Tongariro Power Scheme** provides an object lesson in harnessing the power of water with minimal impact on the environment. Its two powerhouses produce around seven percent of the country's electricity, while the outflows that feed into Lake Taupo add flexibility to the much older chain of eight hydroelectric dams along the Waikato River. Some argue it is unacceptable to tamper with such a fine piece of wilderness but, while there have been some minor environmental impacts, it is surely better than a nuclear power station.

In fact, if it weren't for the scale models in visitor centres and the ugly bulk of the Tokaanu power station, only astute observers would be aware of the complex system of tunnels, aqueducts, canals and weirs unobtrusively going about their business of diverting the waters of the Tongariro River and myriad streams running off the mountain slopes, back and forth around the perimeter of the national park, using modified natural lakes for storage. Mount Ruapehu poses its own unique problems: the threat of **lahars** is ever-present and, after the 1995 eruption, abrasive volcanic ash found its way into the turbines of the Rangipo underground powerhouse, causing an unscheduled seven-month shutdown.

MOUNT RUAPEHU SKI-FIELDS

Mount Ruapehu is home to the North Island's only substantial **ski-fields**, **Whakapapa** and **Turoa**, which attract around two-thirds of the nation's skiers. Every weekend from **late June to mid-October**, cars pile out of Auckland and Wellington (and everywhere in between) for the four-hour drive to Whakapapa, on the northwestern slopes of Mount Ruapehu, or Turoa, on the south side. Both have excellent reputations for pretty much all levels of skier and the orientation of volcanic ridges lends itself to an abundance of dreamy, natural half-pipes for snowboarding.

TICKETS AND EQUIPMENT

Mt Ruapehu (ⓦmtruapehu.com) manages both fields, sells tow tickets ($95/day) and rents gear (skis, boots and poles from $39, boards and boots from $47). For beginners there's a Discover package ($90) including ski or snowboard rental, 1hr 50min lesson and a learners' area lift pass. Several places in National Park, Ohakune and Turangi also offer competitive rates and a wide selection of equipment.

ACCOMMODATION

Neither field has public **accommodation** on site. Ski clubs maintain dozens of chalets at the foot of the main lifts in Whakapapa's Iwikau Village, but casual visitors (unless invited as a guest) have to stay 6km downhill at Whakapapa Village or 22km away at National Park (see p.303). Almost everyone skiing Turoa stays in Ohakune.

SKI AREAS

Whakapapa New Zealand's largest and busiest ski area, with over sixty runs (two beginner, forty intermediate, twenty advanced), a dozen major chairlifts and T-bars and the dedicated learners' area of Happy Valley. It offers 675 vertical metres of piste, plus snow-making equipment, ski schools, a huge gear-rental operation and some café/ bars. Access is along the toll-free, sealed Bruce Road. Tyre chains are not available (see opposite). Shuttle buses run regularly from Whakapapa Village, National Park, Turangi and Taupo. Typically open late June to mid-Oct.
Turoa The country's greatest vertical range of piste (720m) and a skiable area almost as extensive as Whakapapa's, with wide, groomed trails (three beginner, eleven intermediate, over a dozen advanced) particularly aimed at intermediate skiers; it also offers the region's best après-ski at Ohakune. It's usually possible to drive straight up the sealed, toll-free, 17km access road from Ohakune without chains, and park for nothing, but the ski-field operators will fit chains ($30; cash only) when needed. Several shuttle buses run up from Ohakune, charging around $25 return. Typically open mid- to late June to mid-Oct.

Ruapehu Crater Rim hike

5–8hr return From Iwikau Village car park 15km return; 1000m ascent • **From top of Waterfall Express chairlift** 9km return; 650m ascent • Chairlift Jan to mid-March 9am–4pm • $24 return

There's much more of a vertical component to the **Ruapehu Crater Rim hike**, a tough, steep slog made worthwhile by the dramatic silhouettes of Cathedral Rocks and the views west to Mount Taranaki. The walk can be done from the car park at Iwikau Village but is much more appealing from the top of the Waterfall Express chairlift, thereby avoiding a long trudge through a barren, rocky landscape. From the top of the **chairlift** the route is poorly marked, but from Christmas until the first snows, the ascent can usually be made in ordinary walking boots without crampons. Guided crater walks are also available (see opposite).

Iwikau Village

From Whakapapa, SH48 continues as Bruce Road 6km uphill to **Iwikau Village** (known locally as the "Top o' the Bruce"), an ugly jumble of ski-club chalets which from late June through to mid-October becomes a seething mass of wraparound shades and baggy snowboarders' pants. Outside the ski season, the village dies, leaving only a couple of **chairlifts** to trundle up to the shiny-new *Knoll Ridge Café* (see below), from where you can take **guided walks** on the mountain.

ARRIVAL   WHAKAPAPA

By bus The only bus services to Whakapapa are the shuttle buses from Turangi (twice daily) and National Park (3–5 daily), which drop off close to the DOC, plus NakedBus (1 daily on demand).

GETTING AROUND

By car and shuttle No snow chains are available in Whakapapa, so you'll need to bring your own or use one of the shuttle services, which operate from accommodation in the area, or with the hourly or better mountain shuttle (☎0800 117 686).

INFORMATION AND TOURS

DOC SH48 (daily: Dec–Feb 8am–6pm; March–Nov 8am–5pm; ☎07 892 3729, ✉whakapapavc@doc.govt.nz). Contains all the maps and leaflets you'll need, plus has extensive displays on the park, including the tiny Ski History museum and a couple of audiovisual presentations (one for $3, both for $5) shown on demand – one on volcanism hereabouts, the other combining Maori legends surrounding Tongariro with impressive footage of the landscape through the seasons.

Mt Ruapehu guided tours ☎07 892 4000, ⊕mt ruapehu. Guided crater walks (mid-Dec to mid-April daily 9.30am; 6hr; $145 including the lift) provide a commentary on geology, flora and more.

ACCOMMODATION

Whakapapa has limited places to stay, which are often booked out well in advance. Reserve as far ahead as possible through the ski season and over the Christmas and January school holidays.

Chateau Tongariro SH48 ☎0800 242 832, ⊕chateau.co.nz. Whakapapa's most prominent building is this 1929 brick edifice with gracious public areas including a huge lounge with full-size snooker table and great mountain views; it's worth a visit for a Devonshire tea even if you're not staying. Guests have use of the highest nine-hole golf course in New Zealand, tennis courts, gym and a small indoor pool, and stay in fairly anodyne rooms modernized to international hotel standard. If you're after space and good views you'll need one of the premium rooms, mostly in the new wing sympathetically added in 2004. The website often advertises significant discounts in spring and autumn. Standard rooms $195, premium rooms $245

Discovery SH47, 1.1km south of the SH48 turn-off ☎07 892 2744, ⊕discovery.net.nz; one-way village shuttle $15, return ski-field shuttle $35. A five-minute drive northwest of Whakapapa Village, this 10-acre site with views of the Tongariro volcanoes has a wide range of accommodation options. Camping $16, backpacker cabins $60, motel $135, chalet $165

Mangahuia Campsite Off SH47, close to the foot of the Whakapapa access road. Simple, seventeen-pitch streamside DOC campsite with toilets, running water, picnic tables and sheltered cooking area. Operates on a first-come, first-served basis; deposit fee at site registration stand. $4

Skotel 100m up the hill beside the *Chateau Tongariro* ☎0800 756 835, ⊕skotel.com. Hotel with woodsy, three-bunk rooms, doubles, a sauna and a restaurant/bar. Note that rates are hiked considerably in the ski season. Single $40, twin $55, en-suite rooms $140, cabins sleeping four $185

Whakapapa Holiday Park Opposite the DOC office ☎07 892 3897, ⊕whakapapa.net.nz. The budget option, set in a pretty patch of beech forest with tent and powered sites. Camping $19, dorms $25, cabins $79, units $109

EATING AND DRINKING

Fergusson's Café Opposite the DOC office. Start your day with egg-laden breakfasts, fill up on cheap snacks or tuck into filled (and filling) sandwiches for lunch (dishes $6.50–16.50). Daily 7am–6pm.

Knoll Ridge Café ⊕mtruapehu.com This shiny-new café has a very modern design and is New Zealand's highest, perched at 2020m, serving up long views and typical mountain fare such as ham and cheese toasties, panini and caramel slices (dishes $4–9.50). Daily winter and Dec–Easter 9.30am–3.30pm.

Lorenz's Café 5km up the hill from Whakapapa village ⊕mtruapehu.com. Basic café with a range of snacks (pies *et al*), as well as larger meals (mains $10–25). It's at the base of the chairlift that whisks you up to *Knoll Ridge Café*. Daily breakfast and lunch.

Pihanga Café & T Bar Chateau Tongariro ☎0800

242 832. The *Chateau's* budget option, serving pub-style meals that are a cut above: calamari Cajun salad, crispy stir-fries with egg noodles and creamy seafood chowder, all with matching Mac's beer suggestions (mains $12.50–24.50). Daily 11.30am–late.

Ruapehu Room Chateau Tongariro ☏ 0800 242 832. If you want to reward yourself for the successful completion of a major tramp, the *Chateau's Ruapehu Room* has elegant à la carte meals with an emphasis on high-quality meat (prime beef, double lamb, and NZ-farmed venison), at à la carte prices (mains $32–38). You'll need to reserve

ahead for dinner and Sunday lunch, and to dress for the occasion (no jeans or T-shirts). Daily breakfast and dinner, Sun lunch.

The Terrace Restaurant & Bar Skotel ☏ 0800 756 835. Serves good-value bistro meals spanning burgers and grilled polenta to sirloins (mains $14.50–32), and has a lively bar. Daily breakfast, lunch and dinner.

Tussock Pub At the base of the village ☏ 07 892 3809. The cheapest booze and food (mains $15–20) is at the village pub, where the few locals tend to drink and catch sports on the big-screen TV. Daily 3pm–late.

Tramping in Tongariro National Park

Tongariro National Park contains some of the North Island's finest walks, all through spectacular and varied volcanic terrain. The **Tongariro Alpine Crossing** alone is often cited as the best one-day tramp in the country, but there are many longer possibilities, notably the three- to four-day **Tongariro Northern Circuit**. Mount Ruapehu has the arduous but rewarding **Crater Rim Hike** (see p.298) and the **Round the Mountain Track**, a circuit of Ruapehu offering a narrower variety of terrain and sights than the Tongariro tramps, but consequently less used; both are best accessed from Whakapapa.

Tongariro Alpine Crossing

19.4km; 6–8hr; 750m ascent • All shuttles drop off at Mangatepopo Rd End car park between 6–9am and pick up at Ketetahi Rd around 4.30pm

During the summer season (typically mid-Nov to April) the **Tongariro Alpine Crossing** is by far the most popular of the major tramps in the region, and for good reason. Within a few hours you climb over lava flows, cross a crater floor, skirt active geothermal areas, pass beautiful and serene emerald and blue lakes and have the opportunity to ascend the cinder cone of Mount Ngauruhoe. Even without this wealth of highlights it would still be a fine tramp, traversing a mountain massif through scrub and tussock before descending into virgin bush. On weekends and through the height of summer up to seven hundred people per day complete the Crossing: aim for spring or autumn and stick to weekdays. Other ways to **avoid the crush** are to get one of the early shuttles and keep ahead of the crowds, or turn one long, arduous day into a relaxed two-day experience, dawdling behind the mob and staying the night at **Ketetahi Hut** (see p.303).

Mangatepopo car park to Mangatepopo Saddle

Almost everyone walks west to east, saving 400m of ascent. The first hour is gentle, following the Mangatepopo Stream through a barren landscape and passing the

---

TRAMPING IN WINTER

Once the autumn snows arrive (typically in late April) ordinary tramping gear becomes inadequate for doing the Tongariro Alpine Crossing or any of the longer tramps. If you have crampons and an ice axe (and know how to use them) then winter is a great time to get out into the mountains: there are far fewer people, and while the Great Walk huts along the Tongariro Alpine Crossing and Tongariro Northern Circuit lose their cooking facilities they become cheaper ($15.30, instead of $31). Huts along the Round the Mountain Track are the same price year-round. For more information on weather and equipment, see p.303.

For those less experienced, there are **guided walks** (generally June–Oct) along large sections – though not all – of the Tongariro Alpine Crossing, which include basic instruction on how to use the ice axe and crampons provided (see p.303).

Mangatepopo Hut. The track steepens as you scale the fractured black lava flows towards the **Mangatepopo Saddle**, passing a short side track to the **Soda Springs**, a small wildflower oasis in this blasted landscape. The Saddle marks the start of the high ground between the bulky and ancient Mount Tongariro and its youthful acolyte, **Mount Ngauruhoe**, which fit walkers can climb (additional 2km return; 2–3hr; 600m ascent) from here and still make the shuttle bus at the end of the day. The two-steps-forward-one-step-back ascent of this 35-degree cone of red and black scoria is exhausting but the views from the toothy crater rim and the thrilling headlong descent among a cascade of tumbling rocks and volcanic dust make it a popular excursion.

Mangatepopo Saddle to Ketetahi Hut

From the Mangatepopo Saddle, the main track crosses the flat pan of the **South Crater** and climbs to the rim of **Red Crater**, with fumaroles belching out steam, which obscures the banded crimson and black of the crater walls. Colours get more vibrant still as you begin the descent to the Emerald Lakes, opaque pools shading from jade to palest duck-egg, and beyond to the crystal-clear Blue Lake. Sidling around Tongariro's **North Crater**, you begin to descend steeply on golden tussock slopes to **Ketetahi Hut**, a major rest stop with views of Lake Rotoaira and Lake Taupo.

Ketetahi Hut to Ketetahi car park

From Ketetahi Hut you pass close to the steaming Ketetahi Springs, then begin the final descent through cool streamside bush to the car park on Ketetahi Road.

Tongariro Northern Circuit

42km; 3–4 days at a gentle pace • Whakapapa is the main point of access

If the Tongariro Alpine Crossing appeals, but you're looking for something more challenging, the answer is the **Tongariro Northern Circuit**, one of New Zealand's Great Walks. In summer (roughly Oct–April), the huts – Mangatepopo, Ketetahi, Waihohonu and Oturere – are classed as **Great Walk huts** and come with gas cooking stove but not pans or crockery. Campers can use the hut facilities. The circuit is usually done clockwise.

Whakapapa to Mangatepopo

9km; 2–3hr; 50m ascent

This section can be skipped by getting a shuttle to Mangatepopo car park. The track undulates through tussock and crosses numerous streams before meeting the Tongariro Alpine Crossing track close to Mangatepopo Hut. The track can be boggy after heavy rain but is usually passable.

Mangatepopo Hut to Emerald Lakes

6km; 3–4hr; 660m ascent

Follow the Tongariro Alpine Crossing (see opposite); you then have the choice of continuing on the Crossing to Ketetahi Hut (4km; 2–3hr; 400m descent) and returning to this point the next day, or continuing to the right. The track passes black lava flows from Ngauruhoe's eruptions in 1949 and 1954. From the top of Red Crater a poled route (to the left) leads to Tongariro Summit, while the main track continues on past the crater rim.

Emerald Lakes to Oturere Hut

5km; 1–2hr; 500m descent

There are spectacular views of the Oturere Valley, the Kaimanawa Ranges and the Rangipo Desert as you descend steeply through fabulously contorted lava formations from Red Crater's eruptions towards the desert and Oturere Hut.

Oturere Hut to Waihohonu Hut

8km; 2–3hr; 250m descent

You begin this leg by crossing open, rolling country over gravel fields – plant regeneration after volcanic eruptions is a lengthy process – before fording a branch of the Waihohonu Stream. You then descend into the beech forests before a final climb over a ridge brings you to the hut, where you can drop your pack and press on for twenty minutes to the cool and clear Ohinepango Springs.

Waihohonu Hut to Whakapapa

14km; 5–6hr; 200m ascent

The final day cuts between Ngauruhoe and Ruapehu, passing the Old Waihohonu Hut (no accommodation), which was built for stagecoaches on the old road in 1901. The path then continues alongside Waihohonu Stream to the exposed Tama Saddle and, just over 1km beyond, a junction where side tracks lead to Lower Tama Lake (20min return) and Upper Tama Lake (1hr return), both water-filled explosion craters, where you can swim, if you don't need your water warm. It is only around a two-hour walk from the saddle back to Whakapapa, so you should have time to explore Taranaki Falls before ambling back through tussock to the village.

Round the Mountain Track

71km; 4–5 days • Whakapapa is the main point of access

The challenging **Round the Mountain Track** loops around Mount Ruapehu and is most easily tackled from Whakapapa. The track can also be combined with the Northern Circuit to make a mighty five- or six-day **circumnavigation** of all three mountains.

ARRIVAL AND DEPARTURE   **TONGARIRO PARK TRAMPS**

By car Most visitors access both the Tongariro Alpine Crossing and the Tongariro Northern Circuit from the car park at the end of Mangatepopo Rd, off SH47. Car parks at both ends of the Alpine Crossing track have a reputation for break-ins so it's a good idea to leave your vehicle in Ohakune, Turangi, National Park or Whakapapa and make use of the shuttle buses (see below).

GETTING AROUND

By bus and shuttle bus A couple of InterCity bus routes pass through Tongariro National Park but most services are run by smaller companies, many associated with backpacker hostels. If you're staying in any of the towns listed below there'll be a choice of operators offering basically the same service (often with an early bus getting you to the trailhead before the masses). The larger, reliable operators are listed below: your accommodation and the various visitor centres can flesh out the options. Companies generally charge around $35 for combined Tongariro Alpine Crossing drop-off and pick-up.

FROM NATIONAL PARK

Numerous shuttle buses serve the trailheads in summer and ski-fields in winter. Try *Howard's Lodge, The Park* and *YHA National Park Backpackers* (see p.304), who all run their own services.

FROM OHAKUNE

Matai Shuttles ☎ 0800 462 824, ⓦ mataishuttles .co.nz. Runs twice daily in summer calling at National Park (and sometimes Whakapapa) on the way to Mangatepopo car park.

FROM TAUPO

Tongariro Expeditions ☎ 07 377 0435, ⓦ thetongariro crossing.co.nz. Good for getting to the park generally, but to attempt the Crossing from Taupo involves a ridiculously early start and puts you on it at its busiest.

FROM TURANGI

Mountain Shuttle ☎ 0800 117 686, ⓦ tongariro crossing.com. Runs Alpine Crossing and ski-field shuttles year-round. The earliest of the several crossing shuttles available is around 6am.

Extreme Backpackers ☎ 07 386 8949 (see p.296). Also offers Alpine Crossing and ski-field shuttles year-round.

FROM WHAKAPAPA

Several shuttles stop on their way to the Tongariro Alpine Crossing. The most frequent is Mountain Shuttle (see above).

INFORMATION AND TOURS

DOC leaflets The leaflets from i-SITEs in Taupo and Turangi covering the tramps are informative and adequate for most purposes though map fans will want the region's Parkmap ($19).

Weather Mountain weather (ⓦmetservice.co.nz/public /mountain/tongariro.html) is extremely changeable, and the usual provisos apply. Even on scorching summer days, the increased altitude and exposed windy ridges produce a wind-chill factor to be reckoned with, and storms roll in with frightening rapidity. From the end of March through to late November there can be snow on the tracks, so check current conditions.

Equipment Any time of year, it's essential to take warm clothing and rain gear – and if you plan to scramble up and down the steep volcanic cone of Mount Ngauruhoe, take gloves and long trousers for protection from the sharp scoria rock. Water is also scarce on most tracks so carry plenty. For information on tramping in winter, see box, p.300.

GUIDED WINTER WALKS

Tongariro Expeditions ⓣ07 377 0435, ⓦthetongariro crossing.co.nz. Charge $155 from National Park and Turangi for trips across the sections of the Alpine Crossing that are open.

Adrift Outdoors ⓣ07 892 2751, ⓦadriftnz.co.nz. National Park-based operator that offers a winter Alpine Crossing for the same price as Tongariro Expeditions.

ACCOMMODATION

Other than accommodation in Whakapapa (see p.299), the only places to stay are trampers' huts, all of which have adjacent campsites. Hut tickets can be bought in advance from DOC offices in Whakapapa and Ohakune, or the i-SITE in Turangi; if bought from a hut warden you pay an extra $5.

Round the Mountain Track Backcountry hut pass not valid at Waihohonu Hut (Great Walk Hut) but hut bookable online. Backcountry hut pass valid for all other huts. Under-18s free. Huts $\overline{$15}$, Waihohonu hut $\overline{$31}$, camping $\overline{$5}$, Waihohonu camping $\overline{$20.40}$

Tongariro Alpine Crossing The Ketetahi Hut is a Great Walk hut and is bookable online. Backcountry hut pass not valid. Under-18s free. Hut $\overline{$31}$, camping $\overline{$20}$

Tongariro Northern Circuit Mangatepopo, Ketetahi, Waihohonu and Oturere are all Great Walk huts and are bookable online. Under-18s free. Huts $\overline{$31}$, camping $\overline{$20.40}$

National Park

The evocative moniker attached to **National Park**, 15km west of Whakapapa Village, belies the overwhelming drabness of this tiny settlement – a dispiriting collection of A-frame chalets sprouting from a scrubby plain with only the views of Ruapehu and Ngauruhoe to lend it grace. Comprised of a grid of half a dozen streets wedged between SH4 and the parallel rail line, the place owes its continued existence to skiers and trampers bound for the adjacent Tongariro National Park, and paddlers heading for **Whanganui River trips**. With limited accommodation at Whakapapa Village, visitors often stay here, using shuttle buses (see opposite) to get to the slopes and the tramps.

THE 42 TRAVERSE

Near the town of National Park, the **42 Traverse** (46km one-way; 4–6hr) **mountain-bike ride** – often wrongly called the 42nd Traverse – has long been popular with Kiwi riders and is gaining a wider following. It mostly follows a narrow 4WD road through some fairly remote country with great downhills (500m net descent), a couple of stream crossings and lashings of atmospheric native bush.

It isn't a particularly technical ride, but there are 300m of climbing and it will take moderately experienced and fit riders four to six hours to complete. The traverse is best done from National Park where all lodgings will help organize pick-up and drop-off (usually $35 in total). Some lodgings have bike rental.

BIKE RENTAL

Kiwi Mountain Bikes ⓣ0800 562 4537, ⓦkiwi mountainbikes.co.nz. If you don't – or can't – rent a bike from where you're staying, try here; they charge $65 for the 42 Traverse and do guided rides on the mostly downhill Fishers Track (17km; 520m descent; $99) with van pick-up from the bottom.

4

Tupapakurua Falls Track

4–5hr return

When wind and rain tempt you to stay indoors, consider the **Tupapakurua Falls Track** which winds through the bush protected from the worst of the weather. It initially follows the gravel Fisher Road from near the train station then, at a small parking area after 2km (30min), you branch left onto a track to a bench seat (additional 20min) with great views west to Mount Taranaki. A further hour's walk brings you to a small canyon with views of the slender, 50m Tupapakurua Falls.

ARRIVAL AND DEPARTURE — NATIONAL PARK

By train and bus Trains stop beside Station Road. InterCity buses from Taumarunui, Turangi and Ohakune pull up nearby on Carroll Street close to the *National Park Hotel*. Both bus and train tickets can be bought at *Howard's Lodge* (see below).

Train destinations Auckland (3–7 weekly; 5hr 30min); Ohakune (3–7 weekly; 30min); Palmerston North (3–7 weekly; 3hr 30min); Wellington (3–7 weekly; 5hr).
Bus destinations Auckland (2 daily; 5hr 30min); Ohakune (2 daily; 30min).

INFORMATION

Tourist information National Park has no i-SITE but visitor information is available from the *Macrocarpa Café* (see below), which also has postal facilities.

Services There's an ATM in the petrol station on SH4 (generally daily 7.30am–7pm); *Schnapps Bar* (opposite) also has an ATM.

ACCOMMODATION

Accommodation is plentiful except over weekends and school holidays during the **ski season** – when prices generally rise – and from Christmas to the end of January. Half a dozen places have a mixture of backpacker dorms and doubles (some en suite) and everywhere either has its own **track transport** (typically $35 for drop-off and pick-up) or works closely with someone who does.

Howard's Lodge Carroll St ☎ 07 892 2827, ⊛ howards lodge.co.nz. High-standard lodge where those in the en-suite rooms get access to a plusher kitchen and lounge. There's also a spa, and a wide range of rentals including mountain bikes ($60/day), skis ($33) and snowboards ($40). Dorms $26, rooms $75, en suites $105

National Park Hotel Carroll St ☎ 07 892 2805, ⊛ nationalparkhoteltongariro.co.nz. The town's main pub (see below) has old-fashioned yet clean, comfortable dorms, private rooms and backpacker cabins, all with shared facilities. Surprisingly modern amenities include a lounge with big-screen TV and broadband. Dorms $20, backpacker cabins $50, doubles $60

The Park Corner of SH4 and Millar St ☎ 07 892 2748, ⊛ the-park.co.nz. The town's largest lodge is a well-organized 82-room complex with a bar, restaurant and spa pool, though no mountain views from rooms. Dorms $35, en-suite rooms $120, apartments $160

Plateau Lodge Carroll St ☎ 0800 861 861, ⊛ plateau lodge.co.nz. There's a relaxed ski-chalet feel to this wood-panelled lodge with a broad range of accommodation, a hot tub, and freebies including wi-fi and a guest phone. Dorms $28, en-suite rooms $90, apartments $160

Tongariro Crossing Lodge Carroll St ☎ 07 892 2688, ⊛ tongarirocrossinglodge.co.nz. This quaint, colonially furnished, former stagecoach inn has a more private feel than most of the lodges hereabouts, with just six rooms, all of which are en-suite. Breakfast (extra $18) is available. $149

YHA National Park Backpackers Findlay St ☎ 07 892 2870, ⊛ npbp.co.nz. Fairly basic associate YHA with its own indoor climbing wall ($10, plus $3 for boots and harness). Camping $14, dorms $23, rooms $60, en suites $70

EATING AND DRINKING

All the lodges mentioned above offer **self-catering** facilities, and *The Park* has an on-site **restaurant** serving good, pub-style meals.

Macrocarpa Café 3 Waimarino Tokaanu Rd ☎ 07 892 2911. Busy café that serves as the village's post office, visitor centre and general gathering point, dishing up filling fare (mains $8–14.50) such as beer-battered snapper, smoked chicken salad and hot roast beef rolls. Daily 7am–6pm.

National Park Hotel Carroll St ☎ 07 892 2805. Parts of this timber hotel date back to 1913. Its *Mill Bar and Restaurant* (named after the town's former sawmills, with displays in the bar) serves pub fare including a beef and black beer stew and pavlova with kiwifruit for dessert (mains $16.50–24.50). Daily 7am–6pm.

Schnapps Bar SH4 **☎** 07 892 2788, **ⓦ** schnappsbar ruapehu.com. Braised lamb shanks in mint jus is the perennially popular choice at this big, orange pub at the entrance to town, which also serves mountain burgers and huge portions of fish and chips (mains $18.50–22.50). Breakfast is also served on weekends during winter, when, of an evening, there's often live entertainment, quizzes and sport on the big screen year-round. Daily noon–late.

★ The Station At the train station **☎** 07 892 2881, **ⓦ** thestationcafe.co.nz. Worth a trip to National Park in its own right for its big cooked breakfasts, photo-worthy counter food (also available to take away) or hot lunches such as seafood chowder. Exquisite evening meals include sesame-coated salmon, juniper-rubbed venison with dark plum sauce, and feta-filled chicken breast (mains $25.50–36), topped off with scrumptious desserts such as sweet spring rolls (banana and macadamia nuts in crispy pastry with butterscotch sauce) and chocolate parfait (creamy frozen mousse with espresso jelly), paired with suggested wines. Wed–Mon 10am–late, Tues 10am–3pm.

Ohakune

Ohakune, 35km south of National Park, welcomes you with a giant fibreglass carrot, celebrating its position at the heart of one of the nation's prime market-gardening regions. This is easily forgotten once you're in town among the chalet-style lodges and ski-rental shops geared to cope with the influx of winter-sports enthusiasts who descend from mid-June to around the end of October for the ski season. Outside these months Ohakune has traditionally been quiet, but restaurants and bars are increasingly open

---

OHAKUNE OUTDOOR ACTIVITIES

During winter, the most popular activity is **skiing** and **snowboarding** at Turoa (see box, p.298). There are numerous **walks** around Ohakune, most listed in the *Walks in and around Tongariro National Park* brochure ($3); the best are detailed below. Tracks can be slippery, so check conditions in advance, especially in winter. Most tracks are off-limits for **mountain biking**, although you can coast down Ohakune Mountain Rd (1000m descent in 17km).

WALKS

Lake Surprise (9km return; 5hr) Tackle an undulating section of the Round the Mountain track (see p.302) to a shallow lake, from the trailhead at the 15km mark on Ohakune Mountain Road. The hike passes evidence of volcanic debris which swept down the mountain during the 1975 and 1995 eruptions.

Mangawhero Forest Walk (3km loop; 1hr) The pick of Ohakune's shorter trails following a well-marked loop through the bush from the bottom of Ohakune Mountain Road.

Old Coach Road (11km; 3hr one-way) Excellent easy walking and mountain-bike path that combines beautiful native bush, long views over farmland and a disused tunnel with a good deal of history, all explained on wayside panels. From the end of Marshalls Rd, 2km northwest of Ohakune Junction, the route partly follows a track which, for a couple of years from 1906, allowed Auckland–Wellington rail passengers to link up the then incomplete line. Today, a highlight of the road is the spindly 290m-long Hopuruwhenua Viaduct (part of the original rail route but abandoned by line straightening in the 1980s), which was briefly the site of A.J. Hackett's first commercial bungy operation in 1987. The website **ⓦ** ohakune coachroad.co.nz has background information, including some great historic photos. DOC also has information on the route.

Waitonga Falls Walk (4km return; 1hr 20min) Moderate bushwalk to a spectacular 39m waterfall, starting 11km up Ohakune Mountain Road.

HORSE RIDING

Ruapehu Homestead 4km east of town on SH49 **☎** 027 267 7057. If the area's more strenuous activities aren't to your taste, then let horses do the work on rides lasting anywhere from one to two and a half hours. Riders can choose from forest or open farmland routes. Rates start at $40/hr.

MOUNTAIN BIKING

TCB 27 Ayr St **☎** 06 385 8433, **ⓦ** tcbskiandboard .co.nz. Rents mountain bikes from $50/day from Nov–June. Matai Shuttles (see p.302) will take you and your bike to the top for $20.

4

year-round to cater to summer visitors here to **hike** the Old Coach Road, get bussed to the Tongariro Alpine Crossing or prepare for the Whanganui River journey (see p.242).

ARRIVAL AND DEPARTURE   OHAKUNE

By train The Auckland–Wellington rail line passes through Ohakune Junction, at the town's northern edge. The train station is on Thames St.
Destinations Auckland (3–7 weekly; 6hr 30min); Wellington (3–7 weekly; 5hr 30min).

By bus InterCity buses on the Hamilton–Taumarunui–Wanganui run (daily) stop close to the i-SITE in Central Ohakune, 2km to the southwest of the train station.
Destinations Auckland (2 daily; 6hr 30min); Wellington (2 daily; 4hr 30min); see p.302 for regional shuttles.

GETTING AROUND

By shuttle bus Matai Shuttles, 61 Clyde St (☎ 0800 462 824, ⓦ mataishuttles.co.nz), provides transport around town, including a night shuttle during the ski season

between Ohakune town centre and Ohakune Junction (daily 6pm until the last bar shuts; $5 one-way).

INFORMATION

i-SITE & DOC 54 Clyde St (i-SITE daily 9am–5pm; DOC hours vary but it's open at least Wed–Sun 9am–5pm; ☎ 06 385 8427, ⓦ visitruapehu.com).

Services Internet access is available at PeppaTree ($5/hr), opposite the i-SITE.

ACCOMMODATION

Ohakune has stacks of **places to stay**, though several of them close outside the ski season and are packed once the snows arrive; prices get hiked up by around thirty percent more than those quoted here at this time. Many places have a minimum two-night stay, especially during weekends. Those arriving by bus will find it more convenient to stay in the main town rather than Ohakune Junction.

Hobbit Motor Lodge 80 Goldfinch St ☎ 06 385 8248, ⓦ the-hobbit.co.nz. Situated midway between the town and Ohakune Junction, with motel-style amenities, including an outdoor spa. Bed down in backpacker dorms, basic through to en-suite studios, or self-contained units. Dorms $25, studios $85, en-suite cabins $140, motel units $210

Ohakune Top 10 Holiday Park 5 Moore St ☎ 06 385 8561, ⓦ ohakune.net.nz. A well-kept and central campsite with a pleasant bush-girt setting. Camping $30, cabins $67, en-suite cabins $140, motel units $210

Powderhorn Chateau 194 Mangawhero Terrace, at base of Ohakune Mountain Rd, Ohakune Junction ☎ 06 385 8888, ⓦ powderhorn.co.nz. Hotel in an immense log cabin, with spacious, cosy rooms (the best with balcony and forest views), plus a large indoor hot pool. $240

★ **Rimu Park Lodge** 27 Rimu St, Ohakune Junction ☎ 06 385 9023, ⓦ rimupark.co.nz. One of the most comprehensive choices, this 1914 villa contains six-bunk dorms and doubles. Along with a hot tub, the grounds are dotted with simple cabins, en-suite units, two railway carriages fitted out as self-contained units with separate lounge and sleeping quarters, some classy modern apartments and a fully self-contained chalet. Dorms $35, rooms $90, cabins $80, units $130, carriages $190, apartments $170, chalet $320

The River Lodge 206 Mangawhero River Rd ☎ 06 385 4771, ⓦ theriverlodge.co.nz. Appealing lodge rooms and

two cabins (most with mountain views) in a wonderfully peaceful parkland setting with mature native beech trees beside a small trout river. Well-appointed rooms are complemented by lounge areas, DVDs, books and games, and an outdoor spa pool. Continental breakfast is included and, with prior arrangement, you can have dinner ($55 including a glass of wine). Look for signs 5km out on the road to Raetihi. Lodge rooms $120, chalets $160

Station Lodge 60 Thames St ☎ 06 385 8797, ⓦ stationlodge.co.nz. In the heart of the wintertime action at Ohakune Junction, this popular, well-equipped lodge has backpacker dorms through to chalets, and great facilities including an outdoor spa and free town bikes, plus on-site mountain-bike, ski and snowboard rental. Dorms $27, doubles $54, units $100, chalets $200

Whare Ora 1 Kaha St, Rangataua ☎ 06 385 9385, ⓦ whareoralodge.co.nz. Lovely, woodsy B&B with amiable hosts, in a large house 5km east of Ohakune. The downstairs room has a spa bath and overlooks a lovely garden while the immense upstairs suite comes with unsurpassed mountain views. Delicious three-course dinners are available on request ($80 including wine). $255

YHA LKNZ Backpackers 1 Rata St, Ohakune Central ☎ 06 385 9169, ⓦ localknowledgenz.com. Decent YHA-affiliated hostel with all manner of rooms and games areas. The owners are full of enthusiasm for the outdoors and run shuttles to help you access it. Dorms $25, en-suite doubles $79

EATING, DRINKING AND NIGHTLIFE

During the ski season, Ohakune Junction is *the* happening place to spend your evenings, with a string of busy bars, while in summer the focus switches to central Ohakune.

The Bearing Point 55 Clyde St, central Ohakune ☎ 06 385 9006. The locals' hangout, favoured for its internationally inspired dishes such as vegetarian korma, dukkah-coated chicken with couscous and Thai seafood curry (mains $27–38), and its relaxed bar. Tues–Sun 6pm–late.

Cyprus Tree 19a Goldfinch St, central Ohakune ☎ 06 385 8857, ⓦ thecyprustree.co.nz. Leather sofas and a roaring fire set the tone for this café/bar/restaurant doing a modern take on classic Italian dishes – antipasto platters and bruschetta followed by pasta, risotto, pizza (mains $22–31), plus a couple of steak and fish dishes and desserts. Winter: Mon–Thurs dinner from 4pm, Fri & Sat brunch, lunch and dinner from 10am; Summer: Mon, Thurs & Friday dinner from 5pm, Sat & Sun brunch and dinner.

Italian Café & Restaurant 55 Clyde St, central Ohakune ☎ 06 385 8346. Dishes up authentic Italian cuisine, from pastas including cannelloni, linguini and traditional lasagne to *scallopinne masala* (finely sliced pork flambéed in masala wine), chicken cacciatore and daily-changing home-made desserts. Daily 5pm–late.

Matterhorn Powderhorn Chateau (see opposite). The chateau's fine-dining option has beamed ceilings and delivers superb food such as five-spice duck breast (mains $27–36) in a refined but relaxed atmosphere. Seasonally by reservation.

Powderkeg Powderhorn Chateau (see opposite). With a woodsy après-ski feel, this casual (and usually jumping) brasserie/bar is always good for burgers and pizzas, as well as a short but stellar selection of mains ($24–32) including fish and vegetarian options. Daily 7am–late.

Utopia 47 Clyde St, central Ohakune ☎ 06 385 9120. There's a European theme at this casual daytime spot for an extensive range of breakfasts, light lunches such as Portuguese-style sardines and the town's best espresso (mains $9.50–19.50). Daily 9am–3pm.

The Desert Road

South of Turangi, SH1 sticks to the east of the Tongariro National Park running roughly parallel to the Tongariro River. This is the eerily scenic **Desert Road** (SH1), which traverses the exposed and barren Rangipo Desert – not a true desert (it gets too much rainfall), but kept arid by the free-draining blanket of volcanic ash and pumice. Road cuttings slice through several metres of the stuff, leaving a timeline of past eruptions. Snow can close the road in winter – keep tabs on the weather before you set out. The Desert Road and the roads flanking the western side of Ruapehu, Ngauruhoe and Tongariro meet at **WAIOURU**, an uninspiring row of service stations and tearooms perched 800m above sea level on the bleak tussock plain beside New Zealand's major **army base**, home to New Zealand's National Army Museum.

Tree Trunk Gorge

14km south of Turangi, down Tree Trunk Gorge Rd

Tree Trunk Gorge Road leads down to the Tongariro River at a spot where it squeezes and churns through a narrow fissure known as **Tree Trunk Gorge**. Back on the highway you soon climb out of the pine forest for great views of the three volcanoes off to the west and the blasted territory ahead. It is a dramatic scene, somehow made even more elemental by the three lines of electricity pylons striding off across the bleak tussock towards Waiouru.

The National Army Museum

SH1, at Hassett Drive, Waiouru • Daily 9am–4.30pm • $15 • ☎ 06 387 6911, ⓦ armymuseum.co.nz

Concrete bunkers house the **National Army Museum**, where the *Roimata Pounamu* ("Tears on Greenstone") **wall of remembrance** comprises water (symbolizing mourning and cleansing) streaming down a curving bank of heavily veined greenstone tiles while a recorded voice recites the name, rank and place of death of each of the roughly 33,000 New Zealanders who have died in the various wars. The chronologically arranged exhibits are manageable in scale but detailed enough to give coverage of the campaigns, the affecting human stories behind them and the smaller details such as the display on the warrior flags Maori fought under during the New Zealand Wars of the 1860s. Accounts of the bungled Gallipoli campaign of World War I come complete with an instructive model of Anzac Cove. Nursing during World War II gets equal billing with coverage of POWs incarcerated not just in Germany but also Singapore as New Zealand's world focus begins to shift towards Asia, and eventually the Vietnam War. Allow around an hour and a half to take it all in.

There's an interesting **discovery centre** for the kids, and the museum **café** is about the best around.

Taihape and around

In the 30km south of Waiouru you drop down off the volcanic plateau into the farming service town of **TAIHAPE** in the heart of the Rangitikei District. The main reason to stop is its proximity to the hilly country to the east, which hides one of New Zealand's most thrilling whitewater-rafting trips and the North Island's highest bungy jump.

Taihape promotes itself as "New Zealand's Gumboot Capital" with a corrugated iron boot sculpture and an annual **Gumboot Day** (mid-March), a tongue-in-cheek celebration of this archetypal Kiwi footwear with a gumboot-throwing competition.

Gravity Canyon

332 Mokai Rd; turn off SH1 at Utiku and follow signs east; or follow gravel backroads from River Valley • Daily 10am–4pm • Bungy jump $179; bungy lift only $40; flying fox $155; bridge swing $159 • ☎ 0800 802 864, ⓦ gravitycanyon.co.nz

Some adventure seekers may want to skip the rafting thrills nearby and instead head straight to Gravity Canyon. Here you'll find an 80m **bungy jump**, the country's longest and fastest **flying fox** (175m high, 1km long), on which you reach speeds of up to 160km/hr, and a **bridge swing** ($159) offering 50m of freefall. The bungy has a unique and rather pleasant water-powered lift to get you back to the bridge.

ARRIVAL AND DEPARTURE   TAIHAPE

By bus InterCity buses stop on Kuku St, around the corner from the Information Centre, while NakedBus stops at *Gumboot Manor* restaurant at the northern end of town. Destinations Auckland (4 daily; 7hr); Taupo (5 daily; 2hr); Turangi (5 daily; 1hr 10min); Wellington (5 daily; 4hr).

By train The train station is one block west of the Information Centre on Robin St.
Destinations Auckland (3–7 weekly; 7hr 30min); Wellington (3–7 weekly; 4hr 20min).

INFORMATION AND TOURS

Tourist information 90–92 Hautapu St (daily 9am–5pm; ☎ 06 388 0604, ⓦ taihape.co.nz). The Information Centre is inside the library; information on the region is also available at ⓦ rangitikei.com.

RAFTING THE RANGITIKEI RIVER

The Grade V gorge section of the **Rangitikei River** is one of the toughest **whitewater-rafting** rivers in the country, with ten major rapids packed into a two- to three-hour run. Trips are run from Mangaweka (see opposite), or more directly from *River Valley*, an adventure lodge right beside the river.

OUTFITTERS

River Valley 30km east of Taihape ☎ 06 388 1444, ⓦ rivervalley.co.nz. Morning, and occasionally afternoon, trips ($169) are run throughout the year. There are also scenic rafting trips ($169/5hr) down the quieter Grade II section immediately downstream of the lodge, plus a range of multiday trips. For information on accommodation at River Valley, see opposite.

Mangaweka Adventure Company SH1, Mangaweka village ☎ 0800 655 747, ⓦ mangaweka .co.nz. Offers a number of whitewater-rafting and kayaking trips including the Rangitikei Grade V Gorge trip ($180) and a couple of family-oriented rafting trips and multiday trips from ($199 including meals), with camping beside the river. For information on camping here, see opposite.

River Valley ☎ 06 388 1444, ⓦ rivervalley.co.nz. Offers excellent horse-trekking trips ($109/2hr) which head over farmland and provide great views across the rugged country hereabouts.

ACCOMMODATION

★ **River Valley** Pukoekahu ☎ 06 388 1444, ⓦ rivervalley.co.nz. Visitors to the adventure lodge best known for its rafting trips (see box opposite) camp, stay in six-bunk dorms (linen provided), pleasant rooms, or very comfortable en-suite cabins. Kiwi Experience buses call nightly. There's a self-catering kitchen or straightforward low-cost meals (using organic produce from the garden) and a bar. Everyone also has free access to pétanque and volleyball and (for a small fee) a wood sauna, an infrared sauna (with coloured lighting and music), a spa pool with views of the river and massage in summer. Camping $18, dorms $31, rooms $75, en-suite cabins $169

Safari Motel 18 Mataroa Rd ☎ 06 388 1116, ⓦ safarimotel.co.nz. The NakedBus stops opposite this clean, uncluttered motel 1km north of town on SH1, but they'll also pick up from the visitor centre. Larger studios have kitchenettes, as do the one-bedroom apartments. Rooms $80, apartments $120

Taihape Motels Kuku St, at Robin St ☎ 06 388 0456, ⓦ taihapemotels.co.nz. Spotless rooms at this bargain-priced central motel have comfy queen- or king-size beds; there are also three holiday flats sleeping up to eight people (call for rates). Rooms $65

EATING AND DRINKING

Brown Sugar Café Huia St ☎ 06 388 1880. Cottage-like café with a tempting blackboard menu of grilled brie and chicken, vegetable samosas and big Greek salads (dishes $10–17). Daily 7am–3.30pm.

Soul Food Café 69 Hautapu St ☎ 06 388 0176. Big breakfasts (including pancakes, corn fritters and a "farmers brekkie" of mince meat on grain toast with relish) are served all day at this popular spot ($10.50–18.80); salads, pastas, fish and chips and burgers are lunchtime mainstays. Friday night is pizza night. Sat–Thurs 8am–4pm, Fri 8am–8pm.

Mangaweka

SH1, 24km south of Taihape

A DC3 aeroplane (and sign reading "Mangaweka International Airport") marks the dilapidated hamlet of **MANGAWEKA**, headquarters of the Mangaweka Adventure Company, which offers a number of **whitewater-rafting** and **kayaking** trips (see box opposite).

ACCOMMODATION

MANGAWEKA

Mangaweka Adventure Company 1km east of SH1 ☎ 0800 655 747, ⓦ mangaweka.co.nz. A lovely, simple campsite with some riverside pitches, swimming and $2 showers, with accommodation and a bar in the works – check the website for updates. Camping $7, powered camping $9

4

The
Coromandel,
Bay of Plenty
and the
East Cape

314 The Hauraki Plains

319 The Coromandel
Peninsula

343 The Bay of Plenty

360 The East Cape

CATHEDRAL COVE, COROMANDEL PENINSULA

5

The Coromandel, Bay of Plenty and the East Cape

The long sweep of bays and peninsulas east of Auckland is split into three distinct areas, some of the most beguiling coastal strips in the country. Visitors and locals flock to the jagged Coromandel Peninsula, its volcanic spine cloaked in rainforest and its edges nibbled by endless rugged coves and sweeping golden beaches. Its coast blends into the Bay of Plenty, strung by yet more beaches and dotted with islands, notably the fuming, volcanic White Island. Further east, the East Cape is one of the least-visited parts of the country where time virtually stands still and life is measured by the rhythm of the land. This is the most intensely Maori part of the country, but as far away from the performance-and-hangi shtick of Rotorua as you could imagine.

Coromandel-bound from Auckland you'll cut across the dairy country of the **Hauraki Plains** at the foot of the Coromandel Peninsula, with a few pleasant surprises. In the spa town of **Te Aroha** you can luxuriate in a private soda bath, while near **Paeroa** there are walks in the lush **Karangahake Gorge**, once the scene of intensive gold mining.

Jutting north, the only half-tamed **Coromandel Peninsula** is an area of spectacular coastal scenery, offering walks to pristine beaches and tramps in luxuriant mountainous rainforest. Its two coasts are markedly different. The west has a more rugged and atmospheric coastline, and easier access to the volcanic hills and ancient kauri trees of the **Coromandel Forest** – best explored from historic **Thames**, and from quaint **Coromandel**, set in rolling hills beside a pretty harbour. On the east coast, **Whangamata** and **Whitianga** offer a plethora of water activities and long sandy beaches. Whitianga is also handy for **Hot Water Beach**, where natural thermal springs bubble through the sand, and the crystalline **Cathedral Cove Marine Reserve**, ideal for dolphin spotting and snorkelling.

From the open-cast gold-mining town of **Waihi**, at the base of the Coromandel Peninsula, the **Bay of Plenty** sweeps south and east to Opotiki, traced along its length by the Pacific Coast Highway (SH2). The bay earned its name in 1769 from **Captain Cook**, who was impressed by the Maori living off its abundant resources and by the generous supplies they gave him – an era of peace shattered by the **New Zealand Wars** of the 1860s, when fierce fighting led to the establishment of garrisons at Tauranga and Whakatane.

Kauaeranga walks p.325
The Coromandel Walkway p.331
Cook plants the flag p.333
Tours and activities around Whitianga and Mercury Bay p.337
Kiwifruit-picking p.343
Tuhua (Mayor Island) p.344
Activities around Tauranga and Mount Maunganui p.348

Offshore Whakatane p.356
The Hau Hau p.357
Opotiki tours and activities p.359
Legends of the East Cape Maori p.362
East Cape manuka oil p.364
Cape Runaway to Waipiro Bay tours and activities p.365

RUAKOKORE CHURCH, EAST CAPE

Highlights

❶ Te Aroha Rejuvenate in the geyser-fed hot soda springs in this charming Edwardian spa town at the foot of Mount Te Aroha. **See p.317**

❷ Kauaeranga Valley Hike past gold-mining remains as you work your way through a jagged landscape of bluffs and gorges to the Pinnacles overlooking both Coromandel Peninsula coasts. **See p.325**

❸ Driving Creek Railway One man's desire to more easily obtain clay for his pots has turned into this modern narrow-gauge railway through rich Coromandel bush to a wonderful viewpoint. **See p.327**

❹ Hot Water Beach Grab a shovel, stake your spot and dig into the sand to wallow in surfside hot springs. **See p.336**

❺ Glowworm kayaking Take to the water at dusk and paddle into a leafy wonderland gorge studded with pinpricks of blue-green light. **See p.348**

❻ White Island Visit the otherworldly moonscape and sulphur deposits of New Zealand's most active volcano. **See p.356**

❼ The East Cape Rugged, isolated and solidly Maori, this little-visited region is the place to connect with the land and its people. **See p.360**

HIGHLIGHTS ARE MARKED ON THE MAP ON PP.314–315

5

The Bay of Plenty has the best **climate** on the North Island, making it a fertile fruit-growing region (particularly citrus and kiwifruit). The coast, though popular with Kiwi holidaymakers, has remained relatively unspoiled, offering great surf beaches and other offshore activities. The western bay is home to one of the country's fastest-growing urban areas, centred on **Tauranga** and the contiguous beach town of **Mount Maunganui**. The east revolves around **Whakatane**, the launching point for boat excursions to active **White Island**, as well as dolphin swimming and wilderness rafting on the **Motu River**.

Contrasting with these two regions is the rugged and sparsely populated **East Cape**. With a dramatic coastline backed by the **Waiapu Mountains**, a rich and varied Maori history and great hospitality, this isolated region provides a taste of a more traditional way of life.

The Hauraki Plains

The fertile **Hauraki Plains** stretch southeast from the Coromandel Peninsula forming a low-lying former swamp-turned-farming region which, in typically laconic Kiwi fashion, describes itself as "flat out and loving it". The Firth of Thames, the final destination for a number of meandering rivers, borders it to the north.

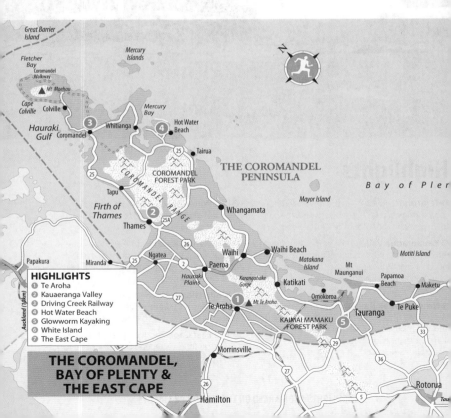

HIGHLIGHTS
1. Te Aroha
2. Kauaeranga Valley
3. Driving Creek Railway
4. Hot Water Beach
5. Glowworm Kayaking
6. White Island
7. The East Cape

THE COROMANDEL, BAY OF PLENTY & THE EAST CAPE

The hub of the plains is **Paeroa**, not much in itself but handy for walks in the magnificent **Karangahake Gorge**, running almost to Waihi.

The real gem hereabouts is **Te Aroha**, a delightful Edwardian spa town (little more than a village) at the southern extremity of the plains, where you can hike Mount Te Aroha and soak afterwards in natural hot soda springs.

Paeroa

PAEROA, 120km southeast of Auckland, is "World Famous in New Zealand" as the birthplace of **Lemon and Paeroa** (L&P), an iconic home-grown soft drink founded in 1907 using the local mineral water (though it is now made elsewhere by Coca-Cola). It's pretty artificial-tasting but more lemony than *Sprite* and the likes. The L&P logo is emblazoned on shopfronts throughout town and there's a giant brown L&P bottle at the junction of SH2 and SH26.

ARRIVAL AND DEPARTURE
PAEROA

By bus InterCity and NakedBus both stop outside the Information Centre on their Auckland–Tauranga run. Turley-Murphy (☎ 07 884 8208) runs a service between Hamilton and Whitianga via Te Aroha, Paeroa and Thames.

Destinations Auckland (2 daily; 2hr 30min); Hamilton (2 daily; 1hr 30min); Te Aroha (daily; 20min); Thames (2 daily; 20min); Whitianga (daily; 2hr 30min).

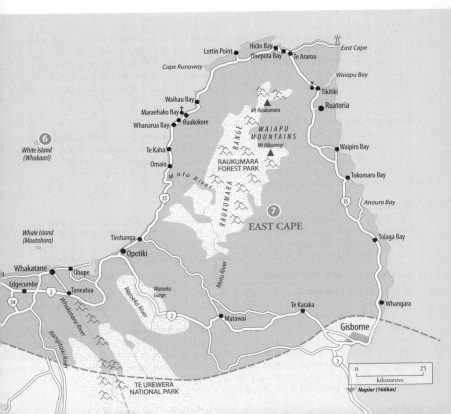

5

INFORMATION

Tourist information The Paeroa Information Centre is on the corner of SH2 and Seymour St (daily 9am–4pm). Apart from telling you how you can spend your time in Paeroa, the information centre also sells L&P souvenirs.

EATING AND DRINKING

L&P Café & Bar Corner of SH2 and Seymour St ☎07 862 7773, ⓦlpcafe.co.nz. Sells L&P-flavoured ice cream as well as filling breakfast, lunch and dinner highway-stop fare such as eggs Benedict ($13.80), Caesar salad ($14.50) and gourmet burgers (from $15.40). Mon–Tues 8.30am–3pm, Wed–Sat 8.30am–8.30pm, Sun 8.30am–8pm.

Karangahake Gorge

SH2, 8km east of Paeroa

Karangahake Gorge was the scene of the Coromandel's first gold rush, though in this leafy cleft it's hard to envisage the frenetic activity that took place around the turn of the twentieth century. The steep-sided gorge snakes along SH2 as it traces the Ohinemuri River to Waihi.

The largest (though still tiny) settlement is **Karangahake**, where a car park marks the start of several excellent walks along the rivers and around old gold-mining ruins. They range from twenty minutes to several hours and are detailed in DOC's *Karangahake Gorge* leaflet. Beyond, minuscule **Waikino** is the western terminus of the Goldfields Railway (see p.342).

Karangahake Tunnel Loop Walk

3km; 45min; mostly flat

At Karangahake, a pedestrian suspension bridge crosses the river to join a **loop walk**, heading upstream beside the Ohinemuri River, past remnants of the gold workings and the foundations of stamper batteries, hugging the cliffs and winding through regenerating native bush. You complete the loop by crossing the river and walking through a 1km-long tunnel (partially but adequately lit), where you can spot glowworms.

Karangahake Gorge Historic Walkway

To explore the length of the gorge, follow the **Karangahake Gorge Historic Walkway** that covers 7km of a former rail line right through the gorge as far east as the *Waikino Station Café*. One section is shared by the Karangahake Tunnel Loop Walk (see above) and the full length has been made suitable for bikes as part of the National Cycle Network though there is no convenient bike rental as yet.

Victoria Battery

The stumpy remains of the **Victoria Battery** mark the eastern end of Karangahake Gorge. The area's gold ore was processed here from 1897 until 1952, using up to 200 stamps to crush 800 tonnes a day, at one stage making it the largest such site in the country. Explanatory panels clarify the mysterious-looking concrete foundations.

ACCOMMODATION AND EATING   KARANGAHAKE GORGE

★ **Bistro at The Falls Retreat** 25 Waitawheta Rd, opposite Owharoa Falls ☎07 863 8770, ⓦfallsretreat .co.nz. Sit in the shade under the trees, or in the rustic modern cottage at this delightfully peaceful café and restaurant that whips up a fine thin-crust, wood-fired pizza ($20), lunches of creamy leek and chicken pie with salad ($16) and dinner mains such as seafood bisque with garlic and chilli poached mussels, shrimps and calamari ($29). Leave space for a delectable dessert. They also have an equally peaceful self-catering cottage. Restaurant: Jan & Feb daily 11am–10pm, March–Dec Wed–Sun 11am–10pm. $125

Golden Owl Lodge 3 Moresby Rd, Karangahake ☎07 862 7994, ⓦgoldenowl.co.nz. Chilled backpackers in a modern house and handy for all the walks, with a spacious lounge, kitchen with dishwasher, book exchange, board games and an assortment of twins and doubles. Dorms $29, room $62, en suite $75

Ohinemuri Estate Winery and Café 21 Moresby St ☏ 07 862 8874, ⓦ ohinemuri.co.nz. Peaceful winery, restaurant and lodging where you can sample the wines (made here with grapes grown elsewhere), tuck into Mediterranean-accented café fare including tasting platters ($40–45), and stay in a self-contained hayloft apartment sleeping four. Restaurant: daily 10am–5pm; closed Mon & Tues in winter. $115

Waikino Station Café SH2, 13km east of Paeroa ☏ 07 863 8640. The original Waikino train station (still served by the Goldfields Railway from Waihi) makes a superb setting for this good café with great old photos and a roaring fire in winter. Expect breakfasts and burgers ($10–16) plus cakes and coffee. Daily 9.30am–4pm.

Te Aroha

On the fringes of the Hauraki Plains, the small town of **TE AROHA**, 21km south of Paeroa, is home to New Zealand's only intact **Edwardian spa**. In a quiet way it is a delightful spot, hunkered beneath the imposing bush-clad slopes of the **Kaimai-Mamaku Forest Park**. The 954m **Mount Te Aroha** rears up immediately behind the neat little town centre, providing a reasonably challenging goal for hikers.

Everything of interest – banks, post office, library – is on or close to Whitaker Street, its old-fashioned feel enhanced by an old air-raid **siren** which sounds daily at 8am, 1pm and 5pm: some people still measure their day by it.

Brief history

The town was founded in 1880 at the furthest navigable extent of the Waihou River. A year later, rich deposits of gold were discovered on Mount Te Aroha, sparking a full-scale **gold rush** until 1921. Within a few months of settlement, the new townsfolk set out the attractive **Hot Springs Domain**, 44 acres of gardens and rose beds around a cluster of **hot soda springs** which, by the 1890s, had become New Zealand's most popular mineral spa complex. Enclosures were erected for privacy, most rebuilt in grand style during the Edwardian years. The fine suite of original buildings has been restored and integrated with more modern pools fed by the springs and nearby **Mokena Geyser**.

Mokena Spa Baths

Hot Springs Domain • Mon–Thurs 10.30am–9pm; Fri–Sun 10.30am–10pm • $18/person for 30min, minimum 2 people; advance bookings essential • ☏ 07 884 8717, ⓦ tearohaspa.co.nz

Te Aroha's centrepiece is the well-signposted **Mokena Spa Baths** where the silky-smooth mineral waters of the Mokena Geyser are channelled into private, enclosed pools, usually kept at 40°C though you can adjust the temperature. Choose a king-size claw-foot slipper bath if you fancy adding aromatherapy oils; otherwise go for one of the six, bubbling cedar tubs good for up to eight. A half-hour soak in the hot, naturally carbonated water is plenty. Not only will your skin feel gloriously soft (don't shower directly afterwards) but it's claimed that the alkaline waters extract polluting heavy metals from your system and ease arthritis. Fear of people fainting and drowning means you're not permitted to enter the baths alone. Assorted pampering and massage treatments are also available.

Te Aroha Leisure Pools

Hot Springs Domain • Mon–Fri 10am–5.45pm, Sat & Sun 10am–6.45pm • $6.50 all day plus $2 for the spa • ☏ 07 884 4498, ⓦ tearohapools.co.nz

There's a family feel to the outdoor **Te Aroha Leisure Pools** where regular town water is chlorinated and kept at around 32°C in the 20m-long main pool and around 38°C in the spa. There's also a toddlers' pool and, nearby, a free 36°C **foot-spa** that's perfect for a bit of pampering at the end of a Mount Te Aroha hike. A decent **café** occupies an adjacent timber cottage with views over the Domain.

Mokena Geyser

Hot Springs Domain

Just uphill from the Mokena Spa Baths is the erratic **Mokena Geyser** – said to be the world's only hot soda geyser – which goes off roughly every forty minutes to a height

5

of four metres – on a good day. Due to its spa-feeding duties it doesn't always spurt to an impressive height – the best time to catch it in action each day is between noon and 2pm.

Te Aroha and District Museum

Daily: Nov– Easter 11am–4pm; Easter–Oct noon–3pm • $4 • ☎ 07 884 4427, ⊕ tearoha-museum.com

An old sanatorium, just below the spa baths in front of the croquet lawn, houses the exhibit-packed town **museum**. Highlights include two finely decorated Royal Doulton Victorian lavatories, a chemical analysis of the local soda water, an early linotype machine, and over three hundred pieces of souvenir porcelain from around the world.

St Mark's Anglican Church

Corner of Church and Kenrick sts • Often open during the day; call ahead • ☎ 07 884 8728

By the Boundary Street exit from the Domain you'll find the 1926 **St Mark's Anglican Church**, insignificant but for the incongruous 1712 organ, brought to New Zealand in 1926 and said to be the oldest in the southern hemisphere. Organ demonstrations can be arranged; ask at the i-SITE or call.

Mount Te Aroha

Immediately east of the Hot Springs Domain

The town edges up onto the lower slopes of **Mount Te Aroha** (952m), the top of which, legend has it, was named by a young Arawa chief, Kahumatamomoe, who climbed it after losing his way in the region's swamp while making for Maketu in the Bay of Plenty. Delighted to see the familiar shoreline of his homeland, he called the mountain Te Aroha, "love", in honour of his father and kinsmen. There are enough **trails** to keep you entertained for a day or so; two of the best are Bald Spur Track and Summit Track.

Bald Spur Track

3km return; 1hr 30min; 900m ascent

The most rewarding short hike is the there-and-back tramp from the Hot Springs Domain up through a lovely puriri and fern grove, climbing fairly steeply to a bench and lookout point known as Whakapipi or Bald Spur. With great views across the town and farmland beyond, it is particularly good before breakfast or towards sunset.

Summit Track

8km return; 4–6hr; 900m ascent

This thigh-burning ascent builds on the Bald Spur walk, continuing steeply up into the Kaimai-Mamaku Forest Park and gradually getting rougher to the TV transmitter at the top. The reward (at least on a fine day) is a 360-degree view, as far as Ruapehu and Taranaki. Return by the same route or the longer **Tui Mine Track** (extra 1–2hr) via old mine workings.

ARRIVAL AND INFORMATION

TE AROHA

By bus Services on Hamilton's Busit network (☎ 0800 428 748, ⊕ busit.co.nz) stop outside the i-SITE.
Destinations Hamilton (2 daily; 1hr 5min); Paeroa (1 daily; 20min).

i-SITE 102 Whitaker St, by the Domain (Mon–Fri 9.30am–5pm, Sat & Sun 9.30am–4pm; ☎ 07 884 8052 ⊕ tearohanz.co.nz). Get local and DOC information here along with leaflets outlining rewarding day walks in the area

GETTING AROUND

By bike Outdoor Adventure, 176a Whitaker St (Mon–Fri 8.30am–5pm, Sat 9am–noon; ☎ 07 884 4545, ⊕ outdoor

adventure.co.nz), rents mountain bikes: $10/hr or $35/day Ask about the fun local MTB trails.

ACCOMMODATION

Aroha Mountain Lodge 5 Boundary St ☎ 07 884 8134, ⓦ arohamountainlodge.co.nz. Opt for comfortable rooms in a pair of villas right next to the Hot Springs Domain, or one of two cottages sleeping six nearby. Go out for breakfast or pay an extra $20 a head to eat in. Doubles $135, cottages $275

Te Aroha Holiday Park 217 Stanley Rd, 3km south, off the road to Hamilton ☎ 07 884 9567, ⓦ tearoha holidaypark.co.nz. Well-maintained site set among shady oaks, with a mineral water rock pool (open evenings), a large summer-only swimming pool and an eclectic range of mis-matched cabins and tourist flats that have accumulated here over the decades. Camping $12, on-site vans $48, cabins $48, tourist flats $85

YHA Te Aroha Miro St, off Brick St ☎ 07 884 8739, ⓦ yha.co.nz. One of the oldest and simplest YHAs in New Zealand, this hostel in a heart-warmingly cosy wooden cottage has remained virtually unchanged since it opened in the early 1960s. Set on the lower slopes of Mount Te Aroha, there are lovely views from the hammocks strung beneath the kanuka trees, and free bikes. Dorms $23, double room $56

EATING

Banco 174 Whitaker St ☎ 07 884 7574. This gracious former bank is an intriguing amalgam of good café, second-hand clothing shop and art gallery. It's always interesting and there's an attractive, sunny courtyard out back. Opt for coffee and cake, or try more substantial meals such as salmon caper pasta ($18) or ribeye fillet with mushroom ragout ($33). Daily 10am–5pm and Fri & Sat 6.30pm–late.

Berlusconi 149 Whitaker St ☎ 07 884 9307, ⓦ tearoha -info.co.nz/berlusconi. Te Aroha's top dining choice with something of a wine-bar atmosphere. Come for evening mains such as pan-fried snapper with vine tomatoes and blood-orange vinaigrette ($33), one of their fine pizzas ($27) or something a little lighter, and cheaper, at lunch. Wed 5.30–10pm, Thurs–Sun 11am–3pm & 5.30–10pm or later.

Ironique 159 Whitaker St ☎ 07 884 8489, ⓦ ironique .co.nz. Filled with quirky iron sculptures, this all-rounder is a good bet for brunches, snacks, and evening meals such as burger and chips ($19) or chicken in a spicy plum sauce ($29). Mon 8am–4.30pm, Tues–Fri 8am–10pm, Sat 9am–10pm, Sun 9am–4.30pm.

The Coromandel Peninsula

The Hauraki Gulf is separated from the Pacific Ocean by the mountainous, bush-cloaked **Coromandel Peninsula**, fringed with beautiful surf and swimming beaches and basking in a balmy climate.

Along the **west coast**, cliffs and steep hills drop sharply to the sea, leaving only a narrow coastal strip shaded by **pohutukawa** trees that erupt in a blaze of red from mid-November to early January. The beaches are sheltered and safe but most are only good for **swimming** when high tide obscures the mudflats. Most people prefer the sweeping white-sand beaches of the **east coast**, which are pounded by impressive but often perilous **surf**.

At the base of the peninsula, **Thames** showcases its gold-mining heritage and is the most convenient place from which to explore the forested **Kauaeranga Valley**'s walking tracks. Further north, **Coromandel town** offers the opportunity to ride the narrow-gauge **Driving Creek Railway** and is close to the scenic trans-peninsular 309 Road. For really remote country, however, head to **Colville** and beyond, to the peninsula's northern tip. The sealed SH25 continues east to **Mercury Bay**, centred on more populous **Whitianga**, near which you can dig a hole to wallow in the surfside hot springs that lure hundreds to **Hot Water Beach**, or snorkel in a gorgeous bay at **Cathedral Cove Marine Reserve**. Yet more beaches string the coast further south around **Whangamata** and **Waihi Beach**, the latter of which is separated from nearby **Waihi** by about 10km of farms and orchards.

If you're here between mid-November and early December you'll come across the **Pohutukawa Festival** (ⓦ pohutukawafestival.co.nz), during which the whole peninsula marks the crimson blooms of these distinctive coastal trees with picnics, wearable art competitions and music: look for posters and leaflets.

5

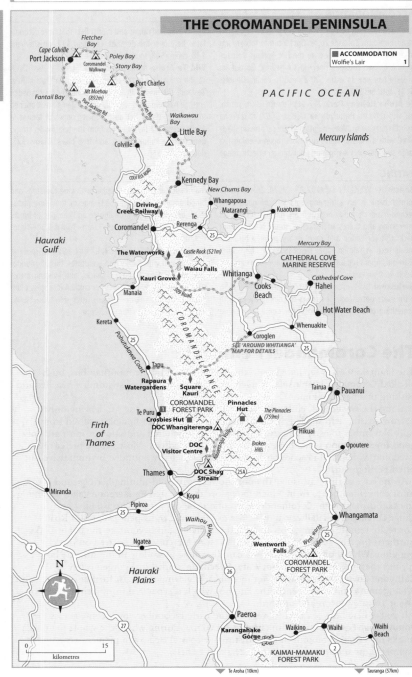

THE COROMANDEL PENINSULA

■ ACCOMMODATION
Wolfie's Lair 1

5

Brief history

The peninsula is divided lengthwise by the **Coromandel Range** – sculpted millions of years ago by volcanic activity, its contorted skyline clothed in dense rainforest. Local Maori interpret the range as a canoe, with **Mount Moehau** (the peninsula's northern tip) as its prow, and Mount Te Aroha in the south as its sternpost. The summit area of Mount Moehau is sacred, Maori-owned land, the legendary burial place of Tama Te Kapua, the commander of one of the Great Migration canoes, *Te Arawa*.

Except for the gold-rush years, the peninsula largely remained a backwater, and by the 1960s and 70s, the low property prices in declining former gold towns, combined with the juxtaposition of bush, hills and beaches, lured hippies, **artists** and New Agers. Most eked out a living from organic market gardens, or holistic healing centres and retreats, while painters, potters and **craftspeople**, some very good, hawked their work (i-SITEs have details of rural craft outlets all over the peninsula). These days much of the peninsula is a more commercial animal: increasingly Aucklanders are finding ways to live here permanently or commute, and are converting one-time *baches* into expensive designer properties, raising both the area's profile and the cost of living.

GETTING AROUND

By car Your own vehicle gives the most flexibility, and although many of the more remote roads are gravel, few pose any real danger. Just take it steady.

By bus The main services are: InterCity (☎ 09 583 5780, ⓦ intercity.co.nz), which provides a regular clockwise loop service from Thames north to Coromandel, across to Whitianga and back south and across to Thames; NakedBus ($2/min charge to call ☎ 0900 62533, ⓦ nakedbus.com), which runs from Whitianga to Ngatea where it connects with their Auckland–Tauranga service;

and Whitianga-based Go Kiwi (☎ 866 0336, ⓦ go-kiwi .co.nz) who run Whitianga to Auckland Airport and Auckland via Hahei, Tairua, Whangamata and Thames, and Whitianga (all 1 daily) then back again; also Fri & Sun between Whitianga and Coromandel and Whitianga to Tauranga and Rotorua (4–7 a week in summer).

By bike An excellent (if tiring) way to explore the Coromandel Peninsula is by bike, making a 3–4 day loop taking plenty of rests for swims. Try Paki Paki Bike Shop for rentals (see p.324).

ACCOMMODATION

Seasons and reservations As one of the North Island's principal holiday spots, the Coromandel Peninsula becomes the scene of frenetic activity from late Dec–Jan with little real relief until the end of March. Finding accommodation can become impossible – book as far ahead as you can, never less than a couple of days. Numbers are more manageable for the rest of the year (though long weekends fill quickly), and in winter much of the peninsula

is deserted, though the climate remains mild.

Camping The whole issue of limiting freedom camping really came to a head on the Coromandel Peninsula and rules are stricter here than elsewhere – and enforced. There are very few places where you can legally camp outside authorized campsites: search for freedom camping at ⓦ tcdc.govt.nz for the latest.

Thames

The Coromandel's gateway and main service hub, the historic former gold town of **THAMES** is packed into a narrow strip between the Firth of Thames and the Coromandel Range. It retains a refreshingly down-to-earth sense of community, and its range of accommodation, eateries, transport connections and generally lower prices make it a good starting point for forays further north.

Its gold legacy forms the basis of the town's appeal and you can spend half a day visiting the several museums, though they're all volunteer-run and, frustratingly, open at different times – summer weekends work out best.

Fans of Victorian **architecture** can spend a happy couple of hours wandering the streets aided by the maps in two free leaflets – *Historic Grahamstown* and *Historic Shortland & Tararu*.

5

Inland, the industrial heritage is all about kauri logging in the **Kauaeranga Valley**, a popular destination for hikers visiting the Coromandel Forest Park and easily accessible from town.

Brief history

Thames initially evolved as two towns: Grahamstown to the north, and Shortland to the south. The first big discovery of gold-bearing quartz was made in a creek-bed in 1867, and by 1871 Grahamstown had become the largest town in New Zealand with a population of around 20,000 and over 120 pubs, only a handful of which remain today. Due to the reliance on machinery (rather than less costly gold-panning), gold mining tailed off during the 1880s and had mostly finished by 1913. Little of significance has happened since, leaving a well-preserved streetscape.

Goldmine Experience

Corner SH25 and Moanataiari Creek Rd • Dec 26–March daily 10am–4pm; April–Dec 24 Sat & Sun 10am–1pm • $15 • ☎ 07 868 8514, Ⓦ goldmine-experience.co.nz

The only way to really get a sense of what it was like to be a miner in Thames is to visit the **Goldmine Experience**, built around an informative 40-minute tour underground along a narrow horizontal shaft originally cut by hand by Cornish miners. Topside, gold ore is crushed and the gold extracted when a stamper battery kicks into deafening gear. You can also pan for gold, while the historically inclined can watch a great video of miners at work, played in the 1914 office building.

School of Mines & Mineralogical Museum

Corner of Cochrane and Brown sts • Jan daily 11am–3pm; Feb–Dec Wed–Sun 11am–3pm • $5 • ☎ 07 868 6227

Adults with little or no mining experience flocked to Thames, and the more ambitious among them attended this **School of Mines**, which operated from 1886 until 1954 and was one of the most important in the country. Enthusiastic volunteers will show you around the ancient chemistry lab with its lovely precision balance and the public assay room – all crucibles, glass jars and a furnace – where miners could bring their ore for quality assessment. Most of what's here has been on-site since the glory days, including the vast collection of geologic samples in rows of glass cases.

Museum of Technology and Thames Historical Museum

Museum of Technology Corner of Bella St and Waiorakaraka Rd • Generally Sat & Sun 10am–3pm • $5 • ☎ 07 868 2141 • **Thames Historical Museum** • Corner of Cochrane and Pollen sts • Daily 1–4pm • $5

The vast machinery may be gone but this 1898 building (a.k.a. the Bella Street Pumphouse Museum) remains largely unchanged from when its pump helped keep most of Thames' mines dry. Excellent models and photos help interpret its pivotal role. Just up the road is the Thames Historical Museum, which covers the town's social history. Rooms in the old schoolhouse are set up as old miners' huts, there are tales of logging days, and a nice 1925 Simplex movie projector.

Butterfly and Orchid Garden

Dickson Holiday Park, 115 Victoria St, just off SH25, 3.5km north • Daily: Nov–Easter 10am–4pm; Easter to mid-June, Sept & Oct 10am–3pm • $11 • ☎ 07 868 8080, Ⓦ butterfly.co.nz

Spend a tranquil half-hour or so inside a tropical hothouse at the magical **Butterfly and Orchid Garden** amid the acrobatics of hundreds of butterflies. At any one time there are around twenty to thirty species here; because of the insects' short lifespan (roughly 2–3 weeks), the garden cycles through over 1000 of these exquisite winged creatures each month, about half imported as pupae, and half bred on-site.

THAMES

COROMANDEL FOREST PARK

1 (1.5km), 2 (2.5km), 3 (11km), Butterfly & Orchid Garden (2.5km), Coromandel (55km) & Whitianga (100km)

Goldmine Experience

WW1 Memorial & lookout

Historical Museum

Museum of Technology

School of Mines & Mineralogical Museum

Organic Co-op

Karaka Bird Hide

Pak 'n Save

Goldfields Mall

Firth of Thames

Kauaeranga Valley (13km)

Kauaeranga River

8 (2km) & 6 (4km)

ACCOMMODATION

Coastal Motor Lodge	1
Cotswold Cottage	8
Cruz 'n' Stop	5
Dickson Holiday Park	2
Gateway Backpackers	6
Rolleston Motel	7
Sunkist Backpackers	4
Wolfie's Lair	3

RESTAURANTS, CAFÉS & BARS

Brew	5
Food for Thought	4
Grahamstown Bar & Diner	3
Kopu Station Hotel	6
Speakeasy	1
Sola Café	2

ARRIVAL AND DEPARTURE

THAMES

By bus NakedBus and InterCity buses stop outside the i-SITE.
Destinations Auckland (5 daily; 2hr); Coromandel (1 daily; 1hr 15min); Tauranga (4 daily; 1hr 45min); Whitianga (2 daily; 1hr 40min).

INFORMATION AND TOURS

i-SITE 206 Pollen St (Nov–April Mon–Fri 8.30am–5pm, Sat & Sun 9am–4pm; May–Oct Mon–Fri 9am–5pm, Sat 9am–1pm, Sun noon–4pm; ☎ 07 868 7284, ⊛ thamesinfo .co.nz). Has internet access and sells bus tickets.

Canyoning To really get off the beaten track consider canyoning down the fabulous Sleeping God canyon with Canyonz (see p.114), whose trips begin in Auckland but pick up in Thames.

Eyezopen Adventure Co ☎ 07 868 9018, ⊛ eyezopen .co.nz. The people to see for local insight, self-guided Coromandel itineraries, guided mountain bike rides in the Kauaeranga Valley, guided overnight tramps to the Pinnacles and lots more.

5

GETTING AROUND

By bike Paki Paki Bike Shop, 535 Pollen St (📞07 867 9026, 🌐pakipakibikeshop.co.nz; Mon–Thurs 9am–5pm, Fri 9am–5.30pm, Sat 9am–1pm), have a couple of hybrid touring bikes ($25/day) ideal for getting around town or further afield (see p.321).

By bus *Sunkist Backpackers* (see below) run a shuttle service to the Kauaeranga Valley road end ($35 return; minimum 2 people).

By car Davy Rentals, 208 Pollen St (📞07 868 7153, 🌐davyrentals.co.nz; Mon–Fri 7.30am–5pm), has budget cars for $40–65/day and allow them onto the peninsula's roughest roads. *Sunkist Backpackers* rent RAV4s for $65/ day or $35/day if you rent for a week.

By taxi Thames Taxis 📞07 868 3100.

ACCOMMODATION

Coastal Motor Lodge 608 Tararu Rd (SH25), 2.5km north of town 📞07 868 6843, 🌐stayatcoastal.co.nz. Well-equipped "cottage" family units and streamlined, spacious black A-frame chalets (all self-contained and designed for two) set in spacious grounds, some with views over the firth. Free wi-fi. Cottages **$135**, chalets **$175**

★ **Cotswold Cottage** 46 Maramarahi Rd, 3km south of town off SH25 📞07 868 6306, 🌐cotswoldcottage.co.nz. Lovingly restored 1920s villa set in mature grounds on the outskirts of Thames with beautiful views of the adjacent river and peninsula hills, a guest spa, sauna and three en-suite rooms. Rates include delicious cooked breakfasts; evening meals are available on request for around $45. **$165**

Cruz 'n' Stop 309 Mary St 📞07 868 9833, 🌐campervan cruznstopcom.com. Basic, paved parking lot right in the centre of town with no dump station but with power hookups, a shower, toilets and a small lounge with TV and magazines. Per van **$30**

Dickson Holiday Park 115 Victoria St, off SH25, 3.5km north of town 📞07 868 7308, 🌐dicksonpark.co.nz. Large, friendly campsite in a pretty valley with good facilities including a pool. There's free pick-up from Thames. Camping **$19**, dorms **$26**, on-site caravans **$62**, cabins **$79**, motel units **$136**

Gateway Backpackers 209 Mackay St 📞07 868 6339. You'll be well looked after at this intimate hostel just a few paces from the i-SITE and bus stop, housed in two wooden buildings linked by a central courtyard with facilities including free bikes. Dorms **$25**, doubles **$62**, en suite **$72**

★ **Rolleston Motel** 105 Rolleston St 📞09 868 8091, 🌐rollestonmotel.co.nz. Classic 1970s motel (though with some units recently remodelled) on a quiet backstreet. Each unit has its own little courtyard and everything is beautifully maintained, including the outdoor pool, hot tub and barbecue area. **$115**

Sunkist Backpackers 506 Brown St 📞07 868 8808, 🌐sunkistbackpackers.com. Atmospheric 1860s former pub, with a wide balcony and hammocks in the garden. Excellent facilities include free bikes and on-site 4WD rental. InterCity buses stop out front on request; free pick-ups can be arranged from the bus station. Camping **$19**, dorms **$25**, doubles **$66**

Wolfie's Lair 11 Firth View Rd, Te Puru, 12km north of town 📞07 868 6339, 🌐wolfieslair.co.nz. Rejuvenating six-bed hostel just back from the firth with accommodation in twins and doubles. Pick-ups from Thames and fishing trips by arrangement. Rooms **$54**

EATING AND DRINKING

Brew 200 Richmond St 📞07 868 5558. Casual daytime café that transforms into a slightly more formal evening restaurant serving high-quality Spanish platters, tapas and Coromandel mussel fritters ($9), plus substantial meals such as herb-crusted venison rack ($34). Mon–Fri 8am–10pm or later, Sat & Sun 9am–10pm or later.

Food for Thought 574 Pollen St 📞07 868 6065. This budget café has taken numerous New Zealand-wide awards for its home-made pies (especially its chicken and vegetable version) and also has a mouthwatering range of cakes, plus excellent coffee. Mon–Fri 6.30am–3.30pm, Sat 7am–1.30pm.

Grahamstown Bar & Diner 700 Pollen St 📞09 868 9178. Popular, polished-wood bar that's fine for a pint or quality meals such as nachos ($14), chicken Caesar salad ($19), eye fillet ($3) or one of their seafood platters ($40 & $70). Mon–Fri 11am–9pm or later, Sat & Sun 9am–9pm or later.

Kopu Station Hotel 1 Kopu Rd, Kopu, 5km south of town 📞07 868 7916. "Te Kopu" is a favourite local watering hole, popular for its regular live bands, a great range of drinks (including lots of specials), grassy beer garden and laidback attitude. Daily 10am–11pm.

Organic Co-op 736 Pollen St 📞07 868 8797. Community-run non-profit place that's good for organic supplies, veggies and eggs. Some of the produce is volunteer-grown at the community garden near the corner of Mackay and Cochrane sts. Mon–Fri 9am–5pm, Sat 9am–noon.

★ **Sola Café** 720b Pollen St 📞07 868 8781, 🌐sola cafe.co.nz. Relaxed bohemian café serving cakes, stellar coffee, salads and vegetarian dishes, from breakfasts and frittatas to wraps and enchiladas (mostly $10); some vegan and wheat-free options are available. There's courtyard seating out back. Daily 8am–4pm.

Speakeasy 746 Pollen St 📞07 868 6994. Low-lit

front-room bar with a 1920s Prohibition-era feel, timber tables and snug booths for supping cocktails and liqueur coffees ($8). Acoustic and low-key bands play Thurs & Sun. Wed–Sat 4pm–1am, Sun 2pm–1am.

Kauaeranga Valley

The steep-sided **Kauaeranga Valley** stretches east of Thames towards the spine of the Coromandel Peninsula, a jagged landscape of bluffs and gorges topped by **the Pinnacles** (759m), with stupendous views to both coasts across native forest studded with rata, rimu and kauri. It's reached along the scenic and mostly sealed Kauaeranga Valley Road snaking 21km beside the river, providing access to some of the finest walks in the Coromandel Range. The road winds through regenerating bush containing scattered "pole stands" of young kauri that have grown since the area was logged a century ago: only a handful in each stand will reach maturity.

The ease of access to these tracks can lead trampers not to take them as seriously as other tramps, but in bad weather the conditions can be treacherous, so go properly prepared (see p.51).

Note that the soil-borne **kauri dieback** disease (see box, p.195) is not present in Coromandel kauri forests. If you've recently visited the Auckland or Northland forests (which do have kauri dieback), be extra vigilant about cleaning your footwear.

INFORMATION
KAUAERANGA VALLEY

DOC visitor centre 14km along Kauaeranga Valley Rd (Oct–Dec 24 daily 9am–4pm; Dec 26–April daily 8.30am–4pm; May–Sept Wed–Sun 9am–3pm; ☎07 867 9080). Superb visitor centre with great displays on early kauri logging in the valley, big maps of the area and a 40min DVD on the history of logging. Pick up the *Kauaeranga Valley Recreation* booklet ($2) that details walks or buy the 1:50,000 *Hikuai Topo50* map BB35 ($9). The office can also store luggage ($2/ small locker). They'll also sell you hut tickets, though it is cheaper if you buy online (via the on-site computer).

ACCOMMODATION

The campsites listed here are the best of eight very similar DOC campsites (⊛doc.govt.nz), all dotted along Kauaeranga Valley Rd 14–23km east of Thames. The two huts are only accessible on foot on the Kauaeranga walks (see box below).

KAUAERANGA WALKS

Cookson Kauri Track (6km return; 3–4hr). Moderate, well-formed track to a couple of large kauri – pretty much the only accessible ones left standing hereabouts. Starts from the Wainora campsite, 7km beyond the DOC office.

Kahikatea Walk (900m return; 20min) Flat walk from the DOC office to a scale model of a kauri driving dam, a type once used extensively in this forest.

Nature Walk to Hoffman's Pool (1.5km loop; 30min) A short, easy loop beginning 1.5km beyond the DOC office. Information panels help make it a classic introduction to the valley's native forest. The track leads to a tranquil sand-edged pool in a river bend, an ideal picnic and swimming spot with a lovely deep swimming hole. You return the same way or in a loop along the road.

Pinnacles Hut–Billygoat Basin Walk (18km loop; 8hr). Typically done as a two-day hike with a night spent at the Pinnacles Hut (see p.326), this is a great way to get a taste of the region. It starts at the road-end and spends the first 2–3hr following Webb Creek along an old packhorse route (steep in places) used by kauri bushmen in the 1920s up to Pinnacles Hut. From the hut there's a steep 50min climb, including some short ladders, to the jagged teeth of the Pinnacles themselves, and wonderful views. On the return, head south from the Hydro junction via Billygoat Basin, with information panels telling the story of the loggers.

Wainora–Booms Flat circuit (15km loop; 7hr). Excellent full-day outing starting along the Cookson Kauri Track then topping out at 549m with great views all around. After following an undulating track to Orange Peel Corner you can descend on the track to Booms Flat or turn this into a two-day walk by overnighting at Crosbies Hut (see p.326) which adds 4hr to the total length. In wet weather, avoid the Booms Flat track.

5

Crosbies Hut Brand-new, ten-bunk hut best accessed on the Wainora–Booms Flat circuit. It comes equipped with mattresses and a wood store but no gas rings. If you're looking for a quieter alternative to the Pinnacles Hut this is it. $\underline{\$15.30}$

Pinnacles Hut and campsite This large and relatively plush eighty-bunk place is one of the most popular of all DOC huts, especially on Saturday nights and during school holidays. It is beautifully sited atop the range, around a 3hr walk from the road end, and there's always a warden present. You can camp here, too, in a wooded streamside setting beside the hut. Book through ⓦ doc.govt.nz;

backcountry hut passes not valid. Hut $\underline{\$15.30}$, camping $\underline{\$5.10}$

Shag Stream 14km along Kauaeranga Valley Rd from Thames. The nearest DOC campsite to Thames is a simple, bush-girt affair right by the DOC visitor centre. It's equipped with vault toilets and has access to stream water (which should be treated). $\underline{\$9}$

Whangiterenga 19km along Kauaeranga Valley Rd from Thames. Marginally the nicest of the roadside campsites and the only one with flush toilets. Water is gathered from the stream and should be treated. $\underline{\$9}$

The Pohutukawa Coast

From Thames, SH25 snakes 58km north to Coromandel town, tracing the grey rocky shoreline of the "**Pohutukawa Coast**" (so called for its abundance of these blazing native trees) past a series of tiny, sandy bays, most with little more than a few houses and the occasional campsite.

Tapu–Coroglen Road

Hills and sand-coloured cliffs rise dramatically from the roadside for the first 19km until you reach **Tapu**, where the **Tapu–Coroglen Road** peels off to the peninsula's east coast. It is a wonderfully scenic 28km run of narrow, unsealed yet manageable driving, leaving behind the marginal farmland on the coast and climbing over the peninsula's mountainous spine. You eventually drop down to Coroglen, linking with the main road between Whitianga and Whangamata.

Rapaura Watergardens

586 Tapu–Coroglen Rd • Daily 9am–5pm • $15 • ☏ 07 868 4821, ⓦ rapaurawatergardens.co.nz

Even if you aren't driving the whole Tapu–Coroglen Road, it's worth making a detour 6km along the road to **Rapaura Watergardens**, a landscaped "wilderness" of bush and blooms, lily ponds and a trickling stream, threaded by paths, with philosophical messages urging you to stop and think. There are a few picnic areas, an excellent summer-only **café** and accommodation (see below).

Square kauri

Tapu–Coroglen Rd, 3km east of Rapaura Watergardens

Near the road's summit, an easily missed signpost points to the "**square kauri**", opposite a rough lay-by and just before a small bridge. Steep steps through bush (175m; 10min) lead to this 1200-year-old giant of a tree (41m high and 9m wide), whose unusual, angular shape saved it from loggers.

Manaia-Kereta Lookout

SH25, 12km north of Tapu

The road lurches inland soon after Kereta, snaking over hills to the roadside **Manaia-Kereta Lookout** (206m), which has great views of the northern peninsula, the majestic Moehau Range and Coromandel Harbour. Beyond, the vertical cliffs of Great Barrier Island may be visible on a clear day. Along the rocky shoreline and blue-green Firth of Thames, SH25 continues for 23km before reaching Coromandel.

ACCOMMODATION	**POHUTUKAWA COAST**

Rapaura Watergardens 586 Tapu–Coroglen Rd ☏ 07 868 4821, ⓦ rapaurawatergardens.co.nz. Choose from an enchanting luxury cottage for two or a serene two-bedroom lodge lined with rimu. Once the day visitors have left you have the watergardens to yourself. Cottage $\underline{\$165}$, lodge $\underline{\$275}$

Coromandel

The peninsula's northernmost town of any substance is charming little **COROMANDEL**, 58km north of Thames, huddling beneath high, craggy hills at the head of Coromandel Harbour.

From the south, SH25 becomes Tiki Road and then splits into two: Wharf Road skirts the harbour while Kapanga Road immediately enters the heart of town, which is made up of photogenic wooden buildings, where all you'll find are a couple of supermarkets and petrol stations, a bank and a cluster of cafés. A couple of blocks further on, it becomes Rings Road, before heading northwards out of town towards the main attractions, the **stamper battery** and the **Driving Creek Railway**.

Brief history

The town and peninsula took their name from an 1820 visit by the British Admiralty supply ship *Coromandel*, which called into the harbour to obtain kauri spars and masts. A more mercenary European invasion was precipitated by the 1852 discovery of **gold**, near Driving Creek.

Driving Creek Railway and Potteries

Driving Creek Rd, 3.5km north of town • **Train trips** Daily 10.15am & 2pm plus up to four additional trips per day during summer; 1hr return • $25 **Pottery** Daily 10am–5pm • Free • ☎ 07 866 8703, ⓦ drivingcreekrailway.co.nz

The ingenious **Driving Creek Railway** is the country's only narrow-gauge hill railway. It was built mostly by hand and is the brainchild of Barry Brickell, an eccentric local potter and rail enthusiast who wanted to access the clay-bearing hills. The track is only 381mm wide and climbs 120m over a distance of about 3km, rewarding you with spectacular views, extraordinary feats of engineering and quirky design; at the end of the line panoramas extend from a specially constructed wooden lodge, the Eyefull Tower. The journey starts and ends at the **workshops**, where you can see various types of **pottery**: stoneware, bricks and earthenware items, and sculptures made from terracotta. There's also a video about Brickell and a sculpture garden in a wildlife sanctuary designed to protect the local and visiting birdlife.

Coromandel Goldfields Centre & Stamper Battery

410 Buffalo Rd, 2km north of town • 1hr guided tours available; check times with the i-SITE • $10

Coromandel's gold-mining history is explained at the **Coromandel Goldfields Centre & Stamper Battery**. Fascinating guided tours flesh out how gold ore was extracted and refined, and they even fire up New Zealand's biggest water wheel which runs the fully functional 1899 stamper battery. It makes quite a racket.

Long Bay Kauri Grove

Wharf Rd, 3km west of town

The attractive beach at **Long Bay** marks the start of a pleasing **walk** through a scenic reserve (40min loop) winding through bush to an ancient kauri tree and on to a small grove of younger ones. Beyond, at the junction with a gravel road, turn right to Tucks Bay to follow the coastal track back. The track starts 100m inside the *Long Bay Motor Camp* where a signpost marks the track.

ARRIVAL AND INFORMATION   **COROMANDEL**

By bus InterCity and NakedBus from Thames (daily; 1hr 15min) and Whitianga (2 daily; 1hr) pull into the car park opposite the i-SITE.

By ferry 360 Discovery (☎ 0800 360 3472, ⓦ 360discovery .co.nz) operate a passenger ferry between Auckland and Hannafords Wharf, 7km south of Coromandel (5–7 weekly;

2hr). The $55 one-way fare includes a bus into town.

i-SITE 355 Kapanga Rd (Nov–Easter daily 9am–5pm; Easter–Oct Mon–Fri 9am–5pm, Sat & Sun 10am–4pm; ☎ 07 866 8598, ⓦ coromandeltown.co.nz). Carries DOC leaflets, Hot Water Beach tide times and has internet access.

5

GETTING AROUND

By car Car rental firms in town include the Coromandel service station at 226 Wharf Rd (☏ 07 866 8736; $65/24hr), which allows its cars onto the unsealed roads north of Colville.

By shuttle bus The Coromandel Discovery shuttle bus to

Fletcher Bay ($95 return; complimentary tea, coffee and biscuits; ☏ 0800 668 175, ⓦ coromandeldiscovery.co.nz) is the best way to reach the Coromandel Walkway (see p.331), dropping off walkers and collecting them at Stony Bay before returning to Coromandel.

ACCOMMODATION

Anchor Lodge 448 Wharf Rd ☏ 07 866 7992, ⓦ anchor lodgecoromandel.co.nz. Modern and well-run motel with heated pool, spa and a wide range of accommodation including a backpacker hostel section and some nice two-bedroom units nestled in the bush. Dorms $25, budget doubles and twins $60, motel units $145, suites $230

★ **Buffalo Lodge** 860 Buffalo Rd ☏ 07 866 8960, ⓦ buffalolodge.co.nz. Artist Evelyne's architecturally designed home is perched high up in the bush north of town, with dizzying gulf views from its three guest rooms (all with private deck). Give two days' notice for superb three-course dinners using organic produce, much of it from Evelyne's garden ($95/person). Not suitable for children. Closed May–Sept. $235

Coromandel Colonial Cottages 1737 Rings Rd ☏ 07 866 8857, ⓦ corocottagesmotel.co.nz. Eight well-kept whitewashed wooden cottages (some sleeping six) neatly arranged in tranquil gardens 1.5km north of town with a big solar-heated swimming pool, a kids' playground and a BBQ area. $150

Coromandel Top 10 Holiday Park 636 Rings Rd ☏ 0800 267 646, ⓦ coromandelholidaypark.co.nz. Sprawling over 3.5 acres a 3min walk north of town, this all-purpose spot combines camping and campervan facilities with a complex range of cabins and well-equipped motel units. All guests have access to the swimming pool and facilities including bike rental. Camping $20, cabins $70, kitchen cabin $80, motel units $140

Jacaranda Lodge 3195 Tiki Rd (SH25) ☏ 07 866 8002, ⓦ jacarandalodge.co.nz. A modern house in farmland 3km south of town offering B&B accommodation in six

comfortable rooms (most en-suite), a stellar collection of New Zealand films on DVD, and delicious continental breakfasts including home-made muesli and juices and jams from the orchards outside. Room $135, en suite $160

Lion's Den 126 Te Tiki St ☏ 07 866 8157, ⓦ lionsden hostel.co.nz. Small, funky hostel beloved by backpackers for its cosy, colourful common areas, tropical gardens, sociable shared-house-style atmosphere and proximity to town and bush walks. Dorms $26, rooms $60

★ **Long Bay Motor Camp** 3200 Long Bay Rd ☏ 07 866 8720, ✉ lbmccoromandel@xtra.co.nz. Laidback beachfront campsite 3km west of town with great sunset views, safe swimming, kayak rental ($10/hr), and bargain fishing and scenic boat trips. There are additional unpowered sites at the secluded Tucks Bay, a 1km drive through the bush or a 5min walk around the headland. Camping $19, cabins $65, kitchen cabins $85

Tidewater Tourist Park 270 Tiki Rd ☏ 07 866 8888, ⓦ tidewater.co.nz. Ultra-comfortable motel and attached associate YHA, 200m from town near the harbour, with BBQ area, bike and kayak rental and spacious cabin-style units sleeping up to six people. Camping $15, dorms $28, rooms $60, motel units $160

Tui Lodge 60A Whangapoua Rd, just off SH25 ☏ 07 866 8237, ⓦ coromandeltuilodge.co.nz. Good-value hostel a 10min walk south of town (and on the InterCity bus route), set in a big rambling house surrounded by an orchard and tranquil garden with a large chill-out gazebo. Free perks include laundry, tea and coffee, fruit (in season), a BBQ and bike use. Camping $15, dorms $25, rooms $60, en-suite rooms $80

EATING AND DRINKING

Little Coromandel has a disproportionate number of places to **eat** and some great seafood vendors for essential supplies.

Coromandel Hotel 611 Kapanga Rd ☏ 07 866 8760, ⓦ coromandelhotel.co.nz. Even farmers and fishermen can barely finish the meals at this traditional boozer known locally as the "Top Pub". Expect the likes of a steak sandwich ($17) or lamb shanks ($15), or grab a drink and sit out in the beer garden. Daily 11am–10pm or later.

Coromandel Mussel Kitchen Corner of SH25 and 309 Rd, 4km south ☏ 07 866 7245, ⓦ musselkitchen.co.nz. Premium mussels are delivered four times a week at this roadside café specializing in mussel pots ($19) with

sourdough bread to dunk into a broth of kaffir lime and coconut curry or cream and garlic. They also dish up mussel chowder and other regular café fare. Sept–June daily 11am–3pm and until 9pm in summer.

Coromandel Oyster Company 1611 Tiki Rd (SH25), 5km south of town ☏ 07 866 8028. Buy mussels, scallops, crayfish and, of course, oysters fresh out of the water. They also sell mussel chowder. Daily 8am–6pm.

Coromandel Smoking Company 70 Tiki Rd ☏ 0800 327 668, ⓦ corosmoke.co.nz. Great shop selling their

5

own smoked fish and shellfish, and particularly notable for mackerel and oysters. A perfect spot to stop for picnic supplies. Daily 9am–5pm.

★ **Driving Creek Café** 180 Driving Creek Rd, 3.5km north of town ☎ 07 866 7066, ⓦ drivingcreekcafe.com. Classic Coromandel: a laidback and welcoming vegetarian (and mostly organic) café that's perfect for great coffee, rich fruit smoothies, breakfasts and dishes such as banana pancakes ($15). There are beautiful hill views from the veranda and garden, occasional acoustic music, free wi-fi and a secondhand bookshop. Daily 9.30am–5pm.

Peppertree 31 Kapanga Rd ☎ 07 866 8211, ⓦ pepper treerestaurant.co.nz. Coromandel's finest dining, serving either indoors – there's an open fire in winter – or in the

garden. Pop in for a salmon bagel brunch ($15) or dinner of eye fillet with bacon-wrapped scallops ($37). Daily 10am–9pm.

Star and Garter 5 Kapanga Rd ☎ 07 866 8503, ⓦ star andgarter.co.nz. Airy wood-lined 1873-built bar and covered beer garden in the centre of town, popular with an urbane, mixed-age crowd for the full range of Monteith's brews and some palatable wines. You can order in food from *Umu* and *Peppertree* next door. Daily 11am–late.

The Success Café & Restaurant 102 Kapanga Rd ☎ 07 866 7100. Relaxed daytime café with a cherry-tree-shaded courtyard. In the evenings it morphs into a bistro/bar serving good Kiwi cuisine such as pork ribs baked in bourbon ($26). Licensed & BYO. Daily 8.30am–10pm or later.

Northern Coromandel Peninsula

The landscape at the tip of the Coromandel is even more rugged than the rest of the peninsula, its green hills dropping to apparently endless beaches, clean blue sea and frothing white surf. The roads are lined with ancient pohutukawa trees, blazing red from early November until January. With its dairy farms long deserted, it's virtually uninhabited and there are **few facilities** except for some superb basic camping: replenish supplies in Coromandel.

The only real settlement is tiny Colville. North of there the road turns to gravel, becoming narrower, rougher and dustier the further north you go: allow an hour to reach Fletcher Bay from Colville in fine weather. Three kilometres north of Colville the road splits, the right fork heading east over the hills to Stony Bay and the southern end of the Coromandel Walkway. The left fork runs 35km north to Port Jackson and Fletcher Bay at the very tip of the peninsula, following the coast all the way.

Colville

From Coromandel town, the road is sealed to just beyond the tiny settlement of **COLVILLE**, a quiet valley comprising little more than a post office, a petrol pump, a café and the Colville General Store (☎ 07 866 6805) where you can stock up on provisions before heading to points north.

Port Jackson

An abandoned **granite wharf** 19km northwest of Colville marks the halfway point on the road to the peninsula tip. The road then cuts inland, over hills rising straight from the shore, to reach **PORT JACKSON**, just two houses and a 1km sandy crescent of beach. It's safe for swimming and is backed by a grassy DOC reserve (ideal for a picnic) and a DOC campsite.

Fletcher Bay

From Port Jackson the road deteriorates on the final 6km stretch to **FLETCHER BAY**, probably the best beach of all, with safe swimming and backed by another DOC campsite and a backpackers. The eastern end of the beach marks the start of the **Coromandel Walkway**.

Stony Bay

Stony Bay, at the southern end of the Coromandel Walkway, is reached by two perilously narrow and twisty gravel roads – one, via Little Bay, across the Coromandel Range from just beyond Coromandel, the other traversing the Moehau Range from just beyond Colville. The latter runs 14km from Colville to the small holiday settlement of **Port Charles**, and a further 6km to Stony Bay, where there's another DOC campsite.

INFORMATION AND ACTIVITIES

NORTHERN COROMANDEL PENINSULA

Driving Before heading out, check on the road conditions at the Coromandel i-SITE, fill up with petrol and be prepared to drive slowly and take your time. There's no hurry up here.

Horse trekking Colville Farm, Colville Rd, 1.5km south of Colville ☎07 866 6820, ⓦcolvillefarmholidays.co.nz. Guided horse trekking with short rides on a sheep and cattle farm and longer treks heading into native bush or out to the beach ($30/hr; $120/5hr).

ACCOMMODATION

With a few exceptions, accommodation is limited to camping. To help deter illegal freedom camping, DOC has opened five waterside campsites around the northern peninsula (see map p.320): three of the best are listed below. For the two weeks after Christmas the campsites are full, but for most of the rest of the year you'll have this unspoilt area to yourself. Expect toilets, cold showers and not much else.

Colville Farm Colville Rd, 1.5km south of Colville ☎07 866 6820, ⓦcolvillefarmholidays.co.nz. Great rural bolt-hole with spots for tents (pay $2 extra to use the backpacker facilities), backpacker beds in a cottage, a couple of rustic bush lodges and two self-contained houses with fabulous views. Camping __$12__, dorm __$25__, lodge __$70__, houses __$110__

Fantail Bay campsite 22km north of Colville ⓦdoc.govt.nz. Fairly small beachfront DOC site surrounded by farmland. There's room for just 100 people, sharing flush toilets, stream water and cold showers. Booking is essential in the summer. __$9__

Fletcher Bay campsite 34km north of Colville ⓦdoc.govt.nz. The most remote of the DOC sites, with views across to Great Barrier and Little Barrier islands. It comes with flush toilets, stream water and cold showers, and, despite its 250-person capacity, booking is essential for the two weeks after Christmas. __$9__

Fletcher Bay Backpackers Fletcher Bay, 34km north of Colville ☎07 866 6685, ⓦdoc.govt.nz. Fairly basic hostel in a superb location on a hill 400m from the beach overlooking the campsite. The four rooms have two bunk beds in each and bedding is provided. __$25__

EATING AND DRINKING

Green Snapper Café Colville ☎07 866 6697, ⓦgreensnappercafe.co.nz. Welcoming café with a fire in winter and outdoor seating in summer. Stop in for breakfast ($10–20), a smoothie ($7), dhal and basmati ($14) or fish burgers ($13) and fab coffee. Christmas to mid-Feb daily 9am–9pm; rest of the year open most days 9am–4pm.

Coromandel to Whitianga

The drive east from Coromandel to Whitianga can be done in under an hour, but you could easily stretch it out longer on either of two highly **scenic roads** that cross the mountains: the snaking **309 Road** (33km, of which 14km are gravel; no public transport) spends much of its time in the bush, twisting across the peninsula's spine and topping out at the 306m-high saddle before descending to Whitianga; the main **SH25** climbs through forested hills before zigzagging down to the coast past the deserted beaches of Whangapoua and Kuaotunu.

THE COROMANDEL WALKWAY

If you're after more exertion than swimming, fishing or lolling about on the beaches, consider hiking from Fletcher Bay to Stony Bay along the gentle **Coromandel Walkway** (11km one-way; 3hr). The walk starts at the far end of the beach in Fletcher Bay and heads off into a no-man's-land, first following gentle coastal hills that alternate between pasture and bush, before giving way to wilder terrain as you head further south past a series of tiny bays. Several hilltop **vantage points** provide spectacular vistas of the coast and Pacific Ocean beyond. **Stony Bay** is a sweep of pebbles with a bridge across an estuary that's safe for swimming. The DOC leaflet *Coromandel Recreation Information* briefly describes the walk and shows a map, but the path is clearly marked.

For information on how to reach the walkway via shuttle bus from Coromandel town, see p.328.

5

Along the 309 Road
The Waterworks
471 The 309 Rd • Daily: Nov–April 9am–6pm; May–Oct 10am–4pm • $18 • ☎ 07 866 7191, ⊚ thewaterworks.co.nz

Set a couple of hours aside to visit **The Waterworks**, 5km along the 309 Road, a rambling garden carved from the bush where you can do fun stuff with water. You are greeted with a waterwheel built from construction helmets, teapots and gumboots, before continuing past a static bicycle shooting a jet of water when you pedal, or a raised waterway where you can play an elaborate form of pooh sticks. The highlight is a huge clock powered by jets playing against a row of empty pop bottles arranged on a pendulum: apparently it keeps remarkably good time unless the wind blows the pendulum off kilter. Bring a swimsuit for a dip in the natural swimming hole.

Castle Rock
100m past The Waterworks • 2km return; 40min–1hr 30min

A rough access road to the north crosses a ford and climbs steeply for 3km to the trailhead for the track to **Castle Rock**, the most easily accessible peak on the Coromandel Peninsula. The climb gets steeper towards the final tree-root claw onto the 521m summit of this old volcanic plug, but your efforts are rewarded by fantastic views to both coasts: the Whangapoua peninsula and the Mercury Islands on the east, and Coromandel and the Firth of Thames on the west.

Waiau Falls and the "Siamese" Kauri
309 Rd, 2.5km southeast of Castle Rock

Though of modest height, **Waiau Falls** still crash over a tiered rock face into a pool below, making this a gorgeous spot to cool off right next to the road. Half a kilometre on, a car park heralds the easy bush track to the towering, magnificent **Kauri Grove** (1km return; 30min) and "**Siamese**" **Kauri** a little further; this is one of the best places in the country to appreciate their immense size.

Along the SH25
Whangapoua and New Chums Beach

From Coromandel, **SH25** traverses lush native forest, passing a couple of isolated but pretty beachside settlements with campsites. About 14km from Coromandel is the 5km turn-off to the secluded village and white-sand beach of **WHANGAPOUA**. At the end of the road (along the right fork into town) a pretty bushwalk over a headland brings you to **New Chums Beach** (accessible at low tide only; 4km return; 1hr), one of New Zealand's finest beaches, recently saved from development.

Kuaotunu

Continuing along SH25, about 30km from Coromandel, you descend to diminutive **KUAOTUNU**, beside a lovely white-sand beach. There's not much to it, but the village is an alluring spot with a few places to stay, a great summer pizza joint and the chance to go sailing with NZ Spirit (see box, p.337) who also pick up in Kuaotunu.

From here, SH25 continues through farmland to Whitianga and Mercury Bay.

ACCOMMODATION AND EATING
KUAOTUNU

Black Jack Lodge SH25 ☎ 07 866 2988, ⊚ black-jack .co.nz. Superb upmarket streamside hostel just steps from the beach with budget bikes and kayaks for rent and a wonderfully relaxed atmosphere. Shares $35, rooms $90, en suite $110

Kuaotunu Bay Lodge B&B SH25 ☎ 07 866 4396, ⊚ kuaotunubay.co.nz. Understated luxury in a modern house with great views from private decks. Everything is

beautifully appointed, there's free wi-fi and they impose a one-night surcharge from Dec–March. $295

Kuaotunu Camp Ground 33 Bluff Rd ☎ 07 866 5628, ⊚ kuaotunumotorcamp.co.nz. Decent campsite with kayak rental and an on-site fish and chip shop. The beach is just across the road but most sites don't have great views. Camping $20, cabins $65, self-contained units $120

Luke's Kitchen 20 Blackjack Rd, off SH25 ☏ 07 866 4480. The only place to eat in Kuaotunu is fairly ramshackle, with most of the seating outside, but the food is superb, especially the pizza ($20). BYO. Daily in summer 8am–9pm.

Whitianga and around

Pretty **WHITIANGA** clusters where Whitianga Harbour meets **Buffalo Beach**, a long curve of surf-pounded white sand on the broad sweep of **Mercury Bay**.

The town is a relaxed place to chill for a day or two, perhaps trying **bone carving** or getting pampered at The Lost Spring **hot pools**. It also makes a central base from which to make a series of half-day and **day-trips** to some of the Coromandel's top spots. A short passenger ferry ride across the narrow harbour mouth to **Ferry Landing** opens up a bunch of **gorgeous beaches** such as Lonely Bay. They're often deserted out of season, though from December to February you'll have to work harder to find tranquillity. By taking a bus from Ferry Landing (or driving south via Whenuakite) you can access **Cathedral Cove**, a stunning geological formation with great swimming, and magical **Hot Water Beach**, where natural hot springs bubble up through the sand.

Offshore, the protected waters of **Te Whanganui-A-Hei (Cathedral Cove) Marine Reserve** offer superb snorkelling and scuba diving. Cathedral Cove, the marine reserve and the extraordinary array of volcanic island and sea caves offshore are the main focus of a range of **boat tours** and **kayak trips** from Hahei and Whitianga. Bottlenose **dolphins** and **orca** are often seen.

Mercury Bay Museum

11 The Esplanade • Daily 10am–4pm • $5 • ☏ 07 866 0730, ⓦ mercurybaymuseum.co.nz

An old butter factory on the Esplanade houses the **Mercury Bay Museum** with plenty on kauri logging, early settlers and big game fishing. The highlight is the coverage of early explorers, particularly Maori pioneer Kupe, who is thought to have landed near here up to a thousand years ago. Captain Cook also gets a look-in.

The Lost Spring

121a Cook Drive • Daily 11am–9pm • $28 for 1hr, $60 all day • ☏ 07 866 0456, ⓦ thelostspring.co.nz

A nondescript patch of suburban Whitianga is the unlikely location for **The Lost Spring**, a slice of Eden in the form of a series of hot pools in lavishly landscaped grounds with Polynesian music playing and cocktails delivered by staff with frangipani flowers behind their ear. The complex is the brainchild of Alan Hopping, who – in an epic series of disasters and ultimate triumph – believed in, searched for, and finally found and tapped a local hot spring to create this extraordinary oasis. Ranging from 33°C–40°C, the pools combine spa kitsch with re-created natural bush splendour. You can dine at the classy on-site **café** and should book ahead for all manner of treatments from a foot massage ($65) to a full-body pampering ($350).

Shakespeare Lookout

1.5km west of Ferry Landing and another 1km uphill • Free

The cliffs below **Shakespeare Lookout** apparently once resembled the Bard's profile, though it is hard to imagine today. It is better to admire the panoramic views from the

---

COOK PLANTS THE FLAG

James Cook effectively claimed New Zealand for King George III, planting the British flag at Cooks Beach in November 1769. Cook spent 12 days anchored here – the longest he spent anywhere on his first voyage around Aotearoa – observing the **transit of Mercury** across the sun on November 9; in doing so he established the exact latitude and longitude of the new-found land and named (or rather re-named) both Mercury Bay and, of course, Cooks Beach.

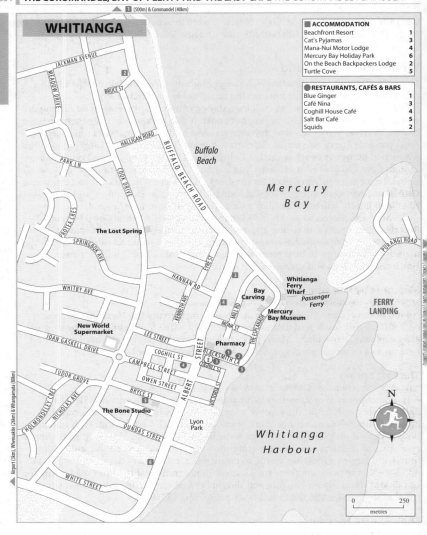

WHITIANGA

■ **ACCOMMODATION**
Beachfront Resort	1
Cat's Pyjamas	3
Mana-Nui Motor Lodge	4
Mercury Bay Holiday Park	6
On the Beach Backpackers Lodge	2
Turtle Cove	5

● **RESTAURANTS, CAFÉS & BARS**
Blue Ginger	1
Café Nina	3
Coghill House Café	4
Salt Bar Café	5
Squids	2

lookout, which stretch east to Cooks Beach and across Mercury Bay, west to Buffalo
Beach, and north towards Mount Maungatawhiri. Signposted tracks (2km one-way;
30min) lead from the car park to the secluded Lonely Bay and on to the popular family
holiday spot of **Cooks Beach**, also accessible from the main road 2km further east.

Hahei
The small beachside community of **HAHEI**, 6km east of Cooks Beach (10km by road),
has a store, a few places to stay and eat, and is the launch site for boat, kayak and dive
trips into **Te Whanganui-A-Hei (Cathedral Cove) Marine Reserve** (see box, p.337), also
accessible via the Cathedral Cove Walk.

Cathedral Cove Walk

5km return; 1hr 30min; 300m ascent on the way back

Almost everybody does the **Cathedral Cove Walk**, a hilly coastal track from a car park on Grange Road. Although steep in places, the route affords great views out to sea. The reward is a perfect pair of beaches backed by white cliffs and separated by an impressive rock arch that vaults over the strand like the nave of a great cathedral.

Steps bring you down onto **Mare's Leg Cove**, a gorgeous swimming beach with composting toilets offering a seat with a view. You need to walk through the arch to reach the second fine beach, **Cathedral Cove**, though rockfall from the ceiling in 2009 has made DOC jittery and there are signs (and sometimes ropes) to discourage people from going through.

To walk from Hahei Beach follow the step at the northern end of the beach: you'll reach the car park at the start of the walk in around twenty minutes.

Gemstone Bay and Stingray Bay

A few minutes' walk along the Cathedral Cove Walk, a five-minute track descends to the rocky **Gemstone Bay**, which is perfect for snorkelling. DOC has set up four buoys in different marine environments between 50m and 150m offshore with panels explaining the undersea wonders. Rent gear from Cathedral Cove Dive (see box, p.337).

Stingray Bay, signposted further along the Cathedral Cove Walk, is a perfect cove of white sand that's often deserted when Cathedral Cove is packed.

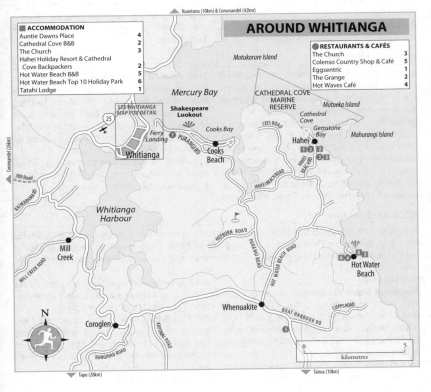

5

Hot Water Beach

15km southeast of Whitianga, but over 30km by road

With the opportunity to dig your own hot pool in the sands next to the breakers, **Hot Water Beach** is understandably one of the most popular destinations on the Coromandel Peninsula. The hot springs which bubble up beneath the sand can only be exploited two hours either side of **low tide** (less in rough weather; check tide times at the Whitianga i-SITE). Wander 100m across the sands to the rocky outcrop that splits the beach in two, dig your hole and enjoy the hot water, refreshed by waves. You'll need a spade to dig your "spa": rent one from your accommodation, the Hot Water Beach Store (daily 9am or earlier–5pm or later depending on low tide times) or *Hot Waves Café* (see p.339) for $5, plus $20 deposit.

The springs have become so popular – up to 500 people crowd the beach at peak times – that some prefer to come at night: bring a spade and a torch. The beach here has a dangerous **tidal rip**: take care when swimming (see box, p.63). For accommodation and a café near the beach, see p.338 & p.339.

ARRIVAL AND INFORMATION

By plane The airport is 4km south of the town centre and is serviced by Sunair (☎0800 786 247, ⊛sunair.co.nz) flights from Auckland and Great Barrier Island. A cab to or from town costs around $15; try Whiti City Cabs (☎07 866 4777).

Destinations Auckland (2 daily; 30min); Great Barrier Island (2 daily; 30min).

By bus NakedBus and InterCity buses drop off at accommodation around town and outside the i-SITE. To

GETTING AROUND

By ferry A passenger ferry between Whitianga Wharf and Ferry Landing (daily: 7.30am–6.30pm, 7.30–8.30pm & 9.30–10.30pm, later in summer; $2 each way) runs roughly every 10min; the crossing takes 3min.

By bus BusIt (☎0800 427 546, ⊛busit.co.nz) runs a regular service ($3 one-way) from Ferry Landing to Cooks Beach, Hahei and Hot Water Beach from Boxing Day until early Feb, with around four buses a day and extra on New Year's Eve. Cathedral Cove Shuttles (☎027 422 5899, ⊛cathedralcoveshuttles.co.nz) is essentially an on-demand taxi service between Ferry Landing, Cooks

WHITIANGA AND AROUND

head down to Tauranga you'll need to change at either Thames (Intercity) or Ngatea (NakedBus).

Destinations Coromandel (1 daily; 1hr); Ngatea (1 daily; 1hr 15min); Tauranga (3 daily; 2–3hr); Thames (2 daily; 1hr 40min).

i-SITE 66 Albert St (Christmas–Jan daily 8am–6pm; Feb–Christmas Eve Mon–Fri 9am–5pm, Sat & Sun 9am–4pm; ☎07 866 5555, ⊛whitianga.co.nz). Internet service is available here.

Beach, Hahei and Hot Water Beach. Go Kiwi (☎0800 446 549, ⊛go-kiwi.co.nz) has an eastern beaches tour from Whitianga ($47) to visit Hahei (for Cathedral Cove) and timed for low-tide at Hot Water Beach. With Tairua Bus Co (☎07 864 7194, ⊛tairuabus.co.nz) you can visit either Hot Water Beach or Hahei from Whitianga for around 4hr before catching the onward bus to Tairua.

By car Getting to Hahei and Hot Water Beach by car takes around half an hour: head 25km southeast on SH2 to Whenuakite and turn north onto minor roads.

ACCOMMODATION

As one of the Coromandel's main tourist centres, Whitianga has plenty of accommodation, augmented by places around Hot Water Beach, Hahei and even Kuaotunu (see p.332), 16km north. In addition to advance bookings in summer, be prepared for higher prices than on the rest of the peninsula (especially anywhere with a sea view) and minimum stays in peak periods.

WHITIANGA

Beachfront Resort 113 Buffalo Beach Rd ☎07 866 5637, ⊛beachfrontresort.co.nz; map p.334. Luxurious yet kid-friendly motel, right on the beach, with eight spacious units with sea views and private balconies. Guests can use the spa pool, BBQ, kayaks, a dinghy, fishing rods and boogie boards. $175

Cat's Pyjamas 12 Albert St ☎07 866 4663, ⊛cats-pyjamas.co.nz; map p.334. Cosy central hostel a 2min

walk from the town centre and beach, with mural-painted common areas, a sunny courtyard and, yes, a resident cat. Dorms $25, rooms $60, en-suite room $70

Mana-Nui Motor Lodge 20 Albert St ☎07 866 5599, ⊛mananui.co.nz; map p.334. A centrally located, comfortable motel with twelve fully self-contained ground-floor units (some of which have two bedrooms), plus a pool and spa. $130

Mercury Bay Holiday Park 121 Albert St ☎07 866 5579,

TOURS AND ACTIVITIES AROUND WHITIANGA AND MERCURY BAY

BONE CARVING

Bay Carving 12 The Esplanade ☎07 866 4021, ⓦbaycarving.com. German carver Roland Baumgart offers short (2–3hr) carve-your-own sessions (from $45) based on set patterns using cattle bone blanks.
The Bone Studio 6b Bryce St ☎07 866 2158,

ⓦcarving.co.nz. Ian Thorne takes only a couple of budding carvers at a time, giving just the right amount of guidance and encouraging self-expression. Bookings essential. $100/full day.

KAYAKING

Cathedral Cove Kayak Tours 88 Hahei Beach Rd, Hahei ☎0800 529 258, ⓦseakayaktours.co.nz. Hahei Beach is the launch pad for professional, guided sea-kayak trips taking a maximum of twenty people on half-day trips ($95) either to Cathedral Cove and the

islands off shore, or into the sea caves to the east. Full-day trips ($150) combine the two, and they offer shorter but wonderful dawn and sunset trips (Dec–Feb only; $75). Free pick-ups from Ferry Landing.

BOAT TRIPS

All trips cover pretty much the same territory, between Whitianga and Hot Water Beach including Cathedral Cove and its marine reserve.

Cave Cruzer Adventures Whitianga Wharf ☎0800 427 893, ⓦcavecruzer.co.nz. RIB tours past Shakespeare Cliff to Cathedral Cove and beyond. The Express tour departs 9.30am & 4.30pm (1hr plus; $50); an extended and more leisurely variation departs 10.30am & 1.30pm (2hr plus; $75).
Glass Bottom Boat Whitianga Wharf ☎07 876 1962, ⓦglassbottomboatwhitianga.co.nz. Two-hour trips ($90) with the chance to see what's below the surface. Departures at 10.30am & 1pm, and more in summer.
Hahei Explorer Hahei ☎07 866 3910, ⓦhahei explorer.co.nz. A rigid-hull inflatable that takes small

groups on exhilarating hour-long sea-cave trips (2–4 departures daily; call ahead for times; $70), visiting Cathedral Cove and an amazing blowhole, with an entertaining commentary.
NZ Spirit ☎021 072 7983, ⓦnzspirit.co.nz. A genuinely relaxed way to get to Mercury Bay's best remote beaches, swimming and snorkelling spots with chilled music, all aboard a modern, 13m catamaran. Go for the half-day Beach Finder ($75), a 2hr sunset cruise ($45), or the full-day Beach Explorer ($150). BYO wine or cocktails encouraged, especially for the sunset cruise. Trips also start from Kuaotunu (see p.332).

DIVING

Scuba diving and snorkelling in Cathedral Cove Marine Reserve and along the coast can be arranged through a couple of companies, both offering first-time dives and full instruction courses.

Cathedral Cove Dive 48 Hahei Beach Rd, Hahei ☎07 866 3955, ⓦhahei.co.nz/diving. Rent snorkelling gear for Gemstone Bay ($20), opt for a boat-based snorkelling trip ($80 with all gear) or take a dive trip (1 dive $115; 2 dives $215; all gear included).

Dive Zone 7 Blacksmith Lane, Whitianga ☎07 867 1580, ⓦdivethecoromandel.co.nz. A wide range of snorkelling and dive trips ($225 for 2 dives with all gear) plus snorkelling or diving from sit-on-top kayaks. It's great fun and prices are usually cheaper than a boat dive.

HORSE RIDING

Twin Oaks Riding Ranch SH25, 9km north of Whitianga ☎07 866 5388, ⓦtwinoaksridingranch .co.nz. Scenic two-hour horse treks, with breathtaking

views of Mercury Bay and the northern Coromandel. Daily 9.30am & 1.30pm, plus twilight trek at 6pm Dec–Feb, $60.

ⓦmercurybayholidaypark.co.nz; map p.334. Sheltered, well-equipped site about 700m from the town centre with barbecues, a pool and free spades for Hot Water Beach. Camping $19, on-site vans $60, units $65, motel units $125
★ **On the Beach Backpackers Lodge** 46 Buffalo Beach Rd ☎07 866 5380, ⓦcoromandelbackpackers .com; map p.334. Whitianga's best hostel, this associate YHA is a 10min walk north of town and a 2min stroll to

the beach across the road and a grassy reserve. A couple of the dorms are en-suite and most of the doubles and twins are in self-contained apartment-style units, each with barbecue. Kayaks, boogie boards and spades for Hot Water Beach are all free, and bike rentals are available. Dorms $25, rooms $70
Turtle Cove 14 Bryce St ☎07 867 1517, ⓦturtlecove .co.nz; map p.334. Just a 5min walk from the beach and

5

town, this is the Kiwi Experience buses' preferred stop. It's noisy but with stylish, contemporary rooms (some en-suite) in the main building and garden-set cabins. The facilities are good and include free local calls and an outdoor bar with pool table. Dorms $27, rooms $65

HAHEI

★ **Cathedral Cove B&B** 14 Cathedral Court ☎07 866 3550, ⓦcathedralcovebandb.co.nz; map p.335. With spades and torches for Hot Water Beach, beach umbrellas for the local beach, a book exchange and all manner of caring touches, the owners of this modern, sustainably minded B&B seem to have thought of everything. Pine-panelled rooms are very comfy and the breakfasts are excellent. Shared bathroom $190, en suite $215

The Church 87 Beach Rd ☎07 866 3533, ⓦthechurch hahei.co.nz; map p.335. Lovely array of handcrafted cottages in a garden setting, all facing the sun, most with leadlight windows and some with wood fires. Continental breakfast trays available. Studios $135, cottages $195

Hahei Holiday Resort & Cathedral Cove Backpackers 41 Harsant Ave ☎07 866 3889, ⓦhaheiholidays.co.nz; map p.335. Located on half a kilometre of beachfront an easy walk from Cathedral Cove and close to restaurants and a shop, the options here range from dorms in a basic backpacker lodge to luxurious self-contained beachfront villas. Camping $19, cabins $70, kitchen cabins $80, self-contained cabins $80, cottages $160, deluxe villas $265

Tatahi Lodge 13 Grange Rd ☎07 866 3992,

ⓦtatahilodge.co.nz; map p.334. Tranquilly set in bush and gardens, just footsteps from cafés and shops and with easy access to Cathedral Cove, your options here comprise self-contained timber-lined units, airy backpacker accommodation, and a tucked-away cottage that sleeps five. Dorms $28, rooms $84, studios $150, units $220, cottage $250

HOT WATER BEACH

Auntie Dawns Place 15 Radar Rd ☎07 866 3707, ⓦauntiedawn.co.nz; map p.335. This hillside house overlooking the beach offers true Kiwi hospitality with two simple yet comfortable self-contained apartments for two just a 3min walk along a hidden track from Hot Water Beach. They've been welcoming guests here for decades, and the home brew (which is regularly shared) is better than ever. $120

Hot Water Beach B&B 48 Pye Place ☎0800 146 889, ⓦhotwaterbedandbreakfast.co.nz; map p.335. Hospitable B&B sited close to the beach with great sea views. The two en-suite rooms have access to sunny decks and there's even a full-sized snooker table. $260

★ **Hot Water Beach Top 10 Holiday Park** 790 Hot Water Beach Rd, Hot Water Beach ☎800 246 823, ⓦhot waterbeachtop10.co.nz; map p.335. Brand-new campsite with friendly owners and state-of-the-art amenities including wi-fi and Sky TV in a sunny glassed-in guest lounge and an on-site shop serving fresh fish and chips in summer. Family campers have a separate area to under-25s. Camping $21, cabins $70, en-suite chalets $150

EATING AND DRINKING

WHITIANGA

Blue Ginger 10 Blacksmith Lane ☎07 867 1777, ⓦblue ginger.co.nz; map p.334. Great little eat-in or takeaway spot serving delectable morsels such as smoked fish wontons ($9), chicken coconut laksa ($16) and beef rendang ($19). Mon 10am–4pm, Tues–Sat 10am–10pm.

★ **Café Nina** 20 Victoria St ☎07 866 5440; map p.334. Café in one of Whitianga's oldest cottages serving made-to-order dishes such as chicken Caesar salad ($15), or vegetarian, vegan and gluten-free options including spanakopita ($8), plus great coffee and home-made carrot cake. Daily 8am–3.30pm or later.

Coghill House Café 10 Coghill St ☎07 866 0592, ⓦcafecoghill.co.nz; map p.334. Relaxing café that's good for breakfast ($10–18), tortilla wraps ($13) and great pies. Ease yourself into the lounging area or outdoor seating. Daily 7am–3pm.

Salt Bar Café Whitianga Marina Hotel, The Esplanade; map p.334. Beachy-chic lunch and dinner café/bar with decking onto the marina. Known for its classical, à la carte evening mains (under $35) such as market fish on saffron pea risotto. Bands sometimes play here in summer. Daily 11am–10pm or later.

Squids 15/1 Blacksmiths Lane ☎07 867 1710; map p.334. Cocktail/wine bar, good for a few drinks and good-value portions (evening mains under $35) such as lamb's fry and bacon, salmon with roast *kumara* and steak with garlic mash. Mon–Sat noon–2pm & 5.30–9pm or later.

FERRY LANDING

★ **Eggsentric** 1049 Purangi Rd, Flaxmill Bay, 1km west of Ferry Landing ☎07 866 0307, ⓦeggsentriccafe.co.nz; map p.335. The chef/owner usually plays a little evening guitar and generally entertains the guests at this quirky place with tables scattered among the sculpture-strewn gardens and in the colourful interior that comes alive in the evenings with acoustic music and poetry readings, particularly on Fridays. Simple but superb lunches might include Rarotongan-style marinated fish salad or macadamia-crumbed scallops ($17) while dinners usually revolve around seafood. Try the platter ($45) with local crayfish, scallops and mussels. Daily except Mon 9am–10pm or later.

HAHEI

The Church 87 Beach Rd ☎07 866 3797, ⓦthechurch restauranthahei.co.nz; map p.335. A wooden former

Methodist church, trucked here from Taumarunui, makes a lovely setting for this classy restaurant where mains include lamb cutlet on a *kumara*, parsnip and mint purée with pomegranate jus ($35), and desserts can come in the form of almond, basil and citrus cake ($15). The wines are excellent, too. Daily 5.30–10pm, but often closed in winter if it is quiet.

The Grange 7 Grange Rd ☎07 866 3502; map p.335. Essentially Hahei's pub, with sports TV, a great range of Mercury Bay wines, and fish and chips ($26). Tues–Sun 5–10pm or later.

HOT WATER BEACH
★ **Hot Waves Café** 8 Pye Place ☎07 866 3887; map

p.335. Stylish licensed café with airy dining areas and an attractive garden setting, serving light meals such as Greek salad or Thai beef noodles ($12–15), snacks and excellent coffee. Free book exchange. Daily 8.30am–4pm.

WHENUAKITE
★ **Colenso Country Shop & Café** SH25, 2km south of Whenuakite ☎07 866 0323, ⓦcolensocafe.co.nz; map p.335. Sit in the delightful gardens, on the sunny deck or inside this excellent café where great care is taken preparing the likes of olive and sundried tomato tarte ($7), Vietnamese chicken salad ($17), toothsome cakes and great coffee. Oct–April daily 10am–5pm; May–July & Sept daily 10am–4pm; closed Aug.

Tairua

Diminutive and pretty **TAIRUA**, 22km south of Hot Water Beach and 44km from Whitianga, nestles between pine-forested hills and the estuary of the Tairua River. Mostly popular with holidaying Kiwis, it's separated from the crashing Pacific breakers by two opposing and almost touching peninsulas: one is covered by the exclusive suburban sprawl of anodyne **Pauanui**; the other is crowned by the impressive volcanic **Mount Paku**, which can be climbed (10min ascent from car park, 30min ascent from beach) for spectacular views over the town, its estuary and beaches.

ARRIVAL AND INFORMATION   TAIRUA

By bus Daily NakedBus and InterCity buses from Auckland, Thames and Whitianga stop at the information centre.
Tourist information 223 Main St (Mon–Fri 9am–5pm,

Sat & Sun 9am–4pm; ☎07 864 7575, ⓦtairua.info). Tairua's information centre can organize accommodation and sells bus tickets.

GETTING AROUND

By ferry A five-minute passenger ferry ride links Tairua and Pauanui (Dec–Easter 9am–5pm every 2hr; $5 return,

$3 one-way; check updated schedules with the information centre).

Opoutere

Around 20km south of Tairua, a 5km side road leads to **Opoutere**, a tiny harbourside retreat at the foot of a mountain with a gorgeous, wild sweep of white-sand **surf beach** backed by pines. The pohutukawa-fringed road hugs the shores of the Wharekawa Harbour where wetlands make good birdwatching spots, mudflats yield shellfish and the calm waters are good for kayaking.

Opoutere Beach
1km east of Opoutere

At the junction of Opoutere and Ohui roads, Opoutere Beach car park has a footbridge leading to two paths, both reaching the beach in ten minutes or so. The left fork runs straight through the forest to the usually deserted **beach**, while the right-hand track follows the estuary to the edge of the **Wharekawa Harbour Sandspit Wildlife Refuge**, where endangered New Zealand **dotterels** breed from November to March. Opoutere Beach can have a strong undertow and there are no lifeguards, so don't swim. It's an unofficial nudist beach, but even if you're clothed, be sure to bring repellent to guard against sandflies.

5

Mount Maungaruawahine

2km return; 40–50min

For a wider view over the estuary and the coastline, tackle the track up **Mount Maungaruawahine**, climbing through gnarled pohutukawa and other native trees to the summit where there are sweeping vistas of the estuary and out towards the coast. The summit track begins by the gate to the YHA (see below).

ARRIVAL AND INFORMATION — OPOUTERE

By bus There's no regular bus service, but drop-offs can be arranged with Go Kiwi (see below).

Groceries You'll need to bring all your food as there is no shop and lodgings offer only basic provisions.

ACCOMMODATION

Opoutere Coastal Camping 460 Ohui Rd, 700m beyond the YHA ☎ 07 865 9152, ⓦ opouterebeach.co.nz. There's direct beachfront access from this well-maintained campsite in a secluded setting amid pines and pohutukawas. There are also rustic cabins with limited facilities but great views, and some more sophisticated chalets. Closed May–late Oct. Camping **$19**, cabins **$100**, chalets **$140**

YHA Opoutere Opoutere Rd ☎ 07 865 9072, ⓦ yha .co.nz. Old-school in both senses, this traditional YHA beside the estuary occupies a 1908 schoolhouse and surrounding wooden buildings amid mature bush alive with the calls of native birds. There's free use of kayaks and the chance for nocturnal glowworm spotting. May–late Oct closed Sun–Thurs. Dorms **$27**, rooms **$80**

Whangamata

The summer resort town of **WHANGAMATA**, 15km south of Opoutere, is bounded on three sides by estuaries and the ocean, and on the fourth by bush-clad hills. **Ocean Beach**, a 4km-long crescent of white sand, curves from the harbour to the mouth of the **Otahu River**. The sand bar at the harbour end has an excellent break that's sought-after by **surfers**.

The main drag, Port Road, runs straight through the small town centre, linking it with SH25.

Wentworth Falls

The track starts at the DOC campsite (see opposite) 5km down Wentworth Valley Rd, which is off SH25 about 2km south of town • Walk: 10km return; 2hr

One of the best ways to pass a couple of hours is to **walk** to **Wentworth Falls** in the Wentworth Valley which cuts into foothills of the Coromandel Range, 7km southwest of town. It is a lovely walk on well-maintained paths winding gradually uphill through regenerating bush past numerous small swimming holes. The route continues into the heart of the mountains, but most turn around at the pretty two-leap 50m falls, best viewed from a small deck.

ARRIVAL AND DEPARTURE — WHANGAMATA

By bus Go Kiwi (☎ 0800 446 549, ⓦ go-kiwi.co.nz) run from Auckland via Thames to Whangamata (Oct–March only).

Destinations Auckland (1 daily; 3hr 20min); Thames (1 daily; 1hr 10min).

INFORMATION AND TOURS

i-SITE 616 Port Rd (Mon–Sat 9am–5pm, Sun 9am–2pm; Sun until 5pm in Oct–March; ☎ 07 865 8340, ⓦ whangamata info.co.nz). Internet available.

Surfboard rental There are a number of surf shops along Port Rd, all of which rent boards and accessories and arrange surf lessons from around $50/hr. Try Whangamata Surf Shop (☎ 07 865 8252; Mon–Fri 9am–5pm; daily in summer) at no. 634.

Kiwi Dundee Adventures ☎ 07 865 8809, ⓦ kiwi dundee.co.nz. Dedicated conservationist Doug Johansen (a.k.a. "Kiwi Dundee") runs a variety of day and multi-day eco-tours incorporating wildlife experiences and paths off the beaten track. Full-day trips, including lunch and pick-ups from accommodation in Tairua, Pauanui and Whangamata, cost $230; book well in advance.

ACCOMMODATION

Breakers Motel 318 Heatherington Rd ☏ 0800 865 8464, ⓦ breakersmotel.co.nz. Modern motel with spacious units, many of which have views over the marina and spa pool. There's also a large swimming pool and breakfast is available. **$160**

Brenton Lodge 2 Brenton Place ☏ 07 865 8400, ⓦ brentonlodge.co.nz. A garden-set retreat with sea views on the edge of Whangamata, with two beautifully decorated cottages (each sleeping four) as well as two suites, as well as a sparkling swimming pool, spa, fresh flowers, home-made chocolates and delicious breakfasts. **$390**

Southpacific Accommodation Corner of Port Rd and Mayfair Ave ☏ 07 865 9580, ⓦ thesouthpacific.co.nz. An immaculate motel (with full kitchens in some rooms) and a separate backpackers lodge with budget twins, doubles and four-shares. Guests have free use of mountain bikes, kayaks and surfboards. Dorms **$24**, backpacker rooms **$126**, units **$147**

Wentworth Valley Campground Wentworth Valley Rd, 7km southwest of Whangamata ☏ 07 865 7032, ⓦ wentworthvalleycamp.co.nz. Chilled DOC campsite with streamside pitches, BBQs and coin-operated hot showers, right by the start of the track to Wentworth Falls. **$9**

EATING

Caffe Rossini 646 Port Rd ☏ 07 865 6117. Contemporary café serving a range of breakfasts, cakes and good coffee. Try the lemon pepper chicken salad ($17) or rack of New Zealand lamb ($29). Tues, Thurs & Sun 9am–4pm, Fri & Sat 9am–8.30pm.

Minato Sushi 713 Port Rd ☏ 07 865 8680. Wonderful sushi spot, with meticulously prepared fish; platters ($38) to share are a speciality. Mon–Sat 8.30–2pm.

Nero's 711 Port Rd ☏ 07 865 6300, ⓦ neros.co.nz. Spot-on pizza and pasta joint that's just the ticket after a day at the beach. Try the spaghetti and meatballs ($24) or a red Thai chicken pizza ($22). Oct–April daily noon–10pm; May–Sept Thurs–Sat 6–10pm.

Waihi and around

SH25 and SH2 meet at the southernmost town on the Coromandel Peninsula, **WAIHI**, 30km south from Whangamata. The small town merits a quick stop to sample its gold mining, both past and present.

Brief history

Gold was first discovered here in a reef of quartz in 1878, but it wasn't until 1894 that a boom began with the first successful trials in extracting gold using cyanide solution. Workers flocked, but disputes over union and non-union labour ensued, and the violent Waihi Strike of 1912 helped galvanize the labour movement and led to the creation of the Labour Party.

Although underground mining stopped in 1952, extraction was cranked up again in 1987 in the open-cast but well-hidden Martha Mine. As the open-cast mine slowly winds down (possibly closing around 2020), recent finds of deep veins have re-focused mining minds on tunnel mining. Current proposals to mine right under the town are likely to be challenged in the Environment Court by concerned residents.

Cornish pumphouse

Seddon St • Free

In the last few years, the hollow concrete shell of a three-storey 1903 **Cornish-style pumphouse** has become the town's icon and most prominent feature. It once kept the mine dry by pumping 300 tonnes of water an hour, then languished in an increasingly precarious position on the edge of the open-cast mine. Then, over a period of three months in 2006, hydraulic rams slid the building 296m on Teflon pads and steel runners to its current central location.

The move was ostensibly to save the historic building, but also allowed the mine to expand into new territory.

5

Mine Viewpoint and the Pit Rim Walkway

Walk behind the Cornish pumphouse to the **mine viewpoint**, where you can peer 260m down into the abyss where 150-tonne dump trucks look like toys. For more pit views follow the **Pit Rim Walkway** (4km loop; 1hr), an almost level track which circumnavigates the mine past a number of explanatory panels and one of the huge dump trucks.

Waihi Arts Centre & Museum

54 Kenny St • Jan daily noon–4pm; Feb–Dec Thurs–Mon 10am–3pm • $5 • ☎ 07 863 8386, ⓦ waihimuseum.co.nz

Mining life, including the 1912 strike, is conjured up evocatively in displays at the **Waihi Arts Centre & Museum**. Check out the diorama of the Victoria Battery and the model of the original fifteen-level deep Waihi mine; only the uppermost eight levels have been chewed out by the current open-cast mine. There's also a small-scale stamper battery, a model of the Cornish pumphouse and a couple of thumbs preserved in formaldehyde; miners once deliberately chopped off a thumb to get £500 compensation – enough to buy a small cottage that they'd otherwise never be able to afford on miners' wages.

Goldfields Railway

End of Wrigley St • Boxing Day–Feb and school holidays daily 10am, 11.45am & 1.45pm; rest of year Fri–Mon 10am, 11.45am & 1.45pm • $15 return • ☎ 07 863 8640, ⓦ waihirail.co.nz

The 1930s diesel engine of the **Goldfields Railway** runs scenic 6km rail trips west to Waikino in the nearby **Karangahake Gorge** (see p.316) along tracks built by a mining company. The whole trip takes about an hour, provides attractive views of the Ohinemuri River and allows a few minutes at the far end to inspect the displays on local history.

Waihi Beach

11km east of Waihi

The 9km-long golden-sand surf beach of **WAIHI BEACH**, 11km east of Waihi, is one of the safest ocean beaches in the country. Although the area has something of a suburban feel, there's an excellent campsite that justifies the detour off SH2.

ARRIVAL AND DEPARTURE   WAIHI AND AROUND

By bus InterCity and NakedBus buses on their Auckland–Tauranga runs stop outside the visitor centre in Waihi.

Destinations Auckland (4 daily; 3hr); Tauranga (4 daily; 1hr).

INFORMATION AND TOURS

Waihi Visitor Centre 126 Seddon St (daily: Oct–April 9am–5pm; May–Sept 9am–4.30pm; ☎ 07 863 6715, ⓦ waihi.org.nz). Information centre in the same building as the mine tour office and mining display (see below). Pay internet available.

Waihi gold mine tours Basement of the visitor centre ☎ 07 863 9015, ⓦ waihigoldminetours.co.nz. As

a complement to the interesting and well-presented (if a little glossy) view of past and present mining techniques in the visitor centre's basement, the mine company offers a two-hour guide tour (Mon–Sat 10am & 12.30pm; $28) visiting three viewpoints around the rim, plus a look at the ore-processing plant and the waste rock embankment.

ACCOMMODATION AND EATING

Bowentown Beach Holiday Park 510 Seaforth Rd, Bowentown Beach ☎ 0800 143 769, ⓦ bowentown .co.nz. A secluded site right at the southern end of the beach with lots of water activities available, as well as bike and kayak rental. Camping $20, cabins $68, kitchen cabins $88, motel units $120, apartments $150

The Porch 23 Wilson Rd, Waihi Beach ☎ 07 863 1330, ⓦ theporch.co.nz. Waihi Beach's dining mainstay for everything from coffee and cake to a sundowner dinner mains such as pork belly on celeriac purée ($29). Mon &

Tues 9am–3pm, Wed–Sun 9am–11pm or later.

Ti-Tree Café 14 Haszard St, Waihi ☎ 07 863 8668. Grab a coffee at this great little café with a wood-floored interior and a garden out back. Food spans the likes of pumpkin feta frittata ($14) and French onion soup to evening wood-fired pizzas ($18–26). Gluten-free options available. Daily 9am–4pm plus Thurs–Sat 6–10pm.

Waitete 31 Orchard Rd, 1.5km west of Waihi ☎ 07 863 8980, ⓦ waitete.co.nz. Combined restaurant, café and ice creamery that serves superb natural ice creams and fat-free sorbets made in the small on-site factory. Lunch is a relaxed affair with dishes such as chicken and chorizo risotto ($17), while dinner is more linen-and-candles formal and features the likes of grilled duck breast with roasted strawberries in balsamic vinegar ($36). Daily 11am–3pm & 6–10pm or later.

Katikati

South of Waihi, the coast begins to curl eastwards into the Bay of Plenty, leaving the bush-clad mountains behind to take on a gentler, more open aspect, with rolling hills divided by tall evergreen shelter belts that protect the valuable kiwifruit vines. In summer, numerous **roadside fruit stalls** spring up, selling ripe produce straight from the orchards, often at knockdown prices.

Some 20km after leaving Waihi you pass **KATIKATI**, an otherwise ordinary town but for the colourful and well-painted **murals** that have sprung up in the last couple of decades to catch passing traffic, many reflecting the heritage of the original Ulster settlers.

The Bay of Plenty

The **Bay of Plenty** occupies the huge bite between the Coromandel Peninsula and the East Cape, backed by rich farmland famous for its kiwifruit orchards. Its western end centres on the prosperous and fast-growing port city of **Tauranga** and its beachside neighbour **Mount Maunganui**. These amorphous settlements essentially form a single small conurbation sprawled around the glittering tentacles of Tauranga Harbour. A combination of warm dry summers and mild winters initially attracted retirees, followed by telecommuters and home-based small businesses.

Both towns have a thriving **restaurant** and **bar** scene, and a number of boats help you get out on the water to **sail**, or **swim with dolphins**. On land, make for Tauranga's modern **art gallery**, or head inland to picnic beside the swimming holes at **McLaren Falls** or paddle to see **glowworms**. With all this, it comes as no surprise that the area is a big draw for Kiwi summer holidaymakers.

Heading southeast along the Pacific Coast Highway (SH2), the urban influence wanes, the pace slows and the landscape becomes more rural, with orchards and kiwifruit vines gradually giving way to sheep country. You'll also find a gradual change in the racial mix, for the eastern Bay of Plenty is mostly **Maori** country; appropriate since some of the first Maori to reach New Zealand arrived here in their great *waka* (canoes). In fact, **Whakatane** is sometimes known as the birthplace of Aotearoa, as the Polynesian navigator **Toi te Huatahi** first landed here. Whakatane makes a great base for forays to volcanic **White Island** or the bird reserve of **Whale Island**. Further east, **Opotiki** is the gateway to the East Cape and to Gisborne, as well as trips on the remote and scenic **Motu River**.

Tauranga

Once you're through the protecting ring of suburbs, it's apparent that rampant development hasn't spoilt central **TAURANGA** ("safe anchorage" in Maori), huddled on a narrow peninsula with city parks and gardens backing a lively waterfront area.

KIWIFRUIT-PICKING

Tauranga is a major centre for **kiwifruit-picking**, a tough and prickly task that generally requires a commitment of at least three weeks. The picking season is late April to mid-June, but pruning and pollen collection also take place from mid-June to early September and again from the end of October to January. You're usually paid by the bin or by the kilo, so speed is of the essence. If this doesn't put you off, you'll find up-to-date information at the backpacker hostels, which will often help you arrange work.

5

You can easily spend half a day checking out the art gallery, strolling along the waterfront or lingering in the shops, restaurants and bars in Tauranga's compact **city centre**, concentrated between Tauranga Harbour and Waikareao Estuary. Come summer, though, you'll soon want to head over to Mount Maunganui (see p.349).

Brief history

In 1864 the tiny community of Tauranga became the scene of the **Battle of Gate Pa**, one of the most decisive engagements of the **New Zealand Wars**. In January the government sent troops to build two redoubts, hoping to prevent supplies and reinforcements from reaching the followers of the Maori King (see p.216), who were fighting in the Waikato. Most of the local Ngaiterangi hurried back from the Waikato and challenged the soldiers from a *pa* they quickly built near an entrance to the mission land, which became known as Gate Pa. In April, government troops surrounded the *pa* in what was New Zealand's only naval blockade, and pounded it with artillery. Despite this, the British lost about a third of their assault force and at nightfall the Ngaiterangi slipped through the British lines to fight again in the Waikato.

The Rena oil spill

In October 2011, the area became the focus of attention when the MV *Rena* container ship grounded on the **Astrolabe Reef**, 20km northeast of Mount Maunganui. Images of crazily tilted stacks of containers on the back of the severely listing ship zipped around the world as rescue crews tried to save the local beaches and birds from the slick of leaking fuel oil. All appears back to normal now, though the ship (now in two parts) remains on the reef.

Tauranga Art Gallery

108 Willow St · Daily 10am–4.30pm · Free · ☏ 07 578 7933, ⓦ artgallery.org.nz

After a determined fifteen-year campaign to give the city a contemporary cultural attraction, the **Tauranga Art Gallery** opened in 2007. A former bank building has been so transformed with layered metal sheets that it has been dubbed "The armadillo". Inside, its series of clean-lined display spaces over two floors house some excellent national and international travelling exhibitions.

TUHUA (MAYOR ISLAND)

The ecotourism-geared **TUHUA (Mayor Island)** is a cone-shaped, dormant volcano protruding from the Bay of Plenty and accessed by boat from Tauranga, 40km to the south. Its crater is virtually overgrown and the whole place is threaded with great **walking tracks** that open up a landscape thick with healthy populations of bellbird, tui, wood pigeon, fantail, grey warbler, waxeye, kingfisher, pied tit, kaka, morepork, shining cuckoo and harrier hawk. As there are no natural predators on the island, the birds are quite fearless and can be viewed at close range. **Wasps** are abundant, however, and anyone allergic to stings should pack medication or stay away. A third of the island's coast has been designated as a **marine reserve**, making for excellent **snorkelling**: many boats will rent snorkelling gear (around $20/day).

TOURS AND ACCOMMODATION

Blue Ocean Charters (☏0800 224 278, ⓦblueocean.co.nz) run day-trips to the island several times a week in summer (7am–5.30pm; $130), giving you around 8hr on land. That's just about enough to fully explore the island, though you'll appreciate it more if you stay overnight in simple cabins ($30; ☏07 578 7677, ✉taurangainfo@doc.govt.nz) or camping ($10/person) at Opo, the bay where you land. Blue Ocean don't charge any extra for overnight stays. To preserve Tuhua's pest-free status, all luggage must be thoroughly checked for stowaways.

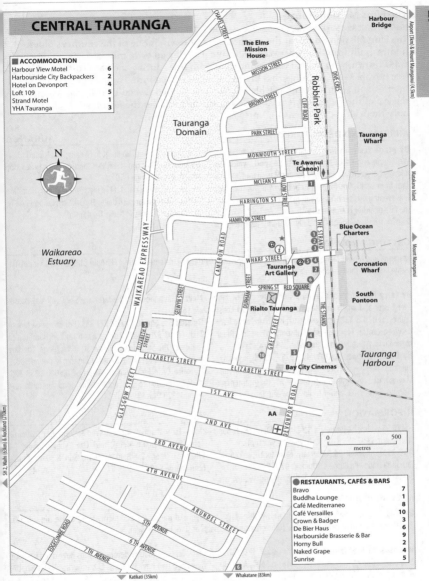

CENTRAL TAURANGA

ACCOMMODATION

Harbour View Motel	6
Harbourside City Backpackers	2
Hotel on Devonport	4
Loft 109	5
Strand Motel	1
YHA Tauranga	3

RESTAURANTS, CAFÉS & BARS

Bravo	7
Buddha Lounge	1
Café Mediterraneo	8
Café Versailles	10
Crown & Badger	3
De Bier Haus	6
Harbourside Brasserie & Bar	9
Horny Bull	2
Naked Grape	4
Sunrise	5

Te Awanui and Robbins Park

The Strand • Free

A protective awning shelters *Te Awanui*, an ornately carved traditional **war canoe** that is still used on ceremonial occasions on the harbour. The Strand continues north to **Robbins Park**, a swathe of green adorned by a rose garden and begonia house with fine views of Mount Maunganui. This was the site of Monmouth Redoubt from the New Zealand Wars (see p.790).

5

The Elms Mission House

Mission St • Wed, Sat & Sun 2–4pm; and by appointment • $5 • ☎ 07 577 9772, Ⓦ theelms.org.nz

The Elms Mission House, at the northern end of town, is one of the country's oldest homes, built from kauri between 1835 and 1847 by an early missionary, Archdeacon A.N. Brown, who tended the wounded of both sides during the **Battle of Gate Pa** (see box, p.344). The house has maintained its original form complete with dark-wood interior and a dining table at which Brown entertained several British officers on the eve of the Battle of Gate Pa, little suspecting that over the next few days he would bury them all.

ARRIVAL AND DEPARTURE
TAURANGA

By plane Daily Air New Zealand flights link Auckland, Wellington and Christchurch with the airport, which lies midway between Tauranga and Mount Maunganui (around 3km from each). Bus #2 goes to both towns but there are few evening bus services so you may want to catch a cab: the fare to either is around $15.
Destinations Auckland (5 daily; 35min); Christchurch

(2 daily; 1hr 50min); Wellington (4 daily; 1hr 10min).
By bus InterCity and NakedBus long-distance buses stop outside the Tauranga i-SITE.
Destinations Auckland (4 daily; 3hr 40min); Hamilton (3 daily; 2hr); Rotorua (8 daily; 1hr 30min); Taupo (5 daily; 2hr 30min); Thames (4 daily; 1hr 45min).

GETTING AROUND

Tauranga and Mount Maunganui are 6km apart, separated by the 3.5km-long Tauranga Harbour Bridge and an industrial estate linked to the Port of Tauranga.

By ferry From just after Christmas until the end of Jan, over Easter and when cruise ships are in port, Kiwi Coast Cruises (☎ 07 579 1325, Ⓦ kiwicoastcruises.co.nz) run a ferry between central Tauranga and Salisbury Wharf in Mount Maunganui, typically with 5 trips daily ($8 each way).
By bus Bayhopper (☎ 0800 422 9287, Ⓦ baybus.co.nz) operates the bus services around Tauranga and Mount Maunganui, covering most places in the immediate vicinity. Routes #1 and #2 run between Tauranga and

Mount Maunganui. Single fares are $2.60; all-day passes are $6.30.
By taxi Use Citicabs (☎ 07 571 8333) or Tauranga Mount Taxis (☎ 07 578 6086). There's a cab rank in Hamilton St (between the Strand and Willow St) in Tauranga. The fare between Tauranga and Mount Maunganui is around $30.
By bike Cycle Tauranga, 50 Wharf St (☎ 0800 253 525, Ⓦ cycletauranga.co.nz), rent hybrids good for town and around ($20/2hr; $49/day).

INFORMATION

i-SITE 95 Willow St (Mon–Fri 8.30am–5.30pm, Sat & Sun 9am–5pm; ☎ 07 578 8103, Ⓦ bayofplentynz.com).
DOC 253 Chadwick Rd, Greerton, 6km south of central Tauranga (Mon–Fri 8am–4.30pm; ☎ 07 578 7677).
Services The library, corner of Wharf and Willow sts

(Mon–Fri 9.30am–5.30pm & Wed to 7pm, Sat 9.30am–4pm, Sun 11.30am–4pm), and City Cyber Lounge, 24 Wharf St (Mon–Sat 8.30am–9pm, Sun 8.30am–6pm), both charge $4/hr.

ACCOMMODATION

Tauranga has numerous hostels and motels within walking distance of the centre, and plenty more out in the suburbs. A plethora of motels line 15th Avenue, some offering good deals at slack times of year.

Ambassador Motor Inn 9 15th Ave ☎ 07 578 5665, Ⓦ ambassador-motorinn.co.nz; map p.351. A 5min drive from the city centre, near the estuary, this has popular, well-equipped budget units and more luxurious options. There's a heated pool, some rooms have a spa bath, while others have river views. $100
★ **Avenue 11 Motel** 26 11th Ave ☎ 07 577 1881, Ⓦ avenue11.co.nz; map p.351. Great-value boutique motel with something of the feel of a B&B in a central but quiet location overlooking a small park. Three of the four

spacious, sumptuously decorated units have good harbour views and two have kitchens. Extra touches include bathrobes, a spa and a helpful host. $129
Bell Lodge 39 Bell St, off Waihi Rd (take Otumoetai exit off SH2) ☎ 07 578 6344, Ⓦ bell-lodge.co.nz; map p.351. Clean, modern and comfortable hostel with mostly en-suite rooms and bargain motel units. It's well set up for job seekers, particularly those after long, hourly paid contracts. It's in a peaceful spot 4km from the centre, with free pick-up and a free daily shuttle to Mount Maunganui

on request. Camping $\overline{\$20}$, dorms $\overline{\$28}$, en-suite doubles $\overline{\$74}$, motel-style units $\overline{\$95}$

Harbour View Motel 7 5th Ave East ☎07 578 8621, ⓦharbourviewmotel.co.nz; map p.345. Quiet and homely, just a 10min walk from town and a stone's throw from the bay. There's a spa and free use of kayaks plus the chance for fishing excursions. Ideal for families. $\overline{\$105}$

Harbourside City Backpackers 105 The Strand ☎07 579 4066, ⓦbackpacktauranga.co.nz; map p.345. Large hostel bang in the middle of the action. The waterfront views and tranquil atmosphere of the roof terrace make up for the basic rooms and noise on Fri and Sat nights (soundproofing from neighbouring bars and rooms at the rear of the building also help). Popular with workers who appreciate the management's good kiwifruit contacts. Dorms $\overline{\$29}$, doubles $\overline{\$74}$, en suite $\overline{\$80}$

★ **Hotel on Devonport** 72 Devonport Rd ☎07 578 2668, ⓦhotelondevonport.net.nz; map p.345. Sleek, modern boutique hotel with 38 rooms, all in muted tones with black-and-white photos on the walls and most with super-king-size beds and a minibar. Higher-priced rooms ($200–230) have city and/or harbour views. $\overline{\$165}$

Just the Ducks Nuts 6 Vale St ☎07 576 1366, ⓦjusttheducksnuts.co.nz; map p.351. A small, friendly hostel 1.5km from the city centre up a very steep driveway. It's popular with workers, has great views of the harbour and the Mount and free pick-ups. Dorms $\overline{\$27}$, doubles $\overline{\$62}$, en suites $\overline{\$74}$

Loft 109 109 Devonport Rd ☎07 579 5638, ⓦloft109.co.nz; map p.345. Slightly cramped but central and friendly hostel in a trendy townhouse-style building with a roof deck and nautical decor. Separate women's dorm. Dorms $\overline{\$28}$, doubles $\overline{\$62}$

Strand Motel 27 The Strand ☎07 578 5807, ⓦstrandmotel.co.nz; map p.345. Aging, budget motel that's central and near the waterfront, but on a fairly noisy corner. You get sea views from the decks of most of the fully equipped units. $\overline{\$95}$

YHA Tauranga 171 Elizabeth St ☎07 578 5064, ⓦyha.co.nz; map p.345. Well-equipped and welcoming hostel in rambling, secluded grounds (slightly marred by the adjacent expressway) a 5min walk from the centre, with BBQ, volleyball, a putting circuit and mini bushwalking trail. Camping $\overline{\$20}$, dorms $\overline{\$29}$, 4-shares $\overline{\$31}$, rooms $\overline{\$74}$

CAMPING

Silver Birch Family Holiday Park 101 Turret Rd ☎07 578 4603, ⓦsilverbirch.co.nz; map p.351. Fairly central campsite right on the river's edge with a family atmosphere, playground and hot mineral pools. Camping $\overline{\$15}$, cabins $\overline{\$50}$, en-suite cabins $\overline{\$90}$, motel units $\overline{\$120}$

EATING

Most of Tauranga's cafés and restaurants are in the centre, notably along Devonport Road and the Strand. Fresh produce is sold at the Saturday-morning farmers' market (8am–noon) at the Tauranga Primary School at 31 5th Ave.

Bravo Red Square ☎07 578 4700, ⓦcafebravo.co.nz; map p.345. Cool, minimalist café and restaurant that spills onto the pedestrianized Red Square for breakfast, gourmet snacks or dinner, with mains such as crispy skinned duck with vincotto poached pear in savoury walnut chutney (mains $30–33). Mon 9am–5pm, Tues–Sat 9am–9pm or later, Sun 9am–5pm.

Café Mediterraneo 62 Devonport Rd ☎07 577 0487; map p.345. Also known as *The Med*, this popular café has good breakfasts, such as three-grain porridge ($9.50), tempting counter food, and specials (written on a giant wall-mounted roll of brown paper) including pan-seared fish on grilled asparagus with toasted brioche (dishes $9–19) and some outdoor seating. Mon–Fri 7am–4pm, Sat 7.30am–4pm, Sun 8am–4pm.

Café Versailles 107 Grey St ☎07 571 1480, ⓦcafeversailles.net; map p.345. Award-winning traditional French restaurant serving a wonderful range of Gallic fare from snails ($18) to boeuf bourguignon ($29), all fabulously presented with a glass of home-grown Cabernet. Mon–Sat 3.30–9pm or later.

★ **De Bier Haus** 109 The Strand ☎07 928 0833, ⓦdebierhaus.com; map p.345. Justifiably popular Belgian brasserie serving snacks such as beer-battered frites with aioli, or soft German-style "Brezels" with garlic butter, balsamic vinegar and olive oil, all washed down with Hoegaarden. Mains (mostly $20–30) are good too, and include salt and pepper squid or sirloin and fries. Top all this off with a cheeseboard, cured figs and walnuts ($16).

★ **Harbourside Brasserie & Bar** Under the railway bridge at the southern end of the Strand ☎07 571 0520, ⓦharboursidetauranga.co.nz; map p.345. Tucked under the rail bridge on the edge of the harbour in a former dinghy storage shed, this fine-dining restaurant presents a short, stellar menu which might include half a dozen oysters in wasabi kelp hollandaise ($20) followed by Chinese roast duck on mushroom risotto ($34). Daily 11.30am–10pm or later.

Sunrise 10 Wharf St ☎07 578 9302, ⓦmillsreef.co.nz; map p.345. Intimate, friendly, funky and very popular licensed café where good breakfast standards vie with tasty chickpea and lentil burgers ($13), salads ($10–14) and home-made cakes and slices. Mon–Fri 7am–4pm, Sat 8am–3pm, Sun 9am–3pm.

5

DRINKING, NIGHTLIFE AND ENTERTAINMENT

Tauranga currently holds the region's clubbing baton, with summer revelry continuing into the wee hours along the Strand.

CLUBS AND BARS

Buddha Lounge 61b The Strand ☎07 928 1516, ⓦ thebuddhalounge.co.nz; map p.345. This small but cool venue with a balcony reverberates to soul, house and drum 'n' bass till late, with alluring sofas upstairs. It can be a bit of a squeeze on a Fri or Sat night. Thurs–Sat 8pm–3am.

Crown & Badger Corner of the Strand and Wharf St ☎07 571 3038, ⓦ crownandbadger.co.nz; map p.345. Lively and sometimes frenetic English-style pub with decent enough beer and great-value pub-style meals such as pepper steak ($22). Daily 9am–10pm or later.

Horny Bull 67 The Strand ☎07 578 8741, ⓦ horny bull.co.nz; map p.345. Texan-style food – think full rack of pork ribs ($28) – keeps energy levels up at this jolly and often-packed bar. Mon–Sat 11am–late, Sun 9am–late.

Naked Grape 97 The Strand; map p.345. Hip wine bar with claret-coloured walls that makes a refreshing change from the pub-style places along the Strand, and also serves classy but surprisingly inexpensive breakfasts (cinnamon pancakes), lunches, and dinners such as lamb rump with roasted red peppers ($30). Mon–Sat 7.30pm–late, Sun 8am–4pm.

ACTIVITIES AROUND TAURANGA AND MOUNT MAUNGANUI

The Tauranga and Mount Maunganui region is great for getting out **on the water**. There's a full range of boats to take you cruising, fishing, sailing, swimming with dolphins and even out to Tuhua (Mayor Island). Tauranga Wharf has recently been overhauled, with a barge converted into a finger pier from which a number of trips depart though others leave from Tauranga Bridge Marina, over on the Mount Maunganui side of the harbour.

CRUISES AND DOLPHIN WATCHING

Butler's Swim with Dolphins ☎0508 288 537, ⓦ swimwithdolphins.co.nz. Book a day or so in advance to head out on the yacht *Gemini Galaxsea* with Skipper Graham Butler, a good-natured sea dog and greenie with a high success rate of finding dolphins, and sometimes whales. Snorkel gear is provided, as is tea, coffee and hot chocolate, but you'll need to bring your own food for the day. Trips (8hr; departing 8.30am;

$135) leave from Tauranga Bridge Marina year-round, but are weather dependent. You can go again if you don't see dolphins.

Dolphin Seafaris ☎0800 326 8747, ⓦ nzdolphin .com. Five-hour trips ($130) in a powerful cruiser with committed anti-whaling crew. Trips generally run Dec–May (weather permitting), leaving at 8am. There's a repeat trip for dolphin no-shows.

FISHING

Blue Ocean Charters Tauranga Bridge Marina ☎0800 224 278, ⓦ blueocean.co.nz. Game fishing for marlin, tuna and kingfish (Dec–April), which involves chartering the boat (from $1250/day), but you can sometimes join an existing charter. Reef fishing for snapper and tarakihi goes for $75–100/person, depending on numbers, with an extra $30 for tackle.

Deep Star Charters ☎07 575 891, ⓦ deepstar charters.co.nz. Regular reef fishing trips ($80/day plus $30 for tackle and bait), plus overnight hapuku trips ($130 breakfast included, tackle $30) which involve reef fishing in the morning then seeking hapuku, blue nose and bass around Mayor Island later on.

SURFING

Discovery Mount Maunganui ☎027 632 7873, ⓦ discoverysurf.co.nz. One of several outfits offering surfing lessons at the Mount, with 2hr starter and

improver group sessions ($80) and 2hr private lessons ($150 for one, $200 for two).

KAYAKING AND GLOWWORM KAYAKING

Canoe & Kayak 5 MacDonald St, Mount Maunganui ☎07 574 7415, ⓦ canoeandkayak.co.nz. Budget, guided kayak trips taking you either Round the Mount (2hr 30min; $89), on Lake McLaren into a beautiful canyon overhung with trees (3hr; 1hr 30min paddling; $89) or the same trip around dusk when the canyon walls are a constellation of glowworms ($89).

Waimarino 36 Taniwha Place, Bethlehem ☎07 576 4233, ⓦ waimarino.com. Offers kayak trips on Tauranga Harbour ($120) and unguided exploration of the placid sections of the Wairoa River ($65), or the iconic Glowworm Tour ($120, $170 with gourmet dinner) to the glowworm canyon on Lake McLaren.

CINEMAS

Bay City Cinemas 45 Elizabeth St ☎ 07 577 0800, ⊕ baycitycinemas.co.nz; map p.345. Smart, multi-screen cinema showing mostly mainstream films with small discounts before 5pm and all day Tues.

Rialto Tauranga 21 Devonport Rd ☎ 07 577 7445, ⊕ rialtotauranga.co.nz; map p.345. Boutique three-screener showing mostly art-house films in plush environs. Also has discounts before 5pm and all day Tues.

Mount Maunganui

Habitually sun-kissed in summer, Tauranga's neighbouring beach resort, **MOUNT MAUNGANUI**, huddles under the extinct volcano of the same name, a modest cone that's a landmark visible throughout the western Bay of Plenty. It was once an island but is connected to the mainland by a narrow neck of dune sand (a tombolo) now covered by "The Mount", as the town is usually known. The sprawl of apartment blocks, shops, restaurants and houses isn't especially pretty but is saved by the 20km-long golden strand of **Ocean Beach**, itself enhanced by a couple of pretty islands just offshore and lined by Norfolk pines. It's wonderful for swimming, surfing and beach volleyball, and there are good restaurants and bars nearby where everyone gravitates for sundowners. Naturally, it is a big draw for Kiwi holidaymakers, some of whom give it a party-town reputation, especially at New Year when the place can be overwhelming and accommodation hard to come by.

Exploring the Mount

Walking track: 3km; 45min • Summit hike: 2km one-way; 1hr

The grassy slopes of the Mount (Mauao in Maori) rise 232m above the golden beach and invite exploration. A mostly level **walking track** loops around the base of the mountain, offering a sea and harbour outlook from under the shade of ancient pohutukawas. The base track links with a **hike to the summit** that is tough going towards the top but well worth the effort for views of Matakana Island and along the coast.

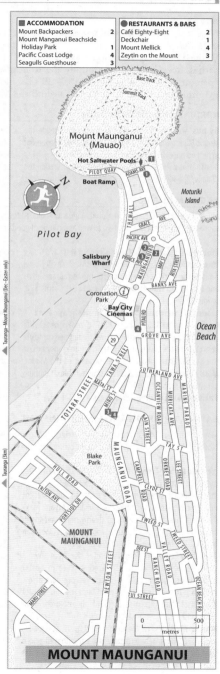

■ ACCOMMODATION	
Mount Backpackers	2
Mount Manganui Beachside Holiday Park	1
Pacific Coast Lodge	4
Seagulls Guesthouse	3

● RESTAURANTS & BARS	
Café Eighty-Eight	2
Deckchair	1
Mount Mellick	4
Zeytin on the Mount	3

MOUNT MAUNGANUI

5

Hot Saltwater Pools

9 Adams Avenue • Mon–Sat 6am–10pm, Sun 8am–10pm • Public pool $10.30; private spa, not including public pool, $23.40/30min • ☎ 07 575 0868, ⊛ tcal.co.nz

Wedged between the shopping strip and the Mount itself, the **Hot Saltwater Pools** harness deep geothermal groundwater to heat seawater, creating family-friendly open-air pools ranging from 33°C– 39°C. Chlorination makes it feel more like a swimming pool, but after a stroll around the Mount a luxuriant soak is well deserved.

ARRIVAL AND INFORMATION

By bus A couple of NakedBus services stop outside the Mount Maunganui i-SITE, but it is often more convenient to pick up buses in Tauranga.
Destinations Auckland (2 daily; 3hr 30min); Wellington (2 daily; 9hr 30min).

MOUNT MAUNGANUI

By plane Mount Maunganui shares an airport with Tauranga (see p.346).
i-SITE Salisbury Ave, just off Maunganui Rd (daily 9am–5pm; ☎ 07 575 5099, ⊛ bayofplentynz.com).

ACCOMMODATION

Much of the accommodation at Mount Manganui is geared towards long-staying Kiwi holidaymakers, but you'll also find short-stay apartments and motels, as well as a couple of good hostels.

Mount Backpackers 87 Maunganui Rd ☎ 07 575 0860, ⊛ mountbackpackers.co.nz; map p.349. A small hostel right in the thick of things, close to the restaurants, bars and beach, and with an on-site internet café. Dorms **$28**, rooms **$72**

Mount Maunganui Beachside Holiday Park 1 Adams Ave ☎ 0800 682 3224, ⊛ mountbeachside .co.nz; map p.349. An extensive, well-equipped campsite very close to the beach in a pleasant, terraced spot beside the hot saltwater pools, right at the foot of the Mount. Mostly camping spots plus a few simple cabins. Camping per site **$35**, cabins **$100**

Pacific Coast Lodge Backpackers 432 Maunganui Rd ☎ 0800 666 622, ⊛ pacificcoastlodge.co.nz; map p.349. Vast hostel with colourful murals on the walls and spacious dorms, plus a large kitchen and BBQ area. The only downside is that it's about a 25min walk from the restaurants and the fashionable end of the beach. Dorms **$26**, rooms **$72**

★ **Seagulls Guesthouse** 12 Hinau St ☎ 07 574 2099, ⊛ seagullsguesthouse.co.nz; map p.349. Clean, neat and immaculately maintained upscale backpackers with well-appointed kitchen, bike rental ($25/day) and continental breakfast ($8). Almost everyone gets a double or twin as there is just one three-bed dorm. Dorm **$30**, doubles **$70**, en suites **$80**, family room **$100**

EATING, DRINKING AND ENTERTAINMENT

Mount Maunganui doesn't have Tauranga's selection or culinary hotspots, but there are plenty of places on the half-dozen blocks of Maunganui Road that make up the centre, or on the waterfront strip by the Mount in the lee of apartment buildings.

★ **Café Eighty-Eight** 88 Maunganui Rd ☎ 07 574 0384; map p.349. It is hard to go past the delectable selection of sandwiches and sweet and savoury muffins at this excellent modern café with a cosy interior and small courtyard. Make the effort though for the likes of creamy mushrooms with crispy bacon ($16) or a chicken and pineapple Jamaican burger ($17). Top coffee, too. Daily 7am–5pm.

Deckchair 2 Marine Parade, under the Twin Towers ☎ 07 572 0942; map p.349. A great place to go for breakfast or morning coffee – when you can gaze across the beach to the ocean in the warming early sun – or for a lunch of Thai chicken salad ($18). Or just drop in for coffee and a muffin. Daily 6am–5pm.

Mount Mellick 317 Maunganui Rd ☎ 07 574 0047; map p.349. Popular and friendly Irish bar with well-priced food such as beef burgers ($20) or steak and Guinness

pie ($23), and a fun calendar of events including courtyard cricket, jam nights, live music, quiz nights and big-screen sports. Daily 11am–1am.

Zeytin on the Mount 118 Maunganui Rd ☎ 07 57 3040; map p.349. Relaxed Turkish restaurant with strong Greek and Italian influences, dishing up an antipasti platter ($28), kebabs ($18), a delicious chicken date and almond tagine ($20), feta, spinach and roasted veggie pizza ($20) or classic cannelloni ($20). Tues–Sun 9am–9pm.

CINEMAS

Bay City Cinemas 249 Maunganui Rd ☎ 07 577 0900, ⊛ baycitycinemas.co.nz; map p.349. Mainstream films in a more laidback environment than the sister location in Tauranga.

Around Tauranga and Mount Maunganui

The fertile countryside inland from Tauranga and Mount Maunganui is backed by the angular peaks of the Kaimai-Mamaku Forest Park. Rivers cascade down the slopes and across the coastal plain, along the way creating McLaren Falls on the Wairoa River, which eventually reaches the sea near the adventure park of Waimarino.

Waimarino

36 Taniwha Place, Bethlehem, 8km west of town • Day pass $40; under-16s $32 • ⓣ 07 576 4233, ⓦ waimarino.com

This fun adventure park beside a tidal section of the Wairoa River is great for kids of all ages with opportunities to swim, work out on an outdoor climbing wall, plummet down New Zealand's only kayak slide, muck around in kayaks and pedalos and get jettisoned off The Blob, a kind of massive cushion that lets you launch your mates sky high. They also run a variety of kayak trips (see box, p.348) and offer kayak rentals.

McLaren Falls

McLaren Falls Rd, off SH29, 18km southwest of Tauranga

A dam normally diverts water away from the 15m **McLaren Falls**, but on certain Sundays (Dec–March weekly; Sept, Oct, April & May every second week) the waters are released, firing up the falls. The **Wairoa River** downstream then becomes the scene of frenetic activity as hundreds of rafters and kayakers congregate to run the Grade IV–V rapids (see box, p.272). On other days the place is the preserve of locals who flock here to soak in a series of shallow pools hewn out of the bedrock. A few minutes' rock hopping should secure you a pool to yourself: bring a picnic and sunscreen.

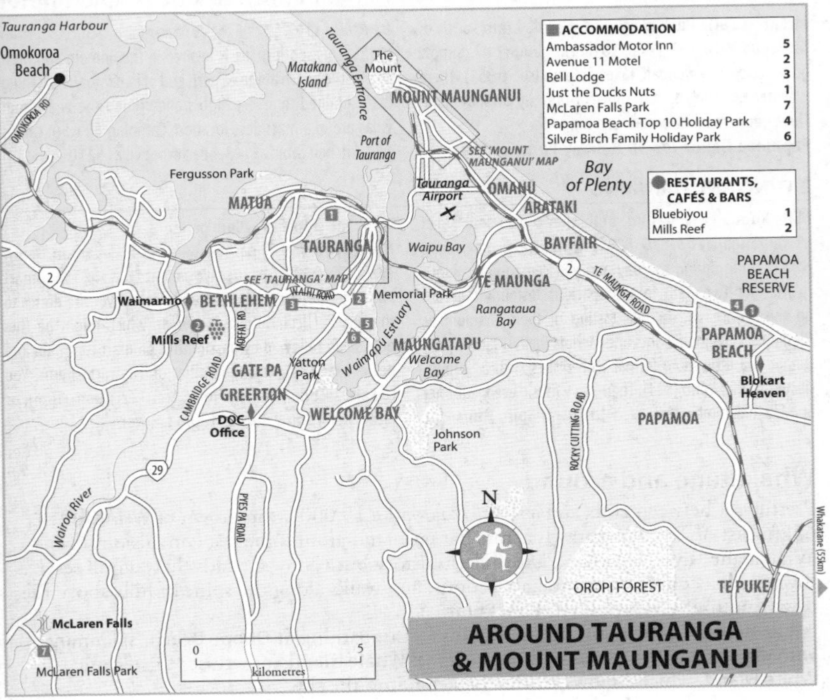

AROUND TAURANGA & MOUNT MAUNGANUI
ACCOMMODATION
Ambassador Motor Inn 5
Avenue 11 Motel 2
Bell Lodge 3
Just the Ducks Nuts 1
McLaren Falls Park 7
Papamoa Beach Top 10 Holiday Park 4
Silver Birch Family Holiday Park 6
RESTAURANTS, CAFÉS & BARS
Bluebiyou 1
Mills Reef 2
Tauranga Harbour
Omokoroa Beach
OMOKOROA RD
Matakana Island
Tauranga Entrance
The Mount
MOUNT MAUNGANUI
Port of Tauranga
SEE 'MOUNT MAUNGANUI' MAP
Bay of Plenty
Fergusson Park
MATUA
Tauranga Airport
OMANU
ARATAKI
TAURANGA
Waipu Bay
BAYFAIR
SEE 'TAURANGA' MAP
WAIHI ROAD
Memorial Park
TE MAUNGA
TE MAUNGA ROAD
PAPAMOA BEACH RESERVE
Waimarino
BETHLEHEM
Mills Reef
MOFFAT RD
Rangataua Bay
Waimapu Estuary
MAUNGATAPU
Welcome Bay
PAPAMOA BEACH
CAMBRIDGE ROAD
GATE PA
Yatton Park
GREERTON
Blokart Heaven
DOC Office
WELCOME BAY
ROCKY CUTTING ROAD
PAPAMOA
Johnson Park
Wairoa River
PYES PA ROAD
N
Whakatane (55km)
OROPI FOREST
TE PUKE
McLaren Falls
McLaren Falls Park
0 5
kilometres

5

McLaren Falls Park

Daily Oct–April 7.30am–7.30pm; May–Sept 7.30am–5.30pm

Just upstream from McLaren Falls, 190 hectares have been turned into a pretty waterside park around **Lake McLaren**, most notable for its campsite (see p.352), the easy Waterfall Track through a glowworm dell and excellent glowworm kayak tours (see box, p.348).

Papamoa Beach

Mount Maunganui's Ocean Beach stretches 20km southeast to **Papamoa Beach**, which is great for surfing and swimming away from the glitz of the Mount.

Papamoa is also home to the world's original purpose-built **blokart speedway track** at Blokart Heaven, 176 Parton Rd (from $30/30min; ☎07 572 4256, ⓦblokartheaven .co.nz): think go-kart with a sail (tuition available). With a fair wind you can get up to 60km/hr; naturally it's weather-dependent, so no wind equals no fun.

Te Puke

Kiwi360 daily: summer 9am–4pm; winter 10am–3pm; café daily 10.30am–3pm • 45min guided tours $20 • ☎07 573 6340, ⓦkiwi360.com

Te Puke, 12km southeast of Papamoa Beach, is New Zealand's kiwifruit capital, as evidenced by **Kiwi360**, 6km east of the town centre. Graced by a surreal giant kiwifruit slice, this massive **orchard and processing plant** operates as a kind of horticultural theme park, running informative tours as well as a souvenir emporium and a café serving kiwifruit muffins, kiwifruit salads, kiwifruit wine and liqueur and full meals.

ACCOMMODATION

AROUND TAURANGA AND MOUNT MAUNGANUI

McLaren Falls Park McLaren Falls Rd, 11km south of Tauranga ☎07 577 7000, ⓦtauranga.govt.nz. Simple grassy sites in a wooded, lakeside park (see p.351). There is water and toilets, but showers only by arrangement. Three-night maximum stay. Camping $\underline{5}$

Papamoa Beach Top 10 Holiday Park 535 Papamoa Beach Rd ☎07 572 0816, ⓦpapamoabeach.co.nz; map p.351. This spotless site is located in the domain and right beside the beach at the eastern end of Papamoa. Everything is maintained to a very high standard and the beachfront villas are in a matchless location. Camping $\underline{21.50}$, cabins $\underline{84}$, kitchen cabins $\underline{143}$, beachfront villas $\underline{210}$

EATING AND DRINKING

Mills Reef 143 Moffat Rd, Bethlehem, 8km southwest of Tauranga ☎07 576 8800, ⓦmillsreef.co.nz; map p.351. Come during the day and you can combine lunch (platter for two $38) in the spacious restaurant or out on the terrace with a free tasting of their Chardonnay, Rieslings, Sauvignon Blancs and Merlots (daily 10am–5pm). Dinner is a little more formal with dishes such as cumin-dusted rack of lamb ($34). There's live music every summer Sunday lunchtime. Mon–Wed 10.30am–3pm, Thurs–Sat 10.30am–3pm & 5–10pm or later.

Bluebiyou 559 Papamoa Beach Rd, Papamoa Beach ☎07 572 2099, ⓦbluebiyou.co.nz; map p.351. Smart and airy café/bar/restaurant with views over the dunes to the sea. Particularly nice for lunch, which might be Thai beef salad followed by passionfruit pannacotta (main and dessert for $30), or any number of à la carte items. You can also just drop in for a drink. Mon–Fri noon–10pm or later, Sat & Sun 9.30am–10pm or later.

Whakatane and around

Prettily set between cliffs and a river estuary, the 15,000-strong town of **WHAKATANE**, 65km east of Te Puke, sprawls across flat farmland around the last convulsions of the Whakatane River. It has had a turbulent history but is now a relatively tranquil service town with a couple of cultural attractions, and walks along the spine of hills above the town and to the viewpoint at **Kohi Point**.

It also makes a great jumping-off point for sunbathing at **Ohope Beach**, **swimming with dolphins**, visits to the bird sanctuary of **Whale Island** and cruises to volcanic **White Island**, which billows plumes of steam into the sky.

Brief history

The area has had more than its fair share of dramatic events. The **Maori** word *Whakatane* ("to act as a man") originated when the women of the *Mataatua* canoe were left aboard while the men went ashore; the canoe began to drift out to sea, but touching the paddles was *tapu* for women. Undeterred, Wairaka, the teenage daughter of a chief, led the women in paddling back to shore, shouting *Ka Whakatane Au i Ah au* ("I will deport myself as a man"); a statue at Whakatane Heads commemorates her heroic act.

Apart from a brief sortie by Cook, the first Europeans were flax traders in the early 1800s. In March 1865, missionary **Carl Völkner** was killed at Opotiki and a government agent, **James Falloon**, arrived to investigate. Supporters of a fanatical Maori sect, the Hau Hau (see p.357), attacked Falloon's vessel, killing him and his crew. In response, the government declared **martial law**, and by the end of the year a large part of the Bay of Plenty had been confiscated and Whakatane was a military settlement. **Te Kooti** (see p.383) chose Whakatane as his target for a full-scale attack in 1869 before being driven back into the hills of Urewera.

5

Pohaturoa
The Strand

Whakatane's defining feature is the large rock outcrop known as **Pohaturoa** ("long rock"). The place is sacred to Maori and the small park surrounding the rock contains carved benches and a black marble monument to Te Hurinui Apanui, a great chief who propounded the virtues of peace and is mourned by Pakeha and Maori alike. The site was once a shrine where Maori rites were performed, and the seed that grew into the karaka trees at the rock's base is said to have arrived on the *Mataatua* canoe.

Wairere Falls
Wairaka Rd

The sea once lapped the cliffs that now hem in the town. Follow them around from Pohaturoa to the base of **Wairere Falls**, nestled in a sylvan cleft. Once the source of the town's water and motive power for mills, they're now free-flowing and an impressive sight after rain.

Te Koputu a Te Whanga a Toi
Kakahoroa Drive • Mon–Fri 9.30am–5.30pm, Sat & Sun 10am–2pm • $5 donation requested • ☎ 07 306 0500, Ⓦ whakatanemuseum.org.nz

Devote a little time to Eastern Bay of Plenty's brand-new cultural focus, Te Koputu a Te Whanga a Toi, with exhibits on early Maori settlement after their arrival in the *Mataatua waka* (canoe). There's plenty of material on the post-colonial era, too, including on the a local Maori rugby team that toured Britain in 1888, and the 1954 Melbourne Cup, won by locally raised horse, Rising Fast.

Mataatua Wharenui
105 Muriwai Drive • Ⓦ mataatua.com

Known as "The House That Came Home", **Mataatua Wharenui** is one of the finest (and largest) carved meetinghouses you'll see. It has a fascinating history. Built locally in 1875 by the Ngati Awa people as a final attempt to restore self-belief after all their land was sold or confiscated, it was removed in 1879 to represent New Zealand at the British Empire Exhibition in Sydney. After a long stint at London's Victoria and Albert Museum, the house was returned to New Zealand in 1925 and spent 70 years in Dunedin before finally being returned to its rightful Ngati Awa owners as part of a Treaty of Waitangi settlement in 1996.

You can see the richly carved exterior of the re-erected house and peer in through the windows, but details of the planned opening as an interactive cultural centre were still not finalized in mid-2012; check with the i-SITE.

River Walk

A walking path follows the levee along the south side of the Whakatane River for 4km to its mouth. The most interesting section runs from the city centre 2km to the heads and makes for a lovely late-afternoon stroll that passes two replicas of the *Mataatua waka* in a reserve, with views across the river to the sprightly bronze statue of Wairaka on a rock. You can also reach the heads by car along Muriwai Drive.

Kohi Point and Ohope Walk
5.5km one-way; 2hr • Details in a free leaflet or the more detailed *Discover the Walks Around Whakatane* booklet ($2) from the i-SITE

The best of the local walks starts in the centre of town and follows the Nga Tapuwae o Toi ("Sacred Footsteps of Toi") Walkway, which traverses the domain of the great chieftain Toi and continues to **Kohi Point**, giving panoramic views of Whakatane, Whale and White islands and Te Urewera National Park. From Kohi Point, continue through Otarawairere Bay (no passage 1hr either side of high tide) and on to Ohope Beach, from where you can return to Whakatane by the Bayhopper bus (see opposite).

Ohope

The tiny settlement of **OHOPE**, 7km east of Whakatane, extends along the beach in a thin ribbon to the entrance of **Ohiwa Harbour**. Ohiwa ("a place of watchfulness") is the site of a natural shellfishery for pipi and cockles, and a place of numerous *pa* sites, signifying the importance of a convenient and renewable food source to the Maori way of life.

Otherwise, this is very much a surf-and-sand beach resort, though it makes a pleasant base from which to explore Whakatane (just $2.60 one-way on the Bayhopper bus) and its surroundings.

ARRIVAL AND DEPARTURE — WHAKATANE AND AROUND

By bus InterCity and NakedBus buses running along SH2 between Rotorua and Gisborne stop twice daily in each direction outside the Whakatane i-SITE. The local Bayhopper (0800 422 928, baybus.co.nz) serves Tauranga, Mount Maunganui, Ohope ($2.60 one-way) and Opotiki (Mon & Wed).

Destinations Gisborne (2 daily; 3hr); Mount Maunganui (Mon–Sat 1 daily; 2hr); Ohope (Mon–Sat 4–6 daily; 30min); Opotiki (2–4 daily; 40min); Rotorua (2 daily; 1hr 30min); Tauranga (Mon–Sat 1 daily; 2hr).

By plane Flights from Auckland and Wellington arrive at Whakatane airport, about 10km west of the centre, connected by the Dial-A-Cab shuttle (around $25; 0800 308 0222).

Destinations Auckland (4 daily; 45min); Wellington (1 daily; 1hr 10min).

INFORMATION AND TOURS

i-SITE Corner of Quay St and Kakahoroa Drive (Mon–Fri 8am–5pm, Sat & Sun 10am–4pm; 07 306 2030, whakatane.com). Well stocked with DOC leaflets (including *Discover the Walks Around Whakatane*) for the local area and offers free internet and wi-fi.

Kiwi Jet Tours 0800 800 538, kiwijetboattours .com. Zoom around on the Rangitaiki River with an ex-world champion jetboat racer who will take you from the Matahina Dam, 25km south of Whakatane, to the beautiful Aniwhenua Falls over a number of modest whitewater sections ($95).

ACCOMMODATION

Whakatane has a sizeable stock of accommodation, with an emphasis on mid-range motels. Also consider Ohope Beach, just over the hill.

Crestwood Homestay 2 Crestwood Rise 07 308 7554, crestwood-homestay.co.nz. Attractive, friendly B&B in a quiet hilltop setting with scenic views and a 20min walk from the town centre. Evening meals ($50 including wine) are available by arrangement. The owner is a radio operator for the Whakatane Coastguard and is happy to show guests around its headquarters. $150

Karibu Backpackers 13 Landing Rd, 1.5km southwest of the centre 07 307 8276, karibubackpackers.co.nz. Suburban house converted into a big, well-maintained and welcoming hostel with an attractive garden for camping. There's off-street parking, plus free use of bikes and free pick-up from the bus stop. Camping $14, dorms $23, rooms $56

Tuscany Villas 57 The Strand 0800 801 040, tuscanyvillas.co.nz. Top-of-the-line motor inn with a range of studios and suites, all fitted out to a high standard with kitchenette. The one-bedroom suites all have a spa bath or hot tub. Double $155, one-bedroom suite $175

Whakatane Holiday Park McGarvey Rd 07 308 8694, whakataneholidaypark.co.nz. A sheltered campsite a 10min walk along the levee from the Strand, with a summertime outdoor pool and basic but well-maintained facilities. Rates go up 15–25 percent from Christmas to early Feb. Camping $15, cabins $60, kitchen cabins $70, self-contained units $85

White Island Rendezvous 15 The Strand East 0800 242 299, whiteisland.co.nz. Spotless, Mediterranean-style multi-level motel opposite the wharf. Some rooms have spa baths, and all are equipped with Sky TV and microwave. There's also a popular on-site café, *PeeJay's Coffee House* (see p.357). Self-contained units $140

OHOPE

Ocean View Motel 18/2 West End, Ohope Beach 07 312 5665, oceanviewmotel.co.nz. Very relaxing motel at the western end of the beach, with safe swimming, bushwalks and free use of bikes, kayaks, boogie boards, surfboards and laundry facilities. All of its self-contained units have sea views. Rooms $120

Ohope Beach Top 10 Holiday Park 367 Harbour Rd, 10km east of Whakatane 0800 264 673, ohopebeach .co.nz. Upmarket holiday park right behind Ohope Beach, with a pool complex including a waterslide and a free summer-time kids' programme. Higher rates apply from Christmas to early Feb. Camping $22, cabins $90, self-contained units $100, motel units $135, luxury apartments $190

5

OFFSHORE WHAKATANE

WHALE ISLAND

Whale Island (Motohora), 10km offshore from Whakatane, is a 2km-by-1km DOC-controlled haven where considerable efforts were made decades ago to eradicate goats and rats. Native bush is rapidly returning and the island has become a bird reserve and safe environment for saddlebacks, grey-faced petrels, sooty shearwaters, little blue penguins, dotterels and oystercatchers, as well as three species of lizard – geckos and speckled and copper skinks – and the reptilian tuatara; occasional visits are made by the North Island kaka and falcon, as well as fur seals.

Access to the island itself is only by a limited number of **guided tours** (Jan & Feb only; contact Whakatane's i-SITE for details and reservations). Expect to pay around $85 for a 4hr trip.

WHITE ISLAND

Whakatane's star attraction is **White Island** (Whaakari), named by Cook for its permanent shroud of mist and steam. Roughly circular and almost 2km across, White Island lies 50km offshore, sometimes a rough ride. Neither this nor its seething volcanism deters visitors, who flock to its desolate, other-worldly landscape, with billowing towers of gas, steam and ash spewing from a crater lake 60m below sea level. Smaller fumaroles come surrounded by bright yellow and white crystal deposits that re-form in new and bizarre shapes each day. The crystal-clear and abundant waters around the island make this one of the best **dive** spots in New Zealand.

Whaakari embodies the ongoing clash between the Indo-Australian Plate and the Pacific Plate that has been driven beneath it for the last two million years. This resulted in the upward thrust of super-heated rock through the ocean floor, creating a massive **volcanic** structure. **Sulphur**, for use in fertilizer manufacture, was sporadically mined on the island from the 1880s, but catastrophic eruptions, landslides and economic misfortune plagued the enterprise. The island was abandoned in 1934, and these days it is home only to 60,000 grey-faced **petrels** and 10,000 **gannets**. You can only land on the island via a guided boat tour or by helicopter.

TOURS AND ACTIVITIES ON AND AROUND THE ISLANDS

Easily the most popular way to experience the islands is with White Island Tours, who get out to White Island whenever the weather plays ball. You can also get out there by helicopter, explore below the surface on dive trips or head out dolphin watching and swimming from December to March – anybody offering to take you outside those months is either wildly optimistic or less than scrupulous.

Whakatane's numerous **fishing** guides predominantly work on a charter basis from the local marina; the i-SITE has a list of operators doing half-day and full-day trips and they can usually hook you up with a boat to suit your needs.

Dive White 186 The Strand ☎0800 348 394, ⓦdivewhite.co.nz. White Island from below is one of New Zealand's top dive destinations. Visibility is commonly around 20m at half a dozen dive sites, encompassing walls, drop-offs, arches and underwater vents surrounded by schools of blue maomao, kingfish, rays and much more. 8hr trips run daily in summer and on demand in winter (two dives including all gear $345).

Dive Works Charters 96 The Strand ☎0800 354 7737, ⓦwhaleislandtours.com. Excellent dolphin and seal swimming (3–4hr; $160) around Whale Island and White Island plus eco-tours onto Whale Island and dive and snorkelling trips.

Vulcan Helicopters ☎0800 804 354, ⓦvulcanheli

.co.nz. See White Island from the air on flights (2hr; $550/person for 2 passengers) that leave from Whakatane airport and include a 1hr walking tour of the island visiting the crater rim, fumaroles and the old sulphur works.

White Island Tours (a.k.a. **"Pee Jay Charters"**) 15 The Strand East ☎0800 733 529, ⓦwhiteisland.co .nz. Book at least a couple of days in advance for this 6hr trip ($185) out to White Island, which offers two hours on the island – including standing on the edge of the crater (with a gas mask on) amid pillars of smoke and steam looking down into the steaming crater lake. You also visit the site of a 1923 sulphur-processing factory that is being gradually eaten away by the corrosive atmosphere.

EATING, DRINKING AND NIGHTLIFE

The Bean 72 The Strand East ☎07 307 0494, ☻the beancafe.co.nz. Laidback daytime café and coffee roastery, so you can be sure of a good hit to go with your bagel or home-style baking. Free wi-fi. Mon–Sat 8am–4pm, Sun 9am–3pm.

The Craíc Whakatane Hotel, 79 The Strand ☎07 307 8670. Atmospheric Irish bar furnished in mellow dark wood and serving tasty fare. Most of the town's nightlife happens here, with live bands on Friday night and some Sunday afternoons, and dancing in the bar. Daily noon–9pm or a lot later.

PeeJay's Coffee House 15 The Strand, inside the White Island Rendezvous Motel ☎07 308 9589, ☻whiteisland.co.nz. Fine espresso helps wash down daytime snacks and light meals. Early opening hours make it a good spot for breakfast before a morning boat trip. Try the mushroom and chorizo-slathered ciabatta ($16) and make use of the free wi-fi. Daily 6.30am–2pm.

Roquette 23 Quay St ☎07 307 0722, ☻roquette -restaurant.co.nz. Whakatane's best restaurant and bar features dishes such as salt and pepper calamari with lemon aioli ($20) and seafood and tomato risotto ($33). Mon–Sat 10am–10pm.

Whakatane Sportfishing Club The Strand East ☎07 307 1573, ☻wsfc.co.nz. Spacious bar with huge windows overlooking the boats and river, great for cheap drinks, good-value bar meals such as seafood chowder ($13) and a seafood platter with salad and chips ($23). It's a private club but visitors can sign in. Daily 11am–10pm or later.

The Wharf Shed 2/2 The Strand East ☎07 308 5698, ☻wharfshed.com. All-day café-cum-restaurant in a converted wooden butter store and a mellow riverside setting. Good for a late breakfast, lunch or watching the sun set over the water while tucking into seafood, including pan-seared salmon ($31). Daily noon–late.

OHOPE

Ohiwa Oyster Farm 11 Wainui Rd, 1km south of Ohope beach on the road to Opotiki ☎07 312 4565. Pick up cheap supplies of fresh seafood, including mussels, oysters and smoked fish, from this shack beside Ohiwa Harbour, with a couple of picnic tables at the water's edge. Daily 9am–8pm.

Toi Toi 19 Pohutukawa Ave ☎07 312 5623, ☻toitoi -ohope.co.nz. Polished concrete floors and white chairs give a somewhat spartan feel to this classy restaurant and bar with a deck out back overlooking Ohope Beach. They still welcome sandy beach bums either for a coffee, a beer or anything from veggie cannelloni ($26) to eye fillet ($36). Acoustic acts often play in summer. Mon–Fri 4–10pm or later, Sat & Sun 10am–10pm or later.

Opotiki

The small settlement of **OPOTIKI**, 46km east of Whakatane (via the Ohope Road), is the easternmost town in the Bay of Plenty and surrounded by lush countryside and beaches. Opotiki also acts as the gateway to (and final supply stop for) the wilds of the East Cape and trips on the remote and scenic Motu River.

The town has few notable sights to delay your departure for the East Cape or Gisborne. From Opotiki, SH2 strikes inland to the more citified opportunities of

---

THE HAU HAU

Zealous missionaries encouraged many Maori to abandon their belief structure in favour of **Christianity** but, as land disputes with settlers escalated, the Maori increasingly perceived the missionaries as agents for land-hungry Europeans.

When **war** broke out and the recently converted Maori suffered defeats, they felt betrayed not only by the Crown but also by their newly acquired god, and some formed the revivalist **Hau Hau** movement, based on the Old Testament. Dedicated to routing the interlopers, disciples danced around *nui* **poles**, chanting for Pakeha to leave the country. The name is derived from the **battle cry** of the warriors, who flung themselves at their enemies with their right arms raised to protect them from bullets, believing that true faith prevented them from being shot. The movement began in 1862 and by 1865, having capitalized on widespread Maori unrest, there was a *nui* pole in most villages of any size from Wellington to the Waikato. The Hau Hau were some of the most feared **warriors** and involved in the bloodiest and most bitter battles, but the movement began to fade after their **leader** and founder, Te Ua Haumene, was captured in 1866. Some of the sect's ideas were **revitalized** when the infamous rebel **Te Kooti** (see p.383) based parts of his **Ringatu** movement on Hau Hau doctrine.

5

Gisborne, while SH35 meanders around the perimeter of **the East Cape**, never straying far from its rugged and windswept coastline.

Opotiki Museum

123 Church St • Mon–Fri 10am–4pm, Sat 10am–2pm • $10

All Opotiki's significant historic buildings cluster around the junction of Church and Elliot streets, including the **Opotiki Museum**, which occupies the whole block between Elliot and Kelly streets. Much of the content is typical small-town museum fare, boosted by the Tanewhirinaki Carvings, a fine collection of Maori sculptures from this area that spent many years as part of the Auckland Museum collection. Be sure to head along to the *Shalfoon & Francis* section at #129, a nostalgic 1870s-established grocery and hardware store that revels in its un-catalogued store of old typewriters, biscuit tins and just about anything you might find in an old hardware store.

St Stephen's Church

Church St, opposite the museum • Mon–Fri 10am–4pm, Sat 10am–2pm; get key from the museum if it isn't open • Free

The innocent-looking white clapboard **St Stephen's Church** was once the scene of a notorious murder, for it was here, in March 1865, that local missionary **Carl Völkner** was allegedly killed by prophet Kereopa Te Rau from the Hau Hau sect (see box, p.357). The case is far from clear-cut: it appears that Völkner had written many letters to Governor Grey espousing the land-grabbing ambitions of settlers, and local Maori claim Völkner was justly executed. Settlers used the story as propaganda, fuelling intermittent skirmishes over the next three years. Nip in and see the gorgeous *tukutuku* panels around the altar. Völkner's gravestone is slotted into the wall of the church around the back.

Hukutaia Domain

Daily dawn–dusk

A welcome retreat into the bush is given by the small and unspoiled **Opotiki (Hukutaia) Domain**, with its understorey of nikau and a grand puriri tree thought to date from 500 BC and once used as a burial tree by local Maori. The bush also contains a good lookout over the Waioeka Valley and a series of short yet interesting rainforest tracks. To get here, head south from the centre of town on Church Street as far as the Waioweka River Bridge, cross it and bear left along Woodlands Road for 7km.

ARRIVAL AND DEPARTURE

OPOTIKI

By bus InterCity and NakedBus buses between Whakatane and Gisborne stop outside the *Hot Bread Shop Café* at the corner of Bridge and St John sts. Bayhopper buses to Whakatane (Mon–Sat) and Tauranga (Mon & Wed only) leave from the corner of Elliot and St John sts in the centre of town. Destinations Gisborne, via SH2 (2 daily; 2hr); Hicks Bay, via SH35 (2 weekly; 3hr); Rotorua (2 daily; 2hr 10min); Whakatane (2–3 daily; 40min).

GETTING AROUND

By bike Travel Shop, 109 Church St (☎07 315 8881, ✉travelshop@xtra.co.nz), rents bikes ($45/day) with drop-offs arranged.

INFORMATION

i-SITE/DOC 70 Bridge St (Christmas–Jan daily 8am–5pm; Feb–Christmas Mon–Fri 9am–4.30pm, Sat & Sun 9am–1pm ☎07 315 3031, ⊛opotikinz.com). The combined i-SITE and DOC office has loads of information about the East Cape plus internet access and pay showers.

ACCOMMODATION

Aurum 213 Ohiwa Beach Rd, 13km west of town ☎07 315 4737, ⊛aurumretreat.co.nz. Three beautifully appointed self-contained rooms, tucked under pohutukawas and with fabulous sea views. The Upper Room is particularly romantic and there's an outdoor wood-fired bath. Breakfast and light meals are available on request. **$200**

Beyond the Dunes 5 Wairakaia Rd, 5km east of town

OPOTIKI TOURS AND ACTIVITIES

Opotiki is all about getting out on the water, either fishing offshore, or exploring the rivers kayaking, jetboating or whitewater rafting.

JETBOATING

Motu AAA Jetboat 📞 027 686 6489. Scenic flat-water jetboating on the lower 20km of the Motu River with the option of taking up an inflatable kayak and paddling back down ($75 with a minimum of 2 people; Dec–April daily, and by arrangement).

FISHING AND KAYAKING

Marine Life Tours 16 Wharf St 📞 027 350 4910, 🌐 marinelifetours.com. Runs simple surfcasting trips ($40/hr for two people, with all gear), but they also organized the construction of the Opotiki Community Reef, designed to maintain fish stocks. Learn about it on a 1hr tour ($15). Best of all, there's also a self-guided 10km drift down an easy section of the Waioeka River known as "Tangle With Taniwha" (3–4hr; $80).

Travel Shop 109 Church St 📞 07 315 8881, 📧 travelshop@xtra.co.nz. Rents kayaks ($45/day) for self-guided tours with drop-offs arranged.

WILDERNESS RAFTING ON THE MOTU RIVER

Some of the best **wilderness rafting** trips in New Zealand are on the Grade III–IV **Motu River**, hidden deep in the mountain terrain of the remote Raukumara Ranges, with long stretches of white water plunging through gorges and valleys to the Bay of Plenty coast. In 1981, after a protracted campaign against hydro-dam builders, the Motu became New Zealand's first designated "wild and scenic" river. Access by 4WD, helicopter and jetboat makes one- and two-day trips possible, but to capture the essence of this remote region you should consider one of the longer trips in which you'll see no sign of civilization for three days – a magical and eerie experience.

Wet 'n' Wild Rafting 📞 0800 462 723, 🌐 wetnwildrafting.co.nz. Rotorua-based company starting trips from Opotiki that range from two days ($995, with helicopter access), to the full five-day adventure ($995, with no helicopter access) from the headwaters to the sea. In all cases transport and gourmet meals are provided; you can bring your own tent and sleeping bag or rent them from Wet 'n' Wild.

📞 07 315 7942, 🌐 bookabach.co.nz. Simple, modern, self-contained, pine-lined *bach* just over the dunes from a sweeping swimming beach. A great spot to hole up for a day or two, though you'll need your own bedding. Price increases to $85 at weekends. $70

Capeview Cottage Tablelands Rd, 8km southeast of town 📞 0800 227 384, 🌐 capeview.co.nz. Very comfortable rimu-lined, fully self-contained cottage on a kiwifruit and avocado orchard with long coastal views, a barbecue on the deck and a broad library. The hosts are eco-minded and very knowledgeable about the area. $145

Central Oasis Backpackers 30 King St 📞 07 315 5165, 📧 centraloasis@hotmail.com. Friendly German-run hostel in a higgledy-piggledy villa right in the centre of town, with one double, one twin and a dorm. Dorm $23, double & twin $56

Ohiwa Holiday Park 380 Ohiwa Harbour Rd, off SH2, 15km west of town 📞 07 315 4741, 🌐 ohiwaholidays.co.nz. Little-known gem of a campsite right on the beach, with safe swimming, kayaks for rent and a "jumping pillow" – massively popular with kids (and a few adults). Two-night minimum at peak times. Camping $17, cabins $55, kitchen cabins $70, flats $100, park motels $120

★ **Opotiki Beach House** 7 Appleton Rd, off SH2, 5km west of town 📞 07 315 5117, 🌐 opotikibeachhouse.co.nz. The pick of Opotiki's hostels is this laidback beachside hangout with free use of kayaks and bodyboards. Dorms $28, rooms $66

EATING AND DRINKING

1759 Masonic Hotel, 121 Church St 📞 07 315 6115. Classic pub meals in a raw brick backroom of this classic pub. Expect dishes such as venison with Jack Daniels sauce and roast veggies ($22). Daily 9am–10pm or later.

Hot Bread Shop & Illy Café 43 St John St 📞 07 315 6795. Mainstream spot for good coffee, yummy cakes and pastries, brunch and snacks. Daily 5am–5pm.

Ocean Seafoods Fish and Chips 90 Church St 📞 07 315 6335. The best chip shop in town, doing fish and chips for around $8, plus burgers and the usual Kiwi chippy staples. In fine weather, grab some and head down to the riverside. Mon–Wed 9am–7.30pm, Thurs–Sun 9am–8.30pm or later.

★ **Two Fish** 102 Church St 📞 07 315 5548. Excellent

5

café with mismatched furniture and a dedication to quality, made-on-the-premises foods; stop in for breakfast, delicious muffins (raspberry and lemon) or quick bites such as chicken wraps. Also has the best espresso around. Mon–Fri 8am–4pm, Sat 8.30am–2pm.

The Waioeka Gorge route

From Opotiki, **SH2** strikes out south to **Gisborne**, 137km away. It's one of New Zealand's great scenic drives, dotted with tiny settlements, weaving up and down steep hills cloaked in bush. The route winds gingerly along the Waioeka River for 30km before tracing the narrow and steep **Waioeka Gorge** then emerging onto rolling pastureland and dropping to the plains around Gisborne, all arrow-straight roads through orchards, vineyards and sheep farms.

The **only petrol** along the route is at Matawai, but opening hours are limited: fill up in Opotiki or, if you're coming from the south, in Gisborne.

Waioeka Gorge walks

Break your journey on the first 72km stretch to Matawai by tackling one of the interesting **walks** on either side of the road. Ten scenic tracks through forest, ranging from fifteen minutes to ten hours one-way, are described in the DOC leaflet *Walks in Waioeka and Urutawa*, available at the Opotiki i-SITE.

The East Cape

Jutting into the South Pacific northeast of Opotiki and Gisborne, the little-visited **East Cape** (also known as Eastland) is an unspoilt backwater that's a reminder of how New Zealand once was. Between Opotiki and Gisborne, the Pacific Coast Highway (SH35) runs 330 scenic kilometres around the peninsula, hugging the rugged coastline much of the way and providing mesmerizing sea views on a fine day.

As soon as you enter the region you'll notice a change of pace, epitomized by the occasional sight of a lone horseback rider clopping along the road. **Maori** make up a significant percentage of the population – over eighty percent of land tenure here is in Maori hands, and locals are welcoming, particularly once you take time to talk to them and adjust to the cape's slower pace.

The **coast** is very much the focus here but there are also **hiking** opportunities, and just about everywhere you go there will be someone happy to take you **horse trekking**, either along the beach or into the bush. The **towns**, such as they are, don't have much to recommend them and you're better off planning to stay at scattered places in between, perhaps by a rocky cove or wild beach.

Inland, the inhospitable **Waiapu Mountains** run through the area, encompassing the northeastern Raukumara Range and the typical native flora of the Raukumara Forest Park. The isolated and rugged peaks of Hikurangi, Whanokao, Aroangi, Wharekia and Tatai provide a spectacular backdrop to the coastal scenery, but are only accessible through **Maori land** and **permission** must be sought.

The East Cape accounts below have been divided into three sections of roughly equal length, with accommodation listings at the end of each section.

GETTING AROUND | **THE EAST CAPE**

By car Although the road is sealed all the way around the East Cape, it twists in and out of small bays so much that it takes a full six hours from Opotiki to Gisborne without any stops. Pumps around the East Cape are relatively few and far between, and some run out of petrol from time to time. Te Araroa, Ruatoria and Tolaga Bay are your best bets, but fill up before you start.

By bus Public transport is limited to infrequent buses and courier services, which also carry passengers. Currently they don't quite overlap, making it difficult to complete the full journey without resorting to hitching. Tour company buses (see opposite) are also an option.

BUS COMPANIES

BayHopper ☎0800 422 928, ⊚baybus.co.nz. Runs from Potaka (just west of Hicks Bay) to Opotiki and back on Tues and Thurs only. No booking needed; pay as you get on. The operators live in Te Araroa so will sometimes drop people off there at the end of their run.

Cooks Couriers ☎06 864 4711. Runs from Te Araroa to Gisborne and back (Mon–Sat only), stopping to pick up parcels.

TOURS

Kiwi Experience ☎09 336 4286, ⊚kiwiexperience .com. Even if backpacker tour buses are not usually your bag, it is worth considering the hop-on-hop-off East As tour ($395), a minimum four-day loop from either Taupo or Rotorua around the East Cape and Gisborne. They stop in great spots that help you catch the spirit of the area.

Stray ☎09 526 2140, ⊚straytravel.co.nz. From Nov–April, Stray's hop-on-hop-off Go East pass (minimum 3 days; $350) covers the cape from Rotorua with stops in Maraehako Bay and Gisborne.

INFORMATION

Tourist information There are no i-SITE offices or formal visitor centres around the East Cape: pick up information in Opotiki or Gisborne.

Services The only banking services around here are a bank and ATM at Ruatoria. Mobile phone coverage is limited to around Opotiki and from Te Araroa to Gisborne (Vodafone), and from Tokomaru Bay to Gisborne (Telecom).

ACCOMMODATION AND EATING

Hostels are scattered along the route, with the occasional motel and B&B, but upmarket accommodation is almost non-existent. Apart from a couple of steak-and-chips places attached to pubs and motels, there isn't anywhere on the East Cape that you'd describe as a real restaurant. Come prepared for self-catering or accept a diet of toasted sandwiches and fish and chips. Self-caterers will find limited grocery shopping, and many places close as early as 5pm.

Camping Campsites are an East Cape staple with several good commercial sites. Free beachside camping is prohibited, but there are six designated "freedom camping" sites, from Waipiro Bay down to the outskirts of Gisborne. These operate from mid-Sept to mid-April and require a permit ($10 for 2 consecutive nights; $25 for 10; $60 for 28; valid for up to 6 people), available from the i-SITEs in Opotiki and Gisborne. Fairly strict (but common sense) rules apply and inspectors periodically enforce them. Fires are not allowed and campers must all have an onboard or chemical toilet.

Opotiki to Waihau Bay

The road from Opotiki to **Waihau Bay** covers 103km, generally sticking close to the sea, but frequently twisting up over steep bluffs before dropping back down to desolate beaches heavy with driftwood. The logs have been washed down from the Raukumara Range by the numerous rivers that reach the sea here, often forming delightful freshwater swimming holes. This is probably the section of the East Cape where you'll want to spend much of your time. You'll find family campsites every few kilometres, none of them far from the beach, with a wealth of aquatic activities on offer – from boogie boards and canoes to half-day fishing and dive trips – along with horse riding and bikes to search out your own secluded cove.

Omaio

Leaving Opotiki, you first pass Tirohanga, the last of the real swimming beaches for some distance. After 40km you cross the **Motu River** where you can pick up jetboat tours (see box, p.359). A further 12km on, **OMAIO** offers a store with a petrol pump and takeaways, and *Hoani Waititi Reserve* (see p.362), one of the East Cape's few free campsites.

Te Kaha

13km east of Omaio

TE KAHA spreads for 7km along the highway in a beautiful crescent shape, with spectacular headlands and a deserted, driftwood-strewn beach that's safe for swimming. Te Kaha is about the closest land to White Island, 50km offshore, and has some good places to stay.

5

LEGENDS OF THE EAST CAPE MAORI

According to legend, a great *ariki* (leader) from the East Cape was drowned by rival tribesmen, and his youngest daughter swore vengeance: when she gave birth to a son called **Tuwhakairiora**, she hoped he would make good her promise. As a young man, Tuwhakairiora travelled and encountered a young woman named **Ruataupare**; she took him to her father, who happened to be the local chief. A thunderstorm broke, signalling to the people that they had an important visitor among them, and Tuwhakairiora was allowed to marry Ruataupare and live in Te Araroa. When he called upon all the *hapu* of the area to gather and avenge the death of his grandfather, many warriors travelled to Whareponga and sacked the *pa* there. Tuwhakairiora became renowned as a warrior, dominating the area from **Tolaga Bay** to Cape Runaway, and all Maori families in the region today trace their descent from him.

Ruataupare, meanwhile, grew jealous of her husband's influence. While their children were growing up, she constantly heard them referred to as the offspring of the great Tuwhakairiora, yet her name was barely mentioned. She returned to her own *iwi* in **Tokomaru Bay**, where she summoned all the warriors and started a war against rival *iwi*; victorious, Ruataupare became chieftainess of Tokomaru Bay.

Another legend that has shaped this wild land is one of rivalry between two students – **Paoa**, who excelled at navigation, and **Rongokaka**, who was renowned for travelling at great speed by means of giant strides. At the time, a beautiful maiden, Muriwhenua, lived in Hauraki and many set off to claim her for their bride. Paoa set off early but his rival took only one step and was ahead of him; this continued up the coast, with Rongokaka leaving huge footprints as he went – his imprint in the rock at Matakaoa Point, at the northern end of Hicks Bay, is the most clearly distinguishable. En route, they created the **Waiapu Mountains**: Paoa, flummoxed by Rongokaka's pace, set a snare for his rival at Tokomaru Bay, lashing the crown of a giant totara tree to a hill; recognizing the trap, Rongokaka cut it loose. The force with which the tree sprang upright caused such vibration that Mount Hikurangi partly disintegrated, forming the other mountain peaks. Finally, Rongokaka stepped across the Bay of Plenty and up to Hauraki, where he claimed his maiden.

Whanarua Bay and Maraehako Bay

White Island remains in view as you continue 16km to the twin communities of **WHANARUA BAY** and **MARAEHAKO BAY**, a pair of rock-fringed coves separated by a craggy headland. With a selection of good accommodation and even a café at *Pacific Coast Macadamias* (see opposite), this makes one of the best places in these parts to base yourself for a couple of days of swimming and exploring.

Ruakokore Church

Still hugging the coast, SH35 winds 13km to **Ruakokore**, not really a place at all, but the memorable site of a picture-perfect, white clapboard Anglican church which stands on a promontory framed by the blue ocean. The church was built in 1894 and is usually open. It has little blue penguins nesting underneath.

Waihau Bay

From Ruakokore Church it's 5km to **WAIHAU BAY**, another sweeping crescent of sand and grass that's ideal for swimming, surfing and kayaking. The film director Taika Waititi thought it ideal too, and in 2010 shot his film *Boy* in the area. The abundance of shellfish and flatfish here might encourage you to sling a line from the wharf beside the combined store, post office and petrol station.

ACCOMMODATION AND EATING	OPOTIKI TO WAIHAU BAY

OMAIO

Hoani Waititi Reserve Omaio Marae Rd, opposite the store. This is a very basic campsite set on a grassy pohutukawa-fringed headland. You'll have to bring your own water and use the public toilets 500m away. **Free**

Oariki Coastal Cottage Maraenui, almost 40km east of Opotiki ☏ 07 325 2678. A self-catering cottage for four, surrounded by native bush and overlooking the sea.

It comes with a log fire and opportunities for jetboating, fishing and diving (dependent upon numbers). Call ahead for directions and to arrange an organic dinner ($35). **$150**

TE KAHA

★ **Chay's @ TK** SH35 ☎07 325 2194, ✉paora @hotmail.com. Super-relaxing hostel at the water's edge with an outdoor spa (on a deck just 1m from the high tide), access to the beach, and opportunities for kayaking, jetskiing and fishing. There's much singing, guitar- and piano-playing and Maori/Irish festivities especially when the Kiwi Experience bus arrives. Along with dorms and a double there's an en suite with a view, a self-catering kitchen and the chance to buy dinner, often with kai moana caught nearby. Dorms **$30**, double **$80**, en suite **$130**

Te Kaha Beach Resort SH35 ☎07 325 2830, ⓦtekaha beachresort.co.nz. There's a very un-East Cape feel to this modern, streamlined 3-storey complex with apartment-style accommodation featuring full state-of-the-art kitchens, as well as a pool, and a restaurant and bar with 180-degree ocean views. **$170**

Tui Lodge 200 Copenhagen Rd ☎07 325 2922, ⓦtui lodge.co.nz. Set within three acres of gardens, this spacious and supremely tranquil B&B in a purpose-built lodge just inland from the *Te Kaha Beach Resort* has en-suite rooms and offers dinner ($35). **$180**

WHANARUA BAY AND MARAEHAKO BAY

★ **Maraehako Bay Retreat** SH35 ☎07 325 2648, ⓦmaraehako.co.nz. Paradisiacal, rustic waterside hostel in a rocky cove with a safe, private swimming beach, free use of kayaks and the chance for fishing, diving, whale and dolphin watching and horse-trekking expeditions. Camping **$20**, dorms **$28**, doubles **$66**

Maraehako Camping Ground SH35 ☎07 325 2901. Simple camping at the eastern end of stony Maraehako Bay, with toilets, solar-heated showers and plenty of space to pitch up. Run by the same welcoming Maori family as Maraehako Bay Retreat. Camping **$12**

Pacific Coast Macadamias SH35 ☎07 325 2960, ⓦmacanuts.co.nz. Simple but superb café amid the nut orchards where you can feast on delicious home-made macadamia products such as muffins and ice cream, as well as good coffee. Oct–April daily 10am–3pm, longer in Jan & Feb.

The Homestead SH35 ☎07 325 2071, ⓦhomestead onthebay.co.nz. An attractive B&B on a sunny clifftop setting with great views. There are only two bedrooms, which share a bathroom, and three-course dinners ($45 with wine) are available on request. **$190**

WAIHAU BAY

Oceanside Apartments Oruaiti Beach, 5km northeast of Waihau Bay ☎07 325 3699, ⓦwaihaubay.co.nz. Two spacious self-contained units (one sleeping seven) just across the road from a safe, sandy beach. Meals are available on request (dinner $35), or you can try and catch your own supper by surfcasting for snapper and kahawai off the beach. Ask about the diving and fishing trips and kayak rental. Three-night minimum from Christmas–Easter. **$130**

Waihau Bay Holiday Park SH35, 3km east of Waihau Bay ☎07 325 3844. Modest campsite across SH35 from the beach, with reasonable facilities and its own camp store. Camping **$14**, on-site vans **$70**, cabins **$80**, units **$100**

Cape Runaway to Waipiro Bay

Beyond Waihau Bay the highway continues close to the water for a few more kilometres before veering inland at **Cape Runaway**, the East Cape's northernmost point. For the next 125km you hardly see the coast again, with the significant exceptions of **Hicks Bay**, **Te Araroa** and **East Cape**.

Hicks Bay

Tiny **HICKS BAY** (Wharekahika), 44km east of Waihau Bay, shelters between headlands and coastal rock bluffs almost halfway along SH35. There's a safe swimming beach at **Onepoto Bay** (the southern corner of the larger Hicks Bay), and the area makes a good base from which to visit the East Cape Lighthouse. Hicks Bay was named after Lieutenant Zachariah Hicks, who sighted it on Cook's *Endeavour* expedition in 1769. There are numerous *pa* sites in the area, in varying states of repair, some of which were modified for musket fighting during the 1860 Hau Hau uprising.

Entering the community along Wharf Road, off SH35, you'll find a general store and takeaway, and not much else.

Te Araroa

From Hicks Bay, SH35 climbs over a hill and drops back to the coast beside the broad surf-washed shore of Kawakawa Bay. At its eastern end, the small village of **TE ARAROA**

5

> ## EAST CAPE MANUKA OIL
>
> Australian tea tree oil is famous for its antimicrobial qualities. The oil of the almost identical New Zealand *manuka* is generally just as good, but in 1992 manuka oil from the East Cape was found to have super-strong antibacterial and antifungal properties. The small factory at 4464 Te Araroa Rd, 2km west of Te Araroa (Nov–April daily 9am–4pm; May–Oct Mon–Fri 9am–4pm; ☎ 0508 626 852, ⊛ eastcapemanuka.co.nz), extracts the essential oils by steam distillation from the twigs of *manuka* trees grown in the surrounding hills. You can't tour the factory, but a wide range of *manuka*-oil soaps, medicinal creams and aromatherapy potions (all exported around the world) is sold in the shop/café where you can also sample *manuka* tea and buy local *manuka* honey.

("long pathway") marks the midway point between Opotiki and Gisborne. Te Araroa was once the domain of the famous Maori warrior Tuwhakairiora and the legendary Paikea, who is said to have arrived here on the back of a whale. Ironically, the first Europeans in the area occupied a **whaling station** not far from the present township. These days the settlement contains little more than a petrol station, two stores and a takeaway selling fresh **fish and chips**. In the grounds of the local school on Moana Parade stands a **giant pohutukawa** tree – so giant that it's easy to believe the claims that it's New Zealand's largest.

East Cape Lighthouse
21km east of Te Araroa along an unsealed road • Follow the sign east along the foreshore

The New Zealand mainland's easternmost point is marked by the **East Cape Lighthouse**. The dramatic coastal run from Te Araroa is along a cliff-clinging road that ends in a car park. From there, you climb 755 steps to the lighthouse perched atop a 140m-high hill – an atmospheric spot with views inland to the Raukumara Range and seaward towards East Island (a bird sanctuary), just offshore.

St Mary's Church
SH35, Tikitiki • Open most days • Free

From Te Araroa SH35 cuts inland through 24km of sheep-farming country before reaching **TIKITIKI** where you should take a peek inside the Anglican **church**, on a rise as you enter the town. It looks very plain from outside, but within hides a treasure-trove of elaborate Maori design, *tukutuku* and carving; unusually, the stained glass is also in Maori designs, and the rafters are painted in the colours of a Maori meeting house. The memorial to the war dead has a very long list for such a tiny community.

Ruatoria

Inland **RUATORIA**, signposted just off the main highway 19km south of Tikitiki, is the largest town since Opotiki (though that's not saying much), with a bank, petrol, a pub, groceries, and a serviceable daytime café as well as evening takeaways from the roadside *Kai Kart* nearby.

Waipiro Bay

At Kopuaroa, around 15km south of Ruatoria, a loop road heads 6km to the broad sweep of **Waipiro Bay**, a busy port in its heyday, but now a beautiful and secluded inlet with just an incongruous brick church, a few houses and a modest sense of past glory. It's a fine spot for a swim, or just sit on the beach watching the breakers.

ACCOMMODATION   **CAPE RUNAWAY TO WAIPIRO BAY**

HICKS BAY
Hicks Bay Motel Lodge 5198 Te Araroa Rd (SH35), 2km east of Hicks Bay ☎ 06 864 4880, ⊛ hicksbaymotel

.co.nz. A complex of comfortable but not over-restored 1960s hotel rooms (some equipped with four bunks, others with motel-style kitchen facilities) set in spacious grounds

CAPE RUNAWAY TO WAIPIRO BAY TOURS AND ACTIVITIES

Spend a little time around the northeastern reaches of the East Cape, either horse trekking, sampling something of the local Maori culture or exploring the slopes of sacred Mount Hikurangi.

Eastender Horse Treks 876a Rangitukia Rd ☎06 864 3033, ⓦeastenderhorsetreks.co.nz. Turn off at St Mary's Church (see opposite) to access the Eastender hostel (see below) and Eastender Horse Treks, which offers some of the best trips in the area, including a gallop along the beach ($85/2hr, $210/4hr).

Matakaoa Cultural Tours 141 Onepoto Rd, Hicks Bay ☎021 885 602, ⓔaniph407@gmail.com. To sample something of what it means to be Maori in Hicks Bay, join this tour which takes you around to points of significance to Maori, and probably will include a few house calls as well (2–3hr; $50).

MOUNT HIKURANGI TREK

The 1754m-high **Mount Hikurangi**, 25km west of Ruatoria, is the North Island's highest non-volcanic peak and the first place on the New Zealand mainland to see the sunrise. Sacred to Maori as the place where Maui (p.800) beached his *waka* after fishing up the North Island, nine giant **carvings** were installed at 1000m to celebrate the new millennium.

This hill country to the west of Ruatoria comes under the jurisdiction of the **Raukumara Conservation Area**, which includes the upper catchments of several rivers that drain into the Bay of Plenty. The desolate terrain and limited access discourage most visitors from exploring the park but it's possible to tackle the **trek** up Mount Hikurangi (20km return; 8–16hr; 1500m ascent) in one long day, although it's really best done over two days with a night in the rustic Mt Hikurangi Hut ($15) partway up.

The Ngati Porou control the land, so you'll need to contact Te Runanga O Ngati Porou, 1 Barry's Ave, Ruatoria (☎06 864 9004, ⓔpbrooking@tronp.org.nz) for track access permission and to pay hut fees. For a cultural perspective, ask about customized **guided trips**.

high on the hill overlooking Onepoto and Hicks bays, with incredible views. There's also a licensed restaurant, a bar and access to a glowworm grotto. Dorms $35, doubles $110, motels $130

TE ARAROA

Te Araroa Backpackers 57 Waione Rd, 1km west of town ☎06 864 4896, ⓦteararoabackpackers.com. Maori-owned backpackers in a two-storey wooden villa in peaceful grounds with separate male and female dorms plus doubles, and access to a cooking area and lounge outside. There's a small Maori art gallery on-site, and if you pre-order dinner ($25) you'll be eating with the family. Dorms $25, doubles $50

Te Araroa Holiday Park 4814 Te Araroa Rd (SH35),

6km west of town ☎06 864 4873, ⓦteararoa holidaypark.co.nz. Campsite with a handy shop and a takeaway van in summer, plus sea kayaks and mountain bikes for rent. Camping $14, cabins $65, flats $100, motels $140

TIKITIKI

Eastender Backpackers Rangitukia Rd, 8km east of SH35 at Tikitiki ☎06 864 3820, ⓦeastender backpackers.co.nz. Remote and friendly hostel with fairly functional dorms and nicer doubles in cabins on the grounds. There are opportunities to try your hand at bone carving, to go eeling and horse trekking (see box above), and to shoot possums. Camping and campervans $10, dorms $25, doubles $60

Tokomaru Bay to Whangara

At **Tokomaru Bay** the road emerges from inland bush and pastoral country to reveal the North Island's east coast in all its glory. For the remaining 80km to Gisborne you stay mostly inland but catch frequent glimpses of yawning bays and crashing surf, accessed directly on SH35 or short side roads leading to little-visited coves.

Tokomaru Bay

TOKOMARU BAY (or just "Toko"), 40km south of Ruatoria, is a gorgeous spot to idle for a day, exploring the steep green hills, rocky headlands and the broad expanse of **beach**, which is dotted with driftwood, pounded by surf, and provides a good spot to swim. The Maori who settled here trace their descent to Toi te Huatahi, the great navigator

5

and the first to arrive from the ancestral home of Hawaiki. In 1865 the Mawhai *pa* was the scene of several attacks by a party of Hau Hau, but a small garrison of old men and women repulsed them.

At the far northern end of town, a long wooden wharf and the ruined buildings of an abattoir testify to the former prosperity of this once-busy port, which thrived until improved road transport forced the factory's closure in 1953.

Anaura Bay

Some 22km south from Tokomaru, a 6km-long sealed side road runs to rugged **ANAURA BAY**, a prized **surf** spot with a broad sweep of sand and jagged headlands. At the north end of the bay, the **Anaura Scenic Reserve** harbours a large area of mixed broadleaf bush noted for its large puriri trees and abundance of native birds. Starting near the end of the road, and signposted to the west by the reserve, the **Anaura Bay Walkway** (3.5km loop; 2hr) follows the course of the Waipare Stream into thick green bush, up a gently climbing valley and out into scrubland before turning back towards the bay and a lookout point with magnificent views.

Tolaga Bay

TOLAGA BAY (Uawa), 36km south of Tokomaru, is the first place you reach since leaving Opotiki that feels like a viable town, its population of six hundred one of the better-serviced communities on the East Cape, with a supermarket, petrol and a clutch of cafés. Once again, rugged headlands enclose the bay, the scene of a 1769 visit by James Cook and his crew. They're commemorated in the town's street names: Banks, Solander, Forester and, of course, Cook. Anchoring to replenish his stocks of food and water, Cook named the bay "Tolaga", a misinterpretation of the Maori name for the prevailing wind (*teraki*).

Tolaga Bay Wharf
Wharf Rd

Tolaga Bay's claim to fame is the 660m-long concrete **Tolaga Bay Wharf**, said to be the longest concrete jetty in the southern hemisphere. Built in the late 1920s to service coastal shipping, it juts out past steep sandstone cliffs into deep water. Its impressive length didn't stop it becoming redundant when coastal shipping ceased here in 1963. Once in a near-ruinous state, some restoration has taken place, and its historic-place ranking has been raised to the highest level, so more will undoubtedly follow. It's no longer strong enough for vehicles, but you can wander to the end for a picturesque picnic.

Cooks Cove Walkway
1km south of town on Wharf Rd • 5.8km; 2hr 30min return

Cooks Cove Walkway is the best of Tolaga Bay's short walks, involving an initial walk across farmland then a steep and often muddy climb through bush and birdlife to a great viewpoint looking down to Cook's Cove. The track heads down to the cove where there's a plaque marking the good captain's visit here in 1769.

Whangara

The 47km stretch from Tolaga Bay to Gisborne becomes both tamer and bleaker the further south you travel, much of the land cleared for farming. The road climbs in and out of more small bays, occasionally providing panoramic vistas of sea and close-ups of the slate-grey rock shelves that characterize this coast. It passes the turn-off to **Whangara**, where the film *Whale Rider* was shot, but, as there's no direct access, there's little to see from the lookout apart from a sweep of sand and an island said to be the fossilized remains of the whale that the legendary Paikea rode all the way from Hawaiki.

For a guided introduction to the area, Tipuna Tours (from $70; ☎027 240 4493, ⓦtipunatours.com) arrange enlightening trips and visit one of the three *marae* at Tolaga Bay.

After Whangara there's little to stop you heading straight for Gisborne except to ride the renowned surf at **WAINUI BEACH**, 9km from the city.

ACCOMMODATION AND EATING
TOKOMARU BAY TO WHANGARA

TOKOMARU BAY

★ **Brian's Place** 21 Potae St ☎06 864 5870, ⓦbrians place.co.nz. A small, friendly spot with loft-style rooms, dorms with a maximum of three guests, and some amazing cabins (one of which is a single), all perched on a hillside with great sea views. Tent sites also have superb views and there are surfboards and bikes for rent ($5; free if you stay a second night). Camping $15, dorms $28, doubles $66, single cabin $45, cabins $66

Te Puka Tavern 153 Beach Road ☎06 864 5466, ⓦtepukatavern.co.nz. New owners are raising the standards at this traditional Kiwi pub, adding espresso, a daytime café, internet and quality meals such as roast beef and apple crumble. It is the only place in town for a drink, so it can get busy at weekends. They also have four brand-new sea-view rooms. Daily 11am–10pm or later, closed Mon & Tues lunch in winter. $160

ANAURA BAY

Anaura Bay campsite Very basic DOC site wonderfully set beside the beach immediately beyond the start of the Anaura Bay Walkway. There's water but no toilets (you'll need a chemical toilet or holding tank), though there is a dump station on-site from Dec–Feb. Closed Easter–late Oct. $15

Anaura Bay Motor Camp ☎06 862 6380. At the south end of the bay, superbly sited beside the beach. Facilities are in the former schoolhouse and there's a store selling essentials. Camping $12, powered sites $14

TOLAGA BAY

Tolaga Bay Holiday Park 167 Wharf Rd ☎06 862 6716, ⓦtolagabayholidaypark.co.nz. Beachfront campsite with a store, barbecue area, kayak rental, great views and a handful of cabins, as well as a few other options. Camping $14, caravans $55, kitchen cabins $55, beachfront deluxe cabin $85

Tolaga Bay Inn 12 Cook St ☎06 862 6856. The Bay's best place to eat, serving enormous slices of home-baked cake, knockout coffee, freshly prepared soups and the likes of chicken focaccia sandwich ($16) or eggs Florentine ($13.50). Tues, Wed and Sun 9am–3pm, Thurs–Sat 9am–8pm.

Poverty Bay, Hawke's Bay and the Wairarapa

372 Gisborne

377 Around Gisborne

378 The road to Napier

380 Te Urewera National Park

385 Napier

392 Cape Kidnappers and the wineries

397 Hastings

401 Southern Hawke's Bay

401 The Wairarapa

VINEYARD AND TE MATA PEAK, HAWKES BAY

Poverty Bay, Hawke's Bay and the Wairarapa

From the eastern tip of the North Island, a mountainous backbone runs 650km southwest to the outskirts of Wellington, defining and isolating the east coast. The Raukumara, Kaweka, Ruahine, Tararua and Rimutaka mountain ranges protect much of the region from the prevailing westerlies and cast a long rain shadow, the bane of the area's sheep farmers, who watch their land become parched, dusty and brown each summer. Increasingly, these pastures are being given over to viticulture, and the regions of Poverty Bay, Hawke's Bay and the Wairarapa are world-renowned for their wine. Any tour of the wineries has to take in Poverty Bay, a major grape-growing region, where the main centre of Gisborne was the first part of New Zealand sighted by Cook's expedition in 1769. Finding little – other than wary local Maori – he named it Poverty Bay and sailed south to an area he later named Hawke Bay, after his boyhood hero Admiral Sir Edward Hawke (the name of the surrounding province has since evolved into Hawke's Bay). Here Cook clashed with Maori at Cape Kidnappers, now the site of an impressive gannet colony.

Hawke's Bay has long been dubbed "the fruit bowl of New Zealand" and its orchard boughs still sag under the weight of apples, pears and peaches. The district is best visited from the waterfront city of **Napier**, famed for its Art Deco buildings, constructed after a massive earthquake flattened much of the city in 1931. Nearby Hastings suffered the same fate and wove Spanish Mission-style buildings into the resulting Art Deco fabric, though these won't delay you long as you head south to the sheep lands of the Wairarapa and the temptingly accessible vineyards surrounding Martinborough.

Access to the mountainous **interior** of this region is limited, with only six roads winding over or cutting through the full length of the ranges. The tortuous but scenic SH38 forges northwest from the small town of **Wairoa**, the gateway to the remote wooded mountains of Te Urewera National Park and beautiful **Lake Waikaremoana**, which is encircled by the four-day Lake Waikaremoana Track tramping route.

GETTING AROUND

By train The only passenger trains in the region are those linking the main Wairarapa towns (including Masterton, Carterton and Featherston) with Wellington.

By bus InterCity (ⓦ intercity.co.nz) run a daily service between Gisborne and Napier, and another south to Wellington, though this goes through Palmerston North,

Gisborne tours and activities p.374
Lake Waikaremoana: short hikes p.382
Te Kooti Rikirangi p.383
Pania of the reef p.386
Art Deco Napier p.387
Napier festivals and events p.392

The Cape Kidnappers gannets p.395
Hawke's Bay wineries p.396
Long names and famous flutes p.402
Golden Shears p.404
Martinborough festivals p.408

ST JOHN'S CATHEDRAL, NAPIER

Highlights

❶ Swim with sharks Take a dip – if you dare – off the coast of New Zealand's easternmost city, Gisborne, or join the sharks in their tank at Napier's National Aquarium. **See p.374 & p.388**

❷ Lake Waikaremoana Take in this picturesque lake on short hikes or while tackling the North Island's most prized multi-day tramp. See p.381

❸ Napier Wander through the world's finest collection of small-scale Art Deco architecture to Napier's pine-shaded seafront promenade. See p.385

❹ Cape Kidnappers Come face-to-beak with residents of the world's largest mainland gannet colony on a tour or under your own steam. **See p.395**

❺ Vineyards Sip to your heart's content in Hawke's Bay Wine Country, or stroll to almost a dozen fine wineries from appealing Martinborough. **See p.396 & p.408**

❻ Pukaha Mount Bruce National Wildlife Centre Observe some of the world's rarest birdlife thanks to the conservation heroics performed at this bushland sanctuary. **See p.402**

HIGHLIGHTS ARE MARKED ON THE MAP ON P.372

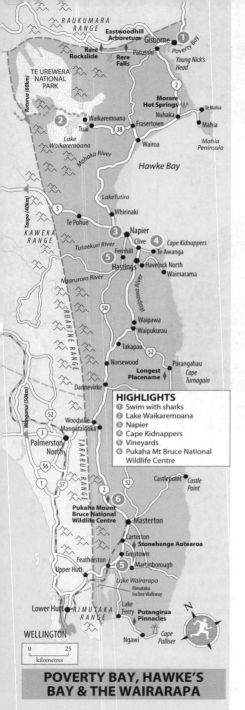

POVERTY BAY, HAWKE'S BAY & THE WAIRARAPA

HIGHLIGHTS
1 Swim with sharks
2 Lake Waikaremoana
3 Napier
4 Cape Kidnappers
5 Vineyards
6 Pukaha Mt Bruce National Wildlife Centre

missing the Wairarapa. NakedBus (ⓦ nakedbus.co.nz) run a daily service from Napier and Hastings to Wellington that also routes via Palmerston North.

Gisborne

New Zealand's easternmost city, **GISBORNE**, is the first to catch the sun each day, and, thanks to the isolating mountain ranges all about it has been spared from overdevelopment. Warmed by long hours of sunshine, broad straight streets are lined with squat weatherboard houses and shops and interspersed with expansive parkland hugging the Pacific, the harbour and three rivers – the Taruheru, Turanganui and Waimata.

Brief history
It was here in October 1769 that **James Cook** first set foot on the soil of Aotearoa, an event commemorated by a shoreside statue. He immediately ran into conflict with local Maori, killing several of them before sailing away empty-handed. He named the landing site **Poverty Bay**, since "it did not afford a single item we wanted, except a little firewood". Despite the fertility of the surrounding lands, the name stuck, though many Maori prefer **Turanganui a Kiwa** – honouring a Polynesian navigator.

Early nineteenth-century Poverty Bay remained staunchly Maori and few Pakeha moved here, discouraged by both the Hau Hau rebellion and Te Kooti's uprising (see box, p.383). It wasn't until the 1870s that **Europeans** arrived in numbers to farm the rich alluvial river flats. After a decent port was constructed in the 1920s, sheep farming and market gardening took off, followed more recently by the grape harvest and the rise of plantation forestry. Today Gisborne's Maori and Pakeha population is almost exactly 50:50, and the city's relaxed pace and easy-going beach culture make it appealing to visitors in search of a little sun and surf.

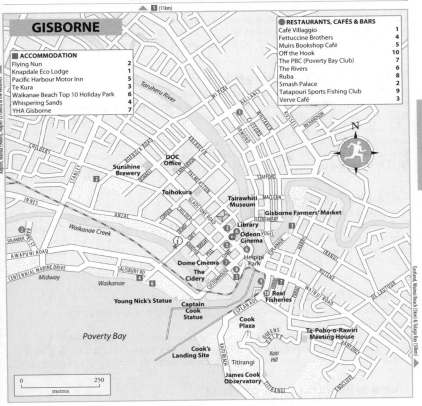

GISBORNE

ACCOMMODATION
Flying Nun	2
Knapdale Eco Lodge	1
Pacific Harbour Motor Inn	5
Te Kura	3
Waikanae Beach Top 10 Holiday Park	6
Whispering Sands	4
YHA Gisborne	7

RESTAURANTS, CAFÉS & BARS
Café Villaggio	1
Fettuccine Brothers	4
Muirs Bookshop Café	5
Off the Hook	10
The PBC (Poverty Bay Club)	7
The Rivers	6
Ruba	8
Smash Palace	2
Tatapouri Sports Fishing Club	9
Verve Café	3

Cook's statue and landing site

Young and Cook's statues are both in the park on the western side of the river mouth • Cook's landing site is on the opposite side of the river, on Kaiti Beach Rd

Almost everywhere in the city is an easy stroll from Midway Beach. Swimming, surfing and sunbathing aside, most of Gisborne's sights are connected in some way to the historical accident of James Cook's landing – and the dynamic between Maori and Pakeha cultures it engendered. The first of Cook's crew to spy the mountains of Aotearoa, a couple of days before the first landing, was 12-year-old surgeon's boy Nick Young. Cook rewarded him by naming the white-cliffed promontory, 10km south of Gisborne across Poverty Bay, on his chart as Young Nick's Head. Young's keen eyes are commemorated by a statue of a youth pointing (hopefully but none too certainly) at the cliffs. Nearby is a **statue of Cook** atop a stone hemisphere. A grey obelisk on the eastern side of the river mouth marks **Cook's landing site**.

James Cook Observatory

Titirangi Drive • Public stargazing every Tues; non-Daylight Saving Time door closes at 7.30pm; during Daylight Saving Time door closes at 8.30pm • $5 • You can access the observatory from Titirangi Domain via a footpath that leads to Titirangi Drive

Behind Titirangi Domain, Titirangi Drive climbs the side of **Kaiti Hill** to **Cook Plaza**, designed around a sculpture intended to represent Cook. Kaiti Hill's highest point has tremendous views across Poverty Bay to the cliffs of Young Nick's Head, and is occupied by the **James Cook Observatory**, which runs public stargazing nights. One of the amateur stargazers who run the observatory recently discovered a planet – indicating they know their stuff, or at least where to look for it.

Te Poho-o-Rawiri Meeting House

Queens Drive • Visits arranged by calling Mihi Aston at ☎ 06 863 2350 • Donation

On the eastern side of the Kaiti Hill lies **Te Poho-o-Rawiri Meeting House**, one of the largest in the country. The interior is superb, full of fine ancestor carvings interspersed with wonderfully varied geometric *tukutuku* (woven panels). At the foot of the two support poles, ancient and intricately carved warrior statues provide a fine counterpoint to the bolder work on the walls. Like most *marae* it is not easily accessible but you may be able to tag on to large pre-arranged tours; book in advance.

Te Tauihu Turanga Whakamana

Heipipi Endeavour Park, corner of Customhouse St and Gladstone Rd

Early Maori explorers are honoured with **Te Tauihu Turanga Whakamana** – a striking wooden sculpture in the centre of town, depicting a Maori *tauihu* (canoe prow) carved with images of Tangaroa (god of the sea), the demi-god Maui, and Toi Kai Rakau (one of the earliest Maori to settle in New Zealand).

Tairawhiti Museum

10 Stout St • Jan daily 10am–4pm, Feb–Dec Mon–Sat 10am–4pm, Sun 1.30–4pm • $5; free on Mon • ☎ 06 867 2728, W tairawhitimuseum.org.nz

Across the river at the **Tairawhiti Museum**, the permanent *Watersheds* exhibit charts the parallel and intertwining lives of Maori and Europeans on the East Coast. There's everything from a whalebone walking stick carved with Maori designs and coverage of

---

GISBORNE TOURS AND ACTIVITIES

Gisborne offers one of New Zealand's few opportunities for heart-pounding **shark encounters**, albeit (thankfully for some) from the safety of a cage. The **reef** is worth a look, too, or you can try your hand at **surfing**. **Wine tours** are also popular, and a good way to see the surrounding countryside.

Dive Tatapouri Tatapouri, 14km northeast of Gisborne ☎ 06 868 5153, W divetatapouri.com. Takes small groups about 15km offshore from where, two at a time, you climb into a tough metal cage, which is partly lowered into water where mako sharks lurk. Standing chest deep, you get around half an hour in the water ($300) – quite long enough – ducking down with a mask and snorkel or regulator to observe these curious 3m-long, 80kg killing machines. They also offer a reef ecology tour ($40) on which you don waders, walk onto the reef at low tide and hand-feed stingrays, kingfish and octopuses. For an extra $30 (book in advance) you can swim with the rays.

Gisborne Wine Tours Shed 3, 50 The Esplanade ☎ 06 867 4085, W gisbornewine.co.nz. This five-hour tour visits three winery cellar doors (locations are changed daily) and the price ($110) includes all wine tastings and an antipasto lunch at one of the stops. It departs daily at 11am from the Gisborne Wine Centre, with a maximum of eight people/trip or minimum of two; book in advance.

Surfing With Frank ☎ 06 867 0823, W surfing withfrank.com. To take advantage of Gisborne's renowned surf, hit the breaks with Frank Russell, who's been at it for years and can get most anyone standing up on a board (private lesson $75; group lesson $50 including board and wetsuit rental, maximum four people/group).

Tipuna Tours ☎ 027 240 4493, W tipunatours.com. One of the best ways to explore the region is with this operator, which runs cultural interpretation tours (from $70) to Whangara (see p.366) visiting the locations where the movie *Whale Rider* was shot.

Cook's arrival to the vibrant painting of early Ngati Porou leader Hinematioro by renowned painter Robyn Kahukiwa.

A maritime wing incorporates the original wheelhouse and captain's quarters of the 12,000-tonne *Star of Canada*, which ran aground on the reef off Gisborne's Kaiti Beach in 1912, along with exhibits on shipping, and a shrine to the local surfing. Several disused buildings from around the region are clustered outside the museum, notably the six-room 1872 **Wyllie Cottage**, the oldest extant house in town, and the **Sled House**, built on runners at the time of the Hau Hau uprising so that it could be hauled away by a team of bullocks at the first sign of unrest.

Toihoukura

Cobden St, near the corner of Gladstone Rd • Mon–Fri 9am–5pm, but during term times by appointment • ☎ 06 868 0847 • Free

A striking modern whale-tail sculpture heralds **Toihoukura**, a school of Maori visual arts and design where existing carvings are restored and students are instructed in the oral history and traditions of Maori design. Interpretations using modern materials and techniques are encouraged, and many vibrant and stunning pieces find their way into the public gallery.

Sunshine Brewery

109 Disraeli St • Mon–Sat 9am–6pm • Free • ☎ 06 867 7777, ⓦ gisbornegold.co.nz

If while sightseeing you've worked up a thirst, repair to the boutique **Sunshine Brewery** for a brief tour of the tiny brewhouse and a sampling of Gisborne Gold lager, pilsner, stout and a delectable English-style ale. The lager is available in bars around town, but the shop prices are cheaper.

The Cidery

91 Customhouse St • Mon–Fri 9am–4.30pm • Free • ☎ 06 868 8300, ⓦ harvestcider.co.nz

The alternative to the relatively small-scale production of boutique beers and lagers (see above) is the more industrial cider production plant run by Harvester at **The Cidery**. Although their product is a much bigger money-spinner, the guys here are refreshingly friendly and the samples they dish out are splendid; try the zingy ciders, local mead, harvest scrumpy and a non-boozy ginger beer.

ARRIVAL AND DEPARTURE

GISBORNE

By bus NakedBus and InterCity buses converge on the i-SITE.

Destinations Auckland (2 daily; 9hr 15min); Hastings (1–2 daily; 5hr); Napier (2 daily; 4hr); Opotiki, via SH2 (2 daily; 2hr); Rotorua (2 daily; 5hr); Wairoa (1 daily; 1hr 30min); Whakatane (2 daily; 3hr).

By plane Direct flights from Auckland and Wellington arrive at Gisborne airport, about 2km west of the town centre, which can be reached by taxi for $20; try Gisborne Taxis (☎ 06 867 2222).

Destinations Auckland (6–7 daily; 1hr); Wellington (3–4 daily; 50min).

GETTING AROUND

By bike Most of the city is easily covered on foot, though rental bikes ($50/day) from Avanti Plus, at the corner of

Gladstone and Roebuck rds (☎ 06 867 4571), are good for a spin round the wineries (see p.377).

INFORMATION

i-SITE 209 Grey St (daily: Nov to Easter 8.30am–5.30pm; Easter to Oct Mon–Fri 8.30am–5pm, Sat 9am–4pm, Sun 11am–3pm; ☎ 06 868 6139, ⓦ gisbornenz.com). Offers internet access, sells Waikaremoana hut passes and has exhibits on local social and natural history.

DOC 63 Carnarvon St (Mon–Fri 8am–4.30pm; ☎ 06 869 0460). Has plenty of information on tramping outside the immediate Gisborne area.

Services Internet at the library, 35 Peel St (Mon & Wed–Fri 9.30am–5.30pm, Tues 9.30am–8pm, Sat 9.30am–1pm).

6

ACCOMMODATION

Despite the huge number of motels – chiefly along the main strip, palm-shaded Gladstone Road, and the waterfront Salisbury Road – accommodation can be hard to come by during the month or so after Christmas.

Flying Nun 147 Roebuck Rd ☎ 06 868 0461. This slightly scruffy, hippyish former convent, a 15min walk from town, is where Dame Kiri Te Kanawa first trained her voice. Some of the spacious dorms front onto broad verandas, and although doubles can be a little cramped, singles are good value. Spacious grounds include a BBQ area and games room. No credit cards. Tents $16, dorms $24, singles $40, doubles and twins $58

★ **Knapdale Eco Lodge** 114 Snowsill Rd, Waihirere, 13km northwest of Gisborne ☎ 06 862 5444, ⓦ knapdale.co.nz. They take their "eco" moniker seriously at this luxurious lodge in a tranquil semi-permaculture farm with chickens, deer and horses. The two rooms are both airy and cosy, and a dawn chorus from the nearby forest alerts you to the sumptuous breakfast. Gourmands should book one of the exquisite dinners ($75/person). Deluxe guest room $398, "Romance" room $472

Pacific Harbour Motor Inn Corner of Reads Quay and Pitt St ☎ 06 867 8847, ⓦ pacific-harbour.co.nz. Glass bricks and panoramic windows – some with harbour views – flood this contemporary motel with natural light. The rooms are large and fully equipped, and some come with balconies and spa baths. Units $130

★ **Te Kura** 14 Cheeseman Rd ☎ 06 863 3497, ⓦ tekura.co.nz. There are just two great-value B&B guest rooms (one with a deep claw-foot bath) in this grand, 1920s, beautifully timbered Arts and Crafts homestead overlooking the Waimata River in central Gisborne. Guests can relax in their own lounge, use the swimming pool and access free wi-fi, and the generous hosts serve full breakfasts. $139

Waikanae Beach Top 10 Holiday Park Grey St ☎ 06 867 5634, ⓦ top10.co.nz. Idyllically sited motorpark right by Gisborne's main beach and a 5min walk from town. Some of the comfortable cabins are en-suite, and there are also self-contained and motel units. Camping $21, standard cabins $60, en-suite cabins $75, self-contained units $110, motel units $135

★ **Whispering Sands** 22 Salisbury Rd ☎ 0800 405 030, ⓦ whisperingsands.co.nz. Great-value beachfront motel with four large, modern units, all with full kitchens; those on the upper level have sea views. The owners are friendly and very helpful. $145

YHA Gisborne 32 Harris St ☎ 06 867 3269, ⓦ yha.co.nz. Spacious, central hostel in a weatherboard homestead with a sunny deck, a cheery paint job and a manager switched on to the local surf hotspots. There are twins, doubles and one en suite. Dorms $26, rooms $58

EATING, DRINKING AND NIGHTLIFE

Café Villaggio 57 Ballance St ☎ 06 863 3895. Casual licensed café/restaurant in a lovely Art Deco house, with seating either on sofas around the fire in winter or spilling outside in summer. It's popular with locals, largely because of dishes such as the mean seafood chowder ($11.50) and smoked salmon filo ($20); most mains $26–32. Sun–Wed 8am–4pm, Thurs–Sat 8am–late.

Fettuccine Brothers 12 Peel St ☎ 06 868 5700. Long-standing Italian restaurant (with adjacent bar), serving a full range of dishes from pasta (around $26) to substantial meat and fish dishes (around $32). Mon–Sat 5pm–late.

Gisborne Farmers' Market Army Hall car park, Corner of Fitzherbert and Stout sts ⓦ gisbornefarmers market.co.nz. A bustling market that's great for fruit and vegetables, as well as all manner of meats, cheeses, organic produce and baked goods. Sat 9.30am–12.30pm.

Muirs Bookshop Café 62 Gladstone Rd. Airy café tucked above Gisborne's best bookshop, adjacent to the secondhand section. From a sun-drenched balcony that overlooks the main street, you can tuck into panini, salads, "bookshop brownies" and "muddy" chocolate cake ($4); most menu items are under $16. Mon–Fri 9.30am–3.15pm, Sat 9am–3pm.

★ **Off the Hook & Real Fisheries** The Esplanade, at Crawford Rd ☎ 06 868 1644. The best fish and chip takeaway in town serves cooked-to-order fresh fish, including snapper, moki, trevally and tarakiki ($10 with chips). Real Fisheries is part of the same operation, and good for those looking for straight-off-the-boat fish. Off the Hook Tues–Thurs 10am–6.30pm, Fri 10am–8pm, Sat noon–6.30pm; Real Fisheries Mon–Fri 8.30am–5pm, Sat 8.30am–12.30pm.

The PBC (Poverty Bay Club) 38 Childers Rd, at Customhouse St, behind the 1874 Café ☎ 06 863 2006, ⓦ thepovertybayclub.co.nz. A cool, intimate bar/club with a great long bar, smooth leather sofas and some classy liquids to partake of while listening to mellow sounds. Wed–Fri 5pm–late, Sat 8pm–late, Sun 5.30pm–late.

The Rivers Corner of Gladstone Rd and Reads Quay ☎ 06 863 3733. Convivial Irish-type bar with good Guinness and a range of hearty meals including steaks, pies, chicken and fish ($16–34) that is now better known for its food than its late-night boozing and noise. Daily 9am–late.

Ruba 14 Childers Rd ☎ 06 868 6516. Stylish, licensed, daytime café, perfect for coffee, warm honey and lemon curd and cream cheese muffins, or lunches such as salt and pepper squid ($16). Most dishes $9–30. Daily 7am–3pm.

★ **Smash Palace Wine Bar** 24 Banks St ☎ 06 867 7769. Wonderfully oddball bar in a corrugated-iron barn, where overalls from the surrounding industrial area rub shoulders with suits. Food basically comprises snacks – favourites include flaming pizzas and nachos flame-toasted with a blowtorch. There's live entertainment, too, from blues to heavy metal, mostly at weekends. Mon–Thurs 3pm–late, Fri–Sun noon–late.

Tatapouri Sports Fishing Club 54 The Esplanade ☎ 06 868 4756. Sociable club right on the wharf with veranda seating for seafood, steaks or gourmet burgers (all under $28). There's cheap beer, and visitors just sign in: ask at the bar. Daily 11am–late.

★ **Verve Café** 121 Gladstone Rd ☎ 06 868 9095. With rotating art exhibitions by up-and-coming local artists, this groovy but low-key daytime café and restaurant serves gorgeous, moderately priced food, from the famous chicken sandwiches ($18) to falafel, steak sandwiches and cakes ($5–$22). Mon–Fri 7.30am–5pm, Sat & Sun 8am–3pm.

CINEMAS

★ **Dome Cinema** The Poverty Bay Club, 38 Childers Rd ☎ 083 243 005, ⓦ domecinema.co.nz. A fabulous, independent screen with bean-bag seating, a bar and an eclectic mix of must-see films, all shown in the old billiard room, with a coloured glass dome in the centre of the ceiling.

Odeon Cinema 79 Gladstone Rd ☎ 06 867 3339. Expect all the usual mainstream blockbusters to be showing at this centrally located cinema.

Around Gisborne

Winery visits, gentle walks and a smattering of specific attractions make a day or so spent in Gisborne's surrounds an agreeable prospect. If you don't have a car and want to get out to the wineries, your best bet is to **bike** (see p.375) out there on the flat roads or opt for a tour (see box, p.374).

Bushmere Estate

166 Main Rd South, 6km northwest of Gisborne • Tastings normally Thurs–Sun; call ahead to check • ☎ 06 868 9317 • ⓦ bushmere.com

Occupying a free-draining alluvial valley in the lee of the Raukumara Range and blessed with long hours of strong sun and cooling sea breezes, Poverty Bay's wineries (ⓦ gisbornewine.co.nz) have traditionally operated as a viticultural workhorse, churning out vast quantities of gluggable Chardonnay. With reduced demand for that grape, small producers are planting better cultivars (along with Viognier and Gewürztraminer) and producing quality wines. The region isn't very well set up for viticultural tourism but many wineries give a personal touch if you call in advance, and a few open for regular tastings in summer. One such is **Bushmere Estate**, with a good café in a pretty vineyard setting and very popular with locals for Sunday lunch.

Millton

199 Papatu Rd, 11km southwest of Gisborne • Tastings daily 10am–4pm • ☎ 06 862 8680, ⓦ millton.co.nz

Millton is one of New Zealand's few organic wineries to apply biodynamic principles. The timing of planting, harvesting and bottling is dictated by the moon's phases to produce some delicious wines (especially Chardonnay, Chenin Blanc and Viognier) that, it is claimed, can be enjoyed even by those who experience allergic reactions to other wines. Bring ingredients for a picnic among the vines and a leisurely game of pétanque on the winery's pitch.

Eastwoodhill Arboretum

Wharekopae Rd, 35km northwest of Gisborne • Daily 9am–5pm • $15 • ☎ 06 863 9003, ⓦ eastwoodhill.org.nz

A bottle of wine tucked under your arm and a groaning picnic hamper is the most conducive way to enjoy New Zealand's largest collection of northern hemisphere vegetation at **Eastwoodhill Arboretum**. It was the life's work of William Douglas Cook, who grew to love British gardens and parks while recuperating in England during

6

World War I. Concerned that war would break up the great estates of Europe and destroy their genetic stock of trees, he imported the best he could. Cook died in 1967 leaving numerous trails threading through a unique mixture of over 3500 species – magnolias, oaks, spruce, maples, cherries – brought together in an unusual microclimate in which both hot- and cold-climate trees flourish.

Rere rockslide

12km past Eastwoodhill Arboretum, accessed of Wharekopae Rd

The Wharekopae River plunges 10m over **Rere Falls**, where you can take a short walk behind the curtain of water, but this is easily eclipsed by the **Rere rockslide**, about 2km upstream, where the river cascades down a 20m-wide and 60m-long rock slope that is smooth enough to provide great sport. In summer there's little water and a lot of algae, making for a super-fast ride down to the pool at the bottom. The extra water in winter makes for a slower, less exciting and colder ride. Bring something to slide on – a boogie board, inner tube or old bit of plastic – and ask locals for advice and safety tips.

The road to Napier

At 213km, the road from Gisborne to Napier is easily manageable in a day, allowing plenty of time to take in the at times spectacular scenery and all the worthwhile stops along the way. South of Gisborne, **SH2 leaves** the Poverty Bay vineyards behind and traverses the hill country of the Wharerata State Forest before reaching **Morere**. From there it's just a short jaunt down SH2 before you can turn east and access the **Mahia Peninsula**. Continuing west on SH2 brings you to Wairoa, from where you can access Te Urewera National Park (see p.380) and Lake Waikaremoana, or continue on to Napier, stopping off to see the **Boundary Scenic Reserve**.

Morere and Morere Hot Spings

SH2, 50km south of Gisborne • Daily 10am–5pm, later in summer if busy • $6; private pools extra $3 for 30min • ☎ 06 837 8856, ⓦ morerehotsprings.co.nz

Tiny **MORERE** is best known for the highly saline and pleasantly non-sulphurous waters – the result of ancient seawater, warmed and concentrated along a fault line – that well up along a small stream at the **Morere Hot Springs**. The immediate area is also one of the east coast's last remaining tracts of native coastal forest, and grassy BBQ areas surrounding the pools form the nucleus of numerous trails that radiate out through stands of tawa, rimu, totara and matai; a short streamside walk (10min) takes you to the Nikau Plunge Pools, where soaking tanks are surrounded by nikau palm groves. Also consider the Mangakawa Track (3km; 2hr), which loops from the springs through gorgeous virgin bush up to a ridge-top beech forest.

ACCOMMODATION

MORERE

Morere Hot Springs Lodge & Cabins SH2 ☎ 06 837 8824, ⓦ morerehotsprings.co.nz. A wonderfully relaxing spot with self-contained accommodation scattered around the well-kept grassy site, all on a working farm with a good swimming hole. You'll need to bring most of the rudimentary supplies with you. Cabins $80, cottage $95

Morere Tearooms & Camping Ground Just west

of Nuhaka on SH2 ☎ 06 837 8792, ⓦ morerea ccommodation.co.nz. A traditional Kiwi campsite surrounded by trees, with good tent sites, basic cabins and limited communal facilities, but more comfortable self-contained units. Limited supplies are available at the tearooms, at a price. Tearoom open daily 8am–5pm, later after Dec. Camping $18.50, cabins $55, self-contained units $95

Mahia Peninsula

At Nuhaka, 8km south of Morere, the highway flirts briefly with the sea before turning sharp right for Wairoa. Nuhaka-Opoutama Road spurs east to the **Mahia Peninsula**, a distinctive high promontory that separates Hawke Bay from Poverty Bay. Surfers make good use of the rougher windward side, while the calmer beaches on the leeward side offer safe bathing and boating. Outside the mad month after Christmas it makes a relaxing place to break your journey. The peninsula's main settlement, **MAHIA BEACH**, lies 15km further on. It was made famous nationally throughout 2008 and 2009 by playing host to Moko, a playful bottlenose dolphin who cavorted daily with swimmers. He moved on late in 2009.

ACCOMMODATION AND EATING   MAHIA PENINSULA

Café Mahia 476 Mahia East Coast Rd. Licensed café serving tempting hogget rolls and flogging home-made jams and relishes. Nothing on the menu is over $20 – you'll find coffee and cake or a sandwich is ambitious enough. Daily 11am–2pm, later in Dec and Jan.

★ **Cappamore Lodge** 435 Mahia East Coast Rd ☎ 06 837 5523, ⓦ cottagestays.co.nz/cappamore/cottage .htm. Over the hill and on the windward side of the island, closer to the surf beaches at tiny Te Mahia, is a marvellous self-contained, handcrafted log house with two large living areas and two separate bedrooms; the owners live in a similar version across the courtyard. $120

Mahia Beach Motels & Holiday Park 43 Moana Drive,

Mahia Beach ☎ 06 837 5830, ⓦ motelscabinscamp mahiabeach.com. Spacious camping, basic tourist cabins and flashier motel units are the order of the day at this simple camp spread out on grassland back from the beach, which gets absolutely stuffed in the summer. The office shop has a small amount of supplies. Camping $18, cabins $90, motel units downstairs $125, motel units upstairs $145

Sunset Sports Bar and Grill 2 Newcastle St ☎ 06 837 5071. Apart from takeaways, eating in Mahia is limited to this lively spot, which does hearty meals such as steak, crayfish, and fish and chips ($15–34). They often have live music at weekends during high season. Daily 10am–late.

Wairoa

Although the official launch pad for trips to Lake Waikaremoana, many trampers prefer to travel from Gisborne or Napier and not disturb the dust at the sleepy farm service community of **WAIROA**, 40km west of the Nuhaka junction. Hugging the banks of the willow-lined Wairoa River a couple of kilometres from its mouth, where ships once entered to load the produce of the dairy- and sheep-farming country all around, the town offers little reason to break your journey, except an intriguing museum and the chance to eat or stock up on provisions for the Waikaremoana Track (see p.381).

Wairoa Museum

142 Marine Parade • Mon–Fri 10am–4pm, Sat 10am–1pm • Donation

The **Wairoa Museum** evokes a picture of the town's more lively history through well-presented displays (including one on the devastating cyclone Bola, which swept through the region in 1988) and contains a beautifully carved Maori figure dating back to the early eighteenth century. Also worth checking out is the information on the Wairoa Bar and the river pilot from 1872 who died at sea; no mention is made of whether he had a locker, but he was called Davy Jones.

ARRIVAL AND INFORMATION   WAIROA

By bus InterCity buses pick up daily at the i-SITE.
Destinations Gisborne (1 daily; 1hr 30min); Napier (1–2 daily; 2hr 30min).
i-SITE Corner of SH2 and Queen St (Nov–March daily 8am–5pm; April–Sept Mon–Fri 9am–4.45pm, Sat & Sun

9.45am–10.45am & 3.15–4pm to coincide with incoming buses; ☎ 06 838 7440, ⓦ wairoadc.govt.nz). Sells DOC hut tickets, arranges Lake Waikaremoana shuttle pick-ups and has internet access.

6

GETTING AROUND

To Lake Waikaremoana The Lake Waikaremoana Shuttle Service (☎06 837 3741) picks up on demand for the trip inland to the lake ($35–50/person, depending on numbers).

ACCOMMODATION

Café 287 3km south of Wairoa on SH2 ☎06 838 6601, ⓦcafe287.com. A large café in a larger car park overlooked by several en-suite cabins from which, in turn, you can just about glimpse the Wairoa River. In the evening the cabins are quiet with the exception of trucks pulling all-nighters on SH2, but at least you can walk to the café (see below). Cabins **$110**

Riverside Motor Camp 19 Marine Parade ☎06 838 6301, ⓦriversidemotorcamp.co.nz. Clean and simple but ageing accommodation in on-site vans, slightly more salubrious cabins, plus flat tent pitches and a very basic backpackers with a wee lounge and deck. It's all on a relatively narrow riverside pitch about a 2min walk from SH2. Camping **$16**, backpacker bunks **$27**, on-site vans **$45**, kitchen cabins **$70**

Vista Motor Lodge SH2 north of the Wairoa bridge ☎0800 284 782, ⓦvistamotorlodge.co.nz. The only worthwhile motel in town is showing its age a little but is still essentially good value with a variety of comfy units, well-kept gardens, a heated pool and a startlingly bright reception area redolent of Hawaii in the 1970s. **$120**

EATING

Café 287 3km south of Wairoa on SH2 ☎06 838 6601, ⓦcafe287.com. Roadside diner with accommodation (see above), dishing up hearty, home-cooked breakfasts, lunches and dinners from fettucini to steaks ($17–25) – although the breakfasts seem to be the most popular choice with the passing trade. Daily 8am–5pm.

Eastend Café 250 Marine Parade ☎06 838 6070. This surprisingly big-town-feeling, sophisticated place is one of the two best spots to eat during the day, serving the likes of Thai chicken and BLT ($8–18) along with delicious cakes and coffee. The café showcases local art and occasionally plays host to local events. Mon–Sat 7.30am–4pm, Sun 8.30am–4pm; closed Sun in the winter.

★ **Osler's Bakery & Café** 116 Marine Parade Try one of the 23 varieties of home-made pie at this local institution. The decor will be a trip down memory lane for anybody who liked the Austen Powers movies. Mon–Fri 4.30am–4.30pm, Sat & Sun 5am–3pm.

Wairoa Home Grown Market The Greenhouse Garden Centre & Café, 21 Mahia Ave (SH2). Wairoa's farmers' market sets up in the garden centre's car park, and is a good place to grab a quick snack or stock up on supplies for the trip to Lake Waikaremoana. Sat 8–11am.

Boundary Stream Scenic Reserve

Off SH2 at Tutira and 15km northwest along Pohakura Rd

From Wairoa south to Napier, SH2 becomes considerably steeper and twistier, so take it slowly and allow about an hour and a half. Make time to visit the wonderful **Boundary Stream Scenic Reserve**; a "mainland island" with great examples of a variety of environments from lowland to mountain forest. The reserve contains North Island brown kiwi, kereru, North Island kaka, shinning cuckoo and, very occasionally, New Zealand falcon. There are several walks, including one to the Bell Rock viewpoint (5km return; 3hr) and, at the far end of the reserve, to Shine Falls, which crashes 58m down onto rocks surrounded by lush vegetation.

Te Urewera National Park

Te Urewera National Park, 65km northwest of Wairoa, straddles the North Island's mountainous backbone and at 2120 square kilometres encompasses the largest untouched expanse of native bush outside Fiordland. Unusually for New Zealand, it is almost completely covered in vegetation; even the highest peaks – some approaching 1500m – barely poke through this dense cloak of primeval forest, whose undergrowth is trampled by deer and wild pigs and whose rivers are filled with trout. One road, SH38, penetrates the interior, but the way to get a true sense of the place is to hike, particularly the celebrated Lake Waikaremoana Track encircling **Lake Waikaremoana**, the "Sea of Rippling Waters" and the undoubted jewel of the park. The lake's deep clear waters, fringed by white sandy beaches and rocky bluffs, are ideal for swimming, fishing and kayaking.

Habitation is sparse, but the Tuhoe people, the "Children of the Mist", still live in the interior of the park (the largest concentration around the village of **Ruatahuna**). Most visitors make straight for **Waikaremoana**, the visitor centre and motor camp on the lakeshore, but immediately south, the quiet former hydroelectric development village of **Tuai** provides some additional basic services. Otherwise you're on your own.

6

Lake Waikaremoana

Shrouded by bushland, **Lake Waikaremoana** fills a huge scalloped bowl at an altitude of over 585m, precariously held back by the Panekiri and Ngamoko ranges. The lake came into being around 2200 years ago when a huge bank of sandstone boulders was dislodged from the Ngamoko range, blocking the river that once drained the valleys. The Maori have a more poetic explanation for the lake's creation. Hau-Mapuhia, the recalcitrant daughter of Mahu, was drowned by her father and turned into a *taniwha*, or "water spirit". In a frenzied effort to get to the sea, she charged in every direction, thereby creating the various arms of the lake. As she frantically ran south towards Onepoto, the dawn caught her, turning her to stone at a spot where the lake is said to ripple from time to time, in memory of her struggle.

Lake Waikaremoana Track

46km; 3–4 days; 1150m ascent

The **Lake Waikaremoana Track** is one of New Zealand's "Great Walks". It is also the most popular multi-day tramp in the North Island and often compared with the South Island's renowned Routeburn and Milford tracks, although, with the exception of an exhausting climb on the first day, this is a much gentler affair, with plenty of opportunities to fish, swim and listen to the plentiful and melodious birdlife.

About sixty percent of walkers prefer to travel clockwise around the lake, getting the challenging but panoramic ascent of Panekiri Bluff over with on the first day, though if the weather looks bad there's no reason why you shouldn't change your bookings (through the Aniwaniwa visitor centre) and go anticlockwise in the hope that it will improve.

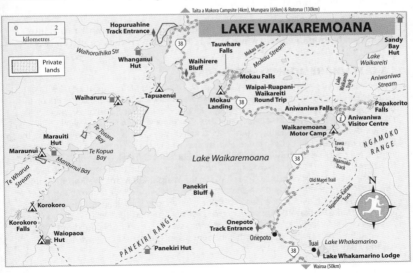

Three days is enough for fit walkers, but it's normally done in four, spending nights in the five Great Walk **huts** or five designated **campsites** (see p.384) scattered around the lakeshore. When tackled clockwise, as outlined below, the first leg is the toughest, so carry plenty of drinking water.

Onepoto to Panekiri Hut

9km; 4–5hr; 750m ascent; 150m descent

The track starts at a shelter by the lakeshore close to SH38 and climbs steeply past the site of a redoubt set up by soldiers of the Armed Constabulary in pursuit of Te Kooti (see box opposite). It then undulates along the ridge top, occasionally revealing fabulous lake views. Wonderfully airy steps up a rocky bluff bring you to the Panekiri Hut, magnificently set on the brink of the cliffs that fall away to the lake far below. Camping in this fragile environment is prohibited; committed campers must press on to Waiopaoa, an exhausting 8hr walk from the start at Onepoto.

Panekiri Hut to Waiopaoa Hut

7.5km; 3–4hr; 600m descent

Setting out from Panekiri Hut, the track descends the ridge then rapidly loses height through an often muddy area where protruding tree roots provide welcome hand-holds. Occasional lake views and the transition from beech forests to rich podocarp woodlands make this an appealing, if tricky, section of track down to the Waiopaoa Hut and campsite.

Waiopaoa Hut to Marauiti Hut

11km; 4–5hr; 100m ascent

The track largely follows the lakeshore, crossing grassland and then kanuka scrub before reaching the Korokoro campsite (1hr 30min from Waiopaoa Hut). A side track leads to the pretty 20m Korokoro Falls (45–60min return). Meanwhile, the main track climbs slightly above the lake past barely accessible bays, eventually reaching the Maraunui campsite and, after ascending the low Whakaneke Spur, descends to the waterside Marauiti Hut.

Marauiti Hut to Waiharuru Hut

6km; 2hr; 150m ascent

From the Marauiti Hut, the track crosses the bridge over the stream that runs into Marauiti Bay, passing the lovely white-sand Te Kopua Bay. It then climbs an easy

---

LAKE WAIKAREMOANA: SHORT HIKES

The Aniwaniwa visitor centre (see p.384) and the *Waikaremoana Motor Camp* (see p.384) are both well set up for helping hikers tackle the Lake Waikaremoana Track. But if you're not up for a three- to four-day trek, the best way to see and get a feel for the place is on one or more of the region's rewarding shorter hikes, detailed in DOC's *Lake Waikaremoana Walks* leaflet ($2.50).

Start off with **Papakorito Falls**, a 20m-wide curtain of water 2km east of the visitor centre, the easy **Hinerau Track** (1km; 20min return; 50m ascent), which starts from the visitor centre and leads to the double-drop **Aniwaniwa Falls**, or the **Black Beech Track** (2km; 30min one-way; 50m descent), which follows the old highway from the visitor centre to the motor camp.

If you've the best part of a day to spare, take on the **Waipai–Ruapani–Waikareiti Round Trip** (17km; 5–6hr; 300m ascent), which starts 200m north of the visitor centre and winds up heading through dense beech forest past the grass-fringed Lake Ruapani to the beautiful and serene **Lake Waikareiti**. You can rent rowboats here (around $20/half-day), though you'll need to plan ahead as the key is held at Aniwaniwa visitor centre. Return down the Waikareiti Track or head on around to the northern side of the lake (3hr one-way) and stay at **Sandy Bay Hut** (18 bunks; $15).

6

TE KOOTI RIKIRANGI

Te Kooti Rikirangi was one of the most celebrated of Maori "rebels", a thorn in the side of the colonial government throughout the New Zealand Wars of the late 1860s and early 1870s. An excellent fighter and brilliant strategist, Te Kooti kept the mountainous spine of the North Island on edge for half a decade, eluding the biggest manhunt in New Zealand's history.

Born near Gisborne around 1830, Te Kooti was not of chiefly rank but could trace his ancestry back to the captains of several *waka* (canoes) that brought the Maori to New Zealand. By the middle of the 1860s, he was fighting for the government against the fanatical, pseudo-Christian Hau Hau cult that started in Taranaki in 1862. The cult spread to the east coast where, in 1866, Te Kooti was unjustly accused of being in league with its devotees. Denied the trial he demanded, he was imprisoned on the Chatham Islands, along with three hundred of his supposed allies. In 1867, he was brought close to death by a fever, but rose again, claiming a divine revelation and establishing a new religion, **Ringatu** ("the uplifted hand"), which still has some sixteen thousand believers today. Ringatu took its cues from the Hau Hau, but developed into a uniquely Maori version of Catholicism, drawing heavily on the Old Testament. Some say Te Kooti saw himself as a Moses figure – apparently given to dousing his uplifted hand in phosphorus so that it glowed brightly in the dim meeting houses.

After two years on the Chathams, Te Kooti and his fellow prisoners commandeered a ship and engineered a dramatic escape, returning to Poverty Bay. He sought safety in the **Urewera Range**, with the Armed Constabulary in hot pursuit. Te Kooti still managed to conduct successful campaigns, exacting revenge against government troops at Whakatane on the Bay of Plenty, Mohaka in Hawke's Bay and at Rotorua. With the end of the New Zealand Wars in 1872, Te Kooti took refuge in the Maori safe haven of the King Country. He was eventually pardoned in 1883, and in 1891 was granted a plot of land near Whakatane, where he lived out the last two years of his life.

saddle before dropping down to Te Totara Bay and follows the lake to the large and modern Waiharuru Hut and campsite.

Waiharuru Hut to Whanganui Hut

5.3km; 2–3hr; 100m ascent

It's a short hike across a broad neck of land to the Tapuaenui campsite and beyond. The track follows the lakeshore to the characterful old Whanganui Hut, which is set in a clearing beside a stream and is fitted with built-in three-tier bunks.

Whanganui Hut to Hopuruahine

5km; 2–3hr; 50m ascent

The final leg of the hike is also the shortest and easiest. The track skirts the lake to the point where water taxis pick up (45min), then follows grassy flats beside the Hopuruahine River before crossing a suspension bridge to the access road to a camping area (free).

ARRIVAL AND DEPARTURE

LAKE WAIKAREMOANA

By bus from Wairoa Lake Waikaremoana is approached most easily by bus from Wairoa along SH38, which continues through the park to Murupara and Rotorua. The Lake Waikaremoana Shuttle Service (see p.379) also services the lake from Wairoa.

By bus from Rotorua Between Lake Waikaremoana and Murupara there is over 60km of tortuous gravel road,

so approaching from the northwest is less than appealing. If you wish to travel this route contact Magic Bus (☏09 358 5600, ⓦ magicbus.co.nz), who currently run the Gisborne–Waikaremoana–Rotorua route on Mon and Fri, or Te Uruwera Shuttles (☏0800 873 937, ⓦ tshuttle.co.nz), who run in both directions between Rotorua and Lake Waikaremoana on Thurs and Sun in summer.

GETTING AROUND

By car You can drive to the trailheads at either end of the Lake Waikaremoana Track, but there are occasional thefts

and most people prefer to park free of charge at the *Waikaremoana Motor Camp* (see p.384) and take a bus or boat to the trailheads.

By bus and boat Homebay Water Taxi & Cruises (☎ 06 837 3826), based at the *Waikaremoana Motor Camp*, operate a reliable, on-demand shuttle-bus service to the trailheads, often supplementing with a water taxi in summer. They charge around $40 (minimum of two people) for a joint drop-off and pick-up package, and they'll also run a water-taxi service to anywhere else you might want to start or finish, enabling you to walk shorter sections by means of pre-arranged pick-ups from specified beaches. Enquire at the *Waikaremoana Motor Camp* about renting kayaks and open canoes for use on the lake.

INFORMATION AND TOURS

Aniwaniwa visitor centre By the lake in the old rangers' house, opposite the former visitor centre, which at the time of writing was undergoing repairs (daily: Oct–April 8am–4.45pm; May–Sept 8am–4.15pm; ☎ 06 837 3803, ✉ teurewerarvc@doc.govt.nz). The DOC-operated visitor centre is the place to come for Lake Waikaremoana Track hut bookings.

DOC leaflets and maps Comprehensive walking information is covered in the *Lake Waikaremoana Track* leaflet, though map enthusiasts might like the two 1:50,000 Topo50 maps that cover the full circuit.

Services The only place that has petrol between Wairoa and Murupara is the *Waikaremoana Motor Camp*.

Weather The winter months (June–Sept) can be cold and wet, making spring and autumn the best times to undertake the walk, though go prepared as it can snow at any point in the year.

Equipment Each hut is supplied with drinking water, toilets and a heating stove, but a cooking stove, fuel and all your food must be carried. Campsites just have water and toilets.

Pack transport Homebay Water Taxi & Cruises (see above) can organize pack transport between most huts, allowing for a largely luggage-free walk, though this is only economical for groups of four or more.

GUIDED HIKES

Walking Legends ☎ 0800 925 569, ✆ walkinglegends .com. Offers four-day walks ($1290), led by enthusiastic and knowledgeable guides, with accommodation in the same DOC huts used by independent walkers. Trips depart from Rotorua, and excellent meals and wine are provided – all you have to do is carry a daypack. The longest day is around seven hours and there's usually enough time to squeeze in a bit of trout fishing.

ACCOMMODATION

LAKE WAIKAREMOANA

Lake Whakamarino Lodge Tuai village, off SH38 15km south of the visitor centre ☎ 06 837 3876. Converted from construction workers' quarters and wonderfully sited beside the trout-filled Lake Whakamarino, the accommodation here is in basic rooms and more upmarket self-contained units; book ahead, as it fills up quickly. Rooms $70, self-contained units $120

Mokau Landing campsite SH38, 11km northwest of the visitor centre. A large, grassy DOC site that sits between the bush and the lake, with running water and toilets. Mokau Falls is just 1.5km away. $7

Te Taita O Makora campsite SH38, 22km northwest of the visitor centre. A very basic ten-pitch DOC site with toilets and a water supply from a nearby stream; it's best to take the necessary precautions in treating any drinking water.

Waikaremoana Motor Camp SH38, 2km south of the visitor centre ☎ 06 837 3826, ✆ lake.co.nz. A well-equipped establishment with camping sites, wooden cabins, larger semi-detached tourist flats and wee individual tin chalets. There is also a store of sorts, a reasonably sized communal kitchen and dining room. Showers are available for non-guests ($5). Camping $15, cabins $55, self-contained chalets $90, tourist flats $90

LAKE WAIKAREMOANA TRACK

DOC huts and campsites Panekiri, Waiopaoa, Marauiti, Waiharuru and Whanganui are all Great Walk huts and must be booked in advance, as must the campsites; you can do so online at ✆ doc.govt.nz, although you'll need to call in at the Aniwaniwa visitor centre to pick up your Great Walk Ticket. Your chances of getting a place are much better outside the busy month or so after Christmas and the week of Easter. Backcountry hut pass not valid. Under-18s free. Huts $30.60, camping $12.20

EATING

Groceries and meals on request The nearest full-time restaurant is over 60km away in Wairoa, so you'll largely have to fend for yourself when it comes to food. There's a reasonable range of groceries at the *Waikaremoana Motor* *Camp*, and meals are sometimes available on request at the *Lake Whakamarino Lodge* (mains around $25), but you're better off relying on your own supplies.

Napier

Laidback, seaside **NAPIER** is Hawke's Bay's largest city (population 54,000) and one of New Zealand's most likeable regional centres, thanks to its Mediterranean climate, affordable prices and the world's best-preserved collection of small-scale Art Deco architecture, built after the earthquake that devastated the city in 1931 (see p.386).

Thanks to the whim of mid-nineteenth-century Land Commissioner Alfred Domett, the grid of streets in the city's Art Deco **commercial centre** bears the names of literary luminaries – Tennyson, Thackeray, Byron, Dickens, Shakespeare, Milton and more. Bisecting it all is the partly pedestrianized main thoroughfare of Emerson Street, whose

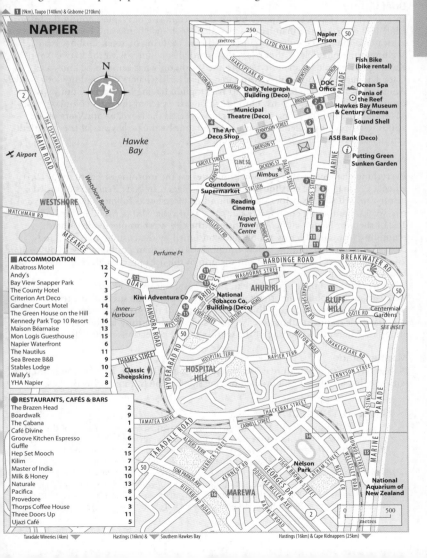

▲ **1** (9km), Taupo (140km) & Gisborne (210km)

NAPIER

N

Hawke Bay

✈ Airport

WESTSHORE

Napier Prison

Fish Bike (bike rental)

Ocean Spa
Pania of the Reef
Hawkes Bay Museum & Century Cinema

Daily Telegraph Building (Deco)

DOC Office

Municipal Theatre (Deco)

Sound Shell

The Art Deco Shop

ASB Bank (Deco)

Putting Green
Sunken Garden

Countdown Supermarket

Nimbus

Reading Cinema

Napier Travel Centre

HARDINGE ROAD

BREAKWATER RD

Perfume Pt

WAGHORNE STREET

QUAY

AHURIRI

BLUFF HILL

Centennial Gardens

SEE INSET

Kiwi Adventura Co

Inner Harbour

National Tobacco Co. Building (Deco)

Classic Sheepskins

HOSPITAL HILL

Nelson Park

National Aquarium of New Zealand

MAREWA

■ ACCOMMODATION	
Albatross Motel	12
Andy's	7
Bay View Snapper Park	1
The County Hotel	3
Criterion Art Deco	5
Gardner Court Motel	14
The Green House on the Hill	4
Kennedy Park Top 10 Resort	16
Maison Béarnaise	13
Mon Logis Guesthouse	15
Napier Waterfront	6
The Nautilus	11
Sea Breeze B&B	9
Stables Lodge	10
Wally's	2
YHA Napier	8

● RESTAURANTS, CAFÉS & BARS	
The Brazen Head	2
Boardwalk	9
The Cabana	1
Café Divine	4
Groove Kitchen Espresso	6
Guffle	2
Hep Set Mooch	15
Kilim	7
Master of India	12
Milk & Honey	10
Naturale	13
Pacifica	8
Provedore	14
Thorps Coffee House	3
Three Doors Up	11
Ujazi Café	5

Taradale Wineries (4km) ▼   Hastings (16km) & ▼ Southern Hawkes Bay   Hastings (16km) & Cape Kidnappers (25km) ▼

terracotta paving and palm trees run from Clive Square – one-time site of a makeshift "Tin Town" while the city was being rebuilt after the earthquake – to the Norfolk pine-fringed **Marine Parade**, Napier's main beach.

Around the northeastern side of Bluff Hill (Mataruahou), about 5km from the city centre, lies the original settlement site of **Ahuriri**, now home to trendy restaurants, cafés, bars and boutiques.

Napier makes a perfect base from which to visit the gannet colony at Cape Kidnappers (see p.394) as well as the vat-load of world-class **wineries** on the surrounding plains (see p.395).

Brief history

In 1769, James Cook sailed past **Ahuriri**, the current site of Napier, noting the sea-girt Bluff Hill linked to the mainland by two slender shingle banks and backed by a superb saltwater lagoon – the only substantial sheltered mooring between Gisborne and Wellington. Nonetheless, after a less-than-cordial encounter with the native Ngati Kahungunu people he anchored just to the south, off what came to be known as Cape Kidnappers. Some thirty years later, when early whalers followed in Cook's wake, Ahuriri was all but deserted, the Ngati Kahungunu having been driven out by rivals equipped with European guns. During the uneasy peace of the early colonial years, Maori returned to the Napier area, which weathered the **New Zealand Wars** of the 1860s relatively unscathed. The port boomed, but by the early years of the twentieth century all the available land was used up.

The earthquake

Everything changed in two and a half minutes on the morning of February 3, 1931, when a 7.9 magnitude **earthquake**, one of the biggest in New Zealand's recorded history, rocked the city. More than six hundred aftershocks followed over the next two weeks, hampering efforts to rescue the 258 people who perished in the Bay area, 162 of them in Napier alone. The centre of the city was completely devastated, crumbling into smouldering rubble and consumed by the ensuing fire. The land twisted and buckled, finding a new equilibrium more than 2m higher, with 300 square kilometres of new land wrested from the grip of the ocean – enough room to site the Hawke's Bay airport and expand the city.

Napier embraced the opportunity to start afresh: out went the trams, telephone wires were laid underground, the streets were widened and, in the spirit of the times, almost everything was designed according to the precepts of the **Art Deco** movement. The simultaneous reconstruction gave Napier a stylistic uniformity rarely seen, ranking it alongside Miami Beach as one of the world's largest collections of Art Deco buildings.

Marine Parade

Napier's most striking feature is **Marine Parade**, a dead-straight 2km of boulevard lined with stately Norfolk pines, bordered on one side by hotels, motels, B&Bs, hostels,

---

PANIA OF THE REEF

Just south of Ocean Spa (see opposite) is a bronze cast of the curvaceous **Pania of the reef**, a siren of local Maori legend. **Pania** was a beautiful sea-maiden who would swim from the watery realm of Tangaroa, the god of the ocean, each evening to quench her thirst at a freshwater spring in a clump of flax close to the base of Bluff Hill before returning to her people each morning. One evening, she was discovered by a young chief who wooed her and wanted her to remain on land. Eventually they married, but when Pania went to pay a farewell visit to her kin they forcibly restrained her in the briny depths and she turned to stone, forming what is now known as **Pania Reef**. Fishers and divers still claim they can see her with her arms outstretched towards the shore.

ART DECO NAPIER

The 1931 earthquake saw Napier rebuilt in line with the times. Although **Art Deco** embraced modernity, glorifying progress, the machine age and the Gatsby-style high life, the onset of the Great Depression pared down these excesses, and Napier's version was informed by the privations of an austere era. At the same time, the architects looked for inspiration to California's Santa Barbara – which, just six years earlier, had suffered the same fate and risen from the ashes. They adopted fountains (a symbol of renewal), sunbursts, chevrons, lightning flashes and fluting to embellish the highly formalized but asymmetric designs. In Napier, what emerged was a conglomeration of early twentieth-century design, combining elements of the Arts and Crafts movement, the Californian Spanish Mission style, Egyptian and Mayan motifs, stylized floral designs and even Maori imagery. For the best part of half a century, the city's residents merely daubed the buildings in grey or muted blue paint. Fortunately, this meant that when a few savvy visionaries recognized the city's potential in the mid-1980s and formed the **Art Deco Trust**, everything was still intact. The trust continues to promote the preservation of buildings and provides funding for shopkeepers to pick out distinctive architectural detail in pastel colours similar to those originally used.

You can get a sense of Art Deco Napier by wandering along the half-dozen streets of the city centre, notably **Emerson Street**. Worth special attention here is the **ASB Bank**, on the corner of Hastings Street. Its exterior is adorned with fern shoots and a mask from the head of a *taiaha* (a long fighting club), while its interior has a fine Maori rafter design. On Tennyson Street, look for the flamboyant **Daily Telegraph** building, with stylized fountains, and the **Municipal Theatre**, built in the late 1930s in a strikingly geometric form.

ART DECO NAPIER TOURS AND TRAILS

Keen observers will find classic Art Deco everywhere but for a systematic exploration of Napier's Art Deco revival try any or a combination of the options listed below.

The Art Deco Shop 163 Tennyson St ☎ 06 835 0022, ⓦ artdeconapier.com. Apart from all the merchandise it sells, the shop also has a free 24min introductory video and sells a leaflet ($7.50) for the self-guided Art Deco Walk, which outlines a stroll (daily 9am–5pm; 1.5km; 1hr 30min–2hr) through the downtown area.

Art Deco Afternoon Walking Tour Dedicated Deco buffs meet at the Art Deco Shop for this tour (April–Sept daily 2pm; Oct–March 5pm; 2hr; $21), which brings 1930s Napier to life through anecdotal patter and gives you the chance to gaze around the interiors of shops and banks without feeling too self-conscious.

Art Deco Morning Walking Tour and Art Deco Evening Walk Both of these tours are shorter than the afternoon walking tour (see above) and start at the i-SITE. Morning tour (1hr; $16) daily 10am; Evening Walk (1hr 30min; $19) daily from the end of Jan–March.

Vintage Deco Car Tours and Deco Tour 163 Tennyson St ☎ 06 835 0022, ⓦ artdeconapier.com. The Art Deco Trust operates both these tours. The car tour (1hr; $140 for a maximum of three people) is subject to availability, while the Deco Tour (daily 11.30am; 1hr 15min; $48) involves a minibus jaunt around Napier's Art Deco attractions outside the city centre.

shops and restaurants and by a dark grey stony beach on the other. The latter is Napier's main beach, but it's unsafe for swimming – for golden-sand swimming beaches head 30km north to Waipatiki or 35km south to Waimarama or Ocean Beach. A popular walking and cycling path links a string of attractions along the seaward edge of Marine Parade, starting by Napier's port at the northern end of town and passing the foot of Bluff Hill before arriving at the Ocean Spa.

Ocean Spa

42 Marine Parade • Mon–Sat 6am–10pm, Sun 8am–10pm • $9 • ☎ 06 835 8553, ⓦ oceanspa.co.nz

A large glass and concrete beachside complex, **Ocean Spa** houses a gym and salt-chlorinated, lido-style complex of hot pools (36–38°C) with bubbles, jets, spouts, steam room, sauna, massages ($35/30min), beauty treatments and a lap pool (26°C), all overlooking the sea. The long hours and warm waters make it a great place for a relaxed summer evening.

6

Hawke's Bay Museum & Art Gallery

65 Marine Parade • ⓦ hbmag.co.nz

Opposite Pania (see box, p.386) stands the bleak body of the **Hawke's Bay Museum & Art Gallery**, once a fabulous venue. At the time of writing, a major expansion was under way but not due for completion until sometime in late 2013. Once it reopens, expect quality exhibits with an emphasis on art, design and decorative arts. Completion will also mean the reopening the excellent on-site art-house cinema.

Opossum World

157 Marine Parade • Mon–Fri 9.30am–5pm, plus Sat & Sun in the summer 9.30am–4pm • Free • ☎ 06 835 7697, ⓦ opossumworld.com

Although you'll have seen the road pizza possum and possibly even heard some crashing about in the bush, you won't really get a sense of what so incenses most Kiwis about the cute little animals until you look through the displays in this shop, which touts itself as a "unique shopping and educational experience". New Zealand's 70 million possums eat 21,000 tonnes of vegetation (mostly native plants) every night, and if they're not treated as pests eventually they'll turn the country into something that looks like the Nevada desert. The displays here cover the lives of the old possum trappers such as Barry Crump (see p.819) and the controversial use of 1080 poison – used to control numbers, it also has a devastating effect on native wildlife. Possum fur has great insulating properties – so much so that it was used to protect the wiring on some of the Apollo Space Program's equipment; the shop sells possum fur hats, gloves, scarves and more.

National Aquarium of New Zealand

546 Marine Parade • Daily 9am–5pm; ocean tank hand-feeding 10am & 2pm; reef tank hand-feeding 10am; swimming with sharks daily 2pm; behind-the-scenes tour daily by reservation • $17.90; behind-the-scenes tour $35.70; snorkelling with sharks $75/30min; scuba diving (for qualified divers only) with sharks $75, or $117 with all gear • ☎ 06 834 1404, ⓦ nationalaquarium.co.nz

Further along the seafront lies the **National Aquarium of New Zealand**, one of the finest in the country, with distinct marine environments from Africa, Asia and Australia, plus a substantial New Zealand section. At the time of writing, a display for penguins rescued from the defunct Marine World was under construction; once open, it should add to the aquarium's already excellent reputation.

The most spectacular section is the **ocean tank**, its Perspex walk-through tunnel giving intimate views of rays and assorted sharks; try to time your visit for one of the hand-feeding sessions. There's more hand feeding at the **reef tank**, plus behind-the-scenes tours and the chance to swim with the sharks in the ocean tank. Within the controlled environment of the tank and without shark cages or nets this is a rare chance to come face to face with these "monsters" of the deep.

There are also excellent non-aquatic sections on New Zealand's reptilian tuatara, and a nocturnal **kiwi house**.

Bluff Hill

The city centre's northern flank butts up against the steep slopes of **Bluff Hill**, a 3km-long hummock of winding streets, home to some of Napier's more desirable suburbs. The primary reason for negotiating the hill is the **Bluff Hill Domain Lookout** (daily 7am–dusk) at the eastern summit, which offers views of Cape Kidnappers to the west and across to the Mahia Peninsula in the east.

Napier Prison Tour

55 Coote Rd • Daily 9am–5pm; guided tour daily 9.30am & 3pm; R16 night tour June–Jan Fri & Sat 7pm • Audio and guided tour $20; R16 night tour $65 with dinner, $25 without • ☎ 06 835 9933, ⓦ napierprison.com

Immediately south of Bluff Hill, **Napier Prison** is an imposing sandstone ex-clink, built in 1862 and decommissioned in 1993. This is no Alcatraz but a very Kiwi jail – all weatherboard and corrugated iron – that, like its inmates, had a chequered career, housing women, children and lunatics as well as hardened male inmates. Several cells are intact, complete with gang graffiti and, reputedly, the ghosts of former inmates. Take either the one-hour audio or guided tour, or join the R16 night tour, which includes spooky interaction and a dinner option.

Ahuriri
5km northwest of the city centre

Napier's European ancestry is all around the harbourside suburb of **Ahuriri**. James Cook found shelter for the *Endeavour* in the Ahuriri Estuary and the fledgling town grew up around the harbour. When the industrial port moved round the headland Ahuriri languished, but in recent years the old wool stores and warehouses around the inner harbour (also known as the Iron Pot), as well as the waterfront strip stretching back to town, have been reborn as home to cavernous bars, a new brewery (see p.392), chic shops, cafés and restaurants, all buzzing from Thursday evening through the weekend.

National Tobacco Company Building
Corner of Bridge and Ossian sts

During the day the Ahuriri district makes for a pleasant place to stroll beside the yachts or peek in to the boutiques. The only real sight, however, is the **National Tobacco Company Building**. Its exterior is the most frequently used image of Art Deco Napier and exhibits a decorative richness seldom seen on industrial buildings, including Art Nouveau motifs of roses and raupo (a kind of Kiwi bulrush).

Sheepskin Tannery
22 Thames St • Tours Mon–Fri 11am & 2pm • Free • ☎ 06 835 9662, ⓦ classicsheepskins.co.nz

Unique behind-the-scenes twenty-minute tours of a **sheepskin tannery** are offered by Classic Sheepskins. You also have the opportunity to buy factory-priced products including Thor boots (the Kiwi equivalent of Ugg boots); they'll even pick you up for free from the city centre.

ARRIVAL AND DEPARTURE
NAPIER

By plane Regular direct flights from Auckland, Wellington and Christchurch arrive at Hawke's Bay Airport, 5km north of town on SH2, where they are met by the Super Shuttle (☎0800 748 885, ⓦsupershuttle.co.nz), which charges $20 to get into town.
Destinations Auckland (7–10 daily; 1hr); Christchurch (2 daily; 1hr 25min); Wellington (4–5 daily; 50min).

By bus InterCity and NakedBus buses pull in outside the i-SITE.
Destinations Auckland (2 daily; 7hr 15min); Dannevirke (4 daily; 2hr); Gisborne (1–2 daily; 4hr); Hastings (Mon–Fri hourly or better, Sat 5 daily; 1hr); Norsewood (4 daily; 1hr 30min); Palmerston North (3 daily; 3hr); Taupo (4–5 daily; 2hr); Wellington (4 daily; 5hr 15min).

GETTING AROUND

By bike Napier's central sights are easily covered on foot, but cycling along the 130km of paths in and around the city is a pleasant way to see the area; try Fish Bike, 26 Marine Parade (daily 9am–5pm, later in summer; ☎06 833 6979, ⓦfishbike.co.nz), who rent out an assortment of bikes for $50/day.
By bus The GoBay local bus services (☎06 878 9250,

ⓦhbrc.govt.nz) are of use primarily for visits to Hastings, Havelock North and the Mission Estate Winery (where they drop off within walking distance).
By car Auto Rental (☎06 834 0045) and Pegasus (☎06 843 7020) both have short-lease vehicles from $60/day.
By taxi Napier Taxis (☎06 835 7777).

INFORMATION AND ACTIVITIES

i-SITE 100 Marine Parade (daily 9am–5pm; ☎06 834 1911, ⓦhawkesbaynz.com). Can advise on tide times for gannet visits, book travel and track/hut tickets and has internet access.
DOC 59 Marine Parade (Mon–Fri 9am–4.15pm; ☎06 834

3111). Has information about walks into the remote Kaweka and Ruahine ranges to the west.
Kiwi Adventure Company Climbing Wall 58 West Quay, ☎06 834 3500, ⓦkiwi-adventure.co.nz. Set close to the water in one of the former wool stores and behind

6

Hep Set Mooch Café (see p.392), this establishment has a good indoor climbing wall ($15 for all day) and will teach all comers of any age, as well as organize kayaking and caving trips locally – although mostly you'll be tagging along with existing groups. Tues–Thurs 3–9pm, Sat & Sun 10am–6pm.

ACCOMMODATION

Apart from the usual shortage of rooms during the month or so after Christmas and the February festivals (see p.392) you should have little trouble finding accommodation in Napier. There are dozens of **motels** around town, many concentrated in Westshore, a beachfront suburb a couple of kilometres from the centre beside SH2. Right in the thick of things, Marine Parade has low-cost backpacker **hostels**, plush motels and classy **B&Bs**.

Albatross Motel 56 Meeanee Quay, Westshore ☎ 0800 252 287, ⓦ albatrossmotel.co.nz. Large, good-value motel beside SH2 but close to Westshore Beach and Ahuriri's restaurants, with a small pool, spa and free wi-fi. Accommodation is in studio units on the ground and first floors, and larger, open-plan deluxe units on the ground only. Studios $119, deluxe $140

Andy's 259 Marine Parade ☎ 06 835 5575, ⓦ andys backpackers.co.nz. An enthusiastically run – if slightly threadbare – little hostel that's been around for a long time. Some rooms have windows facing Marine Parade at street level, while others have (at a stretch) an ocean view. There's also a small but well-equipped kitchen and wee garden area. Dorms $26, rooms $52, ocean aspect $60

Bay View Snapper Park 10 Gill Rd, Bay View, 9km north of Napier ☎ 0800 287 275, ⓦ snapperpark.co .nz; map p.394. Revamped and welcoming, with a jazzy reception and summer-only café, this beachfront campsite provides an antidote to *Kennedy Park's* gulag ambience. A few campervan spots and some units have sea views. Camping $20, cabins $75, self-contained units $135, motel units $150

The County Hotel 12 Browning St ☎ 0800 843 468, ⓦ countyhotel.co.nz. One of the few 1931 earthquake survivors, this elegant, period-decorated business and tourist hotel (in the Edwardian former council offices) has plush rooms, a posh restaurant and wee cocktail bar. $315

Criterion Art Deco 48 Emerson St ☎ 06 835 2059, ⓦ criterionartdeco.co.nz. Central, well-organized 58-bed hostel in an Art Deco building, formerly a hotel. The dorms (some single-sex) and doubles (some en suite) are good value and there are large communal areas but a small kitchen. Guests get free continental breakfast and discounts in *The Cri* café/bar downstairs, which serves cheap standard Kiwi café fare, has pool tables, big-screen TVs and occasional live music. Dorms $23, rooms $65, en suites $85

Gardner Court Motel 16 Nelson Crescent ☎ 0800 000 830, ⓦ gardnercourtmotel.co.nz. Exceptionally welcoming, quiet, clean and reasonably central old-school motel with a solar-heated outdoor pool and simple motel rooms at bargain prices. The place is made by the enthusiasm and friendliness of the long-term owners. $110

The Green House on the Hill 18b Milton Oaks, Bluff Hill ☎ 06 835 4475, ⓦ the-green-house.co.nz. The owner goes to great lengths to make you feel welcome in her vegetarian homestay, surrounded by trees halfway up a hidden urban hill and at the end of a steep drive. Choose from the en suite or two-room suite with a private bathroom, and enjoy the inventive breakfasts and city views. Free wi-fi. $135

Kennedy Park Top 10 Resort Storkey St, off Kennedy Rd ☎ 0800 457 275, ⓦ kennedypark.co.nz. This organized and ultra-efficient campsite on steroids just 2km from the city centre, has acres of powered sites, a pool, BBQ area, kids' playground, restaurant and a huge range of cabins and units. Camping $21.50, cabins $60, kitchen cabins $83, en-suite $92, holiday unit $110, motel units $115

Maison Béarnaise 25 France Rd, Bluff Hill ☎ 06 835 4693, ⓦ maisonbearnaise.co.nz. Enchanting century-old villa that overlooks the town, with a lovely garden and two delightful, airy, en-suite doubles. Free wi-fi and tasty traditional breakfasts, made from seasonally available ingredients, are the icing on the cake. $220

★ **Mon Logis Guesthouse** 415 Marine Parade ☎ 06 835 2125, ⓦ monlogis.co.nz. Century-old wooden house transformed inside by a taste of French chic in the four rooms sharing a balcony with sea views. The friendly and knowledgeable Gallic owner makes every effort to look after you and provides absolutely delicious breakfasts. $180, sea view $240

Napier Waterfront 217 Marine Parade ☎ 06 835 3429, ⓦ napierbackpackers.co.nz. A weatherboard building complete with street-level veranda overlooking Marine Parade. There are cosy dorms, private rooms and good cooking facilities. Regular BBQs in the garden create a relaxed vibe. Dorms $23, rooms $56

The Nautilus 387 Marine Parade ☎ 0508 68 845, ⓦ nautilusnapier.co.nz. Large, modern motel in which all rooms offer sea views, a hot tub, TV and room service. There is also a small on-site restaurant and wi-fi. Studio $175, deluxe and apartments $225

★ **Sea Breeze B&B** 281 Marine Parade ☎ 06 835 8067, ⓔ seabreeze.napier@xtra.co.nz. Unique, seafront Victorian villa with flamboyantly decorated theme rooms; Indian and Turkish share a bathroom, while Asian has an en suite. The owners go to great lengths to ensure you enjoy your stay and provide a guest kitchenette and a lounge with sea views. Breakfast is a generous, self-service continental accompanied by the sound of waves. $130

Stables Lodge 370 Hastings St ☎06 835 6242, ⓦstableslodge.co.nz. Rooms ranged around a central courtyard give this 38-bed hostel an intimate feel and it is all pretty friendly and relaxed. Free internet, hammocks, a book exchange and a BBQ that takes the pressure off the small but well-equipped kitchen add to the communal atmosphere. Dorms $26, rooms $64

Wally's 7 Cathedral Lane ☎06 833 7930, ⓦwallys .co.nz. Central, well organized hostel in a pair of 1920s

villas, plus a cottage used as an eight-bed dorm. Good range of rooms, most reasonably comfortable, huge DVD collection and some off-street parking. Dorms $26, rooms $56, en suite $76

★ **YHA Napier** 277 Marine Parade ☎06 835 7039, ⓦyha.co.nz. The pick of the backpacker options is a homely, central and spotlessly clean hostel spread across three airy historic weatherboard houses on the waterfront. Four-share dorms, doubles, snug singles, twins and a five-bed family room make this a flexible choice, and some rooms have sea views. The sunny courtyard at the back with a BBQ and adequate kitchen space satisfy, even in the busy season. Dorms $30, singles $45, twins and doubles $74

EATING, DRINKING AND ENTERTAINMENT

During the day central Napier boasts a number of good **cafés** for food, a drink or coffee, but once the sun drops below the yardarm you're better off heading for Ahuriri. The surrounding **wineries** (see p.396) do offer fine dining, both day and night, but it comes at a price. There are two large **supermarkets** in the town centre, both on Munroe St: Countdown (daily 6am–midnight) at no. 1, and Pak 'n Save (daily 6am–midnight) at no. 25. It's rare to find any really exciting entertainment, unless you hit town at **festival time** (see box, p.392), but a couple of the **bars** host live music at weekends and when touring bands pass through. Entertainment listings are covered in the weekday-only *Hawke's Bay Today* newspaper, on Thursday and Friday.

CITY CENTRE

The Brazen Head 21 Hastings St ☎06 835 3517. Irish-style pub that is required by law, like all bars, to provide food – but you'll want to skip it here. Instead, come for the live music, themed nights, quizzes and boozy atmosphere at weekends, which all help make up for the nosh. Daily 11am–late.

★ **The Cabana** 11 Shakespeare Rd ☎06 835 1102, ⓦcabana.net.nz. A new version of a once famous in New Zealand venue, this is once again a proper venue for travelling bands and shows that many a larger town would be proud of. A visit to Napier is not complete without at least poking your head round the door. Occasional cover charge applies, depending on the acts ($5–20). Thurs–Sun 4pm–late.

Café Divine 53 Hastings St ☎06 835 6218. Popular spot with locals and travellers alike, living up to its name with enormous slices of healthy home-made quiches, veggie bakes, filos and wraps, delicious seafood chowder ($15.50), and other inexpensive breakfasts and lunches ($9–28). Daily 7am–5pm.

★ **Groove Kitchen Espresso** 112 Tennyson St ☎06 835 8530, ⓦgroovekitchen.co.nz. Cool café with lovely food – including their own bagels – irresistible coffee and great sounds from the speakers or the turntables in the corner. Mains ($18–26) include Sicilian roast fish with lemon, capers and rosemary. On selected evenings in the summer they host live or DJ music and serve curries. Mon–Thurs 8am–around 2pm, Fri 8am–around 2pm & 6.30pm–late, Sat 8.30am–around 3pm & 6.30pm–late, Sun 8.30am–3pm.

★ **Guffle** 29A Hastings St ☎06 835 8847, ⓦguffle .co.nz. Dress up just a little or not at all (depending on your sense of occasion) when you visit this ultra-cool wee cocktail and wine bar, which serves the best drinks in town and has great tunes anytime, plus occasional live music. They can rustle up some chips if you need them but their specialities are the phenomenally good cocktails. Mon–Sat 4pm–late.

Kilim 193 Hastings St ☎06 835 9100. BYO wine without corkage and cheap Turkish grub to eat in or take away make this a local favourite. Mains ($14–16.50) include grilled kofte, falafel and spinach borek. Service is haphazard but the staff are keen and the food is tasty and filling. Sun–Thurs 11am–9pm, Fri & Sat 11am–9.30pm.

Pacifica 209 Marine Parade ☎06 833 6335, ⓦpacifica restaurant.co.nz. A bit too sophisticated for its own good, this restaurant concentrates on fish and seafood dishes, mixed in a confusing consommé of nuevo cuisine and tapas styles at eye-watering prices – particularly if you want a decent feed. Tapas-like mains are $29; try the smoked eel porridge. In fine weather, head for the driftwood-screened garden. Mon–Fri 6pm–late.

★ **Thorps Coffee House** 40 Hastings St ☎06 835 6699. Marvellous old-school eat-in or takeaway build-your-own sandwich place also serving good breakfasts, muffins and great coffee (nothing over $20). The interior features bevelled Art Deco detailing. Mon–Sat 8am–5pm & Thurs–Sat from 6pm.

Ujazi Café 28 Tennyson St ☎06 835 1490. Stylish café serving good breakfasts (including vegetarian) and lunch: quiches, slices, salads, fruit sorbets, strong Fairtrade coffee

NAPIER FESTIVALS AND EVENTS

The Mission Concert Ⓦ missionconcert .co.nz. An outdoor concert at the Mission Estate Winery featuring an internationally famous vocalist – past luminaries include Tom Jones, Eric Clapton and Rod Stewart – and drawing crowds of around 25,000. Usually sometime between January and March.

Art Deco Weekend Ⓦ artdeconapier.com. A celebration of all things Art Deco-related, featuring guided walks, open-house tours of domestic architecture, vintage cars, 1930s-dress picnics, champagne breakfasts, dress balls, silent movies and the like. Usually the third weekend in February.

Deco Decanted Jazz Festival Ⓦ artdeconapier.com. Heading into winter, the festival helps keep Napier's Art Deco spirit alive with the music that defined the era. Usually the third weekend in July.

and particularly good custard squares, all in and around the $15–25 mark. Mon–Fri 8am–5pm, Sat & Sun 8am–3pm.

AHURIRI

★ **Boardwalk** 8 Hardinge Rd ☎ 06 834 1168, Ⓦ boardwalknapier.co.nz. From the outside it looks like a bog-standard beachside bar and café, with the promenade one step from the back-garden seating. In the evening, though, it transforms itself into a surprisingly inventive restaurant featuring some stunning fish dishes as well as great slow-roast pork belly (mains $15–35); try the estuary seafood pasta and the fish platter entrée. Tues–Fri 10am–late, Sat & Sun 8.30am–late.

Hep Set Mooch 58 West Quay ☎ 06 833 6332, Ⓦ shed2 .co.nz/hep_set_mooch. Gaudy, relaxed daytime café in a vast warehouse. The fun and friendly staff serve a wide range of breakfasts (such as steaming porridge with stewed apple), great muffins and a healthy selection of salads, frittatas and filo pies ($5–25). Daily 8am–3pm.

Master of India 79 Ahuriri Shopping Centre ☎ 06 834 3440. Atmospheric curry house with ornate gilded decor and a broad menu of vegetarian delights and goat specialities, all mostly under $25; takeaways available. BYO and licence. Thurs–Sat 11.30am–2pm & 5.30pm–late.

Milk & Honey Crown Hotel, Corner of Bridge St and Hardinge Rd ☎ 06 833 6099, Ⓦ milkandhoney.co.nz. Polished boards, concrete beams and fold-back windows with sea views make this smart restaurant/bar a popular spot, aided by the Mediterranean menu that mostly favours Italian influences (mains around $30) and very considerate service. Try the carpaccio or the affagato and vanilla ice cream, or drop in to browse the foodie books

while sipping a Syrah or a very good espresso. Daily 7am–10pm.

★ **Naturale on the Quay** 419 Nelson Quay ☎ 06 834 3150. A Kent brewer turned bar-keeper with a vision and a passion for his own special brews, including a manuka beer with no hops, Skor lager and a traditional English ale – all great stuff. A 340ml bottle will set you back $6, a 1.25l bottle $15, and you'll find the brews at selected bars in the area. Tues 1–5.30pm, Wed & Thurs 1–7pm, Fri & Sat 1–7.30pm, Sun 2–6pm.

Provedore 60 West Quay ☎ 06 834 0189. Popular café-bar with a sophisticated, European edge, serving tapas ($7–14) and playing some nice DJ sounds plus occasional live music – it all adds up to a fine place to while away an evening. BYO on Sun. Mon–Fri 4pm–late, Sat & Sun 10am–late.

Three Doors Up 3 Waghorne St ☎ 06 834 0835, Ⓦ threedoorsup.co.nz. A licensed fine-dining Italian-influenced restaurant with a cosy atmosphere and affordable prices, hence very popular with the locals. It's open from brunch through dinner but is best visited in the evening, particularly for dishes such as seared scallops (mains $16–35). Wed–Sun 10am–2.30pm, 5.30pm–late.

CINEMAS

Century Cinema 65 Marine Parade, at the Hawke's Bay Museum and Art Gallery (see p.388) ☎ 06 835 7781, Ⓦ hbmag.co.nz. At the time of writing this independent cinema was not open, but it is expected to be up and screening sometime in 2013; call ahead to check the latest. **Reading Cinema** 154 Station St ☎ 06 831 0600, Ⓦ readingcinemas.co.nz. Screens all the latest first-release mainstream films.

Cape Kidnappers and the wineries

No visit to Napier and Hastings is complete without a visit to the world's most accessible mainland gannet colony at **Cape Kidnappers** and an exploration of the region's surrounding seventy or so **wineries**.

FROM TOP GANNETS (P.395); CAPE KIDNAPPERS (P.394) >

Cape Kidnappers
Brief history

After James Cook's ill-starred initial encounter with Maori at Gisborne (see p.372), he sailed to the southern limit of Hawke Bay and anchored off the jagged peninsula known to the Ngati Kahungunu as Te Matua-a-maui, "the fishhook of Maui" – a reference to the origin of the North Island, which was, as legend has it, dragged from the oceans by Maui. Here, Maori traders noticed two young Tahitian interpreters aboard the *Endeavour*, believing them to be held against their will, the traders captured one of them and paddled away. The boy escaped back to the ship but Cook subsequently marked the point on his chart as **Cape Kidnappers**.

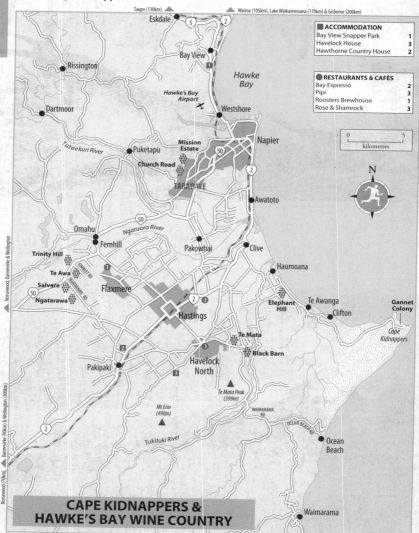

ACCOMMODATION
Bay View Snapper Park	1
Havelock House	3
Hawthorne Country House	2

RESTAURANTS & CAFÉS
Bay Espresso	2
Pipi	3
Roosters Brewhouse	1
Rose & Shamrock	3

CAPE KIDNAPPERS & HAWKE'S BAY WINE COUNTRY

6

THE CAPE KIDNAPPERS GANNETS

Gannets (closely related to boobies) are big birds that can live for as long as thirty years. They're distinguished by their gold-and-black head markings and a complete lack of fear of humans. The birds at Cape Kidnappers start nesting in June, laying their eggs from early July through to October, with the chicks hatching six weeks later. Once fledged, at around fifteen weeks, the young gannets embark on their inaugural flight, a marathon, as-yet-unexplained 3000km journey to Australia, where they spend a couple of years before flying back to spend the rest of their life in New Zealand, returning to their place of birth to breed each year. It is thought that the birds mate for life, using the same or an adjacent nest each year, but recent observation indicates that adultery does occur – usually because of mistaken identity.

During the **breeding season** (July–mid-Oct), the cape is closed to the public. One of the three colonies, the Saddle, is reserved for scientific study and allows no public access. The remaining two colonies, Plateau and Black Reef, are open outside the breeding season, and at the former you will get within a metre or so of the birds. When pairs reunite, after a fishing- or nest-material-gathering trip, you can get close enough to hear their beaks clack together in greeting.

VISITING THE GANNETS

There are three ways to visit the gannets – on foot and with two tours – all starting from Clifton, 20km southeast of Napier and reached from the Napier or Hastings i-SITE offices by Kiwi Shuttle (booking essential; $40 return; ⓣ 06 844 1104). Most tours are tide-dependent and travel to the colony along the beach below rock-fall-prone 100m-high cliffs.

Walking (late Oct–April; roughly 6hr return) The most strenuous but least expensive way to get to the gannets is to walk the 11km along the beach from Clifton. No permits are needed, but you'll need to check tide tables and pick up DOC's useful *Guide to Cape Kidnappers* leaflet either from DOC or the Hastings or Napier i-SITEs. You set off from Clifton between three and four hours after high tide, and head back no more than ninety minutes after low tide. Once at the access point on the beach it's a strenuous 25min climb to the Plateau Colony across private land, though the track is well marked.

Gannet Beach Adventures ⓣ 0800 426 638, ⓦ gannets.com. The traditional gannet trip, aboard tractor-drawn trailers along the beach. The pace and approach give plenty of opportunities to appreciate the geology along the way and observe the birds at close quarters. Tours end near a DOC shelter from where it's a 25min uphill slog to the Plateau, where you'll have half an hour to admire the birds (daily late Oct–early May; 4hr; $39).

Gannet Safaris ⓣ 0800 427 232, ⓦ gannetsafaris.com. If you don't fancy the uphill walk, want more time with the birds and the chance to see and learn about the spectacular Summerlee Station luxury accommodation complex, this is the tour for you. You travel overland by minibus, passing through Summerlee Station, and continue through some stunning scenery and great views to the colonies, where you have 55 minutes or so to gander at the gannets (3hr; $65, or $90 with pick-up from Napier).

Neither Cook nor Joseph Banks, both meticulous in recording flora and fauna, mentioned any gannets on the peninsula's final shark-tooth flourish of pinnacles. However, a hundred years later, twenty or so pairs were recorded, and now there are 20,000 birds – making this the largest mainland **gannet colony** in the world.

Hawke's Bay wine country

Napier and Hastings are almost entirely encircled by the **Hawke's Bay's wine country**, one of New Zealand's largest and most exalted grape-growing regions. Largely the province of boutique producers, it is threaded by the **Hawke's Bay wine trail**, which wends past 35-odd wineries, some offering free tastings and many with a restaurant, or at least the chance to picnic in landscaped grounds.

With a climatic pattern similar to that of the great Bordeaux vineyards, Hawke's Bay produces fine **Chardonnay** and lots of **Merlot**. **Cabernet Sauvignon** is also big but struggles to ripen in cooler summers. Many winemakers are now setting Hawke's Bay

6

HAWKE'S BAY WINERIES

There are over seventy **wineries** in the entire region. Those listed below are recommended, either because they stand out for some particular reason other than wine tastings or because they make good lunch spots. You may find it cheaper to buy the same bottle of wine at a local supermarket than at the cellar door.

Napier's closest wineries are 8km to the southwest in the suburb of **Taradale**. Closer to Hastings, there are clusters outside **Havelock North**, 5km southeast of Hastings, and 10km northwest near **Fernhill** – the fastest-growing wine district in Hawke's Bay. Winery **opening hours** are generally daily 10am–5pm in summer, but they are sometimes closed on Monday, Tuesday and even Wednesday when things are quiet.

The best of the winery restaurants are those at *Black Barn*, *Elephant Hill*, *Mission Estate* and *Te Awa*.

Black Barn Black Barn Rd, Havelock North ☎ 06 877 7985, ⓦ blackbarn.com. Designer winery complex with free cellar door tastings, a lunch bistro and café (mains around $35), art gallery, growers' market and an amphitheatre that hosts a number of outdoor events, including cinema, through the summer. Tastings daily 10am–5pm; bistro and café closed Mon & Tues; growers' market Dec–Feb 9am–noon.

Church Road 150 Church Rd, Taradale ☎ 06 844 2053, ⓦ churchroad.co.nz. Renowned winery with an interesting guided tour ($15), which visits their museum, fashioned from old underground vats. Tastings are free (reserve tastings cost extra) and often include their famed Church Road Chardonnay. Tasting platters for one or two cost $48, cheese boards $28. Tour daily 11am & 2pm; tastings daily 10am–5pm.

Elephant Hill 86 Clifton Rd, Te Awanga ☎ 06 872 6060, ⓦ elephanthill.co.nz. Architecturally dramatic winery with an infinity pool, single vineyard wines and a fine restaurant/bar open for lunch and dinner (mains $30–35). Best known for its Chardonnay, Rose and Syrah; tastings are $5 redeemable on purchase of a bottle. Tastings: daily in winter 11am–4pm; summer 10am–5pm.

Mission Estate 198 Church Rd, Taradale ☎ 06 845 9350, ☎ 06 845 9354 for restaurant bookings, ⓦ missionestate.co.nz. Noted for its pivotal role in the development of the Hawke's Bay's wine industry, New Zealand's oldest winery offers well-organized, free historic tours that culminate in a tasting; tastings-only are also free. There's also an on-site gallery and an à la carte restaurant with lunch and dinner served on the terrace or in the old seminary building; expect dishes such as tea-smoked salmon ($18) and pork sirloin ($32). Tours daily 10.30am & 2pm; tastings Mon–-Sat 9am–5pm, Sun 10am–4.30pm.

Ngatarawa 305 Ngatarawa Rd, Bridge Pa ☎ 06 879 7603, ⓦ ngatarawa.co.nz. A dependable small winery with free tastings of quality tipples in a century-old stable complex overlooking attractive picnic areas and a pétanque pitch. Tastings daily 11am–5pm.

Salvare 403 Ngatarawa Rd, Bridge Pa ☎ 06 874 9409, ⓦ salvare.co.nz. Little more than a one-man operation, this is the place to come for personal service, free tastings and a couple of olive oils and vinaigrettes to try. Tastings: summer daily 10.30am–4.30pm; winter Thurs–Mon 10.30am–4pm, Tues & Wed 10.30am–3pm.

Te Awa 2375 SH50, Fernhill ☎ 06 879 7602, ⓦ teawa .com. Sited near the famed (for wine) Gimblett Road, this winery produces exceptional reds (Merlot and Cabernet Merlot) that are more aromatic and livelier than many of their Hawke's Bay rivals; tastings are free. Lunch in what is one of New Zealand's finest winery restaurants is a treat, dining inside or out on dishes such as beef fillet with butternut pumpkin purée ($34) or *assiette* of seafood including roast snapper, sole fillet and king scallop ($30), all wine-matched, naturally. Tastings daily 10am–4pm.

Te Mata 349 Te Mata Rd, Havelock North ☎ 06 877 4399, ⓦ temata.co.nz. New Zealand's oldest winery on its existing site, now making a fairly small volume of premium handmade wines, notably a Bordeaux-style Coleraine, one of New Zealand's top reds. Free tastings – try the Syrahs and Sav' Blancs – with the added bonus of the architecturally controversial house among the grapes, designed by Ian Athfield. Tastings Mon–Fri 8.30am–5pm, Sat 10am–5pm, Sun 11am–4pm.

Trinity Hill 2396 SH50, Fernhill ☎ 06 879 7778, ⓦ trinityhill.com. Strikingly modern winery in the Gimblett Road area, producing excellent reds and Chardonnay and leading New Zealand's experimentation with the likes of Montepulciano, Tempranillo and Arneis; they even make a port blended from Touriga Nacional. Tastings are free and you can build your own picnic basket for about $25 and eat in the grounds. Tastings daily Oct–April 10am–5pm, May–Sept 11am–4pm.

up to become New Zealand's flagship producer of **Syrah**, a subtler version of the Aussie Shiraz (though it is made from the same grape) that utilises the original European name.

Much of the country covered by the wine trail is also part of the region's **art and food trails** (see below).

Brief history

Hawke's Bay is New Zealand's longest-established wine-growing region: French Marist missionaries planted the first vines in 1851, ostensibly to produce sacramental wine. The excess was sold, and the commercial aspect of the operation continues today as the Mission Estate Winery. Some fifty years later, other wineries began to spring up, favouring open-textured gravel terraces alongside the Tutaekuri, Ngaruroro and Tukituki rivers, which retain the day's heat and are free from moist sea breezes. In this arena the vineyards of the **Gimblett Road** – the so-called **Gimblett Gravels** – produce increasingly world-renowned wines.

6

New Zealand Wine Centre

1 Shakespeare Rd, Napier • Daily: Dec–Feb 10am–7pm; March–Nov 10am–6pm • $29; $14.50 for tasting only; $14.50 for wine adventure only • ☎ 06 835 5326, ⓦ nzwinecentre.co.nz

For the best introduction to what's on offer visit Napier's **New Zealand Wine Centre**, where you are taught how to identify wine flavours, then sit in a small cinema sampling six wines as winemakers on screen enthuse about them. There's also a museum and aroma room.

GETTING AROUND · HAWKE'S BAY WINE COUNTRY

By car You can easily drive yourself around and visit the wineries, but taking a tour obviates the need to find a designated driver.

Wine tours At least half a dozen tours are on offer, most visiting four or five wineries over the course of a morning or afternoon. They're mainly Napier-based but will pick up in Hastings and Havelock North, usually for free. Self-guided bike tours are also available.

Runs half-day trips ($60), visiting four to five wineries and tasting about thirty different wines. Picks up and drops off at accommodation in Napier, Hastings and Havelock.

On Yer Bike 121 Rosser Rd, Hastings ☎ 076 879 8735, ⓦ onyerbikehb.co.nz. A great alternative to the vehicle tours, with a series of easy routes from two wineries in 14km to six in 23km. All-day bike rental (tandems available), route map, emergency mobile phone and a packed lunch are included ($60; $50 without food).

Vince's World of Wine ☎ 06 836 6705. Great fun, with an entertaining, knowledgeable guide and a flexible schedule.

TOUR OPERATORS

Grape Escape ☎ 0800 100 489, ⓦ grapeescape.net.nz.

INFORMATION

Wine leaflets The region's i-SITE offices carry the free *Winery Guide*, which outlines the wineries – for the pick of the bunch, see box opposite.

Arts and crafts leaflets The free *Hawke's Bay Art Guide* directs you to studios, workshops and galleries of painters, sculptors, potters and craftspeople in the region.

Food leaflets The free *Hawke's Bay Food Trail* includes a map showing the location of all manner of quality foodstuffs – everything from chocolate and olive oil to cheese and pepper sauce – along with gourmet cafés and restaurants.

Hastings

Inland **HASTINGS**, 20km south of Napier, was once a rival to its northern neighbour as Hawke's Bay's premier city, buoyed by the wealth generated by the surrounding farmland and orchards. Napier's ascendancy as a tourist destination put Hastings firmly in second place, though it does have an attractive core of buildings, erected after the same 1931 earthquake that rocked Napier. Hastings was saved from the worst effects of the ensuing fires, which were quenched using the artesian water beneath the city before they could take hold.

6

After the earthquake, Hastings embraced the Californian-inspired **Spanish Mission** style of architecture: roughcast stucco walls, arched windows, small balconies, barley-twist columns and heavily overhung roofs clad in terracotta tiles. The finest examples can be seen in an hour or so, using the self-guided *Art Deco Hastings* walk leaflet ($2 from the i-SITE). If time is short, limit your wanderings to Heretaunga Street East, taking in the gorgeous bronzework and sumptuous lead lighting of the **Westerman Building** or, at the corner of Hastings Street, the **Hawke's Bay Opera House** – built fifteen years before the earthquake, but remodelled to create the region's finest Spanish Mission facade.

The city is also at the heart of the wonderful Hawke's Bay wine country, and most of its vineyards are within easy reach. Apples, pears and peaches also continue to be grown in huge quantities, and the harvest provides work (see opposite).

Hastings' more upmarket neighbour is **Havelock North**, 3km southeast and at the foot of the striking ridgeline of **Te Mata Peak**. There isn't a great deal to it, and the only diversion is a drive up the peak, or try out the local bars and cafés that line its cobbled streets.

Hastings City Art Gallery

201 Eastbourne St East • Daily 10am–4.30pm • Free • ☎ 06 871 5095, ⓦ hastingscitygallery.co.nz

Worth a quick look is the **Hastings City Art Gallery**, which hosts travelling and local art exhibitions, the former usually more diverting. There is no local gallery collection

HASTINGS

● **EATING & DRINKING**
Bay Espresso	1
Opera Kitchen	3
Rush Munro's	2
Vidal Estate	4

■ **ACCOMMODATION**
A1 Backpackers	1
Hastings Top 10 Holiday Park	4
The Rotten Apple	3
Travellers Lodge	2

so you're pretty much at the mercy of whatever happens to be touring, or which local schools, colleges or societies have decided to exhibit their work.

Te Mata Peak

Te Mata Peak Rd

Driving from Hastings to Havelock North, the long ridge of limestone bluffs which make up the 399m **Te Mata Peak** looms into view. The ridge is held to be the supine form of a Maori chief, Rongokako, who choked on a rock as he tried to eat through the hill – just one of many Herculean feats he attempted while wooing the beautiful daughter of a Heretaunga chief; according to legend, overcome with grief at her father's death, Rongokako's daughter threw herself off the peak.

Te Mata Peak Road winds up the hill to a wonderful vantage point that's great towards sunset. Views stretch over the fertile plains, north across Hawke's Bay and Cape Kidnappers, and east to surf-pounded Ocean Beach and Waimarama, the main swimming **beaches** for Hastings and Havelock North. A parking area partway up Te Mata Peak Road marks the start of moderate **walking tracks** through groves of native trees and redwoods and a wetland area before reaching the summit (2–3hr return).

ARRIVAL AND DEPARTURE

HASTINGS

By bus Long-distance buses stop at Russell Street North, a few steps from the i-SITE. Local operator GoBay (☎06 878 9250) runs to Napier and Havelock North (Mon–Fri; limited services Sat) from the corner of Eastbourne St East and Russell St.

Destinations Auckland (2 daily; 7hr 30min); Dannevirke (4 daily; 1hr 30min); Gisborne (1–2 daily; 5hr); Napier (Mon–Fri hourly or better, Sat 5 daily; 1hr); Norsewood (3 daily; 1hr 10min); Taupo (4–5 daily; 2hr 30min);

Wellington (3 daily; 4hr 45min).

By plane Regular direct flights from Auckland, Wellington and Christchurch arrive at Hawke's Bay Airport, which is about 20km north of town on SH2, where they are met by the Super Shuttle (☎0800 748 885, ✆supershuttle.co.nz), which charges $43 to get into town.

Destinations Auckland (7–10 daily; 1hr); Christchurch (2 daily; 1hr 25min); Wellington (4–5 daily; 50min).

INFORMATION AND ACTIVITIES

i-SITE 100 Heretaunga St East (Mon–Fri 8.30am–5pm, Sat & Sun 9am–4pm; ☎06 873 0080, ✆visithastings.co.nz). Sells bus tickets and has leaflets on the wineries.

Fruit-picking work The fruit harvest begins in February and lasts three or four months, providing casual, hard-going, low-paid orchard work for those willing to thin, pick or pack fruit. The hostels are a good source of work and

up-to-the-minute information though you'll be competing with locals and itinerant old fruit-picking hands; for more information on working in the region see below.

Airplay Paragliding ☎06 845 1977, ✆airplay.co.nz. Go tandem paragliding from Te Mata Peak, riding the thermals and Pacific winds (15min; $140).

ACCOMMODATION

Availability of budget accommodation in Hastings is affected by the fruit-picking season: from mid-February to May you'll struggle to find cheap rooms, especially if you're looking for self-catering or a long-stay, so book well ahead. Nearby Napier (see p.385) makes a good alternative base if you're able to commute. For more luxurious accommodation, head for Havelock North, where **B&Bs** and swanky self-catering predominate.

A1 Backpackers 122 Stortford St ☎06 873 4285, ✉a1backpackers@xtra.co.nz; map p.398. A1 has less of a work-camp feel than Hastings' other backpackers. It is set in a well-kept peaceful villa and has a helpful owner who offers free local pick-up for two-night stays. The dorms are adequate but the doubles more comfortable. Dorms $24, rooms $60

Hastings Top 10 Holiday Park 610 Windsor Ave ☎0508 427 846, ✆hastingstop10.co.nz; map p.398. Appealing campsite on the edge of Windsor Park, with tent sites and

a range of modern units (the more expensive of which are quite swish) and good facilities, though it does get busy in the fruit-picking season. Camping $19, cabins $70, self-contained units $145, park motel $145, chalets $150

★ **Havelock House** 77 Endsleigh Rd, 3km southwest of Havelock North off Middle Rd ☎06 877 5439, ✆havelockhouse.co.nz; map p.394. Three large guest rooms (two with deep baths) occupy this spacious house in a quiet, woodsy setting. Guests can access a vast lounge

6

equipped with full-size billiard table, a tennis court and an outdoor pool, plus there's a separate two-bedroom house with deck and barbecue. Room $180, suite $180, house $200

★ **Hawthorne Country House** 1420 SH2, 6km southwest of Hastings ☎ 06 878 0035, ⑩ hawthorne .co.nz; map p.394. Beautiful and very welcoming B&B in a grand Edwardian villa surrounded by croquet lawns and farmland. The four en-suite rooms are decorated with understated elegance, while good breakfasts, afternoon teas and drinks with canapés all make for a relaxed atmosphere. $300

The Rotten Apple 114 Heretaunga St East ☎ 06 878 4363, ⑩ rottenapple.co.nz; map p.398. Central hostel with lots of long-stayers, assistance for would-be fruit workers and low weekly rates for the same, all in an old hotel with basic rooms and facilities that just about stand up when the place is full. Dorms $23, rooms $60

Travellers Lodge 608 St Aubyn St West ☎ 06 878 7108, ⑩ tlodge.co.nz; map p.398. Hostel in a pair of suburban houses, with bike rental, wi-fi and off-street parking. There is a range of rooms, all pretty basic, but with lots of beds, mostly seeing an uneven mix of Kiwi labourers and touring foreigners from Nov–May. Facilities are limited. Dorms $25, rooms $60

EATING, DRINKING AND ENTERTAINMENT

For a town of its size, Hastings is relatively poorly supplied with good places to eat, though an ever-expanding selection of places in neighbouring Havelock North bumps up the quota, and lunches at the region's wineries are a good if pricey option (see box, p.396).

★ **Bay Espresso** 141 Karamu Rd, 3km north of Hastings ☎ 06 877 9230, ⑩ bayespresso.co.nz; map p.394. A rustic, daytime café (with plenty of garden seating) that's a locals' weekend home-from-home. Superb coffee and breakfasts are supplemented by light and healthy lunch specials ($14–20). If you're hungry, try the Orchardists Big Breakfast, which boasts chorizo and black pudding. Locations at 19 Middle Rd, Havelock North, and 108 Market St, Hastings. Mon–Fri 7.30am–4pm, Sat & Sun 8am–4pm.

Hawke's Bay Farmers' Market Hawke's Bay Showgrounds, Kenilworth Rd; map p.398. On a fine Sunday morning, skip breakfast and head straight to this market, one of the best on the North Island, where innumerable stalls introduce you to fresh local produce, coffee and pastries while a local musician or two entertains. It's held indoors in winter. Sun 8.30am–12.30pm.

Opera Kitchen 312 Eastbourne St East, Hastings ☎ 06 870 6020, ⑩ operakitchen.co.nz; map p.398. Classy licensed café showcasing local produce through simple but delicious dishes ($9–25) served in stripped-back surroundings. Worth checking out if just for the knitted hats they put on boiled eggs. Sometimes open for pre-theatre dinner or when there's something on at the Opera House; otherwise Mon–Fri 8am–4pm, Sat & Sun 9am–3pm.

★ **Pipi** 16 Joll Rd, Havelock North ☎ 06 877 8993, ⑩ pipicafe.co.nz; map p.394. Impressive in its pinkness, this casual and very popular café, tapas bar and pizza restaurant exudes casual style. Nothing matches but everything fits, and you help yourself from the drinks fridge and tell them what you've had when you pay. The food's great too, offering the likes of fishcakes with rocket and white bean mash ($22), great traditional pizzas (from $16) and a slew of local wines. Tues–Sun 4–10pm.

Roosters Brewhouse 1470 Omahu Rd, 7km west of central Hastings ☎ 06 879 4127; map p.394. Welcoming microbrewery offering traditional natural brews best supped in its pleasant café or outdoors at garden tables while tucking into straightforward hearty dishes at reasonable prices. There's also free tasting of its English ale, lager and dark beers, and you can buy a flagon to take away – a wise move considering the prices elsewhere. Mon–Fri 10am–7pm, Sat 4–7pm.

Rose & Shamrock 15 Napier Rd, Havelock North ☎ 06 877 2999, ⑩ roseandshamrock.co.nz; map p.394. Popular for Sunday roasts with the agricultural and blue-rinse gangs, this fair attempt at a pub has 24 Irish, English and Kiwi beers on tap, plus well-priced bar meals ($18–30), including fish and chips and old Irish sausages with gravy and occasional live Irish folk music. Daily 10.30am–late.

Rush Munro's 704 Heretaunga St West, Hastings; map p.398. A small ice-cream garden that's been packing in the locals for 80 years – even Bill Clinton once stopped in. For the retro experience go for the feijoa peaked cone ($3–8). Mon–Fri 11am–6pm, Sat & Sun 11am–7pm.

Vidal Estate 913 Aubyn St East, Hastings ☎ 06 872 7440, ⑩ vidal.co.nz; map p.398. Ingredients are mostly local and organic in this popular semi-formal restaurant attached to a winery and specializing in pricey (dinner mains $27–40) nosh; try the maple and whiskey hot smoked chicken, new potato, endive and green olive salad ($22.50) for lunch. Book ahead at weekends. Daily 11.30am–late.

OPERA

Hawke's Bay Opera House 101 Hastings St South ☎ 06 871 5280, ⑩ hawkesbayoperahouse.co.nz; map p.398. Plays host to regular shows, including concerts, musicals, stand-up comedy and, of course, opera.

Southern Hawke's Bay

South of Hastings, the main road (SH2) runs through the relentless sheep stations of **Southern Hawke's Bay**, a region uncluttered by places of genuine interest. Small farming towns stand as fitting memorials to the pioneers who tamed the region, particularly Danes and Norwegians who stepped in when the New Zealand Wars of the 1860s discouraged immigration from Britain.

Norsewood

If time isn't too pressing, make a fleeting stop at the "**Scandinavian**" **settlements** such as the village of **NORSEWOOD**, 45km south of Hastings, little more than a quiet street which runs from a replica Norwegian-style stave church, past *Café Norsewood* to a glassed-in boathouse containing the fishing boat *Bindalsfaering*, a gift from the Norwegian government commemorating Norsewood's centenary in 1972.

Dannevirke

The Danish heritage of the farming town of **DANNEVIRKE**, 20km south of Norsewood, is flagged by a modern windmill in Copenhagen Square on the main street, along with cut-out signs of smiling Vikings greeting and farewelling visitors. If you're after sustenance, try the licensed *Black Stump* café, 21 High St (Mon–Fri 9am–late, Sat & Sun 10am–late), or the excellent Granny's Kitchen, 120 High St (Mon–Fri 9am–3pm), who make great pies including an award-winning steak and cheese.

South of Dannevirke, SH2 runs 25km to Woodville, where SH3 strikes west through the Manawatu Gorge to Palmerston North and SH2 heads south into the Wairarapa.

The Wairarapa

Most of the **Wairarapa** region is archetypal Kiwi sheep country, with wool-flecked green hills stretching into the distance. In recent years, however, the southern half of the region has increasingly benefited from free-spending weekenders from Wellington visiting the boutique hotels, innovative restaurants and many wineries surrounding **Martinborough**, the region's current wine capital and, along with Greytown, its most appealing settlement.

North of **Masterton**, the region's main commercial centre, the **Pukaha Mount Bruce National Wildlife Centre** provides a wonderful opportunity to witness ongoing bird conservation work; to the south, **Featherston** is a base for walks up the bed of the Rimutaka Incline Railway.

Back on the coast, the laidback holiday settlement of **Castlepoint** is good for swimming and surfing, and **Cape Palliser** is the ideal spot for blustery mind-clearing walks and dramatic coastal scenery.

Cross the **Rimutaka Range** towards Wellington and you're into the Hutt Valley, full of commuter-belt communities, none of which really warrants a stop until you reach Petone, on the outskirts of the capital.

Brief history

The establishment of New Zealand's earliest sheep station in the 1840s on rich alluvial lands close to present-day Martinborough paved the way for development by the progressive **Small Farm Association** (SFA). This was the brainchild of Joseph Masters, a Derbyshire cooper and longtime campaigner against the separation of landowner and labourer, who sought to give disenfranchised settlers the opportunity to become smallholders. Liberal governor George Grey supported him and in 1853 suggested

6

> ## LONG NAMES AND FAMOUS FLUTES
>
> Visitors in search of the esoteric might want to stray along SH52, which makes a 120km tar-sealed loop east towards the rugged coastline from dull Waipukurau, 50km south of Hastings, re-emerging at Dannevirke. Almost 50km south of Waipukurau (and 6km south of Porangahau, where there is rare coastal access), a sign marks the hill known as Taumatawhakatangihangakoauauotamateaturipukakapikimaungahoronukupokaiwhenuakitanatahu, which, unsurprisingly, rates as one of the world's longest place names; roughly, this mouthful translates as "the hill where Tamatea, circumnavigator of the lands, played the flute for his lover".

the SFA should persuade local Maori to sell land for the establishment of two towns – Masterton and Greytown.

Initially Greytown prospered, and it retains an air of antiquity rare among New Zealand towns, but the routing of the rail line favoured Masterton, famed chiefly today for the annual Golden Shears sheepshearing competition.

Tui Brewery

SH2 Mangatainoka, 10km south of Woodville • Mon–Thurs 10am–4pm, Fri–Sun 10am–5pm; tours daily 11am & 2pm (bookings essential) • Free; beer sampling $15; tours $20 • ☎ 06 376 0815, ⓦ tui.co.nz

The northern half of the Wairarapa is very much a continuation of southern Hawke's Bay, but instead of speeding through this pastoral country, make a brief stop at the **Tui Brewery**, which brews cheap consistent beer that has built an enthusiastic following with its "Yeah. Right" billboard advertisements, seen all over the country. The theme is explored in the small museum adjacent to the café and bar serving good Kiwi tucker. You can sample several beers and keep the glass or join one of the **tours**, which include a visit to the distinctive seven-storey brick brewery, tastings and, again, a glass to keep.

Pukaha Mount Bruce National Wildlife Centre

SH2, 40km south of the Tui Brewery • Daily 9am–4.30pm; long-fin eel feedings daily 1.30pm; kaka feedings daily 3pm; guided tour daily 11am & 1pm; twilight tour Thurs–Sat 7.30pm • $20; guided tour $50 including picnic and park entry; twilight tour $60 including canapé and park entry (BYO wine) • ⓦ mtbruce.org.nz

Pukaha Mount Bruce National Wildlife Centre is one of the best places in the country to view endangered native birds and is staffed by people engaged in bringing those birds back from the edge. Kokako, kakariki, Campbell Island teal, hihi, kiwi, takahe and more can be found in spacious aviaries set along the trails through lowland primeval forest. Beyond the trail several thousand acres of forest are used for reintroducing birds to the wild. The generous size of the cages on the trail and the thick foliage often make the birds hard to spot, so you'll need to be patient.

More immediate gratification comes in the form of a stand of Californian redwoods, a nocturnal **kiwi house**, a new behind-the-scenes kiwi breeding facility, regular kiwi chick feedings (check times on entry), reptilian tuatara (see p.811) and closed-circuit cameras trained on other birds' nests. A twenty-minute audiovisual gives a moving account of the decline of birdlife in New Zealand, or you can watch long-fin eels and kaka being fed. Alternatively, join a two-hour guided tour with a ranger to add context, or a twilight tour to add atmosphere and change perspective. There is also a picnic area and café.

ACCOMMODATION   PUKAHA MOUNT BRUCE NATIONAL WILDLIFE CENTRE

The Hut SH2, first house on the right north of the Wildlife Centre ☎ 06 375 8681, ⓦ thehut.co.nz. High above the wildlife centre, you can stay in a traditional rustic *bach* with an outdoor tub for a romantic bath under the stars and a log burner to cook meals. It's a steep 40min walk, or you can arrange four-wheeler transport with the owners for an additional charge. **$100**

Masterton and around

Though it is Wairarapa's largest town, workaday **MASTERTON**, crouched at the foot of the Tararua Range some 30km south of Pukaha Mount Bruce, is of only passing interest, with a commercial heart strung along the parallel Chapel, Queen and Dixon streets. On the town's eastern side **Queen Elizabeth Park** provides a pleasant opportunity to stroll through formal gardens.

Aratoi

Corner of Bruce and Dixon sts, opposite Queen Elizabeth Park • Daily 10am–4.30pm • Donation • ☎ 06 370 0001, ⓦ aratoi.co.nz

Aratoi is a museum-gallery with a series of semi-permanent insights into the history of the Wairarapa region along with some excellent art exhibitions. Among the subjects are the oldest Maori house site (1180 AD) in New Zealand, part of an archeological exhibition based around findings at Omoekau, Palliser Bay. From the gallery collection the most interesting exhibits are early Lindauer portraits of local Maori, kinetic sculpture by Tony Nicholls, in the style of Len Lye, and a Barbara Hepworth copper and bronze from 1956.

6

Wool Shed

12 Dixon St • ☎ 06 378 8008, ⓦ thewoolshednz.com • Daily 10am–4pm • $8

The **Wool Shed** is an excellent museum on all things woolly. Housed in two century-old shearing sheds relocated from rural Wairarapa, it's filled with everything from sheep pens and shearing handpieces to pressed bales of wool stencilled with the marks of sheep stations. Classic 1957 footage of Kiwi shearing hero Godfrey Bowen shows how it should be done, and there's usually footage of recent Golden Shears finals, perhaps showing the super-fast handiwork of David Fagan, New Zealand's five-time world champ and record-breaking sixteen-time Golden Shears winner.

Tararua Forest Park

Accessed from SH2, 25km west of Masterton

Draped over the hills to the west of town, the **Tararua Forest Park** offers excellent tramping through beech and podocarp forest to the subalpine tops, but be aware that the notoriously fickle weather in this area can be dangerous. Serious walkers should consider the **Powell–Jumbo Tramp**, a highly worthwhile twelve-hour circuit that can be broken down into two or more manageable days by staying at **huts** ($15) evenly spaced along the route. The track starts at the backcountry hut-style *Holdsworth Lodge* (see p.404). Day-trippers can undertake easy riverside walks (1–2hr) or head three hours across easy ground to the cosy Atiwhakatu Hut ($5), which has bunks.

ARRIVAL AND DEPARTURE

MASTERTON AND AROUND

By train TranzMetro (☎ 0800 801 700) runs commuter services from Wellington. The train station is at the end of Perry St, a 15min walk from the centre, or call Masterton Radio Taxis (☎ 06 378 2555).
Destinations Carterton (6 daily; 15min); Featherston (6 daily; 40min); Wellington (4–6 daily; 1hr 30min).
By bus Tranzit buses (☎ 0800 471 227) run north to

Palmerston North, stopping at 316 Queen St, a short walk from the i-SITE.
Destinations Carterton (6 Mon–Fri, 3 Sat & Sun; 25min); Featherston (6 Mon–Fri, 3 Sat & Sun; 1hr); Greytown (6 Mon–Fri, 3 Sat & Sun; 30–40min); Palmerston North (2 Mon–Fri, 1 Sat & Sun; 2hr).

INFORMATION

i-SITE Corner of Bruce and Dixon sts (Mon–Fri 9am–5pm, Sat & Sun 10am–4pm; ☎ 06 370 0900, ⓦ wairarapanz.com).

Has information on local hikes.

ACCOMMODATION

Cornwall Park 119 Cornwall St, 2km west of the town centre ☎ 06 378 2939, ⓦ cornwallparkmotel.co.nz. A

clean, peaceful old-style motel with a pool, spa and free wi-fi. It's all a bit dated-looking, but everything works

6

GOLDEN SHEARS

The town's major event is the annual **Golden Shears** competition (ⓦgoldenshears.co.nz), effectively the Olympiad of all things woolly, held on the three days leading up to the first Saturday in March. Contestants flock from around the world to demonstrate their prowess with the broad-blade handpiece; a top shearer can remove a fleece in under a minute, though for maximum points it must be done with skill as well as speed and leave a smooth and unblemished, if shivering, beast. For a few bucks you can just walk in on the early rounds, but to attend the entertaining finals on Friday and Saturday nights you'll need to book well in advance.

perfectly well and units are undoubtedly great value. $104
Holdsworth Lodge 25km west of Masterton at the end of Norfolk Rd, off southbound SH2. Only those taking on the Powell–Jumbo Tramp (see p.403) will likely be interested in staying at this backcountry hut-style accommodation. Booking in advance with DOC (ⓦdoc .govt.nz) is essential. Tent sites $6, lodge $20

Mawley Park Motor Camp 15 Oxford St ☏06 378 6454, ⓦmawleypark.co.nz. Masterton's best budget accommodation is this riverside spot, which offers decent flat campsites interspersed with trees, some new en-suite units and a range of the more traditional cabins and motel units. Camping $10, standard backpacker cabin (shared) $25, kitchen cabins $60, en suites $75

EATING, DRINKING AND ENTERTAINMENT

★ **Café Strada** 232 Queen St ☏06 378 8450, ⓦcafe strada.co.nz. The best eating, drinking and entertainment option in town. As well as providing tasty meals and counter grub during the day it also stays open for quality, moderately priced dinners ($23–27) featuring dishes such as crispy skinned south island salmon. There's live music

some evenings, too. Licensed. Wi-fi. Daily 8am–late.
Entice At Aratoi, Corner of Bruce and Dixon sts ☏06 370 0001, ⓦaratoi.co.nz. Licensed café at the museum-gallery serving delicious counter food including monster savoury muffins, sandwiches and pleasing coffee, with nothing on the menu over $20. Daily 10am–4.30pm.

Castlepoint

The 300km of coastline from Cape Kidnappers, near Napier, south to Cape Palliser is bleak, desolate and almost entirely inaccessible – except for **CASTLEPOINT**, 65km east of Masterton, where early explorers found a welcome break in the "perpendicular line of cliff". A lighthouse presides over the rocky knoll, which is linked to the mainland by a thin hourglass double **beach** that encloses a sheltered **lagoon** known as the Basin. Wairarapa families retreat here for summer fun and surfers ride the breakers, though when the weather turns it is a wonderfully wild bit of coastline. Unless you are a keen surfer, a day visit will suffice; if you do decide to stay, take all your provisions with you.

ACCOMMODATION   CASTLEPOINT

Castlepoint Holiday Park & Motels ☏06 372 6705, ⓦcastlepoint.co.nz. Wonderfully situated, traditional Kiwi holidaymaker campsite, in the middle of nowhere and within earshot of the crashing waves. The broad range of reasonably kept accommodation includes tent sites, cottages and motel units. Camping $22.50, kitchen cabins $95, garden cottage or sea-view house $140, motel units $170, self-contained cook house $300

Carterton

The service town of **CARTERTON**, 15km south of Masterton, has but one thing to offer: **Paua World**, 54 Kent St (Mon–Fri 8am–5pm, Sat & Sun 9am–5pm; free; ⓦpauaworld.com), an Aladdin's Cave of objects fashioned from this beautiful rainbow-swirled seashell – you can pick up anything from wonderfully kitsch fridge magnets to elegant jewellery here. The factory supplies just about every tourist knick-knack shop in the country and you can take a free self-guided tour to see how the stuff is made.

Stonehenge Aotearoa

12km southeast of Carterton • Feb–April Wed–Sun 10am–4pm; guided tours Sat & Sun 11am, and daily Dec 27–Jan 15 (bookings recommended) • $16; guided tours $16 • ☎ 06 377 1600, ⓦ stonehenge-aotearoa.com

Stonehenge Aotearoa, 12km southeast of Carterton, appears like some vision of Neolithic Britain on a hill amid Wairarapa farmland. Though built on the same scale as its kin on Salisbury Plain, the similarity ends. This is a modern wood and concrete edifice, technically classed as a garden ornament by the local council when planning permission was sought. The resulting "open-sky observatory" is primarily educational and best experienced on the detailed hour-and-a-half tours, which cover a fascinating array of information ranging from pure astronomy through Maori star stories and navigation to astrology and myth-busting comparative religion.

Some 5km south of Carterton, a rough road runs 15km west into the foothills of the Tararua Range to **Waiohine Gorge**, a picturesque chasm that's ideal for picnics.

Greytown

Laid out in 1853, the genteel settlement of **GREYTOWN**, 9km south of Carterton, retains something of its original Victorian feel. Once Wairarapa's main settlement, it declined when the railway bypassed the town and revived only when it became the favoured getaway for weekending Wellingtonians. The two-storey wooden buildings either side of the highway house assorted art galleries, "collectibles" shops, fashion outlets, excellent cafés and chichi B&Bs, whose prices reflect the Wellington clientele – if you're looking for somewhere to stay in the area, better to push on to Martinborough.

EATING   **GREYTOWN**

★ **The French Baker** 81 Main St. Serves delectable breads, sandwiches, pastries, smoked fish pies and cakes (all under $18). Mon–Fri 8am–3pm, Sat & Sun 8am–4pm.

★ **Main Street Deli** 88 Main St. A reliable café that's good for soups and sandwiches ($5–18) as well as larger, moderately priced meals. They also sell a good range of cheeses, which makes for a nice combination with the bread from across the street. Mon–Fri 8am–4pm, Sat & Sun 8am–3pm.

Featherston

The last of the Wairarapa towns before SH2 climbs west over the Rimutaka range, **Featherston**, 13km south of Greytown, is for steam-train buffs, who come from across the country to visit the **Fell Locomotive Museum** on Lyon Street (daily 10am–4pm; $5), which contains the last surviving example of the locos that, for 77 years (until the boring of a new tunnel in 1955), climbed the 265m, one-in-fifteen slope of the Rimutaka Incline.

Rimutaka Rail Trail

Trail starts 10km south of Featherston at Cross Creek • 18km; 4–5hr; 265m ascent

The rails of the Rimutaka Incline have long been pulled up, but you can follow the trackbed on the **Rimutaka Rail Trail**, which passes old shunting yards and steams through the 576m summit tunnel before descending to Kaitoke. To save a long shuttle ride back, most just walk up to the summit and back (4–5hr return), or do the same trip by bike (3hr return); rental bikes are available in Martinborough; ask at the i-SITE.

Martinborough

Over the last couple of decades, little **MARTINBOROUGH**, 18km southeast of Featherston, has been transformed from an obscure farming town into the centre of a compact wine region synonymous with some of New Zealand's finest reds. It's within easy striking distance of Wellington, and weekends see the arrival of the smart set to load up their shiny 4WDs at the cellar doors. On Mondays and Tuesdays much of the town simply shuts down to recover.

Brief history

Martinborough was initially laid out in the 1870s by landowner John Martin, who named the streets after cities he had visited on his travels and arranged the core, centred on a leafy square, in the form of a Union Jack. For over a century the town languished as a minor agricultural centre until the first four wineries – Ata Rangi, Dry River, Chifney and Martinborough (all of which produced their first vintages in 1984) – re-invented it as the coolest, driest and most wind-prone of the North Island's grape-growing regions. With the aid of shelterbelts, strategically planted trees and hedges, that splice the vineyards, the wineries produce some outstanding Pinot Noir, notable Cabernet Sauvignon, rich Chardonnay and richly aromatic Riesling.

Martinborough Wine Centre

6 Kitchener St • Daily 10am–5pm • Donation for tastings • ☎ 06 306 9040, ⊛ martinboroughwinecentre.co.nz

Outside the festival times (see box, p.408), your best starting point is the **Martinborough Wine Centre**, a wine shop offering tastings from a different local winery every month and **bike rental** ($35/day) for a spin round the vineyards.

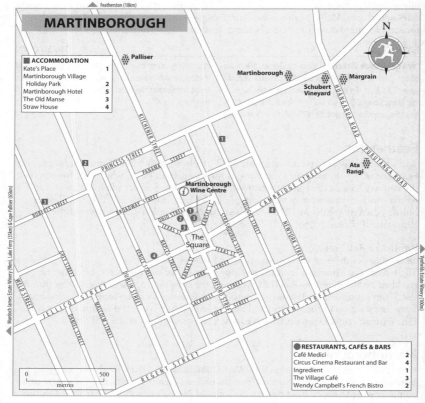

MARTINBOROUGH

ACCOMMODATION
Kate's Place	1
Martinborough Village Holiday Park	2
Martinborough Hotel	5
The Old Manse	3
Straw House	4

RESTAURANTS, CAFÉS & BARS
Café Medici	2
Circus Cinema Restaurant and Bar	4
Ingredient	1
The Village Café	3
Wendy Campbell's French Bistro	2

ARRIVAL AND INFORMATION

By bus and train Tranzit buses (☎0800 471 227) shuttling between Featherston, Masterton and Martinborough meet the TranzMetro commuter trains (☎04 801 7000) from Wellington and drop off diagonally opposite the i-SITE.

i-SITE 18 Kitchener St (Mon–Fri 9am–5pm, Sat & Sun 10am–4pm; ☎06 306 5010, �🌐wairarapa.com). Carries loads of information on the surrounding vineyards, including the *Wairarapa Wine Trail* sheet, can book accommodation and has internet access.

MARTINBOROUGH

Winery information Outside the festival times (see box, p.408), your best starting point is the Martinborough Wine Centre (see opposite), a wine shop offering tastings (for a donation) from a different local winery every month. Over a dozen wineries (see p.408) are accessible on foot or by bike, guided by the free and widely available *Wairarapa Wine Trail* sheet. During the summer places generally open from 11am–4pm at weekends and have shorter hours midweek. They usually charge a $5 tasting fee, refundable with any wine purchase.

ACCOMMODATION

Martinborough's accommodation options lean heavily towards mid- and upper-price B&Bs and homestays, most in rural surroundings, as well as self-contained cottages. Rooms are hard to find during festivals and on summer weekends: weeknights are often a happier hunting ground.

★ **Kate's Place** 7 Cologne St ☎06 306 9935, �🌐katesplace.co.nz. Cosy, laidback homestay/backpacker combo in a cared-for weatherboard cottage on a quiet street. There's just one en-suite double plus a couple of top-quality four-share dorms with super-comfy bunks. Breakfast isn't served, but you can use the kitchen, and there are heaps of books, and wi-fi. Dorms $30, en-suite room $80

Martinborough Village Holiday Park 10 Dublin St West ☎06 306 8946, ⍟martinboroughholidaypark .com. Impeccably maintained campsite a 10min walk from the centre, with tent sites separate from van hook-ups, and cosy cabins. There's a modern kitchen, showers, an intentional absence of TV and bike rental for $35/day. Camping $20, cabins $70, self-contained cabins $115

Martinborough Hotel Memorial Square ☎06 306 9350, ⍟martinboroughhotel.co.nz. The attractively restored grand dame of Martinborough offers rooms

upstairs in the old building with French doors opening onto a veranda, and more contemporary rooms set around the garden; all are serviced, well tended and spacious. There's also a good restaurant and popular bar on site. Veranda rooms $300, garden rooms $320

The Old Manse 19 Grey St ☎06 306 8599, ⍟oldmanse .co.nz. Boutique B&B in a wonderful old villa amid the vines on the edge of town, with a comfortable quiet room and more expansive suite, as well as friendly and helpful owners who will suggest the best local places to frequent. Room $170, suite $225

★ **Straw House** 22–24 Cambridge Rd ☎06 306 8577, ⍟thestrawhouse.co.nz. Choose from the cosy studio or fabulous self-contained two-bedroom house, both built of straw bales, stylishly decorated and very comfortable. Breakfast goodies are generously provided and there's a small reduction for second and subsequent nights. Studio $150, house $270

EATING AND DRINKING

Lunch at a winery restaurant or a platter among the vines is an essential part of the Martinborough experience, though the town also caters to discerning diners with several restaurants charging moderate to high prices, in return for high-quality dishes.

Café Medici 9 Kitchener St ☎06 306 9965. Busy breakfast and lunch café efficiently serving the likes of creamy park vale mushrooms ($17) and tasty counter food (dinner mains $16–30). Daily 8.30am–4.30pm, plus Thurs–Sat 6.30pm–late in summer.

★ **Circus Cinema Restaurant and Bar** 34 Jellicoe St ☎06 306 9442, ⍟circus.net.nz. Try wonderful coffee in the atmospheric bar, plus an unpretentious restaurant serving meze platters, movie-themed pizza – a Ben Hur is smoked ham, mushroom and capsicum – and delicious desserts ($9–29). The place also happens to be a bijou HD cinema with two screens and a penchant for showing

art-house classics. Sit watching the film, sipping your wine, and a tap on the shoulder announces your dessert. Daily 4pm–late.

Ingredient 8 Kitchener St. One of the best places to stock up on gourmet local produce such as wine, olives, cheese and charcuterie. Mon–Fri 9.30am–4pm, Sat & Sun 8.30am–5.30pm.

The Village Café 6 Kitchener St ☎06 306 8814. Daytime café with seating in the rustic-chic barn-like interior and the pergola-covered courtyard. Menu items (all under $25) include tasty brunches, pizzas and salads, and good espresso. Daily 8am–5pm.

6

MARTINBOROUGH FESTIVALS

Toast Martinborough ⓦ toast
martinborough.co.nz. Tickets sell out in
minutes in early October for this wine-
oriented affair with international live acts and
selected vineyards open to ticket holders,
while top Wellington and local restaurants
hawk their wares. Third Sunday in November.

Martinborough Fairs ⓦ martinboroughfair
.org.nz. There's a considerably more
egalitarian feel to the two Martinborough
Fairs – huge country fêtes during which the
streets radiating from the central square are
lined with art and craft stalls. First Saturday in
February and March.

★ **Wendy Campbell's French Bistro** 3 Kitchener St
ⓣ 06 306 8863. Fabulous classic-French inspired
restaurant with an understated frontage and eclectic decor
that give little indication that this is the finest eating in
town. The wonderful food is informed by seasonal Kiwi
produce (mains around $35). Opening hours hardly seem
to matter but try to book ahead, especially at weekends.
Usually Wed–Sun from 6pm.

WINERIES

Ata Rangi Puruatanga Rd ⓣ 06 306 9570, ⓦ atarangi
.co.nz. One of New Zealand's finest Pinot Noir producers
also does the excellent Célèbre Merlot/Syrah blend and
lovely Chardonnay. Central and a great place to start.
Tastings $5. Mon–Fri 1–3pm, Sat & Sun noon–4pm.

Margrain Vineyard Ponatahi Rd ⓣ 06 306 9292,
ⓦ margrainvineyard.co.nz. Good-quality wine from the
relaxed cellar door plus the great little *Old Winery Café*
(generally open noon–3pm) overlooking the vines with
most of the well-priced dishes matched to Margrain wines.

Tastings $5. Labour Day weekend–Easter Fri–Sun
11am–5pm; Jan 1–Feb 6 daily 11am–5pm; Easter–
Labour Day weekend Sat & Sun 11am–5pm.

Martinborough Vineyard Princess St ⓣ 06 306 9955,
ⓦ martinborough-vineyard.co.nz. A Martinborough
original and still one of the largest, producing top-
quality Pinot Noir and Chardonnay. Tastings $5. Daily
11am–4pm.

Palliser Kitchener St ⓣ 06 306 9019, ⓦ palliser.co
.nz. Pioneering Martinborough winery which limits its
impact on the environment while producing premium
wines and running cooking classes. Picnics are encouraged
in the pleasant formal garden. Free tastings. Daily
10.30am–4.30pm.

Vynfields 22 Omarere Rd ⓣ 06 306 9901, ⓦ vynfields
.com. Choose from open lawns, shady bowers or the
elegant villa interior to sample flights of five wines (quarter
glasses $15; half glasses $20) accompanied by antipasto
platters ($32) and terrines ($18) to share. Tastings free.
Wed–Mon 11am–4pm.

Cape Palliser

Cosy, cosmopolitan Martinborough stands in dramatic contrast to the stark, often
windswept coast around **Cape Palliser**, 60km south. The southernmost point on the
North Island, the cape was named in honour of James Cook's mentor, Rear Admiral
Sir Hugh Palliser. Apart from a few gentle walks and the opportunity to observe fur
seals at close quarters, there's not a lot to do out here but clear your head, as swimming
is unsafe and the weather changeable.

Lake Ferry

From Martinborough, a sealed road leads 35km south to **Lake Ferry**, a tiny, comatose
surfcasting settlement on the sandy shores of Lake Onoke. There's not much to do here
but kick back and recharge your batteries, either by staying the night or stopping off
for some food and drink at the *Lake Ferry Hotel* (see opposite).

Putangirua Pinnacles

13km south of Lake Ferry

The Cape Palliser road then twists through the coastal hills until it meets the sea near
the **Putangirua Pinnacles**, dozens of grey soft-rock spires and fluted cliffs up to 50m
high, formed by wind and rain selectively eroding the surrounding silt and gravel.
From the parking area, where there are BBQ areas and a DOC campsite (see opposite),
allow a couple of hours to wander up the easy streambed to the base of the pinnacles,
up to a viewpoint and then back along a pretty, ridge-top bush track.

Ngawi

Beyond the pinnacles, the sealed road hugs the rugged, exposed coastline for 15km to **Ngawi**, a small fishing village where all manner of colourful **bulldozers** grind out their last days, hauling sometimes massive fishing boats up the steep gravel beach. It is five rough kilometres on to the cape proper, where a resurgent **fur seal colony**, right beside the road, is overlooked by the century-old Cape Palliser **lighthouse**, standing on a knoll 60m above the sea at the top of a long flight of some 250 steps. It's easy enough to get within 15m of the seals, but they can become aggressive if they feel threatened, and move surprisingly quickly, given their bulk – keep your distance from pups or their parents will bite you, and don't get between any seal and the sea.

6

ACCOMMODATION AND EATING

CAPE PALLISER

Lake Ferry Hotel 2 Lake Ferry Rd, Lake Ferry ☎ 06 307 7831, ⓦ lakeferryhotel.co.nz. The southernmost hotel on the North Island is a great spot for fish and chips on a sunny afternoon on your way back to Martinborough. There's a traditional Kiwi public bar and garden, overlooking the water, and a slightly more formal restaurant; arrive early to grab a table on fine weekends. Dorms $30, rooms $70, en-suite rooms $90

Lake Ferry Holiday Park, Lake Ferry ☎ 06 307 7873, ⓦ lakeferryholidaypark.co.nz. Dirt-cheap and a little more cramped than the *Lake Ferry Hotel*, but handy for its access to the latter's pub. Accommodation options here include camping, cabins and self-contained units, and there are kitchen facilities, showers, TV and laundry. Camping $12, cabins $60, self-contained units $80

Putangirua Pinnacles campsite Halfway between Lake Ferry and Cape Palliser. A view of the Cook Strait and a pebbly beach across the road are all you get at this DOC site that's within walking distance of the Pinnacles. There's tap water and toilets. Camping $6

Wellington and around

415 Civic Square and around

418 South of Civic Square

421 North of Civic Square

425 The suburbs

430 Wellington Harbour

430 The Hutt Valley

HILLSIDE HOMES IN WELLINGTON

Wellington and around

Understandably, people visiting New Zealand often reject its cities in favour of scenic splendour – with the exception of Wellington. The urban jewel in the country's otherwise bucolic crown, Wellington is by far New Zealand's most engaging and attractive metropolis, a buzzing, cosmopolitan capital worthy of any visitor's attention. Wedged between glistening Wellington Harbour (technically Port Nicholson) and the turbulent Cook Strait, Wellington is the principal departure point to the South Island. But, as the country's only city with a beating heart, it warrants a stay of at least a couple of days – more if you can manage it.

7

Tight surrounding hills restrict Wellington to a compact core, mostly built on reclaimed land. Distinctive historical and modern architecture spills down to the bustling waterfront with its beaches, marinas and restored warehouses, overlooked by Victorian and Edwardian weatherboard villas and bungalows that climb the steep slopes to an encircling belt of parks and woodland, a natural barrier to development. Many homes are accessed by narrow winding roads or precipitous stairways flanked by a small funicular railway to haul groceries and just about anything else up to the house. What's more, "Welly", as it's locally known, is New Zealand's **windy city**, buffeted by chilled air funnelled through Cook Strait, its force amplified by the wind-tunnelling effect of the city's high-rise buildings.

With a population of around 400,000, Wellington is New Zealand's second most populous city. And while Auckland grows more commercially important (and self-important in the eyes of its residents), Wellington reaches for higher ground as the nation's **cultural capital**. Wellingtonians have cultivated the country's most sophisticated **café society, nightlife** and **arts scene**, especially in late summer when the city hosts a series of arts and fringe **festivals** (see box, p.441).

Central Wellington is easily walkable; the heart of the **city centre** stretches south from the train station to Courtenay Place along the backbone of the central business and shopping district, Lambton Quay. The main areas for eating, drinking and entertainment are further south around Willis Street, Courtenay Place, arty Cuba Street, and down to the waterfront at Queens Wharf. From the central **Civic Square**, points of interest run both ways along the waterfront, including the city's star attraction, **Te Papa**, the groundbreaking national museum. Also worth a look is the revamped **Museum of Wellington City and Sea**, which recounts the city's development, Maori history and seafaring traditions. Politicians and civil servants populate the streets of the **Parliamentary District**. Nearby, you can visit **Katherine Mansfield's Birthplace**, the period-furnished childhood home of New Zealand's most famous short-story writer.

The city centre is also the jumping-off point for ambling or cycling along **Oriental Parade** and up to one of the hilltop viewpoints, such as **Mount Victoria**, or catching the stately **Cable Car** to Kelburn. From Kelburn, you can either wander down through the formal **Botanic Gardens** or continue further out to see the ambitious and important

City tours p.415
Cuba Street under threat p.421
Riding the Cable Car p.423
Katherine Mansfield p.425
The best view in Wellington p.425
Walks around Wellington p.428

"Wellywood" p.429
Matiu/Somes Island p.430
Wellington tours and activities p.432
Wellington transport information and
  passes p.433
Welington festivals p.441

WELLINGTON CABLE CAR

Highlights

❶ Te Papa The striking and inventive national museum showcases New Zealand's natural and bicultural history through intriguing exhibits, interactive technology and the nation's premier art collection. **See p.418**

❷ Cuba Street People-watching, café-hopping and window-shopping along the city's hip "alternative" strip give a taste of its divergent lifestyles. **See p.421**

❸ Botanic Gardens Ride the cable car up to Wellington's serene gardens for sweeping views, fragrant roses and the lovely Begonia House. **See p.422**

❹ Parliamentary District Visit the country's seat of power and associated national institutions, and view documents highlighting milestones on the country's road to nationhood including the original Treaty of Waitangi. **See p.423**

❺ Zealandia: the Karori Sanctuary Experience Native birds once again flock around Wellington, thanks to the predator-free environment and regenerating native bush at this unique wildlife sanctuary. **See p.425**

❻ Nightlife Wellington's nightlife surpasses that of anywhere else in New Zealand – from atmospheric theatres and stylish cinemas to cool cocktail bars, bouncy pubs and edgy clubs, alternatives abound. **See p.438**

HIGHLIGHTS ARE MARKED ON THE MAP ON P.414

conservation work at **Zealandia: the Karori Sanctuary Experience**, and **Otari-Wilton's Bush**, the only public botanic garden in the country dedicated solely to native plants. Zealandia and Otari-Wilton's Bush form part of the **Town Belt**, a band of greenery across the hills that encircles the city centre containing several good walks and many of the city's best lookout points. To the east of the city are the quiet suburbs and beaches of the **Miramar Peninsula**, now best known as the home of "Wellywood", the heart of the city's film industry; you can't miss it, thanks to the new Hollywood-style Wellington sign, with the letters symbolically blown along by the wind.

Superb **hiking** opportunities include the seal colony at Red Rocks, or the city's many trails, notably the **Southern Walkway**. And at some point during your stay in this harbour city, you really should get out on the water to the serene wildlife sanctuary of **Matiu/Somes Island**.

Wellington also makes a good base to explore **Kapiti Island** (p.256) and the **Wairarapa** wine district; see box opposite and p.433 for wine tours from Wellington.

Brief history

Maori oral histories tell of the demigod **Maui**, who fished up the North Island, with Wellington Harbour being the mouth of the fish; and of the first Polynesian navigator, **Kupe**, discovering Wellington Harbour in 925 AD and naming the harbour's islands Matiu (Somes Island) and Makaro (Ward Island) after his daughters (see box, p.430). Several *iwi* settled around the harbour, including the Ngati Tara people, who enjoyed the rich fishing areas and the protection the bay offered.

Both Abel Tasman (in 1642) and Captain Cook (in 1773) were prevented from entering Wellington Harbour by fierce winds, and, apart from a few sealers and whalers, it wasn't until 1840 that the first wave of **European settlers** arrived. They carved out a niche on a large tract of harbourside land, purchased by the New Zealand Company,

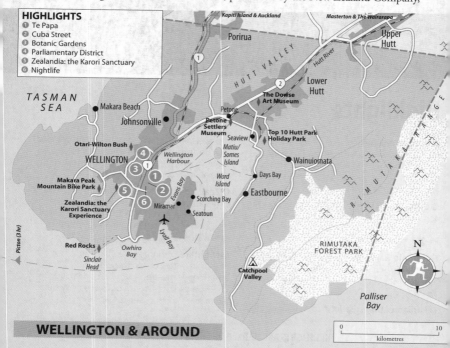

HIGHLIGHTS
1. Te Papa
2. Cuba Street
3. Botanic Gardens
4. Parliamentary District
5. Zealandia: the Karori Sanctuary
6. Nightlife

WELLINGTON & AROUND

CITY TOURS

An ever-increasing number of clued-up local outfits offer entertaining and informative tours of the city; the best are listed below.

Flat Earth ☎ 0800 775 805, ⊛ flatearth.co.nz. Upmarket outfit which takes very good care of you on its range of tours (from $159), including Wellington city highlights, nature and eco tours, and several specialist film tours.

Movie Tours ☎ 027 419 3077, ⊛ adventuresafari .co.nz. Dedicated movie-theme tour options include a Wellington Movie Tour and Weta Cave ($45).

Wairarapa Escape Tours ☎ 06 377 1227, ⊛ tranzit .co.nz. Popular day tours of the Wairarapa (p.401), including a Martinborough Wine Tour ($185).

Wellington Rover ☎ 021 426 211, ⊛ wellington rover.co.nz. Hop-on-hop-off minibus tours making a loop around the city's outer sights – Mount Victoria,

Red Rocks, the zoo and a couple of *LOTR* locations ($50; 3/day), with small discounts for entry to various sights along the way.

Wild About Wellington ☎ 027 441 9010, ⊛ wild aboutwellington.co.nz. Wellingtonian Jennifer Looman's enthusiasm for her city and its artisan produce is infectious, and her daily tours – Sights & Bites (4hr 30min; $205 with lunch) and Wild about Chocolate (4hr 15min; $110) – combine sightseeing with gourmet refuelling stops.

Zest Food Tours ☎ 04 801 9198, ⊛ zestfoodtours .co.nz. Gourmet tours (Mon–Sat; 2hr 30min; from $169) taking in coffee roasteries, chocolate producers, cheese and honey tastings and more.

7

who set up their initial beachhead, named Britannia, on the northeastern beaches at Petone. Shortly afterwards, the Hutt River flooded, forcing the settlers to move around the harbour to a more sheltered site known as Lambton Harbour (where the central city has grown up) and the relatively level land at Thorndon, at that time just north of the shoreline. They renamed the settlement after the Iron Duke and began **land reclamations** into the harbour, a process that continued for more than a hundred years.

In 1865, the growing city succeeded Auckland as the **capital** of New Zealand, and by the turn of the twentieth century the original shoreline of Lambton Harbour had been replaced by wharves and harbourside businesses, which formed the hub of the city's coastal trade; Wellington has prospered ever since.

Civic Square and around

A popular venue for outdoor events, **Civic Square** was extensively revamped in the early 1990s by New Zealand's most influential and versatile living architect, **Ian Athfield**, who juxtaposes old and new, regular and irregular forms and incorporates artwork. The open space is full of interesting sculptures, including Neil Dawson's *Ferns* – interlinking metal fern fronds formed into a ball that appears to float above the square.

Central Library

65 Victoria St • Mon–Fri 9.30am–8.30pm, Sat 9.30am–5pm, Sun 1–4pm

The most arresting building on Civic Square is Athfield's magnificent 1991 **Central Library**, a spacious hi-tech statement in steel, stone, glass and timber with its inner workings – air ducts, water pipes – exposed. Athfield also created the supporting steel nikau palms, which ring the building and provide a link to the rest of Civic Square by continuing out beyond the building itself.

City Gallery Wellington

101 Wakefield St • Daily 10am–5pm • Free; special exhibitions around $10 • ☎ 04 801 3021, ⊛ citygallery.org.nz

The impressive 1939 Art Deco **City Gallery Wellington** hosts touring shows of national and international contemporary works. Most are free, but there's an entry fee for

7

CENTRAL WELLINGTON

■ ACCOMMODATION
Apollo Lodge Motel &	
Majoribanks Apartments	9
Austinvilla B&B	13
Base Wellington	8
Booklovers B&B	14
Cambridge Hotel	10
Downtown Backpackers	1
Halswell Lodge	11
The Mermaid	12
Museum Hotel	4
Nomads Capital	2
Ohotel	5
Trinity Hotel	3
Wellywood Backpackers	7
YHA Wellington City	6

● CAFÉS/DELI
Aro Coffee	18
Fidel's	21
Floriditas	12
Midnight Espresso	15
Mojo	22
Moore Wilson's	3
Nikau Gallery Café	13
Olive	9
Plum	19
Trisha's Pies	

● RESTAURANTS
Beach Babylon	6
Kreuzberg	23
Le Metropolitan	11
Logan-Brown	17
MarLuca	1
Martin Bosley's	4
Masala	10
Matterhorn	7
Oriental Kingdom	8
Ortega	16
Sweet Mother's Kitchen	14
Wellington Trawling	
Sea Market	20
The White House	5

■ PUBS & BARS
Alice	17
The Backbencher Pub	1
Foxglove Bar & Kitchen	8
Kiwi Pub	2
Leuven	10
The Library	4
Mac's Brewery	9
The Malthouse	6
Matterhorn	5
Mighty Mighty	13
Motel	15
S&M's	20
Southern Cross	

■ CLUBS AND LIVE MUSIC VENUES
Bodega	7
Boogie Wonderland	11
Garden Club	14
Happy	19
Medusa	18
San Francisco Bathhouse	16
Sandwiches	12

Town Belt

Matiu/Somes Island

Westpac Stadium

WATERLOO QUAY

Container & Cruise Terminal

Queens Wharf

Ferg's Kayaks

TBS Bank Arena

Damnion Post Ferry Terminal

Museum of Wellington

Cable Car Lower Terminal

THE TERRACE

Old Government Buildings

The Beehive

Parliament House

Parliamentary Library

St Paul's Cathedral

HILL STREET

MOLESWORTH STREET

HAWKESTONE STREET

National Library

Archives New Zealand

Old St Paul's Cathedral

Thorndon Pool

THORNDON

HOBSON STREET

THORNDON QUAY

MURPHY ST

MULGRAVE ST

AITKEN ST

KATE SHEPPARD ST

Lambton Interchange

Train & Bus Station

Long Distance Buses

Bluebridge Ferry Terminal

LAMBTON QUAY

FEATHERSTON STREET

WHITMORE ST

JOHNSTON ST

HUNTER ST

GREY ST

MOTORWAY

WELLINGTON MOTORWAY

GRANT ROAD

PARK ST

GEORGE

HARRIET ST

BOWEN ST

GLENMORE STREET

BOLTON STREET

AURORA TERRACE

CLIFTON TERRACE

EVERTON ST

ASCOT ST

CLERMONT STREET

WESLEY ROAD

Saddon Memorial

Bolton Street Memorial Park

Begonia House

Lady Norwood Rose Garden

Botanic Gardens

Carter Observatory

Cable Car Museum

Katherine Mansfield Birthplace (100m), Interislander Ferry Terminal (700m) & Otari-Wilton Bush (6km)

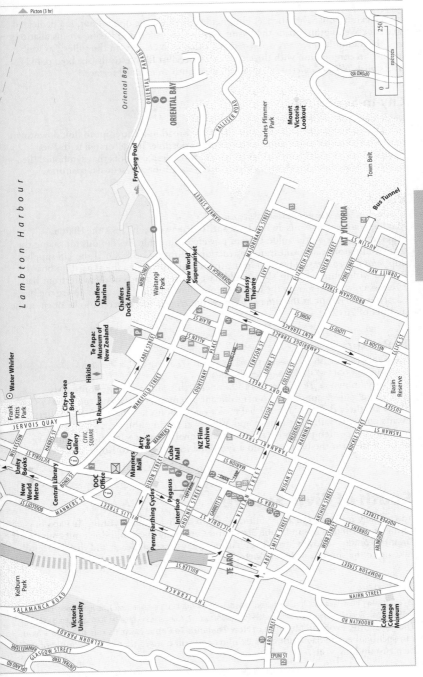

Picton (3 hr)

Oriental Bay

ORIENTAL BAY

Charles Plimmer Park

Mount Victoria Lookout

Town Belt

Lambton Harbour

MT VICTORIA

Bus Tunnel

Freyberg Pool

New World Supermarket

Waitangi Park

Embassy Theatre

Chaffers Marina

Chaffers Dock Atnum

Te Papa: Museum of New Zealand

Hikitia

Water Whirler

City-to-sea Bridge

Te Raukura

Frank Kitts Park

Basin Reserve

JERVOIS QUAY

City Gallery

CIVIC SQUARE

Arty Bee's

Manners Mall

Cuba Mall

NZ Film Archive

Unity Books

Central Library

DOC Office

New World Metro

Penny Farthing Cycles

Pegasus

Interface

TE ARO

Kelburn Park

Victoria University

Colonial Cottage Museum

SALAMANCA ROAD

special exhibitions. The Michael Hirscheld Gallery, on the upper floor, is a dedicated space for Wellington artists, the Deane Gallery has Maori and Pacific art installations and the **auditorium** screens works relating directly to exhibits in the gallery, as well as films in conjunction with the city's many specialist film festivals (see box, p.441). The stylish *Nikau Gallery Café* (p.437) opens onto an external terrace.

City-to-Sea Bridge

Just east of Civic Square, across Jervois Quay

The **City-to-Sea Bridge** was intentionally made broad in an attempt to link downtown to the long-ignored waterfront as seamlessly as possible. It's decorated with Para Matchitt's timber sculptures of birds, whales and celestial motifs that symbolize the arrival of Maori and European settlers and, by extension, present-day visitors.

Hikitia

Southeast of Civic Square along the waterfront • ⓦ hikitia.com

Making your way towards Te Raukura and Te Papa you can't miss the **Hikitia**, believed to be the world's oldest steam-powered crane ship. It's famous for saving the then-Wellington waterfront from destruction. During World War II the US supply ship *John Davenport* was berthed in the inner harbour when a fire started on board. Loaded with munitions, the ship would have destroyed much of the waterfront had *Hikitia*'s crew not removed the deck cargo to allow the fire brigade to dowse the blaze. Closed to the public at the time of writing, the *Hikitia* was expected to be open in the summer of 2012.

Te Raukura

Opposite the Hikitia in Odlins Square, between the City-to-Sea Bridge and Te Papa • Mon—Wed 7am—4pm, Thurs & Fri 7am—late, Sat & Sun 8am—late • Free • ☏ 04 499 8180, ⓦ wharewakaoponeke.co.nz

Formerly known as Te Wharewaka O Poneke, this purpose-built conference centre and gallery contains two magnificent ceremonial *waka* and the *Karaka Café*. There are three distinct areas: Wharewaka (*waka* house), Whare Tapere (gallery, events and entertainment house) and Wharekai (eating house). Throughout the building are contemporary versions of traditional Maori design and carvings, which transform the building into a symbolic *waka* linked to Kupe, the great navigator of Maori legend.

South of Civic Square

You're likely to spend much of your time south of Civic Square visiting **Te Papa** or eating and drinking around **Cuba Street** and **Courtenay Place**, but don't miss out on **Oriental Parade** – a lovely stroll with harbour views, a small beach and the chance to hike up to the summit of **Mount Victoria**.

Te Papa

55 Cable St • Daily 10am—6pm, until 9pm Thurs; guided tours daily: Nov—March 10.15am, 11am, noon, 1pm, 2pm & 3pm; April—Oct 10.15am & 2pm; extra tour at 7pm Thurs both seasons • Free; guided tour $12; audioguide $5 • ☏ 04 381 7000, ⓦ tepapa.govt.nz

The constantly evolving **Museum of New Zealand**, **Te Papa**, rewards repeat visits – you can spend an entire day among the exhibits and still not see them all. A couple of **cafés** help sustain long visits.

This $350-million celebration of all things New Zealand occupies a striking purpose-built five-storey building on the waterfront and was opened in 1998 after extensive consultation with *iwi* (tribes). Aimed equally at adults and children (including hands-on kids' activities in dedicated "discovery" spaces), it combines state-of-the-art technology and dynamic exhibits. Well worth $3 is the *Te Papa Explorer* guide, outlining routes such as "Te Papa Highlights" or "Kids' Highlights". Alternatively, book one of the amazing **guided tours**.

Level 2

The hub of Te Papa is **Level 2**, with its interactive section on earthquakes and volcanoes, where you can experience a realistic quake inside a shaking house, see displays on the fault line that runs right through Wellington, watch Mount Ruapehu erupt on screen and hear the Maori explanation of the causes of such activity. There's also the hi-tech multimedia centre **OurSpace**, where you can project your own text images onto a giant screen, The Wall, and board two **simulator rides** ($10 each, or $18 for both): The High Ride, whirling you through the 3D world of The Wall, and the Deep Ride, journeying into a virtual underwater volcano. Level 2 also provides access to the outdoor **Bush City**, a synthesis of New Zealand environments complete with native plants, a small cave system and swingbridge. From November to March, the hour-long Taste of Treasures tour (11am; tickets must be bought before 10.45am; $24) includes traditional Maori refreshments made from bush plants.

Level 4

The main collection continues on **Level 4**, home to the excellent main Maori section including a thought-provoking display on the Treaty of Waitangi, dominated by a giant glass image of this significant document. There's also an **active marae** with a symbolic modern meeting house quite unlike the classic examples found around the country, protected by a sacred boulder of *pounamu* (greenstone); check behind the cupboard doors at the back for some imagery that shows both a sense of humour and the incredible significance of the place. Temporary exhibitions include displays by different *iwi* showcasing that particular *iwi*'s art and culture.

Adjacent to the *marae*, look out for displays on New Zealand's people, land, history, trade and cultures including Michel Tuffery's bullock made from corned beef cans, and Brian O'Connor's paua-shell surfboard.

Level 5

Level 5 is the home of New Zealand's **national art collection**, displaying a changing roster of works on paper, oils and sculpture representing luminaries of the New Zealand art world past and present; Colin McCahon, Rita Angus, Ralph Hotere, Don Binney, Michael Smither and Shane Cotton are just a few names to watch for.

Oriental Parade

Immediately east of Te Papa, **Waitangi Park** is named after a long culverted stream that has been restored to its natural course, creating a small urban wetland. At the end of Herd Street, the **Chaffers Dock** development incorporates cafés as well as the atrium where Wellington's Sunday-morning farmers' market (see p.436) sets up. The park marks the start of **Oriental Parade**, Wellington's most elegant section of waterfront. Skirting **Oriental Bay**, this Norfolk-pine-lined road curls past some of the city's priciest real estate and even flanks a **beach** installed here in 2003 with sand brought across Cook Strait from near Takaka. Apart from the Freyberg pool (see p.441) and a few restaurants, there are no attractions as such, but you can extend a stroll into a full afternoon by continuing to Charles Plimmer Park and joining the Southern Walkway (see p.428) to the summit of **Mount Victoria**.

CUBA STREET UNDER THREAT

If not the character then certainly the look of some parts of Wellington is set to change. Many of Wellington's older, more atmospheric buildings, primarily along Cuba Street and its surrounds, are under threat, having fallen foul of new legislation on building safety, enacted since the Christchurch earthquakes of 2010 and 2011. The cost of bringing these edifices up to standard is, in some cases, prohibitive and may mean their loss to the wrecking ball. As with Christchurch, this is both an opportunity and a bane, since new buildings will almost certainly be high rent, forcing many of the current quirkier occupants to decamp.

Mount Victoria

At 196m, **Mount Victoria Lookout** is one of the best of Wellington's viewpoints, offering sweeping views of the city, waterfront, docks and beyond to the Hutt Valley; all particularly dramatic around dusk. If you don't fancy the steep but rewarding walk, you can also reach the summit by bus (#20; Mon–Fri), the Wellington Rover (see box, p.415), or by car following Hawker Street, off Majoribanks Street, then taking Palliser Road, which twists uphill to the lookout.

7

New Zealand Film Archive

84 Taranaki St, at Ghuznee St • Mon & Tues 9am–5pm, Wed–Fri 9am–7pm, Sat 4–7pm; evening screenings Wed–Sat 7pm • Free; evening screenings $8 • ☎ 04 384 7647, ⓦ filmarchive.org.nz

The excellent **New Zealand Film Archive** has small film-themed exhibits though the main attraction is the ability to watch just about any New Zealand movie ever made, plus TV programmes, old commercials and assorted home movies on monitors in the media library or in the small viewing room (all free). There are also evening screenings in the cinema, which on Wednesdays will be a New Zealand feature film.

Courtenay Place and Cuba Street

Wellington's entertainment heartland is centred on **Courtenay Place** and adjacent **Cuba Street** (see box above). Named after an emigrant ship (not the island after which the ship was christened, despite the Cuban-themed establishments in this part of town), Cuba Street and its offshoots comprise Wellington's "alternative" district, with secondhand bookshops, vintage record stores, retro and emerging-designer fashion outlets, quirky cafés, and hip bars and restaurants. Between Dixon and Ghuznee streets, Cuba Street's colourful and iconic **Bucket Fountain** was installed in 1969 and still splashes unsuspecting passers-by.

Colonial Cottage Museum

68 Nairn St • Christmas to mid-Feb daily noon–4pm; mid-Feb to Christmas Sat & Sun noon–4pm; guided tours hourly noon–3pm • $8 • ⓦ colonialcottagemuseum.co.nz

Heritage fans may be keen to see the twee **Colonial Cottage Museum**, central Wellington's oldest building. Though dating from 1858 (two decades into Queen Victoria's reign), it's built in late Georgian style, and its decor gives the impression that the family has just left for Sunday church and will be back for lunch.

North of Civic Square

As the city progressively reconnects to the harbour, there's plenty of action around **Queens Wharf**, home to expensive harbour-view apartments, the Museum of Wellington City and Sea and a variety of bars and restaurants, as well as the *Mojo* coffee roastery (see p.437).

The business heart of Wellington beats along Lambton Quay, which runs north to the **Parliamentary District**, the city's administrative and ecclesiastical hub. Parliament marks the southern edge of **Thorndon**, Wellington's oldest suburb and home of the **Katherine Mansfield Birthplace**.

Frank Kitts Park and around

Just north of the Civic Square lies **Frank Kitts Park**, where the mast of the *Wahine* (see below) stands poignant sentinel on the waterfront. A few metres further along is the *Water Whirler*, a kinetic sculpture designed by Len Lye (see box, p.228) and opened in 2006, a quarter of a century after the artist's death. Roughly every hour (10am–10pm but not 2pm; 5–10min), it erupts into a sequence of complex and increasingly energetic gyrations with jets spewing water. Between the sculpture and the museum (see below) is **Plimmer's Ark** (dawn–dusk; free), the resting place of what's left of the *Inconstant*, a wooden sailing ship that was beached and converted to a trading wharf in 1850 by John Plimmer, the father of commercial activity in the burgeoning city.

Museum of Wellington City and Sea

3 Jervois Quay • Daily 10am–5pm; free 30min tours Sun 2pm • Free; Ship 'n Chip tour (5hr) $39 • ☎ 04 472 8904, ⓦ museumswellington.co.nz

Near lively **Queens Wharf**, a Victorian former bond store houses the absorbing **Museum of Wellington City and Sea**. The city's social and maritime history unfolds through well-executed displays on early Maori and European settlement and the city's seafaring heritage. The ground floor offers an easily digestible chronological overview of key events, while the main focus of the first floor is the poignant coverage of the **Wahine disaster**, remembering the inter-island ferry that sank with the loss of 52 lives on April 10, 1968. The *Wahine* foundered in one of New Zealand's most violent storms ever, with 734 people on board. On the top floor, a hologram presentation tells the Maori legends of the creation of Wellington Harbour, while rising up through the centre of the building, a tall screen features a roster of short films. There are also museum tours, including the popular **Ship 'n Chip tour** which involves a ferry trip to Matiu/Somes Island (see box, p.430) and fish and chips for lunch.

Lambton Quay

Now Wellington's main commercial street, **Lambton Quay** formed the original waterfront but was cut off by the docks formed by reclamation. Head straight along Lambton Quay to the Parliamentary District, or detour up the **Cable Car** (see box opposite) and back down through the Botanic Gardens.

The Botanic Gardens

Entrances on Glenmore St, Salamanca Rd, Upland Rd and on the Cable Car • Daily dawn–dusk • Free

A lookout at the top of the Cable Car provides spectacular views over the city. Here, you're also at the highest point of Wellington's **Botanic Gardens**, a huge swathe of green on peaceful rolling hills with numerous paths that wind down towards the city. Pick up the useful free map from the Cable Car Museum.

Lady Norwood Rose Garden and Begonia House

Begonia House daily Oct–March 9am–5pm; April–Sept 9am–4pm • Free

The star in the Botanic Garden's firmament is the fragrant **Lady Norwood Rose Garden**, where a colonnade of climbing roses frames beds of over three hundred varieties set out in a formal wheel shape. The adjacent **Begonia House** is divided into two areas: the tropical, with an attractive lily pond, and the temperate, which has seasonal

RIDING THE CABLE CAR

Even if you never use the rest of Wellington's public transport system, don't miss the short scenic ride up to the leafy suburb of Kelburn and the upper section of the Botanic Gardens on the **Cable Car** (Mon–Fri 7am–10pm, Sat 8.30am–10pm, Sun 9am–10pm; $3.50 one-way, $6 return), installed in 1902. Its shiny red railcars depart every ten minutes from the lower terminus on Cable Car Lane, just off Lambton Quay, and climb a steep, one-in-five incline, making three stops along the way and giving great views over the city and harbour. At the upper terminus on Upland Road, the **Cable Car Museum** (daily: 9.30am–5pm; free) contains the historic winding room with the electric drive motor and a cat's cradle of cables. Two century-old cars are on display along with plenty of background on cable cars around the world. Take time to catch the short movies, particularly the one about the 400-plus mini cable cars people still use to access their properties locally.

displays of begonias and gloxinias in summer, changing to cyclamen, orchids and impatiens in winter.

Carter Observatory

Mon, Wed, Thurs & Fri 10am–5pm, Tues & Sat 10am–9.30pm, Sun 10am–5.30pm; planetarium shows: Mon–Fri 11am, 12.30pm, 1.30pm, 3pm & 4pm, Sat & Sun on the hour; night shows Tues & Sat 6pm, 7pm & 8pm (book ahead) • Exhibition $10; 45min planetarium shows $18 • ☎ 04 910 3140, ⓦ carterobservatory.org

Two minutes' walk from the upper Cable Car terminus is the fabulous, revamped, 1941 **Carter Observatory**, which has illuminating displays on the New Zealand angle on the exploration of the southern skies, from Maori and Pacific Island astronomy and astronavigation through to recent planet searches. Of particular note are a telescope from Captain Cook's era, a piece of moon rock you can touch and the chance to launch a rocket – you man the console, initiate the launch and feel the ground shake as you view the footage of the space-bound projectile. Make time to catch one of the jaw-dropping planetarium shows that include live night sky viewings.

Parliamentary District

The northern end of Lambton Quay marks the start of the **Parliamentary District**, dominated by the grandiose **Old Government Buildings**, which at first glance appear to be constructed from cream stone, but are really wooden. Designed by colonial architect William Clayton (1823–77) to mark the country's transition from provincial to centralized government, the intention was to use stone but cost-cutting forced a rethink. When completed in 1876, it was the largest building in New Zealand, and except for an ornamental palace in Japan remains the largest timber building in the world. It's currently occupied by Victoria University's Law Faculty, but you can usually duck inside, nip up the rimu staircase and see the series of photos of the building as a backdrop to various historical demonstrations and protests.

The Parliament Buildings

Free 1hr guided tours on the hour Mon–Fri 10am–4pm, Sat 10am–3pm, Sun 11am–3pm • ☎ 04 817 9503, ⓦ parliament.nz

Visible across Lambton Quay are the **Parliament Buildings**, the seat of New Zealand's government, a trio of highly individual structures that nonetheless sit harmoniously together. Most distinctive is the modernist **Beehive**, a seven-stepped truncated cone that houses the Cabinet and the offices of its ministers. Designed by British (and Coventry Cathedral) architect Sir Basil Spence in 1964, it was finally completed in 1982, six years after Spence's death. The Beehive is connected directly to the Edwardian Neoclassical **Parliament House**, a grand authoritarian seat of government that stands in stark contrast to the Gothic Revival **Parliamentary Library**, all high church, pomp and whimsy.

Hour-long guided tours start from a visitor centre on the ground floor of the Beehive. Highlights of the tour include the decorative **Maori Affairs Select Committee Room** with its specially commissioned carvings and woven *tukutuku* panels from all the major tribal groups in the land, and the beautifully restored 1899 Victorian Gothic library. You're led through the Debating Chamber when Parliament's not sitting; when it is, check with your guide about watching proceedings from the public gallery.

MPs venture across Molesworth Street to the **Backbencher Pub** (see p.437).

National Library of New Zealand

Corner of Molesworth and Aitken sts, opposite Parliament • Mon–Sat 10am–5pm • Free • ☎ 04 474 3000, ⓦ natlib.govt.nz

At the time of writing, the **National Library of New Zealand**, which is generally off-limits to all but researchers, was closed due to plans to merge with the Archives of New Zealand. By the time you read this, the archives' Constitution Room – a dimly lit climate-controlled vault where the prize exhibit is the original Maori-language Treaty of Waitangi (see p.166 & p.789) – and all the other archives exhibits should have shifted to the national library.

The Treaty of Waitangi barely survived a long spell lost in the bowels of the Old Government Buildings, suffering water damage and the gnawings of rodents before it was rescued in 1908. Various copies of the treaty did the rounds of the country collecting Maori chiefs' signatures, giving a sense of how haphazard the whole process was. Other key documents include the 1835 Declaration of Independence of the Northern Chiefs and Maori petitions dating back to 1909, which complain of broken treaty promises. Look also for the facsimile of the 1893 petition for women's suffrage, put together by New Zealand's iconic suffragette, Kate Sheppard – who features on the $10 note. At this third attempt she managed to amass 32,000 signatures, a quarter of the adult female population, ushering in legislation which made New Zealand the first country to give women the vote.

Old St Paul's Cathedral

Corner of Mulgrave and Pipitea sts • Daily 10am–5pm • Free

From 1866 to 1964 the modest **Old St Paul's** operated as the parish church of Thorndon, but after the houses of the Parliamentary District were taken over by government departments and foreign delegations it was only saved from demolition in the 1960s by sustained public protest. Among the finest European timber churches in the country, its interior is beautiful, crafted in early English Gothic style (more commonly seen in stone) from native timbers that progressively darken with age. Lovely stained-glass windows and the sheen of polished brass plaques on the walls highlight the ranks of dark pews, arches, pulpit and choral area. The church was the major work of an English ecclesiastical architect, Reverend Frederick Thatcher.

St Paul's Cathedral

Corner of Molesworth and Hill sts • Daily 10am–4pm • Free

Old St Paul's could hardly stand in greater contrast to its modern successor, **St Paul's Cathedral**. A mix of Byzantine and Santa Fe styles, it was designed in the 1930s by renowned ecclesiastical architect Cecil Wood of Christchurch. Queen Elizabeth II laid the foundation stone in 1954 but the cathedral wasn't complete until 1998. The cavernous interior dwarfs the dark-wood choir stalls, which look out of place among all the powder-pink concrete. The distinctive pipe organ, built in London, was originally installed in Old St Paul's.

The Katherine Mansfield Birthplace

25 Tinakori Rd • Tues–Sun 10am–4pm • $8 • ☎ 04 473 7268, ⓦ katherinemansfield.com • Bus #14 stops on nearby Park St

A ten-minute walk north from the cathedrals through Thorndon gets you to the **Katherine Mansfield Birthplace**, a modest wooden house with small garden that was Mansfield's (see box opposite) childhood abode. The house has a cluttered Victorian/Edwardian charm and avant-garde decor for its time, inspired by Japonisme and the Aesthetic Movement. An upstairs room is set aside to recount a history of the

KATHERINE MANSFIELD

Katherine Mansfield Beauchamp (1888–1923) is New Zealand's most famous short-story writer. During her brief life, she revolutionized the form, eschewing plot in favour of a poetic expansiveness. Virginia Woolf claimed Mansfield's work to be "the only writing I have ever been jealous of".

Mansfield lived on Tinakori Road for five years with her parents, three sisters and beloved grandmother, and the place is described in some of her works, notably "Prelude" and "A Birthday". The family later moved to a much grander house in what is now the western suburb of Karori until, at 19, Katherine left for Europe, where she lived until dying of tuberculosis in France, aged 34.

author's life and career, with some black-and-white photos of Wellington and the people that shaped her life – and videos including the excellent *A Woman and a Writer*.

The suburbs

Wellington's suburbs are within easy reach of the city centre and contain the ground-breaking **Zealandia: the Karori Sanctuary Experience**, complemented by a fine stand of native bush a few kilometres north at **Otari-Wilson's Bush**. A number of good walks thread through the greenery of the Town Belt or head beyond to the quiet pleasures of **Scorching Bay** on the **Miramar Peninsula**, the hub of Wellington's film industry.

Zealandia: the Karori Sanctuary Experience

31 Waiapu Rd • Daily 10am–5pm; 2hr 30min guided night tours daily 30min before sunset • $28.50; night tour $76.50 including admission (book ahead) • ☎ 04 920 9200 or infoline ☎ 04 920 2222, ⓦ visitzealandia.com • Walk 2km from the Cable Car upper terminus or catch the #3 bus from Lambton Quay or Courtney Place; if you've booked a tour ask about pick-ups from the city centre

Just 3km west of the city centre in the suburb of Karori is a pristine oasis called **Zealandia**, named after the Zealandia microcontinent that broke away from the super-continent of Gondwana some 85 million years ago. Started in the late 1990s, the sanctuary is successfully restoring native New Zealand bush and its wildlife to 2.25 square kilometres of urban Wellington. Sited around two century-old reservoirs that formerly supplied Wellington's drinking water (and still do in times of water shortage), the managing trust first designed an 8.6km-long **predator-proof fence** to keep out all introduced mammals. As well as restocking the area with native trees, eradicating weeds and fostering the existing morepork and tui, the trust has introduced native birds – little spotted kiwi, weka, saddleback, kaka, bellbird, whitehead, North Island robins, takahe and kakariki – plus tuatara (back in a natural mainland environment for the first time in over 200 years) and the grasshopper-like weta to the sanctuary from the overspill of the conservation and restocking programme on Kapiti Island (see p.256).

THE BEST VIEW IN WELLINGTON

If the city panorama from Mount Victoria isn't enough for you, head west to **Brooklyn Hill**, easily identified by its crowning 32m-high **wind turbine**. Fantastic views unfold across the city and south towards the South Island's Kaikoura Ranges as the giant propeller blades whirr overhead. This demonstration turbine has been harnessing Wellington's wind since 1993, providing energy for up to a hundred homes but failing to ignite enough interest to install more. To reach the turbine by car, take Brooklyn Road from the end of Victoria Street and turn left at Ohiro Road, then right at the shopping centre up Todman Street and follow the signposts (the road up to the turbine closes at 8pm Oct–April and 5pm May–Sept). Bus #7 runs up Victoria Street in town and drops you 3km from the summit.

7

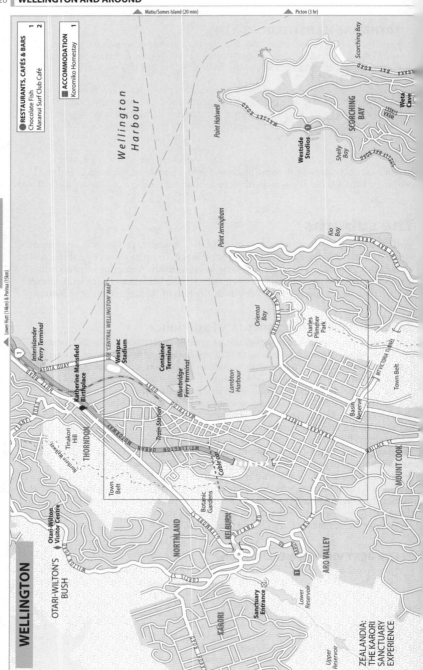

WELLINGTON

▲ Matiu/Somes Island (20 min)   ▲ Picton (3 hr)

● **RESTAURANTS, CAFÉS & BARS**
Chocolate Fish   1
Maranui Surf Club Café   2

■ **ACCOMMODATION**
Koromiko Homestay   1

Wellington Harbour

Scorching Bay

Point Halswell

Westside Studios

Shelly Bay

SCORCHING BAY

Weta Cave

Point Jerningham

Kio Bay

Oriental Bay

Charles Plimmer Park

Town Belt

MOUNT VICTORIA TUNNEL

Interislander Ferry Terminal

AOTEA QUAY

Katherine Mansfield Birthplace

SEE 'CENTRAL WELLINGTON MAP'

Westpac Stadium

Container Terminal

Bluebridge Ferry terminal

Lambton Harbour

Train Station

THORNDON

Tinakori Hill

Northern Walkway

WELLINGTON URBAN MOTORWAY

Basin Reserve

WALLACE ST

MOUNT COOK

Town Belt

Cable Car

Botanic Gardens

KELBURN

NORTHLAND

Otari-Wilton Visitor Centre

OTARI-WILTON'S BUSH

KARORI

Sanctuary Entrance

Lower Reservoir

ARO VALLEY

Upper Reservoir

ZEALANDIA: THE KARORI SANCTUARY EXPERIENCE

▲ Lower Hutt (14km) & Porirua (15km)

▲ Makara Peak (5km)

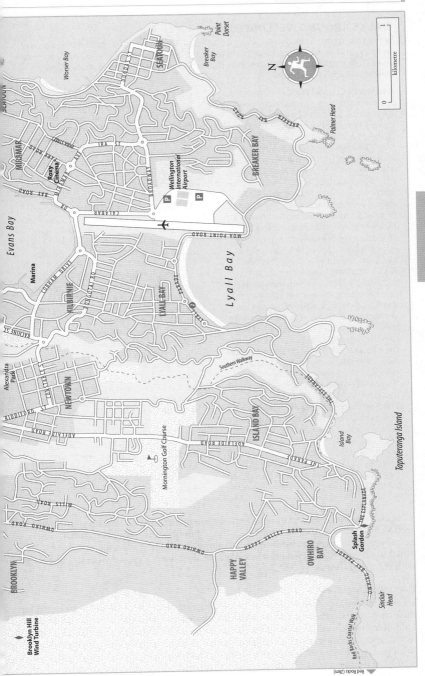

7

7

WALKS AROUND WELLINGTON

With its encircling wooded Town Belt, great city views from nearby hills and the temptation of watching seals along the southern coast, Wellington offers some excellent and easily accessible walking. Pick up free detailed leaflets from the i-SITE (see p.434). For information on walks around Wellington, see box, p.428.

Red Rocks Coastal Walk (4km each way; 2–3hr return). An easy walk that traces Wellington's southern shoreline to Sinclair Head, where a colony of bachelor New Zealand fur seals takes up residence from May–Oct each year. The walk follows a rough track along the coastline from Owhiro Bay to Sinclair Head, passing a quarry and the eponymous Red Rocks – well-preserved volcanic pillow lava, formed about 200 million years ago by underwater volcanic eruptions and coloured red by iron oxide. Maori variously attribute the colour to bloodstains from Maui's nose or blood dripping from a paua-shell cut on Kupe's hand, while another account tells how Kupe's daughters cut themselves in mourning, having given up their father for dead. The track starts around 7km south of the city centre at the quarry gates at the western end of Owhiro Bay Parade, where there's a car park. To get here by bus either take the frequent #1 to Island Bay (get off at the Parade at the corner of Reef Street and walk 2.5km to the start of the walk) or, at peak times, catch #4, which continues to Happy Valley, 1km from the track. Both head east from Courtenay Place.

The Southern Walkway (11km; 4–5hr). Offering excellent views of the harbour and central city, this walk cuts through the Town Belt to the south of the city centre, between Oriental and Island bays. Despite a few steep stretches it's fairly easy going overall. Fantails, grey warblers and wax-eyes provide company, and Island Bay offers some of the city's best swimming. The walk can be undertaken in either direction and is clearly marked by posts bearing orange arrows. To start at the city end, simply walk along Oriental Parade (or take bus #14 or #24) to the entrance of Charles Plimmer Park, just past 350 Oriental Parade. To begin at the southern end, take the #1 bus to Island Bay and follow the signs from nearby Shorland Park.

The Northern Walkway (16km; 4–5hr). Extending through tranquil sections of the Town Belt to the north of the city centre, this panoramic walk stretches from Kelburn to the suburb of Johnsonville, covering five distinct areas – Botanic Garden, Tinakori Hill, Trelissick Park, Khandallah Park and Johnsonville Park – each accessible from suburban streets and served by public transport. Highlights are the birdlife on Tinakori Hill (tui, fantails, kingfishers, grey warblers, silver-eyes); the regenerating native forest of Ngaio Gorge in Trelissick Park; great views across the city and the harbour and over to the Rimutaka and Tararua ranges from a lookout on Mount Kaukau (430m); and, in Johnsonville Park, a disused road tunnel hewn through solid rock. Start at the top of the Cable Car and head north through the Botanic Garden, or join the walk at Tinakori Hill by climbing St Mary Street, off Glenmore Street, and following the orange arrows through woodland. To begin at the northern end, take a train to Raroa station on the Johnsonville line.

This far-reaching project won't be entirely complete until the forest has matured in around 500 years. You can already walk the 35km of paths (some almost flat, others quite rugged) listening to birdsong heard almost nowhere else on the mainland – making it easy to understand why early arrivals to New Zealand were so impressed with the avian chorus.

The sanctuary grounds

It's worth spending at least half a day here wandering past viewing hides, areas noted for their fantails or saddleback, and even the first few metres of a gold-mine tunnel from the 1869 Karori gold rush. Also worthwhile are the guided night tours that give you a chance to watch kaka feeding, see banks of glowworms and hear kiwi foraging for their dinner. With luck you'll even see one or two. The sanctuary is already having a wider effect, with increasing numbers of tui, bellbirds and kaka spotted in neighbouring suburbs.

Admission includes entry to Zealandia's state-of-the-art visitor centre. Spending around an hour touring its interactive exhibits before exploring the sanctuary puts Zealandia's evolution into context. There's also an on-site café serving quality deli-style food.

Otari-Wilton's Bush

160 Wilton Rd, 5km northwest of the city centre • Daily dawn–dusk; visitor centre 9am–4pm • Free • Walk 3km from Zealandia or take the #14 bus from the Lambton Interchange (every 30min)

For a glimpse of the New Zealand bush as it was before humans arrived, head to **Otari-Wilton's Bush**. The remains of the area's original podocarp-northern rata forest were set aside in 1860 by one Job Wilton and form the core of the lush 0.8 square kilometre preserved here.

At the unstaffed visitor centre you'll find a map of the walks, which initially follow a 100m **Canopy Walkway** of sturdy decking high in the trees across a gully. This leads to the **Native Botanic Garden**, laid out with plants from around the country, and the informative **Nature Trail** (30min), a good introduction to the New Zealand forest and its many plants. Assorted trails (all 30min–1hr) wander through the bush, one passing an 800-year-old rimu.

The Miramar Peninsula

Bus #30 serves Scorching Bay daily; Bus #2 goes to the Weta Cave

Around 10km southeast of the city centre, Wellington's airport occupies a narrow isthmus between Evans Bay and Lyall Bay. Making your way there from downtown you'll see a number of sculptures that use the wind to create movement or sound, all part of Wellington embracing its "Windy City" tag. Beyond the airport is the **Miramar Peninsula**, a collection of suburbs and picturesque beaches, including **Scorching Bay**, a crescent of white sand 13km east of the city centre, which has safe swimming and a play area. Miramar is the hub of New Zealand's **film industry** (see box below). You can visit the peninsula as part of a movie tour (see box, p.415).

"WELLYWOOD"

Wellington is the capital of **New Zealand's film industry**, which is increasingly centred on the Miramar Peninsula (see above). During World War II, defence bases were set up here, and the large, long-abandoned buildings were prime for conversion into production company studios. The stunning natural setting has also been used for **film locations** for numerous films including the *Lord of the Rings*, *King Kong*, and the two *Hobbit* films, the first of which is expected to be released in late 2012.

Peter Jackson still lives out this way, and his special effects and entertainment company, Weta, which he co-owns with Richard Taylor, Tania Rodger and Jamie Selkirk, has its base in Miramar. A visit to the workshop's **Weta Cave**, on the corner of Camperdown Road and Weka Street (daily 9am–5.30pm; free; ☏ 04 380 9361, ⓦ wetanz.co.nz), includes an engaging twenty-minute film of behind-the-scenes workshop footage, along with a peek at the small museum, and the chance to buy hand-crafted figurines and limited-edition collectibles at its shop, which also sells movie location guides (from $25). Look for the King Kong footprint in the concrete out front.

Weta partner Jamie Selkirk, along with a number of business partners, had a hand in restoring **The Roxy**, Miramar's Art Deco cinema (see p.440). Some ten different Wellington city tour operators, including those listed on p.415, offer **movie tours** taking in the peninsula's movie-making hotspots.

To learn more about New Zealand's film industry – and to watch New Zealand films on demand for free – stop by the **New Zealand Film Archive** (p.421) in the city centre.

MATIU/SOMES ISLAND

One of Wellington's best day-trips is to **Matiu/Somes Island**, in the northern reaches of the harbour. Legendary navigator Kupe is said to have named it Matiu (meaning "peace") in the tenth century and his descendants lived on the island until deposed by European settlers in the late 1830s. They renamed the island after Joseph Somes, then deputy governor of the New Zealand Company that had "bought" it. For eighty years it was a quarantine station where travellers carrying diseases such as smallpox were held until they recovered or died. During both world wars anyone in New Zealand considered even vaguely suspect – Germans, Italians, Turks, Mexicans and Japanese – was interned on the island until the end of the war, after which it became an animal quarantine station for a number of years.

In the early 1980s its conservation value was recognized, and it is now managed by DOC, which oversees continued efforts to revitalize **native vegetation** and restore the historic buildings. All introduced mammalian predators have now been eradicated and threatened native species are being introduced in an effort to save them from extinction. Already there are six types of lizard, kakariki (the red-crowned parakeet), North Island robins, little blue penguins, the cricket-like weta and the ancient reptilian tuatara. Over fifty of these ancient lizard-like creatures were captive-bred at Wellington's Victoria University and released in 1998. They seem to like it, as numbers are increasing.

ACCESS, INFORMATION AND ACCOMMODATION

Access is on the **Dominion Post Ferry** (3–4 services weekdays, more at weekends; 20min each way; $22 return; ☎04 499 3339, ⓦeastbywest.co.nz) which stops at the island on its cross-harbour journey to Days Bay, enabling you to explore for up to five hours before catching a ferry back to Wellington. Sailings are weather-dependent, so call ahead to confirm departures. From the wharf at the island's northeastern end, a surfaced road runs uphill for 400m to the **DOC field centre** in an old hospital, which has maps of the island, or you can pick one up in advance from the city DOC office (see p.434). A popular option is to take a picnic lunch onto the island. Note that this is a protected reserve and smoking is not allowed. The Museum of Wellington City and Sea (p.422) and Flat Earth (p.415) also run tours here. For information on camping on the island see p.436.

Wellington Harbour

The sight of multicoloured sails scudding across the water should convince you Wellington is at its best when seen from the water. **Wellington Harbour** offers some excellent water-based activities (see box, p.432) that can help you do so, although at the time of writing there were very few sailing opportunities. However, you can hop on the ferry to **Matiu/Somes Island**, isolated in the harbour's northern reaches, for a good look around.

The Hutt Valley

15km northeast of the city centre along SH2

At the northern end of the harbour commuter-land spreads along the Hutt Valley, the largest tract of flat land in these parts, accessible along SH2 and by suburban trains and buses. The original founding of Wellington is remembered in Petone's Settlers Museum, while nearby Lower Hutt has Wellington's closest campsite (see p.436), a great art gallery, and is on the way to the rugged **Rimutaka Forest Park**.

Petone Settler Museum

The Esplanade · Wed–Sun 10am–4pm · Free · ☎ 04 568 8373, ⓦ petonesettlers.org.nz

The suburb of Petone is the site of the first, short-lived European settlement in the Wellington region, and the **Petone Settlers Museum** tells the tale of the early Maori life in the region and the subsequent colonial settlement. The museum is 2.5km east of the Petone train station, so access is easier on buses #81, #83 or the orange Flyer from Courtenay Place and Lambton Quay.

The Dowse Art Museum

45 Laings Rd, 2km west of the Waterloo train station • Mon–Fri 10am–4.30pm, Sat & Sun 10am–5pm; café Mon–Thurs 8am–4.30pm, Fri 8am–7.30pm, Sat 9am–4.30pm, Sun 10am–4.30pm, plus open late first Thurs of each month for live jazz • Free • ☎ 04 570 6500, ⓦ dowse.org.nz • Bus #81, #83 or the orange Flyer from Courtenay Place and Lambton Quay

Some six kilometres north of Petone sprawls **Lower Hutt**, home to **The Dowse Art Museum**, a progressive art museum stunningly redeveloped by Ian Athfield in 2006. It's a well-conceived gallery space filled with travelling shows and occasionally challenging arts and crafts rotated from its permanent collection. While there you'd be wise to visit the on-site licensed café, *Reka*.

Rimutaka Forest Park

Main entrance due south of Lower Hutt and 20km from Wellington along the Coast Rd • 8am–dusk

The **Rimutaka Forest Park** is popular among city-dwellers for its series of easy, short and **day-walks** in the attractive Catchpool Valley; there are also picnic and BBQ facilities, and a well-maintained DOC **campsite** (see p.436). From the signposted main entrance Catchpool Road winds a further 2km up the valley to the car park, the starting point for most of the walks. Keen hikers and campers will want to get as far as the braided Orongorongo River, from where a startlingly grand landscape opens out; camping is free along the riverbanks. There is no convenient bus service, so you'll need to drive or arrange a lift/taxi.

Pick up the *Catchpool Valley/Rimutaka Forest Park* leaflet from DOC in Wellington.

ARRIVAL AND DEPARTURE

WELLINGTON

By plane Wellington International Airport (ⓦ wlg -airport.co.nz), about 10km southeast of the city centre, is an important domestic hub, linking around twenty airports across New Zealand and handling international flights from Australia. Flying avoids the potentially choppy ferry crossing (see below), but you miss cruising through Marlborough Sound. Soundsair (☎ 0800 505 005, ⓦ soundsair.co.nz) flies from Wellington to Picton and Blenheim ($90–100 one-way) and Nelson ($107–117). Air 2 There (☎ 04 904 5130, ⓦ air2there.com) flies between Wellington and Blenheim ($99 one-way).

Destinations Auckland (20–25 daily; 1hr); Blenheim (8–13 daily; 25min); Christchurch (15 daily; 45min); Dunedin (2–4 daily; 1hr 15min); Gisborne (3–4 daily; 1hr); Greymouth (5 weekly; 1hr); Hamilton (7 daily; 1hr); Kaikoura (1–2 daily in summer; 1hr); Napier/Hastings (5 daily; 50min); Nelson (6–10 daily; 35min); New Plymouth (4 daily; 50min); Palmerston North (3 daily; 30min); Picton (6–8 daily; 25min); Rotorua (3 daily; 1hr); Takaka (1 daily; 30min); Taupo (3 daily; 1hr); Tauranga (4 daily; 1hr 10min); Timaru (4 daily; 1hr 10min); Wanganui (4 weekly; 25min); Westport (1 daily Mon–Fri; 55min); Whangarei (1 daily; 1hr 30min).

Getting to/from town Green Cabs (☎ 0508 447 336) use hybrids; Wellington Combined Taxis (☎ 04 384 4444) are

carbon zero-certified; both will cost about $35. The Airport Flyer bus (daily 6.30am–7.45pm; Mon–Fri every 15min, Sat & Sun every 30min) costs $8.50 for the 15min journey to the city centre. Super Shuttle (☎ 0800 748 885 or ☎ 09 522 5100, ⓦ supershuttle.co.nz) charges $15–20 for the first person to a particular destination in the city centre, plus $5 for each extra person travelling to the same place.

By ferry The Interislander terminal (☎ 0800 802 802, ⓦ interislander.co.nz) is 1km north of the train station; the Bluebridge terminal (☎ 0800 844 844, ⓦ bluebridge.co.nz) is opposite the train station. Both companies offer year-round services across the Cook Strait to Picton (6–9 daily; 3hr). The crossing can be choppy, but does afford the chance to see the Marlborough Sounds. Both companies have different fare categories with varying flexibility – check the cancellation policy prior to booking. Interislander fares are around $65–75 one-way for a single passenger, $208–318 for a car and driver, and $15 for bikes. Inter-islander's *Kaitaki* ferry offers the refundable Kaitaki Plus ($45 extra, over-18s only), which includes private lounge and complimentary snacks, drinks, newspapers and internet. Get to the Interislander terminal on either a shuttle bus ($2), which departs from the train station (by Platform 9) 50min before each sailing, or with the backpacker bus ($3) which serves the base and YHA hostels

7

WELLINGTON TOURS AND ACTIVITIES

Wellington harbour's brisk winds make it ideal for **windsurfing** and **kiteboarding** (most of the action centres on Kio and Evans bays), while kayaking and diving are also popular.

On a fine day there's little to beat **cycling** around the coastal roads that follow the bays east of the city. Start by heading east along Oriental Parade and follow the coast as far as you want; even right past the airport and around the northern tip of the Miramar Peninsula to Scorching Bay (see p.429) and Seatoun (25–30km one-way). There is also stacks of **off-road riding**, much of it outlined in the *Mountain Biking in Wellington City* leaflet (available free from the i-SITE), which contains maps of key areas a short ride from the city. Highlights include the coastal track out to Red Rocks (see box, p.428) and the single-track trails around Mount Victoria (see p.421).

Other dry-land pursuits include quad biking, in-line skating and climbing. Ferg's Kayaks (see below) rents **in-line skates** ($15/2hr; $30/3hr), perfect for use in nearby Frank Kitts Park or around Oriental Parade. Ferg's also offers an excellent and very popular **indoor climbing** wall ($15; harness and shoes $4 each).

For information on walks in **Wellington**, see box, p.428.

WATERSPORTS

Wildwinds 36 Customhouse Quay ☎ 04 473 3458, ⓦ wildwinds.co.nz. Offers a two-hour taster windsurf lesson ($110) or a series of two three-hour sessions ($295). Alternatively, opt for two three-hour kiteboard lessons ($195/lesson) or try your hand at stand-up paddleboarding.

Ferg's Kayaks Shed 6 Queens Wharf ☎ 04 499 8898, ⓦ fergskayaks.co.nz. Rents single ($20/2hr) and double ($35/2hr) sit-on-tops, plus single ($25/2hr) and double ($50/2hr) sea kayaks. They also run some fun guided trips, the best being the Lights at Night, a city-illuminated paddle round the bay with great views,

lots of photograph opportunities and a light supper (Tues 6–9pm weather permitting; four or more $85 each; $105 each for 2; book in advance).

Splash Gordon 432 The Esplanade, Island Bay ☎ 04 939 3483, ⓦ splashgordon.co.nz; map pp.426–427. Offers scuba-diving charters on the frigate *Wellington*, scuttled a 5min boat ride off the coast in 21m of water in 2005. Experienced divers can do two dives with all gear ($120); there are also options for people only qualified to 18m, and they run courses for all levels including beginners.

CYCLING AND QUAD BIKING

Makara Peak Mountain Bike Park 116–122 South Karori Rd, about 8km west of the city centre ⓦ makarapeak.org. map p.414. Committed mountain bikers should head to this two-square-kilometre area of forest and farmland centred on the 412m Makara Peak, up behind Karori. There's no entry fee and you'll have the run of some 40km of tracks suitable for all abilities.

Mud Cycles 421 Karori Rd, 2km short of the Makara Peak Mountain Bike Park ☎ 04 476 4961, ⓦ mudcycles.co.nz. Rents hard tail ($30/half-day; $45/day) and full suspension mountain bikes ($45/half-day; $60/day). You can also rent for the weekend or anywhere from three days to a full week. Helmet and trail maps are included. There's also an outlet at *Base*

Wellington (see p.434).

Wellington Adventures 1960 Coast Rd, Wainuiomata ☎ 0800 948 6386, ⓦ wellington adventures.co.nz; map p.414. If you have the urge to push the limit and rack up the kilometres with a few jaw-dropping views along the way, this is the outfit for you. They run one of the best-value and most enjoyable quad bike trips in the country and the views from the farm where it all kicks off are spectacular. After that it keeps getting better as you head through a mixture of coastal scrub, farmland, forest, riverbed and beach on a half- or full-day experience (half-day $219; full day $319). Technically, the trip is reasonably challenging which adds to the awe and wow factor.

(book through the hostels). Bluebridge fares are generally $56–73 one-way for a single passenger, $169–245 for a car (up to 5.5m) and driver, and $10 for bikes. Car rental companies that permit their vehicles on the ferries include Ace, Apex, Maui and Jucy (see p.33 & p.34).

By train and bus The main train station is on Bunny St; the Auckland–Wellington Overlander train (see p.31) runs

once daily Dec–April and Fri, Sat & Sun during the rest of the year. Newmans and InterCity buses terminate nearby, alongside Platform 9.

Train destinations Auckland (1 daily; 12hr); Hutt Central/ Waterloo (every 30min; 20 min); Masterton (2–5 daily; 1hr 30min); National Park (1 daily; 5hr 30min); Otaki (2 daily; 1hr 10min); Otorohanga (1 daily; 8hr 45min); Paekakariki (every 30min; 50min); Palmerston North (2 daily; 2hr–2hr 20min); Paraparaumu (every 30min; 1hr).

Bus destinations Auckland (3–4 daily; 11hr); Masterton via the Hutt Valley (1–2 daily; 2hr); Napier (3–4 daily; 5hr 15min); New Plymouth (3–4 daily; 6hr 30min); Palmerston North (5–7 daily; 2hr); Paraparaumu (10 daily; 50min); Rotorua (5–7 daily; 7hr); Taupo (5–7 daily; 6hr).

By car From the north, SH1 through Porirua and SH2 (part of the grape-signed Classic New Zealand Wine Trail) via Lower Hutt both turn into short urban motorways that merge, running scenically along the harbourside to the city centre. For details of parking, see below. Coming from or heading to the South Island, see p.431 for details of crossing Cook Strait.

GETTING AROUND

By bus Wellington's extensive network of buses and trolley buses operates from Lambton Interchange, just west of the train station.

Bus tickets and passes All tickets and day-passes can be bought direct from the bus driver. One-way fares are $2 within the inner city, beyond which a zone system comes into operation: each extra zone costs an extra $1.50. The After Midnight service (Sat & Sun hourly 1–3am), designed to get the party crowd home safely, is centred on Courtenay Place and costs $6–12. If you intend to use the transport system extensively it's worth getting a Stored Value Card on the first bus you board – it covers all central city bus travel for the day and knocks about $0.50 off each journey.

By train Tranz Metro (☏04 498 3000, ⒲tranzmetro .co.nz) run suburban train services from the station on Bunny St. Trains to the Hutt Valley (see p.430) and the Kapiti Coast (see p.255) leave the train station roughly every half-hour for Waterloo (for Lower Hutt; 20min; $9.50); Porirua (20min; $6); Plimmerton (30min; $7.50); and Paraparaumu (1hr; $11). The Johnsonville line ($4.50) provides handy access for hiking the Northern Walkway (see p.428). It's around thirty percent cheaper if you travel outside peak hours (so not before 9am or from 4–7pm).

Train tickets and passes A one-day Rover ticket ($13) gives you the run of the train network after 9am weekdays and all weekend; up to four people travelling together can save with a group Rover ticket ($35). A three-day weekend Rover ($20) is valid from 4.30am Fri–midnight Sun. Bicycles are free. Tickets can be bought at the Tranz Rail Travel Centre at the main train station or on the train.

By car Making your way around the inner city is simple enough once you get used to the extensive one-way system.

Parking There is no free weekday parking in the city centre, but parking is free for up to 2hr at a time on Sat and all day Sun. Car parks are plentiful, council ones charging around $4/hr during weekdays (generally cheaper at night and on weekends), often with a one-day maximum of $15, assuming you park before 9.30am. The car park by the Te Papa museum is suitable for campervans, and there are several others nearby. If you don't want to bother with moving the vehicle all the time, some places charge $20–25 for a full 24hr.

Parking meters and coupon parking Most inner-city streets have parking meters (usually Mon–Thurs 8am–6pm & Fri 8am–8pm $4/hr; otherwise free) that limit you to a 2hr stay during the metered hours. Slightly further out you get coupon parking (Mon–Fri 8am–4pm) where the first 2hr are free, but to stay longer you have to display a coupon ($7.50 for all day), available from dairies and petrol stations. These areas are also free outside the set hours.

Car rental As well as the companies covered in Basics (see p.33), various local firms offer good deals: Nationwide, 37 Hutt Rd, Thorndon ☏04 473 1165 003, ⒲nationwide rentals.co.nz; Rent-a-Dent, 24 Tacy St, Kilbirnie ☏0800 736 823, ⒲rentadent.co.nz; and Ace Rental Cars, 126 Hutt Rd, ☏0800 535 500, ⒲acerentalcars.co.nz.

By taxi You can hail one almost anywhere in town but there are authorized stands at: the train station; on Whitmore St between Lambton Quay and Featherston St; outside the *James Smith Hotel* on Lambton Quay; off Willis St on the Bond St corner; at the corner of Courtenay Place and Taranaki St; and at the junction of Willis & Aro sts. Try Green Cabs (☏0508 447 336) or Wellington Combined Taxis (☏04 384 4444).

By bike Penny Farthing Cycles, 65 Dixon St (☏04 385 2279, ⒲pennyfarthing.co.nz), rents road bikes for $50/ day. For information on mountain bike rental and Makara Peak Mountain Bike Park, see box opposite.

WELLINGTON TRANSPORT INFORMATION AND PASSES

The useful **Metlink Explorer** ($20) gives one day of unlimited bus and train travel throughout the Wellington region from 9am on weekdays and all day at weekends. You can buy the pass from bus drivers, train staff and from Tranz Metro ticket offices.

For region-wide **train and bus information**, pick up the free *Metlink Network Map* or any of the individual timetables at the visitor centre or train station, or call Metlink (☏0800 801 700, ⒲metlink.org.nz).

INFORMATION

i-SITE Corner of Wakefiled and Victoria sts (daily 8.30am–5.30pm, public holidays 11am–4pm; ☏ 0800 933 536, ⓦ wellington.nz.com). Has all the usual leaflets and maps, plus the handy and free *Wellington: Official Visitor Guide* booklet. The office shares a glass-fronted section of the Civic Centre with a café and internet terminals ($8/hr).

DOC 18 Manners St (Mon–Fri 9am–5pm, Sat 10am–3pm; ☏ 04 384 7770). Has stacks of information on walks in the Wellington region and also sells hut tickets and issues permits for Kapiti Island (both also available online).

Hutt Valley i-SITE 25 Laings Rd (Mon–Fri 9am–5pm, Sat & Sun 9am–3pm; ☏ 04 560 4715, ⓦ huttvalleynz.com).

ACCOMMODATION

Wellington has plenty of accommodation in the city centre, including some excellent **backpacker hostels**. B&Bs are becoming less common, but there's an increasing number of stylish self-catering serviced **apartments**. Breakfasting (or brunching) out is a quintessential Wellington experience, so you might not want a place where breakfast is included. Central **motels** are in short supply, but many business-oriented **hotels** offer good-value deals, especially at weekends. For a little peace and quiet, you might want to stay outside the city centre (see p.258), and drive or take public transport into town. Contact the i-SITE for information on **campervan sites** in central Wellington.

Apollo Lodge Motel & Majoribanks Apartments 49 Majoribanks St ☏ 0800 361 645, ⓦ apollolodge.co.nz; map pp.416–417. Appealing medium-sized renovated motel with modern rooms (some decorated in Edwardian style, others architecturally designed) 200m from Courtenay Place with off-street parking. Its adjacent apartments are well set up for longer stays; call ahead for prices. Motel $140

Austinvilla B&B 11 Austin St, Mount Victoria ☏ 04 385 8334, ⓦ austinvilla.co.nz; map pp.416–417. Two lovely and very private self-contained apartments (one a studio, the other with a separate bedroom and a small garden), both with bathtubs, continental breakfast and off-street parking, in an elegant villa with leafy surrounds a 10min walk from Courtenay Place. Not suitable for young children. Studio $205, one-bedroom $245

Base Wellington 21–23 Cambridge Terrace ☏ 0800 227 369, ⓦ stayatbase.com; map pp.416–417. Slick, well-organized 280-bed hostel converted from an office building. Facilities include cheap internet, lockable cupboards, bike rental and *Basement* bar with theme nights. The women-only "Sanctuary" floor ($3/night extra) includes towels and shampoo. Dorms $29, en suite $99

★ **Booklovers B&B** 123 Pirie St, Mount Victoria ☏ 04 384 2714, ⓦ booklovers.co.nz; map pp.416–417. For charm and comfort you can't do better than this three-bedroom literary B&B in an unfussy Victorian villa a 10min walk from Courtenay Place and Mount Victoria Park. There are books in every room and a full cooked breakfast is served any time within reason. $275

Cambridge Hotel 28 Cambridge Terrace ☏ 0800 375 021, ⓦ cambridgehotel.co.nz; map pp.416–417. Renovated 1930s hotel that operates partly as a backpackers and partly as accommodation for long-stay residents and workers. There's a popular, inexpensive bar and restaurant, the four- to eight-bed dorms are spacious and the hotel rooms, while smallish, are good value. Dorms $29, en suites $105

Downtown Backpackers 1 Bunny St ☏ 04 473 8482, ⓦ downtownbackpackers.co.nz; map pp.416–417. Large hostel in the Art Deco *Waterloo Hotel*, convenient for train, bus and ferry arrivals. Dorms and rooms (some en-suite) are adequate, though there's a bar with cheap beer and a café in this once-grand hotel's former ballroom. Dorms $29, rooms $82, en suites $95

Halswell Lodge 21 Kent Terrace ☏ 04 385 0196, ⓦ halswell.co.nz; map pp.416–417. Comfortable, central and welcoming establishment with simple but good-value hotel rooms, relatively pricey motel units and lovely deluxe rooms (some with spa) in a lodge set back from the street. Free off-street parking. Rooms $100, motel units $145, lodge $165

Koromiko Homestay 11 Koromiko Rd, Highbury ☏ 04 938 6539, ⓦ koromikohomestay.co.nz; map pp.426–427. This homestay for "gay men and their friends" is on a quiet street overlooking the Botanical Gardens and harbour, with two doubles and one single that share a bathroom. There's an outdoor "garden bath" with views of the city, and meals ($25 including wine) are available on request. Single $80, doubles $135

The Mermaid 1 Epuni St at Aro St ☏ 04 384 4511, ⓦ mermaid.co.nz; map pp.416–417. A luxurious women-only guesthouse, set in a restored century-old home where the owner also has a perfume and soap workshop. The four opulently furnished rooms (one with private bathroom) all come with a view of the garden or hills. Everyone has full use of the kitchen. Rooms $100, en suite $150

Museum Hotel 90 Cable St ☏ 0800 994 335, ⓦ museumhotel.co.nz; map pp.416–417. Big, black business hotel with an intimate feel and contemporary New Zealand art on show, locally famous for having been trundled across the street from the Te Papa construction site on rail tracks, hence its nickname, the Museum Hotel de Wheels. Rates are reasonable for the high standards. Rooms $225, harbour view $260

Nomads Capital 118 Wakefield St ☏ 0508 666 237, ⓦ nomadscapital.com; map pp.416–417. Comfy 180-bed

THE PARLIAMENTARY DISTRICT, WELLINGTON (P.423) >

hostel (with vertigo-inducing top bunks) in the city centre with a backpacker bar/café *Blend* attached. Women-only dorms come at no extra charge and there are plush "elite" en-suite doubles. Dorms $29, standard doubles $95, elite doubles $105

★ **Ohotel** 66 Oriental Parade ☎ 04 803 0600, ☯ ohtel .com; map pp.416–417. Chic, sophisticated boutique hotel opposite Waitangi Park at the city end of Oriental Parade, with on-site parking. Each of its ten rooms has decadent bathrooms (two with two-person baths), hi-tech entertainment systems and hand-picked 1950s, 60s and 70s vintage furniture and designer furnishings. $265

Trinity Hotel 166 Willis St ☎ 04 801 8118, ☯ trinity hotel.co.nz; map pp.416–417. A comfortable and well-run budget hotel with sixty rooms, all with phone, Sky TV, tea and coffee. There's an on-site restaurant-bar, plus parking ($15; book ahead). Weekend deals ($120) include a bottle of bubbly, cooked breakfast and late checkout. $109

Wellywood Backpackers 58 Tory St ☎ 0508 005 858, ☯ wellywoodbackpackers.co.nz; map pp.416–417. A zebra-striped building houses this welcoming hostel, which doesn't have its own bar but is just a stone's throw from many. One floor is devoted to common areas (internet and TV lounges, a pool table and an island kitchen), and staff can book you on movie and boat tours. Dorms $28, rooms $72, en suite $82, family room sleeping up to five $145

★ **YHA Wellington City** 292 Wakefield St ☎ 04 801 7280, ☯ yha.co.nz; map pp.416–417. This 320-bedder is one of the best urban hostels in the country, right in the heart of the city with great harbour views from some of the upper-floor rooms. It has spacious common areas including a foosball table and projector-screen TV room, a well-equipped kitchen, bike storage, an info and travel desk and social events such as regular meal nights ($7–10). Many of the doubles, twin, four- and six-share dorms have en suites. Dorms $31, rooms $95, en suite $135

CAMPSITES

Catchpool Valley Rimutaka Forest Park, 30km northeast of Wellington; map p.414. Pleasant drive-in DOC campsite beside the Catchpool stream with hot showers, toilets, water supply and barbecues. The 150 sites are scattered across a green expanse and among tall trees. $10

★ **Matiu/Somes Island** Twelve-person DOC campsite on the Matiu/Somes Island wildlife reserve (see p.414) in the middle of Wellington Harbour with great city views. There are flush toilets, tap water and a camp kitchen with gas stoves, but you need to bring everything else. Book in advance through DOC or contact the Wellington i-SITE for more information/help. $10

Top 10 Hutt Park Holiday Park 95 Hutt Park Rd, Lower Hutt ☎ 0800 488 872, ☯ huttpark.co.nz; map p.414. The capital's closest campsite, 12km north of Wellington on the harbour's northeastern shore. It's near beaches, shops and bushwalks and can be accessed by buses #81 and #83 from Courtenay Place and Lambton Interchange. Camping $32, cabins $63, self-contained units $121, motel units $131

EATING

Wellington has more places to eat per capita than New York and the standard is impressively high, whatever the budget. There's little need to venture much beyond the bounds of the city centre, though a couple of reasons to stray are listed below. As the country's self-professed **coffee** capital (Wellington has no fewer than ten independent roasteries), you'll find the good stuff served up everywhere from cosy spots through to the *très chic*. Gastronomes might want to join a gourmet tour (see box, p.415). If you want to head further off the beaten track, local neighbourhoods worth scouting out include Newtown and the Aro Valley. In the streets around **Courtenay Place** and **Cuba Street** there's a plethora of local and international restaurants – from cheap curry joints and bohemian cafés through to award-winning establishments headed up by some of the finest chefs in the country. During the day many restaurants offer bargain lunch specials. Many pubs and bars (p.439) also serve impressive and generally inexpensive fare. For **groceries** try the three central New World supermarkets: at 68 Willis St; inside the railway station; and the largest, at the eastern end of Wakefield Street. If you're here on a Sunday morning, head down to the car park near Te Papa to the **fruit and vegetable market** and the nearby **farmers' market** in the Chaffers Dock Atrium, with stalls of artisan goods from local producers.

CENTRAL WELLINGTON

Aro Coffee 90 Aro St ☎ 04 384 4970; map pp.416–417. The pick of a village-like cluster of cafés in weatherboard buildings in the Aro Valley, serving its own hand-blended coffee roasted on the premises, along with a short, smart menu of daytime fare such as bubble and squeak with poached eggs and bacon, and home-made pork sausages with white-bean salad (all under $20). Mon–Fri 7.30am–4pm, Sat & Sun 9am–5pm.

★ **Beach Babylon** Ground floor, 232 Oriental Parade ☎ 04 801 7717; map pp.416–417. Ingeniously done out like a retro *bach*, serving everything from casual brunches through to stylish dinners that also incorporate a retro twist: chicken supreme ($26), lamb on coconut rice with harissa couscous ($29), fondue for two ($13) and banana splits ($11) for dessert. Good cocktails, too. Licensed and BYO. Daily 10am–late.

Fidel's 234 Cuba St ☎ 04 801 6868, ☯ fidelscafe.com; map pp.416–417. At the offbeat southern end of Cuba St, this eternally funky, always-busy café is plastered with revolution-era pictures of Castro, and extends into the former barber's next door (in the spirit of Castro they've kept the old Super Cuts sign) and camouflage-netted courtyard. Come for locally roasted Havana coffee, vegan muffins, booze, smoothies, stunning cakes or excellent-value meals (mains $10–26). Mon–Fri 7.30am–late, Sat & Sun 9am–late.

Floriditas 161 Cuba St ☎04 381 2212; map pp.416–417. This light, airy and stylish café is always busy. Wonderful breakfasts range from $15–17.50 and its limited but clever menu includes lunches such as groper and fennel chowder ($13), dinners of char-grilled Angus sirloin ($36) or the house speciality amaretto afogatto ($14.50). Mon–Fri 6.30am–11pm, Sat 7am–11pm, Sun 7.30am–10pm.

Kreuzberg Summer Café 50 Webb St, at Cuba St ☎021 119 6257, ⍟kreuzbergsummercafe.co.nz; map pp.416–417. Black-painted caravan selling Wellington-brewed People's Coffee and snacks such as haloumi or tofu burgers and smoked chicken toasted sandwiches (all under $11) to take away or eat at the striped tables in the former car-yard-turned-urban-garden. Often has live music on summer nights. Licensed. Daily 10am until at least 4pm.

★ **Le Metropolitan** 146 Cuba St ☎04 801 8007, ⍟lemetropolitain.co.nz; map pp.416–417. Of the plethora of French-influenced bistro/restaurant/cafés springing up in town, this is one of the more authentic, right down to the Gallic service. The food is of great quality – think steak frites ($28), escargots ($13), crème brûlée ($13) – and the price is right. Booking is essential. Tues–Sun: brunch Sat & Sun 10am–2.30pm; lunch Tues–Fri noon–2.30pm; dinner 5.30–10pm.

Logan-Brown 192 Cuba St ☎04 801 5114; map pp.416–417. Though no longer the domain of Al Brown (Steve Logan and Brown were Kiwi TV chefs), this Wellington icon of fine dining has hung on to its reputation as one of the best places to spend large wedges of cash in the pursuit of a culinary thrill. Book as far ahead as possible to dine in this colonnaded 1920s former bank. Mains include Hawke Bay lamb rack with pea gnocchi ($48), accompanied by a bottle of 2009 Central Otago Pinot Noir that at $86 provides more of a shock than a thrill. Tues–Sat from 11.30am for lunch; daily for dinner from 6.30pm.

MariLuca 55–57 Mulgrave St ☎04 499 5590, ⍟mariluca.co.nz; map pp.416–417. High-quality, well-priced Italian food with Grandpa's Sicilian maxims writ large on the cream walls: "meat makes meat, bread makes belly, wine makes dance". The menu varies seasonally, almost everything is cooked from scratch using mostly organic ingredients and the wine list extends beyond the horizon with choice. Stop in while touring the Parliamentary District. Lunch Tues–Fri 11am–2pm; dinner Mon–Sat 5.30–11pm.

★ **Martin Bosley's** First floor, 103 Oriental Parade ☎04 920 8302, ⍟martin-bosley.com; map pp.416–

417. Esteemed namesake venue of one of New Zealand's most celebrated chefs serving artistically conceived and presented seafood that complements the views from the upper floor of Port Nicholson Yacht Club. Dinner mains average $50 while the *dégustation* menus ($150) have the option of matched wines ($220). Lunch Mon–Fri & Sun; dinner Tues–Sun.

Masala 2 Allen St ☎04 385 2012; map pp.416–417. Sleek banquettes along with an ambient soundtrack offer a stylish, retro-contemporary alternative to most of Wellington's Indian restaurants. Curries (lunch mains under $13, dinner mains under $20), from the classic to the innovative, are cooked to perfection. Licensed & BYO. Daily 11am–late.

★ **Matterhorn** 106 Cuba St ☎04 384 3359, ⍟matterhorn.co.nz; map pp.416–417. At the end of a long timber-lined corridor in a 1960s coffee house, this establishment is a successful merger of glam bar (see p.439) and fancy restaurant. The beautifully done food (evening mains $29–36) includes twice-baked gorgonzola soufflé, and caramelized slow-cooked pork belly; the Sunday-night roast has cult status. Mon–Fri 3pm–late, Sat & Sun 10am–late.

★ **Midnight Espresso** 178 Cuba St ☎04 384 7014; map pp.416–417. Looking like a bohemian artists' squat, with posters and flyers pinned to the community notice board, artwork and murals covering the walls and a pinball machine and space invaders, this caffeine junkie's heaven serves Havana coffee along with lovely breakfasts, counter food and tasty hot dishes (many veggie or vegan), all under $18. Mon–Fri 7am–3am, Sat & Sun 8am–3am.

Mojo 37 Customhouse Quay ☎04 385 3001, ⍟mojo coffee.co.nz; map pp.416–417. Most days you can watch master roaster Lambros Gianoutsos hand-blending and roasting at the HQ of one Wellington's most successful coffee roasteries. Beans are sold at the shop while the building directly opposite houses *Mojo's* flagship café. Café Mon–Thurs 7am–5pm, Fri 7am–6pm, Sat & Sun 9am–4pm; shop Mon–Fri 8am–4pm.

Moore Wilson's Corner of Tory and College sts; map pp.416–417. Tucked under a parking station opposite the historic Thompson Lewis spring, this superb deli, charcuterie and bakery is the place to come for top-quality picnic supplies, including its own aged cheese. Fill your water bottle from the spring water fountain. Mon–Sat 7.30am–7pm, Sun 9am–5pm.

★ **Nikau Gallery Café** City Gallery Wellington, Civic Square ☎04 801 4168, ⍟nikaucafe.co.nz; map pp.416–417. A stylish, contemporary daytime café with an airy setting and outdoor terrace, plus excellent coffee and a high-quality yet reasonably priced menu: try the kedgeree with house-smoked fish ($22) or one of the lip-smacking desserts such as tangelo jelly, spice figs and orange blossom honey custard ($12). Mon–Fri 7am–4pm, Sat 8am–4pm.

★ **Olive** 170 Cuba St ☎04 802 5266; map pp.416–417. Elegant but relaxed bare-boards, licensed café that sticks mainly to organic produce and is popular with the natives. Great for coffee and cake throughout the day, as well as for delicious breakfasts such as organic porridge, lunches such as pan-fried haloumi and evening meals (mains $23–27) – try the daily changing risotto. BYO Monday. Mon–Fri 8am–9.30pm, Sat 9am–9.30pm, Sun 9am–4.30pm.

Oriental Kingdom Left Bank ☎04 381 3303; map pp.416–417. A simple café beloved by young in-the-know Wellingtonians – so much so that it recently doubled in size to accommodate them. All of its pan-Asian fare is fresh, cheap (mains $9–11) and filling, particularly the laksas and roti. Licensed & BYO. Daily 11am–10pm.

Ortega 16 Marjoribanks St ☎04 382 9559, ⓦortega .co.nz; map pp.416–417. Only steps from Courtenay Place but with the feel of a classy neighbourhood bistro, *Ortega* concentrates on superb seafood served with relaxed panache. Book for dinner (mains around $32) or just drop in for an oloroso sherry at the bar. Tues–Sat 5.30pm–late.

Plum 103 Cuba St ☎04 384 8881, ⓦplumcafe.co.nz; map pp.416–417. Elongated dark-timber, licensed café perfect for cocooning over the paper and a post-hangover "Plumster" breakfast of eggs, sausages, bacon, slow-roasted tomatoes, grilled field mushrooms and more ($19.50), or a veggie Plumster ($15.50). Open Mon–Fri 8am–9pm, Sat & Sun 9am–9pm.

Sweet Mother's Kitchen 5 Courtenay Place ☎04 385 4444, ⓦsweetmotherskitchen.co.nz; map pp.416–417. Breakfast on beignets ($4), tuck into a Po' Boy New Orleans-style baguette ($9), warm up with a bowl of gumbo ($14) or hickory-smoked baby back ribs ($26.50) and finish with a pecan and bourbon pie ($8). Licensed. Daily 8am–late.

Trisha's Pies 32 Cambridge Terrace ☎04 801 5506; map pp.416–417. A traditional Kiwi pie shop and a Wellington institution, serving a vast array of wonderful home-made pies among Wellington's sea of sophisticated dining, and a welcome change it makes. Particular favourites are the steak and cheese, peppered steak, steak and mushroom and veggie, all under $6. Mon–Fri 8.30am–3.30pm, Sat 9am–2pm.

Wellington Trawling Sea Market 220 Cuba St ☎04 384 8461; map pp.416–417. The best fish and chip shop in the city (eat in or take away) also sells wet fish. The fish is cooked to order, and you can complement it with Paua fritters or oysters. Nothing will cost more than $10. Daily 7am–8.30pm.

★ **The White House** First floor, 232 Oriental Parade ☎04 385 8555, ⓦwhr.co.nz; map pp.416–417. Harbour panoramas and exquisite food make *The White House* one of Wellington's best restaurants. The menu offers yellow-fin tuna tartare ($32), cured duck breast, confit of duck leg and orange kumara purée ($50) and vanilla bean panna cotta with raspberries ($19). The *dégustation* menu ($140) is accompanied by paired wines (extra $85). Arrive for an early dinner at 6pm and get the bistro menu at $30 for two courses. BYO wine Sun evenings. Wed–Sun from 11.30am.

THE SUBURBS

Chocolate Fish Café 100 Shelly Bay Rd, opposite Westside Studio, Shelly Bay ⓦchocolatefishcafe.co.nz; map pp.426–427. In its previous Scorching Bay location, the *Chocolate Fish* was famously the *Lord of the Rings* cast and crew hangout. Now at the former Shelly Bay air force base, it has transformed into a fish barbecue with alfresco and indoor seating, seafood, meat and vegetarian sandwiches hot off the grill ($10–14), and delicious home-made muffins, slices and biscuits. They're not licensed, but if you BYO and sit outside, as lots of the locals do, nobody will give you a hard time. Daily 9.30am–late.

★ **Maranui Surf Club Café** Maranui Surf Life Saving Club, The Parade, Lyall Bay ☎04 387 4539, ⓦmaranui cafe.co.nz; map pp.426–427. Situated on the top floor, with a balcony overlooking the beach, sea and approaches to Wellington Airport, this licensed café is an established locals' favourite, with colourful retro beachside decor, generous breakfasts, great coffee and chocolate almond cakes (all under $20). There are few better places to sit and watch the planes go by, particularly at weekends. Daily 7am–5pm.

DRINKING AND NIGHTLIFE

Most **pubs** and **bars** are open daily, from around eleven in the morning until midnight or later. The distinction between bars and **clubs** is often blurred, with many bars hosting free live music and dancing in the evenings, especially at weekends. Resident and guest DJs mix broad-ranging styles to create a party- or club-style atmosphere. Cuba St is home to some of New Zealand's best **nightlife**, with a huge array of late-night cafés, bars and clubs within walking distance of each other.

ESSENTIALS

Gay and lesbian Wellington The scene in Wellington is focused in the inner city, but for the most part it's woven seamlessly into the general café/bar mainstream. In the centre, at least, gay people openly express affection in public, and gays, lesbians, transgender and bi-folk mix

freely together. For the latest information, check out ⓦgaynz.com, or pick up the free, fortnightly *Express* (ⓦgayexpress.co.nz) and *OUT!* (ⓦout.co.nz) magazines. Wellington's big gay event is the annual Pride Week (usually late Sept), with dances, parties, films and art.

★ **Alice** Forresters Lane, off Tory St; map pp.416–417.

At the far end of the same laneway as *Motel* (see below), a neon-lit rabbit disappearing down a hole leads you into this Lewis Carroll-inspired fantasyland where cocktails such as the Mad Hatter's Tea Party (vanilla vodka and iced peppermint tea) are served in teapots and china cups. An internal door connects *Alice* with *Boogie Wonderland* (see below). Wed–Fri 6pm–late, Sat 7pm–5am.

The Backbencher Pub 34 Molesworth St, at Kate Sheppard St ☎ 04 472 3065, ⌨ backbencher.co.nz; map pp.416–417. A favourite with MPs and civil servants for the satirical cartoons and outsized latex puppets of notable local politicians and sportsmen from the 1970s and 80s, and the convivial pub ambience. Try one of the dozen or more draught beers and hearty meals named after current MPs. Daily 11am–11pm.

Foxtail and Foxglove 33 Queens Wharf ☎ 04 460 9410, ⌨ foxtailbar.co.nz; map pp.416–417. *Foxglove* is a popular locals' bar serving decent food with harbour views. What makes it different is the wardrobe on the first floor – when you walk through you enter a cosy little cocktail bar with DJs (though sadly no lion or witch). Tues–Sat 4pm–late.

Kiwi Pub 26 Allen St ☎ 04 385 6908; map pp.416–417. A former English pub that's been stripped out and refitted with Kiwiana, including board games, toys and mismatched furniture. The vibe is laidback and there's a good choice of New Zealand beers on tap. Mon–Sat 11am–late, Sunday 4pm–late.

Leuven 135–137 Featherston St ☎ 04 499 2939, ⌨ leuven.co.nz; map pp.416–417. Belgian-style beer café in the heart of the business district, good for breakfasts of Belgian porridge and fruit ($12) and meals such as its signature 1kg pot of mussels – but especially popular for early-evening tie-loosening sessions over a few Hoegaarden. Mon–Fri 7am–9pm, Sat & Sun 9am–9pm.

★ **The Library** Level 1, 53 Courtenay Place ☎ 04 382 8593, ⌨ thelibrary.co.nz; map pp.416–417. Ultra-cool book-lined cocktail bar with separate rooms (including one that looks like your granny's lounge with a bath in it) and a cornucopia of nooks and crannies where you can sip on excellent drinks and listen to the live music or occasional DJ. Mon–Fri 5pm–late, Sat & Sun 2pm–late.

Mac's Brewbar 4 Taranaki St ☎ 04 381 2282, ⌨ macs brewbar.co.nz; map pp.416–417. Central Wellington's only working brewery, in an 1800s waterfront warehouse, serves classy pub fare along with its excellent brews including Great White (wheat beer), Macs Gold (all-malt lager), Sassy Red (English-style bitter), Black Mac (dark lager), and the knockout Hop Rocker (Pilsner); if you can't decide, order a six-beer tasting tray ($18). Daily 11am–late.

★ **The Malthouse** 48 Courtenay Place ☎ 04 802 5484, ⌨ themalthouse.co.nz; map pp.416–417. In a lounge setting with low sofas, high stools and sleek glossy timber tables, this beer drinker's paradise has thirty different brews

on tap – including some of New Zealand's finest craft brews, such as the Invercargill Brewing Company's Pitch Black – plus some 150 varieties by the bottle. There are detailed tasting notes on each by top Kiwi beer commentator Neil Miller. Sun–Thurs 3pm–late, Fri & Sat noon–3am.

Matterhorn 106 Cuba St ☎ 04 384 3359, ⌨ matterhorn .co.nz; map pp.416–417. Uber-stylish cocktail bar and restaurant (see p.437) with regular live and electronic music. Try the basil and manuka honey Martini at the long bar. Mon–Fri 3pm–late, Sat & Sun 10am–late.

★ **Mighty Mighty** First floor, 104 Cuba St ☎ 04 385 2890, ⌨ mightymighty.co.nz; map pp.416–417. Cool, off-beam late-night bar that more often than not hosts bands of just about any stripe, but might also have a weird play, a pie-eating contest, country ping pong, or hip-hop bowls – you'll just have to go and find out. There's usually a $5–10 cover. Wed–Sat 4pm–3pm.

Motel Bar Foresters Lane ☎ 04 384 9084; map pp.416–417. Accessed off an atmospheric back alley, this New York-style, first-floor bar with a tiny sign, surveillance camera and an intercom to buzz visitors up was once so exclusive it famously turned away Liv Tyler when she was shooting *Lord of the Rings*. It still cuts it, with semi-private booths, cool sounds and serious cocktails. Tues, Wed, Thurs & Sat 6.30pm–3am, Fri 5.30pm–3am.

S&M's 176 Cuba St ☎ 04 802 5335, ⌨ scottyandmals .co.nz; map pp.416–417. A stylish cocktail lounge and bar that is friendly and happening, and features DJs on Fri and Sat, plus the occasional live show. Tues–Sun 5pm–3am.

Southern Cross 35 Abel Smith St ☎ 04 384 9085, ⌨ thecross.co.nz; map pp.416–417. Cavernous bar divided into some cosy spaces with a heated Balinese-style outdoor garden (and hot water bottles and blankets in winter), this charming local hosts everything from a knitting circle (Mon) to music quiz nights (Thurs) and dancing classes (Sun), plus live music at weekends. New Zealand beers are well represented on tap, and the great pub grub includes snacks such as bowls of cheerios (not the breakfast cereal but Kiwi cocktail sausages).

CLUBS AND LIVE MUSIC VENUES

Live bands are a regular fixture, playing in bars, dedicated smaller venues or bigger halls such as the TBS Bank Arena and occasionally free concerts at the waterfront Frank Kitts Park or Civic Square.

Bodega 101 Ghuznee St ☎ 04 384 8212, ⌨ bodega .co.nz; map pp.416–417. New Zealand's longest-running music venue hosts cutting-edge Kiwi bands and the odd offbeat international act. Usually Tues–Sat 4.30pm–3am.

Boogie Wonderland 25 Courtenay Place; map pp.416–417. Wild and wonderfully cheesy, if you love flares, disco and mirror balls this retro joint is for you. Free entry through *Alice* (see above). Cover typically $10–20. Thurs–Sat 9pm–late.

Garden Club 13 Dixon St; map pp.416–417. Atmospheric large live music and show venue and separate smokers' bar. Also plays host to the Carousel Cabaret. Covers $5–45. Wed–Sat 7pm–late.

Happy 118 Tory St, at Vivian St; map pp.416–417. Underground venue with live, electronic and experimental sounds. Most events are free, but there's an occasional charge of $5–15. Wed is jazz night. Tues–Sun from 8pm–late.

Medusa 154 Vivian St; map pp.416–417. A lively, well-respected venue with a tradition of metal gigs plus everything from hardcore and garage punk to drum 'n' bass, from emerging and established artists. Occasional cover $5–10. Wed–Sun 8pm–late.

San Francisco Bathhouse 171 Cuba St ☎ 04 801 6797, ⓦ sfbh.co.nz; map pp.416–417. Not a bathhouse and, obviously, not San Franciscan, but the city's main indie, alternative rock and reggae venue, with a balcony looking out on the assorted life passing along Cuba St. First-rate Kiwi bands are occasionally joined on the bill by international acts. Most gigs $10–50, though some are free. Wed–Sun 7pm–late.

Sandwiches 8 Kent Terrace ☎ 04 385 7698, ⓦ sandwiches.co.nz; map pp.416–417. Posh clubby venue playing mostly drum 'n' bass, with a restaurant attached. Sometimes free, but covers can be up to $45. Daily 11am–late.

ENTERTAINMENT

Performing arts are strong in Wellington, which is home to several professional theatres, the Royal New Zealand Ballet, the New Zealand Symphony Orchestra and assorted opera and dance companies. In addition to its quota of multiplexes, Wellington also has a smattering of art-house cinemas: you can usually save a couple of dollars by going during the day or any time early in the week.

ESSENTIALS

Listings The best introduction is the *Wellington – What's On* booklet, free from the i-SITE and from accommodation around the city. There are also listings in the *Dominion Post* (ⓦ dompost.co.nz) on weekends; the city's free, weekly *Capital Times* (ⓦ capitaltimes.co.nz); and the monthly arts and entertainment guide *Feeling Great* (ⓦ feelinggreat .co.nz).

Tickets Book tickets direct at venues or, for a small fee, through Ticketek (☎ 04 384 3840, ⓦ ticketek.co.nz) which has an outlet at the St James Theatre, 77–87 Courtenay Place.

THEATRES AND CONCERT HALLS

Bats Theatre 1 Kent Terrace ☎ 04 802 4175, ⓦ bats .co.nz. Lively theatre (recently saved from demolition by Peter Jackson) that concentrates on developmental works served up at affordable prices (usually around $15–30), with discounts for backpacker card-holders.

Circa 1 Taranaki St, at Cable St ☎ 04 801 7992, ⓦ circa .co.nz. One of the country's liveliest and most innovative professional theatres, which has fostered the skills of some of the best-known Kiwi directors and actors.

Downstage 12 Cambridge Terrace ☎ 04 801 6946, ⓦ downstage.co.nz. Stages its own productions and the best touring shows: a mix of mainstream and new drama, dance and comedy, with the emphasis on quality Kiwi work.

Opera House 111–113 Manners St ☎ 04 384 4060, ⓦ stjames.co.nz. Hosts touring opera, ballet and musicals.

St James Theatre 77–87 Courtenay Place ☎ 04 802 4060, ⓦ stjames.co.nz. This refurbished theatre in a fine 1912 building is the major venue for the Royal New Zealand Ballet and hosts opera, dance, musicals and plays. It also has a licensed café for pre- and post-performance drinks.

Westpac Stadium (Wellington Regional Stadium) Featherston St ☎ 04 473 3881, ⓦ westpacstadium .co.nz. Dubbed "the cake tin" by its detractors for its iron-clad design, this modern purpose-built stadium is the venue for rugby and cricket as well as occasional rock concerts.

CINEMAS

Embassy 10 Kent Terrace ☎ 04 384 7657, ⓦ deluxe .co.nz. Mainstream and independent movies are shown on a single giant screen at this city-centre cinema.

The New Zealand Film Archive 84 Taranaki St, at Ghuznee St ☎ 04 384 7647, ⓦ filmarchive.org.nz. Runs evening screenings. For more information see p.421.

Paramount 25 Courtenay Place ☎ 04 384 4080, ⓦ paramount.co.nz. Central 1917-established multi-screen showing art and mainstream films with the added indulgence of being able to watch while sipping a beer or wine.

Reading Cinemas 100 Courtenay Place ☎ 04 801 4601, ⓦ readingcinemas.co.nz. Shows mostly main-stream movies with the option of going for their plush Gold Lounge seats (from $25) which come with an in-seat food and drink service.

The Roxy 5 Park Rd, Miramar ☎ 04 388 5555, ⓦ roxy cinema.co.nz. The Roxy has been lovingly refurbished and redesigned in 1930s style. Apart from its two screens, it boasts a glorious cocktail bar and restaurant, *Coco*, where the excellent food is on a par with the surroundings, and jazz bands re-create the feel of a premier on a regular basis. Check out the details, the bronze of Gollum, the light fittings, pillars, door pulls and toilets – a positive Weta dream for anybody who is a fan. Daily 10am–late.

WELINGTON FESTIVALS

Whenever you visit Wellington there's a good chance there'll be some sort of festival happening. The visitor centre has full details; the following are the biggest occasions, listed chronologically.

Summer City Festival (ⓦwellington.govt .nz) A council-sponsored series of free concerts, cultural events and performances around town. January–March.

Wellington Fringe Festival (ⓦfringe .org.nz) Vibrant affair run as a separate and roughly concurrent event to the International Arts Festival, filling the inner city with street and indoor theatre. Usually held in late February or early March.

New Zealand International Arts Festival (ⓦnzfestival.nzpost.co.nz) The country's biggest cultural event lasts a full month and draws top performers from around the world. Fashioned along the lines of the Edinburgh Festival, it celebrates the huge diversity of the arts: classical music, jazz and pop, opera, puppet shows and the Grotesque, cabaret, poetry readings, traditional Maori dance,

modern ballet and experimental works. Most venues are in the city centre. All of March in even-numbered years.

Wellington International Film Festival (ⓦnzff.co.nz) The Wellington leg of the nationwide film tour screens less mainstream offerings at cinemas around town. Tickets $16. Usually late July to early August.

Wellington on a Plate (ⓦwellington onaplate.com) Celebrates the capital's cuisine through tastings, talks and behind-the-stoves tours as well as discounted menus at top restaurants. Last two weeks of August.

World of WearableArt (WOW) (ⓦworld ofwearableart.com) Tickets go like hot cakes for this glorious spectacle of weird costumes which runs like a bizarre fashion show. Last two weeks of September.

SHOPPING

Bookshops Unity Books (Mon–Thurs 9am–6pm, Fri 9am–7pm, Sat 10am–5pm, Sun 11am–5pm; ☎04 499 4245, ⓦunitybooks.co.nz), 57 Willis St, has the best selection of New Zealand and special interest titles, plus more mainstream titles. Other shops include: Whitcoulls with locations at 312 Lambton Quay, 91 Cuba St and 80 Courtenay Place; Borders at 226 Lambton Quay; for secondhand books, try Pegasus at 204a Left Bank Cuba Mall, or Arty Bee's Books, 106 Manners St.

Camping and outdoor equipment Several good shops – Bivouac, Mountain Designs, Fairydown and Kathmandu – cluster around the junction of Willis and Mercer sts.

DIRECTORY

Automobile Association 342–352 Lambton Quay ☎04 931 9999.

Banks and foreign exchange Banks are dotted all over the city centre CBD. To change money head to ANZ at 215–229 Lambton Quay, BNZ at 1 Willis St and Travelex at 120 Lambton Quay.

Embassies and consulates Australia, 72 Hobson St, Thorndon ☎04 473 6411; Canada, 125 The Terrace ☎04 473 9577; UK, 44 Hill St ☎04 924 2888; US, 29 Fitzherbert Terrace, Thorndon ☎04 462 6000; for other countries, check Yellow Pages, under "Diplomatic and consular representatives".

Emergencies Police, fire and ambulance ☎111. Wellington Central Police Station is on the corner of Victoria and Harris sts ☎04 381 2000.

Internet Plenty of places, many along Courtenay Place, generally charge $4–8/hr. Interface, off the Cuba St mall on Left Bank (Mon–Fri 10am–8pm, Sat 10am–6pm), offers a full suite of state-of-the-art facilities. There's free access at the library.

Library Central Library, 65 Victoria St ☎04 801 4040. Mon–Thurs 9.30am–8.30pm, Fri 9.30am–9pm, Sat 9.30am–5pm, Sun 1–4pm.

Medical emergencies For 24hr emergency treatment try the After Hours Medical Centre, 17 Adelaide Rd, Newtown, near Basin Reserve ☎04 384 4944. Wellington Hospital is on Riddiford St, Newtown ☎04 385 5999.

Pharmacy After Hours Pharmacy, 17 Adelaide Rd, Newtown (Mon–Fri 5–11pm, Sat, Sun & public holidays 8am–11pm; ☎04 385 8810), is open late.

Post office Several throughout the city centre; for poste restante go to 43 Manners St.

Swimming Freyberg Pool and Fitness Centre, 139 Oriental Parade (daily 6am–9pm; ☎04 801 4530), has a 33m indoor pool ($5.70 to swim), plus gym, spas, saunas, steam room, fitness classes and massage therapy. Thorndon Pool, 26 Murphy St (Oct–April Mon & Wed 6.30am–8pm, Tues, Thurs & Fri 6.30am–7pm, Sat & Sun 8am–6.30pm; $5.30) is a 30.5m heated outdoor pool near Parliament.

7

Marlborough, Nelson and Kaikoura

447 The Marlborough Sounds

458 Nelson

466 The road to Abel Tasman

473 Abel Tasman National Park and around

480 Golden Bay

489 Nelson Lakes National Park and around

492 The Marlborough Wine Country

498 The road to the Kaikoura Coast

499 Kaikoura

505 South from Kaikoura

SEAWARD KAIKOURA RANGE, KAIKOURA

Marlborough, Nelson and Kaikoura

The South Island kicks off spectacularly. The whole northern section is supremely alluring, from the indented bays and secluded hideaways of the Marlborough Sounds and the sweep of golden beaches around Nelson, to an impressive array of national parks, sophisticated wineries around Marlborough and the natural wonders of Kaikoura. In fact, if you had to choose only one area of New Zealand to visit, this would be a strong contender. Most visitors travel between the North Island and the South Island by ferry, striking land at the town of Picton – drab in the winter, lively in the summer and surrounded by the beautiful Marlborough Sounds. Here, bays full of unfathomably deep water lap at tiny beaches, each with its rickety boat jetty, and the land rises steeply to forest or stark pasture.

To the west, the lively yet relaxed city of **Nelson** is the starting point for forays to wilder spots further north. Some of the country's most gorgeous walking tracks and dazzling golden beaches populate the **Abel Tasman National Park**, while yet further north the relatively isolated **Golden Bay** offers peaceful times in chilled settings with uniformly decent weather. The curve of the Golden Bay culminates in a long sandy bar that juts into the ocean, **Farewell Spit**, an extraordinary and unique habitat. It borders the Kahurangi National Park, through which the rugged and spectacular **Heaphy Track** forges a route to the West Coast.

The least visited of the region's well-preserved areas of natural splendour is the sparsely populated **Nelson Lakes National Park**, principally a spot for tramping to alpine lakes or fishing, though the nearby **Buller River** also attracts raft and kayak rats.

South of Picton, you can slurp your merry way through **Marlborough**, New Zealand's most feted winemaking region centred on the modest towns of **Blenheim** and **Renwick**. A night or two in one of the rural B&Bs and some time spent around the wineries happily balances the more energetic activities of the national parks, and sets you up

Hiking around Picton p.447
Biking the Queen Charlotte Track p.453
Queen Charlotte Sound cruises and tours p.454
The Queen Charlotte Track pp.456–457
Nelson Market p.460
Nelson arts and crafts p.461
Nelson activities p.462
Motueka tours and activities p.470
Activities and tours in Abel Tasman National Park pp.476–477
The road to Collingwood: arts and crafts p.485
Farewell Spit tours p.486

Kahurangi National Park: the Heaphy Track pp.488–489
Nelson Lakes hikes p.491
Rafting and river kayaking in Murchison p.492
Marlborough wine tastings and tours p.496
Marlborough festivals p.498
Driving through Molesworth Station p.499
Walks around Kaikoura p.501
Kaikoura tours and activities pp.502–503
Ski Mount Lyford p.505

LAKE ROTOITI, NELSON LAKES NATIONAL PARK

Highlights

❶ The Queen Charlotte Track This beautiful multi-day hike is made all the more manageable by staying in great backpackers and B&Bs, and having your bags carried for you. **See p.456**

❷ Nelson A vibrant arts community, vineyards on the doorstep, a laidback atmosphere and great weather combine to make Nelson an essential stop. **See p.458**

❸ Abel Tasman National Park Crystal-clear water and golden beaches are rewards for hiking the lush Coast Track or kayaking the myriad inlets and islands. **See p.473**

❹ Farewell Spit tours The original Farewell

Spit Safari takes you to a unique place in New Zealand which you would otherwise not be able to access. **See p.486**

❺ Heaphy Track The huge range of dramatic scenery and final sense of achievement puts this Great Walk up with the best. **See p.488**

❻ Marlborough Wine Country No trip to this area is complete without supping Sauvignon Blanc in New Zealand's most famous wine region. **See p.494**

❼ Kaikoura Whale-watching and dolphin-swimming trips from this pretty town are the highlight of many a visitor's trip. **See p.502**

HIGHLIGHTS ARE MARKED ON THE MAP ON P.446

nicely for a few days of ecotourism in **Kaikoura** where **whale watching** and **swimming with dolphins** and **seals** are the main draws.

The region's **weather** is some of the sunniest in the land, particularly around Blenheim and Nelson, which regularly compete for the honour of the greatest number of sunshine hours in New Zealand.

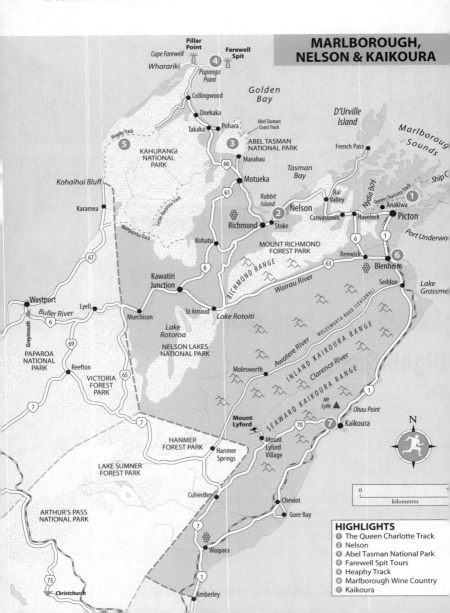

MARLBOROUGH, NELSON & KAIKOURA

HIGHLIGHTS
1. The Queen Charlotte Track
2. Nelson
3. Abel Tasman National Park
4. Farewell Spit Tours
5. Heaphy Track
6. Marlborough Wine Country
7. Kaikoura

GETTING AROUND

By ferry and train You can cross Cook Strait by ferry (see p.431) and link up with the region's only train, from Picton to Christchurch.

By bus Buses fill in the gaps, many doing the same Picton–Christchurch run via Kaikoura with others running to Blenheim and Nelson where there are connections for the Abel Tasman National Park and Golden Bay. The main operators are Southern Link (☎0508 458 835, ⊚southernlinkkbus.co.nz), running between Picton and Christchurch, Atomic Shuttles (☎03 349 0697, ⊚atomictravel.co.nz) and InterCity/Newmans (☎03 365 1113, ⊚intercitycoach.co.nz), who both cover the area extensively.

The Marlborough Sounds

The **Marlborough Sounds** are undeniably picturesque, a stimulating filigree of bays, inlets, islands and peninsulas rising abruptly from the water to rugged, lush green wilderness and open farmland. Large parts are only accessible by sea, which also provides the ideal vantage point for witnessing its splendour. The area is part working farms, including salmon or mussel farms, and part given over to some fifty-odd reserve areas – a mixture of islands, sections of coast and land-bound tracts. The Sounds' nexus, **Picton**, is the jumping-off point for **Queen Charlotte Sound** where cruises and water taxis provide access to the undemanding, varied and scenic **Queen Charlotte Track**. Heading west, Queen Charlotte Drive winds precipitously to the small community of Havelock, New Zealand's green-lipped mussel capital, before exploring the spectacular vistas of Pelorus Sound and perhaps taking the backroads or a boat to view the rich swirling waters of French Pass.

8

Picton

Cook Strait ferries from Wellington arrive in **Picton**, a small harbour and tourist town sandwiched between the hills and the deep, placid waters of Queen Charlotte Sound. Many people stop only for a coffee, looking out over the water before pressing on, but Picton is the best base for exploring the **Queen Charlotte Track**, serviced by several water taxis, and a good spot for getting into the Sounds on **cruises and kayak trips**. The town itself has a few noteworthy attractions and it also makes a decent base for exploring the **wine region** around Blenheim, half an hour's drive to the south.

Brief history

There was a European settlement in the region as early as 1827 when John Guard established a whaling station, but Picton itself didn't come into being until the

---

HIKING AROUND PICTON

The best of the local trails run through Victoria Domain, a mostly bush-clad peninsula immediately east of Picton. Many of the trails link, so pick up one of the several widely available free maps in town.

Bob's Bay Track (1km one-way; 30min; gently undulating). Starting at Shelly Beach near the *Echo*, this extends along the shoreline to a safe swimming and picnicking beach at Bob's Bay providing great views across the water to the ferry terminal and up the Queen Charlotte Sound. From Bob's Bay a short steep path climbs away from the bay to the Harbour View parking area.

The Snout (5km one-way; 1hr 15min; 200m ascent on return). From the Harbour View parking area follow the top of the ridge past the Queen Charlotte View to the tip of the promontory, The Snout, whose evocative Maori name, Te Ihumoeone-ihu, translates as "the nose of the sand worm".

Tirohanga Track (3km one-way; 1hr 15min; 300m ascent). Starting on Newgate Street this is a fairly strenuous walk up the hills behind Picton, passing the lovely Hilltop Viewpoint.

New Zealand Company purchased the town site for £300 in 1848. Picton flourished as a port and **service town** for the Wairau Plains to the south but predominantly as the most convenient port for travel between the islands.

Edwin Fox

Close to the Ferry Terminal • Daily: Dec–March 9am–5pm; April–Nov 9am–3pm • $10

Everything of interest in Picton is along the phoenix-palm-lined waterfront, **Picton Foreshore**. At its western end, close to the ferry terminal, the hulk of the 1600-tonne,

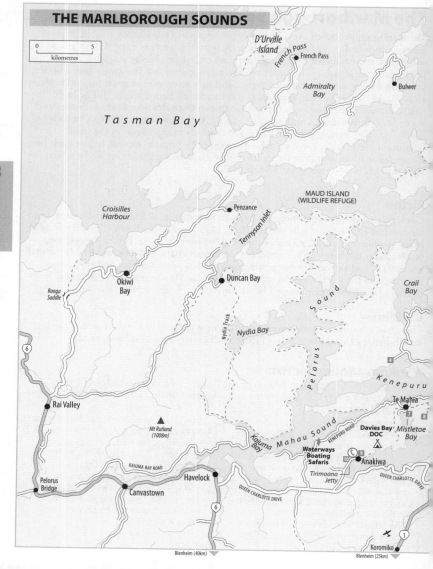

THE MARLBOROUGH SOUNDS

Calcutta-built **Edwin Fox** is the sole survivor of some four thousand "East Indiamen" that once brought migrants to New Zealand. This 1853 example also operated as a troop carrier in the Crimean War, transported convicts to Australia and helped establish New Zealand's frozen meat trade before being towed to Picton in 1967. A small but well-designed museum prepares you for the age-blackened hull itself. Standing on the small part of the lower deck that remains gives a sense of what it must have been like to sail, but the best bit is in the large open hold, all heavy planking, teak ribs and traces of the metal cladding on the external hull.

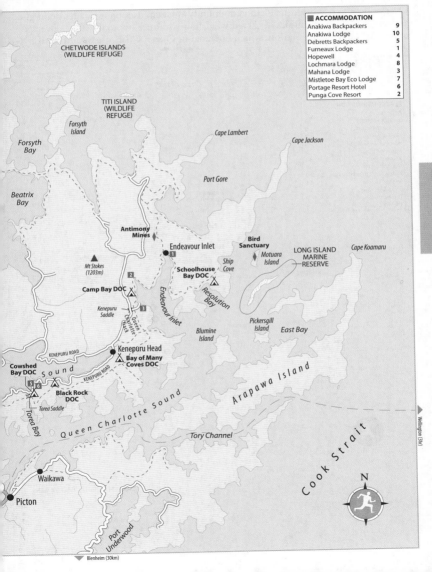

Eco World

Next to the Edwin Fox • Daily: Dec & Feb 10am–7.30pm; March–Dec 10am–5.30pm; feeding at 11am & 2pm • $22 • ⓦ ecoworldnz.co.nz

Eco World offers an insight into the flora and fauna of the Marlborough Sounds with local marine life (including little blue penguins), a few small sharks, a preserved giant squid plus tuatara, including babies, and giant weta. It is best visited during feeding time.

Picton Community Museum

London Quay • Daily 10am–4pm • $5

Overlooking Eco World, the **Picton Community Museum** uses photos, a harpoon gun and some excellent examples of carved whalebone (scrimshaw) to illustrate coverage of the Perano Whaling Station, which operated in Queen Charlotte Sound until 1964.

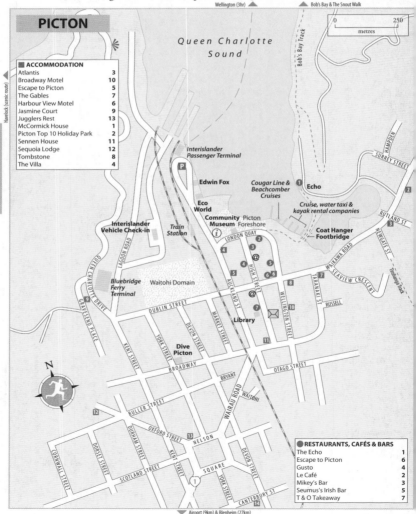

PICTON

Wellington (3hr) ▲   ▲ Bob's Bay & The Snout Walk

Queen Charlotte Sound

0   250
metres

Hawlock (scenic route)

■ ACCOMMODATION	
Atlantis	3
Broadway Motel	10
Escape to Picton	5
The Gables	7
Harbour View Motel	6
Jasmine Court	9
Jugglers Rest	13
McCormick House	1
Picton Top 10 Holiday Park	2
Sennen House	11
Sequoia Lodge	12
Tombstone	8
The Villa	4

8

Bob's Bay Track

HAMPDEN

SURREY STREET

Interislander Passenger Terminal

P

Edwin Fox

Cougar Line & Beachcomber Cruises

❶ **Echo**

Cruise, water taxi & kayak rental companies

RUTLAND ST

NEWGATE ST

Eco World

Community Museum

Picton Foreground

Interislander Vehicle Check-in

Train Station

LAGOON ROAD

ℹ

LONDON QUAY

❸

❷

Coat Hanger — Footbridge

WAIKAWA ROAD

SEAVIEW CRESCENT

Finsbury Track

❹

@

❺

HIGH STREET

❺

❻ ❻

❼

TARANAKI ST

❽

Bluebridge Ferry Terminal

QUEEN CHARLOTTE DRIVE

GRAVESEND PLACE

Waitohi Domain

ALICK ROAD

@

❼

DUBLIN STREET

MARKET STREET

WELLINGTON STREET

✉

❿

RUSSELL

Library

⓫

KENT STREET

YORK STREET

DEVON STREET

Dive Picton

BROADWAY

BRYANT

WAITOHI

OTAGO STREET

N

BULLER STREET

WAIRAU ROAD

⓬

DURHAM STREET

OXFORD STREET

⓭

NELSON

KENT STREET

DEVON STREET

CORNWALL STREET

DORSET STREET

SCOTLAND STREET

SQUARE

YORK STREET

ℹ

CANTERBURY ST

● RESTAURANTS, CAFÉS & BARS	
The Echo	1
Escape to Picton	6
Gusto	4
Le Café	2
Mikey's Bar	3
Seumus's Irish Bar	5
T & O Takeaway	7

▼ Airport (9km) & Blenheim (27km)

At the time of writing, the museum was in the process of a major refurbishment and extension, which should mean that by 2013 they'll be able to display a lot more of their engaging collection.

ARRIVAL AND DEPARTURE — PICTON

By ferry and train Interislander ferry foot passengers disembark close to the town centre, while Bluebridge foot passengers and all vehicles disembark on the western side of town about 1km from the centre; Bluebridge operates a free shuttle bus to the i-SITE. Interislander ferry schedules work in well with the daily *TranzCoastal* train to Christchurch. One-way fares from $99.

Ferry destinations Wellington (3–6 daily).

Train destinations Christchurch, via Blenheim and Kaikoura (1 daily).

By bus Buses stop outside the Interislander ferry terminal and again at the i-SITE.

Destinations Blenheim (8 daily; 30min); Christchurch (4–5 daily; 5hr–5hr 30min); Kaikoura (4–5 daily; 2hr 15min); Nelson (5 daily; 2hr).

By plane Picton airport, 9km south of town, is served by Soundsair (T 0800 505 005, W soundsair.com), with flights from Wellington. A bus ($7 one-way) meets flights and runs into Picton.

Destinations Wellington (10 daily).

GETTING AROUND

By bus Richies (T 03 578 5467) and InterCity go to Blenheim. The 40min run costs $10–16.

By mail bus The Rural Mail Bus Service (T 027 255 8882) is a minivan serving remote spots linking the main post offices in Havelock and Picton, and the southern end of the Queen Charlotte Track at Anakiwa. There are several runs each day. Fares start at $15.

By car Most major international and domestic companies have offices at the ferry terminal or around town. The i-SITE has a free sheet listing them.

By taxi Picton Shuttles T 027 696 5207.

By water taxi A number of companies run services around the sound, as well as cruises (see box, p.454), including: Beachcomber Fun Cruises (T 0800 624 526, W mailboat .co.nz); Cougar Line (T 0800 504 090, W cougarlinecruises .co.nz); Endeavour Express (T 03 573 5456, W boatrides .co.nz); and Kiwi Spirit (T 03 573 6717).

INFORMATION AND ACTIVITIES

i-SITE and DOC On the foreshore, a 5min walk from the ferry terminal (daily 9am–5pm; T 03 520 3113, W destinationmarlborough.com). The combined office is packed with leaflets on the town and the rest of the South Island, including a free Picton and Blenheim map and DOC's free *Queen Charlotte Track* visitor guide. It also has internet access.

Dive Picton Corner of York and Broadway sts T 0800 423 483, W divepicton.co.nz. Offers single dives ($90 with all gear), two-tank dive days ($190–230) and two-tank wreck dive days ($290) on the *Mikhail Lermontov*, a Soviet cruise ship that became the southern hemisphere's largest diveable wreck when it hit rocks in 1986. For the latter you'll need experience at 30m in cold water.

Winery tours Tours of the Marlborough wine country are covered in detail on p.496. Most companies organize Picton pick-ups for around $5 extra.

ACCOMMODATION

Atlantis London Quay T 03 573 7390, W atlantishostel .co.nz. Central hostel, close to ferry with a variety of colourfully decorated dorms, mostly without windows, cosy doubles and free breakfasts in an old diving school, though the communal facilities need a little TLC. Dorms from $20, doubles $55

Broadway Motel 113 Picton High St T 0800 101 919, W broadwaymotel.co.nz. Attractive, relatively modern motel units with large windows and all the usual mod-cons, including Sky TV and wi-fi. Everything is clean and well kept and they have a good recycling policy. $149

Escape to Picton 33 Wellington St T 03 573 5573, W escapetopicton.com. Chic three-suite boutique hotel that's highly professional with everything to the highest standard (including freestanding baths in two suites). Breakfast is served in the restaurant (see p.452). Rates are moveable off-peak. $350

The Gables 20 Waikawa Rd T 03 573 6772, W thegables.co.nz. Pleasant and welcoming B&B with three rooms in the house (one with en suite) and a self-contained cottage out back where breakfast can supplied. Children and dogs welcome. Rooms $170, cottages $175

Harbour View Motel 30 Waikawa Rd T 0800 101 133, W harbourviewpicton.co.nz. Twelve spacious and tastefully appointed self-contained units, each with a balcony and great views over the harbour. Guests are treated to a variety of well-kept clean units with a communal laundry and luggage storarge if you're going on the Queen Charlotte Track. $200

★ **Hopewell** Kenepuru Sound ☎ 03 573 4341, ⓦ hopewell.co.nz. A gorgeous hostel and the best of the accommodation available in the Sounds, in a dreamy setting where even a couple of nights isn't enough to fully appreciate the relaxing surroundings. The hosts are welcoming, there's a waterside hot tub, plus kayaks, fishing and opportunities to visit the local mussel farm or go waterskiing. Access is either on a tortuous 2–3hr drive along Kenepuru Rd, or by a sequence of water taxis from Picton ($60/person each way): call the hostel for details. Closed June–Aug. Dorms $40, rooms $100, en suites $130 s/c cottage sleeping four $170

★ **Jasmine Court** 78 Wellington St ☎ 0800 421 999, ⓦ jasminecourt.co.nz. Top-of-the-line medium-sized motel with luxury units, recently extended and revamped, professionally run by a couple prepared to go that extra mile. Rooms include DVD and CD players, and some have spa baths and verandas. Free email and pay wi-fi. $165

Jugglers' Rest 8 Canterbury St ☎ 03 573 5570, ⓦ jugglersrest.com. Small, very welcoming and relaxed shoes-off hostel about a 10min walk from the ferries, with spacious dorms (no bunks) and a couple of quiet rooms in the grounds. There's a strong recycling ethic, the vegetable garden is open to all and there's home-made jam to spread on fresh bread each morning. Closed June–Sept. Tents $19, dorms $31, rooms $66

McCormick House 21 Leicester St ☎ 03 573 5253, ⓦ mccormickhouse.co.nz. Situated in a half acre of native garden, this atmospheric Edwardian villa has an original rimu-panelled staircase, at the top of which are three luxurious individually decorated rooms. The indulgent breakfasts are made from local produce, and there's a good stock of Kiwi movies and music in the lounge. $350

Picton Top 10 Holiday Park 78 Waikawa Rd ☎ 0800 277 444, ⓦ pictontop10.co.nz. Centrally located camp-site with swimming pool, children's playground, cabins (bedding $5) and motel-style units, in a pleasant spot with sheltering trees. Camping $22, cabins $70, kitchen cabins $95, self-contained units $120

Sennen House 9 Oxford St ☎ 03 573 5216, ⓦ sennenhouse.co.nz. A gorgeous, grand 1886 villa a 10min walk from town that's been tastefully converted into a B&B with five suites, all with kitchen facilities. A welcome wine and a breakfast hamper are supplied. $199

Sequoia Lodge 3 Nelson Square ☎ 0800 222 257, ⓦ sequoialodge.co.nz. Very popular, well-organized hostel shoehorned onto a site that's a 10min walk from the town centre; make use of the free pick-ups. Beds and bunks all come with bed lights and side tables, rooms have heated towel rails, and there's a separate, en-suite female dorm. Breakfast, hammocks, spa, nightly pudding and ice cream, wi-fi and home cinema are all free. Four- to six-bed dorms $22, rooms $60, en suites $72, motel-style units $80, apartment $92

★ **Tombstone** 16 Gravesend Place ☎ 0800 573 7116, ⓦ tombstonebp.co.nz. Wonderfully friendly well-run hostel with a coffin-lid door (it's right by the town cemetery), an easy walk from the port. The purpose-built accommodation block is carpeted and double-glazed, making it super-quiet. The barbecue area, piano, hot tub, bikes and continental breakfast come at no extra charge. Dorms are single-sex, private rooms come with electric blankets and a balcony, and there's a one-bedroom self-contained apartment. Dorms $25, en-suite dorms $30, rooms and en suites $81, apartment $110

The Villa 34 Auckland St ☎ 03 573 6598, ⓦ thevilla .co.nz. Central and youthful hostel set in two houses, one a century old, the other next door and a more modern cottage. When busy it's cramped, but there are all manner of inducements such as free bikes, outdoor spa and gym and apple crumble in winter. Dorms $26, four-bed $30, rooms $62, en suites $76

EATING, DRINKING AND ENTERTAINMENT

★ **The Echo** Picton Marina, East Harbour ☎ 03 573 7498. While this permanently moored top-sail schooner serves food such as a seaman's stack ($19) and a cooked breakfast ($19.50), it's primarily a fine place for a beer on deck. Built in 1905, the *Echo* was the last ship to trade commercially under sail in New Zealand waters and was the subject of a Hollywood film, *The Wackiest Ship in the Army*, starring Jack Lemmon. Check out the displays for more on its colourful past and if you ask nicely they'll show you the movie. Wed–Sun 10am–11pm, kitchen closes at 8pm.

Escape to Picton 33 Wellington St ☎ 03 573 5573. Wine is stored in the vault of this former bank-turned-chic-restaurant, café and bar. You can pop in for a coffee or beer, but this is really about quality dining with dinner mains such as wild mushroom and basil risotto ($36) or 30-day-aged Angus steak with tiger prawns and scallops ($42.50),

all accompanied by lounge music, sometimes live. Mon–Fri 10am–2.30pm & 5pm–late, Sat & Sun 10am–late.

Gusto 33 High St ☎ 03 573 7171. Cosy and popular, this daytime café opens up on to the street and dishes up delicious breakfasts along with a short menu of daily specials including pasta, sandwiches, great steak sandwiches, cakes and good coffee. Summer daily 7.30am–3.30pm; winter Sun–Fri 8am–3.30pm.

★ **Le Café** 14 London Quay ☎ 03 573 5588, ⓦ lecafe picton.co.nz. Bustling, popular and stylish café and bar with pavement seating just across from the Sounds, serving mouthwatering steaks with home-made chutney and all sorts of seafood. Lunch mains around $24, dinner $31. Bands play regularly in the summer. Daily 7am–late.

Mikey's Bar 18 High St ☎ 03 573 5164. Modern bar with very cheap food (all under $22), a pool table, and a barn-like nightclub out back where DJs are interspersed with bands trying to scrape together enough money to play somewhere bigger. Daily 11am–11pm, later at the end of the week and the weekend.

Seumus's Irish Bar Wellington St. Authentically poky Irish bar, known as a local watering hole and for large, inexpensive

and decent bar meals ($20–28). There's outdoor seating and live music several nights a week. Daily noon–late.

T & O Takeaway 85 High St ☎ 03 573 6115. Serves the freshest and best fish and chips in town, plus a variety of other fruits of the sea, all under $10 and usually cooked to order. Daily 11am–2.30pm & 4.30–8pm.

DIRECTORY

Internet Limited free access at the library, plus computers at the i-SITE and at United Video, 63 High St (daily 9am–9pm).

Library 67 High St (Mon–Fri 8am–5pm, Sat 10am–1pm, Sun 1.30–4.30pm).

Luggage storage Most lodgings store luggage while you walk the Queen Charlotte Track. The i-SITE has large luggage lockers ($4/day) and cars can be left securely with Sounds Storage, 7 Market St ($35/first two nights and $10/night after that; ☎ 021 335136).

Queen Charlotte Sound

Picton is a pretty spot, but you've barely touched the region's beauty until you've explored **Queen Charlotte Sound**. This wildly indented series of drowned valleys encloses moody picturesque bays, small deserted sandy beaches, headlands with panoramic views and cloistered islands, while grand lumpy peninsulas offer shelter from the winds and storms, and solitude for the contemplative fisherman or kayaker. For a taste of these labyrinthine waterways, take one of the many **day-cruises** from Picton, but to really appreciate the tranquil beauty you're better off **kayaking** round the bays or **tramping** the Queen Charlotte Track (see box, pp.456–457). The relatively calm waters of the Sounds also give the opportunity for **scuba diving**, checking out the rich marine life of the huge wreck of a Soviet cruise ship (see p.451).

Motuara Island

A couple of sights at the far end of Queen Charlotte Sound crop up on most itineraries, including the DOC-managed **Motuara Island**, a predator-free wildlife sanctuary that is home to the saddleback, South Island bush robin, bellbird and a few Okarito brown kiwi. All the birds are quite fearless and will rest and fly startlingly close to you. Throughout the island little blue penguins choose to nest in boxes provided, rather than build their own, and in spring (Oct–Dec), you can gently lift the top of the box and see the baby penguins.

Just across a channel from Motuara Island, **Ship Cove** marks the bay where Captain Cook spent a total of 168 days during his three trips to New Zealand. A large concrete monument commemorates his five separate visits to the cove.

> ### BIKING THE QUEEN CHARLOTTE TRACK
>
> Though the Queen Charlotte Track (see box, pp.456–457) is primarily for hikers, **mountain bikers** can ride the whole thing in a day or two. There are two steep ascents but it is not overly technical, and with pack transfers and abundant accommodation you won't need to lug heavy panniers. Most of the track is open to bikers year-round, though the northern quarter (Ship Cove–Camp Bay) is off-limits from December to February.
>
> Marlborough Sounds Adventure Company (see box, p.454) operates a three-day Freedom Bike Ride ($755–970) with bike rental, transfers and comfortable accommodation at *Punga Cove* and *Portage Resort*.
>
> Alternatively you cant rent a mountain bike ($50/day from either Marlborough Sounds Adventure or Sea Kayaking Adventure (see box, p.454) and organize your own trip, either camping or staying in cheaper accommodation.

8

QUEEN CHARLOTTE SOUND CRUISES AND TOURS

Water taxis (see p.451) are always flitting about Queen Charlotte Sound taking hikers to the Queen Charlotte Track, or delivering guests to swanky lodges. If you just want to get out on the water this may be all you need, but several companies also run excellent **cruises**.

Beachcomber Fun Cruises ☎0800 624 526, ⓦmailboat.co.nz. Several companies run great cruises around Queen Charlotte and Pelorus sounds, but there is still something unique about the Rural Mail Runs, pulling up at a lonely wharf to deliver the post. The journey includes golden beaches with bush-clad shorelines and dolphins sometimes escort the boat. The downside is that you can't get off for a walk or jump off for a swim. The four-hour magical Mail Run (Mon–Sat 1.30pm; 4hr; $89) leaves from Picton. Three routes are plied on different days of the week, but there's little to choose between them. In summer, all call into Endeavour Inlet, pass a salmon farm and allow fifteen minutes ashore at Ship Cove. Alternative postal routes explore Pelorus Sound from Havelock (see p.455). This operator also offers trips to Ship Cove (3hr; $73) and to Motuara Island (3hr; $73).

Cougar Line ☎0800 504 090, ⓦcougarline.co.nz. The direct competition to Beachcomber Fun Cruises run similar trips, including a Ship Cove Cruise ($75) and scheduled as well as on-demand water taxi services.

Dolphin Watch Ecotours London Quay ☎0800 945 354, ⓦnaturetours.co.nz. Some of the most sympathetic wildlife trips in the Sounds are run by this outfit, which offers dolphin swimming (2–4hr; $165 to swim; $100 to watch) with dusky, common or bottlenose dolphins, as well as sightings of the endemic Hector's dolphins. To combine dolphin watching with the Sounds' other sights, join their trips to either Motuara Island (45min, guided; $110) or Ship Cove (45min, unguided; $110), both of which can also be used as a drop-off for Queen Charlotte Track walkers. The Birdwatchers Expedition (daily 1.30pm; $125) gives you the chance to tick many New Zealand birds off your list – if you're lucky you may get to see an extremely rare king shag. Oct–April only.

Myths and Legends Eco Tours ☎03 573 6901, ⓦeco-tours.co.nz. Run by a sixth-generation local Pakeha and his Maori wife, who tour the bays in their 1930s kauri launch explaining the history and culture of the region ($200/4hr; $250/8hr and lunch; $300 to Cape Jackson at the extreme edge of the Sound; all tours have a two-person minimum).

Queen Charlotte Steam Ship Company ☎03 573 7443, ⓦsteamshipping.co.nz. A variation on the standard cruise from Picton, with hour-long cruises (on the hour from the Short Finger Jetty; $25) puttering about the Sound immediately adjacent to Picton in a small, replica 1920 steel-hull steamboat.

Waterways Boating Safaris 7km along the Kenepuru Rd ☎03 574 1372, ⓦwaterways.co.nz. An unusual way of exploring the Sounds, in the best drive-it-yourself traditions of New Zealand, via guided flotillas of two-person motorboats on amazing excursions round Kenepuru Sound (half-day $100; full day $150). You drive your own boat, designed specifically for the job by Leicester, your guide, following his lead to out-of-the-way bays and bushwalks, as well as getting a view of a local mussel farm.

KAYAKING

Visitors dashing straight to Abel Tasman National Park overlook the breathtaking views to be had kayaking Queen Charlotte Sound, where other floating traffic is virtually non-existent by comparison.

Marlborough Sounds Adventure Company Town Wharf ☎0800 283 283, ⓦmarlboroughsounds.co.nz. Friendly and professional outfit offering a huge range of guided kayaking trips including half-day paddles from Picton (Oct–April daily; 4hr; $85), a gentle one-day trip (7hr; $120), a two-day trip, initially guided then camping out by yourselves and paddling home the next day ($180), and a fully guided three-day trip in the outer sounds ($545); rentals are $60 for one day, $100 for two.

Sea Kayaking Adventure Tours Near the turn-off for Anakiwa ☎03 574 2765, ⓦnzseakayaking.com. Well run and more intimate, with half-day ($75) and full-day ($125) guided trips, a two-day guided and catered trip ($295) and various paddle and walk or bike options. Independent rentals are $60/day, $100/two days and $130/three days.

Queen Charlotte Drive

The 35km Queen Charlotte Drive between Picton and Havelock is a picturesque and spectacular backroad sliding past the flat plain at the head of Queen Charlotte Sound and climbing up the hills overlooking Pelorus Sound before descending to SH6 and Havelock itself. It is a slow and winding drive, but you may want to take it even slower by stopping to wander down to a couple of sheltered coves or up the Cullen Track (a 10min walk yields spectacular views). With water taxis providing convenient access to fabulous out-of-the-way spots, it may seem a little perverse to try to see the Marlborough Sounds by car. Doubly so when you start weaving your way around the narrow and twisting roads – don't expect to average more than 40km/hour, but ultimately it is well worth the effort as the views through the ferns to turquoise bays are magical.

Around 18km west of Picton, a narrow road heads north to **Anakiwa**, the southern end of the Queen Charlotte Track. Here you'll find a wharf used by water taxis taking hikers back to Picton, *Anakiwa Lodge* (see box, pp.456–457) and *Anakiwa Backpackers* (see box, pp.456–457).

Kenepuru Road

A couple of kilometres further along Queen Charlotte Drive, **Kenepuru Road** cuts right and begins its 75km journey out along the shores of Kenepuru Sound. There are many picturesque bays and views along the way and the road provides access to several points along the Queen Charlotte Track, running past a handful of DOC campsites and several places to stay – *Debretts Backpackers* and *Punga Cove* – all listed on p.457, before ending at *Hopewell* backpackers (see p.452).

Havelock and Pelorus Sound

The sleepy town of **HAVELOCK**, 35km west of Picton, is primarily of interest for cruising the stunning **Pelorus Sound**, an intricate maze of steep-sided bays, crescent beaches and sunken sea passages surrounded by forested peaks – the largest sheltered waterway in the southern hemisphere. Almost every bay has a farm for green-lipped mussels, making Havelock the world capital for these choice bivalves: you simply can't leave without tucking into a plateful, Self-caterers can buy fresh mussels from the Four Square supermarket.

Pelorus Mail Boat

$128; under-16s free • ☎ 03 574 1088, 🌐 mail-boat.co.nz

To see an extensive section of Pelorus Sound, get aboard the **Pelorus Mail Boat**, which departs from the marina on Tuesdays, Thursdays and Fridays at 9.30am and follows a different route each day. All the trips are a scenic delight, dropping in on a mussel farm and delivering mail, perishable groceries and even correspondence-school papers to the far-flung residents. Friday's outer sounds trip is the most comprehensive, but the schedule on other days gives more flexibility for dolphin watching and brief time ashore. The trips return late in the afternoon so bring lunch.

Pelorus Bridge Scenic Reserve

18km west of Havelock

The **Pelorus Bridge Scenic Reserve** is a gorgeous forested spot run through by the crystal-clear, trout-filled Pelorus River with sandy beaches, abundant swimming holes and verdant bush enlivened by tui, grey warblers and bellbirds.

The place is understandably popular in summer, particularly the recently revamped but still basic DOC camping area (see p.458) and a DOC office adjoining a modest daytime, licensed café (daily: Nov–March 8.30am–7pm; April–Oct 8.30am–4.30pm), which also rents fishing rods ($25) and sells basic lures.

The **walking tracks** in the reserve are well maintained, fairly flat and clearly marked and there's a swingbridge to add a little extra excitement: the **Totara Walk** (1.5km return; 30min) and **Circle Walk** (1km return; 30min) routes pass through the low-lying woodland for which the area is famous, while the **Trig K Track** (2.5km one-way; 2hr), after a steady climb to 417m, offers stunning views of the whole area.

8

THE QUEEN CHARLOTTE TRACK

The **Queen Charlotte Track** (71km one-way; 3–5 days; year-round) is a stunningly beautiful walk partly tracing skyline ridges with brilliant views across coastal forest to the waters of Queen Charlotte and Kenepuru sounds. It is broad, relatively easy going and distinguished from all other Kiwi multi-day tramps by the lack of DOC huts, replaced by some lovely **accommodation**. Access and egress is generally by boat from Picton. Water taxis can **transport your bags** to your next destination each day. Boats call at numerous bays along the way, so less ambitious walkers can tackle shorter sections, do day-hikes from Picton or take on the track as part of a guided walk (see below).

INFORMATION, COSTS AND ACCESS

The Picton i-SITE can help organize your trip and has the free *Queen Charlotte Track Visitor Guide*; check ⓦdoc.govt.nz or ⓦqctrack.co.nz for more information. Parts of the track cross private land and there is a **fee** for anyone over 15 hiking or biking these sections: Queen Charlotte Track Land Cooperative Passes are sold by DOC, Picton and Blenheim i-SITEs and a number of accommodations on the track. A one-day pass between Anakiwa and Mistletoe Bay costs $6; a pass for up to four consecutive days is $12; an annual pass is $25.

Trampers normally **travel north to south** from Ship Cove to Anakiwa, using **water taxis** to drop them off and pick them up. Sections of the track are accessible from Kenepuru Road, but there is no public transport. There is no overnight parking at Anakiwa, although the Rural Mail Bus Service (see p.451) can take you there.

Water taxi companies (see p.451) all offer a standard package with drop-off at Ship Cove, bag transfers and pick-up at Anakiwa for about $103 (usually in the late afternoon). Endeavour Express ($97) is cheapest but other companies may have more convenient schedules. Bikes cost $5/journey, double kayaks $30. If you fancy just walking a short section of the track and being picked up pretty much anywhere you want, one-way transfers are $40–67.

GUIDED WALKS, COMBOS AND DAY-TRIPS

Marlborough Sounds Adventure Company (see box, p.454) offers **freedom walks** (4-day $695; 5-day $795; packed lunch each day), with nights spent at *Furneaux Lodge*, *Punga Cove Resort* and *Portage Resort Hotel*. Fully catered **guided walks** (4-day $1595; 5-day $1995) include a visit to Motuara Island and optional days spent paddling. To pack in a day each of hiking, biking and paddling, go for the three-day Ultimate Sounds Adventure ($755–970 depending on accommodation). Beachcomber Fun Cruises (see p.454) offer a series of one-day walks ($61–73), while the Cougar Line has walks from one to five hours ($75).

ACCOMMODATION

Booking is essential. Some smaller places don't accept debit or credit cards, so **take plenty of cash**. The six DOC **campsites** cost $6 and have water and toilets but only four have water taxi access. The accommodation below is listed from north to south, with hiking distances measured from Ship Cove.

Furneaux Lodge Endeavour Inlet, Km14 ❶03 579 8259, ⓦfurneaux.co.nz. One of the region's bigger lodges built in attractive grounds around a century-old homestead, with a convivial bar and an excellent restaurant. Rooms range from basic backpackers (bring a sleeping bag) and made-up bunk rooms to self-contained cottages and modern suites. Internet access and phone available. The Croft/bed $38, bunk rooms $45, chalets $169, suites $289

Punga Cove Resort Camp Bay, Km26 ❶03 579 8561, ⓦpungacove.co.nz. A large resort with panoramic views and mountainous tariffs. Facilities include a classy restaurant, pool, spa, sauna, fishing

---

SH6 continues west past the turn-off to French Pass at the small settlement of **Rai Valley** and climbs the hills past Happy Valley Adventures (see box, p.462) to Nelson.

French Pass

Narrow winding roads head north from Rai Valley towards French Pass, a two-hour, 60km drive through pockets of bush locked in sheep country and pine plantations. After tantalizing glimpses of inaccessible bays and coves you're finally rewarded with

gear and kayaks. Dorms (no linen) $\overline{\$42}$, *bach* $\overline{\$180}$, lodge $\overline{\$150}$, chalet doubles $\overline{\$300}$, suites $\overline{\$450}$

Debretts Backpackers Kenepuru Rd, Km51 ☎03 573 4522, ⓦstayportage.co.nz. Tranquil hostel sleeping six, with great views of Portage Bay and Kenepuru Sound. It's a 30min walk from Torea Bay or get them to arrange a taxi. Dorms (linen $5) $\overline{\$45}$, double rooms $\overline{\$80}$

Lochmara Lodge Lochmara Bay, Km58 ☎03 573 4554, ⓦlochmaralodge.co.nz. Beautiful eco-lodge with its own café, restaurant and bar, overlooking Lochmara Bay. There are also free kayaks and snorkelling gear, a bathhouse ($60 for two for 1hr), and massage available. All rooms are en-suite but don't have TV or phone. The lodge is almost an hour's walk off the QCT or a 15min water-taxi ride from Picton ($45; Picton departures daily 9am, 12.15pm, 3.15pm & 5.30pm). Closed June–Aug. Units $\overline{\$90}$, chalets $\overline{\$255}$

MistletoeBay Eco Village Mistletoe Bay, Km65 ☎03 573 4048, ⓦmistletoebay.co.nz. Family-oriented, road-accessible rustic luxury in either the Whare (eight cabins with a communal kitchen), Jo house, a self-contained cottage or the backpackers and campsite with a camp kitchen and coin-op showers ($2). A small store sells home-grown organic produce, meats, eggs and fresh coffee. Camping $\overline{\$16}$, backpackers $\overline{\$30}$, Jo House $\overline{\$140}$, Whare cabins $\overline{\$140}$

★ **Anakiwa Backpackers** Anakiwa, Km71 ☎03 574 1388, ⓦanakiwabackpackers.co.nz. Greatly improved and renovated hostel, with made-up beds, free kayaks, a windsurfer ($25), an espresso machine and a coffee caravan directly opposite. It makes a great base for walking the southern end of the track or just hanging out. There's a four-bed dorm, doubles, and a self-contained apartment sleeping four. Dorms $\overline{\$33}$, rooms $\overline{\$85}$, en suites $\overline{\$105}$, apartment $\overline{\$125}$

★ **Anakiwa Lodge** 9 Lady Cobham Grove, Anakiwa ☎03 574 2115, ⓦanakiwa.co.nz. Around 400m from the end of the track, this comfortable associate YHA sleeps ten and offers internet and wi-fi, pre-prepared dinners ($16), free kayaks and a spa pool. Dorm $\overline{\$33}$, rooms $\overline{\$86}$, en suite $\overline{\$110}$, deluxe $\overline{\$130}$

THE ROUTE

The track passes through some grassy farmland and open gorse-covered hills, but both ends of it are forest reserves. There are a number of **detours** off the main track, including a short walk from Ship Cove to a pretty forest-shrouded waterfall, a scramble down to the Bay of Many Coves, or a foray to the Antimony Mines (where there are exposed shafts – stick to the marked tracks). To do the whole track in three days, get an early start from Ship Cove and plan to hike to Camp Bay. From there you have a fairly long day to Portage, then a relatively easy finish.

Ship Cove to Resolution Bay (4.5km; 1–2hr; 200m ascent). The track climbs steeply away from the shore through largely untouched forest to a lookout with great views of Motuara Island, before dropping down to Resolution Bay, where there's a DOC campsite.

Resolution Bay to Endeavour Inlet (15km; 3–5hr; 200m ascent). Follows an old bridle path over the ridge to *Furneaux Lodge* and *Endeavour Resort*.

Endeavour Inlet to Camp Bay (11.5km; 3–4hr; 100m ascent). Coastal track through regenerating forest packed with birdlife. There's a DOC campsite and several lodges.

Camp Bay to Portage (24.5km; 6–8hr; 650m ascent). The longest stretch without convenient roofed accommodation (just two DOC campsites) is also the most rewarding, mostly following a ridge with views down to the Sounds on both sides.

Portage to Mistletoe Bay (7.5km; 3–4hr; 450m ascent). A steep initial climb is followed by a pleasant ridge walk through manuka, gorse and shrubs with the chance to break the journey at the *Lochmara Lodge*, some 2km off the track.

Mistletoe Bay to Anakiwa (12.5km; 3–4hr; 100m ascent). Follows an old bridle path well above the water with great views, then finishes off through some lovely beech forest.

French Pass itself, a narrow channel between the mainland and D'Urville Island where nineteenth-century French explorer Dumont d'Urville was spun by tumultuous whirlpools. If you're here at mid-tide it is easy to understand why these seething waters were so feared. The maelstrom is best seen from a couple of short tracks in **French Pass Scenic Reserve**, 1km before the road end at **French Pass**. This tiny settlement is little more than a wharf, a shop, DOC's basic *French Pass* campsite (see p.458) and *Sea Safaris & Beachfront Villas* (see p.458).

ARRIVAL AND DEPARTURE

By bus and water taxi Buses between Picton and Nelson all stop at Havelock, while local bus and water taxi

HAVELOCK AND PELORUS SOUND

operators offer services to Kenepuru and Pelorus sounds.

INFORMATION AND ACTIVITIES

Tourist information Rutherford YHA, 46 Main Rd (daily 8.30am–9.30pm; ☎03 574 2104, ⊛ havelockinfocentre .co.nz). The YHA contains the Havelock Info Centre, which can make recommendations and bookings and also acts as the local DOC agent.

Sea Safaris French Pass ☎03 576 5204, ⊛ seasafaris .co.nz. Runs dive trips (from 2hr; $95; own gear required,

can be rented in Nelson; minimum $360 charter) and fishing charters (from 2hr; $95/person; minimum $360), rents sea kayaks ($80/double), and takes groups over to D'Urville Island for mountain biking (bike not supplied) and walking (both $215 for two), wildlife trips ($95), and dolphin and seal swimming (swimming $145; watching $95).

ACCOMMODATION

HAVELOCK

Blue Moon Backpackers 48 Main Rd ☎03 574 2212, ⊜ bookings@bluemoonhavelock.co.nz. The rooms are small but comfortable, and there are good communal facilities in this intimate hostel right in the centre of town, with friendly, very helpful hosts. Dorms $25, rooms $66

★ **Havelock Garden Motel** 71 Main Rd ☎03 574 2387, ⊛ gardenmotels.com. Slightly older, fully self-contained units that are well kept and clean and set in a beautiful green garden with mature trees. The hosts are very helpful. $125

Havelock Motor Camp 24 Inglis St ☎03 574 2339, ⊛ havelockmotorcamp.co.nz. Simple traditional Kiwi campsite with good communal facilities and a good location near the centre of the community, just off Main Road. You'll need to book in the summer. Camping $12, cabins and on-site vans $44

Rutherford YHA 46 Main Rd ☎03 574 2104, ⊛ havelockinfocentre.co.nz. A traditional hostel that

occupies an old schoolhouse where pioneering atomic nucleus discoverer Ernest Rutherford was educated for two years from 1882. Camping $12, dorms $28, rooms $60

PELORUS BRIDGE SCENIC RESERVE

Kahikatea Flat campsite ☎03 571 6019. A recently revamped but still basic DOC camping area that has a fabulously sited kitchen block, plus toilets, hot showers and tap water. Camping $10

FRENCH PASS

French Pass campsite A basic 18-pitch DOC site with tap water, toilets and cold showers. Booking required from Dec 1–Feb 28. Camping $6, camping from Dec 1–Feb 28, plus Easter & Labour weekends $7

Sea Safaris & Beachfront Villas ☎03 576 5204, ⊛ seasafaris.co.nz. B&B beachfront accommodation in self-contained units, all of which have a BBQ and patio. Meals available on request ($42). Closed June–Sept. $220

EATING AND DRINKING

Havelock Hotel 54 Main Rd, Havelock ☎03 574 2412. Serves simple cuisine in massive portions for under $20, including steak and chips, fish and chips and pie and chips, plus the odd non-chip dish. Daily 11am–late, kitchen closes at 9pm.

Slip Inn Havelock Marina ☎03 574 2345, ⊛ slipinn .co.nz. This marina-side establishment does good mussel dishes ($19) topped with the likes of pesto and parmesan

or sweet chilli, or a sampler of seven mussels with different toppings ($10.50), plus cod and chips, steaks or pizzas ($18–30). It's also fine for coffee or a sundowner. Daily 8am–late.

The Wakamarinian 70 Main Rd ☎03 574 1180. Simple café-style food, and particularly recommended for its good pies; try the mussel pie ($8–15). Feb–Nov Mon–Sat 8am–4pm; Dec–Jan daily 8am–4pm.

Nelson

The thriving city of **Nelson**, set on the coast in a broad basin between the Arthur and Richmond ranges, is beguiling. Low rent and rise, it is not much to look at, but its location – supremely placed for accessing Golden Bay, and Abel Tasman, Kahurangi and Nelson Lakes national parks – warm sunny climate, access to good beaches and a cluster of worthwhile wineries in the hinterland are powerful lures to tourists, painters and potters alike, all drawn by the sunlight, the landscape and the unique raw materials for ceramic art that lie beneath the rich green grass. All this makes the city one of the most popular visitor destinations in New Zealand. You can even do an **Abel Tasman day-trip** from Nelson using early buses, which give you enough time for a water taxi ride and a few hours' walking along the Coast Track.

Within central Nelson itself the **Suter Gallery** and the lively **Saturday Market** are good diversions, but you'll soon want to venture further, perhaps to **Tahunanui Beach** or the suburb of **Stoke** for the fascinating **World of WearableArt** museum.

The Nelson Arts Festival (twelve days in mid-Oct; ⓦnelsonfestivals.co.nz) includes theatre, music, readings and street entertainment, much of it either free or costing just a few dollars. The city also hosts the Nelson Jazz & Blues Festival (eight days from Jan 2; ⓦnelsonjazzfest.co.nz) at various venues around the city.

Brief history

Nelson is one of the oldest settlements in New Zealand. By the middle of the sixteenth century, it was occupied by the Ngati Tumatakokiri people, some of whom provided a reception committee for **Abel Tasman**'s longboats at Murderer's Bay (now Golden Bay), where they killed four of his sailors.

By the time Europeans arrived in earnest, Maori numbers had been decimated by internecine fighting and the nearest *pa* site to Nelson was at Motueka, though this did

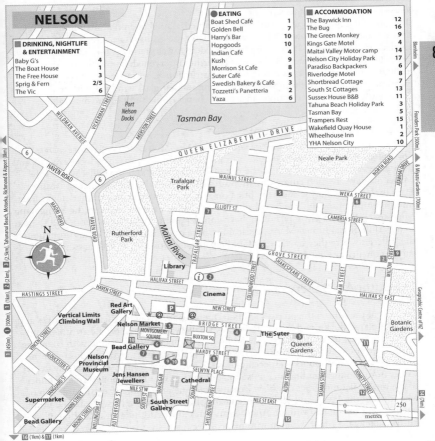

NELSON

◼ DRINKING, NIGHTLIFE & ENTERTAINMENT
Baby G's	4
The Boat House	1
The Free House	3
Sprig & Fern	2/5
The Vic	6

◼ EATING
Boat Shed Café	1
Golden Bell	7
Harry's Bar	10
Hopgoods	10
Indian Café	4
Kush	9
Morrison St Cafe	8
Suter Café	5
Swedish Bakery & Café	3
Tozzetti's Panetteria	2
Yaza	6

◼ ACCOMMODATION
The Baywick Inn	12
The Bug	16
The Green Monkey	9
Kings Gate Motel	4
Maitai Valley Motor camp	14
Nelson City Holiday Park	17
Paradiso Backpackers	6
Riverlodge Motel	8
Shortbread Cottage	7
South St Cottages	13
Sussex House B&B	11
Tahuna Beach Holiday Park	3
Tasman Bay	5
Trampers Rest	15
Wakefield Quay House	1
Wheelhouse Inn	2
YHA Nelson City	10

Port Nelson Docks

Tasman Bay

QUEEN ELIZABETH II DRIVE

Neale Park

WAINUI STREET

Trafalgar Park

WEKA STREET

ELLIOTT ST

CAMBRIA STREET

Rutherford Park

Maitai River

GROVE STREET

SHAKESPEARE STREET

HALIFAX ST EAST

Library

HALIFAX STREET

HAVEN STREET

HASTINGS STREET

Cinema

NEW STREET

Vertical Limits Climbing Wall

Red Art Gallery

Nelson Market

BRIDGE STREET

Botanic Gardens

MONTGOMERY SQUARE

BUXTON SQ.

Bead Gallery

HARDY STREET

The Suter

Queens Gardens

Nelson Provincial Museum

SELWYN PLACE

Jens Hansen Jewellers

Cathedral

NILE ST W

Supermarket

South Street Gallery

NILE ST EAST

Bead Gallery

0   250
metres

◀ 16 (1km) & 17 (1km)

8

Blenheim ▶

Founders Park (500m) ▶ & Miyazu Gardens (700m) ▶

Geographic Centre of NZ ▶

14 (7m) ▶

NELSON MARKET

Saturday morning should involve a pilgrimage to the renowned **Nelson Market** (8am–1pm), which takes over Montgomery Square. Artists are flushed out of their rural boltholes and stalls groan with hand-dipped candles, turned wooden bowls, bracelets made from forks and all manner of produce from the crafts community. Food stalls with mounds of fruit, endless varieties of fresh bread and fish, Thai and vegetarian dishes, preserves, coffee and cakes sustain you while you browse.

little to prevent land squabbles, culminating in the **Wairau Affray** in 1843. Despite assurances from Maori chiefs Te Rauparaha and Te Rangihaeata, that they would abide by the decision of a land commissioner, the New Zealand Company pre-emptively sent surveyors south to the Wairau Plains, the catalyst for a skirmish during which Te Rangihaeata's wife was shot. The bereaved chief and his men slaughtered 22 people in retaliation but the settlers continued their land acquisition after numbers were boosted by a wave of immigrants from Germany.

Christ Church Cathedral

Trafalgar St • Daily 9am–5pm (services permitting) • Free

The glowering, grey-stone Christ Church Cathedral, perched on a small hill peering down Trafalgar Street towards the sea, dominates the grid-pattern streets of Nelson. English architect Frank Peck's original 1924 design was gradually modified over many years due to lack of money; World War II further intervened, and even now the cathedral tower still looks as if it's under construction. Contrasting with the grim exterior, the interior is illuminated by dazzling stained-glass windows with ten particularly noteworthy examples in a small chapel to the right of the main altar.

Nelson Provincial Museum

Corner of Hardy and Trafalgar sts • Mon–Fri 10am–5pm, Sat & Sun 10am–4.30pm • $5 • ☎ 03 548 9588, ⓦ nelsonmuseum.co.nz

The **Nelson Provincial Museum** takes a fresh, multimedia approach to local exhibits and then draws strands from them to the rest of New Zealand and the wider world. The Maori displays are each curated by the various local *iwi* with their choice of treasures from their own *marae*; witness the fine bone club, delicate flax and feather cloak, and interpretation of the designs in *tukutuku* panels. The death masks from the Mangatapu Murders highlight a grisly tale of robbery, murder and betrayal from 1866, and there's a collection of traditional Maori musical instruments whose sounds echo throughout the galleries where they have a new Goldie painting. Upstairs, travelling exhibitions of varying quality and merit take centre stage.

The Suter Art Gallery

208 Bridge St • Daily 10.30am–4.30pm • $3; free on Sat • ⓦ thesuter.org.nz

Just east of the centre, the pretty Victorian **Queens Gardens**, with their mature trees and well-populated duck pond, host **The Suter Art Gallery**. This small public art museum is one of the finest in the South Island and hosts visiting exhibitions along with changing displays from its own extensive collection. During the summer try to catch something of its stock of **watercolours** – especially those of John Gully whose works largely depict scenes from the surrounding area. Also look out for oils by **Toss Woollaston**, a founder of the modernist movement in New Zealand and one of a group of artists and writers who, during the 1930s and 1940s, began exploring notions of a New Zealand culture independent of colonial Britain. Another must is Gottfried Lindauer's painting of Huria Matenga, a Maori woman who helped save many lives from the wreck of the

Delaware in 1863. Posed against a background of the foundering American ship, her status (*mana*) is denoted by feathers, bone, greenstone jewellery and the ceremonial club she holds. The building is also host to a smashing little bijou independent **cinema** which often does art-house movie screenings and foreign films (see p.466).

Botanical Reserve

Accessed from the corner of Milton and Hardy sts • Open access • Free

At the east end of Bridge Street is the **Botanical Reserve**, where New Zealand's first ever rugby game was played in 1870. The hill behind commands a good view over the town and, it is claimed, marks the **geographical centre** of New Zealand.

Founders Park

87 Atawhai Drive • Daily 10am–4.30pm; Miyazu Gardens daily 8am–dusk • $7; gardens free

About 1km north of the Botanical Reserve, **Founders Park** offers a somewhat sanitized version of early colonial history through relocated and replica buildings. Next door, the delightful Japanese-style **Miyazu Gardens** celebrate the relationship between Nelson and its sister city Miyazu. The gardens are a quiet oasis of reflective pools, ornamental cherry trees and traditional bridges.

Tahunanui Beach

4km northwest of central Nelson

Haven Road (SH6) runs northwest out of central Nelson and, after 1km, becomes **Wakefield Quay**, a popular spot for strolling along the waterfront but primarily known for the *Boat Shed Café* jutting picturesquely over the water. Continue 3km along SH6 to reach **Tahunanui Beach Reserve**, a long golden strand backed by grassland and

8

NELSON ARTS AND CRAFTS

Many of the region's artists and craftspeople display at galleries outside Nelson (see p.466) but you can get an idea of what's in store by visiting galleries in town. Good starting points are listed below.

Red Art Gallery 1 Bridge St ☎03 548 2170. Specializes in contemporary New Zealand fine art, glass and jewellery. Mon–Fri 8am–4pm, Sat & Sun 9am–2pm.

Catchment Gallery 255 Hardy St ☎03 539 4100. The emphasis here is on quality painting, sculpture, prints and jewellery. Tues–Fri 10am–5pm, Sat 10am–2pm.

South Street Gallery 10 Nile St. Standing on the corner of South Street, one of Nelson's oldest with a row of pretty workers' cottages, this gallery specializes in local pottery. Mon–Fri 8.30am–4.30pm, Sat & Sun 10am–4pm.

Bead Gallery 157 Hardy St ⓦbeads.co.nz. The Bead Gallery is packed to the rafters with over 10,000 bead styles, all for sale. The idea is simple; you either design your own bead-piece or have one custom-made for you using anything from 10¢ baubles to some of the most exotic anywhere in the world (up to $200 a piece). They have a particularly fine range of psychedelic century-old Venetian glass trade beads from West Africa at relatively modest prices. Mon–Sat 9am–5pm, Sun 10am–4pm.

Stephan Gillberg Bone Carving 87 Green St ☎03 546 4275, ⓦcarvingbone.co.nz. Another opportunity to put your creativity to work comes in the form of bone carving; one-day workshops will see you complete an attractive pendant by the end of the day, have a reasonable understanding of how the process works and know a bit about what the traditional symbols mean. $79 with pick-up from your accommodation at 9.30am.

Jens Hansen 320 Trafalgar Square ⓦjenshansen .com. *Lord of the Rings* fans will want to visit the jeweller's Jens Hansen, who Peter Jackson got to make "The one ring to rule them all", or a few dozen of them to suit various cast members. Replicas are available. Mon–Fri 9am–5pm, Sat 9am–2pm, Sun in summer 10am–1pm.

drifting dunes. It is where Nelson comes to relax on sunny weekends, with safe swimming, a fun park, zoo and children's playgrounds: buses run here frequently along SH6 from the city.

World of WearableArt (WOW)

95 Quarantine Rd • Daily 10am–5pm • $22 • ⓦ wowcars.co.nz

About 3km out of Nelson on SH6, follow signs off the roundabout to the **World of WearableArt and Classic Cars** for a unique theatrical experience. It is primarily a purpose-built showcase for the best designs from the annual WearableArt show, a fashion show with a difference first put on by Suzie Moncrieff in Nelson in 1987 and now held annually in Wellington. Participants from around the world submit sculptures or pieces of art that can be worn as clothes – many made from the most unusual materials such as household junk, food, metal, stone, wood and tyres. A thirty-minute video of past shows sets the scene for the best of the costumes themselves, all theatrically displayed.

NELSON ACTIVITIES

Nelson is the sort of place where sunbathing at Tahunanui might be as active as you want to get, though there is no shortage of energetic diversions.

QUAD BIKING AND THE SKYWIRE

Happy Valley Adventures 194 Cable Bay Rd 17km northeast of Nelson off SH6 ☏ 03 545 0304, ⓦ happyvalleyadventures.co.nz. Explore up to 40km of track on a large forested farm, climbing hills, passing monstrous matai trees, stopping to learn a little about the forest and its stories and eventually reaching a high spot with expansive views of Cable Bay. The most popular trips are the Bayview Circuit (2hr; rider $150; passenger $30), and the Blue Hill Ride (3hr; $160; no passengers) designed for the more skilled and ambitious rider. Happy Valley Adventures also operates the Skywire ($85), a four-seater cable-car chair that swoops almost 1km across a forested valley at speeds of around 80kmph then back to the excellent hilltop café with its panoramic deck. The birds-eye view is spectacular and many people find the return, with your back to the action, a little unnerving.

HORSE RIDING

Stonehurst Farm Horse Treks 17km southwest of Nelson on Haycock Rd ☏ 0800 487 357, ⓦ stonehurstfarm.co.nz. The majority of treks (1hr $70; 2hr 30min $110; 3hr $140) take place in the foothills of the Richmond ranges, offering great views of the coast and beyond.

TANDEM PARAGLIDING AND HANG-GLIDING

Nelson Paragliding ☏ 0508 359 669, ⓦ nelsonparagliding.co.nz. A hair-raising drive up the hill to the launch site reveals a spectacular landscape, before you run like hell then glide off into the quiet up draughts for 15–20min of eerily silent flight. Tandem flights go for $180 and a one-day introductory lesson costs $250.

Nelson Hang Gliding ☏ 03 548 9151, ⓦ flynelson.co.nz. Offers more of a birdlike quality to your flight experience than paragliding (15min tandem flight $185).

KAYAKING AND SAILING

Cable Bay Kayaks ☏ 0508 222 532, ⓦ cablebaykayaks.co.nz. Paddling with this outfit makes a refreshing change from the mayhem around Abel Tasman. They do a half-day trip ($85) and a full-day tour ($145; bring your own lunch) which gives more time for exploring the caves of this beautiful and intricate coastline and doing a little snorkelling. They're based near Happy Valley (see above) and will pick up from Nelson.

Sail Nelson ☏ 03 546 7275, ⓦ sailnelson.co.nz. Runs sailing charters and great, fully catered sailing courses (two-day beginner $500; five-day RYA course $1595) living aboard a 10m yacht, typically around D'Urville Island and Abel Tasman. Courses run on fixed dates for two to four people.

ROCK CLIMBING

Vertical Limits 34 Vanguard St ☏ 0508 837 842, ⓦ verticallimits.co.nz. Indoor rock climbing is ideal for a wet day, and when the weather improves join the full-day climbing trips ($150) to Payne's Ford in Takaka.

ARRIVAL AND DEPARTURE

By plane Flights arrive at Nelson airport, 8km west of the centre. Super Shuttle (☎0800 748 885; $17 one person; $21 for two) meets most flights, or you can grab a taxi (☎03 548 8225; $27).

Destinations Auckland (12 daily; 1hr 20min); Christchurch (4 daily; 50min); Wellington (10 daily; 35min).

By bus Long-distance buses drop you near the centre of the city, within easy walking distance of most accommodation. InterCity and Abel Tasman Coachlines pull in at 27 Bridge St,

while the other companies all stop outside the i-SITE.

Destinations Blenheim (4 daily; 1hr 40min); Christchurch (2 daily; 7–8hr); Collingwood (1 daily; 2hr 45min); Fox Glacier (1 daily; 9hr 30min); Franz Josef (1 daily; 9hr); Greymouth (2 daily; 6–8hr); Heaphy Track (1 daily; 3hr 30min); Kawatiri Junction, for Nelson Lakes (1 daily; 1hr 5min); Motueka (5 daily; 1hr); Murchison (2 daily; 2–4hr); Picton (4 daily; 2hr); Punakaiki (2 daily; 4hr 40min); Takaka (2–3 daily; 2hr–2hr 30min); Westport (2 daily; 3hr).

GETTING AROUND

By bike AvantiPlus, 114 Hardy St (☎03 548 1666), rents bikes from $30/half-day, depending on the type.

By car Daily rates start at about $70; $45/day for week-long rentals. Try: Nelson Car Hire (☎0800 283 545, ⓦnelsoncarhire.co.nz); Ace (☎0800 422 373); Apex (☎03 546 9028); Hardy Cars (☎0800 903 010); Rent-a-Dent (☎03 546 9890); and Thrifty (☎03 547 5563).

By taxi Nelson City Taxis ☎03 548 8225.

By bus SBL buses (☎03 548 1539, ⓦnelsoncoaches.co.nz) run local routes to Tahunanui Beach and Stoke from the terminal at 27 Bridge St, while Abel Tasman Coachlines leaves Nelson at 6.45am daily in summer for Mapua ($10), Marahau ($20) and Totaranui ($45), via Motueka ($12), connecting with launch services deeper into the Abel Tasman National Park. They also run a service to Takaka ($35) in Golden Bay, with links to the Heaphy Track ($33).

INFORMATION

i-SITE and DOC Corner of Trafalgar and Halifax sts (Mon–Fri 8.30am–5pm, Sat & Sun 9am–4pm; ☎03 548 2304, ⓦnelsonnz.com). Nelson's main source of information also contains the DOC (same hours; ☎03 546 9339), which does track bookings and has details on the local national parks, including Abel Tasman tide tables.

Websites Check out ⓦbackpacknelson.co.nz, which has

links to local accommodation, entertainment, seasonal work and much more.

Cycling information Given the opening of the cycleway to Abel Tasman National Park you might want to check out U Bikes (☎0800 282 453, ⓦubike.co.nz) and A2B Ecycle (☎021 222 7260, ⓦa2b-ecycle.co.nz) for information on cycling the tracks and bike hire.

8

ACCOMMODATION

There's a broad range of accommodation, much of it in the centre of town within reach of cultural diversions and nightlife. Classy **B&Bs** and excellent **hostels** are abundant, and there are a couple of campsites close to town, but you may want to save your camping for the prettier areas around Motueka, the national park or Golden Bay.

★ **The Baywick Inn** 51 Domett St ☎03 545 6514, ⓦbaywick.com. Lovely, renovated two-storey 1885 villa, overlooking the Maitai River with luxuriously appointed rooms, two in a new cottage out back. An enthusiastic welcome includes afternoon tea, while the full cooked breakfasts are delicious. Three-course dinners by arrangement ($50–60). Free wi-fi. Room with private bath $\underline{165}$, en suite $\underline{195}$, cottage rooms $\underline{225}$

★ **The Bug** 226 Vanguard St ☎03 539 4227, ⓦthebug.co.nz. Welcoming 46-bed hostel about 1km from the centre of Nelson adorned with VW Beetle paraphernalia. Along with free bikes, free internet and wi-fi and local pick-ups they have a hammock, table football and a female dorm, and make a point of lacking a TV. Dorms $\underline{23}$, rooms $\underline{66}$, en suites $\underline{80}$

★ **The Green Monkey** 129 Milton St ☎03 545 7421, ⓦthegreenmonkey.co.nz. Wonderfully quiet boutique hostel in a converted villa that's beautifully looked after but still has a relaxed atmosphere. Free internet, wi-fi,

bikes and occasional chocolate cake. Book well in advance. Dorms $\underline{26}$, doubles $\underline{68}$

Kings Gate Motel 21 Trafalgar St ☎0800 104 022, ⓦkingsgatemotel.co.nz. Centrally located refurbished motel with spacious, comfortable and well-kept rooms including full kitchens, spa baths and wi-fi access. There's also a pool. $\underline{159}$

Maitai Valley Motor Camp 472 Maitai Valley Rd ☎03 548 7729, ⓦmvmc.co.nz. Bargain basic camping in a quiet, lovely wooded section beside the Maitai River (with good swimming holes) 7km southeast of Nelson. The simple cabins and camp sites are set among mature trees. Camping $\underline{12}$, cabins $\underline{50}$

Nelson City Holiday Park 230 Vanguard Rd ☎0800 778 898, ⓦnelsonholidaypark.co.nz. Small and well-managed campervan park with limited tent space but various grades of accommodation from simple cabins to more salubrious kitchen cabins and one-bed units. Bike rental available for $35/day. Camping $\underline{30}$, powered site

$\underline{\$40}$, cabins $\underline{\$50}$, kitchen cabins $\underline{\$60}$, self-contained units $\underline{\$80}$, one-bed units $\underline{\$110}$

Paradiso Backpackers 42 Weka St ☎03 546 6703 & ☎0800 269 667, ⊕backpackernelson.co.nz. A big hostel set in a converted villa with purpose-designed outbuildings, sleeping around 140. The outdoor pool, spa, sauna, volleyball and free wi-fi attempt to make up in shiny things what it lacks in space, quiet and privacy; the slightly more expensive motel units next door offer more of the last two. Packed in the summer. Dorms $\underline{\$25}$, en-suite share $\underline{\$29}$, rooms $\underline{\$66}$, motels $\underline{\$140}$

Riverlodge Motel 31 Collingwood St ☎03 548 3094, ⊕riverlodgenelson.co.nz. One of the better motels in town, giving good value for money across a range of units, all of which are clean and comfortable with access to a guest laundry. All have Sky TV, good showers and some have spa baths. $\underline{\$150}$

★ **Shortbread Cottage** 33 Trafalgar St ☎03 546 6681, ⊕shortbreadcottage.co.nz. Yummy boutique hostel with polished-wood floors, only thirteen comfy beds, free internet and wi-fi, loads of peace and quiet and lots of home comforts. Book well ahead. Dorms $\underline{\$26}$, rooms $\underline{\$60}$

South St Cottages South St ☎03 540 2769, ⊕cottageaccommodation.co.nz. Three gorgeous 1860s cottages (numbers 1, 3 & 12 in Nelson's prettiest street) are let on a nightly, self-catering basis with breakfast provisions supplied by the knowledgeable hosts. The accommodation is charmingly old-fashioned but with all mod cons. Also on offer is a luxury two-bedroom apartment on the corner of South and Nile sts. $\underline{\$225}$

Sussex House B&B 238 Bridge St ☎03 548 9972, ⊕sussex.co.nz. Charming five-room B&B in a central, 1880s villa featuring honey-coloured rimu floors and welcoming hosts. All rooms are en-suite, except for one with a private bathroom, and two rooms have access to a veranda. The extensive continental breakfasts are great and there's free internet. $\underline{\$180}$

Tahuna Beach Holiday Park 70 Beach Rd, Tahunanui ☎0800 500 501, ⊕tahunabeach.co.nz. Absolutely enormous, sometimes overwhelming, estuary-side campsite a 5min walk from Tahunanui Beach with loads of facilities, including a mini-golf course and kids' playgrounds, and a wide range of accommodation. Book far in advance for the summer. Camping $\underline{\$17}$, cabins $\underline{\$50}$, kitchen cabins $\underline{\$65}$, self-contained units/motels $\underline{\$110}$

Tasman Bay 10 Weka St ☎0800 222 572 ⊕tasmanbaybackpackers.co.nz. A comfortable purpose-built hostel a few minutes from the town centre, with clean, spacious rooms (some en-suite) and enthusiastic, friendly management who ensure you always get more than you pay for. Free bikes, and free chocolate pudding nightly. Camping $\underline{\$18}$, dorms $\underline{\$25}$, rooms $\underline{\$66}$, en suite $\underline{\$85}$

Trampers Rest 31 Alton St ☎03 545 7477. Lovely and cosy backpackers with only eight beds in comparatively small rooms. TV watching is by consensus only, there's free internet and wi-fi, a tuned piano, and the wee garden boasts a hammock, avocado tree and bike storage. There are also free bikes, and the owner, a real tramping enthusiast, is an absolute mine of information. Dorms $\underline{\$29}$, single $\underline{\$48}$, doubles $\underline{\$66}$

★ **Wakefield Quay House** 385 Wakefield Quay ☎03 545 8209, ⊕wakefieldquay.co.nz. Great B&B with stupendous sea views over Haulashore Island. The house is up a steep rise from the busy road. Both rooms are beautifully turned out and come with drinks on arrival plus a tasty breakfast the next day. $\underline{\$325}$

★ **Wheelhouse Inn** 41 Whitby Rd ☎03 546 8391, ⊕wheelhouse.co.nz. The bay views are magical from the picture windows of these five nautically themed, self-catering apartments high on the hill, 2km west of central Nelson. All are very private and come with full kitchen, laundry, TV/DVD, internet and BBQ, but you'll need to book well in advance. The Captain's Quarters is the largest, sleeping up to six. $\underline{\$275}$

★ **YHA Nelson City** 59 Rutherford St ☎03 545 9988, ⊕yha.nelson@yha.co.nz. Purpose-built, this is the best hostel in Nelson, and consequently has the best facilities, including two kitchens, plenty of communal space, informed staff and an infrared sauna. There's a wide range of accommodation, including connecting rooms for families and two disabled-access units. Dorms $\underline{\$29}$, rooms $\underline{\$78}$, en suites $\underline{\$98}$

EATING

Nelson's enviable lifestyle is reflected in the broad choice of eating options within easy reach of the town centre. And when you tire of these, there's always fine food on the waterfront, at Mapua Wharf or at the wineries. Nelson's pubs and bars (see opposite) are also good for a quick snack.

Boat Shed Café 350 Wakefield Quay ☎03 546 9783. Fine views over Tasman Bay make this converted boat shed hanging out over the water a hit, but you also get fabulous, fresh seafood and great concoctions from the best local producers. Perfect for romantic sunset dinners and relaxed lunches. Try the Trust the Chef menu (five small courses $60; add dessert $70). Daily 10am–late.

Golden Bell 104 Hardy St. Top traditional Thai, relaxed and well run and dishing up all your perennial favourites for around $20. BYO. Daily 11.30am–2.30pm and 5pm–late.

★ **Harry's Bar** 296 Trafalgar St ☎03 539 0905. Smooth cocktail bar and Asian restaurant, known these days primarily for good-quality well-priced food, including particularly fine crispy duck, chilli salt squid, fried snapper and kaffir lime tart. At weekends it can also get a bit lively after the plates are stacked. Tues–Sat 4pm–late.

Hopgoods 284 Trafalgar St ☎03 545 7191. Some of Nelson's finest dining is found in this airy restaurant with outdoor streetside tables. Locally sourced, organic produce informs a range of seasonal dishes fashioned by a perfectionist chef into traditional European-influenced gastronomy. Expect the likes of herb roast lamb with potato boulangere, spring carrots, peas and mint gremolata ($36). Mon–Sat 5.30–9.30pm.

★ **Indian Café** 94 Collingwood St ☎03 548 4098. The town's best curry house is set in a historic villa and dishes up all your favourites, plus one or two highly imaginative variations, for around $18, as well as offering a takeaway menu ($9–25). Mon–Fri noon–2pm & daily 5pm–late.

Kush 5 Church St. Funky, licensed coffee house named after the eponymous kingdom in Ethiopia thought to be populated by the world's first coffee drinkers. The decor cashes in on 1970s kitsch with grotesquely upholstered pre-loved sofas and Formica wall units full of interesting books. The real star is the coffee, with a great selection of organic beans and each duty manager roasting their own *in situ*, while keeping the bug-eyed caffeine addicts fuelled on double shots. The counter food is simple but tasty, they do legendary brunches on Sundays, the notice board is full of local gossip and they host tango classes on Sat nights. Mon–Thurs 7.30am–4.30pm, Fri & Sat 7.30am–10pm, Sun 9am–2pm.

Morrison St Cafe 244 Hardy St. Semi-formal café serving extremely good-quality brunches, lunches and snacks, with many dishes dairy or gluten free. Along with the liberal sprinkling of local art adorning the walls there

is outdoor seating, newspapers and magazines, but don't let anything distract you from the food ($9–28), which is rightly popular with the natives, including home-made muesli, *kumara* and leek fritters and excellent coffee. Mon–Fri 7.30am–4.30pm, Sat & Sun 9am–4pm.

Suter Café 208 Bridge St. Daytime licensed café in the Suter Art Gallery with views over the Queens Gardens duck pond. The food is fresh and imaginative ($5–15) and the setting conducive to lounging around for snacks, wine and coffee after an hour wandering the gallery or catching a flick in the cinema. Daily 9am–4pm.

★ **Swedish Bakery & Café** 54 Bridge St. So small you could blink and miss it, but if you do you'll kick yourself. Genuine Danishes, Swedish marzipan treats and sandwiches (including Swedish meatball and beetroot combos) sit beside some classic bakery favourites including a passion fruit and lemon tart that is quite literally the taste of summer. Nothing on the menu is over $15. Mon–Fri 8.30am–3.30pm, Sat 9.30am–1.30pm.

Tozzetti's Panetteria 41 Halifax St. Wonderful little bakery serving freshly cut sandwiches, great pies, muffins, delicious cakes and stupendous bread (all under $12). Go early to get the pies – particularly the fish – and don't be surprised if you leave with more than you intended to buy. Mon–Fri 7am–4pm, Sat 7.30am–noon.

★ **Yaza** Montgomery Square. So hip it'll never need a replacement, this cool licensed café is the epitome of laidback. They serve excellent breakfasts, lunches, coffees and the cheesiest cheese scones around (most items $5–20). It's also worth seeking out for its occasional evening entertainments including poetry, music, DJs and talks. Mon–Fri 8am–5pm, Sat & Sun 8am–4pm.

DRINKING, NIGHTLIFE AND ENTERTAINMENT

While most of its suburban neighbours retire early to sip cocoa, Nelson stays up and parties – at least on Friday and Saturday. For raucous boozing and some dancing head for Trafalgar Street or the half-dozen bars on Bridge Street between Trafalgar and Collingwood streets. Pubs and **bars** of all stripes often have **live music**, karaoke and DJ **nights**; pick up the *Star Times* gig guide flyer to find out **what's on**.

★ **Baby G's** 8 Church St ☎03 545 8957. Nelson's "alternative" venue, with Mon improv night, Thurs open mic evenings and regular burlesque shows at weekends, plus a selection of live music and DJ sounds. Wed–Sat 5pm–late.

The Boat House 326 Wakefield Quay ☎03 548 7646. Just down the road – on the Nelson side – from the more famous *Boat Shed Café* (see opposite), this private licensed club, set up in the 1980s to save the 1906 rowing club building – a large stilted boat shed and ramp hanging over the waves. Open to the public and now a highly regarded live music venue (cover charges $10–20), it's a fabulously atmospheric place to enjoy a gig, a drink and/or some delicious, home-made, high-end bar food (mains $16–22). Wed–Fri 11am–2pm

& Fri 5pm–late.

★ **The Free House** 95 Collingwood St. Brilliant pub in a former church fitted with the only hand pumps in town, perfect for microbrews from around the region and serving a selection of the best. Ask at the bar and they'll order in pizza or a curry from across the street, and there's often live music in the Bedouin-style tent out front. Mon–Thurs 11am–11pm, Fri–Sun 11am–midnight.

★ **Sprig & Fern** 280 Hardy St. Central incarnation of this local institution that started out on Milton St (see p.466), set in a double-fronted shop with LED light decoration at the top of the front windows and a large outdoor courtyard at the back. Great beer on tap (tasting racks of six beers cost $15), good pub surroundings and you can order takeaway to eat in. Popular with the locals, who come along for the chat, the pub quiz and because it's slightly less expensive than *The Free House* (see p.465). Daily 11am–10pm.

Sprig and Fern 134 Milton St. Suburban villa converted into a cosy bar with open fires and a selection of locally brewed, unpasteurized Sprig & Fern beers – crisp lagers and wheat beers to a ruby porter and a delicious pale ale – plus scrumpy, cider and a selection of local wines. Grab fish and chips from next door and bring them over. Daily 11am–10pm.

The Vic 281 Trafalgar St. Quality version of the Mac's brewery pubs that have sprung up all over the country, with a lively atmosphere, decent beer, good-value pub grub ($16–29) and mostly iffy live music with the occasional good band thrown in. Daily 11am–11pm.

CINEMA AND THEATRE

State Cinema 6 91 Trafalgar St ☏03 548 0808, ⓦstatecinemas.co.nz. Screens all the latest mainstream films.

Suter Art Gallery 208 Bridge St ☏03 548 0808, ⓦstatecinemas.co.nz. Screens films of more minority interest, mostly art house and foreign.

Nelson Theatre Royal 78 Rutherford St ☏03 548 3083. Recently renovated, the theatre has traditional touring productions, local shows and vaudeville/cabaret-style shows.

DIRECTORY

Internet Free at the library plus good rates at Aurora, 161 Trafalgar St, and Boots Off Travellers Centre, 53 Bridge St.
Library 27 Halifax St (Mon–Fri 10am–6pm, Sat 10am–1pm, Sun 1–4pm).
Left luggage Limited lockers at Boots Off Travellers Centre, 53 Bridge St.

Medical treatment Nelson Region After Hours and Duty Doctor, 96 Waimea Rd ☏03 546 8881 (daily 8am–10pm).
Pharmacy Prices Pharmacy, corner of Hardy & Collingwood sts. Mon–Fri 8.30am–8pm, Sat 9am–8pm, Sun 10am–6pm.
Post office 209 Hardy St (Mon–Fri 8am–5.30pm, Sat 9.30am–12.30pm).

8

The road to Abel Tasman

A great part of Nelson's charm lies on its doorstep, particularly the excellent **wineries** to the west. Here the vines appreciate the combination of New Zealand's sunniest climate and either the free-draining alluvial gravels of the Waimea Plains or the clay gravels of the Moutere Hills. Wineries are interspersed with the **studios** of a number of contemporary artists working in the Nelson region, many of whom exhibit in their own small **galleries**, showcasing ceramics, glass-blowing, woodturning, textiles, sculpture, installations and painting.

Almost everywhere of interest is located on or just off the much straightened SH60, which runs north from Richmond towards Motueka through rural scenery and sea views. A couple of kilometres north along SH60, the Moutere Highway cuts left for **Upper Moutere**, while Redwood Road turns right past the *Seifried* winery (see p.472) and on to the picture-book-pretty **Rabbit Island**, one of Nelson's most popular beaches.

You can sample the best of the region on an extended drive from Nelson to Motueka, but there's enough on offer to warrant spending a couple of leisurely days. Equip yourself with the *Nelson Wine Guide*, *Nelson Great Beer Trail*, *Nelson's Creative Pathways* and *Nelson Potters* leaflets, all free and available from visitor centres. A few kilometres further north, **Motueka** is the most practical base and provides the easiest access for trips into the Abel Tasman National Park.

Waimea Inlet and around

Höglund Art Glass

Lansdowne Rd • Daily 10am–5pm • ☏03 544 6500, ⓦhoglundartglass.com

Highway 6 runs 15km southwest of Nelson to Richmond where SH60 cuts straight north towards Motueka while its old route runs closer to the shores of **Waimea Inlet**. Roughly 5km along SH60, **Höglund Art Glass** is an international-standard glass gallery displaying a vast array of Scandinavian-influenced work. The bold bright designs work best on bigger pieces with clean lines, but prices start around $49 before swiftly

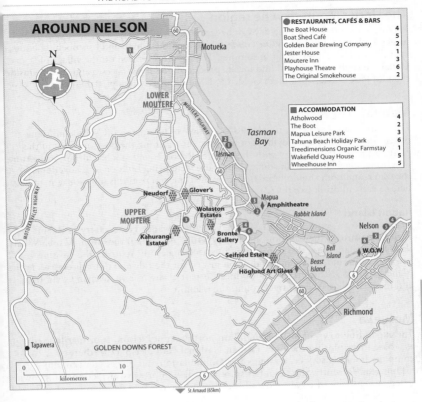

AROUND NELSON

RESTAURANTS, CAFÉS & BARS	
The Boat House	4
Boat Shed Café	5
Golden Bear Brewing Company	2
Jester House	1
Moutere Inn	3
Playhouse Theatre	6
The Original Smokehouse	2

ACCOMMODATION	
Atholwood	4
The Boot	2
Mapua Leisure Park	3
Tahuna Beach Holiday Park	6
Treedimensions Organic Farmstay	1
Wakefield Quay House	5
Wheelhouse Inn	5

8

entering the stratosphere. A glass museum introduces you to the history and techniques of handblown glass manufacture, through works by the Swedish owners Ola and Marie Höglund, and from December to April you can watch live glass-blowing.

Playhouse Café and Theatre

171 Westdale Rd • ☎ 03 540 2985 • Daily 11am–11pm or later • ⓦ playhousecafe.co.nz

Continuing north on SH60, follow the signs from the right-hand turn into Westdale Road and you'll end up at a relatively new curiosity that is well worth at least an hour of your time. The straw-house **Playhouse Café and Theatre** is a live, licensed venue serving interesting grub during the day and hosting an extraordinary array of performances at night. Fast becoming popular with live music acts, the grotto-like interior and Hundertwasser-esque decor plays host to lectures, talks, themed nights, plays, cabaret and travelling shows. The management offers free pick-up and drop-off for Nelson and Mapua, and cover charges apply ($5–15) for live music, depending on the act.

Bronte Gallery

122 Bronte Rd East • Daily 9am–5.30pm • ⓦ brontegallery.co.nz

Back on SH60, head north for Bronte Road East and signs to the **Bronte Gallery** about 1.5km off the highway. On display and for sale are highly individual works by internationally recognized ceramic artist Darryl Robertson and intriguing abstract oils by Lesley Jacka Robertson.

The Upper Moutere wine region

An interesting and rewarding day can be spent touring Nelson's wineries (see p.472), armed with the free *Nelson Wine Guide*, which includes a map and lists opening hours, typically daily 11am–4.30pm in summer. The region is centred on the village of **Upper Moutere**, where you'll find locally produced preserves, cheeses and the like inside the Old Post Office at Moutere Gold, 1381 Moutere Hwy (daily 10am–4pm).

Mapua

On a sunny late afternoon, tiny **MAPUA**, a couple of kilometres off SH60 and some 34km from Nelson, is an idyllic spot with the sun catching the boats moored in the picturesque Waimea Estuary with the pines of Rabbit Island as a backdrop. At the time of writing, a new boardwalk and amphitheatre were being built on a rise overlooking the water, and both should be complete by the time you read this, but you're mainly here to eat and drink (see p.472).

Rabbit Island

Before or after a good munch in Mapua, you might want to take a **ferry** to Rabbit Island (Moturoa). The Flat Bottomed Fairy (☎027 463 3779) runs from Mapua Wharf daily from 10am every two hours until 4pm ($8 single; $12 return). The crossing involves a tour of the channel, and if you just go for the ride and don't disembark at the island it costs $5. The ferry was introduced as part of the Nelson Tasman Cycle Trail, and there is 6.8km of cycle track round the island.

Motueka

The expanding town of **MOTUEKA**, 47km northwest of Nelson, is primarily used as a base for exploring the Abel Tasman National Park (see p.473): there's a complete booking service, a range of accommodation and places you can rent hiking gear. Recently, the town has sprouted a few impressive attractions of its own, based largely around its airfield and including the chance to **fly** microlights and helicopters (see box, p.470).

The name Motueka means "island of the weka", a reference to the abundance of these edible birds, which provided sustenance for Maori. European settlers arrived in 1842 and established a horticulture industry based mainly around hops, since supplemented by pip fruit and grapes, which often need **seasonal workers**, particularly from December to March.

Motueka Quay

Motueka is strung along SH60, with quieter streets spurring off from the main highway. Head 1km down Old Wharf Road to reach **Motueka Quay** where the ghost of this once-busy port lingers among the scant remains of the old jetty. Here lies the rusting hulk of the Scottish-built *Janie Seddon* – named after the daughter of Richard Seddon, prime minister of New Zealand from 1893 until his death in 1906. The hulk provides a fantastic foreground for pictures of the seascape and a great backdrop for picnics.

Motueka District Museum

140 High St • Dec–March Mon–Fri 10am–4pm; April–Nov Tues–Fri 10am–3pm • $2 donation

The tiny **Motueka District Museum** delves into the area's history through a few Maori and European artefacts, as well as the *Motueka Carvings*, a modern four-panel frieze in the foyer that skilfully depicts the livelihoods that have traditionally sustained Tasman Bay.

FROM TOP LITTLE KAITERITERI, TASMAN BAY (P.474); SPLIT APPLE ROCK, TASMIN BAY (P.475) >

MOTUEKA TOURS AND ACTIVITIES

There are some great **hikes** around the Motueka area, but **airborne** activities such as skydiving and tandem paragliding are also very popular.

HIKING

In the hills to the west of Motueka is some of the best subalpine hiking in the north of the South Island, around the 1795m **Mount Arthur** and the associated uplifted plateau, the **Mount Arthur Tablelands**, all detailed in DOC's *The Cobb Valley, Mount Arthur and the Tablelands* leaflet available from the Motueka i-SITE. Traditionally, few visitors have bothered coming up this way, so what company you find will mostly be Kiwis and wildlife.

The principal starting point is the Flora car park, 930m up at the end of Graham Valley Road that leads off SH61 30km southwest of Motueka. A good 2–3hr loop heads up an easy path (1hr) to the Mount Arthur Hut ($15), from where the lowlands spread before you with Mount Arthur dominating the southern skyline. Continue along a ridge and down to Flora Hut (free) then back along a gravel road to the car park. The summit of Mount Arthur can be reached in three hours from the Mount Arthur Hut.

SKYDIVING

Skydive Abel Tasman Motueka airport, 3km southwest of town ☎0800 422 899, ⓦskydive.co.nz. Regarded as one of the ten best drop zones in the world, primarily because it offers jumps from 16,500ft (75 secs freefall; $399) and 13,000ft (50 secs freefall; $299), which is currently longer than most companies, with a backdrop of stunning scenery and helpful parachuting "buddies".

FLYING STUNTS

Uflyextreme Hangar 2, Motueka airport, 3km southwest of town ☎0800 360 180, ⓦuflyextreme .co.nz. Fly a Pitts Special in a 15min aerobatic display including four point rolls, loops and a Cuban eight without any previous training (allow an hour at the airport). In terms of an adrenaline rush, it makes skydiving look like afternoon tea with your granny. You can also take flights with the instructor, who lets you take control soon after take off (15min $299; 15min plus DVD $399; 20min plus DVD $499; 2 15min flights in same day $669). It is money well spent.

HELICOPTER FLIGHTS, MICROLIGHTS AND TANDEM HANG-GLIDING

Uflyheli Queen Victoria St, Motueka airport, 3km southwest of town ☎0800 835 943 ⓦuflyheli .co.nz. After a short briefing and flight you take the controls of an R22, two-seater, entry-level helicopter (30min $350; 1hr $650), practising simple forward flight, auto rotation and hovering.
Tasman Sky Adventures College St, Motueka airport, 3km southwest of town ☎0800 114 386, ⓦskyadventures.co.nz. Take the passenger seat in a microlight for some pulse-quickening thrills, buzzing above the region's glorious scenery (15min $95; 30min taking in parts of Abel Tasman National Park $185). They also offer tandem hang-gliding, towing the rig by microlight to a pre-appointed height before cutting you and your pilot loose (15min $185; 30min $275).

ARRIVAL AND DEPARTURE — THE ROAD TO ABEL TASMAN

Buses do travel along the road to Abel Tasman, but they only stop in Motueka. For all other destinations, you'll need to have your own vehicle or join a guided tour, some of which combine the wineries and art galleries.

By bus Buses pick up and drop off on Wallace St in Motueka, close to the i-SITE.
Destinations Collingwood (1 daily; 1hr 30min); Heaphy Track (1 daily; 2hr 15min); Kaiteriteri (3 daily; 20min); Marahau (4 daily; 40–50min); Nelson (5 daily; 1hr); Takaka (2 daily; 1hr 10min); Totaranui (1 daily; 2hr 15min).
Bay Tours ☎0800 229 868, ⓦbaytoursnelson.co.nz. Offers afternoon trips (3–4 vineyards; $70) or full-day tours (5–6 wineries; $90) among their selection.

INFORMATION

The only i-SITE along the road to Abel Tasman is in Motueka, but you can also check in at the office in Nelson for information on the area before you begin your journey.

i-SITE Wallace St (Dec–March Mon–Fri 8.30am–5.30pm, Sat & Sun 9am–5pm; April–Nov Mon–Fri 9am–4.30pm, Sat & Sun 9am–4pm; ☎03 528 6543, ⓦmotuekaisite .co.nz) Has internet access, can help people find short-term jobs and staff can assist in organizing Abel Tasman National Park and Heaphy Track trips.

Gear rental You can rent gear for camping and tramping from hostels or Abel Tasman Outdoors, 177 High St (Mon–Fri 8.30am–6pm, Sat 9am–2pm, Sun 10am–2pm; ☎03 528 8646), who offer packs ($5/day), two-person tents ($10/day), stove and pots ($10/day) and sleeping bags ($10/day), with discounts for multi-day rentals. They also rent scuba gear.

ACCOMMODATION

MAPUA

Atholwood 118 Bronte Rd East ☎03 540 2925, ⓦatholwood.co.nz. Luxurious accommodation next door to the Bronte Gallery (see p.467), with comfortable rooms, a swimming pool, spa, mature gardens and bush running down to Waimea Inlet. Rates include breakfast and reach around $425. **$350**

The Boot 320 Aporo Rd, 7km north of Mapua at Tasman ☎03 526 6742, ⓦtheboot.co.nz. Attached to the *Jester House* café (see p.472) is *The Boot*, an enormous red fairy-tale boot with a luxurious lounge area, romantic bedroom and a little garden patio. B&B **$300**

Mapua Leisure Park 33 Toru St ☎03 540 2666, ⓦmapualeisurepark.co.nz. A variety of accommodation options, including cabins and motel units, in wonderful surroundings. Stop in at the summer-only *Boatshed Café* and bar. In Feb and March the place is clothing-optional, though plenty of non-nudists still visit. Beachside camping **$22**, beachfront cabins **$74**, kitchen cabins **$95**, motel units **$132**

MOTUEKA

Avalon Manor Motel 314 High St ☎0800 282 566, ⓦavalonmotels.co.nz. A well-equipped 16-unit motel with spacious and comfortable units that come with Sky TV, a well-tended garden, plus free movies and wi-fi. Units start at **$160**

★ **Eden's Edge** 137 Lodder Lane, Riwaka ☎03 528 4242, ⓦedensedge.co.nz. Located on an apple orchard 4km north of town, this purpose-built great-value hostel has a rural but very comfortable feel. There's a garden, pool, bike storage, some nicely appointed rooms (some of which are en-suite) and four-share dorms. Camping **$17**, dorms **$28**, rooms **$68**, en suites **$78**

Equestrian Lodge Motel Tudor St ☎0800 668 782, ⓦequestrianlodge.co.nz. Well-kept upscale motel in a suburban area, only 5min from the centre of town, with comfy units backing onto a large grassy area with a solar-heated pool. **$170**

Hat Trick Lodge 25 Wallace St ☎03 528 5353, ⓦhattricklodge.co.nz. Conveniently located opposite the i-SITE, this purpose-built hostel has high standards,

a spacious and well-equipped kitchen and lounge, bike rental and free gear storage, as well as a separate women's dorm and a family room with its own bathroom and kitchen. Dorms **$27**, rooms **$62**, en suites **$70**

The Laughing Kiwi 310 High St ☎03 528 9229, ⓦlaughingkiwi.co.nz. Friendly, central backpackers spread over two cottages, with spacious dorms and rooms, a self-contained cottage, plus plenty of outdoor seating and a hot tub. Dorms **$27**, rooms **$62**, en suite **$68**, self-contained cottage **$120**

Motueka Beach Reserve Wharf Rd, 4km southeast of town. Council-run waterside parking for self-contained campervans only, with toilets and cold showers nearby, plus BBQs and picnic tables. Maximum two nights. Per night **$5**

Motueka Top 10 Holiday Park 10 Fearon St ☎0800 668 835, ⓦmotuekatop10.co.nz. Plenty of trees and well-kept facilities, including a spa pool, just 1km north of the town centre. Camping/site **$45**, cabins **$65**, units **$125**, motel units **$140**

The Resurgence Riwaka Valley Rd, 12km northwest of town ☎03 528 4664, ⓦresurgence.co.nz. A relaxing boutique lodge tucked away near the resurgence of the Riwaka River from below Takaka Hill. The attention to detail is staggering, from sound eco-credentials to the well-planned meals ($90). Facilities include an outdoor pool and spa, gym and bushwalks. Rooms are in the house or cabins. From **$525**

Rowan Cottage 27 Fearon St ☎03 528 6492, ⓦrowancottage.net. Tastefully styled, small cottage with a lovingly tended garden that holds a self-contained guest room with a private entrance and en suite. Continental breakfasts are optional and everyone can use the barbecue. **$130**

★ **Treedimensions Organic Farmstay** Shaggery Rd, 10km west of town ☎03 528 8718, ⓦtreedimensions .co.nz. Wake up to birdsong and breakfast on the deck of the attractive, great-value self-contained rooms with comfy beds. Sit overlooking an amazing certified organic orchard with 45 types of fruit and 700 species (you can usually try whatever's ripe), explore the grounds on foot or have a chat with the welcoming host, who is the Gandalf of all things organic. **$135**

8

EATING AND DRINKING

UPPER MOUTERE

Moutere Inn 1406 Moutere Hwy ☎03 543 2759, ⓦmoutereinn.co.nz. Established in 1850, the inn has

claims as New Zealand's oldest pub and now expertly balances being a local boozer, brewer and shrine to fine beverages. Alongside the quality pub snacks and main meals ($15–25) you can sip a tasting tray of four beers or a glass of wine – they stock in excess of thirty brews and thirty different wines as well as thirteen single malts and six brands of tequila. Thurs–Sun noon–9pm or later.

UPPER MOUTERE WINERIES

★ **Glover's** Gardner Valley Rd ❶ 03 543 2698, ❻ glovers -vineyard.co.nz. A wonderful small-output, one-man-and-his-cats winery run by the slightly eccentric Dave Glover, once renowned for tucking a Wagner CD into every package destined for overseas. Wagner usually plays in the background while you taste (free) European-structured wines crafted to produce highly tannic reds (Pinot Noir and Cabernet Sauvignon) and acidic whites (Sauvignon Blanc and Riesling) that stand up for themselves. Daily 10am–5pm.

Kahurangi Sunrise Rd ❶ 03 543 2980, ❻ kahurangi wine.com. Respected winery, offering tastings ($2 for four wines) from some of the South Island's oldest commercial vines (though that's only 1973), as well as the estate's own-brand olive oil and a café, popular for wood-fired pizza ($10–18). Daily 10.30am–4.30pm.

Neudorf Neudorf Rd, Upper Moutere ❶ 03 543 2643, ❻ neudorf.co.nz. Relaxed winery in a low-slung wooden building covered by vines with simple outdoor seating in the shade of tall ancient trees. It is a lovely spot for tastings (free), some from the 30-year-old vines on site – splash out ($2.50) to sample the Moutere Chardonnay and the Pinot Noir, two of the country's better. Everything is available by the bottle and glass, so bring a picnic and relax in the garden. Daily 10am–5pm, closed June–Aug.

Seifried Corner of SH60 and Redwood Rd ❶ 03 544 1555, ❻ seifried.co.nz. The area's largest winery offering a wide range of wines to taste ($5); try the Austrian Würzer and Zweigelt varietals, unique within New Zealand. The separately run restaurant fancies itself as fine dining, reflected in the high-end pricing. Daily 11am–3pm.

Woollaston Estates School Rd, Mahana ❶ 03 543 2817, ❻ woollaston.co.nz. Swish, fascinating, certified organic winery landscaped into the Moutere Hills with tussock-roofed buildings where operations are all gravity-fed. Bring a picnic or buy a platter ($30) and enjoy tastings (free) with great views over the vines to the coast. A huge steel sculpture welcomes visitors and the art collections include works by relative Toss Woollaston (see p.460). Daily 11am–4.30pm.

MAPUA

Golden Bear Brewing Company 12 Aranui Rd ❶ 03 540 3210, ❻ goldenbearbrewing.com. Top-class microbrews; elegant lagers and super-hoppy pale ales to take away, or drink in with the brewing tanks as a backdrop. They also dish up some US versions of Mexican food to soak up the ale. Wed & Thurs 4pm–late, Fri 3pm–late, Sat & Sun noon–late.

★ **Jester House** 7km north of Mapua at Tasman ❶ 03 526 6742, ❻ jesterhouse.co.nz. A rewarding licensed daytime café popular for its tasty food, garden seating, rose arbours, giant chess set and tame eels to keep the kids entertained. The food is all home-baked and reasonably priced, and the coffee is strong. Sept–May daily 9am–5pm; May–Aug Thurs–Sun 9am–4.30pm.

★ **The Original Smokehouse** 6 Aranui Rd ❶ 03 540 2280, ❻ smokehouse.co.nz. Sells delicious manuka-smoked fish and mussels, widely acclaimed fish pâtés and lovely traditional fish and chips. Bring along a loaf of bread, a lemon and some wine and enjoy a picnic on a bench at one of the uncluttered ends of the wharf. Daily 11am–7pm.

MOTUEKA

Chokdee 109 High St ❶ 03 528 0318. Reliable Thai cuisine to eat in or take away, with all the usual soups, curries and noodle dishes at modest prices ($9–20). Licensed. Daily 11am–2pm, 5pm–late.

★ **Elevation** 118 High St. Licensed café with the best food in town, including some great breakfasts, mussels Provençal, and spaghetti with pork meatballs – none of it over $25. They also do tasting trays of local beers. Daily 8.30am–late.

Hot Mama's 105 High St. After years of being the coolest place in town they inexplicably switch to becoming a pizza and taco restaurant, although the intention is to retain its reputation as a cool alternative gig venue. Daily 11am–late.

Monkey Wizard 483 Main Rd, Riwaka ❻ monkey wizard.co.nz. A brewery open for tastings and takeaways of their lovingly brewed beers, among which are Brass Monkey lager and Abel Ale, an English-style bitter. Daily 10am–6pm.

★ **Red Beret** 147 High St. Excellent café that draws in locals for a wide range of all-day breakfasts and lunches, from filo wraps and pasta dishes to gourmet burgers, steak sandwiches, excellent fish and chips ($19.50) and delicious monster slices of cake. Daily 7am–4pm.

★ **Resurgence Coffee** Corner of School and Main rds, 7.5km from town. Among all the pre-loved Kiwiana and international kitsch at this retro retailer, located in the old Great Universal Store, are some tables where you can sit and have a paper cup of the fantastic coffee and a cake from the counter. Mon–Thurs 8am–4pm, Fri 8am–6pm, Sat & Sun 8am–2pm.

Smiths Veggie Sales School Rd, Riwaka, on the left heading away from SH60. Mr and Mrs Smith have been selling great fresh veg from their garden to trampers and locals alike for years. Make an effort to stop in – it's well worth the diversion. Mon–Sat 10am–4pm.

Swinging Sultan 172 High St ❶ 03 528 8909. Kebab takeaway with just a couple of tables on the pavement, where you can tuck into chicken and beef kebabs or falafel ($7.50–11). Daily 8am–10pm.

T.O.A.D. Hall 502 High St, 3km south of town. Organic fruit-and-veg vendor and café with a flower-filled garden that's perfect for imbibing delicious made-to-order ice cream, gourmet pies, bagels, Kush (see p.465) coffee and decent breakfasts. Daily 8am–6pm.

Abel Tasman National Park and around

The **Abel Tasman National Park**, 60km north of Nelson, is stunningly beautiful with golden sandy beaches lapped by crystal-clear waters and lush green bushland, interspersed with granite outcrops and inhabited by an abundance of wildlife. Deservedly it has an international reputation that draws large numbers of trampers, kayakers and day-trippers from November to March. But don't be put off. Despite being New Zealand's smallest national park – just 20km by 25km – the Abel Tasman absorbs crowds tolerably well and compensates with scenic splendour on an awesome scale.

Most visitors come to see the coastline. Some come to hike the **Abel Tasman Coast Track** with its picturesque mixture of dense coastal bushwalking, gentle climbs to lookouts and walks across idyllic beaches. Abundant water taxis mean you can pick the sections to hike and get a lift back when you've had enough. Others come to **kayak** the spectacular coastline, spending leisurely lunchtimes on golden sands before paddling off in the late afternoon sun to a campsite or hut. Hiking and kayaking can be combined, and you might even tack on **sailing** the limpid waters or **swimming with seals** to round off the experience. You can stay in the park, either at one of the DOC huts and campsites, or in considerably more luxury at the ever-increasing number of attractive lodges.

With **guided and advanced trip booking** you can be whisked from Nelson straight into the park, missing potentially fascinating nights in the surrounding gateway towns. **Motueka** (see p.468) is best for organizing your own trip, but most kayaks and water taxis leave from tiny **Marahau**, at the park's southern entrance. A few trips depart from diminutive **Kaiteriteri**, where a gorgeous beach tempts many to stay.

The park's northern reaches are accessed from **Takaka** (see p.481) where Abel Tasman Drive leads to Wainui, Awaroa and **Totaranui**, all on the Coast Track.

Brief history

Since around 1500, Maori made seasonal encampments along the coast and some permanent settlements flourished near the mouth of the Awaroa River. In 1642, **Abel Tasman** anchored two ships near Wainui in Golden Bay and lost four men in a skirmish with the Ngati Tumatakokiri, after which he departed the shores. Frenchman **Dumont d'Urville** dropped by in 1827 and explored the area between Marahau and Torrent Bay, but it was another 23 years before **European settlement** began in earnest. The settlers chopped, quarried, burned and cleared until nothing was left but gorse and bracken. Happily, few obvious signs of their invasion remain and the vegetation has vigorously regenerated.

Natural history

Abel Tasman is full of rich and varied **plant life** with beech trees in the damp gullies and kanuka tolerating the wild and windy areas. **Bird** species include tui, native pigeons, bellbirds (their presence betrayed by a distinctive call), fantails that flutter close by feeding off the insects you disturb as you walk through the bush, and bobbing, ground-dwelling weka. Along the coast you might see the distinctive orange-beaked oystercatchers picking their way along the beaches and shags that dive to great depths for fish. Offshore, the **Tonga Island Marine Reserve** is famous for its **fur seal colony**, seabirds and varied and bountiful fish.

8

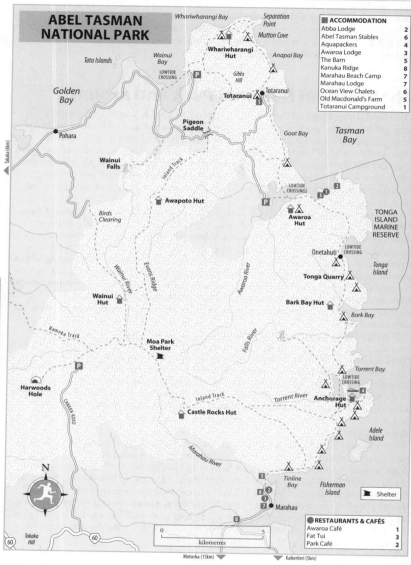

ABEL TASMAN NATIONAL PARK

ACCOMMODATION	
Abba Lodge	2
Abel Tasman Stables	6
Aquapackers	4
Awaroa Lodge	3
The Barn	5
Kanuka Ridge	8
Marahau Beach Camp	7
Marahau Lodge	7
Ocean View Chalets	6
Old Macdonald's Farm	5
Totaranui Campground	1

RESTAURANTS & CAFÉS	
Awaroa Café	1
Fat Tui	3
Park Café	2

8

Kaiteriteri

The tiny resort settlement of **KAITERITERI**, 15km north of Motueka and just south of the Abel Tasman National Park, ranks high in the pantheon of Kiwi summer-holiday destinations and is consequently packed to its limited gills from Christmas through to late January. There's an understandable appeal, with a golden arc of safe swimming beach looking out towards Tasman Bay where a couple of small islands add perspective. With Marahau (see opposite) becoming too congested for some, Kaiteriteri has fashioned itself as an alternative embarkation point for cruises, water taxis and kayaking trips.

Marahau

About 8km north of Kaiteriteri, tiny **MARAHAU** is poised at the southern entrance to the Abel Tasman National Park. All the tours, water taxis and kayak operators not working out of Kaiteriteri or Motueka are based here, making this a very popular last or first night of civilization for national park users.

The beach road runs through the settlement to the **park entrance**, marked by an unstaffed DOC display shelter. A long boardwalk across marshland then leads into the national park.

Exploring Abel Tasman National Park

There is a plethora of ways to explore the Abel Tasman National Park – no matter what combination of activities you'd like to try, there's almost bound to be an operator who'll oblige. Relatively few people tramp the **Inland Track**, and most are keen to stick to the **Coast Track**, with its long golden beaches, clear water, spectacular outcrops and the constant temptation to snorkel in some of the idyllic bays. Unsurprisingly, the coast is where you'll find most of the **accommodation**, ranging from beachside campsites to swanky lodges. **Water taxis** take you virtually anywhere along the coast and as far north as the lovely beach at Totaranui. They usually give a commentary along the way, though there are also dedicated **cruises**, some visiting the seal colony on the **Tonga Island Marine Reserve** and **Split Apple Rock**, a large boulder that has split and fallen into two halves, like an upright neatly cleaved Braeburn.

The intricate details of the coast are best explored by **kayak** (see box, pp.476–477), either on a guided trip or by renting kayaks and setting your own itinerary. Better still, combine kayaking with walking a section of the Coast Track. Water taxi drop-offs and guided kayaking are banned in the section of park north of Totaranui, making this a much **quieter area** to hike and hang out.

Abel Tasman Coast Track

The **Abel Tasman Coast Track** (51km; 2–5 days) is one of the **easiest** of New Zealand's Great Walks, one for people who wouldn't normally think of themselves as trampers, but you should still download or buy DOC's *Abel Tasman Coast Track* leaflet. Lack of fitness is no impediment as huts are never more than four hours apart (campsites 2hr) and you can use water taxis to skip some sections or just pick the bits you fancy walking. In dry conditions you don't even need strong boots – trainers will do. All this combines to make the Coast Track extremely popular, especially from December to the end of February when some sections seem like a hikers' highway, although heading for the section north of Totaranui will often deliver a less frenetic experience.

The **route** traverses broad golden beaches lapped by emerald waters, punctuated by granite pillars silhouetted against the horizon and zigzagging gentle climbs through valleys. The main planning difficulty is coping with two **tide-dependent** sections at Onetahuti and across the Awaroa Estuary. Tide times will help you decide which way you're going to do the track – if there are low tides in the afternoon you'll probably want to head south, if they're in the morning, head north. Even at low tide you can still expect to get your feet wet. Before setting off you should also arrange your transport drop-offs and pick-ups with a water taxi or cruise company (see p.478).

For accommodation along the track, see p.479.

Marahau to Anchorage

12.4km; 4hr

Direct access from Marahau makes this section popular. The bush isn't the most beautiful but the golden crescent beaches are unparalleled. The track follows a wooden causeway across the Marahau Estuary to Tinline Bay before rounding a point overlooking Fisherman and Adele islands just off the coast. As the track winds in and

8

out of gullies the coastal scenery is obscured by beech forest and tall kanuka trees until you emerge at Anchorage, with its hut, campsite and summertime offshore backpackers.

Anchorage to Bark Bay

8.7km; 3hr

Aim to cross Torrent Bay two hours either side of low tide, or be prepared to skirt the bay (adding an hour) to reach the few dozen houses that constitute Torrent Bay. Climb out of the bay through pine trees to the gorgeous Falls River, crossed by a 47m-long swingbridge. The Bark Bay hut and campsites are 1hr ahead.

Bark Bay to Awaroa

11.5km; 4hr

After crossing (or skirting) Bark Bay Estuary you cut away from the coast only to return at Tonga Quarry where there's a campsite and views out to Tonga Island and its associated Marine Reserve. You soon reach the golden beach at Onetahuti. The stream at its northern end is tidal (cross 3hr either side of low tide). The track then climbs to the Tonga Saddle and descends to Awaroa Inlet and the settlement of two dozen houses and a DOC hut with a campsite alongside; *Awaroa Lodge* is within easy walking distance and has a restaurant and bar.

ACTIVITIES AND TOURS IN ABEL TASMAN NATIONAL PARK

Although there are a number of operators offering activities such as **seal swimming**, **scuba diving**, **scenic cruises** and guided **walks**, one of the best ways to explore the park's more remote shores is by **sea kayak**. Some of the best operators for these activities are listed below.

KAYAKING

It's hard to beat gently paddling along, exploring little coves (and possibly being accompanied by seals or dolphins), stopping on a golden beach for a dip and then continuing to a campsite where you can cool a beer in a stream.

Marahau, at the southern end of the park, is the kayaking hot spot for many operators. Most companies offer a broadly similar range of one- to five-day guided trips and kayak rentals, often known as "freedom rentals". The stretch north of Marahau is known as the "Mad Mile", because that's where you'll see the largest concentration of paddlers, but congestion eases further north. Only Golden Bay Kayaks work from the quieter north end of the park.

Guided trips typically combine paddling, water taxis, visiting seals and walking, while **multi-day** guided trips include all that and accommodation, food as well as extra time to explore.

For **freedom rentals** you are typically given shore-based instruction then let loose in a double kayak. You are not allowed to venture north of Abel Head at the north end of the Tonga Island Marine Reserve nor paddle solo. Conditions are generally benign and suitable for relative beginners, though if you've any doubts about your ability, opt for a guided trip. Rental **prices** are around $65 per person for each of the first two days, $45 for the third then $35–40 for each subsequent day. One-way rentals have a fee (around $50) for returning the kayak to base by water taxi. Most companies have a range of camping **gear rental**, will store your vehicle while you're away and operate year-round, though the range of trips is reduced in winter.

ADVENTURE OPERATORS

Abel Tasman Charter ☎0800 223 522, ⓦabeltasmancharters.co.nz. Operates a small cruise boat from near Kaiteriteri, with a flexible itinerary partly determined by the guests. Usually there's seal viewing, a visit to Split Apple Rock, time ashore and a good picnic lunch. Nov–April only ($235).

Abel Tasman Dive Nelson ☎027 155 177, ⓦabeltasmandive.co.nz. Snorkel and scuba-diving trips in the park (from Kaiteriteri) and PADI training courses are all on the agenda. Trips start at $185 for a full day snorkelling and $285 for two scuba dives. All gear provided plus lunch.

Abel Tasman Kayaks Marahau ☎0800 732 529 ⓦabeltasmankayaks.co.nz. Guided kayak trip

---

8

Awaroa to Totaranui

5.5km; 1hr 30min

You must cross the Awaroa Estuary (2hr either side of low tide) to reach Goat Bay then up to a lookout above Skinner Point before reaching Totaranui, with its great arc of beach and extensive campsite.

Totaranui to Whariwharangi

7.5km; 3hr

After rounding the Totaranui Estuary, press on over and around rocky headlands as far as Mutton Cove then wander through alternating shrubland and beaches, preferably making a side trip to Separation Point with its lookout and fur seal colony. Continue to the hut at Whariwharangi, a former homestead.

Whariwharangi to Wainui

5.5km; 1hr 30min

It is an easy walk to the road on the eastern side of Wainui Bay, where buses pick up, but it is also possible to cross Wainui Bay (2hr either side of low tide), or follow the road round the bay. If you follow the road, you can also take in the short hike up to the Wainui Falls, which heads off the road at the base of Wainui Bay.

---

specialists based in Marahau offering half-day ($115) and full-day ($129–225) trips, plus a half-day seal sanctuary tour ($179) – all of which include a water taxi ride around much of the park. They also do gourmet catered overnight trips with luxury camping ($445), and rent freedom kayaks.

Abel Tasman Sailing ☎0800 467 245, ⓦsailinga dventures.co.nz. Offers trips on one of two 13m catamarans, combining sailing with walking, seal watching and kayaking, or you can just sail. They also do overnight trips ($85–175) and boat charters.

Abel Tasman Sea Shuttle ☎0800 732 748, ⓦabeltasmanseashuttles.co.nz. Kaiteriteri-based water taxis and scenic cruises (half-day $55; full day $72), with cruise and walk options (from $62).

Abel Tasman Seal Swim ☎0800 732 529, ⓦsealswim.com. Swimming with seals can be a lot more fun than with dolphins, simply because seals are more manoeuvrable and curious. The water is usually crystal-clear and the impact on the seals is minimized by ensuring that you wait for them to come and swim with you. The seal-swimming branch of Abel Tasman Kayaks gives you about an hour in the water ($179), after a 45min water taxi ride.

Aquataxi ☎0800 278 282, ⓦaquataxi.co.nz. Water taxis from Marahau and Kaiteriteri, plus scenic cruises ($69–81).

Golden Bay Kayaks ☎03 525 9095, ⓦgoldenbay kayaks.co.nz. Highly recommended Pohara-based company who operate in the beautiful north of the park. Offers guided trips (half-day $80) and an unguided overnight trip ($90). Also rents double

(half-day $90; full day $110) and sit-on-top kayaks (1hr $25), plus stand-up paddleboards ($15–20/hr).

Kahu Kayaks ☎03 527 8300, ⓦkahukayaks.co.nz. Marahau-based kayak rentals and guided trips that often come in fractionally cheaper than the opposition. A good all-round taster is the full-day cruise (5hr; $149), which gives you three hours paddling the Mad Mile followed by a water taxi visit to the seal colony, a short coastal walk and a water taxi back to Marahau.

Kaiteriteri Kayaks ☎0800 252 925, ⓦseakayak .co.nz. Guided trips from Kaiteriteri including a half-day paddle to Split Apple Rock ($94); a full-day with a water taxi ride to Onetahuti Beach, paddle to Tonga Island and the seals, lunch, and paddle to Anchorage Bay for water taxi pick-up ($199). Assorted combos also available.

The Sea Kayaking Company 506 High St, Motueka ☎0508 252 925, ⓦseakayaknz.co.nz. Motueka-based operator offering half-day trips (Adele Island $115), multi-day excursions (three days $710) and rentals ($65/ person/day; reducing on subsequent days).

Wilsons ☎0800 223 582, ⓦabeltasman.co.nz. Longstanding operator, offering all manner of trips including: a cruise, seal watch and walk ($64); a half-day Split Apple Rock kayak ($89); a five-day walking trip with three days walking and two days loafing at luxury beachfront lodges ($1910, all food included); cruises from Kaiteriteri to Totaranui and back (3 daily in summer; 4hr; $74) on a spacious and stable catamaran; and a Seals and Beach trip (6–8hr; $64), cruising around the Tonga Island seal colony with plenty of time to walk from Tonga Quarry to Medlands Beach and swim a bit.

8

The Inland Track

The **Inland Track** (42km; 3 days) between Marahau and Totaranui is far less popular than the Coast Track and is strenuous enough to require moderate fitness and decent tramping gear. The track can be combined with the Coast Track to make a six- to seven-day loop and is described in a DOC leaflet.

The route climbs from sea level to **Evans Ridge** past granite outcrops and views of the coast: highlights include the **Pigeon Saddle**, the moorlands of Moa Park and the moon-like Canaan landscape, with an optional side trip to Harwood's Hole (see p.480).

Camping is not recommended on the Inland Track, but there are three, small, first-come-first-served **DOC huts** ($5; backcountry hut passes valid), with water and toilets but no cooking facilities.

ARRIVAL AND DEPARTURE ABEL TASMAN NATIONAL PARK AND AROUND

Access into the park proper is generally on foot or by boat, but a couple of roads extend to the park entrances – principally Marahau in the south and Totaranui in the north.

By bus The best bus service in the region is Abel Tasman Coachlines (Nelson ☎ 03 548 0285; Motueka ☎ 03 528 8850; ⓦ abeltasmantravel.co.nz), which runs two to three times daily between Motueka, Kaiteriteri and Marahau. One service runs from Nelson (6.45am in summer & 7.45am all year) for Motueka (1hr; $12 one-way) and Marahau (1h 45min; $20), connecting with launch services deeper into the park. Connections leave Motueka for Takaka (7.45am in summer; $26) and Totaranui ($36).

GETTING AROUND

By water taxi Water taxis based in Kaiteriteri and Marahau give you the chance to walk a particular section of coast or simply ride to any of six beaches along the coast – Anchorage, Torrent Bay, Bark Bay, Onetahuti, Awaroa and Totaranui. Three main companies do two to five scheduled runs from the south of the park to Totaranui and back, charging virtually the same price – just book whichever is going the right way at the right time or call Aquataxi (☎ 0800 278 282, ⓦ aquataxi.co.nz). Typical one-way fares from Marahau are to Anchorage ($33), Torrent Bay ($33), Bark Bay ($38), Onetahuti ($40), Awaroa ($43) and Totaranui ($45).

INFORMATION

Abel Tasman National Park The main sources of information are the i-SITE offices in Nelson, Motueka and Takaka, all of which will book boats, kayaks, hut and camping tickets, transport and accommodation. There are also unmanned DOC display shelters at the Marahau and Totaranui park entrances, with tide times and safety precautions.

ACCOMMODATION

KAITERITERI

★ **Bellbird Lodge** Sandy Bay Rd ☎ 03 527 8555, ⓦ bellbirdlodge.com. Offers two comfortable suites, great views, first-class care and welcoming hosts, all in the family home where the peace and quiet is only shattered by the inconsiderate local birds. $287

Kaiteriteri Beach Motor Camp ☎ 03 527 8010, ⓦ kaiteribeach.co.nz. The camp is booked solid months in advance from Christmas to early February with holidaying Kiwis, who enjoy the closeness to the beach and variation of good-quality cabins and communal facilities. Bedding for en-suite cabins is $5/bed. Camping $18, cabins $43, en-suite cabins $75

Kaiteri Lodge Inlet Rd, just back from the beach ☎ 03 524 8114, ⓦ kaiterilodge.co.nz. Something between a motel and backpackers, with four-share rooms and en-suite doubles. It is also the primary stop for all the tour buses, including Kiwi Experience, and is right by *The Beached Whale* (see opposite). Dorms $35, en-suite rooms $160

Kimi Ora Spa Resort 99 Martin Farm Rd, signposted 1km back from the beach road ☎ 0508 546 4672, ⓦ kimiora.com. A genuine European spa complex, set in pine forest, with heated indoor and outdoor pools. You can just stay, but the emphasis is on fitness (there's a mountain bike track around the property), therapy and indulgent massage sessions. Rooms $199, suites $279

MARAHAU

Abel Tasman Stables Accommodation 100m along Marahau Valley Rd ☎ 03 527 8181, ⓦ abeltasman stables.co.nz. A two-room B&B homestay, one en-suite, one with a private bathroom, three self-contained studio motel-style units and one self-contained cottage. Room $80, units and cottage $145

The Barn Harvey Rd ☎03 527 8043, ⓦbarn.co.nz. A lively backpackers near the park entrance with an outdoor fireplace and baths in the grounds. Well set up for campers with an outdoor cooking area, the site also has dorms, twins and doubles, mostly in basic cabins. Camping $18, dorms $28, cabins $58, rooms $72

★**Kanuka Ridge** 21 Moss Rd ☎03 527 8435, ⓦabeltasmanbackpackers.co.nz. Peaceful hostel set on a hill back from the beach with a dedicated walking track, just one dorm, several bush-backed rooms, plenty of birdsong and free wi-fi. There's bike rental ($50/day; $30/two days) and the owner can direct you to great tracks and all manner of other cool stuff. Closed June–Sept. Camping $18, dorms $28, rooms $62, en suites $82

Marahau Beach Camp Beach Rd ☎0800 808 018, ⓦabeltasmancentre.co.nz. Unpretentious, well-kept campsite with tent sites, backpackers accommodation and a variety of cabins on a site with good communal facilities. Camping $35, dorms $22, rooms $50, kitchen cabins $70

Marahau Lodge Beach Rd ☎03 527 8250, ⓦabeltasmanmarahaulodge.co.nz. Studio and larger chalets scattered about the lawns give a relaxed feel to this upmarket lodge with outdoor spa, sauna, and breakfast delivered to your room (on request). $175

Ocean View Chalets Beach Rd ☎03 527 8232, ⓦaccommodationabeltasman.co.nz. Open year-round, these ten timber chalets set on a hillside contain spacious comfortable rooms, all with balconies and distant sea views from the beds, which are soft and welcoming. Studio $145, self-contained unit $180

★**Old Macdonald's Farm** Harvey Rd, by the park entrance ☎03 527 8288, ⓦoldmacs.co.nz. Family-run farm with cottages and a self-contained studio, plus camping and a huge wooded area next to a couple of swimming holes. There's also secure parking ($6/night), a well-stocked shop and gear storage. Camping $15, campervans $40, dorms $27, cabins $80, self-contained studio $140

ABEL TASMAN NATIONAL PARK

Unlike many of New Zealand's national parks, the Abel Tasman offers a range of accommodation, accessed either by boat or the Abel Tasman Coast Path. Most people stay at the four DOC huts, spaced around four hours' walk apart along the coast, while hardened trampers will want to camp at some of the eighteen DOC campsites strung along the coast, all either beside beaches or near the DOC huts (whose facilities you are not supposed to use). Bookings are required year-round for all huts and campsites and

should be made at least a week in advance in summer. Book online (ⓦdoc.govt.nz) or at an i-SITE. There are also private accommodation options and multi-day all-inclusive trips to consider; Wilsons (see p.477) run two- to five-day guided walking and kayaking holidays with comfortable accommodation at their two trackside lodges at Torrent Bay and Awaroa.

Huts These come with water, heating, good toilets, basic but comfortable bunks and most have showers, but there are no cooking facilities: bring a sleeping bag, cooking stove, pans, utensils, food and a torch. Two-night maximum stay in summer. Oct–April $35.70, May–Sept $15

Campsites All eighteen DOC sites have a water supply and toilets, but it means carrying more gear and you'll need lots of sandfly repellent. Only the Anchorage and Bark Bay campsites allow campfires. Two-night maximum stay in summer for all campsites. Oct–April $12.20, May–Sept $8

Abba Lodge Awaroa Bay ☎03 528 8758, ⓦabbalodge.co.nz. Newest backpacker accommodation in the park, with nineteen rooms and close to the *Awaroa Lodge* restaurant and bar. Dorms $50, doubles $125

Aquapackers Anchorage ☎0800 430 744, ⓦaquapackers.co.nz. Expensive backpacker accommodation in made-up dorms and doubles aboard two converted boats moored for the summer just off the beach in Anchorage Bay: there's a free ferry from beach to boat. The package includes BBQ dinner, basic breakfast and access to a pay bar. It can feel cramped but the stillness of the park at night and sounds of lapping water make it worthwhile. Sept–May only. Dorms $70, doubles $140, land-based *bach* $195

Awaroa Lodge Awaroa ☎03 528 8758, ⓦawaroalodge.co.nz. Nestled in the bush with great wetland views, this upmarket lodge uses ingredients from its organic garden in its classy restaurant (mains around $40). Hikers and casual visitors can drop in for a coffee or a drink by the enormous fireplace (and access the internet), but it is really aimed at the well-heeled arriving by water taxi or plane to stay in the plush en-suite rooms or suites. Closed June–Aug. Rates begin at $295

★**Totaranui Campground** Totaranui. The only car-accessible accommodation on the Abel Tasman coast, this huge campsite (there's room for 850 people) is so busy in summer that places are obtained by lottery for Christmas to the end of Jan. A booking form (required Dec 10–Feb 10) can be downloaded from ⓦdoc.govt.nz. A separate section for track hikers usually has space, though you might want to press on. $12.50

EATING AND DRINKING

KAITERITERI

The Beached Whale Inlet Rd ☎03 527 8114. Party bar specializing in booze deals, cheap food and live music.

Daily 11am–11pm in summer, 4–11pm in winter.

Kimi Ora 99 Martin Farm Rd ☎0508 546 4672, ⓦkimiora.com. The resort's restaurant serves healthy, vegetarian

8

four-course buffet dinners (around $35; Nov to Easter only), with a small selection of organic wines, beers and juices.

Shoreline Café Corner of Inlet Rd and Kaiteriteri-Sandy Bay Rd ☎03 527 8507. Beach views from the terrace and pretty decent meals, all ranging from $23–30. Daily 9am–10pm in summer, 9am–6pm in winter.

MARAHAU

★ **Fat Tui** 11 Marahau Valley Rd, at Kahu Kayaks. A van selling wonderful takeaway fish and chips and gourmet burgers, all to restaurant standard. Dail dawn–dusk.

★ **Park Café** 1 Harveys Rd ☎03 527 8270 ⊛parkcafe.co.nz. Located by the start of the track, thi place is legendary among appreciative walkers emerging from the park and locals alike. Famed for wholesom lunches, good coffee, restorative beers and a range o delicious dinner mains ($24–30) and desserts ($12) Daily 8am–late.

Golden Bay

Occupying the northwestern tip of the South Island, **GOLDEN BAY** curves gracefully from the northern fringes of the Abel Tasman National Park to the encircling arm of **Farewell Spit**, all backed by the magnificent Kahurangi National Park. With bush-clad mountains on three sides and waves lapping at the fourth, Golden Bay's inaccessibility has helped foster the illusion that if it is not a world apart it is certainly otherworldly.

Wainui Bay, just east of the main town of **Takaka**, is most likely the spot where Abel Tasman first anchored, guaranteeing his place in history as the first European to encounter Aotearoa and its fierce inhabitants. The apparently isolating presence of **Takaka Hill** keeps today's bayside communities from growing virally, though the area has attracted a cross section of immigrants, alternative lifestylers, craftspeople, businessmen and artists, which goes some way to explaining the population's perceived spirit of **independence**. The area has been particularly popular with German-speakers who now constitute ten percent of the five thousand or so residents. Sunny, beautiful and full of fascinating sights, Golden Bay deserves a couple days of your time and has a knack of inducing you to stay longer.

Takaka Hill

The only way to get to Golden Bay by road is on SH60, a normal but very twisty road over the **Takaka Hill** that skirts the inland border of the Abel Tasman National Park. Take it slow and stop frequently at viewpoints with glorious mountain and seascapes from Nelson north to D'Urville Island.

Atop Takaka Hill, some 20km north of Motueka, you can be guided through **Ngarua Caves** (Oct–April daily 10am–4pm; 45min guided tours on the hour; $15), a pleasing show cave with illuminated stalactite formations and skeletons of moa that fell through holes in the cave roof.

Harwoods Hole

Accessed along Canaan Rd, 500m north of Ngarua Caves

The twisting, unsealed Canaan Road runs 11km to a car park with access to **Harwoods Hole**, a huge vertical shaft 176m deep and over 50m in diameter, which links up to a vast cave system below. Reached by an enchanting trail (6km return; 1hr 30min; mostly level) through silver beech forest that follows a dry rock-strewn riverbed, the lip has no viewing platform, so don't go crashing about looking for it or you'll end up in it before you see it. About 30min along the trail a side track (20min return) leads to a **clifftop viewpoint** with stunning views down towards the Takaka Valley and the coast. A spot beside Canaan Road 3km back from the car park was one of several sites in the area used by the **Lord of the Rings** crew and was re-used for *The Hobbit* films.

Rameka Track

5km; 3hr one-way; 750m descent

Mountain bikers are spoilt for choice here, with the excellent new Canaan Downs tracks leading off from the road-end car park, and the clearly signposted **Rameka Track**, which follows one of the earliest surveyed routes down into the Takaka Valley with superb views of the granite outcrops and the surrounding country. Along the way it includes Great Expectations, a section of single-track designed and built by Jonathan Kennett, co-author of New Zealand's mountain bikers' bible (see p.821), on land set aside as a carbon sink, and being planted out in native trees. A visit here works especially well if you can find an amenable driver who can meet you at the bottom, thus avoiding the slog back up SH60 and Canaan Road.

Takaka and around

The small town of **TAKAKA**, almost 60km north of Motueka, is Golden Bay's largest settlement, and one that has increasingly set its cap at the summer tourists, while continuing to cater for the local farming community and barefoot crusties who emerge from their shacks and tipis to sell home-made crafts and natural/spiritual healing services. Immediately north, **Te Waikoropupu Springs** emerge from their underground lair, while to the north yawns a considerable stretch of beautiful bay, running parallel to SH60 as it rolls into Collingwood and Farewell Spit. To the east, Abel Tasman Drive winds past the safe swimming beach at **Pohara** and a few minor sights before heading into the northern section of the Abel Tasman National Park (see p.475). Most of the action in Takaka takes place along Commercial Street (SH60 as it passes through town), where you can quickly get a handle on the spirit of the place by visiting Golden Bay Organics, at no. 47, and the Monza Gallery, at no. 25.

8

Golden Bay Museum

11 Commercial St • Daily 10am–4pm • Free

The **Golden Bay Museum** has a detailed diorama depicting Abel Tasman's ill-fated trip to Wainui Bay in 1642 plus all manner of historic bits and bobs relating to Tasman and the rest of the bay. There's also coverage of local Maori and the area's logging history.

Te Waikoropupu Springs

4km north of Takaka, off SH60

One site not to miss is **Te Waikoropupu Springs**, the largest in New Zealand, set amid old gold workings and regenerating forest. Vast quantities of fresh water well up through at least sixteen crystal-clear vents, one creating Dancing Sands (where the sands, pushed by the surging water, appear to perform a jig). The colourful aquatic plant life can be seen by means of a large reverse periscope on the boardwalk.

Bencarri

McCallum Rd, 6km southeast of Takaka • Late Sept–April daily 10am–5pm • $12 • 📞 03 525 8261

Even if you don't have kids, follow the families flocking to the banks of the Anatoki River, specifically to **Bencarri**, a farm animal park where you can feed and pet the llamas, donkeys, emus, piglets, rabbits and more. Also up for a free lunch are the Anatoki eels, who live wild in the river but have been fed here since 1914. Put some meat (provided) on a stick and the thick black eels will rise out of the water.

Anatoki Salmon

239 McCallum Rd, 6km southeast of Takaka • Daily 9am–4.30pm • Free • 📞 03 525 7251, 🌐 anatokisalmon.co.nz

You can catch your own hatchery-raised fish at **Anatoki Salmon**. They'll provide you with tackle and you only pay for bait and what you catch ($19/kg of live fish). They'll even smoke or barbecue your catch, which you can eat there or pop in a pizza box and go somewhere more scenic.

Abel Tasman Drive

East of Takaka, **Abel Tasman Drive** threads its way past the small waterside settlement of Pohara then splits into three, each road ending at a trailhead for the Abel Tasman Coast Track: Awaroa, Totaranui and Wainui Bay – see map on p.474.

Rawhiti Cave

3hr return • Instruction sheet available from the Takaka i-SITE

Just off Abel Tasman Drive, a poorly signed rough track, which can be perilously slippery in wet weather and crosses a riverbed, leads to a viewing platform over **Rawhiti Cave**, its cavernous mouth hung with myriad pendulous stalactites, transparent stone straws and a discarded billy, now encrusted in rock deposited from the dripping ceiling. Take a torch and spare batteries.

Grove Scenic Reserve

7km from Takaka • Unrestricted access • Free

From Takaka, follow signs to the wonderful **Grove Scenic Reserve**, a mystical place that could have been transplanted straight from Arthurian legend. Massive rata trees sprout from odd and deformed limestone outcrops, and a ten-minute walk takes you to a narrow slot between two enormous vertical cliffs where a lookout reveals expansive views of the coast and beaches around Pohara. Take your camera.

Pohara

Pohara, 10km east of Takaka, has a couple of places to stay (see opposite) and eat (see p.484), a relaxing sandy beach and a working jetty opposite the jarring site of a former cement factory. Among the moored fishing and pleasure boats is *The Espresso Ship* (Dec–Feb daily 10am–4.30pm; BYO food), which roasts, brews and serves excellent organic Fair Trade coffee. The ship is actually Jacques Cousteau's old dive ship, *The Physalie*.

Just round the corner is pretty **Tata Beach** and the trailhead for **Wainui Falls** (40min return), where Nikau palms shade the banks of the river, and a curtain of spray swathes the rather lovely falls.

Tui Community

The Wainui Bay road (now gravel) runs past the **Tui Community** (one of the last of several spiritual and educational trusts started in Golden Bay in the 1970s), and ends at the northernmost access point to the Coast Track. Other roads go to the Awaroa Estuary, and the wonderful golden arc of **Totaranui Beach**. This is a common place to finish the Coast Track, right by the *Totaranui Campground* (see p.479).

ARRIVAL AND DEPARTURE
TAKAKA AND AROUND

By bus Golden Bay Coachlines (⊕03 525 8352, ⓦ gbcoachlines.co.nz) and Abel Tasman Coachlines (⊕03 548 0285, ⓦ abeltasmantravel.co.nz) jointly run from Nelson and continue north to Collingwood and the Heaphy Track, and east to Totaranui. Both drop off outside the Takaka i-SITE on SH60.

Destinations Collingwood (1 daily; 30min); Heaphy Track (1 daily; 1hr); Motueka (2 daily; 1hr 10min); Nelson (2 daily; 2hr 15min); Totaranui (1 daily; 1hr).

GETTING AROUND

By bike Most of the hostels in Takaka have free bikes for guests, and The Quiet Revolution, 11 Commercial St (closed Sat afternoon & Sun; ⊕03 525 9555, ⓦ quietrevolution .co.nz), rents mountain bikes ($25/day; $45/day for off-road use) and sells the *Fat Tyre Fun* ($2) leaflet, containing over a dozen great mountain-bike rides in Golden Bay.

INFORMATION

i-SITE SH60, as you enter Takaka from the south (daily 9am–5pm; ☎03 525 9136, ⓦnelsonnz.com). Carries all DOC information, handles bookings, hut tickets for the national parks and organizes rental cars.

Internet Available at the library, 3 Junction St (Mon–Thurs 9.30am–5pm, Fri 9.30am–6pm, Sat 9.30am–12.30pm), and several commercial outlets on Commerce St.

ACCOMMODATION

Golden Bay is a popular holiday spot for both Kiwis and foreign visitors; as a result there is plenty of good-quality accommodation, from backpackers to swanky lodges. Camping ranges from the enormous DOC campsite at Totaranui to wayside spots where you can park your campervan overnight.

TAKAKA

Annie's Nirvana Lodge 25 Motupipi St ☎03 525 8766, ⓦnirvanalodge.co.nz. Enthusiastically run associate YHA right in town with a homely atmosphere, a nice garden with lots of seating, cheap rental bikes, and private rooms (including three attractive garden doubles). Dorms $25, rooms $63

★ **Autumn Farm Lodge** 3km south of Takaka, off SH60 ☎03 525 9013, ⓦautumnfarm.com. Charming gay-friendly lodge, on a sizeable plot with comfortable rooms, a big bathhouse and a laidback (clothing optional) atmosphere. Also hosts an eight-day annual gay summer camp over New Year. Reservations essential. Camping $20, backpackers $40, B&B $140

Golden Bay Motel 132 Commercial St ☎0800 401 212, ⓦgoldenbaymotel.co.nz. Well-kept little motel with off-street parking and incredibly good-value, spacious, clean, comfy rooms about a 5min walk from the centre of town. $95

Kiwiana 73 Motupipi St ☎0800 805 494, ⓦkiwiana backpackers.co.nz. Beautifully kept and well-run hostel in a large villa where the Kiwiana theme runs to the labelling of the airy rooms – paua, jandals, tiki, etc – and collection of books in the games room where they have pool and table tennis. There's a free hot tub, on-site vans and BBQ in the well-tended garden, plus free bikes. Closed July & Aug. Camping $18, dorms $27, rooms $60, vans $78

Mohua Motels SH60 ☎03 525 7222, ⓦmohuamotels .com. Takaka's newest motel is located at the southern entrance to town and has attractive, well-appointed units, Sky TV and in-room internet. It's all part of a plush package set around a car park about a 5min walk from the local shops. $165

★ **Shady Rest** 139 Commercial St ☎03 525 9669, ⓦshadyrest.co.nz. Lovely central B&B in a historic former doctor's house with comfortable, wood-panelled rooms that are either en-suite or have a private bathroom. A generous breakfast, solar-heated outdoor bath and a lovely garden that runs down to a peaceful creek make this a treat. Rates start at $195

AROUND TAKAKA

★ **Adrift** Tukurua Rd, 17km north of Takaka ☎03 525 8353, ⓦadrift.co.nz. Five gorgeous self-contained cottages (and one studio) decorated in chic, modern style and all with direct access across lawns to the beach. All rooms have a sea view, making them perfect for a leisurely breakfast in bed. With double spa baths, free use of kayaks and a small penguin colony on site you may never want to leave. Studio $250, cottages start at $390

★ **Golden Bay Hideaway** 220 McShare Rd, Wainui Bay, 23km east of Takaka ☎03 525 7184, ⓦgoldenbay hideaway.co.nz. Wonderful spot, close to the northern end of the Abel Tasman Coast Track, comprising an eco-efficient house sleeping two, known as "Little Greenie", and a beautifully crafted house truck. Great views, an outdoor bath and cook-your-own-dinner/breakfast supplies complete the package. Truck $150, hippie house $180, eco house $225

The Nook 678 Abel Tasman Drive, Pohara, 9km east of Takaka ☎03 525 8501, ⓦthenookguesthouse.co.nz. A relaxed eco-backpackers in a lovely wood-floored house where TV and internet are intentionally absent. Apart from the comfy dorms and doubles there's a fairly luxurious, straw-and-plaster cottage, rented as a self-contained unit or two doubles. Free pick-up from Takaka by arrangement, and bikes and a kayak are available. Camping $15, dorms $28, doubles $75, house truck $120, cottage for up to four $180

Pohara Beach Top 10 Holiday Park 809 Abel Tasman Drive ☎0800 764 272, ⓦpoharabeach.com. A popular, well-equipped traditional Kiwi beachfront holiday park with a broad range of accommodation, excellent communal facilities and very helpful owners. Camping $18, cabins $59, en-suite cabins $107, motels $154

★ **Sans Souci Inn** Richmond Rd, Pohara Beach, 10km east of Takaka ☎03 525 8663, ⓦsanssouciinn.co.nz. Endearing Swiss-run inn with a communal feel, set in a mud-brick building with sod roof and handmade floor tiles. The six rooms share one large bathroom with shower stalls, bath and composting toilets, though there's also a self-contained cottage sleeping four and an excellent restaurant (see p.484). Guests can use the kitchen or go for the delicious breakfasts ($9–15). Closed July to mid-Sept. Rooms $115, cottage $160

★ **Shambhala** SH60, 16km north of Takaka at Onekaka ☎03 525 8463, ⓦshambhala.co.nz. Welcoming shoes-off backpackers with a slightly spiritual

8

bent, including yoga classes, located 2km down a track almost opposite the *Mussel Inn* (see below), from where free pick-up can be arranged. Dorms are in the main house, or there are spacious twins and doubles with lovely sea views in a separate block, with solar-heated showers and composting toilets. Lovely wild gardens and beach access. Closed June–Oct. Camping and campervans $18, dorms $28, double rooms $66

Totaranui Campground 26km east of Takaka (see p.479). Large and popular beachside campsite within Abel Tasman National Park, with a shop, running water, toilets, picnic tables and cold showers. Book in advance. $12.50

Waitapu Bridge 4km north of Takaka on SH60. Pleasant riverside freedom site with toilets and river water. For self-contained campervans only. Maximum two-night stay. Free

EATING, DRINKING AND ENTERTAINMENT

Takaka has some good places to eat and there are more a few kilometres out that justify the journey. Drinking and music are best in the *Wholemeal Café*, *Roots*, *The Brigand* and the *Mussel Inn*.

TAKAKA

The Brigand 90 Commercial St ☎ 03 525 9636. Relaxed restaurant-bar serving burgers, ribs, salmon and tempting warm chocolate cake (Mains $24–34) – with lots of outdoor seating and live music several nights a week plus open mic on Thurs. Daily 11am–late.

Dangerous Kitchen 46a Commercial St ☎ 03 525 8686 for takeaway orders. Large, good-value café that's very popular with the locals for eating in, watching the world pass from the pavement seating, or takeaway grub. Exotic pizzas are the mainstay, though they do tasty wraps, good breakfasts and salads ($10–28). Licensed. Daily 9am–9pm, closed Sun Aug & Sept.

Infusion 30 Commercial St. The only German-run teahouse on the South Island, dishing up the best bread (the flour is freshly stone-ground) and pastries in the bay and thirty varieties of loose tea. Mon–Fri 9am–5pm, Sat 9am–3pm.

★ **Roots Bar** 1 Commercial St. Hang out around the open fire tucking into lovingly prepared Kiwi-style tapas (nothing over $20) and sipping Nelson-brewed Sprig and Fern beers and ciders as reggae, roots or drum'n'bass music floats by. DJs and bands often play at the weekends until late. Tues–Sun 4.30pm–late.

Schnapp Dragon 1 Hoody Alley, off Commercial St in the town centre ☎ 03 525 9899, ⌨ schnappdragon .co.nz. An intriguing recent addition to the drinking scene, Takaka's own distillery has an insanely enthusiastic owner who creates world-class whiskey, gin, tequila, vodka, extraordinary liqueurs and champagne from honey. Mon– Fri 9am–5pm, Sat 10am–5pm.

TLC (The Little Café) 65A Commercial St. Tiny coffee house with outdoor seating under a pin oak overlooking the main road, serving the best coffee in the bay and some counter nosh. Mon–Fri 9.30am–4pm.

★ **Wholemeal Café** 60 Commercial St. A Takaka institution that's endearingly sloppy at times, but it's always good value and makes a decent spot to hang out over a good coffee and large cake. Return for pizza, colourful and healthy salads, and assorted fish, meat and veggie dishes ($16–25) in the cavernous interior or on the back deck. Licensed. Daily 7.30am–4.30pm, later for events or concerts and during summer.

AROUND TAKAKA

★ **Mussel Inn** SH60, 18km north of Takaka. Do not miss this place – whether you want to eat, enjoy wine, cider or ale (they brew many varieties of their own, including the manuka-infused "Captain Cooker"), sit and read, play chess or soak up the lively atmosphere of a live band or local event. The building is adorned with local art and clumpy, but comfortable, wooden furniture. You can always get a simple, fresh and wholesome meal; try a plate of the local mussels, a pie, open burger (fish, meat or falafel) or some excellent cake. Daily 11am–late, closed Aug & Sept.

Penguin Café 818 Abel Tasman Drive, Pohara. Spacious café-restaurant and bar that's worth the drive out from Takaka if only to sip a beer or coffee on the roadside deck which catches the sun most of the day and has a water sculpture to keep you amused. Well-presented dishes include Anatoki salmon, seafood pizza and home-made ice cream. Most mains $20–36. Tues–Sun 11am–late, Mon 4pm–late.

Sans Souci Inn Richmond Rd, Pohara Beach, 10km east of Takaka ☎ 03 525 8663, ⌨ sanssouciinn.co.nz. Simple licensed restaurant with a daily set menu of freshly prepared imaginative food that can include hot smoked fish, beef fillets and veggie options (all $29–34). There's also a choice of sumptuous desserts ($11.50). Booking essential. Dinner served at 7pm unless specified.

Collingwood and around

Golden Bay's northernmost settlement of any consequence is laidback **COLLINGWOOD**, the base for tours to **Farewell Spit** (see p.486). The town occupies a thread of land wedged between the sea and Ruataniwha Inlet, a location which was briefly

THE ROAD TO COLLINGWOOD: ARTS AND CRAFTS

Many of the region's best **artists and craftspeople** live and work between Takaka and Collingwood, so the winding roads offer endless opportunities for mooching around country galleries, usually daily between 10am and 4.30pm, armed with the free, widely available *Artists in Golden Bay* leaflet. Two of the best are listed below.

Onekaka Arts 13km north of Takaka ☎ 03 525 7366, ⓦ onekakaarts.co.nz. Hand-crafted silver jewellery by Peter Meares and Grant Muir and jade carved by Geoff Williams. Call ahead for hours.

Estuary Arts 22km north of Takaka ☎ 03 524 8466, ⓦ estuaryarts.co.nz. Rosie Little and Bruce Hamlin produce brightly coloured and Pacific-influenced tableware and handmade low-relief art tiles, plus Little's evocative, almost organic, landscapes and energetic colourful abstracts. Oct to mid-April Wed–Sun 9am–5pm, plus Mon & Tues during holidays.

championed in the 1850s as the site for the nation's new capital; street plans were drawn up, but as the gold petered out, so did the enthusiasm. The details are spelled out in the diminutive **Collingwood Museum** and **Aorere Centre** (both daily 9am–6pm; donation), in adjoining buildings, the former a traditional museum, the latter using multi-media to present information on natural history and cultural heritage and links with various plaques around the town.

Devil's Boots
7km southwest of Collingwood

The Aorere Valley runs southwest of Collingwood towards the start of the Heaphy Track. Call briefly at the **Devil's Boots**, bulbous limestone overhangs on either side of the gravel road that look like two feet protruding from the ground, with trees and shrubs sprouting from their soles.

About 4km on, follow signs to the *Naked Possum café* (see p.486), which marks the beginning of the lovely **Kaituna Track** (2hr return) a bushwalk past old gold workings to the river confluence at Kaituna Forks.

Langford's Store
Bainham, 18km southwest of Collingwood • Thurs–Tues 9am–5pm

The wonderful **Langford's Store** is a combined general store and post office built in 1928 by ancestors of the current owners and seemingly little changed. Wooden shelves are stacked with goods, you can still get an assorted bag of sweets and the hand-cranked Burroughs adding machine is used to tally up your bill. Be sure to stop for coffee and cake.

ACCOMMODATION   COLLINGWOOD AND AROUND

Collingwood Motor Camp 6 William St, Collingwood ☎ 03 524 8149. Traditional but basic campsite, stuffed to the gills in the summer (make sure you book ahead) with a few wooden cabins and some much more swanky self-contained units. Camping $16, cabins $50, self-contained units $80

Collingwood Park Motel 1 Tasman St, Collingwood ☎ 0800 270 520, ⓦ collingwoodpark.co.nz. Good-value units on a site that backs onto the river estuary. The rooms are comfortable, clean and run by friendly people. $120

Somerset House 12 Gibbs Rd, Collingwood ☎ 03 524 8624, ⓦ backpackerscollingwood.co.nz. A low-key backpackers with decent, clean and comfortable rooms in a house with reasonable communal facilities, estuary views, free breakfast and cheap bikes. Dorms $30, rooms $66

EATING

★ **Lady Luck Coffee Caravan** In the car park behind the Collingwood Motor Camp and opposite the public boat ramp. Good grub for under $20, excellent coffee and cakes, a big local following trying to squeeze into this funky retro, blue and grey kai kart, or lounge at the outdoor tables, characterize this recent edition to the canon of weird but great eateries in the bay. Thurs–Mon, 9am–4pm, later in the summer.

8

FAREWELL SPIT TOURS

The trip to Farewell Spit, some 22km north of Collingwood, is an iconic New Zealand journey and shouldn't be missed – if you do nothing else but this in Golden Bay your time will not have been wasted. At the time of writing, only one tour company merited inclusion.

Farewell Spit Eco Tours Tasman St, Collingwood ☎ 0800 808 257, ⓦ farewellspit.com. In operation since 1946, this outfit runs the Farewell Spit Eco Tour (6hr 30min; $145) which heads out along the sands of the spit to its historic lighthouse in a purpose-built 4WD. The trip comes with a bright commentary, peppered with local lore. During the day you'll see vast numbers of birds, seals (plus the occasional sea lion) and fossils, climb an enormous sand dune and maybe see the skeletons of wrecked ships if the sands reveal them. Their more eco-oriented Gannet Colony Tour (6hr 30min; $155) includes most of the above plus a 20min walk to the massive gannet colony towards the very end of the spit. Trips operate year-round with departure times dependent on tides: check the website. On both trips lunch ($10) is optional.

The Naked Possum 14km southwest of Collingwood, signposted 2km along an unsealed road from the Kaituna bridge turn-off ☎ 03 524 8488, ⓦ nakedpossum .com. A daytime café set on the edge of the bush with stacks of outside seating, some under cover around an always-lit roaring fire. High-quality café food is supplemented by wild bush tucker; try a tahr burger or a venison, mushroom and red wine pie washed down with a handle of their exclusive Stunned Possum, a rata honey beer brewed at the *Mussel Inn* (see p.484). The wild berry tart is also famed. Make sure to check out the cushions made from local possum skins. Daily 10am–4pm, later on Fri & Sat evening.

8

The road to Farewell Spit

North of Collingwood the road skirts Ruataniwha Inlet, and, after 10km, passes *The Innlet* (see p.488). The road now follows the coast 11km to **Puponga**, at the northern tip of the South Island, where you can stay at the excellent *Farewell Gardens Motor Camp* (see p.488). Around 2km on is Puponga Farm Park, a coastal sheep farm open to the public; check out the visitor centre (see p.488) for more information.

Farewell Spit

From the Puponga Farm Park, there are great views right along **Farewell Spit** – named by Captain Cook at the end of a visit in 1770 – which stretches 25km east, often heaped with tree trunks washed up from the West Coast. The whole vast sand bank is a **nature reserve** of international importance, with salt marshes, open mudflats, brackish lakes and bare dunes providing habitats for over a hundred **bird species**: bartailed godwit, wrybill, long-billed curlew and Mongolian dotterel all come to escape the Arctic winter, and there are breeding colonies of Caspian terns, and large numbers of black swans. Sadly, the unusual shape of the coastline seems to fool whales' navigation systems and beachings are common.

Short **walks** head to the outer beach (2.5km) and the inner beach (4km); both provide good views of the spit, which is otherwise off-limits except on guided tours from Collingwood (see p.484).

Cape Farewell

Away from Farewell Spit, walks head through the farm park to **Cape Farewell** (the northernmost point on the South Island), the strikingly set **Pillar Point Lighthouse** and to the wave-lashed **Wharariki Beach**. Here, rock bridges and towering arches are stranded just offshore, while deep dunes have blocked rivermouths, forming briny lakes and islands where fur seals and birds have made a home. Visit within a couple of hours of low tide when you can access some sea caves where the seals hang out.

KAHURANGI NATIONAL PARK: THE HEAPHY TRACK

The huge expanse of Kahurangi National Park encompasses 40,000 square kilometres of the northwestern South Island, between the wet and exposed western side of the Wakamarama Range and the limestone peaks of Mount Owen and Mount Arthur. Over half New Zealand's native **plant species** are represented, as are most of its alpine plants, and the remote interior is a haven for wildlife, including rare carnivorous snails and giant cave spiders.

The park's extraordinary landscapes are best seen by walking the **Heaphy Track** (78km; 4–5 days), which links Golden Bay with Kohaihai Bluff on the West Coast. One of New Zealand's Great Walks, it is appreciably tougher than the Abel Tasman Coast Track, though it compensates with beauty and the diversity of its landscapes – turbulent rivers, broad tussock downs and forests, and nikau palm groves at the western end. The track is named after Charles Heaphy who, along with Thomas Brunner, became the first European to walk the West Coast section of the route in 1846, accompanied by their Maori guide Kehu. Maori had long traversed the area heading down to central Westland in search of *pounamu* for weapons, ornaments and tools.

TRAILHEAD TRANSPORT

The western end of the track is over 400km by road from the eastern end, so if you leave gear at one end, you'll have to re-walk the track, undertake a long bus journey, or fly back to your base at Nelson, Motueka or Takaka. Track transport only runs from late October to mid-April: in **winter** everything becomes more difficult, requiring taxis to reach trailheads.

The **east coast end** of the track starts at Brown Hut, 28km southwest of Collingwood. Golden Bay Coachlines run there from Nelson (departing 6.45am; $55), Motueka (8am; $45), Takaka (9.15am; $33) and Collingwood (9.35am; $24). From the **west coast end** of the track, you'll arrive at the Kohaihai shelter, 10km north of Karamea. Even with the best connections you'll need to spend nights in both Karamea and Nelson before returning to Takaka. The operators listed below provide services that can help avoid this.

Trek Express ☏ 0800 128 735, ⓦ trekexpress.co.nz. You'll have to base yourself in Nelson, but they'll run you from there to Brown Hut, pick you up at Kohaihai Shelter several days later, then run you back to Nelson that evening ($110).

Heaphy Track Help Takaka ☏ 03 525 9576, ⓦ heaphytrackhelp.co.nz. Takaka-based Derry Kingston will deliver your car to Karamea ($290 plus fuel costs). He then walks the track, meeting you partway to give you the keys.

Remote Adventures ☏ 0800 150 338, ⓦ remote adventures.co.nz. Flying also gives you the chance to return to your car the same day you finish. This outfit will pick up in Karamea and fly to Takaka ($170/person).

TRAIL INFORMATION AND GUIDED HIKES

Download DOC's *Heaphy Track* brochure, or buy one at an i-SITE. It includes a **schematic map** that is satisfactory for hiking, though it is helpful to carry the detailed 1:150,000 *Kahurangi Park* map ($19).

INFORMATION AND ACTIVITIES

Tourist information The *Paddle Crab Café* (daily 9.30am–5pm; ☏ 03 524 8454), adjacent to Puponga Farm Park, acts as the visitor centre for Farewell Spit. You can also check ⓦ doc.govt.nz, and download the *Farewell Spit and Puponga Farm Park* leaflet for more information.

THE ROAD TO FAREWELL SPIT

Cape Farewell Horse Treks ☏ 03 524 8031, ⓦ horse treksnz.com. Offers some of the most visually spectacular horse riding in the South Island. Trips don't actually go onto Farewell Spit, but visit Pillar Point (90min; $55), Puponga Beach (90min; $65) and Wharariki Beach (3hr; $120).

ACCOMMODATION

★ **Farewell Gardens Motor Camp** 37–39 Seddon St, Puponga ☏ 03 524 8445, ⓦ farewellgardens.co.nz. An idyllic little spot, located beside the sea at the base of Farewell Spit, with a variety of accommodation options for everyone from families to backpackers. Facilities include two camp kitchens, lounge, BBQ, washing machine and dryer and hot showers. Camping $16, en-suite cabin $70,

self-contained apartment $150

The Innlet 839 Pakawau Rd ☏ 03 524 8040, ⓦ goldenbayindex.co.nz. An excellent hostel with delightful garden cottages and several heated outdoor baths in the bush. Camping $21, dorms $29, rooms $65, self-contained cottage $75, studio apartment $96, Ruru cottage $180

Bush and Beyond Guided Walks ⓘ 03 528 9054, ⓦ naturetreks.co.nz. Guided walks along the track – and elsewhere in the park – are admirably handled by this ecologically caring operator, who run five-day trips ($1595).

ACCOMMODATION

Along the route, there are seven **huts** that **must be booked** and paid for year-round (Oct–April $30.60; May–Sept $15.50; book online at ⓦ doc.govt.nz), with heating, water and toilets (mostly flush). All except Brown and Gouland Downs have cooking stoves, but you need to carry your own pots and pans. There are also nine designated **campsites** that also must be booked (Oct–April $12.30, May–Sept $8.60) and are mostly close to huts, though you can't use hut facilities. There is a two-night limit in each hut or campsite. Take all provisions with you, and go prepared for sudden changes of weather and a hail of sandflies.

THE ROUTE

Ninety percent of hikers walk the Heaphy Track from east to west, thereby getting the tough initial climb over with and taking it relatively easy on subsequent days.

Brown Hut to Perry Saddle Hut (17km; 5hr; 800m ascent). A steady climb all the way along an old coach road, passing the Aorere campsite and shelter, and Flanagans Corner viewpoint – at 915m, the highest point on the track.

Perry Saddle Hut to Gouland Downs Hut (7km; 2hr; 200m ascent). It's a very easy walk across Perry Saddle through tussock clearings and down into a valley (passing the famed pole strung with used tramping boots) before crossing limestone arches to the hut. This is a great little eight-bunk hut (no cooking facilities) where you might hear kiwi at night.

Gouland Downs Hut to Saxon Hut (5km; 1hr 30min, 200m descent). Crossing Gouland Downs, an undulating area of flax and tussock.

Saxon Hut to James Mackay Hut (12km; 3hr; 400m ascent). Cross the grassy flatlands, winding in and out of small tannin-stained streams as they tip over into the Heaphy River below.

James Mackay Hut to Lewis Hut (12.5km; 3–4hr; 700m descent). If you have the energy it is worth pressing on to a haven of nikau palms – but sadly also less welcome sandflies.

Lewis Hut to Heaphy Hut (8km; 2–3hr; 100m ascent). It is possible to get from Lewis Hut to the track end in a day but it is more enjoyable to take your time and stop at the Heaphy Hut, near where you can explore the exciting Heaphy rivermouth: its narrow outlet funnels river water into a torrid sea, resulting in a maelstrom of sea and fresh water.

Heaphy Hut to Kohaihai (16km; 5hr; 100m ascent). This final stretch is a gentle walk through forest down the coast until you reach Crayfish Point, where the route briefly follows the beach. Avoid this section within an hour of high tide, longer if it is stormy. Once you reach Scott's Beach, you have only to climb over Kohaihai Bluff to find the Kohaihai Shelter car park on the other side – and hopefully your pre-arranged pick-up from Karamea.

Whariki Holiday Park Whariki Beach, Cape Farewell ⓘ 03 524 8507, ⓦ whararikibeachholiday park.co.nz. Thirty tent sites, a backpacker lodge, on-site caravans, plus a wide range of facilities that includes a communal kitchen, fridge/freezer, BBQ, hot showers (coin-op), laundry, bike rental and a coffee and snacks caravan (daily 8am–8pm in summer). Camping $18, lodge $25, caravans/person $30

Nelson Lakes National Park and around

Two glacial lakes characterize the **Nelson Lakes National Park**, around 120km southwest of Nelson, **Rotoiti** ("little lake") and **Rotoroa** ("long lake"), nestled in the mountains at the northernmost limit of the Southern Alps. Both are surrounded by tranquil mountains and shrouded in dark beech forest and jointly form the headwaters of the Buller River. **Tramping** (see box, p.491) is undoubtedly the main event and you could easily devote a week to some of the longer circuits, though the short lakeside walks are also rewarding.

The park's subalpine rivers, lakes, forests and hills are full of birdlife, but it has offered little solace to humans: Maori passed through the area and caught eels in the lakes, but the best efforts of European settlers and gold prospectors yielded meagre returns. Now, recreation is all.

St Arnaud

ST ARNAUD (pronounced Snt-AR-nard) is a speck of a place scattered around the north shore of Lake Rotoiti, with around a hundred residents but over four hundred houses, mostly used by holidaying Kiwis. The town is largely used as a base for anglers, kayakers and yachties.

ARRIVAL AND DEPARTURE
ST ARNAUD

By bus Access to the region is with Nelson Lakes Shuttles (☎03 521 1900, ⓦnelsonlakesshuttles.co.nz) who offer an on-demand service to and from Nelson ($40/person,

minimum $160 charge) and also connect St Arnaud with the Mount Robert car park ($15/person, minimum $25 charge) and Lake Rotoroa ($30/person, minimum $90 charge).

GETTING AROUND

By water taxi Rotoiti Water Taxis operate on Lake Rotoiti from St Arnaud to the head of the lake ($90 for up to three people, then $25/person; ☎027 702 278,

ⓦrotoitiwatertaxis.co.nz), so if you fancy sections of hiking at the southern end of the lake there's no need to walk the whole way.

INFORMATION AND ACTIVITIES

DOC View Rd (daily 8am–4.30pm extended to 5 or 6pm in summer; ☎03 521 1806). Has all the hiking, biking, fishing and ecology information you could need as well as local accommodation and transport listings.

Rotoiti Water Taxis ☎027 702 278, ⓦrotoitiwater taxis.co.nz. Does scenic cruises around the lake by prior arrangement ($35/person; minimum charge $105) and rents kayaks ($50/half-day) and canoes ($60/half-day; $100/day).

ACCOMMODATION AND EATING

Alpine Lodge Main Rd, opposite the Village Alpine Store ☎03 521 1869, ⓦalpinelodge.co.nz. Dorms, budget rooms and hotel rooms in wooden buildings, with a licensed restaurant, bar and spa pool. The adjacent *Alpine Lodge Café* provides strong coffee, home-made cakes, all-day snacks and summertime dinners such as steak, fish and burgers, all served with chips ($15–30). Dorms $29, budget rooms $69, hotel rooms $150

Kerr Bay campsite On the lakeshore, 500m from the Village Alpine Store. A simple DOC site with pay showers ($1), toilets, tap water, cooking facilities and a BBQ area. $10

★ **Nelson Lakes Motels and Travers-Sabine Lodge** SH63 ☎03 521 1887, ⓦnelsonlakes.co.nz. About 150m up the street from the *Alpine Lodge*, this is the pick of the local places to stay. The *Nelson Lakes Motels* is a mid-sized hostel with some doubles, twins and shared rooms, kitchen, TV and a wealth of information. The *Travers-Sabine Lodge* has a cluster of comfortable, fully self-contained log-built chalets next door. Both have access to a hot tub ($8). Dorms $26, rooms $62, self-contained units $115

St Arnaud Village Alpine Store 75 Main Rd ☎03 521 1854. The hub of the village sells petrol, groceries – including fresh produce – and fish and chips. Daily 7.30am–7.30pm.

★ **Tophouse** Tophouse Rd, 8km northeast of St Arnaud ☎0800 544 545, ⓦtophouse.co.nz. An 1887 former drovers' inn and stagecoach stop that makes for an appealing alternative. Sitting by the fire in this earth-built hotel decorated with Victorian furniture can make you feel like you've slipped back in time. Accommodation is either in shared-bathroom inn rooms or outside in fairly modern motel-style cabins. They also do Devonshire teas, lunches featuring the likes of wild venison and plum pie and chips ($18) or a set evening meal ($49). Don't miss the country's smallest pub – six is a crowd – with excellent local beers. Rooms & cabins $135

West Bay campsite 3km drive from St Arnaud. A basic DOC site with two separate camping areas with some forested pitches, plus tap water, cold showers and toilets. Closed April–Nov. $7

Lake Rotoroa

20km northwest of St Arnaud, approached along the Gowan Valley Rd

Pretty **Lake Rotoroa** feels a good deal more remote than the area around St Arnaud. The lake ends near a DOC **campsite**, from where there are a few short walks. Lake Rotoroa

NELSON LAKES HIKES

With 270km of track served by twenty huts there is no shortage of walking options. For **day-walks**, arm yourself with DOC's *Walks In Nelson Lakes National Park* booklet. The two **multi-day tramps** have their own leaflets supplemented by the 1:100,000 *Nelson Lakes National Park* map ($19).

These are alpine tracks so **go equipped** with good boots, and warm, waterproof clothing – it can snow in almost any month up here – and crampons are likely to be needed from April to November. Both tracks start from the upper Mount Robert car park, 7km by road from St Arnaud.

The following hikes are listed in approximate order of difficulty.

Bellbird Walk Kerr Bay, St Arnaud (10–15min loop; flat). Easy meander through beech forest alive with the sound of tui, bellbirds and fantails thanks to the Rotoiti Nature Recovery Project, an attempt to replicate the successful offshore island pest clearances by concerted trapping and poisoning. Several of these "mainland islands" have been set up across New Zealand since the late 1990s with considerable success. Visit in the early evening when the birds (even reintroduced great spotted kiwi) are particularly noisy and frisky.

Honeydew Walk Kerr Bay, St Arnaud (30–45min loop; flat). An extension of the Bellbird Walk, named for the sweet excretions of the scale insect that burrows into the bark of the beech trees, its produce attracting loads of nectar-loving tui and bellbirds.

Whisky Falls Mount Robert trailhead (10km; 3–5hr return; 100m ascent). From a parking area on the Mount Robert Road, follow the Lakeside Trail to these 40m falls. Often shrouded in mist and fringed by hanging ferns, the falls are particularly grand after heavy rain.

Mount Robert Circuit (9km; 3–4hr loop; 600m ascent). An excellent loop around the visible face of Mount Robert starting at the Mount Robert car park, ascending the steep Pinchgut Track to the edge of the bush then traversing across to Bushline Hut ($15) before zigzagging down Paddy's Track to the start.

Angelus Hut Loop Mount Robert trailhead (28km; 2-day loop; 1000m ascent). One of the most popular overnighters, this loop follows the exposed Robert Ridge to the beautiful Angelus Basin with its shiny new hut (Oct–April bookings required $20, camping $10; May–Sept $15) and alpine tarn. Two common routes complete the loop: the steep Cascade Track and the Speargrass Track, a bad-weather escape route.

Travers-Sabine Circuit (80km; 4–7 days; 1200m ascent). This major tramp is the scenic equal of several of the Great Walks, but without that status it is far less crowded. The track probes deep into remote areas of lakes, fields of tussock, 2000m mountains and the 1780m Travers Saddle. At the height of summer its verges are briefly emblazoned with yellow buttercups, white daisies, sundew and harebells. The circuit requires a good level of fitness, but is fairly easy to follow with bridges over most streams. There are 11 huts ($15), all but one serviced ($10; tickets from DOC), and three campsites – fires are not allowed, so carry a stove and fuel.

8

Water Taxis ply the length of the lake ($50/person, minimum $150; ☎03 523 9199) to Sabine Hut on the Travers-Sabine Circuit (see box above).

Murchison

MURCHISON, 125km southwest of Nelson and 60km west of St Arnaud, is a small, former gold town now favoured by hunting and fishing types as well as rafters and river kayakers. Numerous rivers feed the nearby Buller, providing excellent white water and plenty of opportunities for bagging trout. Once clear of Murchison, SH6 shadows the river through the Buller Gorge to the **West Coast** town of Westport, a route covered in Chapter 12 (see p.634).

Everything of note is on SH6 (Waller St) or Fairfax Street, which crosses it, including the **Murchison Museum**, 60 Fairfax St (daily 10am–4pm; donation requested), in the 1911 former post office with newspaper clippings, photographs and various oddities including gold-rush-era Chinese pottery and opium bottles.

RAFTING AND RIVER KAYAKING IN MURCHISON

With its breathtaking scenery and swift (in places) water the Buller River provides an ideal backdrop for **rafting** and inflatable **kayak** trips, as do the Mokihinui and Karamea rivers.

Ultimate Descents 51 Fairfax St ☎0800 748 377, ⓦrivers.co.nz. During the season (early Sept–late May) this operator runs sections of the Buller River (Grade III–V; 4hr 30min; $130), spending at least two hours on the water. There are also gentler family trips (Grade II; 4hr 30min; $115), and combo trips (Grade II–IV; 8hr; $240) rafting the tougher bits and kayaking down some easier sections. Check the website for helicopter-access and multi-day trips on the Mokihinui and Karamea rivers.

Ultimate Descents also owns the other rafting company in town, White Water Action.

New Zealand Kayak School 111 Waller St ☎03 523 9611, ⓦnzkayakschool.com. Those keen to learn whitewater kayaking or just brush up on some skills should visit this internationally respected school, which offers four-day courses ($895, including lodging at the school's hostel) that are worth every cent. Oct–April.

ARRIVAL AND DEPARTURE

MURCHISON

By bus Buses stop at the visitor centre or along Waller and Fairfax sts.

Destinations Greymouth (2 daily; 4hr); Nelson (2 daily;

2hr); Punakaiki (2 daily; 2hr 30min); Westport (2 daily; 1hr 30min).

INFORMATION AND ACTIVITIES

Tourist information 47 Waller St (Oct–Easter daily 10am–5pm; Easter–Sept daily 11am–3pm; ☎03 523 9350). The Murchison visitor centre does bookings and stocks gold pans ($10) and the *Recreational Gold Panning* leaflet – the town is one of the few places in the country with public gold panning.

Services At the time of writing, an ATM was expected to

be installed; check with the visitor centre.

Day walks The visitor centre also stocks DOC's *Murchison Day Walks* leaflet featuring the Skyline Walk (3km return; 1hr 30min), which climbs through the native forest to the skyline ridge above Murchison with views of the confluence of the Buller, Matakitaki, Maruia and Matiri rivers. The track starts from the junction of SH6 and Matakitaki West Bank Rd.

ACCOMMODATION AND EATING

Commercial Hotel 37 Fairfax St ☎03 523 9696, ⓦthecommercialhotel.co.nz. A fairly standard Kiwi drinkers' bar with a separate restaurant/café that serves generous bar meals. Bar Mon–Fri 4pm–late, Sat & Sun 3pm–late. Restaurant daily 5–8.30pm.

Kiwi Park 170 Fairfax St, 1km south of town ☎03 523 9248, ⓦkiwipark.co.nz. Family-run holiday park with farm animals to keep the kids quiet and a range of well-kept cabins as well as good communal facilities. Camping $15, cabins $60, motel units $100, luxury cottages $225

Lazy Cow 37 Waller St ☎03 523 9451, ⓔlazycow @xnet.co.nz. A cosy hostel in the centre of town with a convivial atmosphere, clean and snug rooms, nightly meals ($12) and a spa bath. Dorm $28, rooms $74, en suite $84

Mataki Motel 34 Hotham St ☎0800 279 088, ⓦmataki motel.co.nz. Clean and quiet motel clearly signposted about 1km from town, with comfortable and spacious rooms that are reasonably cosy. Some units have a full kitchen. $100

Murchison Lodge 15 Grey St ☎0800 523 9196, ⓦmurchisonlodge.co.nz. Comfortable and convivial eco-conscious lodge with airy rooms, welcome drinks and a full breakfast including eggs laid in the grounds, where you'll also find a few cows and pigs. Free wi-fi. Private bathroom $190, en suite $215

Rivers Café 51 Fairfax St ☎03 523 9009, ⓦrivers cafemurchison.co.nz. Serves pretty good coffee and substantial main meals such as ribeye ($30), salmon ($34) and green been and haloumi salad ($25) in comfortable laidback surroundings. Daily 9am–8.30pm.

Riverview Holiday Park SH6, 1.5km east of town ☎03 523 9591. Simple campsite with lots of pitches, good communal facilities, a variety of well-kept, good-value cabins, a café and helpful owners. It's all located by the gurgling Buller River and is much frequented by kayakers and rafters. Camping $14, cabins $40, tourist flat $100, motel unit $110

The Marlborough Wine Country

In July 1972, Marlborough County Council Livestock Instructor, S.G.C. Newdick, wrote "Vineyards: in regard to these, as there is a glut on the market of grapes there does not appear to be any likelihood of vineyards starting up in Marlborough in the foreseeable future." In the intervening years **Marlborough Sauvignon Blanc** single-handedly put the New Zealand wine industry on the world map, and made the Marlborough Wine Country the largest wine region, with almost sixty percent of the national grape crop.

Many wineries go all out to attract visitors, using distinctive architecture, classy restaurants, art and gourmet foodstuffs. The profusion of weekend visitors from Nelson, Wellington and further afield has spawned a number of smart B&Bs throughout the district, trying to out-luxury one another. If this is what you're after there's little need to bother with **Blenheim** itself, particularly since most of the vineyards are closer to the small, equally unremarkable town of **Renwick**, 10km to the west.

Blenheim

In the early 1970s, **BLENHEIM**, 27km south of Picton, was a fairly sleepy service town set amid pastoral land: now it is a fairly sleepy service town completely surrounded by some of the most fecund and highly regarded vineyards in the land. It is also much visited and as a result has developed a passable café culture, but most of the attractions of note are beyond its rather conservative town limits.

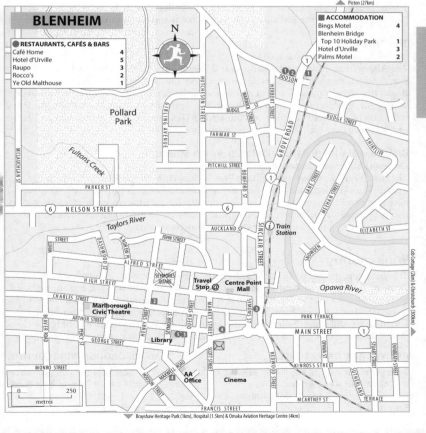

Omaka Aviation Heritage Centre

79 Aerodrome Rd, 4km southwest of town • Daily 10am–4pm • $25 • ⓦ omaka.org.nz

With the exception of the wineries, Blenheim is light on sights. Easily the most diverting is the **Omaka Aviation Heritage Centre**, located beside an airfield. Two large hangars contain 21 World War I planes, some original and still airworthy, others authentic replicas, and many set in amazingly realistic dioramas made by film-maker Peter Jackson's Weta Workshop. Indeed, Jackson, who is a huge World War I buff, owns much of the collection and chairs the trust, which set the place up and will guide its growth over the next few years. The planes are fine examples of their kind, and some, such as the German Halberstadt D.IV and the American Airco DHS, are unique. Check out the crash-landing scene depicting the death of Manfred von Richthofen complete with an original fabric cross from the plane, and a group of Australian soldiers souveniring his boots. A collection of the Red Baron's own memorabilia is displayed nearby. Elsewhere there's the flight suit of US ace Eddie Rickenbacker and a mass of models, badges and love letters – the collection of an obsessive. Everything is made more poignant when you chat to the guides and interpreters, who are mostly former aviators.

Omaka Car Collection

79 Aerodrome Rd, 4km southwest of town • Daily 10am–4pm • $12.50 (pay in the Aviation Heritage Centre) • ⓦ omakaclassiccars.co.nz

One man's obsession with automobiles, classics and otherwise, from the 1950s to the 1980s, plus a couple of spanky motorbikes. The collection totals over 100; just over half are out at any time and all are renovated, taxed and ready to roll.

The Argosy

760 Middle Renwick Rd, at Caldwell • Daily 10am–8pm • $2

The Argosy is an Armstrong passenger and freight aircraft, the last of its kind in the world, which flew with the now defunct Safe Air Ltd, servicing the Chatham Islands. Board the plane for a look round and to watch the documentary about the winding up of Safe Air, the last flight of the Argosy, and sit in the cockpit and listen to an authentic recording of the night the plane encountered a UFO in the vicinity of Kaikoura. Entry to the plane is through *The Argosy* restaurant (see p.497).

Brayshaw Heritage Park and Marlborough Museum

New Renwick Rd, 2.5km south of Blenheim • Museum daily 10am–4pm • $10

The best bit of the **Brayshaw Heritage Park** is the **Marlborough Museum**, which has a small Maori collection and an interesting wine exhibit, covering the region's wine heritage, *terroir*, technology and how pruning techniques have been adapted to match the local conditions. The rest of the park is given over to old buildings, vehicles and equipment and only comes to life during reconstruction days.

Wine country

The gravel plains that flank the Wairau River around the towns of Blenheim and Renwick form some of New Zealand's most prized **wine country**. The region, sheltered by the protective hills of the Richmond Range, basks in around 2400 hours of sunshine a year, making it perfect for ripening the grapes for its esteemed Sauvignon Blanc. Chardonnay and Pinot Noir grapes also grow well (guaranteeing tasty bubbly), as do olives, used for light golden olive oils. The best of the local wineries are listed on p.497.

ARRIVAL AND DEPARTURE   **MARLBOROUGH WINE COUNTRY**

By train and bus Trains and long-distance buses stop at the Blenheim i-SITE at the rail station.

Train destinations Christchurch via Kiakoura (1 daily); Picton (1 daily).

Bus destinations Christchurch (4–5 daily; 4hr 45min–5hr 30min); Nelson (4 daily; 1hr 45min); Picton (8 daily; 30min).

By plane The airport is 7km west of town. Marlborough

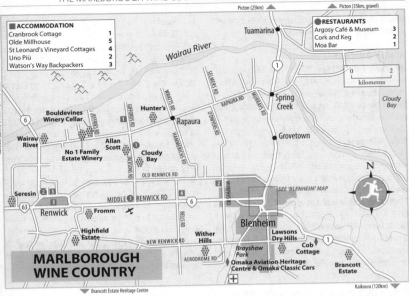

ACCOMMODATION
Cranbrook Cottage	1
Olde Millhouse	5
St Leonard's Vineyard Cottages	4
Uno Più	2
Watson's Way Backpackers	3

RESTAURANTS
Argosy Café & Museum	3
Cork and Keg	2
Moa Bar	1

MARLBOROUGH WINE COUNTRY

Taxis (☎ 03 577 5511) charge $35 into town.
Destinations Auckland (4 daily; 1hr 20min); Christchurch (3 daily; 50min); Wellington (10 daily; 25min).

GETTING AROUND

By bike There's bike rental at several hostels in Blenheim. AvantiPlus Cycle, 61 Queen St (☎ 03 578 0433), rent bikes for $40/half-day.

INFORMATION

i-SITE In the Blenheim train station on Sinclair St (Mon–Fri 9am–5.30pm, Sat & Sun 9am–4pm; ☎ 03 577 8080, ⓦ lovemarlborough.com). Stocks an assortment of leaflets including the *Marlborough Wine Trail* map and the *Art and Craft Trail* brochure (both free). Internet is free at the library, 33 Arthur St (Mon–Fri 9am–6pm, Sat 10am–1pm, Sun 1.30–4.30pm), and cheap enough at the i-SITE or the Travel Stop Cyber Café, 17 Market St (Mon–Sat 10am–9pm, Sun 10am–4pm). All have wi-fi.

ACCOMMODATION

As befits a major wine region there's an abundance of high-priced luxury accommodation, plus more modest places in town. Budget places mostly cater to seasonal workers, though there is one exceptional hostel in Renwick. During the first full week of February nearly all accommodation is booked far in advance for the festival season (see box, p.498), so either plan well ahead or steer clear of the region.

BLENHEIM

Bings Motel 29 Maxwell Rd ☎ 0800 666 999, ⓔ email @bingsmotel.co.nz. Classic older-style motel that used to be an old military barracks, close to the centre of Blenheim with plenty of space, low rates and run by a pleasant owner. $94

Blenheim Bridge Top 10 Holiday Park 78 Grove Rd ☎ 0800 268 666, ⓦ blenheimtop10.co.nz. Sited a little too close to the main road and railway line but it is central and has all the expected facilities as well as good camp sites and comfortable units and cabins. Camping/site $35, cabins $78, kitchen cabins $90, self-contained units $125

★ **Hotel d'Urville** 52 Queen St ☎ 03 577 9945, ⓦ durville.com. This former bank right in the centre of town has been turned into a chic and stylish small hotel with a restaurant and cocktail bar. The best – some say the only – place to stay in town, and a good place to eat and party. $290

Palms Motel 68 Charles St ☎ 0800 256 725, ⓦ blenheimpalmsmotel.co.nz. Nicely decorated central motel with Sky TV and a range of individually styled units,

8

most of which are spacious, and some of which come with spa bath. Cooked breakfast available ($12). $150

WINE COUNTRY

★ **Cranbrook Cottage** 145 Giffords Rd, about 9km northwest of Blenheim ☎ 03 572 8606, ⓦ cranbrook .co.nz. Romantic, picture-book 1860s self-contained cottage sleeping four, set in a tree-filled paddock amid the vines. Breakfast – delivered to your door in a basket – is to die for. Two-night minimum. $210

Olde Millhouse 9 Wilson St, Renwick ☎ 0800 653 262, ⓦ oldemillhouse.co.nz. Lovely three-room B&B set among cottage gardens where a continental breakfast can be served. There is bike rental (also available to non-guests), a spa pool, free wi-fi and free bus transfers. $145

St Leonard's Vineyard Cottages 18 St Leonard's Rd ☎ 03 577 8328, ⓦ stleonards.co.nz. A broad range of former farm buildings beautifully converted into rustically luxurious self-contained quarters, with access to a solar-heated pool, free bikes, barbecue areas and grounds amid the vines. Choose from The Old Dairy (max 2), Shearers

Quarters (max 3), the Stables (max 2), the Cottage (max 3) and the Woolshed (max 5), which comes with an outdoor bath. Breakfast ingredients are supplied, often with home-laid eggs. Old Dairy $115, Shearers Quarters $150, Stables $185, Cottage $210, Woolshed $310

★ **Uno Più** 75 Murphys Rd ☎ 03 578 2235, ⓦ unopiu .co.nz. Run by friendly, former Italian restaurant-owner, Gino, who makes this homestay magical. It's hard to imagine being looked after any better, either in the 1917 homestead or out in the modern mud-brick self-catering cottage. Breakfasts are great and excellent dinners ($80) are available by arrangement. Book in advance. Homestead $430, cottage $470

★ **Watson's Way Backpackers** 56 High St, Renwick ☎ 03 572 8228, ⓦ watsonswaybackpackers.co.nz. Easily Marlborough's best hostel: a very comfortable spot in the shade of large trees in a wonderful garden, with a public tennis court over the fence, snug rooms, made-up doubles, easy access to the wineries, low-cost bikes, an outdoor bath, BBQ and owners who can't do enough for you. Closed Sept. Tents $15, dorms $30, rooms $66, en suites $76

8

MARLBOROUGH WINE TASTINGS AND TOURS

Tastings and tours are the best way to experience the region. Don't be tempted to cram too many tastings into a day; most vineyards are more suited to leisurely tastings than whistle-stop guzzling. Most of the wineries will also ship cases of wine anywhere in the world, but shipping costs and high import duties mean that it seldom makes financial sense to do so – better to just drink the stuff on picnics and at BYO restaurants.

TASTINGS

Around fifty wineries have cellar-door **tastings** (mostly for a small charge, which is deducted from subsequent purchases). Some add a short tour, tack on a restaurant or even link up with outlets hawking olive oil, fruit preserves and the like. Most of the notable wineries are around Renwick or immediately north along Raupara Road, all listed on the free *Marlborough Wine Trail* sheet (along with their opening hours and facilities), and most also feature on the more detailed *Marlborough Wineries & Wines* fold-out map ($2). **Opening hours** are generally 10am–4pm or 5pm daily, though much reduced in winter.

Armed with leaflet and map you're ready for a day among the vines, preferably with lunch at one of the winery restaurants. Few wines are available for much under $20 a bottle, and wineries like to show off with their restaurants, so although it will almost certainly be a pleasurable experience it won't be cheap.

WINE TOURS

To avoid having to designate a driver, take an organized wine tour.

Highlight Wine Tours ☎ 03 577 9046, ⓦ highlight winetours.co.nz. A low-key locally owned and operated business, running afternoon ($55), half-day ($65) and full-day ($75, including two lunch stops but not the cost of lunch) tours.

Marlborough Wine Tours ☎ 03 578 9515, ⓦ marlboroughwinetours.co.nz. Offers some of the cheapest tours, including jaunts of three ($45), five ($60) and seven hours ($80), with time for lunch at one of the wineries (not included).

Sounds Connection ☎ 0800 742 866, ⓦ sounds connection.co.nz. Specializes in half-day tours visiting four or five wineries ($75), and also offers a full-day circuit of six or seven wineries ($99, excluding lunch).

Wine Tours by Bike ☎ 03 577 6954, ⓦ winetours bybike.co.nz. Rents bikes (half-day $40; full day $60) but the cost includes accommodation pick-ups and they will come and rescue you if you have a mechanical breakdown.

EATING AND DRINKING

A few hours spent visiting vineyards should be accompanied by lunch at one of the wineries — especially *Highfield Estate*, *Hunter's* and *Wairau River*. A few are also open in the evenings, but for dinner you may prefer to head into Blenheim.

BLENHEIM

★ **The Argosy** 760 Middle Renwick Rd ☎03 572 7388, ⓦargosy.net.nz. A fabulous traditional restaurant offering great value, generously portioned fish and chips, platters, scallops, breakfasts, roast dinners (mains $9–32) and all manner of snacks. Licensed. Mon–Fri 10am–8pm, Sat & Sun 10am–9pm.

Café Home 1c Main St. Primo espresso alongside fresh sandwiches, frittata slices and cakes in minimalist surroundings ($9–20). Mon–Fri 8am–5pm, Sat 9am–2pm.

Hotel d'Urville 52 Queen St ☎03 577 9945, ⓦdurville .com. Classy restaurant with stylish modern decor and exemplary cuisine, making the best of seasonal produce (mains $38–42). Book in advance. Daily for lunch and dinner.

Moa Bar 258 Jackson Rd ☎03 572 5149. Brilliant little traditional bar serving the full range of ten beers and two ciders from the Moa brewery. They also dish up brewer's and cheese platters. Daily 11am–late.

★ **Raupo** 2 Symons St ☎03 577 8822, ⓦraupocafe .co.nz. Great café with a terrace overlooking the Opawa River, serving superb lunches (mostly $18), bistro-style dinners ($26–33) and high tea, both morning and afternoon ($15). Daily 9am–11pm.

★ **Rocco's** 5 Dodson St ☎03 578 6940. Enjoyable authentic Italian restaurant that could unabashedly sit on a New York or Rome street. For a blowout, order the awesome chicken Kiev alla Rocco — chicken breast filled with ham, garlic butter and cheese, all wrapped in a veal schnitzel ($28) — or the fillet alla Rocco. Fresh pasta is made daily. Dinner only. Mon–Sat 6pm–late.

Ye Old Malthouse 1 Dodson St ☎03 577 8348. Convivial bistro, wine and alehouse dishing up tasty pizzas ($18–24) and offering à la carte options. Wash these down with Renaissance beers brewed on site, including a Scotch ale and a superbly hoppy American-style pale ale. Mon–Sat 11am–11pm.

RENWICK

Cork and Keg Inkerman St. Friendly English-style local with traditional games like dominoes and a good selection of South Island craft beers including those from the local Moa stable. All-day pub meals from $16.50–23. Daily midday–11pm.

THE WINERIES

Bouldevines Wine Cellar 193 Rapaura Rd ☎03 572 8444, ⓦbouldevines.co.nz. Single vineyard boutique wines in a shop-like cellar door, reasonably priced and covering the range of grape varieties on offer in the area. Daily 10am–5pm.

Brancott Estate 180 Brancott Rd, 5km south of Blenheim on SH1 ☎03 520 6975, ⓦbrancottestate .com. A good starting point for your exploration of the region. Montana effectively kicked off the wine region in the early 1970s and now operates the country's largest winery, a favourite with coach parties. Come for free tasting, the café or the winery tour (daily 11am, 1pm & 3pm; 50min; $15.50), which includes a little wine appreciation, a short movie and structured tasting. Also worth a look is the newly constructed, hill-top restaurant and heritage centre, where you can get good food and views — as well as an advertorial video presentation and the one hour Living Land Experience Tour ($40). Encompassing human and natural history, the tour ends with a tasting, but the highlight is the chance to see a very rare New Zealand falcon — a guilty nod to the fact that wineries and winemaking are half the reason the birds are endangered in this area. Cellar door daily 10am–4.30pm.

Cloudy Bay Jacksons Rd ☎03 520 9197, ⓦcloudybay .co.nz. Marlborough Sauvignon Blanc put New Zealand on the world wine map in the late 1980s and the Cloudy Bay Sauvignon was its flagship. It is still drinking so well today that they can't keep up with demand; it can be tasted ($5) along with their other top-notch wines. Cheese and charcuterie platters are $25. Daily 10am–5pm.

Fromm Godfrey Rd ☎03 572 9355, ⓦfrommwineries .com. A vineyard that is turning winemakers' heads with a very hands-on approach, producing organic, predominantly red, wine, including an excellent Pinot Noir, a peppery Syrah, and a Riesling with echoes of the best German efforts. Visit if you're serious about the subject and you'll taste ($5) a product that's a match for anywhere in the world. Daily 11am–5pm.

Highfield Estate Brookby Rd ☎03 572 9244, ⓦhighfield.co.nz. Easily recognizable by its Tuscan-inspired tower, which you can climb for excellent views, *Highfield* offers free tastings and lays on some of the best food in the region, with mains ($19–35) and antipasto platters ($67) that will easily feed two, plus cheese boards ($20) and delectable desserts ($13), all served overlooking the vines. Daily 10am–5pm.

Hunter's Rapaura Rd ☎03 572 8489, ⓦhunters.co.nz. Jane Hunter is recognized as one of the world's top female winemakers. Drop by to taste (free), visit the art gallery or eat in the family-friendly restaurant, which does platters ($25–35) plus more formal dinners Wed–Sat. Cellar door daily 9.30am–4.30pm.

8

MARLBOROUGH FESTIVALS

Blenheim springs to life during February, with two major festivals.

Blues, Brews and BBQs (Ⓦbluesbrews.co
.nz). The month kicks off at the Blenheim
A&P Showground with a combination of
musicians and brewers from all over the
country. This is mixed in a heady cocktail
with some good old-fashioned Kiwi BBQ
food, as well as some more adventurous
fare. First Saturday in February.
Marlborough Wine Festival (Ⓦwine
-marlborough-festival.co.nz). Various arts
and crafts demonstrations, exhibitions,
markets and special events pad out the

week of the Blues, Brews and BBQs festival,
but this is Blenheim's big event. Around
8,000 people flock to the *Montana Brancott*
winery, where a vast field of marquees
contain local wines and food for purchase
and consumption and throb with the sound
of live music. Tickets are $48, and include
a glass. Richies (☎03 578 5467) run buses
to the festival site from the town and the
airport ($12.50 return), as well as from Picton
($25 return). Second Saturday in February
10.30am–6pm.

★ **Lawsons Dry Hills** Alabama Rd ☎03 578 7674,
Ⓦlawsonsdryhills.co.nz. Established vines produce stunning wines in this multi-award-winning winery, well worth
visiting for the Pinot Gris, Gewürtztraminer and Sauvignon
Blanc if nothing else. Tastings are free, and you can sample
cheese boards ($14–22). Cellar door daily 10am–5pm.
No 1 Family Estate 196 Rapaura Rd ☎03 572 9876,
Ⓦno1familyestate.co.nz. Home of the area's best-known
and most accomplished maker of bubbles. Free tastings.
Daily 10.30am–4.30pm.
Seresin Bedford Rd ☎03 572 9408, Ⓦseresin.co.nz.

Stylish winery with a distinctive primitivist "hand" logo
perched on a rise overlooking the vines. Largely organic,
estate-grown grapes interact with wild yeast to produce
world-class wines, and they produce some killer olive oil.
Tastings $5. Daily 10am–4.30pm.
Wither Hills 211 New Renwick Rd ☎03 520 8270,
Ⓦwitherhills.co.nz. A striking, roadside winery that's all
concrete and tussock. Nip in for tastings ($5) of the popular
Chardonnay, Pinot Noir and Sauvignon Blanc (including
the fine single-vineyard Rarangi). Daily 10am–4.30pm.

The road to the Kaikoura Coast

The 130km between the coast and the brooding Seaward Kaikoura Range from
Blenheim to Kaikoura is one of the most spectacular coastal roads in New Zealand.
It is best to allow plenty of time for frequent stops along the gorgeous stretches of
coastline. Around 20km south of Blenheim a sign points inland towards **Molesworth
Station** (see box opposite) and **Hanmer Springs**.

Lake Grassmere, 50km south of Blenheim, is a vast shallow salt lake, which annually
produces 70,000 tonnes a year of table salt. **Cyclists** may want to overnight 20km south
of the salt works at *Pedallers Rest Cycle Stop* (see opposite).

From Lake Grassmere, you're now following the coast, with grey gravel beaches all
the way and accessible at various points. Almost 90km out of Blenheim, the rocky
Kekerengu Point juts out and makes a great place to watch the crashing waves while
stopping in at *The Store* (see opposite) for a bite to eat.

Ohau Point

35km south of Kekerengu Point

Ohau Point marks the best stretch of coastline – a wonderful rocky, surf-lashed strip
that continues for around 30km to Kaikoura then 20km beyond. Ohau Point is home
to the South Island's largest seal colony with dozens (if not hundreds) of seals lolling
on the rocks not more than 20m away. Immediately before Ohau Point, Ohau Stream
Walk (15min return) weaves through the bush to a nice waterfall and pool where in
October and November seal pups can be seen playing in the pools during the day.
Approach quietly.

DRIVING THROUGH MOLESWORTH STATION

Timing is everything if you want to drive (or ride) the Acheron Road through **Molesworth Station**, at 1800 square kilometres New Zealand's largest farm. The central 59km section of road is only open to traffic for a few weeks each summer (late Dec–March). It is an impressive run through New Zealand's most accessible high country, passing historic cob houses with towering mountains all around. The drive from Blenheim to Hanmer Springs (190km) takes over five hours, a couple of them on gravel. There are no services so make sure your tank is topped up. **Camping** is only permitted at *Molesworth Cob Cottage* and *Acheron Accommodation House* (both $6). For the latest information obtain DOC's *Molesworth* leaflet ($2) and check ⓦ doc.govt.nz.

Molesworth Tour Company ☏ 03 577 9897, ⓦ molesworthtours.co.nz. Access is also possible from Oct–May with this operator, which explores the region on one-day (from $190), overnight ($748), three-day ($1235) and four-day ($1655) trips, as well as cycle tours, which come in a bit cheaper.

The coastline around here is a perfect habitat for **crayfish**, which are sought by the locals and sold roadside, notably at Rakautara (see below).

ACCOMMODATION AND EATING

Cay's Crays and Nin's Bins Rakautara, 3km south of Ohau Point. Two roadside caravans hawking delicious cooked crayfish for around $35–55.

Pedallers Rest Cycle Stop Lake Grassmere, 1.5km off SH1 ☏ 03 575 6708, ✉ pedallers@ruralinzone.net. A small but comfy spot that's frequented by cyclists, but welcomes most everyone. There's a small on-site shop. To

THE ROAD TO THE KAIKOURA COAST

get there, look for the water tank and sign beside the road. Bunks $18, camping $14

The Store Kekerengu Point ☏ 03 575 8600, ⓦ the-store.co.nz. A great spot to tuck into burgers ($21.50), fish and chips ($20), cakes and coffee. It's licensed, and is popular with the passing tour bus trade. Daily 8am–7pm.

Kaikoura

The small town of **KAIKOURA**, 130km south of Blenheim and 180km north of Christchurch, enjoys a spectacular setting in the lee of the Kaikoura Peninsula, wedged between the mountains and the ocean. Offshore, the sea bed drops away rapidly to the kilometre-deep Kaikoura Canyon, a phenomenon that brings sea mammals in large and varied numbers. **Whale watching** and **swimming with dolphins** are big business here, and the presence of expectant tourists has spawned a number of eco-oriented businesses offering swimming with seals, sea kayaking and hiking.

Brief history

Kaikoura got its name when an ancient **Maori** explorer who stopped to eat crayfish found it so good he called the place *kai* (food) *koura* (crayfish). Maori legend also accounts for the extraordinary coastline around Kaikoura. During the creation of the land, a young deity, Marokura, was given the job of finishing the region. First, he built the Kaikoura Peninsula and a second smaller peninsula (Haumuri Bluff). Then he set about creating the huge troughs in the sea between the two peninsulas, where the cold waters of the south would mix with the warm waters of the north and east. Realizing the depth of Marokura's accomplishment, the god Tuterakiwhanoa said that the place would be a gift (*koha*) to all those who see its hidden beauty – and it is still known to local Maori as Te Koha O Marokura.

The Ngai Tahu people harvested the wealth of the land and seas until Te Rauparaha and his followers decimated them, in around 1830. The first **Europeans** to settle were whalers who came in the early 1840s, swiftly followed by farmers. The trials and tribulations of their existence are recorded in the Kaikoura Museum and the more evocative Fyffe House. Kaikoura ticked on quietly until the late 1980s

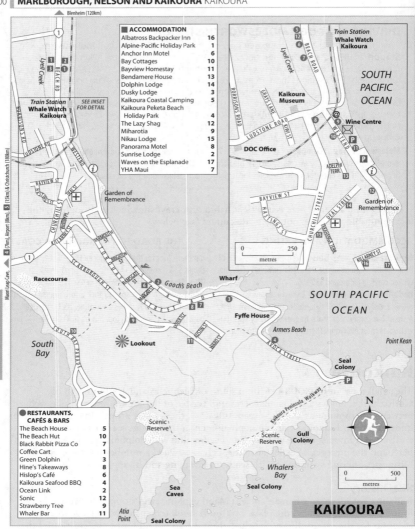

ACCOMMODATION

Albatross Backpacker Inn	16
Alpine-Pacific Holiday Park	1
Anchor Inn Motel	6
Bay Cottages	10
Bayview Homestay	11
Bendamere House	13
Dolphin Lodge	14
Dusky Lodge	3
Kaikoura Coastal Camping	5
Kaikoura Peketa Beach Holiday Park	4
The Lazy Shag	12
Miharotia	9
Nikau Lodge	15
Panorama Motel	8
Sunrise Lodge	2
Waves on the Esplanade	17
YHA Maui	7

RESTAURANTS, CAFÉS & BARS

The Beach House	5
The Beach Hut	10
Black Rabbit Pizza Co	7
Coffee Cart	1
Green Dolphin	3
Hine's Takeaways	8
Hislop's Café	6
Kaikoura Seafood BBQ	4
Ocean Link	2
Sonic	12
Strawberry Tree	9
Whaler Bar	11

KAIKOURA

when whale watching really took off and put the place on the tourism map. Since then it has steadily expanded, becoming more commercial, though without losing its small-town feel.

Kaikoura Museum

14 Ludstone Rd • Mon–Fri 10am–4.30pm, Sat & Sun 2–4pm • $5

Soon to be moved to a new, purpose-built location opposite the i-SITE in the centre of town, the **Kaikoura Museum** currently makes the best of its old site, where a large rock contains the fossilized ribcage of a Cretaceous-period plesiosaur. The Maori collection illustrates the stages needed to convert a mussel shell into effective fishhooks, while out back there's an early 1900s jailhouse (complete with padded cell) that was used in Kaikoura until 1980.

Fyffe House

62 Avoca St • Oct–April daily 10am–5.30pm; May–Sept Thurs–Mon 10am–4pm • $9

Out on the peninsula, don't miss the town's oldest building, **Fyffe House**, an original whaler's cottage resting on whalebone foundations. The house began life as part of the Waiopuka Whaling Station that was founded by Robert Fyffe in 1842 and was originally an unprepossessing two-room cooper's cottage. Extended by George Fyffe in 1860, some rooms look now much as they did then, while others reflect the condition of the place when the last resident moved out in 1980. Avoca Street follows the edge of the peninsula round to a car park (the start of the Kaikoura Peninsula Walkway; see box below) where fur **seals** often lounge on flat, sea-worn rocks watching the plentiful birdlife.

WALKS AROUND KAIKOURA

Kaikoura isn't all about spending money watching marine mammals. There's plenty to be seen on foot, best accessed on two local walks and two longer tramps.

DAY WALKS

Kaikoura Peninsula Walkway (11km loop; 3hr; undulating). A superb circuit of the peninsula covered on DOC's *The Peninsula Walkway* leaflet. Pick it up at the i-SITE and follow the route along the Esplanade past Fyffe House to the seal colony. From here it loops over the grassy cliffs to South Bay, with views down to the seals lolling on the rocks below. Several options follow paths back over the peninsula to the i-SITE. Chances are you'll see red-billed and black-backed gulls, oystercatchers, herons and shags: be warned that gulls nesting during September and October are likely to attack if they feel that their nests are threatened: steer well clear.

Also worth a look is the small reserve, behind a predator-proof fence, set aside for Hutton's Shearwaters who were damaging themselves trying to land in the town.
Mount Fyffe (16km return; 6–8hr; 1400m ascent). Several walks close to town are outlined in DOC's *Mount Fyffe and the Seaward Kaikoura Range* leaflet. The most immediately appealing is this tough hike to the 1602m summit of Mount Fyffe. Starting at a poorly signposted car park 12km northwest of town, the route climbs steadily up a 4WD road to the summit with its glorious views over the Kaikoura Peninsula and coast.

MULTI-DAY WALKS

Kaikoura Wilderness Walks T 0800 945 337, W kaikourawilderness.co.nz. Offers a delightful combination of guided walk in gorgeous, wild country up behind Kaikoura and a night in the luxury *Shearwater Lodge* – far from everything on the bushline at 1000m, but with crisp sheets in en-suite rooms and three-course meals. After a Kaikoura pick-up and short drive, day one (8.5km one-way; 6hr; 700m ascent) involves a steady ascent to the lodge where you're served refreshments by a roaring fire, followed by dinner. The hills above the lodge are explored on the second day (optional), before wandering back to the valley on the final day (two-day option $1195; three-day option $1595). Oct–March.
Kaikoura Coast Track T 03 319 2715, W kaikoura track.co.nz. The mixture of wild beach scenery, farmland and regenerating bush makes for a pleasant and

very manageable walk, but the real pleasure in this self-guided, private walk (37km; 3 days; 600m ascent; $215) is in experiencing country life and chatting to the farming families at the two overnight stops. This walk starts and ends 50km south of Kaikoura at the backpacker-style *Staging Post*, 75 Hawkeswood Rd, Hawkeswood (Atomic buses stop within 1km), then climbs the Hawkeswood Range with spectacular views of the Seaward Kaikoura mountains. Walker numbers are limited, so book in advance. The fee covers track maintenance, bag transport (so you only need carry a daypack), and three nights' accommodation in warm cottages with bunk beds, fully equipped kitchens and showers as well as fresh farm produce, milk, bread and home-cooked meals by arrangement. *Staging Post*: dinner $55; camping $26, powered sites for two $38, cabins/couple $60, B&B rooms/couple $95

8

KAIKOURA TOURS AND ACTIVITIES

Just 1km off the Kaikoura Peninsula the coastal shallows plummet into the 1000m-deep Kaikoura Canyon, a network of undersea troughs that funnel warm subtropical waters and cold sub-Antarctic flows into a nutrient-rich upwelling. This provides an unusually fecund habitat supporting an enormous variety of marine life, including fourteen species of whale. Marine mammals come for an easy meal, and tourists come to watch. You can expect to see gigantic sperm **whales** (year-round), **dolphins** (year-round), migratory humpback whales (June–July) and **orca** (Dec–Feb). Book well in advance, though rough seas often lead to **cancellations** so allow yourself a couple of days' flexibility.

WHALE WATCHING

Whale Watch Kaikoura The Whaleway Station, Whaleway Rd ☎ 0800 655 121, ⓦ whalewatch.co.nz. Kaikoura's flagship activity is conducted by this Maori-owned and operated company. You meet at the office at the train station and are bussed around to South Bay where a speedy catamaran whisks you a few kilometres offshore (2hr 30min; $145). There are typically one or two whale sightings along with dolphins and seabirds; if you see no whales there's an eighty percent refund. The office sells pills and bands to alleviate sea sickness – a wise investment, particularly for afternoon trips.

Wings Over Whales ☎ 0800 226 629, ⓦ whales .co.nz. An alternative to on-the-water viewing is aerial whale watching. This outfit offers 30min flights ($165). There's a shuttle service ($5/person each way) between the town and the airport. Bring binoculars.
Kaikoura Helicopters ☎ 03 319 6609, ⓦ worldof whales.co.nz. Offers a 30min flight (2 people $325 each), a 40min flight (2 people; $395 each) and a 50min coastal flight (2 people; $435). Bring binoculars.

SWIMMING WITH DOLPHINS AND SEALS

Dolphin Encounter 96 The Esplanade ☎ 0800 733 365, ⓦ dolphin.co.nz. Runs highly professional trips (5.30am, 8.30am & 12.30pm; swimming $165; watching $80), which you'll get the most out of if you're a reasonably confident swimmer; the more you duck-dive the more eager the dolphins will be to investigate. They seem to find it attractive listening to you humming through your snorkel – any tune will do. Don't get too carried away though: dolphins have a penchant for swimming in ever decreasing circles until lesser beings are quite dizzy and disorientated. Book three to four weeks in advance for the Dec–Feb peak season (though standbys do become available at short notice).

Seal Swim Kaikoura 58 Westend ☎ 0800 732 579, ⓦ sealswimkaikoura.co.nz. Seal swimming is just as much fun as dolphin swimming (and some might say equally moving), as seals tend to be even more curious than dolphins. This operator offers shore-based trips

Maori Leap Cave

2km south of town on SH1 · 35min tours daily on the half-hour 10.30am–3.30pm · $15 · ☎ 03 319 5023

The sea-formed **Maori Leap Cave** is named after a Maori warrior who jumped to his death from the hills above the cave to escape capture by another tribe. Stalagmites and stalactites sprout from the floor and ceiling of the cave, and translucent stone straws seem to defy gravity by maintaining their internal water level. There are also examples of cave coral and algae that survive in the dank cave by turning darkness into energy.

ARRIVAL AND DEPARTURE

KAIKOURA

By bus InterCity and Atomic buses on the Picton–Blenheim–Christchurch run all drop off on Westend, in the town car park near the visitor centre.
Destinations Christchurch (4–5 daily; 2hr 30min); Picton (4–5 daily; 2hr 15min).

By train The *TranzCoastal* train between Picton and Christchurch arrives at the station on Whaleway Station Rd. Destinations Christchurch (1 daily); Blenheim (1 daily); Picton (1 daily).

GETTING AROUND

By taxi Most places in town are within walking distance, though since the town is increasingly spread out you may find use for a taxi; try Kaikoura Shuttles ☎ 03 319 6166.

By bike R&R Sport, 14 Westend (☎ 03 319 5028), charges $20 for a half-day and $30 for a full day.

($70) and better, more flexible trips by boat (2–2hr 30min total; $110). There's a fair bit of swimming involved so it helps if you've snorkelled before. Oct–May only.

BIRDWATCHING, SEA KAYAKING AND SCUBA DIVING

Albatross Encounter 96 The Esplanade ☎ 0800 733 365, ⓦ albatrossencounter.co.nz. Travel a kilometre or two offshore in a small boat and for the chance to see some endangered seabirds (2–3 trips daily; 2–3hr; $110). Bait is laid to attract all manner of species – shags, mollymawks, gannets, petrels and a couple of varieties of albatross come amazingly close.

Kaikoura Kayaks ☎ 0800 452 456, ⓦ kaikourakayaks .co.nz. Operates year-round and often runs trips when others don't. You'll learn most (and probably see more

wildlife) on the half-day Seal Kayaking guided trips ($95), though suitably skilled paddlers can rent kayaks ($70/half-day; $85/full day). In summer, try guided sit-on-top kayak fishing trips ($120/ half-day).

Dive Kaikoura 13 Yarmouth St ☎ 0800 348 352, ⓦ divekaikoura.co.nz. Get a close look at temperate kelp forests, nudibranchs and sponges, plus the odd crayfish and seal on scuba-diving tours, including two-tank trips for certified divers ($250) and introductory dives for novices.

MAORI CULTURE AND STARGAZING

Maori Tours Kaikoura ☎ 0800 866 267, ⓦ maori tours.co.nz. Offers emotionally engaging half-day tours ($125), guided by an ex-whale-watch boat driver and his family, that give a real taste of *Maoritanga* and the genuine hospitality it demands. Tours take in various local sights, storytelling, explanations of Maori ways and medicines, cultural differences, and involve learning a song, that you then surprise yourself by singing.

Kaikoura Night Sky ☎ 03 319 6635, ⓦ kaikoura nightsky.co.nz. Once the sun goes down, crystal-clear nights offer a great chance to experience the night sky with small groups clustered around a mobile 20cm telescope in the fields away from the bright lights of Kaikoura. The planets, moon craters and distant galaxies come alive with tales of celestial navigation and what the southern sky means to Maori. (Nov–April; 1hr–1hr 30min; $50).

FLIGHTS AND SKYDIVING

Pilot a Plane Kaikoura Airfield, SH1 ☎ 03 319 6579, ⓦ airkaikoura.co.nz. Aspiring fliers get to take off and then take the controls for 20min ($120). It's a great adrenaline buzz and comes with even better scenery. The company also runs various charter-plane whale-

watching options.

Skydive Kaikoura Kaikoura Airfield, SH1 ☎ 0800 843 759, ⓦ skydivekaikoura.co.nz. Offers personal tandem skydiving trips (13,000ft; $380), a world away from the conveyor-belt skydiving in Taupo.

8

INFORMATION

i-SITE On Westend (daily 9am–5pm; ☎ 03 319 5641, ⓦ kaikoura.co.nz). Apart from regular i-SITE duties, the office also handles most DOC enquiries and stores luggage

for $2.

Services There's internet access at Global Gossip, 19 Westend ($4/hr), with plenty of machines and wi-fi.

ACCOMMODATION

There's a fair range of accommodation, most of it strung out along SH1 (Beach Road) immediately north of the centre, along the Esplanade or on the peninsula east of town.

★ **Albatross Backpacker Inn** 1 Torquay St ☎ 0800 222 247, ⓦ albatross-kaikoura.co.nz. A cool, spacious converted post office and telephone exchange with unusual Turkish-style decor in some rooms. Well-tended grounds make it especially good on fine days and they love their music. Dorms $29, rooms $69

Alpine-Pacific Holiday Park 69 Beach Rd ☎ 0800 692 322, ⓦ alpine-pacific.co.nz. This central, shaded park maintains high standards, offers a range of accommodation and has an outdoor pool and spa. Camping $20, cabins $70, en-suite cabins $115, motel units $130

Anchor Inn Motel 208 The Esplanade ☎ 0800 720 033, ⓦ anchorinn.co.nz. Luxurious motel with tastefully decorated, self-contained units that come with every convenience (some with spa bath) plus wi-fi. Standard $185, sea view $210

★ **Bay Cottages** 29 South Parade, South Bay ☎ 03 319 5506, ⓦ baycottages.co.nz. Purpose-built self-contained motel-style units in a quiet spot 2km from the town centre on the south side of the peninsula. The owner is exceptionally friendly and takes guests out crayfishing and for a buzz round the bays (free) for breakfast. Free laundry. Basic $\overline{\$100}$, standard $\overline{\$130}$

Bayview Homestay 296 Scarborough St ☏ 03 319 5480, ⓦ bayviewhomestay.wordpress.com. Margaret Woodill, who has lived in this house for almost all of her seventy-odd years, and her daughter really make this traditional B&B homestay a complete delight. Garden and swimming pool are for guests' use and rooms are simple with external access and either an en suite or a private bathroom. It's all that was great about staying with your granny. $\overline{\$130}$

Bendamere House 37 Adelphi Terrace ☏ 0800 107 770, ⓦ bendamere.co.nz. Five high-standard rooms, all with kitchenettes, in the grounds of a large villa on the hill. There are great sea views and hearty breakfasts, and it's all within walking distance of the town. $\overline{\$200}$

Dolphin Lodge 15 Deal St ☏ 03 319 5842, ⓦ dolphin lodge.co.nz. Small hostel with a garden (complete with spa and hammock) overlooking the sea that offers dorms (with few bunks) and cosy doubles, plus bikes ($10/day). Dorms $\overline{\$25}$, rooms $\overline{\$60}$

Dusky Lodge 67 Beach Rd ☏ 03 319 5959, ⓦ dusky lodge.com. Well-organized hostel sleeping 120-plus with sauna, spa, swimming pool and a restaurant along with log fires and a big terrace. One level is devoted to deluxe en suites with flat-screen TVs and their own upscale lounge and kitchen. Popular with the Magic Bus patrons. Dorms $\overline{\$26}$, rooms $\overline{\$56}$, en suites $\overline{\$70}$, deluxe en suites $\overline{\$80}$

Kaikoura Coastal Camping SH1, 15km south of town ☏ 03 319 5348, ⓔ goosebay@ihug.co.nz. A string of appealing, family-oriented campsites, three of which are beachside. The northernmost, Paia Point, has no power, while the others have powered sites and showers. Paia Point $\overline{\$10}$, other sites $\overline{\$13}$

Kaikoura Peketa Beach Holiday Park 665 SH1, 8km south of Kaikoura ☏ 03 319 6299, ⓦ kaikoura peketabeach.co.nz. Peaceful beachside campsite that's popular with surfers who make use of the excellent waves on the doorstep. The surroundings are quiet (apart from the crashing of waves), there's lots of birdlife, and

accommodation is in comfortable cabins, or you can camp. Camping $\overline{\$16}$, cabins $\overline{\$62}$

The Lazy Shag 37 Beach Rd ☏ 03 319 6662, ⓔ lazy -shag@hotmail.com. Purpose-built hostel where guests' comfort is the priority. Rooms are warm and quiet, common rooms are spacious and well equipped, and all dorms, twins and doubles are en suite. Dorms $\overline{\$25}$, rooms $\overline{\$66}$

Miharotia 274 Scarborough St ☏ 03 319 7497, ⓦ miharotia.co.nz. Classy B&B in a plush home with three rooms, all beautifully appointed, with deck access to the outside hot tub. Sea and mountain views are great and the hosts (one a former paua diver) serve an excellent full breakfast. From $\overline{\$410}$

Nikau Lodge 53 Deal St ☏ 03 319 6973, ⓦ nikaulodge .com. Five of the seven en-suite rooms in this lovely, wooden, 1925 house have mountain or sea views, plus there's free wi-fi, an outdoor spa pool and good breakfasts. $\overline{\$190}$

★ **Panorama Motel** 266 The Esplanade ☏ 0800 288 299, ⓦ panoramamotel.co.nz. There are superb views from the stripped-pine units with a chalet feel; you'll pay $10 extra for better views from the upper floor, and the whole shebang is run by a helpful owner. $\overline{\$150}$

Sunrise Lodge 74 Beach Rd ☏ 03 319 7444, ⓔ sunrise hostel@xtra.co.nz. Small hostel, just a 2min walk from Whale Watch, offering a maximum of three to a room (no bunks), plus free orientation bus trips at sunset (on request) and free bikes. The separate self-contained flat sleeping four is good for families. Dorms $\overline{\$28}$, rooms and en suite $\overline{\$89}$

Waves on the Esplanade 78 The Esplanade ☏ 0800 319 589, ⓦ kaikouraapartments.co.nz. Luxurious two-bedroom, motel-style apartments with balconies, sea views, full kitchen, laundry and access to a spa pool. $\overline{\$270}$

★ **YHA Maui** 270 The Esplanade ☏ 03 319 5931, ⓔ yha.kaikoura@yha.co.nz. Comfortable and good-value hostel with the best sea and mountain views in town – from the kitchen/diner and lounge – plus well-informed, knowledgeable staff. Dorms $\overline{\$32}$, rooms $\overline{\$90}$, en suite $\overline{\$110}$

EATING AND DRINKING

Kaikoura is small but the steady flow of tourists helps keep a decent selection of cafés and restaurants alive. Prices are a little on the high side, especially if you're keen to sample the local crayfish, though if that's your aim, you might want to buy them ready-boiled from one of the kai caravans north of town (see p.499).

The Beach House 39 Beach Rd. Kaikoura's cool set hangs out here, despite the dreadful service, imbibing coffee over extended breakfasts ($10–18), or lunches, which include seafood chowder and panini from the cabinet. *The Beach Hut*, a small outlet on the Esplanade opposite the car park, is owned by the same people and, surprisingly, is better value and more lively. Beach House daily 8.30am–3pm.

Black Rabbit Pizza Co 17 Beach Rd ☏ 03 319 6360. Quality pizzas, pasta dishes, and desserts to take away,

though there are three tables. Try a spicy Red Hot Rascal ($13). Daily 5pm–late.

Coffee Cart 72 Beach Rd. Serves some of the best coffee in town plus muffins and free wi-fi. Mon–Sat 9am–4pm.

Green Dolphin 12 Avoca St ☏ 03 319 6666, ⓦ green dolphinkaikoura.com. Large windows and sea views, professional service and tasty food from a short but well-chosen contemporary menu that usually includes a half-crayfish ($60 plus), along with mains half that price and a fab fish stew. Daily 5pm–late.

Hine's Takeaways 18 Westend. Top fish, chip and crayfish dinners – perfect for sunset on the waterfront or picnics. Daily noon–8.30pm.

★ **Hislop's Café** 33 Beach Rd ☎03 319 6971, ⚟hislops -wholefoods.co.nz. The pick of the cafés in Kaikoura, a lovely wooden-floored villa that's a must for coffee and cakes, inside or out, as well as organic meals (some vegetarian or gluten-free), tasty seafood and toothsome daily fresh-baked bread. Wine by the glass, including vegan and many organic varieties. Open for breakfast, lunch (salads and sandwiches) and dinner. Daily 9am–9pm.

Kaikoura Seafood BBQ Armers Beach ☎0327 376 3619. A few tables scattered roadside and a takeaway cart make a great setting for simple seafood, all served with salad and rice. Daily 11am–dusk.

★ **Ocean Link** Corner of Margate St and the Esplanade, overlooking the beach. The best of the seafood kai karts in Kaikoura, offering fresh-caught local fish, fish burgers, scallops, whitebait and cray, as well as salmon, all at great-value prices, plus some delicious seafood chowder. Lip-smacking for picnics – just bring a bottle and go find a quiet corner of the beach. Late Sept–March daily 11am–dusk.

Strawberry Tree 21 Westend ☎03 319 6451. Convivial Irish-styled bar that's usually busy with a mix of locals and travellers. There's a seafood-heavy menu. Daily 11am–11pm.

Whaler Bar and Restaurant 49–51 West End ☎03 319 3333. Bar serving cheap, generous grub, a range of ales and providing live music during the summer. Daily 11am–11pm.

South from Kaikoura

South of Kaikoura, it's a two- to three-hour run down SH1 to Christchurch with relatively minor points of interest along the way. The road initially follows a 20km stretch of delightful rocky coastline then ducks inland through farming country for most of the rest of the way. Hikers should consider putting three days aside for the Kaikoura Coast Walk (see box, p.501), while wine drinkers will want to stop at the hamlet of **Waipara**, 130km south of Kaikoura, where paddocks full of vines announce one of New Zealand's fastest-growing viticultural regions. Thanks to its long warm days, combination of alluvial gravels and limestone clays, and protection from cooling sea winds, the area produces quality wines, particularly Pinot Noirs and Riesling. As a wine destination it is very much in its infancy: a dozen places offer tastings and several have restaurants, but there isn't much else.

8

EATING AND DRINKING   **SOUTH FROM KAIKOURA**

The vineyards are all within 5km of Waipara at the junction of SH1 and SH7 to Hanmer Springs and the Lewis Pass.

Pegasus Bay 4km south of the junction, then 3km east ☎03 314 6869, ⚟pegasusbay.com. There's an upscale tenor here, where contemporary artworks surround diners in what is one of the finest winery restaurants in the country. Nip in to taste some of the delicious wines or stay for lunch when each course is matched with an appropriate wine. Winery 10.30am–5pm; restaurant daily noon–4pm.

Waipara Springs 4km north of Waipara ☎03 314 6777, ⚟waiparasprings.co.nz. The vineyard here was first planted in 1982. The family-oriented garden restaurant (mains $20–35; platter for three $50) always has wholesome fresh-baked bread to go with the daily specials. Tastings $4. Daily 11am–5pm.

SKI MOUNT LYFORD

In winter, consider following the scenic SH70 inland from Kaikoura and skiing **Mount Lyford** (mid-June to mid-Oct; ⚟mtlyford.co.nz), which offers some of the best skiing in the upper South Island. It's a small field and has limited lift facilities ($70/day), but caters for a broad range of abilities (3 beginner runs, 11 intermediate, 6 advanced) and is rarely crowded.

Mount Lyford Lodge 10 Mount Lyford Forest Drive ☎03 315 6446, ⚟mtlyfordlodge.co.nz. The best option if you're going to ski at Mount Lyford, with space for campervans, plus dorms and rooms. There's also a welcoming restaurant and bar. Campervans $35, dorms $30, rooms $90

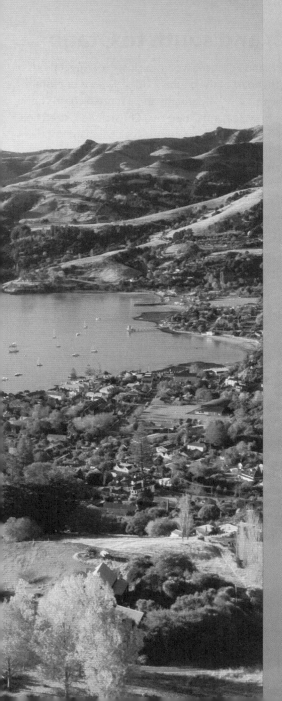

Christchurch and south to Otago

508 Christchurch

525 North of Christchurch

525 Banks Peninsula

535 South to Otago

AKAROA HARBOUR, BANKS PENINSULA

9

Christchurch and south to Otago

In many ways, the South Island's east coast comes closer to expectations of New Zealand than any other part of the country. Huge sweeps of pastoral land come wedged between snowy mountains and a rugged coast. The main hub of the region is New Zealand's third city, Christchurch, stretched out between the Pacific Ocean and the agriculturally rich flatlands of the Canterbury Plains. Tragically, this stately city was severely damaged by a series of devastating earthquakes in 2010 and 2011, and recovery will take years (see box, p.511). The beach suburb of Sumner, within easy reach of the city, was also badly damaged, as was the port town of Lyttelton, just over the bald Port Hills. However, locals' resilience and initiative have seen some creative innovations in the area while repairing and rebuilding takes place.

South of Christchurch, the coastline of the **Banks Peninsula** is indented with numerous bays and harbours. The peninsula's largest settlement is the quaint "French village" of **Akaroa**. Unaffected by the quakes, it makes an ideal base for exploring this picturesque region.

Continuing south from the Banks Peninsula, the main road (SH1) forges across the Canterbury Plains, a patchwork of fertile fields and vineyards bordered by long shingle beaches littered with driftwood. Further south the countryside again changes character, with undulating coastal hills and crumbling cliffs announcing the altogether more rugged terrain of North Otago. Historic settlements dotted along the coast attest to the wealth that farming brought to the region. The first significant town is the workaday port of **Timaru**, close to a series of Maori rock paintings, evidence of a far longer history than the imposed European feel would have you believe. Further south, **Oamaru** is much more beguiling, with wonderfully accessible penguin colonies and an impressive core of nineteenth-century mercantile buildings in the process of being restored. Beyond, routes lead on towards Dunedin and the south, passing the unearthly Moeraki Boulders – huge, perfectly spherical rocks formed by a combination of subterranean pressure and erosion.

Christchurch

Despite a population decline following the devastating 2010 and 2011 earthquakes (see box, p.511), **CHRISTCHURCH** is the largest city on the South Island, with around 350,000 people, and capital of the Canterbury region. Founded as an outpost of Anglicanism by its first settlers, the city was named after an Oxford college. To some extent it pursues an archetype – the boys at Christ's College still wear striped blazers, and punts glide along the winding River Avon – but in recent years the city's traditional conservatism developed a youthful and more multicultural edge, balanced by laidback beach life at the Pacific Ocean suburb of **Sumner**.

Christchurch earthquakes p.511
Tours and activities in and around Christchurch p.515
The TranzAlpine p.517
The Banks Peninsula Track p.528

Akaroa tours and activities pp.532–533
Maori rock art p.537
Oamaru whitestone p.539
Blue penguins p.544

PUNTING ON THE AVON, CHRISTCHURCH

Highlights

❶ Hagley Park Christchurch's Hagley Park is the city's communal backyard, and incorporates New Zealand's "Garden City's" magnificent botanic gardens. **See p.514**

❷ Ballooning The Canterbury Plains are one of the best ballooning spots in the world, with spectacular views to the Southern Alps and up and down South Island. **See p.515**

❸ Akaroa Stay in a romantic B&B in this French-influenced village on the Banks Peninsula, dine at its excellent restaurants and swim with Hector's dolphins. **See p.529**

❹ Timaru Learn about local Maori rock art at the new Te Ana Rock Art Centre, or take a fascinating guided tour to see it in its original setting. **See p.536**

❺ Oamaru The fine core of Neoclassical buildings in the slowly gentrifying Historic District makes this a perfect base for spotting both blue and yellow-eyed penguins. **See p.539**

❻ Moeraki Boulders Watch the surf crash about these extraordinary 2m spherical boulders artfully littering the tide line. **See p.546**

HIGHLIGHTS ARE MARKED ON THE MAP ON P.510

9

Until the quakes, Cathedral Square was the heart of the city, and a new green space is planned here once the future of the ruined early 1900s cathedral is clear. Historic building to have survived the quakes include the Italianate 1879 **Old Post Office** and the adjacent 1901 Palladian-style former **Government Building**. Other surviving buildings include the neat rows of pastel-painted 1930s Spanish Mission-style buildings along **New Regent Street** and, along Victoria Street, the Victorian **clock tower**, which houses a clock originally imported from England in 1860 to adorn the government buildings.

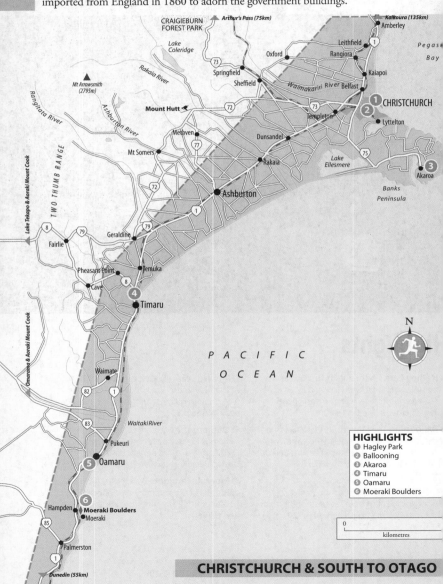

HIGHLIGHTS
1. Hagley Park
2. Ballooning
3. Akaroa
4. Timaru
5. Oamaru
6. Moeraki Boulders

0
kilometres

CHRISTCHURCH & SOUTH TO OTAGO

CHRISTCHURCH EARTHQUAKES

The 7.1 magnitude earthquake that hit Christchurch on September 4, 2010 marked the start of a series of tectonic events – including some 2500 aftershocks within a year – that would have a dramatic, deadly effect on the city, changing it irrevocably. The aftershock of February 22, 2011 killed 185 people and badly damaged or destroyed many buildings in the city centre, while one more person died in the June 14, 2011 aftershock. Still reeling from the devastation, the city was struck again on December 23, 2011, this time by 5.8 and 6 magnitude quakes.

At the time of writing, parts of the city centre within the Four Avenues – Moorhouse, Fitzgerald, Bealey and Deans – were still cordoned off. Some will remain inaccessible to the general public until structural safety has been ascertained and it's known which buildings require demolition, and the timeframe during which this will happen. Christchurch's iconic neo-Gothic buildings fared particularly badly, including its landmark cathedral, the geographic and, for many, spiritual heart of the city. In early 2012 it was announced that the cathedral could not be saved and would be demolished. Authorities are considering installing a temporary "cardboard cathedral" – check ⓦ christchurchcathedral.co.nz for updates. The Port Hills were also roadblocked at the time of writing, and parts of the beachside suburb of Sumner were stacked with shipping containers to protect against further land slippage. For residents, it remains an uncertain time as they await news of insurance and authorities' plans for rebuilding the city, while contending with ongoing seismic activity.

But there is good news: as plans for rebuilding unfold, some businesses remain or have since reopened, and others have relocated or are intending to do so, either temporarily or permanently, to unaffected suburbs. These suburbs have experienced a renaissance as people who once frequented the city centre are seeking out eating, drinking and entertainment venues further afield. And spirited locals are creating pop-up bars, shops, restaurants and cafés (many housed in shipping containers) as well as new long-term establishments, while working to repair and reopen businesses where possible. See p.523 for websites listing gap fillers and permanent venues. Key areas affecting visitors are as follows:

ESSENTIALS

Information Watch out for websites and brochures that haven't been updated since the quakes. Contact companies directly, or check with the i-SITE (p.521), which can provide updates on what's open during your stay and which roads are or are not safe to travel on. Information is also available from the Canterbury Earthquake Recovery Authority (CERA; ⓦ cera.govt.nz).

Accommodation Due to the number of lodgings damaged in the city centre – along with the number of visiting surveyor and construction workers, and residents staying in tourist accommodation while their homes are undergoing repairs – accommodation in the city and its surrounds is tight. Book as far ahead as possible.

Eating A major reduction of places to eat means advance reservations are recommended, even for simple cafés.

Transport Christchurch's airport was unaffected by the quakes. For details of long-distance buses and local transport, see p.520.

Even while rebuilding takes place, Christchurch still works as a base for exploring further afield, with a plethora of companies offering **activities** such as rafting, ballooning and high country tours in the surrounding countryside (see box, p.515), and is also within a two-hour drive of several good **ski-fields** to the west.

Brief history

Maori occupied scattered settlements around the region before the first Europeans arrived, establishing Lyttelton as a whaling port in the 1830s. By 1843, the Scottish Deans brothers (see p.516) were farming inland, but the real foundations of Christchurch were laid by the **Canterbury Association**, formed in 1849 by members of Oxford's Christ Church College, and with the Archbishop of Canterbury at its head. The association had the utopian aim of creating a middle-class, Anglican community in which the moralizing culture of Victorian England could prosper.

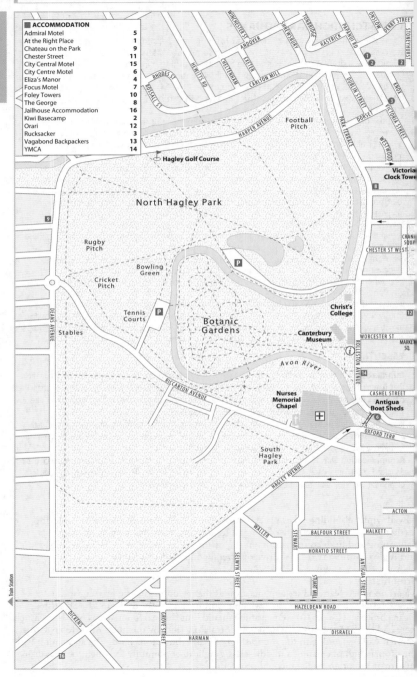

ACCOMMODATION	
Admiral Motel	5
At the Right Place	1
Chateau on the Park	9
Chester Street	11
City Central Motel	15
City Centre Motel	6
Eliza's Manor	4
Focus Motel	7
Foley Towers	10
The George	8
Jailhouse Accommodation	16
Kiwi Basecamp	2
Orari	12
Rucksacker	3
Vagabond Backpackers	13
YMCA	14

CENTRAL CHRISTCHRUCH

SPRINGFIELD RD
DURHAM ST NORTH
CALEDONIAN RD
SHERBORNE STREET
BISHOP ST RD
PACK EST
GERALDINE ST
CHAMPION ST

After Hours Surgery

BEALEY AVENUE

DOLLANS
OTLEY STREET
AMURI PK
CHURCHILL

PEACOCK STREET
MELROSE STREET
EVERIDGE STREET
MOA PL
COLOMBO STREET

CONFERENCE
GRACEFIELD
ABERDEEN STREET
ELY STREET
WILLOW

AIREDALE
ULSTER
MADRAS STREET

BANGOR

MANCHESTER STREET
HURLEY

SALISBURY STREET

DURHAM STREET
PETERBOROUGH LA.

PETERBOROUGH STREET

KILMORE STREET

CHESTER ST WEST
CAMBRIDGE TERR
OXFORD TERR
CHESTER STREET

VICTORIA SQUARE

ARMAGH STREET

NEW REGENT

ST

GLOUCESTER STREET

Christchurch Art Gallery
CHANCERY LA
LATIMER
WORCESTER STREET
BARBADOES STREET

THE STRIP
OXFORD TERR
SQUARE

HEREFORD STREET
LIVERPOOL
WOOLSACK

CAMBRIDGE TERR
HIGH STREET
CASHEL STREET

BEDFORD ROW
CLARKSON
GILMOUR
FITZGERALD AVENUE

MANCHESTER STREET
HIGH ST
LICHFIELD STREET
POPLAR
ASH
DUKE

City Bus Exchange
TUAM STREET

MOLLETT STREET

COLOMBO STREET
ST ASAPH STREET

DURHAM S STREET
WELLES STREET
QUILL
ALFRED

WALKER STREET
WINCHCOMBE
SOUTHWARK
WILLIAMS

WILMER STREET
AVCESTER
ATLAS
ALLEN STREET
COVENTRY
FERRY RD

BATH STREET
DUNDAS STREET
EATON
ROPE

MOORHOUSE AVENUE
MORTIMER

N

CARLYLE

CASS

SANDYFORD
BYRON

0   250
metres

●**EATING, DRINKING & ENTERTAINMENT**

Antigua Boatshed Café	6
Beat Street Café	5
Keo Thai	1
Pomeroy's Old Brewery Inn	4
Sophie's	2
Vic's Café	3

9

It was at Lyttelton that four ships containing nearly eight hundred **settlers** arrived in 1850, bound for the new city of Christchurch. The earliest settlers weren't all Anglicans by any means, and the millenarian aspirations upon which the city was founded soon faded as people got on with the exhausting business of carving out a new life in unfamiliar terrain. Nevertheless, the association's ideals had a profound effect on the cultural identity of the city, and descent from those who came on the "four ships" still carries social cachet among members of the Christchurch elite.

Earthquakes in 2010 and 2011 severely affected the city, destroying many of its renowned buildings, but local and national authorities and residents are committed to planning and rebuilding a new, revitalized city.

Christchurch Art Gallery

Corner of Worcester Blvd and Montreal St • Due to reopen sometime in 2013 • ☎ 03 941 7300, ⓦ christchurchartgallery.org.nz

Behind a striking frontage of curving glass intersecting at odd angles, a grand staircase inside the **Christchurch Art Gallery** leads to the historical, twentieth-century and contemporary collections. New Zealand works are the strongest, particularly those by Christchurch and Canterbury artists. Most of the collections survived the quakes, and the gallery is also purchasing new works.

Canterbury Museum

Rolleston Ave • Daily: Oct–March 9am–5.30pm; April–Sept 9am–5pm • Free • ☎ 03 366 5000, ⓦ canterburymuseum.com

Opposite the earthquake-damaged Arts Centre, an 1870 neo-Gothic structure houses the **Canterbury Museum**, founded by archeologist Julius Haast who supplied the museum with an Egyptian mummy bought for $24 in 1886. Christchurch's association with the Antarctic is explored with a flimsy unreliable motor tractor from Shackleton's 1914–17 expedition, a Ferguson tractor that became the first vehicle to reach the Pole as part of Edmund Hillary's push in 1958, and the far more robust Sno-Cat used by Brit Vivian Fuchs on the same expedition. Charmingly retro dioramas of penguins and Weddell seals set the tone for the Maori collection, full of great carvings but also featuring dioramas of bronzed natives going about their daily lives. Look out for **Fred and Myrtle's Paua Shell House**, a shrine to kitsch Kiwiana modelled on a house in Bluff where the famed Fluteys plastered their home with polished paua shells. After their deaths in 2000 and 2001, the contents were shipped here and reassembled.

Next door stands **Christ's College**, the city's most elite private school. Its Victorian architecture was damaged, but the school is still operating.

Hagley Park

Sprawling **Hagley Park** contains the spectacular Botanic Gardens, a golf course and playing fields, and at weekends it seems like the entire population of Christchurch is here, strolling around or playing some form of sport.

Botanic Gardens

Rolleston Ave gate • Daily 7am until 30min after sunset • Free

One corner of Hagley Park is devoted to the **Botanic Gardens**, which help Christchurch live up to its "Garden City" moniker with a collection of indigenous and exotic plants and trees unrivalled on the South Island. From summer to autumn, perennials give a constant and dazzling display of colour, the herb garden, containing a variety of culinary and medicinal plants, exudes aromatic scents, and, from December, the rose garden blooms with over 250 varieties. Above all, though, it's just a great place to hang out on a sunny day.

River Avon

Antigua Boat Sheds 2 Cambridge Terrace • Daily: Oct—March 9.30am—5.30pm; April—Sept 9.30am—4.30pm • Paddleboat $20/30min for two; single canoe $10/hr; double canoe $20/hr; rowboat $30/hr • ☎ 03 366 5885, ⓦ boatsheds.co.nz • **Punting on the Avon** $25/person/30min • ☎ 03 366 0337, ⓦ punting.co.nz

The Botanic Gardens are enclosed by a loop of the River Avon, which you can explore by heading along to the **Antigua Boat Sheds** and renting a paddleboat, canoe, or rowboat. Adjacent **Punting on the Avon** supplies a guide, nattily dressed in a blazer and straw boater, to **punt** you along the river.

Nurses' Memorial Chapel

Riccarton Ave • Mon—Sat 1—4pm • Free • ☎ 03 389 3318, ⓦ cnmc.org.nz

On the southern borders of Hagley Park, Christchurch Hospital almost engulfs the tiny brick-and-slate 1928 **Nurses' Memorial Chapel**, dedicated to nurses who served in

TOURS AND ACTIVITIES IN AND AROUND CHRISTCHURCH

Christchurch makes a good base for exploring the immediate vicinity and beyond. Here are some of the more diverting activities and tours.

BALLOONING

Up Up And Away ☎ 03 381 4600, ⓦ ballooning .co.nz. A romantic and gentle way to get airborne, with peaceful early-morning flights over Christchurch's surrounds and spectacular views from mountains to coast for $360.

Aoraki Balloons ☎ 0800 256 837, ⓦ nzballooning .co.nz. This Methven-based operator offers great "Premier Plains" trips across the patchwork fields of the Canterbury Plains followed by a champagne picnic breakfast in a field for $385.

CYCLING

Christchurch Bike Tours ☎ 0800 733 257, ⓦ chch biketours.co.nz. A city bike tour that takes you through quiet streets around Christchurch. On Saturdays, there's

also a "farmers market" option to the Riccarton Farmers Market (p.516), returning through Mona Vale estate. Two-hour tours $40/person.

HIGH COUNTRY TOUR

Hassle-free Tours ☎ 0800 148 686, ⓦ hasslefree .co.nz. If you want to ride the *TranzAlpine* train (see box, p.517) but don't fancy a whole day on board, try Hassle-free's Alpine Safari (10hr; $395), which includes

jetboating the Waimakariri River, going off-road in a 4WD across a high-country sheep and cattle station and returning by the *TranzAlpine* from Arthur's Pass.

SURFING

aumoana 9 Wakefield Ave, Sumner ☎ 03 326 7444, ⓦ aumoana.co.nz. Rents and sells boards (2hr $20, half-day $40, full day $50) and wetsuits (2hr to half-day $5, free with full-day board hire). Daily 10am—5.30pm.

Aaron "Lockie" Lock ⓦ surfcoach.co.nz. Local surf guru who offers lessons from the beach in Sumner, starting from $70 for 2hr.

TANK DRIVING

Tanks for Everything 980 McLeans Island Rd, near the airport ☎ 03 359 1007, ⓦ tanksforeverything .co.nz. As unlikely as it may seem, you can drive your own tank. You get a 45-minute tour of the vehicles, which include armoured patrol carriers, a Russian Cold

War-era tank and a Centurion tank, followed by 15—25 minutes of instruction and time at the controls. Prices depend on vehicle; driving costs $100—450 (some with a car crush option costing an extra $395), while riding only is $35—350 depending on numbers.

WHITEWATER RAFTING

Rangitata Rafts ☎ 0800 251 251, ⓦ rafts.co.nz. There are no big rivers near Christchurch, but this outfitter (see p.568) runs one of the most satisfying

trips in New Zealand on the Grade IV—V Rangitata River with pick-ups from Christchurch for $218.

9

World War I. It was constructed after the death of three Christchurch-trained nurses aboard a torpedoed troopship in 1915, and contains four stained-glass windows by the English glass artist Veronica Whall, with an uneven texture and a variety of colours set off by the otherwise dark, low-ceilinged interior.

Mona Vale

63 Fendalton Rd • Grounds open daily 8.30am to just before dusk • Free

Inspired by a couple of hours spent in the Botanic Gardens, you might fancy a stroll across North Hagley Park to the beautiful precincts of **Mona Vale**. Originally part of the Deans' estate (see below) and now tended by the Canterbury Horticultural Society, the gardens have majestic displays of roses, dahlias, fuchsias and irises, as well as magnolias, rhododendrons and herbaceous perennials. The old homestead is closed for post-quake repairs until approximately late 2013.

Riccarton Bush

Off Kahu Rd • Daily dawn–dusk • Free • **Deans Cottage** Daily 9am–dusk • Free • **Riccarton House** Closed for repairs at time of writing • ☏ 03 341 1018, ⓦ riccartonhouse.co.nz • **Farmers' market** Sat 9am–noon, plus Nov–April Wed 4–7pm • ⓦ christchurchfarmersmarket .co.nz • Take bus #24 to get to Riccarton Bush

Southwest of the city centre in the suburb of Riccarton, **Riccarton Bush**, a.k.a. **Deans Bush**, is an area of native forest containing several 500-year-old kahikatea trees. The survival of this valuable area of forest is largely due to Scottish brothers William and John Deans, who came here to farm in 1843 and somehow resisted the temptation to put all their property to immediate agricultural use. Today a concrete path navigates the bush, with signs pointing out the various species. The tiny black-pine **Deans Cottage** was built by the Deans brothers on their arrival, and is furnished as it would have been when they lived there. Their descendants built the adjacent, grand Victorian **Riccarton House**, all oak panelling and stag heads. There's a **Farmers' Market** here on Saturday morning year-round and a popular Wednesday-evening Farmers' Market in the warmer months, where you can buy local produce direct from growers, bakers, brewers and more.

International Antarctic Centre

38 Orchard Rd • Daily: Oct–April 9am–7pm; May–Sept 9am–5pm; penguin feedings at 10.30am, 1.30pm & 3.30pm • $55; students and seniors $46 • ☏ 03 357 0519, ⓦ iceberg.co.nz

Beyond Deans Bush, Memorial Avenue runs northwest to the airport and the **International Antarctic Centre**, a well-presented and dynamic exhibit concentrating on New Zealand's involvement in Antarctica. It is pricey, but you could easily spend half a day here. Since the mid-1950s, Christchurch airport has been the base of the US Antarctic programme that sponsors over 140 flights a year to its base at McMurdo Sound, and the neighbouring New Zealand outpost at Scott Base. There's stacks here on Antarctic exploration and the fragile polar ecosystem, with video presentations, digital photos emailed daily from the ice at Scott Base, recordings of current weather conditions and a habitat for little blue **penguins**, which you can see being fed. In the Snow & Ice Experience you can don a down jacket and experience a snowy environment at -5°C. Every half-hour a fairly naff simulated Antarctic storm increases the wind chill to -18°C, though the fury is mostly in the soundtrack. Your entry ticket allows you unlimited turns on the fifteen-minute **Hägglund Ride** (every 20min), on which a five-tonne tracked polar buggy is put through its paces over an obstacle course.

Orana Wildlife Park

McLeans Island Rd, 20km west of the city centre • Daily 10am–5pm; lion encounter daily 2.15pm (book ahead) • $25; lion encounter $30 • 03 359 7109, ⓦ oranawildlifepark.co.nz

Drivers can skirt round the northern perimeter of the airport – follow Russley Road then McLeans Island Road – to **Orana Wildlife Park**, a well-organized, open-range zoological park strong on African savannah animals. Feeding times are staggered throughout the day, with something to see every half-hour. You can even hand-feed a giraffe and join the **lion encounter**, touring the lion enclosure on the caged back of a truck. New Zealand is represented by kiwi, tuatara, an active aviary and a gecko house where the little beasties are perfectly camouflaged in the foliage.

Willowbank Wildlife Reserve

60 Hussey Rd • Daily 9.30am–7pm • $25 • ☎ 03 359 6226, ⓦ willowbank.co.nz • Bus #11, every 30–60min from central Christchurch

Although nowhere near as exciting as Orana Park, the smaller and more intimate **Willowbank Wildlife Reserve** has some good displays of native birds including a kiwi house where they incubate eggs and raise chicks. This is also the site of the Ko Tane Maori Experience (see p.524).

Air Force Museum

45 Harvard Ave, Wigram, 7km west of the city centre • Daily 10am–5pm; 45min tours daily 11am, 1.30pm & 3pm • Free; flight simulators $5/5min; tours $10 • ☎ 03 343 9532, ⓦ airforcemuseum.co.nz

On the former Wigram RNZAF base, the **Air Force Museum** presents two dozen aircraft including a Dakota converted for use on the British queen's state visit in 1953, and a Spitfire among several World War II veterans. Flight simulators will keep the (big) kids happy, particularly the one simulating the World War II Mosquito as it engages in combat in the Norwegian fjords, while enthusiastic volunteer guides conduct assorted tours, including one of the restoration and storage hangars.

THE TRANZALPINE

One of the most popular day-trips from Christchurch is to ride the *TranzAlpine* **train** (4hr 30min each way; book well ahead for discounted prices; full rate $185 one-way, $399 day return, ⓦ tranzscenic.co.nz), a tourist-oriented trip across to Greymouth on the West Coast (an extension to Hokitika is under consideration). It's a gorgeous 231km journey – with numerous viaducts and nineteen tunnels – all seen from the train's large viewing windows and open-sided observation car. Christchurch's industrial suburbs give way to the farmland of the Canterbury Plains before climbing through braided river valleys and open tussock country into the Southern Alps. There's a pause at the beech-forest high point of Arthur's Pass before descending through the 8.5km-long Otira Tunnel that burrows under the 920m pass itself to the West Coast.

The train leaves Christchurch train station at 8.15am every morning and nominally returns by 6.05pm, though years of under-funding mean that delays are fairly common. Levels of comfort and catering are also below par for what is essentially a tourist attraction, though standards are improving.

If you travel in December you will see red and white rata in bloom, but the trip is at its romantic, snow-cloaked best in the winter months (June–Aug). A good strategy for those with a vehicle is to catch the train at Darfield, 45km west of Christchurch, allowing a later start in return for missing Christchurch's industrial suburbs and a few farms. It's also worth considering alighting at Moana for a relaxed three-hour lakeside lunch before boarding for the return journey. It beats a hurried snack in Greymouth.

The trip can also form part of a high-country tour (see box, p.515).

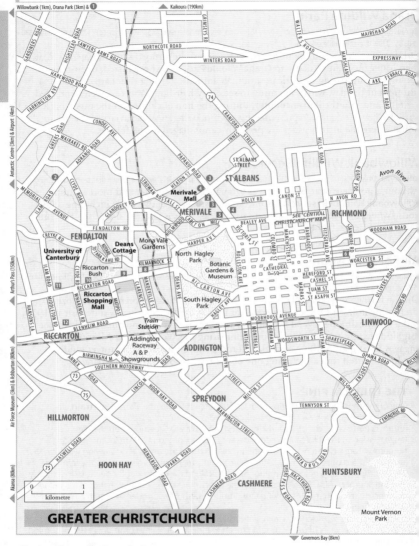

GREATER CHRISTCHURCH

Christchurch Gondola

10 Bridle Path Rd, 15min drive from the city centre • Closed for repairs at the time of writing • ☎ 03 384 0310, ⓦ gondola.co.nz • Served by Lyttelton bus #28 and some tours

The **Christchurch Gondola**, located by the entrance to the Lyttelton tunnel, whisks you to the upper station on the 945m summit of **Mount Cavendish**, where you can admire the 360-degree views of Christchurch, the Canterbury Plains, the volcanic outcrops of the Banks Peninsula and the Southern Alps. The gondola is expected to have reopened by the time you're reading this – check the website or with the i-SITE (see p.521).

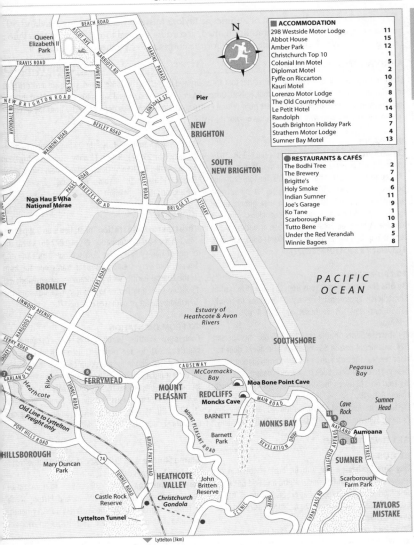

■ ACCOMMODATION	
298 Westside Motor Lodge	11
Abbot House	15
Amber Park	12
Christchurch Top 10	1
Colonial Inn Motel	5
Diplomat Motel	2
Fyffe on Riccarton	10
Kauri Motel	9
Lorenzo Motor Lodge	8
The Old Countryhouse	6
Le Petit Hotel	14
Randolph	3
South Brighton Holiday Park	7
Strathern Motor Lodge	4
Sumner Bay Motel	13

● RESTAURANTS & CAFÉS	
The Bodhi Tree	2
The Brewery	7
Brigitte's	4
Holy Smoke	6
Indian Sumner	11
Joe's Garage	9
Ko Tane	1
Scarborough Fare	10
Tutto Bene	3
Under the Red Verandah	5
Winnie Bagoes	8

Sumner

13km southeast of central Christchurch • Bus #3 from the City Exchange bus station

Estuary beaches become sea beaches at **Sumner**, a Norfolk pine-backed strip of shops, restaurants, cafés, wine bars and surf shacks fronting a broad patch of golden sand. Named after Dr J.B. Sumner, Archbishop of Canterbury and president of the Canterbury Association in the 1850s, the suburb was also affected by the earthquakes, particularly that of February 2011, which knocked the top off the beach's highlight, the striking **Cave Rock** (peppered with little caves like an enormous Swiss cheese), reducing its size by half. However, there are still plenty of people soaking up the sun and sea atmosphere. For information on surfing in Sumner, see box, p.515.

9

The best **surfing** is 2km south of Sumner at **Taylor's Mistake** (reached along Nayland St), a narrow beach and small community named, according to local lore, after a captain who ran aground here after mistaking the bay for the entrance to Lyttelton Harbour.

ARRIVAL AND DEPARTURE   CHRISTCHURCH

Christchurch is the hub of air, road and rail routes for Canterbury and the rest of the South Island. There are direct **flights** to Blenheim, Dunedin, Hokitika, Invercargill, Nelson, Queenstown, Wanaka and several North Island cities. Most intercity journeys are best done by **bus**. All depart from central Christchurch, and some also depart directly from the airport – confirm departure points with the companies or with the i-SITE.

BY PLANE
Christchurch Airport The airport (☏ 03 358 5029, ⓦ christchurchairport.co.nz) is 10km northwest of the city centre and is open 24hr. It has ATMs, foreign-exchange booths and a new i-SITE office open for all arriving international flights. There's also a free-phone board for accommodation and car-rental bookings, plus left luggage at Luggage Solutions (suitcase or backpack $10 for one day, $20 overnight; daily 4.30am–6pm, and until 11.30pm Fri & Sat; ☏ 03 358 8027).

TO/FROM TOWN
By bus The City Flyer bus runs from the airport to central Christchurch approximately every 30 minutes to hourly ($7.50 one-way), as do buses #3, #10 & #29 ($7.50 one-way).
By shuttle Super Shuttle (☏ 0800 748 885; first person $24, additional person $5) operates a frequent door-to-door service. They pick up at most accommodation when heading to the airport; book the evening before.
By taxi Taxis between the airport and central Christchurch charge $40–50.
Destinations Auckland (24 daily; 1hr 20min); Blenheim (3 daily; 50min); Dunedin (8 daily; 1hr); Hokitika (3 daily;

35min); Invercargill (6 daily; 1hr 20min); Napier/Hastings (2 daily; 1hr 25min); Nelson (4 daily; 50min); Palmerston North (4 daily; 1hr 10min); Queenstown (5 daily; 50–60min); Rotorua (4 daily; 1hr 40min); Wanaka (1–2 daily; 1hr); Wellington (16 daily; 45min).

BY TRAIN
Christchurch train station The station is on Troup Drive, Tow Junction (train information ☏ 0800 872 467), near the corner of Hagley Park, over 2km southwest of Cathedral Square. Two very scenic passenger trains operate from it: the Coastal Pacific (with panoramic viewing windows) to Picton (meeting ferries to the North Island), and the TranzAlpine to Greymouth (see box, p.517).

TO/FROM THE STATION
Canterbury Shuttles (☏ 0800 021 682, ⓦ canterbury shuttles.co.nz) do free central Christchurch pick-ups for ticket holders. Phone for a pick-up or check the website for their standard pick-up loop (mostly hostels). Post-train journey drop-offs around the city centre cost $5.
Destinations Arthur's Pass (1 daily; 2hr 15min); Blenheim (1 daily; 4hr 45min); Greymouth (1 daily; 4hr 30min); Kaikoura (1 daily; 3hr); Picton (1 daily; 5hr 20min).

GETTING AROUND

BY BUS
City Bus Exchange The hub for bus services run by several companies unified under Metro and Red Bus (info desk Mon–Fri 7.30am–6pm, Sat & Sun 9.30am–5.30pm; ☏ 03 366 8855, ⓦ metroinfo.org.nz, ⓦ redbus.co.nz) is at 46–50 Lichfield St.
Fares and cards With the exception of the airport City Flyer bus (see above), the fare anywhere in the city's zone one, including Sumner and Lyttelton, is $3.20. If you're here for a few days, save money by buying a Metrocard from the Bus Exchange (min $10). Standard fares drop to $2.30, and once you've paid for two fares on a certain day subsequent journeys are free. Most routes run from 6.30am until around midnight.

BUS COMPANIES
Akaroa French Connection ☏ 0800 800 575, ⓦ akaroa bus.co.nz. To Akaroa daily at 8.45am (and more in summer).

Akaroa Shuttle ☏ 0800 500 929, ⓦ akaroashuttle.co.nz. To Akaroa 2–3 times daily.
Atomic Shuttles ☏ 03 439 0697, ⓦ atomictravel .co.nz. North to Kaikoura, Blenheim and Picton; south to Timaru, Oamaru and Dunedin; west to Greymouth and inland through Geraldine and Twizel to Wanaka and Queenstown.
Hanmer Connection ☏ 0800 242 663, ⓦ atsnz.com. Twice daily to Hanmer Springs.
Hanmer Shuttle ☏ 0800 800 575, ⓦ akaroabus.co.nz. Departs daily at 9.45am to Hanmer Springs.
InterCity/Newmans ☏ 03 365 1113, ⓦ intercitycoach .co.nz. North to Kaikoura, Blenheim, Picton and Nelson; south to Timaru, Oamaru, Dunedin and Invercargill; and inland to Methven, Aoraki Mount Cook, Wanaka and Queenstown.
Knightrider ☏ 0800 317 057, ⓦ knightrider.co.nz. Thrice-weekly evening/night trips to Dunedin.

Methven Travel ☎0800 684 888 or ☎03 302 8106, 🖰methventravel.co.nz. Daily to Methven.

NakedBus 🖰nakedbus.com. Services operated by Atomic; same destinations.

Southern Link ☎0508 458 835, 🖰southernlinkbus .co.nz. Daily services to Dunedin, Queenstown and Picton.

West Coast Shuttle ☎03 768 0028, 🖰westcoastshuttle .co.nz. Once daily to Greymouth.

Destinations Akaroa (2–3 daily; 1hr 30min); Aoraki Mount Cook (1 daily; 5hr 20min); Arthur's Pass (2 daily; 2hr 30min); Blenheim (3–5 daily; 4hr 45min–5hr 30min); Dunedin (5–6 daily; 6hr); Geraldine (4 daily; 2hr); Greymouth (2 daily; 4hr); Hanmer Springs (3 daily; 2hr); Hokitika (1 daily; 4hr 30min); Kaikoura (3–5 daily; 2hr 30min); Lyttelton (every 15–30min; 35min); Methven (3–7 weekly; 1hr 30min); Oamaru (5–6 daily; 4hr); Picton (3–5 daily; 5hr–5hr 30min); Queenstown (5–6 daily; 7–8hr); Tekapo (4–5 daily; 3–4hr); Timaru (5–6 daily; 2hr 30min); Twizel (4–5 daily; 4–5hr); Wanaka (4–5 daily; 7–8hr).

BY CAR AND TAXI

Driving in Christchurch remains straightforward despite the quakes, with road closures well signposted.

Parking Most central spaces are metered Mon–Sat 7am–6pm (otherwise free). There's convenient parking in the centre of Hagley Park (Armagh St entrance); it's free for the first hour and all day at weekends.

There are dozens of car and van rental places in Christchurch, mostly based at the airport. For more on car rental, see Basics, p.33.

Taxis Try Blue Star (☎03 379 9799) or Gold Band (☎03 379 5795).

BY BIKE

Given Christchurch's relatively quiet roads and flat terrain, cycling is an ideal way of exploring some of the more out-of-the-way suburbs. Check with the i-SITE for rental outlets.

INFORMATION

i-SITE Rolleston Ave, next to the Canterbury Museum (daily: Nov to mid-Jan 8.30am–6pm; mid-Jan to March 8.30am–7pm; April–Oct 8.30am–5pm; ☎03 379 9629, 🖰christchurchnz.com). Stocks all manner of useful leaflets, can handle bookings for much of the South Island, has the latest on festivals and has exclusive specials on accommodation and activities. It's also the first port of call for tramping information.

ACCOMMODATION

Convenient **motels** are mostly strung out along Papanui Rd to the northwest of the city centre, and Riccarton Rd to the west of Hagley Park. Most **campsites** are within walking distance of a bus stop. Christchurch's 24hr airport means most places (including hostels) accommodate **late arrivals** and early departures: when making a reservation, double-check your date of arrival has been understood, especially if you're arriving around midnight. Particularly since the earthquakes, accommodation should be booked well ahead.

CENTRAL CHRISTCHURCH

Admiral Motel 168 Bealey Ave ☎03 379 3554, 🖰admiralmotel.co.nz; map pp.512–513. Great-value motel with a BBQ, picnic tables and kids' play area in the flowering gardens, spotless rooms and friendly bilingual French/English owners. Doubles **$100**

At the Right Place 85–87 Bealey Ave ☎03 366 1633, 🖰atrp.co.nz; map pp.512–513. Set back from the street along a 70m driveway, this quiet budget property has backpacker accommodation with modern kitchen facilities and a Sky TV lounge, and light-filled motel rooms. Dorms **$29**, doubles **$75**, studios **$109**

Chateau on the Park 189 Deans Ave ☎0800 808 999, 🖰chateau-park.co.nz; map pp.512–513. A two-hundred-room hotel, memorable for its lovely surroundings on the edge of Hagley Park, with an outdoor pool, restaurants and cocktail bar. Doubles **$190**

Chester Street 148 Chester St East ☎03 377 1897, 🖰chesterst.co.nz; map pp.512–513. With just fourteen beds this is the city's smallest hostel and feels more like a shared house with comfy, colourful doubles and a three-bed dorm. There's limited off-street parking and a pleasant garden; the owner also has a range of campervans for sale. Dorms **$30**, doubles **$66**, self-contained cottage **$130**

City Central Motel Apartments 252 Barbados St ☎0800 309 0540, 🖰citycentral.co.nz; map pp.512–513. Modernized motel with flat-screen-TV-equipped, stylish rooms, free wi-fi and parking. It's on a busy intersection but the windows are double-glazed. Doubles **$135**

City Centre Motel 876 Colombo St ☎0800 240 101, 🖰citycentremotel.co.nz; map pp.512–513. Plush, modern, very quiet motel with contemporary furnishings in autumnal colour schemes, flat-screen TVs and off-street parking – and an electric back massager on request. Doubles **$175**

Eliza's Manor 82 Bealey Ave ☎03 366 8584, 🖰elizas .co.nz; map pp.512–513. Luxury B&B in a grand 1861 house with eight rooms, all period furnished, and with heat pump temperature control. It's worth splurging on the spacious but pricier Heritage rooms. Doubles **$230**

Foley Towers 208 Kilmore St ☎03 366 9720, 🖰bbh .co.nz; map pp.512–513. A Christchurch backpacking original from the mid-1980s; built around a couple of old houses, which manages to maintain an intimate feel thanks to attentive staff, attractive gardens and an abundance of doubles and twins. Dorms $27, doubles $64, en-suite doubles $70

Focus Motel 344 Durham St North ☎03 943 0800, ⌨focusmotel.com; map pp.512–513. Stylish, central motel with modern studios and larger units, some with spa baths and all fitted out with leather sofas, classy bed linen with foliage prints and kitchen facilities. Doubles $140

The George 50 Park Terrace ☎0800 100 220, ⌨thegeorge.com; map pp.512–513. One of the country's finest urban boutique hotels, renovated with considerable panache. There's great art, a cool bar and the chic *Pescatore* restaurant overlooking Hagley Park. Check for internet specials. Doubles $506

★ **Jailhouse Accommodation** 338 Lincoln Rd ☎03 982 7777 & ☎0800 524 546, ⌨jail.co.nz; map pp.512–513. A jail as recently as 1999, this Victorian Gothic prison in the thriving suburb of Addington has been imaginatively turned into an atmospheric hostel with mostly double and twin-bunk rooms plus some bunk-free dorms, all kauri-floored. Whimsical touches include barbed-wire inlaid toilet seats and a couple of cells left as they were. Helpful owners, a free Kiwi and prison-related DVD library, free pool table and good espresso. Bus #7 drops off at the door. Dorms $30, doubles $85

Kiwi Basecamp 69 Bealey Ave ☎0800 505 025, ⌨kiwibasecamp.com; map pp.512–513. One of the cheapest hostels in town but still maintaining a high standard. Set in a two-storey villa, it's a relaxed spot with free bikes, free shuttle service around town (from 8am–8pm, including the train station and airport) and free breakfast. Dorms $25, doubles $70

Orari 42 Gloucester St ☎03 365 6569, ⌨orari.net.nz; map pp.512–513. An informally run and art-adorned B&B in a large 1893 home. Ten bright, sunny rooms all have artworks and either en suites or private bathrooms (one with a tub). Rates include wine on arrival and a full breakfast. Doubles $165

Rucksacker 70 Bealey Ave ☎03 377 7931, ⌨rucksacker.com; map pp.512–513. In a century-old traditional timber house, this cheerful hostel has a sociable garden and BBQ area, cheap bike rental and limited off-street parking, as well as the option of female-only dorms for no extra cost. Dorms $23, doubles $58

Vagabond Backpackers 232 Worcester St ☎03 379 9677, ⌨bbh.co.nz; map pp.512–513. Very friendly place with only thirty beds, some in an annexe at the back of the house; all are well kept, quiet and clean. There's off-street parking, a BBQ and a lovely garden area. There are also two doubles in a self-contained apartment. Dorms $26, doubles $60, apartment doubles $89

YMCA 12 Hereford St ☎0508 962 224, ⌨ymcachch.org.nz; map pp.512–513. State-of-the-art YMCA with spartan dorms, singles, basic doubles and deluxe en-suite doubles with phone, tea and coffee; and TV. Guests get significant discounts at the fitness centre, gym, squash courts, climbing wall and sauna, and there's an on-site café. Dorms $30, doubles $80, en-suite doubles $110

GREATER CHRISTCHURCH

298 Westside Motor Lodge 298 Riccarton Rd ☎0800 200 371, westsidemotorlodge.co.nz; map pp.518–519. Free airport transfers are part of the deal at this contemporary, well-equipped motor lodge, which offers a variety of room sizes and units for travellers with limited mobility. Doubles $115

Colonial Inn Motel 43 Papanui Rd ☎0800 111 232, ⌨colonialinnmotel.co.nz; map pp.518–519. Modern, streamlined motel with clean, comfortable units, including some huge two- and three-bedroom units, and undercover parking. Upper-level units open onto a communal balcony. Doubles $120

Diplomat Motel 127 Papanui Rd ☎0800 109 699, ⌨diplomatmotel.co.nz; map pp.518–519. Situated in the heart of Merivale, this smart motel has large self-contained units with separate kitchens, a large outdoor swimming pool and spa and free wi-fi. Doubles $125

Fyffe on Riccarton 208 Riccarton Rd ☎0800 341 3274, ⌨fyffeonriccarton.co.nz; map pp.518–519. All rooms at this stylish motorlodge have super-king-size beds, double-glazed windows, DVD players and coffee plungers; higher-priced executive studios also have spas. Doubles $135

Kauri Motel Corner of Kauri St and Riccarton Rd ☎03 341 5865, ⌨kaurimotel.com; map pp.518–519. Across the road from Riccarton Shopping Mall, this unadorned but bright and clean motel has neutral-toned rooms and free bikes for guest use. Doubles $120

Lorenzo Motor Lodge 36 Riccarton Rd ☎0800 456 736, ⌨lorenzomotorlodge.co.nz; map pp.518–519. Quality linens, passes to the gym across the road and free wi-fi are among the highlights of this smart motel, which has good-sized studio units plus suites with double spas. Doubles $145

The Old Countryhouse 437 Gloucester St ☎03 381 5504, ⌨oldcountryhousenz.com; map pp.518–519. One of Christchurch's most peaceful backpacker hostels, fashioned from a couple of wood-floored villas with bold decor and spacious dorms. Take bus #21. Dorms $30, doubles $90, en-suite doubles $110

Randolph 79 Papanui Rd ☎0800 537 366, ⌨randolphmotel.co.nz; map pp.518–519. Excellent modern motel in grounds overshadowed by a huge copper beech tree. Rooms are extremely well equipped with cooking facilities, TV/DVD, stereo and in-room laundry. Deluxe rooms come with double spa baths and there's even a small gym. Doubles $150

Strathern Motor Lodge 54 Papanui Rd ☎0800 766 624, ⌨strathern.co.nz; map pp.518–519. Spacious and well-presented modern units with kitchenette or full kitchen and free wi-fi. The "honeymoon" unit has its own spa bath. Doubles $140

SUMNER

The beachside suburb of Sumner has a selection of appealing places to stay, all accessible on fast and frequent city buses.

Abbott House 104 Nayland St ⊕0800 020 654, ⊚abbotthouse.co.nz; map pp.518–519. Attractively restored 1870s villa set a block back from the beach with accommodation in either a studio with kitchenette, or in a suite with large lounge, kitchen and laundry. Both have TV/DVD, private entrances and continental breakfast ingredients are supplied. Doubles $120

★ **Le Petit Hotel** 16 Marriner St ⊕03 326 6675, ⊚lepetithotel.co.nz; map pp.518–519. Boutique B&B with French-themed decor and breakfast (served alfresco in fine weather), airy rooms with balconies or terraces, and hi-tech facilities including plasma satellite TVs and free wi-fi. Doubles $145

Sumner Bay Motel 26 Marriner St ⊕0800 496 949, ⊚sumnermotel.co.nz; map pp.518–519. Stylish motel a block from the beach, with a range of studios and apartments all with a balcony or courtyard, Sky TV and DVD player. Doubles $159

CAMPSITES

Christchurch's campsites are well set up for tents and campervans, and offer good deals on cabins.

Amber Park 308 Blenheim Rd, Upper Riccarton ⊕03 348 3327, ⊚amberpark.co.nz; map pp.518–519. Spacious, grassy site with all the expected features just 4km south of the city (bus #5 stops right outside), and handy for the train station. Camping $40, en-suite cabins $72, motels $116

Christchurch Top 10 39 Meadow St, Papanui ⊕0800 396 323, ⊚meadowpark.co.nz; map pp.518–519. Situated 5km north of central Christchurch on SH74 (reached by buses #11, #12 & #13), this large campsite, close to supermarkets and restaurants, has a full range of facilities including a heated indoor pool. Camping $38, cabins $83, self-contained chalets $98, motels $99

South Brighton Holiday Park 59 Halsey St, South New Brighton ⊕03 388 9844, ⊚southbrightonmotor camp.co.nz; map pp.518–519. Handily sited near the beach 7km east of central Christchurch, this medium-sized site has good facilities including free wi-fi and a limited range of cabins and flats. Camping $30, cabins $48, self-contained cabins $80

EATING, DRINKING AND ENTERTAINMENT

Most restaurants offer BYO with corkage charges ranging from around $3 to $7 – confirm when you book. The website ⊚dineout.co.nz updates the opening status of Christchurch's eateries. The Go Guide in Friday's *The Press* newspaper covers entertainment **listings including live music** for the whole week. For a general idea of who's playing, spinning or mixing, check out the fortnightly *JAGG* club guide (⊚jagg.co.nz), available free in bars. Good websites tracking post-quake openings and events include ⊚neatplaces.co.nz, ⊚gapfiller.co.nz and ⊚manuka.co.nz. There is also a varied programme of music events in Hagley Park throughout the summer; check ⊚summertimes.org.nz.

CENTRAL CHRISTCHURCH

The shipping container-fashioned Re:START mall (see p.524) has an open-air food court with sushi, ice cream, coffee, hot dogs and more, as well as a couple of good cafés, *Hummingbird* and *Crafted Coffee Company*. If you're self-catering, head for the New World supermarket at 555 Colombo St.

Antigua Boatshed Café 2 Cambridge Terrace ⊕03 366 6768, ⊚boatsheds.co.nz; map pp.512–513. Adjoining its punting operation (p.515), this green-and-white-striped 1882 boatshed is a serene riverside spot for dishes including a fish of the day (mains $17.50–26.50), and can also pack picnic hampers (per person $14.50) to take on board the boats. Daily 7am–5pm.

★ **Beat Street Café** Corner Armagh and Barbadoes sts ⊕03 366 6324; map pp.512–513. A welcome newcomer, this groovy café on the site of a former bike shop serves delicious all-day breakfasts, including a veggie deluxe eggs Benedict, loaded with roast zucchini, mushrooms, tomatoes and capsicum on sourdough, on brightly coloured china plates (dishes $8–16.50). Daily 7am–5pm.

Keo Thai 4 Papanui Rd ⊕03 355 6229, ⊚keothai .co.nz; map pp.512–513. Authentic Thai food is served

in an elegant dining room recessed behind a plant- and table-filled courtyard. Mains ($19–27) range from mild pad thai to a fearsomely hot *yum nua* (traditional beef salad). Great wine list. Daily 5pm–late.

Pomeroy's Old Brewery Inn 4 Papanui Rd ⊕03 355 6229, ⊚pomeroysonkilmore.co.nz; map pp.512–513. This heritage inn in central Christchurch is a charmer, with Kiwi craft beers such as Emerson's Bookbinder Bitter on tap and a cosy restaurant (mains $20.50–32.50); Pub Tues–Thurs 3pm–late & Fri–Sun noon–late; restaurant Fri–Sun noon–4pm, Tues–Sun 4–10pm.

Sophie's Café 8 Papanui Rd ⊕03 355 2133, ⊚sophies café.co.nz; map pp.512–513. Plastered in photos of the stars who have eaten at this lively steakhouse or otherwise rubbed shoulders with its legendary founder, *Sophie's* serves huge burgers and platters to share and enormous steaks (mains $17.50–36), as well as locally brewed Matson's beer. Mon 8am–2.30pm & 5.30pm–late, Tues–Thurs 7.30am–2.30pm & 5.30pm–late, Fri 7.30am–late, Sat & Sun 8.30am–late.

Vic's Café 132 Victoria St ⊕03 366 2054, ⊚vics.co.nz; map pp.512–513. Contemporary and sleek, *Vic's* is a relaxed spot for breakfast (served until 2pm), bagels,

9

panini and sandwiches (dishes $5.50–19.50) served on its home-baked bread, which you can buy in-store at its bread shop. Mon–Fri 7am–4pm, Sat & Sun 7.30am–4pm.

GREATER CHRISTCHURCH

The Bodhi Tree 397 Ilam Rd ☎03 377 6808, ⊚thebodhitree.co.nz; map pp.518–519. Relocated Burmese place that's enormously popular for entrée-size dishes to share such as tea-leaf salad, fish fillet with tamarind, coriander, chilli and tomato, tempura whitebait on mango salad and yellow split-pea tofu salad (dishes $12.50–20). Tues–Sun from 6pm.

★ **The Brewery** 3 Garlands Rd, Woolston ☎03 389 5359, ⊚casselsbrewery.co.nz; map pp.518–519. Also known as *Cassel & Sons*, this old tannery-turned-brewery has awesome ales, craft beers and lagers made using a wood-fired kettle, regular live entertainment and DJs, and some of the best food in town, including lager-battered blue cod (mains $19.50–28.50). Daily 7am–late.

Brigittes Hawkesbury Building, Aikmans Rd, Merivale ☎03 355 6150, ⊚brigittes.co.nz; map pp.518–519. Trendy café and wine bar in villagey Merivale, serving everything from a mushroom brioche breakfast to prawn filo twisters and aged ribeye on roast garlic mash (mains $18–38). There's a snazzy courtyard with wooden couches and iridescent cushions. Mon 8am–5pm, Tues–Sat 8am–late, Sun 9am–5pm.

★ **Holy Smoke** 650 Ferry Rd, Woolston ☎03 943 2222, ⊚holysmoke.co.nz; map pp.518–519. Even if you don't dine on this smokehouse's sublime salmon for breakfast, lunch or dinner (mains $24–29) in its industrial-chic warehouse-like surrounds, it's worth stopping in to pick up vacuum-packed salmon for sandwich fillings or salads. Daily 9am–late.

Indian Sumner 11a Wakefield Ave, Sumner ☎03 326 4777, ⊚sumnertoferrymead.co.nz; map pp.518–519. Good name, great curries. Dine outside on the pavement, take away or try to get into the cramped but atmospheric interior for something from the small but well-chosen selection of mains ($15–18). Tues–Sun 5pm–late.

Joe's Garage 19 Marriner St, Sumner ☎03 962 2233, ⊚joes.co.nz; map pp.518–519. Funky café alive with folk

getting their caffeine jolt from great espresso while huddled over a laptop (free wi-fi) or tucking into dishes such as crumbed beef schnitzel with chips and tomato herb sauce (dishes $6.80–23). Daily 7am–late.

Ko Tane: The Maori Experience Willowbank Wildlife Reserve, 60 Hussey Rd ☎03 359 6226, ⊚kotane.co.nz; map pp.518–519. If you've missed your chance in Rotorua, you can catch a Maori concert and *hangi* evening here. Packages include a cultural performance, tour and four-course dinner ($105); with the option of a Kiwi wildlife tour ($135). Daily by reservation.

Scarborough Fare 147 Esplanade, Sumner ☎03 326 7923, ⊚scarboroughfare.co.nz; map pp.518–519. Complete with surf boards hung on the walls, this quintessential beach hangout is great for replenishing post-surf brekkies and contemporary dishes such as Sumner Bay scallops (dishes $11.90–19.90) to eat indoors or on the terrace overlooking the waves. Mon–Fri 8.30am–5pm, Sat & Sun 8am–5pm.

Tutto Bene 192 Papanui Rd, Merivale ☎03 355 4744, ⊚tuttobene.co.nz; map pp.518–519. Outstanding Italian restaurant where hearty portions of pizza, pasta and risotto along with traditional meat-, poultry- and seafood-based mains (mains $32.90–35.40) are dished up on gingham tablecloths. Daily 5pm–late.

★ **Under the Red Verandah** 502 Worcester St ☎03 381 1109, ⊚utrv.co.nz; map pp.518–519. Cottage-housed café with fantastic breakfast/brunch and lunch menus (mains $17.50–24), as well as great counter food like blue cheese tart, pumpkin and corn cakes, bacon and *kumara* frittata, organic breads and coffee served in the bare-boards interior or in the sunny courtyard. Pick up gourmet goodies such as preserves and infused olive oils at its in-house deli. Mon–Fri 7.30am–4pm, Sat & Sun 8.30am–4pm.

Winnie Bagoes 2 Waterman Pl, off Ferry Rd, Ferrymead ☎03 376 4900, ⊚winniebagoes.co.nz; map pp.518–519. This much-loved central Christchurch institution has relocated and is open for business in Ferrymead. Its signature gourmet pizzas ($17.50–33) come with toppings such as chicken, cranberry and brie; live music and DJs (usually Thurs–Sun) keep the bar hopping. Daily 11.30am–late.

SHOPPING

Ballantynes Corner of Cashel and Colombo sts, diagonally opposite the Re:START mall ⊚ballantynes.com. This branch of the venerable department store is up and running once more, post-earthquake.

Re:START shopping mall Cashel St, between Oxford Terrace and Colombo St ⊚restart.org.nz. Testament to the resilience and ingenuity of Christchurch locals, Re:START, is a new shopping area in Cashel Mall that's a lot more interesting than what it replaced, populated with

brightly coloured shipping containers fashioned into shops and cafés. Kathmandu is here, along with Trelise Cooper and several other Kiwi fashion icons. Secondhand bookshop Scorpio Books has opened an outlet, as has another Christchurch stalwart Johnson's Grocers – far different from their ancient premises but still stocking an eclectic range of otherwise hard to obtain groceries. Mon–Sat 10am–6pm, Sun 10am–5pm.

DIRECTORY

Banks and exchange A couple of banks have opened temporary outlets in the new Re:START mall (see opposite). Most banks have branches in the suburbs; try the Riccarton Shopping Mall on Riccarton Rd.

Left luggage (see p.520 for airport storage). Most hostels offer a left-luggage facility at usually no more than $5/day.

Medical treatment In emergencies call ☎111. For a doctor at any time call The 24 Hour Surgery (☎03 365 7777; no appointment necessary), at the corner of Bealey Ave and Colombo St. Christchurch Hospital (☎03 364 0640) is at the corner of Oxford Terrace and Riccarton Ave.

Pharmacies The 24 Hour Surgery (☎03 366 4439) stays open daily until 11pm.

Police Central Police Station (☎03 363 7400) is at the corner of Hereford St and Cambridge Terrace.

Post office There's a post office in Merivale Mall, off Riccarton Rd.

North of Christchurch

There's not much of note to the north of Christchurch, and most visitors zip along SH1 on their way to the northern end of the South Island – specifically to the increasingly popular wine-growing centre of Waipara (see p.505) or on to Kaikoura for whale-watching and dolphin-swimming trips. There are, however, a few worthy places to stop in for sustenance, the best of which are listed below.

EATING AND DRINKING

NORTH OF CHRISTCHURCH

★ **Brew Moon** 150 Ashworths Rd (SH1), Amberley, 47km north of Christchurch ☎03 314 8030, ⓦbrew mooncafe.co.nz. This wonderful brewery/café produces four beers at its on-site brewery, best sampled with a tasting tray ($10). It also cooks delicious breakfasts, counter food, lunches and dinners (mains $20–35) from scratch on the premises, including gourmet pizzas such as blue cheese and truffle oil. The rustic garden is idyllic on a summer's day or evening. Daily 11am–8pm, longer in midsummer.

Nor'wester Café 95 Main Rd North, Amberley, 40km north of Christchurch ☎03 314 9411, ⓦnorwestercafe .co.nz. Stop for brunch, a snack, lunch or dinner at this licensed café, which is renowned for its fresh, uncomplicated, European-influenced dishes, great coffee and long wine list. Daily from 9am.

Pukeko Junction Café & Deli 458 Ashworths Rd (SH1), Leithfield, 42km north of Christchurch ☎03 314 8834, ⓦpukekojunction.co.nz. Stop for local Hummingbird plunger coffee or dine on "real food made with love", such as breakfast pancakes with bacon and maple syrup, and lunch choices including kumara, cream cheese and cashew nut filo wraps or smoked salmon fish cakes (dishes $8–18.50). You can also pick up takeaway treats for a picnic. Daily 9am–4.30pm.

Banks Peninsula

Flying into Christchurch you'll be struck by the dramatic contrast between the flat plains of Canterbury and the rugged, fissured topography of **Banks Peninsula**, a volcanic thumb sticking out into the Canterbury Bight. When James Cook sailed by in 1769 he mistakenly charted it as an island and named it after his botanist, Joseph Banks. His error was only one of time, as this basalt lump initially formed an island, only joined to the land as silt sluiced down the rivers from the eastern flanks of the Southern Alps.

The fertile **volcanic** soil of the peninsula's valleys sprouted totara, matai and kahikatea trees that, along with the abundant shellfish in the bays, attracted early Maori around a thousand years ago. The trees progressively succumbed to the Maori fire stick and European timber-milling interests, and the peninsula is now largely bald, with patches of tussock grass and small pockets of regenerating native bush.

Today, the two massive drowned craters that form Banks Peninsula are key to the commerce of the region. Lyttelton Harbour protects the port town of **Lyttelton**, disembarkation point for countless European migrants. Lyttelton is the only town on the Banks Peninsula to have been severely affected by the 2010 and 2011 earthquakes, and numerous buildings had been demolished or were undergoing major repairs at the time of writing.

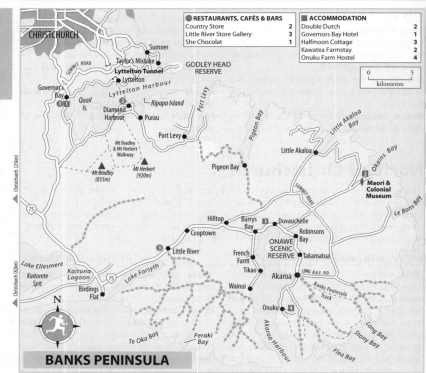

● RESTAURANTS, CAFÉS & BARS	
Country Store	2
Little River Store Gallery	3
She Chocolat	1

■ ACCOMMODATION	
Double Dutch	2
Governors Bay Hotel	1
Halfmoon Cottage	3
Kawatea Farmstay	2
Onuku Farm Hostel	4

BANKS PENINSULA

There's a refined tone to the picturesque and visitor-oriented town of **Akaroa**, lent a gentle French influence by its founders. Elsewhere on the peninsula, a network of narrow, twisting roads winds along the crater rims and dives down to gorgeous, quiet bays once alive with whalers, sealers and shipbuilders, but now seldom visited except during the peak of summer. Despite the denuded grassland of much of the landscape, Banks Peninsula is very popular for relatively easy scenic **walks**, with panoramic views, ancient lava flows and relics from the earliest Maori and European settlers.

GETTING AROUND   **BANKS PENINSULA**

By car and bike To reach the smaller communities tucked into the bays you'll need your own transport. If you're planning on cycling, bear in mind that the peninsula is extremely hilly, and the routes linking the Summit Road with the various bays below can be steep.

Lyttelton

Just 12km southeast of Christchurch city centre, **LYTTELTON** is hemmed in by the rocky walls of the drowned volcanic crater that forms **Lyttelton Harbour**. This working and cruise port town's attractive setting drew a coterie of city escapees to its offbeat cafés and restaurants. Sadly, it was severely affected by the 2010 and 2011 earthquakes, particularly the earthquake of June 13, 2011, losing many of its historic sites, restaurants and bars. However, Lyttelton's strong community spirit is evident in its community garden, and in gap-filling innovations such as the "Lyttelton Petanque Club: Established 2011" on a razed building site.

ARRIVAL AND INFORMATION

By bus The quickest way from Christchurch to Lyttelton is through the 2km Lyttelton Tunnel. The #28 bus from central Christchurch leaves every 15–30min ($2.80), takes about 35min and makes stops at various spots around town, the easiest of which to recognize is Lyttelton School on Oxford St.

Tourist information At Port-A-Com, 65 London St (Mon–Fri 11am–3pm, Sat 10am–1pm, Sun 11am–2pm; ☏ 03 328 9093, ⓦ lyttletonharbour). Another good source of information on the town is ⓦ lyttelton.net.nz.

ACCOMMODATION

Dockside 22 Sumner Rd ☏ 027 448 8133, ⓦ dockside .co.nz. One very pleasant studio with sky-blue decor, cooking facilities and a private garden, plus two larger apartments with similarly artistic decor, fully equipped kitchens and large decks, all overlooking the docks. Studio **$90**, apartment **$120**

Governors Bay Hotel Main Rd, Governors Bay, 8km west of Lyttelton ☏ 03 329 9433, ⓦ governorsbayhotel .co.nz; map p.526. This large colonial hotel has been entirely renovated but retains simple (yet pricey) bathroom-less rooms above the bar with a shared balcony and great harbour views. Double **$100**

EATING AND DRINKING

Wander along London Street to check for post-quake temporary and permanent openings, including funky shipping-container-housed venues. If you're here on Saturday morning, call in to the small **Farmers' Market** in the school grounds on Oxford Street.

Fisherman's Wharf Norwich Quay ☏ 03 328 7530, ⓦ lytteltonwharf.co.nz. Bouillabaisse risotto, seafood baskets and daily catches are among the fish dishes served all day at this airy harbourfront restaurant (mains $9–18), but there are also huge salads and steaks. Wed–Sun 11am–late.

Governors Bay Hotel Main Rd, Governors Bay, 8km west of Lyttelton ☏ 03 329 9433, ⓦ governorsbayhotel .co.nz; map p.526. Sophisticated pub grub at this historic hotel ranges from gourmet salads to rosemary lamb shanks (mains $20–33), which you can enjoy on the outdoor terrace with a pint. Mon–Fri 11am–late, Sat & Sun 9.30am–late.

★ **She Chocolat** 79 Main Rd, 8km west of Lyttelton at Governors Bay ☏ 03 329 9825, ⓦ shechocolat.com; map p.526. Not only does this chocolaterie serve decadently thick hot chocolate, but you can buy its chocolates to take away, watch them being made through the kitchen's viewing window, or even attend its chocolate school (from $195 for a full-day course). Its on-site restaurant (mains $15.90–29) has tables inside and scattered around the garden, all with views straight down Lyttelton Harbour to the sea. Mon–Fri 10am–5pm, Sat & Sun 9am–5pm.

Lyttelton Harbour

Boats reach **Lyttelton Harbour** through "the heads". The spectacular DOC-administered **Godley Head** was closed at the time of writing, due to post-quake safety issues – check the DOC website (ⓦ doc.govt.nz) for updates. Across the harbour, the main destinations are the small community of **Diamond Harbour**, and **Quail Island**, a haven for birds.

Diamond Harbour

Ferries every 30–60min; 10min journey • $5.60 each way • ⓦ diamondharbour.org.nz

In bright sunlight the water sparkles like a million gems at **Diamond Harbour**, directly across the water from Lyttelton. Passenger **ferries** make the run across the harbour arriving at the Diamond Harbour wharf. You can generate a thirst with a 500m walk uphill, then slake it at the *Country Store* (☏ 03 329 4854; daily 8.30am–6pm), where snacks include muffins and toasted sandwiches.

Quail Island

Black Cat Ferries sail to the island Oct–April daily 12.20pm; additional boat Dec–March at 10.20am • $25 return; cash only • ☏ 03 304 7641

Set in mid-harbour, the 0.86-square-kilometre **Quail Island** was known by the local Maori as Otamahua, meaning "place where children collected seabirds' eggs". From 1907 to 1925 it housed a small leper colony, and in the early days of Antarctic exploration Shackleton and Scott quarantined their dogs there before venturing to

9

the South Pole. These days it's a venue for day-trips, swimming and walking: pack food, plenty of drinking water and rain gear. Two circular **walking tracks** (1hr & 2hr 30min) start from the island's wharf and visit safe swimming beaches, along with several shipwrecks that can be seen at low tide.

Lake Ellesmere and Little River

Lake Ellesmere (Waihora), 30km south of Christchurch, is a vast expanse of fresh water separated from the Pacific Ocean by the 30km-long Kaitorete spit, jutting southeast from Banks Peninsula to rejoin the mainland. At the base of the spit is **Birdlings Flat**, a narrow shingle bank that has traditionally been a rich source of food for local Maori, who were granted protected fishing rights here in 1896; the accumulated shingle of the sheltering bank also provides a fossicking ground for greenstone and gems. Birdlings Flat separates the sea from **Lake Forsyth** (Wairewa), a long finger of water skirted by SH75 on the way to the tiny community of **Little River**, 53km from Christchurch, notable mainly for the *Little River Store & Gallery* (ⓦ littlerivergallery.com; Mon–Fri 7.30am–4.30pm, Sat & Sun 7.30am–5pm), an excellent café, bar and bakery (dishes $6.30–9.50).

THE BANKS PENINSULA TRACK

The private **Banks Peninsula Track** (35km; 4-day option $255, 2-day option $165; closed May–Sept; ⓦ bankstrack.co.nz) makes a wonderful alternative to DOC tracks and Great Walks. As well as a lovely combination of coastal cliff walking, volcanic landscapes, sandy swimming beaches, lush native bush and harbour views, you get to stay in some delightful, rustic accommodation and meet the locals. It's not a tramp for route-march aficionados, more a social hike best done over four days with friends keen to partake in a little botanizing, some swimming and much lazing around. Only twelve people are allowed to start the track each day on the four-day walk, and four people on the two-day version, so **book** well in advance.

You need to be reasonably fit, but because you're guaranteed a bunk each night you can walk at your own pace. The fee includes transport to the start from Akaroa and accommodation along the way in lodging with showers, full kitchen, electricity and limited food supply. Standby rates ($195 & $125 respectively) are available within five days of starting the track.

You'll need to bring a good pair of boots, sleeping bag and all-weather gear. You should also carry provisions for at least the first two days, although it's possible to buy food at small shops at Stony Bay and Otanerito Beach. There's limited scope for having your pack transported to your destination each night: see website for details.

THE ROUTE

The first evening you are driven 5km south of Akaroa to Onuku where you spend the night in **Onuku hut** or in one of the stargazer huts with a view of the heavens. A home-cooked meal ($28) is available. The track proper starts the next day.

Onuku to Flea Bay (11km; 3hr 30min) A steady climb to 700m, where there are great views, followed by a descent past a series of small waterfalls, one of which you can walk behind. Accommodation at Flea Bay is in a charming 1850s cottage with a veranda overlooking the beach. Penguin colony viewing (free) and sea kayaking around the Pohatu Marine Reserve ($25) are available.
Flea Bay to Stony Bay (8km; 2hr 30min) An exposed hike along coastal cliffs, with a seal colony providing lunchtime distraction. The night is spent in one of the gorgeous huts/cottages, where there's a fire bath under the stars, indoor/outdoor shower, a small shop selling bread, tinned food, beer and wine, and a few short tracks exploring the bay.
Stony Bay to Otanerito Bay (6km; 2hr) Another short day, with comfortable accommodation in a farmhouse with a great swimming beach, run by author Fiona Farrell and her husband.
Otanerito Bay to Mount Vernon (10km; 3hr; 600m ascent) The final day's walk heads inland through Hinewai Nature Reserve past several small waterfalls and back to Akaroa.

For a little exercise in these parts, consider the **Little River Railtrail** (ⓦlittleriverrailtrail .co.nz), which currently runs for 24km along Lake Forsyth and Lake Ellesmere and will eventually link to Christchurch. Natural High, at 58 McDonalds Rd, Lincoln (ⓣ03 982 2966, ⓦnaturalhigh.co.nz), has bike rental from $60 per day.

Barry's Bay

From Little River, SH75 climbs over the hills that separate Akaroa Harbour from the rest of Banks Peninsula and down to the tiny community of **BARRY'S BAY**, home to **Barry's Bay Cheese**, where you can tuck into free samples, and watch cheese being made in season or a video presentation on its production (daily 9am–5pm; cheese-making season Oct–May; call for cheese-making days; ⓣ03 304 5809, ⓦbarrysbaycheese.co.nz).

ACCOMMODATION	BARRY'S BAY
Halfmoon Cottage SH75, just east of Barry's Bay ⓣ03 304 5050, ⓦhalfmoon.co.nz; map p.526. A small and wonderfully relaxed hostel in an 1896 villa set in a	pretty garden just across from the beach. It offers free bikes and broadband, and rents kayaks. Closed June–Aug. Dorm $30, double $75

Akaroa

The small waterside town of **AKAROA** ("Long Bay"), on the eastern shores of Akaroa Harbour, 85km southeast of Christchurch, comes billed as New Zealand's **French settlement**. Certainly the first settlers came from France, some of their architecture survives and the street names they chose have stuck, but that's about as French as it gets. Nonetheless, the town milks the connection with a couple of French-ish restaurants, some French-sounding boutique B&Bs and a tricolour fluttering over the spot where the first settlers landed.

Still, it is a pretty place, strung along the shore in a long ribbon easily seen on foot, with attractive scenery all around, plus a smattering of low-key activities including a unique dolphin swim, and easy access to the **Banks Peninsula Track** (see box opposite). But Akaroa primarily pitches itself to those looking for gentle strolls followed by good food and wine before falling into a comfy bed. These factors make the town a popular Kiwi holiday destination; some two-thirds of its houses are *baches* (holiday homes), leaving only around 550 permanent residents.

Brief history

The site of Akaroa was originally the domain of the Ngai Tahu paramount chief, Temaiharanui. In 1838, French Commander Jean Langlois traded goods for what he believed to be the entire peninsula and returned to France to encourage settlers to populate a new French colony. Meanwhile, the British sent William Hobson to assume the role of lieutenant-governor over all the land that could be purchased; and just six days before Lavaud sailed into the harbour, the British flag was raised in Akaroa. Lavaud's passengers decided to stay, which meant that the first formal settlement under **British sovereignty** was comprised of 63 French and six Germans.

Akaroa Museum

71 rue Lavaud • Daily: Oct–April 10.30am–4.30pm; May–Nov 10.30am–4pm • $4 • ⓣ03 304 1013

Opposite the visitor centre the **Akaroa Museum** stands head and shoulders above most small-town museums. Several interesting Maori artefacts and a twenty-minute film account of the remarkable history of settlement on the peninsula are backed up by a display illustrating the differences between the English version of the Treaty of Waitangi and a literal English translation of the Maori-language document signed by Maori chiefs all over Aotearoa. Other exhibits deal with the peninsula's whaling history and fascinating albums full of photographs of the original French and German settlers.

9

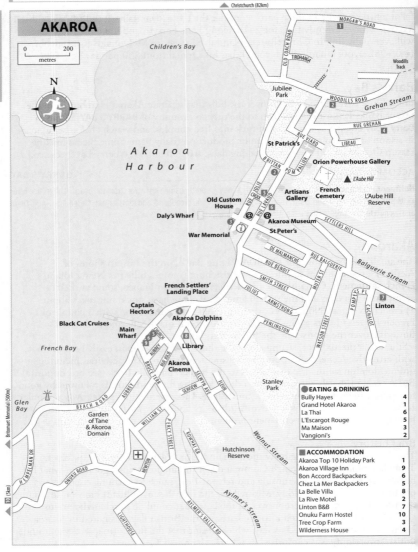

Look, too, for displays on local son **Frank Worsley**, who captained Shackleton's ship *Endurance* to Antarctica and, after disaster struck, the *James Caird* to South Georgia and safety.

The museum incorporates the early 1840s **Langlois-Eteveneaux Cottage**, thought to have been partly constructed in France before being shipped over, and now filled with nineteenth-century French furniture. Also associated with the museum is the town's former **Court House**, with its original dock and bench, and the tiny **Custom House**, across rue Lavaud next to Daly's Wharf, from which spy-glass-wielding officials once kept watch on the port below.

French Cemetery

The **French Cemetery** at the northern end of town is reached by a footpath that leads from rue Pompallier into the L'Aube Hill Reserve. The first consecrated burial ground in Canterbury, the cemetery was sadly neglected until 1925, when the bodies were reinterred in a central plot marked by a single monument.

Linton (The Giant's House)

68 rue Balguerie • Daily: Christmas–March noon–5pm; April–Christmas 2–4pm • $20 • ⓦ thegiantshouse.co.nz

One place you shouldn't miss is **Linton**, home of sculptor Josie Martin and a working testament to her art. Known locally as "The Giant's House", every room, the garden and even the drive to the garage have become a canvas on which she can display her talents. Huge mosaics, concrete figures and sculpted seats tucked away in garden nooks all have an overriding spirit of fun.

Orion Powerhouse Gallery

1 rue Pompallier • Oct–April Mon–Fri 1–4pm, Sat & Sun 11am–4pm • Donation requested • ⓣ 03 304 7245

Akaroa became one of Canterbury's first towns in Canterbury to have a supply of electricity when a small hydro power station was commissioned in 1911. The former plant now houses the **Orion Powerhouse Gallery**, a venue for local art and craft exhibitions, as well as concerts of acoustic music on Sundays, plus a small technology museum.

Tree Crop Farm

2km up rue Grehan • Daily 10am–5pm; closed in inclement weather • $10 • ⓣ 03 304 7158, ⓦ treecropfarm.com

With the feel of a managed wilderness, private lifestyle property **Tree Crop Farm** has clichéd but cute aphorisms – such as "the best plastic surgery is to cut up your credit cards" – written everywhere imaginable. You can wander along its farm tracks and garden paths or book into rustically romantic huts (see p.533).

ARRIVAL AND DEPARTURE

AKAROA

By car From Christchurch, the main route to Akaroa is SH75, via Lake Ellesmere and Little River. Before the earthquake the Summit Rd from Sumner via Lyttelton, along the Port Hills and ridges of the peninsula, was a more leisurely way to approach Akaroa, but you'll need to check with the i-SITE in Christchurch about its condition and how safe it is – or isn't – before setting off this way.

By bus Akaroa Shuttle (Nov–April three daily; May–Oct one daily; $50 return; ⓣ 0800 500 929, ⓦ akaroashuttle .co.nz) and Akaroa French Connection (one daily; $45 return; ⓣ 0800 800 575, ⓦ akaroabus.co.nz) pick up at central Christchurch accommodation for the 90min run to Akaroa. Both services drop off outside the combined post office-visitor centre.

INFORMATION

Tourist information 80 rue Lavaud (daily: Nov–April 9am–5pm; May–Oct daily 10am–4pm; ⓣ 03 304 8600, ⓦ akaroa.com). The visitor centre shares space with the post office, and has pack storage ($1/hr, $5/day). It's also the place to pick up the *Akaroa Historic Village Walk* booklet

($10), a guide to the town's architectural and cultural gems; audioguides ($10) are also available.
Services There's a BNZ bank (Mon–Fri 9.30am–4.30pm) with an ATM across the street from the visitor centre.

ACCOMMODATION

Akaroa's best **accommodation** caters to the weekend getaway set and there are some gorgeous B&Bs, lodges and high-quality hotels and motels. Staying in one of these seems to suit the spirit of Akaroa, and it is worth stretching the budget if you can.

Akaroa Top 10 Holiday Park 96 Morgan's Rd, off the Old Coach Rd ⓣ 0800 727 525, ⓦ akaroa-holidaypark .co.nz; map p.530. Sprawling across a terraced hillside overlooking the harbour and the main street, this site has modern facilities, including a swimming pool. Arriving from the north, look for the small, blue caravan sign indicating the turn-off about 500m before you reach the main village. Camping $35, cabins $70, self-contained units $118

AKAROA TOURS AND ACTIVITIES

If you want to do more than sip Pinot Gris and mooch around the galleries, there is no shortage of diversions in Akaroa. Choose from swimming with the world's smallest breed of dolphin, kayaking, harbour cruises, jetboating, wildlife viewing, and even going along on the local mail run. Dolphin-swimming trips are also available from *Onuku Farm Hostel* (see p.533).

MAIL RUNS

Akaroa Harbour Scenic Mail Run ☏ 03 304 7573, ⓦ akaroamailrun.com. Visits settlements around the inner harbour (5hr; $50) during postal deliveries in a small minibus. Mon–Sat 9am.

Eastern Bays Scenic Mail Run ☏ 03 304 8526. Marginally preferable to the Akaroa Harbour Scenic Mail Run, this minibus mail service covers Okains and Le Bons bays and more (5hr; $60). Mon–Fri 9am.

SWIMMING WITH DOLPHINS, CRUISES, SAILING AND JETBOATING

Black Cat Main Wharf Beach Rd ☏ 03 304 7641, ⓦ blackcat.co.nz. Runs 3hr dolphin-swimming trips (Oct–April 6am, 8.30am, 11.30am, 1.30pm & 3.30pm; May–Sept 11.30am; swimming $139, spectators $72), offers partial refunds if you don't get to swim with the dolphins, and has dry suits in winter. Also runs 2hr harbour cruises (year-round at 1.30pm, plus Nov–March 10.30am; $68) visiting the mouth of the harbour and back via a beautiful high-walled volcanic sea cave, colonies of spotted shags and cormorants, and caves where blue penguins can sometimes be spotted.

Akaroa Dolphins 65 Beach Rd ☏ 0800 990 102, ⓦ akaroadolphins.co.nz. Operates harbour cruises

(daily: Nov–April 10.15am, 12.45pm & 3.15pm; May–Oct 12.45pm; $70) that include birdwatching; expect to see black-backed gulls, red-billed gulls, shearwaters, terns, prions, mollymawks and more.

Fox II Sailing Adventures Leaving from Daly's Wharf ☏ 0800 369 7245, ⓦ akaroafoxsail.co.nz. An atmospheric alternative in the form of sailing trips ($70) on a wooden 1922 ketch to the outer bays of Akaroa Harbour, with an excellent chance of seeing dolphins.

Akaroa Jet Adventures 61B Beach Rd ☏ 03 304 7092, ⓦ akaroajet.co.nz. Get an adrenaline rush whizzing around Akaroa Harbour on a 50min jetboat ride (Oct–April; $50).

KAYAKING

Captain Hector's Canoe & Boat Hire 65 Beach Rd ☏ 03 304 7866. If you're just after splashing around in boats, Captain Hector's rents sea kayaks (single kayak $60/person/day, double $120/person/day) paddleboats, canoes and rowboats.

Akaroa Guided Sea Kayaking Safari Meets at

By The Green café; 37 rue Lavaud ☏ 021 156 4591, ⓦ akaroakayaks.com. Provides small group-guided kayaking trips (Nov–April only; full day $195), with swimming, a good chance of encountering dolphins, and lunch is included. Anyone can join the trips from *Onuku Farm Hostel* (see p.533).

PENGUIN AND SEAL VIEWING

Akaroa Seal Colony Safari ☏ 03 304 7255, ⓦ seal tours.co.nz. Runs air-conditioned 4WD vehicles to view

fur seals, on the eastern tip of the peninsula. Tours (daily 9.30am & 1pm; $70) last over 2hr 30min and are

---

Akaroa Village Inn 81 Beach Rd ☏ 0800 695 1111, ⓦ akaroavillageinn.co.nz; map p.530. A rambling complex with probably the widest range of accommodation in town, a variety of decors and lots of self-catering apartments, several with two bedrooms and some good harbour views. Studio units $195, apartments $240, luxury apartments $350

Bon Accord Backpackers 57 rue Lavaud ☏ 03 304 7782, ⓦ bon-accord.co.nz; map p.530. Small, friendly hostel fashioned from two houses, with a large garden. Slippers and hot water bottles are provided and there are free bikes, fishing rods and off-street parking. Dorms $27, rooms $60

Chez La Mer Backpackers 50 rue Lavaud ☏ 03 304 7024, ⓦ chezlamer.co.nz; map p.530. High-quality budget accommodation in a homely 1871 house complete

with a lovely garden, hammock and outdoor cooking area. The staff are helpful, and offer free use of bikes and fishing rods and useful maps of local walks and points of interest. Dorms $25, rooms $70, en suites $80

La Belle Villa 113 rue Jolie ☏ 03 304 7084, ⓦ labelle villa.co.nz; map p.530. B&B in a lovely 1870s wooden house set in flower-filled gardens with spacious, light en-suite rooms, frilly bedspreads and alfresco breakfasts in summer. Doubles $170

La Rive Motel 1 rue Lavaud ☏ 0800 247 651, ⓦ larive .co.nz; map p.530. Large motel with a conical tower alluding to French chateau architecture, with a tranquil garden setting and eight units, all containing full kitchens and TVs. Particularly good for groups. $125

limited to six people, departing from the Akaroa visitor centre (see p.531).

Pohatu Penguins 🕿 03 304 8552, 🌐 pohatu.co.nz. Shireen and Francis Helps have been looking after white-flippered penguins on their farm at Flea Bay on the Banks Peninsula Track (see p.528) for decades. You can see the birds close up on three different tours: "standard" penguin viewing (2–3hr; $70); the chance to take part in penguin monitoring on 4WD nature tours ($90); and getting a glimpse of the birds swimming or sitting on the rocks during breeding and moulting seasons while you sea kayak around Flea Bay and the Pohatu Marine Reserve ($80). Prices include pick-ups from Akaroa; there are cheaper options if you can drive to the farm, but the road is 4WD-only and steep.

WALKING

For those who lack the time or inclination to tackle the Banks Peninsula Track (see box, p.528), there are equally rewarding shorter walks.

Round the Mountain Walk (10km; 4hr return) The best of Akaroa's walks circumnavigates the hills above the town via the Purple Peak Road; get a map from the visitor centre in town.

Beach Road–Glen Bay–Red House Bay (5km one-way; 1hr 15min) Stroll along waterfront Beach Road towards Glen Bay and the nineteenth-century red-and-white wooden lighthouse that used to stand at Akaroa Head before being moved to its current location in 1980. Continue towards Akaroa Head for about fifteen minutes and you'll come to Red House Bay, the scene of a bloody massacre in 1830, when the great northern chief Te Rauparaha bribed the captain of the British brig *Elizabeth* with flax to conceal Maori warriors about the vessel and then to invite Te Rauparaha's unsuspecting enemies (led by Temaiharanui) on board, where they were slaughtered. Te Rauparaha and his men then feasted on the victims on the beach.

Onuku Road (5km one-way; 1hr 15min) Follow this inland road to Onuku, where you'll find the *Onuku Farm Hostel* (see below) and Onuku Marae with a pretty little nineteenth-century church.

HORSE RIDING

Kate Tapley Horse Treks Brocherie's Rd 🕿 03 329 0160, 🌐 akaroariding.co.nz. Located about a 15min drive east of Akaroa via Long Bay Rd, the treks here (from $110/2hr) run along trails with panoramic views of the farmland, coastal forest and sparkling bays.

FISHING AND DIVING

Akaroa Fishing and Dive Charters Daly's Wharf 🕿 03 304 7220, 🌐 akaroafishing.co.nz. Offers various fishing trips (from $90 for up to 3hr of harbour fishing including gear, bait and fish cleaning and packing) and dive and snorkelling charters.

Linton B&B (The Giant's House) 68 rue Balguerie 🕿 03 304 7501, 🌐 thegiantshouse.co.nz; map p.530. Stay in a living art gallery (see p.531) built in and around this 1881 house. The large rooms (some en-suite) are all wildly decorated, with, say, a boat bed or a greenhouse conservatory. A delicious continental breakfast is served and there are big reductions for multi-night stays. Doubles **$270**

★ **Onuku Farm Hostel** 6km south of town on the Onuku Rd 🕿 03 304 7066, 🌐 onukufarm.com; map p.526. On a hill above a bay, this wonderfully secluded spot on a sheep farm centres on the cosy main house where there are doubles and dorms (including a 6-bunk en-suite girls' dorm with hairdryer). There's no TV, and internet access is hidden away. Outside there's accommodation in a lovely brick cottage and a network of bush and farmland tracks, some leading to the hammock-strung campsite equipped with outdoor kitchens and showers, plus several huts and stargazers – rather like wooden tents. The hostel also runs 3–4hr guided kayaking ($45), and summer dolphin-swimming trips ($100; max 6), and encourages fishing and mussel collecting. Free pick-up around 12.30pm from Akaroa. Cash only. Closed June–Sept. Camping and small campervans per person **$15**, dorms **$25**, rooms **$72**

Tree Crop Farm 2km up rue Grehan 🕿 03 304 7158, 🌐 treecropfarm.com; map p.530. The four "love shacks" are the only place to stay if you're looking for the sort of rustic romance that secluded candle-lit shacks hung with mirrors and supplied with outdoor fire-heated bush baths

9

offer. It's not for everyone but is a unique experience, and checkout isn't until noon or later. Doubles **$200**

★ **Wilderness House** 42 rue Grehan ☎ 03 304 7517, ⓦ wildernesshouse.co.nz; map p.530. Lovely and welcoming B&B in a fine old home with four tastefully decorated rooms, each with en suite or private bath (one with a deep tub). There's a sumptuous guest lounge with port, and in good weather delicious breakfasts are served on the terrace overlooking semi-formal grounds with English roses. To top it all off, they even have their own small vineyard. Doubles **$295**

EATING, DRINKING AND ENTERTAINMENT

Akaroa has some outstanding places to eat. **Expensive** establishments predominate, but there's also a bakery, takeaways and cheaper cafés, mostly along Beach Road, as well as a couple of lively pubs. Many places cut back their hours, or even close completely, during winter.

★ **Bully Hayes** 57 Beach Rd ☎ 03 304 7533, ⓦ bully hayes.co.nz; map p.530. Named after the 1800s American pirate William Henry "Bully" Hayes, who frequented the waters hereabouts, this always-busy place cooks up big breakfasts and casual lunches, and serves sensational seafood platters (including succulent Foveaux Strait oysters – and Akaroa salmon, of course) as well as high-end evening fare like truffle-butter roasted chicken (mains $19.80–42). Daily 8am–late.

Grand Hotel Akaroa 6 rue Lavaud ☎ 03 304 7011, ⓦ grandhotelakaroa.co.nz; map p.530. The village's communal lounge room, this lovely old pub has top-quality meals (mains $18.95–29) at both lunch and dinner every day and a sunny beer garden. Daily 10am–late.

La Thai 69 Beach Rd ☎ 03 304 8060. Aromatic curries, Thai salads, stir-fries and whole fish (steamed or deep fried) are decent value for money at this smart Thai restaurant (mains $21–28). Thurs–Mon lunch & dinner.

L'Escargot Rouge 67 Beach Rd ⓦ lescargotrouge .co.nz; map p.530. "Parisian" breakfast choices at this chic spot include a baguette, croissant and pain au chocalat, croque monsieur (brioche with Dijon mustard, ham and cheese) and croque madame (like a croque monsieur but topped with an egg); during the day there's a tempting selection of deli-style counter food (dishes $3.50–10). Daily 7.30am–5pm.

Ma Maison 2 rue Jolie ☎ 03 304 7668, ⓦ mamaison .co.nz; map p.530. A lovely setting overlooking Daly's Wharf makes this a great spot for an early-evening drink though it's equally tempting for quality brunches from 10am, then classy, slightly French-influenced dinners (mains $28.50–35). Mon–Fri 11.30am–3pm & 5.30pm–late, Sat & Sun 10.30am–late.

Vangioni's 40f rue Lavaud, entrance on rue Britain ☎ 03 304 7714, ⓦ vangionis.co.nz; map p.530. On a Mediterranean-like evening the garden here is a great place to dine on excellent trattoria fare, delicious tapas and great pizza (mains $15–33). When the weather is inclement, retreat to the cosy, casual bar area. Mon–Fri 5pm–late, Sat & Sun 11am–late.

CINEMAS

Akaroa Cinema Corner of rue Jolie and Selwyn Ave ☎ 03 304 7678, ⓦ cinecafé.co.nz; map p.530. For non-blockbuster movies, check out this boutique cinema, which plays art, foreign, classic and new films. It's got an on-site café, and you can take your glass of wine into the theatre with you.

Around Akaroa

A day is well spent exploring the bays around Akaroa. Twisting roads drop down to gems of bays with deserted beaches and the remains of once thriving towns where the school or store just about hangs on. With few connecting roads between the bays, exploring the region is likely to take longer than you might expect; check road conditions with the Akaroa visitor centre (see p.531).

Le Bons Bay

Verdant **LE BONS BAY** is a small peaceful community with a number of holiday homes ranged behind a gorgeous sandy **beach**, framed on two sides by cliffs. Head here for moody walks along the beach and safe swimming (after checking road conditions in Akaroa before you set out).

Okains Bay

OKAINS BAY has a tiny permanent population but swells with Christchurch family holidaymakers in January. The beach and the placid lagoon formed by the **Opara Stream** are excellent for swimming and boating, but the museum is the real reason to visit.

Okains Bay Maori and Colonial Museum

Okains Bay Rd · Daily 10am–5pm · $10 · ⓦ okainsbaymuseum.co.nz

The **Okains Bay Maori and Colonial Museum**, housed in a former cheese factory, contains one of the most remarkable collections of Maori artefacts in the South Island.

Originally amassed by a local collector, Murray Thacker, the collection includes a great collection of *hei tiki* (a pendant with a design based on the human form) in different styles from around Aotearoa, plus a valuable example returned here from an English collection. There's a "god stick" dating back to 1400, a war canoe from 1867 and greenstone adze heads. There's also a beautiful meeting house, with fine symbolic figures carved by master craftsman John Rua. Within the same compound, several outbuildings contain more traditional exhibitions relating to European settlement, including a "slab" stable and cottage – constructed from large slabs of totara wood.

ACCOMMODATION
OKAINS BAY

Double Dutch 32 Chorlton Rd ☎03 304 7229, ⓦ doubledutch.co.nz; map p.526. Wonderfully relaxing upscale hostel in a very spacious modern house with just seven beds – which makes it feel more like a friendly share house than a hostel. Closed June–Aug. Dorms $30, doubles $70

Kawatea Farmstay 1048 Okains Bay Rd ☎03 304 8621, ⓦ kawateafarmstay.co.nz; map p.526. Century-old homestead set in lush gardens bordered by 5km of scenic coastline, with welcoming hosts, three rooms and a lovely loft. Dinners are available on request ($35, including New Zealand wines). Doubles $125, en-suite doubles $155

South to Otago

Heading south from Christchurch, SH1 forges straight across the **Canterbury Plains** connecting small farming service towns. Aside from the occasionally magnificent views of the snowcapped **Southern Alps** to the west, the drive south is through a monotonous landscape broken only by the broad gravel beds of braided rivers, usually little more than a trickle spanned by a kilometre-long bridge.

As the road passes the pottery town of **Temuka** and reaches the southern end of the Canterbury Plains, hills force it back to the shoreline at mundane **Timaru**. From here, SH8 strikes inland towards Fairlie, Lake Tekapo and Aoraki Mount Cook.

The coastal highway continues south through rolling hills to the architecturally harmonious city of **Oamaru**, and the unique and fascinating **Moeraki Boulders**. This is **penguin** country, with several opportunities to stop off and spy blue and yellow-eyed penguins. From Moeraki there is little to delay you on your progress toward Dunedin, except maybe the small crossroads town of **Palmerston**, where SH85, "The Pigroot" to **Central Otago**, leaves SH1, providing another opportunity to forsake the coast and follow a historical pathway to the now defunct goldfields inland.

Rakaia

Gradually leaving the suburbs of Christchurch behind, around 60km south you cross the longest bridge in New Zealand, the 1.8km-long Rakaia River Bridge. It leads into the tiny salmon-fishing and sheepshearing settlement of **Rakaia**, where a minor road called Thompson's Track heads inland towards Methven, Mount Hutt and Mount Somers. You can see live salmon at **Salmon Tales**, which has an interpretive visitor centre and craft shop at Railway Terrace East (daily 8am–5pm; ⓦ salmontales .co.nz), and taste it at its café (Mon–Wed 8am–5pm, Thurs–Sun 8am–late) in dishes including cured salmon salad or pan-fried salmon of the day (dishes $7.50–29.50, dinner mains $21–33).

9

Temuka

Temuka, 150km south of Christchurch, takes its name from the Maori for "fierce oven" – and indeed, a large number of Maori earth ovens have been found in the area. In the twentieth century, fierce ovens were used to fire **pottery**, which became a local industry following the arrival of immigrants from the "Potteries" area around Stoke-on-Trent in England. Recently, **Temuka Pottery** has revived the tradition in its new premises inside Temuka's historic Mendelson Barn, on the SH1 bypass (Mon–Fri 9am–5pm, Sat & Sun 10am–4pm; ⓦtemukapottery.co.nz).

Timaru

The 28,000-strong port city of **TIMARU**, 18km south of Temuka, is at the end of a straight and flat two-hour drive from Christchurch. The city isn't a vastly compelling place to stop, though it's enlivened by the new **Te Ana Maori Rock Art Centre**, the **Aigantighe Art Gallery** and the **South Canterbury Museum**. On a fine day, it's worth spending a quiet hour ambling around the **Botanical Gardens**, entered via Queen Street (daily 8am–dusk; free), or strolling along the new **boardwalk** along Caroline Bay and the low cliffs north past the wooden 1878 **Blackett's Lighthouse** to Dashing Rocks.

Brief history

The name Timaru comes from *Te Maru*, Maori for "place of shelter", as it provided the only haven for *waka* paddling between Banks Peninsula and Oamaru. In 1837

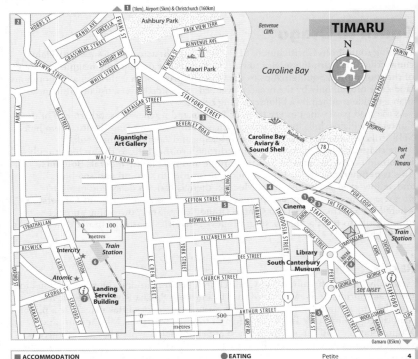

■ ACCOMMODATION				● EATING			
Panorama Motor Lodge	4	Timaru Top 10		Arthur St Café	5	Petite	4
Pleasant View	1	Holiday Park	2	Ginger and Garlic	1	Pukeko Café and Deli	2
Sefton Homestay	5	Wanderer Backpackers	3	Off the Rails Café	6	Speights Ale House	7
				Sukhothai	3		

European settlement was initiated by Joseph Price, who set up a **whaling** station south of the present city at Patiti Point. A large part of today's commercial and pastoral development was initiated by Yorkshiremen **George and Robert Rhodes**, who established the first cattle station on the South Island in 1839 and effectively founded Timaru. Land reclamation created a harbour in 1877 and helped form the fine sandy beach of Caroline Bay. For a time, Timaru became a popular seaside resort, and its annual two-week **summer carnival**, starting on Boxing Day, is still a highlight.

Landing Service Building and Te Ana Maori Rock Art Centre

2 George St • Daily: Nov–April 10am–5pm; May–Oct 10am–3pm • 1hr guided tour $20; 3hr guided tour of rock art sites Nov–April $125 (including transport and refreshments; book ahead) • ☎ 027 231 6937, ⓦ teana.co.nz

Timaru's business district centres on the 1876 **Landing Service Building**, a volcanic "bluestone" former store where goods were unloaded from the small boats that were winched up onto a shingle beach in front. It contains the i-SITE (p.538), as well as the new **Te Ana Maori Rock Art Centre** with state-of-the-art multimedia displays as well as **rock drawings** found in the vicinity. Te Ana also offers guided tours of rock art sites (see box below).

South Canterbury Museum

Perth St • Tues–Fri 10am–4.30pm, Sat & Sun 1.30–4.30pm • Free • ☎ 03 687 7212, ⓦ timaru.govt.nz

The **South Canterbury Museum** contains good displays on the life of local Maori (who lived a much more hunter-gatherer lifestyle than their northern kin) and on the whaling station that occupied Patiti Point in the late 1830s and early 1840s. Hanging over the main hall of the museum is a reconstruction of the 1902 **aircraft** used by Temuka lad **Richard Pearse** in his attempt to notch up the world's first powered flight, some months in advance of the Wright brothers. Many locals claim he succeeded, and indeed his plane was technically far ahead of that of his rivals, but Pearse himself did not believe his flight – a rather desperate 100m, followed by an ignominious plunge into gorse bushes – was sufficiently controlled or sustained to justify this claim. He was a lifelong tinkerer and inventor, and his drawings are displayed along with rusty engine parts. There's a memorial to Pearse at the site of the legendary flight, about 13km west of Temuka on the way to Waitohi.

Aigantighe Art Gallery

49 Wai-iti Rd • Tues–Fri 10am–4pm, Sat & Sun noon–4pm • Free • ☎ 03 688 4424, ⓦ timaru.govt.nz/artgallery

A grand 1908 house known as Aigantighe (Gaelic for "at home"; their sign's suggested pronunciation is "egg-and-tie") is occupied by the **Aigantighe Art Gallery**. Original features of the house provide a suitable setting for a diverse and rotating permanent collection including five major works by native son Colin McCahon. Other artists to look out for are Frances Hodgkins, C.F. Goldie and the prolific landscape Realist,

---

MAORI ROCK ART

Around five hundred years ago, Maori moa hunters visited the South Canterbury and North Otago coastal plain, leaving a record of their sojourn on the walls and ceilings of open-sided limestone rock shelters. There are more than three hundred **rock drawings** around Timaru, Geraldine and Fairlie; the faded charcoal and red ochre drawings depict a variety of stylized human, bird and mythological figures and patterns. The best of the cave drawings can be seen in the region's museums, notably Timaru's new Te Ana Maori Rock Art Centre (see above) and the North Otago Museum in Oamaru (see p.540). Around 95 percent of those remaining *in situ* are on private land and are often hard to make out, and what is visible is often the misguided result of nineteenth-century repainting. The best destination is Frenchman's Gully, where moa and a stylized birdman figure can be seen. Contact the Te Ana Maori Rock Art Centre for guided tours.

9

Austen Deans. At the back of the gallery, the **sculpture garden** is dominated by the results of a 1990 symposium when Kiwi, Japanese and Zimbabwean sculptors carved thirteen works from soft Mount Somers stone, which has weathered nicely. Look out for *Baboon*, carved with power tools by a Zimbabwean who had only ever carved by hand.

ARRIVAL AND DEPARTURE   TIMARU

By bus InterCity buses stop outside the train station (not served by passenger trains), NakedBus stops across the road from the station, and Atomic buses stop outside the i-SITE. Destinations Christchurch (5–6 daily; 2hr 30min); Dunedin

(5–6 daily; 3hr 30min); Oamaru (5–6 daily; 1hr).
By plane Timaru's airport is 13km north of the town centre on Falvey Rd.
Destinations Wellington (2–3 daily; 1hr 10min).

GETTING AROUND

By bus Timaru's Metro bus service (📞 03 688 5544, 🌐 metro info.org.nz) has a flat rate of $1.70 for all journeys around the city, and $4 to Temuka. Tickets are sold in the i-SITE.

By bike Rent bikes from The Cyclery, 106 Stafford St (📞 03 688 8892), for $35/day.
By taxi Timaru Taxis 📞 03 688 8899.

INFORMATION

i-SITE 2 George St, inside the Landing Service Building (Mon–Fri 8.30am–5pm, Sat & Sun 10am–3pm; 📞 03 687 9997, 🌐 southcanterbury.org.nz).
Services There's internet access ($6/hr) at *Off the Rail Café*

(see below) and free access at the library on Sophia St (Mon, Wed & Fri 9am–8pm, Tues & Thurs 9am–6pm, Sat 10am–1pm, Sun 1–4pm).

ACCOMMODATION

Panorama Motor Lodge 52 The Bay Hill 📞 0800 103 310, 🌐 panorama.net.nz. Striking and hospitable motel with spacious units and all the usual facilities, as well as a sauna, spa baths, gym, off-street parking and great views over Caroline Bay. Doubles $135
Pleasant View 2 Moore St 📞 03 686 6651, 🌐 pleasant view.co.nz. A stylish, modern house with two en-suite rooms, one of which has great sea views, plus a living area for all guests. Doubles $95
★ **Sefton Homestay** 32 Sefton St 📞 03 688 0017, 🌐 seftonhomestay.co.nz. Great-value B&B in a lovely 1920s house set in leafy grounds. One room is an en suite, while the other is equally attractive with a private guest bathroom fitted with a deep tub. There's free wired internet

and wi-fi plus a dedicated guest lounge and discounts for cyclists. Doubles $125
Timaru Top 10 Holiday Park 154a Selwyn St 📞 0800 242 121, 🌐 timaruholidaypark.co.nz. Well-kept, very high-standard holiday park offering a range of accommodation, close to the golf course and within walking distance of Maori Park. Camping $32, cabins $57, self-contained units $100, motel units $120
Wanderer Backpackers 24 Evans St 📞 03 688 8795, 🌐 bbh.co.nz. Small roadside backpackers that's relatively close to town, has off-street parking, free bus pick-ups, free bikes, a dishwasher and no check-out time. There are even occasional hunting trips. Ask about tent sites. Dorms $23, doubles $56

EATING, DRINKING AND ENTERTAINMENT

Arthur St Café 8 Arthur St 📞 03 688 9449. Great little café spread across several cosy rooms with tables outside. Excellent breakfasts include toasted bagels with olive tapenade and pan-fried mushrooms, sweet donuts with scrambled eggs, and French toast, but there's also veggie filo wraps, cute cakes and coffee (dishes $6–18.50). Mon–Fri 7.30am–5.30pm, Sat 9am–3pm.
★ **Ginger and Garlic** 335 Stafford St 📞 03 688 3981, 🌐 gingerandgarlic.co.nz. Timaru's premier fine-dining restaurant is romantically set in a beautiful old building with sweeping views over Caroline Bay. Starters such as hand-crafted bread rolls with garlic butter, cold-pressed olive oil and aged balsamic vinegar or oysters are followed by mains such as duck breast with wasabi spiced onion bhaji and

honeyed onion broth, or Antarctic scallops and chorizo with blue cheese risotto (mains $26–36). Save room for desserts, too: try the caramel wontons with vanilla ice cream and chocolate ganache. Mon–Fri lunch, Mon–Sat dinner.
★ **Off the Rail Café** 22 Station St 📞 03 688 3594. Groovy retro licensed café, housed in a 1967 former train station waiting room, with original booths, a jukebox, a white leather sofa and a good selection of value-for-money food such as pies, lasagne and burgers (dishes $7–16) and zingy coffee. Mon–Fri 7.30am–5pm, Sat & Sun 9am–5pm plus 7.30–8.30pm Fri & Sun.
Petite 16 Royal Arcade 📞 03 688 3981. Atmospheric cocktail bar with a vast range of concoctions along with wine by the glass and light bites such as antipasto platters

for two. Tues–Sat 4pm–midnight.
Pukeko Café and Deli 333 Stafford St ☎03 688 4484.
Funky, upbeat café with a tempting range of deli counter
items to take away and delicious daily specials to eat in,
such as hot smoked salmon, chicken and mango nachos
and steak stacks (dishes $16–23). Mon–Fri 7am–3pm,
Sat 9am–2pm.
Speights Ale House 2 George St ☎03 686 6030,
ⓦtimarualehouse.co.nz. Popular, cavernous bar in the
Landing Service Building, offering generous pub-style

lunches and dinners (mains $14.50–32.90), plus occasional
weekend live music. Daily 11.30am–late.
Sukhothai 303 Stafford St ☎03 688 4843. Good Thai
restaurant serving old favourites (mains $17–30) plus $10
lunch specials. Tues–Sun lunch and dinner.

CINEMAS

Movie Max 5 Corner of Canon and Sophia sts ☎03 684
6987, ⓦmoviemax5.co.nz. Screens first-run Hollywood
movies. Free parking.

Oamaru

The former port town of **OAMARU**, 85km south of Timaru, is one of New Zealand's
most alluring provincial cities, and a relaxed place to spend a day or two. The most
immediate attraction is the presence of both blue and yellow-eyed **penguin colonies**
on the outskirts of town, but the town itself has a well-preserved **Historic District**, a core
of nineteenth-century buildings built of the distinctive cream-coloured local limestone
that earned Oamaru the title "The Whitestone City". At the turn of the twentieth
century it had a reputation as being the most attractive city in the South Island – a
status it's regaining thanks to ongoing restoration.

The best times to visit Oamaru are from November to January when penguins are
in their greatest numbers, and for the **Victorian Heritage Celebrations** over the third
weekend in November when the streets of the historic district become a racetrack for
penny-farthings, cheered on by local residents in Victorian attire.

Brief history

The limestone outcrops throughout the area once provided shelter for Maori and later
the raw material for ambitious European builders. As a commercial centre for gold-rush
prospectors, and shored up by quarrying, timber and farming industries, Oamaru grew
prosperous. The port opened for **migration** in 1874, although many ships foundered on
the hostile coastline and in the late nineteenth century wrecks littered the shore. After
this boom period Oamaru declined, times evocatively recorded in work by local writer
Janet Frame. It's only in recent years that the town has begun to come alive again.

Thames Street

Thames Street – home to the majority of civic buildings including the 1906 Opera House,
Palladian Courthouse and classically proportioned Athenaeum building (now home to
the North Otago Museum) lined up along one side – and the knot of streets around Tyne,
Itchen and Harbour streets define Oamaru's **Historic District**, a dense cluster of grand civic
and mercantile buildings that sets the town centre apart from any other in the land.

OAMARU WHITESTONE

The key to Oamaru's distinctive look is whitestone, a "free stone" which is easily worked with
metal hand tools when freshly quarried but hardens with exposure to the elements. While
keeping the prevailing Neoclassical fashion firmly in mind, the architects' imaginations ran riot,
producing deeply fluted pilasters, finely detailed pediments and elegant Corinthian pillars
topped with veritable forests of acanthus leaves. Oamaru was given much of its character by
architect R.A. Lawson and by the firm Forrester and Lemon who together produced most of
the more accomplished buildings between 1871 and 1883. Oamaru stone is still used in
modern buildings such as the Waitaki Aquatic Centre in Takaro Park. Enthusiasts can visit the
source of Oamaru stone at the Parkside Quarry (Mon–Fri 9am–4.30pm; free; guided tours $10;
☎03 433 9786, ⓦoamarustone.co.nz), 7km west of town.

OAMARU

▲ **1** (1km), **2** (1.7km), **3** (2km), **1** (18km) & Timaru (84km)

■ ACCOMMODATION

Café 469 & Motels	2
Alma Motels	8
Alpine Motel	4
Chillawhile	1
Criterion Hotel	11
Kiwiana Cottage	10
Northstar	3
Oamaru Creek	5
Oamaru Top 10 Holiday Park	7
Old Bones Backpackers	9
YHA Red Kettle	6

Historic District

Glen Waren Reserve

Glen Eden Reserve

Janet Frame's House

Cinema

Former Train Station

SOUTH PACIFIC

YARE ST

FORRESTER DR

DEVON

YARE ST

CHELMER STREET

Oamaru Gardens

ISIS STREET

STOUR STREET

SEVERN STREET

DOUGLAS

ALAMEIN

ITCHEN ST

WANSBECK STREET

URE STREET

ARUN STREET

TWEED

TEST STREET

AVON STREET

TAMAR STREET

TOWEY STREET

MERSEY STREET

LUNE STREET

TILL STREET

GRETA STREET

HULL STREET

WHARF ST

TEES ST

UPPER URE ST

■ MUSIC VENUE/CLUB

Penguin Club	1

● EATING & DRINKING

Criterion Bar	6
Dilaans	4
Loan & Merc	7
Portside	5
Riverstone Kitchen	1
Short Black	2
Whitestone Cheese	3

ROYAL TERR

TRENT STREET

NEN STREET

EXE STREET

TORRIDGE

DEE STREET

USK STREET

RIBBLE STREET

SEVERN ST

SEE INSET FOR DETAIL

STEWARD ST

MEDWAY ST

MEEK ST

THAMES ST

Oamaru Creek

WEAR ST

COQUET STREET

EDEN STREET

WARREN STREET

ALN STREET

REED STREET

DEE STREET

WARBUST

CROSS STREET

HOOKE ST

CHESS

WANSBECK STREET

MARINE PARADE

TYNE ST

Historic Train

WATERFRONT ROAD

Friendly Bay

Lookout

Blue Penguin Colony

King George Park

SELWYN ST

BUSH ST

BRINKBURN ST

BYWELL ST

KENNET

INSET (metres 0–100):

SEVERN ST

The Court House

North Otago Museum

STEWARD ST

MEDWAY ST

THAMES STREET

HUMBER STREET

MEEK ST

Former Post Office

National Bank

Forrester Gallery

First Post Office

Historic Train Station

ITCHEN ST

Steampunk HQ

St Luke's

TEES ST

Woolstore Complex

Bookbinde

Harbour Board Office

Smith's Grain Store Bookshop

HARBOUR ST

Whisky Art

WANSBECK STREET

0 — 500 metres

◄ **8** (5km), Totara Estate (8km) & Dunedin (115km)

i 03 433 0852, northotagomuseum.co.nz

North Otago Museum

60 Thames St • Mon–Fri 10am–4.30pm, Sat & Sun 1–4pm • Free • **①** 03 433 0852, **Ⓦ** northotagomuseum.co.nz

The colonnaded 1882-built Athenaeum building last served as a subscription library before providing a home for the **North Otago Museum**, with its modest selection of displays on North Otago history, the area's geology incorporating early Maori rock art and Temuka pottery, as well as the life of local novelist Janet Frame.

The Former Post Office

Thames St

The Former Post Office originally came without the tower, which was added by the architect's son, Thomas Forrester, in 1903. This building replaced the adjacent 1864 First Post Office, an Italianate structure which predates all the other whitestone work.

It's the town's only remaining example of the work of Australian-born architect W.H. Clayton (1823–77), who trained in England and emigrated to New Zealand in 1863, designing Dunedin's All Saints' Church and Edinburgh House before being appointed the country's first – and only – Colonial Architect, during which time he designed the Old Government Buildings in Wellington.

The Forrester Gallery

9 Thames St • Daily 10.30am–4.30pm • Free • ☎ 03 434 1463, ⓦ forrestergallery.com

Directly opposite the one-time post offices are two of Lawson's buildings: the imposing **National Bank** has perhaps the purest Neoclassical facade in town; its grander neighbour now operates as the **Forrester Gallery**. This features touring exhibitions of contemporary and traditional art, plus a basement of works by iconic Kiwi artist Colin McCahon and local painter Colin Wheeler, whose cityscapes are dominated by the colour of Oamaru stone.

Tyne–Harbour Street Historic District

Continuing towards the waterfront from Thames Street, you enter Oamaru's original commercial quarter, full of whitestone flamboyance. Gentrification is taking its time, but this is gradually becoming the place to hang out, perhaps grabbing a coffee or a beer in between browsing the shops, art galleries and minor museums.

Woolstore Complex and the Oamaru Auto Collection

1 Tyne St • Oamaru Auto Collection daily 10am–4pm; Sunday market 10am–4pm • $8

Follow Itchen Street east and as you round the corner into Tyne Street you'll spot the **Woolstore Complex**, housing boutiques, galleries and the *Woolstore Café*, and the **Oamaru Auto Collection**, with a collection of some thirty vintage, classic and historic motorsport vehicles that any car enthusiast won't want to miss.

Union Offices

7 Tyne St • Mon–Fri 2–6pm or by appointment • Free • ☎ 03 434 9277

Oamaru's elegant old **Union Offices**, built in 1877, are now the atmospheric home of a traditional bookbinder's workshop. You can stop by or call ahead to watch local character Michael O'Brien binding and restoring rare books and also see examples of old printing and letterpress machines.

Smiths Grain Store and around

Next to the Union Offices

The stately **Smiths Grain Store**, built in 1882 by stonemason James Johnson, is considered to be the most ornamental of its kind in the country. The first floor is now used as an art gallery. Further along you'll find Slightly Foxed, 11 Tyne St, which buys and sells a wonderful array of quality secondhand and classic **books**.

Harbour Board Office

Harbour Street runs parallel to Tyne Street and is lined by more rejuvenated mercantile buildings. The 1876 Venetian Renaissance-style **Harbour Board Office** was one of the first public buildings designed by the prolific Forrester and Lemon. Interpretation panels on the ground floor relate the history of Oamaru Harbour and the architects' influence on Oamaru.

Whisky Art

14 Harbour St • Daily 11am–5pm • Free

On the second floor of the 1882 **Loan & Mercantile** wool and grain store (once the largest in New Zealand), which until recently was home to New Zealand's only producer of single-malt whisky and now houses the fabulous *Loan & Merc* carvery

9

restaurant (p.545), this cavernous, bare-boards open space has been transformed into a **gallery** for independent jewellery, visual and textile artists. Don't miss the views over the harbour and surrounding streets from its enormous windows.

Steampunk HQ

1 Itchen St • Daily 10am–4pm • Free • Ⓦ steampunknz.co.nz

Fans of the sub-genre of science fiction, fantasy, alternative history and speculative fiction "steampunk" – and anyone fascinated by the pseudo-Victorian mechanical-style sculptures, artworks, photography and even fashion – should make time to visit **Steampunk HQ** gallery, fronted by a surreal retro-futuristic steam engine.

Oamaru Gardens

Entrances off Severn St (SH1) and Chelmer St • Daily dawn–dusk; glasshouses 9am–4pm • Free

Five minutes' walk west of the Historic District, **Oamaru Gardens** offer manicured natural beauty in a streamside setting. The rhododendron dell, fragrant garden and Victorian summerhouse give a sense of the wealth the town once enjoyed.

Janet Frame House

56 Eden St • Nov–April daily 2–4pm • $5; 2hr guided walking tour $50 (includes entry to Janet Frame House) can be booked at the i-SITE

On the gardens' southern edge, the **Janet Frame House** was the modest childhood home of one of New Zealand's greatest writers. She lived here from early school days to leaving for higher education: "I wanted an imagination that would inhabit a world of fact, descend like a shining light upon the ordinary life of Eden Street..."

Even before her death in 2004 the house was being restored to 1930s style; you can explore it, get some insight from the custodian and listen to a marvellous recording of the author reading an extract from *Owls Do Cry*, about the very sofa you'll be sitting on.

Fans of her work may want to follow the **Janet Frame Trail** (free leaflet available from the i-SITE), taking you to locations used in varying degrees of disguise in her books – the former subscription library in the Athenaeum that featured in *Faces In The Water*, or the rubbish dump that formed the symbolic centre of *Owls Do Cry*. Alternatively, the knowledgeable and entertaining local tour guide leads Janet Frame **walking tours** (see p.544).

The penguin colonies

Penguins Crossing bus ($50 for 2hr 30min–3hr; ☎ 0800 304 333, Ⓦ penguinscrossing.co.nz)

Oamaru is unique in having both yellow-eyed and blue **penguin colonies** within walking distance of the town centre. It is usually possible to see both colonies in one evening, since the yellow-eyes tend to come ashore earlier than the blues. Penguins are timid creatures and easily distressed, so keep quiet and still, and do not encroach within 10m of the birds. Once disturbed, the penguins may not return to their nests for several hours, even if they have chicks to feed.

To facilitate your penguin watching, use the door-to-door **Penguins Crossing**, a bus tour with commentary that visits the yellow penguins first, getting you to the blue penguins (entry included) in time for their arrival.

Blue penguin colony

The colony is 15min southeast of the town centre, along Waterfront Rd • Daily: best visited just before dusk; self-guided tour daily 10am–2hr before dark • $25; tour $12; entry/tour combo $32

Blue penguins nest under most of the waterside buildings, and if you sit along the shoreline around dusk you'll probably see a few waddle past. More formal and informative viewing takes place at the **Blue penguin colony**. In the visitor centre there's a chance to see an infrared 24-hour monitor in one of the nest boxes and videos on

9

BLUE PENGUINS

Blue penguins, the smallest of their kind, are found all around the coast of New Zealand, and along the shores of southern Australia, where they are known as little penguins. White on their chests and bellies, they have a thick head-to-tail streak along their back in iridescent indigo-blue. Breeding takes place from May to January, and the parents take it in turns to stay with the eggs during the 36-day incubation period. The newly hatched chicks are protected for the first two or three weeks before both parents go out to sea to meet the increasing demand for food, returning full of fish, which they regurgitate into the chick's mouth. At eight weeks the chicks begin to fledge, but sixty percent die in their first year; the juveniles that do survive usually return to their birthplace. At the end of the breeding season the birds fatten up before coming ashore to moult: over the next three weeks their feathers are not waterproof enough for them to take to the sea and they lose up to half their bodyweight.

blue penguins before being deprived of your cameras and videos and led out to the 350-seat grandstand. Come during the breeding season (June–Dec) and you'll see chicks – and hear them calling to their parents out at sea, hunting for food. When the parents return around dusk, travelling in groups known as rafts, they climb the steep harbour banks and cross in front of the grandstand to their nests. Outside the breeding season, penguins indulge in much less toing and froing, but provide an engaging spectacle nevertheless. In the peak season (Nov to mid-Feb) you might hope to see two hundred penguins in a night, though this might drop to a dozen or so in March, June and August. It can all seem a bit of a circus, so, if you'd prefer a more intimate encounter, try the self-guided **Behind the Scenes** tour, which visits the breeding colony where you should see birds inside nesting boxes, maybe with chicks.

Yellow-eyed penguins
Bushy Beach, reached along Bushy Beach Rd

The much larger **yellow-eyed penguins** nest in smaller numbers but keep more sociable hours, usually coming ashore in late afternoon or early evening; they're best seen between October and February. The birds mainly arrive 2km away at **Bushy Beach**, where a hide enables you to see them making their way across the beach in the morning and early evening.

ARRIVAL AND DEPARTURE
OAMARU

By bus Buses drop off at the corner of Eden and Thames sts.
Destinations Aoraki Mount Cook (3 weekly; 3hr); Christchurch (5–6 daily; 4hr); Dunedin (7–9 daily; 2hr); Omarama (3 weekly; 1hr 45min); Tekapo (4 weekly; 3hr); Timaru (5–6 daily; 1hr); Twizel (7 weekly; 2hr).

INFORMATION AND TOURS

i-SITE 1 Thames St (mid-Dec to March daily 9am–6pm; April to mid-Dec Mon–Fri 9am–5pm, Sat & Sun 10am–4pm; ☎03 434 1656, ⓦvisitoamaru.co.nz). Stocks useful free leaflets and can organize walking tours (see below).
Services There's internet access ($3/hr) at the i-SITE and free access at the Oamaru Public Library, 62 Thames St (Mon–Fri 9.30am–5.30pm, Sat 10am–12.30pm).
Ralph's Rambles ☎03 434 7337. This irrepressible guide leads amusing and highly informative 90min walking tours ($25; 24hr notice needed) of Oamaru; he also runs the Janet Frame walking tour (see p.542).

ACCOMMODATION

Oamaru and the area south towards Dunedin have a wealth of great hostels, and even motel B&B prices are cheaper than many other places in the South Island. Finding any **style of accommodation** is seldom difficult, but it pays to book a day or two ahead from December to March.

Alma Motels SH1, 5km south of town ☎0800 000 644, ⓦalmamotels.co.nz. Ageing motel with functional units and all the expected facilities (electric blankets, a guest laundry, and a trampoline). A bargain. Doubles **$80**

Alpine Motel 285 Thames St ☎0800 272 710, ⓦalpineoamaru.co.nz. Comfortable motel close to the town centre, with ten spacious, updated studio units, some with full kitchens, making them a good choice for families. Doubles $85

Café 469 & Motels 469 Thames Hwy ☎03 437 1443. Set back from the busy approach road to Oamaru behind a traditional daytime café, these three snug one-bedroom motel units have Art Deco styling, off-street parking and free laundry facilities. All rooms open to a flower-filled garden set with picnic tables. Doubles $85

★ **Chillawhile** 1 Frome St ☎03 437 0168, ⓦchillawhile.co.nz. There's a loose, chilled feel to this arty hostel in a rambling house 2km north of the centre. Rooms are dedicated to playing music (with guitar and organ), painting and drumming workshops. Pot-luck dinners are encouraged and dorms are set up with a small sitting area to encourage sociability. Free light breakfast and bus pick-ups. Dorms $29, doubles $58

Criterion Hotel 3 Tyne St ☎0800 259 334, ⓦcriterion .net.nz. Charming Victorian-styled boutique B&B in an atmospheric 1877 pub right in the heart of the historic district, complete with guest kitchen and lounge. A sizeable breakfast is included. Doubles $105, en-suite doubles $135

Kiwiana Cottage 9 Itchen St ☎03 434 5246. If you'd prefer to be self-sufficient, this simple, super-central 1854-built cottage comes with full kitchen facilities and a cosy lounge area. There are reduced rates for longer-term bookings – call ahead or contact the i-SITE for bookings. Cottage $85

Northstar 495a SH1 ☎03 437 1190, ⓦnorthstarmotel .co.nz. Sparkling revamped motel 3km north of the centre with stylish, new units and its own excellent restaurant (lunch/dinner mains $18/29), also open to non-guests. Doubles $120

★ **Oamaru Creek** 24 Reed St ☎03 434 1190, ⓦoamarucreek.co.nz. Warm, friendly homestay B&B in a former maternity home, with spacious and tastefully decorated rooms (some en-suite), fantastic professionally cooked organic breakfasts and sociable owners who will try to put you on the right trail to a good time. Doubles $130, en-suite doubles $140

Oamaru Top 10 Holiday Park 30 Chelmer St ☎0800 280 202, ⓦoamarutop10.co.nz. In a lovely sheltered setting close to Oamaru Gardens with a good range of accommodation. Camping $40, cabins $65, motels units $105

★ **Old Bones Backpackers** Beach Rd, Kakanui ☎03 434 8115, ⓦoldbones.co.nz. Gorgeous, purpose-built, upscale backpackers on the coast 6km south of town (follow Wharfe Rd) with just eight doubles and twins opening onto a spacious, comfortable and TV-free lounge/kitchen. Everything is to the highest standard, and there's free internet and underfloor heating in the bedrooms. Closed May–Sept. Singles $45, doubles $90

YHA Red Kettle 2 Reed St ☎03 434 5008, ⓦyha.co.nz. Small and pleasant old-style hostel close to the town centre with five-bed dorms and a couple of private rooms. Closed May–Sept. Dorms $28, doubles $56

EATING, DRINKING AND ENTERTAINMENT

Most of Oamaru's **eating and drinking** takes place on and around Thames Street. If you're planning an outing to Moeraki Boulders, don't miss dining at the fabulous *Fleur's Place* (p.547). Heading north, try lunch at the *Riverstone Kitchen* (p.546). Oamaru's farmers' market (Sunday 9.30am–1pm; ⓦoamarufarmersmarket.co.nz) is held opposite the *Loan & Merc* (below).

Criterion Bar Criterion Hotel, 3 Tyne St ☎0800 259 334, ⓦcriterion.net.nz. With the tenor of a Victorian English pub there's a long wooden bar, some good old-fashioned beer (notably London Porter and Emersons traditional ale), plus filling, inexpensive food, including bangers and mash and blue cod (mains $12.50–23.50). Daily lunch & dinner.

Dilaans 263 Thames St. Good-value Turkish takeaway and café. Slather a couple of sauces over the chicken shish and wash it down with an apple tea (dishes $10–21). Tues–Sun 11am–10.30pm.

★ **Loan & Merc** 14 Harbour St ☎03 434 9905, ⓦloanandmerc.co.nz. The historic Loan & Mercantile building (p.541) is a magnificent backdrop for this carvery restaurant newly opened by Kiwi restaurateur Fleur Sullivan, who put the area on the dining map with *Fleur's Place* (p.547) at Moeraki. Ploughman's lunches are the focus during the day, while the night-time carvery includes

three daily roasts as well as fish (mains $20–32.50). Both include home-made chutneys, pickles and preserves which you can also buy to take away. Daily lunch & dinner.

★ **Penguin Club** Emulsion Lane ⓦthepenguinclub .co.nz. A legendary back-alley venue bar hosting Friday jam nights (from 8pm), poetry, theatre and gigs by Kiwi touring bands ($10–30 cover charge): almost everyone of note in the Kiwi music biz has played here. From the *Criterion Hotel*, walk down Harbour St, and turn left down an unprepossessing alley. Entry price is low, and if you pick up a programme of events from the i-SITE you'll be let in at the members' price. Hours vary.

Portside 2 Waterfront Rd ☎03 434 3400. Stylish, modern restaurant/bar by the blue penguin colony where the airy interior is a fine place to dine, particularly on seafood dishes such as salmon bouillabaisse (mains $19.50–29.50). Or just come for a sundowner on the deck overlooking the sea. Thurs–Tues 11am–late.

9

Short Black 45 Thames St ☎ 03 434 6406. Contemporary café serving superbly thick, ice-cold smoothies (including with soy milk) and generously proportioned all-day breakfasts and lunchtime fare such as BLTs (dishes $5.50–16.50). Mon–Fri 7am–4pm, Sat 8.30am–3pm.

★ **Riverstone Kitchen** 1431 SH1, 19km north of Oamaru, 66km south of Timaru ☎ 03 431 3505, ⓦ riverstonekitchen.co.nz. Some of the finest café food around, served in an uncluttered country setting with it's own produce-filled gardens. It's best for lunch when you're passing and/or browsing its deli, though they also serve sumptuous bistro dinners, such as deep-fried zucchini flowers with four cheeses, a ribeye with sautéed potatoes and tea-smoked almonds, and drunken chocolate torte with rum and raisin ice cream (mains $28–29). Daily lunch, Thurs–Sun dinner.

Whitestone Cheese 3 Torridge St ☎ 03 434 8098 ⓦ whitestonecheese.co.nz. This cheese factory has a viewing gallery at the back (best Mon–Fri before noon) and offers five-cheese tasting platters for $5 as well as free samples of its daily specials. In addition to its café (dishes $4–12), its shop sells picnic supplies including Whitestone's famed soft, creamy Windsor Blue cheese. Café daily 8.30am–2pm, shop daily 9am–5pm.

Totara Estate

SH1, 8km south of Oamaru • Daily Sept–May 9am–5pm • $9 • ☎ 03 434 7169, ⓦ totaraestate.co.nz

It's worth taking half an hour or so to look around **Totara Estate**, the birthplace of the New Zealand meat industry. Until the early 1880s New Zealand was a major wool exporter, but no one knew what to do with all the surplus meat. Meanwhile, Britain's burgeoning industrial cities were on the brink of starvation. The solution came when the Australian and New Zealand Land Company pioneered refrigeration on a sailing ship, and, in 1882, the three-masted *Dunedin* was refitted with coke-driven freezers and filled with lamb from Totara Estate. The estate is now a grassy historic park built around solid whitestone buildings containing a small museum along with a harness room, stables, granary barn and blacksmith's forge. The foundations and partial remains of the original slaughterhouse and carcass shed form the basis of a modern reconstruction that gives an idea of what work was like here.

Moeraki Boulders

SH1, 40km south of Oamaru • Access to the boulders is either by a 300m walk along the beach from a DOC parking area, or more immediately via a short private trail ($2 in the honesty box at any hour), though it's free for patrons of the adjacent café (daily: Oct–April 8am–6pm; May–Sept 9am–5pm)

The large, grey spherical **Moeraki Boulders** (some almost 2m in diameter) lie partially submerged in the sandy beach at the tide line, about 2km before you hit Moeraki village. Their smooth skins hide honeycomb centres, which are revealed in some of the broken specimens. The boulders once lay deep in the mudstone cliffs behind the beach and, as these were eroded, out fell the smooth boulders, with further erosion exposing a network of surface veins. The boulders were originally formed around a central core of carbonate of lime crystals that attracted minerals from their surroundings – a process that started sixty million years ago, when muddy sediment containing shell and plant fragments accumulated on the sea floor. They range in size from small pellets to large round rocks, though the smaller ones have all been taken over the years, leaving only those too heavy to shift.

Maori named the boulders Te Kaihinaki (food baskets), believing them to have been washed ashore from the wreck of a canoe whose occupants were seeking *pounamu*. The seaward reef near Shag Point (see opposite) was the hull of the canoe, and just beyond it stands a prominent rock, the vessel's petrified navigator. Some of the Moeraki Boulders were *hinaki* (baskets), the more spherical were water-carrying gourds and the irregular-shaped rocks farther down the beach were *kumara* from the canoe's food store. The survivors among the crew were transformed at daybreak into hills overlooking the beach.

Moeraki village

The picturesque and tranquil fishing village of **MOERAKI** offers boulder access along the beach (they're 2km to the north) and a chance to see yellow-eyed penguins up close. Drive to the white wooden lighthouse (1km off SH1 then 5km along an unsealed road) then follow signs down a path which leads to a hide, overlooking the beach where yellow-eyed penguins emerge after a hard day's fishing (3.30pm–nightfall), and seals loll. A second path leads to a *pa* site, its importance explained on a panel nearby.

ARRIVAL
MOERAKI VILLAGE

By bus Most buses will drop you on SH1, 1.5km from the village, but Coastline Tours (📞 03 434 7744) will drop you in the centre on their Oamaru–Dunedin run.

ACCOMMODATION

Moeraki Beach Motels Corner of Beach and Haven sts 📞 03 439 4862, 🌐 moerakibeachmotels.co.nz. The four units here face the bay, and the owners also manage a number of holiday homes in the village. Doubles $100
Moeraki Village Holiday Park 114 Haven St 📞 03 439 4759, 🌐 moerakivillageholidaypark.co.nz. Well located above the boat harbour and just a 50m walk to the beach, this campsite has a range of accommodation options. Camping $29, cabins $55, tourist flats $95, motel units $108
Olive Grove Lodge & Holiday Park SH1, 11km north of Moeraki Boulders 📞 03 439 5830, 🌐 olivebranch .co.nz. Family-run and TV-free, *Olive Grove* occupies a bend in a river with good swimming holes. Along with a hot tub, infrared sauna and hammocks there's a selection of brilliantly decorated rooms and plenty of riverside space. Closed June–Aug. Camping/person $12, dorms $25, doubles $60, en-suite doubles $70
Three Bays 39 Cardiff St 📞 03 439 4520, 🌐 threebays .co.nz. A delightful self-contained unit set high on the hill with great long views over the town towards the Moeraki Boulders and ocean. Unit $170

EATING

⭐ **Fleur's Place** The Old Jetty 📞 03 439 4480, 🌐 fleursplace.com. By far the best eating in Moeraki is at this marvellous converted corrugated-iron shack, which lures sophisticates from Dunedin (plus the likes of Gwyneth Paltrow and Rick Stein) for exceptional seafood meals with fish straight off the boat (mains $30–38), a good wine selection or an excellent coffee. Dinner bookings are essential and this could be your chance to sample muttonbird. Alternatively, dine outside by the waterfront on dishes including fish and chips with shoestring fries and home-made tartare sauce, or opt for a phenomenal seafood chowder in its own bread basket "bowl" from Fleur's on-site takeaway caravan (dishes $12–16). Wed–Sun 9am–11pm.

Shag Point and the Matakaea Scenic Reserve

Just over 10km south of Moeraki village, a side road runs 3km to the windswept promontory of **Shag Point** and the **Matakaea Scenic Reserve**, where the rocks are often slathered with seals and a viewing platform allows distant views of yellow-eyed penguins.

Palmerston

The small town of **PALMERSTON**, 9km south of Shag Point, is home to not much more than a hilltop monument that marks the work of **John McKenzie**, the minister of Lands, Agriculture and Immigration in the early 1890s, who laid the groundwork for modern farming by breaking up the vast holdings of absentee landlords, making them available to new immigrants.

Palmerston marks the junction of two routes: the "Pigroot" (SH85) inland to the Maniototo and the historic goldfield heartland of Central Otago; and SH1 running 52km south to Dunedin.

Central South Island

553 Hanmer Springs and the Lewis Pass

556 Porter's Pass and the Craigieburn Range

560 Arthur's Pass National Park

563 The South Canterbury foothills

569 The Mackenzie Country

BOULDERS AT KURA TAWHITI

Central South Island

The Central South Island is one of the most varied and visually stunning areas in New Zealand, with expansive pasturelands, dense native forests and a history rich in tales of human endeavour, tinged with the toughness and idiosyncrasies of the area's settlers. The region's defining feature is the icy, white sawtooth ridge of the Southern Alps that forms the South Island's central north–south spine and peaks at New Zealand's loftiest summit, 3754m Aoraki/Mount Cook. Summers are generally hot and dry with long days that sear the grasslands a tinder-dry yellow-brown. In winter, snow supplies numerous ski-fields. These alpine conditions foster unique plants and wildlife, including the Mount Cook lily, the largest white mountain daisy in the world, and the mischievous kea – the world's only alpine parrot.

From Christchurch to Westport, the forested **Lewis Pass** road provides access to the tranquil spa town of **Hanmer Springs** before passing the more rustic hot pools at **Maruia Springs**. Further south, both road and rail head through the spectacular **Arthur's Pass National Park**, with its abundance of day-walks and longer trails.

South of Christchurch, roads lead across the Canterbury Plains towards the small foothill settlement of **Methven**, the base for **Mount Hutt**-bound skiers and summertime walkers exploring **Mount Somers** – often dry when Arthur's Pass is wet and enveloped in cloud.

The southern half of the region leaves behind the rolling hills for the sun-scorched grasslands of the **Mackenzie Country**, an area renowned for massive sheep runs and the unearthly blues of its glacier-fed lakes, **Tekapo** and **Pukaki**. The mightiest of the Southern Alps form an imperious backdrop. **Aoraki/Mount Cook Village**, huddled at the foot of the mountain, is the starting point of numerous walks, glacial lake trips and heli-trekking and heli-skiing. An alternative base for forays to Aoraki/Mount Cook is the former hydro construction town of **Twizel**, less than an hour's drive south, surrounded by dams, control gates and water channels.

Yet further south, the road toward Wanaka and Queenstown passes through New Zealand's gliding capital, **Omarama**, before heading over the dramatic Lindis Pass.

GETTING AROUND

By bus Bus routes centre on Christchurch with services north to Hanmer Springs (but not onwards over Lewis Pass to Nelson), west to Arthur's Pass and Greymouth and southwest to Methven. Atomic, InterCity/Newmans/Grea Sights, NakedBus and Southern Link (☎0508 458 835 ⊕ southernlinkbus.co.nz) thread down through the

Hanmer Springs outdoor activities p.555
Ski-fields along the Arthur's Pass road p.557
Craigieburn hikes p.559
Kea: New Zealand's alpine trickster p.560
Walks and tramps around Arthur's Pass p.562
Activities around Methven p.565
Mount Somers Track p.567

Searching for Edoras p.568
James McKenzie p.570
Skiing in the Mackenzie Country p.572
Tours and activities in Tekapo p.573
Sir Edmund Hillary p.576
Aoraki/Mount Cook tours and activities pp.578–579
The Waitaki hydro scheme p.581
Gliding around Omarama p.583

AMONG THE ICEBERGS AT TASMAN GLACIER

Highlights

❶ Skiing the Central South Island Mount Hutt is a great starting point for some of the country's best, most reasonably priced and least-crowded slopes. **See p.557 & p.564**

❷ Hiking around Arthur's Pass Walking in this wild, rugged national park offers a jaw-dropping insight into a uniquely beautiful alpine landscape. **See p.562**

❸ Rafting the Rangitata Raft some of the best and bounciest white water in the country on trips from Peel Forest, Geraldine or Christchurch. **See p.568**

❹ Stargazing above Lake Tekapo After taking in the lake's incredible opaque blue waters, gaze up at the astonishingly clear star-filled night sky from Mount John Observatory. **See p.573**

❺ Exploring Aoraki/Mount Cook's glacial lakes Get up close to the icebergs with a boat cruise or closer still on a kayak trip on the glacial lakes beneath the country's highest peak. **See p.578**

❻ Gliding over Omarama Experience the thrill of silent flying at New Zealand's gliding capital, Omarama. **See p.583**

HIGHLIGHTS ARE MARKED ON THE MAP ON P.552

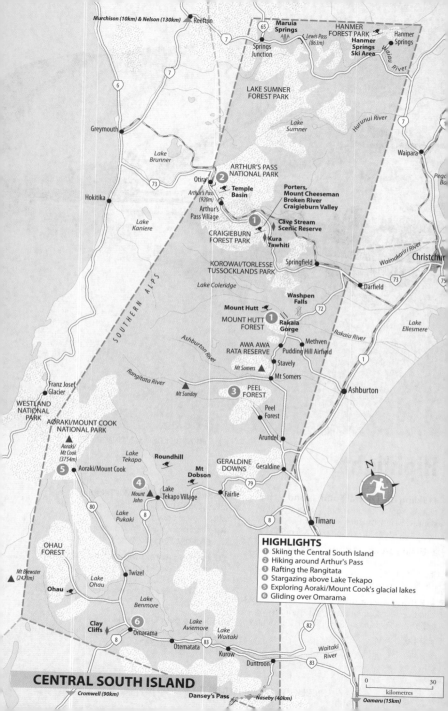

CENTRAL SOUTH ISLAND

Murchison (10km) & Nelson (130km)
Reefton

Maruia Springs
65
Springs Junction
7
Lewis Pass (863m)

HANMER FOREST PARK
Hanmer Springs Ski Area
Hanmer Springs
Waiau River

LAKE SUMNER FOREST PARK
Lake Sumner
Hurunui River
7
Waipara
Pegc Ba

Greymouth

Lake Brunner
73

Hokitika
Lake Kaniere

Otira
2
ARTHUR'S PASS NATIONAL PARK
Temple Basin
Arthur's Pass (920m)
Arthur's Pass Village
1
Porters, Mount Cheeseman Broken River Craigieburn Valley
Cave Stream Scenic Reserve
CRAIGIEBURN FOREST PARK
Kura Tawhiti
Springfield
Waimakariri River
Christchur
73

KOROWAI/TORLESSE TUSSOCKLANDS PARK
Lake Coleridge
Darfield
75

SOUTHERN ALPS

Mount Hutt
Washpen Falls
72
1
MOUNT HUTT FOREST
Rakaia Gorge
Methven
Rakaia River
Lake Ellesmere

AWA AWA RATA RESERVE
Ashburton River
Pudding Hill Airfield
Stavely
Mt Somers
Mt Somers
1

Franz Josef Glacier
Rangitata River
Mt Sunday
3
PEEL FOREST
Peel Forest
Ashburton

WESTLAND NATIONAL PARK

Arundel

AORAKI/MOUNT COOK NATIONAL PARK
Aoraki/Mt Cook (3754m)
5
Aoraki/Mount Cook
Lake Tekapo
Roundhill
GERALDINE DOWNS
Geraldine

Mt Dobson
4
Mount John
Lake Tekapo Village
Fairlie
79

80
Lake Pukaki
8
N

OHAU FOREST
Mt Brewster (2428m)
Twizel
8
Timaru

Ohau
Lake Ohau
Lake Benmore

Clay Cliffs
6
Omarama
Lake Aviemore
Lake Waitaki
82

8
Otematata
83
Kurow
Waitaki River
Duntroon
83

Cromwell (90km)
Dansey's Pass
Naseby (40km)
Oamaru (15km)

HIGHLIGHTS
1 Skiing the Central South Island
2 Hiking around Arthur's Pass
3 Rafting the Rangitata
4 Stargazing above Lake Tekapo
5 Exploring Aoraki/Mount Cook's glacial lakes
6 Gliding over Omarama

0   30
kilometres

ackenzie Country towards Wanaka and Queenstown. nly Great Sights goes directly to Aoraki/Mount Cook so it often more convenient (and usually cheaper) to travel to ekapo and change onto The Cook Connection (☎ 0800 266 26, ⓦ cookconnect.co.nz) which links Aoraki/Mount Cook

with Twizel and Lake Tekapo.

By train The wonderfully scenic *TranzAlpine* (see box, p.517) is the only train serving the region. It traverses the mountains daily travelling from Christchurch to Greymouth via Arthur's Pass in 4hr 30min.

Hanmer Springs and the Lewis Pass

he most northerly of the cross-mountain routes, SH7, crosses the **Lewis Pass** following n ancient Maori and early Pakeha trade route. A side road spurs off to the spa town of **Hanmer Springs**, which is also a popular base for summer walks and winter sports at he nearby **Hanmer Springs Ski Area**. Some 60km further west, you cross the **Lewis Pass** nd drop down to the steaming thermal waters of **Maruia Springs**.

Hanmer Springs

bout 140km north of Christchurch, a side road heads 9km north off SH7 to **HANMER SPRINGS** at the edge of a broad, fertile plain snuggled against the Southern lps foothills. Rainwater seeping through fractures in the rocks of the Hanmer Mountains absorbs various minerals and is warmed by the earth's natural heat, before ising to the surface as the springs that made the town famous. Everything centres on ak-lined Amuri Avenue, which runs past the springs, the i-SITE, shops and the shady ark that gives the town its quiet, sheltered feel.

Hanmer Springs Thermal Pools and Spa

Amuri Ave • Daily 10am–9pm; café Mon–Fri & Sun 10am–5.30pm, Sat 10am–8pm • Pools $18; two pool entries on same day $23; wel rental $5; waterslides $10 extra for unlimited rides; private pools $28 each for 30min (minimum 2 people, including general entry) • ☎ 03 315 0000 for pools, ☎ 03 315 0029 for The Spa, ⓦ hanmersprings.co.nz

Whatever the weather, it's a pleasure to wallow at this modernised open-air complex where you can lounge on the lawns around twelve landscaped thermal pools ranging rom 33°C to 42°C, as well as two freshwater swimming pools kept around 29°C. rtificial streams link the pools, providing great places to relax. Add in three waterslides one that swirls you around what looks like a giant toilet bowl), half a dozen private ools and the *Garden House Café* and you could stay all day. It's at its best in the evening hen the crowds thin and the sun sets. Next door, the stylish **Spa**, New Zealand's rgest, offers pampering treatments including water exfoliation (40min; $140).

Queen Mary Hospital Historic Reserve

ain entrance on Amuri Ave • Open access; guided 1hr tours Nov–March Sun at noon • Free; guided tours $2

o older Kiwis "I'm off to Hanmer" may mean a day at the hot pools, but could equally efer to time spent drying out at the Queen Mary Hospital, New Zealand's most famous esidential alcohol and drugs rehab centre, which closed in 2003. It started life helping ecuperate shell-shocked soldiers during World War I and spent time as a voluntary ental institution. The buildings are closed to the public but you can wander round he leafy grounds admiring ghostly buildings such as the original **Soldiers Block**, where sunlight and fresh air" were considered key to recovery, the Art Deco **Rutherford Ward**, nd the 1928 **Nurses' Hostel**, still with an "Out Of Bounds To Clients" sign on the door.

Hanmer Springs Ski Area

f Clarence Valley Rd, 17km north of Hanmer Springs • Generally open mid-July to Sept • Tows $60 • ⓦ skihanmer.co.nz

he tiny **Hanmer Springs Ski Area** has just one rope tow and New Zealand's longest oma-style lift, with one beginner run, six intermediate and five advanced runs. The ccess road is notoriously dicey, so take the **shuttle bus** ($99 return) operated by

Hanmer Adventure (see box opposite), where you can also rent ski gear. On the mountain, **Robinson Lodge** (see opposite) has gear rentals and basic accommodation. The **Mount Lyford Ski-field** (see box, p.505), 60km to the northeast, is also accessible from Hanmer via SH70.

ARRIVAL AND DEPARTURE   HANMER SPRINGS

By bus Buses stop on Amuri Ave close to the i-SITE. The most reliable services are Hanmer Backpackers & Shuttle (☎03 315 7196, ⓦhanmerbackpackers.co.nz) who run to both Christchurch (twice daily; $25) and Kaikoura (Mon, Wed & Fri; $25). Hanmer Connection (☎0800 242 663,

ⓦatsnz.com) also run between here and Christchurc twice daily ($33). At the time of writing there were n bus services over the Lewis Pass to Nelson.

Destinations Christchurch (4 daily; 2hr); Kaikoura (3 weekl 2hr).

INFORMATION

i-SITE 40 Amuri Ave, next to the hot pools (daily 10am–5pm; ☎03 315 0020, ⓦhanmersprings.co.nz). Helpful for local information and bookings, and to obtain the excellent *Hanmer Springs Walks* and *Hanmer Springs*

Mountain Bike Tracks leaflets ($3 each).

Services The i-SITE contains a small bank (Mon–F 10am–2pm), and there's an ATM on Amuri Ave outsid the 4 Square supermarket.

ACCOMMODATION

The town has a good spread of accommodation but is a popular weekend getaway so year-round it's worth booking ahead.

★ **Cheltenham House** 13 Cheltenham St ☎03 315 7545, ⓦcheltenham.co.nz. The best B&B in town, with four large, gracious rooms set in a 1930s house with a snooker room, and two cottages in the lovingly tended garden. Evening drinks, spa and wi-fi are all included, and an excellent breakfast is served in your room. They also

have a separate modern self-contained four-bedroor house. B&B double $235, house $330

Greenacres 84 Conical Hill Rd ☎0800 822 26 ⓦgreenacresmotel.co.nz. There's a slightly retro qualit to this very quiet motel at the foot of Conical Hill. One and two-bedroom chalets come ranged around a centr

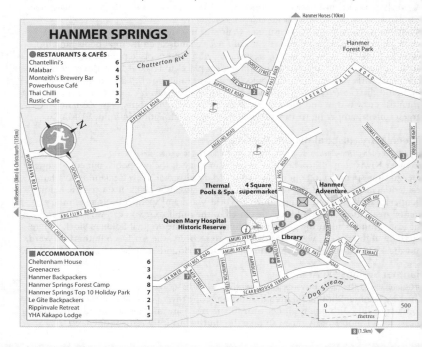

HANMER SPRINGS

● RESTAURANTS & CAFÉS	
Chantellini's	6
Malabar	4
Monteith's Brewery Bar	5
Powerhouse Café	1
Thai Chilli	3
Rustic Cafe	2

■ ACCOMMODATION	
Cheltenham House	6
Greenacres	3
Hanmer Backpackers	4
Hanmer Springs Forest Camp	8
Hanmer Springs Top 10 Holiday Park	7
Le Gite Backpackers	2
Rippinvale Retreat	1
YHA Kakapo Lodge	5

HANMER SPRINGS OUTDOOR ACTIVITIES

Hanmer has plenty to keep you entertained, most conveniently on the edge of town, where black pines, Norway spruce, Douglas firs and assorted deciduous trees of the **Hanmer Forest Park** offer great hiking and biking. Slightly further afield there's great horse riding and a bunch of activities at Thrillseekers on SH7.

HIKING

Conical Hill (2km return; 1hr; 150m ascent). A fairly easy but rewarding walk through exotic forest to a great viewpoint over town and the surrounding hills.
Waterfall Track (2.5km return; 2hr 30min; 400m ascent). An attractive walk through mountain beech forest climbing fairly steeply to the 41m-high Dog Stream Waterfall. The path starts at the end of Mullans Rd.

BIKING

Hanmer Adventure 20 Conical Hill Rd ☎ 0800 368 7386, ⓦ hanmeradventure.co.nz. Rents bikes ($45/day) to explore the forest's gravel roads and twisting singletrack. Alternatively, the centre can transport you to the top of Jacks Pass for a self-guided, mostly downhill ride back with only a slight ascent over Jollies Pass ($99, including a hot pools pass).

BUNGY JUMPING, RAFTING AND JETBOATING

Thrillseekers Near the turn-off from SH7, 9km south of town ☎ 03 315 7046, ⓦ thrillseekers.co.nz. The Waiau Ferry Bridge is home to all manner of activities including scenic two-hour-plus rafting trips through the Grade II Waiau River Canyon (70–90min on the water; $149), jetboat rides through the steep-sided gorges of the Waiau River (30min; $115), bungy jumps ($169 including T-shirt) from a 35m platform midway across the Waiau Ferry Bridge, and quad biking (2hr; $129), with combo packages available.

HORSE RIDING

Alpine Horse Safaris Hawarden, 60km southwest of town ☎ 03 314 4293, ⓦ alpinehorse.co.nz. Short rides are available (2hr for $65, 4hr for $95) but this is really a place for serious 3–10-day cross-country trips (from $938) across a working high-country station and even down to Tekapo, often staying in musterers' huts and eating around a camp fire. Check the website for trip schedule.
Hanmer Horses 187 Rogerson Rd, 5km northwest of town off Jacks Pass Rd ☎ 0800 873 546, ⓦ hanmerhorses.co.nz. You'll often need to cross a couple of streams to access rides ($59/hr, $99/2hr 30min), which are customized to the group's ability.

lawn, there's a hot tub ($4/person) and free internet in the office (and pay wi-fi throughout). $125
★ **Hanmer Backpackers** 41 Conical Hill Rd ☎ 03 315 7196, ⓦ hanmerbackpackers.co.nz. Heart-warmingly cosy A-frame chalet-style hostel bang in town with a snug, book-filled, TV-free lounge, hot water bottles, spotless facilities, sociable BBQ patio and lots of free treats such as fresh fruit. Limited camping $16, camping for two $25, dorms $27, doubles $58, en suites $70
Le Gîte Backpackers 3 Devon St ☎ 03 315 5111, ⓦ legite.co.nz. Relaxed and tastefully decorated hostel in a couple of converted houses and a modern chalet, around a 10min walk from the centre, opening to a large garden with a giant swing-sofa. There's plenty of space for tents and campervan parking. Camping $15, dorms $28, doubles $64, en suites $76
Rippinvale Retreat 68 Rippingale Rd ☎ 0800 373 098, ⓦ hanmersprings.net.nz. Upmarket lodge on the edge of town with just two suites, both beautifully furnished and each with private courtyard and fresh flowers. Breakfast (with mostly home-grown and organic ingredients) is served in your room and there's a spa pool and outdoor fireplace in the spacious grounds. $355
Robinson Lodge Hanmer Springs Ski Area ⓦ ski hanmer.co.nz. During the season, ski-field visitors can stay in the simple backpacker accommodation in the lodge that also offers cooking facilities. Bring all your food and bedding with you. Per person $30
YHA Kakapo Lodge 14 Amuri Ave ☎ 03 315 7472, ⓦ kakapolodge.co.nz. Large, sun-filled modern associate YHA hostel opening to communal balconies and courtyard areas. It's welcoming but a little stark. Dorms $28, rooms $66, en suites $90, motel units $100

CAMPING

Hanmer Springs Forest Camp 243 Jollies Pass Rd, 2km east of town ☎ 03 315 7202, ⓦ hanmerforestcamp .co.nz. A community campsite with no powered sites, but plenty of well-maintained budget cabins, plus space for tents. Camping $12, cabins $30

10

Hanmer Springs Top 10 Holiday Park 5 Hanmer Springs Rd ☎0800 904 545, ⓦmountainviewtop10.co.nz. The closest holiday park to the town centre, with a range of roofed accommodation, and tent sites overlooking a riverside reserve. Camping $16, cabins $75, kitchen cabins $85, self-contained units $138, motel units $160

EATING AND DRINKING

★ **Chantellini's** 11 Jollies Pass Rd ☎03 315 7667, ⓦchantellinis.com. With French kitchen and front-of-house staff, this classy but relaxed café and restaurant is open in the day for the likes of eggs Benedict ($16) and *croque monsieur* ($12), either in the garden or the elegant rooms. The table d'hôte lunches (not Sat; $30) and dinners (not Sat; $30 or $50) are excellent, and in winter you shouldn't miss high tea ($25; with champagne $30), served on three-tier plates. Daily 10am–10.30pm.

Malabar 5 Conical Hill Rd ☎03 315 7754, ⓦmalabar.co.nz. Flashy fusion restaurant with an adventurous menu featuring modern twists on dishes from Asia and the subcontinent such as rack of Indian lamb ($36) or five-spice pork belly ($33). Breakfast and lunch are in a more standard Kiwi style though they do an Indian breakfast of vegetable curry, two parathas and a lassi ($19). Daily 8.30am–10pm or later.

Monteith's Brewery Bar 47 Amuri Ave ☎03 315 5133, ⓦmbbh.co.nz. The town's liveliest bar, all timber and river stones, with reliable meals such as warm spinach and feta salad ($22) and lamb marinated in red wine ($32). Daily 9am–10pm or later.

★ **Powerhouse Café** 8 Jacks Pass Rd ☎03 315 5252. Funky modern café in a 1926 building that once housed a diesel generator, serving the best coffee in town (organic Christchurch-roasted Hummingbird), mouth-watering and often gluten-free counter food (the Thai fishcakes are a house speciality), decadent brunches of French toast, kedgeree, oatmeal and lemon pancakes with hazelnut syrup ($14–18), and filling lunches such as tropical bouillabaisse with coconut milk, and calamari salad on organic soba noodles ($22). Daily 8am–3pm & Sat 6.30–10pm.

Rustic Café 8 Conical Hill Rd ☎03 315 7274. Great little tapas restaurant with small plates of tasty treats such as pan-fried chorizo with roasted capsicum, battered monkfish or mini samosa ($11 each or four for $40). Daily 9.30am–9.30pm; closed Tues & Wed in winter.

Thai Chilli 12a Conical Hill Rd ☎03 315 5188. Budget Thai in quantities large enough to take away for later. Mains $15–20, and $10 lunch specials such as Penang curry. No licence or BYO. Mon–Sat 11am–2pm & 4.30–9.30pm.

Lewis Pass

West of the Hanmer Springs turn-off, SH7 continues its climb towards the 907m **Lewis Pass**, 65km to the west, with low-yielding grassland with broom (blazing yellow in the summer), spiky matagouri, manuka and kanuka giving way to red and silver beech forest. To explore the area on foot, pick up DOC's *Lake Sumner/Lewis Pass Recreation* leaflet from the Hanmer Springs i-SITE, which outlines almost two dozen day and multi-day **walks**.

Maruia Springs

SH7, 75km northwest of Hanmer Springs • Daily 8am–7.30pm • Pools $19; private baths $26/45min; towel rental $6 • ☎03 523 8840, ⓦmaruiasprings.co.nz

West of Lewis Pass it's a further 8km to **Maruia Springs**, a blissful spa grouped around Japanese-style men's and women's bathhouses, private bathhouses and natural-rock outdoor **hot pools**, whose steaming mineral waters range from black to milky white.

ACCOMMODATION

LEWIS PASS

Maruia Springs Resort ☎03 523 8840, ⓦmaruiasprings.co.nz. Simple but well-equipped rooms opening to shared or private balconies overlooking the gardens and mountains. Rates include access to the springs and its restaurant serves Japanese- and European-style meals (breakfast $11–19; dinner mains mostly $20–30). $180

Porter's Pass and the Craigieburn Range

Both the *TranzAlpine* train and the SH73 (promoted as the Great Alpine Highway) from Christchurch to Arthur's Pass and the West Coast thread across the fertile Canterbury Plains beside the braided Waimakariri River before crossing Porter's Pass and dropping into a beautiful region alongside the Craigieburn Range. The road then passes the otherworldly boulders of **Kura Tawhiti** (Castle Hill Conservation Area) and the **Cave Stream** tunnel walk, while side roads wind up to various club-style ski-fields.

Springfield

From Christchurch the route is virtually flat for 70km west to **SPRINGFIELD** a lowland village that's the main base for four nearby ski-fields (see box below), as well as high-speed boat trips down the narrow, clear waters and waterfalls of **Waimakariri Gorge**.

10

Rewi Alley Memorial Park

SH73 • Open access • Free

A Chinese-style garden **memorial** beside SH73 remembers Springfield's best-loved son, writer, social reformer and unofficial ambassador for China, **Rewi Alley** (1897–1987).

SKI-FIELDS ALONG THE ARTHUR'S PASS ROAD

The five ski-fields listed below (from east to west along SH73) are easily accessible from the highway, four of them in the Craigieburn Range and one, Temple Basin, around 50km further west above Arthur's Pass. They predominantly offer traditional, inexpensive, Kiwi ski-club-style winter sports with spectacular views, reliable snow and virtually no queues. There are no gondolas, cable cars or chairlifts: T-bars, platter lifts and "nutcracker" rope tows are the go. Most have **equipment rental** and some offer on-field **accommodation**. The season generally runs from July to September, although October is often good; for snow conditions check ⓦ snow.co.nz.

TICKETS, PASSES AND TRANSPORT

All fields offer their own season tickets, though many go for the multi-mountain **Chill6 Pass** ($1195; $770 if bought before May; ⓦ chillout.co.nz), which covers all the fields below plus Mount Olympus. The Chill11 Pass ($1395; $855 if bought before May) additionally covers Hanmer Springs, Mount Lyford, Roundhill and three other fields. *Smylies* (see p.558) in Springfield runs regular **shuttles** to Porters and other fields; check their website for prices.

THE SKI-FIELDS

Porters 96km west of Christchurch, off SH73 via a 6km unsealed road ⓣ 03 318 4002, ⓦ skiporters .co.nz. The region's main commercial field with the longest single run in the southern hemisphere, easy access and good learners' packages. A free shuttle runs from the chain-fitting area to the main car park (bookings essential). Expansion plans (to be developed 2013 onwards) look set to make this the biggest field in the northern South Island with a sealed road, alpine village and gondola lift opening up Crystal Valley. Runs: 2 beginner; 3 intermediate; 9 advanced. Lift pass $82

Mount Cheeseman 112km from Christchurch along SH73 ⓣ 03 344 3247, ⓦ mtcheeseman.co .nz. Well-appointed family-oriented field with good facilities, a friendly atmosphere and a wide variety of runs for intermediates, plus off-piste for those with greater experience. Runs: 2 beginner; 3 intermediate; 8 advanced. Lift passes $69

Broken River 120km from Christchurch at the end of a 6km access road, off SH73 ⓣ 03 318 8713, ⓦ brokenriver.co.nz. An excellent intermediate field with good powder until late in the season, occasional night skiing and fine boarding. Runs: 2 beginner; 7 intermediate; 10 advanced. Lift passes $65, night pass $40. A free inclinator (passenger-carrying goods lift) runs from the car park to the ticket office. It's possible to ski between Broken River and Craigieburn.

Craigieburn Valley 120km out of Christchurch and another 6km up a side road ⓣ 03 318 8711, ⓦ craigieburn.co.nz. This thrill-seeking field has three rope tows accessing the mostly steep runs. No ski hire. Runs: 0 beginner; 6 intermediate; 15 advanced. Lift passes $68

Temple Basin SH73, 4km west of Arthur's Pass ⓣ 03 377 7788, ⓦ templebasin.co.nz. Renowned among snowboarders for its 430m drop and great off-piste for those who know their stuff. Floodlit for night skiing, it offers a variety of runs and basic, on-field accommodation. From the car park it's an hour's walk up to the ski-field, though there's a goods lift for your gear. The *Mountain House* (p.561) runs shuttles here ($25 one-way for 1–6 people). Runs: 6 beginner; 10 intermediate; 8 advanced. Lift passes $67

He spent 60 years in China where he is much revered for starting the Gung Ho ("working together") cooperative movement. His life story is told (in English and Mandarin) in a small pavilion.

INFORMATION AND ACTIVITIES

Tourist information The Station 73 Café (see below) acts as an ad-hoc information centre.

Rubicon Valley Horse Treks ☎ 0508 257 222 or ☎ 03 318 8886, ⓦ rubiconvalley.co.nz. Offers some of the best-value horse trekking around, from a gentle farm trek (1hr; $50) to a mountain trail ride following a musterers' trail (4hr 30min; $250). Pick-ups in Springfield.

Waimak Alpine Jet Rubicon Rd ☎ 0800 263 626,

ⓦ waimakalpinejet.co.nz. Shallow braided sections, the narrow Waimakariri Gorge, 360-degree spins and a good deal of local lore make these jetboat trips excellent value for money. The route partly follows the *TranzAlpine* train line. Advance bookings essential (online). The Canyon Safari (1hr; $115) is the one to go for, but the Adventure Tour (30min; $85) covers the essentials.

ACCOMMODATION AND EATING

Kowai Pass Reserve Campground Domain Rd ☎ 03 818 4887. Basic and peaceful with powered and standard sites in a sheltered spot with coin-operated showers. Sign in with the caretaker signposted on the opposite side of SH73. $7

Smylies SH73 ☎ 03 318 4740, ⓦ smylies.co.nz. Welcoming Japanese/Dutch-run associate YHA and motels with free Japanese baths (daily in winter, on request in summer), a wood-fire-warmed lounge, slightly creaky rooms and delicious Japanese- or Kiwi-style evening meals ($20) and

continental, cooked, or Japanese-style breakfasts ($10–15), as well as ski-shuttle services (see box, p.557) and bouldering mat rental. Dorms $29, doubles $66, motel units $85

★ **Station 73 Café** King St, signposted 500m off SH73 ☎ 03 318 4000. A slice of ginger crunch and a cuppa seems just about right in this simple but well-kept café in the Springfield train station with mountain views and walls lined with railway ephemera. They also serve toasted sandwiches, gourmet pies and good espresso. Daily 8.30am–3pm, later in summer.

Porter's Pass

About 10km west of Springfield, the highway neatly bisects the 2.1-square-kilometre **Korowai/Torlesse Tussocklands Park**, New Zealand's first conservation park designed to protect the unique and quickly disappearing tussock grasslands of the eastern South Island. The road peaks at **Porter's Pass**, which at 932m is marginally higher than Arthur's Pass further west.

Kura Tawhiti (Castle Hill Conservation Area)

Over Porter's Pass you drop down into the Castle Hill basin, hemmed in by the ski-field-draped Craigieburn Range. The grassy lower slopes are peppered by clusters of grey limestone outcrops up to 30m high that have become a magnet for **world-class bouldering** and a regular stop for top international rock climbers.

Boulderers make for scattered locales such as **Flock Hill** (where large portions of *The Lion, The Witch and the Wardrobe* were filmed), Spittle Hill and Quantum Field, but everyone else stops at **Kura Tawhiti**, often known as **Castle Hill** for its fort-like larger formations. It is a place of spiritual significance to Maori, with mountain daisies and Castle Hill buttercups blooming in summer. From a parking area, a number of easy paths wind among the rocks and tussock-covered hills. Allow an hour or bring a picnic and stay for the afternoon.

Cave Stream Scenic Reserve

6km west of Kura Tawhiti

Cave Stream Scenic Reserve nestles among limestone outcrops with views of the Craigieburn and Torlesse ranges and offers a rare opportunity for an unguided **walk/wade** exploration of a **limestone cave**. Cave art, signs of seasonal camps and the discovery of an ancient wooden-framed flax backpack and other artefacts over 500 years old indicate that Maori visited the area extensively. The cave contains bones as well as providing a home for large but harmless harvestman spiders and young eels that wriggle along the walls.

The cave "walk"

The 594m cave traverse takes about an hour: take a companion, dress warmly, be sure to carry at least one torch each and have something dry to change into afterwards. After entering at the downstream end, you wade through a deep pool. If the water is above waist-high, fast-flowing, foaming or discoloured, do not attempt the walk. As you work your way upstream there are only two major obstacles apart from the dark and cold: a 1.5m rockfall about halfway through that funnels the water and so can be quite hard to climb, and a 3m waterfall at the very end. The latter (within sight of the cave exit) is negotiated by climbing up a ladder of iron rungs embedded in the rock and crawling along a short, narrow ledge while holding onto an anchored chain.

10

ACCOMMODATION AND EATING

Craigieburn Shelter campsite SH73, 5km north of Cave Stream Scenic Reserve. A small and pretty DOC site beside a stream (you'll have to treat the water) with long-drop toilets and a day-use shelter. $6

Flock Hill Lodge SH73, 10km north of Cave Stream Scenic Reserve ☏ 03 318 8196, ☻ flockhill.co.nz. Accommodation on a high-country sheep station that's handy if you're bouldering, skiing, mountain biking or

CAVE STREAM SCENIC RESERVE

tramping hereabouts. There are backpacker bunkrooms sleeping four (linen $5 extra), a separate kitchen/dining room with coin-op internet (also used by campers), plus motel units and some attractive wood-panelled self-contained cottages. All accommodation is self-catering and there's a restaurant serving the likes of chicken burgers ($18) and venison and Guinness hotpot ($23). Camping $15, dorms $31, motel $140, cottages $155

Craigieburn Forest Park

5km west of Cave Stream Scenic Reserve

The Broken River ski-field road marks the Craigieburn Shelter (see above) and the access point for the **Craigieburn Forest Park**. The park is dominated by alpine scrub, tussock grasslands and dense, moss-covered mountain beech forest sprinkled with scarlet native mistletoe flowers from December to February. A variety of native birds squawk through the forest, including bellbird, rifleman, silver eye and kea, and, between October and February, long-tailed and shining cuckoos join the throng.

CRAIGIEBURN HIKES

DOC's *Craigieburn Forest Park Day Walks* leaflet, available from the local visitor centres, details eleven walks in the park. Some are quite short while others can involve overnight stays.

Bealey Spur (9km return; 4–6hr; 500m ascent). When it is wet in Arthur's Pass it is often dry on Bealey Spur, a long steady ridge hike through mountain beech forest that's never too tough but still rewards with fabulous views of the Waimakariri Basin. It ends at an old sheep musterers' hut (6 bunks; free) set amid subalpine scrub and tussock grasslands. The track starts at the end of Cloudesley Rd, near *Bealey Hotel*, 14km south of Arthur's Pass Village.

Cass–Lagoon Saddle Track (33km; 2 days; 1300m ascent). Rugged hikers might fancy this lovely mountain loop with an overnight

stop at Hamilton Hut (20 bunks; $15) almost exactly halfway. It starts at the east end of Cass Rd bridge and finishes beside SH73, 11km further west: infrequent buses can be used to complete the loop. DOC publish a handy leaflet, downloadable from ☻ doc .govt.nz.

Lyndon Saddle (6km; 3–4hr; 500m ascent). Fun loop from Craigieburn Shelter up through regenerating mountain beech to the superb viewpoint of Helicopter Hill (1262m). Continue along glacial terraces to the Broken River ski-field road then back beside Cave Stream to the start.

Arthur's Pass National Park

The most dramatic of the three Southern Alps crossings links Christchurch with Greymouth, via **Arthur's Pass**, traversed by a scenic rail line and the equally breathtaking SH73.

The pass is surrounded by the 950-square-kilometre **Arthur's Pass National Park**, a remarkable alpine landscape with some superb easy walks and tough tramps. The park centres on diminutive **Arthur's Pass Village**, nestled along SH73 at 737m above sea level in a steep-sided, forest-covered U-shaped valley. Because the park spans the transition zone between the soggy West Coast and the much drier east, Otira, just west of the pass, gets around 6m of rain a year, while Bealey, 15km to the east, gets only 2m. Consequently, Arthur's Pass Village is often shrouded in mist, providing a moody contrast with the rich vegetation of the valley floor and slopes. The village offers a slim range of lodging and even more limited eating: stock up beforehand if you're planning to spend time in the area. Nights are often chilly and snow occasionally blocks the pass.

Arthur's Pass itself is 4km west of the village and, at 920m, is almost 200m higher. It's marked by a large obelisk dedicated to Arthur Dudley Dobson (see below). Naturally, there are great views here and the Dobson Nature Walk (see box, p.562).

Immediately west of the pass, the road drops away dramatically across the **Otira Viaduct**, a huge concrete gash built in 1999 to span the tumbling river below. Side streams carry so much water that one is diverted over the roadway in a kind of artificial waterfall. A small lookout provides the best view.

Brief history

Arthur's Pass was named after civil engineer **Arthur Dudley Dobson**, who heard about the route from local Maori (who had traditionally used it as a highway), and surveyed it in 1864. By 1866 horse-drawn coaches were using it to access the Westland goldfields.

Arthur's Pass Village sprung up in the early 1900s to provide shelter for tunnel diggers and railway workers. The rail line's completion in 1923 coincided with the boom in alpine tourism worldwide, and the village ticks by on summer hikers, winter skiers and the daily *TranzAlpine* train visits.

KEA: NEW ZEALAND'S ALPINE TRICKSTER

One of the most enduring memories of a visit to Arthur's Pass and many other alpine areas of the South Island is the sight of a bright green **kea** mischievously getting its beak into something, or simply posing for the camera. With their lolloping sideways gait and inexhaustible curiosity, the world's only alpine parrots are endearing: at backcountry huts you might find kea sliding down the corrugated-iron roofing or pulling at the nails holding the roof on. Be careful where you leave your hiking boots – trampers have been known to wake up to a pile of leather strips and shredded laces.

With these playful scavenging tendencies it's hardly surprising kea traditionally got the blame for attacking sheep, and for many years were routinely shot by farmers. Recent research seems to indicate kea only attack already-weakened sheep, and shooting has long since stopped as the birds are now fully protected.

These days, however, their greatest threat is human food. These kleptomaniacs can be persistent – you'll hear the ruffle of feathers, see the flash of red beneath their wings and they'll be tearing at your lunch just out of reach. But **feeding** them is forbidden as it reduces their ability to forage for themselves in winter when the summertime walkers have left town, and draws them towards the road where many are run over. As a result, the kea population is estimated to be as low as 1000–5000 birds. For more information visit Ⓦ keaconservation.co.nz.

ARRIVAL AND DEPARTURE

By train The *TranzAlpine* (see box, p.517) stops in the centre of the settlement, which is a short walk from everything.
Destinations Christchurch (1 daily; 2hr 10min); Greymouth (1 daily; 2hr).

By bus West Coast Shuttle (☏ 03 768 0028, ☷ westcoast shuttle.co.nz) run a fast service from Greymouth (8am) to Christchurch (noon), returning 3–7pm. Atomic Shuttles (☏ 03 349 0697, ☷ atomictravel.co.nz) do the opposite going from Christchurch (7.30am) to Greymouth (11.15am) and Hokitika (noon) then back to Christchurch (5.15pm).
Destinations Christchurch (2 daily; 2hr 30min); Greymouth (2 daily; 1hr 30min); Hokitika (1 daily; 2hr 15min).

INFORMATION

DOC office SH73 (daily: Nov–April 8am–5pm; May–Oct 8.30am–4.30pm; ☏ 03 318 9211, ☷ arthurspass.com). Excellent information centre with extensive displays on wildlife, plants, geology and local history, and plays a video about the trail blazed by the stagecoaches and the railway on request ($2). The latest weather report is posted outside.

Services There are no banks or ATMs in Arthur's Pass. The single petrol pump here is the only one between Springfield and the West Coast.

ACCOMMODATION

Good-value accommodation is strung out along the main road. Places fill up quickly during the high season (Dec–March).

Alpine Motel 52 Main Rd (SH73) ☏ 03 318 9233, ☷ apam.co.nz. These old but well-kept chalet-style motel units come with kitchen and DVD players, and family units have a fireplace. $\overline{115}$, family units $\overline{135}$

Arthur's Pass Village B&B Homestay 72 School Terrace ☏ 03 318 9183, ☷ arthurspass.org.nz. A cosy cottage that's very much a homestay, thanks in part to the warm welcome from the owners. The two comfortably appointed rooms share a guest bathroom and breakfasts are largely organic with home-made bread and raspberry jam from local fruit. $\overline{130}$

Arthur's Pass Village Motel SH73 ☏ 03 318 9235, ☷ apmotel.co.nz. Just two simple but comfortable, modern studio units with kitchenettes, queen beds and satellite TV, all in the heart of the village. $\overline{145}$

Bealey Hotel SH73, 12km east of Arthur's Pass Village ☏ 03 318 9277, ☷ bealeyhotel.co.nz. High on a knoll, this historic hotel has motel-style rooms with great views of a broad expanse of the Waimakariri River. The restaurant/ bar is filled with memorabilia of the hotel's early role as a stop-off point for Cobb & Co coaches and of claimed moa sightings hereabouts in recent decades (hence the life-size moa sculptures standing sentinel in the grounds). Lodge rooms $\overline{80}$, motel units $\overline{150}$

★ **Mountain House** ☏ 03 318 9258, ☷ trampers .co.nz. Two associate YHA hostels in one, offering the largest number and widest range of beds in the village. The gleaming, state-of-the-art main hostel is supplemented by a pair of two- and three-bedroom self-contained 1920s railway workers' cottages and in, summer (normally Dec–March), the owner opens the "Historic Lodge", New Zealand's original 1950s YHA, with bags of old-school character. Also limited camping and van hookups. **Camping** $\overline{20}$, dorms $\overline{29}$, budget doubles $\overline{70}$, cottage room $\overline{82}$

Rata Lodge SH73, Otira, 15km west of the village ☏ 03 738 2822, ☉ rata.lodge@xtra.co.nz. Spacious and chilled forest-girt hostel on the western edge of the national park. There's a four-bunk dorm, two en-suite doubles with TV, and a little bush walk with glowworms. Bring food to self-cater. Dorms $\overline{28}$, doubles $\overline{69}$

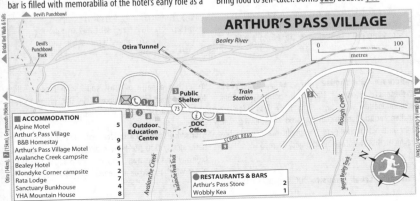

ARTHUR'S PASS VILLAGE

■ **ACCOMMODATION**

Alpine Motel	5
Arthur's Pass Village B&B Homestay	9
Arthur's Pass Village Motel	6
Avalanche Creek campsite	3
Bealey Hotel	1
Klondyke Corner campsite	2
Rata Lodge	7
Sanctuary Bunkhouse	4
YHA Mountain House	8

● **RESTAURANTS & BARS**

Arthur's Pass Store	2
Wobbly Kea	1

10

WALKS AND TRAMPS AROUND ARTHUR'S PASS

Apart from a few easy walks around Arthur's Pass Village, the national park is substantially more rugged than most in New Zealand, making it suitable only for moderately to highly experienced trampers.

SAFETY, INFORMATION AND EQUIPMENT

Most walks involve route finding (bring a compass) and unbridged river crossings – make adequate preparations (see Basics, p.51), and record your intentions through ⓦadventure smart.org. The free *Tramping in Arthur's Pass National Park* leaflet assigns Route Guide numbers (RG) to the major tramps, covered on specific leaflets downloadable from ⓦdoc.govt.nz. You'll also need 1:50,000 topographic **maps**, available for sale ($9 each) or rent ($1 plus $20 deposit) at the DOC office, which also sells gas canisters, and offers secure gear storage ($2/item/day).

ACCESS AND ACCOMMODATION

The *Mountain House* (see p.561) operates a taxi-style **Trampers shuttle service** to the trailheads: a joint drop-off and pick-up service for the Mingha–Deception route costs around $100 for up to 6 people. A couple of hikes involve stays in **DOC huts** which can't be booked. You can obtain hut tickets from the DOC office in Arthur's Pass or use an Backcountry Hut Pass.

Avalanche Peak Track (5km return; 6–8hr; 1000m ascent). Strenuous day-hike that offers wonderful views of the surrounding mountains. Parts of the route are exposed; it should only be attempted by well-equipped, experienced trampers in reasonable weather. The best way is going up the spectacular Avalanche Peak Track and making a circuit by returning on the Scotts Track.

Bridal Veil Nature Walk (2.5km return; 1hr 30min; 50m ascent). Lovely walk that ascends through mountain beeches then crosses the Bridal Veil Creek before returning the same way.

Casey Saddle to Binser Saddle (RG10: 40km; 2 days; 400m ascent). Demanding loop with great views as you cross easy saddles on well-defined tracks through open beech forest, staying overnight in Casey Hut (16 bunks; $15).

Devil's Punch Bowl (2km return; 1hr; 100m ascent). The village's most popular short walk, following an all-weather climb and descent to the base of a 131m waterfall, crossing two footbridges and zigzagging up steps.

Dobson Nature Walk (1km return; 30min). Easy graded walk at the crest of Arthur's Pass with panels explaining subalpine herbs, tussock and shrubs, best seen Nov–Feb when they're in bloom. The nature walk can be reached on foot from Arthur's Pass Village (4km each way) along a lively bush walk that also visits Jack's Hut, a green corrugated-iron shed once used by roading crews.

Mingha–Deception (RG6: 25km; 2 days; 400m ascent, 750m descent). A great overnighter that traces the route used for the mountain-run stage of the arduous Coast to Coast race (see p.661). Long sections are easy to follow, but there are unmarked areas requiring route finding, and 36 unbridged river crossings, so watch the water levels. If you're feeling particularly fit, add on a side trip to Lake Mavis (500m ascent), a high mountain tarn with some lovely views. You can use either the Goat Pass Hut (20 bunks; $5) or the Upper Deception Hut (6 bunks; free) and ponder how mad you'd have to be to run the route competitively.

Sanctuary Bunkhouse SH73 ☎03 942 2230, ⓦthesanctuary.co.nz. Unstaffed dorm-style bunk accommodation with just eight beds. Has adequate kitchen facilities, plus coin-operated hot showers and 24hr internet available to the public via honesty box payment. Bike rental can be arranged. Dorms $18

CAMPING

Avalanche Creek campsite DOC site that's not much more than a patch of grass and a gravel parking lot for campervans directly opposite the DOC office. There's potable water, toilets and a dry day-use shelter. Camping $6

Klondyke Corner campsite 8km east of the village. Basic, grassy DOC site fairly peacefully set between the highway and the river with long-drop toilet and river water, which should be treated. Camping $6

EATING AND DRINKING

Arthur's Pass Store SH73 ☎ 03 318 9235. The best place to fuel up for a hike or replenish afterwards. It serves breakfasts, pies, sandwiches and excellent coffee, and has fairly limited groceries, a bottle store and internet access ($2/30min). Daily 8am–5.30pm, later in summer.

Wobbly Kea SH73 ☎ 03 318 9101, ⍟ wobblykea.co.nz.

The village linchpin for steaming hot chocolate, smooth coffee and imaginative lunches, and meat and fish dinners in hearty portions: the $28 pizzas are big enough for two modest appetites. Also doubles as a busy bar hosting occasional live gigs. Mon–Thurs & Sun 8am–8pm, Fri & Sat 8am–9pm.

10

The South Canterbury foothills

The **South Canterbury foothills** mark the transition from the flat Canterbury Plains to the rugged and spectacular Southern Alps. The area is primarily known for the winter resort town of **Methven**, which serves the ski slopes of **Mount Hutt**. In summer, an array of activities includes skydiving, jetboating and some wonderful **walking** around Mount Somers.

The main **route** through the area is SH72, dubbed the "Inland Scenic Route".

Washpen Falls

590 Washpen Rd, Windwhistle, 25km north of Methven • Self-guided walk $10 • ☎ 03 318 6813, ⍟ washpenfalls.co.nz

One of the area's lesser-known gems, the private family farm of **Washpen Falls** offers a wonderfully diverse meander through native bush and farmland for anyone of moderate fitness. The **walking track** heads up to a point, and offers spectacular views of the Canterbury Plains. Along the way there's a canyon formed by an ancient volcano (used by Maori to trap moa), great examples of native-bush regeneration and, of course, the cascading falls. The office (a corrugated-iron shed) has leaflets outlining the track's highlights. The walk is short but steep in places: set aside 2hr and take your time or spin it out over a picnic.

ACCOMMODATION

WASHPEN FALLS

Washpen Chalet 590 Washpen Rd, Windwhistle, 25km north of Methven ☎ 03 318 6813, ⍟ washpenfalls.co.nz. This wonderfully homely three-bedroom 1960s chalet on the Washpen Falls farm overlooks the surrounding farmland and hills. It's not flash but there's a great spirit to the place, and firewood is included. Bring food to self-cater. Extra adults cost $25. **$100**

Rakaia Gorge

15km north of Methven

The turquoise Rakaia River emerges onto the Canterbury Plains from the **Rakaia Gorge**, created by an ancient lava flow and now lined in many places with regenerating forest. **Maori history** tells how a *taniwha* (water spirit) lived nearby, hunting and eating moa and weka; his possessions, because of his status as a spirit, were *tapu*. While he was away searching for a hot spring one cold day the northwest wind demon flattened his property. To prevent this happening again, the *taniwha* collected large boulders and stones from the mountains to block the course of the demon and so narrowed the Rakaia River, making it flow between the rocky walls. The heat from his body melted the snow and ice on the mountains, and his perspiration fell on the rocks and formed crystals in the riverbed.

The gorge can be explored by jetboat (see p.565). Downstream, the river fans out into a classic example of the braided rivers so common on the eastern side of the South Island.

Rakaia Gorge Walkway

15km; 3–4hr return

The *taniwha*'s sweaty work can be seen from the **Rakaia Gorge Walkway**, which starts where SH72 crosses the river. The path leads through several forest stands and spectacular geological areas, past hardened lava flows of rhyolite, pitchstone and andesite, to the upper gorge lookout. The less committed should walk as far as a fenced viewpoint high on a bluff above the river (1hr return).

ACCOMMODATION

RAKAIA GORGE

Rakaia Gorge campsite SH72, 15km north. Peaceful campsite high on the south bank of the Rakaia with views out across the plains. Comes equipped with toilets (year-round) and hot showers (mid-Oct to April). <u>$7.50</u>

10 Mount Hutt ski-field

22km northeast of Methven • Lift pass $91; full ski/board rental from $48 • ☎ 03 308 5074, ⓦ nzski.com

Mount Hutt is widely regarded as one of the best and most varied ski-fields in the land, with a vertical rise of 683m, a variety of runs (two beginner, eight intermediate and thirty advanced) and, generally, the longest season (roughly June–Oct). All this is served by a triple, a quad and a six chairlift, and plenty of snowmaking. Rentals are available on the mountain, but there's no accommodation here, so most people **stay** in Methven, from where there are frequent **shuttle buses** (all around $18 return; 45min to the ski-field): buy a ticket on board or from the i-SITE, from where most of the shuttles depart.

Methven

A hundred kilometres west of Christchurch on SH77, **METHVEN** is Canterbury's winter-sports capital and the accommodation and refuelling centre for the **Mount Hutt**

ACTIVITIES AROUND METHVEN

Aoraki Balloon Safaris ☎0800 256 837, ⓦnzballooning.com. Hot-air balloon rides above the patchwork quilt of the Canterbury Plains and the magnificent Southern Alps – particularly scenic in winter. Sunrise trips (4hr; $385) include bubbly and breakfast back on land.

Discovery Jet ☎03 318 6943, ⓦdiscoveryjet.co.nz. Great-value, high-octane jetboating to the top end of the Rakaia Gorge. Either go for the full 30min round trip ($75), or opt for a 15min spin ($40) with a drop off at the Rakaia Gorge Walkway then walk back – take a picnic to make an afternoon of it.

Skydiving NZ Pudding Hill Airfield, 10km northwest of town ☎0800 697 593, ⓦskydivingnz.com. Very professional outfit offering magical mountain views from tandem jumps (12,000ft for $335; 15,000ft for $440) with free pick-ups from Methven.

ski-field during the busy June to October **ski season**. Outside those months it can be pretty quiet, though summer visitors often base themselves here to explore the nearby **Rakaia Gorge** and **Washpen Falls** to the north, and **Mount Somers** to the south. It's not a big place but the small centre has banks, post office and camping supplies.

NZ Alpine & Agriculture Encounter

Methven Heritage Centre, 160 Main St • Daily 10am–5pm • $17.50

Methven celebrates its position at the intersection of plains and mountains in this new, interactive museum focusing on winter sports and agriculture. A massive combine harvester recalls the historic importance of arable farming while a working cross section of a model cow celebrates the big bucks that dairying is now bringing in. You can even try your hand spinning some merino or play on the digger simulator – trying to dig a trench and fill a truck is a lot harder than you might think.

A collection of historic skis and some great old footage herald a section on avalanche control and the building of the Mt Hutt ski-field, including the original hut used by Willi Huber to winter on the site while assessing its skiing potential – two mice kept him company through the lonely snowy months.

ARRIVAL AND INFORMATION

METHVEN

By bus Methven Travel runs buses from Christchurch (four weekly in summer; four daily in ski season; 1hr 15min; $38 one-way) and stop centrally on Main St (SH77). Numerous shuttles serve the ski-field (see opposite).

i-SITE Methven Heritage Centre, 160 Main St (mid-Oct to May Mon–Fri 9am–5pm, Sat & Sun 10am–3pm; June to mid-Oct daily 8.30am–5.30pm; ☎03 302 8955, ⓦamazingspace.co.nz). Has internet access ($2/20min) and wi-fi ($5/hr).

Ski and bike rental Jace's Hutt, 30 Forest Drive (May–Oct daily 7.30am–7pm; ☎03 302 9553, ⓦskitrader .co.nz), rents and sells skis and other ski equipment. Big Al's, corner of Forest Drive and Main St (Nov–May Mon–Fri 3–5.30pm; June–Oct daily 7.30am–7.30pm; ☎03 302 8003, ⓦbigals.co.nz), rents skis and boards, and bikes (hardtail $40/day; full suspension $59/day) in the summer. Has information on an easy town loop and the Mount Hutt Bike Park.

ACCOMMODATION

Abisko Lodge & Camp Ground 74 Main St ☎03 302 8875, ⓦabisko.co.nz. Excellent establishment in the town centre incorporating Methven's most central campsite. Camping/site $25, powered site $37, doubles $126, one-bedroom apartments $190

★ **Beluga** 40 Allen St ☎03 302 8290, ⓦbeluga.co.nz. Luxurious en-suite rooms in a beautifully kept villa that has retained its original charm, with an outdoor hot tub in its tranquil gardens and an honesty bar. There's also a private "garden suite", and a delightfully renovated self-catering cottage sleeping up to four (minimum three nights in winter, two in summer). Winter rates start at $230. B&B $165, garden suite B&B $200, cottage $275

Central Luxury Apartments 6 Methven Chertsey Rd ☎03 302 8829, ⓦcentralapartmentsmethven.co.nz. These new and classy self-contained units come complete with a big TV, laundry and full kitchen. $165, ski season $270

The Lodge 1 Chertsey Rd ☎0800 128 829, ⓦthe lodgenz.com. Generously sized, contemporary rooms, some with spa baths, and a popular on-site bistro and bar (below). Doubles $105, ski season $135

10

Mount Hutt Bunkhouse 8 Lampard St ☏ 03 302 8894, Ⓦ mthuttbunkhouse.co.nz. Comfortable, proudly TV-free backpackers spread over two adjacent houses with a large garden (including volleyball court) and log fires. Dorms $28, rooms $64

Skibo House 82 Forest Drive ☏ 03 302 9493, Ⓦ skibo house.com. Friendly B&B in a modern house where most rooms have great mountain views, though they share a bathroom. Excellent breakfasts might include Bircher muesli and porridge, and there's an outdoor hot tub. B&B

$100, self-contained units $120

Snow Denn Lodge Corner of McMillan and Banks sts ☏ 03 302 8999, Ⓦ methvenaccommodation.co.nz. Welcoming associate YHA hostel spanning two adjoining A-frame buildings (one with comfy dorms, and the other a private-room "flashpackers"), each with spacious lounges and well-equipped kitchens. Freebies include a good continental breakfast, use of bikes, plus internet and wi-fi. Dorms $25, doubles $70, en suites $80

EATING, DRINKING AND ENTERTAINMENT

The Blue Pub 1 Barkers Rd ☏ 03 302 8046, Ⓦ thebluepub.co.nz. Popular with the après-ski crowd and locals, this 1918-built cobalt-painted hotel has a lively bar hosting bands and weekend DJs. The café/restaurant dishes up hearty meals such as Thai beef salad ($20) and porterhouse steak with egg and chips ($26). Daily noon–10pm or later.

Café 131 131 Main St ☏ 03 302 9131. Airy wood-floored Art Deco café that's perfect for people-watching over Methven's best coffee. There's an array of cakes and counter food, all-day breakfasts, filling, inexpensive lunches (BLT and fries $17) and a book exchange. Daily 7.30am–5.30pm.

The Last Post 116 Main St ☏ 03 302 8259. In a former post office with a roaring open fire, Methven's finest dining features the likes of home-made cornbread and dips followed by almond-crusted yellow-fin tuna or Asian-steamed salmon parcels ($37). You can also just drop in for a cocktail. Mon–Sat 5–11pm or later.

LT's @ The Lodge 1 Chertsey Rd ☏ 03 303 2000. Bistro fare and great gourmet pizzas (small $16; large $24), such as apricot chicken, served in a cosy room with a stone-walled fireplace. The attached bar hosts events including

beach parties with trucked-in sand. Daily 4.30–10pm or later; closed Mon outside the ski season.

★ **Primo Caffe** 38 McMillan St ☏ 03 302 9060. Wonderfully quirky café in an antique/vintage clothing/junk shop (everything is for sale), serving all-day breakfast ($10–16), good coffee, delectable home-made cakes and a range of meals which might include soup, savoury crepes and shepherd's pie. There's outside seating in the back. Daily 7am–5pm.

Thai Chilli Corner of Main Rd and Forest Drive ☏ 03 303 3038. It's not every day you hear Louis Armstrong cranked out of an old gramophone in purple-painted surroundings while tucking into authentic Thai dishes, prepared and served with care. There's a short menu of pad Thai, green curry, beef satay and more, and nothing is over $18. Daily 5–9pm in ski season; closed Sun & Mon rest of year.

CINEMA

Cinema Paradiso 112 Main St ☏ 03 302 1957, Ⓦ cinemaparadiso.co.nz. Wonderful bijou digital cinema, with two tiny rooms showing a roster of mostly art-house flicks.

Mount Somers and Staveley

The 1687m **Mount Somers** rises from the flatlands above the villages of **Mount Somers**, 21km southwest of Methven, and **Staveley**, 8km further south The mountain is encircled by the **Mount Somers Track**, which is conveniently in the rain shadow of the mountains and is often above the bushline – when it's raining in Arthur's Pass and Mount Cook is clagged in, there's still a chance you'll be able to get some hiking in here. The terrain, gentle by South Island standards, incorporates patches of regenerating beech forest and open tussock pocked by outcrops of rock. Large areas of low-fertility soil subject to heavy rainfall turn to bog, and as a result you'll find bog pine, snow totara, toatoa, mountain flax and maybe even the rare whio (blue duck).

If you don't fancy a long walk, just go as far as **Sharlpin Falls** (about 1hr return) or go riding with Staveley Horse Treks.

INFORMATION AND ACTIVITIES

MOUNT SOMERS AND STAVELEY

Information The stores in Staveley and Mount Somers have good local information, or check out Ⓦ mtsomers.co.nz.
Staveley Horse Treks 191 Flynns Rd ☏ 03 303 0809,

✉ brucegray@clear.net.nz. Runs some of the South Island's best – and cheapest – horse treks (from $35/hr; minimum two people; bookings essential).

MOUNT SOMERS TRACK

The strenuous but exhilarating Mount Somers Track (25km loop; 2–3 days; 1000m ascent) makes a subalpine loop round the mountain, passing abandoned coal mines, volcanic formations and a deep river canyon.

The **entire loop** is best tackled anticlockwise from Staveley. However, roads meet the loop in the west at Woolshed Creek (accessed from Mount Somers) and in the east at Sharplins Falls car park (accessed from Staveley), so if you don't fancy the whole thing you can **walk either half** and get your vehicle shuttled.

10

TICKETS AND EQUIPMENT

There is no booking system. Buy DOC hut tickets ($15.30 for each hut) before you start at the stores in Staveley or Mount Somers, or from i-SITEs or DOC offices. You'll need to carry a cooking stove, pots and all your food; water at the huts should be treated. Marker poles point the way adequately in most conditions but the rolling country on top of the hills is subject to disorientating fog, so bring a map and compass.

TRANSPORT

Staveley Horse Treks (☎03 303 0809, ✉brucegray@clear.net.nz) do vehicle shuttles for $35. After dropping you at the Woolshed Creek trailhead, they keep your vehicle safe near Sharplin Falls car park ready for your emergence from the wilds. Methven Travel (☎03 302 8106) operates an on demand shuttle service from Methven to Woolshed Creek car park ($140 for 1–4 people) or Sharplin Falls car park ($80 for 1–4 people).

THE ROUTE

Sharplin Falls Car Park to Pinnacles Hut (5km; 3hr 45min; 470m ascent). The most popular section of the track is the first 2km to Sharplin Falls, a modest cascade in a pretty canyon. There are lots of steps but they're even and well cared for. The route then climbs steadily through beech forest, reaching the tree line at Pinnacles Hut (19 bunks), nestled below rock monoliths frequently used by climbers.

Pinnacles Hut to Woolshed Creek Hut (6.2km; 3hr; 265m ascent). Climb towards the 1170m saddle, now through treeless tussock with wide views into the mountains and back to the plains. On the descent, take the 5min side trip to the Water Caves, where a stream courses below a rockfall of house-sized boulders. It is then only 10min to the modern Woolshed Creek Hut (26 bunks), a good place to stay a couple of nights, spending the

intervening day exploring the little valleys and canyons hereabouts.

Woolshed Creek Hut to the Sharplin Falls car park (13.5km; 8hr; 400m ascent). The tramp follows the South Face Route around the mountain and feels quite different. There's a less isolated feel as you gaze across the Canterbury flatlands towards the distant coast. The terrain is a mix of high-country scrub (somewhat exposed at times) and beech forest. Soon after leaving the hut, the Howden Falls side track is worth a quick look. You then climb a ridge before traversing tussock-covered flats, passing a new day-shelter at about the halfway point. After a steep climb up through beech forest you begin the long descent, first on a ridge with great views then down into the bush to Sharplin Falls car park.

ACCOMMODATION AND EATING

STAVELEY

Ross Cottage Flynns Rd ☎03 303 0880, ⊛nature .net.nz. A delightful 130-year-old self-catering cottage operated by Tussock and Beech Ecotours, who offer a variety of eco-focused guided tours. $135

Staveley Village Store 1 Burgess Rd ☎03 303 0859. A local store in the best tradition: a place for great coffee, simple breakfasts and lunches, ice cream, limited groceries and eight different kinds of superb sausage rolls including leek and mushroom. Daily 9am–5pm.

Topp Lodge 12 Burgess Rd ☎03 303 0955, ⊛topplodge .co.nz. Lynda Topp, one half of New Zealand's best-known lesbian yodelling cowgirl twins, the Topp Twins, runs this quirky B&B right in Staveley. The rooms are peaceful and very comfortable and come with full breakfast, dinner is available ($45) and there's a full liquor licence. $120

MOUNT SOMERS

Mt Somers Domain Hoods Rd, 1km off SH72 ☎021 176 0677. Cheap camping next to the local swimming pool

10

SEARCHING FOR EDORAS

Go searching for Edoras and you won't find it. Though the crew of *Lord of the Rings: The Two Towers* spent the best part of a year erecting the Rohan capital city, everything was removed after filming. What you do get is Mount Sunday, a 100m-high glacially levelled outcrop (roche moutonnée) surrounded by open river flats a 48km drive west from the village of Mount Somers. Over half of the journey is on rough gravel but it is a beautiful drive, bounded by big, grassy, round-shouldered hills sheltering a flat valley, with the main icy backbone of the Southern Alps up ahead.

You should put an hour aside to wander across the fields (and cross a couple of streams) to get to Mount Sunday. Once you're standing on top surveying the grasslands all about, you can imagine the bleats of the sheep are the battle cries of…well, maybe not.

Hassle-free Tours (**☏**0800 427 753, **☒**hasslefree.co.nz) run fun day-trips here from Christchurch ($235 including a café lunch).

---

with a basic toilet and shower block and little else. Camping/site $12, powered $18

Mount Somers Holiday Park Hoods Road, 1km off SH72 **☏**03 303 9719, **☒**mountsomers.co.nz. Comfortable tree-filled campsite with powered sites, simple cabins (with bedding for rent) and fully made-up en-suite cabins. Camping/site $22, cabins $54, en-suite cabins $79

Mount Somers Store 59 Pattons Rd **☏**03 303 9831. Another classic country store selling DOC hut tickets, ice cream, sausage rolls and a reasonable range of groceries. Mon–Sat 8am–6pm, Sun 9am–5pm.

Stronechrubie SH72 1km south of Mount Somers **☏**03 303 9814, **☒**stronechrubie.co.nz. Beautiful self-contained chalets in a lovely rural setting, as well as the only real restaurant in these parts: expect local beef ($38) or baked salmon ($33) and an excellent wine selection. Good-value dinner and bed and breakfast packages. Book for meals Wed–Sat 6.30–10pm, Sun noon–2pm. $120

Peel Forest

The tiny hamlet of **PEEL FOREST**, 12km west of SH72 and 35km south of Mount Somers, is the hub of **Peel Forest Park**, one of the eastern South Island's last remaining patches of original native bush, which is threaded with **walking tracks**. Come for easy walks, horse trekking and the superb **whitewater rafting** trips through the Rangitata Gorge.

INFORMATION AND ACTIVITIES

Peel Forest Store **☏**03 696 3567, **☒**peelforest .co.nz. Peel Forest revolves around this great old store, which acts as visitor centre (pick up DOC's *Peel Forest Park leaflet* outlining walks from 30min to 6hr), post office, campsite office, takeaway and local bar. On Fri & Sat nights it serves restaurant meals such as Tuscan lamb salad ($23). Mon–Thurs & Sun 9am–6.30pm, Fri & Sat 9am–9pm.

Peel Forest Horse Trekking **☏**0800 022 536, **☒**peelforesthorsetrekking.co.nz. Runs excellent treks that range from a stroll along the river (1hr; $55) to a

PEEL FOREST

full-day trek up Mt Peel ($380 including lunch), plus multi-day trips.

Rangitata Rafts 14km north of Peel Forest Store **☏**0800 251 251, **☒**rafts.co.nz. This highly professional outfit runs some of New Zealand's best whitewater rafting trips on the Grade IV–V high-sided gorge section of the Rangitata River. Trips (Oct–April daily 10.30am; $198) include two and a half hours on the water – with a nerve-testing optional 10m cliff jump – as well as lunch and a barbecue dinner. Pick-ups from nearby Geraldine, or from Christchurch (add 2hr at either end), cost just $20 extra.

ACCOMMODATION

Peel Forest Camp Ground **☏**03 696 3567. A lovely wooded DOC-run family campsite set beside the Rangitata River, with tent and powered sites ($5/site extra) and four simple cabins. Camping $12, cabins $44

Rangitata Rafts 14km north of Peel Forest Store

☏0800 251 251, **☒**rafts.co.nz. Even if you're not rafting, this is a great spot away from the crowds. Tent, park your camper (no powered sites) or stay in the backpacker-style accommodation. Camping $10, dorms $25, doubles $60

Geraldine

The prosperous farming town of **GERALDINE**, 45km south of Mount Somers and 35km north of Timaru, rewards a brief stop for a couple of **attractions** and to browse its smattering of **craft shops**, **galleries**, and **food stores** specializing in gourmet picnic ingredients such as local cheeses, pickles, jams, wine and chocolates.

Giant Jersey and Bayeux Tapestry

10 Wilson St • Mon–Fri 9am–5pm, Sat & Sun 10am–4pm • Giant jersey donation; tapestry $2 • T 03 693 9820, W giantjersey.co.nz and W 1066.co.nz

The whopping 5.5kg jersey here ranks among the **world's largest**. You might have more time for the array of heraldic mosaics, and a 42m-long half-scale **tableau of the Bayeux Tapestry** made entirely from 1.5 million tiny pieces of spring steel broken from knitting machines – the last 8m are artists' Michael and Rachael Linton's interpretation of how the missing final section of the original might have looked, and work continues on a new tableau extending the history back to King Harold's troubles with Norwegian invaders immediately before the Battle of Hastings.

ARRIVAL AND INFORMATION — GERALDINE

By bus Intercity/Newmans/Great Sights, Atomic and Southern Link buses all drop off outside Geraldine's i-SITE, as do Budget Shuttles (T 03 615 5119, W budgetshuttles .co.nz) on their Christchurch to Timaru run.

Destinations Aoraki/Mount Cook (1 daily; 2hr 30min); Christchurch (6–7 daily; 2hr); Queenstown (5 daily; 5–6hr); Timaru (1–2 daily; 30min).

i-SITE Corner of Talbot and Cox sts (Dec–March Mon–Fri 9am–5pm, Sat & Sun 10am–4pm; April–Nov Mon–Fri 9am–5pm, Sat & Sun 10am–3pm; T 03 693 1006, W southcanterbury.org.nz).

ACCOMMODATION

Geraldine Holiday Park 39 Hislop St T 03 693 8147, W geraldineholidaypark.co.nz. Well-tended campsite surrounded by sheltering trees where guests can rent cheap bikes for knocking about town. Camping/site $32, cabins $47, self-contained units $78, motel units $125

Rawhiti Backpackers 27 Hewlings St, 1km southwest of the centre T 03 693 8252, W rawhitibackpackers .co.nz. Peaceful hostel in an artistically decorated 1924-built former maternity hospital, with spotless rooms and common areas and expansive gardens. Dorms $32, doubles $72

EATING AND ENTERTAINMENT

Café Plums 44 Talbot St T 03 693 9770. Ordinary-looking café that produces delicious made-on-the-premises Swiss chocolates and cakes such as raspberry linzer torte and honey-and-nut cake. Mon–Fri 8am–5pm, Sat 9am–2pm.

Verdé Café Deli 45c Talbot St T 03 693 9616. Café in a secluded rose-clambered cottage garden a block back from the main road, where classy café fare spans a great selection of counter food plus a tempting brunch menu: think pea, asparagus and haloumi paella, or salmon on a feta potato cake (both $16). Daily 9am–4pm.

CINEMA

Geraldine Cinema 84 Talbot St T 03 693 8118, W nzcinema.co.nz. Wonderful reinvented movie house with sofas, beanbags and cosy duvets in winter. It occasionally plays host to live bands and even opera. Typically open Thurs–Sun.

The Mackenzie Country

The Canterbury Plains and the central South Island's snow-capped peaks frame the **Mackenzie Country**, a dramatic region of open sheep-grazed grasslands that shimmer green in spring but dry off through summer to a golden brown. It is all beautifully set off (in Nov and Dec) by stands of purple, pink and white **lupins** – regarded as weeds but much loved nonetheless.

Light reflected from microscopic rock particles suspended in glacial meltwater lends an ethereal opaque hue to the region's **mesmerizingly blue, glacier-fed lakes**, notably

10

JAMES MCKENZIE

A Kiwi folk hero, James McKenzie lends his name (well, close enough anyway) to the **Mackenzie Country**, a 180km crescent of rolling dry grassland between Fairlie and Kurow (to the south on SH83). A Gaelic-speaking Scottish immigrant of uncertain background, McKenzie is believed to have spent only a couple of years in New Zealand but his legend lives on. He was arrested in 1855 for stealing over 1,000 sheep, most of them from the Rhodes brothers' Levels Run station near Timaru, and grazing them in the basin of rich high-country pastureland, with the assistance of a single dog, Friday. McKenzie escaped from prison three times during the first year of his five-year sentence, and when holding him became too much trouble, he was given a free pardon, after which he quietly disappeared, some say to America, others to Australia.

A poem commemorates the man and his dog in the visitor shelter at Lake Pukaki near the turn-off to Aoraki/Mount Cook.

Tekapo, Pukaki and Ohau, which all form part of the **Waitaki hydro scheme** (see box, p.581). At 700m above sea level, the region has some of the **cleanest air** in the southern hemisphere, and on a good day the sharp edges and vibrant colours make this one of the best places to photograph the Southern Alps, particularly around **Tekapo**.

The region encompasses New Zealand's highest peak, **Aoraki/Mount Cook**, accessed from **Aoraki/Mount Cook Village**, a perfect spot for alpine hiking and glacier skiing.

Sadly, this iconic and beautiful landscape is under threat as high international milk prices are driving the conversion of sheep stations into dairy farms, the necessary lush grass being grown on fields moistened using massive irrigation arms that create kilometre-wide **green circles of grass** amid the otherwise brown landscape. They're particularly intrusive around Twizel and Omarama.

Tekapo

The **Godley** and **Cass** rivers feed into the 83-square-kilometre **Lake Tekapo** which spills into the **Tekapo River** then wends its way across the Mackenzie Basin.

On Lake Tekapo's southern shore, the burgeoning village of **TEKAPO** revolves around a roadside ribbon of cafés and gift shops surrounded by new housing developments. Its name derives from the Maori *taka* ("sleeping mat") and *po* ("night"), suggesting that this place has long been used as a stopover. It still is, with visitors keen to spend a sunny afternoon picnicking on the lakeshore, enjoying the sunset from a hot pool then stargazing after dark.

Church of the Good Shepherd
Pioneer Drive • Daily 9am–5pm • Donation

Everyone's first stop is the tiny lakeside **Church of the Good Shepherd**, an enchanting little stone church built in 1935 as a memorial to the Mackenzie Country pioneers. Behind the rough-hewn Oamaru stone altar, a square window perfectly frames the lake and the surrounding hills and mountains. About 100m east, the **Collie Dog Monument** was erected in 1968 by local sheep farmers to honour the dogs that make it possible to graze this harsh terrain.

Alpine Springs
6 Lakeside Drive • Daily 10am–9pm • $18 • ☎ 0800 235 382, ⓦ alpinesprings.co.nz

To simply unwind, head to this outdoor complex which combines beautiful, state-of-the-art hot pools (each subtly shaped like local lakes, with heated alpine water ranging from 32°C to 40°C) with a day spa. Treatments include a hot-stone massage (90min, $195). There's also a summertime in-line skating rink ($8), and a winter park with ice-skating ($16) and snow tubing (from $19).

FROM TOP CHURCH OF THE GOOD SHEPHERD (P.570); APPROACHING PINNACLES HUT, MOUNT SOMERS TRACK (P.567) >

10

SKIING IN THE MACKENZIE COUNTRY

Along with the glacier skiing at Aoraki/Mount Cook the Mackenzie basin offers club skiing at three fields, all generally open from late June to late September.

Mount Dobson 28km east of Tekapo along SH8 then 15km north along a gravel access road ☎ 03 685 8039, ⓦ dobson.co.nz. Renowned for its powder snow, long hours of sunshine and uncrowded fields, Mt Dobson's four beginner, six intermediate and four advanced runs cater for all levels. There's a platter lift, T-bar and a triple chair, and a weekend and holiday shuttle connects to Fairlie – contact the ski office for seasonal schedules. Lift ticket $72.

Ohau 9km west of Lake Ohau Lodge ☎ 03 438 9885, ⓦ ohau.co.nz. This small, high-country ski-field has reliable powder snow and uncrowded slopes, with three beginner, seven intermediate and five advanced runs. Equipment rental is available at the field. Lift tickets $63.

Roundhill 32km north of Tekapo along Lilybank Rd ☎ 03 680 6977, ⓦ roundhill.co.nz. Families flock to this relaxed field where you'll find one long T-bar and two learner tows plus the world's longest and steepest rope tow, giving a total vertical of 783m – the greatest in the country. Most of the terrain is gentle and undulating, though the rope tow gives access to four black runs. Lift passes cost $72, and there are good ski and board rental and instruction packages, plus tobogganing for $15/day.

Mount John

9km northwest of Tekapo • ☎ 03 680 6960, ⓦ earthandsky.co.nz

Minimal light pollution presents perfect conditions for observing the night skies, and the 1000m summit of **Mount John**, 9km northwest of Tekapo, has sprouted telescope domes operated by the University of Canterbury and astronomical institutions around the world. There's an excellent hike up here (see box opposite) and great reward in the form of *Astro Café*, though the star attraction is the range of observatory and night sky tours (see box opposite).

ARRIVAL AND DEPARTURE
TEKAPO

By bus Buses linking Christchurch and Queenstown all stop in the village centre: NakedBus, Southern Link and InterCity/Newmans/Great Sights outside Lake Tekapo Tavern; Atomic outside the Shell petrol station; and Cook Connections pick up from accommodation.
Destinations Aoraki/Mount Cook (1–2 daily; 1hr 30min); Christchurch (5 daily; 3–4hr); Queenstown (5 daily; 3–4hr); Twizel (5 daily; 30min).

INFORMATION

i-SITE SH8 (Dec–March 9am–7pm; April–Nov 9am–5pm; ☎ 03 680 6579, ⓦ mtcooknz.com).

Services There is no bank. The ATM in the Shell petrol station accepts most (but not all) cards.

ACCOMMODATION

Most accommodation in this tourist-oriented village is on the expensive side, with the few budget options often oversubscribed – book ahead.

The Chalet Boutique Motel 14 Pioneer Drive ☎ 0800 843 242, ⓦ thechalet.co.nz. Six individually decorated, self-contained apartments, some overlooking the lake, in a pretty spot footsteps from the Church of the Good Shepherd. $185
Lake Tekapo Motels and Holiday Park 2 Lakeside Drive ☎ 03 680 6825, ⓦ laketekapo-accommodation .co.nz. Situated at the southwestern end of Tekapo 1km from town, this large, well-equipped campsite overlooks the lake. Camping $15, basic cabins $70, en-suite cabins $115, motel units $130
Lakefront Lodge Backpackers Lakeside Drive ☎ 0800 840 740. Light-filled modern chalet-style hostel with lake views from the spacious lounge and some rooms. There's bike ($25/half-day) and kayak rental ($25/hr). Dorms $28, doubles $80

★ **Merino Country Farmstay** SH8, 13km east of Lake Tekapo Village ☎ 03 685 8670, ⓦ merinocountry farmstay.co.nz. Traditional Kiwi hospitality on a working sheep farm running 5,000 merinos, with romantic accommodation in the 1924-built homestead and exquisite evening meals ($50; on request). Continental breakfast Is included, or you can upgrade to a cooked breakfast ($16 extra) made with produce from the vegetable garden and orchard as well as freshly laid eggs. $150

Peppers Bluewater Resort ☎ 0800 275 373, Ⓦ peppers.co.nz/bluewater. Classy collection of small hotel rooms and stylish, larger villas (up to three bedrooms), most with great lake and mountain views. The landscaped grounds include a good restaurant and bar. Doubles $145, deluxe doubles $270, villas $325

Tailor-made-Tekapo Backpackers 9 Aorangi Crescent ☎ 03 680 6700, Ⓦ tailor-made-backpackers.co.nz. A 5min walk from the bus stop and shops, this friendly 1950s hostel lacks a view but does have comfy rooms with beds (no bunks) plus well-kept grounds with a BBQ area. Dorms $27, doubles $66, en suites $76

10

TOURS AND ACTIVITIES IN TEKAPO

Mount John, immediately north of Tekapo, is the destination for a couple of nice **walks** which can be combined as a loop (probably taking the longer, gentler route up), and for superb skywatching **observatory tours**. The magnificent scenery all around provides a great backdrop to some fine boat trips, horse rides and flightseeing.

WALKS

Mt John Summit (1km one-way; 1hr; 300m ascent). Short, sharp ascent from beside the Alpine Springs up through larch forest full of birds.

Mt John Lakeshore & Summit (6km one-way; 2hr; 300m ascent). Easy stroll north along the lakeshore then gradually up a long ridge with ever longer views.

OBSERVATORY TOURS

Book early if you don't want to be shunted onto an even later tour, and **dress warm**: they equip you with enormous red parkas and feed you hot chocolate but it can still be cold. Most tours start from the office in town; a free shuttle bus takes you to the hilltop.

Observatory Day Tour (daily 10am–4pm on request; 30min; $50). If you've driven or walked to the summit of Mount John, consider this tour, which starts at the *Astro Café*. They'll show you the inside of some of the observatory domes and, if clear, look at the sun through a solar telescope.

Observatory Night Tour (daily after nightfall, approx 8pm in winter, 10pm in summer; 2hr; $105). Easily the most popular tour, you'll get to look through the largest telescopes available (up to 61cm) at whatever's up: the Southern Cross, the Large Magellanic Cloud, nebulae, and perhaps the glorious Jewel Box. They'll show you how to get the best star photos (even with a

point-and-shoot), and if the night is cloudy you'll delve into the life of an astronomer and the work being done by the universities of Canterbury and Nagoya.

Sunset Tour (daily at dusk; 2hr; $105). If you can't face the late finish of the night tour, go for this option where you'll get a (hopefully) great sunset followed by telescope viewing of the darkening sky.

Cowan's Hill Star Tour (nightly after dark on clear nights; 1hr 30min; $65). Budget tour that doesn't visit Mt John conducts viewing from a telescope on a hill away from the (admittedly minimal) lights of Tekapo. This is the only tour that offers a full refund if it is cloudy.

BOAT TRIPS

Cruise Tekapo ☎ 027 479 7675, Ⓦ cruisetekapo .co.nz. Speedboat lake trips ranging from a spin around

the highlights (20min; $40) to a visit to Motuariki Island with a barbecue salmon meal (2hr; $110).

FLIGHTSEEING

Air Safaris ☎ 0800 806 880, Ⓦ airsafaris.co.nz. Take the "Grand Traverse" (50min; $325) which swoops across the Main Divide to the West Coast, providing views of the Franz Josef and Fox glaciers, the Tasman and Muller glaciers and Aoraki/Mount Cook.

Tekapo Helicopters ☎ 0800 359 835, Ⓦ tekapo helicopters.co.nz. Various flights, all including a snow landing: visit the Ben Ohau Range (25min; $195), Mount Cook (45min; $330) or over the range to Franz Josef and Fox glaciers (70min; $550).

HORSE RIDING

Mackenzie Alpine Trekking ☎ 0800 628 269, Ⓦ maht.co.nz. One-hour ($50) or 3hr 30min ($140) guided horse riding in dramatic alpine scenery where

you really get a sense of how tough it was to tame this land. Operates Nov–April.

YHA Lake Tekapo 3 Simpson Lane ☎03 680 6857, ⓦyha.co.nz. One of the best YHAs around, full of life and with a common room heated by a log-burner and framed by a floor-to-ceiling lake-view window. Camping $18, dorms $38, double $96

CAMPING

Lake McGregor 1km west of Tekapo then 9km north. Simple DOC-style camping in open country beside a pretty lake, with a vault toilet and tap water. Reached along a mostly gravel road. $5

EATING AND DRINKING

★ **Astro Café** Mt John summit. With stupendous lake and mountain views, this café atop Mt John serves cakes, sandwiches, soup ($10) and stellar espresso. Daily 10am–5pm.

★ **Kohan** SH8 ☎03 680 6688, ⓦkohannz.com. The surroundings are functional, but there's a great view and superb sashimi that won't break the bank. The bento box will set you back $24. BYO & licensed. Daily 11.30am–2pm & 6–9pm.

Reflections SH8 ☎03 680 6234, ⓦreflections restaurant.co.nz. Local salmon, rack of lamb and peppered venison all get a run on the wide-ranging menu at this reliable restaurant that opens out to a terrace at the lake's edge, though there are few-to-no vegetarian options. Try the chicken breast sandwich ($16) or salmon in lemon caper beurre blanc ($28). Daily 7am–9pm or later.

Run 77 SH8 ☎03 680 6900. Classy store selling elegant merino-wool clothing and gourmet deli goods (including local organic wines) and also housing the village's best daytime café, with great coffee and freshly baked sweet and savoury treats. Daily 9am–5pm.

Lake Pukaki

47km southwest of Tekapo

From Tekapo, SH8 heads to the southern shores of the 30km-long **Lake Pukaki**, another intensely opaque blue glacial lake backed by the glistening peaks of the Southern Alps. A roadside parking area is the spot to pull over and admire fabulous views across the lake to Aoraki/Mount Cook and its icy attendants.

Peters Lookout

A kilometre on from the viewing area, SH80 branches north towards Aoraki/Mount Cook. This good, fast and virtually flat road runs for 55km from the Lake Pukaki junction along the tussocklands of Lake Pukaki's western shore, passing, after 12km, **Peters Lookout**, another popular lakeside viewing point.

ACCOMMODATION   LAKE PUKAKI

The Pines SH8, 12km north of Twizel. A vast and unsigned camping area with long-drop toilets, a water tap and fabulous lake and mountain views from spots along the waterfront. **Free**

Aoraki/Mount Cook

New Zealand's highest mountain, the spectacular 3754m **Mount Cook** is increasingly known by its Maori name, **Aoraki**, meaning "cloud piercer" – and the two names are often run together as Aoraki/Mount Cook. It commands the 700-square-kilometre **Aoraki/Mount Cook National Park**, which was designated a UNESCO World Heritage Site in 1986. With 22 peaks over 3000m, the park contains the lion's share of New Zealand's highest mountains, mostly made of greywacke (a type of rock common in New Zealand) laid in an ocean trench 250–300 million years ago.

Aoraki/Mount Cook is at the heart of a unique mountain area whose rock is easily shattered in the cold, leaving huge amounts of gravel in the valley floors. The tussock-cloaked foothills, where Mount Cook lilies, summer daisies and snow gentians thrive, contrast with the inhospitable ice fields of the upper slopes.

All this is easily accessible on walks to great viewpoints and even to the base of the 27km-long **Tasman Glacier**, fed by icefalls tumbling from the heavily glaciated surrounding peaks.

10

The **weather** here is highly changeable, often with a pall of low-lying cloud liable to turn to rain, and the mountain air is lung-searingly fresh. On windy days, an atmospheric white dust rises from the plain at the base of the mountain.

Brief history

Maori tell how Aoraki came to be. Both the sky father (Raki) and the earth mother (Papa-tua-nuku) already had children by previous unions. After their marriage, some of the sky father's children came to inspect their father's new wife. Four brothers, Ao-raki, Raki-roa, Raki-rua and Raraki-roa, circled around her in a canoe called Te Waka-a-Aoraki, but once they left her shores disaster befell them. Running aground on a reef, the canoe was turned to stone. The four occupants climbed to the higher western side of the petrified canoe, where they too were transformed: Ao-raki became Aoraki/Mount Cook, and his three younger brothers formed flanking peaks – Mount Dampier, Mount Teichelmann and Mount Tasman.

Geologists claim that about two million years ago the **Alpine Fault** began to lift, progressively pushing the rock upwards and creating the Southern Alps. These days the process continues at about the same rate as erosion, ensuring that the mountains are at least holding their own – if not getting bigger.

Mount Cook was named in honour of the English sea captain in 1851. Its summit was first reached in 1894 but, because of the peak's sacredness to Maori, climbers are asked not to step on the summit itself.

Aoraki/Mount Cook Village

The only habitation in the national park is at the tiny **AORAKI/MOUNT COOK VILLAGE**, set at 760m and encircled by a horseshoe of mountains topped by Aoraki/Mount Cook itself. Almost everything is run either by *The Hermitage* hotel (which operates the Sir Edmund Hillary Alpine Centre) or DOC (who have a fascinating visitor centre). Mostly, though, you'll be wanting to get outdoors.

DOC visitor centre

Daily: Dec–Feb 8.30am–6pm; March–Nov 8.30am–5pm • Free • ☏ 03 435 1186

Not just a place to get tramping and weather info and buy maps but a window on the wondrous natural and social history of the region – a natural complement to what's on show at the Sir Edmund Hillary Alpine Centre. Set an hour aside to delve into displays spread across two floors exploring climate, glacier dynamics, climbing history and the region's relevance to early explorers, scientists and cartographers. There are wonderful old photos of Victorian women climbers in full-length dresses, a helpful relief model of the mountains, material on the history of *The Hermitage* and on the development of mountain huts (especially the Mueller Hut). Outside,

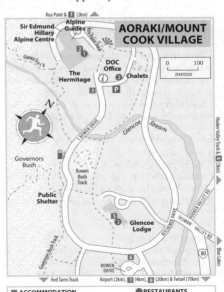

■ ACCOMMODATION		■ RESTAURANTS,
Aoraki Mount Cook Alpine Lodge	3	CAFÉS & BARS
Glentanner Park Centre	8	Chamois Bar & Grill	3
The Hermitage	2	The Hermitage	1
Mt Cook Backpacker Lodge	5	The Old Mountaineers	2
Unwin Lodge	7	
White Horse Hill campground	1/4	
YHA Mt Cook	6	

10

> ## SIR EDMUND HILLARY
>
> Sir Edmund Hillary has long been the most famous and admired New Zealander, and his death in 2008, aged 88, has probably raised his profile further. His ascent of Mount Everest in 1953 with Tenzing Norgay was undoubtedly an impressive achievement, and his humanitarian work in the villages of Nepal was widely lauded, but above all, Hillary embodied the qualities Kiwis hold most dear: hard-working, straight-talking, honest and, most of all, modest. As he famously said on his return from the successful summit attempt, "Well George, we knocked the bastard off". That's what gets your face on every $5 note in the country.
>
> Though he grew up near Auckland, Sir Ed did much of his early climbing around Aoraki/Mount Cook Village, where a **bronze statue** of a youthful Hillary stands outside *Sir Edmund Hillary Alpine Centre*.

the old six-bunk Empress Hut (relocated from the slopes of Aoraki/Mount Cook) gives a sense of mountain life that isn't much changed today.

Sir Edmund Hillary Alpine Centre

Inside *The Hermitage* • Daily 7.30am–8.30pm • Free; movies and planetarium $16 for one show, $27 for all six • ☎ 0800 686 800, ⓦ hermitage.co.nz

The history of *The Hermitage* hotel and its place in Kiwi climbing history is told in this small museum which also showcases the development of the region and the climbing life of its namesake, including a replica of the tractor he used to get to the South Pole in 1956. It is interesting enough but the emphasis is on a state-of-the-art **3D theatre** and **planetarium** which plays a near continuous roster of shows, such as: *Mount Cook Magic*, which whizzes you through the geographical, cultural and sporting evolution of the mountains using a blend of authentic footage and computer graphics; *Hillary on Everest*; and Black Holes, *Tycho to the Moon*, one for the kids. Profits from the centre help fund Hillary's Himalayan Trust.

Tramping and walking in Aoraki/Mount Cook National Park

Scenic **walks** in the park range from gentle day-hikes on the fringes of the village to spectacular alpine treks. DOC's *Walks around Aoraki/Mount Cook Village* leaflet lists eleven excellent shorter walks (10min–5hr) which can be extended by those with relevant experience. Don't walk on the surface of any of the glaciers unless you know what you're doing, or are in the company of someone qualified.

Blue Lakes and Tasman Glacier View

1km return; 40min; 100m ascent

A fairly gentle walk with good views of the lower sections of the Tasman Glacier, which is 600m deep at its thickest point, 3km across at its widest and moves at a rate of 20cm a day. The walk starts at the Blue Lakes shelter, 8km drive up the Tasman Valley Road, but you'll need your own vehicle as there are no shuttles.

Governors Bush Walk

1hr return from the village; 2km

The easiest of the local walks, this trail leads through a small stand of silver beech with abundant birdlife. You gradually climb to a lookout with views back towards Aoraki/Mount Cook. It is sheltered enough to make it viable in poor weather.

Hooker Valley Track

9km return from Whitehorse Hill campsite; 3hr; 200m ascent

You don't really need to do all of this popular and superb there-and-back hike; just go as far as you want, perhaps to the Alpine Memorial with views of the western side of Aoraki/Mount Cook or across a couple of swingbridges beside pretty Mueller Lake to

Hooker Lake at the base of the Hooker Glacier. Allow an extra hour if you start from and return to the village.

Kea Point Walk

2hr return from the village; 7km; negligible ascent

For great views with relatively little effort, follow this path through gentle grasslands to a viewpoint on the moraine wall of the Mueller Glacier. Here you can look down into Mueller Lake, up the valley to the Hooker Glacier and above you to the hanging glaciers and icefalls of Mount Sefton.

10

Mueller Hut Route

10km return from the village; 6–8hr; 1000m ascent

This challenging route leaves the Kea Point Track just before its arrival at the glacier and climbs steeply westwards up the Sealy Tarns Track. From the tarns the route to the hut is marked by orange triangles guiding you up the final assault on loose gravel to a skyline ridge and the modern Mueller Hut (see p.580). At 1800m the views are quite startling and you're engulfed by almost perfect silence, interrupted only by the murmur of running water and squawking kea. The track requires crampons, ice axes and winter

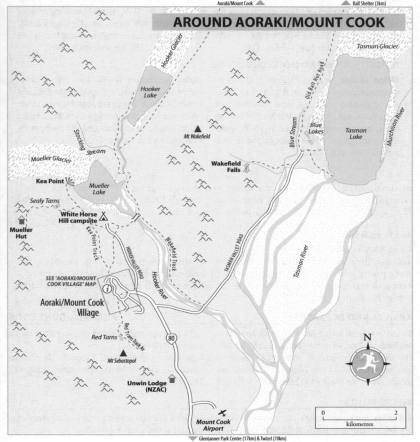

10

AORAKI/MOUNT COOK TOURS AND ACTIVITIES

As long as the weather plays ball, it would be hard to be bored around Aoraki/Mount Cook Village. As well as cruising or paddling a glacier lake you can hike to places you never thought you'd go, ride horses and off-road vehicles in spectacular scenery or spend an hour gazing at the night sky.

Scenic flights offer glimpses of areas you could never dream of reaching on foot. Book a few days ahead, but be prepared to be flexible as flights are cancelled in high winds or poor visibility. The peak season is November–March, but in winter (June & July) the weather's often clearer and the views more dramatic.

There are no developed ski-fields in the Aoraki/Mount Cook area, but choppers open up the Tasman Glacier and surrounding mountains for guided **heli-skiing and heli-snowboarding**. During the **season** (July–Sept or Oct), steep, untouched runs cater for those with strong intermediate skills or better.

BOATING AND KAYAKING

Glacier Explorers ☎ 0800 686 800, ⊛ glacier explorers.co.nz. Spend an eerie hour chugging around on Tasman Lake among detached icebergs turned grey by the presence of ground-down rock that reflects the light. Examining chunks of fallen ice up close reveals beautiful honeycombed cells. Wrap up warmly for the trips, which incorporate a 15min shuttle from the village, a half-hour moraine walk then the boat ride. Trips run mid-Aug to late May (3–7 daily; $140).

Glacier Sea Kayaking ☎ 03 435 1890, ⊛ mtcook .com. There's a real sense of being dwarfed by icebergs when you're at water level on unique and fascinating paddling trips aboard outrigger-stabilized kayaks with enthusiastic guides. The biggest bergs are on Tasman Lake (2 daily; 4hr; $145), reached by minibus ride then a 30min moraine walk, but you get better views of Aoraki/ Mount Cook from trips on the less exposed Mueller Lake (2–3 daily; 3hr; $130). Trips run early Oct–April.

GUIDED HIKING AND MOUNTAINEERING

Alpine Guides The Hermitage ☎ 03 435 1834, ⊛ alpineguides.co.nz. The main resource for experienced climbing guides and rental equipment such as crampons and ice axes ($10/item/day). There are regular mountaineering courses (6 days; $2025), winter ski-touring trips and custom private guiding on snow and rock. Daily 8am–5pm.

Alpine Recreation ☎ 0800 006 096, ⊛ alpine recreation.com. Professional guiding company best known for its high-altitude trek across Ball Pass ($1080) which involves a three-day alpine crossing reaching 2130m close to Aoraki/Mount Cook and staying in the comfortable, private Caroline Hut.

mountaineering experience in the colder months but is generally ice-free from November to mid-April. At any time of year, consult DOC's *Mueller Hut Route* leaflet ($2), and sign the intentions book before you set out.

Red Tarns Track

4km return from the village; 2hr; 300m ascent

This excellent and very achievable walk has one short, steep section but rewards with some pretty pools coloured by the red pond weed that gives them their name. From here uninterrupted views stretch across the village towards Aoraki/Mount Cook and along the Tasman Valley.

ARRIVAL AND DEPARTURE AORAKI/MOUNT COOK

By bus Great Sights make a daily run from Christchurch to Aoraki/Mount Cook, while the Cook Connection (☎ 0800 266 526, ⊛ cookconnect.co.nz; mid-Sept to May only) links Aoraki/Mount Cook with Twizel and Tekapo. All bus services call at *Glentanner Park Centre*, *Unwin Lodge* and *YHA Mt Cook* on request, before dropping off at the car park near *The Hermitage*.

Destinations Christchurch (1 daily; 5hr 30min); Lake Tekapo (1–3 daily; 1hr 30min); Queenstown (1 daily; 4hr); Twizel (1–3 daily; 1hr).

INFORMATION

DOC office and visitor centre 1 Larch Grove Rd (daily: Dec–Feb 8.30am–6pm, March–Nov 8.30am–5pm; ☎ 03 435 1186, ⊜ mtcookvc@doc.govt.nz). All the information you need on walks, huts and the village.

10

SCENIC FLIGHTS

Helicopter Line Glentanner Park, 20km south of the village ☎0800 650 651, ⓦhelicopter.co.nz. Three scenic helicopter trips with opportunities to hover along the valley walls and peaks, or view the tumbling blocks of the Hochstetter Icefall; all include brief snow landings. Choose from the Alpine Vista (20min; $215), Alpine Explorer (30min; $295) and Mountains High (45min; $399), which circumnavigates Aoraki with views down to the West Coast.

Mount Cook Ski Planes ☎0800 800 702, ⓦmtcookskiplanes.com. Flights from the company that helped develop the technology for snow landings and have been operating memorable flights from the Mount Cook Airfield since 1955. Prices are the same for fixed-wing or helicopter flights – from $275 for 25min, up to the Grand Circle (55min; $530), which loops around Aoraki, briefly crossing the Main Divide, hugging the immense valley walls and then landing on the silent Tasman Glacier to wander on the breathtaking footprint-free snow.

FOUR-WHEEL DRIVING

Tasman Valley 4WD & Argo Tours ☎0800 686 600, ⓦmountcooktours.co.nz. The Hermitage operates this good rainy-day alternative (year-round; 2–5 trips daily; 90min; $75) involving riding around the Tasman moraine in an eight-wheeler Argo stopping at otherwise inaccessible viewpoints.

SKIING AORAKI/MOUNT COOK

Alpine Guides ☎03 435 1834, ⓦalpineguides.co.nz. Offers multi-day ski-touring and ski-mountaineering trips plus the only access to heli-skiing in the park (July–Sept; 5 runs for $950, plus equipment).

Southern Alps Guiding ☎03 435 1890, ⓦmtcook .com. All-day guided trips including lunch and two very long wilderness runs (8–10km; $830), or one run on the Tasman and one on the even less visited Murchison Glacier ($925). You can also heli-ski the Ben Ohau range (four runs; $825).

HORSE RIDING

Glentanner Park Centre SH80, 20km south of the village ☎03 435 1855, ⓦglentanner.co.nz. One-hour ($70) or two-hour ($90) panoramic horse trekking tours on easy to moderate terrain. Nov–April only.

STARGAZING

Big Sky The Hermitage ☎0800 686 800, ⓦhillary centre.co.nz. A brief planetarium primer is followed by an outdoor examination of the southern sky. Departures after dark all year (2hr; $50).

Services The unstaffed petrol station accepts New Zealand cards (international credit card users need to organize it via The Hermitage hotel desk for a $5 fee). Most accommodation and The Old Mountaineers have pay internet. There's no bank or ATM but cash is often available on NZ EFTPOS cards at The Hermitage reception.

ACCOMMODATION

Book early from Oct–April, when the village often fills to capacity. Prices drop considerably during the rest of the year.

Aoraki/Mount Cook Alpine Lodge 101 Bowen Drive ☎0800 680 680, ⓦaorakialpinelodge.co.nz. Great accommodation at a realistic price, with comfy twins and doubles, a lounge with a fantastic view, a fully equipped kitchen, a deck with barbecue, and pay internet. Doubles $159, family rooms $220

Glentanner Park Centre SH80, 20km south of the village ☎03 435 1855, ⓦglentanner.co.nz. Well-equipped site with sheltered camping, dorm-style accommodation (bring or rent bedding) and cabins with views of the mountains and Tasman Valley, a panoramic sheltered barbecue area and a café. Camping $17, dorms $28, basic cabins $95, self-contained en-suite cabins $155

The Hermitage ☎0800 686 800, ⓦhermitage.co.nz. Vast hotel and restaurant complex approached through an impressive foyer – the third incarnation since the first premises opened in 1868. Rooms and suites in the main building (all of which have a balcony, many with fine views) are supplemented by chalets and motel units scattered nearby. Double $210, motels & chalets $270, Mt Cook view double $330, suite $470

Mt Cook Backpacker Lodge ☎0800 100 512, ⓦmountcookbackpackers.co.nz. Smart hostel fashioned from former staff accommodation with a self-catering kitchen and the Chamois Bar on site. Quad dorms mostly lack the views and balconies enjoyed by the en-suite doubles and private units with their own kitchen. Dorms $35, doubles $125, suites $170

10

Unwin Lodge Near the airport turn-off, 4km from the village ☏ 03 435 1100, ⒲ alpineclub.org.nz/hut/unwin. Newly rebuilt Alpine Club hut that gives priority to NZAC members and climbers but is open to all, with simple bunkroom accommodation and a massive common area with kitchen. Laundry and internet available. Non-members $30

⭐ **YHA Mt Cook** 1 Bowen Drive ☏ 03 435 1820, ⒠ yhamtck@yha.co.nz. Excellent 76-bed hostel in a cosy wooden building with modern well-kept facilities, bike rental ($30/half-day), free evening saunas and a fairly well-stocked shop. Dorms $36, doubles $118

CAMPSITES AND HUTS

Mueller Hut Only hikers tackling the Mueller Hut Route (see p.577) will want to stay the night at this 28-bunk hut, which cannot be booked in advance. Sign in at the visitor centre and pay your fee before you go – places are allocated on a first-come-first-served basis. Hut $36, camping outside $15

White Horse Hill campsite Hooker Valley Rd, 2km north of the village. A serene and informal first-come-first-served DOC camping area with stony ground and treated water in summer. Accessible by road or a 20min walk along the Kea Point Track. $6

EATING AND DRINKING

Groceries don't come cheap here and the range is very limited: bring what you need from Twizel or further afield.

Chamois Bar & Grill Mt Cook Backpacker Lodge. Straightforward boozing bar with pretty ordinary pub meals such as fish and chips, pasta and pizza, all around $18. Daily 11am–11pm.

The Hermitage ☏ 0800 686 800, ⒲ hermitage.co.nz. The hotel has dining for every taste with the *Sir Edmund Hillary Café & Bar* serving light meals from a deep Mount Cook-view terrace. The *Alpine Restaurant* serves all-you-can-eat buffets for breakfast (continental $19; cooked $27), lunch ($39) and dinner ($57), while the *Panorama Room* offers swanky à la carte dining with matchless views (mains around $40), with priority given to hotel guests. Lastly, the *Snowline Lounge* has deep leather sofas and magic views. Sir Edmund Hillary Café & Bar daily 10am–4.30pm; Alpine Restaurant 6.30–10am, noon–2pm & 6–9.30pm; Panorama Room 6–10pm; Snowline Lounge 3–11pm or later.

⭐ **The Old Mountaineers** ☏ 03 435 1890, ⒲ mtcook.com. A little pricey, but undoubtedly the best place to hang out, with a log fire, real mountain-lodge feel, comfy chairs with wonderful mountain views, an internet lounge, outstanding café-style meals including hearty veggie burgers ($21) and scrumptious soups ($13) plus great coffee, beer and wine. Daily 10am–9.30pm; winter daily 11am–8pm.

Twizel

TWIZEL (rhymes with bridle), 70km south of Aoraki/Mount Cook and 9km south of the junction of SH8 and SH80, began life in 1966 as a construction village for people working on the Waitaki hydro scheme (see box, p.581). The town was due to be bulldozed flat after the project finished in 1985. Some think this would have been a kinder fate, but enough residents wanted to stay that their wishes were granted, and it's now a low-key summertime base for forays to Aoraki/Mount Cook (a 45min drive away), scenic Lake Ohau and gliding at Omarama.

Kaki/Black Stilt visitor hide

SH8, 3km south of Twizel • 1hr guided tours late Oct to mid-April daily 9.30am & 4.30pm • $15 • ☏ 03 435 3124

Twizel's main attraction is the DOC-run **Kaki/Black Stilt visitor hide**, which is attempting to preserve the world's rarest wading bird from extinction by hatching eggs in captivity and raising the chicks before releasing them into the wild. Numbers plummeted following habitat loss due to introduced plant species, the Waitaki hydroelectric project and introduced mammalian predators, reaching a 1970s low of just 23 birds. But things are looking up and there are now over 80 breeding adults in the wild.

Access is solely on guided tours, which must be booked through the Twizel information centre.

ARRIVAL AND DEPARTURE

TWIZEL

By bus Atomic, NakedBus, InterCity/Newmans/Great Sights and Southern Link buses stop beside the car park by Market Square on their Queenstown–Christchurch runs. Cook Connection links to Tekapo and Aoraki/Mount Cook.

THE WAITAKI HYDRO SCHEME

The Waitaki hydro scheme provides a fifth of the nation's power from twelve power stations scattered along the Waitaki River and its headwaters around lakes Tekapo, Pukaki and Ohau. The scheme has its origins in the work of the engineer Peter Seton Hay, who in 1904 submitted a report to the New Zealand government indicating the extraordinary hydroelectric potential of the region. Construction began with the Waitaki power station in 1935 and continued through to 1985, when the commissioning of the Ohau C station completed one of the largest construction projects in New Zealand.

Throughout the region water is diverted along a network of canals to fill a long sequence of storage lakes held back by impressive dams, particularly the 100m-high earth-built **Benmore Dam**, 32km from Omarama in the Waitaki Valley, off SH83 en route to the east coast. You can walk or drive to the top of the dam, or take a short loop track with distant views of Aoraki/Mount Cook.

10

Destinations Aoraki/Mount Cook (1–3 daily; 1hr); Christchurch (5 daily; 4–7hr); Omarama (4 daily; 30min); Queenstown (5 daily; 3hr); Wanaka (4 daily; 2–3hr).

INFORMATION AND TOURS

Tourist information 61 Mackenzie Drive (Nov–March daily 9am–5pm; April–Oct Tues–Sat 10am–4pm; ☎03 435 3124, ⓦ twizel.info). The Twizel information centre has all the local information you need plus bookings for the Black Stilt tours.

Services There's a post office and bank (with an ATM) in the Market Place Shopping Centre.

Gear rental Twizel Adventures (☎03 435 0760, ⓦ twizeladventures.com) rent just about everything from jet skis ($120/4hr), to kayaks ($25/4hr) and mountain bikes ($25/4hr).

The Helicopter Line ☎0800 650 652, ⓦ helicopter .co.nz. Does chopper flights over/around Aoraki/Mount Cook ($230–535): they're more expensive than those from Aoraki/Mount Cook Village, but you get more time in the air.

Lord of the Rings Tour Discovery Tours ☎0800 213 868, ⓦ discoverytours.co.nz. This outfit gets you out of unlovely Twizel onto the gorgeous surrounding plains which were used for filming the battle scenes on the Pelennor Fields (daily at 9am & 1.30pm; 2hr; $79).

ACCOMMODATION

Twizel has a good range of accommodation but its proximity to Aoraki/Mount Cook means it's essential to book ahead from Christmas to at least the end of February.

Aoraki Lodge 32 Mackenzie Drive ☎03 435 0300, ⓦ aorakilodge.co.nz. Tasteful and welcoming B&B in the centre of town with four en-suite rooms, all with separate access, and a pretty garden. $210

High Country Lodge & Backpackers 23 Mackenzie Drive ☎03 435 0671, ⓦ highcountrylodge.co.nz. This huge former hydroelectric workers' camp is like a village within a village. It sleeps up to 280 in barrack-style timber buildings and newer motels, but still gets booked solid in summer. Dorms $32, rooms $78, en-suite rooms $88, motel units $125

Mountain Chalet Motels Wairepo Rd ☎0800 629 999, ⓦ mountainchalets.co.nz. Great-value collection of light-filled, self-contained A-frame chalets and an adjacent lodge offering simple, comfortable backpacker accommodation. Dorms $28, dorms with own bedding $25, chalets $110

★ **Omahau Downs** SH8, 2km north of town ☎03 435 0199, ⓦ omahau.co.nz. Lovely combination of four modern B&B rooms with great Aoraki/Mount Cook views, and three self-catering cottages in a rural setting. All share access to an outdoor wood-fired bath ($20). Closed June–Aug. B&B $165, self-contained cottage $125

Twizel Holiday Park 122 Mackenzie Drive ☎03 435 0507, ⓦ twizelholidaypark.co.nz. Large campsite with tent and powered sites plus some motel units and en-suite rooms that use a separate kitchen from campers. Camping/site $36, dorms $30, rooms $90

EATING AND DRINKING

Hunters Café Bar 2 Market Place ☎03 435 0303. Family-friendly spot serving generous lunches (under $20) and evening mains such as beer-battered fish and locally farmed salmon (under $30). Daily 11am–9.30pm or later.

★ **Poppies** 1 Benmore Place ☎03 435 0848, ⓦ poppiescafe.com. Elegant wine-red space with polished concrete floors and shelves of gourmet deli goods, serving classy café fare, as well as beautifully cooked lunches such as ham and asparagus tart ($16), with lots of organic produce straight from the owners' garden. Dinners might stretch to local salmon on a lemon and herb risotto ($32). Daily: Dec–March 8am–10pm; April–Nov 10am–9pm.

Shawty's 4 Market Place ☎ 03 435 3155, ⊛ shawtys .co.nz. Restaurant and lounge bar where good coffee,

tasty breakfasts and sizeable lunches are served with care in the casual interior or overlooking the village green. Dinners include ribeye on mash with grilled field mushrooms ($30), and they do a fine line in gourmet pizzas including chorizo ($17) and chili bean and jalapeño ($26). Daily 8.30am–10pm, shorter hours in winter.

10 Lake Ohau

The narrow Lake Ohau Road runs 25km west of Twizel to idyllic **Lake Ohau**, secluded among beech forest with distinctive natural features including kettle lakes (small depressions left when blocks of glacial ice melt) and terracing on its banks that reflects the light of summer sunsets. Northwest of the lake, the **Ohau Forests** are crisscrossed by numerous tracks (30min–4hr), outlined in DOC's *Ruataniwha Conservation Area* leaflet, available from *Lake Ohau Lodge*. In winter, the Ohau ski-field (see box, p.572) is in full swing.

ACCOMMODATION AND EATING   LAKE OHAU

Lake Ohau Lodge Lake Ohau Rd ☎ 03 438 9885, ⊛ ohau.co.nz. Though popular on summer tour-bus itineraries, this 72-room hotel is saved by its wonderful setting and super-peaceful evenings. There's no self-catering, but guests and visitors can book ahead for

breakfast (continental $15; cooked $21) and dinner ($42) from a set menu, or drop by for a drink at the well-stocked bar. The lodge also has petrol, and organizes a ski-shuttle service ($25 return). Camping $\overline{12}$, doubles $\overline{105}$

Omarama

SH8 traverses tussock and sheep country 30km south from Twizel to the junction settlement of **OMARAMA** (Maori for "place of light"), best known for the **Clay Cliffs** just outside town and its wonderful conditions for **gliding**.

Omarama Hot Tubs

25 Omarama Ave (SH8) • Daily 10am–10pm • Hot tubs $30/person for 90min; hot tub & sauna $125 for two including towels • ☎ 03 438 9703, ⊛ hottubsomarama.co.nz

There are no hot springs at **Omarama Hot Tubs**, just chemical-free mountain water heated in ten exquisitely landscaped private outdoor tubs overlooking the mountains. Though it feels very open, no one can overlook your idyll.

Totara Peak Gallery

Chain Hills Hwy (SH83) • Sept to mid-June daily 9am–5.30pm • Free • ☎ 03 438 9757, ⊛ omaramaantiques.com

It would be easy (but wrong) to pass the Western-style frontage of this movie-museum-cum-collectables-shop. Come to browse the secondhand books, old hand tools, ceramics, jewellery and classic cars but mostly to ogle the random collection of original props and costumes from shows such as *Xena: Warrior Princess*.

Clay Cliffs Scenic Reserve

10km west of SH8, 5km north of Omarama • Open access • $5; pay at the Omarama Hot Tubs

A rough side road leads to the **Clay Cliffs Scenic Reserve** where the braided Ahuriri River provides a picturesque backdrop to eerie badlands of bare pinnacles and angular ridges separated by narrow ravines and canyons. They were created when a 100m uplift caused by the Ostler Fault exposed gravels that responded individually to the weathering process.

The Maori name for the clay cliffs is *Paritea*, meaning white or light-coloured cliff, and they were so named by Araiteuru, who brought *kumara* (sweet potatoes) from

GLIDING AROUND OMARAMA

Prevailing westerly winds rising over the Southern Alps create a unique air-wave across the Mackenzie Country's flatlands, making Omarama New Zealand's gliding capital. Its airfield was the one-time playground of Dick Georgeson, pioneer of New Zealand aviation and the South Island's first glider pilot, back in 1950. You can follow his lead with Southern Soaring (☎0800 762 746, ⓦ soaring.co.nz) who let you take the front seat on spectacular two-seater glider flights, with a chance to take the controls and get great views of Aoraki/Mount Cook on a good day. The 30min trip ($325) is a great taster, but if you can, upgrade to the 1hr ($395) or the 2hr ($595), which will probably head over to the mountains and may require supplementary oxygen. Most trips run October and March.

10

Hawaiki. The cliffs provided natural shelter for moa hunters, with several surviving earth ovens indicative of early Maori settlement.

ARRIVAL AND INFORMATION

OMARAMA

By bus Buses stop centrally from Christchurch (5 daily; 5–7hr); Queenstown (5 daily; 2hr 15min); Twizel (5 daily; 30min).

Tourist information Omarama Hot Tubs (daily 10am–10pm; ☎03 438 9703) has a small information centre and does bookings.

ACCOMMODATION AND EATING

Ahuriri Bridge campsite SH8, 3km north of town. A pretty and peaceful, willow-shaded DOC campsite beside the Ahuriri River that's perfect for tenters and those in campervans. Comes with long-drop toilets and river water. Free

★ **Buscot Station** SH8, 8km north of town ☎03 438 9646. This merino sheep farm is the most peaceful place to stay in the area, in a cosy homestead surrounded by a beautifully kept garden; they'll arrange pick-ups if you book ahead. Dorms $22, doubles $55

Omarama Top 10 Holiday Park 1 Omarama Ave ☎0800 662 726, ⓦ omaramatop10.co.nz. Quality camping and cabins right in the centre of town. Camping/site $32, cabins $55, kitchen cabins $75, en suites $110

Sierra Motels 22 Omarama Ave ☎0800 743 772, ⓦ omarama.co.nz. Friendly motel with a mixture of older and newer units all with Sky TV, kitchenette or full kitchen plus its own fishing tackle shop. $120

The Wrinkly Rams 24 Omarama Ave (SH8) ☎03 438 9751, ⓦ thewrinklyrams.co.nz. Licensed local landmark that offers Omarama's best café and pub-style fare, along with live sheep-shearing shows. Expect all-day breakfast ($19) and Caesar salad ($16). Daily 8am–8pm or later.

Dunedin to Stewart Island

588 Dunedin

600 Port Chalmers and around

603 The Otago Peninsula

609 The Catlins Coast

618 Gore

620 Invercargill

624 Bluff

626 Stewart Island

TAIERI GORGE RAILWAY

Dunedin to Stewart Island

The southeastern corner of the South Island contains some of the least-visited parts of New Zealand, yet packs in the gems. The darkly Gothic harbourside city of Dunedin is a seat of learning and culture, influenced by the country's oldest university and thriving Scottish immigrant traditions. Elsewhere it is all about wild nature. On Dunedin's doorstep, the windswept Otago Peninsula is a phenomenal wildlife haven, mostly farmland but fringed with opportunities to see yellow-eyed and blue penguins, fur seals and albatrosses within 5km of each other. South of Dunedin there are yet more exemplary opportunities to see wildlife at its primal best along the dramatic Catlins Coast. Provincial Invercargill is the gateway to Stewart Island, New Zealand's third island and superb territory for stepping back a few years and spotting kiwi.

11

The "Edinburgh of the South", **DUNEDIN** takes its name from the Gaelic translation of its Scottish counterpart, with which it shares street and suburb names. Founded by Scottish settlers, its heyday was in the 1860s and 1870s as the commercial centre for the gold-rush towns of inland Central Otago. This left an enduring legacy of imposing **Gothic Revival architecture** fashioned from volcanic bluestone and creamy limestone.

On Dunedin's outskirts, **Port Chalmers** hangs onto a slightly bohemian, rough-around-the-edges feel, repaying a quick visit by combining it with the nearby **Orokonui Ecosanctuary**. Across the harbour, the **Otago Peninsula** packs in the wildlife highlights with penguins, albatrosses and seals all competing for attention with **Larnach Castle** and its fine grounds.

To the south, the pace slows along the untamed **Catlins Coast**, with yet more wonderful opportunities for spotting marine wildlife, but in an altogether wilder setting. Hills cloaked in native forest come right down to a shoreline indented with rocky bays, long sweeps of sand and spectacular geological formations.

New Zealand's southernmost city is **Invercargill**, bordered by the rich pastureland of Southland's farming communities. The city is the springboard for **Bluff**, the country's oldest European town, and magical **Stewart Island**. Relatively few visit New Zealand's third island, but those who do are rewarded by the extraordinary birdlife, particularly in **Mason Bay** and on **Ulva Island**.

Kiwis from more northern parts delight in condemning the **climate** of the southern South Island, and it's true that the further south you go the wetter and more

Dunedin tours and activities p.595
Rugby in Dunedin p.599
Dunedin festivals p.600
Riding Dunedin's scenic railways p.601
Dunedin and Otago Peninsula nature tours p.603
Walks around Dunedin and the Otago Peninsula p.605
Observing wildlife p.606
The yellow-eyed penguin p.607
The royal albatross p.608

The Catlins Top Track p.615
The New Zealand sea lion and Hector's dolphin p.618
Burt Munro – Invercargill's local hero p.620
Foveaux Strait, Bluff oysters and muttonbirds p.626
Short walks around Oban p.629
Stewart Island adventure trips and tours p.630

CAREY'S BAY, OTAGO HARBOUR

Highlights

❶ Dunedin Soak up the Gothic architecture of New Zealand's "Scottish city" while sampling the galleries, museums and frenetic student scene. See p.588

❷ Taieri Gorge Combine a train trip winding through the rugged Taieri Gorge with cycling the Otago Central Rail Trail. See p.601

❸ Otago Peninsula Whether you choose to paddle, cruise or drive around this stunning coastline you'll get amazingly close to all sorts of wildlife. See p.603

❹ Curio Bay Survey a fossilized forest along the shoreline, watch yellow-eyed penguins come ashore and see Hector's dolphins surfing the waves of the wild Catlins Coast. See p.617

❺ Invercargill Inspect a tuatara, see Burt Munro's record-breaking motorcycle and sample the fine produce of the Invercargill Brewery. See p.620

❻ Stewart Island You'll slip straight into Rakiura's island vibe as soon as you step ashore – but make the effort to rouse yourself for superb birdwatching, great kayaking and rugged tramps. See p.626

❼ Mason Bay Tramp to Stewart Island's windswept west coast for a chance to spot rare kiwis in the wild. See p.629

HIGHLIGHTS ARE MARKED ON THE MAP ON P.588

changeable it gets. Come between November and April and you'll experience daytime highs approaching 20°C and catch the best of the wildlife during the breeding season.

Dunedin

The darkly Gothic harbourside city of Dunedin is the largest city in the southern half of the South Island, its population of around 120,000 bolstered by 25,000 students from the **University of Otago** – New Zealand's oldest tertiary institution

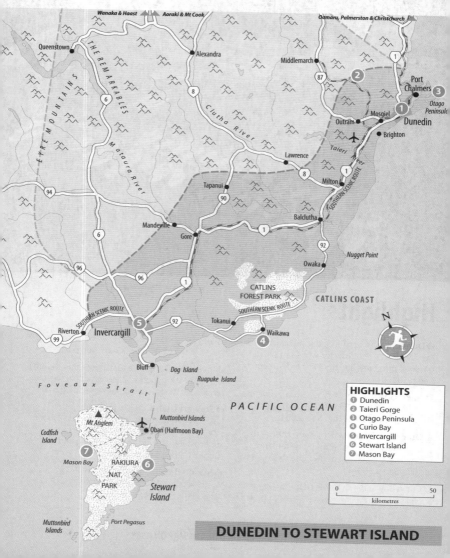

HIGHLIGHTS
1. Dunedin
2. Taieri Gorge
3. Otago Peninsula
4. Curio Bay
5. Invercargill
6. Stewart Island
7. Mason Bay

DUNEDIN TO STEWART ISLAND

– who contribute to a strong **arts scene**, as well as vibrant **nightlife**, during term time at least.

The university aside, the city hasn't had a lot of investment in recent decades and while some sections can feel a bit shabby it does mean that classic buildings remain unaffected by recent architectural meddling, giving a harmonious uniformity.

Although Dunedin spreads beyond the suburb-strung hills and surf beaches, the city has a compact and manageable heart, centred on **The Octagon**. This manicured, tree-lined green space is bordered by the **art gallery**, the Neoclassical **Municipal Chambers** and the schizophrenic **St Paul's Cathedral**. Further afield, the newly revamped **Otago Settlers Museum** is sure to impress, while the **Chinese Gardens** offer contemplative calm. It is worth a look in the nearby **Dunedin Railway Station** even if you're not making a journey on the time-warped **Taieri Gorge Railway**.

Beer and chocolate are always winners, best experienced on the **Cadbury World** tour and **Speight's Brewery Tour**. Towards the north of the central city, **Olveston** gives a taste of Dunedin life from its heyday, a topic treated more formally in the **Otago Museum**. The **Botanic Garden** climbs up to the memorial on **Signal Hill** where you can look down on **Otago Harbour**, a sheltered inlet 22km long and no wider than a river in places. The harbour is protected from the ocean by the wonderful **Otago Peninsula** (see p.603).

Local buses get you quickly to Baldwin Street, the world's steepest, and to the sandy beaches of **St Clair** and **St Kilda**, the former with a classy hotel and cluster of cafés.

Brief history

From around 1100 AD, **Maori** fished the rich coastal waters of nearby bays, travelling inland in search of moa, ducks and freshwater fish, and trading with other *iwi* further north. Eventually they formed a settlement around the harbour, calling it Otakou (pronounced "O-tar-go") and naming the headland at the harbour's entrance after their great chieftain, Taiaroa – today a *marae* occupies the Otakou site. By the 1820s European whalers and sealers were seeking shelter in what was the only safe anchorage along this stretch of coast, unwittingly introducing foreign diseases. The local Maori population was decimated, dropping to a low of 110, but subsequent intermarriage bolstered numbers.

The Scots arrive

The New Zealand Company selected the Otago Harbour for a planned **Scottish settlement** as early as 1840 and purchased land from local Maori, but it wasn't until 1848 that the first migrant ships arrived, led by Captain William Cargill and the Reverend Thomas Burns, nephew of the Scottish poet Robert Burns. With the arrival of English and Irish settlers the following year, the Scots were soon in the minority, but their national fervour still stamped its distinct character on the town.

The prospectors arrive

In 1861, a lone Australian prospector discovered **gold** at a creek near present-day Lawrence, about 100km west of Dunedin. Within three months, diggers were pouring in from Australia, and as the main port of entry Dunedin found itself in the midst of a gold rush. The port was expanded, and the population doubled in six months, trebled in three years and made the city New Zealand's most important. This new-found wealth spurred a building boom that resulted in much of the city's most iconic architecture, including the university.

By the 1870s gold mania had largely subsided, but the area sustained its economic primacy through **shipping**, railway development and farming. Decline began during the early twentieth century, when the opening of the Panama Canal in 1914 made Auckland a more economic port for British shipping. In the 1980s, the improvement in world gold prices and the development of equipment enabling large-scale recovery of gold from low-yielding soils re-established **mining** in the hinterland. Today you can visit the massive operation at Macraes (see p.747), an hour's drive from Dunedin.

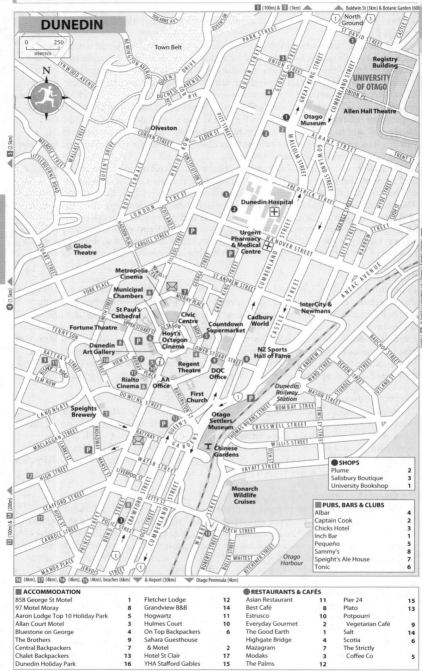

DUNEDIN

■ SHOPS

Plume	2
Salisbury Boutique	3
University Bookshop	1

■ PUBS, BARS & CLUBS

Albar	4
Captain Cook	2
Chicks Hotel	3
Inch Bar	1
Pequeño	5
Sammy's	8
Speight's Ale House	7
Tonic	6

■ ACCOMMODATION

858 George St Motel	1	Fletcher Lodge	12
97 Motel Moray	8	Grandview B&B	14
Aaron Lodge Top 10 Holiday Park	5	Hogwartz	11
Allan Court Motel	3	Hulmes Court	10
Bluestone on George	4	On Top Backpackers	6
The Brothers	9	Sahara Guesthouse	
Central Backpackers	7	& Motel	2
Chalet Backpackers	13	Hotel St Clair	17
Dunedin Holiday Park	16	YHA Stafford Gables	15

● RESTAURANTS & CAFÉS

Asian Restaurant	11	Pier 24	15
Best Café	8	Plato	13
Estrusco	10	Potpourri	
Everyday Gourmet	2	Vegetarian Café	9
The Good Earth	1	Salt	14
Highgate Bridge	4	Scotia	6
Mazagram	7	The Strictly	
Modaks	3	Coffee Co	5
The Palms	12		

The Octagon

Dunedin's diminutive central plaza is **The Octagon**, laid out in 1846 and ringed by a blend of well-preserved buildings and more modern additions. The sloping site is presided over by a **statue of Robert Burns**, symbol of Dunedin's Scottish origins. Every Friday (10am–4pm), the area spills over with **market** stalls selling local crafts, and at all times there'll be people huddled over phones and laptops making use of The Octagon's **free wi-fi**.

Dunedin Public Art Gallery

30 The Octagon • Daily 10am–5pm • Free • ☎ 03 477 4000, ⓦ dunedin.art.museum

Though the **Dunedin Public Art Gallery** is the oldest in the country, founded in 1884, the current incarnation is the work of Dunedin City Council architects in 1996. They fashioned this gleaming space out of six Victorian buildings, all elegantly refurbished to create a light, modern split-level space with several exhibition areas. In the polished-wood foyer a spiral staircase from the department store which once occupied the site winds up to Neil Dawson's *Cones*, five of them chasing each other across the roof space. The gallery hosts a rotating collection of early and contemporary New Zealand pieces and temporary international travelling shows, alongside an extension of Wellington's **New Zealand Film Archive** (see p.421), where you can watch Kiwi movies, documentaries and TV programmes on individual computer screens.

Municipal Chambers

The Octagon is dominated by the 1880 **Municipal Chambers**, a grand, classical structure with a clock tower, all constructed from limestone dramatically offset against volcanic bluestone. It's a fine example of the handiwork of Scottish architect **Robert A. Lawson**, whose influence can be seen in the design of many of Dunedin's public buildings.

St Paul's Cathedral

Daily 10am–4pm • Free

Beside the Municipal Chambers rise the twin white-stone spires of **St Paul's Cathedral**, one of Dunedin's finest buildings and the seat of Anglican worship in the city. The 20m-high, stone-vaulted Gothic Revival nave, entirely constructed from Oamaru stone, was consecrated in 1919. The vaulted ceiling is the only one of its kind in New Zealand, and much of the stained glass in the impressive windows is original. The Modernist chancel and large organ were added in 1971.

Regent Theatre

18 The Octagon • ☎ 03 477 8597, ⓦ regenttheatre.co.nz

Across The Octagon from St Paul's a fine 1874 facade announces the **Regent Theatre**, originally a hotel, then a cinema and finally a theatre. The theatre hosts international shows and the Royal New Zealand Ballet, as well as live music. Inside, elaborate nineteenth-century plasterwork and marble staircases are juxtaposed with 1920s stained-glass windows and geometric balustrades.

First Church of Otago

Moray Place • Heritage Centre Oct–May Mon–Fri 10am–4pm, Sat 10am–2pm; June–Sept Mon–Sat 10.30am–2.30pm • Free

The 54m-high stone spire of the **First Church of Otago** is visible throughout the city. Robert A. Lawson's neo-Gothic building is generally recognized as the most impressive of New Zealand's nineteenth-century churches, with particular praise given to the wooden gabled ceiling and, above the pulpit, a brightly coloured rose window.

Behind the altar, the **Heritage Centre** explores the history of the church and its prime movers.

Otago Settlers Museum

31 Queens Gardens · Reopening December 2012; probably daily 10am–5pm · Free · ☎ 03 477 4000, ⓦ otago.settlers.museum

A major $38 million redevelopment programme will see the **Otago Settlers Museum** reopening in a stylishly upgraded and expanded form across three main buildings: the original neo-Georgian brick heritage building, a 1939 Art Deco former bus garage and the new glass-walled entrance foyer containing *Josephine*, a restored 1872 double-ended Fairlie steam engine that is the oldest in the country.

The museum covers almost 250 years of colonial and social history in Dunedin and Otago, drawing on an exhaustive collection of artefacts, paintings and photographs and an extensive transport section. New exhibits will almost certainly make this an essential stop.

Chinese Gardens

Corner of Rattray and Cumberland sts · Daily 10am–5pm and Wed 7–9pm; 1hr guided tour 10am & 2pm · $9; tour $20 · ☎ 03 477 3248, ⓦ dunedinchinesegarden.com

Dunedin's **Chinese Gardens** opened in 2007, the culmination of a major project marking the contribution of the Chinese gold miners and their descendants to the life of the city. It is one of only three Ming Dynasty scholars' gardens outside China and everything – from the 900 tonnes of limestone to the prefabricated mortise-and-tenon jointed buildings – was shipped here from Shanghai. Ranged round a contemplative pool, it feels a world away from the surrounding city, enhanced by the opportunity to drink tea and eat steam buns and dumplings in a pavilion. You might even catch Tai Chi sessions or mah-jong lessons.

Dunedin Railway Station

22 Anzac Ave

Impossible to miss thanks to its towers, turrets and minarets, the resplendent **Dunedin Railway Station** was constructed on reclaimed swampland in 1906. The walls of its exquisitely preserved **foyer** glisten with green, yellow and cream majolica tiles made especially for New Zealand Rail by Royal Doulton, and the mosaic floor celebrates the steam engine and consists of more than 700,000 tiny squares of porcelain. Upstairs on the balcony, a stained-glass window at each end depicts an approaching train, whose headlights gleam from all angles.

The station no longer sees regular passenger services, though it is the terminus for the Taieri Gorge Railway (see p.601).

New Zealand Sports Hall of Fame

Daily 10am–4pm · $5 · ☎ 03 477 7775, ⓦ nzhalloffame.co.nz

The station's upper floor houses a hagiographic collection of memorabilia relating to the 140 members of the **New Zealand Sports Hall of Fame**: sainted rugby loose forward Colin Meads; 1954 world record long jumper Yvette Williams; late 1950s world champion sheep shearer Godfrey Bowen; mountaineer Edmund Hillary; fast bowler Richard Hadlee; yachtsman Peter Blake; middle-distance runners Jack Lovelock, Dick Quax, Rod Dixon and John Walker; and many, many more.

Hocken Library

90 Anzac Ave · Mon–Fri 9.30am–5pm, Tues until 9pm, Sat 9am–noon · Free · ☎ 03 479 8874, ⓦ library.otago.ac.nz/hocken

The **Hocken Library** is the university's extensive research facility, built around an impressive New Zealand and Pacific collection assembled by Dr Thomas Morland Hocken, a Dunedin physician and one of the country's first historians. The collection is housed in an Art Deco former butter factory – the foyer usually has fascinating top-class temporary exhibits.

Cadbury World

280 Cumberland St • Mon–Fri for 75min tours, Sat & Sun, plus public holidays and Christmas to mid-Jan when production lines not running for 45min tours; book ahead for both tours • 75min tours $20; 45min tours $14 • ☎ 0800 424 6286, ⓦ cadburyworld.co.nz

Diverting displays on the history of chocolate and a chance to nibble on cacao beans (bitter and highly caffeinated but not unpleasant) set the scene for tours enthusiastically led by guides clad in bright purple. In the factory you'll see lines producing chocolate buttons, boxed assortments, Easter eggs and the like. A rather gratuitous "chocolate waterfall" set up for visitors will entertain the kids, and everyone gets liberally showered with free samples.

Speight's Brewery Tour

200 Rattray St, 500m southwest of The Octagon • Mon–Thurs 10am, noon, 2pm, 6pm & 7pm, Fri–Sun 10am, noon, 2pm, 4pm & 6pm • $23 • ☎ 03 477 7697, ⓦ speights.co.nz

New Zealand's "liquid gold", Speight's Gold Medal Ale, has been brewed in Dunedin since the late 1880s, and remains one of the country's biggest-selling beers. Sample it at its best at the end of the **Speight's Brewery Tour**, an informative 1hr 30min meander around one of New Zealand's oldest breweries, established in 1876. Much of the brewery building is from 1940 in industrial Art Deco style, while the brick chimney (topped by a stone beer barrel) is visible from across the city.

The tour entry point is beside a **water spigot** fed by the same sweet-tasting artesian liquid that is used to brew the beer. Locals stop by regularly to fill water bottles.

Olveston

42 Royal Terrace, 10min walk northwest of The Octagon • Daily 9.30am, 10.45am, noon, 1.30pm, 2.45pm & 4pm for 1hr guided tours only; maximum 15 people/tour so book ahead in summer • $17 • ☎ 0800 100 880, ⓦ olveston.co.nz

Dunedin's showpiece historic home is **Olveston**, a fine Edwardian four-storey manor built of Oamaru limestone around 1906 for Jewish importer, David Theomin. The last-surviving family member, his daughter Dorothy, lived there until her death in 1966, after which the house was bequeathed to the people of Dunedin. It remains just as she left it: you could easily imagine her walking in through the door as you tour the house, which is a treasure trove of art and antiques. The family were passionate about travel, art and music and their tastes are reflected in everything from the Arts and Crafts fireplaces, English oak panelling and Venetian glassware to the Japanese and Delft porcelain. A kosher kitchen, elegant gardens and David Theomin's 1921 Fiat Tourer complete the scene.

Otago Museum

419 Great King St • Daily 10am–5pm; highlights tour daily 11.30am; Southern Land, Southern People tour daily 3.30pm • Free; Highlights tour $12; Southern Land, Southern People tour $12; Tropical Forest $10 • ☎ 03 477 7474, ⓦ otagomuseum.govt.nz

The star attraction of the absorbing **Otago Museum** is the fascinating "Southern Land, Southern People" gallery covering aspects of life and natural history in the southern half of the South Island and the sub-Antarctic islands. Large boulders give an idea of the rock that underlies the region in displays that also draw in a fossilized plesiosaur skeleton and the influence of Oamaru stone on the region's architecture. Everything is knitted neatly together, with a discussion on climate illustrated by a Maori flax rain cape, and coverage of the region's fish calling on the experience of whitebaiters.

Elsewhere look out for the Animal Attic, a deeply Victorian amalgamation of macabre skeletons and stuffed beasts – the chickens have even escaped to roost among the rafters. Maori artefacts in the Tangata Whenua gallery are as good as almost anywhere, and the humid, 28°C **Tropical Forest** section is a great place to escape a cold Dunedin day among a thousand butterflies.

University of Otago

Campus accessed from the corner of Cumberland and Union sts

New Zealand's oldest university, the **University of Otago** was founded by Scottish settlers in 1869. Based on the design of Glasgow University, it quickly expanded into a complex of imposing Gothic bluestone buildings, foremost among them the registry building with its **clock tower**. A stroll through the campus from Union Street to Leith Street will take you past the best bits, though if you're here in summer (Dec–Feb) you'll miss the usual studenty vibe.

Dunedin Botanic Garden

Accessed from corner of Great King St and Opoho Rd • Sunrise–sunset • Free

The serene **Dunedin Botanic Garden** was established in 1863 at the foot of Signal Hill. The steep Upper Garden contains the expansive Rhododendron Dell, where established specimens grow among native bush. There's also an arboretum, a native plant collection and an aviary, home to native birds such as kea and kaka.

Lower Garden

Information centre & Winter Garden Glasshouse daily 10am–4pm; Alpine House daily 9am–4pm • ☎ 03 471 9275

The flat Lower Garden features exotic trees, Winter Garden conservatories, rose, Mediterranean and South African gardens and a playground. A volunteer-run information centre lies between the tea kiosk and the Winter Garden. Access to the Lower Gardens car park is from Cumberland Street.

Signal Hill

Accessed from Opoho Rd • The Opoho bus from The Octagon Stand #7 goes to within 1km of the summit, passing the north end of the Botanic Garden. You can also walk to Signal Hill from the garden (6km return; 1hr 30min)

The 393m summit of **Signal Hill**, just north of the Botanic Garden, is crowned by a scenic reserve with magnificent views over Dunedin, the upper harbour and the sea from the Centennial Memorial. Apparently the nation's only monument commemorating one hundred years of British sovereignty (1840–1940) following the signing of the Treaty of Waitangi, the memorial is flanked by two powerful bronze figures symbolizing the past and the future. Embedded in the podium is a tribute to Dunedin's namesake: a chunk of the rock upon which Edinburgh Castle was built.

Baldwin Street

5km north of the city centre: follow Great King St until it becomes North Rd then look for the tenth road on the right. The Normanby–St Clair bus (#9 & #28) from The Octagon stops at the foot of Baldwin St. Buses #8 & #29 head back downtown

Dunedin rejoices in the world's steepest street, the dead-straight **Baldwin Street**, which, with a *Guinness Book of Records*-verified maximum gradient of 1 in 2.66, has a slope of almost 19 degrees. The views from the top aren't bad, but the highlight is walking up, something achieved in about five minutes, under the bemused gaze of locals. During the annual "Gutbuster" event (generally held in late Feb as part of the Dunedin Summer Festival), contestants run to the top and back down again – the current record is one minute 56 seconds.

St Clair Beach

4km south of the city centre

The contiguous suburbs of St Kilda and St Clair back a long, wild sweep of sand enclosed by two volcanic headlands. **St Clair Beach** is excellent for surfing (see box opposite) and can be accessed on frequent buses from The Octagon.

St Clair Hot Salt Water Pool

The Esplanade • Oct–March Mon–Fri 6am–7pm, Sat & Sun 7am–7pm • $5.70 • ☎ 03 455 6352

St Clair beach meets the cliffs at its western end beside the **St Clair Hot Salt Water Pool**, the last remaining open-air pool of its kind in the country. Filled with seawater heated to 28°C, it has a real community feel with all sorts of folk down for their constitutional. The small café has the best views along the beach.

St Kilda Beach and Tomahawk Beach

About 1km east of the salt-water baths, St Clair morphs into **St Kilda Beach**, which is reasonably safe for swimming as long as you keep between the flags; it is patrolled in summer.

At the beach's eastern end, a headland separates St Kilda from the smaller **Tomahawk Beach** (not safe for swimming), often dotted with horses and buggies preparing for trotting races at low tide.

ARRIVAL AND DEPARTURE

DUNEDIN

11

By plane Dunedin airport, 30km south of town then 5km off SH1, is served by domestic flights as well as direct international flights from Australia. Shuttle buses, including Super Shuttle (☎ 0800 748 885, ⓦ supershuttle .co.nz; $25 for 1, $35 for 2), drop off at city-centre accommodation. A taxi is about $80.
Destinations Auckland (3 daily; 1hr 50min); Christchurch (6–8 daily; 1hr); Wellington (5–6 daily; 1hr 15min).

By train Dunedin has no main-line passenger trains, just the Taieri Gorge Railway (see box, p.601).
Destinations Middlemarch (summer Fri & Sun only 1 daily; 2hr 30min); Pukerangi (1–2 daily; 2hr).
By bus Dunedin is a regional hub for bus services. Atomic/NakedBus run (from Dunedin Railway Station) to Christchurch, Invercargill, Queenstown and Wanaka; Catch-A-Bus South (☎ 03 479 9960, ⓦ catchabussouth.co.nz) link

---

DUNEDIN TOURS AND ACTIVITIES

Dunedin's guided and self-guided **walks** are a great way to get to know another side of the city. On the city fringes, there's **surf** at St Clair and the best **swimming** is at Brighton, a blend of sand and rocky outcrops, 15km southwest of Dunedin: catch the Brighton/Green Island bus from Stand 5 on Cumberland Street between Hanover and St Andrew streets ($6.30).

Dunedin has forested **mountain bike** trails right on its doorstep in the form of Signal Hill Reserve, just 3km northeast of The Octagon (free trail map from bike rental shops; see p.596), and half- and full-day cross-country routes listed in the free *Fat Tyre Trails* leaflet, some of them accessible from the city centre.

TOURS

City Walks ☎ 0800 925 571, ⓦ citywalks.co.nz. Guided heritage walks around the city centre (10.30am; 2hr; $30), around the university (1.30pm; 90min; $30) or a heritage walk with breakfast (9am; 1hr; $30).
Dunedin Literary Walk ☎ 03 470 1109, ⓦ research write.co.nz/LiteraryWalk. The enthusiastic Jennie Coleman leads these 2hr explorations (daily 10.15am &

2.15pm; £30) of the city's literary heritage.
Hair Raiser Tours ☎ 0800 428 683, ⓦ hair raisertours.com. Entertainingly spooky walking tours such as the Underbelly Crime Walk (Mon–Fri 10.30am & 8pm; $30), the Ghost Walk (daily: Oct–March 8pm; April–Sept 6pm; $30) and a graveyard tour (daily: Oct–March 9.30pm; April–Sept 8pm; $30).

SWIMMING AND SURFING

Esplanade Surf School Eastern end of the Esplanade, by the St Clair Surf Rescue Station ☎ 03 455 8655, ⓦ espsurfschool.co.nz. Cool-water

surfing lessons with wetsuit and board supplied (3–6-person group lessons $60/90min; 90min one-on-one lessons $120).

MOUNTAIN BIKING

Offtrack ☎ 03 453 6582, ⓦ offtrack.co.nz. Half-day guided rides on some of Dunedin's finest singletrack and 4WD tracks ($55), plus very scenic day rides in the

Catlins ($99) and an excellent day-trip ($120) on the Dunstan Road in the Maniototo (see box, p.746).

to Gore and Invercargill (not Sat); InterCity/Newmans go from 205 St Andrew's St to Queenstown via Alexandra and Cromwell, Christchurch via Oamaru and Timaru, Invercargill and Te Anau; Knightrider (☎03 342 8055, ⓦknightrider.co.nz) runs to Christchurch; and Wanaka Connexions run from Dunedin Railway Station to Wanaka and Queenstown.

Destinations Alexandra (4 daily; 3hr); Balclutha (4–5 daily; 1hr 30min); Christchurch (5–6 daily; 5–6hr); Cromwell (4 daily; 3hr 30min); Gore (4–5 daily; 2hr 30min); Invercargill (4–5 daily; 3hr 30min); Lawrence (4 daily; 1hr 30min); Oamaru (5–6 daily; 2hr); Queenstown (4 daily; 4–5hr); Te Anau (1 daily; 4h 30min); Wanaka (2–3 daily; 4hr).

GETTING AROUND

By bus The city has an efficient, if initially confusing, bus system (generally Mon–Fri 7.30am–11pm, Sat & Sun limited services; ⓦorc.govt.nz). Buses are numbered but are usually identified by their destination: the most useful is the Normanby–St Clair run, which goes from the beach right through the city, past the Botanic Garden, to the foot of Baldwin Street and beyond.

Bus fares Fares are zoned: the central city is Zone One ($1.90), Portobello is Zone Seven ($6.40). All buses except those to Port Chalmers and Otago Peninsula start or pass through the centre of town, stopping at different stands around The Octagon.

By car Dunedin operates a one-way system running north–south through the city and affecting Cumberland, Castle, Great King and Crawford sts.

Parking Parking is seldom a problem, with inexpensive meters and restricted zones in the centre and free long-term street parking a few hundred metres outside.

Car rental The international and nationwide agencies are complemented by good local companies such as Rhodes, 124 St Andrew St (☎0800 746 337, ⓦrhodesrentals.co .nz), and Ace (☎0800 502 277, ⓦacerentalcars.co.nz).

By taxi The handiest taxi ranks are in The Octagon, between George and Stuart sts, or call Dunedin Taxis (☎03 477 7777).

By bike Cycle World, 67 Stuart St (☎03 477 7473), rents bikes from $25/half-day or $40/day ($5 extra with panniers). Offtrack (☎03 453 6582, ⓦofftrack.co.nz) will supply hardtail mountain bikes for $35/day.

INFORMATION

i-SITE 26 Princes St (Dec–March Mon–Fri 8.30am–6pm, Sat & Sun 8.45am–6pm; April–Nov daily 8.30am–5pm; ☎03 474 3300, ⓦisitedunedin.co.nz). Handles transport, accommodation and trips, and stocks walking and cycling

leaflets including *Walk the City* ($4), detailing points of interest around central Dunedin, and *A Walking Guide to Dunedin* ($5) for longer walks.

DOC 77 Stuart St (Mon–Fri 8.30am–5pm; ☎03 477 0677).

ACCOMMODATION

There's a broad choice of accommodation in Dunedin, most of it in or near the city centre. If you prefer something more rural, consider the **Otago Peninsula** (see p.603). **Freedom camping** is allowed in Dunedin City Council car parks all over the region provided you are self-contained and there are no more than two campervans in a 50m radius.

CENTRAL DUNEDIN

858 George St Motel 858 George St ☎0800 858 999, ⓦ858georgestreetmotel.co.nz. A beautifully executed modern motel with a design based on Victorian houses, divided into thirteen big, luxurious units and larger suites. Studios $130, suites $160

97 Motel Moray 97 Moray Place ☎0800 909 797, ⓦ97motel.co.nz. Very central hotel/motel that's better than it looks from the street, with 40 cheerful rooms either in the motel itself or the high-rise former student accommodation behind with rooftop views. Good beds, good bathrooms, great value and plenty of off-street parking. $120

Allan Court Motel 590 George St ☎0800 611 511, ⓦallancourt.co.nz. Central and well-kept 1980s motel with spacious, mostly one- and two-bedroom apartments and some deluxe units with spa bath. $145

★ **Bluestone on George** 571 George St ☎03 477

9201, ⓦbluestonedunedin.co.nz. Fifteen classy studio apartments with state-of-the-art kitchens, stylish bathrooms, in-room laundries and tasteful understated decor. There's even a small gym and lounge. $170

★ **The Brothers** 295 Rattray St ☎03 477 0043, ⓦbrothershotel.co.nz. Stylish fifteen-room boutique hotel tastefully converted from a 1920s Christian Brothers' residence. Pared-down contemporary decor and friendly service set the tone, with many of the rooms opening onto verandas with splendid city views; one is in the former chapel. A spacious lounge has more city views, Sky TV, free wi-fi and broadband. Parking and continental breakfast are included. $160

Central Backpackers 243 Moray Place ☎0800 423 687. Welcoming and efficiently run forty-bed hostel with a mixed clientele. Along with free wi-fi and a DVD lounge with Playstation there are backpack-size security lockers and a friendly cat. Dorms $27, twins $66, doubles $70

Chalet Backpackers 296 High St ☎0800 242 538, ⓦchaletbackpackers.co.nz. Light fills the mostly four-bed (no bunks) dorms at this comfortable hostel with pleasing harbour views, good kitchen and dining facilities, comfy singles and doubles, plus a pool table and piano room. Phone ahead in winter. Dorms $26, rooms $60

Fletcher Lodge 276 High St ☎0800 843 563, ⓦfletcherlodge.co.nz. Attention is devoted to guests' comfort at this elaborate lodge set in an English baronial-style home built in 1924 for leading Kiwi industrialist Sir James Fletcher. The five rooms and suites are complemented by an adjacent pair of fully equipped apartments reflecting the owner's Polish origins – you get independence but miss out on the splendour of the main house. Doubles $335, apartments $650

Grandview B&B 360 High St ☎03 472 9472, ⓦgrandview.co.nz. Very welcoming B&B in an 1860s house with great views over the city and seven rooms, three of which are en-suite. A good continental breakfast is included but there's also a full guest kitchen, an honesty bar and barbecue on the deck plus an infrared sauna ($5). Doubles $115, en suites $165

★ **Hogwartz** 277 Rattray St ☎03 474 1487, ⓦhogwartz.co.nz. Lovely welcoming hostel in the former Catholic bishop's residence close to the centre of town and with free parking. There are no bunks, but some rooms have city views and there are also nicely modernized self-contained units in the adjacent Stables and Coach House. It has all the facilities you'll need and they'll even do your laundry ($6–8/load). Occasional winter closures. Dorm $28, doubles $68, en suite $82, studios $106

Hulmes Court 52 Tennyson St ☎0800 448 563, ⓦhulmes.co.nz. The style of this pair of houses (one Edwardian, the other a grander 1860 Victorian affair) is a bit higgledy-piggledy but the price is right. Just a short climb from The Octagon with big, individually themed rooms (several en-suite), off-street parking, free internet, and a continental breakfast served in the sunny drawing room. Rooms $110, en suites $140

On Top Backpackers Corner of Filleul St and Moray Place ☎0800 668 672, ⓦontopbackpackers.co.nz.

Purpose-built 100-bed hostel with a lively atmosphere aided by the associated bar and pool hall. Along with six- to eight-bed dorms there are a number of en-suite doubles, plus a TV, BBQ terrace and a light, open-plan kitchen/common room. A basic continental breakfast is included. Dorms $26, doubles $64, en suites $90

Sahara Guesthouse & Motel 619 George St ☎03 477 6662, ⓦdunedin-accommodation.co.nz. Roomy 1863 guesthouse with mostly shared facilities, plus ten standard motel units with basic kitchen facilities and some new comfortable deluxe studios. It's all pragmatic rather than romantic but does have off-street parking. Shared bath $70, en suite $80, deluxe $135

YHA Stafford Gables 71 Stafford St ☎03 474 1919, ⓔyhadndn@yha.co.nz. Atmospheric hostel in a rambling 1902 building with a rooftop garden overlooking the city, and a clued-in staff. Three- to six-bed dorms (some with balconies), doubles and twin rooms are generally large and there's an apartment with its own kitchen. Dorms $32, doubles $85, apartment $110

ST CLAIR

Hotel St Clair 24 Esplanade ☎03 456 0555, ⓦhotelstclair.co.nz. This modern, stylish 26-room hotel and its *Pier 24* restaurant have become the focal point for St Clair, with smart clean lines, luxury fittings and some wonderfully spacious seaview apartments. Doubles $195, seaview $250

CAMPSITES AND HOLIDAY PARKS

Aaron Lodge Top 10 Holiday Park 162 Kaikorai Valley Rd, 2.5km west of the city centre ☎0800 879 227, ⓦaaronlodgetop10.co.nz. A sheltered, fairly spacious and well-tended site in the hills. Camping/site $44, cabins $60, self-contained units $96, motels $140

Dunedin Holiday Park 41 Victoria Rd ☎0800 945 455, ⓦdunedinholidaypark.co.nz. Lying alongside St Kilda Beach, this well-appointed park is a 5min drive from the city centre and served by the Brockville–St Kilda bus: pick it up at The Octagon, Stand 1. Camping/site $36, cabins $50, en-suite cabins $91, motel units $127

EATING

Dunedin packs in a pretty decent range of places, from cafés to fine restaurants, mostly around The Octagon and along George Street. Interesting outliers can be found in suburban Roslyn and beachy St Clair. For staples, stop by the central Countdown supermarket at 309 Cumberland St.

CENTRAL DUNEDIN

Asian Restaurant 43 Moray Place ☎03 477 6673. Nothing flash, but zingy, fun and always busy, dishing up the classics such as combination fried noodles ($6, large $9), spicy duck with tofu ($7/11). Licensed and BYO. Mon–Sat noon–2pm & 5–10pm or later, Sun 5–10pm.

Best Café 30 Lower Stuart St ☎03 477 8059.

Time-warped Dunedin stalwart where mains are served with bread, curled butter and no frills. The menu has expanded to eight species of fresh fish, served with chips and coleslaw (1 piece for $9–12; 3 pieces for $19–23), and there's also tasty seafood chowder ($14) plus oysters and whitebait patties in season. Licensed and BYO. Mon–Thurs 11.30am–2.30pm & 5–8pm, Fri & Sat 11.30am–2.30pm & 5–9pm.

11

Etrusco First floor, 8 Moray Place ☏03 477 3737, ⓦetrusco.co.nz. Cheap, cheerful and hugely popular Italian-run crispy pizza and pasta restaurant (medium dishes $15–20; large $20–26) somewhat ostentatiously located in an airy and lovingly restored building. Feels like it has barely changed since the 1980s – in a good way. Daily 5.30–10pm or later.

Everyday Gourmet 466 George St ☏03 477 2045, ⓦeverydaygourmet.net.nz. A great relaxed spot for a light breakfast or lunch of fresh salads, bagels, gourmet pies, delectable cakes and the likes of baked salmon risotto ($14). Also shelves of gourmet foodstuffs. Mon–Fri 7.30am–5.30pm, Sat 8am–3pm.

The Good Earth 765 Cumberland St ☏03 471 8554. Art adorns the white walls of this predominantly organic and Fairtrade café with park views through big windows. Stop in for a coffee and a melt-in-your-mouth sun-dried tomato, feta and rocket scone ($4), or lunches such as lightly curried cauliflower soup with focaccia ($12) or Moroccan chicken on couscous and preserved lemon salad ($16). Mon–Fri 7am–5pm, Sat & Sun 9am–5pm.

Mazagram 36 Moray Place ☏03 477 9959. If immaculate espresso is your goal head straight for this tiny café for bean freaks where everything is roasted on the premises. The barista decides which blend to use every morning and you can buy a dozen styles of freshly roasted beans. Mon–Fri 8am–5pm, Sat 10am–2pm.

★ **Modaks** 337 George St ☏03 477 6563. Edgy and funky café with local pop art lining the walls, plus great espresso and chewy cinnamon pinwheel scones. The menu is laden with vegetarian and vegan dishes: try their Mexican eggs breakfast ($16) that comes with delicious gluten-free jalapeño bread. Mon–Fri 7.30am–6pm, Sat & Sun 8am–6pm.

Otago Farmers' Market Dunedin Railway Station car park ⓦotagofarmersmarket.org.nz. Every weekend morning the station car park comes alive with fruit, veg and tasty morsel vendors from around the district at this always-popular market. Saturday 8am–noon.

The Palms 18 Queens Gardens ☏03 477 6534, ⓦpalmsrestaurant.co.nz. Friendly local favourite with picture windows overlooking Queens Gardens and a menu ranging from lamb rump with crispy polenta and aubergine purée ($34) to roast garlic risotto ($32). Mon–Fri noon–2pm & 6–10pm or later, Sat & Sun 6–10pm or later.

★ **Plato** 2 Birch St ☏03 477 4235, ⓦplatocafe.co.nz. Dunedin's cooler grown-ups find their way across the overpasses and railway tracks to this consistently excellent casual bistro in a 1960s former seafarers' hostel – a low rectangular room with acoustic tiles. Naturally, the constantly

changing menu is strong on seafood, so try the green-lipped mussels in beer and caramelized onion broth ($18), then fish curry with spinach, coconut and prawns ($33). Mon–Sat 6–10pm or later, Sun 11am–10pm.

Potpourri Vegetarian Cafe 97 Stuart St ☏03 477 9983. You don't need to be veggie to appreciate this established vegetarian café where the bare brick walls are decorated with botanical etchings. Delicious seed-and-fruit slices and muffins complement daily soups and the likes of bean burrito and salad ($14). Mon–Fri 8.30am–3pm, Sat 9am–3pm.

★ **Scotia** 199 Upper Stuart St ☏03 477 2993, ⓦscotiadunedin.co.nz. The cosy ambience of a converted Victorian terraced house feels an appropriate setting for this restaurant and bar with a distinct Scottish angle. There's Emerson's on tap, a fine collection of over 300 whiskies, friendly efficient service and Kiwi bistro food with nods to Scottish culinary origins such as potted hough (ham hock, chutney and oatcakes; $9), cullen skink (a smoked seafood chowder; $15), and haggis, neeps and tatties (entrée $16; main $26). The desserts are sumptuous. Mon–Fri 10am–11pm, Sat 3–11pm.

The Strictly Coffee Co 23 Bath St ☏03 479 0017, ⓦstrictlycoffee.co.nz. If not the best coffee in town then in company with it, sold by the cup or the kilo in an industrial-chic, cherry-red daytime café filled with chrome coffee grinders. Enjoy the great crusty rolls and wraps and the little courtyard. Mon–Fri 7.30am–4pm.

ROSYLN

★ **Highgate Bridge** 300 Highgate ☏03 474 9222. Known to most of its devoted fans as "The Friday Shop" for its limited opening hours, this bakery sells superb pastries, tarts, almond croissants and the exalted Rachel Scott bread. Fri 7.30am–4pm.

ST CLAIR

Pier 24 24 Esplanade ☏03 456 0555, ⓦhotelstclair.co.nz. Chic modern restaurant that ranks as one of Dunedin's finest with wonderful views out to the St Clair surf. Casual enough to nip in for a coffee or a beer, but it's really about Michael Coughlin's food: sesame-crusted tuna with shaved fennel ($21) followed by roast chicken and chorizo on grilled polenta and slow-roasted tomatoes ($36). Daily 7am–9pm or later.

Salt 240 Forbury Rd ☏03 455 1077, ⓦsaltbar.co.nz. Casual Art Deco-styled bar and restaurant with a fire in winter and streetside eating when it's warm. Lunch on chicken Caesar salad ($18) or dine on tiger prawn linguine ($25). Mon–Fri 10am–10pm, Sat & Sun 9am–10pm.

DRINKING, NIGHTLIFE AND ENTERTAINMENT

Like all good university cities, drinking is taken seriously here. A number of the city's dozens of **pubs** and **bars** serve English- and German-style beers from Dunedin's premier micro-brewery, Emerson's. Local **bands** play at weekends (at the

RUGBY IN DUNEDIN

There's no surer way to get a real taste of Dunedin in party mode than to attend a **rugby match** at the new 30,000-seater Forsyth Barr Stadium (Ⓦforsythbarrstadium.co.nz) at 130 Anzac Avenue, 2km east of The Octagon. The city is proud of having the world's only fully roofed, natural-turf stadium, but its $200 million construction (in time for the 2011 Rugby World Cup) was controversial and put huge strains on the local ratepayers. Highlanders Super 15 games are held every second weekend during the season (late Feb–July) and there are occasional All Black Games (generally May–Oct). For free schedules and ticket sales visit The Champions of the World shop, 8 George St (Mon–Fri 9am–5.30pm, Sat & Sun 10am–4pm; Ⓣ03 477 7852).

places below and *Chicks* in Port Chalmers), although once the students head home for the summer holidays (late Nov–early March) the dancefloors can look forlorn. For information, pick up the free *Ink* weekly entertainment guide from the i-SITE, cafés and venues.

PUBS, BARS AND CLUBS

Albar 135 Stuart St Ⓣ03 479 2468. Inviting, popular Scottish-themed bar with a good selection of whiskies, European and Kiwi bottled beers and plenty of Kiwi craft beers on tap. The otherwise authentic tapas menu ($5–8) includes an unusual haggis option. Celtic acoustic music on Tues nights and occasional whisky tastings. Mon–Sat 11am–midnight or later, Sun noon–10pm.

Captain Cook Tavern 354 Great King St Ⓣ03 474 1935. If you've got the stomach for it, this black cavern roughhouse bar is an essential part of the Dunedin experience. Young students are lured by cheap food, cheaper drinks and grotesque entertainments: "The Cook" reputedly has NZ's highest beer consumption and its own Speight's rip-off ale Cook Draught, Pride of the Cook, brewed by the conglomerate opposition. Has to be done. Daily noon–3am.

Inch Bar 8 Bank St Ⓣ03 473 6496. For a change from the downtown vibe, head for this intimate neighbourhood watering hole with speciality beers (including several Emerson's on tap) and a select range of tapas from paprika squid ($15) to a big bowl of *patatas bravas* ($10). Daily 3–11pm or later; closed Mon in winter.

★ **Pequeño** Down the alley beside 12 Moray Place Ⓣ03 477 7830, Ⓦpequeno.co.nz. All low lighting, leather sofas and banquettes around the fire. Excellent wine and cocktails and Thurs-night live jazz (usually swing or funk). Mon–Fri 5pm–1am or later, Sat 7pm–3am or later.

Sammy's 65 Crawford St Ⓣ03 477 2185. Live music and DJ venue, more cutting-edge than most, with open-mic nights, installations and exhibitions as well as touring acts from across the globe. Doesn't get going until late; covers apply depending upon the act. Daily 11pm–late.

Speight's Ale House 200 Rattray St Ⓣ03 471 9050, Ⓦthealehouse.co.nz. Popular and spacious Speight's-owned pub right by the brewery with good beer and food served in rural-kitsch decor. Daily 11.30am–10pm or later.

Tonic 138 Princes St Ⓣ03 471 9194, Ⓦtonicbar.co.nz. With a beer from every decent Kiwi micro-brewery you can think of, Emerson's on tap, a decent wine list, antipasto platters ($18) and friendly regulars, this wonderful little bar will bring a tear to your eye. Tues–Thurs 4–11pm, Fri 3.30pm–1am, Sat 6pm–1am.

THEATRE, CINEMA AND CLASSICAL MUSIC

In addition to its festivals, Dunedin has a lively year-round theatre scene. Public recitals are held by the music department of the University of Otago (check with the i-SITE).

CINEMAS

Hoyts Octagon 33 The Octagon Ⓣ03 477 3250, Ⓦhoyts.co.nz. Multiplex screening all the latest mainstream films.

Metropolis Cinema Town Hall, Moray Place Ⓣ03 471 9635, Ⓦmetrocinema.co.nz. With only 56 seats this is a delightful place to watch art-house and more commercial movies for just $13. Popcorn is out, but you're welcome to take your coffee in with you. Book ahead.

Rialto 11 Moray Place Ⓣ03 474 2200, Ⓦrialto.co.nz. Another run-of-the-mill but perfectly good cinema that screens mainstream films.

THEATRES

Allen Hall 90 Union St East Ⓣ03 479 8896. Campus theatre that showcases the talents of the university's drama students. Shows are often of an alternative bent and don't cost much.

Fortune Theatre 231 Stuart St Ⓣ03 477 8323, Ⓦfortunetheatre.co.nz. Converted from a neo-Gothic church, the Fortune divides its programme between new works by Kiwi playwrights, fringe theatre, popular Broadway-style plays and occasional musicals. Tickets around $40. Closed Jan to mid-Feb.

Globe 104 London St Ⓣ03 477 3274, Ⓦglobetheatre.org.nz. This small and intimate venue features contemporary plays, classical drama and experimental works. Tickets $20.

11

DUNEDIN FESTIVALS

Dunedin Summer Festival All manner of local events, including a trolley derby, street races and the Baldwin St Gutbuster. Mid-February.

Fringe Festival ⓦ dunedinfringe.org.nz. Ten-day arts and culture festival with street performers, short films, comedy and exhibitions. Generally takes place in mid-March.

New Zealand International Film Festival ⓦ nzff.co.nz. The usual mix of oddball and pre-release mainstream movies. Early to mid-August.

Otago Festival of the Arts ⓦ otagofestival .co.nz. Mid- to high-brow arts festival with opera, plays and plenty of music. Late September to early October every even year.

Scottish Week Daily concerts, pipe bands and Highland dancing, all in the name of celebrating the city's cultural roots. Late September.

Mayfair Theatre 100 King Edward St ☎ 03 455 4962, ⓦ mayfairtheatre.co.nz. Home to the Dunedin Opera Company who stage two or three productions a year.

Regent 17 The Octagon ☎ 03 477 6481, ⓦ regent theatre.co.nz. The city's largest and most ornate theatre, hosting musicals, ballets, touring plays, comedians, the New Zealand Symphony Orchestra, Dunedin's Southern Sinfonia and the city's film festival.

SHOPPING

Bivouac 171 George St ☎ 03 477 3679, ⓦ bivouac .co.nz. Quality selection of tramping, mountaineering and skiing gear for rent and for sale. Mon–Fri 9.30am–5.30pm, Sat & Sun 10am–4pm.

Plume 310 George St ☎ 03 477 9358. Top women's fashion store run by Margi Robertson, founder of top Kiwi label Nom*D. Everything from Workshop to Comme des Garçons along with local labels Zambesi and, naturally Nom*D. Check out the superb leadlight entrance. Mon–Thurs 9am–5.30pm, Fri & Sat 9am–6.30pm, Sun 10am–4pm.

R & R Sport 70 Stuart St ☎ 03 474 1211, ⓦ rrsport .co.nz. Outdoor equipment shop with Dunedin's biggest range of camping, skiing, cycling and general sporting equipment. Mon–Thurs 9am–5.30pm, Fri 9am–6pm, Sat 9.30am–4pm, Sun 10.30am–4pm.

★ **Salisbury Boutique** 104 Bond St ☎ 03 477 3933, ⓦ salisburyboutique.co.nz. Cool designer shop in an upcoming part of town, good for designer clothes, jewellery and art. Thurs & Fri 4–8pm, Sat 11am–8pm.

University Bookshop 378 Great King St, opposite the Otago Museum ☎ 03 477 6976, ⓦ unibooks.co.nz. Comprehensive independent bookshop covering two floors, with the bargains located upstairs. Mon–Fri 8.30am–5.30pm, Sat 9.30am–3pm, Sun 11am–3pm.

DIRECTORY

Banks and foreign exchange The major banks are clustered on George and Princes sts, all with ATMs. On Saturday try the ANZ, corner of George and Hanover sts, which is open 10am–2pm. On Sundays and public holidays you can change money at the i-SITE.

Internet access Free access in the library (below) and around The Octagon.

Library Dunedin Public Library, corner of John and Stewart sts (Mon–Fri 9.30am–8pm, Sat & Sun 11am–4pm; ☎ 03 474 3690), has newspapers and free internet.

Medical treatment Dunedin Hospital, 201 Great King St (☎ 03 474 0999); emergencies only. After-hours doctors are available at 95 Hanover St (daily 8am–11.30pm; ☎ 03 479 2900).

Pharmacy After-hours service at Urgent Pharmacy, 95 Hanover St (daily 10am–10pm; ☎ 03 477 6344).

Post office 233 Moray Place.

Travel agents Flight Centre, 373 George St (Mon–Fri 9am–5.30pm, Sat 10am–4pm; ☎ 03 479 0020).

Port Chalmers and around

Container cranes loom over the small, quirky town of **PORT CHALMERS**, 12km northeast of Dunedin and reached along the winding western shore of Otago Harbour. Arranged on hills around a container port and cruise-ship berth, the town has a vibrant artistic community, headed by celebrated New Zealand painter and sculptor **Ralph Hotere**. The whole place has a delightfully run-down, lost-in-time feel, though a modest amount of renovation of many of the fine nineteenth-century buildings

RIDING DUNEDIN'S SCENIC RAILWAYS

Dunedin's dramatic railway station marks the start of two wonderfully scenic train trips, both run by the Taieri Gorge Railway (**☎**03 477 4449, **🌐** taieri.co.nz). One threads inland through the Taieri Gorge itself while the other winds along a spectacular coastal route north to Palmerston.

THE TAIERI GORGE ROUTE

The Taieri Gorge journey stretches 77km northwest from Dunedin through rugged hill country. Constructed between 1879 and 1921, the line once carried supplies a total of 235km from Dunedin to the old gold town of Cromwell, returning with farm produce, fruit and livestock bound for the port. Commercial traffic stopped in 1990, and much of the route was turned into the Otago Central Rail Trail (see box, p.743), but the most dramatic section – through the schist strata of the Taieri Gorge – continues to offer a rewarding journey at any time of year.

Most trains run as far as **Pukerangi** (58km from Dunedin), a lonely wayside halt near the highest point of the track (250m) where you wait a few minutes then head back. Some services continue a further 19km to the old gold town of **Middlemarch** (see p.747).

RIDING THE TAIERI GORGE

The air-conditioned train is made up of a mix of modern steel carriages with large panoramic windows and nostalgic, **refurbished 1920s wooden cars**. Storage is available for backpacks and bicycles, and there's a licensed snack bar on board.

Trains run up the Taieri Gorge on a fairly complex **timetable**. In summer there are usually two trains a day from Dunedin to Pukerangi and back (Sept Sat & Sun at 9.30am & 12.30pm; Oct–April daily except Fri & Sun 9.30am & 2.30pm; $86 return; $57 one-way; 4hr return). Two days a week in summer the train continues beyond Pukerangi to Middlemarch (Oct–April Fri & Sun 9.30am & 2.30pm; $99 return; $66 one-way; 6hr return).

TAIERI GORGE AND RAIL TRAIL COMBOS

As well as the day-trips, the Taieri Gorge trip makes an excellent way to start your journey inland towards Wanaka and Queenstown ($138). Buses meet the train at Pukerangi or Middlemarch and head through the Maniototo (see p.742) to Queenstown ($148): book through the Taieri Gorge Railway.

Cyclists can take the train (bikes go free, though they need to be booked) then hop straight onto the Otago Central Rail Trail. If you don't have your own bike, get in touch with Offtrack (see box, p.595) or one of the rail trail specialists (see box, p.743).

THE SEASIDER

A completely different but equally picturesque rail journey, the *Seasider*, leaves Dunedin Railway Station and runs along the main northbound line 66km up the coast to Palmerston. It initially follows the flank of Otago Harbour then winds through Port Chalmers to Blueskin Bay with tunnels, bridges and great coastal views all the way. The train ($86 return; $57 one-way; 4hr return) runs sporadic days throughout the year (check the website for times) and stops for 30min for coffee in Palmerston.

along George Street, the main drag, has left a framework for a few cool shops and cafés. Two late Victorian churches vie for attention with the cranes: the elegant stone-spired Presbyterian **Iona Church** on Mount Street, and the nuggety bluestone Anglican **Holy Trinity**, on Scotia Street, designed by Robert A. Lawson.

For a little exercise tackle **Back Beach Walk** (4km loop; 1hr; mostly flat) with views across to Goat Island and Quarantine Island in the harbour with the Otago Peninsula beyond: pick up a map from the library.

Brief history

Chosen in 1844 as the port to serve the proposed Scottish settlement that would become Dunedin, Port Chalmers became the embarkation point for several **Antarctic expeditions**, including those of Captain Scott, who set out from here in 1901 and again for his ill-fated attempt on the Pole in 1910. The first trial shipment of **frozen meat** to Britain was sent from Port Chalmers in 1882 and today the export of wool, meat and timber, and reception of cruise ships is its chief business.

Regional Maritime Museum

19 Beach St • Mon–Fri 9am–3pm, Sat & Sun 1.30–4.30pm • Donation

George Street meets the port at the small **museum** housed in an 1877 former post office. Brimming with maritime artefacts, models and local settler history, museum highlights include a display of navigational equipment and a working electric model of a **gold dredge**, built in 1900 by an apprentice boilermaker, who along with his brothers installed the first electric power system in the region, after a few shocks.

Orokonui Ecosanctuary

600 Blueskin Rd, 3.5km north of Port Chalmers • Daily 9.30am–4.30pm; 1hr guided tour daily 11am; 2hr guided tour daily 11.30am; after dark tour Tues & Sun at dusk • $15.90; 1hr tour $30; 2hr tour $45; after dark tour $69 • ☏ 03 482 1755, ⊛ orokonui.org.nz

Modelled on the Zealandia: the Karori Sanctuary Experience attraction in Wellington (see p.425), the **Orokonui Ecosanctuary** is a welcome addition to the pantheon of wildlife activities within easy reach of Dunedin. Start at the visitor centre, all eco-designed using secondhand shipping containers and wood milled on-site. Solar panels heat roof rainwater for washing, and centre waste is treated and used for irrigation. The place is packed with information and the café offers wonderful views of the valley, but the real treats are just the other side of the 8.7km predator-exclusion fence, protecting three square kilometres of regenerating bush, some of it over a century old, containing reintroduced native birds, tuatara and skinks. Among the birds you are likely to encounter are tomtit, South Island riflemen, grey warbler, brown creeper, saddleback, bellbird, tui, fantail and kaka.

You can take a self-guided walk through the sanctuary, but will learn (and probably see) more on a guided tour with the freedom to roam afterwards. Either drive here (30min from Dunedin) or come on a wildlife tour (see box opposite). No public buses visit.

Aramoana

The tiny settlement of **Aramoana**, on a sand dune spit at the mouth of Otago Harbour 12km north of Port Chalmers, was catapulted into the Kiwi psyche in 1990 when one David Gray shot 13 of his neighbours before being shot by police. The story of the massacre is told in Robert Sarkies' 2006 film *Out of The Blue*. Pop out there if you fancy a walk on wild, often deserted **beaches** with views across the mouth of Otago Harbour towards Taiaroa Head and the possibility of seeing yellow-eyed penguins and sea lions.

ARRIVAL AND INFORMATION

PORT CHALMERS AND AROUND

By bus The #13 & #14 buses run between Dunedin and Port Chalmers, leaving from Stand 4 opposite the Countdown supermarket in Cumberland St, dropping you off in George St about 25min later (sporadic service on Sun).

Tourist information The library, 20 Beach St (Mon–Wed & Fri 9.30am–5.30pm, Thurs 9.30am–8pm, Sat 11am–2pm; ☏ 03 474 3690), has local leaflets and free internet.

ACCOMMODATION AND EATING

As well as the places to eat listed below you'll find several scenic picnic spots dotted along Peninsula Beach Road, just around from the harbour.

★ **Billy Browns** 423 Aramoana Rd, Hamilton Bay, 5.5km north of Port Chalmers ☏ 03 472 8323, ⊛ billy browns.co.nz. Quirkily designed first-class hostel isolated on farmland in an area where you probably wouldn't stay were the accommodation not so brilliant. It has stunning views, a log fire, stacks of vinyl, and made-up beds but no TV or internet. It sleeps just nine, so book ahead. Dorms $28, rooms $70

DUNEDIN AND OTAGO PENINSULA NATURE TOURS

Even if you have your own wheels there's a lot to be said for exploring the area on an informative guided tour.

4 Nature Tours ☎03 472 7647, 🌐4nature.co.nz. Nature and wildlife oriented tours focused on the western side of Otago Harbour, such as their Ecosanctuary and Wading Birds Tour (4–5hr; $90) visiting Orokonui.

Elm Wildlife Tours ☎0800 356 563, 🌐elm wildlifetours.co.nz. Excellent, ecologically minded guided bus tours (usually 5–6hr; $99) leave Dunedin in the afternoon and visit the Albatross Centre, catching sight of lots of wildlife. Trips can include an Albatross Centre tour ($125), an hour-long Monarch Cruise ($148), or everything combined (8hr; $208). Families, backpackers and students save $10 on all trips.

Monarch Wildlife Cruises & Tours 20 Fryatt St, Dunedin ☎0800 666 272, 🌐wildlife.co.nz. A converted fishing boat with licensed galley is put to good use running short cruises around Taiaroa Head

(summer 5 daily; winter 1–2 daily; 1hr; $49) from the Wellers Rock jetty, near the tip of the Otago Peninsula. This can be combined with a trip to the Albatross Centre ($80). If you're not planning to drive out along the peninsula, opt for the Wildlife Tour (9am & 3.30pm; 3hr 30min; $89), which leaves from the wharf in Dunedin, cruises around Taiaroa Head then drops you at Wellers Rock and returns to Dunedin by bus. Various albatross and penguin centre combos are available.

Wild Earth Adventures ☎03 489 1951, 🌐wild earth.co.nz. For an often magical perspective on the coast and its wildlife, take a sea-kayaking tour around Taiaroa Head or Portobello (both 4hr; $115), spending around two hours on the water. Among the other trips a particular favourite is the Twilight Tour (Oct–March; 3–5hr; $115), with wildlife, quiet and the lights of Dunedin in the background.

11

Carey's Bay Historic Hotel 17 Macandrew Rd, 1km north of town ☎03 472 8022, 🌐careysbayhotel.co .nz. Maritime bar in an 1874 bluestone building with a restaurant specializing in seafood; try the great chowder ($16) or platters laden with scallops, mussels, squid and prawns ($24–42). Occasional live music. Daily 10.30am–10pm, with winter evening closures.

Chicks Hotel 2 Mount St ☎03 472 5074. Top live music venue and pub, in an atmospheric 1876 stone building with a hanging sign depicting a skull and crossbones.

Generally open if a band is playing and for jam sessions. A bit of a schlep from Dunedin, but well worth it. Open most Fri & Sat nights.

★ **Port Royale** 10 George St ☎03 472 8283. Cool spot looking out onto the main street, a great place to enjoy excellent coffee and a muffin or for simple lunches such as pea, ham and potato pie with salad ($12) or a BLT ($10) and a beer in the sheltered courtyard. Mon–Fri 8am–4.30pm, Sat & Sun 8.30am–4.30pm.

The Otago Peninsula

The 35km-long crooked finger of the **OTAGO PENINSULA**, running northeast from Dunedin, divides Otago Harbour from the Pacific Ocean. With sweeping views of the harbour, the sea and Dunedin against its dramatic backdrop of hills, the peninsula offers outstanding year-round **marine wildlife viewing** that's probably the most condensed and varied in the country.

The prime wildlife viewing spots are concentrated at the peninsula's tip, **Taiaroa Head** (less than an hour's drive from Dunedin), where cold waters forced up by the continental shelf provide a rich and constant food source. The majestic **royal albatross** breeds here in what is the world's only mainland albatross colony. Also concentrated on the headland's shores are **penguins** (the little blue and the rare yellow-eyed) and **southern fur seals**, while the cliffs are home to other seabirds including three species of **shag**, **muttonbirds** (sooty shearwaters) and various species of gull. New Zealand **sea lions** sometimes loll on beaches, while offshore, orca and **whales** can be seen. Other than taking one of the excellent wildlife tours, the best opportunities for seeing animals are on some of the beaches. **Sandfly Bay** (see box, p.605) welcomes yellow-eyed penguins home in the late afternoon, then **Pilots Beach** sees the arrival of blue penguins around dusk.

11

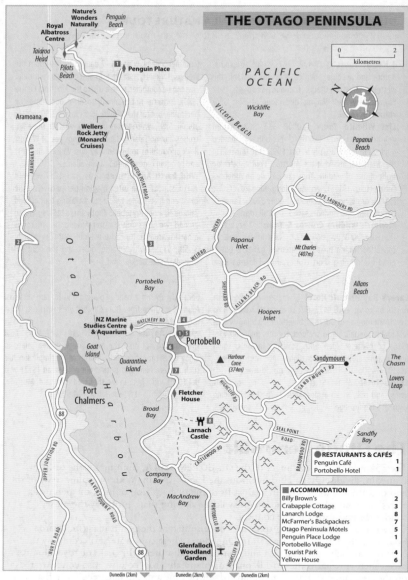

THE OTAGO PENINSULA

RESTAURANTS & CAFÉS
Penguin Café   1
Portobello Hotel   1

ACCOMMODATION
Billy Brown's   2
Crabapple Cottage   3
Lanarch Lodge   8
McFarmer's Backpackers   7
Otago Peninsula Motels   5
Penguin Place Lodge   1
Portobello Village
 Tourist Park   4
Yellow House   6

Around the head of Otago Harbour, **Portobello Road** shakes off Dunedin's southern suburbs and begins to weave its way along the peninsula's shoreline past little bays, many dotted with stilt-mounted boathouses. Beyond the accommodation and eating nexus of **Portobello**, Harington Point Road continues to Taiaroa Head.

Apart from wildlife spotting there's appeal in the beautiful woodland gardens of **Glenfalloch**, the excellent **Marine Studies Centre & Aquarium**, the exemplary grounds of

Larnach Castle and several **scenic walks** to spectacular views and unusual land formations created by lava flows.

GETTING AROUND AND INFORMATION | THE OTAGO PENINSULA

By car The peninsula is best accessed with your own wheels, either via Portobello Road, which snakes along the western shoreline, or the inland Highcliff Road, which winds up and over the hills.

By bus The Peninsula bus (3–9 daily; $6.30) from Stand 5 on Cumberland Street in Dunedin runs halfway along the peninsula, as far as Portobello (35min), from where it's another 14km to Taiaroa Head. On weekdays a couple of services continue to Harington Point, within 2km of Taiaroa Head.

Tourist information Pick up the free *Visitor's Guide to the Otago Peninsula* from the Dunedin i-SITE (see p.596).

Glenfalloch Woodland Garden

430 Portobello Rd, 11km east of Dunedin • Daily dawn–dusk • $5 • ☎ 03 476 1006, ⓦ glenfalloch.co.nz

The peaceful **Glenfalloch Woodland Garden** contains 1.2 square kilometres of mature garden and bush, surrounding a homestead built in 1871 and accessed by a small licensed café. Between mid September and mid-October the garden is ablaze with rhododendrons, azaleas and camellias.

Larnach Castle

145 Camp Rd, Company Bay • Daily 9am–5pm; gardens daily Oct–March 9am–7pm; April–Sept 9am–5pm • Castle and gardens $28; gardens only $12.50 • ☎ 03 476 1616, ⓦ larnachcastle.co.nz • Take the Peninsula bus either to Company Bay, from where it's a 5km signposted walk uphill, or to Broad Bay and a steeper 2km walk

At **Company Bay**, Castlewood Road runs 4km inland to the 1871 Gothic Revival **Larnach Castle**, which sits high on a hill commanding great views across the harbour to

---

WALKS AROUND DUNEDIN AND THE OTAGO PENINSULA

The *Otago Peninsula Tracks* leaflet (free from the Dunedin i-SITE or DOC office) briefly describes two dozen walks on the peninsula (including the first two below), most of them well defined but pretty steep in places. The weather here can turn cold or wet very quickly, even on the sunniest days, so come prepared.

Lovers Leap and the Chasm (3km; 1hr; closed Aug–Oct). Wonderfully accessible peninsula walk, forming an easy loop which crosses farmland to sheer cliffs dropping 200m to the sea, where you'll see collapsed sea caves and rock faces of layered volcanic lava flows. The track begins from the end of Sandymount Road, 8km south of Portobello (a 25min drive from Dunedin).

Sandfly Bay (3km return; 1hr). Pleasant walk across farmland then down the dunes to the beach, a wonderful place to watch yellow-eyed penguins come ashore in the late afternoon. Make for the colony at the south end where there's a hide and, in summer, a DOC ranger to make sure people don't disturb the birds. Start at the end of Seal Point Rd, 7km southwest of Portobello.

Tunnel Beach (1.5km return; 1hr; 140m ascent on the way back; closed Aug–Oct for lambing). One of the best local walks is also the shortest and least strenuous, yet offers breathtaking coastal views of creamy sandstone cliffs and islets weathered into curious shapes. Untouched by lava flows, it gives a glimpse of Dunedin's geology before the volcanic eruptions that changed the landscape. A steep path drops through farmland to impressive sandstone clifftops and a magnificent sea arch. Additionally, at mid-tide and lower, you can walk down the steps of a short tunnel carved through the cliff in the 1870s, which leads to a pretty sandy beach on the other side with sandstone buttresses towering above – an atmospheric spot for a picnic.

The route starts from the car park at the end of Tunnel Beach Road, 7km southwest of central Dunedin. The Corstophine bus (Octagon Stand 1) will drop you 1.7km from the start of the walk; get off at Stenhope Crescent.

Dunedin. More château than fort, this sumptuous residence was designed by Robert A. Lawson for Australian-born banker, politician and importer William Larnach. Materials were shipped from all over the world then punted across the harbour and dragged uphill by ox-drawn sleds. Its outer shell took three years to complete, with the ornate interior taking another nine.

After years of neglect the castle was rescued by the Barker family in the late 1960s and has since been progressively restored while remaining their home. Check out the concealed spiral staircase in the corner of the third floor, which leads up to a terraced turret.

The castle's magnificent manicured **grounds**, divided into nine gardens, are of national significance and quite beautiful; keep an eye out for the handful of *Alice in Wonderland* statues, such as one of the Cheshire cat hiding in an ancient Atlas cedar tree.

You can refresh yourself at the café in the former ballroom, or stay overnight (see p.608).

11

The Fletcher House

727 Portobello Rd, 15km northeast of Dunedin • Christmas–Easter daily 11am–4pm; Easter–Christmas Sat & Sun 11am–4pm • $4 • T 03 478 0180, W fletchertrust.co.nz

As you head along Portobello Road towards the tip of the peninsula, devote a few minutes to **The Fletcher House**, a small Edwardian villa built by James Fletcher, founder of the Fletcher construction conglomerate. Built entirely of native wood, with rimu ceilings and floors, in 1909, it became the family home of the Broad Bay storekeeper and has now been lovingly restored to its original state.

NZ Marine Studies Centre & Aquarium

Hatchery Rd, Portobello • Daily 10am–4.30pm; guided tours daily 10.30am; fish feeding Wed & Sat 2–3pm • $12.50; guided tours $21.50 including admission • T 03 479 5826, W marine.ac.nz

From the village of Portobello, the gravel Hatchery Road leads 2km along a headland to this working marine laboratory (run by the University of Otago), a great spot that can easily take up half a day. Don't miss the "virtual submersible" which mimics a bathyscaphe descent to the bottom of the 1200m-deep canyon that lies 10km offshore.

Although staff are around to answer your questions, you're better off on the **tour**, which often stretches beyond the allotted hour; it includes history, fish watching and sticking your hands in "touch tanks" to feel the small sea creatures and, if you keep exploring after the tour, participating in the **fish feeding**.

Penguin Place

45 Pakihau Rd, off Harington Point Rd, 3km south of Taiaroa Head • Oct–March 10.15am–dusk every 30–60min & April–Sept 3.15–4.45pm as required for 90min tours; bookings essential • $49 • T 03 478 0286, W penguinplace.co.nz

The wonderful **Penguin Place** penguin-conservation project gives you the rare privilege of entering a protected nesting area of around forty yellow-eyed penguins.

OBSERVING WILDLIFE

When **observing wildlife**, respect the animals by staying well away from them (at least 10m), and keeping quiet and still. **Penguins** are especially frightened by people and they may be reluctant to come ashore (even if they have chicks to feed) if you are on or near the beach and visible. In summer, keep to the track as they're extremely vulnerable to stress while nesting and moulting. Never get between a **seal** or **sea lion** and the sea; these animals can be aggressive and move quickly.

THE YELLOW-EYED PENGUIN

Found only in southern New Zealand, the endangered **yellow-eyed penguin**, or *hoiho*, is considered the most ancient of all living penguins but today numbers only around four thousand. It evolved in forests free of predators, but human disturbance, loss of habitat and the introduction of ferrets, stoats and cats have had a devastating effect. The small mainland population of just a few hundred occupies nesting areas dotted along the wild southeast coast of the South Island (from Oamaru to the Catlins), while other smaller colonies inhabit the coastal forest margins of Stewart Island and offshore islets, and New Zealand's sub-Antarctic islands of Auckland and Campbell.

Male and female adults are identical in colouring, with pink webbed feet and a bright yellow band that encircles the head, sweeping over their pale yellow eyes. Standing around 65cm high and weighing 5–6kg – making them the third-largest penguin species after the Emperor and the King – they have a **life expectancy** of up to twenty years. Their **diet** consists of squid and small fish, and hunting takes them up to 40km offshore and to depths of 100m.

Maori named the bird **hoiho**, meaning "the noise shouter", because of the distinctive high-pitched calls (an exuberant trilling) it makes at night when greeting its mate at the nest. Unlike other penguins, the yellow-eyed does not migrate after its first year, but stays near its home beach, making daily fishing trips and returning as daylight fails.

The penguins' **breeding season** lasts for 28 weeks, from mid-August to early March. Eggs are laid between mid-September and mid-October, and both parents share incubation duties for about 43 days. The eggs hatch in November and for the next six weeks the chicks are constantly guarded against predators. By the time the down-covered chicks are six or seven weeks old, their rapid growth gives them voracious appetites and both parents must fish daily to satisfy them. The fledglings enter the sea for the first time in late February or early March and journey up to 500km north to winter feeding grounds. Fewer than fifteen percent of fledged chicks reach breeding age, but those that do return to the colony of their birth.

Carefully controlled and informative tours begin with a talk about penguins and their conservation, then a guide takes you to the beachside colony where well-camouflaged trenches lead to several hides among the dunes. These allow extraordinary proximity to the penguins and excellent photo opportunities. Proceeds from the tours are used to fund the conservation unit that looks after injured penguins. You can also **stay** overnight (see p.609).

Taiaroa Head

The world's only mainland albatross colony occupies **Taiaroa Head**, a wonderland of wildlife that also served as a fortified outpost against threats imagined and real.

Royal albatross can be spied in flight all year round from anywhere on the headland, and a short signposted walk from the Royal Albatross Centre car park leads to a **cliff-edge viewing area** with spectacular views of a spotted shag colony.

Royal Albatross Centre

1260 Harington Point Rd • Daily: Nov 24–March 10am–7.30pm; April–Nov 23 10am–5pm • Free; 45min Classic Tour $40; 75min Unique Taiaroa Tour $50; bookings recommended • ☎ 0800 528 767, ⊛ albatross.org.nz

To see interesting displays on local wildlife and history (or just to grab a coffee) head into the **Royal Albatross Centre**. You can buy tickets here for the excellent **Classic Albatross Tour** which includes an introductory film and time to view the birds from an enclosed area in the reserve (binoculars provided), where there is also a closed-circuit TV of the far side of the colony. The **best months** for viewing are generally January and February, when the chicks hatch, and April to August, when parent birds feed their

---

THE ROYAL ALBATROSS

The majestic **albatross**, one of the world's largest seabirds, has long been the subject of reverence and superstition: the embodiment of a dead sea captain's soul, condemned to drift the oceans forever. A solitary creature, the albatross spends most of its life on the wing or at sea.

Second only to size to the wandering albatross, the graceful **royal albatross** has a wingspan of up to 3m. They can travel 190,000km a year at speeds of 120kph, and have a life expectancy of 45 years. The albatross mates for life, but male and female separate to fly in opposite directions around the world, returning to the same breeding grounds once every two years, and arriving within a couple of days of one another. The female lays one egg (weighing up to 500g) per breeding season, and the parents both incubate it over a period of eleven weeks.

Once the chick has hatched, the parents take turns feeding it and guarding it against stoats, ferrets, wild cats and rats. Almost a year from the start of the breeding cycle, the fledgling takes flight and the parents leave the colony and return to sea only to start the cycle again a year later.

11

chicks. By September the chicks and adults are ready to depart and new breeding pairs start to arrive.

Fort Taiaroa

30min guided tour daily on demand • $20

The Royal Albatross Centre is the starting point for tours around **Fort Taiaroa**, a historic warren of tunnels and gun emplacements originally built in 1885 when an attack from Tsarist Russia was feared, and re-armed during World War II. The main attraction is the restored Disappearing Gun (operated by hydraulics), visited on either the basic tour or as part of the centre's Unique Taiaroa Tour.

Pilots Beach

Blue Penguin Encounter: Oct–April nightly at dusk • Check website for prices • ☎ 03 476 1775, ⊛ bluepenguins.co.nz

For many summers, visitors after a free wildlife encounter have headed down to **Pilots Beach**, on the western side of Taiaroa Head (follow the main road to the shore as it snakes past the Royal Albatross Centre), where southern fur seals loll on the shore and little blue penguins (perhaps 70 or more) can be seen coming ashore around dusk.

From September 2012, evening access will only be possible by joining the **Blue Penguin Encounter**, a short guided walk from the Albatross Centre (where tickets will be sold) down to a couple of low-impact viewing platforms among the sand dunes. Numbers will be restricted to 100 visitors per night.

Natures Wonders Naturally

Taiaroa Head, 1.5km past the Albatross Centre • Daily 10.15am until 1hr before sunset for 1hr tours • $55 • ☎ 0800 246 446, ⊛ natureswondersnaturally.com

The peninsula road ends at **Natures Wonders Naturally**, a headland farm which endlessly enthusiastic owner, Perry Reid, has turned into one of the finest opportunities to see wildlife up close. There's no animal feeding or nesting boxes, just wild nature sometimes literally within arm's reach. The 8WD amphibious vehicles used to transport you around the 6km of often-steep farm tracks seem a little incongruous but get you to a fabulous viewing spot for cliff-dwelling spotted shags, right in among a fur seal colony and to a hide above a completely untouched beach where yellow-eyed penguins waddle up to their sand dune nests at just about any time of day.

ACCOMMODATION

THE OTAGO PENINSULA

Crabapple Cottage 346 Harington Point Rd ☎ 03 478 0103, ⊛ crabapple.co.nz. Stay close to Taiaroa Head in a rustic 1870s one-bedroom cottage that's delightfully restored within and comes with microwave, toaster and kettle. Breakfast goodies can be supplied ($20 for two people). $140

Larnach Lodge and **Camp Estate Country House** Larnach Castle ☎ 03 476 1616, ⊛ larnachcastle.co.nz.

Cosy up in the converted stables, containing six shared-bath rooms, or in the twelve individually decorated grander rooms in the *Lodge*. Just outside the grounds the modern *Camp Estate* offers glam rooms in a modern house designed like a Scottish manor house, with long harbour views. All overnight guests get free castle admission, breakfast and the chance to book a three-course dinner in the castle's grand dining room ($65/person plus wine). Stables $155, lodge $260, Camp Estate $380

McFarmer's Backpackers 774 Portobello Rd 03 478 0389, otago-peninsula.co.nz/mcfarmers .html. Excellent harbourside backpackers with a relaxed atmosphere, nice three-share, plus a queen and a twin. There is no Sky TV, no computers and no phone, and they often close in winter. Dorm $31, doubles $71

Otago Peninsula Motel 1724 Highcliff Rd, Portobello 03 478 0666, otagopeninsulamotel.co.nz. A modern comfortable motel in the heart of the village.

The units at the front have harbour views, and there's free wi-fi. $140

Penguin Place Lodge 45 Pakihau Rd 03 478 0286, penguinplace.co.nz. This simple, comfy backpackers has harbour views from many of its doubles and twins. You can rent bedding ($5/stay/bed) or use your own. Per person $25

Portobello Village Tourist Park 27 Hereweka St, Portobello 03 478 0359, portobellopark.co.nz. Modest campsite with simple but well-kept facilities, budget rooms and more upscale tourist flats with bathroom, TV and kitchenette. Linen $5/person/night. Camping $16, doubles $55, tourist flats $108

Yellow House 822 Portobello Rd, 1km southwest of Portobello 03 478 1001, yellowhouse.co.nz. Classy B&B with one beautiful airy room and a separate suite in its own wing. There are fine harbour views, two cats and an excellent full breakfast. Double $195, suite $240

EATING

Penguin Café 1726 Highcliff Rd, Portobello 03 478 1055, penguincafe.net.nz. Newish café with excellent Mazagran coffee and a wide range of teas, delicious cakes, plenty of counter food and lunch dishes such as fish pie and BLT (mostly around $15). Internet and wi-fi are available. Daily 8.30am–4pm.

Portobello Hotel 2 Harington Point Rd, Portobello 03 478 0759. Classic Kiwi pub where you sit in the bar for a beef burger and chips ($15) or the slightly more salubrious dining conservatory, tucking into fish and chips ($26) or Moroccan lamb salad ($26). Daily 11.30am–10pm or later.

The Catlins Coast

The rugged coastal route linking Dunedin and Invercargill is one of the less-travelled highways on the South Island, traversing some of the country's wildest scenery along the **Catlins Coast**. It is part of the **Southern Scenic Route** (southernscenicroute.co.nz), which continues on to Te Anau in Fiordland.

The region is home to swathes of native forest, most protected as the **Catlins State Forest Park**, consisting of rimu, rata, kamahi and silver beech. Roaring southeasterlies and the remorseless sea have shaped the coastline into plunging cliffs, windswept headlands, white-sand beaches, rocky bays and gaping caves, many of which are accessible. **Wildlife** abounds, including several rare species of marine bird and mammal, and the whole region rings with birdsong most of the year.

The best way to enjoy the **Catlins Coast** is to invest at least a couple of days and take it easy. From Nugget Point in South Otago (just southeast of Balclutha) to Waipapa Point in Southland (60km northeast of Invercargill), the wild scenery stretches unbroken, dense rainforest succumbing to open scrub as you cut through deep valleys and past rocky bays, inlets and estuaries. The coast is home to **penguins** (both blue and yellow-eyed), **dolphins**, several species of seabird and, at certain times of year, migrating **whales**. Elephant **seals**, fur seals, and increasingly, the rare New Zealand **sea lion** are found on the sandy beaches and grassy areas, and **birds** – tui, resonant bellbirds, fantails and grey warblers – are abundant in the mossy depths of the forest. Even colourful rarities such as kakariki and mohua can be seen if you're patient.

| GETTING AROUND | THE CATLINS COAST |

By car and tour The region is linked by SH92, which is sealed all the way, though virtually all the Catlins'

attractions are on gravel roads. Without your own transport, visit on one of the guided tours.

11

TOURS

Bottom Bus ☎ 03 477 9083, ⓦ travelheadfirst.com. Hop-on-hop-off service offered (three times a week in summer) as a supplementary trip by Kiwi Experience (though it attracts less of the booze-bus crowd). It loops from Queenstown to Dunedin, Invercargill via the Catlins then back to Queenstown over 3–7 days ($299). You can start anywhere, and there are Milford Sound and Stewart Island add-ons. Sector fares are also available.

Catlins Coaster ☎ 03 477 9083, ⓦ catlinscoaster.co.nz. A hop-on-hop-off, small-bus tour from Dunedin straight to Invercargill then along the Catlins Coast, either done in a single 12hr day ($195) or spread over multiple days ($210) using subsequent Coasters to move you on to the next spot. Also available as a one-way tour from Invercargill to Dunedin ($175) plus links to Te Anau,

Queenstown and Stewart Island.

Catlins Wildlife Trackers Mohua Park ☎ 0800 228 5467, ⓦ catlins-ecotours.co.nz. Entertaining and inspirational tours led by committed conservationists sharing in-depth knowledge about the local ecology, history and geology. The intimate two-day Catlins Ecotour ($730), for groups of up to eight, explores remote beaches and rich rainforest from their tranquil house at Mohua Park. Drive there or be picked up from Balclutha on demand. All meals, accommodation in their eco-cottages (see p.614), transport and equipment are provided. They also offer the Catlins Traverse (Nov–March on demand; 26km; six people maximum; $800), a two-day guided trek with all accommodation, food and transport included. With only light packs to carry it is suitable for anyone of moderate fitness. Advance bookings essential.

INFORMATION

i-SITE 4 Clyde St, Balclutha (roughly Nov–March Mon–Fri 8.30am–5pm, Sat & Sun 9.30am–3pm; April–Oct Mon–Fri 8.30am–5pm, Sat & Sun 10am–2pm; ☎ 03 418 0388, ⓦ cluthacountry.co.nz). There is no i-SITE in the Catlins, so if you're approaching from the north, make full use of this i-SITE in the gateway town of Balclutha, 83km southwest of Dunedin. It has all the usual information and booking facilities plus internet access.

Services There are no banks or ATMs within the Catlins; many places accept credit and debit cards but bring cash.

There are very few gas stations, and pumps close at around 5pm; fill up before you set off, then at Owaka (card operated), Papatowai or Tokanui. Mobile phone coverage is poor. Telecom have coverage around Owaka. At the time of writing, there was no Vodafone coverage anywhere (though there may soon be around Papatowai).

Opening hours Lodging and restaurant opening hours vary seasonally and from year to year; check direct or with the visitor centres.

ACCOMMODATION

Outside the main settlement of Owaka you'll only find a smattering of places to stay, the best of them listed in the text.

Freedom camping Travellers in campervans have traditionally appreciated the abundance of peaceful wayside spots for sneaky overnight stays, but a combination of sheer numbers and misuse of these sites means freedom camping is now banned in the area. Instant fines have been imposed.

EATING

Self-catering Throughout the region you'll find very few worthwhile restaurants and cafés. It pays to bring your own supplies and self-cater where possible. You can get groceries in Owaka and there are small general stores at Kaka Point and Papatowai plus limited supplies at Curio Bay Holiday Park (see p.617).

Brief history

The Catlins, one of the last refuges of the flightless moa, was a thriving hunting ground for **Maori** but by 1700 they had moved on, to be supplanted by European **whalers and sealers** in the 1830s. Two decades later, having decimated marine mammal stocks, they too departed. Meanwhile, in 1840, Captain Edward Cattlin arrived to investigate the navigability of the river that bears his (misspelt) name, purchasing a tract of land from the chief of the Ngai Tahu. Boatloads soon followed, lured by the great podocarp forests. Cleared valleys were settled and bush millers supplied Dunedin with much of the wood needed for housing – in 1872 more timber was exported from the Catlins than anywhere else in New Zealand. From 1879 the rail line from Balclutha began to extend into the region, bringing sawmills, schools and farms with it. Milling continued into the 1930s, but gradually dwindled and today's tiny settlements are shrunken remnants of the once-prosperous logging industry.

THE CATLINS COAST

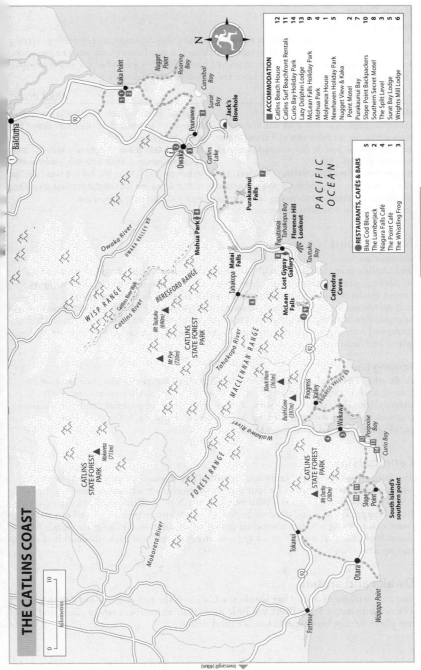

■ ACCOMMODATION	
Catlins Beach House	12
Catlins Surf Beachfront Rentals	11
Curio Bay Holiday Park	14
Lazy Dolphin Lodge	13
McLean Falls Holiday Park	9
Mohua Park	4
Molyneux House	1
Newhaven Holiday Park	5
Nugget View & Kaka	
Point Motel	2
Purakaunui Bay	7
Slope Point Backpackers	10
Southern Secret Motel	8
The Split Level	3
Surat Bay Lodge	5
Wrights Mill Lodge	6

● RESTAURANTS, CAFÉS & BARS	
Blue Cod Blues	5
The Lumberjack	4
Niagara Falls Café	2
The Point Café	1
The Whistling Frog	3

PACIFIC OCEAN

11

Invercargill (40km) ▶

Kaka Point

22km south of Balclutha

The first stop inside the Catlins is **Kaka Point**, a tiny holiday community with golden sands patrolled by lifeguards in summer, making it a good swimming and surfing spot. Just behind the township a scenic reserve of native forest is accessible on an easy loop track (2.5km; 30min; signposted from the top of Marine Terrace).

ACCOMMODATION AND EATING KAKA POINT

Molyneux House 2 Rimu St ☎03 412 8002, ⓦmolyneuxhouse.co.nz. Very comfy B&B in a modern house offering just one deluxe suite with its own kitchen and great sea views from the deck. Continental breakfast ingredients provided. $190

Nugget View & Kaka Point Motels 11 Rata St ☎0800 525 278, ⓦcatlins.co.nz. Comfortable place with a range of spacious units, almost all with decking and wonderful ocean views. The owner also offers intimate tours ($35; $30 for guests; 2hr 30min) along the point to see penguins and seals and get a taste of the local history. Budget $95, studios $130, spa units $155

The Point Café & Bar 58 Esplanade ☎03 412 8800. This decent-enough café/pub is the only spot for a coffee, seafood chowder ($16) or blue cod and chips ($18), but works best for a beer while watching the breakers or sitting in the garden bar. Daily 11am–10pm.

Nugget Point

9km south of Kaka Point

The Catlins proper kicks off with a bang at dramatic **Nugget Point**, a steep-sided, windswept promontory rising 133m above the sea. Just offshore lie **The Nuggets**, jagged stacks of wave-pounded rock whose layers have been tilted vertical over time. It is an impressive sight, visited on an easy, 900m track (30min return) which ends at a still-functioning 1870 lighthouse, from where you can gaze down on lively groups of honking southern fur seals. Gannets, spoonbills and three species of shag wheel overhead.

Roaring Bay

At **Roaring Bay** you can watch **yellow-eyed penguins** as they leave their nests at sunrise and descend the steep grassy cliffs to the sea or as they return two hours before dark. Their progress is slow, so you need plenty of patience, and binoculars come in handy. A modern viewing hide is accessed along a 500m path from a parking area just before the road end.

Cannibal Bay

The long crescent of sand known as **Cannibal Bay** (named by an early explorer who thought human bones he found here were evidence of human feasting; in fact it was a Maori burial site) is a haul-out spot for New Zealand sea lions. To reach it from Nugget Point you'll need to backtrack a few kilometres then head out to the coast again (along a narrow, winding gravel road), then stroll along the beach for a closer look. Keep at least 10m away from any sea lions and back off quickly if they rear up and roar.

Owaka and around

The only settlement of any size within the Catlins is the farming town of **OWAKA**, 18km southwest of Kaka Point and little more than a crossroads where you'll find a few places to stay, three restaurant/cafés and petrol.

Owaka Museum

10 Campbell St · Mon–Fri 9.30am–4.30pm, Sat & Sun 10am–4pm · $5 · ☎ 03 415 8323, ⓦ nzmuseums.co.nz

A well-curated local museum with evocative exhibits on the area's significance to Maori and the coast's shipwrecks as well as sealer and whaler Captain Cattlin. The Owaka library is on site and the staff can supply advertising and walks leaflets for the area.

Jack's Blowhole

10km southeast from Owaka

A gravel waterside drive runs to Jack's Bay, from where a farmland track (20–30min each way) leads to **Jack's Blowhole**, an impressive 55m-deep hole in the ground, which connects with the sea through a 200m tunnel. Effectively the collapsed roof of a cave, the bottom of the hole is washed by surf at high tide when plumes of spray waft up.

Mohua Park

744 Catlins Valley Rd, 10km southwest of Owaka then 7.5km inland · Daily 9am–5pm · Donations welcome · ☎ 03 415 8613

Spend an hour or so checking out this delightful, remnant patch of forest in a transition zone where beech forest meets native podocarp, with patches of regenerating bush thick with native fuchsia. Nip into the 1920s homestead to pick up a leaflet detailing several trails that are typically alive with native birds. Engaging and knowledgeable owners Fergus and Mary Sutherland have displays on rat and stoat control and particularly on efforts to help the endangered **mohua** further establish itself in the area. If he's available, Fergus may even show you around.

Purakaunui Falls

Purakaunui Falls Rd, 17km southwest of Owaka · 20min return walk

If there has been a good bit of rain recently (not uncommon in the Catlins) don't miss this gorgeous 20m-high, three-tiered waterfall in a scenic reserve of silver beech and podocarp. It is well signposted off the main road and is accessed along a pleasant nature trail to a picnic area and viewing platform.

Matai Falls

Papatowai Hwy, 18km southwest of Owaka · 20–30min return walk

The easy walk to **Matai Falls** is as much a reason to visit as the fairly modest but pretty falls themselves. It winds through Table Hill Scenic Reserve among 10m-high native fuchsia trees, easily identified by their peeling pinkish bark and, in early summer, small red-and-blue trumpet flowers.

INFORMATION

Tourist information Catlins Information Centre, inside the Owaka Museum, 10 Campbell St (Mon–Fri 9.30am–4.30pm, Sat & Sun 10am–4pm; ☎ 03 415 8371, ⓦ catlins.org.nz). Dispenses useful updates on eating and sleeping options, as well as DOC information.

OWAKA AND AROUND

ACCOMMODATION

★ **Mohua Park** 744 Catlins Valley Rd, 10km southwest then 7.5km inland ☎ 03 415 8613 & 0800 CATLINS, ⓦ catlinsmohuapark.co.nz. Four magically peaceful eco-cottages isolated on the edge of bush overlooking farmland. The cottages are self-catering, so bring supplies, or join owners Fergus and Mary Sutherland for home-cooked breakfast ($20) or dinner ($70, including wine). They also rent low-cost mountain bikes and kayaks from their house on the coast. One-night surcharge $30. $170

★ **Newhaven Holiday Park** 324 Newhaven Rd, Surat Bay, 5km east of Owaka ☎ 03 415 8834, ⓦ newhavenholiday.com. Small and delightful campsite bordering the estuary and just a 2min walk from the beach. Simple cabins and self-contained tourist flats come ranged around a central grassy area. Camping $15, cabins $60, flats $100

Purakaunui Bay Purakaunui Bay Rd, 17km south of Owaka. A DOC toilets-and-water site right on the coast, with views of the cliffs, good surfing and Cosgrove Island nature reserve just offshore. $6

The Split Level 9 Waikawa Rd ☎ 03 415 8304, ⓦ thesplitlevel.co.nz. There's little advantage to staying

THE CATLINS TOP TRACK

One of the most varied walks in the region is the private **Catlins Top Track** (Nov–April only; 22km loop; ☎03 415 8613, ⓦcatlins-ecotours.co.nz), which begins and ends at Papatowai and crosses sweeping beaches, farmland, privately owned bush and even a stretch of disused railway line, delivering fascinating geology, a great variety of flora and fauna and true tranquillity. It can be walked in a day (9–10hr; $25) but is better appreciated in two leisurely days ($45 including accommodation; $85 including pack transport), spending the night in a converted 1960s trolley bus high up on a spectacular viewpoint; the bus comes equipped with one double bed and four single bunks, electric lighting, a gas camping stove with cutlery and dishes, a gas heater in winter, and its own water supply – there's even a separate loo with a view. All walkers are given an excellent booklet that details each section of the walk accompanied by a map. Bring your own food, drinking water and sleeping bag.

right in Owaka, but if you need to then try this warm and spacious 1970s house with a quad-share dorm, a twin and a double, all a decent distance from the well-appointed kitchen/lounge. There are also en-suite motel units in a separate building. Dorm $30, doubles $68, units $76

Surat Bay Lodge Surat Bay Rd, 5km east of Owaka ☎03 415 8099, ⓦsuratbay.co.nz. Backpacker beds in a peaceful spot, where the Catlins Estuary meets the beach. The owners will pick you up for free from Owaka and there's bike or kayak rental. Dorms $29, rooms $68

11

EATING

The Lumberjack 3 Saunders St ☎03 415 8747, ⓦlumberjackbarandcafe.co.nz. This establishment is probably the best of Owaka's middling trio of places to eat and drink. It's pretty old-fashioned but good enough for a

decent ribeye steak with a choice of three sauces plus veg ($29) beside the big open fire. Daily 10am–9pm or later, some winter closures.

Papatowai and around

Heading southwest through the Catlins on the Papatowai Highway (SH92) you cross the McLennan River into the small settlement of **PAPATOWAI**, 26km south of Owaka, with its general store, quirky gallery and a couple of good walks.

Lost Gypsy Gallery

Papatowai Hwy • Sept–April generally daily 10am–5pm, though often closed Wed • Free; "theatre" $5

Wild nature aside, the real highlight of the Catlins is the **Lost Gypsy Gallery**, a cheerful old bus beside the main road containing a wonderland of Blair Somerville's animatronics – machines and toys ingeniously constructed from recycled materials and old electrical components. Almost everything in the bus is for sale (from teabag dunkers to dancing penguins) but Somerville showcases his best work in the **Winding Thoughts Theatre … of Sorts**, just behind the bus. This highly amusing treasure trove of wacky and often interactive home-made inventions includes: a pedal-powered TV; a paua-shell waterwheel; a wonderful organ with each key activating sounds from a car radio, an old phone, an electric toothbrush, a cymbal and more; and bits of old TVs, egg beaters, wooden tennis racquets and just about anything imaginable in who-would-ever-think-of-that combinations. There's also an entertaining toilet for paying customers and a welcome coffee kiosk on site.

Florence Hill Lookout

Papatowai Hwy, 2.5km southwest of Papatowai

Stop briefly at the roadside **Florence Hill Lookout**, which presents a fabulous panoramic view of Tautuku Bay, a magnificent crescent of pale sand backed by extensive forest. At the far end you can pick out the **Frances Pillars**, wave-lashed rock pinnacles made of conglomerate rock.

Tautuku Boardwalk and Lake Wilkie

Papatowai Hwy, 5km southwest of Papatowai

Birders will appreciate a stroll along the **Tautuku Boardwalk** (20–30min return), a raised walkway nature trail over some estuarine marshes into fernbird territory. Others might prefer the walk to **Lake Wilkie** (20min return) through mature forest with interpretative signs explaining forest succession. The lake is a glacial remnant that has gradually shrunk as the forest has encroached.

Cathedral Caves

Papatowai Hwy, 10km southwest of Papatowai • Accessible 2hr either side of low tide, unless temporary closures are in place • $5

The ever-popular **Cathedral Caves** are the grandest of the fifteen or so caves that punctuate this part of the coast, with soaring walls created by furious seas. Unfortunately, in recent years there have often been long periods when natural changes to the beach and coastline make access impossible: ask at local visitor centres, or check the sign at the entrance.

11

McLean Falls

Rewcastle Rd, 11km southwest of Papatowai then 3km off the main road • 30–40min return walk

The picturesque 22m-high **McLean Falls** are the most impressive of the falls hereabouts and reached along an uphill rainforest walk through podocarps and fuchsia. The falls are best visited in the late afternoon when sun strikes the forest around the main cascade. The falls were named after an early settler who apparently used to bathe here.

ACCOMMODATION AND EATING   **PAPATOWAI**

★ **McLean Falls Holiday Park** 27 Rewcastle Rd ☎ 03 415 8338, ⓦ catlinsnz.com. Excellent and professionally run complex with sheltered campsites and plenty of firm powered sites, all accessing barbecue areas, and a TV lounge. Backpackers get use of cute twin cabins, each with its own table and chairs on the tiny porch. There are also slightly more plush Kiwiana cabins with doubles available, nicely appointed motel units and purpose-built one-bedroom chalets. Camping $20 shares $32, cabins $75, Kiwiana cabins $85, motels $135, chalets $195
Southern Secret Motel 2510 Papatowai Hwy, Papatowai ☎ 03 415 8600, ⓦ homepages.ihug.co.nz /~aikman. Though it looks like an ordinary home on the outside, this motel has four fabulous rooms done out in Pacific colours with mosquito-net-draped wrought-iron beds and a free library of over 300 videos. The same people

offer *Erehwon*, a self-contained cottage with two doubles just up the road. Motels $99, self-contained cottage $125
The Whistling Frog 27 Rewcastle Rd ☎ 03 415 8338, ⓦ whistlingfrogcafe.com. Some of the best dining in the Catlins is at this cosy and welcoming café and bar at the McLean Falls Holiday Park. As well as the standard range of Kiwi breakfasts, expect the likes of soup ($12.50), spit-roasted lamb sandwich ($17) and chicken enchiladas ($25), and nothing deep-fried. There's wine by the glass and Emerson's on tap. Sept–May daily 8.30am–9pm.
Wrights Mill Lodge 865 Tahakopa Valley Rd, 9km northwest of Papatowai ☎ 03 204 8424, ⓦ catlins accommodation.co.nz. Upscale backpackers set amid beautiful gardens in a tranquil valley. The four rooms (no dorms) are in a century-old house with a sunny veranda and barbecue area. Double $76, en suite $86

Waikawa

There's not much to the fishing village of **WAIKAWA**, 38km west of Papatowai – just a few houses, the pretty, white former Waikawa St Marys Anglican Church and a museum.

Waikawa Museum

604 Niagara Waikawa Highway • Daily 10.30am–4.30pm • Donation • ☎ 03 246 8464

To learn something of the seafaring and logging life hereabouts, visit the small **Waikawa Museum** which also has a small case containing a bible with a bullet hole and the bullet, which penetrated the unfortunate World War I rifleman carrying it. The museum also doubles as the area's visitor centre, with material on the Hector's dolphins (see box, pp.532–533) that come in close to the shore at nearby Curio Bay.

Blue Cod Blues Niagara Waikawa Rd, Waikawa. Top-quality burgers ($6–8) and blue cod and chips ($7) from a nicely kitted-out wayside caravan with the odd table or two outside. Generally Mon 11am–2pm, Fri–Sun 11am–2pm & 4.30–7pm; daily in high summer.

★ **Niagara Falls Café** 256 Niagara Waikawa Rd, 4km north of Waikawa ☎03 246 8577, ⓦniagarafallscafe .co.nz. Great licensed café in Niagara's refurbished old schoolhouse surrounded by gardens and lawns. Everything is prepared on site from natural ingredients and generally cooked as plainly as possible to bring out the pure flavours. Stop in for superb coffee and carrot cake, a whitebait entrée ($20; available all year), blue cod with salad and house-baked bread ($26) or rack of lamb ($35). Wheat- and dairy-free options are available and select Kiwi wines all come by the glass. Pay wi-fi and internet available. Daily 9am–11pm, but check for winter closures.

Curio Bay and Porpoise Bay

5km southwest of Waikawa

Contrasting seascapes come together at a windswept headland that separates two of the most beautiful bays in this region packed with such things. To the north, the beautiful sandy curve of **Porpoise Bay** forms superb rolling breakers where **Hector's dolphins** love to surf. To the south, the rocky wave-cut platform of **Curio Bay** is littered with the remains of a **petrified forest**, its fossilized Jurassic trees clearly visible at low tide. Over 170 million years ago, when most of New Zealand still lay beneath the sea, this would have been a broad, forested floodplain. Today, the seashore, composed of several layers of forest buried under blankets of volcanic mud and ash, is littered with fossilized tree stumps and fallen logs. Steps lead to a beach where, in places, you can even pick out ancient tree rings. Return at sunrise or just before dusk when up to a dozen **yellow-eyed penguins** stagger ashore to their burrows in the bushes at the back of Curio Bay. If you want to get in the surf, contact Catlins Surf (☎03 246 8552, ⓦcatlins-surf .co.nz), who rent boards ($40/3hr), offer **surfing lessons** ($50/90min) and give you a chance to try **stand-up paddleboarding** ($75/2hr 30min). The nearest place to eat is *Niagara Falls Café* (see above).

11

★ **Catlins Beach House** 499 Curio Bay Rd ☎03 246 8340, ⓦcatlinsbeachhouse.co.nz. Step off the lawn onto the beach at this wonderfully chilled-out hostel in a self-contained house with a pot-belly log burner and room for just nine in two doubles (one en suite) and a bunkroom. Dorms $25, double $70, en suite $95
Catlins Surf Beachfront Rentals ☎03 246 8552, ⓦcatlins-surf.co.nz. A selection of fully self-contained beachside holiday homes all available by the night and all with linen and towels provided. Prices range up to $250. $110
Curio Bay Holiday Park 601 Curio Bay Rd ☎03 246 8897, ⓔvalwhyte@hotmail.com. Wonderfully sited campsite where tent and powered sites come nestled into dense flax enclaves that protect you from the sometimes ferocious winds. There are views across both Porpoise Bay and Curio Bay, and a tiny store sells supplies. Showers are $2. Camping/site $16, powered sites $27
Lazy Dolphin Lodge 529 Curio Bay Rd ☎03 246 8579, ⓦlazydolphinlodge.co.nz. Spacious and beautifully sited hostel on dunes from where you can watch dolphins frolicking in the surf. All beds (no bunks) are made up and they have towels for rent ($3). Dorms $33, doubles $72

Slope Point

6km west of Curio Bay, but 16km by gravel road

Slope Point is the southernmost land on the South Island, some 7km further south than Bluff. A walk through sheep paddocks (40min return) brings you to a wind-lashed promontory that's totally exposed to the southern ocean. A sign advises that it is still 4803km to the South Pole.

The **western continuation** of the **Southern Scenic Route**, from Invercargill to Te Anau via Tuatapere, is covered in the Fiordland chapter (see p.778).

THE NEW ZEALAND SEA LION AND HECTOR'S DOLPHIN

Two extremely rare species – the **New Zealand sea lion** (*Phocarctos hookeri* a.k.a. *Hooker's sea lion*) and **Hector's dolphin** (*Cephalarhynchus hectori*) – are found only in New Zealand waters.

New Zealand sea lions mostly live around the sub-Antarctic Auckland Islands, 460km south of the South Island, but some breeding also takes place on the Otago Peninsula, along the Catlins Coast and around Stewart Island. The large, adult male sea lions are black to dark brown, have a mane over their shoulders, weigh up to 400kg and reach lengths of over 3m. Adult females are buff to silvery grey and much smaller – less than half the weight and just under 2m. Barracuda, red cod, octopus, skate and, in spring, paddle crabs make up their diet, with New Zealand sea lions usually diving 200m or less for four or five minutes – although they are capable of achieving depths of up to 500m. Pups are born on the beach, then moved by the mother at about six weeks to grassy swards, shrubland or forest, and suckled for up to a year.

Sea lions prefer to haul out on sandy beaches and in summer spend much of the day flicking sand over themselves to keep cool. Unlike seals they don't fear people. If you encounter one on land, give it a wide berth of at least 10m (30m during the Dec–Feb breeding season), and if it rears up and roars, back off calmly but quickly – they can move fast.

The **Hector's dolphin**, with its distinctive black and white markings, is the smallest dolphin in the world and, with a population around 7,000, is also one of the rarest. It's only found in New Zealand inshore waters – mostly around the coast of the South Island – with eastern concentrations around Banks Peninsula, Te Waewae Bay and Porpoise Bay, plus western communities between Farewell Spit and Haast. They roam up to 8km from shore in winter but in summer prefer shallow waters within 1km of the coastline, catching mullet, arrowsquid, red cod, stargazers and crabs. Female dolphins are typically a little larger than the males, growing to 1.2–1.4m and weighing 40–50kg. They give birth from November to mid-February, and calves stay with their mothers for up to two years.

In summer and autumn, the tiny resident population at Porpoise Bay regularly enters the surf zone and even comes within 10m of the beach. Hector's dolphins are shy and being disturbed can impact on feeding, which in turn affects their already low breeding rate. If you're spending time around them, be sure to follow DOC rules (posted locally), which essentially forbid touching, feeding, surrounding and chasing dolphins and encourage you to keep a respectful distance. Swimming around pods with juveniles is also forbidden, and in summer most pods will have juveniles.

ACCOMMODATION

SLOPE POINT

Slope Point Backpackers 164 Slope Point Rd ☏ 03 246 8420, ⓦ slopepoint.co.nz. Friendly and great-value hostel on a working sheep farm where kids (of all ages) are welcome to check out the animals. There's a selection of doubles, dorm rooms and a self-contained unit, plus camping and a couple of powered sites. Camping $12, dorms $22, doubles $47, unit $87

Waipapa Point

26km west of Curio Bay

Waipapa Point is the site of New Zealand's worst civilian shipwreck, in 1881, when 131 lives were lost on SS *Tararua*. The lighthouse that now stands on the point was erected soon after and you may now see fur seals and sea lions on the golden beach and rocky platform at its foot.

Gore

The quiet Southland farming town of **GORE**, 70km west of Balclutha and 70km northeast of Invercargill, is a pleasant transit point at the intersection of routes from Dunedin to Te Anau and Invercargill. Dominated by the Hokonui Hills, Gore spans the Mataura River ("reddish swirling water"), and claims to be the **brown trout capital** of the world – celebrated by an enormous fish statue in the town centre. It also claims to be New Zealand's home of **country music** (not that anyone is fighting them for the honour), a scene that is most accessible during **Gold Guitar Week** (late May and early June; ☎03 208 1978, �🌐goldguitars.co.nz) when hundreds of would-be country stars and a few established performers roll into town for five days of low-key entertainment.

Hokonui Moonshine Museum

Hokonui Heritage Centre, 16 Hokonui Drive • Mon–Fri 8.30am–5pm, Sat 9.30am–4pm, Sun 1–4pm • $5

The entertaining **Hokonui Moonshine Museum** details decades of illicit whisky distillation deep in the local bush-covered hills. This began in 1836 and reached a peak during a regional fifty-year-long local Prohibition from 1903. Alcohol freedom is still restricted in these parts, with all liquor sales governed by a licensing trust. Fortunately, the visit ends with a dram of whisky loosely based on the Hokonui recipe. If you're around in late February, check out the **Hokonui Moonshine Festival** (�🌐hokonuimoonshinefest.co.nz).

Eastern Southland Art Gallery

14 Hokonui Drive • Mon–Fri 10am–4.30pm, Sat & Sun 1–4pm • Free

Art lovers shouldn't miss the **Eastern Southland Art Gallery** with its nationally significant collection of art bequeathed by expat Kiwi sexologist, Dr John Money. Among the majestic African carvings are some horsemen and a pair of life-size Bambara ancestral figures. Local interest focuses on richly coloured oils by Rita Angus, works by Dutch émigré Theo Schoon, who incorporated Maori iconography into his painting long before it was fashionable, and career-spanning pieces from the private collection of arguably New Zealand's top living painter, Ralph Hotere. Temporary exhibitions, usually by notable Kiwi artists, justify repeat visits.

Old Mandeville Airfield

1558 Waimea Hwy (SH94), 17km west of Gore • Museum daily 10am–5pm • $5; flights from $60/10min–$220/30min • ☎03 208 9755, �🌐croydonaircraft.com

Fans of vintage aircraft shouldn't miss the **Old Mandeville Airfield**, where you can watch the restoration of vintage planes, take to the air in a Tiger Moth, Fox Moth or Dragonfly, and have a leisurely wander around the brand-new **museum** containing all sorts of beautiful aeroplanes. An on-site café provides sustenance.

ARRIVAL AND DEPARTURE   GORE

By bus Gore lies on the major bus route between Dunedin, Invercargill and Te Anau. Buses drop off at the visitor centre.

Destinations Dunedin (4–5 daily; 30min); Invercargill (4–5 daily; 1hr); Te Anau (1 daily; 1hr 45min).

INFORMATION AND ACTIVITIES

Tourist information 16 Hokonui Drive, inside the *Hokonui Heritage Centre* (Mon–Fri 8.30am–5pm, Sat 9.30am–4pm, Sun 1–4pm; ☎03 203 9288, �🌐gorenz .com).

Trout fishing During the fishing season (Oct–April) you can pit your wits against a brown trout with tackle rented from B&B Sports, 65 Main St (☎03 208 0801); they also sell fishing licences ($23/day).

ACCOMMODATION

Fire Station Backpackers 19 Hokonui Drive ☎03 208 1925, ⍾thefirestation.co.nz. This comfortable hostel has two doubles and two quad-share bunkrooms, all of which come with linen. There's also a full kitchen and lounge, plus coin-op internet and wi-fi. Dorms $28, doubles $65

Wentworth Heights 86a Wentworth St, 3km northeast of town ☎03 208 6476, ⍾wentworthheights .co.nz. Very comfortable semi-rural B&B with fabulous breakfasts, dinners by arrangement and a warm welcome that few can match. Host Barry Perkins is also a fishing guide with great local knowledge. $160

EATING

Casa Bella 81 Hokonui Drive, 1km north ☎ 03 208 0154. Gore's top dining, in a grand Victorian villa. The menu (mains mostly $35) leans towards Italian with everything made from scratch. Tues–Sat 5.30–10pm.

The Green Room 59 Irk St ☎ 03 208 1005, ✉ thegreenroom@ispnz.co.nz. Casual wood-floored café that's good for soup, quiches, frittatas or just a coffee and a slice of cake. Mon–Sat 7.30am–4.30pm.

The Thomas Green 30 Medway St ☎ 03 208 9295, ⓦ tommyg.co.nz. City style comes to eastern Southland at this flash restaurant of mirrors, smart lighting and green and black chesterfields tucked behind the facade of a heritage building. The food is upscale pub style with the likes of beetroot-cured salmon gravalax ($12) followed by ribeye with a mushroom sauce ($31). Daily 10.30am–10pm or later.

Invercargill

Many visitors pass straight through **INVERCARGILL**, regarding it as little more than a waystation en route to Stewart Island or the Catlins Coast. But the city warrants a little more time. Settled in the mid-1850s, it sprawls over an exposed stretch of flat land at the head of the New River Estuary. In 2000, community contributions allowed its main centre of learning, the Southern Institute of Technology (SIT), to offer free tuition for New Zealand and Australian residents (with lower than usual fees for international students) on all of its courses. As a result, Invercargill's population swelled to 50,000, and its arts scene and nightlife gained new life. More recently, the discovery of a possible oil source nearby has led to some new investment in the town, and the prospect of more to come.

To the south, at the tip of a small peninsula, lies **Bluff**, the departure point for ferries to **Stewart Island** (see p.626).

Southland Museum and Art Gallery

108 Gala St, beside Queens Park • Mon–Fri 9am–5pm, Sat & Sun 10am–5pm • Free • ☎ 03 219 9069, ⓦ southlandmuseum.com

Invercargill's chief attraction is the **Southland Museum and Art Gallery**, a giant white pyramid housing a well-laid-out collection over two storeys. Upstairs, the fascinating "Beyond the Roaring Forties" exhibit focuses on New Zealand's **sub-Antarctic islands**, tiny windswept clusters lying hundreds of kilometres apart between New Zealand and the Antarctic. They're the only obstacles in the way of the westerly gales that rage through these latitudes, earning them the names Roaring Forties and Furious Fifties. Displays cover the shipwreck victims who have clung on to the islands, sometimes for years, sealers who subsisted while almost wiping out their quarry, meteorological teams that have weathered the storms with the albatrosses and penguins, and plants from the daisy, lily and carrot families which have adapted to form swathes of gigantic **megaherbs**.

Southland's history is also imaginatively and comprehensively treated, while downstairs, Maori artefacts include a post-European-contact carved figure with a top

---

BURT MUNRO – INVERCARGILL'S LOCAL HERO

Few New Zealanders, let alone anyone in the rest of the world, knew about Burt Munro (1899–1978) until Roger Donaldson's *The World's Fastest Indian* hit movie screens in 2005. All of a sudden everyone had heard of this eccentric Invercargill mechanic who, in 1967, aged 68, set the under-1000cc speed record of 295kph (183mph) on a 1920 Indian Scout bike. He had spent years modifying the bike and testing it at Oreti Beach.

His stock has been rising around Invercargill ever since the movie's release, with a display in the museum, a statue outside Queens Park, the original bike in E. Hayes and Sons Ltd shop, and the annual Burt Munro Challenge, four days of speedway and street racing, a hill climb and, of course, beach racing each November.

INVERCARGILL

● RESTAURANTS, CAFÉS & BARS

The Batch	1
Duo	7
Kings Fish Supply	8
The Rocks	3
The Seriously Good Chocolate Company	2
Three Bean	6
Tillermans Music Lounge	5
Waxy O'Shea's	4

■ ACCOMMODATION

295 on Tay	5
Admiral Court Motor Lodge	6
Invercargill Top 10 Holiday Park	2
Safari Lodge	1
Southern Comfort	3
Tuatara Lodge	4

11

hat and a couple of intricately carved *waka huia* treasure boxes. Burt Munro's exploits (see box opposite) get hagiographic coverage along with a replica bike made for *The World's Fastest Indian*.

Don't miss the **tuatara** – small, dinosaurian reptiles found nowhere else in the world – including Henry, who is thought to be well over 100 years old. You can observe them through windows running along the back of the museum facing the park: they usually come out of their burrows on sunny days in the afternoon.

Queens Park

Main entrance on Gala St

The vast **Queens Park** is Invercargill's prime green space and has been a public reserve since 1869. Today there are lovely formal gardens and a walk-through aviary, among other delights. The park's main entrance has a new **statue of Burt Munro** cocooned in streamlined fairings of his 1920 Indian motorcycle.

The water tower

Corner of Doon and Leet sts · Sun & public holidays 1.30–4.30pm · $2 · ☎ 03 211 1679

Invercargill's eastern skyline is dominated by the ornate 40m-high brick **water tower**, a Romanesque, polychrome edifice that's surely far grander than it really needed to be. It was completed in 1889 and stairs inside allow you to experience the city's best view.

11

E. Hayes and Sons Ltd

168 Dee St · Mon–Fri 7.30am–5.30pm, Sat & Sun 9am–4pm · Free · ☎ 03 218 2059, ⓦ ehayes.co.nz

Among the retail section of wrenches and hedge trimmers in Invercargill's premier hardware and homeware store, **E. Hayes and Sons Ltd**, there's an odd little find. Fascinating classic cars and historic motorbikes are dotted among the paint tins and hedge trimmers. Star attraction is the record-breaking bike ridden by Burt Munro (see box, p.620) at Bonneville, accompanied by some of his other bikes, British thumpers from the 1950s and 1960s, gleaming T-Birds and Corvettes and the shop's own nicely restored 1956 Morris-Commercial delivery van. There's also a functioning petrol engine made, for a £20 bet, from detritus found in a garage. After two years the bet was won and if you ask nicely they'll prove it to you.

Invercargill Brewery

8 Wood St · Mon–Thurs 11am–5.30pm, Fri 11am–6.30pm, Sat 11am–4pm · ☎ 03 214 5070, ⓦ invercargillbrewery.co.nz

Connoisseurs of fine beer won't want to miss out on the **Invercargill Brewery**. There are no tours but you can cut to the chase in the tasting room where you can sample up to six brews at no charge as long as you buy something at the end. Brewer Steve Nally makes half a dozen varieties, including B.Man, specially created to pair with spiced curries, and Pitch Black, with coffee aromas, as well as limited seasonal productions such as boysenberry and the *Smokin' Bishop*, a smoky-tasting bock.

Anderson Park Art Gallery

SH6, 7km north of the city centre · Daily 10.30am–5pm · Free · There is no bus service here; take a taxi ($25 one-way) or rent a bike (see opposite)

On the outskirts of Invercargill, the beautiful grounds of **Anderson Park** provide the setting for the atmospheric **Anderson Park Art Gallery**, housed in a 1925 neo-Georgian mansion built for local businessman Robert Anderson. Designed by Christchurch architect Cecil Wood, it was constructed from reinforced concrete and set against a backdrop of forest. During October a spring exhibition of recent Kiwi art replaces the permanent collection, which is one of the country's most interesting independent collections of traditional and contemporary New Zealand art, including Ralph Hotere, Colin McCahon, Don Binney and Dick Frizzell. Behind the gallery, **The Maori House**, built in the early 1920s and used for dances, has a doorway and porch decorated with carvings by Tene Waitere, a renowned Rotorua carver.

Oreti Beach

10km west of town, along Dunns Rd

The road from Invercargill to **Oreti Beach** literally finishes on the beach. Continuing isn't recommended, especially since this will invalidate any rental agreement, but locals drive out there all the time, either taking the dog for a high-speed walk or doing doughnuts in their hot Japanese cars.

This beautiful broad expanse of fine sand sweeps 30km right around to the seaside resort of Riverton to the west, and gives great views of Stewart Island and Bluff. Burt Munro used the beach for many of his speed motorbike trials. In summer, it's popular for swimming (surf patrols operate when busy), yachting and waterskiing, but windy days can cause violent sandstorms.

ARRIVAL AND DEPARTURE   INVERCARGILL

By plane Stewart Island planes and Air New Zealand flights from Wellington and Christchurch land at Invercargill's airport, 2.5km southwest of the city centre. For transport into town use Blue Star taxis (☎ 03 217 7777; $20) or Executive Rental Cars (☎ 03 214 3434; $15/group to the same address). Airport parking costs $6 for 24hr plus $2/each extra day.

Destinations Christchurch (5–7 daily; 1hr 15min); Stewart Island (3 daily; 20min); Wellington (1–2 daily; 1hr 50min).
By bus InterCity and Atomic/NakedBus stop outside the i-SITE. Catch-A-Bus South (☎ 03 479 9960, ⓦ catchabus south.co.nz) do pick-ups from accommodation.
Destinations Dunedin (4–5 daily; 3hr 30min); Gore (4–5 daily; 1hr); Queenstown (1 daily; 3hr).

GETTING AROUND

By bus At the i-SITE, pick up the *Invercargill City Bus Timetable* outlining the city's dozen bus routes (Mon–Sat only; ☎ 03 218 7170, ⓦ icc.govt.nz), which mostly make loops out from the centre and are free Mon–Fri 9am–2.30pm and all day Sat. There are also a couple of bus circuits which are always free,

the most useful being the Freebie (every 15min), which loops around the centre passing the i-SITE.
By bike Rental is cheapest from the i-SITE ($10/4hr), but you'll get good-quality mountain bikes from Cycle Surgery, 2l Tay St (☎ 03 218 8055), for $30/day.

INFORMATION

i-SITE 108 Gala St (Mon–Fri 8am–5pm Sat & Sun 8.30am–4pm; ☎ 03 211 0895, ⓦ southlandnz.com). Excellent visitor centre in the foyer of the Southland Museum, where you can pick up the *What's On* guide (good for local events listings) and the *Invercargill Heritage Trail*

leaflet, which details some distinctive architecture around the city centre.
DOC Level 7, 33 Don St (Mon–Fri 9am–4.30pm; ☎ 03 211 2400). Information and track booking for walks and wildlife in the Catlins, Stewart Island and Fiordland.

ACCOMMODATION

Accommodation prices this far south are reasonable, and there's a fair choice close to the transport links. Weeknights fill up quickly when business reps converge on town. **Freedom camping** is not allowed in town or anywhere nearby; the nearest is Colac Bay.

295 on Tay 295 Tay St ☎ 0800 295 295, ⓦ 295ontay .co.nz. Modern and palatial motel with all mod cons including full kitchens, heated towel rails, electric blankets and hairdryers. Some studios and one-bedroom units have spa baths. **$125**

Admiral Court Motor Lodge 327 Tay St ☎ 0800 111 122, ⓦ admiralcourt.co.nz. Seventeen spotless, fully self-contained units with extras, including breakfast delivered to your door, plungers with freshly ground coffee, free wi-fi, and transport to and from the airport. A handful of units also have spa baths. **$100**

Invercargill Top 10 Holiday Park 77 McIvor Rd, 9km north of the city centre ☎ 0800 486 873, ⓦ invercargilltop10.co.nz. Upscale parkland campsite

with the typically high-standard Top 10 facilities. Camping **$19**, cabins **$78**, en-suite units **$98**

Safari Lodge 51 Herbert St ☎ 0800 885 557, ⓦ safari lodge.co.nz. Swanky four-room B&B in a 1902 mock-Tudor mansion, full of mementos of the owner's Mozambique travels. The rooms are tastefully decorated and all have four-poster beds, while amenities include a large billiard table and hot tub. Be sure to check out the lovely vintage cars in the garage. **$280**

Southern Comfort 30 Thomson St ☎ 03 218 3838, ⓔ coupers@xtra.co.nz. Suburban hostel in a neatly kept Victorian villa set among manicured lawns where a kids' playhouse has been put to use as a cute, small double. There's a modern kitchen and free luggage storage for

11

those tramping on Stewart Island. Linen for dorm beds costs $2. Dorms $\overline{28}$, playhouse $\overline{46}$, double $\overline{66}$

Tuatara Lodge 30 Dee St ☎0800 488 282, ⓦtuataralodge.co.nz. Friendly spacious hostel in a converted bank building, right in the heart of town. The rooms are immaculate (although some are without windows) and there's a lounge with a circular pool table and piano, plus an excellent café on the ground floor. Limited off-street parking. Dorms $\overline{25}$, doubles $\overline{69}$, en suites $\overline{80}$

EATING AND DRINKING

Invercargill specializes in wholesome food in farmhand quantities, though a little delicacy is beginning to show through. If you're self-catering, look out for local **seafood**, including excellent Bluff oysters (fresh April–Oct) and blue cod, as well as **muttonbird**. A number of the city's **bars** transform into dance venues as the evening wears on, though the town is usually quiet until Thursday night, and liveliest during university term time.

★ **The Batch** 173 Spey St ☎03 214 6357. Invercargill's smartest modern café is in a light airy space with sofas and comfy chairs. They serve great coffee and muffins, and brunches such as *kumara* and coconut fritters with streaky bacon ($16), poached eggs with chorizo on ciabatta ($15), and bok choy, pineapple and pear salad ($15), plus Friday-evening platters with fresh local produce. Free wi-fi and use of iPad. Mon–Thurs 7.30am–4.30pm, Fri 7.30am–7.30pm, Sat & Sun 8am–4pm.

Duo 16 Kelvin St ☎03 218 8322. With professional but relaxed service and some of the best food around, *Duo* is a cut above the Invercargill mean. Try a herb pork steak ($35) followed by crème brûlée with tamarillos ($12). Tues–Sat 11.30am–2pm & 5.30–10pm.

King's Fish Supply 59 Ythan St. You can buy the fresh seafood on display to take away (priced by weight) or have it cooked to order while you wait (extra $1); they also do incredibly cheap, delicious fish and chips ($6). Mon–Tues 8.30am–7.30pm, Wed–Sat 8.30am–8.30pm, Sun 4–8.30pm.

The Rocks Courtville Place, 101 Dee St ☎03 218 7597. Long-time locals' favourite with bare brick walls and varied menu stretching from seafood chowder ($15) to chicken focaccia melt ($18) and blueberry and port venison ($35). Tues–Sat 11am–2pm & 5–10pm or later.

The Seriously Good Chocolate Company 147 Spey St ☎03 2218 8060, ⓦseriouslygoodchocolate.com. This tiny café is a good spot for a sausage roll, frittata and assorted counter food (all made on-site from scratch) but it's really a place to indulge your chocolate passion. Sup on a super-rich hot chocolate while you choose from their fabulous selection of inventive creations all made out back. The packets of chocolate include those flavoured by Central Otago wines, or with a Kiwiana theme (chocolate in the shape of a muttonbird and flavoured with caramel and salt). The variations are endless. Mon–Fri 8am–5.30pm, and in summer Sat 9.30am–2pm, Sun 10.30am–3pm.

Three Bean 73 Dee St ☎03 214 1914. Popular breakfast and lunch café dishing up zingy coffee and a well-made bacon and egg bagel ($13) along with excellent cakes, scones and muffins. Good magazines and free wi-fi. Mon–Fri 7am–4pm, Sat 8.30am–2pm.

Tillermans Music Lounge 16 Don St ☎03 218 9240, ⓦfacebook.com/tillermans. Popular bar with pool tables, and a focal point for (often fairly offbeat) live music. Fri & Sat 9pm–3am.

Waxy O'Shea's 90 Dee St ☎03 214 0313, ⓦwaxys.co .nz. Convivial and more convincing-than-average Irish bar with good – and occasionally live – music. They do a decent bangers and mash for $18. Daily 11am–10pm or later.

DIRECTORY

Internet Wired ($2 for 30min) and wi-fi ($5/hr) access at the i-SITE, and the library (free).

Left luggage The i-SITE will hold bags during the day but not overnight (free).

Library 50 Dee St (Mon–Fri 9am–8pm, Sat 10am–1pm, Sun 1–4pm; ☎03 218 7025).

Medical treatment Southland Hospital, on Kew Rd (☎03 218 1949), has a 24hr accident and emergency department. For illness and minor accidents outside surgery hours, contact the Urgent Doctor Service, 40 Clyde St (☎03 218 8821; Mon–Fri 6pm–6am; Sat & Sun 9am–4pm).

Pharmacy Inside the Countdown supermarket (Mon–Thurs & Sat–Sun 8.30am–8pm, Fri 8.30am–9pm).

Police 117 Don St (☎03 211 0400).

Post office 51 Don St, near the junction with Kelvin St (Mon–Fri 8.30am–5pm, Sat 10am–12.30pm).

Bluff

The small but busy fishing town and port of **BLUFF**, 27km south of Invercargill, occupies a slender-waisted peninsula with its man-made harbour on one side and wild Foveaux

Strait on the other. Continuously settled since 1824, Bluff is the oldest European town in New Zealand and it is showing its age a little. Parts look decidedly run-down and most visitors are here to hop on the ferry to **Stewart Island**, but the place has a great setting, a long history and some fine short walks. Unless you have your own vehicle, seeing the town will involve a good deal of walking, as it spreads along the shoreline for about 6km.

Bluff's famous oysters (see box, p.626) are celebrated at the annual **Bluff Oyster & Food Festival** (third weekend in May; ⓦ bluffoysterfest.co.nz), an event the local organizers claim is "unsophisticated and proud of it".

Bluff Maritime Museum

241 Foreshore Rd, 1km north of the ferry dock • Mon–Fri 10am–4.30pm, Sat & Sun 1–5pm • $2

Bluff's small **Bluff Maritime Museum** contains historical displays focusing on whaling, the harbour development, oyster harvesting and shipwrecks. Pride of place is given to a triple-expansion steam engine and the 1909 oyster boat, *Monica II*, which sits outside the building.

Stirling Point

SH1, 2km south of the ferry dock

State Highway 1 ends at **Stirling Point**, not the South Island's most southerly point (that's Slope Point in the Catlins), but a fine spot with a multi-armed signpost that balances Cape Reinga's at the other end of the country. It marks the distance to major cities around the world, as well as the equator (5133km) and the South Pole (4810km). This is also the southern limit of the Te Araroa long-distance path from Cape Reinga. For something much more manageable, Stirling Point is the start of a couple of short **walks** (see below).

Nearby, a massive **anchor chain sculpture** disappears into the sea, symbolically linking Stirling Point with Russell Beck's near-identical sculpture at Lee Bay on Stewart Island. In Maori lore, the South Island is demi-god Maui's canoe, and Stewart Island is *Te Punga o Te Waka a Maui*, "The Anchor Stone of Maui's Canoe".

There are a couple of good walks from the car park at Stirling Point. The Foveaux Walkway (6.6km; 2hr one-way; mostly flat) loops back towards town and has great coastal views. The Topuni Track (2km one-way; 45min; 265m ascent) is fairly steep and climbs to Bluff Hill Lookout for 360-degree views encompassing Stewart Island, 35km away. The lookout is also accessible by road from Bluff: follow Lee Street, opposite the ferry wharf, for 3km.

ARRIVAL AND INFORMATION   BLUFF

By bus Stewart Island Experience (☎ 0800 000 511, ⓦ stewartislandexperience.co.nz) runs a regular bus service from Invercargill ($22 each way), to connect with the ferry. For details on ferry sailings to Stewart Island, see p.626.

Tourist information Bluff's maritime museum acts as a de facto visitor centre. Check out ⓦ bluff.co.nz and pick up a *Bluff Heritage Trail* leaflet at Invercargill's i-SITE.

ACCOMMODATION AND EATING

Bluff Homestead 90 Bann St ☎ 03 212 8800, ⓦ bluffhomestead.co.nz. The three delightful rooms in this grand 1873 timber house on a hill all come with great views from their sun porch or bay window. In addition there's an en-suite cabin with a double bunk, campervan parking, free wi-fi for all and breakfast on request ($15–20). Campervans/person $15, cabin $75, doubles $150

Bluff Lodge 120 Gore St ☎ 03 212 7106, ⓦ blufflodge .co.nz. Super-handy for the Stewart Island ferries, this

1899 former post office now has five- and seven-bed dorms (no bunks) and three doubles, all sharing kitchen and bathroom facilities. There's also a separate three-bedroom house down the road. Linen is $5/person extra. Dorms $18, doubles $45, house $100

Johnson's Oysters 8 Foreshore Rd ☎ 03 212 8665. Between June and August you can buy Bluff oysters direct at factory prices from several spots on Bluff's waterfront including this venerable establishment. Daily 9am–4pm.

11

FOVEAUX STRAIT, BLUFF OYSTERS AND MUTTONBIRDS

Foveaux Strait, between the South Island and Stewart Island, has a fearsome reputation as a rough stretch of water, right in the path of the Roaring Forties with no land east or west until you hit South America. Mostly flat-floored and just 20–30m deep, this causes waves to rear up and further compound the discomfort of ferry passengers and those out harvesting the strait's bounty.

The best-known foodstuff pulled from the waters hereabouts is the sweet **Bluff oysters**, a highly sought-after delicacy dredged from April until September then processed in local oyster sheds before being sent all over the country.

Foveaux Strait is also home to a cluster of overgrown rocks known as the Titi or **Muttonbird Islands**, where local Maori have the traditional right to harvest sooty shearwater chicks in April and early May. These muttonbirds (*titi* in Maori) are regarded as a delicacy, though the anchovy-duck flavour is something few Pakeha acquire.

Stewart Island

Foveaux Strait (see box above) separates the South Island from New Zealand's third main island, **STEWART ISLAND**, a genuinely special place of rare birds, bountiful seas and straight-talking people.

Most of Stewart Island is uninhabited and characterized by bush-fringed bays, sandy coves, windswept beaches and a rugged interior of tall rimu forest and granite outcrops. It is known in Maori as Rakiura ("The Land of Glowing Skies"), although the jury is still out on whether this refers to the aurora australis – a.k.a. **southern lights** – occasionally seen in the night sky throughout the year, or the fabulous sunsets. With the creation of **Rakiura National Park** in 2002 a full 85 percent of the island is now protected.

Almost the entire population of 400 lives in the sole town, **Oban**, where boats dock, planes land and the parrot-shriek of kaka provides the soundtrack. There's not much to do in town, but the slow island ways can quickly get into your blood and you may well want to stay longer than you had planned, especially if you're drawn to serious wilderness **tramping**, abundant **wildlife** in unspoilt surroundings and sea **kayaking** around the flooded valley of **Paterson Inlet**.

Brief history

Maori had been here for centuries before Captain Cook came by in 1770 and erroneously marked Rakiura as a peninsula on his charts. The island was later named after William Stewart, the first officer on a sealing vessel that visited in 1809. With the arrival of Europeans, felling rimu became the island's economic mainstay, supporting three thousand people in the 1930s. Now almost all of Stewart Island's residents live from **conservation** work, **fishing** (crayfish, blue cod and paua), **fish farming** (salmon and mussels) and tourism.

Oban (Halfmoon Bay)

Scattered around Halfmoon Bay, **OBAN** (also commonly known as Halfmoon Bay) comprises little more than a few dozen houses, a visitor centre, a tiny museum, a couple of stores and cafés, and a hotel with a bar. More houses straggle away up the surrounding hills, surrounded by bush alive with native birds. Without even trying, you'll see tui and kereru and small flocks of squawking **kaka**, large rusty-brown native parrots that are almost never seen elsewhere in the country.

Rakiura Museum

9 Ayr St • Oct–May Mon–Sat 10am–1.30pm, Sun noon–2pm; June–Sept Mon–Fri 10am–noon, Sat 10am–1.30pm, Sun noon–2pm • $2 • ☎ 03 219 1221

Devote a few minutes to the **Rakiura Museum**, which focuses on local history including an 1816 globe still showing Stewart Island attached to the South Island, as Cook had depicted it. The small Maori collection contains a rare necklace made from several hundred dolphin teeth, while two giant sperm whale teeth add bite to a whaling display that includes delicate examples of scrimshaw.

Observation Rock

Excelsior Rd, 25min walk from central Oban

A short path through the bush leads to **Observation Rock**, a hilltop clearing with a wonderful panorama of Paterson Inlet and the island's highest peak,

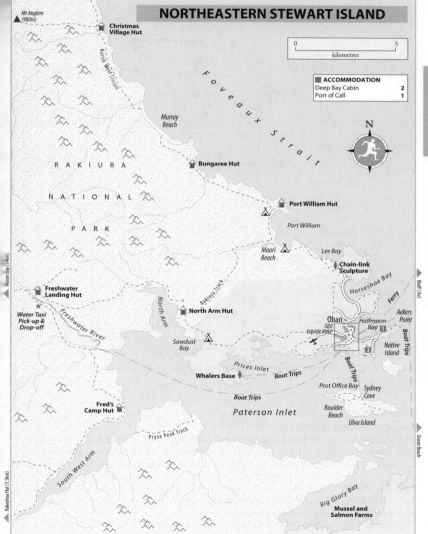

NORTHEASTERN STEWART ISLAND

0 — 5 kilometres

■ **ACCOMMODATION**
Deep Bay Cabin — 2
Port of Call — 1

Mt Anglem (980m)

Christmas Village Hut

North West Circuit

Murray Beach

Foveaux Strait

R A K I U R A

N A T I O N A L

P A R K

Bungaree Hut

Port William Hut

Port William

Lee Bay

Chain-link Sculpture

Maori Beach

Horseshoe Bay

Ferry

Bluff (1hr)

Ackers Point

Oban
SEE OBAN MAP

Halfmoon Bay

Native Island

Boat Trips

Freshwater Landing Hut

Water Taxi Pick-up & Drop-off

Mason Bay (14km)

Freshwater River

North Arm

Rakiura Track

North Arm Hut

Sawdust Bay

Whalers Base

Prices Inlet

Boat Trips

Boat Trips

Post Office Bay

Sydney Cove

Boulder Beach

Ulva Island

Fred's Camp Hut

Paterson Inlet

Pryse Peak Track

South West Arm

South West River

Rakeahua Hut (1.5km)

Big Glory Bay

Mussel and Salmon Farms

Ocean Beach

11

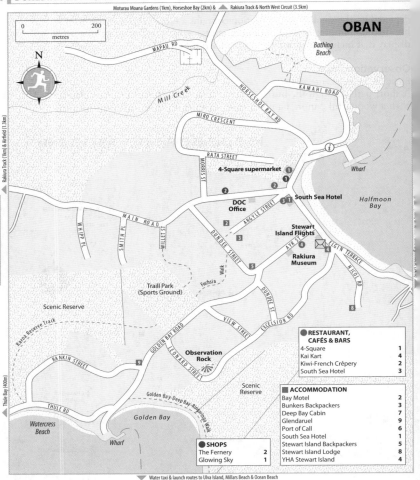

Moturau Moana Gardens (1km), Horseshoe Bay (2km) & Rakiura Track & North West Circuit (3.5km)

OBAN

RESTAURANT, CAFÉS & BARS

4-Square	1
Kai Kart	4
Kiwi-French Crêpery	2
South Sea Hotel	3

ACCOMMODATION

Bay Motel	2
Bunkers Backpackers	3
Deep Bay Cabin	7
Glendaruel	9
Port of Call	6
South Sea Hotel	1
Stewart Island Backpackers	5
Stewart Island Lodge	8
YHA Stewart Island	4

SHOPS

The Fernery	2
Glowing Sky	1

Water taxi & launch routes to Ulva Island, Millars Beach & Ocean Beach

Mount Anglem. As the sun sets you may be treated to a dozen or so kaka screeching and flying about.

Ulva Island

Paterson Inlet, 2km offshore • Daylight hours • Free

The birdlife in Oban is pretty special, but it pales next to that on the 2km-long, low **Ulva Island** – an open wildlife sanctuary that's been cleared of introduced predators through sustained local effort. On a series of easy walks to secluded beaches you'll see more native birdlife than almost anywhere else in New Zealand. The place is full of birdsong, its dense temperate rainforest alive with endangered saddleback, bellbirds, kaka, yellow- and red-crowned parakeets, tui, fantails, pigeons and robins, who approach visitors with fearless curiosity.

Everyone lands at **Post Office Bay**, whose former post office, over 100 years old, is a remnant from the days when Ulva Island was the hub of the Paterson Inlet logging

---

SHORT WALKS AROUND OBAN

Over a dozen short walks around Oban are covered in the DOC's *Day Walks* leaflet ($2); a couple of the nicest are right in town.

Fuchsia and Raroa Reserve Track
(2km one-way; 30min). This little-used trail winds through fuchsia forest filled with tui, bellbirds, kaka and pigeons then comes out at Trail Park. Cross this and head down through rimu forest to reach Golden Beach.

Golden Bay–Deep Bay–Ringaringa
(6km loop; 1hr 30min–2hr). Skirting east from Golden Bay, the track follows the coast to Deep Bay and then over the hill to Ringaringa Beach. From here, follow the signs over a stile to Ringaringa Point and the graves of early missionaries.

Harrold Bay and Ackers Point Lighthouse (3km return; 40min). An easy, well-graded coastal walk that will provide the chance to see little blue penguins and muttonbirds returning to their nests at dusk (Nov–Feb). Near the start of the track, you can follow a brief diversion to Harrold Bay, the site of a simple stone house built in 1835, making it one of the oldest European buildings in New Zealand. The main track continues through coastal forest to a lighthouse and lookout point from where you can watch the penguins make the arduous climb to their nests hidden in the bush. You'll need a torch to find your way around after dusk, but it's important to keep the beam pointed to the ground to avoid disturbing the birds. Follow the signs from Leask Bay, 2.5km east of town.

11

community. Armed with DOC's *Ulva Island: Te Wharawhara* booklet ($2), you can find your own way along trails, though naturalist guidance on one of the tours (see box, p.630) means you'll spot a lot more. There's a pleasant picnic shelter beside the sand beach at **Sydney Cove**.

For information on how to get to the island see p.631.

Whalers Base

On the shores of Paterson Inlet, 7km west of Oban

Whalers Base is another wildlife-rich destination that can be included on boat and guided **kayaking trips**. A one-time over-wintering spot for Norwegian whalers, it is accessed via **Millars Beach**, from where an easy twenty-minute coastal walk heads north from the beachside picnic shelter through native bush. Several eerie relics remain from 1924–32 when a fleet of Antarctic whaling ships was repaired here, and the beach is littered with objects left behind: old drums, cables, giant iron propellers, a boiler out in the water and, at the far end, a wrecked sailing ship deliberately sunk by the whaling company to create a wharf.

If you're not visiting as part of a guided trip, catch a water taxi (around $50 return): most operators will leave you there for a few hours and pick you up later.

Mason Bay

Stewart Island has become synonymous with **kiwi spotting** in the wild, something that is difficult to do on mainland New Zealand. Tours from Oban include kiwi spotting, but most people are keen to get to **Mason Bay**, on the west coast, where they stay overnight in the DOC hut (see p.632) and head out after dark in the hope of finding these elusive creatures. You'll almost certainly hear them, and have a fair chance of seeing them provided you don't go crashing about in the bush: just pick a spot and wait. Take a torch, but keep the beam pointed to the ground to avoid disturbing the birds.

For hardy visitors, the cheapest way to visit is to **walk** (38km one-way; 13–15hr) along the southern leg of the North West Circuit (see p.631), probably staying

11

STEWART ISLAND ADVENTURE TRIPS AND TOURS

The dispersed nature of the sights on Stewart Island makes it well suited to guided trips and tours. Both **Ulva Island** and **Whalers Base** form part of various tours and kayak trips that take in Paterson Inlet and beyond. Adventurous visitors can explore more thoroughly by sea kayaking around the scattered inlets and islands. On extended trips you can even paddle out to the four water-accessible DOC huts around the inlet. Bottlenose dolphins and fur seals are frequent visitors and the tidal flats attract wading birds. There's also a chance to see kiwi in the wild without having to cross the island to Mason Bay.

The waters around Stewart Island are changeable, and May to August brings the most settled weather; only extremely experienced kayakers should venture into these waters unaccompanied.

Stewart Island Experience 03 219 0034, stewartislandexperience.co.nz. The main player on the island runs a number of trips and offers small discounts to those taking multiple trips. Their Marine Nature Cruise (Nov–March daily at noon; 2hr 30min; $85) visits the outer bays, where you can spot seabirds and seals. You can also spend 30–45min in a semi-submersible exploring the undersea life of Jacky Lee Island, 7km northeast of Half Moon Bay. Along with bladder kelp, blue cod, moki and curious filter-feeding animals, you may well see seals swimming by. The Paterson Inlet Cruise (Oct–April 1–3 daily; 2hr 30min; $85) journeys around the outer reaches of the inlet and includes a 45min guided nature walk around Ulva Island. The Village and Bays Tour (2–3 daily; 1hr 30min; $45) gets you onto a minibus and gives you the lie of the land.

Bravo Adventure Cruises 03 219 1144, kiwispotting.co.nz. Evening trips geared around spotting the Stewart Island brown kiwi (a subspecies of the mainland birds). Four-hour trips ($140) leave from the Oban wharf around dusk bound for Glory Bay (35min), from where you walk across an isthmus to the dark, windswept Ocean Beach where the birds often forage for tiny crustaceans. Great care is taken to avoid disturbing these timid birds. Trips are weather dependent and extremely popular, so reserve well ahead. You'll need warm clothing, sturdy footwear and reasonable fitness as there's about 2hr of walking.

Rakiura Kayaks 03 219 1137, rakiura.co.nz. Excellent paddling trips around Paterson Inlet or along the coast north of Halfmoon Bay. Explore narrow inlets overhung by bush and see plenty of birdlife on the Discoverer (2hr 30min; $65); catch similar sights plus blue penguins in the long southern evening on the Twilighter (2hr 30min; $65); or head to Ulva Island or Whalers Base on the Adventurer (6hr; $105). All trips have a $10 lunch option, and there is also kayak rental: half-day single $45, double $65; full day $60/$80.

Ulva's Guided Walks 03 219 1216, www.ulva .co.nz. Ulva Goodwillie was named after the island she now visits regularly on excellent 3–4hr guided walks ($115) which include plenty of botanizing and local Maori stories. Ulva also leads half-day trips to the former Maori settlement and early sealing site at Port William with lots of seabird spotting, and teams up with other companies to offer the Birding Bonanza (5hr; $150) combining Ulva island with seabird spotting and an evening kiwi-spotting expedition (generally Tues; full day; $380).

overnight at Freshwater Hut (see p.632). You can save a lot of time by catching a **water taxi** (see opposite) from Oban to Freshwater Landing Hut ($55 each way; 40min) then walking to Mason Bay (15km; 3–4hr; flat but often flooded – check conditions before you head out).

Stewart Island Flights offer a "Coast to Coast" **loop**, flying from Oban to the beach at Mason Bay (not at high tide), staying a night or two there, walking to Freshwater Landing, then getting a water taxi back to Oban (or vice versa). It costs $215 for the flight and water taxi combo (hut accommodation extra), with a three-adult minimum: call them as they can often hook you up with others to make up numbers.

Rakiura Track

36km loop; 2–3 days

Stewart Island's most popular overnight track is the relatively gentle **Rakiura Track**, one of New Zealand's Great Walks. This makes a circuit from Oban, though you can shave

7km off the route by getting someone to drop you off and pick you up at the road-ends. DOC's *Rakiura Track* leaflet is adequate for route finding; for information on accommodation along the track, see p.633.

You can walk in either direction at any time of the year and there is no limit on the number of nights you can stay, but the majority of people walk anticlockwise. This gets the best coastal walking in early around Maori Bay and Port William, site of the first hut. The track then contours around a forested ridge to reach Paterson Inlet and the North Arm hut before the final push back to Oban.

North West Circuit

125km; 8–12 days

It is a very big step up from the Rakiura Track to the **North West Circuit** around the island's northern arm: only the hardiest (masochistic) trampers should consider attempting it. The boggy terrain is energy sapping even in good weather: thigh-deep mud is not uncommon. And unless you organize a boat or charter flight to drop food at one of the coastal huts, you'll have to carry all your supplies.

The track itself alternates between open coast and forested hill country, offering a side trip (11km return; 6hr) to the 980m summit of Mount Anglem. DOC's *North West and Southern Circuit Tracks* leaflet gives a good overview, pinpointing the **ten huts** (see p.632) which are mostly sited on the coast; there are no campsites.

11

ARRIVAL AND DEPARTURE   STEWART ISLAND

By plane Many people choose to fly to Stewart Island from Invercargill, which avoids the nasty sea crossing but can still be a bumpy ride. Stewart Island Fights (☎03 218 9129, ⓦstewartislandflights.com) has return flights for $195, or $175 for BBH, YHA and student-card holders. You can also go standby ($120 return); put your name down on the list first thing on the day you want to fly to stand the best chance. Flights land 3km west of town; transfer between Oban's airfield and the centre of town is included in the price of your ticket. The luggage allowance is 15kg/person; camping gas and fuels aren't allowed.
Destinations Bluff (on demand; 20min); Invercargill (3 daily; 20min).
By helicopter Rakiura Helicopters (☎03 212 7700,

ⓦrakiurahelicopters.co.nz) has flights between Bluff and Oban for $250 one-way: prices vary for other destinations.
By ferry Foveaux Strait has a reputation for trying the stomachs of even the hardiest sailors, but if you're bringing a lot of luggage, want to carry camping stove fuel or just need to save money it is the way to go. Stewart Island Experience (☎0800 000 511, ⓦstewartislandexperience .co.nz) has fast catamarans ($69 each way) running between Bluff and the wharf in central Oban, leaving Bluff at 9.30am and in the late afternoon, with extra services in summer. A connecting bus picks up from Invercargill city and airport, and costs $22 each way. There's secure parking at the Bluff terminal for around $8/night.
Destinations Bluff (2–4 daily; 1hr).

GETTING AROUND

Oban is a pleasant place to **walk** around, and unless you are staying in one of the more distant lodges you won't need any land transport. There are no roads outside the immediate vicinity of Oban, so straying further afield requires flying, taking a water taxi or walking.

By car and bike Stewart Island Experience (☎0800 000 511, ⓦstewartislandexperience.co.nz) rent small cars ($80/4hr; $120/8hr); scooters ($70/day) and basic mountain bikes ($29/4hr; $39/8hr).
By boat Water taxis (typically speedboats with powerful outboard motors, carrying six to ten people) give great flexibility. A handful of companies offer a broadly similar

service, including Ulva Island Ferry (☎03 219 1013) who operate a regular service to Ulva Island (Mon–Sat only departing Golden Bay Wharf at 9am, noon and 4pm; departing Ulva at noon, 4pm and 6pm; $20 return). All other companies run to Ulva Island on demand ($25 return; 10min) and to pretty much anywhere else you want to go: try Stewart Island Water Taxi (☎03 219 1394, ⓦportofcall.co.nz).

INFORMATION

DOC office/Rakiura National Park Visitor Centre Main Rd, Oban (Boxing Day–April daily 8am–5pm;

May–Oct Mon–Fri 8.30am–4.30pm, Sat & Sun 10am–2pm; Nov–Dec 24 Mon–Fri 8am–5pm, Sat & Sun

9am–4pm; ☎03 219 0009, ⓦdoc.govt.nz). As well as all the usual DOC information there are excellent displays on the island's tracks, natural history, pioneering life on the island, pest control on Ulva Island and some fascinating movies.

Oban Visitor Centre The Wharf (daily: Nov–April 7.30am–6.30pm; May–Oct 8am–5pm; ☎03 219 0056). General island information with an emphasis on Stewart Island Experience trips and ferry crossings.

Weather and equipment Year-round, come prepared for all weather (often in the same day). This is particularly true for trampers who need to be ready for whatever the Stewart Island weather conjures up: winds come straight across the southern ocean from Antarctica. Take several layers of clothing to cope with sun and rain, and don't forget sandfly repellent.

ACCOMMODATION

The island is never crowded (with only around 35,000 overnight visitors a year), but if you visit between mid-December and mid-February book in advance. Huts can be busy from November through to March, so it's a good idea to bring a tent.

OBAN

Oban's range of accommodation is broadish, although finding a place in high season can be difficult: book before you arrive.

Bay Motel 9 Dundee St ☎03 219 1119, ⓦbaymotel .co.nz. Top-class motel with each fully self-contained unit having a large deck with views over town and the bay. Quality furnishings and great service. $165

★ **Bunkers Backpackers** 13 Argyle St ☎03 219 1160, ⓦbunkersbackpackers.co.nz. The shoes-off policy gives a relaxed and welcoming feel to this hostel in a large double-fronted villa where everyone hangs out discussing plans in the lounge or around the barbecue. As well as comfy shared-bath doubles and twins there are four- and seven-bed dorms. Amenities include free wi-fi and internet, free local calls and stacks of DVDs. Dorms $30, doubles $76

Deep Bay Cabin 22 Deep Bay ☎03 219 1219, ⓔwanjengell@xtra.co.nz. Snug self-contained wooden cabin hidden in the bush with four bunks, kitchen and shower, and a year-round pot-bellied stove. Roughly a 20min walk from town and a great spot for resting after the longer tracks. $60

★ **Glendaruel** 38 Golden Bay Rd ☎03 219 1092, ⓦglendaruel.co.nz. Comfortable and welcoming B&B a 10min walk from town, surrounded by native bush. The three rooms are all en-suite, including a single charged at half the double rate. Guests get their own lounge with telescope, and the owner will do her best to ensure you have a great time on the island. $230

★ **Port of Call** Jensen Bay, 2.5km east of town ☎03 219 1394, ⓦportofcall.co.nz. Choose from a boutique B&B with just one room in a large, sun-filled, contemporary house overlooking the bay, a self-catering *bach* just across the road sleeping three with a full kitchen, iPod dock and courtesy transfers into town, or the rustic and romantic, self-contained Turner Cottage, enveloped in bush on the hill above Oban. B&B $385, bach $260, cottage $190

South Sea Hotel 25 Elgin Terrace ☎03 219 1059, ⓦstewart-island.co.nz. Century-old waterfront pub containing old-fashioned shared-bath rooms with TV and a nice shared lounge overlooking the wharf; some rooms have sea views but others are directly above the noisy bar. There are also four shared-bath rooms in a cottage out back and nine more modern motel units. Doubles $85, sea-view doubles $110, en-suite units $159

Stewart Island Backpackers 18 Ayr St ☎03 219 1114, ⓦstewartislandbackpackers.com. The island's largest hostel, with large communal areas, ranks of comfortable-enough shared-bath doubles and twins and four-share dorms ranged around a central courtyard. Also has camping with use of hostel facilities. Camping $18, dorms $30, doubles $70

Stewart Island Lodge 14 Nichol Rd ☎0800 656 501, ⓦstewartislandlodge.co.nz. You're really looked after at this very well-appointed lodge with five rooms all opening out onto a deck with superb views over Halfmoon Bay. The vistas are matched by those from the guest lounge where pre-dinner drinks and canapés and breakfast are served. Free wi-fi. Closed June–Aug. Shoulder season rates ($290) in Sept, Oct, April & May. $390

YHA Stewart Island 44 Elgin Terrace ☎03 249 7847, ⓦyha.co.nz. This former postmaster's house is a bit like staying at your grandmother's place, with three rooms, sleeping up to seven. There are full self-catering facilities and great harbour views from the chintzy lounge. The YHA has been planning to open a new 52-bed eco-hostel next door for some time: check their website for progress. Whole house rental only. First two nights $165, extra nights $25

DOC HUTS

Freshwater On the North West Circuit and handy on the way to Mason Bay this 16-bunk hut is accessible by water taxi from Oban. No bookings; buy hut tickets from DOC in Oban. $5

Mason Bay Kiwi-spotters base themselves at this twenty-bunk hut tucked in behind the dunes, with heating and camping outside. No bookings; buy hut tickets from DOC in Oban. Hut $5, camping free

North West Circuit There are ten huts accessible along the North West Circuit including the two on the Rakiura Track (see p.630). The remaining eight huts (including Freshwater; see above) cost $5 a night (DOC backcountry hut pass valid) or you can buy a North West Circuit Pass ($35), which entitles you to ten hut nights in all huts except those on the Rakiura Track. Huts $5

Rakiura Track Hikers must book and pre-pay for the two huts (Port William and North Arm) and three campsites (Maori Beach, Port William and Sawdust Bay). Book online

(there is a free computer for this in the Oban DOC office) or get DOC staff to do it for you ($2 booking fee). The huts are equipped with mattresses, wood stoves for heating only, running water and toilets, so you'll need your own cooker. Huts $20.40, camping $5.10

EATING AND DRINKING

4-Square 20 Elgin Terrace ☎03 291 1069. Mid-sized general store with the essentials for self-catering. They do a packed lunch deal consisting of a sandwich, sliced fruit and drink ($11; book a day ahead). Daily 7.30am–7pm.

★ **Kai Kart** Ayr St ☎03 219 1225. Billy Connolly once stopped by this fabulously quirky old Pie Kart, a glorified caravan decked out with leadlights and decoupaged tables. You can order superb blue cod fish and chips ($9.50) or burgers ($8–15) to eat inside or at the outdoor picnic tables, or take them to the adjacent beach. Nov–Easter daily 11.30am–2.30pm & 5–9pm.

Kiwi-French Crêpery 6 Main Rd ☎03 219 1422. The KFC is a cosy little café/restaurant dishing up French-style

buckwheat crêpes in a range of Kiwi-fied fillings such as chicken, pesto and camembert ($19), artichoke, toasted seeds and cheese ($20), or Nutella ($12). They also have espresso and cake. Oct–May daily 9am–6pm or to 8.30pm if there are bookings.

South Sea Hotel 25 Elgin Terrace ☎03 219 1059. The island's pub is very much its social centre. Muffins, coffee, soups and snacks are served during the day, while early evening meals consist of dishes such as green-lipped mussels ($15) followed by stuffed filo chicken breast ($27). The lively bar has a Sunday pub quiz that shouldn't be missed. Daily 7am–10pm or later.

11

SHOPPING

The Fernery 20 Main St ☎03 219 1453. This large shop is a cornucopia of souvenirs and gifts inspired by the island and handmade by New Zealand artists and craftspeople. Everything is made in New Zealand. Sept–May daily 10.30am–5pm.

Glowing Sky Elgin Terrace ☎03 219 1518, ⓦ glowingsky.co.nz. The original outlet of this premier

maker of stylish New Zealand merino wool gear, perfect for outdoor pursuits and the street. They now have outlets in Wanaka, Waiheke Island, Dunedin and Invercargill (where the stuff is now made), but this is where it all started. Prices are fab, and if you need something to keep warm on the tracks these are the folks to see. Daily 10am–5pm, later in summer.

DIRECTORY

Banks There are no banks or ATMs. Most business take credit and debit cards, but bring plenty of cash. You can sometimes get cash from the 4-Square shop or *South Sea Hotel*.

Internet Wi-fi for guests at most accommodation. Coin-op internet at the *South Sea Hotel* ($8/hr).

Left luggage Available at the DOC (small $10, rucksack size $20; no time limit).

Phone coverage Telecom is good in Oban, fair around the bays to the northeast of Oban right to the island's northern tip, and sporadic elsewhere on the island. Vodafone are promising Oban coverage soon.

Post office Stewart Island Flights depot, Elgin St (Oct–March Mon–Fri 7.30am–5.30pm, Sat & Sun 8.30am–4.30pm; April–Sept daily 8.30am–4.30pm).

The West Coast

639 North along the Buller and Grey rivers

644 Westport

648 Westport to Karamea

649 Karamea

651 The Oparara Basin

652 Kohaihai River

652 Paparoa National Park and around

657 Punakaiki to Greymouth

657 Greymouth

662 Hokitika

666 Lake Kaniere

666 Hokitika Gorge

666 From Hokitika to the glaciers

669 The glaciers

676 South Westland and the Haast Pass

PANCAKE ROCKS, PUNAKAIKI

The West Coast

The Southern Alps run down the backbone of the South Island, both defining and isolating the West Coast. A narrow, rugged and largely untamed strip 400km long and barely 30km wide, the West Coast is home to just 32,000 people. Turbulent rivers cascade from the mountains through lush bush, past crystal lakes and dark-green paddocks before spilling into the Tasman Sea, its coastline fringed by atmospheric, surf-pounded beaches and backed by the odd tiny shack or, more often, nothing at all.

What really sets "the Coast" apart is the interaction of settlers with their environment. **Coasters**, many descended from early gold and coal miners, have long been proud of their ability to coexist with the landscape – a trait mythologized in their reputation for independent-mindedness and intemperate drinking, fuelled by Irish migrants drawn to the 1860s gold rushes. Stories abound of late-night boozing way past closing time, and your fondest memories of the West Coast might be chance encounters in the pub.

No discussion of the West Coast would be complete without mention of the torrential **rainfall**, which descends with tropical intensity for days at a time; waterfalls cascade from rocks and the bush becomes vibrant with colour. Such soakings have a detrimental effect on the soil, retarding decomposition and producing a peat-like top layer with all the minerals leached out. The result is **pakihi**, scrubby, impoverished and poor-looking paddocks that characterize much of the West Coast's cleared land. The downpours alternate with abundant sunshine, while today's "gold rushes" occur during the springtime rush to catch **whitebait**, when anglers line the riverbanks on rising tides trying to net this epicurean holy grail.

The boom-and-bust nature of the West Coast's mining has produced scores of ghost towns and spawned its three largest settlements – **Westport**, **Greymouth** and **Hokitika**. The real pleasure of the West Coast, though, lies in smaller places, where the Coasters' indomitable spirit shines through: places such as **Karamea**, on the southern limit of the Kahurangi National Park, or **Okarito**, by a seductive lagoon. With the exception of a couple of decent museums and a handful of sights, the West Coast's appeal is in its scenic beauty – the drive, either up or down the coast, is iconic, matching any great road trip in the world. The **Oparara Basin**, near Karamea, and the **Paparoa National Park**, south of Westport, exhibit some of the country's finest limestone formations, including huge arched spans and the famous Pancake Rocks, while in the Westland National Park the frosty white tongues of the **Franz Josef** and **Fox glaciers** poke down the flanks of the Southern Alps toward dense emerald bush and the sea.

Westland's endangered forest p.641
Blackball: birthplace of New Zealand's labour movement p.642
The Croesus Track p.644
The Denniston Self-Acting Incline p.648
Paparoa walks and the Inland Pack Track p.655
Rafting the wild West Coast rivers p.659
Greymouth tours and activities p.660
The Coast to Coast Race p.661

Greenstone p.664
Wildfoods Festival p.665
Okarito tours and activities p.668
Glaciers explained p.669
Franz Josef Glacier tours and activities pp.672–673
Fox Glacier tours and activities p.675
Welcome Flat Hot Springs hike p.677
Gillespie Pass: the Wilkin and Young valleys circuit pp.680–681

Highlights

❶ Oparara Basin Set a day aside to explore this remote area's caves harbouring moa bones, vast limestone arches and placid streams that are great for cooling off. **See p.651**

❷ Pancake Rocks Layered like a stack of pancakes, this geological curiosity is gorgeous at any time but it's especially spectacular when high seas set the blowholes into action. **See p.656**

❸ Hokitika Gorge Stroll through pristine bush to a swing bridge spanning the exquisite turquoise-blue waters of Hokitika Gorge. **See p.666**

❹ Okarito The tiny settlement that inspired Keri Hulme's Booker Prize-winning novel *The Bone People* offers a rare opportunity to spot the national symbol, with Okarito Kiwi Tours, in the wild, with a 98 percent success rate, and/or kayak with Okarito Nature Tours on the seductive lagoon. **See p.667**

❺ Glacier adventures Hiking out onto icy glaciers is an awe-inspiring experience, and expeditions are run with great enthusiasm at both Fox and Franz Josef. **See p.672 & p.675**

HIGHLIGHTS ARE MARKED ON THE MAP ON P.638

Since this is New Zealand there's no shortage of **activities**, including thrilling fly-in **rafting** trips down the West Coast's steep rivers. The limestone bedrock makes for some penetrative adventure **caving**, and there's plenty of **hiking**, with the Heaphy Track to the north, the Inland Pack Track near Punakaiki and a stack of tramps around the glaciers.

Most people visit from November to April, but in **winter** temperatures are not too low, there are greater numbers of cloud-free days and pesky **sandflies** are less active. The West Coast never feels crowded but in the off season accommodation is more plentiful, although many adventure trips and scenic **flights**, which require minimum numbers to operate, may be harder to arrange. Motels in particular are generally substantially more expensive than elsewhere on the South Island, and the Coast's laissez-faire attitude means that even on a chilly winter's night you're unlikely to be able to get a discount on a room, even if the motel is resoundingly empty. The area's relative remoteness also means that food and other prices tend to be somewhat higher – consider stocking up on basics before heading here.

GETTING AROUND

By car and bike The simplest and most rewarding way to see the West Coast is with your own vehicle. The prevalent northerly wind makes cycling a chore but that said the distances between towns aren't off-putting and there's plenty of accommodation including campsites.

By train and bus Public transport is fairly restrictive: trains only penetrate as far as Greymouth, while bus services are few and though they call at all the major towns they won't get you to most of the walks. However, with patience and forward planning to work in with bus schedules, it's possible to see much of interest, especially if you're prepared to walk from bus drop-off points. The main West Coast bus route is the InterCity/Newmans service from Nelson to Fox Glacier via Westport, Greymouth, Hokitika and Franz Josef. A second service starts in Franz Josef and stops in Fox Glacier, Haast and Makarora on the way to Wanaka and Queenstown. This setup enforces a night in either Franz Josef or Fox. To travel straight through, go with Atomic (ⓦ atomictravel .co.nz), who run daily between Greymouth and Queenstown. Several other companies service smaller places.

Brief history

Westland has a long history of Maori habitation around its coastal fringes, river mouths and sheltered bays. The main settlement is believed to have been the Hokitika area, with its abundant *pounamu* (greenstone), where communities lived on fish and forest birds. Beaches, river valleys and mountain passes provided the main access, as the Tasman Sea made canoe journeys hazardous.

European arrival and the gold rush

Captain Cook sailed up the West Coast in 1770, describing it as "an inhospitable shore ... As far as the eye could reach the prospect was wild, craggy and desolate". Little here then for early **European explorers** such as Thomas Brunner and Charles Heaphy, who made forays in 1846–47, led by Kehu, a Maori guide. They returned without finding the cultivable land they sought, and after a shorter trip in 1861 Henry Harper, the first bishop of Christchurch, wrote, "I doubt if such a wilderness will ever be colonized except through the discovery of **gold**". Prophetic words: within two years reports were circulating of flecks in West Coast rivers and a year later Greymouth and Hokitika were experiencing gold rushes. The boom was soon over but mining continued into the twentieth century with huge dredges working their way up the gravel riverbeds by the spent tailings.

Coal and environmental awareness

As gold was worked out, **coal** took its place and laid the foundation for more permanent towns; the West Coast still produces half the country's output. Kiwis and immigrants alike also took advantage of the abundant open space and relatively low land prices nurturing a thriving **alternative culture**. Recent decades, however, have seen a greater awareness of the Coast's fragile **ecosystems** – a situation that gave rise to tension between the Coasters and the government, particularly regarding native timber felling and its impact on the area's unique environment.

12

North along the Buller and Grey rivers

Stretching 169km from its source at Lake Rotoiti in the Nelson Lakes National Park to its mouth at Westport, the **Buller River**'s blue-green waters reflect sunlight dappled through riverside beech forests as they swirl through one of the grandest of New Zealand's river gorges. The Maori name for the Buller is Kawatiri, meaning "deep and swift", qualities which lure rafters to several stretches. Gold was discovered along the Buller in 1858, sparking a gold rush centred on **Lyell**, now a ghost town whose outlying remains can be visited on the **Lyell Walkway**.

The Buller lies between the Lyell and Brunner ranges, and is traced by SH6 from Kawatiri Junction to Westport through Inangahua Junction, where Greymouth-bound travellers turn south towards **Reefton**. From Reefton, SH7 hugs the **Grey River**, a far less dramatic watercourse, as it flows through a wide valley to the east of the granite tops of the Paparoa Range past more evidence of the gold and coal industries, principally at **Blackball** and the **Brunner Industrial Site**.

The Buller Gorge

The Buller River runs through the pine and fern bushland of the Buller Gorge from Lake Rotoiti to the Tasman Sea at Westport. The river was used as a thoroughfare by Maori, who helped early European explorers and gold miners to safely navigate its rapids. SH6 from Nelson passes through Murchison (see p.491) and follows the river 11km to **O'Sullivan's Bridge**, where you turn right to remain on SH6 as it enters the Upper Buller Scenic Reserve.

Buller Gorge Swingbridge

6km past O'Sullivan's Bridge on SH6 • Daily: summer 8am–7pm; winter 9am–5.30pm; jetboats in summer hourly 10am–4pm; in winter by reservation • Bridge $5; Flying Fox $30–60; gold panning $12.50; jetboat $75/45min • ☎ 03 523 9809, ⓦ bullergorge.co.nz

The **Buller Gorge Swingbridge** is an adventure heritage park hybrid, accessed by New Zealand's longest (110m) pedestrian swingbridge. Crossing high above the river, it parallels a fun 160m-long **flying fox** (zipwire) on which you can ride sitting, tandem, or horizontal, Superman-style. On the far side of the swift-flowing water, the heritage park has a variety of **bushwalks** (15min–2hr) taking in an earthquake fault line, gold mine workings and the Ariki Falls (1hr return). You can also pan for gold or catch a jetboat ride, taking in the bridge.

Lyell and the Lyell Walkway

20km southwest of Buller Gorge Swingbridge, on SH6

The grassy site of the former gold-mining town of **Lyell** sits high above the Buller River on flats beside Lyell Creek. In its 1890s heyday it supported five hotels, two banks, two churches and a newspaper, all serving a population of three thousand. Fires and the gradual decline in gold mining saw off the settlement but the few remains can be visited via the short but strenuous **Lyell Walkway**, which passes terraces where huts stood, sobering slabs askew in the cemetery (15min return), and the ten-hammer Croesus quartz stamping battery (1hr 30min return). The roadside site of the former township itself is now a peaceful DOC **campsite** ($6).

The Lower Buller Gorge

At **Inangahua Junction**, 17km west of Lyell, SH69 cuts south to Reefton, while SH6 continues west towards Westport through the **Lower Buller Gorge**, the narrowest and most dramatic section. The road hugs the cliff face in places, most notably at **Hawks Crag**, where the rock has been hewn to form a large overhang – the fact that the water level rose several metres above this carved-out section during a 1926 flood will give you some idea of the volume of water that can surge down the gorge.

Reefton

Located beside the Inangahua River at the intersection of roads from Westport, Greymouth and Christchurch, **REEFTON** owes its existence to rich gold-bearing quartz reefs. These were exploited so heavily in the 1870s that some considered Reefton "the most brisk and businesslike place in the colony". It was also the first place in New Zealand, and one of the first in the world, to install electric street lighting powered by a hydroelectric generator. Such forward thinking abated and Reefton weathered poorly, though the reopening of an old gold mine on the outskirts of town has brought new hope and money. Still, once you've undertaken the town's historic walks and peeked at the museum you'll probably want to head for Waiuta or press on down the Grey Valley.

The Historic and Powerhouse walks

Two walks link the specific points of interest around town, both the subject of brochures ($1 each) available from the i-SITE visitor centre. The elegiac **Historic Walk** (40min) meanders around Reefton's grid of streets, visiting once-grand buildings – some ripe for preservation, others partway there. In the centre of town, on the corner of Walsh Street and Broadway, the so-called "Bearded Miners" entertain visitors at an old **miner's cottage** and smithy (daily, pretty much when they feel like it; donation) by firing up the forge and helping you pan for gold. The pleasant **Powerhouse Walk** (40min) is slightly more uplifting in recalling an illustrious past, perhaps because of its course along the Inangahua River.

The informative *Walks in the Murray Creek Goldfield* leaflet, available in the Blacks Point Museum and at the i-SITE, details nearby **mining trails**.

Blacks Point Museum

Blacks Point, on SH7 towards Springs Junction • Oct–April Wed–Fri & Sun 10am–noon & 1–3pm, Sat 1–4pm • $5

The water for Reefton's original hydroelectric scheme was diverted 2km from Blacks Point, where the **Blacks Point Museum** occupies a former Wesleyan Chapel. The museum charts the district's cultural and mining history and shows a DVD, on request, promoting the modern mining operation, namechecking the **guided mine tour** (see below). Outside, an ancient five-hammer stamper battery is cranked into action, also on request.

ARRIVAL AND DEPARTURE   REEFTON

By bus East West Coaches (☎ 03 789 6251) on their Sun–Fri Westport–Christchurch run stop on Broadway, Reefton's main street, within site of the i-SITE and DOC office; ask at

the i-SITE about seasonal services to Nelson.

Destinations Christchurch (6 weekly; 3hr 30min); Nelson (seasonal; 3hr); Westport (6 weekly; 1hr).

INFORMATION AND TOURS

i-SITE/DOC 67–69 Broadway (daily: Nov–June Mon–Fri 8.30am–5pm, Sat & Sun 9.30am–4.30pm; July–Oct Mon–Fri 9am–5pm, Sat & Sun 10am–3pm; ☎ 03 732 8391, ⓦ reefton.co.nz). The combined i-SITE and DOC office has internet access ($6/hr), a small replica gold mine

(admission by donation) and rents gold pans and shovels ($5/day).

Guided mine tour The i-SITE will book you a spot on this tour (12.30pm; 3hr; $55), which explores the working gold mine on the outskirts of town.

ACCOMMODATION

The Old Bread Shop 155 Buller Rd ☎ 03 732 8420, ⓦ reeftonbackpackers.co.nz. Cosy backpackers in an early 1900s former bakery with loads of DVDs and free internet terminals and wi-fi. The owner can arrange fly fishing lessons and point guests to prime fishing locations on the surrounding rivers. No credit cards; linen costs $2, showers cost $3. Dorms <u>$18</u>, doubles <u>$50</u>

The Old Nurses Home 104 Shiel St ☎ 03 732 8881, ⓔ reeftonretreat@hotmail.com. Popular with Kiwi tourists,

Reefton's rambling and atmospheric former nurses' home offers a wide range of twins and doubles with communal bathrooms. Twins & doubles <u>$80</u>

Reef Cottage B&B Inn 51–55 Broadway ☎ 0800 770 440, ⓦ reefcottage.co.nz. The best and friendliest place to stay in town, with four beautifully decorated Victorian- and 1920s-style doubles (two en-suite, two with separate bathrooms) and an appealing café (see p.642). Doubles <u>$100</u>

12

WESTLAND'S ENDANGERED FOREST

If gold and coal built the West Coast's foundations, the **timber industry** supported the structure. Ever since timber was felled for sluicing flumes and pit props, Coasters relied on the seemingly limitless forests for their livelihood. Many miners became loggers, felling trees which take from three hundred to six hundred years to mature and which, according to fossil records of pollen, have been around for 100 million years.

Few expressed any concern for the plight of Westland's magnificent stands of **beech** and **podocarp** until the 1970s, when environmental groups rallied around a campaign to save the Maruia Valley, east of Reefton, which became a touchstone for forest conservation. It wasn't until the 1986 **West Coast Accord** between the government, local authorities, conservationists and the timber industry that some sort of truce prevailed. In the 1980s and 1990s most of the forests were selectively logged, often using helicopters to pluck out the mature trees without destroying those nearby. While it preserved the appearance of the forest, this was little comfort for New Zealand's endangered **birds** – particularly kaka, kakariki (yellow-crowned parakeet), morepork (native owl) and rifleman – and long-tailed **bats**, all of which nest in holes in older trees.

In 1999, Labour leader Helen Clark honoured her election pledge and banned the logging of beech forests by the state-owned Timberlands company. Precious West Coast jobs were lost and the government stepped in with the $100 million fund, which helped restart the local economy. Thousands still felt betrayed in this traditionally Labour-voting part of the world, but a resurgent farming sector, higher property prices and increased tourism gave Clark breathing space, until the economic downturn and 2008 general election, when she lost government to the National Party's John Key. All logging of native forest on public land throughout New Zealand has remained banned since 2000.

Reefton Domain Motor Camp 1 Ross St, at the top of Broadway ☎ 03 732 8477. This central campsite has hook-ups and is an ideal spot for swimming in the Inangahua River. Camping **$20**, cabins **$76**

Slab Hut Creek 1km off SH7, 10km south of Reefton. The primitive Slab Hut Creek DOC campsite is situated south on SH7 down the Grey Valley and 1km east in a former gold mining area where you can try your luck fossicking. **$6**

EATING

Alfresco's 16 Broadway ☎ 03 732 8513. Welcoming place serving locally named dishes such as "Snowy Battery" (seared ribeye steak topped with crumbed mussels) and "Prohibition Pork" (hot sliced ham with pineapple sauce), plus equally aptly named pizzas, including the seafood-topped "Quartz Reef" (mains $22.50–30). **Daily lunch & dinner.**

Miner's Crib 54 Broadway ☎ 03 732 8458. Dependable fare includes all-day breakfasts (complete with hash browns), a good range of seafood (blue cod, John Dory and turbot, plus seafood baskets) and steaks (mains $19–26). Mon 4.30–8pm, Tues–Thurs 11.30am–8pm, Fri–Sun 11.30am–9pm.

Reef Cottage Café 51–55 Broadway ☎ 03 732 8440. Warmed by an open fire, this timber cottage is an atmospheric spot for full cooked breakfasts (until 1pm), light meals and daily specials such as home-made soup, quiches and crispy bacon butties (dishes $4.50–13.50). **Daily breakfast & lunch.**

The Grey Valley

Southwest of Reefton, SH7 follows the Grey Valley, cut off from the Tasman Sea by the rugged Paparoa Range and hemmed in by the Southern Alps. From both sides, the bush is gradually reclaiming the mine workings that once characterized the region. Nothing has stepped in to replace them, however, and yet the small communities continue to tick over, eking a living from inquisitive tourists keen to explore the former mining towns of **Waiuta** and **Blackball** and to walk the **Croesus Track**.

Waiuta

Along the Grey Valley from Reefton, the first diversion of any consequence is 21km south, where **Hukarere** marks the junction for **WAIUTA**, a ghost town seventeen partly sealed kilometres east. This was the last of the West Coast's great gold towns, reaching a population of 6000 in the 1930s.

Its end came when a mineshaft collapsed in 1951, burying large deposits of gold-bearing reef-quartz, almost 900m down, where it was uneconomic to extract them. Miners left for jobs on the coast, Australian companies bought most of the mining equipment and many houses were carted off, but the town wasn't completely abandoned; a few cottages are still occupied and there are several more buildings scattered around, including the original post office. The rolling country, pocked by waste heaps, is slowly being colonized by gorse and bramble, but the cypresses and poplars that once delineated gardens and the fruit trees that filled them remain; sadly the rugby field, whippet track, croquet lawns and swimming

---

BLACKBALL: BIRTHPLACE OF NEW ZEALAND'S LABOUR MOVEMENT

During the first three decades of the twentieth century, the whole of the Grey Valley was a hotbed of doctrinaire socialism, as organizers moved among the towns, pressing unbending mine managers to address atrocious working conditions. An impasse resulted in the crippling 1908 "cribtime strike", when Pat Hickey, Bob Semple and Paddy Webb requested an extension of their "crib" (lunch) break from fifteen to thirty minutes. Management's refusal sparked an illegal ten-week **strike** – the longest in New Zealand's history – during which the workers' families were fined £75 for their action. None could pay, and although the bailiffs tried to auction their possessions, the workers banded together refusing to bid – one then bought all the goods for a fraction of their worth and redistributed them to their original owners. This spirit eventually won the day: the workers returned to the mine and crib time was extended, but the £75 was extracted from their subsequent wages. The struggle led to the formation of the **Miners' Federation**, which later transformed itself into the **Federation of Labour**, the country's principal **trade union organization**. Eric Beardsley's historical novel *Blackball 08* gives an accurate and passionate portrayal of the strike.

ool fared less well. It's wonderfully atmospheric for just mooching around, guided by the nvaluable **Waiuta** leaflet (from the Reefton i-SITE) and strategically placed interpretive panels – you can see the lot in a couple of hours.

Blackball

Both the Grey River and SH7 meander through inconsequential small towns until they reach **Stillwater**, 11km short of Greymouth, where side roads lead to Blackball and Lake Brunner.

Languid **BLACKBALL** is a former gold- and coal-mining village spread across a plateau at the foot of the Paparoa Range, 11km northeast of Stillwater. Here, commuters, neo-hippies and gnarled part-time hunters and prospectors coexist. Blackball owes its existence to alluvial gold discovered in Blackball Creek in 1864, but gold returns diminished and it was left to coal to save the day. This supported Blackball until the mine's closure in 1964, along the way staking the town's place in New Zealand's history as a birthplace of the **labour movement** (see box opposite).

These days – apart from its famous Blackball salami (see p.644) – Blackball's rustic tranquillity is its main draw, along with excellent walking through the gold workings of Blackball Creek and up onto the wind-blasted tops of the Paparoa Range along the **Croesus Track** (see p.644).

Moana and Lake Brunner

From SH7 near Blackball, the sealed Arnold Valley-Lake Brunner road runs 55km southeast to link up with SH73 between Greymouth and Arthur's Pass. Along the way, the road passes Lake Brunner (Moana Kotuku), a filled glacial hollow celebrated for its trout fishing. The shoreline village of **MOANA** is popular with holidaying Kiwis and second-home owners but not brimming with diversions (or facilities). By late summer the lake is surprisingly warm and makes for good **swimming**, or you can head out on foot along a couple of easy paths. At the end of town, a slender swingbridge over the fledgling Arthur River provides access to the riverside **Rakaitane Track** (30min return) and the **Lake Side Track** (20–60min return), with good mountain views.

Brunner Industrial Site

SH7, 2km past Stillwater

A tall brick chimney marks the **Brunner Industrial Site** (unrestricted access). Recently smartened-up roadside information panels mark the path to a fine old suspension bridge (now strengthened and refurbished but still only open to foot traffic), which crosses the swirling river to the remaining buildings and the ruins of the skilfully crafted beehive coking ovens.

On his explorations in the late 1840s, Thomas Brunner noted a seam of riverside coal, and by 1885 the site was producing twice as much as any other mine in the country and exporting firebricks throughout Australasia. In 1896 New Zealand's worst mining disaster (with 69 dead) heralded its decline. The site was finally abandoned in the 1940s and only exhumed from dense bush in the early 1980s.

ARRIVAL AND DEPARTURE

THE GREY VALLEY

By train and bus The TranzAlpine train (see p.517) stops twice a day at Moana's lakeshore station on Ana St: once at 11.47am from Christchurch to Greymouth, and again at 2.42pm from Greymouth to Christchurch.

Christchurch–Greymouth buses run by Atomic Shuttles also stop here once daily in each direction. With no regular public transport, you'll have to find your own way to and from Blackball.

ACCOMMODATION

Formerly The Blackball Hilton 26 Hart St, Blackball ☎ 0800 425 225, ⓦ blackballhilton.co.nz. The last of the mining-era hotels, this local social gathering spot

opened as the *Dominion* in 1910, and subsequently operated as the *Hilton* – ostensibly named after the former mine manager remembered in Hilton St nearby –

THE CROESUS TRACK

Prospectors seeking new claims gradually pushed their way up Blackball Creek. The scant remains of decades of toil now provide the principal interest on the **Croesus Track**, the first half of which is easily explored in a day from Blackball. The whole track over the 1200m Paparoa Range to Barrytown, on the coast 30km north of Greymouth, takes two gentle days or one eight-hour slog. DOC's informative *Central West Coast* leaflet shows adequate detail for walkers.

ACCESS AND ACCOMMODATION

The track **starts** at Smoke-ho car park, at the end of a rough but passable road 7km north of Blackball, and **finishes** opposite the *All Nations Tavern* on SH6 in Barrytown, where buses pass twice daily in each direction. The most convenient approach is with Kea Tours (T 0800 532 868) who do a Blackball drop-off and Barrytown pick-up combo for $40 (minimum 2). The only hut is the first-come-first-served **Ces Clarke Hut** (24 bunks; $15), with panoramic views and a coal-burning stove.

THE TRACK

Much of the track was designed to accommodate tramways, so you get a gentle, steady grade as you wind through native podocarps interspersed with ferns, mosses and vines, gradually giving way to hardier silver beech and eventually alpine tussock and herbfields above the tree line. Sea mist commonly cloaks the tops during the middle of the day. Half an hour from the Smoke-ho car park, a side path (10min return) leads to the former site of the **Minerva Battery**. Immediately after the junction, the main path crosses Clarke Creek on a modern wire bridge above the remains of an old wooden bridge. Another half-hour on, a detour leads to two clearings that once contained **Perotti's Mill** (10min return) and the **Croesus Battery** (50min return). After almost an hour, another side path leads to the primitive **Garden Gully Hut** (5min return) and the **Garden Gully Battery** (40min return). The main track turns sharply west before reaching the **Ces Clarke Hut**, on the tree line: fill your water bottles here, as there is no other supply. The top of the ridge near Mount Ryall (1220m) lies two undulating hours beyond, a little more if you run off to climb **Croesus Knob** (1204m). The broad ridge offers wonderful views of the coast, reached in under three hours by a steep but well-marked path diving into the bush.

until challenged by the international hotel chain of the same name. Apart from lively drinking with locals, the hotel offers the annual World of Unwearable Arts Exhibition (dates vary), Blackball's cheeky riposte to The World of WearableArt (see p.441), plus basic but spacious doubles and twins with old-fashioned furnishings and shared bathrooms. Rates include breakfast. The restaurant serves coffee, lunches and dinner (mains $20–30), which might include Blackball salami, and is open to non-guests. Doubles $110

Lake Brunner Resort Ahau St, Moana T 03 738 0083, W lakebrunnerresort.net.nz. Block of swanky modern units, some with lake views. Studios $145, two-bedroom units $240

EATING

★ **Blackball Salami Co** 11 Hilton St, Blackball T 03 732 4111, W blackballsalami.co.nz. For picnic supplies, call in at this excellent shop to feast on delicious venison sausages, chorizo, various salamis (of which 150 go to Antarctic bases every year) and other delectable morsels. Mon–Fri 8am–4pm, Sat 9am–2pm.

Station House Café 34 Koe St, Moana T 03 738 0158, W keothai.co.nz. The best eating around, this licensed restaurant/café opens onto a timber deck with umbrella-shaded tables and stunning lake and mountain views. It serves a tempting range of lunches and dinners by reservation (mains around $30). Daily lunch & dinner.

Westport

Like a proud fly caught in amber, **WESTPORT**, despite government and tourist money and the council's zealous desire to modernize, remains fixed in time. Diversions are scarce, except at the seal colony at **Cape Foulwind**, on the brain-clearing walk to the old lighthouse beyond or exploring the ghostly former coal towns of the **Rochford Plateau**. Were Westport – once known as "Worstport" – not a transport interchange, few would ay in this workaday fishing port as the temptations of the Heaphy Track (see box, p.488–489) and Karamea, 100km north, are too strong. However, stay some must, nd time here is made tolerable by good-value accommodation, an engaging museum, ome adventure activities and an outstanding restaurant, *The Town House* (p.647), that ould hold its own in Auckland, Wellington and well beyond.

Almost everything of consequence in Westport is around Palmerston Street. For tours o the nearby former coal-mining town of Denniston, see p.647.

3rief history

Westport was the first of the West Coast towns, established by one **Reuben Waite** in 1861 as a single store beside the mouth of the Buller River. He made his living provisioning Buller Gorge prospectors in return for gold, but when the miners moved on to richer pickings in Otago, Waite upped sticks and headed south to help found Greymouth.

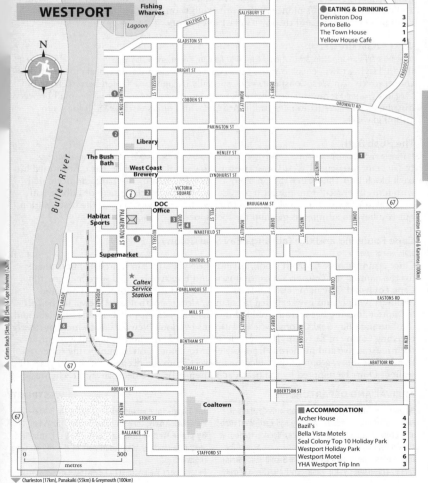

Westport turned to coal and, while the mining towns to the north were becoming established, engineers channelled the river to scour out a **port**, which fast became the largest coal port in the country, but now lies idle. Westport battles on, with a respectable-sized fishing fleet and the odd ship laden with the produce of New Zealand's largest cement works, at Cape Foulwind, fuelled by coal from the opencast mine at Stockton.

Coaltown

165 Queen St • Daily: Nov–April 9am–4.30pm; May–Oct 10am–4pm • $12.50 • ☎ 03 789 8204

Westport's coal-mining past is brought to life at **Coaltown**, where imaginatively presented and engaging exhibits concentrate on the Buller coalfield. Scenes of the workings in their heyday pack two interesting videos, complemented by remnants salvaged from the site: a coal wagon on tracks angled as it was *in situ* at an unsettling 45 degrees, a huge braking drum and a mock-up of a mine tunnel, complete with musty smells. Fascinating photos of the tramways in operation, a scale model of the plateau and a collection of miners' hats and lamps round things out. The museum also records the region's pioneer past, with exhibits on gold dredging, the Buller earthquakes, brewing and the town's maritime history.

West Coast Brewery

10 Lyndhurst St • Mon–Fri 9.30am–5pm, Sat noon–4pm • ☎ 03 789 6201, ⓦ westcoastbrewing.com

Before leaving town, check out the preservative- and chemical-free beers made by the cooperatively run **West Coast Brewery**, especially its signature Green Fern Certified Organic Super Premium Lager, better known simply as Green Fern. The small brewery distributes its wares nationally and in Australia, and offers tastings ($10 for seven 100ml glasses).

The Bush Bath

114 Palmerston St • Mon–Fri 9am–5pm, Sat 10am–2pm • Double bath $40 for 1hr 15min • ☎ 03 789 8828, ⓦ thesoapbox.co.nz

In true entrepreneurial West Coast spirit the owner of a soap shop has transformed his back block into **The Bush Bath**, an open-air area screened by dry bark and decorated with ferns imported from the bush outside town. Prices include soap or bubble bath plus a glass of wine, but you'll need to bring your own towel. It's not the best location but you have to admire his gall and the locals love it.

Cape Foulwind and the Tauranga Bay Seal Colony

12km west of town

Once again we have Captain Cook, battling heavy weather in March 1770, to thank for the naming of Westport's most dramatic and evocatively titled stretch of coastline, **Cape Foulwind**. The name also lends itself to the undulating 4km Cape Foulwind Walkway, which runs over exposed headlands, airing superb coastal views. It's perfect for sunset ambling between the old lighthouse, a replica of Abel Tasman's astrolabe and the **Tauranga Bay Seal Colony**, where platforms overlook New Zealand's most northerly breeding colony of fur seals. The animals, at the southern end of the walkway, are at their most active and numerous from October to January, often numbering four hundred or more, a sign of the welcome recovery from the decimation of 150 years of sealing. Don't be tempted by the beach at Tauranga Bay, it's deceptively treacherous.

ARRIVAL AND DEPARTURE · WESTPORT

By bus Karamea Express buses stop outside the i-SITE. Atomic Shuttles, NakedBus, InterCity and East–West drop off outside the i-SITE and the Caltex service station at 197 Palmerston St.

Destinations Greymouth (2 daily; 1hr 30min–2hr 15min); Karamea (5–6 weekly; 1hr 40min–2hr); Murchison (2 daily; 1hr 15min–1hr 45min); Nelson (2 daily; 3hr 30min–4hr); Punakaiki (2 daily; 1hr); St Arnaud (1 daily; 1hr 45min).

By plane Westport's airport (☎ 03 788 9111, ⓦ bullerdc.govt.nz/airport) is 14km southwest of the city on Cape Foulwind.

Destinations Wellington (1–2 daily; 50min).

INFORMATION AND TOURS

i-SITE 1 Brougham St (Oct–Apr Mon–Fri 9am–5pm, Sat & Sun 10am–4pm; May–Sept 9am–4.30pm, Sat & Sun 10am–pm; ☎03 789 6658, ⓦ westport.org.nz). The office has internet access, and you can book your Heaphy Track (see box, pp.488–489) tickets here for $5 (or book them online for free).

DOC 72 Russell St (Mon–Fri 8am–noon & 1–5pm; ☎03 788 8008). Has information on less-walked tracks.

Outwest Tours ☎0800 688 937, ⓦ outwest.co.nz. Offers a tour (by reservation at the i-SITE; $105; minimum four people) of nearby Denniston, a former mining community and now semi-ghost town (see p.648), and the surrounding Rochford Plateau.

GETTING AROUND

By foot Westport is compact enough to cover by walking, though to reach the nearby attractions you'll need your own transport.

By taxi Buller Taxis (☎03 789 6900).

By bike Habitat Sports, 204 Palmerston St (☎03 788 8002), rents bikes for $35/3hr 30min and $60/day.

ACCOMMODATION

Book ahead if you're going to be here on the weekend after February 6, when the town hosts the Buller Marathon.

Archer House 75 Queen St ☎03 789 8778, ⓦ archer house.co.nz. A lovely 1890 villa set in beautiful gardens, and retaining many of its ornate Victorian details including a wraparound veranda. Two rooms are en-suite, while one has a private bathroom; rates include continental breakfast. Doubles **$170**

Bazil's 54 Russell St ☎03 789 6410, ⓦ bazils.com. Cosy backpackers with doubles and twins (some en-suite) and a pleasant garden including a covered BBQ area. Camping **$15**, dorms **$28**, doubles **$68**, family rooms **$90**

Bella Vista Motels 314 Palmerston St ☎0800 235 528, ⓦ staybellavista.co.nz. A modern, businesslike motel taking the identikit form of other Bella Vista Motels around the country. Sky TV and limited cooking facilities available. Studios **$115**, spa units **$145**

Seal Colony Top 10 Holiday Park Marine Parade, Carters Beach, 6km west of town ☎0508 937 876, ⓦ top10westport.co.nz. Spacious, fully equipped site, with cabins and comfortable motel units, situated just a stone's throw from a broad beach. Camping **$36**, cabins **$70**, motel units **$105**

Westport Holiday Park 31 Domett St ☎03 789 7043, ⓦ westportholidaypark.co.nz. Smallish, low-key site partly hemmed in by native bush and surrounded by suburbia, a 10min walk from the town centre. Camping **$30**, cabins **$65**, en-suite chalets **$95**, motel units **$125**

Westport Motel 32 The Esplanade ☎0800 805 909, ⓦ westportmotel.co.nz. New owners have jazzed up the place, which has a relaxed, welcoming atmosphere befitting its off-the-main-drag location and luxurious touches including New Zealand-made natural skincare products. Doubles **$95**

YHA Westport Trip Inn 72 Queen St ☎03 789 7367, ⓦ tripinn.co.nz. Friendly owners and an energetic refurbishment policy have breathed new life into this rambling YHA Associate backpackers. Quiet and relaxed with a great deck, BBQ, well-equipped kitchen, home cinema, internet terminals and wi-fi. Camping **$20**, dorms **$27**, rooms **$66**

EATING, DRINKING AND NIGHTLIFE

Local **pubs** serve meals. Be aware that at weekends pubs adhere to the West Coast tradition of aggressive edginess. **Nightlife** of any quality is absent since the council demolished the atmospheric, historic cinema, but *The Town House* (see below) is a sophisticated spot for cocktails.

Denniston Dog 18 Wakefield St ☎03 789 8885. The only café/bar that isn't just a pub with a percolator offers a good range of beers, coffee and some excellent light and main meals ($16–34). Try the Flintstone ribeye, the Prospector rump steak or the Miner's Wife lamb rump. Daily lunch & dinner.

Porto Bello 62 Palmerston St ☎03 789 8885. A classy bar and grill serving $10 lunchtime pizzas and evening meals (mains $14–24) spanning Cajun chicken salad to ribeye steak and seafood, plus Sunday roasts. Daily lunch & dinner.

★ **The Town House** Corner of Cobden and Palmerston sts ☎03 789 7133, ⓦ thetownhouse.co. World-class café/restaurant serving great coffee, breakfast, brunch, lunch and excellent evening meals (mains $24–32) utilizing produce from small, local producers and its own restaurant garden. Dishes include lemon and herb roast chicken with goat's cheese and bacon stuffing, veggie options such as potato ravioli with wild mushrooms and truffle oil, and mouthwatering desserts. It's all served up in the stylish wallpapered interior or on the sunny deck. Mon–Fri 10am–late, Sat & Sun 9am–late.

Yellow House Café 243 Palmerston St ☎03 789 8765. Don't let the bright yellow and red walls of this converted

12

house put you off; instead, decorate your own paper tablecloth with crayon and tuck into delicious cakes during the day and the likes of artichoke dip and aubergine pastas in the evening (mains $14–25), all cooked to order from mostly local ingredients. Licensed. Mon–Wed 3pm–late, Thurs–Sun noon–late.

Westport to Karamea

The Karamea Road (also known as SH67) runs north from Westport to Karamea, parallel to the coast and pinched between the pounding Tasman breakers and bush-clad hills. The journey takes almost two hours if you don't stop, and passes through meagre hamlets with barely a shop or a pub. However, there are some interesting diversions – not least the coal towns around Westport such as Denniston – and rustic accommodation en route. North of the **Mokihinui River**, the road leaves the coastal strip, twisting and climbing over **Karamea Bluff** before descending again into a rich apron of dairying land. Rainfall begins to drop off and humidity picks up, promoting more subtropical vegetation characterized by marauding cabbage trees and nikau palms. At the foot of the bluff, **Little Wanganui** marks the turn-off for the start of the **Wangapeka** and **Leslie–Karamea** tracks (jointly 52km; 3–5 days), which traverse the southern half of the Kahurangi National Park (see box, pp.488–489) to Tasman Bay near Motueka.

Charles Heaphy and Thomas Brunner surveyed the region in 1846, paving the way for European and Chinese gold miners, who came twenty years later. Pioneers established themselves at **Karamea**, now the base for visiting the fine limestone country of the **Oparara Basin** and the final stretch of the **Heaphy Track** (see box, pp.488–489).

Note that there's **no fuel** between Westport and Karamea and that the only fuel in Karamea is available from the Karamea visitor centre, so fill up before leaving Westport. Note too that mobile phone coverage in this area is intermittent at best.

Denniston

Museum/visitor centre Jan daily & year-round by appointment 11am–3pm • Donation • ☎ 03 789 9755

Westport historically thrived on supplying inhospitably sited coal-mining towns where fresh vegetables were hard to grow and sheep almost impossible to raise. Foremost among them was the now semi-ghost town of **DENNISTON**, 9km east of Waimangaroa off SH67, the setting for Jenny Pattrick's 2003 bestselling historical novel *The Denniston Rose*, located high on the Rochford Plateau and once famous for its gravity-powered tramway (see box below).

The region peaked at around 2500 inhabitants in 1910, but the accessible coal eventually played out in the late 1960s. Since then, houses have been carted away and the bush has rapidly engulfed what remains – a post office, a fire station, half a dozen scattered houses (three or four of them occupied) and a treasure-trove of industrial

---

THE DENNISTON SELF-ACTING INCLINE

John Rochford discovered the rich Coalbrookdale Seam in 1859 and the plateau was soon humming with activity, spurred on by the construction of the Denniston Self-Acting Incline in 1879. This impressive, gravity-powered tramway was the steepest rail-wagon incline in the world, lowering coal-filled wagons 518m over 1.7km and hauling up empty ones. Throughout its 88-year lifespan, over a thousand tonnes of coal a day would rattle at a prodigious 70km/hr down to Conn's Creek for the trip into Westport. Initially goods, machinery and even people came up the incline, but after four unfortunates were flung to their death, a path was constructed in 1884, easing some of the hardship of living on the plateau.

The incline closed in 1967, but fit and ambitious visitors can still get an idea of what was involved by tackling the **Denniston Incline Walk** (2km one-way; 3hr up, 2hr down), which follows the 1884 path roughly parallel to the incline; the route begins at Conn's Creek, 2km inland from Waimangaroa.

rcheology centred on a gaunt winding derrick. The views are great in fine weather, but blanket of cloud and damp fog adds a suitably ethereal quality.

Apart from these, the only real sight of note is the old schoolhouse, which has been urned into a small "Friends of the Hill" **museum** and **visitor centre**, containing historical photos and old mining machinery. It all comes alive when you talk to curator Gary James, who is usually happy to open up. For guided tours of Denniston, see p.647.

Granity

The tiny community of Granity, 7km north of Waimangaroa, makes for a good place to break your journey as you head further north on SH67. Stop in at the dark, rustic *Granity Drifter's Café* (⊕03 782 8808; daily noon–late), 97 Torea St, which has internet access and regular gigs, or play an outsized game of **chess** on a giant community board in the rotunda (⊕03 782 8080; $10 deposit).

Ngakawau and around

About 9km north of Waimangaroa a coal depot in Ngakawau, which merges imperceptibly with Hector, just across the Ngakawau River, signals the start of the lovely **Charming Creek Walk** (5km one-way; 2hr; 100m ascent), which follows an old railway, used for timber and coal extraction between 1914 and 1958. The first half-hour is dull, but things improve dramatically after the S-shaped Irishman's Tunnel, which has great views of the boulder-strewn river below and, after a swingbridge river crossing, the Mangatini Falls. From here to the picnic stop by the remains of Watson's Mills is the most interesting section of the walk and is as far as most people get (2–3hr return).

12

ACCOMMODATION
WESTPORT TO KARAMEA

GRANITY

Granity Sands Backpackers 94 Torea St ⊕03 782 8558. Arty, eco-conscious backpackers footsteps from the beach, with board games, books, comfy sofas ranged around a huge fireplace, and rambling gardens. Watch out for the "guard frog". Dorms $20, doubles $50

NGAKAWAU AND AROUND

The closest accommodation around Ngakawau is actually either in or just north of Hector, which is just across the river.

Gentle Annie 15km north of Hector on SH67 and 3km down a side road ⊕03 782 1826, ⊚gentleannie .co.nz. Relaxed, beautifully sited spot near the mouth of the Mokihinui River, beside Gentle Annie Beach.

Accommodation ranges from camping to well-equipped, romantic, self-contained cottages with sea or river views; the on-site *Cowshed Café* (open busy periods only) also rents sit-on-top kayaks ($30/half-day). Camping $12, dorms $25, doubles $120, cottages sleeping 6 $150

The Old Slaughterhouse 2km north of Hector, just off SH67 ⊕03 782 8333, ⊚oldslaughterhouse.co.nz. A relaxing hostel in a lovely wooden house perched on the hillside with vast ocean views, welcoming hosts, good bushwalks and Hector's dolphins regularly playing in the surf below. It would be a crime to shatter the peace with TV, internet, washing machines or hairdryers, so they don't. Access is via a steep 10min walk off SH67, though the owners will carry your bags on a quad bike. Dorms $36, doubles $80

Karamea

Despite its isolation, virtually at the end of the road (to continue any distance north you'd have to go on foot along the Heaphy Track), there's no shortage of things to do in **KARAMEA**, 100km north of Westport. The southern section of the **Kahurangi National Park** easily justifies a day or two and the **Oparara Basin** (see p.651) rewards exploration.

Back in 1874, this was very much **frontier territory**, with the Karamea River port providing the only link with the outside world. Settlers eked a living from **gold** and **flax**, but after a couple of fruitless years realized that the poorly drained *pakihi* soils would barely support them. They pushed on, opening up the first road to Westport just in time for the upheavals of the 1929 Murchison **earthquake**, which altered the river flow and permanently ruined the harbour. Logging finally ceased in 2000, leaving tourism, agriculture and fruit-growing as the town's lifeblood.

ARRIVAL AND DEPARTURE

KARAMEA

By bus Karamea Express bus services ply the Karamea–Westport route (Nov–March Mon–Sat; April–Oct Mon–Fri; $30 each way; ☎ 03 782 6757), running south to Westport at 7.20am from the information centre and setting off at 11.30am for the return journey. Buses connect with

ongoing services in Westport. Karamea Express also serves the Heaphy Track trailhead at Kohaihai (Nov–March daily around 2pm; $15; in winter on demand) and drops off at the Wangapeka trailhead on the Karamea–Westport run.

INFORMATION

Tourist information Market Cross, 2km east of the centre (Jan–April daily 9am–5pm; May–Dec Mon–Fri 9am–5pm, Sat & Sun 9am–1pm; ☎ 03 782 6652, ⓦ karameainfo.co.nz). Has internet access, and you can

book huts for the Heaphy Track online here, or get staff to do it for you for $5 extra. The Heaphy Track is generally walked from north to south and is covered on p.488.

ACCOMMODATION

Karamea Domain On SH67 between The Last Resort and the Karamea Village Hotel ☎ 03 782 6069. Basic site utilizing the showers and toilets of the town's sports field. Camping $15, hook-ups $16, dorms $12

Karamea Farm Baches 17 Wharf Rd ☎ 03 782 6838, ⓦ karameamotels.com. Run by the same people as *Rongo* backpackers (see below), about 100m toward the estuary and just 150m from the *Karamea Village Hotel*. Quirky, colourful motel-style units are equipped with full kitchens and spacious bedrooms. Doubles $75

The Last Resort 71 Waverley St (SH67) ☎ 0800 505 042, ⓦ lastresort.co.nz. Based around an imaginatively styled main lodge with an on-site restaurant and bar, comfortable accommodation in dorms (no bunks, no linen: bring a sleeping bag), simple but attractive lodge rooms (some en-suite), motel-style studios and well-appointed "cottages" sleeping four. Dorms $38, lodge doubles $78, en-suite lodge doubles $98, studios $130, cottages $155

Market Cross Homestay B&B 14 Bridge St ☎ 03 782 6604, ⓦ marketcross.co.nz. Pleasantly old-fashioned rooms in a comfortable house with an open fire, kitchen facilities, and cooked breakfasts ($15) on request, plus a

babysitting service if you're travelling with little ones. Doubles $120

Riverstone Restaurant Chalets 3.5km south of Karamea's centre on the main road, just after the river bridge ☎ 03 782 6640, ⓦ rivstone.co.nz. Purpose-built, comfortable chalet accommodation behind and up the hill from the restaurant (see below), with good views of the river. Chalets $180

Rongo 130 Waverley St (SH67) ☎ 03 782 6667, ⓦ living inpeace.com. Rainbow-painted, timber-floored hostel in sprawling grounds with an organic veggie garden, cactus garden and a (very) rustic bush bath. Art and music play a big part in the hostel's daily life – it even runs a community radio station (107.5FM). If you stay three nights you get the fourth free. Dorms $32, doubles $75

Wangapeka Backpackers Retreat and Farmstay Wangapeka Rd ☎ 03 782 6663, ⓦ wangapeka.co.nz. Cosy homestay on a working farm with native bush and welcoming, well-informed hosts, who will ensure you make the most of the beautiful surroundings. Dorms $20, dorms with breakfast & dinner $45, doubles $70, doubles with breakfast & dinner $120

EATING AND DRINKING

Apart from the *Karamea Village Hotel*'s legendary fish and chips, Karamea's **eating** options are limited and there's only one small **supermarket** at Market Cross.

★ **Karamea Village Hotel** Corner of Waverley St and Wharf Rd ☎ 03 782 6800. Karamea's revamped pub is the best place to eat in town thanks to its enormous pub meals (mains $17.50–29), and, especially, its pheno-menal fish and chips, served with zingy home-made tomato sauce, which justify the trip from Westport alone. Daily 7am–3am.

The Last Resort 71 Waverley St (SH67) ☎ 0800 505 042, ⓦ lastresort.co.nz. Sleek, semi-formal dining with

good-value burgers and steaks (mains $16–29) and a relaxing bar. Bookings advised. Daily 7am–late.

★ **Riverstone Restaurant** 3.5km south of Karamea's centre on the main road, just after the river bridge ☎ 03 782 6640, ⓦ rivstone.co.nz. Fine dining comes to town in style with this superbly sited restaurant with river views and a mouthwatering menu (mains $24–33), including duck confit, spiced lamb salad, and home-made cheeses. Tues–Sat 5–10pm.

The Oparara Basin

Kahurangi's finest limestone formations lie east of the Karamea–Kohaihai Highway in the **Oparara Basin**, a compact area of **karst** topography characterized by sinkholes, underground streams, caves and bridges created over millennia by the action of slightly acidic streams on the jointed rock. This is home to New Zealand's largest native **spider**, the harmless, 15cm-diameter gradungular spider (found only in caves in the Karamea and Collingwood area, where it feeds off blowflies and cave crickets), and to a rare species of ancient and primitive carnivorous **snail** that grows up to 70mm across and dines on earthworms. Tannin-coloured rivers course gently over bleached-white boulders and, in faster-flowing sections, the rare whio (blue duck) swims for its supper. If your interest in geology is fleeting, the Oparara Basin still makes a superb place for day **walks** or a **picnic**.

Honeycomb Hill Caves

10km north of Karamea and then 14km east along McCallums Mill Rd • **Honeycomb Hills Cave Tour** daily 10am; 2hr 30min; minimum 2 people • $95 • **Arch Kayak Tour** mid-Dec to Aug; book one day prior • $95 • ☎ 03 782 6652, ⊛ oparara.co.nz

The Oparara Basin is home to the **Honeycomb Hill Caves**, which have become a valuable key to understanding New Zealand's fauna. The sediment on the cave floor has helped preserve the ancient skeletons of birds, most of them killed when they fell through holes in the roof. The bones of over fifty species have been found here, including those of the Haast eagle, the largest eagle ever known, with a wingspan of up to 4m.

The cave system can only be visited on the excellent and educational **Honeycomb Hill Caves Tour** which explores just some of the 15km of passages. Tours depart from the end of McCallums Mill car park, close to the cave. If you don't have your own transport, a ride can be organized for $25 return. Cave trips can be combined with the **Honeycomb Hill Arch Kayak Tour**, a gorgeous paddle through bush and under a broad limestone arch.

Crazy Paving and Box Canyon caves

Accessed via a 5min track from the McCallums Mill car park

As is common in limestone areas, the watercourses alter frequently, leaving behind dry caves such as the **Crazy Paving and Box Canyon caves** (about 10min return) near the Honeycomb Caves. Both are good for spider- and fossil-spotting: take a torch each, and mind the slippery floors.

KARAMEA & THE OPARARA BASIN

7 (10km) & Westport (100km)

■ ACCOMMODATION		● EATING & DRINKING	
Karamea Domain	2	Karamea Village Hotel	1
Karamea Farm Baches	5	The Last Resort	2
The Last Resort	3	Riverstone Restaurant	3
Market Cross Homestay B&B	4		
Riverstone Restaurant Chalets	6		
Rongo	1		
Wangapeka Backpackers Retreat and Farmstay	7		

12

Oparara Arch and Moria Gate Arch

Signposted from a car park 3km back down the road towards Karamea

The two most spectacular examples of limestone architecture lie at the end of beautiful short bushwalks nearby. The largest is the **Oparara Arch** (40min return), a vast two-tiered bridge 43m high, 40m wide and over 219m long, which appears magically out of the bush but defies any attempt at successful photography. The lovely **Moria Gate Arch** was named decades before *Lord of the Rings* movie fever swept the land. It's reached on a track (1hr return) through the untouched, high-canopy native forest then through a short cave (torch handy but not essential). This can be combined with a visit to peaceful **Mirror Tarn** (90min for both).

Kohaihai River

17km north of Karamea

Visitors with no aspirations to tramp the full length of Heaphy Track can sample the final few coastal kilometres from the mouth of the Kohaihai River, where there's river (but not sea) swimming, a beautifully sited DOC **campsite** ($6) and an abundance of maddening sandflies (consider buying sandfly "armour" – close-weave mesh jackets, from $30 – and a range of other protective gear from Westport's i-SITE). In the heat of the day, you're much better off across the river in the cool of the **Nikau Walk** (30–45min loop), which winds through a shady grove dense with nikau palms, tree ferns and magnificent gnarled old rata dripping in epiphytes. When it cools off, either continue along the Heaphy to **Scott's Beach** (1hr 30min return), or stick to the southern side of the Kohaihai River and the **Zig-Zag Track** (35min return), which switchbacks up to an expansive lookout.

Paparoa National Park and around

South of Westport, SH67 crosses the Buller River and picks up the SH6, the main West Coast road. This stretch of coast is home to the Paparoa Range, a 1500m granite and gneiss ridge inlaid with limestone that separates the dramatic coastal strip from the valleys of the Grey and Inangahua rivers. In 1987, the coastal limestone country was designated the **Paparoa National Park**, one of the country's smallest and least-known parks. The highlight is undoubtedly **Pancake Rocks**, where crashing waves have forced spectacular blowholes through a stratified stack of weathered limestone. But to skip the rest would be to miss out on a mysterious world of disappearing rivers, sinkholes, caves and limestone bluffs best seen on the **Inland Pack Track**, but also accessible on shorter walks.

Maori often stopped while travelling the coast in search of *pounamu* (greenstone), and early **European explorers** followed suit seeking agricultural land. Charles Heaphy, Thomas Brunner and two Maori guides came through in 1846, finding little to detain them, but within twenty years this stretch was alive with **gold** prospectors at work on the black sands at **Charleston**.

Visitor services are centred on **Punakaiki**, close by the Pancake Rocks, where bus passengers get a quick glimpse and others pause for the obligatory photos. A couple of days spent here will be well rewarded with a stack of wonderful walks, horse riding or canoeing up delightful limestone gorges.

Mitchells Gully Gold Mine

SH6, 23km south of Westport • Usually 9am–4pm • $10 • ☏ 03 789 6257

Mitchells Gully Gold Mine, a historic, family-run mine dating back to 1866, demonstrates the time-honoured methods used to extract fine gold held in a cement-like mass of oxidized ironsand. Along with mining paraphernalia, you can see a

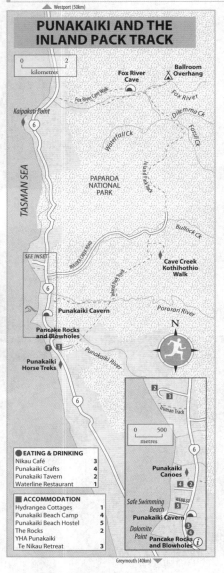

PUNAKAIKI AND THE INLAND PACK TRACK

12

● **EATING & DRINKING**
Nikau Café	3
Punakaiki Crafts	4
Punakaiki Tavern	2
Waterline Restaurant	1

■ **ACCOMMODATION**
Hydrangea Cottages	1
Punakaiki Beach Camp	4
Punakaiki Beach Hostel	5
The Rocks	2
YHA Punakaiki	
Te Nikau Retreat	3

restored overshot wheel driving a stamping battery, and working water races and tunnels.

Charleston and Underwater Adventures

SH6, 26km south of Westport • Nile River Rainforest Train (3–4 daily) $20; Underworld Rafting caving trip (4hr) $165; Glowworm Cave Tour (3hr) $105; Adventure Caving (5hr) $330 • ☎ 03 788 8168, ⓦ caverafting.com

The most intensive mining in this region went on at **CHARLESTON**, once a rollicking boomtown of around 18,000 people, but now a one-horse town without the horse. Instead, it's the base for Underworld Adventures. Tours in the surrounding area include the adult- and child-pleasing **Nile River Rainforest Train**, a 25-minute interpretive journey on a modern narrow-gauge bush train through native bush, masking interesting limestone features. The train journey forms part of the hugely enjoyable Underworld Rafting **caving trip**, incorporating a bushwalk through a dramatic valley of limestone bluffs before delving underground decked out in wetsuit and caver's helmet accompanied by a rubber inner tube. An informative guided walk through the Metro cave system finishes through fabulously illuminated, flooded, glowworm cave and out to a gorgeous ravine into the Nile River, where depending on water levels you can shoot the rapids or just drift. For the more timid there's the **Glowworm Cave Tour**, while adrenaline seekers should opt for the full-on **Adventure Caving**, which explores the Te Tahi cave system by means of a 30m abseil, plus numerous tight squeezes, scrambles and climbs.

ACCOMMODATION

Beaconstone Birds Ferry Rd, off SH6 9km north of Charleston ☎ 027 431 0491, ⓦ beaconstone.co.nz. One of the best hostels on the West Coast, set in 120 acres of native bush threaded by walking trails.

Great-value accommodation includes a separate cottage with mountain views, while eco-friendly features include composting toilets and solar power. Closed June–Sept Dorms $25, doubles $66, cottage $70

PAPAROA WALKS AND THE INLAND PACK TRACK

The best way to truly appreciate the dramatic limestone scenery of the Paparoa is on the **Inland Pack Track** (27km; 2–3 days; see map opposite), but this should only be undertaken by folk with plenty of hiking experience. Most of the terrain is easy going, but there are no bridges for river crossings, and while the water barely gets above your knees in dry periods, the rivers can become impassable after rain. With less time or greater demand for comfort, some of the best sections can be seen on two day-walks.

SHORTER WALKS

Punakaiki–Pororari Rivers Loop (12km; 3hr 30min; 100m ascent) A delightful route that follows the initial stretch of the Inland Pack Track as far as the Pororari River, which is then followed downstream between some magnificent limestone cliffs to return to Punakaiki.

Fox River Cave Walk (10km; 2hr 30min; 100m ascent) This walk traces the last few kilometres of the Inland Pack Track from the Fox Rivermouth as far as the caves and returns the same way.

INLAND PACK TRACK PRACTICALITIES

The Inland Pack Track starts 1km south of the Punakaiki visitor centre beside the south bank of the Punakaiki River. DOC's *Inland Pack Track* leaflet provides enough information for the tramp; the 1:50,000 *Paparoa National Park* map is also very handy.

The track is best walked south to north, which eliminates the risk of missing the critical turn-off up Fossil Creek. There are no huts along the way, just a massive rock **bivvy** known as the Ballroom Overhang at the end of a long first day. You're advised to carry a **tent** for protection from voracious sandflies, and to avoid a wet night in the open if the rivers flood. **Campfires** are permitted at the Ballroom Overhang, but DOC recommends carrying a stove as most of the usable wood has already been burned. Be sure to check the **weather** forecast with DOC and fill out an **intentions form**.

Punakaiki River to Bullock Creek (9.5km; 4hr; 220m ascent, 100m descent) The track rises to a low saddle then descends to ford the Pororari River, continuing with views inland to the Paparoa Range before reaching Bullock Creek. This should be forded with care – in flood conditions it is impassable.

Bullock Creek to Fox River (10km; 3–4hr; 100m ascent, 150m descent) This section sees you skirt swampland then climb to a ridge before descending gradually to Fossil Creek, which is followed wading from pool to pool, occasionally clambering over fallen tree trunks. After half an hour of this, Fossil Creek meets the main tributary of the Fox River, Dilemma Creek, by a small sign – keep your eyes peeled. This is the most dramatic section of the trip but potentially the most dangerous, with eighteen fords to cross between gravel banks in the bed of Dilemma Creek: if you have any doubts about the first crossing, turn back, as they only get worse. The lower river has carved out a deep canyon between gleaming white vertical cliffs and, if you can find a patch of sun, this makes a great place to rest. The track resumes by a sign on the true left bank just above the confluence with the Fox River; a steep bluff on the right makes a useful landmark.

Fox River to Ballroom Overhang (1km; 30min each way; negligible ascent) A signposted track crosses to the true right bank of the Fox River below the confluence, then crosses several more times to the vast limestone **Ballroom Overhang** with its 100m-long lip. It could easily provide shelter for a hundred or more campers, and has a long-drop toilet.

Fox River to Fox Rivermouth (5km; 2hr; 100m descent) From the Ballroom Overhang, return the same way you came, back to the river confluence. From there, the track runs to the Fox Rivermouth. A short distance along, a sign points across the river to the interesting Fox River Cave (30min). Meanwhile, the Inland Pack Track crosses to the car park by the Fox Rivermouth, some 12km by road from your starting point; southbound **buses** currently pass around 11.45am and 3.55pm.

12

Te Miko

SH6, 20km south of Charleston

The 50m-high cliffs of Te Miko were tagged Perpendicular Point by Charles Heaphy, who in 1846 recorded climbing the cliff on two stages of ladders constructed of shaky and rotten rata vines while his dog was hoisted on a rope. Te Miko remained an impenetrable barrier to pack animals until 1866, when a new Westport–Greymouth telegraph line prompted the forging of the **Inland Pack Track** (see box, p.655). The coast road, finally completed in 1927, now climbs over Te Miko, passing the **Iramahuwhero Point Lookout**, with stupendous views along the coast past the layered rocks of the Te Miko cliff.

Punakaiki and the Pancake Rocks

SH6, 22km south of Charleston

The **Pancake Rocks** and blowholes at **PUNAKAIKI** are often all visitors see of the Paparoa National Park, as they tumble off the bus opposite the twenty-minute paved loop track which leads to the rocks. Layers of limestone have weathered to resemble an immense stack of giant pancakes, the result of **stylobedding**, a chemical process in which the pressure of overlying sediments creates alternating durable and weaker bands. Subsequent uplift and weathering has accentuated this effect to create photogenic formations. The edifice is undermined by huge sea caverns where the surf surges in, sending spumes of brine spouting up through vast **blowholes**: high tide with a good swell from the south or southwest sees the blowholes at their best.

More shapely examples of Paparoa's karst landscape are on show on a number of walks. Inside the **Punakaiki Cavern**, 500m to the north, you'll find a few glowworms (go after dark: torch essential), and, 2km beyond that, the **Truman Track** (30min return) runs down from the highway to a small beach hemmed in by wave-sculpted rock platforms.

Apart from the rocks, there's good **river swimming** in the Pororari and Punakaiki rivers, and **sea bathing** at the southern end of Pororari Beach, a section also good for point-break **surfing**.

ARRIVAL AND INFORMATION   PUNAKAIKI

By bus North- and south-bound buses run by InterCity and Atomic stop for half an hour opposite the Pancake Rocks, by DOC/i-SITE, allowing enough time for a quick look.

DOC/i-SITE SH6 (daily: Dec–April 9am–6pm; May–Nov 9am–4.30pm; ☎ 03 731 1895, ⍉ doc.govt.nz). DOC's Paparoa National Park visitor centre is also an i-SITE, with displays on all aspects of the park, information on activities, walking maps, leaflets and staff who can help with bookings.

Services Punakaiki has no fuel and no ATMs, so come prepared.

TOURS

Punakaiki Canoes SH6, 1km north of the Pancake Rocks ☎ 03 731 1870, ⍉ riverkayaking.co.nz. Rents kayaks ($35/2hr, $55/day) from their base beside the Pororari River and runs guided trips by arrangement (from $70).

Punakaiki Horse Treks SH6, 600m south of the Pancake Rocks ☎ 03 731 1839, ⍉ pancake-rocks.co.nz. Organizes bush, river and beach horse riding from Oct–April (2hr 30min; $125).

ACCOMMODATION

Hydrangea Cottages SH6 ☎ 03 731 1839, ⍉ pancake-rocks.co.nz. Four gorgeous cottages set above the road, most with sea views. The real appeal, though, is the self-catering cottages themselves (studio, one- & two-bedroom), all constructed with native timbers and local stone. Studios $140, suites $295

Punakaiki Beach Camp SH6 ☎ 03 731 1894, ⍉ nzcamping.co.nz. Attractive, grassy campsite roamed by wekas, with a range of tent sites and campervan

hook-ups plus a handful of cabins. It's handily positioned close to the beach and Punakaiki Tavern. Camping $15.50, cabins $182, kitchen cabins $112

Punakaiki Beach Hostel 4 Webb St ☎ 03 731 1852, ⍉ punakaikibeachhostel.co.nz. Breezy timber beachhouse-style backpackers right by the sand with great communal areas, board games and a TV-free policy. Camping $20, dorms $27, doubles $65

The Rocks Hartmount Place ☎ 03 731 1141,

therockshomestay.com. Welcoming homestay, with three comfortable en-suite rooms, all with bush or sea views, and a lounge with a broad seascape and free wi-fi. Rates include breakfast. **$220**

★ **YHA Punakaiki Te Nikau Retreat** Hartmount Place, 200m north of the Truman Track and 3km north of the i-SITE ☎ 03 731 1111, tenikauretreat.co.nz. Associate YHA hostel which must rank as one of the most relaxing backpackers in the country, carved out of bush peppered with nikau palms. The smattering of buildings includes small dorms, rooms, separate houses, rustic en-suite cabins for couples and a beneath-the-stars "stargazer tent" option (like a wooden sleeping bag with a glass roof); you can buy fresh bread, muffins and eggs on site. Camping **$15**, stargazer tent **$45**, dorms **$27**, doubles **$71**, en-suite doubles **$86**, cabins **$110**

EATING

Punakaiki has a limited supply of **eating** options. There's no shop for supplies, so if you're self-catering, bring everything.

Nikau Café SH6, by the i-SITE. Popular with the tour buses, this place serves "West Coast" breakfasts (bacon, eggs, sausages, hash browns and toast), pancakes with hot cherries and cream, home-made pies, and daily specials such as ground beef lasagne (mains $12.50–18.50). Daily summer 8am–5pm, winter 8am–4pm.

Punakaiki Crafts SH6, by the i-SITE. Craft shop with a small café serving coffee, tea, cakes and slices. Daily 9am–at least 4pm.

Punakaiki Tavern SH6, 1km north of the i-SITE ☎ 03 731 1188, punakaikitavern.co.nz. No-frills pub with good-value, simple, well-portioned meals (mains $16.50–26). Daily 8am–late.

Waterline Restaurant Punakaiki Resort, SH6, 700m south of the i-SITE ☎ 03 731 1167, punakaiki -resort.co.nz. Easily the swankiest place in Punakaiki, overlooking the sea, with elegantly presented fare such as scallops in white wine and cream sauce, followed by venison medallions with potato gratin (mains $28–38). Daily lunch & dinner by reservation.

12

Punakaiki to Greymouth

Punakaiki to Greymouth is a spectacular drive, pushed onto the sea cliffs by the intrusive ramparts of the Paparoa Range. Tragedy struck the area in 2010 when explosions rocked the Pike River coal mine, 46km north of Greymouth, trapping and killing 29 miners inside.

Photos aside, the only reasons to stop are to visit the **Barrytown knife maker**, 2662 Coast Rd/SH6, who will guide you through the intricacies of making your own blade, from hot steel to honed slicer, in a day ($140; around 9am–4pm; ☎ 03 731 1053, barrytownknifemaking.com). Tiny **RAPAHOE**, 30km south of Punakaiki, has about the safest bathing beach on the coast and a reputation for gemstones. Follow the track to the excellent vantage point of **Point Elizabeth** (2hr return).

Greymouth

The Grey River forces its way through a break in the coastal Rapahoe Range and over the treacherous sand bar to the sea at **GREYMOUTH**, the West Coast's largest settlement. The drab, workaday town is not the highlight of most visitors' itineraries, but is the end of the line for the *TranzAlpine* Railway (an increasing number of people take the train from Christchurch and pick up a rental car here) and a convenient stop for drivers. Greymouth, like Hokitika, has a reputation for high-quality greenstone carving (see box, p.664). Once you've checked out the greenstone galleries, adventure activities and brewery tours, do what you came for and move on, particularly in winter when **The Barber**, a razor-sharp cold wind whistling down the Grey Valley, envelops the town in thick icy fog.

Brief history

Greymouth began to take shape during the early years of the **gold rush** on land purchased in 1860 by James Mackay, who bought most of Westland from the Poutini Ngai Tahu people for 300 gold sovereigns. The town's defining feature is the river, which is deceptively calm and languid through most of the summer but awesome after

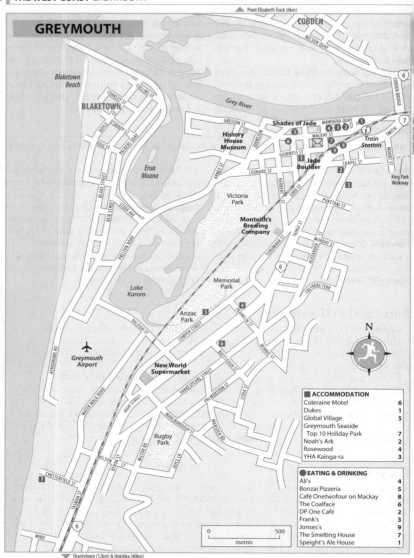

GREYMOUTH

ACCOMMODATION

Coleraine Motel	6
Dukes	1
Global Village	5
Greymouth Seaside	
Top 10 Holiday Park	7
Noah's Ark	2
Rosewood	4
YHA Kainga-ra	3

EATING & DRINKING

Ali's	4
Bonzai Pizzeria	5
Café Onetwofour on Mackay	8
The Coalface	6
DP One Café	2
Frank's	3
Jonses's	9
The Smelting House	7
Speight's Ale House	1

heavy rains. Devastating **floods** swept through Greymouth in 1887, 1905, 1936, 1977 and 1988; since the last great flood, the Greymouth Flood Protection Scheme has successfully held back most of the waters.

Jade Boulder

1 Guinness St • Oct–April Mon–Fri 8.30am–5.30pm, Sat & Sun 9am–5pm • Free • Ⓦ ianboustridge.com

Some of Greymouth's finest greenstone carvings are found at the **Jade Boulder**, a gallery, studio and shop with a variety of works, including some by master carver Ian Boustridge. Even if you have no intention of buying, pop in to watch the cutting, grinding and polishing and visit the **Jade Trail**, which tells the parallel stories of jade from a Maori mythological and geological perspective.

Shades of Jade
16 Tainui St • Mon–Fri 8.30am–5pm, Sat 10am–2.30pm, Sun noon–2.30pm • Ⓦ shadesofjade.co.nz

Another of the town's jade gallery/shops well worth a visit is the tiny **Shades of Jade**, a charming spot where the local carvers keep the prices down because they own the shop and make their own stock using New Zealand *pounamu*. There's jade carving daily and they'll often show you stones they've picked up on the beaches and in the rivermouths.

History House Museum
Gresson St • Mon–Fri 10am–4pm • $6 • ☎ 03 768 4028, Ⓦ greydc.govt.nz/council-services

Greymouth's **History House Museum** does a good job of relating the Grey District's history, particularly prior to 1920, through maritime, gold and coal mining and timber milling memorabilia and a stack of photos depicting the town's heyday. The townspeople's long struggle to combat the floods is also given a thorough going over.

Monteith's Brewing Company
Corner of Turumaha and Herbert sts • Brewery tours daily • Call for prices • ☎ 03 768 4149, Ⓦ monteiths.co.nz

Undergoing major renovations at the time of writing, Monteith's Brewing Company is due to have reopened for tours (including tastings) by the time you're reading this;

12

RAFTING THE WILD WEST COAST RIVERS

In recent years kayakers and rafters have realized that some of the most thrilling and scenic whitewater trips are on New Zealand's West Coast, where dramatically steep rivers spill out of the alpine wilderness, fed by the prodigious quantity of rain that guarantees solid flows most of the time. The steepness of the terrain means you're in constantly thrilling if not downright scary territory (rivers in this area are mostly Grade IV, sliding either one up, or down). If you enjoy rafting and want more, this is a good place to come.

ACCESS

Few of these rivers had been kayaked or rafted until the 1980s, when helicopters were co-opted to reach them. Most rafting trips still require **helicopter access**, so costs are relatively high, and what you pay will often depend on numbers, so getting, say, six people together will save you a packet.

BOOKING AND SEASONS

Though their popularity is increasing, trips are still relatively infrequent and you should **book** as far in advance as possible. The main **season** is November to April, though rafting is generally possible from early September to late May, and there is a minimum age of 13 years (15 for some of the more frightening runs).

RIVERS

The **most commonly rafted rivers** are (from north to south) the Karamea (Grade III+), the Mokihinui (Grade IV), the Arahura (Grade IV), the Whitcombe (Grade V), the Hokitika (Grade III–IV), the Wanganui (Grade III), the Perth (Grade V) and the Whataroa (Grade IV).

OUTFITTERS

Eco-Rafting Franz Josef ☎ 03 755 4254, Ⓦ eco rafting.co.nz. Uses rafting to introduce customers to the nature and social history of the various rivers it rafts on the West Coast, including the Whataroa River near Franz Josef. Drive-in rafting trips start from $110; a full-day heli-raft starts from $450.

Ultimate Descents 51 Fairfax St, Murchison ☎ 0800 748 377, Ⓦ rivers.co.nz. One-day heli-rafting trips on the Karamea ($500) and two-day trips on the Mokihinui ($900), among others.

Wild West Adventures Greymouth ☎ 0508 286 877, Ⓦ fun-nz.com. Offers a wide range of trips, from hardcore heli-rafting (from $485) to relatively tame rafting ($175), on most of the rivers listed above.

GREYMOUTH TOURS AND ACTIVITIES

Activities around Greymouth are predominantly aquatic, subterranean or both.

Kea Tours ☎03 768 9292, ⓦkeatours.co.nz. Operates tours to the Pancake Rocks (2.15pm; 2hr 30min; $98) and will pick up/drop off at local accommodation or the i-SITE/travel centre.

Wild West Adventures 8 Whall St ☎0800 223 456, ⓦfun-nz.com. Runs some of the best activities in town, notably Taniwha Cave Rafting (5hr; 90–120min underground; $165), an undemanding caving trip where wetsuits and cavers' lamps are the order of the day because of long sections on inner tubes under glowworms. They also offer even gentler, family-friendly Rain Forest Boat Cruising (3hr; $160), plying placid waterways with kayaks and pontoons dressed up like jungle canoes. They also do a bunch of rafting and heli-rafting trips.

Air West Coast Greymouth Airport, 2km south of town ☎03 738 0524, ⓦairwestcoast.co.nz. A nice

change of pace, with scenic flights (minimum two people; from $320) past Mt Cook, the glaciers and Milford Sound.

On Yer Bike 511 SH6, 5km north of Greymouth ☎0800 669 372, ⓦonyerbike.co.nz. Offers adrenaline-charged activities including "extreme off-roading" in 8WD amphibious tank-style Argos (from $50/30min), quad bikes ($115/hr) and go-karts, with free transport from Greymouth.

Shantytown Rutherglen Rd, Paroa, 12km south of town ☎03 762 6634, ⓦshantytown.co.nz. If you're travelling with kids, you might want to consider a visit to this re-created gold-rush village heritage park ($30) where activities include a steam train and panning for gold. Return transfers from Greymouth cost an additional $26. Daily 8.30am–5pm.

book ahead and be sure to wear closed footwear. Age-old recipes have been revived to produce flavoursome brews popular New Zealand wide.

Point Elizabeth Track
6km north of town • 5km return; 90min

Choose a fine evening for a pleasant walk: the **Point Elizabeth Track** follows the coast through stands of nikau to a lookout. You can continue another 3km to Rapahoe (see p.657) and pick up a bus from there back to town (2 daily).

ARRIVAL AND DEPARTURE   GREYMOUTH

By train The *TranzAlpine* train (see box, p.517) is Greymouth's only passenger service, and pulls in at the station on Mackay St. Destinations Arthur's Pass (1 daily; 2hr 15min); Christchurch (1 daily; 4hr 20min).

By bus InterCity and Atomic buses running south to Hokitika and Franz Josef, or north to Westport and Nelson, meet the *TranzAlpine* train on arrival. An Atomic bus also finishes its daily run from Picton here, but doesn't

synchronize with the trains.
Destinations Arthur's Pass (2 daily; 1hr 30min); Christchurch (2 daily; 4hr 30min); Fox Glacier (2 daily; 3hr 45min–4hr 30min); Franz Josef (2 daily; 3hr–3hr 30min); Hokitika (3–5 daily; 30min); Murchison (1 daily; 2hr 15min); Picton (1 daily; 7hr); Punakaiki (2 daily; 30min); Queenstown (2 daily; 9–10hr); Wanaka (2 daily; 8hr–8hr 30min); Westport (2 daily; 1hr 30min–2hr 15min).

GETTING AROUND

By car All the major companies have car-rental offices either at the train station or nearby.

INFORMATION

Tourist information Inside the train station on Mackay St (Nov–Easter Mon–Fri 8.30am–6pm, Sat 9am–5pm, Sun 10am–4pm; Easter–Oct Mon–Fri 8.30am–5.30pm, Sat & Sun 9am–4pm; ☎03 768 5101, ⓦgreydistrict.co.nz). The

combined i-SITE and West Coast Travel Centre has internet access ($3/30min), and provides the *Grey District* visitor guide, containing a good street map.

ACCOMMODATION

Greymouth has many good **backpackers** but few other standout **places to stay**. **Book** a couple of days ahead when local events pack out the town: the Kumara Races (second weekend in Jan), the Coast to Coast Race (second weekend in Feb; see box opposite), Hokitika's Wildfoods Festival (second weekend in March) and the Around Brunner Cycle Race (third weekend in April).

Coleraine Motel 61 High St ☎0800 270 077, ⓦcolerainemotel.co.nz. Units in this sparkling motel come with Sky TV, CD/DVD players, double glazing to keep the road noise down, and some have spa baths. Units $155, executive units $185

Dukes 27 Guinness St ☎03 768 9470, ⓦduke.co.nz. Smoothly organized, vibrantly colourful hostel in the centre with an intimate bar, well-equipped doubles, comfortable beds and knowledgeable and helpful hosts who make tasty soup nightly. Dorms $29, doubles $66, en-suite doubles $80

Global Village 42 Cowper St ☎03 768 7272, ⓦglobalvillagebackpackers.co.nz. Light and spacious, well-equipped hostel backing onto parkland and a river. The rooms are imaginatively decorated in tribal themes with artefacts from around the world, the bathrooms have recently been decorated with large colourful mosaics, and there's a range of tempting activities: free bikes and kayaks, low-cost sauna, spa and small gym, and a BBQ out back most fine evenings. All beds are made up and there are some single-sex dorms. Camping $16, dorms $27, rooms $66

Greymouth Seaside Top 10 Holiday Park 2 Chesterfield St ☎0800 867 104, ⓦtop10greymouth .co.nz. The more central and better of the two motor parks, right by the beach with very good facilities. Camping $40, cabins $57, kitchen cabin $90, motels $100

Noah's Ark 16 Chapel St ☎0800 662 472, ⓦnoahs arkbackpackers.co.nz. Large but homey hostel in a two-storey villa with great verandas and a spacious lounge with Sky TV. Rooms and dorms are lavishly decorated with animal themes and there are free bikes and a spa. Camping $19, dorms $24, doubles $56

★ **Rosewood** 20 High St ☎0800 185 748, ⓦrosewoodnz.co.nz. Appealing B&B in a beautiful two-storey 1920s home – all wood panelling, leadlight windows and tasteful decor. Rooms are en-suite or have private bathroom; rates include cooked breakfasts. Doubles $185

YHA Kainga-ra 15 Alexander St ☎03 768 4951, ⓦyha .co.nz. Former priest's residence, now a relaxed, quiet hostel with excellent facilities, including a well-informed booking office, a selection of dorms, twins and doubles, and views over the town. Dorms $29, doubles $25, en-suite doubles $95

EATING AND DRINKING

Ali's 9 Tainui St ☎03 768 5858. Unpretentious, licensed café serving snacks, lunches and dinners including burgers, sweetcorn fritters, salmon patties and steak and fries (mains $18.50–27). Food is hit-and-miss depending on the kitchen staff – stop by first; if it's busy it's a good sign. Mon–Fri 10am–late, Sat 11am–late, Sun 11am–3pm.

Bonzai Pizzeria 31 Mackay St ☎03 768 4170, ⓦbonzai.co.nz. Cheerful licensed restaurant (mains

$16–23) with tearoom staples through the day, including pastries and quiches and a broad range of reasonably priced and tasty pizzas served daytime and evening. Mon–Sat 7am–late, Sun 3pm–late.

Café Onetwofour on Mackay 124 Mackay St. Great lamb burgers and a tempting range of pastas (mains $18–24.50). Mon–Fri 9am–late, Sat 10am–late.

The Coalface 29 Boundary St ☎03 768 9223. Slice and sear your own meals including meat, fish and vegetarian

12

THE COAST TO COAST RACE

Kiwis are mad on multisport and punch above their weight on the international circuit, and every weekend you'll see scores of people honing their biking, running and paddling skills. The ultimate goal of all true multisporters is the gruelling 243km **Coast to Coast Race** (second weekend in Feb; ⓦcoasttocoast.co.nz), which requires a pre-dawn start from the beach near Kumara Junction, 15km south of Greymouth. A 3km run leads to a 55km cycle uphill to Otira where jelly-kneed contenders tackle the most gruelling section, a 33km run up and down the boulder-strewn creek beds of the Southern Alps, before kayaking for several hours down Canterbury's braided Waimakariri River and then cycling the final stretch to Sumner.

From humble beginnings in 1983 – when it was the world's first major multisport event – the Coast to Coast has blossomed into a professional affair with over a thousand competitors. Serious contenders engage a highly organized support crew and specialized gear; only the most high-tech bikes will do and designers build racing kayaks especially for Waimakariri conditions. Most competitors take two days, but around 150 elite triathletes compete in "The Longest Day", tackling the same course in under 24 hours. Mere mortals – though admittedly extremely fit ones – can also compete by forming two-person teams sharing the disciplines.

The event remains largely a macho spectacle that draws considerable press interest and correspondingly generous sponsorship – a vehicle manufacturer is usually coaxed into offering a car or truck to the winner if they break a certain time. The course record is an astonishing 10hr 34min and 37 seconds, set in 1994.

options (mains $15.50–29.50) on heated stones at your table at this stylish spot, or choose from an inventive range of pizzas, pastas and whitebait delicacies. Daily lunch & dinner.

DP One Café 126 Mawhera Quay. Cool café, with internet access, serving snacks (dishes $8–15) and tasty coffee. Daily 9.30am–4pm.

★ **Frank's** 115 Mackay St ☎ 03 768 9075. Funky first-floor late-night lounge with inventive nibbles such as Momo dumplings, Thai chicken curry and Blackball salami (mains $18–29). Live music, comedy, poetry and art events mix things up. Thurs–Sat 5pm–late.

Gaalburn Dairy Goat Farm 18km south of Greymouth ☎ 03 736 9784, ⓦ gaalburncheese.co.nz. If you have a hankering for some unique and delicious goat's cheese, head to this farm shop, where they make fabulous saanen, a sort of cheddar, among others. Call ahead for hours.

★ **Jones's** 37 Tainui St ☎ 03 768 6464. Smooth spot with above-average café/bar food (mains $16.50–34.50)

such as crumbed camembert with cranberry jelly, pumpkin, hazelnut and blue cheese-filled cannelloni, and mussels steamed with cider. There's also live blues and jazz on weekends. Mon–Fri 10am–2pm & 5.30pm–late, Sat 5.30pm–late.

The Smelting House 102 MacKay St ☎ 03 768 0012. This smashing little café serves daily-changing hot dishes (most around $10) and counter food including enormous sausage rolls, blueberry and boysenberry muffins, kumara, spinach and feta fritters and tasty veggie pies. Mon–Fri 8am–4pm.

Speight's Ale House 130 Mawhera Quay ☎ 03 768 0667, ⓦ greymouthspeights.co.nz. Big and bustling restaurant/bar in a 1909 Edwardian Baroque former government building with a good menu of hearty dishes (mains $17–32) such as whitebait patties, "great mates drunken steak" (rump steak) and Stewart Island battered blue cod, mostly matched to beers from the Speight's range.

Hokitika

South from Greymouth, SH6 hugs a desolate stretch of coast with little of abiding interest until **HOKITIKA**, 40km away. "Hoki" is infinitely more interesting than Greymouth, due to its location on a long, driftwood-strewn beach, some engaging activities – including the strangely seductive sock-making machine museum and an atmospheric glowworm dell – and proximity to good bushwalks in the surrounding area, not least of which is the spectacular Hokitika Gorge (see p.666).

Despite its beautiful beach, the town is primarily renowned for its crafts scene, and is becoming something of an artists' enclave, with a slew of studios, galleries and shopfronts where you can see weaving, carving (greenstone or bone) or glass blowing in action or buy the high-quality results of the artists' labours. The National Kiwi Centre, a privately run aquarium and nocturnal house combination, is also here, but it's difficult to justify the high admission price.

Brief history

Like other West Coast towns, Hokitika owes its existence to the **gold rushes** of the 1860s. Within months of the initial discoveries near Greymouth in 1864, fields had been opened up on the tributaries of the Hokitika River, and Australian diggers and Irish hopefuls all flogged over narrow passes from Canterbury to get their share. Within two years Hokitika had a population of 6000 (compared with today's 4000), streets packed with hotels, and a steady export of over a tonne of gold a month, mainly direct to Melbourne. Despite a treacherous bar at the Hokitika rivermouth, the **port** briefly became the country's busiest, with ships tied up four deep along Gibson Wharf. As gold grew harder to find and more sluicing water was needed, the enterprise eventually became uneconomic and was replaced by dairying and the timber industry. The port closed in 1954, only to be smartened up in the 1990s as the focus for the town's Heritage Trail.

Hokitika Museum

Carnegie Building, on the corner of Tancred and Hamilton sts • Mon–Fri 9am–5pm, Sat & Sun 10am–2pm • $5 • ☎ 03 755 689

Hokitika's leading role in the West Coast gold rushes rightly occupies much of the **Hokitika Museum**. The photos depicting the dangers of crossing the Hokitika River bar and the pleasures of the hundred or so bars of a different kind that once lined Tancred Street are also highlights.

HOKITIKA

1 (2km), **2** (5km), **3** (12km), Greymouth (40km) & Christchurch (260km)

■ ACCOMMODATION	
252 Beachside	4
Awatuna Homestead	3
Beachfront Hotel	7
Beach Walk Motor Camp and Motels	2
Birdsong	1
Koru Cottage	6
Mountain Jade	9
Shining Star	5
Teichelmann's B&B	8

● EATING & DRINKING	
Café de Paris	4
Fat Pipi	3
Ocean View	1
Stations Inn	5
West Coast Wine Co.	2

TASMAN SEA

Glowworm Dell
Cemetery

Signal Station Lookout

Vintage Sock Knitting Machine Museum
Bonz 'n' Stonz
Crooked Mile Cinema
iaNZart
Hokitika Glass Studio
Hokitika Museum
Custom House

Supermarket
National Kiwi Centre
Ruby Rock Gallery
The Regent Cinema
Clock Tower
Westland Greenstone
Mountain Jade
CASS SQUARE

Hokitika River

12

0   500
metres

SH6, Lake Mahinapua (10km), The Glaciers (135km) & Haast (280km)

Vintage Sock Knitting Machine Museum

75 Revell St • Daily 9am–5pm • Free • ☎ 03 755 7251

For an entirely different, charming and quirky experience pop into the **Vintage Sock Knitting Machine Museum**, which doubles as a commercial outlet for all things woolly. The friendly, knowledgeable staff will give you a rundown on the largest collection of fully restored sock knitting machines known to man, some capable of knocking up ten pairs in an hour.

ARRIVAL AND DEPARTURE   HOKITIKA

Fuel gets more expensive south along the coast, so fill up before leaving Hokitika.

By plane Air New Zealand flys daily to Hokitika from Christchurch, arriving 2km east of the centre.
Destinations Christchurch (2–4 daily; 35min).
By bus Buses from Christchurch and along the coast stop at the i-SITE and outside the National Kiwi Centre at 64 Tancred St. Atomic buses stop outside the i-SITE and the

museum (see opposite).
Destinations Arthur's Pass (1 daily; 1hr 45min); Christchurch (1 daily; 4hr 30min); Fox Glacier (2–3 daily; 3hr); Franz Josef (2–3 daily; 2hr 30min); Greymouth (3–5 daily; 30min); Ross (2–3 daily; 25min); Whataroa (2–3 daily; 1hr 30min).

INFORMATION AND TOURS

i-SITE 36 Weld St (Dec–March daily 8.30am–8pm; April–Nov Mon–Fri 8.30am–6pm, Sat & Sun 10am–4pm;

☎ 03 755 6166, ⓦ hokitika.org). Does DOC bookings, and is your best source of information about the new Westland

GREENSTONE

Maori revere **pounamu** (hard nephrite jade) and **tangiwai** (softer, translucent bowenite), usually collectively known as **greenstone**. In Aotearoa's pre-European culture, it took the place of durable metals for practical, warfaring and decorative uses: adzes and chisels were used for carving, *mere* (clubs) for combat, and pendants were fashioned for jewellery.

In Maori, the entire South Island is known as **Te Wahi Pounamu**, "the place of greenstone", reflecting the importance of its sole sources, the belt from Greymouth through the rich Arahura River area near Hokitika south to Anita Bay on Milford Sound – where the beautifully dappled *tangiwai* occurs – and the Wakatipu region behind Queenstown. When the Poutini Ngai Tahu arranged to sell most of Westland to James Mackay in 1860, the Arahura River, their main source of *pounamu*, was specifically excluded.

Greenstone's value has barely diminished. Mineral claims are jealously guarded, the export of greenstone is prohibited and no extraction is allowed from national parks; penalties include fines of up to $200,000 and two years in jail. **Price** is heavily dependent on quality, but rates of $100,000 a tonne are not unknown – and the sky's the limit when the stone is fashioned into sculpture and jewellery. Many of the cheaper specimens are quite crude, but pricier pieces (a minimum of $100 for something aesthetically pleasing, and over $1000 for anything really classy) exhibit accomplished Maori designs; at the other end of the scale, pendants can be picked up for as little as $20.

Hokitika is the main venue for greenstone shoppers: keep in mind that the larger **shops** and **galleries** are firmly locked into the tour-bus circuit so prices are high. Big shops are fine for learning about the quality of the stone and competence of the artwork but smaller places have more competitive deals. Buyers should ask about the origins of the raw material – insiders suspect that lots of greenstone sold in New Zealand is cheaper jade sourced overseas.

HOKITIKA ARTS AND CRAFTS

Pick up a free city map from the i-SITE showing the locations of Hokitika's growing collection of art and craft shops, studios and galleries; **greenstone** in particular is big business. The places listed below are some of the best places to see artisans at work, and do a bit of shopping.

Bonz 'n' Stonz Carving Studio 16 Hamilton St ☎0800 214 949. If you want to carve a piece of greenstone for yourself, pop along to this excellent studio where you can learn to carve; the friendly and estimable Steve Gwaliasi guides you through the design and execution in what is a personal and very memorable experience (6hr; jade $150; bone $85; shell $75).

Hokitika Glass Studio 9 Weld St ☎03 755 7775, ⓦhokitikaglass.co.nz. Glass-blowing is another longstanding Hoki tradition, best seen on weekdays at this studio. 9am–5pm.

Ruby Rock Gallery 23 Tancred St ☎03 755 7448, ⓦnzrubyrock.com. To learn about New Zealand's only precious stone, Goodletite rock, containing ruby, sapphire and tourmaline crystals, stop by this gallery. Not found anywhere else in the world, the glistening rock is worked here by master gem-cutter Gerry Commandeur into jewellery.

Wilderness Trail, a four-day, off-road cycle trail linking Greymouth and Ross, sections of which should be completed by the time you're reading this.

Services Banks in Hokitika are the last before Wanaka, more than 400km southeast over the Haast Pass, although Franz Josef has an ATM.

Wilderness Wings ☎0800 755 8118, ⓦwildernesswings .co.nz. Airport-based operator offering a number of scenic flights, including over the glaciers (35min; $285; minimum two people).

Hokitika Heritage Walk Grab the free, eponymous leaflet from the i-SITE and head out on a self-guided tour of the town's historic landmarks, including the Gibson Quay area, a restored former riverside dock that makes for a pleasant evening stroll; go from the spit-end Signal Station Lookout to the 1897 Custom House, via a memorial to ships lost on the bar.

ACCOMMODATION

Accommodation in Hokitika is seldom hard to find, though you should book ahead during the Kumara Races (second weekend in Jan), for all of February including around the Coast to Coast race (see box, p.661) and during the Wildfoods Festival (see box opposite).

252 Beachside 252 Revell St ☎ 0508 252 252, ⓦ 252beachside.co.nz. Spacious motel and campervan park across the road from the beach with a swimming pool, spa and enclosed kids' play area, offering a range of comfortable units. The friendly owners have reams of information on activities in and around town. Van sites $32, cabins $65, studios $125

★ **Awatuna Homestead** SH6, 13km north of Hokitika ☎ 0800 006 888, ⓦ awatunahomestead.co .nz. Welcoming B&B with three tasteful, comfortable rooms and one self-catering apartment. A relaxing spot with assorted animals, home-grown veggies, plenty of books, outdoor bath, a track down to the beach and evening storytelling sessions; evening meals by arrangement. Rooms $290, apartment $370

Beachfront Hotel 111 Revell St ☎ 03 755 8344, ⓦ beachfronthotel.co.nz. A broad range of rooms but the pick of the bunch are the first-floor, beach-facing variety with full wall-windows and balconies just 50m from the water's edge. Doubles $135, ocean-view doubles $332

Beach Walk Motor Camp and Motels 8 Greyhound Rd, off SH6, 5km north of Hokitika, just after the Arahura road/rail bridge ☎ 03 755 6550, ⓦ jacquie grantsplace.com. Small, simple and well kept with fabulous, good-value, relatively new motel units. Van hook-ups and tent sites $15, motels $75

Birdsong 124 SH6, 3km north of town ☎ 03 755 7179, ⓦ birdsong.co.nz. The pick of the local hostels is this small, friendly laidback spot, each brightly decorated room featuring a painting of the bird it's named after. Dorms $29.50, doubles $65, en-suite doubles $89

Koru Cottage 195 Sale St ☎ 03 755 7636, ⓦ koru cottage.co.nz. Pretty self-catering cottage sleeping up to four that comes with TV/DVD, barbecue and full kitchen. They'll even loan you a whitebait net to try your hand during the season (Sept to mid-Nov). $155

Mountain Jade 41 Weld St ☎ 03 755 8007, ⓦ mountain jadebackpackers.co.nz. Central, cheap hostel above the jade studio of the same name with a couple of comfortable doubles out back, overlooking the car park. Dorms $26, doubles $58, en-suite doubles $85

Shining Star 16 Richards Drive ☎ 03 755 8921, ⓦ accommodationwestcoast.co.nz. There's no road between you and the beach at this excellent site. Its stylized geometric log cabins are all equipped with en suites and offer stunning sea views; some have cooking facilities. Van sites $25, cabins $90

Teichelmann's B&B 20 Hamilton St ☎ 03 755 8232, ⓦ teichelmanns.co.nz. Comfortable and well appointed, this history-filled central B&B has friendly hosts, a range of en-suite rooms and a romantic garden cottage with double spa bath. A hearty breakfast is served. Doubles $225, cottage $255

12

EATING, DRINKING AND ENTERTAINMENT

For free evening entertainment, stroll to the **Glowworm Dell** about 1km north of the centre beside SH6. The *Hokitika Guardian*, free from the i-SITE and around town, has entertainment listings.

Café de Paris 19 Tancred St ☎ 03 755 8933. Extensive selection of moderately priced breakfasts, lunches and more formal dinners based on a French theme (mains $22–34). Book in the evenings. Daily 7.30am–late.

★ **Fat Pipi** 83a Revell St. This takeaway hole-in-the-wall's locally famed pizzas include "Greenpiece" (zucchini, spinach, mushrooms, feta, olives and roast red pepper pesto), and its whopping "Whitebait", topped with a quarter-pound of whitebait folded into a beaten egg, with mozzarella, capers and lemon (pizzas $20–26). Thurs–Sun 5pm–late.

Ocean View 111 Revell St ☎ 03 755 8344. *Beachfront*

Hotel restaurant with classy à la carte evening fare such as cider-glazed pork (mains $28.30–35) and great sea views from window tables and the deck. Daily 4.30–9.30pm.

★ **Stations Inn** Blue Spur Rd ☎ 03 755 5499, ⓦ stationsinnhokitika.co.nz. Hokitika's best gourmet dining is 5km west of town on the way to Hokitika Gorge. Chef Stuart Perry creates intricate dishes from Kiwi produce, such as braised rabbit in a pastry shell with bacon chips and kumara mash, house-cured Marlborough salmon with home-made rye bread, and multi-award-winning beef and lamb dishes (mains $26.50–38.50). Tues–Sat 6pm–late.

WILDFOODS FESTIVAL

In the last decade or so, Hokitika has become synonymous with the annual Wildfoods Festival (second Sat in March; advance tickets $30; ⓦ wildfoods.co.nz), when the population quadruples to celebrate bush tucker. Around fifty stalls in Cass Square sell delicacies such as marinated goat kebabs, smoked eel wontons, huhu grubs, "mountain oysters" (a.k.a. sheep's testicles) and, of course, whitebait, washed down with home-brewed beer and South Island wine. The feasting is followed by an evening hoedown, the Wildfoods Barn Dance ($10) and bonfires on the beach.

★ **West Coast Wine Co.** 108 Revell St ☎ 03 755 5417, ⓦ westcoastwine.co.nz. Tiny bar in a wine shop with a delightful courtyard, where good wine is complemented by excellent coffee and supplemented by moreish cheese and meat platters and very un-"Yorkshire Pork Pies" (dishes $4.80–18.50). Tues–Fri 11am–late, Sat noon–late.

CINEMAS
The Regent 23 Weld St ☎ 03 755 8101, ⓦ hokitika regent.com. A 1935 Art Deco theatre – with "cutting-edge technology" – screening mainstream movies.
Crooked Mile Talking Movies 36 Revell St ☎ 03 755 5309, ⓦ crookedmile.co.nz. Screens art-house and alternative films.

Lake Kaniere

18km east of Hokitika

Some of the best bush scenery and **walks** around Hokitika are 30km inland where the dairying hinterland meets the foothills of the Southern Alps. Minor roads (initially following Stafford Street out of town) make a good 70km scenic drive, shown in detail on DOC's **Central West Coast: Hokitika** leaflet ($2). The road passes the fishing, waterskiing and tramping territory of **Lake Kaniere**, a glacial lake with fantastic reflections of the mountains in the crystal water, several picnic sites and primitive camping ($6) along its eastern side. The most popular walk is the **Kaniere Water Race Walkway** (9km one-way; 3hr; 100m ascent), starting from the lake's northern end and following a channel that used to supply water to the goldfields, through stands of regenerating rimu.

Hokitika Gorge

35km east of Hokitika

Lake Kaniere's eastern-shore road passes the magical **Dorothy Falls**, with giant moss-covered boulders in unearthly shades of green, and continues to a side road leading to the dazzling **Hokitika Gorge**, where a gentle path leads to a swingbridge over the exquisite turquoise-coloured Hokitika River.

From Hokitika to the glaciers

The main highway snuggles in close to the Southern Alps for most of the 135km to the glacier at Franz Josef. The journey through dairy farms and stands of selectively logged native bush is broken by a series of small settlements – **Ross**, **Pukekura** and **Harihari**. The most popular attractions along the way are **Whataroa**, to visit the **White Heron** colony, and **Okarito**, where the relaxed charms of the lagoon and **kiwi-spotting** trips may give you pause.

Immediately **south** of Hokitika, it's 5km along SH6 to a relatively hidden landing where gentle paddleboat **cruises** (daily, departure times vary; 90min; $30; ☎ 03 755 7239) take you along the Mahinapua Creek to the lake. A couple of kilometres on, the **Mahinapua Walkway** (16km return; 4hr; mainly flat; DOC leaflet from the Hokitika i-SITE, $2) offers easy walking with picnic opportunities at a lakeside beach. A further 2km south along SH6 the **Mananui Bush Walkway** (30min return) leads through coastal forest remnants to dunes and there's a particularly nice basic **camping** spot at **Lake Mahinapua**, accessed off SH6 1km south ($6).

Ross

At the tiny village of **ROSS**, 30km south of Hokitika, a lake-filled hole is all that remains of the rich opencast mine that sought alluvial **gold** until 2004. The mining company has moved to a new site nearby, but would dearly love to get at the gold-bearing gravels underneath the town.

Leave time for the well-signposted **Water Race Walk** (4km loop, 1hr), and check out the Jade Studio at 23 St James St (daily noon–5pm), one of the best small **jade** galleries around.

Miner's Cottage

Bold St • Daily: Dec–March 9am–4pm; April–Nov 9am–3pm • Free

Though Ross had over 3000 residents at its gold-rush peak, things had slowed considerably by 1909, when a couple of diggers prospecting less than 500m from the current visitor centre turned up the largest gold nugget ever found in New Zealand, the 3.1kg **"Honourable Roddy"**, named after the then Minister of Mines. The nugget was bought by the government and given as a coronation gift in 1910 to Britain's George V, who melted it down to make royal tableware. A replica of the fist-sized lump resides in the 1885 **Miner's Cottage**, surrounded by gold-rush photos.

Pukekura

Bushman's Centre daily 9am–5.30pm • Free; museum $4 • ☎ 03 755 4144, ⓦ pukekura.co.nz

A giant model sandfly at the hamlet of **PUKEKURA**, aka "Puke", 23km south of Ross, marks the **Bushman's Centre**. The centre's **museum** takes a light-hearted approach to timber milling, live deer capture, possum trapping and harvesting sphagnum moss for East Asian orchid growers. The highlight for many is the centre's **café** (see below), but the rest areas around beautiful (and often warm) **Lake Ianthe**, 6km to the south, make good picnic stops.

Harihari

Tiny **HARIHARI**, 17km south of Pukekura, was the marshy landing site of **Guy Menzies**, who flew solo from Sydney to New Zealand in 1931, becoming the first to do so. Menzies ended up strapped in upside down in the mud of La Fontaine swamp, 10km northwest of town, a site now marked by explanatory panels. A replica of Menzies' plane resides near the southern entrance to town in **Guy Menzies Park**. You might also want to turn onto Whanganui Flat Road and drive 20km (partly gravel) coastwards past the Menzies' landing site to the delightful **Hari Hari Coastal Walkway** (8km loop; 2–3hr; negligible ascent), which runs past elaborate whitebaiting stands to the Doughboy Lookout (60m) with great views of the coast and the Southern Alps. After a short stretch of dramatic coastline you return though kahikatea forest and along the line of a tram track once used by loggers.

Whataroa and the Waitangiroto Nature Reserve

SH6, 30km south of Harihari • White Heron Sanctuary Tours Oct–Feb 3–6 daily; 2hr 30min • $120; booking advised • ☎ 0800 523 456 or ☎ 03 753 4120, ⓦ whiteherontours.co.nz

From October to late February, New Zealand's entire adult population of the graceful white heron (*kotuku*) arrives to breed at the Waitangiroto Nature Reserve near **WHATAROA**. Sitting across the river, in a hide, gazing on forty or so nesting pairs of herons (plus slightly larger numbers of royal spoonbills) going about their daily business of preening, fishing and mating is a truly memorable if slightly surreal experience that ends all too quickly. The only way to visit is with the highly professional **White Heron Sanctuary Tours**, in the centre of Whataroa. The trip includes a scenic jetboat ride on the pretty Waitangiroto River and about half an hour ogling the birds; binoculars are provided.

Okarito

In 1642, Abel Tasman became the first European to set eyes on Aotearoa at **Okarito**, 15km south of Whataroa and 10km off SH6, now a secluded hamlet dotted round the southern side of its eponymous lagoon. The discovery of gold in the mid-1800s sparked an eighteen-month boom that saw fifty stores and hotels spring up along the lagoon's shores. Timber milling and flax production stood in once the gold had gone, but the community foundered, leaving a handful of holiday homes, a few dozen permanent residents and a lovely beach and lagoon, used as the setting for much of Keri Hulme's Booker Prize-winning novel, *The Bone People*.

12

OKARITO TOURS AND ACTIVITIES

Nature-based kayaking trips and cruises departing from Okarito offer the chance for close encounters with the area's seventy species of birdlife including the kotuku (white heron) and royal spoonbill, while bushwalking tours have an excellent success rate for spotting kiwi. The area's operators are listed below.

WALKS

Okarito Trig Walk (1hr 30min return; 200m ascent) This route begins at the southern end of town, climbing to a headland with fabulous mountain and coastal views.

Pakihi Walk (2km return; 20–30min; 50m ascent) Head 5.5km back towards SH6 and look for the good gravel path – it leads to a lookout with long views of Okarito Lagoon.

TOUR OPERATORS

Okarito Nature Tours ☎03 753 4014, ⓦokarito .co.nz. Runs great-value guided kayaking trips (2hr; $75; minimum two people) and rents double kayaks (half-day $40; full day $60; overnight camping at remote beach $80). Call first to check tide conditions, but plan to go out early in the morning when the water is calmest and the birds are active and abundant.

Experience Okarito Boat Tours ☎03 753 4223, ⓦokaritoboattours.co.nz. If you don't want to paddle, opt for one of these leisurely cruises through the lagoon and its feeder streams. Early tours (2hr; $85)

concentrate on spotting birds while later tours (1hr; $45) mainly focus on the seductive scenery.

Okarito Kiwi Tours 53 The Strand ☎03 753 4330, ⓦokaritokiwitours.co.nz. Wildlife of a different feather can usually be seen on these excellent, low-impact trips into the bush for kiwi spotting (2–3hr; $75). If it goes well you'll start about ninety minutes before sunset and catch a glimpse of some of the extremely rare Okarito brown kiwi. To maximize the already high (98 percent) success rate, wear quiet clothes and sturdy boots.

INFORMATION

Tourist information 4 Aylmer St, Ross (daily: Dec– March 9am–4pm; April–Nov 9am–3pm; museum $2; ☎03 755 4077, ⓦross.org.nz). The visitor centre-museum shows an interesting audiovisual presentation (included

in admission) on the 1865 gold rush and rents gold pans ($10) in addition to offering on-site gold panning with a guaranteed strike ($10.50).

ACCOMMODATION AND EATING

PUKEKURA

Bushman's Centre Café ☎03 755 4144, ⓦpukekura .co.nz. Serves a "roadkill menu" that includes possum pies (technically paid for "by donation" since possums have been banished from Kiwi menus).

Puke Pub SH6 ☎03 755 4008, ⓦpukekura.co.nz. Across the road from the Bushman's Centre and run by the same owners, the pub has a fabulous wild game menu (mains $20–27) that includes New Zealand wallaby. There's also on-site accommodation in the form of camping or double rooms with shared bathroom and kitchen facilities. Pub daily 3pm–late. Camping $10, doubles $45

HARIHARI

Flaxbush Motel SH6 ☎03 753 3116, ⓔflaxbush123 @xtra.co.nz. What with the park and the coastal walkway you may decide to stay, in which case treat yourself to this very welcoming spot, which is a Noah's ark for unwell and injured wildlife and home to a variety of farm animals. Motel studios $90, cottages $120

OKARITO

There are no cafés or shops in Okarito, so bring provisions.

MacDonalds Creek Campsite SH6, 4km south of the Okarito junction. Easily accessible along a gravel road, this basic DOC campsite is situated by the shore of Lake Mapourika, offering trout fishing and swimming opportunities. Camping $6

Okarito Beach House & Royal Hostel The Strand ☎03 753 4080, ⓦokaritobeachhouse.com. This huddle of buildings, which include comfy rooms and a romantic self-contained cottage, offers the settlement's widest range of accommodation. Dorms $20, doubles $60, en-suite doubles $80, cottage $80

The School House The Strand ☎03 752 0796, ⓦdoc .govt.nz. A memorial commemorating Tasman's sighting stands next to this DOC-managed 1860 former schoolhouse. Rates are for one or two people for the whole place, but there's no shower so you'll need to wander across the street to the shady campsite (no powered sites), where showers take $1 coins. Closed June–Aug. Camping $10, schoolhouse $60

The glaciers

Around 150km south of Hokitika, two white rivers of ice force their way down towards the thick rainforest of the coastal plain – ample justification for the region's inclusion in Te Wahipounamu, the South West New Zealand World Heritage Area. The glaciers form a palpable connection between the coast and the highest peaks of the Southern Alps. Within a handful of kilometres the terrain drops from over 3000m to near sea level, bringing with it **Franz Josef glacier** and **Fox glacier**, two of the largest and most impressive of the sixty-odd decent-sized glaciers that creak off the South Island's icy spine, together forming the centrepiece of the rugged **Westland National Park**. Legend tells of the beautiful Hinehukatere who so loved the mountains that she encouraged her lover, Tawe, to climb alongside her. He fell to his death and Hinehukatere cried so copiously that her tears formed the glaciers, known to Maori as Ka Riomata o Hinehukatere – "The Tears of the Avalanche Girl".

The area is also characterized by the West Coast's prodigious **precipitation**, with upwards of 5m being the typical yearly dump. These conditions, combined with the rakish angle of the western slopes of the Southern Alps, produce some of the world's fastest-moving glaciers; stand at the foot for half an hour or so and you're bound to see a piece peel off. But these phenomenal speeds haven't been enough to counteract melting, and both glaciers have receded over 3km since Cook saw them at their greatest recent extent, soon after the Little Ice Age of 1750. Glaciers are receding worldwide, but the two here sometimes buck the trend by advancing from time to time, typically around five years after a particularly big snowfall in the mountains.

The glaciers were already in full retreat when travellers started to battle their way down the coast to observe these wonders of nature. They were initially named "Victoria" and "Albert" respectively but, in 1865, geologist Julius von Haast renamed Franz Josef after the Austro-Hungarian emperor, and following a visit by prime minister William Fox in 1872, the other was bestowed with his name.

Activity in the glaciers focuses on two small **villages**, which survive almost entirely on tourist traffic. Both lie close to the base of their respective glaciers and offer excellent plane and helicopter **flights**, guided **glacier walks** and **heli-hiking**. With your own

12

GLACIERS EXPLAINED

The existence of a **glacier** is a balancing act between competing forces: snowfall at the **névé**, high in the mountains, battles with rapid melting at the **terminal** lower down the valley, the victor determining whether the glacier will advance or retreat. Snowfall, metres thick, gradually compacts to form clear **blue ice**, accumulating until it starts to flow downhill under its own weight. Friction against the valley walls slows the sides while ice in the centre slips down the valley, giving the characteristic scalloped effect on the surface, which is especially pronounced on such vigorous glaciers as Franz Josef and Fox. Where a riverbed steepens, the river forms a rapid: under similar conditions, glaciers break up into an **icefall**, full of towering blocks of ice known as **seracs**, separated by **crevasses**.

Visitors familiar with grubby glaciers in the European Alps or American Rockies will expect the surface to be mottled with **rock debris** which has fallen off the valley walls onto the surface; however, the glaciers here descend so steeply that the cover doesn't have time to build up and they remain pristine. Rock still gets carried down with the glacier though, and when the glacier retreats, this is deposited as **terminal moraine**. Occasionally retreating glaciers leave behind huge chunks of ice which, on melting, form **kettle lakes**.

The most telling evidence of past glacial movements is the location of the **trim line** on the valley wall, caused by the glacier stripping away all vegetation. At Fox and Franz Josef, the advance associated with the Little Ice Age around 1750 left a very visible trim line high up the valley wall, separating mature rata from scrub.

transport, it makes sense to base yourself in one of the two villages and explore both glaciers from there. If you have to choose one, Franz Josef has a wider range of accommodation, restaurants, and offers the most comprehensive selection of trips, while Fox is quieter.

Franz Josef Glacier

FRANZ JOSEF GLACIER (Waiau) is the slightly larger of the two glacier villages. The glacier almost reaches the fringes of the village, the Southern Alps tower above and developers have done what they can to create an alpine character with steeply pitched roofs and pine panelling. It's an appealing place, and small enough to make you feel almost like a local if you stay for more than a night or two – something that's easily done, considering the number of fine walks and the proximity of the glaciers.

In Franz Josef you can hike to the glacier, join a guided walk on the glacier, kayak on a nearby lake or take a scenic flight. Guided glacier walks and kayaking take place in most weather conditions, but on misty and very wet days you'll find that scenic flights and heli-hikes are cancelled and alternatives limited.

Glacier Hot Pools

Cron St • Daily noon–10pm; last entry 9pm • Main pools $23; private pool $42/45min • ☎ 0800 044 044, ⊛ glacierhotpools.co.nz

When the weather's wet, the best bet is a soak in the new, specially constructed **Glacier Hot Pools**. Artificially heated to 36°C, 38°C and 40°C respectively, the three public

12

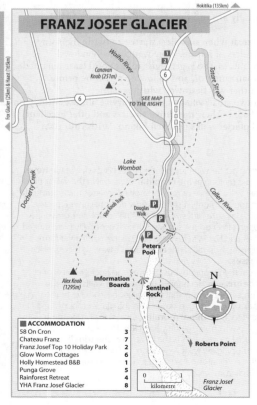

FRANZ JOSEF GLACIER

Hokitika (135km)

Waiho River

Canavan Knob (251m)

For Glacier (25km) & Haast (165km)

SEE MAP TO THE RIGHT

Tatare Stream

Lake Wombat

Docherty Creek

Alex Knob Track

Callery River

Douglas Walk

Peters Pool

Alex Knob (1295m)

Information Boards

Sentinel Rock

N

Roberts Point

0   1
kilometre

Franz Josef Glacier

■ **ACCOMMODATION**

58 On Cron	3
Chateau Franz	7
Franz Josef Top 10 Holiday Park	2
Glow Worm Cottages	6
Holly Homestead B&B	1
Punga Grove	5
Rainforest Retreat	4
YHA Franz Josef Glacier	8

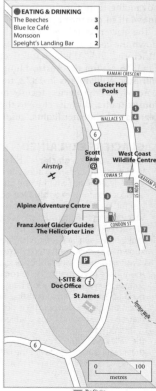

● **EATING & DRINKING**

The Beeches	3
Blue Ice Café	4
Monsoon	1
Speight's Landing Bar	2

KAMAHI CRESCENT

Glacier Hot Pools

WALLACE ST

Scott Base

West Coast Wildlife Centre

Airstrip

COWAN ST

GRAHAM PL

CRON ST

Alpine Adventure Centre

Franz Josef Glacier Guides The Helicopter Line

CONDON ST

i-SITE & Doc Office

St James

Terrace Walk

0   100
metres

The Glacier

pools are covered in semi-porous canopies and surrounded by native bush, most of which has been transported to the site. Private pools come with cabana-type sheds containing showers. The pools' restorative qualities come into their own when you need to banish the aches of hiking or yomping about on a guided glacier walk; combo deals are available with Franz Josef Glacier Guides (see box, pp.672–673).

West Coast Wildlife Centre

Corner of Cowan and Cron sts • Daily from 9am; call for seasonal closing times • $25; valid for 24hr; "backstage pass" $40 • ☎ 03 752 0600, ⓦ wildkiwi.co.nz

The enormous building that once housed the Hukawai Glacier Centre is now home to the state-of-the-art **West Coast Wildlife Centre**, where you can see New Zealand's rarest kiwis, the rowi and Haast tokoeka. Part of BNZ Operation Nest Egg (see box, p.806), from approximately July to February, you'll also see chicks incubating, and, from around September to March, see them brooding. Tickets are valid for 24 hours; a "backstage pass" includes a half-hour behind-the-scenes tour.

ARRIVAL AND DEPARTURE   FRANZ JOSEF

By bus InterCity and Atomic buses stop on the main road in the village (SH6; known here as Main Rd) by the combined i-SITE and DOC office.
Destinations Fox Glacier (3 daily; 30min); Haast (3 daily;

3hr–3hr 30min); Greymouth (3 daily; 3hr–3hr 30min); Hokitika (3 daily; 2hr 30min); Makarora (3 daily; 4hr 20min– 5hr); Queenstown (2 daily; 7–8hr); Wanaka (3 daily; 6–7hr).

GETTING AROUND

By shuttle bus Glacier Valley Eco Tours (☎ 0800 999 739, ⓦ glaciervalley.co.nz) offer a shuttle service to the glacier

road-end ($12.50 return). Fox Bus (☎ 0800 369 287) run shuttle services on demand.

INFORMATION

i-SITE/DOC SH6 (daily: Nov–March 8.30am–6pm; April–Oct 8.30am–noon & 1–5pm; ☎ 03 752 0796, ⓔ westlandnpvc@doc.govt.nz). The excellent combined office has stacks of leaflets on walks in the area and first-class glacier and geology displays. The centre also gets

weather reports twice daily, so check with them before starting any serious walks.
Services There is an ATM but no banks. Internet access is most reliable at Scott Base on SH6 (daily 9am–6pm; $4/hr).

ACCOMMODATION

With the region's popularity and a bus schedule that forces many people to overnight here, accommodation in Franz Josef is tight throughout the summer. Between November and March (and particularly February), you should aim to make **reservations** at least a week in advance, more like six months for swankier places.

58 On Cron 58 Cron St ☎ 03 752 0627, ⓦ 58oncron .co.nz. Stylish units decorated with Italian fabrics and equipped with queen- or super-king-size beds; some rooms have spa baths. Guests have access to gas BBQs amid native bush gardens. Doubles $175, spa studios $230
Chateau Franz 8 Cron St ☎ 0800 728 372, ⓦ chateau franz.co.nz. A wide range of accommodation, from budget dorms and smaller en-suite dorms to full-blown motel units. Free spa, free soup nightly and TVs and VCRs everywhere (with free popcorn, too). Dorms $23, doubles $55, en-suite doubles $95, motel units $95
Franz Josef Top 10 Holiday Park SH6, 1km north of town ☎ 0800 467 897, ⓦ mountainviewtop10.co.nz. High-spec rural campsite with a good range of tent and powered sites, cabins and units. Camping $40, cabins $75, kitchen cabins $90, units $145

Glow Worm Cottages 27 Cron St ☎ 0800 151 027, ⓦ glowwormcottages.co.nz. Small, homely hostel owned by the same crew as *Chateau Franz* with a well-equipped kitchen, six-bed dorms and four-shares with their own bathrooms, plus comfy motel-style rooms. Free soup and spa. Dorms $26, en-suite doubles $110
★ **Holly Homestead B&B** SH6, 1.5km north of town ☎ 03 752 0299, ⓦ hollyhomestead.co.nz. Comfort, to the point of indulgence, in an attractive two-storey 1920s home with five en-suite rooms (one with bathtub). The owners are welcoming, there's a deck with mountain views and rates include a delicious full breakfast. The caveats: it's only suitable for those 12 and over and is closed outside summer (call for seasonal openings). Doubles $265
Punga Grove 40 Cron St ☎ 0800 437 269, ⓦ punga grove.co.nz. Stylish, modern luxury motels, all nicely

12

FRANZ JOSEF GLACIER TOURS AND ACTIVITIES

It's possible to walk to the face of the Franz Josef glacier independently, but to walk on the ice you'll need to take a guided glacier-walking trip. On any fine day the skies above Franz Josef are abuzz with choppers and light planes. Kayaking trips are also on offer.

WALKS

Glacier car park to glacier face (6km return; 1hr 30min) This route is at the top of everyone's list of walks and starts at the car park 5km south of the village. The rough track crosses gravel beds left behind by past glacial retreats, giving you plenty of opportunity to observe small kettle lakes, the trim line high up the valley walls and a fault line cutting right across the valley (marked by deep gullies opposite each other). One of the best viewpoints is from the top of the glacier-scoured hump of Sentinel Rock, a ten-minute walk from the car park.

Douglas Walk (1hr) Reached off the access road, this circular walk passes Peter's Pool, a serene lake left by a retreat in the late eighteenth century.

Roberts Point Track (12km return; 5hr 30min; 950m ascent) One for the more adventurous, this track carries on from a point on the Douglas Walk loop past the Hendes Hut (a good lunch stop) to Roberts Point, high above the ice with stunning views. It's a bit of a slog and often slippery but well worth the effort.

Alex Knob Track (12km return; 8hr; 1000m ascent) Located on the other side of the glacial valley, this route climbs high above the glacier through several vegetation zones and offers more fine views up the valley.

HIKING, HELI-HIKING AND ICE CLIMBING

Glacier Valley Eco Tours 📞 0800 999 739, 🌐 glacier valley.co.nz. Runs a series of local nature tours, including three-hour Franz Josef ($70) and Fox Glacier ($75) tours to the glacier terminals (the front of the glaciers) as well as tours to Lake Matheson (3hr; $70) and a Lake Matheson-Fox glacier combo (5hr; $120).

Franz Josef Glacier Guides SH6 📞 0800 484 337, 🌐 franzjosefglacier.com. A half-day trip (2–3 daily; $123) involves a hike across the braided riverbed below the glacier, fitting your crampons, then a little over an hour on the ice, snaking up ice steps cut by your guide. The full-day trip ($180) gives up to five hours on the ice,

furnished and with Sky TV. Rainforest studios back onto the bush and come with gas fires, underfloor heating and spa bath. Doubles $190

Rainforest Retreat 46 Cron St 📞 0800 873 346, 🌐 rainforestretreat.co.nz. Large lodge and campervan park with gravel pads (good for campervans; just OK for tents) and access to a communal lodge. Also has backpacker dorms and en-suite rooms, spacious studio motel units, atmospheric log cabins on stilts, luxurious lodges, a spa and sauna. Camping $15–19.50, dorms $27, en-suite

four-shares $27, doubles $112, motels $155, log cabins $185, lodges $215

★ **YHA Franz Josef Glacier** 2–4 Cron St 📞 03 752 0754, ✉ yha.franzjosef@yha.co.nz. Modern, well-run hostel on the edge of town with the southernmost rooms overlooking bushland, where you'll hear a joyful dawn chorus. A spacious kitchen, clean comfortable rooms (some en-suite), BBQ area and free sauna make it the best value around. Dorms $23, doubles $72, en-suite doubles $90

EATING, DRINKING AND ENTERTAINMENT

Franz Josef's relatively remote location keeps prices high. Even if you're self-catering you can expect to pay over the odds for a limited stock of **groceries**.

The Beeches Main Rd, between Cowan and Condon sts 📞 03 752 0721. Quality café good for coffee and lunches during the day and a broad range of reasonably priced evening meals (mains $14.95–30.95) such as lamb sausages and mutton shanks; all available indoors or out. Daily lunch & dinner.

Blue Ice Café Main Rd, between Cowan and Condon sts 📞 03 752 0707. The modern and airy restaurant at street level serves imaginative and tasty mains ($20.50–36) and a range of gourmet pizzas to take away or eat in the unreconstructed upstairs bar, where the free pool table and rowdy music draws in a lively crowd most nights. Daily

hopefully finding ice tunnels to explore, deep blue crevices into which to stare and a general sense of wonder and otherworldliness. They also offer heli-hiking (1–2 daily; 3hr; $399), which combines a short helicopter flight with a couple of hours on a fascinating section of ice caves, pinnacles and seracs that you couldn't hope to reach on foot in a day. Try to be clear about your aspirations and abilities and you can be matched up with a party of like-minded folk. You can also go ice climbing (7–8hr; $256) – an instructional roped-up and tiring undertaking on steep ice.

SCENIC FLIGHTS AND SKYDIVING

Safety demands that specific flight paths must be followed, limiting what can be offered and forcing companies to compete on price; ask for youth, student, YHA, BBH, senior or just-for-the-sake-of-it discounts, most readily given if you can band together in a group of four to six and present yourselves as a ready-to-go plane or chopper load. Most people go by helicopter, with all operators regularly landing on a snowfield high above the glacier where the rotors are left running – hardly serene. Planes give you a longer flight with greater range for less money while a ski-plane landing on a snowfield is very rewarding, particularly the silence after they switch the engine off.

Fox & Franz Josef Heliservices Alpine Adventure Centre, Main Rd ☎ 0800 800 793, ⓦ scenic-flights .co.nz. The cheapest operator hereabouts, offering one glacier and landing (20min; $190), two glaciers and landing (30min; $260), and two glaciers, landing and Mount Cook (30min; $260).

Air Safaris 6 Main Rd ☎ 0800 723 274, ⓦ airsafaris .co.nz. A smidgen cheaper than some other operators, but they don't do landings. Try their Grand Traverse (50min; $295).

Skydive Franz Main Rd, across from the bus stop ☎ 0800 458 677, ⓦ skydivefranz.co.nz. For the ultimate aerial adventure, book a tandem skydive (3660m $299; 4570m $399; 5490m $549).

KAYAKING

Glacier Country 20 Cron St ☎ 0800 423 262, ⓦ glacier kayaks.com. Offers marvellous guided kayaking trips, the most popular of which ($90) is on the black waters of the kahikatea- and flax-fringed Lake Mapourika, 8km north of town. Trips run in the morning, afternoon and early evening, spending about three hours on the water, with loads of photo opportunities in sun and/or rain. There's also a heli-paddle option ($450).

12

lunch & dinner, bar open until late.
Monsoon 46 Cron St ☎ 0800 873 346, ⓦ rainforest retreat.co.nz. Convivial café/bar at the *Rainforest Retreat* (see opposite), serving inspired dishes such as Tuscan lamb salad, and great burgers (mains $18–29.50) plus a wide selection of drinks (its motto: "it rains, we pour"). Daily 4.30pm–late; happy hour 7–9pm.

★ **Speight's Landing Bar** Corner of Main Rd and Cowan St ☎ 03 752 0229. Super-popular, swish-looking café/bar, with loads of outdoor seating (plus blankets and a fire pit in chilly weather), serving substantial mains ($13.50–39) including a great range of vegetarian options, lighter meals such as mussels steamed in white wine, and, of course, its eponymous ale. Daily 11am–late.

Fox Glacier

The village of **Fox Glacier**, 25km south of Franz Josef, is scattered over an outwash plain of the Fox and Cook rivers, and services the local farming community and passing sightseers. Everything of interest is beside SH6 or Cook Flat Road, which skirts the scenic Lake Matheson on the way to the former gold settlement and seal colony at Gillespies Beach. The foot of the glacier itself is around 6km away.

ARRIVAL AND DEPARTURE

FOX GLACIER

By bus InterCity and Atomic buses stop by Fox Glacier Guides on Main Rd.
Destinations Franz Josef (3 daily; 30min); Greymouth (3 daily; 3hr 45min–4hr 30min); Haast (3 daily; 2hr 40min–3hr); Hokitika (3 daily; 3hr); Makarora (3 daily; 4hr 30min); Queenstown (3 daily; 6hr–7hr 30min); Wanaka (3 daily; 5–6hr).

GETTING AROUND

By shuttle bus Fox Glacier Shuttles & Tours (☎0800 369 287) goes to the glacier (from $13 return) and Lake Matheson (from $17 return). They also go to Gillespies Beach for a look at the seal colony (price on demand, depending on numbers).

INFORMATION

DOC SH6 (Mon–Fri 9am–noon & 1–4.30pm; ☎03 751 0807, ✉foxsouthwestlandao@doc.govt.nz). The office has displays concentrating on lowland forests and glaciation.

ACCOMMODATION

Fox's range of places to stay is more limited than Franz Josef's; **book** as far ahead as you can and be prepared for resort prices. The basic and free DOC **campsite** at Gillespies Beach (see box opposite) is popular in summer.

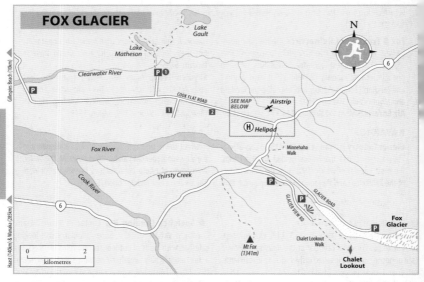

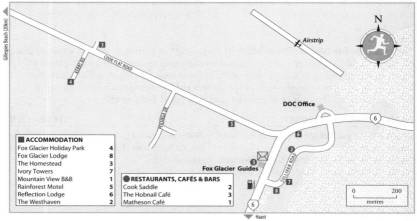

■ ACCOMMODATION

Fox Glacier Holiday Park	4
Fox Glacier Lodge	8
The Homestead	3
Ivory Towers	7
Mountain View B&B	1
Rainforest Motel	5
Reflection Lodge	6
The Westhaven	2

● RESTAURANTS, CAFÉS & BARS

Cook Saddle	2
The Hobnail Café	3
Matheson Café	1

12

FOX GLACIER TOURS AND ACTIVITIES

Fox glacier is accessed from the side, giving more immediate access to crevasses and seracs. As on Franz Josef, glacier walking on the Fox glacier gets better the longer you spend on the ice. The Fox Glacier airport and helipad are slightly less busy than those at Franz Josef, but a similar range of flights is on offer.

WALKS

It would be a shame to miss the Fox glacier just because you've already seen Franz Josef: the approach walks are different and their characters distinct, the Fox valley being less sheer but with more impressive rockfalls.

To Fox glacier The approach, imaginatively named Glacier Road, crosses the wide bed left by glacial retreats and is occasionally re-routed as "dead" ice under the roadway gradually melts. From the car park, 6km from the town, a track leads to the foot of the glacier in half an hour, crossing a couple of small streams en route.

River Walk (2km; 30min) Partway back along Glacier Road, this walk crosses a historic swingbridge to the Glacier Valley Viewpoint on Glacier View Road, which runs 3km along the south side of the Fox River.

Chalet Lookout Walk (4km; 1hr 30min return; 150m ascent) From the Glacier Valley Viewpoint, this route climbs relatively moderately for stupendous glacier and mountain views.

Lake Matheson Walk and Peak Viewpoint (5km west of town along Cook Flat Rd; 1hr) It's difficult to imagine a New Zealand calendar or picture book without a photo of Mount Cook and Mount Tasman mirrored in Lake Matheson. A well-signposted boardwalk through lovely native bush encircles the lake, which was formed by an iceberg left when the Fox glacier retreated 14,000 years ago, giving everyone a chance for that perfect image, especially those who venture out for sunrise. The *Matheson Café* (p.676), by the Lake Matheson car park, serves superb food. About 5km beyond Lake Matheson, Peak Viewpoint is ideal for fabulous fine-day views of the top of the Fox glacier and the snowcapped mountains.

Walks from Gillespies Beach Continue 10km further along Cook Flat Road to reach Gillespies Beach, a former gold-mining settlement with a small cemetery and a primitive DOC campsite. From the campsite an excellent walk threads north parallel to the beach, past the scant remains of an old gold dredge (30min return) to Gillespies Lagoon (1hr 15min return), a short Miners' Tunnel (1hr 40min return) and the Galway Beach Seal Colony (3hr 30min return).

Minnehaha Walk (1km; 20min loop) Back in Fox, fill an empty half-hour with a stroll around this flat walk, which winds through lush bush that's cool and shady on a summer day, or dank and brooding in the rain. Come after dark to see glowworms.

GLACIER HIKING, HELI-HIKING AND ICE CLIMBING

Fox Glacier Guides 44 Main Rd/SH6 ☏ 0800 111 600, ⊕ foxguides.co.nz. A smaller concern than the outfits operating on Franz Josef glacier, which means there are fewer people on the ice at any one time. Still, half-day walks (2–4 daily; $99) only allow an hour on the ice so it's worth stepping up to a full-day trip ($149), with over three hours. They also offer heli-hiking ($399), with two and a half hours of icy hiking, and ice climbing (8–9hr; $245).

SCENIC FLIGHTS AND SKYDIVING

Fox & Franz Josef Heliservices Alpine Adventure Centre, Main Rd, Franz Josef ☏ 0800 800 793, ⊕ scenic -flights.co.nz. Offers the same deals as in Franz Josef (see box, pp.672–673).

Skydive NZ ☏ 0800 751 0080, ⊕ skydivingnz.co.nz. Offers tandem skydives from 3660m ($299) and 4877m ($399).

Fox Glacier Holiday Park Kerrs Rd ☏ 0800 154 366, ⊕ foxglacierholidaypark.co.nz. Comprehensive campsite with a wide range of tent and powered sites, cabins and spacious self-contained units and great mountain views. Camping $39, cabins $68, units $165

Fox Glacier Lodge Sullivan Rd ☏ 0800 369 800, ⊕ foxglacierlodge.co.nz. A pine-lined alpine chalet with attractively furnished en-suite rooms sharing a communal kitchen, and self-contained apartments. A buffet breakfast is included, and there are campervan hook-ups. Doubles $99, apartments $250

The Homestead Cook Flat Rd, 700m off SH6 ☏ 03 751 0835, ✉ foxhomestead@slingshot.co.nz. A friendly homestay in a pleasant old house on a 115-year-old,

2200-acre sheep, beef and cattle farm within walking distance of town. You get occasional views of Mount Cook, pleasant en suites and a continental and/or cooked breakfast (from $7). Doubles **$140**

Ivory Towers Sullivan Rd ⊕ 03 751 0838, ⓦ ivorytowerslodge.co.nz. Fox's only genuine backpackers is friendly, clean and colourfully decorated. Most dorms have both beds and bunks, while doubles all have TV. The kitchen has plenty of elbow room, there's a sauna and a small cinema for those rainy afternoons and bikes to rent. Dorms **$28**, doubles **$73**, en-suite doubles **$87**

Mountain View B&B 1 Williams Drive, 2km off SH6 ⊕ 03 751 0770, ⓦ foxglaciermountainview.co.nz. Welcoming modern B&B with three en suites and a separate self-contained cottage in its own grounds on the edge of town with great mountain views. You get tasteful decor in well-equipped rooms, plus a full breakfast. Doubles **$180**

Rainforest Motel 15 Cook Flat Rd, 200m off SH ⊕ 0800 724 636, ⓦ rainforestmotel.co.nz. Log cabin with attractive and well-priced studios and larger one bedroom units, two of which have fully equipped kitchen with ovens. Studios **$145**, units **$160**

Reflection Lodge Cook Flat Rd, 1.5km off SH6 ⊕ 0. 751 0707, ⓦ reflectionlodge.co.nz. So named because o the glorious reflection of the mountains in the large garde pond, this romantic homestay offers reasonably pricec accommodation in comfortable, spacious and friendly surroundings. Dinner by arrangement. Doubles **$210**

The Westhaven SH6 ⊕ 0800 369 452, ⓦ thewesthaven.co.nz. Central motel with contemporary queen, king and deluxe units; the latter have super king-size beds and spa baths. All units also come with wi-fi and underfloor heating. Doubles **$185**

EATING AND DRINKING

12

Cook Saddle SH6 ⊕ 03 751 0700. A local favourite, this Western-inspired, all-wood saloon dishes out massive portions of good-quality food (mains $12–27) from lentil burgers to pork spare ribs. There's regular live music in the summer. Daily noon–late.

The Hobnail Café 44 Main Rd/SH6 ⊕ 03 751 0825. In the alpine-chalet surroundings of Fox Glacier Guides, this workaday café has unfortunate New Zealand tearoom tendencies, but offers a wide selection of cheapish breakfasts, salads, sandwiches, soups and burgers (dishes $14–18). Daily 7.30am–4pm.

★ **Matheson Café** Cook Flat Rd ⊕ 03 751 0878, ⓦ lakematheson.com. Architecturally stunning café at the start of the walk around Lake Matheson, with mountain views through big picture windows. Fabulous breakfasts ($7.50–19.50) such as the salmon bagel benedict reward an early walk, while lunches include a particularly fine lamb burger and chorizo linguini. Afternoon coffee and cake usually coincide with the sun catching the mountains. Book ahead for summertime evening meals (mains $27.50–35) such as slow-cooked lamb shoulder with kumara mustard rosti. Daily 8am–3pm plus 6pm–late early Nov–Mar.

South Westland and the Haast Pass

South of the glaciers, the West Coast feels even wilder. Many visitors do the run from the glaciers to Wanaka or Queenstown in a day, missing out on some fine remote country. Facilities aren't completely absent: many accommodation and eating places are clustered around **Haast**, and there's an increasing number of other pit stops along the way. There wasn't a road through here until 1965 and the final section of tarmac wasn't laid on the Haast Pass until 1995.

SH6 mostly runs inland, passing the start of the hike to the **Welcome Flat Hot Springs** (see box opposite) and through kahikatea and rimu forests as far as **Knight's Point**, where it returns to the coast along the edge of the Haast Coastal Plain, whose stunning **coastal dune systems** shelter lakes and some fine stands of kahikatea. The plain continues south past the scattered township of Haast to the site of the short-lived colonial settlement of **Jackson Bay**. From Haast, SH6 veers inland over the Haast Pass to the former timber town of **Makarora**, not strictly part of the West Coast but moist enough to share some of its characteristics and a base for the excellent **Gillespie Pass** Tramp.

Bruce Bay

SH6, 45km south of Fox Glacier

One place you might like to break your journey is **Bruce Bay**, where the road briefly parallels a long driftwood-strewn beach perfect for an atmospheric stroll. Recently tour bus drivers have been stopping long enough for their occupants to erect small cairns, most of which are thankfully obliterated by high tide or good wind.

WELCOME FLAT HOT SPRINGS HIKE

The most popular two-day hike in the region is the in-and-back jaunt to the **Welcome Flat Hot Springs**, a series of open-air pools where you're bound to find a spot that's just the right temperature for easing those bones. Almost everyone spends the night at DOC's adjacent **Welcome Flat Hut** (31 bunks; $15, camping $5; annual pass not valid). It should be bookable online by the time you're reading this.

The track (detailed on DOC's *Copland Track* leaflet) starts by a car park on SH6, 26km south of Fox Glacier: Atomic and InterCity **buses** will drop off, and pick up pre-booked customers. From **SH6 to Welcome Flat** (17km; 6–7hr one-way; 450m ascent) is a fairly tough tramp (far less defined than any of the Great Walks) following the true right bank all the way to Welcome Flat, crossing numerous creeks by hopping from rock to rock or wading. If the creeks are high, as they commonly are, you may have to use the flood bridges, which will add an hour or so. After heavy rain, the track becomes impassable: take plenty of extra supplies in case you get held up for a day or two.

Paringa River and Lake Paringa
SH6, 17km south of Bruce Bay

Where SH6 crosses the **Paringa River** a plaque marks the southern limit of Thomas Brunner's 1846–48 explorations. Buses stop nearby at the *Salmon Farm* on SH6 for an overpriced snack or lunch. A better bet is to pick up some delicious hot or cold smoked salmon to take away and continue 8km south to the northern shores of trout-filled **Lake Paringa** and DOC's simple but beautifully sited Lake Paringa **campsite** ($6).

The Monro Beach Walk
SH6, 18km south of Lake Paringa • 5km; 1hr 30min return

The **Monro Beach Walk** leads through lovely forest to a spot where you might see rare **Fiordland crested penguins** in the surf and on the beach, particularly in early morning and late afternoon. They're mainly around during the breeding season (July–Dec), but also occasionally in February, when they come ashore to moult. Even in the absence of penguins the scenery and serenity justify taking the walk.

Knight's Point and Ship Creek
Knight's Point is on SH6, 23km south of Lake Paringa

The highway finally returns to the coast at **Knight's Point**, where a roadside marker commemorates the linking of Westland and Otago by road in 1965. Ahead lies the **Haast Coastal Plain**, which kicks off at the tea-coloured **Ship Creek**, 10km on, where a picnic area and information panels by a beautiful long surf-pounded beach mark the start of two lovely twenty-minute (return) walks: the **Kahikatea Swamp Forest Walk** up the river through kahikatea forest to a lookout, and the wheelchair-accessible **Mataketake Dune Lake Walk** along the coast to the dune-trapped Lake Mat.aketake.

From Ship Creek it's only another 15km to the 700m-long Haast River Bridge, the longest single-lane bridge in the country, immediately before Haast Junction.

Haast

Haast is initially a confusing place, with three tiny communities all taking the name: **Haast Junction**, at the intersection of SH6 and the minor road to Jackson Bay, **Haast Beach**, 4km along the Jackson Bay Road (see p.678), and **Haast Township**, the largest settlement, 3km along SH6 towards Haast Pass and Wanaka.

ARRIVAL AND INFORMATION	HAAST

By bus InterCity and Atomic buses stop outside the *Fantail Café*, but you really need your own vehicle to get around.

DOC Visitor Centre Corner of SH6 and Jackson Bay Rd, Haast Junction (daily: early Nov–April 9am–6pm; rest of year 9am–4.30pm; ☎ 03 750 0809, ⦿ doc.govt.nz). Has informative displays on all aspects of the local environment, plus the 20-minute *Edge of Wilderness* film (shown on demand; $3).

Website Information is also available at ⦿ haastnz.com.

12

TOURS

Waiatoto River Safaris Hannahs Homestead, Jackson Bay Rd ☎0800 538 723, ⓦriversafaris.co.nz. Does jetboat safaris (daily Oct–late April, on demand; $199) comprising a 2hr wilderness ride from the coast into the heart of the mountains, with the emphasis firmly on appreciating history and scenery.

Haast River Safari ☎0800 865 382, ⓦhaastrive .co.nz. Operates cruises (2–3 daily; $139).

Waana Go Fishing Charters ☎03 750 0134, ⓦwann gonz.com. Runs half-day (from $220/person) and full-day ($250/person) charters for a minimum of four people.

ACCOMMODATION AND EATING

Haast gets busy from Christmas to the end of February so book accommodation ahead. There's a small and fairly expensive supermarket for supplies. Opening times for Haast's eating establishments can vary.

Collyer House B&B Nolans Rd, Okuru, off SH6, 13km south of Haast Junction ☎03 750 0022, ⓦcollyerhouse .co.nz. Welcoming luxury accommodation with four modern en suites, all with distant sea views and sizeable cooked breakfasts. Doubles **$250**

Fantail Café Marks Rd, Haast Township ☎03 750 0055. Buzzing little café spread across several cosy rooms with tables outside. Excellent breakfasts (including toasted bagels with olive tapenade and pan-fried mushrooms, sweet donuts with scrambled eggs, and French toast), veggie filo wraps, cute cakes and coffee (dishes $6–17.50). Hours can vary. Daily 8am–4pm.

Haast Beach Holiday Park Jackson Bay Rd, Okuru, 15km south of Haast Junction ☎03 750 0860, ⓦhaast beachholidaypark.co.nz. Simple holiday park close to the beach and the Hapuku Estuary Walk. Tents **$15**, dorms **$27**, cabins **$65**, kitchen cabins **$75**, motel units **$90**

Hard Antler Bar Marks Rd, Haast Township ☎03 750 0034. Locals' favourite, with ample bar meals (mains $20–30) including a hearty venison casserole, and cheap beers poured from antler-topped tap handles. Daily 11am–9pm.

Heritage Park Lodge Marks Rd, Haast Township ☎03 750 0868, ⓦheritageparklodge.co.nz. The pick of places to stay in the township, this well-tended motel offers comfortable studios with pure-wool blankets, some with self-catering facilities. Doubles **$85**

Wilderness Accommodation Haast Township ☎03 750 0029, ⓦwildernessaccommodation.co.nz. Welcoming, great-value spot combining a backpacker hostel with four-shares and a series of motel studio units, all with access to a wilderness-themed common area and kitchen. They also have scooter rental – ideal for trips to Jackson Bay. Dorms **$28**, doubles **$65**, motel units **$140**

The road to Jackson Bay

A modest number of inquisitive tourists make it 50km south of Haast to the fishing village of Jackson Bay. Leaving Haast Junction, the canopies of windswept roadside trees bunch together like cauliflower heads down to and beyond **Haast Beach**, 4km south, where there's a small shop and fuel.

Hapuku Estuary Walk and around

10km from Haast Beach

Opposite the *Haast Beach Holiday Park* (see above), the **Hapuku Estuary Walk** (20min loop) follows a raised boardwalk over a brackish lagoon and through kowhai forest that gleams brilliant yellow in October and November. Sand dunes support rimu and kahikatea forest, and there are occasional views to the **Open Bay Islands**, now a **wildlife sanctuary** and a major breeding colony for fur seals and Fiordland crested penguins. Turn off after crossing Arawhata Bridge and follow the unsealed road for 5km to the new, easy one-hour return walk around **Lake Ellery**.

Jackson Bay

JACKSON BAY, 50km south of Haast on the Haast-Jackson Bay Road, is a former sealing station tucked in the curve of Jackson Head, which protects it from the worst of the westerlies. In 1875 it was chosen as the townsite to rival Greymouth and Hokitika. Assisted migrants – Scandinavians, Germans, Poles, Italians, English and Irish – were expected to carve a living from tiny land allocations, with limited and irregular supplies. Sodden by rain, crops rotted, and people soon left in droves; a few stalwarts stayed, their descendants providing the core of today's residents, who eke out a meagre living from lobster and tuna fishing.

Try the **Wharekai Te Kou Walk** (40min return) across the low isthmus behind Jackson Head to a beach where Fiordland crested penguins may be seen from July to November. The **Smoothwater Track** (3hr return) has great coastal views on the way to the Smoothwater River.

EATING AND DRINKING JACKSON BAY

The Cray Pot There are no facilities in Jackson Bay, except for this rustic diner in an old railway carriage. It doesn't sell crayfish, but it does dish up fantastic fresh-cooked fish (usually blue cod) and chips, seafood chowder and the like (mains $19.50–27.50) and mugs of tea or coffee. It's a great place to get away from the sandflies and gaze at the sea-tossed fishing boats through fake leadlight windows. Mid-Sept–April noon–6.30pm; seasonal openings can vary.

Haast Pass
SH6, east of Haast

From Haast it's nearly 150km over the **Haast Pass** (lower than both Arthur's Pass and Lewis Pass) to Wanaka – a journey from the rain-soaked forests of the West Coast to the parched, rolling grasslands of Central Otago. Ngai Tahu used the pass as a greenstone-trading route and probably introduced it to gold prospector Charles Cameron, the first Pakeha to cross in 1863; he was closely followed by the more influential **Julius Von Haast**, who modestly named it after himself.

The road starts beside the broad **Haast River**, which, as the road climbs, narrows to a series of churning cascades. Numerous short and well-signposted walks, mostly to waterfalls on tributaries, spur off at intervals. The most celebrated are the **Thunder Creek Falls**, the roadside **Fantail Falls**, and the **Blue Pools Walk**, where an aquamarine stream issues from a narrow, icy gorge: swim if you dare. Though there are few specific sights, it is a great area to linger awhile, **camping** in one of the DOC's toilets-and-water sites ($6/person): *Pleasant Flat*, 45km from Haast, or *Cameron Flat* 10km short of Makarora.

Makarora

Comprising a smattering of buildings, the hamlet of **MAKARORA**, midway between Haast and Wanaka, lies on the northern fringe of Mount Aspiring National Park.

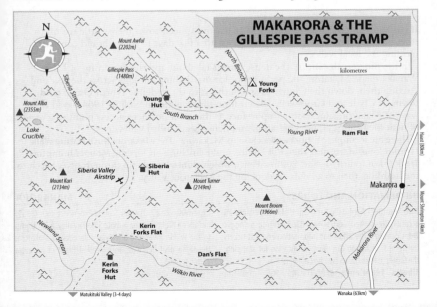

GILLESPIE PASS: THE WILKIN AND YOUNG VALLEYS CIRCUIT

This tramp over the 1490m Gillespie Pass links the upper valley of the **Young River** with that of the **Siberia Stream** and the **Wilkin River**. The scenery is a match for any of the more celebrated valleys further south, but is tramped by a fraction of the folk on the Routeburn or the Greenstone tracks.

The creation of a lake behind a potentially unstable landslip in late 2007 left the Young Valley temporarily **closed to trampers**, but it is now open on the proviso that all trampers must avoid it in the event of heavy rain. The new **Blue-Young Link Track**, an extension of the Blue Pools Track, now provides alternative access to the Young Valley when the river is high. DOC's *Gillespie Pass, Wilkin Valley Tracks* leaflet has all the detail you need for the walk, though the 1:160,000 *Mount Aspiring Parkmap* and the 1:50,000 *Wilkin* **maps** are useful. The route can be divided up into smaller chunks, using Siberia Experience's planes and jetboats (see below), but the full circuit (58km) takes three days.

ACCESS AND ACCOMMODATION

All the **huts** ($15.30; no advance booking) in the Wilkin and Young valleys are equipped with mattresses and heating (but not cooking) stoves; hut **tickets** and Backcountry hut **passes** are available from the DOC office in Makarora (see below). The walk is typically done up the Young Valley and down the Wilkin. **Access** at both ends of the walk is a question of **wading** the broad, braided **Makarora River**, something not advised unless you have river-crossing experience. Someone dies almost every year.

It's a good idea to use the Blue-Young Link Track to access the walk and arrange a **pick-up** by jetboat from Kerin Forks at the far end of the walk, unless you want to take your chances with river crossings or a stand-by backflight out of Siberia Valley.

THE ROUTE

Day 1: Young and Makarora rivers confluence to Young Hut (20km; 6–7hr; 500m ascent) Start from the Blue Pools car park, heading through forest and open country, with bridges crossing the Makarora and Blue rivers and the Ore and Leven streams. The Young Valley is signposted on the left of SH6. Cross the stile and follow orange poles to the confluence of the Young and Makarora rivers. From the confluence to Young Hut, the track traces the true left bank through beech forest to

---

If you're aching for the comforts of Wanaka and Queenstown there's little reason to stop, but casual hikers and keen trampers with a few days to spare should consider tackling the local walks.

In the nineteenth century the dense **forests** all about and the proximity of Lake Wanaka made Makarora the perfect spot for marshalling cut logs across the lake and coaxing them down the Clutha River southeast to the fledgling North Otago **gold towns** of Clyde and Cromwell. The creation of the national park in 1964 paved the way for Makarora's increasing importance as the main northern access point to a region of majestic beauty, alpine vegetation and dense beech-filled valleys.

There are a couple of **short walks** close to Makarora. The **Makarora Bush Nature Walk** (15min loop) starts near the DOC office, and branching off it is the **Mount Shrimpton Track** (5km return; 4–5hr; 900m ascent), which climbs steeply up through silver beech to the bushline, then to a knob overlooking the Makarora Valley.

INFORMATION AND TOURS

MAKARORA

DOC SH6 (Dec–April daily 8am–5pm; May–Nov Mon–Fri occasionally staffed; ☎03 443 8365, ✉mtaspiringgvc @doc.govt.nz). The office has information and hut tickets for tramps, including the main justification for stopping, the Gillespie Pass tramp (see box above).
Siberia Experience ☎0800 345 606, ⍟siberia

experience.co.nz. The 4hr Siberia Experience tour ($355) includes a flight into the remote Siberia Valley, a 3hr tramp to the Wilkin River and a jetboat ride back to Makarora; the same deal but with an extended flight of an extra 25min is $455.

Young Forks, where there is a campsite (free). After the fork, the track follows the South Branch, climbing steeply (100m), before traversing a series of unstable slips to reach Stag Creek. From here it's a steady climb up through forest to the new Young Hut (20 bunks).

Day 2: Young Hut to Siberia Hut (12km; 6–8hr; 700m ascent, 1000m descent) You've another strenuous day ahead, first up to the tree line overlooked by the 2202m Mount Awful, apparently named in wonder rather than horror. Then it's over the Gillespie Pass, a steep and lengthy ascent eventually following snow poles to a saddle; it'll take three hours to reach this fabulous, barren spot with views across the snowcapped northern peaks of the Mount Aspiring National Park. Grassy slopes descend steeply to Gillespie Stream, which is followed to its confluence with the Siberia Stream, from where it's a gentle, undulating hour downstream to Siberia Hut (expected to have been rebuilt by the time you're reading this after the previous hut burnt down; check with DOC for updates). Keen trampers might tag on a side trip to Lake Crucible (4–5hr return) before cantering down to the hut. You can spend two nights at Siberia Hut and do the Lake Crucible side trip on the spare day.

Lake Crucible side trip (13km; 6–7hr return; 500m ascent) From the Siberia Hut, follow the true left bank of the Siberia Stream a short distance until you see Crucible Stream cascading in a deep gash on the far side. Ford Siberia Stream and ascend through the bush on the true right bank of the stream. It is hard going, and route-finding among the alpine meadows higher up can be difficult, but the deep alpine lake tucked under the skirts of Mount Alba and choked with small icebergs is ample reward. Planes fly in and out of the Siberia Valley airstrip, and you can take your chance on "backloading" flights out.

Day 3: Siberia Hut to Kerin Forks (8km; 2–3hr; 100m ascent) Enter the bush at the southern end of Siberia Flats on the true left bank of Siberia Stream and descend away from the stream then zigzag steeply down to the Wilkin River and the Kerin Forks Hut (10 bunks), where many trampers arrange to be met by a jetboat. If it has rained heavily, fording the Makarora lower down will be impossible, so don't forgo the jetboat. The alternative is to walk from Kerin Forks to Makarora (17km; 5–6hr; 100m ascent, 200m descent), following the Wilkin River's true left bank, then crossing the Makarora upstream of the confluence.

12

ACCOMMODATION AND EATING

Boundary Creek SH6. At the head of Lake Wanaka right by the lakeshore, this peaceful campsite, with 40 tent sites, is basic but idyllically situated, with walking trails fanning out around the lake from the campsite. $6

Kidds Bush Meads Rd, 32km north of Wanaka. Tucked away 6km down a side road off SH6 at The Neck, where lakes Wanaka and Hawea almost meet, this basic DOC campsite sits beside Lake Hawea. $6

Makarora Tourist Centre SH6 ☎03 443 8372, ⓦmakarora.co.nz. Makarora's epicentre is this friendly jack-of-all-trades. The shop sells fuel, has limited grocery supplies, and there's a wood-beamed café/bar serving breakfast, sandwiches and buffet lunches (dishes $10.90–18.90), plus basic steak, chicken and veggie evening meals (mains $20–30). There's also a range of good-value accommodation. Camping/person $12, dorms $30, doubles $70, kitchen cabins $85, chalets $125

Central Otago

689 Queenstown

705 Around Queenstown

708 Arrowtown and around

713 Gibbston

715 Glenorchy

718 The Routeburn Track

722 Greenstone and Caples tracks

724 Rees–Dart Track

725 Wanaka and around

736 Along the Clutha River

742 The Maniototo

LAKE WAKATIPU, CECIL PEAK AND WALTER PEAK, QUEENSTOWN

13 Central Otago

Wedged between the sodden beech forests and plunging cliffs of Fiordland, the snowcapped peaks of the Southern Alps, the fertile plains of south Canterbury and the sheep country of Southland lies Central Otago, a region of matchless beauty with cold, glacier-carved lakes, barren hills and clear skies. The hub of "Central", as it is known to locals, is Queenstown, a flawed jewel with a legendary setting looking across Lake Wakatipu to the craggy heights of the Remarkables range. It has become New Zealand's adventure capital, offering the chance to indulge in just about every adrenaline-fuelled activity imaginable. Near neighbour Wanaka is Queenstown's more restrained cousin, draped around the placid waters of its eponymous lake. The whole region is riddled with the detritus of its nineteenth-century gold rushes, particularly around Cromwell and amid the big-sky landscapes of the Maniototo.

Central Otago is shaped by its rivers and lakes. Meltwater and heavy rains course out of the mountains into the 70km lightning bolt of **Lake Wakatipu**, draining east through the Kawarau River, which carves a rapid-strewn path through the Kawarau Gorge. Along the way it picks up the waters of the Shotover River from the goldfields of Skippers.

With a legendary setting looking across Lake Wakatipu to the craggy heights of **The Remarkables** range, **Queenstown** fills many roles. Bungy jumping, jetboating, rafting, skydiving, mountain biking, paragliding and many more activities have been honed into well-packaged, forcefully marketed products. But you don't need to do any of that. Many are happy to relax along the waterfront and dine at the best cafés and restaurants around. The scenery is particularly wonderful, as acknowledged by film-makers who have flocked here over the years to shoot major feature films: several scenes from *The Lion, The Witch and The Wardrobe*, the highest concentration of locations from the *Lord of the Rings* trilogy and, more recently, large sections of *The Hobbit*.

Neighbouring **Arrowtown** wears its gold heritage well. There is something to delay most folk amid quaint streets, intimate restaurants, cool bars, indie cinema, historic Chinese gold settlements and day-long walks to the defunct gold mines around **Macetown**. All this provides a welcome break from Queenstown's high-pitched ambience but perhaps the perfect antidote is the great outdoors. Some of the country's most exalted multi-day tramps start from nearby **Glenorchy**, springboard for the

Gold from dirt p.689
Information on Queenstown activities p.690
Walks around Queenstown p.692
Bungy jumping p.694
Watersports in and around Queenstown pp.696–697
Winter in Queenstown p.700
The Kingston Flyer p.707
Arrowtown's hidden Chinese history p.709
Arrowtown and Macetown walks p.711

Glenorchy activities p.717
Tramping the Routeburn and Greenstone/Caples from The Divide p.722
Winter in Wanaka p.727
Walks around Wanaka p.729
Walks in the Matukituki Valley p.731
Wanaka festivals p.736
Otago Central Rail Trail p.743
Grahame Sydney p.744
Exploring the Old Dunstan Road p.746

OTAGO CENTRAL RAIL TRAIL

Highlights

❶ Nevis Highwire Bungy Test your nerve on the Nevis, at 134m New Zealand's highest bungy, done from a hut suspended high above a canyon. **See p.694**

❷ Shotover River Take a jetboat ride or rafting trip down through an iconic part of the New Zealand adventure landscape. **See p.696**

❸ Ride Queenstown Pootle beside the lake as the sun drops, hurtle through the forest at Queenstown Bike Park or splash out on a wonderful heli-biking trip. **See p.699**

❹ Wineries Over twenty Central Otago wineries offer tastings, particularly of sublime Pinot Noir, in the world's most southerly wine-growing area. **See p.713 & p.738**

❺ The Routeburn Track Lush bush and alpine scenery combine to make this one of New Zealand's best tramps. **See p.718**

❻ Canyoning Get intimate with one of the Matukituki Valley's verdant canyons, jumping, sliding and abseiling – about the most fun you can have in a wetsuit. **See p.732**

❼ Otago Central Rail Trail Absorb the rural pleasures of the Maniototo region on a gentle three-day cycle ride, taking in old tunnels and viaducts. **See p.743**

HIGHLIGHTS ARE MARKED ON THE MAP ON P.686

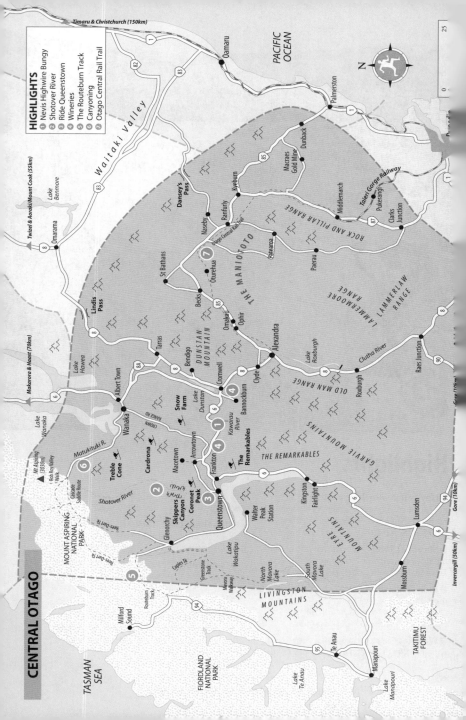

CENTRAL OTAGO

HIGHLIGHTS
1. Nevis Highwire Bungy
2. Shotover River
3. Ride Queenstown
4. Wineries
5. The Routeburn Track
6. Canyoning
7. Otago Central Rail Trail

TASMAN SEA

PACIFIC OCEAN

Timaru & Christchurch (150km)

Twizel & Aoraki/Mount Cook (55km)

Makarora & Haast (70km)

Invercargill (50km)

Gore (100km)

Dunedin

Oamaru

Palmerston

Dunback

Macraes Gold Mine

Kyeburn

Ranfurly

Taieri Gorge Railway

Pukerangi

Middlemarch

Clarks Junction

Paerau

Patearoa

Naseby

Dansey's Pass

St Bathans

Oturehua

Otago Central Rail Trail

Becks

Omakau

Ophir

Alexandra

Lake Roxburgh

Clutha River

Clyde

Bannockburn

Roxburgh

Raes Junction

Lindis Pass

Omarama

Lake Benmore

Waitaki Valley

Waitaki Valley

Lake Hawea

Tarras

Bendigo

Cromwell

Lake Dunstan

DUNSTAN MOUNTAIN

THE MANIOTOTO

ROCK AND PILLAR RANGE

LAMMERLAW RANGE

LAMMERMOORE RANGE

OLD MAN RANGE

GARVIE MOUNTAINS

Kawarau River

Albert Town

Lake Wanaka

Wanaka

Snow Farm

Macetown

Arrowtown

Frankton

The Remarkables

THE REMARKABLES

Treble Cone

Cardrona

Coronet Peak

Queenstown

Skippers Canyon

Shotover River

Glenorchy

Lake Wakatipu

Walter Peak Station

Kingston

Fairlight

EYRE MOUNTAINS

Lumsden

Mossburn

Mt Aspiring (3030m)

Rob Roy Valley Walk

Cascade Saddle Route

Matukituki R.

MOUNT ASPIRING NATIONAL PARK

Rees-Dart Tk

Caples Tk

Greenstone Track

Mavora Walkway

North Mavora Lake

South Mavora Lake

LIVINGSTON MOUNTAINS

Routeburn Track

Milford Sound

FIORDLAND NATIONAL PARK

Te Anau

Manapouri

Lake Te Anau

Lake Manapouri

TAKITIMU FOREST

N

25
0

13

magnificent **Routeburn Track**, the match of any in the country; the green and beautiful **Caples** and **Greenstone** tracks (combined to make a satisfying five-day circuit); and the rugged **Rees–Dart Track**, which opens the challenging Cascade Saddle Route.

Glacially scoured, the three-sided pinnacle of Mount Aspiring, "the Matterhorn of the South", forms the centrepiece of the **Mount Aspiring National Park**. Permanently snowcapped, this alpine high country is linked by the alluring Matukituki Valley to the small resort town of **Wanaka** on the shores of **Lake Wanaka**. The town's laidback atmosphere stands in marked contrast to frenetic Queenstown, though there's no shortage of adventure operators vying to thrill you.

Lake Wanaka and Lake Wakatipu both ultimately feed the Clutha River which threads its way to the coast south of Dunedin passing through land transformed by New Zealand's first gold rushes. Most of the gold has long since gone and the area is largely deserted, but there are numerous interesting relics around the modest centres of **Cromwell**, **Alexandra** and **Roxburgh**. Gold miners fanned out to found tiny towns in the Maniototo: **St Bathans** and **Naseby** are particularly enjoyable places to idle among the boom-time remains.

From June to October the region's focus switches to **skiing**, with Queenstown acting as a base for the downhill resorts of **Coronet Peak** and the **Remarkables**, while Wanaka serves the **Cardrona** and **Treble Cone** fields, as well as the **Snow Farm** Nordic field.

Brief history

Early Maori certainly occupied Central Otago but numbers were small by the time Europeans first came to buy land for grazing in the 1830s. There was increased Pakeha interest in the area after the settlement of Dunedin in 1848, but everything turned around in 1861 when Gabriel Read, an Australian, kicked off New Zealand's greatest **gold rush** by unearthing a few flakes beside the Tuapeka River, south of Lawrence. Within weeks Dunedin had all but emptied and thousands were camping out on the **Tuapeka goldfield** around **Gabriels Gully**. In the winter of 1862 Californian prospectors Horatio Hartley and Christopher Reilly teased their first flakes out of the Clutha River, bagging a 40kg haul in three months. This sparked off an even greater gold rush, this time centred on **Cromwell**, which mushroomed.

Gold in the Shotover

In 1862, Thomas Arthur and Harry Redfern struck lucky at what is now Arthur's Point, on the Shotover River 5km north of Queenstown. Word spread that prospectors were extracting over 10kg a day, and within months thousands were flocking from throughout New Zealand and Australia to work what was soon dubbed "The Richest River in the World".

The mother lode resides under **Mount Aurum**, tributaries of the Shotover carrying the ore down to the goldfields. The river-edge gravels had been all but worked out by 1864, necessitating ever more sophisticated extraction techniques (see box, p.689).

As mining continued in **Skippers Canyon** gold was found in what is now **Arrowtown**, the last of the major gold towns. Within a few years returns had dwindled, and as traders saw profits diminishing, **Chinese miners** were co-opted to pick over the tailings (discarded bits of rock and gravel) left behind by Europeans.

After the gold rush

Though the boom-and-bust cycle was rapid, some form of mining continued for the best part of forty years and the profits fuelled a South Island economy, which dominated New Zealand's exchequer. Dunedin's economy boomed, and the golden bounty funded the majority of the grand civic buildings there.

Eventually many **claims were abandoned** – not for lack of gold, but because of harsh winters, famine, war, a dip in the gold price, lack of sluicing water, or just lack of interest. The miners left behind a landscape littered with abandoned mines,

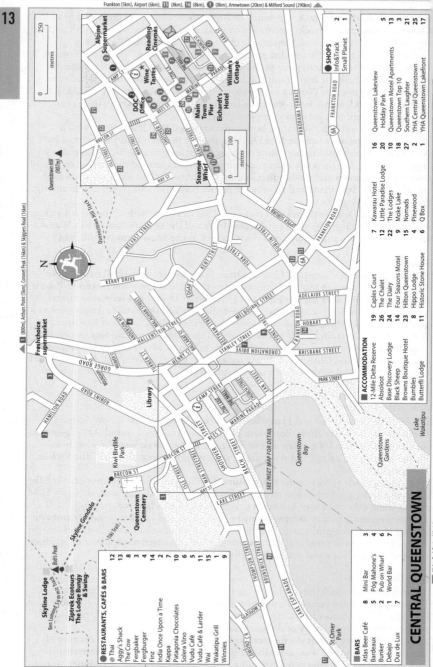

CENTRAL QUEENSTOWN

Frankton (5km), Airport (6km), **15** (8km), **16** (8km), **1** (8km), Arrowtown (20km) & Milford Sound (290km)

1 (800m), Arthur's Point (5km), Coronet Peak (16km) & Skippers Road (16km)

Freethchoice supermarket

Ben Lomond (1748m) Trail

Skyline Lodge
Ziptrek Ecotours
The Lodge Bungy & Swing

Bob's Peak

Skyline Gondola

Kiwi Birdlife Park

Queenstown Cemetery

Library

Lake Wakatipu

Queenstown Bay

Queenstown Gardens

St Omer Park

SEE INSET MAP FOR DETAIL

Walter Peak Station (40min)

16 (9km), **15** (10km), **20** (25km) & Glenorchy (50km)

Queenstown Hill (907m)

Alpine Supermarket
Reading Cinemas
Wine Tastes
DOC Office

William's Cottage
Eichardt's Hotel
Main Town Pier

Steamer Wharf

Panorama Terrace
Frankton Road

● **RESTAURANTS, CAFÉS & BARS**
@ Thai	12
Aggy's Shack	13
The Cow	8
Fergbaker	3
Fergburger	4
Finz	14
India Once Upon a Time	2
Kappa	7
Patagonia Chocolates	10
Solera Vino	6
Vudu Café	5
Vudu Café & Larder	11
Wai	15
Wakatipu Grill	1
Winnies	9

■ **BARS**
Atlas Beer Café	8
Bardeaux	5
Bunker	2
Debajo	1
Dux de Lux	7
Mini Bar	3
Pog Mahone's	4
Pub on Wharf	6
World Bar	7

■ **ACCOMMODATION**
12-Mile Delta Reserve	19
Absoloot	26
Base Discovery Lodge	24
Black Sheep	14
Browns Boutique Hotel	23
Bumbles	8
Butterfli Lodge	11
Caples Court	19
The Chalet	26
The Dairy	24
Four Seasons Motel	14
Hilton Queenstown	23
Hippo Lodge	8
Historic Stone House	11
Kawarau Hotel	7
Little Paradise Lodge	12
The Lodges	22
Moke Lake	9
Nomads	15
Pinewood	4
Q Box	6
Queenstown Lakeview	16
Holiday Park	20
Queenstown Motel Apartments	10
Queenstown Top 10	18
Southern Laughter	27
YHA Central Queenstown	2
YHA Queenstown Lakefront	1

● **SHOPS**
Info&Track	2
Small Planet	1

GOLD FROM DIRT

The classic image of the felt-hatted old-timer panning merrily beside a stream is only part of the story of gold extraction, but it's a true enough depiction of the first couple of years of the Otago gold rush. Initially all a miner needed was a pick and shovel, a pan, and preferably a special wooden box known as a "rocker" for washing the alluvial gravel. As the easily accessible gravel beds were worked out, all manner of ingenious schemes were devised to gain access to fresh pay dirt. The most common technique was to divert the river, and some far-fetched schemes were hatched, especially on the Shotover River: steel sheets were driven into the riverbeds with some success, landslides induced to temporarily dam the flow, and a tunnel was bored through a bluff.

When pickings got thinner miners turned to **sluicing guns** that blasted the auriferous gravel free, ready for processing either by traditional hand-panning or its mechanical equivalent, where "riffle plates" caught the fine gravel and carpet-like matting trapped the fine flakes of gold. Eventually the scale of these operations put individual miners out of business and many pressed on to fresh fields.

To get at otherwise inaccessible gravel stock, larger companies began building **gold dredges**, great clanking behemoths anchored to the riverbanks but floating free on the river. Buckets scooped out the river bottom, then the dredge processed the gravel and spat the "tailings" out of the back to pile up along the riversides.

Otago's alluvial gold starts its life underground embedded in quartz reefs, and when economic returns waned, miners sought the mother lode. **Reef quartz mining** required a considerable investment in machinery and whole towns sprang up to tunnel, hack out the ore and haul it on sledges to the stamper batteries. Here, a series of water-driven (and later steam-powered) hammers would pulverize the rock, which was then passed over copper plates smeared with mercury, and onto gold-catching blankets, before the remains were washed into the berdan – a special kind of cast-iron bowl. Gold was then separated from the mercury, a process subsequently made more efficient by using cyanide.

Although returns are far from spectacular, small-time panners still extract "colour" from the streams all over the province. There's very little appliance of science: instinct counts for much and fancy mining theories not at all. Bigger capital-intensive companies occasionally gauge the area's potential, and as one mining engineer pithily put it, "there's still a shitload of gold out there".

perilous shafts and scattered bits of mysterious-looking machinery. For decades these just rusted elegantly as sheep farming and fruit growing became the mainstay of the economy. Now they have become one of the focal points for the all-important tourist industry.

Queenstown

Queenstown is New Zealand's premier commercialized resort town, superbly set by deep-blue Lake Wakatipu and hemmed in by craggy mountains. Kiwis and visitors complain that the town is too loud, crowded, expensive, big for its boots and the victim of devil-may-care development. There's some truth in this, with the faint screams of adrenaline activity junkies piercing the tranquillity and the base thump of music and shrill whistle of the TSS *Earnslaw* providing the backdrop, but somehow Queenstown retains the air of a small-town idyll. Furthermore, it offers a great selection of restaurants, some of the flashiest accommodation in the country, and nightlife that will either suck you in or drive you away.

Best taken in small doses, Queenstown is well worth using either as a base from which to plan lengthy forays into the surrounding countryside, or as a venue for sampling all manner of adventure activities. The most prominent of these is undoubtedly **bungy jumping** at three of the world's most gloriously scenic bungy sites,

13

INFORMATION ON QUEENSTOWN ACTIVITIES

Queenstown is a fabulous place just to hang out, soaking in the scenery and eating well, but to fully appreciate the place you need to get active. And there can be few places in the world with such an amazing choice of things to do. You'll find information in boxes for walks around Queenstown (p.692), bungy jumping (p.694), winter activities (p.700) and water-based pursuits (p.696). All the other thrills Queenstown offers – on land and in the air – are listed from p.696.

With so much on offer, it's tempting to be frugal elsewhere and blow the budget in Queenstown, but in reality most activities here are more **expensive** than in other parts of the country. To get the most action for the least money, check out one of the numerous **combination deals** knitting together two to five adventure trips. For example, the Awesome Foursome ($624) combines the 134m Nevis Bungy, the Shotover Jet, a helicopter flight and rafting the Shotover. **Prices** don't generally vary much, but check for backpacker discounts and deals. Some operators may offer a small discount for booking directly with them rather than through the numerous booking agents (who all take their cut).

---

visited either in isolation or as part of a package, perhaps including **whitewater rafting** and **jetboating** on the Shotover River.

Visitors after a more sedate time plump for easy **walks** around lakeshore gardens and to hillside viewpoints; **lake cruises** on the elegant TSS *Earnslaw*, the last of the lake steamers; a **gondola ride** to Bob's Peak, which commands magnificent vistas from a cable car over Queenstown and the Remarkables range; and **wine tours** around some of the world's most southerly vineyards (see p.699). **Milford Sound** can be visited from Queenstown (see p.769).

Frantic summers are nothing in comparison to winter, when Kiwi and international skiers descend on **Coronet Peak** and **the Remarkables**, two fine ski-fields within half an hour of Queenstown, particularly during the annual **Queenstown Winter Festival**, late June and early July.

The lakefront

Beside Marine Parade

On a warm day there's nothing better than chilling out by the lakeside. Every fine afternoon the grassy reserve beside Marine Parade is alive with people sunbathing, slack-lining, eating fish and chips with a beer and maybe even taking a chilly dip, though the summer peak water temperature around 11°C deters most. Watch the afternoon parasailers then stick around as the sun sets over the mountains and the *Earnslaw* steams towards Walter Peak for the last time that day.

Marine Parade continues east to **Queenstown Gardens**, an attractive parkland retreat that covers the peninsula separating Queenstown Bay from the rest of Lake Wakatipu.

Eichardt's Hotel

2 Marine Parade

Central Queenstown has relatively little to show for its gold-rush past, though the waterfront **Eichardt's Hotel** was Queenstown's original hotel catering to gold prospectors, parts of it dating back to 1871. Until the mid 1990s you could still prop up the rough bar here over a few beers, but it is a now a super-expensive boutique hotel. Opposite is a statue of Queenstown founder, William Rees, with a ram.

Just along the street, **Williams Cottage** is the oldest house in Queenstown, built in 1864 by boatman John Williams. It retains many original features and now operates as a shop and café.

JETBOATING ON THE SHOTOVER RIVER (P.696) >

13

Wine Tastes

14 Beach St · Daily 10.30am–10pm · ☎ 03 409 2226, ⓦ winetastes.co.nz

If you don't have time to head out to the wineries in Gibbston (see p.713) or Bannockburn (see p.738), call in at **Wine Tastes**, where over eighty wines are dished out by sophisticated vending machines. Simply obtain a charge card or run a tab, try what you fancy in sample (mostly $2–5), half-glass ($5–18) or full-glass quantities ($10–35), then hang out on the leather chairs, perhaps while snacking on a cheeseboard ($28–34).

Queenstown Cemetery

North of town, along Brecon St

As you make your way towards Bob's Peak, you'll pass Queenstown's **cemetery** – the final resting place of Queenstown pioneers Nicholas von Tunzelmann (who opened up the first pastoral lease in the area), hotelier Albert Eichardt and Henry Homer, discoverer of the Homer Saddle on the Milford Road.

Kiwi Birdlife Park

Brecon St, at the base of Bob's Peak · Daily: Nov–Feb 9am–6pm; March–Oct 9am–5pm; conservation show daily 11am & 3pm; kiwi feeding 10am, noon, 1.30pm & 4.30pm · $38 including audio tour, valid all day; combo with Skyline gondola $59 · ☎ 03 442 8059, ⓦ kiwibird.co.nz

The expanse of ponds, lawns, native bush and aviaries at the **Kiwi Birdlife Park** houses some of New Zealand's rarest birds. Though more zoo than wildlife park, it does a good job of presenting morepork, kea, kereru (native pigeons), kakariki (native parakeets) and black stilt, the latter one of the world's most endangered bird species (see p.580 &

WALKS AROUND QUEENSTOWN

When hard-sell adventure activities in Queenstown get a bit oppressive, a few hours away can be wonderfully therapeutic. The majority of the walks outlined below – listed in ascending order of difficulty – are well covered by DOC's *Wakatipu Walks* brochure (downloadable from ⓦ doc.govt.nz). Serious multi-day tramps in the region are centred on Wanaka (see p.730) and Glenorchy (see p.715).

One Mile Creek Walkway (50m ascent; 6km return; 1hr 30min). Fairly easy walk heading through a gully filled with beech forest before following a 1924 pipeline from Queenstown's first hydroelectric scheme. The route starts on the lakefront by the Fernhill roundabout and offers an opportunity to acquaint yourself with fuchsia, lancewood and native birds – principally fantails, bellbirds and tui.

Queenstown Hill Walk (500m ascent; 5km return; 2–3hr). Starting from the top of Belfast Street, this is a fairly steep climb through mostly exotic trees to panoramic views from the 907m Queenstown Hill.

Ben Lomond Summit Track (1400m ascent; 11km return; 6–8hr). A full-day tramp scaling Ben Lomond, one of the highest mountains in the region (1748m) and consequently subject to inclement

weather, especially in winter when the track can be snow-covered. Start by the One Mile Creek Walk or use the Skyline Gondola and walk up past the paragliding launch site to join the track, which climbs through alpine tussock to reveal expansive views. Gentler slopes approach Ben Lomond Saddle, from where it's a steep final haul to the summit.

Ben Lomond–Moonlight Track (1400m ascent; 16km one-way; 8–10hr). A demanding, difficult-to-follow route (especially in snow) combining the ascent to Ben Lomond Saddle with a poled sub-alpine route to the site of the former gold town of Sefferstown and the eastern section of the Moonlight Track to Arthur's Point. Organize someone to pick you up at Arthur's Point or endure a 5km slog back to Queenstown.

box, pp.810–811), alongside the products of captive-breeding programmes for the North Island brown kiwi. Time your visit to coincide with the thirty-minute **Conservation Show**, when you get up close and personal with kereru, kea and tuatara, or the fifteen-minute kiwi feeding.

Bob's Peak

The Skyline Gondola and the Tiki Trail are both accessed from the end of Brecon St • Gondola: daily 9am–9.30pm • $25 return • ☎ 03 441 0101, ⓦ skyline.co.nz

For easy access to superb views of Queenstown, Lake Wakatipu, the Remarkables and Cecil and Walter peaks, head up to **Bob's Peak** whose conifer-clad slopes rise immediately behind the town. The sedate **Skyline Gondola** whisks you up 450m, depositing you at the Skyline Complex, base for a number of activities. In addition to those covered below there's fantastic mountain biking in **Queenstown Bike Park** (see box, p.699).

Activities based at Bob's Peak don't include the gondola ride in their prices. If you'd rather save money and get some exercise, follow the steep **Tiki Trail** (1hr; 450m ascent) up through the trees.

If all this kick-starts your appetite the complex has a café and a buffet-style "taste of New Zealand" restaurant (lunch $39, dinner $59, both cheaper if bought with the gondola ride).

Tandem paragliding

G Force Paragliding • Daily 9am–5pm or later • $199; at 9am $179, both excluding gondola ride • ☎ 0800 759 688, ⓦ nzgforce.com

Most fine days, the sky above Queenstown is dotted with paragliders, sometimes up to a dozen of them wheeling gracefully back to earth from their launch pad on Bob's Peak. Call in advance if you want to fly at a particular time, but otherwise just get yourself to the top station of the gondola (extra charge) and wait your turn – like a taxi rank. How many acrobatic manoeuvres are executed during the ten to fifteen minutes you're airborne is largely down to you, your jump guide and the conditions. If you don't see anyone in the air during the main operating times, don't bother with the gondola ride, as the weather's probably being uncooperative.

Skyline Luge

Daily 9am–dusk • Gondola plus: 1 ride $33; 2 rides $38; 5 rides $48; gondola price included

Excellent fun can be had following this 800m-long twisting concrete track on a wheeled plastic buggy with a primitive braking system. Take it easy on your first run which takes you about a quarter of the way down the hill. A chairlift whips you back to the top where you can let rip on subsequent runs once you've got the hang of it. Helmets are provided.

The Ledge Bungy and Ledge Swing

Summer generally 1–7pm; winter 4–9pm • Ledge Bungy $180; Ledge Swing $150 • ☎ 0800 286 495, ⓦ bungy.co.nz

Launching yourself off a 47m platform near the top of the Skyline Gondola feels like you are diving out over Queenstown. Unlike at other sites, you're fitted with a body harness allowing you to do a running jump, and if they aren't too busy you may be able to jump with all manner of "toys" (surfboards, bikes and the like) to add that extra dimension. There are also winter night jumps and you get a free T-shirt. Follow the Tiki Trail to the bungy site or catch the Skyline Gondola.

The Ledee Swine is the shortest of Queenstown's swings at 47m, but handily sited in a spectacular setting high above the town. Photos (downloadable from the web) are included in the price.

13

BUNGY JUMPING

Even visitors who had no intention of parting with a large wad of cash to dangle on the end of a thick strand of latex find themselves bungy jumping in Queenstown. A combination of peer pressure, magnificent scenery and zealous promotion gets to most people and, let's face it, historic bridges high above remote rivers beat a crane over a supermarket car park any day. The sport's commercial originator **AJ Hackett**, at the corner of Camp and Shotover streets (☎ 0800 286 495, ⊛ bungy.co.nz), runs all three Queenstown-area bungy jumps: the original 43m Kawarau (see p.714); the 47m Ledge (see p.693) and the mighty Nevis. There are several bungy and swing combos (all three bungy jumps for $465, for example). If you want a record of your fifteen minutes of hair-raising fame you can pay to download photos or a film from the company's website (some free, others $15–20).

Nevis Highwire (134m; several Queenstown departures daily 8.40am–2.40pm). Some say that with bungy jumping it is only the first metre that counts, but size does matter and the Nevis is New Zealand's highest, with eight seconds of freefall. Jumpers launch from a partly glass-bottomed gondola strung way out over the Nevis River, a tributary of the Kawarau 32km east of Queenstown. Access is by 4WD through private property so spectators have to fork out $50, though this does give you a ride out to the launch gondola and a wonderful view. Free T-shirt but jump photos are extra. $260.

Ziptrek Ecotours

2hr Moa tour several times daily; 3hr Kea tour several times daily • Moa tour $129; Kea tour $179 • ☎ 0800 947 8735, ⊛ ziptrek.co.nz

One way to get down from Bob's Peak is with **Ziptrek Ecotours**, a slightly odd synthesis of soft adventure – a series of ziplines (flying foxes) through the Douglas firs – combined with instruction on ecological awareness. If you're already a convert to the church of sustainability then it can all seem a bit unnecessary, and if you're not then it is plain preachy. Still, there's no doubting the eco-credentials of the company, and zipping through the trees and learning to flip upside down can be fun.

The **Moa** uses the first four lines (three of 100m and one of 300m) and finishes a short walk from the gondola top terminal. The **Kea** adds two much longer and steeper ziplines and finishes near the bottom terminal of the gondola. Wear closed shoes, and even in the middle of summer you should take a jacket.

TSS Earnslaw

Steamer Wharf • late June–late May mostly from 10am–6pm; 3–6 1hr 30min sailings daily • Cruise-only $52 • ☎ 0800 656 501, ⊛ realjourneys.co.nz

The coal-fired **TSS Earnslaw**, the last of the lake steamers, is one of Queenstown's most enduring images. Wherever you are, the encircling mountains echo the shrill sound of the steam whistle as the beautifully restored relic slogs manfully out from Steamer Wharf.

Launched in 1912 (with centenary celebrations in October 2012), the 51m-long craft was the largest and most stately steamer to ply the lake. Burnished brass and polished wood predominate even around the gleaming steam engine, which is open for inspection. Crowds usually cluster around the piano at the back of the boat for a surprisingly popular music-hall singsong that can make the return journey a delight (or seem interminable, depending on your persuasion).

Walter Peak High Country Farm

Farm tour 2–3 daily; 3hr 30min; $77 including cruise • **Farm tour and BBQ lunch** 1–2 daily 3hr 30min; $98 including cruise • **Evening dining** 2–3 daily; 3hr 30min; cruise and dinner $98; cruise and buffet $118 • **Horse trekking** 3 daily; 3hr 30min; $113 including cruise • **Guided cycling** daily; 7hr 30min; $205 • **Independent cycling** daily; $72

Earnslaw cruises all head across the lake to **Walter Peak High Country Farm**, a tourist enclave nestling in the southwestern crook of Lake Wakatipu. The Walter Peak homestead, a convincing replica of the original which burnt down in 1977, is beautifully sited among lawns that sweep down to the lakeshore, and plays host to a farm tour and various activities, all of which can be added to your cruise.

Most people take the **farm tour** – an entertaining if sanitized vignette of farm life, with demonstrations of dog handling and sheepshearing. This comes with tea and scones on the lawn, or you can upgrade to a **BBQ lunch**. The boat trip itself can be combined with forty minutes of **horse trekking** plus tea and scones, or gentle **guided cycling** along the gravel road to Mavora Lakes and past old musterers' huts. There's a guide and sag wagon in attendance allowing you to cycle as much or as little as you wish (15–35km), and lunch and afternoon tea included. **Independent cycling** gives you free rein along the Von River and to Mavora Lakes with a map and food/drink voucher included. Alternatively you can just take the cruise and pay $5 each way for your bike. It is even possible to cycle to Fiordland joining SH94 at Burwood, 27km east of Te Anau. Lastly there are **evening dining** cruises with the choice of a roast dinner or a carvery buffet.

ARRIVAL AND DEPARTURE   QUEENSTOWN

By plane Queenstown's airport (ⓦqueenstownairport .co.nz) is at Frankton, 7km northeast of the city. Most flights are met by the door-to-door Super Shuttle ($16 for one person; $21 for two). You can also get into town using the Connectabus (see below). Blue Bubble Taxis (ⓣ03 450 3000) charge around $35 for the ride into town. Most major car rental companies have offices at the airport.

Destinations Auckland (5–6 daily; 1hr 50min); Christchurch (6 daily; 1hr); Wellington (1 daily; 1hr 45min).

By bus Buses arrive close to the junction of Camp and Shotover sts from where it's less than 100m to the i-SITE and barely a 15min walk to most hotels and hostels.

Bus services Atomic runs to Christchurch, Dunedin and up the coast to Greymouth; InterCity/Newmans operates the most extensive services to all major destinations; Southern Link (ⓣ0508 458 835, ⓦsouthernlinkbus.co.nz) runs to Christchurch; Topline Tours (ⓣ03 249 8059, ⓦtoplinetours

.co.nz) run to Te Anau in summer; and both Wanaka Connexions (ⓣ03 443 9120, ⓦalpinecoachlines.co.nz) and Connect Wanaka (ⓣ0800 405 066, ⓦconnectabus .com) go to Wanaka. The latter travels over the spectacular Crown Range. Trampers are well served by: Tracknet (ⓣ03 249 7777, ⓦtracknet.net) who run fairly frequently to Te Anau, Milford Sound and the Milford Track, the Routeburn Track and Invercargill; and Info&Track (ⓣ0800 462 248, ⓦinfotrack.co.nz) who serve Glenorchy, the Rees–Dart, Greenstone/Caples and Routeburn tracks.

Destinations Alexandra (4 daily; 1hr 30min); Aoraki/Mount Cook (1 daily; 4–5hr); Arrowtown (13 daily; 40min); Christchurch (5 daily; 7–11hr); Cromwell (8 daily; 1hr); Dunedin (4 daily; 4–5hr); Franz Josef Glacier (2 daily; 7–8hr); Glenorchy (2–5 daily; 1hr); Greymouth (1 daily; 10hr); Invercargill (1 daily; 3hr); Te Anau (3 daily; 2hr 15min); Tekapo (5 daily; 3–4hr); Wanaka (10 daily; 1hr 30min).

GETTING AROUND

Everywhere you are likely to want to go in central Queenstown can be reached **on foot**. Most activities take place out of town but operators run courtesy buses to the sites, usually picking up centrally or from accommodation en route.

By bus Connectabus (ⓣ03 441 4471, ⓦconnectabus.com) operates limited services from O'Connells Mall on Camp St. The most useful service goes from Queenstown to Frankton (every 15min; 10min) and on to the airport (5min). From Frankton there's a service to Arrowtown (12 daily; 15min), and a bus runs from Queenstown to Arthur's Point (every 30–60min; 15min). One-way fares from Queenstown are: airport ($6), Arrowtown ($8), and an all-day-pass ($17) and seven-day pass ($40) can be bought on board.

By car Drivers will have no problem negotiating

Queenstown's streets. Parking can be tight in the centre of town, though you'll usually find a free all-day spot a few streets away. Numerous car rental companies around town and at the airport offer good deals: look for advertised rates.

By taxi There are taxi ranks on Camp St, at the top end of the Mall, and on Shotover St. Alternatively, book with Blue Bubble Taxis (ⓣ03 450 3000).

By bike One of the best ways to explore the area is by bike. The massive range of opportunities is listed on p.699.

INFORMATION

i-SITE Corner of Camp and Shotover sts (daily: Dec–March 8am–7pm; April–Nov 8am–6.30pm; ⓣ03 442 4100, ⓦqueenstowninformation.co.nz). There are numerous visitor centre-cum-booking offices along Shotover St, all

with products to push, but only the i-SITE offers impartial advice and bookings for just about everything.

DOC On the first floor of the Outside Sports shop, 36 Shotover St (Oct–April daily 8.30am–6pm; May–Sept daily

13

WATERSPORTS IN AND AROUND QUEENSTOWN

Some of the most thrilling activities around Queenstown take place on or in the water – sometimes a bit of both. You'll almost certainly get splashed during 360-degree spins when **jetboating** and punching through big waves **whitewater rafting**. You're almost always in the water when **river surfing**, **sledging** and **canyoning**, and only **family rafting** gives you much chance of a dry run.

JETBOATING

There are strong arguments for spending your jetboating dollar on better-value wilderness trips elsewhere – the Wilkin River Jet, Waiatoto River Safaris and trips down the Wairaurahiri River spring to mind – but Queenstown does offer the scintillating Shotover Jet and the thrilling, scenic and historic Skippers Canyon Jet.

Shotover Jet Corner of Camp and Shotover sts ☎ 0800 746 868, ⊛ shotoverjet.com. Slick, touristy and pricey but the thrills come thick and fast. Courtesy buses take you out to Arthur's Point, 5km north of Queenstown, where super-powerful jetboats thrust downstream along the Shotover Canyon. Perilously close shaves with rocks and canyon walls plus several 360-degree turns and periodic dousings guarantee that a twenty-minute trip is enough for most (daily 8.30am–5pm; $119).

Skippers Canyon Jet ☎ 0800 226 966, ⊛ skippers canyonjet.com. A great way to combine exploring the Skippers Road (see p.707) with jetboating among the ancient gold workings of the upper Shotover River. Trips (3 daily; 3hr 30min with 30min jetboating) cost $129 and there are various combos, perhaps the most logical being with a rafting trip down the Shotover River ($309), which doesn't save you much money but helps pack in the thrills.

WHITEWATER RAFTING

Queenstown's adventure stalwart is whitewater rafting, which takes place locally on the **Kawerau River** and the **Shotover River**, and infrequently in the remote **Landsborough River**. Although there appear to be three whitewater rafting companies in town, each with assorted packages and combo deals, all rafts are in fact operated by Queenstown Rafting, 35 Shotover St (☎ 0800 723 8464, ⊛ rafting.co.nz).

Kawarau River (Grade II–III; 4hr with around 1hr on the water). With its large volume, this is the more reliable of the two rivers. The 7km "Dog Leg" section negotiates four rapids (exciting but not truly frightening), ending with the potentially nasty Chinese Dog Leg, said to be the longest commercially rafted rapid in New Zealand. Being lake-fed, its flow is relatively steady, though it peaks in spring and drops substantially towards the end of summer. $195; heli-rafting $279.

Shotover River (Grade III–IV; 5hr with almost 2hr on the water). More demanding than the Kawarau, with rapids revelling in names such as The Squeeze, The Anvil and The Toilet. They reach their apotheosis in the Mother-in-Law rapid, usually bypassed at low water by

diverting through the 170m Oxenbridge Tunnel (see p.707). The 14km rafted section flows straight out of the mountains and its level fluctuates considerably. In October and November, snowmelt ensures good flows and a bumpy ride; by late summer low flows can make it a bit tame for hardened rafters, though it is still scenic and fun for first-timers. In winter the lack of sunlight reaching the depths of the canyon makes it too cold for most people, though you can elect to do a much shorter trip by accessing the rapids by helicopter. $195; heli-rafting $279.

Landsborough River (Grade III; mid-Nov to April Friday departures; 3 days). Fly-in wilderness trip ($1495) with camping beside the river – it's more about the whole experience than the whitewater.

8.30am–5.30pm; ☎ 03 442 7935, ✉ queenstownvc@doc .govt.nz). The place to go for all tramping, Great Walks and National Park information.
Tourist publications Seek out the free *iTAG* guide

(⊛ itag.co.nz) with all the latest trip prices, and the *Mountain Scene* newspaper for an insight into what's currently making Queenstown tick.

TOURS AND ACTIVITIES

Queenstown is packed with things to do, with everything from walking (see box, p.692) to bungy jumping (see box, p.694) plus some stupendous water-borne activities (see box, pp.696–697) and winter sports (see box, p.700). The rest

FAMILY RAFTING

Whitewater rafting is usually limited to those aged 13 and older, but all ages can manage the gentler (Grade I–II) stretches.

Family Adventures ☎ 0800 472 384, ⊛ family adventures.co.nz. A dramatic drive into Skippers Canyon is followed by an hour and a half floating in rafts down the upper Shotover River past gold mining relics. You don't even need to paddle. 5hr total; adults $179; kids $120.

KAYAKING

Kayak Adventures Queenstown ☎ 027 455 5993, ⊛ kayakadventuresqueenstown.com. Spend time paddling on Lake Wakatipu either renting a kayak ($35/hr; $45/3hr) or on a guided half-day trip ($129) exploring parts of the lake only accessible from the water.

RIVER SURFING AND WHITEWATER SLEDGING

While rafters bob around high on their inflatable perches, river surfers and sledgers get right in the thick of it in a wetsuit, a helmet and fins, being encouraged to view their independence and freedom of movement as virtues rather than hazards. What look like ripples to rafters become huge waves: things work best if you are both confident in water and a decent swimmer. There isn't a lot to choose between **river surfing** (using a foam boogie board and surfing as many of the rapids' standing waves as possible), and **whitewater sledging** (where you snuggle your arms and upper body into a plastic "sledge", gaining manoeuvrability in return for more difficulty surfing waves.

Frogz Whitewater Sledging ☎ 0800 437 649, ⊛ frogz.co.nz. Whitewater sledging making two runs down the Roaring Meg section of the Kawarau with Queenstown and Wanaka pick-ups. Two trips daily; 5hr with 2hr on the water; $175.

Mad Dog River Boarding 37 Shotover St ☎ 0508 623 364, ⊛ riverboarding.co.nz. Usually the cheapest of the river boarding companies, running once down the Roaring Meg section and adding in some big cliff jumps and mucking around being towed behind a jetski. Nov–April 1–2 daily; $169.

Serious Fun River Surfing ☎ 0800 737 468, ⊛ riversurfing.co.nz. River levels determine whether you run the Dog Leg or two runs down the Roaring Meg section of the Kawarau River. Either way, the 4hr trips give around 2hr on the water. Nov–April 1–2 daily; $175.

CANYONING

Fans of river surfing and whitewater sledging will love **canyoning**, in which small groups are led down narrow canyons to walk in streams, swim across pools, slide down rocks and jump off cliffs, protected only by a wetsuit, helmet and climbing harness.

Canyoning.co.nz ☎ 03 441 3003, ⊛ canyoning.co .nz. Queenstown's only canyoning company runs trips down three canyons in the area, the easiest of which is the Queenstown Canyon option (Oct–April 2 daily; 3hr, 2hr in the canyon; $185) involving morning and afternoon trips to Twelve Mile Delta just out of town. For a longer day out requiring a bit more commitment, go for the Routeburn Canyon trip (Oct–April 1 daily; 7hr with up to 3hr in the canyon; $240; $210 from Glenorchy) which involves walking the first twenty minutes of the Routeburn Track then launching yourself into a water-sculpted, narrow canyon full of jumps and slides. It is then a big leap up to the Earnslaw Heli-Canyon trip (Oct–April on demand; full day with 5–6hr in the canyon; heli-access from Queenstown $1500; walk-in $800) with groups of two to four people doing stacks of serious abseils in a remote location.

of the (by no means inferior) tours and activities are covered below, divided into airborne and land-based subsections and listed alphabetically.

AIRBORNE TOURS AND ACTIVITIES

SWINGING

Swinging presents an alternative to bungy jumping but still includes that stomach-in-your-mouth freefall sensation, with the bonus of a massive swoop through the air on the end of a rope.

Canyon Swing ☎ 0800 279 464, ⊛ canyonswing.co.nz. With a total of 60m fall in a huge sweeping arc over the Shotover River and the chance to impress the rafters below, this is a winner. You launch yourself forwards, backwards,

seated in a chair or even with a bin over your head. 109m; 7–10 departures daily; allow 2hr; $199, second swing $39.
Nevis Swing ☎ 0800 286 495, ⊛ bungy.co.nz. Adjacent to the Nevis bungy is the world's highest swing, a massive thrill, though the launch options are way more limited. 120m; 2 daily; allow 4hr; $180; $160/person in tandem.

PARAGLIDING, HANG-GLIDING AND PARASAILING
A fine day with a little breeze is all it needs to fill the skies above Queenstown with tandem paragliders descending from Bob's Peak (see p.693). You get longer flights (paragliding and hang-gliding) from Coronet Peak, 10km northeast of town 700m down to the Flight Park on Malaghans Road, and there are less scary parasailing trips on Lake Wakatipu.
Coronet Peak Tandems ☎ 0800 467 325, ⊛ tandemparagliding.com. Fly with a four-time New Zealand champion and his crew ($185).
Extreme Air ☎ 0800 727 245, ⊛ extremeair.co.nz. If pretending to be a bird becomes addictive, learn how to paraglide or hang-glide properly. Day courses from $300.
Skytrek ☎ 0800 759 873, ⊛ skytrek.co.nz. There's more of a birdlike quality to hang-gliding with progressively steeper turns as you soar ($220).
Paraflights Town Pier ☎ 0800 225 520, ⊛ paraflights .co.nz. Great views of Queenstown and the surrounding mountains from 200m above Lake Wakatipu as you and your parachute are towed behind a boat and winched out on a rope. After 10min admiring the scenery, you're winched back in again, still dry. Solo $139, tandem $109 each, triple $89 each.

SKYDIVING AND AEROBATICS
NZone 35 Shotover St ☎ 0800 376 796, ⊛ nzone.biz. Queenstown is an expensive place to go tandem skydiving, but the fabulous views over Lake Wakatipu and the jumps site at the foot of the Remarkables do compensate considerably. Jumps from 12,000ft (45 seconds freefall; $329) and 15,000ft (65 seconds; $429).
Aerostunts ☎ 0800 788 687, ⊛ aerostunts.co.nz. Feel the G-force on a 15min spin (literally) in a Pitt Special biplane, with all manner of loop the loops ($310).

SCENIC FLIGHTS AND BALLOONING
Numerous companies offer scenic flights, either fixed-wing or in a helicopter. Adventure combos often link the activities with a chopper flight, and both modes are used to reach Milford Sound. If neither of these satisfies consider a stand-alone flight. For something far more sedate, opt for early morning ballooning.
Alpine Choppers ☎ 0800 801 3019, ⊛ alpinechoppers .co.nz. Scenic flights with a landing at the top of the Remarkables (20min; $200), or Milford Sound (1.5–2hr 20min; $725).

Sunrise Balloons ☎ 0800 468 247, ⊛ ballooningnz .com. Gorgeous daybreak flights climbing as high as 2000m to gawp at the mountain scenery (on a clear day you can see Aoraki/Mount Cook) before landing for a champagne breakfast (3hr including around 1hr flight time; $445).

LAND-BASED TOURS AND ACTIVITIES
LORD OF THE RINGS TOURS
Queenstown and the surrounding area boast the country's highest concentration of *Lord of the Rings* film locations – some instantly recognizable, others so digitally manipulated you'll really need to stand there with a still from the film to work out just what was and wasn't used. The memory of the trilogy still supports an entire tour industry that will almost certainly get a fillip when *The Hobbit* movies come out at the end of 2012 and 2013. Just about anyone who runs adventure trips into the countryside will tag on "as seen in The Lord of the Rings" or "venturing into Middle-Earth" in their promotional material, but if you really want to stand where Frodo stood you need to join a specialist tour with one of the operators listed below.
Dart River Jet Safaris ☎ 0800 327 853, ⊛ dartriver .co.nz. Glenorchy-based jetboat trips with a significant *LOTR* component (see box, p.717).
Glenorchy Air ☎ 03 442 2207, ⊛ trilogytrail.com. The main company who flew *LOTR* cast and crew offers a One Ring Trilogytrail (3hr 30min; $148), comprising a minibus tour of sites around Queenstown; a Two Ring Trilogytrail (2–3hr; $370) flying past locations; and a Three Ring Trilogytrail (7hr including 2hr 30min of flying; $850), with landings at three locations.
Heliworks ☎ 03 441 4011, ⊛ heliworks.co.nz. These folk did the chopper flying for the cast and now run a wide range of *LOTR* scenic flights, starting at $450 for 45 minutes, including one landing.
Info&Track 37 Shotover St ☎ 03 442 9708, ⊛ infotrack .co.nz. Their budget 4WD Paradise Safari (4hr 30min; $135) includes Maori legends and gold-mining history as they uncover parts of Lothlórien, Isengard and so forth.
OffRoad Adventures ☎ 0800 633 762, ⊛ offroad4x4 .co.nz. A good range of 4WD scenic tours, many visiting *LOTR* locations and often undercutting the opposition.
Nomad Safaris ☎ 0800 688 222, ⊛ nomadsafaris .co.nz. Major 4WD operator offering several *LOTR* trips under their Safaris of the Scenes banner, with frequent stops to envisage *LOTR* scenes being shot. Tour either the Wakatipu Basin around Queenstown (4hr; $165) or Glenorchy (4hr; $165) with fewer but arguably more spectacular sites. The drivers, who were often involved as extras, offer good background.
Southern Lakes Sightseeing ☎ 03 338 0982, ⊛ lord oftheringstours.co.nz. Wanaka and Queenstown pick-ups are available for three *LOTR* tours, including helicopter

options and the excellent Trails Of Middle Earth (full-day; $299), on which you get to visit twenty locations and pose for photos with swords and other props.

OFF-ROAD AND 4WD TOURS

Either ride yourself across barren Central Otago uplands, or let someone else take the strain on informative tours often visiting *LOTR* locations.

Nomad Safaris ☎ 0800 688 222, ⓦ nomadsafaris .co.nz. Easily the biggest 4WD tour operator, Nomad run Land Rovers on several *LOTR*-oriented trips (see opposite), trips into Macetown (see p.710) and trips into Skippers Canyon (see p.707). They'll also let you get behind the wheel of a Land Rover for some real off-roading ($265; passengers $165) and drive a quad bike (3hr 30min; 1hr riding; $245) with everyone riding at the same pace.

Off Road Adventures 61a Shotover St ☎ 0800 633 7623, ⓦ offroad.co.nz. Not just pootling along in a line of quad bikes, this is serious off-road fun on a variety of terrains. Packages range from straightforward, family-oriented quad bike trips (3hr; 1hr riding; $189) to the tougher Adventure Tour (3hr; 1hr 30min riding; $249), taking motorbikes on steep trails on a 15,000-acre high-country station.

Skippers Canyon Jet ☎ 0800 226 966, ⓦ skippers canyonjet.com. Their Land Tour is the best way to fully experience Skippers, with guides whose family have lived here since the gold era. You'll get to see the recently expanded Winky's Museum of gold era relics, see a sluicing gun in operation and try a little panning (4hr 30min; $149).

WINE TOURS

Appellation Central Wine Tours ☎ 03 442 0246, ⓦ appellationcentral.co.nz. To really learn about the area's wines and winemakers, join these informative and fun small-group tours calling at wineries in Gibbston and around Bannockburn and Cromwell. Their afternoon Boutique Wine Tour (noon–5pm; $175) includes lunch at one of the four wineries, but enthusiasts will want to go for the more leisurely, full-day Gourmet Wine Tour (9.30am–4.30pm; $215) taking in five vineyards, a mid-morning cheese tasting, lunch at one of the wineries plus the Gibbston Valley cave tour (see p.714). They pick up from Queenstown and Arrowtown.

MOUNTAIN BIKING

Queenstown is fast becoming a major cycling destination. There have always been great rides here, but with the opening up of gondola access to downhilling in the Queenstown Bike Park (see below), the sterling track-building efforts of the Queenstown Mountain Bike Club (ⓦ queenstownmtb.co.nz), and the imminent completion of the Queenstown Trail, part of the New Zealand Cycle Trail (ⓦ wakatiputrails.co.nz) everything is coming together. Whether you're after a gentle lakeside ride, steep downhill or a multi-night adventure,

there's something for you, and the whole Queenstown region is heli-biking heaven. All the bike shops rent suitable machines and are staffed by keen riders who will point to the best Queenstown has to offer. There's lots more great information at ⓦ ridequeenstown.co.nz.

Fat Tyre ☎ 0800 328 897, ⓦ fat-tyre.co.nz. Guided ride specialist with a variety of single-track mountain-biking packages with up to five hours in the saddle, including an excellent trip in the Dunstan Mountains above Cromwell (5hr; $199). Also all-day heli-rides ($390–499) that are scenic, challenging and great fun. Mostly Oct–May.

Outside Sports 36 Shotover St ☎ 03 441 0074, ⓦ outsidesports. Major bike rental operation with everything from simple hardtails good for lakeside trails (half-day $29; full day $49) through full suspension bikes ideal for the Queenstown Bike Park trails (half-day $49; full day $79) to serious downhillers (half-day $75; full day $110) and high-spec demo machines (half-day $100; full day $150). Check out their rental-plus-gondola packages (half-day $120; full day $160). Daily 8.30am–6pm or later.

Queenstown Bike Park Bob's Peak ⓦ skyline.co.nz /queenstown/MTB. If you've got your own bike, head straight to this lift-assisted bike park where new single-track runs (some moderate, most steep, some death-defying) are being created all the time. Bikes are hooked onto the gondolas (10am–dusk, though they sometimes suspend bike transport around 6–8pm) and a half-day pass ($45) should get you four to six runs. Vertigo offer bike rental at the top station of the gondola. Sept 17–Dec 24 & Jan 8–April; closed over Easter.

R&R Sport Corner of Camp and Shotover sts ☎ 03 409 0409, ⓦ rrsport.co.nz. Decent rental bikes at modest prices: hardtail (half-day $29; full day $49); full suspension (half-day $49; full day $69); downhill (half-day $69; full day $99). Daily 8.30am–8.30pm.

Revolution Tours ☎ 0800 274 334, ⓦ revolutiontours .co.nz. Experience backcountry riding on a four-day three-night trip on the western side of Lake Wakatipu and up to Paradise, with nights in homesteads ($1685).

Vertigo 4 Brecon St ☎ 0800 837 8446, ⓦ vertigobikes .co.nz. Competitive bike rental in town and at the top of the gondola, plus an intro to the bike park with two guided runs ($159) and guided rides down Skippers pack track on a full-suspension bike, descending almost 600m down a narrow track which, until a better road was pushed through in 1888, was the only route into Skippers Canyon (2hr 30min; $169). Also heli-biking (4hr; $399). Daily 8am–6pm.

VIA FERRATA AND ROCK CLIMBING

Climbing Queenstown 36 Shotover St ☎ 0800 254 6246, ⓦ climbingqueenstown.com. If the mountains around Queenstown look tempting but you don't have the skills to go rock climbing, you can get a sense of the experience on some via ferrata (daily 9am & 1.30pm; 4hr; $139), a system

13

WINTER IN QUEENSTOWN

Two ski-fields – **Coronet Peak** and the smaller **Remarkables** – within easy reach of numerous quality hotels, good restaurants and plenty of après-ski combine to make Queenstown New Zealand's premier **ski destination**. The highlight of the season is the ten-day **Queenstown Winter Festival** (w winterfestival.co.nz), around the end of June or early July, which, as well as all the conventional ski/snowboard events, has snow sculpture, ski-golf and great entertainment. Of the various other events, the family-oriented **Remarkables Spring Fling**, in the first week of the September school holidays, is one of the best.

INFORMATION AND PASSES

Both ski areas (and Mount Hutt) are run by the same company, whose website (w nzski.com) has snow reports and plenty of other practical information. One-day lift passes are specific to each area, but a **season ticket** ($999) covers all three fields.

ACCOMMODATION AND EQUIPMENT

Neither ski area has **accommodation** on site, but frequent shuttle buses run to and from Queenstown ($12), where the supply is plentiful – except during school holidays. For **ski rental** visit the excellent (if pricey) Browns, 39 Shotover St (t 03 442 4003, w brownsnz.com), who charge $46/day for mid-range skis, boots and poles or board; or Outside Sports, 36 Shotover St (t 03 441 0074, w outsidesports.co.nz), who offer slightly cheaper deals.

Coronet Peak (t 03 442 4640). First opened in 1947, Coronet Peak, 18km north of Queenstown, became New Zealand's first true ski destination. The most sophisticated snow-making equipment in Australasia extends its season into spring, when cobalt blue skies and stunning scenery earn it an enviable reputation. Its range of runs (3 beginner, 16 intermediate, 12 advanced) for skiers and riders of all abilities, and over 400 vertical metres of skiing, only add to its popularity. Throughout the season, which typically starts in early June and sometimes makes it into October, buses from Queenstown shuttle back and forth along the sealed access road (no toll). Passes for daytime skiing (9am–4pm) cost $95; floodlit skiing (July–Sept Fri & Sat 4–9pm) goes for $49.

The Remarkables (t 03 442 4615). This hill, 28km east of Queenstown, occupies three mountain basins tucked in behind the wrinkled face of the Remarkables. It is best known for learner and intermediate terrain, but there are also good runs (3 beginner, 8 intermediate, 18 advanced) for advanced skiers, and rapid access to some excellent country for off-piste ski touring. Though the bottom of the lifts is 500m higher than at Coronet Peak, more snow is required to cover the tussock, giving a slightly shorter season (late June to early Oct). At 320m, the total vertical descent from the lifts is also less than at Coronet, but you gain an extra 120m by taking the Homeward Run – a long stretch of off-piste with sparkling scenery – to the 14km unsealed access road (no toll), where frequent free buses shuttle you back up to the chairlift. A day pass costs $91.

originally used in Europe to move troops quickly across mountainous terrain during the two world wars. Suitably harnessed up, you make your own way up a trail of steel rungs drilled into a series of cliff faces just above Queenstown, clipping yourself into a long steel cable, which runs beside the rungs. Previous experience isn't necessary, and more demanding routes are available for the gung-ho. The company also offers more conventional rock-climbing trips and courses.

HORSE RIDING

Ben Lomond Station t 0800 236 566, w nzhorsetreks .co.nz. Backcountry horse trekking for those with a little experience. Great scenery and fun riding on trips ranging from an easy trek around Moke Lake (1hr 30min; $80) to the gold-mining heritage of the Ride into the Past (3hr; $150). Daily Nov–April.

ACCOMMODATION

Queenstown has the widest selection of places to stay in this corner of New Zealand, but such is the demand in the middle of summer or at the height of the ski season, that rooms can be hard to come by and prices high. Reserve several days ahead from Christmas to the end of February, longer if you're particular about where you stay. Accommodation at both ends of the spectrum is excellent, with abundant **boutique lodges**, classy **hotels** and budget **hostels**. Things are tougher in the middle where there are few modestly priced, convenient **motels** and **B&Bs**. Some hotels offer good deals in what passes for Queenstown's off season (essentially April, May & Nov) and the i-SITE is a good bet for **accommodation deals** year-round. Almost everywhere is close to the centre, though you might fancy staying at one of the classy hotels at Kawarau Falls, out towards Glenorchy or even in **Arrowtown**.

CENTRAL QUEENSTOWN

Absoloot 50 Beach Rd ☎03 442 9522, ⓦabsoloot .co.nz; map p.688. Lively hostel right in the centre with a lounge and some rooms sporting excellent lake views. Dorms are mostly six-bunk with bathroom, TV and fridge: doubles and queens are en-suite and there's free wi-fi. Regular poker nights, pool competitions, backpacker bar discounts and bike and board storage. Dorms $29, four-share $35, double $90, en-suite queen $110

Base Discovery Lodge 49 Shotover St ☎03 441 1185, ⓦstayatbase.co.nz; map p.688. Massive (300-plus beds) lively hostel with an inadequate kitchen, but that doesn't matter because you'll probably end up eating and drinking in their bar and booking your tours at their travel desk. Dorms have secure lockers, a toilet and shower, women can stay in the Sanctuary section and there's a decent range of en-suite doubles and twins with TV. Dorms $26, Sanctuary $28, doubles $78, en suites $108

Black Sheep 13 Frankton Rd ☎03 442 7289, ⓦblack sheepbackpackers.co.nz; map p.688. Long-established hostel in a converted motel that's great value, particularly in the off-season (April–June & Sept–Dec) when all accommodation is $5/person cheaper. Most dorms are six-bed and there's a great deck with barbecue, spa pool and a relaxed atmosphere. Dorms $25, doubles $70, deluxe $80

Browns Boutique Hotel 26 Isle St ☎03 441 2050, ⓦbrownshotel.co.nz; map p.688. Close to town and yet in a peaceful setting, all ten rooms at this classy lodge have great views from their small balconies across town to the Remarkables. Everything is beautifully appointed, including the luxurious guest lounge with an open fire and the terrace where breakfast is served in summer. $345

Bumbles 2 Brunswick St ☎03 442 6298, ⓦbumbles backpackers.co.nz; map p.688. Refurbished hostel nicely set just across the road from the lakefront, close to town and offering great views from most rooms and common areas, a spacious kitchen, a BBQ area and off-street parking. Dorms $29, doubles $62

Butterfli Lodge 62 Thompson St ☎03 442 6367, ⓦbutterfli.co.nz; map p.688. Million-dollar views from a small house high on the hillside overlooking the lake. It's a bit of a slog up from town but the accommodation is cosy and intimate and the atmosphere is friendly. Book early; two-night minimum. Also a couple of tent sites. Camping $15, dorms $26, doubles $62

Caples Court 20 Stanley St ☎0800 282 275, ⓦcaples court.co.nz; map p.688. Delightful, comfortable motel with more spirit to its decor than most, and each room done in a different style. Most have a kitchen and a balcony and seven of the ten units have views over the town and/or

lake. The others are tucked peacefully away beside a quiet garden. Two-night minimum at busy times. Garden units $130, lake view $170

★ **The Chalet** 1 Dublin St ☎03 442 7117, ⓦchalet queenstown.co.nz; map p.688. Swiss cottage from the outside, stylish boutique B&B within, this quiet seven-roomer is a great choice. Furnishings are high quality but understated, all rooms have little balconies and some overlook the lake and onto the mountains. Undoubtedly one of the best around. $250

The Dairy 10 Isle St ☎03 442 5164, ⓦthedairy.co.nz; map p.688. There's a refined air to this thirteen-room boutique hotel with delightful common areas hung with quality New Zealand artworks (several original) where you might sup something delightful from the extensive honesty bar. The rooms (some with bathtubs) are well appointed and tastefully decorated in modern styles. Breakfast and afternoon tea are served in the original dairy (corner shop). Pay the extra few dollars for a lake view. $465

Four Seasons Motel 12 Stanley St ☎03 442 8953, ⓦqueenstownmotel.com; map p.688. Upgraded down-town motel with off-street parking, good kitchens, mountain views, a spa and one of the very few outdoor motel swimming pools in town (unfortunately beside the main road). $160

Hippo Lodge 4 Anderson Heights ☎03 442 5785, ⓦhippolodge.co.nz; map p.688. A peacefully set couple of suburban houses imaginatively converted into four sections, each with its own bathroom, kitchen and living area. Several of the rooms and lounges have fabulous views over Queenstown. They're one of the few hostels to offer work (2–3hr/day) for accommodation. Camping $19, dorms $28, doubles $68, en suite $88

Historic Stone House 47 Hallenstein St ☎03 442 9812, ⓦhistoricstonehouse.co.nz; map p.688. Sister to *The Chalet*, this relaxing historic stone getaway has a pair of one-bedroom self-contained apartments and one three-bedroom apartment sleeping six with an open log fire. Stylish decor and a peaceful location. $225

The Lodges 8 Lake Esplanade ☎0800 284 356, ⓦthelodges.co.nz; map p.688. Recently renovated lakeside apartments (from studios to three-bedroom) with kitchen, laundry and parking. Most have good lake views. $185

Nomads 5–11 Church St ☎03 441 3922, ⓦnomads queenstown.com; map p.688. Massive, modern hostel right in the heart of things, built to a high standard. The kitchen is piddly, but the stylish en-suite double rooms with TV are excellent and there's a female-only area. Lounges are spacious and there's central parking. Dorms $29, en-suite doubles $130

13

★ **Pinewood** 48 Hamilton Rd ☏0800 746396, ⊚pinewood.co.nz; map p.688. An extensive collection of new and older renovated self-contained buildings (all surrounded by lawns) a 10min walk from the centre, this friendly hostel has a spa bath with views ($10/30min) and en suites that collectively have their own kitchen and lounge areas. There's bike rental (from $29 half-day) and *The Hub*, which serves breakfast and pizza. Dorms $25, doubles $60, en suites $100

★ **Queenstown Motel Apartments** 62 Frankton Rd ☏0800 661 668, ⊚qma.co.nz; map p.688. Well-managed and good-value motel close to town with functional older units (some with good lake views) and eighteen newer ones, all pale wood, bold colours and tasteful artworks. There's a strong environmental stance, with energy-saving light bulbs, double glazing and recycling bins in the kitchenettes. Old units $95, new units $165, new units with lake view $195

Southern Laughter 4 Isle St ☏03 441 8828, ⊚kiwi-backpackers.co.nz; map p.688. Split over three buildings, this rabbit warren of a hostel has a wide variety of rooms (some sharing separate kitchen facilities) and a free spa, and makes up for not being that flash by being friendly. Dorms $26, rooms $68, en suite $78

YHA Central Queenstown 48 Shotover St ☏03 442 7400, ⊚yha.co.nz; map p.688. Among the action this YHA is more like a small hotel, with all rooms en-suite, even the dorms. Adequate kitchen facilities beside a lounge with nice lake views. Dorms $38, doubles $110

YHA Queenstown Lakefront 88 Lake Esplanade ☏03 442 8413, ⊚yha.co.nz; map p.688. One of New Zealand's flagship YHA hostels, in an excellent quiet location a 7min walk from town. The feel is surprisingly homely and accommodation is in spacious, mostly four- to eight-bed dorms plus twins, doubles and one two-bedroom apartment; many of the options have good lake views. Excellent kitchen and separate TV and quiet lounges. Dorms $33, doubles $87, apartment $195

KAWARAU VILLAGE

Hilton Queenstown Peninsula Rd ☏03 450 9400, ⊚queenstown.hilton.com; map p.706. Elegant five-star hotel 8km by road from Queenstown but only 10min by water taxi (10 daily; $15 return), which leaves the hotel's wharf frequently. Rooms are of various sizes and levels of comfort, are beautifully appointed and many have views across the lake towards Coronet Peak. Along with a pool, health spa, deli, pub and a couple of cafés there's also the excellent *Wakatipu Grill* (see p.704). $240

Kawarau Hotel Peninsula Rd ☏03 450 9400, ⊚kawarau.hilton.com; map p.706. Managed by the adjacent *Hilton*, this sister hotel doesn't get quite the fabulous views but guests can access the same restaurants and facilities and stay in stylish rooms, each with

kitchenette, for far less. Rates very flexible with demand check for bargains. $125

TOWARDS GLENORCHY

★ **Little Paradise Lodge** Meilejohn Bay, 28km along Glenorchy Rd ☏03 442 6196, ⊚littleparadise.co.nz; map p.706. Eccentric, alternative and charming guesthouse close to the lake amid Little Paradise Gardens (see p.705). The owner has lined the walls with stone and timber patterns including a frieze depicting New Zealand wildlife. Most of the furniture is handcrafted, goat-skins cover the floor and the toilet cistern is a fish tank. Accommodation is in a three-share room, standard doubles and an en-suite chalet. You can cook for yourself, and there's kayak rental ($10) and free fishing gear. Dorms $45, doubles $140

CAMPING AND HOLIDAY PARKS

Freedom camping is banned in town and its immediate surroundings, but the Queenstown district has a few compact campsites with attendant cabins and several simple DOC sites that get pretty busy in Jan, Feb and March.

12-Mile Delta Reserve 11km west of Queenstown towards Glenorchy ☏03 428 4289, ⊚12miledelta.co.nz; map p.706. Lakeside DOC camping with room for 100 tents or vans, plus vault toilets and tap water amid regenerating scrub. Not the prettiest but good mountain views and lake access. $7

Moke Lake 6km towards Glenorchy then 4km up Moke Lake Rd; map p.706. Peaceful lakeside DOC campsite with eighteen sites, lake water and vault toilets. Moke Lake is an excellent spot for kayaking, swimming and fishing. $7

Q Box 21 Bowen St ☏03 441 1567, ⊚qbox.co.nz; map p.688. Despite being tucked into a light industrial area this new and compact campsite is an appealing streamside place with lots of campervan spots (and a few marginal tent sites) ranged around showers, kitchen and lounge stylishly built into a corral of black shipping containers. Laundry, wi-fi and hook-ups available. Camping/site $30, powered sites $35

Queenstown Top 10 Holiday Park Creeksyde 54 Robins Rd ☏0800 786 222, ⊚camp.co.nz; map p.688. Well-organized, spotlessly clean holiday park a 10min walk from the lake with shaded sites, many used by campervans. A central building houses a spa bathroom and sauna ($15), a ski store and drying rooms. Camping $22.50, shared-bath doubles $72, en suites $120, self-contained units $125, motels $205

Queenstown Lakeview Holiday Park 45 Brecon St ☏0800 482 735, ⊚holidaypark.net.nz; map p.688. Enormous, high-standard site that sprawls over the base of Bob's Peak with grassy (though not well-shaded) tent and van sites plus kitchen-less en-suite studios, fully self-contained units and relatively luxurious tourist flats. Showers $2. Camping $20, studios $125, units $145, flats $160

EATING

Queenstown is blessed with the best range of eating places in this corner of New Zealand, and many are increasingly making the most of the town's climate and spilling out onto the pedestrianized streets and along the waterfront, where you can sit and watch the *Earnslaw* glide in. **Breakfast** and **snack** places generally close by 6pm, though some serve early **dinners**, while restaurants often double as bars as the evening wears on. For **groceries**, try the Alpine Supermarket, 6 Shotover St (Mon–Sat 7am–10pm, Sun 9am–10pm), or Fresh Choice, 64 George Rd (daily 7am–midnight).

★ **@Thai** Third Floor, 24 Church St ☎ 03 442 3683, ⓦ atthai.co.nz; map p.688. Flavours zing around your mouth with every bite at this Thai restaurant that does all your curry and noodle favourites wonderfully. They also dish up the likes of prawn salad with chilli jam and cashew ($23) and *choo chee* – deep-fried blue cod topped with creamy red curry paste and kaffir lime leaves ($28). Smiling service too. Daily 11.30am–10pm.

Aggy's Shack Corner of Marine Parade and Church St ☎ 03 442 4076; map p.688. You'll get the best fish and chips in town ($12) as well as local smoked eel, marinated raw fish, sea urchin and even muttonbird and chips ($20) to enjoy at outdoor benches or on the grassy lakeshore. Daily 11am–10pm or later.

The Cow Cow Lane ☎ 03 442 8588, ⓦ thecowrestaurant .co.nz; map p.688. Be prepared to share a table at this longstanding stone-built pizzeria offering straightforward pasta dishes ($19–21) and traditional pizzas ($30 for a massive one). BYO & licensed. Daily noon–midnight.

Fergbaker 40 Shotover St ☎ 03 441 1206; map p.688. The perfect accompaniment to *Fergburger* next door, with everything from ready-made sandwiches and the likes of couscous and chickpea salads to gourmet pies ($6), delectable breads, blueberry danishes, jalapeño bagels and chocolate éclairs. Everything to go including the espresso. Sun–Wed 7am–10pm, Thurs–Sat 7am–5am.

Fergburger 42 Shotover St ☎ 03 441 1232, ⓦ fergburger .com; map p.688. There's always a cluster of hungry punters outside the swift and sweaty takeaway that has become something of a gold standard for Kiwi burgers. It dispenses massive, broad-ranging variations on meat in a bun (or non-meat in a bun) plus fries and/or a beer or plonk. The bacon, egg and hashbrowns Dawn Horn ($13) is a great kick-start to the day. Limited inside seating. Daily 8.30am–5am.

Finz Steamer Wharf ☎ 03 442 7405, ⓦ finzdownunder .co.nz; map p.688. Cheaper cousin of *Wai*, this semi-formal restaurant offers great lake views and good-value seafood such as seafood chowder ($18), green-lipped mussels ($28) and a seafood platter for two ($90). Daily 5–10pm.

India Once Upon a Time 15 Shotover St ☎ 03 442 5335, ⓦ indiaonceuponatime.com; map p.688. The most reliably authentic curry place in town, serving a delicious royal *patiala* chicken (with black cumin and cardamom; $20) and an extensive Maharaja banquet for $35. Daily 11.30am–2.30pm & 5–11pm.

★ **Kappa** Upstairs at 36a The Mall ☎ 03 441 1423; map p.688. Cheapish, no-nonsense Japanese place that's perfect

for a sushi combo ($10), a bowl of soba or udon noodles ($10–15), a bento box lunch (from $13) or one of the specials – perhaps nori-flavoured blue cod and asparagus tempura ($16). Daily noon–2.30pm & 7.30–10pm.

Patagonia Chocolates 50 Beach St ☎ 442 9066, ⓦ patagoniachocolates.co.nz; map p.688. Waterside café notable for rich hot chocolate drinks (ginger, lavender, chilli), luscious cakes, delectable gelato (from $6) and handmade chocolates. Free wi-fi daily 9am–6pm. Daily 9am–10pm.

Remarkables Market Hawthorn Drive, Frankton ⓦ remarkablesmarket.co.nz; map p.688. See what the locals get up to while checking out the local produce at this farmers' market-style affair with loads of good food, arts and crafts. Late Oct–early April Sat 8am–1pm.

★ **Solera Vino** 25 Beach St ☎ 03 442 6082, ⓔ dine @soleravino.co.nz; map p.688. Despite the Spanish name, this small, fine-dining restaurant offers superb, predominantly French Mediterranean fare in elegant but understated surroundings. Lunch dishes hover around $15 and dinner mains are mostly $35, but specials ($10–20) make this place accessible for almost everyone. Book ahead for dinner. Daily 11am–3pm & 6–11pm.

★ **Vudu Café** 23 Beach St ☎ 03 442 5357, ⓦ vudu .co.nz; map p.688. It's seen many a worthy challenger come and go but this relaxed café remains the town's best. The booths are comfy, there are magazines to pore over and the food is great, whether an inexpensive breakfast, quiche, scrumptious muffins and good coffee, or more substantial offerings such as a bean and lentil bowl ($17) or a venison burger ($17) – the breakfast quesadilla ($15) is a local favourite. Daily 8am–5pm.

Vudu Café & Larder 16 Rees St ☎ 03 441 8370, ⓦ vudu.co.nz; map p.688. Larger and more urban chic sister of its original up the street, adorned with a big photo of Queenstown in the 1950s and with limited lakeside seating. Great juices, smoothies and organic coffee, plus the likes of free-range eggs with haloumi, *dukkah* and rocket ($16), broadbean falafel ($16) and a Reuben sandwich ($15). Daily 7.30am–6pm.

Wai Steamer Wharf ☎ 03 442 5969, ⓦ wai.net.nz; map p.688. Waterfront, fine-dining restaurant with outdoor seating on the wharf and some of the most exquisite food in town. Expect the likes of grouper with crisp polenta, scallops and lime oil ($43) or lamb loin with mint yogurt and goat's cheese ($45). Consider setting the evening aside for the wonderful *dégustation* menu ($138; $215 with wine matches). Daily 6–10pm.

13

★ **Wakatipu Grill** Peninsula Rd ☎ 03 450 9400, ⓦ queenstown.hilton.com; map p.706. Make a special journey (perhaps by water taxi) to this fine restaurant inside the *Hilton Queenstown*. Settle into booths or grab a terrace table overlooking the lake and tuck into half a dozen Stewart Island oysters ($25) perhaps followed by Perendale lamb with caramelized fennel and semi-dried Pinot Noir grapes ($38). Lunch specials ($30) include a glass of wine and a small sampling of some of the menu's finest. Daily 6am–11pm.

Winnies 7 The Mall ☎ 03 442 8635, ⓦ winnies.co.nz; map p.688. Popular for pasta and gourmet pizzas (large $28) made from local ingredients, with a better-than-average à la carte and blackboard menu and reasonable prices, this is a decent spot with balcony seating and friendly service. Daily noon–1am or later.

DRINKING, NIGHTLIFE AND ENTERTAINMENT

Queenstown is still essentially a small town with plenty of backpackers binge drinking in bar/clubs that border on being cattle markets. Decent touring bands are rare, movies are mostly mainstream and there's no highbrow culture. Still, if you are in the mood, it can be fun. Pick up *The Source* entertainment monthly (free) to find out what's on.

★ **Atlas Beer Café** Steamer Wharf, Beach St ☎ 03 442 5995; map p.688. Cosy bar popular with the locals who sit in its windows to watch the *Earnslaw* as she comes in to dock. Enjoy excellent tap beers, including Emerson's, and some inventive tapas such as Vietnamese chicken salad wonton or Moroccan meatballs (both $7.50). Daily 10am–2am.

★ **Bardeaux** 5 Eureka Arcade ☎ 03 442 8284, ⓦ goodgroup.co.nz; map p.688. Seductive little cocktail bar, with big sofas, a roaring fire and a broad selection of excellent whisky and wine. Relaxed early on, but picks up big time after 11pm. Daily 4am–4pm.

The Bunker Cow Lane ☎ 03 441 8030, ⓦ thebunker .co.nz; map p.688. A stylish upstairs cocktail bar with cool music – anything from jazz to ambient. Daily 5pm–4am.

Debajo Cow Lane ☎ 03 442 6099. Catholic-icon-filled late-night Spanish bar that likes to bill itself as Queenstown's home of underground music. Killer cocktails, too. Thurs & Sun midnight–4am, Fri & Sat 11pm–4am.

★ **Dux de Lux** 14 Church St ☎ 03 442 9688, ⓦ thedux .co.nz; map p.688. The only brewpub in town, serving half a dozen excellent beers and good pizzas ($17–27), preferably taken in their garden bar which catches the late afternoon sun. There's live local music (mostly rock, reggae and blues) from Thurs–Sun and an entertaining Tues night quiz. Daily 11am–2.30am.

Mini Bar Eureka Arcade ☎ 03 441 3212, ⓦ goodgroup .co.nz; map p.688. Personable little bar serving an enormous selection of beers from all over the known universe. Daily 4pm–4am.

Póg Mahone's 14 Rees St ☎ 03 442 5382, ⓦ pog mahones.co.nz; map p.688. One of the better Irish bars you'll come across, typically crowded with folk clamouring for draught Guinness and hearty bar meals such as twice-cooked pork belly ($29) and Irish stew with soda bread and veg ($20): check the blackboards outside for all manner of midweek two-for-one discounts and happy hours. Warm yourself by the open fire, soak up the sun on the lakeside or come for live music (Tues–Sat from 9pm). Daily 11.30am–1am or later.

Pub on Wharf 88 Beach St ☎ 03 441 2155, ⓦ pubon wharf.co.nz; map p.688. Busy boozer, particularly early in the evening for good wharf-watching over a beer and one of the $20 mains – try the beef Wellington or bacon hock with bubble 'n' squeak. Frequent live music. Daily 10am–10pm or a lot later.

World Bar 27 Shotover St ☎ 03 442 6757, ⓦ theworld bar.co.nz; map p.688. The longstanding mainstay of the backpacker late-night bar/clubs in town, this is the one place that keeps going until the very end of the night – or beginning of the next day. Daily 4pm–4am.

MAORI PERFORMANCES AND CINEMA

Kiwi Haka Bob's Peak Complex ☎ 03 441 0101, ⓦ skyline.co.nz; map p.688. This half-hour Maori concert performance takes place daily at 5.15pm, 6pm, 7.15pm & 8pm. $59, including gondola ride. Reservations essential.

Reading Cinemas 11 The Mall ☎ 03 442 9990. Screens the usual mainstream films. Head to Arrowtown (see p.708) if you're after something more arty.

SHOPPING

Info&Track 37 Shotover St ☎ 03 442 9708, ⓦ infotrack .co.nz; map p.688. Rents gear such as packs ($7/day), sleeping bags ($7/day) and two-person cooksets ($5/day) but not tents. Daily: Nov–May 7.30am–8pm; June–Oct 6.45am–9pm.

Small Planet 17 Shotover St ☎ 03 442 6393, ⓦ small planetsports.co.nz; map p.688. Carries new and used gear, including snowboards, ski gear, climbing, camping and tramping stuff and books – all at good prices and with competitive buy-back deals. The staff are all qualified guides, and, if you've got something to get rid of, will hawk it for 25 percent commission. The company also does rentals including tents ($12/day), climbing harnesses ($8/day), crampons ($10/day) and avalanche transceivers ($10/day). Daily 9am–8pm.

DIRECTORY

Banks and exchange All major banks have a branch and ATM around the centre.

Internet Several places along Shotover St with long hours, fast connections and good rates (around $3/hr) including Global Gossip, 27 Shotover St (☎ 03 441 3018). There's also (paid) access at the library.

Library 10 Gorge Rd (Mon–Sat 10am–5pm; ☎ 03 441 0600).

Luggage storage Many lodgings will hold gear for you while you're away from Queenstown, especially if you're staying on your return. Info&Track, 37 Shotover St (☎ 0800 462 248, ⓦ infotrack.co.nz), charge $5/item/night.

Luggage transfer Topline Tours (☎ 0508 249 8059, ⓔ topline@teanau.co.nz) will transfer luggage between Queenstown and Te Anau (backpacks $10–15; bikes $10–15) or Queenstown and Milford Sound ($20–25).

Medical treatment Mountain Lake Medical Centre, 38b Gorge Rd (☎ 03 442 7188).

Pharmacy Wilkinsons Pharmacy, corner of The Mall and Rees St (daily 8.30am–10pm, ☎ 03 442 7313).

Police 11 Camp St (☎ 03 441 1600).

Post office 13 Camp St (Mon–Fri 8.30am–5.30pm, Sat 9am–4pm). Has poste restante facilities.

Around Queenstown

The commercial pressures of Queenstown drop away as soon gets a few kilometres out of town. Heading towards Glenorchy, pause a while beside the lake at **Bob's Cove** and admire the quirky plantings at **Little Paradise Gardens**. There's more rugged exploration beside the churning **Shotover River**, once the scene of frenetic gold mining. The early gold discoveries were here, and the tourist motherlode is now mined through rafting trips, jetboating, mountain bike rides and 4WD tours. The Shotover rises in the Richardson Mountains north of Queenstown and picks up speed to surge through its deepest and narrowest section, **Skippers Canyon**, and into the Kawarau River downstream from Lake Wakatipu. The Skippers Road, which follows the Shotover River only in its upper reaches, branches off Coronet Peak Road 12km north of Queenstown. It is approached along Malaghans Road through **Arthur's Point**.

Bob's Cove

Glenorchy Rd, 14km west of Queenstown

The lakeside road from Queenstown to Glenorchy is one the best of the many excellent drives in the district. After shaking off the suburbs of Queenstown the first stop is **Bob's Cove**, the best place to observe the lake's **seiche**, a poorly understood phenomenon (rare but not unknown elsewhere in the world) which causes the lake level to fluctuate by around 150mm every five minutes. Place a stick at the water's edge and watch the change.

A short **nature walk** (30–40min return) leads through bush that's alive with bellbirds to the remains of an 1870s lime kiln.

Little Paradise Gardens

Glenorchy Rd, 30km west of Queenstown • Roughly 9am–5pm; if the sign is out they're open • $6 including tea or coffee and a biscuit • ☎ 03 442 6196, ⓦ littleparadise.co.nz

If you're headed for Glenorchy, or just fancy a gorgeous lakeside drive, make for this semi-wild little haven where everything is made and tended by Swiss owner Thomas Schneider, who has a fine sense of the oddball. Full of roses, lilies, daffodils, plum trees and any plant that takes Schneider's fancy, the place is almost always a riot of colour, but there's nothing sterile or formal here, just grassy paths weaving past the frog and lily pond, a stream threading among concrete sculptures in yoga positions and the home-made fountain sundial. Check out the intriguing signpost to various countries showing how close all the people of that country would have to stand to make a line from here to there. It stands right on the 45th parallel, equidistant from the equator and the South Pole.

13

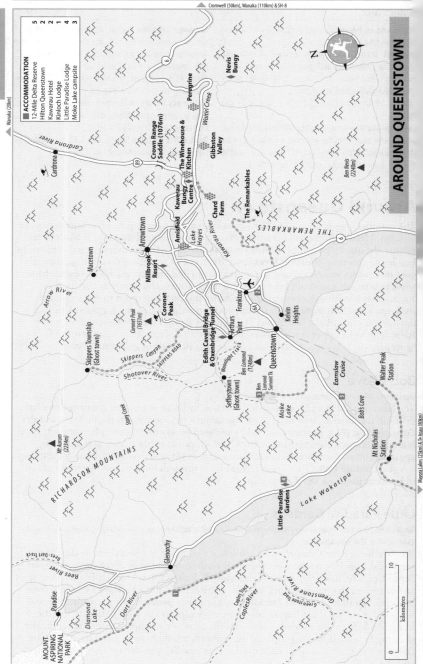

Cromwell (50km), Wanaka (110km) & SH-8

AROUND QUEENSTOWN

■ ACCOMMODATION
12-Mile Delta Reserve 5
Hilton Queenstown 2
Kawarau Hotel 1
Kinloch Lodge 4
Little Paradise Lodge 1
Moke Lake campsite 3

Wanaka (20km)

Cardrona River

Cardrona

Crown Range Saddle (1076m)

Kawarau Bungy Centre

The Winehouse & Kitchen

Gibbston Valley

Peregrine

Waitiri Creek

Nevis Bungy

Ben Nevis (2240m)

Arrowtown

Amisfield

Lake Hayes

Chard Farm

Kawarau River

The Remarkables

THE REMARKABLES

Millbrook Resort

Macetown

Arrow River

Skippers Township (Ghost town)

Skippers Canyon

Shotover River

Coronet Peak (1651m)

Coronet Peak

Edith Cavell Bridge & Oxenbridge Tunnel

Arthurs Point

Frankton

Kelvin Heights

Moonlight Track

Ben Lomond (1748m)

Queenstown

Sefferstown (Ghost town)

Ben Lomond Summit Trk

Moke Lake

Stony Creek

Mt Aurum (2234m)

RICHARDSON MOUNTAINS

Earnslaw Cruise

Bob's Cove

Walter Peak Station

Mt Nicholas Station

Lake Wakatipu

Little Paradise Gardens

Mavora Lakes (25km) & Te Anau (80km)

Glenorchy

Rees-Dart Track

Rees River

Dart River

Diamond Lake

Paradise

MOUNT ASPIRING NATIONAL PARK

Caples Track

Caples River

Greenstone Trk

Greenstone River

Routeburn Shelter

The Divide

0 ————— 10 kilometres

Arthur's Point

Gorge Road leaves central Queenstown through a small light industrial area bound for Arthur's Point, 5km north of Queenstown, where the parabolic concrete Edith Cavell Bridge spans the Shotover River. The Shotover Jet (see box, pp.696–697) performs its antics in the gorge below, and Shotover rafting trips finish here.

Oxenbridge Tunnel
Oxenbridge Tunnel Rd, Arthur's Point

The finale of a Shotover rafting trip is a passage through the 170m-long Oxenbridge Tunnel, which was dug around 1911 to divert the river's flow and allow panning of the gold-bearing riverbed. After three years of drilling the miners reaped meagre rewards, returning only 2.5kg of gold. The tunnel exit can be reached along Oxenbridge Tunnel Road.

The Skippers Road

Rental vehicles are not insured on the treacherous Skippers Road, a narrow, winding ribbon of dirt track that locals tend to hare around, leaving little space for oncoming traffic. That's a shame, because it accesses a wonderful area of gold-rush relics that are well worth exploring. You'll get a bit of flavour of the area on Shotover rafting and Skippers Canyon Jet trips (see box, pp.696–697), since both start up the Skippers Road, but full exploration is better on historically oriented 4WD tours (see box, p.699).

From the start near Coronet Peak, the Skippers Road descends numerous hairpin bends to the river, then shadows it, negotiating Pinchers Bluff, where Chinese and European navvies cut the road from a near-vertical cliff face, to what remains of Skippers township. There are no shops, cafés or much else along the whole route.

Brief history

As the gold-panners gave way to gravity-fed water chutes, mechanical sieves and floating dredges, the construction of a decent road became crucial. From 1863, Chinese navvies spent over twenty years hacking away with pick and shovel at the Skippers Road; those who stuck out the harsh conditions began building quarters more substantial than the standard-issue canvas tents. Meanwhile, entrepreneurially minded pioneers began to exploit the boom, building 27 hotels along the 40km of road, and selling fresh fruit and vegetables at extortionate prices to miners often suffering from scurvy.

By the turn of the twentieth century the river was worked out, though a few miners stayed on. Even today a couple of die-hards make a living from gold panning and sluicing, and in 1999, for a few days after flooding, happy prospectors were panning up to $600 worth in a couple of hours.

Skippers township
29km north of Queenstown

The Skipper Road wends its way upstream to the 1901 Skippers Bridge, the first high-level bridge to be built over the Shotover, and consequently the only one to survive the winter floods, which had swept away past efforts.

THE KINGSTON FLYER

Fiordland-bound drivers have a chance to sample a slice of bygone New Zealand in the form of the **Kingston Flyer** (Oct–April 3 daily • $35 • ☏ 0800 4FLYER, ⦿ kingstonflyer.co.nz). After a few years in retirement, this steam train is back, running along 14km of preserved track from Kingston, 47km south of Queenstown, to Fairlight. From the 1890s until 1957, the Otago rail network terminated at Kingston, and Wakatipu steamers (such as the TSS *Earnslaw*) completed the journey to Queenstown. Gleaming black 1920s locos haul old-time wooden carriages on the two-hour round trip.

13

Just over the bridge you'll find the remnants of **Skippers township**, which once had a population of 1500, though they all legged it once the gold ran out. The **old schoolhouse** has been restored and there are ruins of a few more buildings scattered around, making it a bleak, haunted place.

ACCOMMODATION   THE SKIPPERS ROAD

Skippers campsite Simple DOC campsite occupying a remote and grassy site near the old schoolhouse and cemetery with great views of the surrounding hills. There are toilets (flush in summer) and tap water but you'll need to bring everything else with you. **$7**

Arrowtown and around

ARROWTOWN, at the confluence of the Arrow River and Bush Creek 23km northeast of Queenstown, still has the feel of an old gold town, though on busy summer days any lingering authenticity is swamped by the tourists prowling the sheepskin, greenstone and gold of its souvenir shops. Nonetheless the town is very much a living community, with grocers' shops, pubs and a post office and a great range of accommodation and

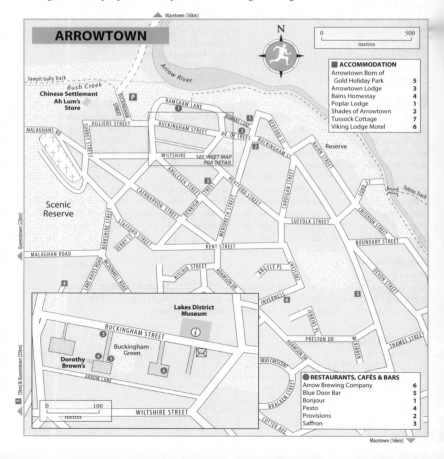

ARROWTOWN'S HIDDEN CHINESE HISTORY

The initial wave of miners who came to Arrowtown in the early 1860s were fortune-seekers intent on a fast buck. When gold was discovered on the West Coast, most of them hot-footed it to Greymouth or Hokitika, leaving a much-depleted community that lacked the economic wherewithal to support the businesses which had mushroomed around the miners.

The solution was to import **Chinese labour**; the first Chinese arrived in Otago in 1866, their number reaching 5000 by 1870. The community settled along Bush Creek, its **segregation** from the main settlement symptomatic of the inherent racism of the time – something that also manifested itself in working practices that forced the Chinese to pick over abandoned mining claims and work the tailings of European miners. Even Chinese employed on municipal projects such as the Presbyterian church got only half the wages paid to Europeans doing the same job.

A ray of light is cast amid the prevailing bigotry by contemporary newspaper reports, which suggest that many citizens found the Chinese business conduct "upright and straightforward" and their demeanour "orderly and sober" – perhaps surprisingly in what was an almost entirely male community. Most came with dreams of earning their fortune and returning home, so, initially at least, few came with their families; a process of chain **migration** later brought wives, children and then members of the extended family. Few realized their dreams, but around ninety percent did return home, many in a box, sent to an early grave by overwork and poor living conditions. Many more were driven out in the early 1880s when recession brought racial jealousies to a head, resulting in the enactment of a punitive poll tax on foreign residents. There was little workable gold by this time and those Chinese who stayed mostly became market gardeners or merchants and drifted away, mainly to Auckland, though the Arrowtown community remained viable into the 1920s. Once the Chinese had left or died, the Bush Creek settlement was abandoned and largely destroyed by repeated flooding.

places to eat. Arrowtown has a permanent (and increasingly wealthy) population of around 2400, but in summer, when holiday homes are full and tourists arrive in force, it comes close to regaining the 7000-strong peak attained during the **gold rush**.

The best way to appreciate Arrowtown is to linger on after the crowds have gone. If you're visiting from Queenstown and not staying over, consider coming for lunch, spend the afternoon hiking, swimming in the river or biking up to the former mining settlement of **Macetown**, then catch a movie and dinner, making sure you get the last bus back.

If you can, visit in late April when the town is at its best, the trees golden and the streets alive during the ten-day **Autumn Festival** (@arrowtownautumnfestival.org.nz), with all manner of historic walks, street theatre and hoedowns.

Brief history

There is considerable doubt as to whether American William Fox was actually the first to discover alluvial gold in the Arrow River in 1862, but he dominated proceedings, managing to keep the find secret while recovering over 100kg. Jealous prospectors tried to follow him to the lode, but he gave them the slip, on one occasion leaving his tent and provisions behind in the middle of the night. The town subsequently bore his name until Foxes gave way to Arrowtown. The Arrow River became known as the richest for its size in the world – a reputation that drew scores of Chinese miners (see box above), who lived in the now partly restored **Arrowtown Chinese Settlement**. Prospectors fanned out over the surrounding hills, where brothers Charley and John Mace set up **Macetown**, now a ghost town.

Avenue of Trees

Twin rows of sycamores and oaks, planted in 1867, have grown to overshadow the tiny miners' cottages along the photogenic **Avenue of Trees**, Arrowtown's defining image. Most of the sixty or so cottages were built towards the end of the nineteenth century

13

and they're unusually small and close together, the chronic lack of timber undoubtedly being a factor. The sheltering hills give Arrowtown parched summers and snowy winters, thrown into sharp relief by autumn, when the deciduous trees planted by the mining community cast golden shadows on a central knot of picturesque miners' cottages. A few have been turned into boutique businesses and cafés.

Lakes District Museum

49 Buckingham St • Daily 8.30am–5pm • $8 • ☎ 03 442 1824, ⓦ museumqueenstown.com

Artefacts found during the 1983 Chinese Settlement dig are displayed inside the **Lakes District Museum**, which covers the lives of the gold miners and their families, with a particular emphasis on the Chinese community. There's also a feature on opium smoking, which remained legal in New Zealand until 1901, some twenty years after games of chance – *fantan* and *pakapoo* – were proscribed. Technophiles also get a look-in, with displays on the quartz-reef mining used at Macetown and on one of the country's earliest hydro schemes, which once supplied mining communities in Skippers and Macetown with power. Down in the basement are displays on the old brewery, a bakery, a print room and a school room.

Arrowtown Chinese Settlement

Western end of Buckingham St • Open entry • Free

A visit to the Lakes District Museum is the best preparation for a stroll around the **Arrowtown Chinese Settlement**, a string of heavily restored buildings, hugging a narrow willow-draped section of Bush Creek. This is easily the best preserved of New Zealand's Chinese communities, and provides an insight into a fascinating, shameful episode in the country's history. Many of the buildings were intended as temporary retreats – with tin, sod and timber the principal materials – only becoming permanent homes as miners aged. Little was left standing when an archeological dig began in 1983, and many of the dwellings languish in a state of graceful decay. Some schist, mortar and corrugated-iron buildings fared rather better and several of these have been restored, fleetingly brought back to life by interpretation panels.

Ah Lum's Store

The best-preserved Chinese building is **Ah Lum's Store**, built in typical Canton delta style in 1883 for Wong Hop Lee and leased from 1909 to 1927 to Ah Lum, one of the pillars of the Chinese community in its later years. By this time integration was making inroads: Ah Lum sold European as well as Chinese goods, and operated an opium den and bank.

Macetown

16km north of Arrowtown, accessed on foot, bike or 4WD road

As gold fever swept through Otago in the early 1860s, prospectors fanned out, clawing their way up every creek and gully in search of a flash in the pan. In 1862, alluvial gold was found at Twelve Mile, sparking the rush to what later became known as **Macetown**, now a ghost town and a popular destination for mountain bikers, horse trekkers and trampers.

Macetown's story is one of boom and bust. At its peak, it boasted a couple of hotels, a post office and a school, but when the gold ran out, it couldn't fall back on farming in the way that Arrowtown and Queenstown did and, like Skippers (see p.707), it died. All that remains of the town are a couple of stone buildings – the restored schoolmaster's house and the bakery – and a smattering of wooden shacks. The surrounding creeks and gullies are littered with the twisted and

ARROWTOWN AND MACETOWN WALKS

Pick up the free *Discover Arrowtown: Maps and Walking Guides*, which illustrates all the walks listed below. They fan out from Arrowtown into country where gold mining communities once sprang up along the river, but were abandoned just as suddenly. Telltale poplar, rowan and willows in the valleys are relics of these settlements, and at abandonned cottage sites **fruit trees** have colonized the riverbanks. In autumn apples, pears and plums weigh down the branches, and bushes of blackberry, blackcurrant, gooseberry, raspberry and elderberry become rampant. There are few specific sights, but you can spend a lazy afternoon gorging on fruit and trying to identify the overgrown sites of houses. The surrounding hills are speckled with **rose bushes**: according to folklore, these were planted by miners seeking vitamin C (rosehips are one of the richest sources); others contend that they were planted primarily for their root systems, which could be fashioned into briar pipes.

Bush Creek (3km return; 1hr; gentle). Easy bush walk initially passing the site of one of Arrowtown's old ice rinks and then following an old irrigation pipe parallel to Bush Creek. Turn around at the 1881 water intake for the irrigation pipe.

Macetown Circuit (8hr loop; 32km; 700m ascent). This strenuous loop combines several local walks and is best done between Christmas and April after the melting snows have subsided, making the 22 river crossings on the Arrow Creek a little easier, though even in summer, access can be problematic after rain. Either make it one long day or spread over two, camping at Macetown. The walk follows the north bank of Bush Creek then skirts the base of German Hill, branching up Sawtooth Gully and following the Big Hill Trail with its expansive views back to Lake Hayes and the Remarkables. The route then drops steeply

towards Eight Mile Creek, the path becoming indistinct as it traverses soggy and potentially ankle-twisting country. After three or four hours, you stumble across the Arrow Creek road, just 2km short of Macetown. The way back follows the Arrow Creek road back to Arrowtown. For respite from the dust, you can occasionally divert onto paths that run parallel to the road.

Sawpit Gully (5km loop; 2–3hr; 300m ascent). You'll need reasonable fitness for Arrowtown's classic loop hike, best done anticlockwise. Along the way beech forest turns to subalpine tussock and back to forest as you pass decayed evidence of gold mining, broken-down water races, mine tailings and the odd stone hut. Views of the Remarkables and Lake Hayes are stunning. You initially follow the Arrow River Trail parallel to the Macetown road then turn left into Sawpit Gully and loop back to Arrowtown.

rusting remains of gold batteries, making a fruitful hunting ground for industrial archeology fans

On first acquaintance, it isn't massively exciting, but the grassy plateau makes a great camping spot. Indeed, arriving for a couple of days with a tent and provisions is the best way to experience Macetown's unique atmosphere.

ARRIVAL AND DEPARTURE

ARROWTOWN

By bus Connectabus (☎0800 405 066, ⓦconnectabus .com) operates services throughout the Wakatipu basin with Frankton as its hub. Catch the #11 from the top of the Mall on Camp St in Queenstown to Frankton then the #10 on to Ramshaw Lane in Arrowtown. A day-pass costs $17 (seven-day visitor transport card $40) and the last bus back to Queenstown leaves at 10.25pm.

Destinations Queenstown (13 daily; 40min).

MACETOWN

By bike Rent a bike from Arrowtown or Queenstown and head up the 4WD road along the Arrow River (requiring

ARROWTOWN AND AROUND

22 fords) or the single-track which parallels it for much of the way, which avoids some of the river crossings. Allow 2hr each way.

Nomad Safaris ☎0800 688 222, ⓦnomadsafaris .co.nz. Trips from Queenstown (4hr; $165) head up the Arrow River, crossing it over twenty times on the rough road into Macetown. Arrowtown pick-ups available.

Southern Explorer ☎0800 493 975, ⓦsouthern explorer.co.nz. Small company specializing in Arrowtown and Macetown exploration offering Macetown trips (4hr; $150) with the option of riding a mountain bike back, almost all downhill. They also offer an overnight trip camping in Macetown ($279).

INFORMATION AND TOURS

ARROWTOWN

i-SITE 49 Buckingham St, inside the Lakes District Museum (daily 8.30am–5pm; ☎ 03 442 1824, ⓦ museumqueenstown .com). Pick up the *Historic Buildings of Arrowtown* booklet ($2), and the informative *Arrowtown Chinese Settlement* booklet ($4). It also has internet access.

Southern Explorer ☎ 0800 493 975, ⓦ southern explorer.co.nz. Small company specializing in Arrowtown and Macetown exploration. Their Arrowtown tour (2hr; $65) includes gold panning and visiting *LOTR* locations.

MACETOWN

Tourist information The area is covered in some detail in the *Macetown and the Arrow Gorge* booklet ($4), available from the i-SITE in Arrowtown.

GETTING AROUND

By bike Arrowtown Bike Hire (☎ 03 442 1466) offer mountain bike rental from their stand on Ramshaw Lane ($35/half-day; $49/8hr).

ACCOMMODATION

ARROWTOWN

Most of Arrowtown's accommodation is of a high standard and usually less busy than in Queenstown.

Arrowtown Born of Gold Holiday Park 12 Centennial Ave ☎ 03 442 1876, ⓦ arrowtownholidaypark.co.nz. Spacious campsite with a tennis court near the community swimming pool. It has a modern kitchen and ablutions block. Camping $18, studios $120, self-contained flats $140

★ **Arrowtown Lodge** 7 Anglesea St ☎ 03 442 1101, ⓦ arrowtownlodge.co.nz. Four comfortable and tastefully furnished cottages built from recycled nineteenth-century mud bricks. Each is en-suite and offers mountain views. A continental breakfast can be served out on the sunny deck, and transport to Macetown and the airport can be arranged. $180

Bains Homestay 32 Butel Rd ☎ 03 442 1270, ⓦ bainshomestay.co.nz. Set in peaceful green surroundings just off the Arrowtown–Lake Hayes road, 300m out of town, accommodation is in a spacious self-contained apartment with a lovely balcony. The apartment can sleep up to four and continental breakfast is included. $140

Poplar Lodge 4 Merioneth St ☎ 03 442 1466, ⓦ poplar lodge.co.nz. Homely, shoes-off backpackers spread over two buildings with small, neat dorms, downstairs rooms with doors opening outside and a couple of separate en-suite units. The owners are friendly, and the rose garden is a nice touch. Dorms $29, doubles $70, en-suite units $99

Shades of Arrowtown 9 Merioneth St ☎ 03 442 1613, ⓦ shadesofarrowtown.co.nz. Tastefully decorated modern motel set in leafy surrounds in the heart of town. There's a good range of units (most with kitchenette or full kitchen), plus a self-contained cottage sleeping six. Units $100, cottage $175

★ **Tussock Cottage** 48 Rutherford Rd, beside Lake Hayes 5km southwest of town ☎ 03 442 1449, ⓦ tussockcottage.co.nz. A fabulous, romantic and luxuriously equipped two-room self-contained straw-bale cottage with a tussock-covered roof. There are bikes and kayaks for guests' use and the hosts are welcoming and informed. $225

Viking Lodge Motel 21 Inverness Crescent ☎ 0800 181 900, ⓦ vikinglodge.co.nz. One of Arrowtown's best-value motels, featuring an outdoor pool and a cluster of one- and two-bedroom A-frame chalets with well-equipped kitchens and Sky TV. There's also a children's play area featuring a trampoline. $139

MACETOWN

Macetown Historic Reserve 15km up the Arrow River from Arrowtown. A grassy DOC-run campsite among gold town remains sheltered by low, stone walls and willow, sycamore and apple trees. Facilities are limited to long-drop toilets, and you'll have to get your water from a stream. Free

EATING, DRINKING AND ENTERTAINMENT

All the places listed below are in Arrowtown.

★ **Arrow Brewing Company** Royal Oak Arcade, 48–50 Buckingham St ☎ 03 409 8849, ⓦ arrowbrewing .co.nz. Sink into deep red couches around the flame-effect fire, or catch the evening breeze in the courtyard at this modern take on a traditional local. Superb craft beers (a fruity Pilsener, a malty dark ale, a seasonal cherry ale and many more) are made on the premises and make a perfect accompaniment to gourmet pies (try a pie and pint for $15), and freestyle pizza ($22). Daily 11am–10pm or later.

Blue Door Bar 18 Buckingham St ☎ 03 442 0885. Stylish, intimate and cool (but not particularly cheap) bar in a 130-year-old cellar with a log fire. It's all rather informal and there's occasionally live jazz, blues and folk. Daily 5pm–late.

Bonjour 25 Ramshaw Lane ☎03 409 8946, ⓦbonjour arrowtown.com. Almost all the staff are French and this great little crêperie and *epicerie* where tables with gingham cloths spill out onto Ramshaw Lane to catch the morning sun. Come for a coffee and a pain aux raisin, a sweet crêpe ($6–13) or savoury *gallete* ($10–18) or something more substantial such as steak frites with salad ($19), duck a l'orange ($31) or a winter fondue ($28). Daily 8.30am–9pm.

★ **Pesto** 18 Buckingham St ☎03 442 0885, ⓦpesto .co.nz. Gourmet pizza and pasta restaurant with mains under $25. If they're busy they'll retrieve you from the *Blue Door Bar* (which they also own), when your table's ready. Daily 5–10pm or later.

★ **Provisions** 65 Buckingham St ☎03 442 0714, ⓦprovisions.co.nz. Delightful little café in a historic miner's cottage with a sunny terrace and garden. Mouthwatering counter food (mostly using their own range of chutneys, vinegars and sauces) is supplemented by the likes of devilled kidneys on toast ($15) or seasonal salads. The sticky buns and gingerbread are legendary. Licensed. Daily 9am–5pm.

Saffron 18 Buckingham St ☎03 442 0131, ⓦsaffron restaurant.co.nz. Arrowtown's finest restaurant (owned by the same folk as *Pesto*) is classy without being overformal and specializes in South Island produce cooked to perfection. Menu items include the likes of lamb sweetbreads with bone-marrow dumplings ($29) followed by confit of rabbit and black sausage in puff pastry ($40). Daily noon–10pm or later.

CINEMA

★ **Dorothy Brown's** Off Buckingham St ☎03 442 1964, ⓦdorothybrowns.com. This wonderful little twoscreen independent cinema is almost too good to be true. Watch mainstream and more arty films from stupendously comfortable seats (40-seat theatre $18.50; 15-seat theatre $15.50) and you can take your wine and snacks in with you.

Gibbston

The **Kawarau River** flows out of Lake Wakatipu near the *Queenstown Hilton* and winds its way past Queenstown's airport before picking up the waters of the Shotover River and plunging into the **Kawarau Gorge**. The river stays confined for the next 30km before spilling into Lake Dunstan by Cromwell's Goldfields Mining Centre (see p.737).

The valley is a major destination for Queenstown's whitewater rafting, sledging and bungy operators, but **Gibbston**, essentially the first 12km of the gorge, has gained an enviable reputation for its wineries. It is only since the 1980s that **grapes** have been grown commercially in Central Otago, one of the world's most southerly wine-growing regions. The vineyards lie close to the 45th parallel in a landscape detractors poohpoohed as too cold for wine production, despite the fact that the Rhône Valley in France lies on a similar latitude. A continental climate of hot dry summers and long cold winters prevails, which tends to result in low yields and high production costs, forcing wineries to go for quality boutique wines sold at prices which seem high (mostly $25–40) until you taste them.

Pioneer winemakers initially experimented in Gibbston, and although far more grapes are now grown around 30km west near Cromwell and Bannockburn (see p.737), Gibbston remains a wine showcase. Half a dozen places have cellar doors open for tasting, several with superb restaurants.

You can drive to them all, but you'll appreciate the experience a lot more if you join one of the **wine tours** that depart from Queenstown (see box, p.699).

Brief history

The steep schist and gravel slopes on the southern banks of the **Kawarau River** were recognized as potential sites for vineyards as early as 1864, when French miner Jean Désiré Feraud, bored of his gold claim at Frenchman's Point near Clyde, planted grapes from cuttings brought over from Australia. His wines won awards at shows in Australia, but by the early 1880s he'd decamped to Dunedin. No more grapes were grown until 1976, when the Rippon vineyard was planted, outside Wanaka (see p.725). It was another five years before the Kawarau Gorge was recognized as ideally suited to the cultivation of Pinot Gris, Riesling and particularly Pinot Noir grapes, with Alan Brady

13

releasing the first commercial wines from Gibbston Valley Wines in 1987. Since then, local winemakers have garnered several shelves full of awards, especially for the elegant, fruit-driven Pinot Noirs.

As an added bonus, the dry conditions inhibit growth of fungus and mildew; the dreaded phylloxera has been kept at bay so far.

Kawerau Bungy Centre

SH6, 23km east of Queenstown • Daily 9am–5pm • Free; bungy jump $180; bungy trampoline adults $20 (kids $15) • ☎ 0800 286 495, ⊕ bungy.co.nz

Almost everyone stops in to at least watch the antics at the Kawarau Bungy Centre, right beside SH6. The original road through the gorge crossed the river here on the 1880 **Kawarau Gorge Suspension Bridge**, which in 1988 became the world's first commercial bungy site. It remains the most frequently jumped site, and the only place hereabouts where you can get dunked in a river. The scene, at busy times, is a ghoulish production line of bungy initiates being trundled out and tour buses disgorging spectators to fill the viewing platforms.

If you're going to bungy anywhere (and are not too bothered that at 43m this is nowhere near the highest jump) then this is the one to do. The location is superb and you've always got an audience. You get a bragging T-shirt and free transport from Queenstown if needed. Kids and anyone not up for the real thing can go on the **bungy trampoline**.

EATING AND DRINKING   GIBBSTON

The following wineries all have **tastings**, and some have excellent on-site **restaurants**. They're listed in increasing distance from Queenstown.

Amisfield 10 Lake Hayes Rd ☎ 03 442 0556, ⊕ amisfield .co.nz; map p.706. Chic modern winery, artfully combining local schist with big windows and recycled timbers. Either taste four wines ($5) or step up to six premium wines ($12) including their renowned estate-grown Amisfield Pinot Noir. Put a few hours aside for lunch at their gorgeous bistro and courtyard, perhaps going for the popular "trust the chef" option with seven dishes served over three courses ($55; with wine match and dessert $100). The Connectabus between Frankton and Arrowtown passes right outside. Tastings daily 10am–6pm; bistro daily 11am–8pm (last booking 6pm).

Chard Farm 205 Chard Rd ☎ 03 442 6110, ⊕ chardfarm .co.nz; map p.706. Free tasting of a wide range of wines – notably Chardonnay, Pinot Noir and Pinot Gris – at one of the Gibbston originals. It's reached down a precipitous 2km dirt road off SH6 opposite the Kawarau Bungy. Mon–Fri 10am–5pm, Sat & Sun 11am–5pm.

Peregrine SH6 ☎ 03 442 4000, ⊕ peregrinewines .co.nz; map p.706. Nestled under a huge steel and plastic structure designed to mimic both the peregrine's wing and the angled layering of the local schist, this stylish winery has free tastings with views of the elegantly industrial barrel room. Superb wine too. Daily 10am–5pm.

Gibbston Valley 1820 Gibbston Valley Hwy (SH6) ☎ 03 442 6910, ⊕ gvwines.co.nz; map p.706. The original and most highly evolved of the region's wineries, with tasting ($5 for three tastes) plus a couple of wine tours which visit a "cave" blasted 80m into the hillside in the late 1980s: The Cave Tour (hourly 10am–4pm; 30min; $15) explores the "cave" and includes some tasting, while the Cave Tour Select (daily 11am & 2pm; $25) upgrades the wines tasted and the quality of the interpretation. There's also a popular daytime garden and conservatory restaurant offering a set menu for two ($46 including wine) along with platters and the likes of pork and puy lentils with pilaf ($29). Don't miss the adjacent cheesery to sample their wine-washed Monk's Gold and signature Pecorino-style Balfour. Daily: Dec–Feb 10am–6pm; March–Nov 10am–5pm.

The Winehouse & Kitchen 1693 SH6 ☎ 03 442 7310, ⊕ winehouse.co.nz; map p.706. Relatively new winery and restaurant by the Kawarau Bungy Centre and owned by AJ Hackett Bungy co-founder Henry van Asch. Call in for an extensive selection of tastings or linger over lunch in their casual but classy restaurant with dishes such as chilli squid and mango salad ($27). The interior is decorated with kitsch Kiwi icons, while outside there's a shady terrace with a big fireplace and a potager garden planted with things that influence the taste of their main wines, such as gooseberry, plum and assorted herbs. Daily 10am–5pm.

Glenorchy

13

The tiny mountain-girt village of **GLENORCHY**, at the head of Lake Wakatipu 50km northwest of Queenstown, is quiet and supremely picturesque, making it a perfect retreat. For many, it is simply a staging post en route to some of the finest **tramping** in New Zealand – a circuit of the Rees and Dart rivers, the Routeburn Track and the Greenstone and Caples tracks.

While a fair number of tourists pass through each day (many to ride the Dart River Jet), Glenorchy remains small, with just a petrol station, a post office, a couple of pubs and cafés, some accommodation and a grocery shop. Just about every local operator plasters its promotional material with *Lord of the Rings* location imagery, as several movie scenes were shot hereabouts. Indeed, the area has been deemed stunning enough to act as movie backdrops for the Rockies and the European Alps and in movies as diverse as *The Chronicles of Narnia: The Lion, the Witch and the Wardrobe*, Peter Jackson's *The Lovely Bones* and *X-Men Origins: Wolverine*. Naturally, Peter Jackson returned in late 2011 to film segments for *The Hobbit* movies. If you need to see specific shooting sites, join the Queenstown-based Safari of the Scenes trips run by Nomad Safaris (see p.698).

Brief history

The Glenorchy region's fantastic scenery owes a debt to beds of ancient sea-floor sediments laid down some 220–270 million years ago and metamorphosed into the grey-green schists and *pounamu* (greenstone) of the Forbes and Humboldt mountains. The western and northern flanks of the Forbes Mountains were shaped by the Dart Glacier, now a relatively short tongue of ice which, at its peak 18,000 years ago, formed the root of the huge glacial system that gouged out the floor of Lake Wakatipu. For a map of the area, see p.716.

In pre-European times the plain beside the combined delta of the Rees and Dart rivers was known as **Kotapahau**, "the place of revenge killing", a reference perhaps to fights between rival *hapu* over the esteemed *pounamu* which littered an area centred on the bed of the Dart River. There's still greenstone up there, but most is protected within the bounds of the Mount Aspiring National Park.

The first **Europeans** to penetrate the area were gold prospectors, government surveyors and nearby run-holders in search of fresh grazing. The fledgling community of Glenorchy served these disparate groups, along with teams of sawmillers and workers from a mine extracting scheelite, a tungsten ore used in armaments manufacture. Despite the lack of road access, **tourists** began to arrive early in the twentieth century, cruising across Lake Wakatipu on the TSS *Earnslaw* before being decanted into charabancs for the 20km jolt north to the Arcadia homestead at **Paradise** – an admittedly beautiful spot, though the name apparently comes from the abundance of paradise ducks in the area. The **road from Queenstown** was eventually pushed through in 1962, opening up a fine lakeside drive.

ARRIVAL AND DEPARTURE	GLENORCHY

By car and bus It is a beautiful drive from Queenstown to Glenorchy, and you can continue from there to the major trailheads (which all have parking areas). But many hikes end a long way from where they start so it makes sense to leave your vehicle in either Queenstown or Glenorchy and use shuttle buses to get to the trailheads.

Bus destinations Dart trailhead (1–2 daily; 40min); Greenstone/Caples trailhead (1–2 daily; 50min); Queenstown (2–4 daily; 1hr); Rees trailhead (1–2 daily; 40min); Routeburn Shelter (2–3 daily; 30min).

BUS/TRANSPORT COMPANIES

Buckley Transport ☎03 442 8215, ⓦbuckley transport.co.nz. Track transport getting you to Routeburn Shelter for an early start (9.15am; $45 from Queenstown; operates all year).They also run a service from the far end of the Routeburn Track to Queenstown (departs The Divide at 2pm; $90) and offer a round-trip package for $125.

Info&Track ☎0800 462 248, ⓦinfotrack.co.nz. The main tramp trailhead operator running between Queenstown and Glenorchy ($20 each way) and continuing to the trailheads

ROUTEBURN, GREENSTONE, CAPLES AND REES-DART TRACKS

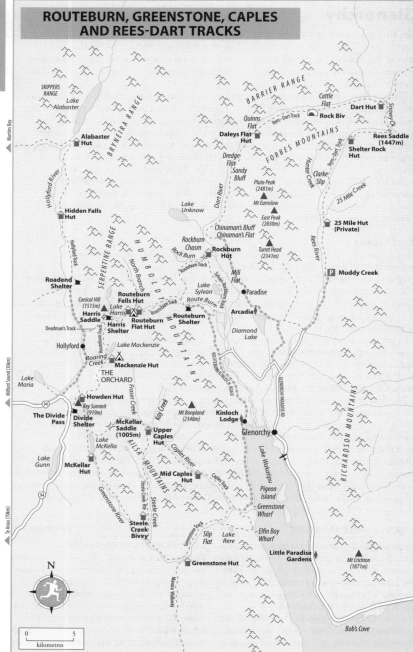

SKIPPERS RANGE

Lake Alabaster

BRYNEIRA RANGE

BARRIER RANGE

Cattle Flat

Dart Hut

Snowy Ck

Quinns Flat

Rock Biv

Rees-Dart Track

Alabaster Hut

Daleys Flat Hut

FORBES MOUNTAINS

Rees Saddle (1447m)

Shelter Rock Hut

Dredge Flat

Sandy Bluff

Hunter Creek

Clarke Slip

Rees-Dart Track

Hollyford River

Hidden Falls Hut

Lake Unknow

Dart River

Pluto Peak (2481m)

Mt Earnslaw

25 Mile Creek

25 Mile Hut (Private)

SERPENTINE RANGE

Hollyford Track

Conical Hill (1515m)

North Branch

HUMBOLDT

Chinaman's Bluff

Chinaman's Flat

East Peak (2830m)

Rees River

Rockburn Chasm

Rock Burn

Rockburn Hut

Turret Head (2341m)

Muddy Creek

Roadend Shelter

Routeburn Track

Mill Flat

Routeburn Falls Hut

Lake Harris

Lake Sylvan

Route Burn

Paradise

Harris Saddle

Harris Shelter

Routeburn Flat Hut

Routeburn Shelter

Arcadia

Sylvan-Rockburn Track

Deadman's Track

Routeburn Track

Diamond Lake

Hollyford

MOUNTAINS

Lake Mackenzie

Lake Maria

Roaring Creek

Mackenzie Hut

THE ORCHARD

Lake Gunn

94

Howden Hut

Key Summit (919m)

Fraser Creek

Mt Bonpland (2348m)

Kinloch Lodge

ROUTEBURN-KINLOCH ROAD

GLENORCHY PARADISE RD

RICHARDSON MOUNTAINS

The Divide

Divide Shelter

Pass

McKellar Saddle (1005m)

Upper Caples Hut

Kay Creek

Glenorchy

Lake Wakatipu

AILSA MOUNTAINS

Lake McKella

Caples River

McKellar Hut

Mid Caples Hut

Caples Track

Pigeon Island

94

Greenstone River

Steele Creek Trk

Steele Creek

Greenstone Wharf

Mt Crichton (1871m)

Steele Creek Bivvy

Greenstone Track

Slip Flat

Lake Rere

Elfin Bay Wharf

Little Paradise Gardens

Greenstone Hut

Mavora Walkway

Bob's Cove

N

0   5
kilometres

Mavora Lakes

Martins Bay

Milford Sound (30km)

Te Anau (70km)

GLENORCHY ACTIVITIES

Almost all the activities in and around Glenorchy are pitched at the Queenstown crowd, but you can always link up with groups when they arrive in town. Durations and prices quoted here are from Glenorchy; most companies charge around $20–30 for transport to and from Queenstown and Queenstown-based trips are two hours longer.

WALKING

Glenorchy Walkway (2km loop; 30–40min; flat). To get a feel for the area, follow the pleasant stroll from the wharf at the end of Islay Street along the edge of Lake Wakatipu and through the wetlands around the lagoon.

JETBOATING

Dart River Jet Safaris Mull St, Glenorchy ☎ 0800 327 853, ⓦ dartriver.co.nz. Busloads are transported from Queenstown for the excellent jetboating on the Dart River, which fully utilizes the vessel's shallow-water capabilities, picking routes through braided riverbeds amid grand snowcapped mountains on the edge of Mount Aspiring National Park. Their Wilderness Safari (3hr from Glenorchy; 6hr from Queenstown; $219 from either town) involves an hour and a half jetboat ride, a bushwalk and a ride in a 4WD coach through some magnificent scenery, including *Lord of the Rings* and *The Hobbit* locations. You can also combine an upstream jetboat ride with canoeing downstream in their Funyak Safari (7hr from Glenorchy, 9hr from Queenstown; $289) in two- or three-person inflatable canoes. Suitable even for absolute beginners, this is a gentle trip with no rapids and little likelihood of an enforced swim. The highlight is the brief stop to walk into Rockburn Chasm, where a small tributary of the Dart has carved out a narrow, twisting canyon filled with calm, clear water. Open year-round.

HORSE RIDING

High Country Horses Priory Rd, 10km north of town ☎ 03 442 9915, ⓦ high-country-horses.co.nz. Glenorchy has always been a horsey town, and although it isn't the cheapest place to ride, the scenery is matchless. Join the River and Willows ride (2hr riding; $125) with a couple of river crossings, the Paradise View ride (3hr riding; $160) with lots of *LOTR* locations, or the more committing Mountain High, River Deep (5–6hr riding; $295). Trips run all year; add $10–20 for Queenstown pick-ups.

BIKING

Revolution Tours ☎ 0800 274 334, ⓦ revolution tours.co.nz. For easy riding and great scenery join the Pedal to Paradise (9hr ex-Queenstown; $220) exploring the flat gravel roads of the Dart Valley with lunch and refreshments provided. The same trails are included as part of their four-day Wakatipu circuit (see p.699).

LAND-ROVER TOURS

Mountainland Rovers 37 Mull St ☎ 03 441 1323, ⓦ mountainlandrovers.co.nz. See the local area on Land-Rover tours (3hr; $139), head up the Rees Valley to the spectacular Lennox Falls or hit the much-viewed *LOTR* circuit. The emphasis is on appreciating the scenery and history of the area, and driver Dick Watson spins a good yarn.

KAYAKING

Kinloch Kayaks ☎ 03 442 4900, ⓦ kayakkinloch .co.nz. Guided sit-on-top kayaking trips on moody Lake Wakatipu are run from *Kinloch Lodge*. Explore the quiet braids of the Dart River (1hr at sunrise or sunset; $40), or stay on the lake for two-hour paddles (10am & 2pm; $80) that include a visit to the site of the region's original sawmill and delicious home baking, topped off with a dip in the outdoor hot tub. It is also possible to kayak to the lodge from Glenorchy (30–40min paddle; $60 one-way, luggage transferred by road).

---

for the Dart ($50); Greenstone/Caples ($35), Rees ($35) and Routeburn ($25). Their Routeburn Track loop package costs $116. Operates late Oct–late April only.
Kinloch Lodge ☎ 03 442 4900, ⓦ kinlochlodge.co.nz. Runs a bus from Glenorchy to their lodge ($15) with links to the Routeburn and Greenstone/Caples trailheads.
Glenorchy Journeys ☎ 03 409 0800, ⓦ glenorchy journeys.co.nz. Glenorchy-based operator linking all the trailheads to Glenorchy and Queenstown at very competitive prices.

13

INFORMATION

Tourist information Glenorchy General Store, 2 Oban St ☎ 03 441 0303. The shop has unstaffed DOC displays, limited groceries, internet and wi-fi ($6/hr).

ACCOMMODATION

Glenorchy Holiday Park 2 Oban St ☎ 03 441 0303. Well-organized site with spacious tent and powered sites, plus cabins sleeping up to four. Non-residents can shower here for $5. Camping $15, dorms $20, cabins $48

Glenorchy Lake House 13 Mull St ☎ 03 442 4900, ⓦ glenorchylakehouse.co.nz. Central two-room lodge with sumptuous fittings and bedding, deep baths, a spacious lounge with mountain views and a big hot tub outside. Guests have the place to themselves but someone will miraculously appear to cook a delicious breakfast and you can even organize gourmet caterers to turn up and prepare a feast ($55–95/person). Room with private bath $325, en suite $380

Kinloch Foreshore Recreation Reserve A small and very pleasant lakeside DOC campsite tucked away in the trees by *Kinloch Lodge*, with a toilet, BBQ area, picnic table and stream water (which should be treated). $7

★ **Kinloch Lodge** 862 Kinloch Rd, 26km by road from Glenorchy ☎ 03 442 4900, ⓦ kinlochlodge.co.nz. Located across the head of the lake from Glenorchy but close to the trailheads for the Greenstone, Caples and Routeburn tracks, this fine spot makes an excellent, peaceful retreat before or after some hard tramping, not least because of the free spa with great lake views ($10 for non-guests, including a shower). Enthusiastically run, the original 1868 Heritage Lodge (free internet) houses small but comfortable Victorian-styled rooms with shared bathrooms and a lovely deck that catches the morning sun. Rooms around a pleasant lawn constitute the adjacent Wilderness Lodge, a self-catering backpacker section (and associate YHA) with bunks and neat rooms, one of which is en-suite. They can arrange boat transport from Glenorchy ($15/person each way; minimum two people between Glenorchy and the lodge), bike rental ($10/hr; $50/day), fishing rod rental ($15/day), guided kayak trips and transport to the track ends. Routeburn and Greenstone/Caples track transfers are free if you stay two nights. Dorms $33, backpacker double $90, backpacker en suite $132, three-course dinner B&B rooms/person $139

Mount Earnslaw Motels 87 Oban St ☎ 03 442 6993, ⓦ mtearnslawmotel.co.nz. Glenorchy's only motel has well-kept and spacious studio units with super-king beds, double-glazed windows, free wi-fi and access to a laundry for that post-tramp clean-up. $120

Sylvan campsite 23km northwest of Glenorchy. Simple but very pleasant DOC campsite beside the burbling Route Burn with BBQ pits, picnic tables and a vault toilet. Camp in the shade of beech trees, gather stream water (which should be treated) and don't miss the easy walk to Lake Sylvan. $7

EATING

Café at The Trading Post 13 Mull St ☎ 03 442 7084, ⓦ glenorchytradingpost.co.nz. Organic Fairtrade coffee, restorative fruit smoothies ($7) and delightful high teas ($20) are just the ticket at this friendly little shop. Eat in or out on the grass. Mon–Sat 10am–4pm.

Glenorchy Café & Bar 27 Mull St ☎ 03 442 9978. Convivial café in the former post office that's very popular for breakfasts, soups, flat breads, gourmet pizzas (Sat evenings only) and other home-made treats; check out the ludicrously large cookies. Also has a stylish wee bar out back. Daily 8.30am–5pm, and until 10pm on Sat in summer.

Harry's Bar & Restaurant Kinloch Lodge ☎ 03 442 4900, ⓦ kinlochlodge.co.nz. The heart of the lodge, this cosy spot with a lake-view deck serves a great range of breakfasts and the likes of wild venison burger and fries ($20). Dinner is either quality bar meals or a full three-course meal ($45; booking required). Summer daily 8–9.30am, noon–3pm & 6.30–7.30pm; closes at 5pm in winter.

The Routeburn Track

The fame of the **Routeburn Track** (32km; 2–3 days) is eclipsed only by that of the Milford Track (see p.771), yet arguably it is superior, with better-spaced huts, more varied scenery and a route mostly above the bushline, away from sandflies. The Routeburn is one of New Zealand's Great Walks, and one of the finest of them, straddling the spine of the Humboldt Mountains and providing access to many of the southwestern wilderness's most archetypal features: forested valleys rich with birdlife (including the rare yellow-headed mohua) and plunging waterfalls are combined with river flats, lakes and spectacular mountain scenery. The nature of the terrain means that

FROM TOP ARROWTOWN (P.708); THE TSS *EARNSLAW* (P.694) >

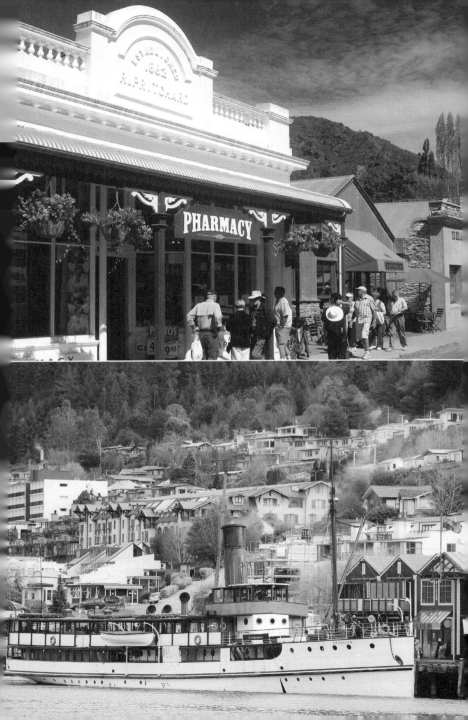

13

the Routeburn is usually promoted as a moderate tramp and the short distance between huts eases the strain. Anyone of moderate fitness who can carry a backpack for five or six hours a day should be fine. That said, the track passes through subalpine country and snowfall and flooding can sometimes close it, even in summer. Fit hikers might consider doing it in two long days, though that doesn't leave much time for soaking up the scenery.

Most people walk the Routeburn Track westwards from Glenorchy to The Divide. To return to Queenstown from here is a journey approaching 300km, so to avoid backtracking anyone with a day or two to spare should consider a **Routeburn combo** with the Greenstone Track or Caples Track to make a three- to five-day loop. In **winter** the Routeburn takes on a different character and becomes a much more serious undertaking. The track is often snowbound and extremely slippery, the risk of avalanche is high and the huts are unheated. Return day-trips from Routeburn Shelter to Routeburn Falls Hut and from The Divide to the Lake Mackenzie Hut are much better bets.

Routeburn Shelter to Routeburn Flats Hut

7km; 1hr 30min–2hr 30min; 250m ascent

The route follows Route Burn steadily uphill on a metre-wide track, though it's never strenuous and has an even shingle surface. Because Route Burn is a tributary of the Dart River, you are following a side valley and will have experienced a wide variety of scenery – river flats, waterfalls and open beech forest – by the time you reach the Routeburn Flats Hut (20 bunks). The nearby *Routeburn Flats* campsite is superbly sited on the edge of wide alluvial flats, at the end of a short path a couple of hundred metres beyond the hut. Only a few tents are permitted and campers can make use of an open fireplace and a small shelter, the run-off from which provides water for cooking.

Routeburn Flats Hut to Routeburn Falls Hut

2km; 1hr–1hr 30min; 300m ascent

Hut users are better off making the first day a little longer and tackling this next leg, which is considerably steeper and rougher, the extra exertion rewarded by a stay at the magnificently sited Routeburn Falls Hut (48 bunks), perched on the bushline above a precipice with eastward views looking back to Routeburn Flats and Sugar Loaf (1329m).

Routeburn Falls Hut to Lake Mackenzie Hut

11km; 4–6hr; 300m ascent, 350m descent

This is the longest stretch and covers the most exposed section of the track. Most of the day is spent above the bushline among the subalpine snow tussock of the Harris Saddle (1255m) and passing through bog country, where sundews, bladderworts and orchids thrive. You might even catch sight of chamois clambering on the rocks to either side of the saddle. The track climbs gradually enough to the Harris Saddle Shelter (2–3hr), which offers respite from the wind and has toilets; on a clear day, drop your pack here and climb up to the 1515m summit of **Conical Hill** (2km return; at least 1hr; 260m ascent) for superb views down into the Hollyford Valley and along it to Martin Bay and the Tasman Sea. Continuing from the Harris Saddle Shelter, you cross from the Mount Aspiring National Park into the Fiordland National Park and skirt high along the edge of the Hollyford Valley, before switchbacking down through silver beech, fuchsia and ribbonwood to Lake Mackenzie Hut (50 bunks). The campsite is a short way from the hut, near the lake.

Lake Mackenzie Hut to Howden Hut

13

9km; 3–4hr; 250m descent

The track continues along the mountainside through a grassy patch of ribbonwood, known as The Orchard, and past the cascading Earland Falls to the Howden Hut (28 bunks) at the junction of three tracks. The Greenstone and Caples tracks (handy for turning the tramp into a five-day Glenorchy-based circuit) head south, while the Routeburn continues.

Howden Hut to The Divide

3km; 1hr–1hr 30min; 50m net descent

This stretch initially climbs for twenty minutes to a point where you can make a half-hour excursion to Key Summit for views of three major river systems – the Hollyford, the Eglinton and the Greenstone. From the **Key Summit** (919m) turn-off, the track descends through silver beech to the car park and shelter at The Divide.

ARRIVAL AND DEPARTURE

THE ROUTEBURN TRACK

Trailhead transport You can drive to the Routeburn Shelter trailhead, but unless you're doing a day walk it makes sense to use the trailhead buses (see p.715). These drop off at Routeburn Shelter at around 7.30am, 10am and 2pm, giving flexibility to hike to either Routeburn Flats hut or continue to Routeburn Falls huts, and even offering ample opportunity to explore the north branch of Route Burn. Routeburn Shelter drop-offs cost $25 from Glenorchy and $45 from Queenstown. At The Divide (the western end of the Routeburn Track) catch one of the several buses running between Te Anau and Milford Sound. The best bet is Tracknet (☎ 0800 483 262, ⊛ tracknet.net) with services to Te Anau (10.15am, 3.15pm & 5.45pm; and 1.30pm on demand; $38) and to Milford Sound (8.15am, 10.45am & 2.15pm; $33).

INFORMATION AND TOURS

Seasons The Routeburn can be hiked all year, though the main hiking season is Oct–late April.

Leaflets and maps DOC's *Routeburn Track* brochure is adequate but the 1:65,000 *Routeburn, Caples & Greenstone Parkmap* ($19) is better.

Weather and track conditions DOC in Queenstown will have the latest weather forecast and track conditions; check ⊛ doc.govt.nz/routeburntrack.

Safety DOC do not track trampers' whereabouts. Let someone know your intentions through ⊛ adventuresmart .org.nz.

Luggage transfer Some hotels/hostels in Queenstown provide a transfer service; see p.705.

Car relocation service For two or more people wanting to walk the Routeburn and return to Queenstown it may be cheaper and more convenient to use Routeburn Relocators (☎ 021 048 8698, ⊛ routeburntrack.info; $250/vehicle) who drive your vehicle from Routeburn Shelter to The Divide so it's there for you when you finish – they then run the Routeburn to get back to their own vehicle.

GUIDED WALKS

Ultimate Hikes ☎ 0800 659 255, ⊛ ultimatehikes.co .nz. If you want to walk the track in comfort with excellent interpretation, this is the outfit for you. They offer return transport from Queenstown, three days' guided walking, all meals, hot showers and two nights in lodges equipped with four-share shared-bath rooms, duvets and a pay bar (Dec–March $1270; Nov & April $1125). The pace is fairly leisurely and walkers only carry their personal effects (no food or camping equipment); daily hikes are typically 5–6hr, occasionally on rough terrain, so anyone unused to hill walking should still do a good deal of preparatory hiking. If you don't fancy the whole three-day hike and the tyranny of shuttle buses but still want to sample the track, consider the Routeburn Encounter day-hike (Nov– late April daily; 10hr; $169), which includes transport from Queenstown, a walk to Routeburn Flats or Routeburn Falls, gear and lunch. Ultimate also offers: a Grand Traverse (multi-share room: Dec–March $1765; Nov & April $1560), a five-day, six-night walk combining the Routeburn and Greenstone tracks; a Routeburn/Milford Track combo (multi-share room: Dec–March $3265; Nov & April $2955).

ACCOMMODATION

Booking There's a compulsory system for booking accommodation for the huts and campsites for the duration of its tramping season. The system (which guarantees you a bed) allows people to walk in either direction, retrace their steps and stay up to two nights in a particular hut. Numbers are limited, so book as far ahead as possible

13

– three months if you need a specific departure date or are part of a large group. It is easiest to book online (🌐 doc .govt.nz) from July 1 for the following season, though it is also possible to book by mail and in person at DOC visitor centres. If the track is closed due to bad weather or track conditions, full refunds are given; however, new bookings can only be made if there is space. Changes can be made to existing bookings ($10 fee) before you start, again, if space allows.

Huts The four huts along the track are equipped with flush toilets, running water (which must be treated), and gas

rings: you'll need to carry your own pans, plates and food. Huts are unheated and have no gas outside the main season. During the main Oct–late April season the huts are staffed by a warden, and the Backcountry Hut Pass is not valid. In winter, huts cannot be booked, but the pass is valid. Per person/night Oct–late April $51.50, per person/ night in winter $15

Camping A limited number of campsites with pit toilets and water exist close to the Routeburn Flats and Lake Mackenzie huts; campers are not allowed to use hut facilities. $15.30

Greenstone and Caples tracks

The **Greenstone Track** (36km; 2–3 days) and **Caples Track** (27km; 2 days) run roughly parallel to each other. Both are easy, following gently graded, parallel river valleys where the wilderness experience is moderated by grazing cattle from the high-country stations along the Lake Wakatipu shore. The Greenstone occupies the broader, U-shaped valley carved out by one arm of the huge Hollyford Glacier. The Caples runs over the subalpine McKellar Saddle and down the Caples Valley, where the river is bigger and the narrow base of the valley forces the path closer to it.

The Greenstone and Caples can be done as a loop from Greenstone car park, 6km south of *Kinloch Lodge*, but more commonly people combine the Routeburn Track with either the Greenstone or the Caples: we've described both tracks as a follow-up to the Routeburn. In **winter**, the lower-level Greenstone and Caples tracks also make a less daunting prospect than the Routeburn: the McKellar Saddle is often snow-covered but at least the huts are heated (see opposite).

Along the Greenstone

Howden Hut to McKellar Hut
7km; 2hr–2hr 30min; 50m descent

After 20min the track passes the primitive but free *Greenstone Saddle* campsite. The Greenstone continues beside Lake McKellar to McKellar Hut (24 bunks), just outside the Fiordland National Park.

McKellar Hut to Greenstone Hut
17km; 4hr 30min–6hr 30min; 100m descent

This easy track starts by crossing the Greenstone River and follows the true left bank down a broad, grazed valley mostly along river flats and through the lower slopes of the beech forests. A swingbridge then crosses Steele Creek, and the track continues for two more hours to the Greenstone Hut (20 bunks), a good base for exploring the gentle **Mavora Walkway** to the south. It will take you 2–3 days, passing through

---

TRAMPING THE ROUTEBURN AND GREENSTONE/CAPLES FROM THE DIVIDE

Our coverage of the Routeburn, Greenstone and Caples tracks assumes you're starting from Glenorchy, but it's also possible to hike the Greenstone/Caples and Routeburn combination from The Divide (north of Te Anau) with the luxury of a mid-tramp break at *Kinloch Lodge* (see p.718) which runs transport from the Greenstone car park to the lodge then on to Routeburn Shelter.

open tussock country and beech forest, to reach Mavora Lakes; a couple of huts ($5) provide accommodation en route.

Greenstone Hut to Greenstone car park
10km; 3–5hr; 100m descent

The track follows the true left bank as the valley narrows and the river heads into a long gorge. The river soon meets the Caples River, an enticing series of deep pools that make great swimming holes. A swingbridge gives access to the left bank of the Caples River and the Caples Track; turn right to Greenstone car park (20–30min), or left to Mid Caples Hut (see below).

Along the Caples
Howden Hut to Upper Caples Hut
14km; 6–8hr; 500m ascent, 550m descent

A pretty long day that includes a very steep bush-clad zigzag up to McKellar Saddle (1005m). Unfortunately, you can't shorten the day since camping is not allowed on the fragile bogland and open tussock of McKellar Saddle. The descent mostly follows snow poles, crossing and re-crossing the infant Caples River before regaining beech forest and the Upper Caples Hut (12 bunks).

Upper Caples Hut to Mid Caples Hut
7km; 2hr–2hr 30min; 50m descent

On this stretch you mainly cross grassland to the hut (12 bunks). Greenstone Wharf is within a day's walk of here, though you can break it into two sections, starting with this one.

Mid Caples Hut to Greenstone car park
7km; 2–3hr; 100m descent

The path reaches a short but dramatic gorge, crosses it and follows the true left bank, continuing alongside the bush edge and crossing grassy clearings before arriving at the junction with the Greenstone Track, from where it is only 20min to Greenstone Wharf car park.

ARRIVAL AND DEPARTURE   GREENSTONE AND CAPLES TRACKS

Trailhead transport There's a car park near Greenstone Wharf which is useful if you're planning a Greenstone & Caples loop. If you're combining with the Routeburn you'll want to use the trailhead buses (see p.715). Info&Track and Kinloch Lodge both call by at noon while Glenorchy Journeys visit at 7am, 9am and on demand. All charge $35 to/from Glenorchy and $50 to/from Queenstown: book ahead if you're coming off the track and hope to be picked up.

INFORMATION

Seasons The tracks are open and hut booking details remain constant year-round.

Leaflets and maps Use DOC's *Greenstone and Caples Tracks* leaflet, together with the 1:65,000 *Routeburn, Caples & Greenstone Parkmap* ($19).

Weather and track information DOC in Queenstown will have the latest weather forecast and track conditions; check ⊚ doc.govt.nz.

Safety Let someone know your intentions through ⊚ adventuresmart.org.nz.

ACCOMMODATION

Booking These tracks are far less popular than the Routeburn so reservations are neither necessary nor possible.

Huts The Greenstone and Caples tracks have two huts each. The huts are heated by wood-burning stoves but there are no gas rings so you'll need a cooking stove as well as pots and food. The Backcountry Pass is valid, or bring backcountry hut tickets. **$15**

Camping Campers are encouraged to camp next to the huts and use the outside facilities. Free camping is allowed in both valleys along the fringes of the bush, at least 50m away from the track and not on the open flats. **$5**

13 Rees–Dart Track

The **Rees–Dart Track** (58km; 3–4 days) is the toughest of the major tramps in the area, covering rugged terrain and requiring six to eight hours of effort each day. It follows the standard Kiwi tramp formula of ascending one river valley, crossing the pass and descending into another, but adds an excellent side trip to the Cascade Saddle.

Muddy Creek car park to Shelter Rock Hut

17km; 6–7hr; 400m ascent

The track follows a 4WD track across grass and gravel flats on the true left bank of the braided lower Rees and requires a couple of foot-soaking stream crossings. Press on past the Rees Valley Station's Twenty-five Mile Hut (private and dilapidated), across Twenty-five Mile Creek and over more river flats for another hour or so, with Hunter Creek and the peaks of the Forbes Mountains straight ahead. Just past Hunter Creek, the Rees Valley steepens appreciably and becomes cloaked in beech forests, which continue sporadically until just below the tree line, where the path passes the site of the old Shelter Rock Hut. Head on for 1km until you hit tussock country, where one final crossing of the Rees River, now a large stream, takes you back to the left bank and the Shelter Rock Hut (22 bunks).

Shelter Rock Hut to Dart Hut

9km; 4–6hr; 600m ascent, 450m descent

The second day is the shortest but one of the toughest, scaling the 1447m Rees Saddle. Stick to the true left bank of the Rees, traversing subalpine scrub and gravel banks for a couple of kilometres, before crossing the river and climbing to a tussock basin and the saddle. Descend across snow grass beside Snowy Creek, which churns down a narrow gorge to your right. A kilometre or so later the track crosses a swingbridge to the true right bank, commencing a loose and rocky descent past a long series of cascades to another crossing of Snowy Creek, just above its confluence with the Dart River. There are camping spots in the grassy areas on the true right bank and accommodation at Dart Hut (32 bunks); many stay two nights here, giving time to explore the Cascade Saddle route (see box, p.731).

Dart Hut to Daleys Flat Hut

16km; 5–7hr; 450m descent

The track from Dart Hut climbs high above the river and stays there for 3km, passing through beech forest before dropping to Cattle Flat, 5km of grassed alluvial ridges traced by a winding and energy-sapping but easy-to-follow route. At the end of Cattle Flat, the track returns to the bush and runs parallel to the river until it reaches the beautiful grassy expanse of Quinns Flat (lovely in late-afternoon light), where the track turns inland. Within half an hour you reach the sandfly-ridden Daleys Flat Hut (20 bunks), redeemed by its pleasant location on the edge of a clearing.

Daleys Flat Hut to Chinaman's Bluff

16km; 5–6hr; 100m ascent, 150m descent

The walk skips through the bush for around 4km until Dredge Flat, where you make your own track, looking for markers on the left that indicate where you re-enter the bush. The track then climbs steeply over Sandy Bluff before dropping to river level for an easy walk across the flats and along the river to Chinaman's Bluff. Track Transport pick up from here, though you can continue on foot from Chinaman's Bluff to Paradise car park (6km; 2hr; negligible descent) along a 4WD track.

ARRIVAL AND DEPARTURE

Trailhead transport You can drive to the Rees trailhead at Muddy Creek car park, 22km north of Glenorchy, and to the Dart trailhead at Paradise car park, 23km north of Glenorchy. A 4WD road continues to Chinaman's Bluff, 30km north of Glenorchy. It is generally easier to get a shuttle bus from either Queenstown or Glenorchy (see p.715), and bus timetables make it most convenient to tramp up the Rees and down the Dart. Info&Track will get you to the Rees trailhead around 10am and pick up from the Chinaman's Bluff at 2pm. Glenorchy Journeys drop at the Rees at 8am & 10am and pick up at Chinaman's Bluff on demand. Both companies charge $35 from Glenorchy and $50 from Queenstown to each of the trailheads.

INFORMATION

Seasons Commonly hiked Nov or Dec–April: the Rees–Dart in winter is really only for mountaineers.

Leaflets and maps DOC's *Dart and Rees Valleys* leaflet and *Mount Aspiring Parkmap* are good, but the more detailed 1:50,000 *Lake Williamson* and *Glenorchy* Topomaps are better.

Weather and track information DOC in Queenstown will have the latest weather forecast and track conditions; check ⓦ doc.govt.nz.

Safety Let someone know your intentions through ⓦ adventuresmart.org.nz.

ACCOMMODATION

Booking Reservations are currently neither necessary nor possible, though DOC plans to require campers and hut users to book in Jan and Feb from 2013 onwards.

Huts The three huts come with heating stove but no gas rings. Bring all cooking gear. Hut wardens are present from Nov–April. The Backcountry Pass is valid, or bring backcountry hut tickets. $15

Camping Permitted outside all huts and anywhere along the track (free) except for the fragile, subalpine section between Shelter Rock Hut and Dart Hut. $5

Wanaka and around

Pronounced evenly as Wa-Na-Ka, **WANAKA**, only 55km northeast of Queenstown (but over an hour by road), is kind of like its laidback cousin. There is a similar combination of beautiful lakeshore surroundings and robust adventure activities, but Wanaka remains an eminently manageable place, with the tenor of a village and a feeling of light and spaciousness – an excellent place in which to chill out for a few days.

There's no beating the setting, draped around the southern shores of **Lake Wanaka** at the point where the hummocky, poplar-studded hills of Central Otago rub up against the dramatic peaks of the Mount Aspiring National Park.

Although central Wanaka is a pleasant place to café cruise or relax on the foreshore, there are no sights as such. For **attractions** you'll either need to head 2km east to Puzzling World or a further 7km to the museums, a micro-brewery and airborne adventure activities around the airport. Alternatively, head 3km west to the delightful Rippon Vineyard. A half-day around the sights will leave plenty of time to go kayaking, jetboating, rock climbing or, best of all, canyoning.

With the jagged summits of the Southern Alps mirrored in Lake Wanaka's waters, the lure of **Mount Aspiring National Park** is strong and Wanaka makes a perfect base for easy walks and hard tramps.

During the winter months, Wanaka's relative calm is shattered by the arrival of skiers and snowboarders eager to explore the downhill **ski-fields** of **Treble Cone** and **Cardrona**, and the Nordic terrain at the **Snow Farm** (see box, p.727).

Brief history

Founded in the 1860s as a service centre for the local run-holders and itinerant gold miners, the town didn't really take off until the prosperous middle years of the twentieth century, when camping and caravanning Kiwis discovered its warm, dry summer climate. Though still only home to around 7000 people, it is now one of New Zealand's fastest-growing towns, with extensive developments and new housing subdivisions popping up everywhere.

WANAKA

0 — 500 metres

● RESTAURANTS, CAFÉS & BARS
Barluga — 6
Kai Whaka Pai — 7
The Landing — 3
Relishes — 5
Sasanoki — 4
Soul Food Organic Café — 1
Urban Grind — 2
White House Café & Bar — 8

● SHOPS
Hamills — 1
Outside Sports — 2

■ ACCOMMODATION
Albert Town Campground — 4
Altamont Lodge — 7
Base Wanaka — 11
Clearbrook — 12
Glendhu Bay Lakeside
  Holiday Park — 6
Lake Outlet Holiday Park — 2
Matterhorn South — 10
Mountain Range — 16
Peak Sportchalet — 1
Renmore House B&B — 14
River Run — 5
Te Wanaka Lodge — 9
Wanaka Bakpaka — 3
Wanaka Lakeview
  Holiday Park — 8
Wanaka Springs Lodge — 15
YHA Wanaka Purple Cow — 13

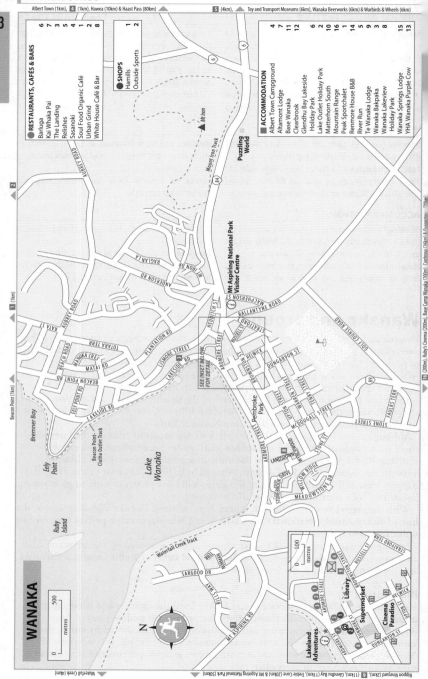

Albert Town (1km), ◀ 4 ▶ (1km), Hawea (10km) & Haast Pass (80km) ▲

5 (4km), ▲ Toy and Transport Museums (6km), Wanaka Beerworks (6km) & Warbirds & Wheels (6km)

Mt Iron

Puzzling World

Mt Aspiring National Park Visitor Centre

Lake Wanaka

Ruby Island

Eely Point

Bremner Bay

Beacon Point (1km) ◀

1 (1km) ▲

2

Pembroke Park

SEE INSET BELOW FOR DETAIL

Waterfall Creek Track

Lakeland Adventures

Library
Supermarket
Cinema Paradiso

0 — 100 metres

N

Rippon Vineyard (2km), 6 (11km), Glendhu Bay (11km), Treble Cone (20km) & Mt Aspiring National Park (50km) ▲

16 (200m), Ruby's Cinema (200m), Base Camp Wanaka (700m), Cardrona (26km) & Queenstown (70km) ▶

Waterfall Creek (4km) ▲

WINTER IN WANAKA

In June Wanaka gets geared up for winter, mountain-bike rental shops switch to ski rental (see p.732), watersports instructors don baggy snowboarder pants and frequent shuttle buses run up to the ski-fields. If you plan to drive up to the ski-fields, you'll need tyre chains, which can be rented at petrol stations in Wanaka.

DOWNHILL AND CROSS-COUNTRY SKIING

Cardrona Alpine Resort Reached by a 12km unsealed toll-free access road branching off 24km south of Wanaka, near Cardrona ☎03 443 7411, ⓦcardrona.com. Predominantly family-oriented field sprawled over three basins on the southeastern slopes of the 1934m Mount Cardrona. Expect dry snow and an abundance of gentle runs (five beginner, thirteen intermediate, nine advanced). There are quads and several learner tows, and a maximum vertical descent of 390m and everyone has the run of three terrain parks. You'll need snow chains to negotiate the access road to the base facilities halfway up the field. Non-drivers can get buses from Wanaka, and from Queenstown, an hour and a half away. There's limited accommodation on the mountain – in luxury, fully self-contained studios for two ($220), or two- and three-bedroom apartments which sleep up to eight ($490–620). Lift pass $95. Late June–early Oct.

Treble Cone 22km west of Wanaka, accessed by a 7km toll-free road ☎03 443 7443, ⓦtreblecone .co.nz. More experienced skiers tend to frequent the steep slopes here. Its appeal lies in open uncrowded runs (four beginner, sixteen intermediate, nineteen advanced) spectacularly located high above Lake Wanaka, and a full 700 vertical metres of skiing with moguls, powder runs, gully runs and plenty of natural and created half-pipes. Three new groomed trails make it much better for beginners than previously and snowboarders will have a ball. Morning buses leave from Wanaka, and a shuttle bus takes skiers from the start of the access road on Mount Aspiring Road up to the tows. Backcountry tours are also available from Treble Cone, with Aspiring Guides (☎03 443 9422, ⓦaspiringguides.com; $195). Lift pass $95. Late June–early Oct.

Snow Farm Across the valley from Cardrona, 24km south of Wanaka, then 13km up a winding dirt road ☎03 443 7542, ⓦsnowfarmnz.com. With so many Kiwi skiers committed to downhill, it comes as a surprise to discover a cross-country ski area. At $40 for access to the field and $30 for ski rental, it's an inexpensive way to get on the snow, negotiating the 55km of marked Nordic trails. July–Sept.

HELI-SKIING

Heli-skiing is not cheap, but there's no other way of getting to runs of up to 1200 vertical metres across virgin snow on any of six mountain ranges.

Harris Mountains Heli-Ski ☎03 442 6722, ⓦheliski.co.nz. Offers almost 400 different runs on 150 peaks – mainly in the Harris Mountains between Queenstown's Crown Range and Wanaka's Mount Aspiring National Park. Strong intermediate and advanced skiers get the most out of the experience, where conditions are more critical than at the ski-fields, but on average there's heli-skiing seventy percent of the time, typically in four- to five-day weather windows. Of the multitude of packages, the most popular is "The Classic" ($845), a four-run day.

Lake Wanaka waterfront

One of the real pleasures of Wanaka is spending time simply chilling out on the waterfront, a kilometre or so of grassy reserve-backed soft-gravel beach with wonderful mountain views. In summer it is full of people sunbathing, picnicking, feeding the ducks and renting various watercraft such as sit-on-top kayaks and pedal boats.

Rippon Vineyard

246 Mount Aspiring Rd, 3km west of town • Daily: Dec–April 11am–5pm; July–Nov noon–5.30pm • ☎03 443 8084, ⓦrippon.co.nz • Drive from Wanaka or walk in 40min alongside the lakeside Waterfall Creek Track, then uphill through the vines

To taste interesting wines in a stupendously scenic setting, make straight for **Rippon Vineyard**, Central Otago's oldest winery, established in 1982. Views from the modern, exposed-concrete-and-timber hilltop tasting room sweep down across the vines towards the lake with the mountains behind. Managed on organic and biodynamic principles,

13

the estate produces very good Pinot Noir sampled at free tastings. Also try their Riesling and the rare Osteiner Riesling hybrid.

You'll struggle to find a more spectacular picnic spot, so pack some tasty goodies and sit back in the sun as you sample the wares.

Stuart Landsborough's Puzzling World

188 SH84, almost 2km east of town • Daily: Nov–April 8.30am–6pm; May–Oct 8.30am–5pm • $12 for the maze or the illusion rooms; $15 for both • ☎ 03 443 7489, ⓦ puzzlingworld.co.nz

A line of monkey puzzle trees heralds **Stuart Landsborough's Puzzling World**, where the star attraction is "The Great Maze", a complex wooden structure comprising 1500m of dead-end passageways packed into a dense labyrinth, with overhead bridges linking the two halves. Your mission is to reach all four corner towers, either in any order (30min–1hr) or in a specific sequence (at least 1hr), then find your way out again. Much of the rest of the place delights in optical illusions, including the "Hall of Following Faces", an octagonal room with seven of the sides made up by arrays of moulded images of famous people. As you walk around, the faces – Einstein, Mother Teresa etc – appear to turn towards you. Yet more fun can be had, and some of Peter Jackson's hobbit-realizing tricks understood, in the Ames Forced Perspective Room, which has been carefully manipulated to make you appear either ent- or hobbit-sized. Yet more illusions are in the pipeline, but leave time to play with the frustrating puzzles in the café.

National Transport and Toy Museum

891 Wanaka–Luggate Hwy (SH6), 9km southeast of town • Daily 8.30am–5pm • $12; family $30 • ☎ 03 443 8765, ⓦ nttmuseum.co.nz

There's a heck of a lot of stuff at the **National Transport and Toy Museum** – hangars full of everything from 500 Barbie dolls and Meccano sets to jet fighters, an impressive *Star Wars* collection, a shiny row of British Seagull outboard motors and an astonishing hoard of cars, trucks and bikes preserved by Wanaka's dry climate. Some machines are well-kept examples of stuff still puttering around New Zealand roads, but there's also exotica such as a Centurion tank, Velocette and BSA bikes, a yellow-fur-covered Morris Minor and the Solar Kiwi Racer, an aluminium and glass-fibre bullet-shaped car powered by solar panels on its roof.

There's little effort to bring the vehicles up to concourse condition: the emphasis is on arresting any decay and providing something for everyone, from little kids to grandparents.

Wanaka Beerworks

891 Wanaka–Luggate Hwy (SH6), 9km southeast of town • Daily 11am–4pm; tours daily 2pm • Free • ☎ 03 443 1865 • ⓦ wanakabeerworks.co.nz

Having Belgian brewer Dave De Vylder at the helm ensures excellent brews at **Wanaka Beerworks**, oddly located by Wanaka's airport. Time your visit to coincide with the simple tour or call by to sample their regular brews – a golden malt, a pilsner and a dark ale. They also produce three bottle-conditioned seasonal brews, such as cherry wheat beer, that change four times a year. A tasting tray of three beers of your choice and some nibbles is $10. You'll find the brews in bars and restaurants around Central Otago.

Warbirds & Wheels

11 Lloyd Dunn Ave, Wanaka Airport, 9km southeast of town • Daily 9am–5pm • $20 • ☎ 03 443 7010, ⓦ warbirdsandwheels.com

The year-round face of the Warbirds over Wanaka festival (see box, p.736), **Warbirds & Wheels**, displays several warplanes in half a hangar, among them a Strikemaster training plane, a World War II hurricane and a Skyhawk that did service in the New Zealand

13

WALKS AROUND WANAKA

There are some great walks and more serious hikes around Wanaka, and these are some of the best; no special gear is required, just robust shoes, wet-weather gear, sun protection and DOC's *Wanaka Outdoor Pursuits* leaflet ($3.50), which has a good map.

Mount Iron Track (4.5km return; 1hr 30min; 240m ascent). The most accessible of Wanaka's hilltop walks climbs a 549m glacially sculpted outcrop, its western and northern slopes ground smooth by the glacier that scoured its southern face. The path through farmland and the bird-filled manuka woodland of the Mount Iron Scenic Reserve starts 1500m east of Wanaka on SH84, climbing the steep southern face to the summit. Here you can enjoy magnificent panoramic views, before following the path down the east face of Mount Iron towards the entrance to Puzzling World (see opposite).

Roy's Peak Track (11km; 4–6hr; 1100m ascent). A more challenging prospect, winding up to the summit (1578m), for wonderful views over Lake Wanaka and surrounding glaciers and mountains. The path starts 7km west of Wanaka on the Mount Aspiring Rd, but is closed during the lambing season (Oct 1–Nov 10).

Diamond Lake Track (7km; 2hr 30min; 400m ascent). A fine local walk with great lake and mountain views, starting at the car park 18km west of Wanaka on the Mount Aspiring Rd. There are a couple of short variations, but to get the views you'll need to tackle the summit of Rocky Mountain (775m).

Beacon Point–Clutha Outlet Circuit (16km; 3–5hr; mostly flat). Long but undemanding riverbank and lakeside walk which starts from Wanaka and follows the shore to Eely Point (15min), a sheltered bay popular for boating and picnics. Beyond Eely Point is Bremner Bay and the continuation of the waterfront path to Beacon Point (a further 30min). Either return the same way or continue along Beacon Point Road to the *Lake Outlet Holiday Park* and pick up the Outlet Track, which runs 4km to Alison Avenue, then down to SH6 not far from the Albert Town bridge. By following SH6 this can be turned into a loop back to Wanaka, passing the base of Mount Iron.

Waterfall Creek Track (2.5km one-way; 35min; negligible ascent). The westbound equivalent of the Beacon Point–Clutha Outlet Circuit leaves Roy's Bay, heading through Wanaka Station Park and past Rippon Vineyard to a car park at Waterfall Creek. From here the path continues as the Millennium Walkway (5km each way; 1hr; 100m ascent), following lakeside terraces to Ironside's Hill. Both of these are open to bikers.

Air Force. The museum honours the festival's founder, aircraft owner and originator of the 1980s live-deer-capture industry, **Sir Tim Wallis**, whose colourful life story is told.

The other half of the hangar houses 25 classic cars. Displays change every six months (check the website for details) and you can usually see restoration going on in the workshop. Don't dismiss the slightly random **Visual Arts Gallery**, which has a fine collection of New Zealand painting that forms part of Fiona Campbell's art-to-the-people Real Art Roadshow (ⓦrealartroadshow.co.nz).

The Cardrona Valley

William Fox's unwitting discovery of gold at Arrowtown in 1862 quickly brought prospectors along the Crown Range and into the **Cardrona Valley**, where gold was discovered later that year. Five years on, the Europeans legged it to new fields on the West Coast, leaving the dregs to Chinese immigrants, who themselves had drifted away by 1870.

Tiny **CARDRONA**, 25km south of Wanaka, comprises little more than a few cottages, a long-forgotten cemetery, the *Cardrona Hotel* (see p.735) and the similarly ancient former post office and store.

South from here, the road twists over the **Crown Range Road** (SH89), the quickest and most direct route from Wanaka to Queenstown, though it is tortuous enough in

13

places to discourage anyone towing a caravan or trailer. Reaching an altitude of 1076m, it is one of New Zealand's highest public roads and is sometimes closed by snow in winter. Nonetheless, on a fine day the drive past the detritus of the valley's gold-mining heyday is a rewarding one, with views across bald, mica-studded hills to the tussock high country beyond. At the pass, a great **viewpoint** overlooks Queenstown and Lake Wakatipu, before it switchbacks down towards SH6 and Queenstown.

The Matukituki Valley and Mount Aspiring National Park

The **Matukituki Valley** is Wanaka's outdoor playground, a 60km tentacle reaching from the parched Otago landscapes around Lake Wanaka to the steep alpine skirts of Mount Aspiring, which at 3033m is New Zealand's highest mountain outside the Aoraki/Mount Cook National Park. Extensive high-country stations run sheep on the riverside meadows, briefly glimpsed by skiers bound for Treble Cone, rock climbers making for the roadside crags, Matukituki-bound kayakers, and trampers and mountaineers hot-footing it to the **Mount Aspiring National Park**.

The park, mooted in 1935 but not created until 1964, is one of the country's largest, extending from the Haast Pass, where there are tramps around Makarora (see p.679), in the north to the head of Lake Wakatipu (where the Rees–Dart Track and parts of the Routeburn Track fall within its bounds) in the south. The pyramidal Mount Aspiring forms the centrepiece of the park, rising with classical beauty over the ice-smoothed broad valleys and creaking glaciers. It was first climbed in 1909 using heavy hemp rope and without the climbing hardware used by today's mountaineers, who still treat the mountain as one of the grails of Kiwi mountaineering ambition.

Travelling along the unsealed section of the Mount Aspiring Road beside the Matukituki River, you don't get to see much of Aspiring, as Mount Avalanche and Avalanche Glacier get in the way. Still, craggy mountains remain tantalizingly present all the way to the **Raspberry Creek**, where a car park and public toilets mark the start of a number of magnificent tramps (see box opposite) into the heart of the park. For information on how to get to the park, see below.

ARRIVAL AND DEPARTURE   WANAKA AND AROUND

By bus Buses all stop outside the i-SITE. Wanaka Connexions (☏ 03 443 9120, ⒲ alpinecoachlines.co.nz) link Dunedin and Queenstown with connections at Cromwell, while Connect Wanaka (☏ 0800 405 066, ⒲ connectabus .com) link to Queenstown over the Crown Range: both call at Queenstown airport. Atomic run to Dunedin and up the West Coast to Greymouth in one day. Catch-A-Bus (☏ 03 449 2024, ⒲ trailjourneys.co.nz) run daily to Dunedin via the Maniototo. Southern Link (☏ 0508 458 835, ⒲ southernlinkbus.co.nz) run daily to Christchurch via Tekapo. Intercity/Newmans pass through on their Queenstown–Cromwell–Franz Josef run but not on their Queenstown–Christchurch run (though you can join it at Cromwell or Tarras, a $90 taxi ride away).
Destinations Christchurch (3 daily; 7–8hr); Cromwell

(5 daily; 45min–1hr); Dunedin (2–3 daily; 4hr–4hr 30min); Franz Josef Glacier (1–2 daily; 7hr); Queenstown (10 daily; 1hr 30min).
By plane Air New Zealand fly into Wanaka airport on SH6, 9km east of the centre, though it is usually much cheaper to fly into Queenstown and bus here from there. Alpine Coachlines meet Wanaka flights ($15; ☏ 0800 754 926). Destinations Christchurch (1 daily; 1hr).

MOUNT ASPIRING NATIONAL PARK

By bus Alpine Coachlines (☏ 03 443 9120, ⒲ alpinecoachlines.co.nz) run the 55km along Mount Aspiring Rd to the national park's main trailhead at Raspberry Creek once or twice daily from Nov–April. Bookings essential. $35 each way.

GETTING AROUND

Wanaka is compact and you can walk everywhere in the centre. Most accommodation is less than fifteen minutes away on foot, but you may want transport for longer excursions.

By bike Many hostels and B&Bs have bikes for guests' use and there are several rental shops including: Thunderbikes,

48 Helwick St (Mon–Fri 8.30am–6pm, Sat & Sun 9am–4pm; ☏ 03 443 2558), who have hardtails ($20/4hr,

WALKS IN THE MATUKITUKI VALLEY

DOC's *Matukituki Valley Tracks* ($2) and *Dart & Rees Valleys* ($2) leaflets are recommended for these walks, along with the detailed *Mount Aspiring National Park* map ($19). The routes are manageable for fit and experienced trampers, but the climatic differences in the park are extreme – the half-metre of rain that falls each year in the Matukituki Valley does not compare with the six metres that fall on the western side of the park, so go prepared. The hikes start at the Raspberry Creek car park, about an hour's drive from Wanaka.

Several huts in this area are owned by the New Zealand Alpine Club (NZAC) but are open to all: pay at the DOC visitor centre in Wanaka.

Raspberry Creek to Aspiring Hut (9km one-way; 2hr 30min–3hr; 100m ascent). A popular and mostly pastoral day-walk starting along a 4WD track which climbs from the Raspberry Creek car park beside the western branch of the Matukituki River, only heading away from the river to avoid bluffs en route to Downs Creek, from where you get fabulous views up to the Rob Roy Glacier and Mount Avalanche. Bridal Veil Falls is a brief distraction before the historic Cascade Hut, followed 20min later by the relatively luxurious stone-built Aspiring Hut (NZAC; 38 bunks; $25, with gas), a common base camp for mountaineers off to the peaks around Mount Aspiring. There's camping ($5) near the hut.

Rob Roy Valley Walk (10km return; 3–4hr; 300m ascent). This justly popular there-and-back hike is shorter and steeper than the walk to Aspiring Hut and more spectacular, striking through beech forest to some magnificent alpine scenery, snowfields and glaciers. From the Raspberry Creek car park, follow the true right bank of the Matukituki for 15min to a swingbridge; cross to the true left bank that leads on to the Rob Roy stream, which cuts through a small gorge into the beech forest. Gradually the woods give way to alpine vegetation – and the Rob Roy Glacier nosing down into the head of the valley. Eco Wanaka Adventures (☎ 0800 926 326, ⓦ ecowanaka.co.nz) run an all-day guided trip here including a picnic lunch ($235).

Aspiring Hut to Pearl Flat (5km; 1hr 30min; 100m ascent) For an excellent day out from Aspiring Hut, explore the headwaters of the Matukituki River to the north. Follow the river as it weaves in and out of the bush to Pearl Flat. Return from here or continue to the head of the valley (see below).

Pearl Flat to the head of the valley (3.2km; 2hr; 250m ascent). Pearl Flat follows the river's right bank, crosses a huge avalanche chute off the side of Mount Barff and climbs high above the river. Scott Rock Bivvy, marked on some maps, is little more than a sheltering rock 50m east of the river, reached by a bridge.

Aspiring Hut to French Ridge Hut (7.2km; 4–5hr; 1000m ascent); the hut (NZAC; 20 bunks; $20) This arduous but spectacular hike ascends very steeply from the valley and offers great mountain views but is normally only snow-free from December to March.

Cascade Saddle Route (4–5 days one-way). One of the most challenging of the local tramps connects the Matukituki Valley's Aspiring Hut to Glenorchy's Rees–Dart Track (see p.724), via a magnificent alpine crossing with panoramic views of the Dart Glacier and the Barrier Range. Ideally you should have some alpine experience, and don't attempt the long stretches of exposed high country in adverse weather. Cascade Saddle can normally only be negotiated without specialized mountaineering equipment from January to March, and you should always carry full waterproofs. A tent gives you the option of breaking the longest day by spending a night on a glacial bench above Dart Glacier. Check ⓦ doc.govt.nz for the latest info and a downloadable leaflet. From Aspiring Hut to Dart Hut (17km; 8–11hr; 1350m ascent), you rise above the tree line onto the steep tussock and snow-grass ridge, which is treacherous when wet or snowy. The route is marked by orange snow poles, which lead you to a steel pylon (1835m) that marks the top of the ridge, down to Cascade Creek and across it, before climbing gently to the meadows around Cascade Saddle. There is a toilet at Cascade Creek for campers. Non-campers will have to press on another four or five hours past the rubble-topped Dart Glacier, where chunks of ice periodically crash into the milky river that surges beneath it. You eventually reach Dart Hut where you join the Rees–Dart Track for the last two days back to Glenorchy. Note that Dart Hut and others on the Rees–Dart circuit may need to be booked in advance in Jan and Feb from 2013 onwards.

13

$40/day) and long-travel fully sprung models ($50/$75); and Outside Sports, 17–23 Dunmore St (daily 8am–8pm in peak season; ☎ 03 443 7966, ⓦ outsidesports.co.nz), who offer a similar range and prices.
By car Wanaka Rentacar, 2 Brownston St (☎ 03 443 6641,

ⓦ wanakarentacar.co.nz), have the cheapest range of vehicles, starting at around $40/day, with unlimited kilometres for longer rentals.
By taxi Wanaka Taxis (☎ 0800 272 700).

INFORMATION

i-SITE 100 Ardmore St (daily: Dec–March 8.30am–6pm; April–Nov 8.30am–5.30pm; ☎ 03 443 1233, ⓦ lakewanaka .co.nz).

DOC Mount Aspiring National Park visitor centre Corner of SH84 and Ballantyne Rd, 500m east of central Wanaka (Nov–Easter daily 8am–5pm; Easter–Oct Mon–Fri 8.30am–5pm, Sat 9.30am–4pm; ☎ 03 443 7660,

ⓔ mtaspiringvc@doc.govt.nz).

Services There are several banks around town with ATMs and foreign exchange.

Racers Edge 99 Ardmore St ☎ 03 443 7882, ⓦ racers edge.co.nz. Rents skis ($38–55/day) and snowboards ($35), and also runs a ski-tuning and repair service.

TOURS AND ACTIVITIES

The absence of Queenstown-style hard sell and conveyor-belt tourism gives Wanaka a more relaxed feel. Magnificent scenery, clear skies and competitive prices make it an excellent place to get airborne, and with a beautiful lake and a number of decent rivers there's plenty of opportunity for getting wet in style. Most accommodation and numerous agents around town handle **bookings**, or you can contact the activity operator direct. Some Queenstown operators (such as Frogz **whitewater sledging**) do Wanaka pick-ups at no extra cost.

CANYONING
Deep Canyon 103 Ardmore St ☎ 03 443 7922, ⓦ deepcanyon.co.nz. Experienced guides take small groups into narrow canyons following a creek downstream with heaps of jumps, rockslides and abseils. Warm, protective clothing helps ease the sense of vulnerability, and the day is rounded off with a bush picnic. First-timers should opt for Niger Stream (7–8hr; $240), down a gorgeous stream with plenty of jumping into deep pools. Abseiling experience ensures you get the best from Big Nige (8hr; $305), which covers the same territory as the Niger Stream trip but starts further upstream with some big rappels. The more advanced Leaping Burn (8hr; $430) involves a greater sense of commitment and exposure and some massive waterfall abseils. Plan ahead to get on one of the Wilkin Wilderness-Wai Rata trips (12hr; $960), a magical combination of a helicopter flight, a fabulous canyon and jetboating out along the Wilkin River. Trips daily from early Oct–March.

ROCK CLIMBING AND MOUNTAINEERING
Basecamp Wanaka 50 Cardrona Valley Rd, 2km south of town ☎ 03 443 1110, ⓦ basecampwanaka.co.nz. Two climbing experiences in one. Inside is the child-oriented Clip 'N Climb ($20/hr; kids $8–16; bring trainers), where an auto-belay system allows you to climb against the clock, do a face-to-face race, or climb in the dark with UV-lit holds. The superbly sculpted outdoor wall ($20; $15 with your own gear) is pretty close to climbing on real rock. Lessons available. Mon–Fri noon–8pm, Sat, Sun & all public and school holidays 10am–8pm.
Wanaka Rock Climbing ☎ 03 443 6411, ⓦ wanaka

rock.co.nz. Wanaka's dry, sunny climate is ideal for rock climbing, and these guys run full-day introductory courses involving top-roping, seconding and abseiling for two to four people (half-day $140 each; full day $210), and lead private trips ($345/day).
Adventure Consultants ☎ 03 443 8711, ⓦ adventure consultants.co.nz. Professional mountaineering with five-day ascents of Mount Aspiring ($4100) as well as excellent seven-day mountaineering courses ($2550) including ice climbing, snow-cave building and all the basic skills, plus several summit ascents.

SKYDIVING AND PARAGLIDING
Skydive Lake Wanaka Wanaka Airport ☎ 0800 786 877, ⓦ skydivewanaka.com. A 10min scenic flight can be combined with 45–60 seconds of freefall on a wonderful tandem skydive ($299 from 12,000ft; $399 from 15,000ft).
Wanaka Paragliding ☎ 0800 359 754, ⓦ wanaka paragliding.co.nz. A gentle but spectacular approach to viewing the tremendous scenery is a tandem flight from high on Treble Cone ski-field down to the lakeside (800m descent) with 15–20min in the air. Trips ($199) take 2hr from Wanaka and transport is included.

SCENIC FLIGHTS
Scenic flights from Wanaka to Milford Sound tend to be a few dollars more expensive than those from Queenstown, but they do spend half an hour more flying over a wider range of stunning scenery, including Mount Aspiring, the Olivine Ice Plateau and the inaccessible lakes of Alabaster, McKerrow and Tutoko. Most local accommodation receives daily bulletins on Milford weather and flight conditions.

Alpine Helicopters ☎03 443 4000, ⊛alpineheli
.co.nz. Milford Sound flights with one or two landings
(2hr; $795).
Wanaka Flightseeing ☎03 443 8787, ⊛flightseeing
.co.nz. Various fixed-wing flights including around Mt
Aspiring (50min; $200) and to Milford Sound (4hr; $460).

BIKING

Wanaka abounds with shops (see p.730) renting bikes and
selling the *Lake Wanaka Cycling Map* ($2), which details local
off-road rides. The lakeside tracks (see box, p.729) are open to
riders, and the "Sticky Forest" has a dense knot of excellent
single track. Alternatively get out to the Dirt Park in the
Cardrona Valley (day pass $30), right by the Snow Farm (see
box, p.727), where there's chairlift access to freestyle terrain.
Freeride NZ 17 Dunmore St ☎0800 743 369,
⊛freeridenz.com. Great guided off-road rides from
relatively low-grade cross country rides (4hr; $185) to
major downhill on singletrack and 4WD roads (5hr; $195)
and heli-biking (5hr; $439).

CRUISES, KAYAKING, RAFTING AND JETBOATING

Alpine Kayak Guides ☎03 443 9023, ⊛alpinekayaks
.co.nz. Fun, self-paddle, half-day kayaking trips ($149) on
the Grade II Clutha River: trips run from Oct–April and
depart from the i-SITE in Wanaka.
Eco Wanaka Adventures ☎0800 926 326, ⊛eco
wanaka.co.nz. A wonderfully informative and scenic
cruise (daily 9am & 1.30pm; 4hr; $180) across Lake Wanaka
to the Mou Wahu island nature reserve complete with its
population of buff weka. The nature walk highlight is "high
tea" overlooking the island's picturesque lake-within-a-
lake, and you can even plant a tree, helping Mou Wahu's
regeneration.
Lakeland Adventures In the i-SITE building ☎03 443
7495, ⊛lakelandadventures.co.nz. Has all manner of
waterborne activities including a gentle cruise to
Stephensons Island (2hr; $85) where you can stroll briefly.
Pioneer Rafting ☎03 443 1246, ⊛ecoraft.co.nz.
Rafting trips (daily Sept–April; half-day $145) pitched at
families. Bobbing along choppy water the emphasis is on
appreciating the scenery and gold panning as you drift
down the Grade II Upper Clutha.
Wanaka Kayaks ☎0800 926 925, ⊛wanakakayaks
.co.nz. Lakeshore kayak rentals (sit-on-tops $12/hr; singles
$18; doubles $30) perhaps heading to Ruby Island (2hr
return) plus guided paddling trips to Ruby Island (3hr; $75)
or around Glendhu Bay (4hr; $115).
Wanaka River Journeys ☎0800 544 555, ⊛wanaka
riverjourneys.co.nz. Great-value jetboating tours (Sept–
May two daily; 3hr; $240) which thunder up the Matukituki
River, providing great views of Mount Aspiring, the
Avalanche Glacier, Mount Avalanche and the rest, with a
knowledgeable guide and bushwalk.

FISHING

Lake Wanaka and nearby lakes and rivers are popular
territory for quinnat salmon and brown and rainbow trout
fishing. There's a maximum bag of six fish per day and you'll
require the sport fishing licence ($23/day, $116 for the
season), obtainable direct (⊛fishandgame.org.nz) or from
tackle shops. Unless you really know your bait, you'll have
a better chance of catching your supper with a fishing
guide – but they don't come cheap; check with the i-SITE
for names.

HORSE RIDING

Timber Creek Equestrian Centre Off Mt Aspiring Rd
around 4km west of Wanaka near the entrance to
Rippon Vineyard ☎03 443 2933. Their Vineyard Trail Ride
(1hr 45min; $89) is a very civilized, scenic ride through the
country and vines, followed by a wine tasting (optional)
and then a gentler still ride back.

ACCOMMODATION

For a diminutive place, Wanaka has a great range of accommodation, particularly luxury lodges. **Rates** are marginally
lower than Queenstown, but reflect the town's resort status. You should have no problem finding a bed, except during the
peak months of January, February, July and August, and during events (see box, p.736) when **booking** is essential and
prices rise. **Freedom camping** is not allowed in town or along the lakefront.

Altamont Lodge 121 Mount Aspiring Rd, 2km west of
Wanaka ☎03 443 8864, ⊛altamontlodge.co.nz. For
hostel prices without the dorms or backpacker vibe, head
for this tramping-cum-ski lodge with a pine-panelled
alpine atmosphere, communal cooking and lounge areas,
a spa pool, drying rooms, spacious lawns, tennis court
and ski-tuning facilities. Twins, doubles and triples are
fairly functional, with shared bathrooms. Singles stay for
$49. **$69**

Base Wanaka 73 Brownston St ☎03 443 4291,
⊛stayatbase.co.nz. New-ish, purpose-built hostel in the
heart of town with its own bar serving budget meals. You
may not feel a need to brave the sometimes cramped
kitchen, though the airy deck makes it feel bigger than
it really is. The rooms are smart and there are upscale
women-only dorms. Has internet and a busy booking
desk. Dorms **$26**, women's-only dorms **$31**, en-suite
doubles **$82**

13

Clearbrook 72 Helwick ☎0800 443 441, ⓦclearbrook .co.nz. Afternoon sun streams in to the studios, one- and two-bedroom apartments at this classy motel with tastefully decorated luxury units ranged along the burbling Bullock Creek. All units have TV, stereo, full kitchen with dishwasher, laundry and balconies with mountain views. All are great value including the separate three-bedroom houses sleeping six ($385). $155

Matterhorn South 56 Brownston St ☎03 443 1119, ⓦmatterhornsouth.co.nz. Combined hostel and budget lodge, with an appealing backpacker section featuring dorms of various sizes and an appealing garden shed. The more upmarket lodge section has modern, en-suite four-shares with TV and fridge, and access to an excellent kitchen and comfortable lounge. Dorms $26, doubles $68, lodge en-suite doubles $95

★ **Mountain Range** Heritage Park 2km along Cardrona Valley Rd ☎03 443 7400, ⓦmountainrange .co.nz. Idyllic and peaceful seven-room luxury lodge amid tussock on the edge of town. The spacious rooms are simply but tastefully decorated with New Zealand artworks and there's an understated, informal air to the place. Hot tub, hammocks, welcome drinks and marvellous breakfasts round out a fine experience. $320

Peak Sportchalet 36 Hunter Crescent, 2km north of town ☎03 443 6990, ⓦpeak-sportchalet.co.nz. Purpose-built self-contained studio and two-bedroom chalet in a peaceful part of town, run by a charming German couple who provide a buffet breakfast ($10 extra). There's an individual touch to the decor, bathrooms get under-floor heating and everywhere is super-insulated. The studio is great for couples; the chalet for a family or two couples. Studio $135, one-bedroom chalet $155, two-bedroom chalet $220

Renmore House B&B 44 Upton St ☎03 443 6566, ⓦrenmore-house.co.nz. Large purpose-built house, centrally located beside the burbling waters of Bullock Creek, with three plush en-suite rooms all fitted out to a high standard. There are bikes for guests' use and the hosts are genial and welcoming. $245

★ **River Run** 86 Halliday Rd, 5km east of Wanaka ☎03 443 9049, ⓦriverrun.co.nz. Stylish lodge sited on ancient river flats with trails leading down to the Clutha River. The thoughtfully conceived modern house uses lots of recycled timber and contains five well-appointed en-suite rooms, sunny verandas and a common dining area where most guests stay for three-course dinners ($90) that are the match of any restaurant in Wanaka. Rates include breakfast and pre-dinner drinks. $400

★ **Te Wanaka Lodge** 23 Brownston St ☎0800 926 252, ⓦtewanaka.co.nz. Welcoming thirteen-room lodge built around a large walnut tree. Comfortable rooms all have private entrances and Sky TV. A cedar hot tub shares the peaceful garden with a delightful small cottage. There's

a hearty breakfast served around a communal table and even an honesty bar with a good wine selection. The owners are friendly and highly knowledgeable about all things outdoors. $195

★ **Wanaka Bakpaka** 117 Lakeside Rd ☎03 443 7837, ⓦwanakabakpaka.co.nz. Beautifully maintained low-key hostel a 5min walk from town, with great lake and mountain views, a peaceful atmosphere, summer BBQs and bike rental ($28/day). Plenty of room for sitting out in the afternoon sun. Dorms $27, doubles $68, lakeview en-suite $80

Wanaka Springs Lodge 21 Warren St ☎0800 171 252, ⓦwanakasprings.com. Classy, purpose-built, boutique lodge with comfortable, beautifully decorated rooms, stylish communal areas, free liqueurs and a spa pool in the native garden. The hosts have good local knowledge. $330

★ **YHA Wanaka Purple Cow** 94 Brownston St ☎03 443 1880, ⓦyha.co.nz. Large and inviting hostel with dorms of up to six beds, many in separate blocks with their own lounge, bathroom and TV. Also several en-suite doubles, some with lake view and TV/DVD, and a couple of deluxe motel units complete with iPod dock. Sit and gaze at the fabulous lake view through the big picture windows, play pool (free), watch the nightly movie or rent a bike. Dorms $28, doubles $86, en suites $102, lakeview en suites $110, units $130

CAMPSITES AND HOLIDAY PARKS

Albert Town Campground SH6, 6km northeast of Wanaka. Open, informal camping area on the banks of the swift-flowing Clutha River with tap water and flush toilets. There's plenty of shade but it gets very busy for four weeks from Boxing Day. $7

Glendhu Bay Lakeside Holiday Park Camp 1127 Mount Aspiring Rd, 12km west of Wanaka ☎03 443 7243, ⓦglendhubaymotorcamp.co.nz. Beautifully situated family campsite with numerous pitches strung along the lakeshore and fabulous views across to Mount Aspiring. Facilities include a popular boat ramp. Camping $16, bunks $20, cabins $50

★ **Lake Outlet Holiday Park** 197 Lake Outlet Rd, 6km from Wanaka ☎03 443 7478. Spacious and stunningly sited campsite at the point where Lake Wanaka becomes the Clutha River, in a great position for strolls along the lake or river frontage. Along with tent and powered sites there are simple cabins, some with a lounge. Rent a bike ($15 for 3hr) and ride the Outlet Track. Camping $14, cabins $50

Wanaka Lakeview Holiday Park 212 Brownston St ☎03 443 7883, ⓦwanakalakeview.co.nz. The closest campsite to town is a 10min walk from the centre and has tent sites, rooms in a lodge that has bathrooms and kitchen under the same roof, and self-contained tourist flats. Camping $17, dorms $20, standard cabins $50, flats $100

EATING AND ENTERTAINMENT

skiers and the healthy influx of summer tourists have determined the style and number of places to eat and drink in Wanaka. Unless you strike it lucky and catch a band passing through, entertainment extends to movies and one nightclub.

Barluga Post Office Lane ☏ 03 443 5400. Little wine bar with leather sofas, armchairs, a log fire and courtyard, with a broad range of quality local wine and cocktails and the occasional DJ and acoustic gig. Daily 4pm–2.30am.

Kai Whaka Pai Corner of Ardmore & Helwick sts ☏ 03 443 7795. Wanaka's liveliest daytime eating spot is a favourite with locals who come for chocolate cookies, breakfasts and fine coffee. On summer evenings the emphasis is on beer and wine, seated at tables on the street perhaps eating Thai beef salad ($18). Daily 7am–11pm.

The Landing 80 Ardmore St ☏ 03 443 5099, ⓦmissyskitchen.com. Fine dining, with a select menu and an extensive wine list that is best appreciated on the balcony on balmy summer nights. Expect pork belly with black pepper caramel and mashed aubergine or risotto Milanese with scallops ($34). Daily 4–10pm or later.

★ **Relishes** 99 Ardmore St ☏ 03 443 9018, ⓦrelishescafe.co.nz. Longstanding, pretension-free Wanaka favourite that's always good for coffee and cake but serves lunches such as caponata and fresh bocconcini on crostini ($16) and dinner mains such as chargrilled loin with herbed polenta cake and rosemary and confit garlic demi-glaze ($32). Don't skimp on dessert. Daily 8am–10pm or later.

Sasanoki 139 Ardmore St ☏ 03 443 6474. Eat in or take away from this modest Japanese kitchen, serving excellent udon noodles, sashimi and donburi, mostly $10–14. Grab a large bento box and a sake for under $35. Daily 11.30am–2.30pm & 5.30–9pm.

Soul Food Organic Café 74 Ardmore St ☏ 03 443 7885. Unpretentious indoor and courtyard eating in this café and wholefood shop specializing in vegetarian, dairy- and gluten-free dishes. Drop by for excellent coffee and muffins, bacon, eggs and mushrooms breakfasts ($14), winter soups, summer salad bar and tasty juices and smoothies. Mon–Fri 8am–6pm, Sat & Sun 8am–4pm.

Urban Grind 72 Ardmore St ☏ 03 443 6748. Smart modern bare-brick café with outsized lampshades. Dishes include baked eggs with saffron, chickpeas and spinach ($14), classic pizzas ($16–19) and evening tapas such as grilled ox tongue with corn and black bean salsa ($9) or truffle fries with aioli ($7.50). Often a DJ for their summer sessions on Sunday afternoon. Daily 8.30am–11pm.

★ **White House Café & Bar** 33 Dunmore St ☏ 03 443 9595. The owner sometimes rubs people up the wrong way, and building maintenance is a little lax, but these are easily outweighed by the wonderful meals when it's on form. A lot of love goes into loosely Mediterranean-influenced dishes such as mackerel, olive, new potato and avocado salad ($35), or ribeye with beetroot relish, silverbeet and fried potato ($40). Leave room for dessert, which might be ginger loaf with figs and blue cheese. Daily 6–10pm or later.

THE CARDRONA VALLEY

Cardrona Hotel Cardrona ☏ 03 443 8153, ⓦcardronahotel.co.nz. Stop for a bite or a beer at this 1863 hotel that survived the floods of 1878, which destroyed most of the old town, battling on until 1961. After years of neglect it was reopened in 1984, and although the frontage is held in a state of arrested decay, the interior has been spruced up. In winter, skiers sink into the chesterfields around the fire, while in summer the beer garden bursts into life. There's a great range of drinks, meals such as lamb and mint burger with mash and peas ($19) or salmon on lemon couscous ($27), plus B&B accommodation Restaurant and bar daily 10am–10pm or later.

CINEMAS AND CLUBS

Cinema Paradiso 66 Brownston St ☏ 03 443 1505, ⓦparadiso.net.nz. By late 2012, this longstanding, quirky cinema should be newly sited in a former Catholic church. The screens might have gone digital but you still sit in sagging old sofas, armchairs, airline seats or even a bisected Morris Minor. The films range from Hollywood to art house, and there's always an interval during which everyone tucks into cookies, ice cream, coffee or booze from the on-site café. Adults $16.

Ruby's 50 Cardrona Valley Rd, 2km south of town ☏ 03 443 6901, ⓦrubyscinema.co.nz. A chic pair of mini, digital cinemas (36-seat & 14-seat) entered through an intimate cocktail bar with Loren, Newman and Hepburn on the wall. Grab yourself a cocktail, wine or craft beer and a few tapas and repair to the cinemas' huge leather recliners. Adults $18.50.

SHOPPING

Hamills 10 Helwick St ☏ 03 443 8094. Rents a fishing tackle package ($20/day) and sell licences.

Outside Sports 17 Dunmore St ☏ 03 443 7966, ⓦoutsidesports.co.nz. Stocks pretty much everything, including backpacks ($10/day), sleeping bags ($10), jackets ($10), hiking books ($8) and cooking stoves ($5).

13

WANAKA FESTIVALS

New Year's Eve The one-time youthful revelry has been curtailed in recent years, and the new year is welcomed in with a family-oriented celebration.

Rippon Festival (ⓦripponfestival.co.nz). One-day rock, roots and reggae festival with a top Kiwi line-up and a magical setting with superb lake and mountain backdrop. There's always a lively after-party. Tickets around $135. First Saturday in February every even-numbered year.

A&P Show (ⓦwanakashow.co.nz). Town meets country at Wanaka's showgrounds on the lakefront with everything from calf-wrangling demos and biggest pumpkin competitions to the perfect Victoria sponge and a Jack Russell race in which up to 100 dogs chase a rabbit dragged around behind

a man on a horse. Heaps of food, drink and fun, but accommodation is hard to come by. Second weekend in March.

Warbirds over Wanaka (ⓣ0800 224 224, ⓦwarbirdsoverwanaka.com). Wanaka airport plays host to New Zealand's premier air show – three days of airborne craft doing their thing watched by over 60,000 people. Tickets: Fri $50; Sat $75; Sun $75; three days $170. Easter every even-numbered year.

Festival of Colour (ⓦfestivalofcolour .co.nz). A biennial celebration of visual art, dance, music, theatre and the like, with top Kiwi acts, including the symphony orchestra, performing all over town and at Hawea. Lots of free stuff, or buy tickets for individual performances. Mid-April in odd-numbered years

DIRECTORY

Internet Wanaka Web, 3 Helwick St (generally daily 9am–9pm; ⓣ03 443 7429), charge $5/hr for a super-fast connection and the ability to log out and back in without losing time or data allowance.

Medical treatment Wanaka Lakes Health Centre, 23 Cardrona Valley Rd (ⓣ03 443 7811). Clinic Mon–Fri

8.30am–6pm plus 24hr emergency care.

Pharmacy Wanaka Pharmacy, 33 Helwick St (Mon–Sat 8.30am–7pm; ⓣ03 443 8000).

Post office 39 Ardmore St (Mon–Fri 8.30am–5.30pm, Sat 9am–noon).

Along the Clutha River

Lake Wanaka is drained by the **Clutha River**, New Zealand's highest volume river, and the second longest – the mouth at Balclutha, south of Dunedin, is 338km from its source. Its flow is interrupted along the way by major dams at Clyde and Roxburgh as the river and SH8 (the fastest route from Queenstown to the coast) squeeze between the Old Man Range to the east, and the Knobby Range to the west.

The Clutha's middle reaches flow through the **Central Otago goldfields**, a fascinatingly historic region, southeast of Queenstown and Wanaka, where the barren and beautiful high country is peppered with gold-town ruins from the 1860s.

The boomtowns were mostly moribund by the early twentieth century, but a few struggled on, mostly growing **stone fruit** and, later, grapes for what has become a burgeoning **wine region** full of unique flavours (see p.739). With wine comes food and the region is increasingly establishing itself as a **foodie** haven. The range of activities seems pale compared to Queenstown or Wanaka, but **mountain biking** is hitting its straps with great rides all over the place and a few operators keen to rent you a bike or lead superb tours.

The reconstructed nineteenth-century boomtown of **Cromwell**, 50km east of Queenstown, probably won't delay you long, but is a good jumping-off point for the former mining settlement of **Bendigo** and the wineries of **Bannockburn**. The twin towns of **Clyde** and **Alexandra** have fashioned themselves as bases for the popular Otago Central Rail Trail, while **Lawrence** relishes is position as the gold rush's home town.

SH8 follows the Clutha River pretty closely and is typically plied by four buses a day running between Dunedin and Queenstown.

Cromwell

The uninspiring service town of **CROMWELL**, 60km east of Queenstown via the Gibbston wine region, does its best to celebrate its gold-mining roots while hopping on the back of the region's food and wine renaissance. Sadly, almost all of Cromwell's historic core is waterlogged below the shimmering surface of the **Lake Dunstan** reservoir, formed by the Clyde Dam, 20km downstream (see p.739). But the immediate surrounds are beginning to find their place on the tourist map, thanks to the cluster of quality wineries, fruit orchards and old gold diggings.

Cromwell may only be 120km from the coast, but this is as far from the sea as you can get in New Zealand, something that gives the area something of a continental climate that's perfect for fruit growing. A 13m-high, fibreglass **fruit sculpture** beside the highway highlights the long-time importance of nectarines, peaches, apples and pears, though these days cherries and grapes are probably more important.

Brief history

Soon after Hartley and Reilly's (see p.687) 1862 discovery of **gold** beside the Clutha River, a settlement sprouted at "The Junction" at the fork of the Kawarau and Clutha rivers. Local stories tell that it was later renamed when a government survey party dubbed it Cromwell to spite local Irish immigrant workers. Miners low on provisions planted the first fruit trees in the region, little expecting Cromwell to become the centre of the Otago **stone fruit** orchard belt.

Old Cromwell Town

Melmore Terrace

Lake Dunstan laps at the toes of **Old Cromwell Town**, a short street of restored old shopfronts, most of which would now be submerged had they not been dismantled and rebuilt on the water's edge. It all feels a bit fake, but on a fine day you can spend a happy hour browsing the art, craft and gourmet food shops before retiring for a libation to the *Grain & Seed Café*.

Goldfields Mining Centre

SH6, 7km west of Cromwell • Daily 9am–5.30pm; self-guided tour departs on the hour • $20; guided tour $25 • ☎ 0800 111 038, Ⓦ goldfieldsmining.co.nz

A footbridge accesses the **Goldfields Mining Centre**, a former mine site scattered along a terrace above the Kawarau River. Among the old huts, flumes and rusty machinery, the most engaging part of the centre is the Chinese Village, ironically constructed as a film set in the early 1990s. You can talk a **self-guided tour** in an hour or so, but it is far more informative to join the one-hour **guided tour** on which you get to handle some large gold nuggets, see a stamper battery cranked up using a water-powered Pelton wheel and try your hand at extracting a flake or two.

The site is also home to **jetboat** rides (see p.738) and the *Wild Earth* restaurant and wine tasting (see p.738).

ARRIVAL AND DEPARTURE   CROMWELL

By bus Cromwell acts as a hub for Intercity/Newmans, Wanaka Connexions, Atomic, NakedBus, Southern Link and Catch-A-Bus, all stopping centrally on Lode Lane right by The Mall. You may well have to change buses here.

Destinations Alexandra (4 daily; 30min); Dunedin (4 daily; 3hr 30min); Lawrence (4 daily; 2hr); Queenstown (7 daily; 1hr); Wanaka (5 daily; 45min).

INFORMATION AND ACTIVITIES

i-SITE 47 The Mall (daily: Nov–March 9am–6pm; April–Oct 9am–5pm; ☎ 03 445 0212, Ⓦ centralotagonz.com). The region's main visitor centre provides the free and comprehensive *Discover Cromwell* and *Walk Cromwell*

leaflets and contains a small museum packed with gold-mining memorabilia. By the middle of 2013 the i-SITE should move to Murray Terrace, beside the fruit sculpture, though the museum will stay here.

13

Goldfields Jet Goldfields Mining Centre ☎ 03 445 1038, ⓦ goldfieldsjet.co.nz. Runs jetboat rides on the deep and swirling waters of the Kawarau River to the base of the Staircase rapid. The 40min trips run on demand and cost $9⬤

ACCOMMODATION

Burn Cottage Retreat 168 Burn Cottage Rd, 3km north of town ☎ 03 445 3050, ⓦ burncottageretreat .co.nz. Three high-standard self-contained cottages plus one B&B room, peacefully set surrounded by vineyards and a hosta garden. Cottages have sunny decks with barbecue and there's always a bowl of walnuts from their trees. B&B $165, cottages $185

Cromwell Top 10 Holiday Park 1 Alpha St ☎ 0800 107 275, ⓦ cromwellholidaypark.co.nz. Large, quality campsite on the edge of town. Facilities include hot tub, TV room and kids' playground with jumping pillow. Camping/sit⬤ $40, cabins $75, en-suite cabins $100, motel units $135

Rosewood Accommodation 102 Barry Ave ☎ 03 44⬤ 1260, ⓦ rosewoodcromwell.co.nz. New and enthusiasti⬤ management look set to turn this spacious and somewha⬤ run-down 1970s former workers' camp into a quality⬤ campsite and backpackers. There are no dorms, jus⬤ doubles and twins. Already popular with fruit pickers, i⬤ should get better and better. Bike rental $10/day. Camping⬤ $15, doubles $62

EATING AND DRINKING

A Drop of Red SH6, 4km southwest of town ☎ 03 445 4151, ⓦ adropofred.com. A wonderfully relaxed café and bistro where you can read magazines and play Scrabble all day over a coffee or get into the 300 Central Otago wines available from 74 wineries. There's always something interesting by the glass and they'll open any bottle as long as you order two glasses. Croque Monsieur ($16), Mediterranean salad ($15) and American beef sloppy Joe ($19) should fortify. Tues–Sun 11.30am–5.30pm and evenings if there are bookings.

Grain & Seed Café Melmore Terrace, Old Cromwell Town ☎ 03 445 1077. With tables overlooking Lake Dunstan and inside an old grain store, this is a good spot for a light lunch (BLT for $12) or a coffee. Free wi-fi. Daily 9am–5pm.

Jones' Fruit Orchards SH6, 5km west of town ☎ 03 445 0275, ⓦ mrsjonesorchard.co.nz. Tour buses disgorge at the half-dozen fruit stalls that encircle Cromwell, but especially at this place, which is stacked with fresh and dried fruit, the former blended to make wonderful fruit ice creams, best consumed in the adjacent rose garden. Daily 8am–5pm or later.

WINERIES

★ **Northburn Station** 45 Northburn Station Rd, off SH8, 4km north of town ☎ 03 445 1743, ⓦ northburn.co.nz. Great winery restaurant in a lovely garden setting on a station where they grow merino wool for New Zealand's iconic Icebreaker clothing. Their signature platters – terrines, relishes, cheeses, salmon and bread ($25/person) – and Mediterranean lamb salads ($23) are superb and helped down by wines grown on the property. Straight wine tasting costs $5. Daily 10.30am–4.30pm.

Wild Earth Restaurant Goldfields Mining Centre ☎ 03 445 4841. You don't need to be visiting the mining centre – just stroll over the bridge across the Kawarau River to access this tasting room for top-quality Wild Earth wines, particularly Pinot Noir. Wine-matched meals charcoal smoked in old Pinot Noir barrels are served on the grass overlooking the river. Try the mussels on the half-shell ($15), tequila-cured salmon ($16) or grilled haloumi stack with aubergine ($16). Daily 10am–5pm.

Wooing Tree 7 Westmorland Place ☎ 03 445 4142, ⓦ wooingtree.co.nz. Casual little family-run winery right in Cromwell where everything is done by hand. Tastings ($5) include excellent Pinot Noir (particularly Beetle Juice) some lunch-friendly rosés, and Blondie, an unusual Blanc de Noir white wine made from Pinot Noir grapes. Daily 10am–5pm.

Bannockburn

There are remote clusters of cottage foundations and sluicings all over Central Otago, and dedicated ruin hounds can poke around the detritus in places such as the **Nevis Valley** and **Bendigo** (ask locally), but the most extensive workings are found at **BANNOCKBURN**, a scattered hamlet 9km southwest of Cromwell that's now more famous for its wineries.

Bannockburn Sluicings

Felton Rd • Open access • Free

Armed with the *Walk Cromwell* leaflet from the Cromwell i-SITE, make for the **Bannockburn Sluicings**, a tortured landscape that was once home to two thousand people, washing away the land to reveal the gold-rich seams below. New interpretive signs punctuate a two-hour **self-guided trail** that starts 1500m along Felton Road and weaves up to Stewart Town, home to dilapidated mud-brick huts and ageing pear and apricot trees.

The Wineries

Exploring mine workings is thirsty work, and you'll welcome the chance to sample the Bannockburn **wineries**. Since the early 1990s, the warm, north-facing hillsides around the sluicings have been increasingly planted with grape vines. The wines – primarily Pinot Noir and Pinot Gris – have quickly established themselves as some of New Zealand's best. Almost a dozen wineries are open for tasting (call in advance if you're visiting in winter), all listed on the free *Central Otago Wine Map*. For informed guidance, join Queenstown-based Appellation Central Wine Tours (see p.699).

EATING AND DRINKING   BANNOCKBURN

Carrick 247 Cairnmuir Rd ☎03 445 3480, ⓦcarrick .co.nz. Fully organic winery overlooking Bannockburn Inlet that's good for tastings of their excellent wines ($5) or lunch of pan-seared duck livers on roasted nectarine, walnuts and witloof ($19). Expect sophisticated Pinot Noir, and estate-grown Chardonnay, Riesling, Pinot Gris and even (unusually this far south) Sauvignon Blanc. Daily 11am–5pm.

Mt Difficulty 73 Felton Rd ☎03 445 3445, ⓦmtdifficulty.co.nz. Great wines and a perfect place to taste them, either at the cellar door or in the restaurant overlooking the vines and the sluicings. Sample their platters ($28 & $50) or mains such as harissa-rubbed pork belly on a chickpea, aubergine and coriander salad ($30). Tasting daily 10.30am–4.30pm. Restaurant daily noon–3pm.

Clyde

SH8 cuts southeast from Cromwell through 20km of the bleak and windswept **Cromwell Gorge**, hugging the banks of Lake Dunstan to peaceful **CLYDE**. With several good places to stay and eat, this small former gold town makes a good base for forays around the region and on to the Otago Central Rail Trail (see box, p.743).

Since the mid-1980s, Clyde has been dominated by the giant grey hydroelectric **Clyde Dam**, 1km north of town, which generates five percent of New Zealand's power and provides water for irrigation. Initially controversial, the dam is nevertheless considered something of an engineering marvel, with special "slip joints" providing the dam wall with flexibility in case of earthquakes.

Clyde's original 1864 stone courthouse is flanked by the **Clyde Museum**, 5 Blyth St (Tues–Sun 2–4pm; $3), worth a peek for its intriguing coverage of Clyde's botched Great Gold Robbery of 1870 when one George Rennie tried to make off with £13,000 in bullion and banknotes.

The **Herb Factory Museum**, 10 Fache St (Tues–Sun 2–4pm; $3, $5 combination ticket with Clyde Museum), was established in the 1930s as New Zealand's first **herb factory**, and thrived by making use of the common thyme that still grows wild in abundance hereabouts.

ARRIVAL AND DEPARTURE   CLYDE

By bus Buses stop in Clyde on demand, pulling up on Sunderland St, which is where you'll find many of the

town's accommodation, restaurants and amenities.

ACCOMMODATION

Clyde Holiday and Sporting Complex Whitby St ☎03 449 2713, ⓔcrrc@ihug.co.nz. Basic campsite surrounding a sports ground, with fully self-contained cabins and several on-site caravans, plus a pool. Camping $18, cabins $45

Dunstan House 29 Sunderland St ☎03 449 2295, ⓦdunstanhouse.co.nz. Comfy B&B in a former stagecoach stop with bags of character. Rooms are imaginatively decorated (half en suite and some with claw-foot bath), some opening out onto a wraparound veranda on the first

13

floor, where miners once rode their horses, after a glass or two. There's plenty of bike storage, and a piano in the lounge. Shared bath $120, en suite $160

★ **Olivers** 34 Sutherland St ☎ 03 449 2600, ⓦ olivers centralotago.co.nz. Don't pass up the opportunity to stay in this gorgeous eleven-room reworking of a former homestead right in the heart of town. Five of the rooms

are in the former stables, which open out into a central courtyard, and all are completely different – schist wall half-tester bed, clawfoot bath – while maintaining the same balance of modern comfort with period style. The five wonderfully spacious premium rooms (some in the house, some in the stables) are especially appealing. Superb cooked breakfast included. $195, premium $315

EATING

The Bank Café 31 Sunderland St ☎ 03 449 2955. Streetside tables catch the morning sun at this central café, offering great coffee, eggs Benedict ($14) and chicken pesto pita pocket with salad ($14) and a friendly smile. Daily 9am–4pm.

The Packing Shed 68 Boulton Rd, Earnscleugh, 4km south of town ☎ 03 449 2757. Semi-formal, rural café in a large garden serving delicious lunches for under $20. To

get there, head across the river bridge opposite the *Post Office Café* and follow Earnscleugh Rd. Oct–March Thurs–Sun 10am–4pm.

Post Office Café & Bar 2 Blyth St ☎ 03 449 2488. This 1865 former post office serves the Post Office dark ale in its bar, but the place is best for its peaceful garden where you can tuck into hearty dishes such as nachos ($11) or lamb fillet crêpe with vegetables ($31). Daily 10am–10pm.

Alexandra

A large white clockface – visible from as far away as 5km – looms out of the cliff backing **ALEXANDRA** (affectionately known as Alex), 10km southeast of Clyde. Alexandra sprang up during the 1862 gold rush, and flourished for four years before turning into a quiet prosperous service town for the fruit-growers of Central Otago. Throughout the summer you'll find fruit stalls selling some delectable apricots, peaches and nectarines, and in December and January some of the world's finest cherries.

Central Stories

21 Centennial Ave • Daily 9am–5pm • Donation • ☎ 03 448 6230, ⓦ centralstories.co.nz

A huge water wheel marks the fascinating **Central Stories**, a social and natural history museum covering everything from the creation of the region's distinctive schist tors to viticulture in the world's southernmost wine region. Learn about the heart-rending mystery of James Horn, whose father's deathbed letter will bring a lump to your throat, and the sorry tale of the rabbits, introduced into the area in 1909, which did what rabbits do – so well that they became a menace throughout the South Island. To combat the problem, the town holds an **Easter Bunny Shoot** every year, and hunters from all over New Zealand congregate on Good Friday for the slaughter.

Shaky Bridge

In the early years, the only way across the Manuherikia River was by punt, but in 1879 the town built the **Shaky Bridge**, a suspension **footbridge**, which connects with the *Shaky Bridge Café* (see opposite) and a **lookout point** (2km one-way; 40min) high above the town on Tucker Hill, affording great views of the whole area.

ARRIVAL AND DEPARTURE

ALEXANDRA

By bus InterCity, Atomic and Wanaka Connexions all stop outside the i-SITE. Catch-A-Bus picks up wherever you want.

Destinations Dunedin (4 daily; 3hr); Lawrence (4 daily; 1hr 15min); Queenstown (4 daily; 1hr 30min); Ranfurly (1–2 daily; 1hr).

INFORMATION AND ACTIVITIES

i-SITE 21 Centennial Ave in Central Stories (daily: Nov–Easter 9am–6pm; Easter–Oct 9am–5pm; ☎ 03 448 9515, ⓦ centralotagonz.com).

Altitude Adventures 88 Centennial Ave ☎ 03 448

8917, ⓦ altitudeadventures.co.nz. An abundance of treeless hills makes Alex a good base for mountain biking. There's also more low-key riding along the Clutha Gold Trail, which follows the river and will eventually go all the way to awrence. Altitude Adventures rent mountain bikes from 35/day to get you out on the singletrack, and staff have the expertise for getting you on the Otago Central Rail Trail (see box, p.743). They also run guided singletrack tours requiring intermediate skills or better: probably the best is the half-day Knobby Range ($175) across high-country tussock and down steep rocky trails with a ride to the start minimising the amount of climbing. Mon−Fri 9am−5pm.

ACCOMMODATION

117 Avenue Motels 117 Centennial Ave ☎ 0800 758 399, ⓦ avenue-motel.co.nz. Very comfortable and central motel with tastefully decorated units and suites (some with spa bath and Xbox). Units $125, suites $145
Marj's Place 5 Theyers, 1km northwest St ☎ 03 448 7098, ⓦ marjsplace.co.nz. Marj is the mother hen at this very welcoming hostel-cum-homestay in two houses on a quiet street. Homestay guests share a bathroom but get robes, a sauna and a spa bath plus access to a well-equipped kitchen with dishwasher. Most backpackers stay across the road, and there are great long-stay rates for fruit pickers. Dorms $25, doubles $70

EATING

★ **Courthouse Café** 8 Centennial Ave ☎ 03 448 7818. Licensed café in (and on the sunny lawns around) Alex's 1878 former courthouse, serving delicious home-baked food such as veggie lasagne with one of their excellent salads ($12) or pork belly ficelle with plum sauce ($10). Mon−Sat 7.30am−4.30pm.
Golden Cobweb 55 Tarbert St ☎ 03 448 8891. Chinese-run chippy that's perfect for great-value blue cod and chips

for under $10. Daily 6−10pm.
Shaky Bridge Café Graveyard Gully Rd ☎ 03 448 5111, ⓦ williamhill.co.nz/cafe.html. Casually sophisticated café close to the Shaky Bridge. Good for coffee and muffins, contemporary brunches and sumptuous dinners with wines from the adjacent vineyard. Mon−Fri 9am−4pm, Sat & Sun 9am−5pm.

Roxburgh

The bland former gold town of **Roxburgh**, 40km south of Alexandra, sits hemmed in by vast orchards that yield bountiful crops of peaches, apricots, apples, raspberries and strawberries, all harvested by an annual influx of seasonal pickers. The season's surplus is sold from a phalanx of roadside stalls from early December through to May.

ACCOMMODATION AND EATING   ROXBURGH

Jimmy's Pies 143 Scotland St ☎ 03 446 8596. Here since 1960, Jimmy's makes pies found all over the South Island, though you'll have to come to home base to sample their gourmet versions ($4.50−6) with fillings such as lamb shank or venison and redcurrant. Also sandwiches, rolls, cake slices and espresso to go. Mon−Fri 7.30am−5pm.
Lake Roxburgh Lodge SH8, 8km north ☎ 03 446 8220, ⓦ lakeroxburghlodge.co.nz. If you decide to stop, head for this welcoming lodge with comfortable rooms each with their own deck all set in peaceful grounds. There's a quality restaurant on site, plus bike and kayak rental (each $30/half-day). Restaurant daily 8−10am, 11am−3pm & 6−9pm. $125

Lawrence

From Roxburgh, SH8 runs 60km southeast to **LAWRENCE**, Otago's original 1861 gold town where, in May 1861, Australian Gabriel Read struck pay dirt. Twelve thousand gold-seekers scrambled to try their luck in the gold-rich Gabriel's Gully but the boom was over in barely a year. Its legacy is a sleepy farming town of barely 550 souls and a smattering of Victorian buildings, hastily constructed in a variety of materials and styles. A few have now been converted into chichi **galleries** that provide some reason to linger.

Gabriel's Gully Historic Reserve

3.5km north along Gabriel's Gully Rd • Open access • Free

Gabriel's Gully Road leads 3.5km north of Lawrence to **Gabriel's Gully Historic Reserve**, where a series of plaques explaining the old workings should take you an hour or so to explore. A climb up the steep rise of **Jacob's Ladder** gives a good view of the gully, long since filled with tailings that reach nearly 20m in depth. It is possible to visit

13

Gabriel's Gully as part of a farmland loop walk from town (8.5km loop; 2hr 30min), returning along a ridge.

By bus InterCity, Atomic and Wanaka Connexions all stop in the centre of town.
Destinations Alexandra (4 daily; 1hr 15min); Cromwell (4 daily; 2hr); Dunedin (4 daily; 1hr 20min).
Tourist information Goldfields Museum, 17 Ross Place

(daily 9.30am–4.30pm; ☎03 485 9222, ⓦlawrence.co .nz). A combined information centre and museum that brings something of the heady early gold-rush days to life through imaginative displays. They also have free wi-fi.

The Maniototo

The most interesting route to the east coast from Alexandra is through the **Maniototo**, a generic name for the flat high country shared by three shallow valleys – the Manuherikia River, the Ida Burn and the Taieri River – and the low, craggy ranges that separate them. Despite easy road access, the Maniototo feels like a windswept and ambient world apart.

The region's big draw is cycling the **Otago Central Rail Trail** (see box opposite), but former gold-mining communities such as **St Bathans** and **Naseby** are worth sampling for their calm seclusion and subtle reminders of how greed transforms the land. Much of the area's pleasure is in even smaller places – the post office at **Ophir** or the old engineering works in the **Ida Valley** – and in the dozens of small cottages, many abandoned – a testimony to the harsh life in these parts.

Brief history

Predictably, Europeans first came to the area in search of gold. They found it near **Naseby**, but returns swiftly declined and farming on the plains became more rewarding. This was especially true when **railway** developers looking for the easiest route from Dunedin to Alexandra chose a way up the Taieri Gorge and across the Maniototo. In 1898, the line arrived in **Ranfurly**, which soon took over from Naseby as the area's main administrative centre. With the closure of the rail line in 1990 an already moribund area withered further until the **Otago Central Rail Trail** caught on. In recent years, environmentalists have battled to save the landscape from **Project Hayes**, what would have been New Zealand's largest wind farm, a battle only won when the power company Meridian Energy backed down in early 2012.

By car and bike Driving or riding is the best way to see the Maniototo as public transport is very limited.
By train The Taieri Gorge Railway (see box, p.601) runs daily from Dunedin to the Otago Rail Trail. On Fri and Sun it stops in Middlemarch, but on other days it turns around at Pukerangi and you'll have to cycle the 18km along the road to reach Middlemarch.
By bus Catch-A-Bus service (☎03 449 2024, ⓦtrailjourneys

.co.nz) runs daytime (Mon–Fri & Sun, plus Sat in high summer) services from Dunedin to Cromwell then back with stops in Middlemarch, Ranfurly, Alexandra, Clyde and Cromwell; Fri and Sun services continue to Wanaka. The Dunedin Connexions bus (☎03 443 9120, ⓦalpinecoachlines .co.nz) will also pick up from the train at Pukerangi or Middlemarch and run through the Maniototo to Wanaka and Queenstown, but only if they have bookings.

Omakau and Ophir

Heading northeast from Alexandra, you climb quickly through inconsequential hamlets onto the high-country plain. After 25km, turn down Ophir Bridge Road which crosses a nice little **suspension bridge** across the Manuherikia River and continues 1km to **Ophir**, the region's original gold town. It still has its imposing and operational 1886 **Post & Telegraph Office** (Mon–Fri 9am–noon). **Omakau**, 2km to the north, has basic services.

OTAGO CENTRAL RAIL TRAIL

One of the finest ways to explore the Maniototo is on the Otago Central Rail Trail, a largely flat 150km route from Clyde to Middlemarch that passes through all the main towns except for St Bathans and Naseby. Open to walkers, cyclists and horse riders, it follows the trackbed of the former **Otago Central Branch railway line** and includes modified rail bridges and viaducts (several spanning over 100m), beautiful valleys and long agricultural plains.

Passenger trains ran through the Maniototo until 1990, a continuation of what is now the Taieri Gorge Railway (see box, p.601), but it wasn't until early 2000 that the trail opened, galvanizing a dying region. Most people **cycle**, and all sorts of accommodation has sprung up to cater to bikers' needs. Pubs and cafés located where the trail crosses roads aren't shy to advertise the opportunity to take a break.

The route is generally hard-packed earth and gravel, making it possible to ride most bikes, though fat tyres make for a more comfortable journey. Combining the ride with the **Taieri Gorge Railway** makes a great way to travel between Clyde and Dunedin. The trail takes most people three days.

If you're just out to pick the **highlights** (or are walking and don't fancy the whole thing) aim for a couple of 10km stretches, both with tunnels, viaducts and interesting rock formations: Lauder–Auripo in the northern section, and Daisybank–Hyde in the east. A torch is handy (though not essential) for the tunnels.

TRAIL INFORMATION

The widely available *Otago Central Rail Trail* leaflet (free) outlines the route; Brian and Diane Miller's *Otago Central Rail Trail* ($15) is a great pocket-sized companion with elevation profiles; and Gerald Cunningham's *Guide to the Otago Central Rail Trail* ($31) adds great history and context. The most comprehensive information on the web is at Ⓦ otagocentralrailtrail.co.nz, though a couple of commercial sites offer good practical information; try Ⓦ otagorailtrail.co.nz and Ⓦ railtrail.co.nz.

BIKE RENTAL AND PACKAGES

There's a huge range of options from simple bike rental to full accommodation and transport packages with luggage delivery. The main players are listed below.

Altitude Adventures 88 Centennial Ave ☎ 03 448 8917, Ⓦ altitudeadventures.co.nz. Alexandra-based operator offering a one-day, 47km highlights package with transport and bike rental ($89), a fully supported 4-day package including B&B accommodation ($680) and all manner of freedom ride, bike rental and customized packages.

Cycle Surgery ☎ 0800 292 534, Ⓦ cyclesurgery .co.nz. Middlemarch-based company offering just about everything you might want to do from bike rental ($35/ day; tandems $70; panniers $5) and minibus shuttles to custom packages possibly including Taieri Gorge tickets, accommodation, bag transfers and meals. They cater for a wide range of budgets.

Trail Journeys ☎ 0800 RAIL TRAIL, Ⓣ trailjourneys .co.nz. Based in Clyde, this operator does self-guide trips (from $299 for 2 days with bike rental, transport, accommodation and baggage transfer) but specializes in packages combining cycling and sightseeing such as 5 days cycling and wine tasting from Queenstown ($1795).

ACCOMMODATION AND EATING   **OMAKAU AND OPHIR**

Flannery Lodge 1 MacDonald St, Ophir ☎ 03 447 3222, Ⓦ ophir.co.nz. Upscale backpackers in a very peaceful spot with five-bed dorms and en-suite doubles in pretty cottages. Camping $25, dorms $44, doubles $125

Muddy Creek Café 2 Harvey St, Omakau ☎ 03 447 3344. Good casual café with fish and chips ($15), pumpkin lasagne ($13), espresso and cakes, plus takeaway burgers and toasted sandwiches. Mon–Thurs 9am–7pm, Fri & Sat 8.30am–8pm, Sun 10am–8pm.

The Ida Valley

The main SH85 avoids the Ida Valley, but it is worth turning off at Omakau and detouring past a couple of the Maniototo's most interesting historical sights.

13

GRAHAME SYDNEY

Many New Zealanders only know the Maniototo through the works of Dunedin-born realist painter **Grahame Sydney** (⒲ grahamesydney.com), who spends much of his time in the region. His broad, big-sky landscapes of goods sheds amid parched fields and letterboxes at lonely crossroads are universally accessible, and instantly recognizable to anyone visiting the region.

Prints and postcards of his work are found throughout the Maniototo and beyond, and originals hang in most of the country's major galleries. At first glance many of the works are unemotional renditions, but reflection reveals great poignancy. As he says, "I'm the long stare, not the quick glimpse".

Hayes Engineering Works

Hayes Rd, Oturehua • Sept–May daily 9am–5pm; Aug Sat & Sun 9am–5pm • $9; guided tours by arrangement for groups of 12 or more $12 • ☎ 03 444 5801, ⒲ hayesengineering.co.nz

All over the world, wire fences are still tensioned by parallel wire strainers designed by Ernest Hayes in 1906 at the **Hayes Engineering Works**, a site based around a frozen-in-time corrugated-iron workshop. Everything is as it was in 1952 when the company decamped to Christchurch – in the gloom, cutters and drill presses are linked by belts and pulleys to overhead shafts originally driven by wind, then hydro power and now the power-takeoff from an ancient tractor (still fired up for guided tours).

Alongside the workshop stands the original 1895 mud-brick **cottage** the family lived in (now a small museum and café) and the somewhat idiosyncratic house they designed and built, decked out precisely as it was in the 1920s. They were engineers, not carpenters, so broken doors are fixed with metal bracing and one doorjamb was fitted with steel springs to prevent the door slamming shut.

Gilchrist's General Store

3355 Ida Valley Rd, Oturehua • Mon–Fri 7.30am–5.30pm, Sat & Sun 8am–5.30pm • Free • ☎ 03 444 5808

Poke your head in to this working museum, a still operational 1929 grocery shop and post office lined with the original wooden shelving laden with ancient groceries. The place was once the hub of the valley, with twelve staff, but saw hard times and almost closed before being revived. Buy a pie, browse the books or just wander in and have a chat.

EATING   THE IDA VALLEY

★ **Ida Valley Kitchen** 3407 Ida Valley Rd ☎ 03 444 5030. Stop for an excellent coffee or a huge chunk of wonderful carrot cake at the region's best café. Sausage rolls and the likes of satay chicken wrap ($14) are served in the smart interior or sunny garden. Sept–May daily 9am–4pm.

St Bathans

The minute former gold town of **ST BATHANS** is out on a limb 80km north of Alexandra and accessed 17km along St Bathans Loop Road from Becks. St Bathans boomed in 1863, but when the gold ran out in the 1930s everything went with it. These days it's virtually a ghost town, with just six residents and an attractive straggle of ancient buildings along the single road.

Blue Lake

The prettiest thing about the area is the striking **Blue Lake** right beside the town, where mineral-rich water has flooded a crater left by the merciless sluicing of Kildare Hill, once 120m high but now entirely washed away. A short track leads from the *Vulcan* to a vantage point over the azure lake, now used for waterskiing, swimming and picnics.

Vulcan Hotel Loop Rd ☎ 03 447 3629. Atmospheric 1882 hotel where local farmers and visitors prop up the wooden bar, which serves St Bathans Gold, a single malt once bottled on the premises. Grab a BLT ($14) or dine on venison in port with cranberry sauce ($36), either in the dark bar or shady garden. You can also stay, though the nicest room (#1) is reputed to be haunted. Bar/restaurant daily 9am–9pm or later. **$100**

Naseby

The small settlement of **NASEBY**, 25km east of St Bathans and 9km off SH85, clings to the Maniototo some 600m above sea level. At its 4000-strong peak in 1865, Naseby was the largest gold-mining town hereabouts, but today numbers have dropped to around 200 huddled in a collection of small houses (many of them originally built of sun-dried mud brick by miners), with a shop, a garage, a couple of pubs, a café and a campsite.

The story of the town and wider region is told through the tiny **Maniototo Early Settlers Museum**, corner of Earne and Leven streets (Dec–April Tues–Sun 1–4pm; $2), which is packed with black-and-white photos of past residents and also contains a small collection of items left by Chinese miners.

Across the street, the Jubilee Museum (daily 10am–5pm; included with Early Settlers Museum entry or $2 token from the general store across the street) houses the remains of an old watchmaker's shop together with displays on the local gold rush of the 1860s and 1870s.

Tourist information 16 Derwent Street (daily: Christmas to mid-Jan 10am–4.30pm; rest of year 11am–2pm; ☎ 03 444 9961). Located in the former post office this volunteer-run place has the *A Walk Through History* map of town and walking maps of the forest.

One Tree Hill Track The visitor centre has maps showing three local walks, the best being this one (1600m; 1hr return), which starts on Brooms St in town and snakes uphill along the eastern side of Hogburn Gully, past dramatic honey-coloured cliffs entirely carved by water.

Mountain Bike Naseby ☎ 03 444 9555, ⊛ mtbnaseby .co.nz. Naseby Forest contains loads of great single-track mountain biking, mostly undulating without seriously steep climbs. This shop rents bikes (mostly hardtail; $40/half-day; $70/full-day) and has trail maps.

Naseby Curling International 1057 Channel Rd ☎ 03 444 9878, ⊛ curling.co.nz. Naseby is New Zealand's home of curling. This occasionally takes place outside on cold winter days but most activity is at this indoor year-round venue where instruction is usually available ($20/hr). Daily 9am–5pm.

ACCOMMODATION AND EATING

Black Forest Café 3 Derwent St ☎ 03 444 7826. Cosy café with good coffee and muffins, great cheese scones and light meals such as eggs Benedict ($16) and frittata ($10). Evening meals by arrangement. Daily 9am–4pm.

Larchview Holiday Park 8 Swimming Dam Rd ☎ 03 444 9904, ⊛ larchviewholidaypark.co.nz. Pretty and tranquil forest campsite a 5min walk from town and across the road from the popular swimming dam complete with springboard. Camping $13, cabins $45, self-contained house $81

Naseby Trail Lodge Corner of Derwent and Oughter sts ☎ 03 444 8374, ⊛ nasebylodge.co.nz. A delightful modern cluster of mud-brick and corrugated-iron one-and two-bedroom self-contained units clustered around *The Falconer*, a quality, straw bale-built restaurant where you might dine on duck breast with creamed saffron leeks ($32). Restaurant: Christmas–April Mon–Sat roughly 6–10pm; rest of year Fri & Sat 6–10pm. $160

Old Doctors Residence 58 Derwent St ☎ 03 444 9775, ⊛ olddoctorsresidence.co.nz. A fabulous B&B where the customers get treated like prodigal children. Luxurious accommodation is in the mud-brick former dairy or a suite comprising the former doctor's surgery and the waiting room. There's a cosy guest lounge and wine tasting with food matches each evening. Sumptuous meals on request. $275

Dansey's Pass

The gravel Kyeburn Diggings Road runs east out of Naseby over **Dansey's Pass** to Duntroon, about 65, mostly winding, gravel kilometres to the north. The first 16km

13

to Kyeburn Diggings is fairly easy going, but beyond the *Dansey's Pass Coach Inn* the road is narrow and not suitable for medium and large campervans. The route is narrow, barren and beautiful, one of the last untouched high country passes with open hillsides covered in tussock. It is sometimes closed by snow between June and September: check in Naseby before setting out.

Old gold workings are visible from the roadside, where water-jets from sluices have distorted the schist and tussock landscape, leaving rock dramatically exposed.

ACCOMMODATION   **DANSEY'S PASS**

★ **Dansey's Pass Coach Inn** Kyeburn Diggings, 16km east of Naseby ☎ 03 444 9048, ⓦ danseyspass.co.nz. Charming wayside inn with a bit of wild west feel that's the only relic of the once 2000-strong gold-rush community. It was built from local schist stone in 1862 (the stonemason was reputedly paid a pint of beer for each stone laid). Stop in for a beer on leather sofas around the fire, grab lunch (perhaps grilled salmon on potato cake; $18) on the grass across the road or stay for dinner of lamb backstrap with Moroccan chutney ($28) in the conservatory restaurant. Aging gold-panner Des frequently props up the bar and spins a good yarn. The nineteen rooms are Victorian styled and there's free wi-fi. Daily 8am–10pm or later. Double **$140**, en suite **$160**

Ranfurly

RANFURLY is the largest settlement on the Maniototo, though that's still not saying much. It has enjoyed a resurgence, thanks to being roughly midway along the rail trail and a rather desperate attempt to brand itself as New Zealand's **Rural Art Deco** centre. In truth, there's only a handful of noteworthy buildings – the *Ranfurly Lion Hotel* and the Ranfurly Auto Repairs shop both exhibit a few Art Deco features, but elsewhere much is achieved with imaginative paint jobs and period signage. Ranfurly goes all out to make the best of what it has, particularly during the **Rural Art Deco Weekend** at the end of February.

The Art Deco Gallery
1 Charlemont St East • Tues–Sun 1–3.30pm • $2 donation

The town's finest period building houses the **Art Deco Gallery**, which contains all manner of Art Deco furnishings and homeware, but the star is the building itself, the 1948 Centennial Milk Bar.

INFORMATION   **RANFURLY**

i-SITE 3 Charlemont St East (daily: Oct–May 8.30am– 5.30pm; June–Sept 9am–5pm; ☎ 03 444 1005, ⓦ maniototo.co.nz). Visitor centre housed in the former train station which has a free audiovisual show on the region and pictorial displays tracing the history of the town and the Otago Central Railway.

ACCOMMODATION AND EATING

E-Central Café 14 Charlemont St East ☎ 03 444 8300. Decent café that does bikers' breakfasts, decent coffee and a range of light meals such as pasta of the day ($12). Daily 9am–3.30pm.

EXPLORING THE OLD DUNSTAN ROAD

In summer, anyone with a 4WD or high-clearance vehicle can set out from Ranfurly to explore part of the magnificent **Old Dunstan Road** (closed June–Sept), the original route to the Central Otago goldfields across the Rock and Pillar and Lammerlaw ranges. Ask for directions and current conditions if you're going it alone, or join Dunedin-based Offtrack (☎ 03 453 6582, ⓦ offtrack.co.nz) who ride the track and include bike rental, pick-up and lunch ($120). You'll need some fitness and intermediate mountain-bike ability but are rewarded with great riding in magnificent country. If you fancy something with more commitment, go for Offtrack's 5-day Dunstan Trail ($1400) between Lawrence and Tarras with 6–7 hours riding a day over rough, steep terrain across private land and nights spent at high-country stations.

Komako 634 Waipiata-Naseby Rd, 3km south of town ☎ 03 444 9324, ⓦ komako.net.nz. Peony garden blooming Oct–Dec) with three gorgeous cabins right by the Rail Trail and surrounded by great views. Accommodation and dinner deals ($100/person), which could be a gourmet barbecue or a roast. $120

Old Post Office Backpackers 11 Pery St ☎ 03 444 9588, ⓦ oldpobackpackers.co.nz. Central hostel sleeping twenty in a variety of rooms and four- to five-bed dorms. Continental breakfast ($10) available and other meals by arrangement. Dorms $28, rooms $65

Ranfurly Holiday Park Corner of Reade and Pery sts ☎ 0800 726 387, ⓦ ranfurlyholidaypark.co.nz. Relaxed, spacious and central campsite. Camping $13, powered/site $30, cabins $40, motel units $95

Ranfurly Lion Hotel 10 Charlemont St East ☎ 03 444 9140, ⓦ ranfurlyhotel.co.nz. A good hotel restaurant in Art Deco surroundings serving the likes of roasts ($20), and fish and chips ($25). Daily 7.30am–11pm.

Middlemarch

At Kyeburn, 15km east of Ranfurly, the slow route to Dunedin (SH87) branches south off SH85 and twists through the eastern Maniototo, a barren yet scenic landscape squeezed between the towering Rock and Pillar Range and the Taieri River. Fifty kilometres south of Kyeburn you'll reach the tiny community of **MIDDLEMARCH** (ⓦ middlemarch.co.nz), at the end of the Rail Trail and the Friday- and Sunday-only terminus of the **Taieri Gorge Railway** (see box, p.601). There's not much to it, but a number of local farms provide B&B accommodation, mostly for rail trailers.

ACCOMMODATION AND EATING	MIDDLEMARCH

Gladbrook 860 Gladbrook Rd, 9km southwest of town ☎ 03 464 3888, ⓦ gladbrookstation.co.nz. Delightful, rural B&B with antique-furnished rooms in a grand home-stead (sharing bathrooms, one with a clawfoot bath). Afternoon tea, breakfast, tennis and croquet are included. Also two nearby self-contained cottages with great views and breakfast. Cottages $120, homestead $170

Kissing Gate Café 2 Swansea St (SH87) ☎ 03 464 3224. Enjoy a coffee or a light lunch at this pretty café in an old wooden cottage and its surrounding garden. Daily 8.30am–5pm.

The Lodge 24 Conway St ☎ 027 228 4789, ⓔ enquiries @thelodge-middlemarch.co.nz. Modest but comfortable B&B accommodation in a central old villa with continental breakfast included. Double $100, en-suite doubles $140

Macraes Gold Mine

Macraes Rd, 55km southeast of Ranfurly • Tours most days 10am & 2pm; call for reservations • $30 • ☎ 0800 465 386, ⓦ oceanagoldtours.com

The most renowned of Otago's operating gold mines, the huge opencast **Macraes Gold Mine**, lies on windswept hills between Ranfurly and Palmerston and can be visited on a two-hour tour that also takes in a historic reserve and a fully operational stamper battery.

Fiordland

753 Te Anau

759 The Kepler Track

761 Milford Road

765 Milford Sound

771 The Milford Track

774 Manapouri and Lake Manapouri

776 Doubtful Sound

778 Dusky Sound

778 The Southern Scenic Route

HALL ARM, DOUBTFUL SOUND

Fiordland

For all New Zealand's grandeur, no other region matches the concentration of stupendous landscapes found in its southwestern corner, Fiordland. Almost the entire region (and most of the area covered in this chapter) falls within the 12,500-square-kilometre Fiordland National Park, which stretches from Martins Bay, once the site of New Zealand's remotest settlement, to the southern forests of Waitutu and Preservation Inlet, where early gold prospectors set up a couple of short-lived towns. It embraces a raw, heroic landscape, with New Zealand's two deepest lakes, its highest rainfall, fifteen hairline fiords and some of the world's rarest birds. Such wonder is acknowledged by the United Nations, who gathered the park – along with Mount Aspiring National Park, parts of Westland and the Aoraki/Mount Cook area – into the Te Wahipounamu World Heritage Area.

14

One persistent feature of Fiordland is the **rain**. Milford Sound is particularly favoured, being deluged with up to 7m of rainfall a year – one of the highest in the world. Fortunately the area's settlements are in a rain shadow and receive less than half the precipitation of the coast. Despite its frequent soakings, **Milford Sound** sees the greatest concentration of traveller activity – in fact, the Sound is particularly beautiful when it's raining, with ribbons of water plunging from hanging valleys directly into the fiords where colonies of red and black coral grow and dolphins, fur seals and Fiordland crested penguins cavort. Many visitors on a flying visit from Queenstown see little else, but a greater sense of remoteness is gained by driving there along the achingly scenic **Milford Road** from the lakeside town of **Te Anau**. Better still, hike the **Milford Track**, widely promoted as the "finest walk in the world", though others in the region – particularly the **Hollyford Track** and the **Kepler Track** – are equally strong contenders.

A second lakeside town, **Manapouri**, is the springboard for trips to the West Arm hydroelectric power station, **Doubtful Sound** and the isolated fiords to the south. From Manapouri, the **Southern Scenic Route** winds through the western quarter of Southland via minor towns along the southwestern coast. The main stops here are Tuatapere, base for the excellent **Hump Ridge Track**, and pretty coastal **Riverton**.

Brief history

Fiordland's complex geology evolved over the last 500 million years. When thick layers of sea-bed sediment were compressed and heated deep within the earth's crust,

Tu-to-Raki-whanoa and Te Namu p.753
The takahe p.755
Te Anau tours and activities p.756
Shortening the way to Milford p.761
Milford Road safety p.762
Hikes from the Milford Road p.763
The Hollyford Track p.764
Milford's fragile ecosystem p.766
Coach, cruise and flight combos to Milford Sound p.769

Milford Sound cruises and activities p.770
Electricity, aluminium and brickbats p.775
Manapouri walks p.776
Doubtful Sound cruises and kayak trips p.777
Jetboating trips around Lake Hauroko p.779
The Hump Ridge and South Coast Tracks pp.780–781

LAKE TE ANAU

Highlights

❶ Te Anau Watch the inspirational film *Ata Whenua: Shadowlands*, shot from a helicopter above the region's landscapes, then book a heli-flight to see for yourself. **See p.753**

❷ Milford Sound Experience Milford's world-famous waters on a kayak trip, overnight cruise or a dive beneath the surface to see rare red and black coral. **See p.771**

❸ The Milford Track Brave the rain and the sandflies to find out why this beautiful four-day tramp was billed "The Finest Walk in the World". **See p.771**

❹ Doubtful Sound Experience scenic grandeur and superb wildlife from a kayak or small cruise boat, without the tourist bustle of Milford Sound. **See p.776**

❺ Hump Ridge Track Combine pristine tramping in this little-visited area with jetboating on the Wairaurahiri River. **See p.780**

HIGHLIGHTS ARE MARKED ON THE MAP ON P.752

crystalline granite, gneiss and schist were formed. As the land and sea levels rose and fell, layers of softer sandstone and limestone were overlaid; during glacial periods, great ice sheets deepened the valleys and flattened their bases to create the classic U shape which was invaded by the sea.

After experiencing the challenging ambience created by Fiordland's copious rainfall and vicious **sandflies** (*namu*), you'll appreciate why there is little evidence of permanent Maori settlement, though they spent summers hunting here and passed through in

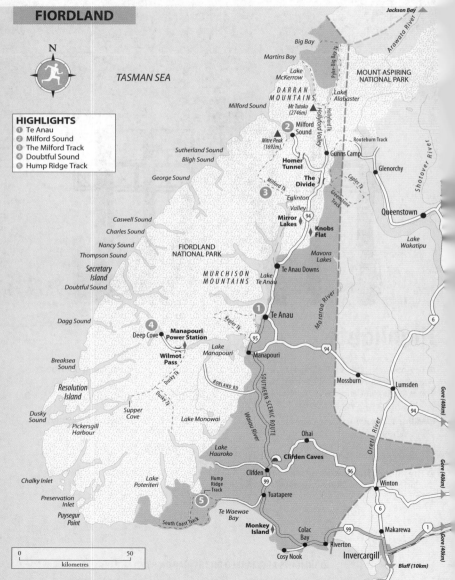

FIORDLAND

N

TASMAN SEA

HIGHLIGHTS
1. Te Anau
2. Milford Sound
3. The Milford Track
4. Doubtful Sound
5. Hump Ridge Track

Jackson Bay
Arawata River
Big Bay
Martins Bay
Lake McKerrow
Pyke-Big Bay Tk
MOUNT ASPIRING NATIONAL PARK
DARRAN MOUNTAINS
Lake Alabaster
Milford Sound
Mt Tutoko (2746m)
Hollyford Tk
Hollyford Valley
Milford Sound
Routeburn Track
Mitre Peak (1692m)
Gunns Camp
Glenorchy
Sutherland Sound
Bligh Sound
Homer Tunnel
The Divide
Caples Tk
Greenstone Track
Shotover River
George Sound
Milford Tk
Eglinton Valley
Mirror Lakes
94
Knobs Flat
Queenstown
Caswell Sound
Charles Sound
Nancy Sound
Thompson Sound
FIORDLAND NATIONAL PARK
Mavora Lakes
Lake Wakatipu
Secretary Island
MURCHISON MOUNTAINS
Lake Te Anau
Te Anau Downs
Doubtful Sound
Dagg Sound
Deep Cove
Manapouri Power Station
Te Anau
Mararoa River
6
Wilmot Pass
Lake Manapouri
95
Breaksea Sound
Dusky Tk
Manapouri
94
Resolution Island
Dusky Tk
BORLAND RD
SOUTHERN SCENIC ROUTE
Mossburn
Lumsden
94
Dusky Sound
Supper Cove
Lake Monowai
Waiau River
Gore (40km)
Pickersgill Harbour
Ohai
Oreti River
Chalky Inlet
Lake Poteriteri
Lake Hauroko
Clifden Caves
96
Winton
Preservation Inlet
Hump Ridge Track
Clifden
99
Gore (40km)
Puysegur Point
South Coast Track
Tuatapere
6
Te Waewae Bay
Monkey Island
Colac Bay
99
Makarewa
Cosy Nook
Riverton
Invercargill
1
Bluff (10km)
Gore (40km)

0   50
kilometres

TU-TO-RAKI-WHANOA AND TE NAMU

In Maori legend Fiordland came into being when the great god **Tu-te-raki-whanoa** hewed the rough gashes of the southern fiords around Preservation Inlet and Dusky Sound, leaving Resolution and Secretary islands where his feet stood. He honed his skill as he worked north, reaching perfection with the more sharply defined Milford Sound (Piopiotahi).

After creating this spectacular landscape, he was visited by Te-Hine-nui-to-po, goddess of death, who feared the vista created by Tu was so wonderful that people would want to live here forever. To remind humans of their mortality, she freed *namu* (**sandflies**), at Te Namu-a-Te-Hine-nui-te-po (Sandfly Point), at the end of the Milford Track. And the pesky bugs have certainly had the desired effect. In 1773, when Cook entered Dusky Sound, he was already familiar with the sandfly:

The most mischievous animal here is the small black sandfly which are exceedingly numerous and are so troublesome that they exceed everything of the kind I ever met with… The almost continual rain may be reckoned another inconvenience attending this Bay.

14

---

search of greenstone (*pounamu*). **Cook** was equally suspicious of Fiordland when, in 1770, he sailed up the coast on his first voyage to New Zealand: anchorages were hard to find; the glowering sky put him off entering Dusky Sound; slight, shifting winds discouraged entry into what he dubbed Doubtful Harbour; and he missed Milford Sound altogether.

Paradoxically for a region that's now the preserve of hardy trampers and anglers, the southern fiords region was once the best charted in the country. Cook returned in 1773, after four months battling the southern oceans, and spent five weeks in Dusky Sound. His midshipman, George Vancouver, returned in 1791, with bloodthirsty sealers and whalers hot on his heels. Over the mountains, **Europeans** seized, or paid a pittance for, land on the eastern shores of Lake Te Anau and Manapouri though it offered meagre grazing, while **explorers** headed for the interior, conferring their names on the passes, waterfalls and valleys they came across – Donald Sutherland lent his name to New Zealand's highest waterfall and Quintin McKinnon scaled the Mackinnon Pass (but failed to persuade cartographers to spell his name correctly).

GETTING AROUND

By bus Almost all buses in Fiordland ply the corridor from Queenstown through Te Anau to Milford Sound: most are tour buses, stopping at scenic spots and regaling passengers with a jocular commentary; others are scheduled services that disgorge trampers at the trailheads. Unless you are very pushed for time don't be persuaded to visit Milford from Queenstown, as it is an arduous journey that will lessen the Milford Sound experience – it's much better to stay overnight in Milford, if you can, or visit from Te Anau.
By plane The only flights you are likely to take are scenic jaunts (see p.769) to Milford Sound from Queenstown or Wanaka.

Te Anau

Ringed by snowcapped peaks, the gateway town to Fiordland, **TE ANAU** (pronounced Teh AHN-ow), stretches along the shores of its eponymous lake, one of New Zealand's grandest and deepest. To the west, the lake's watery fingers claw deep into bush-cloaked mountains so remote that their most celebrated inhabitant, the **takahe**, was thought extinct for half a century. Civilization of sorts can be found on the lake's eastern side, home to a population of under 2000.

The main way-station on the route to Milford Sound, Te Anau is an ideal base and recuperation spot for the numerous tramps, including several of the most famous and worthwhile in the country. Top of most people's list is the **Milford Track**, which starts at the head of the lake, while the **Kepler Track** (see p.759) starts closer to town.

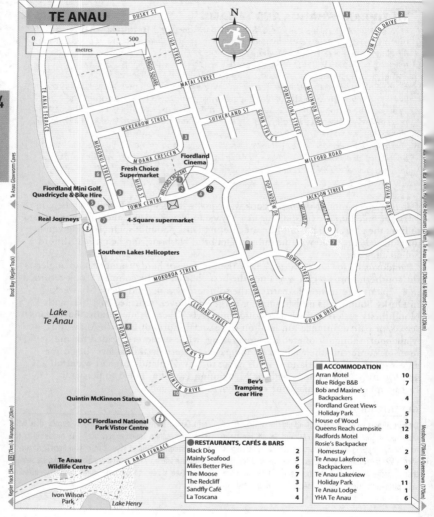

Fiordland Cinema

7 The Lane • Daily 10am–9pm; 5–10 screenings daily • $10; $1 off with voucher from the i-SITE • ☎ 03 249 8844, Ⓦ fiordlandcinema .co.nz

Don't leave town without visiting the **Fiordland Cinema**, which presents the 32-minute *Ata Whenua: Shadowlands*. Filmed mostly from a helicopter, it shows Fiordland at its majestic best throughout the seasons with wonderful cinematography, an original soundtrack and no ponderous voiceover. You'll want to go straight out for a heli-flight (bookable in the foyer). Screenings are interspersed with a selection of mainstream movies, the chairs are big and comfy and you can take espresso, beer or a wine in with you.

Te Anau Wildlife Centre

SH95 • Open access • $1–2 donation

At DOC's **Te Anau Wildlife Centre** you can amble through the park-like setting, getting the chance to glimpse some of New Zealand's rarest birds, most of which are injured or captive-bred. Look out for kakariki (parakeets), whio (blue duck), kea and kaka (indigenous parrots). There is a plan to have a couple of takahe (see box below) foster parents raise a new takahe chick each year from around mid-December.

Te Anau Glowworm Caves

Daily tours: Nov–March 2pm, 5.45pm, 7pm & 8.15pm; April–Sept 2pm, 7pm and some additional tours; 2hr 15min • $70 • ☎ 0800 656 601, ⓦ realjourneys.co.nz

If you're not planning to visit the far more impressive underground attractions at Waitomo, head to **Te Anau Glowworm Caves**. The town's full Maori name, Te Ana-au, means "cave with a current of swirling water" and it was a search for the town's namesake which led to their rediscovery in 1948. The tour feels a little processed but includes a pretty cruise to the western side of Lake Te Anau from the jetty adjacent to the visitor centre. Guides then lead you underground in small groups, spending thirty minutes in a 200m length of the Aurora cave system, followed by a short underground boat ride through glittering glowworms and a couple of noisy waterfalls.

ARRIVAL AND DEPARTURE   TE ANAU

By bus InterCity/Newmans run Queenstown–Te Anau–Milford and back daily; Te Anau–Gore–Balclutha–Dunedin daily. Tracknet (☎ 0800 483 262, ⓦ tracknet.net) run Queenstown–Te Anau–Milford and back three times daily plus Kepler Track shuttles and an Invercargill service (summer only). Buses pick up and drop off at central accommodation. Topline Tours (☎ 03 249 8059,

ⓦ toplinetours.co.nz) serve the Kepler Track, Manapouri and Queenstown.

Destinations The Divide (3–4 daily; 1hr); Dunedin (1 daily; 4hr 30min); Invercargill (1 daily; 4hr); Manapouri (2 daily; 20min); Milford Sound (at least 7 daily; 2hr 15min–2hr 45min); Queenstown (at least 7 daily; 2hr 15min); Tuatapere (2 weekly in summer; 1hr 30min).

THE TAKAHE

For half a century the flightless blue-green **takahe** (*Notornis mantelli*) was thought extinct. These plump, turkey-sized birds – close relatives of the pukeko – were once common throughout New Zealand but after the arrival of Maori their territory became restricted to the southern extremities of the South Island, and by the time Europeans came only a few were spotted, by early settlers in Fiordland. No sightings were recorded after 1898; the few trampers and ornithologists who claimed to have seen its tracks or heard its call in remote Fiordland valleys were dismissed as cranks.

One keen birder, **Geoffrey Orbell**, pieced together the sketchy evidence and concentrated his search on the 500 square kilometres of the **Murchison Mountains**, a virtual island surrounded on three sides by the western arms of Lake Te Anau and on the fourth by the Main Divide. In 1948, he was rewarded with the first takahe sighting in fifty years. However, the few remaining birds seemed doomed: deer were chomping their way through the grasses on which the takahe relied. Culling the deer averted the immediate crisis but did not halt the decline caused by stoats and harsh winters.

Takahe often lay three eggs but seldom manage to raise more than one chick. By removing any "surplus" eggs and hand-rearing them (often using hand-puppets to stop the chicks imprinting on their carers), DOC were able to gradually increase the population. In addition, DOC has established several populations on predator-free sanctuary islands – Maud Island in the Marlborough Sounds, Mana Island and Kapiti Island northwest of Wellington, Maungatautiri near Hamilton and Tiritiri Matangi and Motutapu in Auckland's Hauraki Gulf – where the birds are breeding well. These efforts have helped bring the total population to 250.

The focus is now on boosting chicks' genetic quality, identifying new large breeding sites and fine-tuning management of the wild population. It is hoped that takahe can be removed from the critically endangered list in the next ten years.

14

TE ANAU TOURS AND ACTIVITIES

Kicking around Te Anau before a big tramp provides a good opportunity to explore some of the local **short walks** or get out **on the lake**. Short cruises access the Kepler or Milford tracks (see p.760 & p.774), and if you're not up to a multi-day hike then consider a one-day guided walk along them, though walks along the Milford Road are equally rewarding (see box, p.763).

DAY-WALKS FROM TE ANAU

DOC visitor centre to Control Gates (4km one-way; 50min; flat). Easy lakeside walk past the Te Anau Wildlife Centre to the point where the Waiau River leaves Lake Te Anau for Lake Manapouri. The Control Gates mark the start of the Kepler Track (see p.759).

Brod Bay to Kepler summit (20km return; 7–9hr; 1000m ascent) Catch the Kepler Water Taxi across the lake to Brod Bay ($25) then the first third of the Kepler Track past Luxmore Hut to the summit of Mt Luxmore (1472m), then return, probably walking all the way back to Te Anau. A full but rewarding day.

Control Gates to Brod Bay (5km one-way; 1hr 30min; gently undulating). The first section of the Kepler Track goes to Dock Bay (30min) where there's good swimming, and

on through mountain and silver beech forest, past some limestone bluffs, to the campsite at Brod Bay (which has boat access).

Control Gates to Rainbow Reach (9.5km one-way; 2hr 30min–3hr 30min; mostly flat). Follow the course of the upper Waiau River through red and mountain beech. By using the Tracknet buses to the Control Gates and back from Rainbow Reach (see p.760) you can make this walk over 5–7hr, perhaps going 3km beyond Rainbow Reach to a wetland viewing platform.

Milford Track Day Walk Ultimate Hikes (see p.774) run easy day-walks beside the Clinton River at the start of the Milford Track. Trips ($195) involve a bus to Te Anau Downs, boat to Glade Wharf, 5–6hr hiking and relaxing including lunch at Clinton Hut and return.

LAKE CRUISES, JETBOATING AND KAYAKING

Cruise Te Anau ☎ 03 249 8005, ⟨w⟩ cruiseteanau .co.nz. Scenic cruises aboard a restored kauri motor launch (summer daily 10am, 1pm & 5pm; 2hr 30min; $90) plus overnight cruises including dinner and breakfast (4pm–9.30am; $275).

Luxmore Jet ☎ 0800 253 826, ⟨w⟩ luxmorejet.co.nz. One-hour jetboat ride ($99) past three *Lord of the Rings* locations on the placid Waiau River. Several departures daily ($99).

FLIGHTS

Air Fiordland ☎ 03 249 7505, ⟨w⟩ airfiordland.com. One of the best deals offered by this company is bus to Milford Sound, a cruise and a flight back over the Milford Track (9hr; $520).

Southern Lakes Helicopters 79 Lake Front Drive ☎ 0508 249 7167, ⟨w⟩ southernlakeshelicopters.co .nz. Helicopter flights from a waterside heli-pad start at $195 for 25min and range up to a couple of hours, including flights to Milford, Doubtful and Dusky sounds with landings in a narrow canyon or on snow high in

the hills. They also do heli-hikes and offer drop-offs for the tracks.

Wings & Water Lake Front Drive ☎ 03 249 7405, ⟨w⟩ wingsandwater.co.nz. Floatplane flights are ideal for an aerial view of southern Fiordland. Local loops (10min; $95), Kepler Track overflights (20min; $225) and Doubtful Sound overflights (40min; $310) are among the options. One worthwhile combo involves jetboating down the Waiau River to Lake Manapouri and then flying back to Te Anau via the hidden lakes (1hr; $240).

QUAD BIKING AND HORSE RIDING

Highride Adventures ☎ 0508 444 474, ⟨w⟩ highride .co.nz. Three-hour quad-biking rides taking in the high country and stunning views of lakes Manapouri and Te Anau from their base 27km north of town. No

prior experience is necessary, and a shuttle from Te Anau is included ($155). They also offer horse-riding trips that take about three hours, including the shuttle from Te Anau ($95).

SKY-WATCHING

Astronomy Fiordland ☎ 0508 267 667, ⟨w⟩ astronomy fiordland.co.nz. Excellent trips to the dark skies just out of town using a mobile telescope to view planets, distant

galaxies and all manner of astronomical curiosities. Trips ($45) start just after dark (around 10.30pm in mid-summer) and last an hour and a half.

GETTING AROUND

By bus There's a plethora of transport to the local trailheads, mostly with Tracknet and Topline Tours (see p.755).

By bike Rentals are available from backpackers, Fiordland Mini Golf, Quadricycle & Bike Hire, 7 Mokonui St ($24/half-day; $30/day; ☎ 03 249 7211), and Outside Sports, 38 Town Centre ($30/half-day, $50/day; ☎ 03 249 8195, ⓦ outside sports.co.nz).

By car For Milford trips, rent a car from Rent-a-dent ($80–90/day), at Parklands Motel, 16 Mokoroa St (☎ 0800 727 552, ⓦ teanaucarrentals.co.nz).

INFORMATION AND TOURS

i-SITE Corner of Town Centre and Lake Front Drive (daily 8.30am–5.30pm; ☎ 03 249 8900, ⓦ fiordland.org.nz). The best source of general information is run in conjunction with the booking office of Real Journeys.

Fiordland National Park Visitor Centre Lake Front Drive, 500m south of town (daily: mid-Dec to mid-March 8am–6pm; Oct to mid-Dec & mid-March to April 8am–5pm; May–Sept 8.30am–4.30pm, ⓔ fiordlandvc@doc.govt.nz). Stacks of track and hut information, including a Great Walks booking desk (☎ 03 249 8514, ⓔ greatwalksbooking@doc.govt.nz). Also check out its summer-visitor programme of talks and full-day, conservation-themed trips in the forests (book in advance; prices begin at about $10 but depend greatly on length, transport and who is giving them). Outside stands a statue of Milford Track explorer Quintin McKinnon.

Outdoor gear rental Available from several places including Bev's Tramping Gear Hire, 16 Homer St (☎ 03 249 7389, ⓦ bevs-hire.co.nz; Mon–Sat 9am–noon & 5.30–7pm, Sun 5.30–7pm). Individual items are charged by the day (pack $15, sleeping bag $15 etc) but it often works out better going for the Great Walks Package ($150), which contains everything you need, except boots and food, for 3–4 days. Outside Sports, 38 Town Centre (☎ 03 249 8195, ⓦ outsidesports.co.nz), compete strongly with a full range of gear including tents, backpacks and sleeping bags ($30 each for 4 days).

Heritage Tales of the Fiordland Region ☎ 0508 267 667. Even if you never normally go on a guided tour, consider taking this quirky and highly entertaining two-hour introduction to the region. They go pretty much on demand and the mini-bus only takes eight, so there's plenty of chance for questions and photos. ($40).

ACCOMMODATION

Motels dominate the length of Lake Front Drive and Quintin Drive, a block back. At most accommodation **rates** drop dramatically between June and August, and may be negotiable in the shoulder seasons (mid-April to May & Sept). **Freedom camping** is banned within 10km of Te Anau and there are No Camping signs in likely-looking parking spots well beyond that. There are, however, a couple of cheap DOC sites.

Arran Wines Motel 64 Quintin Drive ☎ 0800 666 911, ⓦ arranmotel.co.nz. Attractive studios, one- and two-bedroom units, some with cooking facilities, plus free wi-fi. Continental breakfast available. $155

Blue Ridge 15 Melland Place ☎ 03 249 7740, ⓦ blueridge.cnet.nz. Classy B&B on the peaceful fringes of Te Anau with one suite in the owners' house and three studios with kitchenettes next door, linked by a pretty garden complete with hot tub. There's a good DVD library, free wi-fi, and an excellent freshly cooked breakfast is served. $275

Bob and Maxine's Backpackers 20 Paton Place ☎ 03 931 3161, ⓔ bob.anderson@woosh.co.nz. Somewhat barn-like purpose-built backpackers in a new suburb on the edge of town with simple but spacious six-bunk dorms and one en-suite twin. Bonuses include stacks of DVDs, free national landline calling and dirt-cheap track drop-offs. Dorms $31, twin $82

House of Wood 44 Moana Crescent ☎ 03 249 8404, ⓦ houseofwood.co.nz. Alpine chalet-style B&B a 2min walk from the town centre with timber-lined en-suite rooms, a cosy lounge shared with the hosts, free use of

bikes, and filling breakfasts with home-made jams. $145

Radfords Motel 56 Lakefront Drive ☎ 0800 782 972, ⓦ radfordslakeviewmotel.co.nz. Modern, scrupulously clean and well-managed motel with everything done to the highest standard. Some units have great views, plus there's free wi-fi and 50 Sky TV channels. $200

★ **Rosie's Backpacker Homestay** 23 Tom Plato Drive ☎ 03 249 8431, ⓦ rosiesbackpackers.co.nz. This small, relaxed and welcoming backpackers sleeps just twelve in a family home with lake and mountain views. Playing the piano, guitars and clarinet is encouraged. Book early as it fills up fast. Closed June & July. Dorms $31, doubles $74

Te Anau Lakefront Backpackers 48 Lake Front Drive ☎ 03 249 7713, ⓦ teanaubackpackers.co.nz. Ageing but friendly and well-organized 110-bed hostel spread across three buildings centred on a former motel. Dorms mostly come with their own bathroom and kitchen and some have great lake views. Pairs of doubles and twins generally share a kitchen and there's a good barbecue area, which helps reduce pressure on the main kitchen. They're well set up for trampers, with $5 gear storage. Camping $18, dorms $28, doubles $74, en suites $86

14

Te Anau Lodge 52 Howden St ☎03 249 7477, ⓦteanaulodge.com. Extremely comfortable accommodation in a former convent moved to the site in the late 1990s and substantially upgraded. Rooms, many with superb mountain views, are styled in keeping with its 1920s origins and all are quite different. A very good breakfast is served in the wood-panelled former chapel, complete with organ keyboard. $240

YHA Te Anau 29 Mokonui St ☎03 249 7847, ⓔyha .teanau@yha.co.nz. Modern and comfortable two-storey hostel close to the town centre with large three- to eight-bed dorms, doubles, free gear storage, helpful staff, separate TV lounge and BBQ area. There's even a self-catering family cottage with double and twin rooms rented separately or together. Dorms $33, doubles $98, en suites $110

CAMPSITES

Fiordland Great Views Holiday Park SH94, 2km east of town ☎03 249 7059, ⓦfiordlandgreatviewsholiday park.co.nz. The cheapest of Te Anau's big holiday parks is set well back from the lake but has good long mountain views from some of the sites. Facilities are pretty good, the owner does free Kepler Track transport and even offers guests a day-trip to Milford ($145) that includes a good cruise, underwater observatory and lunch. Camping $14, cabins $54, self-contained units $100, motels $120

Queens Reach campsite Queens Reach Rd, 8km south of Te Anau off SH95 (towards Manapouri). Find yourself a site among the long grass and manuka scrub at this large, scattered DOC site beside the Waiau River with boat ramp, vault toilets and river water. Free

Te Anau Lakeview Holiday Park 77 Manapouri Rd, 1km south ☎0800 483 2628, ⓦteanau.info. Vast and very well-equipped complex with spacious tent and campervan areas, the *Steamers Beach* backpackers, lots of single rooms, modern facilities including a sauna, and a wide range of cabins and units including some gorgeous new *Marakura* rooms with matchless lake views. Camping $17, dorms $29, singles $36, doubles $70, kitchen cabin $84, en-suite cabins $109, tourist flats $125, motel units $135, *Marakura* $200

EATING AND DRINKING

Eating options are improving in Te Anau, while self-caterers have two well-stocked supermarkets to explore. Given that many visitors are embarking on or coming off tramps, drinking is low-key.

Black Dog 7 The Lane ☎03 249 8844. City-slicker cocktail bar in little old Te Anau. Dress up a little and go for one of the weekly cocktails ($10). Happy hour 5.30–6.30pm. 5.30–10pm or later.

★ **Mainly Seafood** Te Anau Terrace ☎027 516 5555, ⓦmainlyseafood.co.nz. The blue cod burger ($10) from this takeaway mobile burger van slips down a treat especially on a fine evening when you can tuck in watching the sun set over the lake. The venison burger ($10) is equally good and the mixed seafood Fisherman's Basket ($18) could be shared unless you've just finished a big hike. Daily noon–8pm.

Miles Better Pies 2 Milford Rd ☎03 249 9044. Pretty decent pies with fillings such as venison, steak and pepper, and Thai chicken ($6) to eat in or take to the lakefront. Daily 6.30am–3pm or so.

The Moose 84 Lakefront Drive ☎03 249 7100. Rambunctious locals' haunt with low-cost drink deals, plus live music on summer evening weekends. Standard Kiwi pub meals extend to BLT and fries ($18) and monkfish with salad ($28). Daily 10am–10pm or later.

★ **The Redcliff** 12 Mokonui St ☎03 249 7431. This cosy timber cottage houses a semi-formal restaurant that keeps producing the best meals in Fiordland and a welcoming bar with seating in the garden out front and a nice little window nook. Dinner might be lamb cutlet served with lamb & kidney hotpot, creamy mash and pea pesto ($36) or wild hare backstrap ($37). There's a snack menu in the bar. Sept or Oct–May daily 6–10pm.

Sandfly Café 9 The Lane ☎03 249 9529. The best of Te Anau's not particularly inspiring range of cafés is laidback and has heaps of sunny, roadside seating. They serve good coffee and the likes of steak sandwich ($12) and Caesar salad with chicken ($14). Daily 7am–4pm or later.

La Toscana 108 Town Centre ☎03 249 7756. Empty wine bottles line the walls of this old-school pizzeria and spaghetteria where everything is done simply but well. Expect pizzas (medium $13–19; large $17–27), pasta with vodka-flamed pancetta in a creamy sauce ($17 or $21) and tiramisu ($9). Licensed and BYO. Daily 6–10pm.

DIRECTORY

Banks Banks with ATMs are along Town Centre.

Left luggage While away on the tracks, trampers can usually store gear (for a small fee) at their accommodation, though it helps if you're staying there on your return. *Lakeview Holiday Park* offer luggage storage at $10/locker for as long as you need.

Vehicle storage Safer Parking, 48 Caswell Rd (☎03 249 7198, ⓦsaferparking.co.nz), offer secure parking ($9/night) while you're on a tramp. Tracknet and Real Journeys can pick up here for Milford Track, Milford Sound and Doubtful Sound transfers.

The Kepler Track

The **Kepler Track** (45–70km; 3–4 days) was created in 1988 and designated as one of New Zealand's Great Walks. It was intended to take the load off the Milford and Routeburn tracks and has been so successful it has become equally popular. Tracing a wide loop through the Kepler Mountains on the western side of Lake Te Anau, the track has one full day of exposed subalpine ridge walking, some lovely virgin beech forest and has the advantage of being accessible on foot from Te Anau. Typically walked **anticlockwise**, getting most of the climbing out of the way early, the track ranges from as little as 45km – if you use boats and buses – to 70km for the full Te Anau–Te Anau walk.

Well graded and maintained throughout – to the extent that you barely need to look where you are treading – it is still lengthy and strenuous, particularly the long haul up to Luxmore Hut. Some sections can be closed after snowfall.

Top athletes complete the **Kepler Challenge** (first Sat in Dec), a run around the track, in under five hours. The current record, set by Phil Costley in 2005, is 4:37:41.

14

Te Anau to Control Gates

5km; 1hr; flat

Most people get the bus to the Control Gates, but it is possible to walk, first heading south along Lake Front Drive, then right and following the lakeshore until the final right-turn to the Control Gates. It's not a particularly interesting walk, but pretty enough.

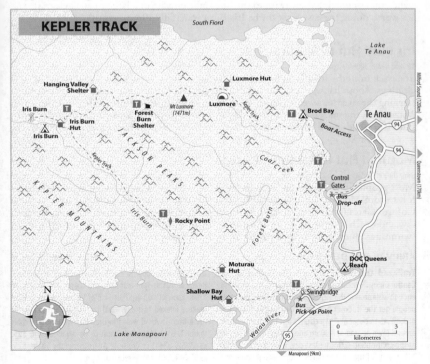

Control Gates to Brod Bay

5.6km; 1hr–1hr 30min; flat

The track follows the lakeshore around Dock Bay and over Coal Creek, passing through predominantly beech and kamahi forests but with a fine stand of tree ferns. Brod Bay has good swimming off a sandy beach and makes a lovely place to camp.

Brod Bay to Luxmore Hut

8.2km; 3–4hr; 880m ascent

Non-campers must press on from Brod Bay, following a signpost midway along the beach. The path climbs fairly steeply; after a couple of hours you sidle below limestone bluffs, from where it is almost another hour to the bushline and fine views over Te Anau and Manapouri lakes and the surrounding mountains. The hut is almost one hour beyond the bushline. A 10min side trip from Luxmore Hut visits the short and fairly dull Luxmore Cave.

Luxmore Hut to Iris Burn Hut

14.6km; 5–6hr; 300m ascent, 900m descent

An exposed, high-level section where any hint of bad weather should be treated seriously. The track climbs to just below the summit of Mount Luxmore (from where you can hike up to the 1471m peak), then descends to Forest Burn Shelter before following a ridge to Hanging Valley Shelter and turning sharply south to trace another open ridge towards Iris Burn – reached by zigzagging west into the forested Hanging Valley then following the stream to the hut and campsite in a large tussock clearing. It's worth doing the easy walk to the Iris Burn waterfall (40min return).

Iris Burn Hut to Moturau Hut

16.2km; 4–6hr; 300m descent

The track from the Iris Burn Hut descends steadily through beech forest and riverside clearings. About halfway you pass toilets at Rocky Point, then enter a short gorge before hugging the river for several magical kilometres. Just before Iris Burn spills into Lake Manapouri, the track swings east and skirts Shallow Bay to the pleasant lakeside Moturau Hut. If you're doing the track in three days, press on to the bus pick-up at Rainbow Reach.

Moturau Hut to Rainbow Reach

6km; 1hr 30min; flat

Most people finish their walk at Rainbow Reach, an easy walk through gentle beech forest from Moturau Hut. Keen trampers might want to continue on foot back to the Control Gates (additional 9.5km; 2–3hr; negligible ascent) on a track through mature lowland beech forest beside the Waiau River. There are opportunities for fishing and swimming, but the river flows swiftly, so pick your spot carefully.

ARRIVAL AND DEPARTURE

THE KEPLER TRACK

Trailhead transport The Kepler Track starts at the Control Gates, 5km southwest of Te Anau. It is a pleasant enough walk around the southern end of the lake, but most people get the Tracknet bus (Oct–April only; $6; ☎ 0800 483 262, ☎ tracknet.net), which picks up at accommodation around town at around 8.30am and 9.30am and drops off at the Control Gates. On the last day, most trampers stop 11km short of the Control Gates at the swingbridge over the Waiau's Rainbow Reach. Tracknet pick up at Rainbow Reach at 10am, 3pm and 5pm and charge $10 back to Te Anau. You can skip another 5km of lakeside walking (and make a relaxed first day start) by boating across Lake Te Anau from Te Anau wharf to Brod Bay with either Kepler Water Taxi (8.30am & 9.30am or by arrangement; $25; ☎ 03 249 8364) or Cruise Te Anau (generally 10am; $25; ☎ 03 249 8005, ☎ cruiseteanau.co.nz).

INFORMATION

Seasons During the season (late Oct–late April) booking is required (see below).

Leaflets and maps DOC's *Kepler Track* brochure (free) is adequate, though for detailed information consult the 1:60,000 *Kepler Track Parkmap* ($20).

Weather and track conditions DOC in Te Anau have the latest weather forecast and track conditions; check ⓦ doc .govt.nz/keplertrack.

Safety DOC do not track trampers' whereabouts. Let someone know your intentions through ⓦ adventuresmart.org.nz.

ACCOMMODATION

Booking During the tramping season there's a compulsory booking system for the huts and campsites, which guarantees you a place. You can walk in either direction, retrace your steps and stay up to two nights in a particular hut. Book as far ahead as possible – three months if you need a specific departure date or are part of a large group. It is easiest to book online (ⓦ doc.govt.nz) from July 1 for the following season, though it is also possible to book by mail and in person at DOC visitor centres ($2). If the track is closed due to bad weather or track conditions, full refunds are given; however, new bookings can only be made if there is space. Changes can be made to existing bookings before you start ($10/booking).

Huts The three main huts – Luxmore (55 bunks), Iris Burn (50 bunks) and Moturau (40 bunks) – have a warden, gas rings and flush toilets: you'll need to carry your own pans and plates. Trampers are discouraged from using the simple and very small Shallow Bay Hut, just off the track beside Lake Manapouri. During the main season the Backcountry Hut Pass is not valid. Outside the main season, the huts lose their warden and gas rings and go back to pit toilets, but the Backcountry Hut Pass is valid. Per person/night late Oct–April $51.50, per person/night off season $15

Camping Campers are forced to tackle the Kepler as one very short and two very long days using the two campsites at Brod Bay and Iris Burn. Both have 15 sites, pit toilets and water. $15.30

Milford Road

The 120km **Milford Road** (SH94), from Te Anau to Milford Sound, is one of the world's finest. This two-hour drive can easily take a day if you grab every photo opportunity, and longer if you explore some of the excellent hiking trails outlined on the *Milford Road* leaflet, available free from the i-SITE in Te Anau. Anywhere else the initial drive beside Lake Te Anau would be considered gorgeous, but it is nothing compared to the Eglinton Valley, where the road penetrates steeper into bush-clad mountains, winding through a subalpine wonderland to the bare rock walls of the seemingly impassable head of the Hollyford River. The Homer Tunnel cuts through to the steep Cleddau Valley before the road descends to Milford Sound.

SHORTENING THE WAY TO MILFORD

Everyone wants to go to Milford Sound, but it is a long way from the rest of the country, so boosters are forever promoting ways to shorten the journey.

The original "Southland–Westland Link" intended to put a road in from Jackson Bay on the West Coast to Milford via the Hollyford Valley. The current **Hollyford Valley Road** was approved in 1936, but only 16km of it was built. Some believe an 80km toll road connecting this with Jackson Bay is the region's infrastructure key.

In the 1990s the Ngai Tahu *iwi* hoped to install a monorail along the Greenstone Valley, the shortest route from Queenstown to The Divide, just 40km east of Milford Sound. An alliance of greenies and outdoor enthusiasts raised enough public concern to scupper that.

Recently, a $160-million, 11km-long **tunnel** has been proposed from near the start of the Routeburn Track to the Hollyford Valley. The cost will be a barrier, but this scheme perhaps has more legs than others. Passengers will be able to stay on the same vehicle (diesel-electric hybrid buses are suggested) all the way from Queenstown to Milford Sound and the one-way journey time would be halved to a little over two hours.

For every supporter of these ventures in Queenstown, there is an opponent in Te Anau – a town that relies heavily on Milford-bound traffic for its livelihood.

14

There's very little habitation along the way, no shops or petrol, but lots of great camping.

Brief history

Maori parties long used the Milford Road route on their way to seek *pounamu* at Anita Bay on Milford Sound, but no road existed until two hundred unemployment-relief workers with shovels and wheelbarrows were put on the job in 1929. The greatest challenge was the Homer Tunnel, which wasn't finally completed until 1953.

Eglinton Valley

Heading north from Te Anau, there's little reason to stop in the first 30km to the harbour at **Te Anau Downs**, where boats leave for the start of the Milford Track. The road then cuts east away from the lake, before veering north into the **Eglinton Valley** through occasional stands of silver, red and mountain beech, interspersed with open flats of red tussock grass. Once grazed, these plains are now returning to their natural state with bush regenerating at the margins, though in November and December the flats are ablaze with pink, purple and white lupins – a pest, but a beautiful one.

Mirror Lakes

Particularly picturesque mountains hem the valley and, when the weather is calm, are reflected in the roadside **Mirror Lakes**, 58km north of Te Anau. Even without the reflective stillness it is a beautiful spot with boardwalks leading down to flax-fringed waters, originally the bed of the Eglinton River.

Around 20km north, the *Cascade Creek* campsite marks the start of the **Lake Gunn Nature Walk**.

The Divide

84km north of Te Anau

As you get nearer to the head of the valley the road steepens to **The Divide**, which at 532m is the lowest east–west crossing of the Southern Alps. This is the start/finish of the Greenstone, Caples and Routeburn tracks, the last of which can be followed to Key Summit (see box opposite). The car park has toilets and a walkers' shelter with a notice board advertising the times of passing buses to Milford Sound (4 daily; 1hr 15min) and Te Anau (3 daily; 1hr), although it is better if hikers prearrange a pick-up.

HIKES FROM THE MILFORD ROAD

Old-timers grumble about tourists wasting their time, effort and money on prize tramps like the Milford and the Routeburn when so many excellent, easily accessible walks are on the Milford Road.

Lake Gunn Nature Walk (3km loop; 45min; negligible ascent). Wheelchair-accessible nature walk with interpretive panels. Starts 75km north of Te Anau.

The Divide to Key Summit (5km return; 2–3hr; 400m ascent). Panoramic views (when it's not raining) over three valley systems are the reward for this tramp along the western portion of the Routeburn Track. Starts 84km north of Te Anau.

Lake Marian (5km return; 2–3hr; 400m ascent). Picturesque ascent to a scenic alpine lake, passing pretty cataracts

(30–40min return), where boardwalks are cantilevered from the rock. Starts 1km along Lower Hollyford Rd, 88km north of Te Anau.

Homer Hut to Gertrude Saddle (10km return; 3–5hr; 600m ascent). This hike starts relatively gently up the dramatic Gertrude Valley, ringed by sheer rock walls. The track then becomes a steep route marked by snow poles and cairns up the final ascent to the saddle where there's a wonderful view of Milford Sound and the 2756m Mount Tutoko, Fiordland's highest peak. Starts 98km north of Te Anau, just by the Homer Hut.

14

Pressing on a couple of kilometres towards Milford, you descend into the valley of the Hollyford River, best seen from a popular **viewpoint** just before the Hollyford Road shoots off north.

The Hollyford Valley

The Milford Road drops down from The Divide into the **Hollyford Valley**, which runs 80km from its headwaters in the Darran Mountains north to the Tasman Sea at Martins Bay. The 16km gravel Lower Hollyford Road provides access to the Hollyford Track, the Lake Marian walk and the tiny settlement of **Gunns Camp** (aka Hollyford Camp), 8km along the valley road. This former roading camp and long-time home of eccentric Murray Gunn now has simple accommodation (see p.765), a museum and a **shop** selling trampers' supplies, postcards, books, maps and some rare bowenite greenstone pendants and souvenirs. The road runs 8km beyond Gunns Camp to the Road End – the beginning of the Hollyford Track. It is also the start of a shorter walk to **Humboldt Falls** (20–30min return), a three-step cascade tumbling 200m.

Gunns Camp Museum

Daily: Oct–March 8am–8pm; April–Sept 9am–7pm • $1, free to guests

If you're at all interested in the region's history, set half an hour aside for this small but fascinating collection of pioneer artefacts, intriguing paraphernalia relating to the one-time community at Martins Bay, stuff on the devastating floods that periodically afflict the region and the building of the Milford Road and the Homer Tunnel. A nice shot shows owner (but no longer resident) Murray Gunn sitting in his kitchen back in 1989.

Homer Tunnel

After the Hollyford turn-off, the Milford Road continues west towards the Hollyford's source, climbing all the while through ever more stunted beech trees to the huge glacial cirque of the Gertrude Valley at over 900m. It is a magnificent spot, frequently strung with waterfalls and resounding to the sound of curious **kea**: do not feed them, as human food can kill them.

The road then cuts to the sea via the 1200m-long **Homer Tunnel**, which punctures the headwall of the Hollyford Valley. Construction was started in 1935, but was badly planned from the start. Working at a one-in-ten downhill gradient, the builders soon

14

THE HOLLYFORD TRACK

Long, but mostly flat, the Hollyford Track (56km; 3–4 days one-way) runs from the end of the Hollyford Valley road to Martins Bay following Fiordland's longest valley. It is essentially a fiord that never quite formed and was never flooded by the sea.

The joy of the Hollyford is not in the sense of achievement that comes from scaling alpine passes, but in the appreciation of the dramatic mountain scenery and the kahikatea, rimu and matai **bush** with an understorey of wineberry, fuchsia and fern. At Martins Bay, Long Reef has a resident **fur seal** colony, and from September to December you might spot rare Fiordland crested **penguins** (tawaki) nesting among the scrub and rocks.

The track is a one-way tramp, requiring three to four days' backtracking – unless you're flash enough to fly out from the airstrip at Martins Bay or tough enough to continue around a long, difficult and remote loop known as the **Pyke–Big Bay Route** (9–10 days total; consult DOC's *Pyke–Big Bay Route* leaflet for details).

SEASONS AND SAFETY

The track is open year-round, but muddy in winter. Jetboats (see below) only run on Lake McKerrow during the guided walk season. Pick up DOC's *Hollyford Track* leaflet and visit DOC in Te Anau for the latest conditions. DOC do not keep track of trampers' whereabouts; let someone know your intentions through ⓦadventuresmart.org.nz.

ACCESS, ACCOMMODATION AND GUIDED WALKS

Access the Hollyford Road end from Te Anau with Tracknet **buses** (Nov–April Mon, Wed & Fri; $52; ☎0800 483 262, ⓦtracknet.net). Guided walkers **fly** out from Martins Bay over spectacular mountains to Milford Sound. You can join them, or get back-flights into Martins Bay, with several companies (see p.769). You can avoid most of the long day's walk beside the attractive but samey Lake McKerrow with Hollyford Track's **jetboat service** between Martins Bay and the head of Lake McKerrow (late Oct to mid-April; around $110).

There is no **booking** system for the track. The six DOC **huts** all cost $15/night and the Backcountry Hut Pass is valid. All have twelve bunks except Alabaster Hut (26 bunks) and Martins Bay Hut (24 bunks). Carry a cooking stove and pots. **Camping** ($5) is permitted next to all huts.

Trips & Tramps ☎0800 305 807, ⓦtripsandtramps .com. The handiest access package is with this outfit, who will book your flight and organize transport between Milford Sound airport and your vehicle at the Hollyford Road end ($195). The same thing done from Te Anau costs $260. **Hollyford Track Guided Walk** ☎0800 832 226, ⓦhollyfordtrack.com. Perfect if you hate carrying a big pack and prefer comfortable lodgings and having hearty meals cooked for you. Knowledgeable guides lead small groups on these three-day hikes with nights spent at the relatively luxurious *Martins Bay Lodge* and the *Pyke River Lodge*. The price ($1795) includes a jetboat journey along Lake McKerrow, avoiding the toughest section, and a flight out of Martins Bay. Late Oct to mid-April.

THE ROUTE

Road End to Hidden Falls Hut (9km; 2–3hr; negligible ascent). The track follows a disused section of road that crumbles into track and then some riverbank before arriving at Hidden Falls Hut.

Hidden Falls Hut to Alabaster Hut (10km; 3–4hr; 100m ascent). Keen walkers may want to push on from Hidden Falls Hut through ribbonwood and beech to Little Homer Saddle and past Little Homer Falls.

Alabaster Hut to Demon Trail Hut (15km; 3–4hr; negligible ascent). Leaving Alabaster Hut, you pass a side track to the nicely sited McKerrow Island Hut, before continuing beside Lake Alabaster to Demon Trail Hut.

Demon Trail Hut to Hokuri Hut (10km; 5–6hr; 100m ascent). Easily the toughest day on the walk, following the shore of Lake McKerrow on rough, undulating ground (a former cattle track) with some tricky stream crossings, to the twelve-bunk Hokuri Hut.

Hokuri Hut to Martins Bay Hut (13km; 4–5hr; negligible ascent). Passing the scant remains of Jamestown, a cattle-ranching settlement that prospered in the 1870s, and the small airstrip served by Hollyford Track's flights, you'll stumble across some of the dozen dwellings that comprise Martins Bay; whitebaiters and hunters stay here occasionally, although there are no permanent residents. Continuing parallel to Martins Bay, and occasionally glimpsing the Hollyford River through wind-shorn trees, you reach the Martins Bay Hut.

nit water and were forced to pump out continuously; a pilot tunnel allowing the water to drain westwards was finished in 1948. After a concerted push, the tunnel was completed in 1953, opening Milford Sound to road traffic for the first time. Each April, uninhibited locals compete in a race through the tunnel naked (apart from running shoes).

Despite recent improvements, the tunnel remains rough-hewn, narrow and dark. During peak periods in the summer **traffic lights** dictate one-way traffic (expect a wait of up to 15min), but for the rest of the time you'll need to look out for oncoming vehicles.

14

The Chasm

The Homer Tunnel emerges at the top of a series of switchbacks down to the Cleddau River. Almost 10km on from the tunnel all buses stop at **The Chasm**, while their passengers stroll (15min return) to the near-vertical rapids where the Cleddau has scoured out a deep, narrow channel. Tantalizing glimpses through the foliage reveal sculpted rocks hollowed out by churning water or eroded into freestanding ribs that resemble flying buttresses. From here it is another 8km to Milford Sound.

ACCOMMODATION	**MILFORD ROAD**

Campers will want to spend a night or two in one of the dozen simple DOC **campsites** along the Milford Road either on the grassy flats of the Eglinton Valley or the bush nearby. All have vault toilets and giardia-free stream water, and most have fireplaces. All are outlined in DOC's free *Conservation Campsites* booklet: some of the best are listed below, in order of distance from Te Anau.

Henry Creek SH94, 25km north of Te Anau on the Milford Rd. The first of the Milford Road DOC sites is attractive with (almost) lakeside sites well spaced along the lakeshore and sheltered camping among the beech trees. Vault toilets and lake water. $5

Walker Creek SH94, 49km north of Te Anau. Small DOC site with valley views just 2km inside the national park. There's stream water, picnic tables and plenty of room for campervans in secluded spots $5

Knobs Flat SH94, 52km north of Te Anau ☎03 249 9122, ⓦknobsflat.co.nz. Six very comfortable motel-style units in a remote location with great valley views from the verandas, and no TV or mobile phone reception. Facilities include all you need for cooking, but no oven. Guided nature walks through the Eglinton Valley are available ($20/hr; $75/half-day) and there's camping (no powered sites) with showers and a well-equipped camp kitchen. Camping $15, doubles $130

Totara SH94, 53km north of Te Anau. DOC campsite with large grassy areas sheltered by clumps of beech, with picnic tables, simple barbecues and fire grates. $5

Deer Flat SH94, 62km north of Te Anau. The pitches at this DOC campsite are scattered around, tucked into patches of beech on the edge of grassy flats. $5

Cascade Creek SH94, 77km north of Te Anau. The closest DOC site to Milford Sound that's suitable for campers – still over 40km away. Fly-fishing possible. $5

Gunns Camp 8km along Lower Hollyford Rd ⓔgunns camp@ruralinzone.net. The only accommodation in these parts is this huddle of simple 1930s cabins that served as married families' quarters for the long-suffering road-builders. An ongoing sympathetic revamp includes a modern lounge and kitchen block, but the place retains its spirit – old, pretty basic but with bags of character. Cabins generally have single beds or six-berth bunk rooms, linked by a kitchen/lounge with a wood fire or a coal range. There's generator power (7.30–10am & 6–10pm) but no refrigeration, no mobile coverage and no internet. Bring food but you can top up at the small shop. Some campervan sites. Camping $12, bunks $20, twin & double cabins $55

Milford Sound

The most northerly and celebrated of Fiordland's fifteen fiords is **Milford Sound** (Piopiotahi) with its vertical sides towering 1200m above the sea and waterfalls plunging from hanging valleys. Some 15km long and mostly less than 1km wide, it is also one of the slenderest fiords – and yes, it is mis-named. Sounds are drowned river valleys whereas this is very much a glacially formed fiord.

14

MILFORD'S FRAGILE ECOSYSTEM

The predations of today's influx of visitors and the operation of a small fishing fleet have necessitated strategies to preserve the **fragile ecosystem**. Like all fiords, Milford Sound has an entrance sill at its mouth, in this case only 70m below the surface – by comparison, the deepest point is almost 450m. This minimizes the water's natural recirculation and hinders the mixing of sea water and the vast quantities of fresh water that pour into the fiord, creating the strange phenomenon of **deep water emergence**. The less-dense tannin-stained fresh surface layer (generally 2–6m deep) builds up, further diminishing the penetration of light, which is already reduced by the all-day shadow cast by the fiord walls. The result is a relatively barren inter-tidal zone that protects a narrow – but wonderfully rich and extremely fragile – band of light-shy red and black **corals**; these normally grow only at much greater depths, but thrive here in the dark conditions. Unfortunately, Milford's fishing fleet use crayfish pots, which tend to shear off anything that grows on the fiord's walls. A marine reserve has been set up along the northeastern shore, where all such activity is prohibited, but really this is far too small and conservation groups are campaigning for its extension.

It is a wondrous place, though it is difficult to grasp its heroic scale unless your visit coincides with that of one of the great cruise liners – even these formidable vessels are totally dwarfed.

Perhaps counter-intuitively, Milford is at its best in the rain, something that happens on over 180 days a year giving a massive 7m of **annual rainfall**. Within minutes of a torrential downpour every cliff-face sprouts a waterfall and the place looks even more magical as ethereal mist descends. Indeed, Milford warrants repeated visits: in bright sunshine (yes, it does happen), on a rainy day and even under a blanket of snow.

None of the other fiords quite matches Milford for its spectacular **beauty**, but what makes Milford special is its **accessibility**. The tiny airport hardly rests as planes buzz in and out, while busloads of visitors are disgorged from buses onto cruises – all day in the summer and around the middle of the day in spring and autumn.

The crowds can certainly detract from the grandeur, but don't let that put you off. Driving to Milford Sound and admiring it from the land just doesn't cut it; you need to get out on the water, either on a cruise or kayaking.

Brief history

Maori know Milford Sound as **Piopiotahi** ("the single thrush"), and attribute its creation to the god Tu-te-raki-whanoa, who was called away before he could carve a route into the interior, leaving high rock walls. These precipitous routes are now known as the Homer and Mackinnon passes, probably first used by Maori who came to collect *pounamu*. The first European known to have sailed into Piopiotahi was sealer John Grono who, in 1823, named the fiord Milford Haven after his home port in south Wales. The main river flowing into the Welsh Milford is the Cleddau, so naturally the river at the head of the fiord is so named.

The earliest settler was Scot **Donald Sutherland**, who arrived with his dog, John O'Groat, in 1877; he promptly set a series of thatched huts beside the freshwater basin of what he called the "City of Milford", funding his explorations by guiding small numbers of visitors who had heard tell of the scenic wonder.

All visitors arrived by boat or walked the Milford Track until 1953 when the road through the Homer Tunnel was finally completed, paving the way for the phalanxes of buses that disgorge tourists onto cruises.

MITRE PEAK, MILFORD SOUND (P.765) >

Milford Sound village

The settlement of Milford Sound is tiny, comprising little more than a small airstrip, fishing harbour, outsized cruise terminal, post office, pub/café and a couple of lodges.

You're pretty much surrounded by water here, and should waste little time getting out on it, but if tales of his pioneering days have inspired you, pay homage at **Donald Sutherland's grave**, hidden among the staff accommodation behind the pub. Alternatively take a five-minute **walk** up to a lookout behind *Mitre Peak Lodge*, or the **Piopiotahi Foreshore Walk**, which leads from the car park to the settlement along the edge of the fiord (5–10min; flat).

Mitre Peak

The view of Milford Sound is dominated by the iconic, triangular, glaciated pinnacle of **Mitre Peak** (1692m), named for its resemblance to a bishop's mitre. It actually doesn't look much like one, but pioneering Victorians were undoubtedly desperate to find an alternative to its Maori name, *Rahotu*, which some translate as "member of upstanding masculinity" (though it really doesn't look much like one of those either).

Sinbad Gully

The left side of Mitre Peak plunges into **Sinbad Gully**, a vast hanging valley that was the last Fiordland refuge of the world's largest parrot, the **kakapo**. A handful were found here in 1981 and added to the genetically limited Steward Island kakapo, now all protected on predator-free islands. A stoat-trapping programme hopes to make Sinbad Gully safe enough to one day release kakapo back into the wild here.

Lady Bowen Falls and Stirling Falls

After heavy rain, Milford Sound can feel like a chasm of waterfalls but there are really only two major falls that keep going long after the rain stops – both best seen from the water. Right by Milford Sound village, the 164m **Lady Bowen Falls** is an impressive sight at any time, but truly thunders after heavy rain sending a vast spume of spray over any who approach.

Halfway along the fiord, the 155m **Stirling Falls** is almost as impressive and features on most cruise-boat itineraries and some kayak trips.

Milford Discovery Centre and Underwater Observatory

Harrison Cove, accessed on various cruises, but mostly those run by Southern Discoveries; 30–45min stop • $36 more than the equivalent non-observatory cruise • ☏ 0800 246 536, ⦿ southerndiscoveries.co.nz

About a third of the way along the fiord is the recently revamped **Milford Discovery Centre and Underwater Observatory**, a floating platform moored to a sheer rock wall in a marine reserve. A spiral staircase takes you 8m down through the relatively lifeless freshwater surface layer to a circular gallery where windows look out into the briny heart of the fiord. Sharks and seals occasionally swim by, but most of the action happens immediately outside in window-box "gardens", specially grown from rare locally gathered **coral** and plant species. Lights pick out colourful fish, tubeworms, sea fans, huge starfish and rare red and black coral (the latter actually white when alive). Unless you're an experienced diver this is the only chance you'll get to see these corals, which elsewhere in the world grow only at depths greater than 40m.

Topside, there's diverting interpretation on the Milford Road, the construction of the Homer Tunnel and the building of the centre in the mid-1990s.

ARRIVAL AND DEPARTURE | **MILFORD SOUND**

Milford Sound is on most visitors' itineraries, and during the season (Oct–April) there are plenty of operators to get you there from almost anywhere in the country. You can drive yourself along the Milford Road (see p.761), catch a bus the same way (see below) or fly direct from Queenstown or Wanaka (see below). Several companies combine forces offering coach/cruise/flight combos (see box below).

BY BUS

Numerous luxury tour buses make the 5hr journey from Queenstown to Milford Sound via Te Anau (complete with frequent photo stops and a relentless commentary). They then disgorge passengers for a cruise on the fiord and transport them back to Queenstown – a hurried twelve- to thirteen-hour day usually starting at 7am. Most trips pick up in Te Anau, but it is more pleasurable to base yourself in Te Anau and catch a bus from there – a leisurely eight hours, allowing you to concentrate on the most interesting section of the Milford Road and usually include a cruise on the sound. The cheapest are those that don't include cruises – good value if you're going kayaking.

Destinations The Divide (4 daily; 1hr 15min); Queenstown (at least 7 daily; 4hr 45min–5hr 30min); Te Anau (at least 7 daily; 2hr 15min–2hr 45min).

BUS COMPANIES

BBQ Bus ☎ 03 442 1045, ⓦ milford.net.nz. The best-value backpacker-oriented trip from Queenstown, with stops for short bushwalks, a BBQ in the Hollyford Valley and a Milford cruise (or flight option). Oct–April daily; May, Aug & Sept four weekly ($182). Also available from Te Anau ($152).

Fiordland Tours ☎ 0800 247 249, ⓦ fiordlandtours .co.nz. Te Anau-based owner-operator running small-bus tours to Milford Sound with accommodation pick-ups, good commentary, cruise and home baking ($169; lunch $20 extra).

Jucy ☎ 0800 500 121, ⓦ jucycruize.co.nz. Budget trip from Queenstown for late-ish risers. Departs 8.15am, joins the 3.15pm Jucy Cruise and stops for a quick meal in Te Anau on the way back, returning 9pm ($159).

Milford Sound Select ☎ 0800 477 479, ⓦ milford soundselect.co.nz. Mid-sized glass-roofed coaches are a nice touch on these very competitively priced coach/cruise/coach tours from Queenstown ($149).

Real Journeys ☎ 0800 656 501, ⓦ realjourneys.co.nz.

Upmarket coach/cruise/coach tours from Queenstown using wedge-shaped, glass-roofed coaches with slightly angled seats that give the best all-round views, and wi-fi. There's good interpretation and a multilingual commentary. Operates all year ($198) with pick-ups in Te Anau ($175).

Tracknet ☎ 03 249 7777, ⓦ tracknet.net. Budget transport between Te Anau and Milford Sound, though you'll have to put up with detours to the trailheads. Oct–April twice daily ($49 each way).

Trips & Tramps ☎ 0800 305 807, ⓦ tripsandtramps .co.nz. Te Anau-based, small-bus interactive, nature-oriented trips include a basic coach and cruise with several short walks (9hr; $165); their Big Day Out (10hr; $173) adding time for a self-guided 2hr hike or a short guided walk along the Hollyford Track; and an overnighter (2 days; $330) with an additional half-day sea kayaking and a night at Milford Sound Lodge. Some trips operate all year.

BY PLANE

Visitors really pushed for time can do a simple overflight of Milford Sound from either Queenstown or Wanaka (typically around $350), but you really should land and take a cruise. Flights are, of course, weather dependent and operators won't fly you in to Milford unless they are fairly confident of getting you out again.

Air Fiordland ☎ 0800 103 404, ⓦ airfiordland.com. Queenstown-based airline doing 4hr fly/cruise/fly trips ($445).

Real Journeys ☎ 0800 656 501, ⓦ realjourneys.co.nz. Major Fiordland operator flying from Queenstown and using their own cruise boats ($438).

Wanaka Flightseeing ☎ 03 443 8787, ⓦ flightseeing .co.nz. Fly/cruise/fly trips from Wanaka give especially good views of Mt Aspiring and the Olivine Ice Plateau en route (4hr; $460).

Destinations Queenstown (at least 20 daily; 35min); Wanaka (2–3 daily; 40min).

14

COACH, CRUISE AND FLIGHT COMBOS TO MILFORD SOUND

If you can't face a full-day coach/cruise/coach trip from Queenstown to Milford Sound, and want a superb flight over the South Island's icy spine as well as seeing the gorgeous Milford Road from the ground, opt for a fly/cruise/coach or coach/cruise/flight combo. Flights are far more likely to get cancelled due to bad weather so if the morning is looking fine it makes sense to fly in and coach out. Many operators offer such combos that, perhaps counter-intuitively, cost more than flying both ways. Typical prices are: Air Fiordland ($520), Milford Sound Select ($495) and Real Journeys ($568).

14

MILFORD SOUND CRUISES AND ACTIVITIES

There's little point visiting Milford Sound and not spending time on the water, and fortunately there are numerous worthwhile ways to do just that.

DAY CRUISES

The dramatic view from the shore of Milford Sound pales beside the spectacle from the water. The majority of cruises explore the full length of Milford Sound, all calling at waterfalls, a seal colony and overhanging rock faces; at **Fairy Falls**, boats nose up to the base of the fall, while suitably attired passengers are encouraged to edge out onto the bowsprit and collect an earful of water.

The simplest option is one of the 1.5–3hr **day cruises** (summer 20-plus daily; winter 10 daily; best booked a few days in advance in Jan, Feb & March) either on one of the large, fast and comfortable boats or one of the more intimate small boats. Most cruise companies vary their **fares** during the day, with those leaving between 11am and 2pm around 20–30 percent more expensive than those at say 9am or 3pm. Otherwise, costs vary according to the size of boat, duration of trip, degree of interpretation and quality of food (if any), but all offer the same scenery.

Jucy Cruise ☎ 0800 500 121, 🌐 jucycruize.co.nz. Fun, budget-oriented cruises ($65–75) on a relatively small (100 passenger) boat. Light lunch available on board.

Mitre Peak Cruises ☎ 03 249 8110 & 0800 744 633, 🌐 mitrepeak.com. With the smallest boats and more personal service, there's undoubted appeal to these 2hr cruises ($68–80).

Real Journeys ☎ 0800 656 501, 🌐 realjourneys.co.nz. The biggest cruise operator with a wide range of boats and professional service. Choose a basic cruise (1hr 40min; $68–90) or a more leisurely nature cruise (2hr–2hr 30min; $75–95): lunches ($17 & $32) available, but Indian and o-bento meals must be pre-ordered.

Southern Discoveries ☎ 0800 264 536, 🌐 southern discoveries.co.nz. Mainstream cruises ranging from a basic cruise (1hr 45min; $65–90) to their Discover More cruise (3hr; $115) with a buffet lunch and a visit to the Milford Discovery Centre.

OVERNIGHT CRUISES

Overnight cruises are all run by Real Journeys (☎0800 656 501, 🌐realjourneys.co.nz), who operate two motor cruisers each offering a slightly different experience. Both operate daily in season from around 4.30pm–9.15am and involve a leisurely cruise around Milford Sound, usually anchoring for a while in **Anita Bay** (Te-Wahi-Takiwai, "the place of Takiwai"), a former greenstone-gathering place at the fiord's mouth, but still sheltered from the wrath of the Tasman Sea. There's a chance to go kayaking, good meals and a night spent at anchor in some sheltered cove. Add $60–80 for return coach transfer from Te Anau, $135 from Queenstown.

Milford Wanderer The 28 berths in this backpacker-oriented boat are mostly in cramped twin rooms that share bathrooms (though there are also a couple of quad-shares). All are equipped with sheets, duvets and towels, and a hearty three-course set meal (drinks extra) helps iron out the kinks.

Nov–March twin-share $325, quad-share $260; April twin-share $228, quad-share $182.

Milford Mariner Fairly luxurious 60-berth boat with comfortable twin-share en-suite cabins and a high-quality buffet meal. Nov–March $495; Sept, Oct & April to mid-May $347.

KAYAKING AND SCUBA DIVING

The elemental nature of Milford Sound can best be appreciated by **kayaking**, possibly seeing wildlife up close and even paddling in the spray from waterfalls. If you'd rather go below surface (and are PADI- or SSI-certified), join a fascinating **scuba diving** trip seeking out black coral, brachiopods (ancient shellfish), purple and white nudribranchs, scarlet wrasse and telescope fish, all visible at modest depths.

★ **Rosco's Milford Sound Sea Kayaks** 72 Town Centre, Te Anau ☎ 03 249 8500 & 0800 476 726, 🌐 roscomilfordkayaks.com. Extensive range of Milford Sound-based kayaking trips with expert and characterful guides, including the wonderful Morning Glory (6hr; $175), with a dawn start, long paddle then a water taxi back. The afternoon Twilighter (5hr; $155) follows a similar format, will probably involve more wind and waves and usually has smaller groups. They even do a paddle and stroll along the Milford Track (4hr; $99) and various combos. Trips are mostly mid-Oct to mid-April, though the Sunriser (5hr; $130) runs year-round.

Tawaki Dive ☎ 0800 829 254, 🌐 tawakidive.co.nz. Two guided dives ($159; $189 including transport from Te Anau; gear rental $99 extra) as part of a 4hr cruise.

ACCOMMODATION AND EATING

The following covers all the lodging, eating and drinking options in Milford Sound.

Blue Duck Bar SH94 ☎03 249 7982. Fairly uninspiring pub with pool tables, sports TV and a short menu of pizzas, chicken burger and chips and spaghetti Bolognese (all around $19). Meals served 5–9pm. Daily 4–11pm or so.

Blue Duck Café SH94 ☎03 249 7982. Get a corner seat for views of Mitre Peak (or to watch the weather sweeping along the fiord) from this café that's good for espresso, muffins, sandwiches, pies and ice cream, though the buffet lunches ($17–21) are less tempting. Daily: Nov–March 8.30am–4.30pm; April–Oct 9am–4pm.

Milford Sound Lodge 1.5km back from the wharf ☎03 249 8071, ⊛milfordlodge.com. Book well in advance to stay at this well-run backpackers with spacious dorms, twins and doubles (with shared bathrooms), a

cramped kitchen, bar, comfortable lounge and pricey shop. Along the riverside are four beautiful units with large windows, plush bathrooms and TV. Camping $18, dorms $30, four-shares $33, doubles $85, units $250

Mitre Peak Lodge ☎03 249 7907. Milford Track guided walkers get priority at (and largely fill) this prominent 35-room 1950s hotel. Others can phone to fill any remaining rooms, which are a bit dated, though those with great Mitre Peak views also have modernized bathrooms. Guests can relax in the lounge bar, have a three-course dinner ($50), buy a cooked breakfast ($15) and even make their own packed lunch ($10). Checkout time is 8.30am. Only open Nov to mid-April. $160, fiord-view $210

The Milford Track

More than any other Great Walk, the **Milford Track** (54km; 4 days) is a Kiwi icon. Its exalted reputation is part accident and part history but there's no doubt that the Milford Track is wonderful and includes some of Fiordland's finest scenery. The track starts at the head of Lake Te Anau and follows the Clinton River into the heart of the mountains, climbing over the spectacular Mackinnon Pass before tracing the Arthur River to Milford Sound.

Some disparage the track as over-regimented, expensive and not especially varied, while others complain that the huts are badly spaced and lurk below the tree line among the sandflies. While these criticisms aren't unfounded – the tramp costs around $340 in hut and transport fees alone – the track is well managed and maintained, the huts clean and unobtrusive, and because everyone's going in the same direction you can charge ahead (or lag behind) and hike all day without seeing a soul. The Milford is also tougher than many people expect, packing the only hard climb and a dash for the boat at Milford Sound into the last two days.

Brief history

It is likely that **Maori** paced the Arthur and Clinton valleys in search of *pounamu*, but there is little direct evidence. The first **Europeans** to explore were Scotsmen Donald Sutherland and John Mackay who in 1880 blazed a trail up the Arthur Valley from Milford Sound. The story goes that while working their way up the valley they came upon the magnificent Mackay Falls and tossed a coin to decide who would name it, on the understanding that the loser would name the next waterfall. Mackay won the toss but rued his good fortune when, days later, they stumbled across the much more famous and lofty Sutherland Falls. They may well have climbed the adjacent Mackinnon Pass, but the honour of naming it went to **Quintin McKinnon** who, with his companion Ernest Mitchell, reached it in 1888 after having been commissioned by the Otago Chief Surveyor, C.W. Adams, to cut a path up the Clinton Valley.

Tourists arrive

The route was finally pushed through in mid-October 1888 and the first **tourists** followed a year later, guided by McKinnon. The greatest fillip came in 1908 when a writer submitted her account of the Milford Track to the editor of

London's *Spectator*. She had declared it "A Notable Walk" but, in a fit of editorial hyperbole, the editor re-titled the piece "The Finest Walk in the World". From 1903 until 1966 the government held a monopoly on the track, allowing only guided walkers; the huts were supplied by packhorses, a system that wasn't retired until 1969.

Wider **public access** was only achieved after the Otago Tramping Club challenged the government's policy by tramping the Milford in 1964. Huts were built in 1966 and the first independent parties came through later that year.

14

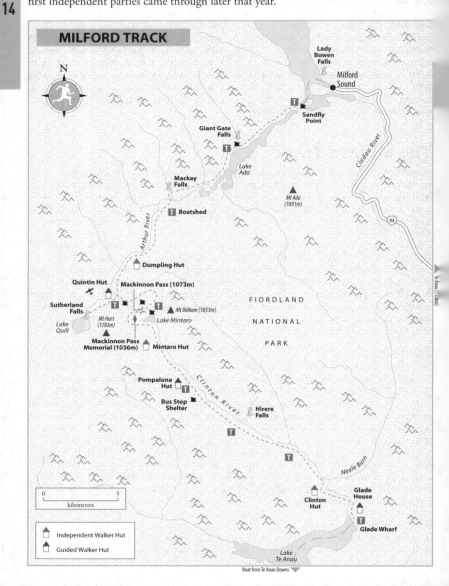

MILFORD TRACK

N

Lady Bowen Falls

Milford Sound

Sandfly Point

Giant Gate Falls

Lake Ada

Cleddau River

Mackay Falls

Mt Ada (1891m)

Boatshed

94

Arthur River

Te Anau (170km)

Dumpling Hut

Quintin Hut

Mackinnon Pass (1073m)

FIORDLAND

Sutherland Falls

Mt Hart (1783m)

Mt Balloon (1853m)

NATIONAL

Lake Quill

Lake Mintaro

Mackinnon Pass Memorial (1036m)

Mintaro Hut

PARK

Pompalona Hut

Clinton River

Bus Stop Shelter

Hirere Falls

Neale Burn

Glade House

Clinton Hut

Glade Wharf

0   5
kilometres

Lake Te Anau

⬆ Independent Walker Hut

⬆ Guided Walker Hut

Boat from Te Anau Downs ▽

Glade Wharf to Clinton Hut

km; 1–1hr 30min; 50m ascent

The first day is a doddle, starting along a 2km 4WD track that serves Glade House (guided walkers only). The path then crosses a swingbridge to the right bank of the gentle, meandering Clinton River; keen anglers can spend an hour or two fishing for trout in the deep pools. The track runs through dense beech forest, only occasionally giving glimpses of the mountains ahead beyond Clinton Hut.

Clinton Hut to Mintaro Hut

16.5km; 4–7hr; 350m ascent

The track follows the true right bank of the Clinton River to its source, Lake Mintaro, right by the Mintaro Hut. Again, it's easy going and by the time you reach a short side track to Hidden Lake, Mackinnon Pass should be visible. The track steepens a little to Bus Stop Shelter, flattens out to Pompolona Hut (guided walkers only), and is a further hour to Mintaro Hut where, if it looks like it will be a good sunset, you should drop your pack and head up Mackinnon Pass.

Mintaro Hut to Dumpling Hut

14km; 5–7hr; 550m ascent; 1030m descent

The walk to this point does little to prepare you for the third day. Though the surface of the broad path is firm and well graded, less experienced bushwalkers will find the haul up to Mackinnon Pass (1hr 30min–2hr) very strenuous. Long breath-catching pauses provide an opportunity to admire the wonderful alpine scenery, notably the headwall of the Clinton Valley, a sheer glacial cirque of grey granite. As the bush drops away behind you, the slope eases to the saddle at Mackinnon Pass, a great place to eat lunch, though you'll have the company of kea and the incessant buzzing of pleasure flights from Milford. A memorial to McKinnon and Mitchell marks the low point of the saddle, from where the path turns east and climbs to a day shelter (with toilets and, in summer, a gas ring) just below the dramatic form of Mount Balloon. From here it's all downhill, and steeply too, initially skirting the flank of Mount Balloon then following the path beside the picturesque Roaring Burn and down to the Arthur River. The confluence is marked by Quintin Hut (guided walkers only), which was originally built by the Union Steamship Company as an overnight shelter for sightseers from Milford visiting the Sutherland Falls. Though it remains a private hut, toilets and shelter are provided for independent walkers – who mostly dump their packs for the walk to the base of the 560m Sutherland Falls (4km return; 1hr–1hr 30min; 50m ascent), the highest in New Zealand. Dumpling Hut is another hour's walk from Quintin Hut.

Dumpling Hut to Sandfly Point

18km; 5–6hr; 125m descent

You're in for an early start and a steady walk to meet your launch or kayak at 2 or 3.15pm. After rain this can be a magnificent walk, the valley walls streaming with waterfalls and the Arthur River in spate. The track follows the tumbling river for a couple of hours to the Boatshed (toilets), before crossing the Arthur River by swingbridge and cutting inland to the magnificent MacKay Falls. More a steep cascade than a waterfall, they are much smaller than the Sutherland Falls but equally impressive, particularly after rain. Don't miss Bell Rock, a water-hollowed boulder that you can crawl inside. The track subsequently follows Lake Ada, created by a landslip 900 years ago, and named by Sutherland after his Scottish girlfriend. A small lunch shelter midway along its shore heralds Giant Gate Falls, which are best viewed from the swingbridge that crosses the river at the foot of the falls. From here it is roughly an hour and a half to the shelter at Sandfly Point.

ARRIVAL AND DEPARTURE — MILFORD TRACK

Trailhead transport Both ends of the Milford Track can only be realistically approached by boat, and arrangements must be made at the same time as accommodation passes are issued. Independent walkers need to catch the Tracknet bus (30min; $23) from Te Anau to the harbour at Te Anau Downs, 30km north of Te Anau, then the Real Journeys launch across Lake Te Anau to Glade Wharf (1hr 30min; $75). There are early departures, but since the first day's walk is very easy, it makes sense to make a late start using the 1.15pm bus and the 2pm launch. At the Milford end of the track, catch the launch from the aptly named Sandfly Point to Milford Sound (Nov–April daily 2pm & 3.15pm; 20min; $39). Tracknet buses back to Te Anau can be picked up at 9.30am, 2.30pm and 5pm (2hr; $49). An off-season option is with Cruise Te Anau ☎ 03 249 8005, ⓦ cruiseteanau.co.nz) who offer a full transportation package for $180 (April–Nov only).

INFORMATION AND TOURS

Seasons During the main hiking season (late Oct–late April) there are strict booking conditions (see below). Hiking the track at other times is not recommended since transport to and from the track is very limited, some footbridges are removed and huts have no heating. Still, bookings are not required and the Backcountry Hut Pass is valid.

Leaflets and maps DOC's *Milford Track* brochure (free) is adequate, though for detailed information consult the 1:70,000 *Milford Track Parkmap* ($20).

Weather and track conditions DOC in Te Anau have the latest weather forecast and track conditions; check ⓦ doc.govt.nz/milfordtrack.

Safety DOC do not keep track of trampers' whereabouts. Let someone know your intentions through ⓦ adventure smart.org.nz. Due to the presence of avalanche zones along the track, anyone walking out of season should check conditions with DOC before setting out.

GUIDED WALKS

Milford Track Guided Walk ☎ 0800 659 255, ⓦ ultimate hikes.co.nz. For many years, the only way to walk the Milford Track was on a guided walk. Some argue that this is still the best approach, with just your personal effects to carry and comfortable beds in clean, plain huts with hot showers, duvets on the bunks, three-course dinners with wine and cooked breakfasts. Accommodation is in shared bunkrooms or double en-suites. Staff prepare the huts, cook the meals, make up the lunches and tidy up after you. The five-day, four-night package includes a pre-track briefing in Queenstown, transport from there to the trailhead, accommodation and food on the track, a night at Milford Sound's *Mitre Peak Lodge*, a Milford Sound cruise and a return bus ride to Queenstown (Nov–April daily departures). The same company runs a variety of other guided walks including the Routeburn Track. A single-room supplement of $600 applies. Bunk/person $1195, double/person $2405

ACCOMMODATION

Booking There's a rigid system of advance hut booking during the main season. You can only walk the track from south to north, spending the first night at Clinton Hut, the second at Mintaro and the third at Dumpling. No backtracking or second nights are allowed. It is easiest to book free online (ⓦ doc.govt.nz) from July 1 for the following season, though it is also possible to book by mail and in person ($2) through the Great Walks Booking Desk (PO Box 29, Te Anau ☎ 03 249 8514, ✉ greatwalksbooking @doc.govt.nz). Pick up your accommodation passes from DOC in Te Anau before 11am on the day of departure. Numbers are limited to forty per day, so you'll need to book well in advance; a couple of months if you are adaptable, six if you need a specific departure date or are part of a large group. If the track is closed due to bad weather or track conditions full refunds are made.

Huts and camping During the season, the three 40-bunk huts all have wardens and are equipped with flush toilets, running water (which must be treated), heaters and gas rings, but not pans and plates; the cost is $153 for the three nights, and family discounts of twenty percent apply throughout the season. Outside the main season these huts lose their warden and gas rings, go back to pit toilets and cost $15. There is no camping on the Milford Track.

Manapouri and Lake Manapouri

Even among New Zealand's bountiful supply of beautiful lakes, **Lake Manapouri** shines, its long, indented shoreline contorted into three distinct arms and clad with thick bush tangled with ferns. The lake sits at 178m and has a vast catchment area, guzzling all the

ELECTRICITY, ALUMINIUM AND BRICKBATS

Lake Manapouri's **hydroelectric** potential had long been recognized, but nothing was done until the 1950s. Consolidated Zinc Pty of Australia wanted to smelt their Queensland bauxite into **aluminium** – a power-hungry process – as cheaply as possible, and alighted upon **Lake Manapouri**. They approached the New Zealand government, who agreed to build a power station on the lake, at taxpayers' expense, while Rio Tinto's subsidiary Comalco built a smelter at Tiwai Point, near Bluff, 170km to the southeast.

The scheme entailed blocking the lake's natural outlet into the Lower Waiau River and chiselling out a vast powerhouse 200m underground beside Lake Manapouri's West Arm, where the flow would be diverted down a 10km tailrace tunnel to Deep Cove on Doubtful Sound. By the time the fledgling **environmental movement** had rallied its supporters, the scheme was well under way, but the government underestimated the anger that would be unleashed by its secondary plan to boost water storage and power production by raising the water level in the lake by more than 8m. The threat to the natural beauty of the lake sparked **nationwide protests**, though the 265,000-signature petition prepared by the "Save Manapouri Campaign" failed to change the government's mind. It was only after the 1972 elections, when Labour unseated the National Party, that the policy was changed and the lake saved. The full saga is recounted in Neville Peat's *Manapouri Saved* (see p.821).

The **Manapouri Underground Power Station** took eight years to build. Completed in 1971, it remains one of the most ambitious projects ever carried out in New Zealand. Eighty percent of its output goes straight to the **smelter** – which consumes around fifteen percent of all the electricity used in the country, and it is widely perceived to be an unnecessary drain on the country's resources. Because of the unexpectedly high friction in the original tailrace tunnel the power station had always run below 85-percent capacity, and to boost power production a second parallel tailrace tunnel was built in the late 1990s.

water that flows down the Upper Waiau River from Lake Te Anau and unwittingly creating a massive hydroelectric generating capacity – something that almost led to its downfall (see box above).

The small village of **Manapouri**, 20km south of Te Anau, wraps prettily around the shores of the lake at the head of the Waiau River, which the hydroelectric shenanigans have turned into a narrow arm of the lake now known as Pearl Harbour.

Apart from cruises and kayak trips, the only thing to do in Manapouri is to saunter along a few minor walks: accommodation and eating options are very limited.

Manapouri Underground Power Station

Oct–April daily at 12.30pm • 3–4hr • $70

Real Journeys (see box, p.777) are the only ones with access to the impressive, if controversial, Manapouri Underground Power Station. After a lake cruise, you can get a sense of the scale of the place by a scale model in the visitor centre, then a bus takes you down a narrow, 2km-long tunnel to a viewing platform in the Machine Hall. All you see are the exposed sections of seven turbines and panels assaulting you with statistics before you're whisked back to the bus.

ARRIVAL AND INFORMATION   MANAPOURI

By bus Topline Tours (☎0508 249 8059, ✉topline @teanau.co.nz) run between Te Anau and Manapouri (Oct–April daily around 10.30am & 4pm; $20 for one person; $30 for two). Real Journeys buses from Te Anau connecting with boats to West Arm and Doubtful Sound may also take extras ($15), but only if their cruise passengers don't fill the bus.

Destinations Te Anau (1–2 daily; 20min).
Tourist information Pearl Harbour (daily: Nov–Feb 8am–8pm; March–Oct 8am–5.30pm; ☎0800 656 501, ✉realjourneys.co.nz). The Real Journeys booking office for Doubtful Sound trips also has some local information.

14

14

MANAPOURI WALKS

The following are covered in more depth in DOC's *Fiordland National Park Day Walks* booklet. See "Getting around" for boat access to the Hope Arm and Circle tracks.

Circle Track (7km; 3–4hr loop; 330m ascent). Manapouri's most popular walk contours the lake before turning southeast to climb the ridge to a point with stupendous views over the lake, then heads north back to the start.

Hope Arm and Back Valley loop (15km loop; 5–8hr; 200m ascent). Lovely exploration of the podocarp and beech forest west of

Manapouri, with great lake views and an optional side trip to Lake Rakatu (extra 2hr). Best done as an overnight, sleeping in either Hope Arm Hut (12 bunks; $5).

Pearl Harbour to Fraser's Beach (20min one-way). Easy lakeshore track through beech forest, partly following the Old Coach Road Walk with fantails and silvereye flitting about the undergrowth.

GETTING AROUND

By boat You can get around Manapouri on foot, but to access the best walking tracks you need to get across the Waiau River, which is less than 100m across.

Adventure Kayak & Cruise 33 Waiau St, next to the Mobil station ☎0800 324 966, ⍟fiordlandadventure .co.nz. Rents rowboats for $10, with an extra charge to stay on the other side overnight. They also rent single and

double kayaks (1 day $50/person; 3 days $125). Oct–April daily 9am–4.30pm.

Adventure Manapouri ☎03 249 8070, ⍟adventure manapouri.co.nz. Runs a regular water taxi across the Waiau (Oct–April daily at 1am, 3pm & 6.30pm; $15 return) and shuttle on demand ($20 return).

ACCOMMODATION

★ **Freestone Backpackers** 270 Hillside Rd (SH99), 3km east of Manapouri ☎03 249 6893, ⍟freestone .co.nz. With its hillside setting, fabulous lake and mountain views, horses and chickens and accommodation mostly in comfy wooden chalets (one en suite), this doesn't really feel like a hostel. Chalets have a pot-bellied stove, veranda and basic cooking facilities. There's also a deluxe en suite in the main house with the fanciest bath/shower you've ever seen, and the friendly hosts sometimes lay on classical recitals. Dorms $20, doubles $66, en suite $76, deluxe $150

★ **Manapouri Lakeview Motor Inn** 68 Cathedral Drive ☎0800 896262, ⍟manapouri.com. An eye for

colour and a sensitivity towards its late-1960s origin informs the gradual upgrading of this classic Kiwi motor lodge with great mountain views from just about every room. Modernized motel-style rooms are nothing flash but very comfortable, and it is hard to beat sitting on the veranda with a beer watching the sun set over the lake. Most rooms are $125 or $140. Budget rooms $96

Possum Lodge 13 Murrell Ave ☎03 249 6623, ⍟possumlodge.co.nz. An appealingly old-fashioned, peaceful and well-maintained campsite and hostel among beech trees where the Waiau River meets the lake. Some powered sites plus retro 1940s motel units. Camping $17, dorms $23, doubles & cabins $55, motel units $105

EATING

Cathedral Café 29 Waiau Drive ☎03 249 6619. Dairy, post office and functional licensed café serving good-value breakfasts ($9–15) and light meals ($10–24). Daily: Nov–Easter 7am–8pm; Easter–Oct 7am–6pm.

Lakeview Café 68 Cathedral Drive, at the Manapouri Lakeview Motor Inn ☎03 249 6652. True to its name,

there are great vistas across Lake Manapouri from the picture windows and benches on the lawn outside this fairly traditional Kiwi pub. Expect chicken quesedilla lunches ($15) and dinner mains such as Thai chicken curry ($21) and Fiordland venison ($34). Also fish, chips and burgers to take away. Meals served daily 11am–9.30pm.

Doubtful Sound

It was the building of the Manapouri hydro scheme that opened up **Doubtful Sound** to visitors. What was previously the preserve of the odd yacht and a few deerstalkers and trampers is now accessible to anyone prepared to take a boat across Lake Manapouri and a bus over the Wilmot Pass. Amid pristine beauty, wildlife is a major attraction, not least the resident pod of sixty-odd **bottlenose dolphins**, who frequently come to play around ships' bows and cavort near kayakers. **Fur seals** slather the outer islands, **Fiordland crested penguins** come to breed here in October and November, and the bush, which comes right down to the water's edge, is alive with kaka, kiwi and other rare bird species.

Like Milford, Doubtful Sound gets a huge amount of **rain**, but don't let that put you off – the place is at its best when the cliffs spring waterfalls everywhere you look after a downpour.

Though the rock architecture is a little less dramatic than Milford Sound, it easily makes up for this with its isolation and far fewer visitors. Travel between Manapouri to Doubtful Sound takes two hours, so to fully appreciate the beauty and isolation of the area it really pays to maximize your time there by staying overnight. Costs are unavoidably high and you need to be self-sufficient, but any inconvenience is easily outweighed by the glorious isolation – you'll see very few other boats or people out here.

14

Brief history

Cook spotted Doubtful Sound in 1770 but didn't enter, as he was "doubtful" of his ability to sail out again in the face of winds buffeted by the steep-walled fiord. The breeze was more favourable for the joint leaders of a Spanish expedition,

---

DOUBTFUL SOUND CRUISES AND KAYAK TRIPS

Spending the day (or preferably a couple of days) on Doubtful Sound is an unmissable experience, and the overall quality of the kayak and cruise operators makes it even more pleasurable.

Adventure Kayak and Cruise ⊕ 0800 324 966, ⓦ fiordlandadventure.co.nz. Good-value kayak trips such as a full-day guided trip ($239) giving over 4hr paddling on Doubtful Sound and an overnighter ($375) camping beside the fiord. A great combo ($269) includes the guided day on Doubtful Sound then on the way back you set up camp beside Lake Manapouri, the guide leaves and next day you paddle yourselves back to Manapouri. Extra days of kayak rental on Lake Manapouri are $35. Operates late Sept–early May.

Deep Cove Charters ⊕ 0800 249 682, ⓦ doubtful -sound.com. For a small-boat overnight experience opt for excellent trips aboard the twelve-berth *Seafinn*, a modern cruiser with lots of space and a dedicated crew. As well as exploring the fiord and watching wildlife you can kayak and fish. Chris, the skipper, will probably check his crayfish pots and any catches will likely end up on the lunch table. All meals are included and accommodation is in slightly cramped doubles/twins with shared bathroom. Operates mid-Oct to March, but is around 10 percent cheaper Oct–Dec. Per adult prices: Bunk $500, twin-share $550, double $600.

Fiordland Wilderness Experiences ⊕ 03 249 7700, ⓦ fiordlandseakayak.co.nz. Now part of the Real Journeys empire, these energetic and awe-inspiring overnight kayaking trips give you maximum time on the water with 4–6hr days paddling quality fibreglass sea kayaks either side of a night spent at a simple bush camp beside the fiord. No experience is needed but the minimum age is 16 and you'll need to bring your own food. Mid-Oct to April 3–7 trips weekly; $399. They also do occasional yacht-supported six-day/ five-night kayaking trips to Dusky Sound ($2650) – a real wilderness experience.

Real Journeys Overnight Cruise ⊕ 0800 656 501, ⓦ realjourneys.co.nz. Spend the night anchored in Doubtful Sound aboard the *Fiordland Navigator*, a modern cruiser sleeping up to 70 that's designed to look like a traditional sailing scow. The trip doesn't visit the power station but you're away from Manapouri for a full 24hr, time enough to immerse yourself in this extraordinary landscape by joining a nature walk, kayaking or even swimming. Food and accommodation are excellent. Operates Mid-Sept to mid-May. Rates are 15 percent higher in Feb, 25 percent less in Sept and there's a ten-percent YHA discount. Per adult prices: quad-share $386, double or twin-share $695, single $1216.

Real Journeys Wilderness Cruise ⊕ 0800 656 501, ⓦ realjourneys.co.nz. The cheapest way to experience Doubtful Sound involves a boat trip across Lake Manapouri, a visit to the underground power station and a bus ride to Deep Cove. You then board a three-hour cruise out to the mouth of the fiord (where fur seals loll on the rocks), and into serene Hall Arm (where bottlenose dolphins sometimes congregate) before the bus and boat trip back. Year-round; 1–2 daily; cruise $265; pre-ordered lunch $17.

Malaspina and Bauza, who in 1793 sailed in and named Febrero Point, Malaspina Reach and Bauza Island. Sealers soon decimated the colonies of fur seals and few people visited the area until the 1960s when the hydro scheme required the construction of the 21km gravel **Wilmot Pass** supply road, which links Manapouri's West Arm with Doubtful Sound's Deep Cove.

14 Dusky Sound

Captain Cook spent five weeks in **Dusky Sound**, 40km south of Doubtful Sound, on his second voyage in 1773, while his crew recovered from an arduous crossing of the Southern Ocean. Time was mostly spent at Pickersgill Harbour where, at Astronomer's Point, it is still possible to see where Cook's astronomer had trees felled so he could get an accurate fix on the stars. Not far from here is the site where 1790s castaways built the first European-style house and boat in New Zealand. Marooned by the fiord's waters, nearby Pigeon Island shelters the ruins of a house built by **Richard Henry**, who battled from 1894 to 1908 to save endangered native birds from introduced stoats and rats.

Very few trips come down this way, making it all the more rewarding if you make the effort. The Milford Wanderer Discovery tour (☎0800 656 501, ⓦrealjourneys.co.nz; book well in advance; from $1850) plies Dusky Sound in winter (and goes further south to Preservation Inlet and Stewart Island) on five- to seven-day cruises, some with helicopter transfer to the boat.

The Southern Scenic Route

While in Fiordland, don't miss out on the beautiful fringe country, where the fertile sheep paddocks of Southland butt up against the remote country of Fiordland National Park. The region's towns are linked by the underrated, pastoral charms of the **Southern Scenic Route** (ⓦsouthernscenicroute.co.nz), a series of small roads where sheep are the primary traffic hazard. From Te Anau it runs via Manapouri to SH99, following the valley of the Waiau River to the cave-pocked limestone country around **Clifden**. A minor road cuts west to Lake Hauroko, access point for the Dusky Track, while the Southern Scenic Route continues south through the small service town of **Tuatapere** (the base for hiking the Hump Ridge and South Coast tracks), to estuary-side **Riverton** and on to Invercargill.

Clifden

CLIFDEN, 85km south of Te Anau, is barely a town at all but is of passing interest for the historic **Clifden Suspension Bridge**, one of the longest in the South Island, built over the Waiau River in 1899 and in use until the 1970s. Sadly you are no longer allowed to walk across.

Clifden Caves

1km along Clifden Gorge Road · Open access · Free

Maori once camped on summer foraging trips at the **Clifden Caves**, which are signposted around 1km north of the bridge along SH96. With no one to guide you there's a palpable sense of adventure when tackling this 300m-long labyrinth lined with flowstone and stalactite formations and dotted with glowworms. The passages are not too tight but you'll need to crouch, scramble and climb three short ladders, following a series of reflective strips; modest scrambling skills are handy. Let someone know your intentions, and go with at least one other person. Wear clothes you don't mind getting dirty and take at least two torches.

JETBOATING TRIPS AROUND LAKE HAUROKO

To explore the beautiful wilderness area around Lake Hauroko, engage one of the companies running wilderness **jetboating trips** on the lake and along the 27km of the Grade III **Wairaurahiri River** down to the coast. Both companies listed below only run when numbers demand, so call several days ahead and hope to hook up with others.

Hump Ridge Jet ☎ 0800 270 556, ⓦ humpridgejet .com. Runs a full-day sightseeing trip down to the coast ($210; BBQ lunch $25 extra) with around 3hr of jetboating, some short walks and plenty of tales of hunting, fishing and live-deer capture back in the 1980s. You can use them as pick-up or drop-off for the South Coast Track ($170 one-way).

Wairaurahiri Jet ☎ 0800 376 174, ⓦ wjet.co.nz. There's a more polished feel to trips run by this operator, who do a full-day trip to the coast with a barbecue lunch at Waitutu Lodge ($225), tramper transport ($169) and summer twilight trips (6–9pm; $179) going part way down the Wairaurahiri River and including a barbecue tea.

14

Lake Hauroko

Lake Hauroko, at the end of a mostly dirt road, 32km west of Clifden, is New Zealand's deepest lake (462m), and far enough off the beaten track (20km of gravel road) that you can skinny dip. Low bush-clad hills surrounding the lake create the "sounding winds" immortalized in its name. The lake forms one end of the epic **Dusky Track** – one of the longest and most remote in New Zealand, and much tougher than any of the Great Walks. Experienced trampers considering tackling it should obtain information and condition reports from DOC offices in the region. At First Bay, the road-end, there's just a parking area and toilets, though you can **camp** some 7km back from the lake at DOC's *Thicket Burn* campsite (free), just a grassy field with toilets and tap water.

Tuatapere

TUATAPERE, thinly spread on the banks of the Waiau River 14km south of Clifden, is the largest town in southwestern Southland (though that's not saying much) and makes a good base for exploring the southern limits of Fiordland. It was once a major sawmilling town, but a single sawmill and one stand of beech/podocarp forest is the only evidence that the town could once have justified its epithet of "The Hole in the Bush". As logging declined, the community banded together to create the **Hump Ridge Track**, to encourage travellers to the area. The South Coast Track visits some of the same area, and both can be combined with jetboating along the Wairaurahiri River and Lake Hauroko.

The bush makes a last stand at a riverside clump of beech, kahikatea and totara on The Domain – staff at the information centre will point the way.

Brief history

Maori legend records the great war canoe *Takitimu* being wrecked on the Waiau River bar at Te Waewae Bay some six hundred years ago. Maori set up summer foraging camps along the river and used these as way-stations on the route to the *pounamu* fields around Milford Sound, but Tuatapere only came into being when European **pioneers** arrived around 1885. By 1909 the **railway** had arrived from Invercargill, bringing with it increasingly sophisticated steam-powered haulers that made short work of clearing the surrounding bushland. More recently, foresters' attention shifted west to the fringes of the Fiordland National Park where, in the 1970s, the Maori owners proposed clear felling stands of rimu. Environmentalists prevailed upon the Conservation Minister who eventually, in 1996, agreed to pay compensation in return for a sustainable management policy.

14

THE HUMP RIDGE AND SOUTH COAST TRACKS

Tuatapere is the base for two excellent and markedly different hiking experiences: the traditional **South Coast Track** and the **Hump Ridge Track**, with its engaging combination of coastal walking, historic remains, subalpine country and relatively sophisticated huts. Both are covered on DOC's *Southern Fiordland Tracks* **leaflet**.

Both tracks share historically interesting kilometres of coastal walking, following a portion of the 1896 track cut 100km along the south coast to gold-mining settlements around the southernmost fiord of Preservation Inlet. This paved the way for woodcutters, who arrived en masse in the 1920s. Logs were transported to the mills on tramways, which crossed the burns and gullies on viaducts – four of the finest have been faithfully restored, including the 125m bridge over Percy Burn that stands 35m high in the middle. The remains of the former mill village of **Port Craig** – wharf, rusting machinery, crumbling fireplaces – are equally fascinating.

The **trailhead** for both tracks is the Rarakau car park, 20km west of Tuatapere, accessible by bus ($25 one-way) organized through the Hump Ridge Track office; there's secure parking here ($5/day).

Jetboat operators (see box, p.779) will pick up and drop off at the Wairaurahiri rivermouth ($170/person one-way), allowing you to walk sections of the tracks combined with a ride on the Wairaurahiri River.

THE SOUTH COAST TRACK

The **South Coast Track** slices through the largest area of lowland rainforest in New Zealand. Although it is easy going it takes the best part of four days to reach Big River and you'll just have to turn around and walk back unless you prearrange a jetboat out up the Wairaurahiri River. A popular alternative is to make a three-day excursion, staying at DOC's Port Craig School Hut ($15.30), and exploring the environs. Three more huts ($5.10 each) spaced four to seven hours' walk apart provide accommodation, and camping is free.

Rarakau to Port Craig School Hut (17km; 5–7hr; negligible ascent). The first leg follows either the old logging road or, tide permitting, the beach – which should shave half an hour off your walking time.

Port Craig School Hut to Wairaurahiri Hut (16km; 4–6hr; 200m ascent). Here the track follows the old tramway, crossing all four of the restored viaducts, before dropping down to the Wairaurahiri River. Alternatively, stay on the banks of the Wairaurahiri River at the private *Waitutu*

Lodge (book through the Tuatapere information centre; $30; ⊛ waitutu.co.nz): take sleeping bag and food.

Wairaurahiri Hut to Waitutu Hut (13km, 4–6hr, negligible ascent). This section of the path largely follows the coastal flats across Maori land. Fit and experienced trampers with camping equipment might want to continue from Waitutu Hut to the end of the track at Big River (12km; 5–7hr; negligible ascent), where DOC's Westies Hut ($5.10) nestles in the mouth of a cave.

THE HUMP RIDGE TRACK

The privately managed 53km Hump Ridge Track (book in advance ☎ 0800 486 774, ⊛ humpridgetrack.co.nz or at the office in Tuatapere, see opposite) is done in three days with nights spent at two comfortable 32-bunk lodges equipped with lights, gas cookers, cooking pots and eating utensils, eight-bunk rooms, a beer and wine licence (you can't bring your own), flush toilets, porridge cooked by the lodge manager and hot showers ($10). There's even helicopter **bag transfer** (max 15kg; $70/leg), that's especially good for the first leg, saving you the biggest ascent when the bag is heaviest.

ARRIVAL AND DEPARTURE · TUATAPERE

By bus Trips & Tramps (☎ 0800 305 807, ⊛ tripsandtramps .com) run the region's only bus service, operating between Te Anau and Tuatapere (Nov–late April Mon & Thurs only).

There is no bus between Tuatapere and Invercargill. **Destinations** Manapouri (2 weekly; 1hr 15min); Te Anau (2 weekly; 1hr 30min).

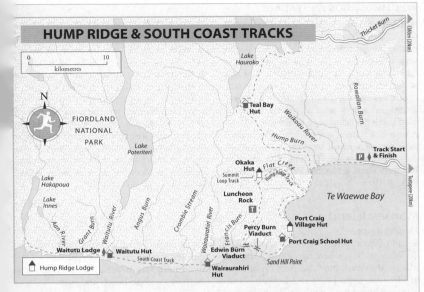

HUMP RIDGE & SOUTH COAST TRACKS

The tramp is occasionally muddy in places and when off the boardwalks it feels like a real "trampers" track. It requires a good level of fitness and it isn't for beginners or under 10s. Everyone walks the track in the same direction, starting at Rarakau.

Summer **season** (late-Oct to mid-April) accommodation packages range from the tramping-style **Freedom Walk** ($130; bring sleeping bag and food) which includes one night in each lodge, upgradable to a double or twin with sheets and duvets (add $100/room). To add a night in Tuatapere, first day heli-packing and hot showers go for Freedom Plus ($350), or opt for a four-day **guided walk** ($1395; typically departs Wed), with meals, a short chopper flight, full heli-packing, a private room at the lodges and a night's B&B accommodation in Tuatapere. **Outside the season** lodge facilities are cut back and heli-packing is not available.

Rarakau to Okaka Lodge (18km; 6–9hr; 900m ascent). After great coastal walking you turn inland along boardwalks through open forest with a thick undergrowth of crown ferns. Glimpse views through the beech forest as you climb steeply up a ridge to the open tops with fabulous views back the way you came. Allow time to explore the adjacent Summit Loop Track (30min) along boardwalks past picturesque sandstone tors and lovely alpine plants.

Okaka Lodge to Port Craig Lodge (19km; 6–9hr; 100m ascent; 900m descent). The track follows the Hump Ridge, staying high for several hours with magical views before descending to the South Coast Track by Edwin Burn Viaduct. You then follow an old tramway to the majestic Percy Burn Viaduct and on to Port Craig.

Port Craig Lodge to Rarakau (17km; 5–7hr; undulating). Wanders through towering coastal rimu and down on to sandy beaches, and back to Rarakau.

INFORMATION

Hump Ridge Track booking office and information centre 31 Orawia Rd (Dec–March Mon–Fri 9am–5.30pm, Sat & Sun 3–5pm; Oct, Nov & April Mon–Fri 9am–5pm; ☎ 03 226 6739). Primarily set up for Hump Ridge Track hikers. They can store valuables while you're on the tramp, but will also help with local accommodation and transport. Its Bushman's Museum (free) gives a rose-tinted version of pioneer history.

14

ACCOMMODATION AND EATING

★ **Last Light Lodge & Café** 2 Clifden Hwy ☎ 03 226 6667, ⊕ lastlightlodge.com. This former forestry camp is getting a major makeover and may well help keep the sleepy town going. Rooms are small and pretty basic but the beds are new and the dorms only have three beds, so often you'll get one to yourself. The focus is the smart café and bar with plenty of seating outside, book exchange, internet and a great range of excellent food which might include Thai green curry ($15) or mussel and bacon chowder ($10). Gardens have been planted and much of the produce will be organic. Dinners by arrangement. Café daily 8am–5pm. Camping $15, dorms $30, doubles $66

Tuatapere Motel & Shooters Backpackers Holiday Park 73 Main St ☎ 0800 009 993, ⊕ tuatapere accommodation.co.nz. Slightly soulless but well-equipped combination of four spacious modern motel units, a backpackers with spa pool ($25/hr for up to 8) and some tent sites and hook-ups. Camping $15, doubles $60, motels $120

★ **Yesteryear Café** 3a Orawia Rd ☎ 03 226 6682. The owner whips up delightful home-made food in this former bakery decked out with a cornucopia of early twentieth-century kitchenware and tea services – a tribute to her and her husband's grandmothers, whose four jam pots hang on the wall. She'll even fire up the old coal range for pikelets with raspberry jam and cream. Otherwise there are pies, mince on toast ($9) and lots of home baking, all accompanied by albums your gran would like on the 1970s turntable. Oct–April daily 7am–5pm.

Monkey Island

23km south of Tuatapere

South of Tuatapere, SH99 follows the wind-ravaged cliffs behind the wide and moody Te Waewae Bay, where fierce southerlies have sculpted the much-photographed macrocarpa trees into compact cauliflower forms. About 3km beyond the small town of Orepuki, signs point to Monkey Island where there's a good beach and basic camping (free) with vault toilets nearby.

Cosy Nook

29km south of Tuatapere

A further 4km south along SH99, signs point 3km west to **Cosy Nook**, a wonderfully picturesque cove hemmed in by granite boulders, which looks quite unlike anywhere else in the country – you could easily imagine it along Scotland's west coast. Indeed, it was named Cozy Neuk by Scot George Thomson as it reminded him of his home village. You'll see a huddle of rustic holiday homes and perhaps a couple of sheltering fishing boats.

Colac Bay

37km southeast of Tuatapere

The highway regains the coast at the quiet community of **Colac Bay**, a name eighteenth-century whalers derived from the name of the local Maori chief, Korako. Apart from swimming and a nationally renowned surf break the only reason to stop is to eat.

Self-contained **campervans** are allowed to park overnight on Colac Foreshore Rd between the boat ramp and shelter shed (2 nights max; free).

Riverton

RIVERTON (Aparima), 12km east of Colac Bay, is one of the country's oldest settlements. Frequented by whalers as early as the 1790s, the town was formally established in 1836 by another whaler, John Howell – who is also credited with kick-starting New Zealand's now formidable sheep-farming industry. Strung along a spit between the sea and the Jacob's River Estuary (actually the mouth of the Aparima and Pourakino rivers), where fishing boats still harbour, Riverton has a blissfully relaxed feel.

Beyond Riverton, SH99 heads into the hinterland of Invercargill, 40km away.

Te Hikoi: Southern Journey

172 Palmerston St • Daily: Oct–March 10am–5pm; April–Sept 10am–3.30pm • $6 • ☎ 03 234 8260, ⓦ tehikoi.co.nz

If you've any interest in the cultural history of the south coast, devote an hour to this well-presented, modern museum, which kicks off with an excellent fifteen-minute movie focusing on the unsettling times of early European contact. The tableau of a Maori muttonbirders' camp isn't entirely convincing but the tales of harvesting on the Titi Islands and the Maori seasonal food-gathering calendar show just how tough it was in these southern climes. Europeans didn't have it much easier, sealing, whaling and hacking out a living from the bush, erecting tramways to extract the straight rimu trunks. To ease the hardship, some brewed rum from cabbage trees. There's also coverage of the Chinese gold-mining community at Round Hill, and old-timers reminiscing about leaving the area to go to World War II.

14

Fiordland Gift Studio

35 Bath Rd • Sept–April Mon–Fri 9am–5pm, Sat & Sun 10am–5pm; May–Aug Mon–Fri 9am–4pm • Free • ☎ 03 234 8825, ⓦ paua.net.nz

A 5m-high paua shell (made from concrete though lined with real paua) at the eastern entrance to town underlines Riverton's reputation as a paua capital. Fiordland Gift Studio is perhaps the best of several shops selling the polished shells by the score, either whole or fashioned into jewellery, and has some great bargains.

EATING	**RIVERTON**

Beach House Café 126 Rocks Hwy ☎ 03 234 8274. With sweeping sea views and a cosy timber-lined dining room warmed by an open fire you can't go far wrong at this quality café and restaurant. Drop in for coffee and cake, a lamb burger with kumara fries ($25) or Stewart Island salmon on pea risotto ($30). **Daily 10am–9pm or later.**

★ **Mrs Clark's Café** 108 Palmerston St ☎ 03 234 8600. The best coffee and cakes in town, served in lively surroundings with interesting music and a glorious display of toast racks around the walls. Try the home-style baked beans with hollandaise on wholegrain toast ($12) or the blue cod fishcakes with fresh salad ($17). Free wi-fi. **Daily 7am–4pm.**

The **eastern continuation** of the **Southern Scenic Route**, along the Catlins Coast to Dunedin, is covered in the Dunedin to Stewart Island chapter, p.609.

MAORI CARVING

Contexts

785 History

799 Maoritanga

806 Landscapes and wildlife

815 Film and music

818 Books

822 Language

825 Glossary

History

Many New Zealanders of European descent have long thought of their country as a model of humanitarian colonization. Maori often take a different view, however, informed by the repeated theft of land and erosion of rights that were guaranteed by a treaty. Schoolroom histories have generally been faithful to the European view, even to the point of influencing Maori mythology. In the last couple of decades, however, revisionist historians have largely discredited what many New Zealanders know as fact. Much that is presented as tradition turns out to be the late-nineteenth-century scholarship of historians who bent research to fit their theories and, in some cases, even destroyed evidence. What follows is inextricably interwoven with Maori legend and can be understood more fully with reference to the section on *Maoritanga* (see p.799).

Pre-European history

It's thought that the ancestors of modern **Maori** arrived from Polynesia in double-hulled canoes between 1200 and 1300 AD. Their journey was planned to the extent that they took with them the *kuri* (dog) and food plants such as taro (a starchy tuber), yam and *kumara* (sweet potato). The notion of a legendary "**Great Fleet**" of seven canoes arriving in 1350 AD seems most likely to be a Victorian adaptation of Maori oral history, which has been readopted into contemporary Maori legend.

The Polynesians found a land so much colder than their tropical home that many of their crops and plants wouldn't grow. Fortunately there was an abundance of marine life and large flightless birds, particularly in the South Island, where most settled. The people of this **Archaic Period** are often misleadingly known as "Moa Hunters" and while some undoubtedly lived off these birds, the moa wasn't present in other areas. By around 1350 settlements had been established all around the coast, but it was only later that there's evidence of horticulture, suggesting a later migration bringing plants for cultivation, or the beginning of successful year-round food storage, allowing a settled living pattern rather than the earlier hunters' short-lived campsites.

Either way, this marks the beginning of the **Classic Period** when *kainga* (villages) grew up close to the *kumara* grounds, often supported by *pa* (fortified villages) where the people could retreat when under attack. As tasks became more specialized and hunting and horticulture took up less time, the arts – particularly carving and weaving (see pp.802–804) – flourished and warfare became endemic. The decline of easily caught birdlife and the relative ease of growing *kumara* in the warmer North Island marked the beginning of a northward population shift. When the Europeans arrived,

1200–1300 AD	c.1350	1642
Arrival of first Polynesians.	The traditional date of arrival of the "Great Fleet" from Hawaiki.	Dutchman Abel Tasman sails past the West Coast.

> ## POLYNESIAN MIGRATION
>
> Modern scholarship suggests that humans from Southeast Asia first explored the South Pacific around five thousand years ago, gradually evolving a distinct culture as they filtered down through the Indonesian archipelago. A thousand years of progressive island-hopping got them as far as Tonga and Samoa, where a distinctly **Polynesian** society continued to evolve, honing seafaring skills to the point where lengthy sea journeys were possible. Around a thousand years ago, Polynesian culture reached its classical apotheosis in the **Society Islands** west of Tahiti, widely thought to be the hub for a series of migrations heading southwest across thousands of kilometres of open ocean, past the Cook Islands, eventually striking land in what is now known as New Zealand (Aotearoa).

95 percent of the population was located in the North Island, mostly in the northern reaches, with coastal settlements reaching down to Hawke's Bay and Wanganui.

European contact and the Maori response

Many **Europeans** were convinced of the existence of a *terra australis incognita*, an unknown southern land that counterbalanced the northern continents. In 1642, the Dutch East India Company, keen to dominate any trade with this new continent, sent Dutchman **Abel Tasman** to the southern oceans where he became the first European to catch sight of Aotearoa. He anchored in Golden Bay, where a small boat being rowed between Tasman's two ships was intercepted by a Maori war canoe and four sailors were killed. Without setting foot on land Tasman turned tail and fled up the west coast of the North Island, going on to add Tonga and Fiji to European maps. He named Aotearoa "Staten Landt", later renamed Nieuw Zeeland after the Dutch maritime province.

Nieuw Zeeland was ignored for over a century until 1769, when **James Cook** (see box opposite) paid the first of three extensive visits. Cook and his crew found Maori a **sophisticated people** with a highly formalized social structure and skills to turn stone and wood into fabulously carved canoes, weapons and meeting houses – yet they had no wheels, roads, metalwork, pottery or animal husbandry. After an initial unfortunate encounter near Gisborne (see p.372) and another off Cape Kidnappers, near Napier (see p.385), Cook managed to strike up friendly, constructive relations. The original settlers now found that their tribal allegiance wasn't enough to differentiate them from the Europeans and subsequently began calling themselves **Maori** (meaning "normal" or "not distinctive") while referring to the newcomers as **Pakeha** ("foreign").

Offshore from the Coromandel Peninsula, Cook deviated from instructions and unfurled the British flag, claiming formal possession without the consent of Maori, but was still able to return twice in 1773 and 1777. The French were also interested – on his 1769 voyage Cook had passed **Jean François Marie de Surville** in a storm without either knowing of the other's presence.

The establishment of the Botany Bay penal colony in neighbouring Australia aroused the first commercial interest in New Zealand and from the 1790s to the 1830s New Zealand was part of the Australian frontier. By 1830 the coast was dotted with semi-permanent **sealing** communities which, within thirty years, had almost clubbed the seals into extinction. The British navy rapidly felled giant kauri trees for its ships' masts, while

1769	1830s	1835
Englishman James Cook circumnavigates both main islands.	Sealing and whaling stations dotted around the coast.	Independence of the United Tribes of NZ proclaimed.

others supplied Sydney shipbuilders. By the 1820s **whalers** had moved in, basing themselves at Kororareka (now Russell), where they could recruit Maori crew and provision their ships. This combination of rough whalers, escaped convicts from Australia and assorted miscreants and adventurers combined to turn Russell into a lawless place populated by what Darwin, on his visit in 1835, found to be "the very refuse of Society".

Before long, the Maori way of life had been entirely disrupted. **Inter-tribal fighting** soon broke out on a scale never seen before. Hongi Hika (see box, p.788) was the first off the mark, but the quest for new territory also fuelled the actions of Ngati Toa's **Te Rauparaha** (see p.256), who soon controlled the southern half of the North Island.

The huge demand for **firearms** drove Maori to sell the best of their food, relocating to unhealthy areas close to flax swamps, where flax production could be increased. Even highly valued tribal treasures – *pounamu* (greenstone) clubs and the preserved heads of chiefs taken in battle – were traded. European **diseases** swept through the Maori population, European-introduced alcohol and tobacco became widespread, Maori women were prostituted to Pakeha sailors, and the tribal structure began to crumble.

Into this scene stepped the **missionaries** in 1814, the brutal New South Wales magistrate **Samuel Marsden** arriving in the Bay of Islands a transformed man with a mission to bring Christianity and "civilization" to Maori, and to save the souls of the sealers and whalers. Subsequently Anglicans, Wesleyans and Catholics all set up missions throughout the North Island, ostensibly to protect Maori from the worst of the exploitation and campaigning in both London and Sydney for more policing of Pakeha actions. In exchange, they destroyed fine artworks considered too sexually explicit and demanded that Maori abandon cannibalism and slavery; in short, Maori were expected to trade in their *Maoritanga* and become "**Europeans**". By the 1830s, self-confidence and the belief in Maori ways was in rapid decline: the *tohunga* (priest) was powerless over new European diseases which could often be cured by the missionaries, and some Maori had started to believe Pakeha that the Maori race was dying out.

The push for colonization

Despite Cook's discovery claim in 1769, imperial cartographers had never marked New Zealand as a British possession and it was with some reluctance – informed by the perception of an over-extended empire only marginally under control – that New South Wales law was nominally extended to New Zealand in 1817. The effect was

---

JAMES COOK

Yorkshireman Lieutenant (later Captain) **James Cook** was a meticulous **navigator** who sailed the *Endeavour* into the Pacific to observe the transit of Venus across the sun. Following Admiralty instructions he then continued west, arriving at "the Eastern side of the Land discover'd by Tasman" where he observed the "Genius, Temper, Disposition and Number of the Natives" and encouraged his botanists, Banks and Solander, to collect numerous samples.

On three voyages between 1769 and 1777 Cook spent a total of ten months around the coast of Aotearoa, leaving his mark with numerous place names. Some of his **charts** were in use well into the twentieth century, and his only significant errors were showing Banks Peninsula as an island and Stewart Island as a peninsula.

1840	1840s	1852
Treaty of Waitangi. Capital moved from Kororareka to Auckland.	Cities of Auckland, Christchurch, Dunedin, Nelson, New Plymouth, Wanganui and Wellington established.	NZ becomes a self-governing colony divided into six provinces.

HONGI HIKA

Hongi Hika from Ngapuhi *iwi* of the Bay of Islands was the first Maori chief to appreciate the value of firearms, and had already acquired several when missionary Thomas Kendall met him in 1814. By this time he was encouraging his people to grow crops that could be traded with Pakeha for guns.

In 1820 Hongi Hika travelled to England with Thomas Kendall to work on *A grammar and vocabulary of the language of New Zealand*. While he was there he briefly became the toast of London society and was presented to George IV as an "equal". Having little use for most of the gifts showered upon him, he traded them for 300 muskets. Eager to emulate the supreme power of the imperial king, Hongi Hika set about subduing much of the North Island, using the often badly maintained and inexpertly aimed guns to rattle the enemy, who were then slaughtered with the traditional *mere*. Warriors abandoned the old fighting season – the lulls between hunting and tending the crops – and set off to settle old scores, resulting in a massive loss of life.

minimal; the New South Wales governor had no official representation on this side of the Tasman and was powerless to act. Unimpressed, by 1831 a small group of northern Maori chiefs decided to petition the British monarch to become a "friend and the guardian of these islands", a letter that was later used to justify Britain's intervention.

Britain's response was to send the less-than-competent **James Busby** as British Resident in 1833, with a brief to encourage trade, stay on good terms with the missionaries and Maori, and apprehend escaped convicts for return to Sydney. Convinced that New Zealand was becoming a drain on the colony's economy, the New South Wales governor withheld guns and troops, and Busby was unable to enforce his will. Busby was also duped by Baron de Thierry, a Briton of French parents, who claimed he had bought most of the Hokianga district from Hongi Hika and styled himself the "sovereign chief of New Zealand", to "save" Maori from the degradation he foresaw under British dominion. In a panic, Busby misguidedly persuaded 35 northern chiefs to proclaim themselves as the "**United Tribes of New Zealand**" in 1835. As far as the Foreign Office was concerned, this allowed Britain to disclaim responsibility for the actions of its subjects.

By the late 1830s there were around two thousand Pakeha in New Zealand, the largest concentration around Kororareka in the Bay of Islands. Most were British, but French Catholics also consolidated their tentative toehold, and in 1839 British-born James Clendon was appointed American consul. Meanwhile, **land speculators** and colonists began taking an interest. The Australian emancipationist, William Charles Wentworth, had "bought" the South Island and Stewart Island for a few hundred pounds (the largest private land deal in history, subsequently quashed by government order) and British settlers were already setting sail. The British admiralty finally took notice when the Australian convict settlements, originally intended simply as an out-of-sight, out-of-mind solution to their bulging prisons, looked set to become a valuable possession.

A combination of these pressures and Busby's exaggeration of the Maori inability to manage their own affairs goaded the British government into action. The result was the 1840 **Treaty of Waitangi** (see box opposite & p.166), a document that purported to guarantee continued Maori control of their lands, rights and possessions in return for their loss of sovereignty, a concept open for misinterpretation. The annexed lands became a dependency of New South Wales until New Zealand was declared a separate colony a year later.

1858	1860–65	1860s	1865
Settlers outnumber Maori.	New Zealand Wars between Pakeha and Maori.	Major gold rushes in the South Island.	Capital moved from Auckland to Wellington.

Settlement and the early pioneers

Even before the Treaty was signed, there were moves to found a settlement in Port Nicholson, the site of Wellington, on behalf of the New Zealand Company. This was the brainchild of **Edward Gibbon Wakefield**, who hoped to stem American-style egalitarianism and use New Zealand as the proving ground for his theory of "scientific colonization". This aimed to preserve the English squire-and-yokel class structure but ended up encouraging absentee landlordism.

Between 1839 and 1843 the New Zealand Company dispatched nearly 19,000 settlers to "**planned settlements**" in Wellington, Wanganui, Nelson and New Plymouth. This was the core of Pakeha immigration, the only substantial non-Wakefield settlement being **Auckland**, a scruffy collection of waterside shacks which, to the horror of New Zealand Company officials, became the capital after the signing of the Treaty of Waitangi.

The company couldn't buy land direct from Maori, but the government bought up huge tracts and sold it on, often for ten or twenty times what they paid for it. In 1850 the New Zealand Company foundered, leaving settlements which, subject to the hard

---

THE TREATY OF WAITANGI

IN ENGLISH

The main points set out in the **English treaty** are as follows:
• The chiefs cede sovereignty of New Zealand to the Queen of England.
• The Queen guarantees the chiefs the "full exclusive and undisturbed possession of their Lands and Estates Forests Fisheries and other properties which they may collectively or individually possess".
• The Crown retains the right of pre-emption over Maori lands.
• The Queen extends the rights and privileges of British subjects to Maori.

IN MAORI

However, the **Maori translation** presents numerous possibilities for misunderstanding, since Maori is a more idiomatic and metaphorical language, where words can take on several meanings. The main points of contention include the following:
• The preamble of the English version cites the main **objectives** of the treaty being to protect Maori interests, to provide for British settlement and to set up a government to maintain peace and order. On the other hand, the main thrust of the Maori version is that the all-important rank and status of the chiefs and tribes will be maintained.
• The concept of **sovereignty** in the Maori version is translated as *kawanatanga* (governorship), a word Maori linked to their experience of the toothless reign of James Busby (see opposite). It seems unlikely that the chiefs realized just what they were giving away.
• In the Maori text, the Crown guaranteed the *tangata whenua* (people of the land) the possession of their properties for as long as they wished to keep them. In English this was expressed in terms of **individual rights** over property. This is perhaps the most wilful mistranslation and, in practice, there were long periods when Maori were coerced into selling their **land**, and when they refused, lands were simply taken.
• **Pre-emption** was translated as *hokonga* – a term simply meaning "buying and selling", with no explanation of the Crown's exclusive right to buy Maori land, which was clearly spelled out in the English version. This has resulted in considerable friction over Maori being unable to sell any land that the government didn't want, even if they had a buyer.
• The implications of **British citizenship** may not have been well understood: it is not clear whether Maori realized they would be bound by British law.

1867	1870s	1876
Maori men given the vote.	Wool established as the mainstay of the NZ economy.	Abolition of provincial governments. Power centralized in Wellington.

realities of colonial life, had failed to conform to Wakefield's lofty theories and were filled with sturdy workers from labouring and lower-middle-class backgrounds.

In 1852 New Zealand achieved self-government and divided the country into six **provinces** – Auckland, New Plymouth, Wellington, Nelson, Canterbury and Otago. In addition to taking over land sales, it encouraged migrants with free passage, land grants and guaranteed employment on road construction schemes – a call heeded by those hoping for a better life away from the drudgery of working-class Britain. Maori still held the best land, growing potatoes and wheat for both local consumption and export to Australia, where the Victorian gold rush had created a huge demand. Pakeha were barely able to compete, and the slump in export prices in the mid-1850s saw many look to **pastoralism**. The Crown helped by halving the price of land, allowing poorer settlers to become landowners but simultaneously paving the way for the creation of huge pastoral runs and putting further pressure on Maori land.

Maori resistance and the New Zealand Wars

The first five years after the signing of the Treaty were a disaster, first under Governor Hobson then the ineffectual FitzRoy. Relations between Maori and Pakeha began to deteriorate immediately, as the capital was moved from Kororareka to Auckland and duties were imposed in the Bay of Islands. The consequent loss of trade from passing ships precipitated the first tangible expression of dissent, a famous series of incidents involving the Ngapuhi leader **Hone Heke**, who repeatedly felled the most fundamental symbol of British authority, the flagstaff at Russell. The situation improved to some degree with the appointment of **George Grey**, the most able of New Zealand's governors, who did more than anyone else to shape the country's early years. Soon Maori began to adapt their culture to accommodate Pakeha – selling crops, operating flour mills and running coastal shipping. Grey encouraged the process by establishing mission schools, erecting hospitals where Maori could get free treatment, and providing employment on public works. In short, he upheld the spirit of the Treaty, thereby gaining enormous respect among Maori. Sadly, he failed to set up any mechanism to perpetuate his policies after he left for the governorship of Cape Town in 1853.

Under **New Zealand's constitution**, enacted in 1852, Maori were excluded from political decision-making and prevented from setting up their own form of government; although British subjects in name, they had few of the practical benefits and yet were increasingly expected to comply with British law. By now it was clear that Maori had been duped by the Treaty of Waitangi: one chief explained that they thought they were transferring the "shadow of the land" while "the substance of the land remains with us", and yet he now conceded "the substance of the land goes to the Europeans, the shadow only will be our portion". Growing **resistance** to land sales came at a time when settler communities were expanding and demanding to buy huge tracts of pastoral land. With improved communications Pakeha became more self-reliant and dismissive of Maori, who began to lose faith in the government and fell back on traditional methods of handling their affairs. Self-government had given landowners the vote, but since Maori didn't hold individual titles to their land they were denied suffrage. Maori and Pakeha aspirations seemed completely at odds and there was a growing **sense of betrayal**, which helped replace tribal animosities with a tenuous unity. In 1854, a month before

1882	1893	1910s
First refrigerated meat shipment to Europe. Lamb becomes increasingly important.	Full women's suffrage; a world first.	Rise of organized labour under the socialist Red Federation. Strikes at Blackball, Waihi and Auckland.

New Zealand's first parliament, Maori held inter-tribal meetings to discuss a response to the degradation of their culture and the rapid loss of their land. The eventual upshot was the 1858 election of the ageing **Te Wherowhero**, head chief of the Waikatos, as the Maori "King", the leader of the **King Movement** (see box, p.216) behind which Maori could rally to hold back the flood of Pakeha settlement. Most were moderates making peaceful overtures that Pakeha chose to regard as rebellious.

Matters came to a head in 1860, when the government used troops to enforce a bogus purchase of land at Waitara, near New Plymouth. The fighting at Taranaki soon consumed the whole of the North Island in the **New Zealand Wars**, once known by Pakeha as the Maori Wars and by Maori as *te riri Pakeha* (foreigners' anger). Maori were divided, with some settling old grievances by siding with the government against their traditional enemies. Through the early 1860s the number of Pakeha troops was tripled to around 3000, providing an effective force against less coordinated Maori forces. Though there were notable Maori successes, the final result was inevitable. Fighting had abated by the end of the 1860s but peace wasn't finally declared until 1881.

British soldiers had been lured into service with offers of land and free passage and, in a further affront to defeated Maori, many were settled in the solidly Maori Waikato. Much of the most fertile land was **confiscated** – in the Waikato, the Bay of Plenty and Taranaki – with little regard to the owners' allegiances during the conflict. By 1862 the Crown had relinquished its right of pre-emption and individuals could buy land directly from Maori, who were forced to limit the stated ownership first to ten individuals and later to just one owner. With their collective power smashed, voracious land agents lured Maori into debt then offered to buy their land to "save" them.

Between 1860 and 1881, the **non-Maori population** rose from 60,000 to 470,000, swamping and marginalizing Maori society. An Anglo-Saxon worldview came to dominate all aspects of New Zealand life, and by 1871 the Maori language was no longer used for teaching in schools.

Meanwhile, as the New Zealand Wars raged in the North Island, **gold fever** had struck the South, with discoveries near Queenstown in 1861 and later along the West Coast. For the best part of a decade, gold was New Zealand's major export, but its most noticeable effect was on population distribution: by 1858 the shrinking Maori population had been outstripped by rapidly swelling Pakeha numbers, most settling in the South Island where relations with Maori played a much smaller part.

Consolidation and social reform

The 1870s were dominated by the policies of Treasurer Julius Vogel, who started a **programme of public works** funded by borrowing on a massive scale. Within a decade previously scattered towns in separately governed provinces were transformed into a single country unified by improved roads, an expanding rail system, 7000km of telegraph wires and numerous public institutions. Almost all the remaining farmable land was bought up or leased from Maori and acclimatization societies sprang up with the express aim of anglicizing the New Zealand countryside and improving **farming**. With no extensive market close enough to make perishable produce profitable, **wool** became the main export, stimulated by the development of the Corriedale sheep, a Romney-Lincoln cross with a long fleece. Wool continued as the mainstay until 1882,

1914–18	1917	1920s
NZ takes part in World War I with terrible loss of life.	Temperance Movement closes pubs at 6pm. Only repealed in 1967.	Initial prosperity evaporates as the Great Depression takes hold.

when the first **refrigerated meat shipment** left for Britain, signalling a turning point in the economy and the establishment of New Zealand as Britain's offshore larder, a role it maintained until the 1970s.

From 1879 until 1896 New Zealand slid into a "long depression", mostly overseen by the conservative "Continuous Ministry" – the last government composed of colonial gentry. During this time **trade unionism** began influencing the political scene and bolstered the Liberal Pact (a Liberal and Labour alliance). In 1890 the alliance wrested power and ushered in an era of unprecedented social change. Its first leader, **John Ballance**, firmly believed in state intervention and installed socialist **William Pember Reeves** as his Minister of Labour. Reeves was instrumental in pushing through sweeping reforms to working hours and factory conditions that were so progressive that no further changes were made to labour laws until 1936. When Ballance died in 1892 he was replaced by **Richard "King Dick" Seddon**, who introduced a graduated income tax and repealed property tax, hoping to break up some of the large estates. New Zealand was already being tagged the "social laboratory of the world", but more was to come.

In 1893, New Zealand was the first nation in the world to enact full **female suffrage**, undoubtedly in line with the liberal thinking of the time, but apparently an accident nonetheless (see box below). In 1898 Seddon further astonished the world by weathering a ninety-hour continuous debate to squeeze through legislation guaranteeing an **old age pension**. Fabian Beatrice Webb, in New Zealand that same year, declared that "it is delightful to see a country with no millionaires and hardly any slums".

By the early twentieth century, the Pakeha standard of living was one of the highest in the world. But things were not so rosy for Maori, whose numbers had plummeted from an estimated 200,000 at Cook's first visit to around 50,000 in 1896. However, as resistance to European diseases grew, numbers started rising, accompanied by a new confidence buoyed by the rise of Maori parliamentary leadership. **Apirana Ngata, Maui**

ACCIDENTAL SUFFRAGE

In 1893, New Zealand became the first nation on earth to grant women the vote. Other territories (South Australia, Wyoming etc) had led the way with limited **women's suffrage**, but New Zealand threw the net wider. It is something New Zealanders are inordinately proud of even though it came about more by accident than any free-thinking principle.

When a radical electoral reform bill was up for consideration, Prime Minister Seddon let an amendment pass on the assumption that it would be rejected by the Legislative Council (an upper house which survived until 1950). Seddon then ordered a Liberal Party councillor to change his vote, his interference causing the ire of two other councillors who then voted for the bill, allowing it to pass by twenty votes to eighteen. It's also contended that female suffrage was approved in response to the powerful quasi-religious temperance movement, which hoped to "purify and improve the tone of our politics"; effectively giving married couples double the vote of the unmarried man, who was often seen as a drunken layabout. Regardless of the rationale, New Zealand set a precedent and other major Western nations eventually followed suit – Finland in 1906, all Australian states by 1908, Britain in 1918, and the US in 1920. It wasn't until 1919, however, that New Zealand women were given the right to stand for parliament, and they were not eligible to be appointed to the New Zealand Legislative Council until 1941.

1935	1941	1947
M.J. Savage's Labour government ushers in the world's first Welfare State.	Bombing of Pearl Harbor and World War II begins New Zealand's military realignment with the Pacific region.	Full independence from Britain.

Pomare and **Te Rangi Hiroa** (**Peter Buck**), all alumni of Te Aute College, an Anglican school for Maori, were committed to working within the administrative and legislative framework of government, convinced that the survival of *Maoritanga* depended on shedding those aspects of the traditional lifestyle that impeded their acceptance of the modern world.

Seddon died in 1906 and the flame went out of the Liberal torch, though the party was to stay in power another six years. This era saw the rise of the "**Red Feds**", international socialists of the Red Federation who began to organize Kiwi labour. They rejected the arbitration system that had kept wage rises below the level of inflation for a decade, and encouraged **strikes**. The longest was at Blackball on the West Coast, where prime movers in the formation of the Federation of Miners, and subsequently the Federation of Labour, led a three-month stoppage.

The 1912 election was won by William Massey's Reform Party, with the support of the farmers or "cow cockies". Allegiances were now substantially polarized and 1912 and 1913 saw bitter fighting at a series of strikes at the gold mines of Waihi, the docks at Timaru and the wharves of Auckland. As workers opposed to the arbitration system withdrew their labour, owners organized scab labour, while the hostile Farmers' Union recruited mounted "special constables" to help the government. Protected by naval and military forces, they decisively smashed the Red Feds. The Prime Minister even handed out medals to strike-breaking dairy farmers.

Coming of age

Though New Zealand had started off as the unwanted offspring of Mother England, it had soon transformed itself into a devoted daughter who could be relied upon in times of crisis. New Zealand had supported Britain in South Africa at the end of the nineteenth century and was now called upon to do the same in **World War I**. Locally born Pakeha now outnumbered immigrants and, in 1907, New Zealand had traded its self-governing colony status for that of a Dominion. This gave the country control over its foreign policy, but did not stop New Zealanders flocking to the war effort. Altogether ten percent of the population was involved, 100,000 fighting in the trenches of Gallipoli, Passchendaele and elsewhere. Seventeen thousand were killed.

At home, the **Temperance Movement** was back in action, attempting to curb vice in the army brought on by drink. Plebiscites in 1911, 1914 and 1919 narrowly averted national prohibition but the "wowsers" succeeded to the point that from 1917 pubs would close at 6pm for the duration of the war, though it wasn't repealed until 1967. This "**Six o'clock swill**" – frenetic after-work consumption in which the ability to tank down as much beer as possible was raised to an art form – probably did more to hinder New Zealand's social development than anything else (and the emphasis on quantity over quality encouraged breweries to churn out dreadful watery brews).

The wartime boom economy continued until around 1920 as Britain's demand for food remained high. Pakeha **returned servicemen** were rehabilitated on newly acquired farmland; Maori returned servicemen got nothing.

New Zealand continued to grow, with ongoing improvements in infrastructure – hydroelectric dams and roads – and enormous improvements in farming techniques, such as the application of superphosphate fertilizers, sophisticated milking machines

1950	1951	1960s
Parliament's upper house abolished.	NZ joins ANZUS military pact with the US and Australia.	Start of immigration from Pacific Islands. Major urbanization of Maori population.

and tractors. Yet it was ill-prepared for the **Great Depression**. The already high national debt skyrocketed as export income dropped and the Reform government cut pensions, health care and public works' expenditure. The budget was balanced at the cost of producing huge numbers of unemployed. Prime Minister Forbes dictated "no pay without work" and sent thousands of men to primitive rural relief camps for unnecessary tasks such as planting trees and draining swamps, resulting in lines of ragged men awaiting their relief money, malnourished children in schools and former soldiers panhandling in the streets.

Throughout the 1920s the Labour Party had watered down some of its socialist policies in an attempt to woo the middle-ground voter. In 1935 it was swept to power and ushered in New Zealand's second era of massive social change, picking up where Seddon left off. Labour's leader **Michael Joseph Savage** felt that "Social Justice must be the guiding principle and economic organization must adapt itself to social needs", a sentiment translated by a contemporary commentator as aiming "to turn capitalism quite painlessly into a nicer sort of capitalism which will eventually become indistinguishable from socialism". Salaries reduced during the depression were restored; public works programmes were rekindled, with workers on full pay rather than "relief"; income was redistributed through graduated taxation; and in two rapid bursts of legislation Labour built the model **Welfare State**, the first in the world and the most comprehensive and integrated. State houses were built and let at low rental, pensions were increased, a national health service provided free medicines and health care, and family benefits supplemented the income of those with children.

Maori welfare was also on the agenda to raise living standards to the Pakeha level, partly achieved by increasing pensions and unemployment payments. Legal changes paved the way for Maori land to be farmed using Pakeha agricultural methods, while maintaining communal ownership. In return, the newly formed **Ratana Party**, who held all four of the Maori Parliamentary seats, supported Labour, keeping them in office until 1949.

New Zealand's perception of its world position changed dramatically in 1941 when the Japanese bombed Hawaii's Pearl Harbor. The country was forced to recognize its position half a globe away from Britain and in the military sphere of America. As in World War I, large numbers of troops were called up, amounting to a third of the male labour force, but casualties were fewer and on the home front the economy continued to boom. By the 1940s New Zealand was the world's most prosperous country, with an enviable quality of life and welfare safety net.

More years of prosperity

The Reform Party and the remnants of the Liberals eventually combined to form the National Party which, in 1949, wrested power from Labour. With McCarthyite rhetoric, National branded the more militant unionists as Communists and succeeded in breaking much of the power of the unions during the violent 1951 **Waterfront Lock-out**. From the late 1940s until the mid-1980s, **National** became New Zealand's main party of government, interrupted only by two three-year stints with Labour in power. The country's underlying conservatism had now found its expression. Most were happy with the government's strong-arm tactics, which emasculated the militant unions.

1972–75	1975	1970s–80s
NZ economy struggles to cope with huge oil price hikes and Britain's entry into the Common Market.	Waitangi Tribunal established to consider Maori land claims.	Contentious sporting relations culminate in massive protests as a racially selected South African Springbok rugby team tours NZ.

Notions of the prosperous "Kiwi ideal" had huge appeal for Brits still suffering rationing after World War II, and between 1947 and 1975, 77,000 British men, women and children became "**ten pound poms**", making use of the New Zealand government's assisted passage to fill Kiwi job vacancies.

By most measures New Zealand's wealth was evenly spread, with few truly rich and relatively few poor. The exception were Maori. Responding to the urban labour shortages and good wages after World War II, many now took part in a **Maori migration** to the cities, especially Auckland. Yet by the 1970s, unemployment, unrest and a disproportionate prison population were exposing weaknesses in the widely held Pakeha pride in Maori bravery, skill, generosity, sporting prowess and good humour that nonetheless did not set aside the discrimination which kept Maori out of professional jobs.

On the economic front, major changes took place under **Walter Nash**'s 1957–60 Labour government, when New Zealand embarked on a programme designed to relieve the country's dependence on exports. A steel rolling mill, oil refinery, gin distillery and glass factory were all set up and an aluminium industry was encouraged by the prospect of cheap power from a hydroelectric project on Lake Manapouri (see box, p.775). When **Keith Holyoake** helmed the next National government, in 1960, Britain was still by far New Zealand's biggest export market but was making overtures to the economically isolationist European Common Market. Britain was no longer the guardian she once was and in the **military** sphere New Zealand began to court Pacific allies, mainly through the ANZUS pact, which provided for mutual defence of Australia, New Zealand and the US.

Dithering in the face of adversity

In 1972 Britain finally joined the Common Market. Some other export markets had been found but New Zealand still felt betrayed. Later the same year **oil prices** quadrupled in a few months and the treasury found itself with mounting fuel bills and decreasing export receipts. The Labour government were defeated in 1975 by National's obstreperous and pugnacious **Robert "Piggy" Muldoon**, who denounced Labour's borrowing and then outdid them. In short order New Zealand had dreadful domestic and foreign debt, unemployment was the highest for decades, and the unthinkable was happening – the standard of living was falling. People began to leave in their thousands and the "brain drain" almost reached crisis point. Muldoon's solution was to "**Think Big**", a catch-all term for a number of capital-intensive petrochemical projects designed to utilize New Zealand's abundant natural gas to produce ammonia, urea fertilizer, methanol and synthetic petrol. It made little economic sense. Rather than use local technology and labour to convert vehicles to run on compressed natural gas (a system already up and running), Muldoon paid international corporations to design huge prefabricated processing plants which were then shipped to New Zealand for assembly, mostly around New Plymouth.

Factory outfalls often jeopardized traditional Maori shellfish beds, and a new **spirit of protest** saw *iwi* win significant concessions. Throughout the mid-1970s Maori began to question the philosophy of Pakeha life and looked to the Treaty of Waitangi to correct their grievances. These were aired at occupations of traditional land at Bastion

1984	1985	1987
The "Hikoi" land march brings Maori grievances into political focus.	French secret service agents bomb Greenpeace flagship the *Rainbow Warrior* in Auckland Harbour.	New Zealand becomes a Nuclear-Free Zone.

Point in Auckland and at Raglan, and through a petition delivered to parliament after a march across the North Island.

Maori also found expression in the formation of **gangs** – particularly Black Power and the Mongrel Mob – along the lines graphically depicted in Lee Tamahori's film *Once Were Warriors* (see p.816), which was originally written about South Auckland life in the 1970s. Fortified suburban homes still exist and such gangs continue to be influential among Maori youth.

Race relations were never Muldoon's strong suit and when large numbers of illegal **Polynesian immigrants** from south Pacific islands – particularly Tonga, Samoa and the Cook Islands – started arriving in Auckland he responded by instructing the police to conduct random "dawn raids" checking for "over-stayers", many of whom were deported.

Muldoon took a hands-off approach when it came to sporting contacts with apartheid South Africa and in 1976 let rugby administrators send an All Blacks team over to play racially selected South African teams. African nations responded by boycotting the Montréal Olympics, making New Zealand an international pariah. New Zealand signed the 1977 Gleneagles Agreement requiring it to "vigorously combat the evil of apartheid" and yet in 1981 the New Zealand Rugby Union courted a **Springbok Tour**, which sparked New Zealand's greatest civil disturbance since the labour riots of the 1920s.

Economic and electoral reform

Muldoon's big-spending economic policies proved unsuccessful, and in 1984 Labour was returned to power under **David Lange**. Just as National had eschewed traditional right-wing economics in favour of a "managed economy", Labour now changed tactics, addressing the massive economic problems: the dollar was devalued by twenty percent, exchange controls were abolished, tariffs slashed, the maximum income tax rate was halved, a Goods and Services Tax was introduced and state benefits were cut. Unemployment doubled to twelve percent, a quarter of manufacturing jobs were lost, and the moderately well-off benefited at the expense of the poor; nevertheless, **market forces** and enterprise culture had come to stay. As one of the world's most regulated economies became one of the most deregulated, the long-standing belief that the state should provide for those least able to help themselves was cast aside.

In other spheres Labour's views weren't so right-wing. One of Lange's first acts was to refuse US ships entry to New Zealand ports unless they declared that they were nuclear-free. The Americans refused and withdrew support for New Zealand's defence safety net, the **ANZUS** pact. Lange also gave **legal recognition to the Treaty of Waitangi**, for the first time since the middle of the nineteenth century. Now, Maori grievances dating back to 1840 could be addressed.

The rise in apparent income created consumer confidence and the economy boomed until the stock market crash of 1987, which hit New Zealand especially hard. In 1990 National's **Jim Bolger** took the helm, and throughout the deep recession National continued Labour's free-market reforms, cutting welfare programmes and weakening the unions by passing the **Employment Contracts Act**, which established the pattern of individual workplaces coming to their own agreements on wages and conditions. By the middle of the 1990s the economy had improved dramatically and what for a time had

1990–96	1997	1999
Continuation of free-market reforms and further dismantling of the welfare state.	National's Jenny Shipley becomes NZ's first female prime minister.	Labour's Helen Clark becomes NZ's second female prime minister, and the first elected in her own right.

een considered a foolhardy experiment was seen by monetarists as a model for open economies the world over. Meanwhile, the gap between rich and poor continued to widen.

Political change

In 1996, New Zealand experienced its first MMP election (see box below), which brought a new Maori spirit into parliament, with far more Maori MPs than ever before.

Bolger's poor handling of the first MMP coalition government saw his support wane, and he was supplanted in a palace coup, with **Jenny Shipley** becoming New Zealand's first female prime minister. In the 1999 election, the **Green Party** came out of left field, long-sidelined but newly resurgent under MMP. They racked up six seats and helped form a government with Labour and the Alliance under **Helen Clark** – the first female prime minister to win an election in her own right. The 1999 election brought New Zealand's first Rastafarian MP, **Nandor Tanczos**, resplendent in waist-length dreads and a hemp suit, and **Georgina Beyer**, the world's first transgender MP.

The Labour-led coalition stopped logging of West Coast beech forests and replaced the Employment Contracts Act with more worker-friendly legislation but failed to deliver on education and health care. Still, Labour was returned with an increased majority after the 2002 election.

Labour's popularity remained high until the 2003 **foreshore and seabed debate** in which Labour forced through legislation ostensibly guaranteeing beach-access to all,

---

FIRST-PAST-THE-POST, MMP AND MAORI SEATS

Ever since New Zealand achieved self-government from Britain in 1852, it had maintained a first-past-the-post Westminster style of Parliament, with the exception of the scrapping of the upper house in 1950.

In the troubled economic times of 1993, when dissatisfaction with both major parties was running high, New Zealand voted for **electoral reform**. They chose Mixed Member Proportional representation (MMP), a system the country still struggles to fully understand. The debate as to how well it works continues, but it does give smaller parties an opportunity to have a greater influence, and New Zealand's Parliament has become all the more colourful for it.

Of the 120 MPs elected, around half represent their own area of the country ("electorate" or "seat") and half are elected from party lists. Voters get **two votes**. The first is for a person, who you hope will become your electorate MP. The second is for a party and is generally considered the more important as it determines the overall make-up of Parliament. A party's representation in Parliament is made up from the number of electorate seats they win plus a number of their list MPs determined by their percentage of the party vote.

To get any seats at all, small parties must exceed the threshold of five percent of the party vote, or win a constituency seat. If they win a seat, their representation is proportional to their party vote even if it's under five percent.

To further complicate matters, Maori voters can choose to vote either within the general system described above, or for one of the seven **Maori seats** which cover the country. All parties are entitled to field candidates in both general and Maori constituencies, though parties championing Maori concerns tend to win.

A **referendum** on New Zealand's electoral system was held at the same time as the 2011 general election, during which Kiwis resoundingly voted to retain the MMP system.

2003	2003	2008
Privy Council in London replaced by a Supreme Court as NZ's highest legal body.	Continued immigration from East Asia brings the Asian population up to ten percent of the nation.	National's John Key forms a minority government with the support of the Maori Party, ACT New Zealand and United Future.

by declaring that the land in question was owned by the Crown. Maori perceived this high-handed action as an affront to their sovereignty, and traditionally Labour-supporting Maori voters turned to the July 2004-established **Maori Party**, co-led by former Labour MP **Tariana Turia**. In November 2004, the Foreshore and Seabed Act was passed into law, and at the 2005 election the Maori Party won four of the seven Maori seats. Still, Labour was able to cobble together a coalition without Maori Party support, and continue in power though with a much reduced majority.

This, combined with the perception of the Labour government having outstayed its welcome after nearly a decade in power, saw a resurgent National Party, under former currency trader **John Key**, form a coalition government following the 2008 election, with the support of the Maori Party (which repeated its electoral success of 2005 and picked up a fifth seat), as well as ACT, New Zealand First and United Future. Labour's **Phil Goff**, who held a number of ministry portfolios under his party's previous government including Defence, took over the leadership of the Labour opposition.

Key's government **repealed the Foreshore and Seabed Act** in April 2011. Shortly afterwards, Maori Party MP Hone Harawira resigned from the Maori Party and formed the Mana Party, after the Maori Party recommended his expulsion due to his opposition to its position on the foreshore and seabed issue.

The November 2011 general election attracted the lowest voter turnout since 1887 (74.21 percent), and saw the National Party re-elected under the widely popular Key. Though the National Party fell two seats short of an outright majority, it formed a coalition government with the Maori Party, ACT and United Future.

Responding to adversity

Although New Zealand has generally weathered the effects of the recent global financial crisis better than many other nations, it has experienced economic difficulties and challenges through natural disasters in recent years.

At 4.35am on September 4, 2010, a 7.1 magnitude **earthquake** struck the Canterbury region near Christchurch. Damage was significant, but miraculously, no one was killed. However, severe **aftershocks** from the quake proved deadly. The worst of these struck Christchurch on February 22, 2011 at 12.51pm. The magnitude 6.3 quake caused widespread damage (including buildings already weakened by the September 2010 quake) and killed 185 people. The February 2011 quake was by far the costliest natural disaster in New Zealand's history, with rebuilding estimated at around $15–16 billion. A third major quake, also 6.3, occurred in Christchurch at 2.20pm on June 13, 2011, killing one person, and compounding the damage to many buildings and demolishing others, as well as increasing rebuilding costs by $6 billion. The quakes damaged over 100,000 homes and ruined much of the city's once-picturesque central district. Non-fatal quakes also struck in December 2011, in addition to several thousand smaller aftershocks that continue to rattle the city. At the time of writing, thousands of residents had permanently relocated to other parts of New Zealand and to Australia, but authorities have continued to affirm their commitment to rebuilding the city, and pop-up and gap-filling enterprises highlight citizens' creativity and spirit. For more detail on the Christchurch earthquakes, see p.511.

2010–11	2011	2011
Christchurch struck by severe earthquakes. The most devastating, in February 2011, killed 185 people.	New Zealand hosts – and wins – the Rugby World Cup.	National re-elected under John Key, forming a minority government with the support of the Maori Party, ACT New Zealand and United Future.

Maoritanga

When the Pakeha first came to this Island, the first thing he taught the Maori was Christianity. They made parsons and priests of several members of the Maori race, and they taught these persons to look up and pray; and while they were looking up the Pakehas took away our land.

Mahuta, the son of the Maori King Tawhiao, addressing the New Zealand Legislative Council in 1903.

The term Maoritanga embodies Maori lifestyle – the Maori way of doing things, embracing social structure, ethics, customs, legends, art and language. Despite New Zealand's Anglo-European-dominated society, contemporary Maori culture has seen a dramatic resurgence in recent decades. Maori make up around fifteen percent of the population. Maori–Pakeha marriage since the early nineteenth century has created a complex interracial pool – a fact that led one academic to speculate "race relations will be worked out in the bedrooms of New Zealand". Many Kiwis are of mixed descent with innumerable Pakeha claiming Maori forebears. Maori ancestry remains the foundation of Maoridom but a sense of belonging is increasingly important.

Maori in the modern world

New Zealand's Maori make up a vital part of all walks of life – as lawyers, MPs, university lecturers, sporting, musical and media identities and even as the Governor-General. That said, average incomes are lower than those of Pakeha, almost half of all prison inmates are Maori and only around a quarter of Maori achieve post-school qualifications. These, along with disproportionate health statistics, are among the imbalances that activists and politicians are working to redress.

Many Pakeha have long cited scenes of Maori and Pakeha elbow-to-elbow at the bar and Maori rugby players in the scrum alongside their Pakeha brothers as evidence of a harmonious existence. Yet this has ignored an undercurrent of Maori dissatisfaction over their treatment since the arrival of Europeans; the policy of **assimilation** relied on Maori conforming to the Pakeha way of doing things, making no concession to *Maoritanga*. Maori adapted quickly to European ways but were rewarded with the near-loss of their language and the loss of their **land**. It is impossible to overestimate the importance of this: Maori spirituality invests every tree, hill and bay with a kind of supernatural life of its own, drawn from past events and the actions of the ancestors. It is by no means fanciful to equate the loss of land with the diminution of Maori life force.

It's only really since the 1980s that the paternal Pakeha view has been challenged, with the country adopting **biculturalism**. As Maori rediscover their heritage and Pakeha comprehend what has been around for generations, knowledge of *Maoritanga* and some understanding of the language is considered desirable and advantageous. Recent governments have increasingly fostered a take-up in the learning of Maori language, resurgence in Maori arts and crafts and a growing pride in the culture by both Maori and Pakeha.

The sluggish pace of change led to an increase in Maori activism. The debate effectively led to the birth of the Maori Party, which is growing in strength and influence, and more recently the Mana Party. This change is too little for some, as evidenced by the 2007 raids of an alleged paramilitary training camp in the North

Island. A group of mostly Maori activists led by Tame Iti were arrested as terrorists, although the charges were commuted to firearms offences. The reaction of the then-Labour government, including the "lock-down" of the community at nearby Ruatoki, heightened calls for greater self-determination.

Maori legend

Maori culture remains primarily oral with chants, storytelling and oratory central to ceremonial and daily life. Different tribal groups had different sets of stories, or at least variations on common themes, but European historians with pet theories often distorted the tales they heard and destroyed conflicting evidence, creating their own Maori folklore. Over time many of these stories have been taken back into Maori tradition, resulting in a patchwork of authentic and bowdlerized legends and helping create a common Maori identity.

Creation

From the primal nothingness of **Te Kore** sprang **Ranginui**, the sky father, and **Papatuanuku**, the earth mother. They had numerous offspring, including: **Haumia Tiketike**, the god of the fern root and food from the forest; **Rongo**, the god of the *kumara* and cultivation; **Tu Matauenga**, the god of war; **Tangaroa**, the god of the oceans and sea life; **Tawhirimatea**, the god of the winds; and **Tane Mahuta**, the god of the forests. Through long centuries of darkness the brothers argued over whether to separate their parents and create light. Tawhirimatea opposed the idea and fled to the skies where his anger is manifested in thunder and lightning, while Tane Mahuta succeeded in parting the two, allowing life to flourish. Ranginui's tears filled the oceans, and even now it is his grief that brings the dew, mist and rain.

Having created the creatures of the sea, the air and the land, the gods turned their attentions to humans and, realizing that they were all male, decided to create a female. They fashioned clay into a form resembling their mother and **Tane** breathed life into the nostrils of the Dawn Maiden, **Hinetitama**.

Maui the trickster and Kupe the navigator

Maori mythology is littered with demigods, none more celebrated than **Maui-Tikitiki-a-Taranga**, whose exploits are legend throughout Polynesia. With an armoury of spells, guile and boundless mischief, Maui gained a reputation as a trickster, using his abilities to turn situations to his advantage. Equipped with the powerful magic jawbone of his grandmother, he set about taming his world, believing himself invincible. He even took on the sun, which passed so swiftly through the heavens that people had no time to

---

MAUI FISHES UP THE NORTH ISLAND

Maui's greatest work was the creation of **Aotearoa**. Because of his reputation for mischief, Maui's brothers often left him behind when they went fishing, but one morning he stowed away, revealing himself far out to sea and promising to improve their catch. Maui egged them on until they were beyond the normal fishing grounds before dropping anchor. In no time at all Maui's brothers filled the canoe with fish, but Maui still had some fishing to do. They scorned his hook (secretly armed with a chip of his grandmother's jawbone) and wouldn't lend him any bait, so Maui struck his own nose and smeared the hook with his blood. Soon he hooked a fabulous fish that, as it broke the surface, stretched into the distance all around them. Chanting an incantation, Maui got the fish to lie quietly and it became the North Island, Te ika a Maui, the fish of Maui. As Maui went to make an offering to the gods, his brothers began to cut up the fish and eat it, hacking mountains and valleys into the surface. To fit in with the legend, the South Island is often called Te waka a Maui, the canoe of Maui, and Stewart Island the anchor, Te punga o te waka a Maui.

end their fields. Maui, with the aid of his older brothers, plaited strong ropes and tied them across the sun's pit before dawn. The sun rose into the net and Maui beat the sun with his magic jawbone, imploring it not to go so fast. The sun weakened and agreed to Maui's request. Maui's legendary antics extend to the creation of Aotearoa (see box opposite).

Maori trace their ancestry back to **Hawaiki**, the source of the Polynesian diaspora, for which the Society Islands and the Cook Islands are likely candidates. According to legend, the first visitor to Aotearoa was **Kupe**, the great Polynesian navigator. He was determined to kill a great octopus that kept stealing his bait; drawn ever further out to sea in pursuit, he finally reached landfall on the uninhabited shores of Aotearoa, the "land of the long white cloud". He named numerous features of the land before returning to Hawaiki with instructions for retracing his voyage.

Social structure and customs

Maori society is **tribal**, though the deracination resulting from the move from tribal homelands to cities has eroded many close ties. In urban situations the finer points of *Maoritanga* have been rediscovered and the basic tenets remain strong, with formal protocol ruling ceremonies from funeral wakes to meetings.

The most fundamental grouping in Maori society is the extended family or **whanau** (literally "birthing"), spanning immediate relatives to cousins, uncles and nieces. A dozen or so *whanau* form localized sub-tribes or **hapu** (literally "gestation or pregnancy"), comprising extended families of common descent. *Hapu* were originally economically autonomous and today continue to conduct communal activities, typically through *marae* (see p.802). Neighbouring *hapu* are likely to belong to the same tribe or **iwi** (literally "bones"), a looser association of Maori spread over large geographical areas. The thirty-odd major *iwi* are tenuously linked by common ancestry, traced back to semi-legendary canoes, or *waka*. In troubled times, *iwi* from the same *waka* would band together for protection. Together these are the **tangata whenua**, "the people of the land", a term that may refer to Maori people as a whole, or just to one *hapu* if local concerns are being aired.

The literal meanings of *whanau*, *hapu* and *iwi* can be viewed as a metaphor for the Maori view of their relationship with their ancestors or **tupuna**, existing through their genetic inheritors, the past forming part of the present. Hence the respect accorded the **whakapapa**, an individual's genealogy tracing descent from the gods via one of the migratory *waka* and through the *tupuna*. The *whakapapa* is often recited on formal occasions such as **hui** (meetings).

Maori traditional life is informed by the parallel notions of **tapu** (taboo) and **noa** (mundane, not *tapu*). This belief system is designed to impose a code of conduct: transgressing *tapu* brings ostracism, ill fortune and sickness. Objects, places, actions and people can be *tapu*, demanding extra respect; the body parts of a chief, especially the head, menstruating women, sacred items, earrings, pendants, hair combs, burial sites, and the knowledge contained in the *whakapapa* are all *tapu*. The productivity of fishing grounds and forests was traditionally maintained by imposing *tapu* at critical times. The direct opposite of *tapu* is *noa*, a term applied to ordinary items that, by implication, are considered safe; a new building is *tapu* until a special ceremony renders it *noa*.

People, animals and artefacts, whether *tapu* or *noa*, possess **mauri** (life force), **wairua** (spirit) and **mana**, a term loosely translated as prestige but embodying wider concepts of power, influence, charisma and goodwill. Birthright brings with it a degree of *mana* that can then be augmented through brave deeds or lost through inaction. Wartime cannibalism was partly ritual and by eating an enemy's heart a warrior absorbed his *mauri*. Likewise personal effects gain *mana* from association with the *mana* of their owner, accruing more when passed to descendants. Any slight on the *mana* of an individual was felt by the *hapu*, who must then exact **utu** (a need to balance any action with an equal reaction), a compunction that often led to bloody feuds, sometimes escalating to war and further enhancing the *mana* of the victors. Pakeha found this a hard concept to grasp and deeds that they considered deceitful or treacherous could be considered correct in Maori terms.

The responsibility for determining *tapu* falls to the **tohunga** (priest or expert), the most exalted of many specialists in *Maoritanga*, conversant with tribal history, sacred lore and the *whakapapa*, and considered to be the earthly presence of the power of the gods.

Marae

The rituals of *hapu* life – *hui*, **tangi** (funeral wakes) and **powhiri** (formal welcomes) – are conducted on the **marae**, a combined community, cultural and social centre where the cultural values, protocols, customs and vitality of *Maoritanga* find their fullest expression. Strictly, a *marae* is a courtyard, but the term is often applied to a whole complex, comprising the **whare runanga** (meeting house, or *whare nui*), *whare manuhiri* (house for visitors), *whare kai* (eating house) and an old-fashioned **pataka** (raised storehouse). *Marae* belonging to one or more *hapu* are found all over the country, while pan-tribal urban *marae* exist to help Maori who have lost their roots.

Visitors, whether Maori or Pakeha, may not enter *marae* without invitation, so unless you're personally invited, you're most likely to visit on a commercially run **tour** (see box, p.804). Invited guests are expected to provide some form of **koha** (donation) towards the upkeep of the *marae*, usually included in tour fees. Remember, the *marae* is sacred and due reverence must be accorded the **kawa** (protocols).

Arts and crafts

The origins of **Maori art** lie in eastern Polynesia but half a millennium of isolated development has resulted in unique forms of expression. Eastern Polynesia has no suitable clay, so Maori forebears had no skills for pottery and focused on wood, stone and weaving, occasionally using naturalistic designs but more often the **stylized forms** that make Maori art unmistakable.

As with other *taonga* (treasures), many examples were taken by Victorian and later collectors, but there is determined effort by *iwi* and Te Puni Kokiri (the Ministry of Maori Development) to restore *taonga* to New Zealand, including severed heads scattered through museums around the world – some were recently returned by London's Victoria & Albert Museum.

Woodcarving

Maori handiworks' greatest expression is **woodcarving**. The essence of great Maori woodcarving is that as much care is given to the production of a humble water bailer as to the pinnacle of Maori creativity, *waka* (canoes) and *whare whakairo* (carved houses). Early examples of woodcarving feature the sparse, rectilinear styles of ancient eastern Polynesia, but by the fifteenth century these were replaced by the cursive style, employed by more traditional carvers today. In Northland, kauri wood was used, while elsewhere durable, easily worked totara was the material of choice. Carvers worked with shells and sharp stones in the earliest times, but the artist's scope increased with the invention of tools fashioned from **pounamu** (greenstone, a form of jade; see box, p.664). Some would say that the quality of the work declined after European arrival: not just through the demand for quickly executed "tourist art", but as a consequence of pressure to remove the phallic imagery found obscene by missionaries. As early as 1844, carving had been abandoned in areas with a strong missionary presence, and it continued to decline until the 1920s when Maori parliamentarian Apirana Ngata established Rotorua's pan-tribal **Maori Arts and Crafts Institute** – a foundation on which *Maoritanga* could be rebuilt.

WHARE

Originally the chief's residence, the *whare* gradually adopted the symbolism of the *waka* – some incorporated wood from *waka*. Each meeting house is a tangible manifestation of the *whakapapa*, usually representing a synthesis of the ancestors: the ridge-pole, the backbone; the rafters, the ribs; the interior, the belly; the gable, the head; and the barge-boards, the arms, often with finger-like decoration. Inside, all wooden surfaces are carved and the spaces filled with intricate woven-flax panels, *tukutuku*.

The role of carver has always been highly respected, with seasoned and skilled exponents having the status of *tohunga* and travelling the country to carve and teach. The work is *tapu* and *noa* objects must be kept away – cooked food is not allowed nearby, and carvers have to brush away shavings rather than blow them – though women, previously banned, can now become carvers.

Maori carving exhibits a distinctive **style**. Relief forms are hewn from a single piece of wood with no concession to natural form, shapes or blemishes. Landscapes are symbolized not actually depicted, perspective is not represented, and figures stand separately. Unadorned wood is rare, carvers creating a stylistic bed of swirling spirals, curving organic forms based on fern fronds or seashells and interlocking latticework. Superimposed on this are key elements, often inlaid with paua shell.

The most common is the ancestor figure, the **hei tiki**, a distorted human form, either male, female or of indeterminate gender. Almost as common is the mythical *manaia*, a beaked birdlike form with an almost human profile. Secondary motifs include the *pakake* (whale) and *moko* (lizard).

While the same level of craftsmanship was applied to all manner of tools, weapons and ornaments, it reached its most exalted expression in *waka taua* (**war canoes**), the focus of community pride and endeavour. Gunwales, bailers and paddles are fabulously decorated but the most detailed work is reserved for the prow and sternpost, usually a matrix of spirals interwoven with *manaia* figures. As guns and the European presence altered the balance of tribal warfare in the 1860s, the *waka taua* was superseded in importance by the *whare whakairo* (carved meeting house).

Greenstone carving

Maori carvers also work in **pounamu** (greenstone), supplied by pre-European trade routes originating in the West Coast and Fiordland; indeed, the South Island became known as Te Wai Pounamu, the Greenstone Water. The stone was fashioned into adzes, chisels and clubs for hand-to-hand combat; tools that took on a ritual significance and demanded decoration. *Pounamu*'s hardness dictates a more restrained carving style and *mere* and *patu* tend to be only partly worked, leaving large sweeping surfaces ending in a flourish of delicate swirls. Ornamental pieces range from simple drop pendants worn as earrings or neck decoration to *hei tiki*, worn as a breast pendant. Like other personal items, especially those worn close to the body, an heirloom *tiki* possesses the *mana* of the ancestors and absorbs the wearer's *mana*, becoming *tapu*.

Tattooing

A stylistic extension of the carver's craft is exhibited in *moko*, ornamental and ceremonial **tattooing** that almost died out with European contact. Women had *moko* on the lips and chin, high-ranking men had their faces completely covered, along with their buttocks and thighs; the greater the extent and intricacy of the *moko*, the greater the status. A symmetrical pattern of traditional elements, crescents, spirals, fern fronds and other organic forms, was gouged into the flesh with an *uhi* (chisel) and mallet, then soot rubbed into the wound. In the last couple of decades the tradition of full-face *moko* has been revived, as a symbol of *Maoritanga* and an art form in its own right; since 1999, *moko* artists have been eligible for government funding.

EXPERIENCING MAORI CULTURE

The most direct and popular introduction to Maori culture is a **concert and hangi** (feast). Virtually all visitors to Rotorua attend one of these generally authentic and entertaining gigs and it's also possible to visit one in Christchurch or Queenstown.

Both the concert and *hangi* usually take place on a traditional *marae* (some cheaper versions are held at hotels). *Kawa* (*protocols*) governing behaviour dictate that *manuhiri* (visitors) must be challenged to determine friendly intent before being allowed onto the *marae*. As visitors, you elect a "chief" who represents you during this *wero*, where a fearsome warrior bears down on you with twirling *taiaha* (long club), flicking tongue and bulging eyes. Once a ritual gift has been accepted, the women make the *karanga* (welcoming call), breaking the *tapu*, followed by their *powhiri* (sung welcome). This acts as a prelude to ceremonial touching of noses, *hongi*, binding the *manuhiri* and the *tangata whenua* physically and spiritually.

And so begins the concert, performed in traditional costume. Highlights are the men's *haka* and the women's *poi* dance, in which tennis-ball-sized bulrush clumps are twirled rhythmically. The concert is followed by the *hangi*, a feast traditionally steamed in an earth oven or, in Rotorua, over a geothermal vent. Typically visits include learning at least a few words of the Maori language.

Beyond commercial concert and *hangi* ensembles, the following tours and lodgings offer opportunities to dig deeper into Maori culture. The website ⓦ inz.maori.nz is also a handy resource to find Maori tourism operators around the country.

Footprints Waipoua Northland. See p.193.
Kapiti Island near Wellington. See p.256.
Maori Tours Kaikoura. See p.503.
TIME Unlimited tours Auckland See p.81.

Maraehako Bay Retreat East Cape. See p.363.
Tipuna Tours East Cape. See p.374.

Weaving and clothing

While men carved, women concentrated on weaving and producing clothing. When Polynesians arrived in these cool, damp islands their paper mulberry plants didn't thrive and they were forced to look for alternatives. They found *harakeke* (New Zealand **flax**), the foundation of Maori fibre-work. The long, strong and pliable fibres, growing on marshy land all over the country, were used as fishing lines, as cordage for axe-heads and as floor matting. With the arrival of the Pakeha, Maori adopted European clothes, but they continued to wear cloaks on formal occasions and today these constitute the basis for contemporary designs.

Used in something close to their raw form for *raranga* (plaiting), they made *kete*, handle-less baskets for collecting shellfish and *kumara*, triangular canoe sails, sandals and *whariki*, patterned floor mats still used in meeting houses. For finer work, trimming, soaking and beating flax, a laborious process, produced stronger and more pliable fibre.

Most flax was neutral but Maori design requires some **colouring**: black is achieved by soaking in a dilute extract of *hinau* tree bark then rubbing with a black swamp sediment, *paru*; red-brown ranges of colours require boiling in dyes derived from the tanekaha tree bark and fixing by rolling in hot ashes; while the less popular yellow tint is produced from the bark of the Coprosma species. Today synthetic dyes are used to create green.

Natural and coloured fibres are both used in *whatu kakahu* (**cloak-weaving**), the crowning achievement of Maori women's art, the finest cloaks ranking alongside prized *taonga*; the immense war canoe now in the Auckland Museum was once exchanged for a fine cloak. The technique is sometimes referred to as finger-weaving as no loom is used. The women work downwards from a base warp strung between two sticks. Complex weaving techniques produce a huge array of different textures, often decorated with *taniko* (coloured borders), cord tags tacked onto the cloth at intervals and, most impressively, **feathers**. Feather cloaks (*kahu hururu*) don't appear to have been common before European contact, though heroic tales often feature key players in iridescent garments. The appeal of the bright yellow feathers of the huia probably saw to its demise, and most other brightly coloured birds are now too rare to use for cloaks, so new feather cloaks are rarely made.

You'll come across some fine examples in museums, the base cloth often completely covered by a dense layer of kiwi feathers bordered by zigzag patterns of tui, native pigeon and parakeet. More robust, *para* (rain capes) were made using the water-repellent leaves of the cabbage tree and a form of coarse canvas that could reportedly resist spear thrusts was used for *pukupuku* (war cloaks). Some *pukupuku* were turned into *kahu kuri* (dog-skin cloaks) with the addition of strips of dog skin, arranged vertically so that the natural fur colours produced distinctive patterns.

Weaving and plaiting are again popular; cloaks are an important element of formal occasions, whether on the *marae* for *hui* and *tangi*, or elsewhere for receiving academic or state honours. Old forms are reproduced directly or raided as inspiration for contemporary designs that interpret traditional elements in the light of modern fashion.

The haka, Maori dance and Maori music

The use of the *haka* (see box below) by what are often predominantly Pakeha sides might seem inappropriate but it is entrenched in Kiwi culture; there was a considerable backlash in 1996 when the All Blacks coach suggested the *haka* should be changed to mollify those Maori *iwi* who had been decimated by Te Rauparaha. The new, specially written *Kapa O Pango haka* was unveiled in 2005 but it hasn't completely replaced the Te Rauparaha version.

The drums of eastern Polynesia didn't make it to New Zealand, so both chants and the *haka* go unaccompanied. Along with the traditional bone flute, Pakeha added the guitar to accompany **waiata** (songs), relatively modern creations whose impact comes from tone, rhythm and lyrics. The impassioned delivery can seem at odds with music that's often based on Victorian hymns: perhaps the best known are *Pokarekare ana* and *Haere Ra*, both post-European-contact creations. Outside the tourist concert party, Maori music has developed enormously in recent years to the point where there are tribal and Maori-language music stations almost exclusively playing music written and performed by Maori, often with a hip-hop or R & B influence and a Pacific twist. For more on music, see box, p.817.

THE HAKA

Before every international rugby match, New Zealand's All Blacks put the wind up the opposition by performing an intimidating thigh-slapping, eye-bulging, tongue-poking chant. Traditionally this has been the Te Rauparaha *haka*, just one of many such Maori posture dances, designed to display fitness, agility and ferocity. The Te Rauparaha *haka* was reputedly composed early in the nineteenth century by the warrior Te Rauparaha (p.256), who was hiding from his enemies in the *kumara* pit of a friendly chief. Hearing noise above and then being blinded by light he thought his days were numbered, but as his eyes became accustomed to the sun he saw the hairy legs of his host and was so relieved he performed the *haka* on the spot.

Touring teams have performed the *haka* at least since the 1905 All Blacks tour of Britain, and since the 1987 World Cup for home matches as well. The performance is typically led by a player of Maori descent chanting:

Ringa pakia Slap the hands against the thighs
Uma tiraha Puff out the chest
Turi whatia Bend the knees
Hope whai ake Let the hip follow
Waewae takahia kia kino Stamp the feet as hard as you can

After a pause for effect the rest of the team join in with:

Ka Mate! Ka Mate! It is death! It is death!
Ka Ora! Ka Ora! It is life! It is life!
Tenei te ta ngata puhuru huru This is the hairy man
Nana nei i tiki mai Who caused the sun to shine
Whakawhiti te ra Keep abreast!
A upane ka upane! The rank! Hold fast!
A upane kaupane whiti te ra! Into the sun that shines!

Landscapes and wildlife

Despite its size, New Zealand is bursting with enormous diversity: subtropical forests, volcanic basins, boiling mud pools, geysers, rugged white-silica and gold-sand fringed coastlines and spectacular alpine regions. These landscapes support an extraordinary variety of animals and plant life, with almost ninety percent of the flora not found anywhere else in the world. Many habitats, plants and wildlife are easily accessible, protected within national parks and scenic reserves.

The Shaky Isles

The earliest rocks are thought to have originated in the continental forelands of Australia and Antarctica, part of Gondwanaland, a massive supercontinent to which New Zealand belonged. Oceanic islands were created by continental drift, the movement of the large plates that form the earth's crust, which created an island arc and oceanic trench about 100 million years ago.

Roughly 26 million years ago, New Zealand rose further from the sea and today's landscape evolved, through **volcanic** activity and continuous movement along fault lines, particularly the Alpine Fault of the South Island. On the boundary between the Australian and Pacific tectonic plates, New Zealand's North Island has the two plates crashing into one another, the Pacific plate pushed beneath the Australian to produce prolific volcanic activity. Conversely under the South Island the Pacific plate rides over the Australian, causing **mountain building** and creating the Southern Alps. This unique island combination generates about four hundred **earthquakes** a year, although only a quarter are big enough to be noticed, and has earned New Zealand the nickname "the Shaky Isles". In 2010 and 2011, severe quakes struck the Canterbury region around Christchurch, causing extensive damage and loss of life (see box, p.511). The volcanoes on the North Island periodically become impressively active: White Island (just off the coast of the Bay of Plenty) blows steam, while Mount Ruapehu erupted in 2006 and 2007. In 2011 Mount Ruapehu's Volcanic Alert Level was elevated to level 1 (signs of volcanic unrest), but at the time of writing, it was not affecting visitors.

The end of isolation

New Zealand's flora and fauna evolved untouched until the first human reached Aotearoa, reportedly around a thousand years ago. Before the arrival of Maori, the land was covered in thick **forest** composed of hundreds of tree species, and the only mammals were seals, whales and dolphins round the coast, and a couple of types of **bat**. Land mammals were non-existent, a unique situation, which allowed **birds** to take

---

CONSERVATION AND WILDLIFE ORGANIZATIONS AND WEBSITES

Department of Conservation Ⓦ doc.govt.nz. Government department charged with conserving New Zealand's natural and historic heritage.
Forest and Bird Protection Society Ⓦ forestandbird.org.nz. New Zealand's leading independent conservation organization.

NZ Birds Ⓦ nzbirds.com. Comprehensive site on everything feathery.
Save The Kiwi Ⓦ savethekiwi.org.nz. Department of Conservation and Bank of New Zealand effort to save this iconic bird from extinction.

THE SCOURGE OF THE BUSH: MAMMALIAN PESTS

Since human habitation began, 43 indigenous bird species have become extinct and New Zealand is now home to about eleven percent of the world's most endangered species. Settlement and the introduction of non-native plants and animals are responsible for devastating this country's unique ecosystem.

POSSUMS

Visitors to New Zealand soon become familiar with the nocturnal **possum**, if only as road-kill. Live specimens usually show up when you are tramping, their eyes reflecting your torchlight around huts at night. Although they look cute they are a pest, causing enormous damage to flora and fauna, stunting trees by munching new shoots, eating native birds' eggs and killing chicks. Consequently, New Zealanders have an almost pathological hatred of this introduced Australian marsupial, and greenies who would never dream of wearing any other fur happily don possum garments.

Before the start of controlled European migration in 1840, enterprising individuals were liberating **brushtail opossums** (*Trichosurus vulpecula*, more commonly known as **possums**) in New Zealand, with the aim of establishing a fur industry. Releases stopped around 1930 but control measures were not introduced until 1951, when a bounty was paid on all possums with their skins intact. Until the late 1980s possums were killed for their fur, but successful anti-fur lobbying saw prices plummet. Hunting tailed off and possum numbers skyrocketed. There are now in excess of **seventy million** possums, who currently eat their way through some 21,000 tonnes of vegetation every night, and are known carriers of bovine TB – endangering the dairy, beef and deer industries.

Possums are so widespread that hunting barely has any effect and the government is forced to spend around $100 million a year on possum control. The most cost-effective is aerial drops of **1080 poison**, a controversial substance banned in almost every other country in the world. Farmers claim it kills their stock and the native birds it is designed to protect. Certainly native birds do die, but the decimation of the possum population allows such an increase in avian breeding success that bird numbers exceed their pre-poisoning levels.

WILD PIGS, DEER, TAHR AND CHAMOIS

When James Cook sailed around New Zealand in the 1770s he released **pigs** so that on return voyages there would be something tasty to eat. These feral pigs (known as "Captain Cookers") are still rooting up the ground, although pig hunting keeps numbers down.

Seven **deer** species were successfully established for sport from 1851 up to the 1930s, and even today there are illegal releases of deer by hunters. Authorities are reluctant to advocate complete removal because of the political strength of the hunting lobby. In the first half of the twentieth century, the government also introduced the Himalayan **tahr**, a goat-like animal, and European **chamois**, both of which inhabit the high country of the South Island.

RABBITS AND MUSTELIDS

Rabbits were introduced to New Zealand from the 1840s, and though they don't pose a particular threat to native wildlife, the means used to try and stem the population certainly does. In the 1880s **ferrets** were introduced, but instead of targeting rabbits, these members of the mustelid family found the flightless birdlife easier prey. Along with **weasels**, **stoats** were also introduced to combat the rabbit plague, but instead they became the number one enemy of native species.

DOGS, CATS, RATS AND MICE

Uncontrolled **dogs** can't resist playing with any flightless birds they might come across, and studies suggest they are responsible for 76 percent of adult brown kiwi deaths alone. There are an estimated 1.2 million **cats** in New Zealand, a quarter of them feral, and they kill numerous birds and lizards.

The *kiore* or Polynesian **rat** has been largely displaced by more aggressive Norway and ship rats, living everywhere from the treetops to the leaf litter, who ravage small bird and insect populations as well as devouring plant seeds and suppressing growth in the bush. **Mice** play a similarly devastating role.

their place in the food chain; with no predators, many gradually lost the ability to fly. When Maori came, with their dogs and rats, and then Pakeha, with all their introduced species, the birds could not compete. Those that survived (see box, pp.810–811) now cling precariously to existence.

Maori impact pales in comparison with the devastation wreaked by **Europeans**. Cook's first exploratory visits left a legacy of wild pigs, sheep and potatoes, while in the early 1800s whalers and sealers bloodied the coastal waters, while logging campaigns cleared vast tracts of native trees for grazing cattle. Pioneers continued to tamper with the delicately balanced ecosystem in an attempt to create a "New England". **Acclimatization societies** sprung up in the late 1800s to introduce familiar animals and plants from settlers' European homelands – New Zealand would never have become the successful pastoral nation it is without the grasses, pollinating birds, bees and butterflies, sheep and cattle. But many releases were disastrous, either out-competing native plants and birds or killing them.

The lowlands

Archetypal paddocks full of **sheep**, often backed by shelter belts of macrocarpa trees, are within sight of the airports. Sheep number about 40 million, roughly half the population of thirty years ago, with much of their grazing land turned over to other uses: dairying, deer farming or, less commonly, ostriches. Elsewhere, land has been redeveloped for horticulture or **vineyards**, which continue to crop up, particularly around Gisborne, Hastings, Martinborough, Blenheim, Nelson, Waipara and Cromwell. Vintners are co-producing **olives** – with increasing success – and optimistic souls plant oak and hazel trees in the hope of creating a truffle industry.

Throughout both farmed and forested New Zealand you'll see native **cabbage trees** (*ti kouka*) with thin grey trunks (up to 10m high) topped by spear-shaped leaves and clusters of white flowers. Captain Cook and his men ate the leaf shoots, finding them vaguely cabbage-like.

Lowland forests

Much of the thick forest that greeted Maori and early settlers was burned, logged, or cleared for farming, but pockets of **native bush** survive. The forests of Northland, the Coromandel Peninsula, the west coasts of both islands, around Wellington and on Stewart Island contain a wonderful variety of native trees. There are also sixty endemic native flowering plant species in lowland areas, whose blooms are almost all white or yellow. With no pollinating bees to attract there was little need for vibrant petals.

New Zealand's best-known tree, the **kauri**, is found in mixed lowland forest, particularly in Northland. With a lifespan of two to four thousand years, this magnificent king of the forest rises to 30m, two-thirds of it straight, branchless trunk. Greatly revered by Maori canoe-builders, who enacted solemn ceremonies before hacking them down, and European shipbuilders, who used them for masts and timbers, many kauri were more prosaically turned into frames, cladding and floorboards for wooden houses. The tree is also the source of kauri gum, dug and exported in the late nineteenth and early twentieth centuries.

Open spaces along forest edges and riverbanks are often alive with tui (see see box, p.811) sucking nectar from golden clusters of **kowhai**, the national flower, which hang from trees, whose wood was once fashioned into Maori canoe paddles and adze handles.

The North Island and the top third of the South are home to New Zealand's only native palm, the **nikau**. Its slender branchless stem bears shiny leaves, up to 30cm, long pink spiky flowers and red berries, used by European settlers as pellets in the absence of ammunition.

Irregularly branched, growing to 20m, the **pohutukawa** is found as far south as Otago, in forests around the coast and at lake edges. Typically it bears festive bright crimson blossoms

THE KIWI

Flightless, dull brown in colour and distinctly odd looking, the kiwi is New Zealand's much-loved national symbol. Stout, muscular, shy and nocturnal, it is a member of the ratite family – which includes the ostrich, emu, rhea, cassowary and the long-extinct moa – and is one of the few birds in the world with a well-developed sense of **smell**. At night you might hear them snuffling around, using the nostrils at the end of their bill to detect earthworms, beetles, cicada larvae, spiders and koura (freshwater crayfish), berries and the occasional frog. Armed with sensitive bristles at the base of its bill and a highly developed sense of hearing, the kiwi can detect other birds and animals on its territory and will readily attack them with its claws. The females are bigger than the males and lay huge eggs, weighing a fifth of their body weight. After eighty days, the eggs hatch and the chicks live off the rich yolk; neither parent feeds them and they emerge from the nest totally independent. They sleep for up to twenty hours a day, which explains why they normally live to the age of 20 or 25.

Sadly there are probably fewer than 70,000 birds left and numbers in the wild are dropping. Kiwi are most easily seen in **kiwi houses** around the country in places such as Auckland Zoo, Otorohanga, Napier, Wellington and Hokitika. The best opportunities for seeing **kiwi in the wild** are:

Trounson Forest Northland (see p.196).
Tiritiri Matangi Auckland (see p.136).
Kapiti Island near Wellington (see p.256).

Okarito near Franz Josef (see p.667).
Mason Bay Stewart Island (see p.629).

KIWI SPECIES

Kiwi have traditionally been divided into three species – brown, little spotted and great spotted – but genetic research in the 1990s subdivided three new species off from the brown kiwi.

Great spotted kiwi Going by the Maori name *roa*, this is the largest kiwi species, with adult males averaging 2.4kg and females 3.3kg. They are the most rugged kiwi, and are happiest in subalpine regions with wet, mossy vegetation. Smaller birds range down into lowland and coastal beech forests. European explorers told stories of kiwi the size of turkeys with powerful spurs on their legs, whose call was the loudest. Their harsh home has also helped keep them relatively safe from mammalian pests. Numbers seem fairly stable around 17,000 birds, mostly in the northern half of the South Island.

Little spotted kiwi Also known as Kiwi Pukupuku, this is the smallest of the kiwi, with adults weighing 1100–1300g. The main population (around 1000 birds) is on Kapiti Island. Mellow and docile by nature, pairs often share daytime shelter, going their separate ways to feed, grunting to one another as they pass. They rarely probe for food, instead finding prey on the ground or in the forest litter. The best time to hear them is just after dark from high points around an island. Listen carefully for the male's shrill whistle and the female's gentle purr.

Brown kiwi These medium-sized kiwi are the most widespread, particularly in the central and northern North Island. They are famous for their big nose, bad temper and for being tough fighters of intruders on their territory. They live in a wide range of vegetation, including exotic forests and rough farmland on the North Island.

Rowi (aka Okarito brown). Originally considered a subspecies of the brown kiwi, this is the rarest kiwi, with only around 250 surviving in the wild, all in the 25,000-acre south Okarito Forest in South Westland. They're greyish in colour, often with patches of white feathers on their face. Males and females share incubation – unlike most kiwi, where the male does the lion's share.

Haast tokoeka These very rare birds only number around 300, unsurprisingly mostly around Haast in south Westland. They range from the shoreline to alpine tops but are most common around the bushline and in subalpine grasslands, even digging their burrows in snow.

Southern tokoeka Totalling around 30,000 and the most common kiwi, with a stable population on Stewart Island where there are no mustelids. Also found in Fiordland, they are one of the most primitive and the most communal, sometimes seen poking about along the tideline within a few metres of one another.

around Christmas. Another well-known red-blooming tree is the gnarled **rata**, found mostly in South Island forests but occasionally popping up around the North Island.

New Zealand is also known for its unusual family of pine species, or **podocarps**. One such is the majestic **rimu** (red pine), which grows to 60m, with small green flowers, red cones and tiny green or black fruit. It was heavily milled for its timber (the charcoal was mixed with oil and rubbed into Maori tattoo incisions) but is still widespread throughout mixed forests. Other podocarps include **matai** (black pine), **miro** (brown pine), **kahikatea** (white pine), and **totara**, which grow for up to a thousand years. The trunks were used by Maori to make war canoes while strips of the thick brown bark were woven into baskets.

Below the canopy of these trees you'll find an enormous variety of **tree ferns**, many hard to tell apart. The most famous, adopted as the national emblem, is the **ponga** (silver fern). Reaching about 10m in height, its long fronds are dull green on top and silvery white underneath.

The lowland forest is prime habitat for the bulk of New Zealand's endangered birds (see box below).

NEW ZEALAND'S RARE AND ENDANGERED WILDLIFE

New Zealand has 43 animals and many more plants on the IUCN Red List of Globally Threatened Species compiled by Birdlife International (🔾 redlist.org). Among developed countries, only the United States has more. Of the birds, some 22 percent of New Zealand species (the world's highest percentage) are regarded as globally threatened, including the following.

BIRDS

Bellbird (*korimako*) Relatively common in forest and shrub, the shy, pale green bellbird is noted for its distinctive musical call.

Black stilt (*kaki*) This thin black bird with round eyes and long red legs is incredibly shy – if you do see one in the wild, keep well away. It is one of the world's rarest wading birds. Usually found in swamps and beside riverbeds, the best place to see them is in the specially created reserve near Twizel (see p.580).

Blue duck (*whio*) Uniquely among ducks, the *whio* (sometimes known as the torrent duck) spends most of its time in mountain streams, where it dives for food. One of four endemic species with no close relatives anywhere in the world, you can spot it by its blue-grey plumage, with chestnut on both breast and flanks. It also has an unusual bill with a black flexible membrane along each side, and yellow eyes (as seen on the $10 note). Its Maori name represents the male bird's call.

Fantail (*piwakawaka*) Relatively common forest dweller, seen constantly opening and closing the tail that gives it its name. It often flies alongside walkers on trails, not out of a desire for company but to feed on the insects disturbed.

Kaka Large parrot closely related to the kea, though it does not venture from its favoured lowland forest environments. You can

recognize the bird by its colour: bronze with a crimson belly and underside of the tail and wings.

Kakapo The world's only flightless parrot, kakapo were once so widespread they were kept as pets. Now there are fewer than a hundred birds left, all on a couple of predator-free islands off the coast of Fiordland (off-limits to tourists).

Kakariki Bright green parakeets that come in yellow-crowned, red-crowned and the newly identified orange-crowned varieties. Found at most wildlife sanctuaries and on offshore Islands.

Kea The world's only alpine parrot. See box, p.560.

Kereru (a.k.a. *kukupa*) With adults weighing in at around 650g, this is the world's second-largest pigeon. Its metallic green, purple and bronze colouring and pure white breast is often seen flashing through low-lying forests with its distinctive noisy wing-slaps. It is a very ancient New Zealand species, which seems to have no relatives elsewhere.

Kiwi See box, p.809.

Kokako Rare slate-grey bird with distinctive blue wattles (patches of skin) on each cheek. An abysmal flyer, it lives mainly in protected forests and mainland islands where trapping keeps predator numbers

Rivers, lakes and wetlands

High mountains and plentiful rain mean that New Zealand is not short of rivers. Canterbury and the Waitaki sport distinctive **braided rivers**, their wide shingle beds and multiple channels providing a breeding ground for many birds, insects, fish and plants. Numerous lakes provide rich habitats; many of New Zealand's **wetlands**, on the other hand, have been drained for agriculture and property development, although some are preserved as national parks and scenic reserves. It's in low wetland areas that you're likely to come across the tallest of the native trees, the kahikatea (white pine), which reaches over 60m.

One bird you're bound to see in the vicinity of a lake is the **pukeko** (swamp hen), a bird still in the process of losing the power of flight. Also found in parts of Australia, the pukeko is mostly dark and mid-blue with large feet and an orange beak, and lets out a high-pitched screech if disturbed.

New Zealand is renowned for its freshwater fishing, with massive brown and rainbow **trout** and **salmon** swarming through the fast-flowing streams. All introduced species,

low. Closely related to the saddleback (see below) and featured on the $50 note.

Morepork (*ruru*) New Zealand's only native owl, this small brown bird is usually heard in the bush at night, and occasionally in town and city gardens. Both Maori and Pakeha names are supposed to represent its call.

New Zealand falcon (*karearea*) Seen occasionally in the north of the North Island but more often in the high country of the Southern Alps, Fiordland and the forests of Westland. New Zealand's only native raptor has a heavily flecked breast, chestnut thighs and a pointed head (as seen on the $20 note). Conservationists and winegrowers hope to reintroduce it to the Marlborough Plains where it may deter smaller, nuisance birds.

Robin There are three species of native robin, all glimpsed as they flit around the forest, often fearlessly pecking the dirt around your feet. They range from black with a cream or yellow breast to all black. Their prolonged and distinctive song lasts for up to thirty minutes, with only brief pauses for breath.

Saddleback (*tieke*) This rare but pretty thrush-sized bird is mostly black except for a tan-coloured saddle.

OTHER SPECIES

Tuatara This nocturnal lizard-like creature is a throwback to the age of dinosaurs and remains little changed over 260 million years. The tuatara lives on insects, small mammals and birds' eggs, a diet that sees them grow to 60cm in length and keeps them alive for well over a hundred years. Best viewed in a zoo or kiwi house.

Weta A relatively common grasshopper-like

Stitchbird (*hihi*) Small with a slightly curved beak and distinctive yellow and white patches on its sides. There are thought to be a few left, some on Kapiti Island and Tiritiri Matangi where you can see them using the feeding stations.

Takahe Rare turkey-sized bird once thought extinct (see p.755).

Tui With its white velvet throat and mostly green and purple velvet-like body, the tui is renowned for mimicking the calls of other birds and for its copious consumption of nectar and fruit. Its song has greater range than the bellbird and contains rather unmusical squeaks, croaks and strangled utterances.

Weka About the most common flightless native, the weka is a little like a kiwi but slimmer, far less shy, and generally dark brown with marked golden flecks, especially on its heavily streaked breast. Like the kiwi, the weka grubs around at dusk but can be seen regularly during the day: many are bold enough to approach trampers and take titbits from their hands. The bird's whistle is a loud and distinctive "kooo-li". There are four subspecies found in a variety of habitats throughout the country.

insect that has lived in lowland forests for 190 million years. Several species live in the bush but they're hard to spot so you're most likely to see them in caves or zoos. The most impressive species is the giant weta (*wetapunga*), which ranks as the heaviest insect in the world, weighing up to 71g, and is said to have been the inspiration for Ridley Scott's *Alien*.

these fish have adapted so well to their conditions that they grow much larger here than other places in the world; as a result, many native species have been driven out. Another delicacy found in New Zealand's waters is native **eels**, which, despite spending most of their lives in New Zealand rivers, migrate over 2000km to breed in the waters off Fiji.

Keeping anglers company along the riverbanks of the Mackenzie country and Canterbury are the perilously rare **black stilts** (see box, pp.810–811). The **common pied stilt**, a black-and-white bird, has been more successful in resisting introduced predators.

Another inhabitant of the Canterbury braided riverbank is the **wrybill**. This small white and grey bird uses its unique bent bill to turn over stones or pull out crustaceans from mud. The wrybill's close cousin, the **banded dotterel**, favours riverbanks, lakes, open land with sparse vegetation and coastal lagoons and beaches. A small, brown and white bird with a dark or black band around its neck, it breeds only in New Zealand, though it does migrate to Australia. Around fast-flowing streams you might see the increasingly rare **blue duck** (see box, pp.810–811).

The highlands

With most of the lowland forests cleared for farming, you need to get into the hills to appreciate the picture that greeted Maori and early European immigrants. The best bets are the Tongariro, Whanganui, Taranaki, Nelson Lakes, Arthur's Pass and Aoraki/ Mount Cook national parks – all cloaked in highland forests, particularly native beech trees, which, unlike northern hemisphere varieties, are evergreen. The 20m-high **mountain beech** (*tawhairauriki*) grows close to the top of the tree line and has sharp dark leaves and little red flowers. Also at high altitudes, often in mixed stands, are **silver beech** (*tawhai*), whose grey trunks grow up to 30m. Slightly lower altitudes are favoured by black and red beech. Often mixed in with them, the thin, straggly **manuka** (tea tree) grows in both alpine regions and on seashores.

New Zealand has five hundred species of flowering alpine plant that grow nowhere else in the world. Most famous is the large white-flowered yellow-centred **Mount Cook lily**, the world's largest buttercup. It flowers from November to January. On the high ground of the South Island is the **vegetable sheep**, a white hairy plant that grows low along the ground and, at a great distance, could just about be mistaken for a grazing animal.

Among alpine caves and rock crevices you might come across the black **alpine weta** (also known as the "Mount Cook flea"). Fewer species of birds inhabit the high country, but those that do are fascinating. In the Southern Alps you'll hear and see the raucous **kea** and perhaps the **New Zealand falcon** (for both see box, pp.810–811). Subalpine areas host smaller birds like the yellow and green **rock wren** and the **rifleman**, a tiny green and blue bird with spiralling flight. Such areas are also the natural home of two of the country's rarest birds, the **takahe** and the **kakapo** (see box, pp.810–811), neither seen outside tightly controlled areas.

The coast, islands and sea

New Zealand's indented coastline, battered by the Tasman Sea and the Pacific Ocean, is a meeting place for warm and cold currents, which makes for an environment suited to an enormous variety of fish. The warm currents, populated by hoki, kahawai, snapper, orange roughy and trevally, attract tropical fish like barracuda, marlin, sharks and tuna. The cold Antarctic currents bring blue and red cod, blue and red moki, and fish that can tolerate a considerable range of temperatures, such as the tarakihi, grouper and bass.

Marine mammals also grace these waters: the rare **humpback whale** is an occasional visitor to Kaikoura and Cook Strait, while **sperm whales** are common year-round in the deep sea trench near Kaikoura. **Orca** are seen regularly wherever there are dolphins, seals and other whales. Another frequent visitor is the **pilot whale**: up to two hundred pass by Farewell Spit each year; they're also seen in Cook Strait and the Bay of Plenty.

Common dolphins congregate all year round in the Bay of Plenty, Bay of Islands and around the Coromandel Peninsula. Of the three other species seen in New Zealand, **bottlenose dolphins** hang around Kaikoura and Whakatane most of the year, while **dusky dolphins**, the most playful, can be spotted near the shore of the Marlborough Sounds, Fiordland and Kaikoura from October to May. At any time of year you might get small schools of tiny **Hector's dolphins** accompanying your boat around Banks Peninsula, the Catlins and Invercargill.

Until recently there were few opportunities to see the Hooker's (or "New Zealand") **sea lion** except on remote Antarctic islands, but these rare animals, with their round noses and deep, wet eyes, now appear around the Catlins and Otago Peninsula. The larger New Zealand **fur seal** is in much greater abundance around the coast. You're most likely to come across them in the Sugar Loaf Marine Reserve off New Plymouth, around the Northland coast, in the Bay of Plenty, near Kaikoura, around the Otago Peninsula and in the Abel Tasman National Park. Both seals and sea lions can become aggressive during the breeding season (Dec–Feb), so remember to keep your distance (at least 30m). **Elephant seals** still breed in the Catlins; more extensive colonies exist on the offshore islands.

Also drawn by the coast's fish-rich waters are a number of visiting and native sea birds, the most famous being the graceful and solitary **royal albatross**, found on the Otago Peninsula and, just offshore, the smaller **wandering albatross**. A far more common sight is **little blue penguins**, which you'll see on any boat journey. The large **yellow-eyed penguin** is confined to parts of the east coast of the South Island, from Christchurch to the Catlins, while the **Fiordland crested penguin**, with its thick yellow eyebrows, is rarely seen outside Fiordland and Stewart Island. Other common seabirds include **gannets**, their yellow heads and white bodies unmistakable as they dive into shoals of fish; and **cormorants** and **shags** (mostly grey or black), usually congregating on cliffs and rocky shores. On and around islands you're also likely to see the **sooty shearwater, titi** (also known as "muttonbirds"), while the **black oystercatchers** and the black-and-white **variable oystercatchers**, both with orange cigar beaks and stooping gait, can be spotted searching in pairs for food on the foreshore.

SANCTUARIES, PARKS AND RESERVES

NORTH ISLAND

Bushy Park Wanganui (see p.238)
Goat Island Marine Reserve Northland (see p.145)
Kapiti Island near Wellington (see p.256)
Parry Kauri Park Northland (see p.154)
Poor Knights Islands Marine Reserve Northland (see p.157)
Pukaha Mount Bruce National Wildlife Centre Wairarapa (see p.402)

Rangitoto and Motutapu Islands Auckland (see p.121)
Tiritiri Matangi Auckland (see p.136)
Waipoua and Trounson Kauri Forests Northland (see p.196)
Zealandia: The Karori Sanctuary Experience Wellington (see p.425)

SOUTH ISLAND

Abel Tasman National Park (see p.473)
Aoraki/Mount Cook National Park (see p.574)
Fiordland National Park (see p.748)
Kura Tawhiti Castle Hill Reserve (see p.548)
Mason Bay Stewart Island (see p.629)

Motuara Island Marlborough Sounds (see p.453)
Oamaru Blue Penguin Colony (see p.542)
Orokonui Eco Sanctuary near Dunedin (see p.602)
Ulva Island off Stewart Island (see p.628)

Green issues

New Zealand comes with an enviable reputation for being **clean and green**, but this is more by accident than design. With a population of just over four million and a relatively short recorded history, you might expect human impact to be limited, but in less than a thousand years (mostly the last 150) humans have converted three-quarters of the land to farming and commercial forestry. Just ten percent of native forest remains, while generous winds and flushing rainfall conveniently dispose of much of the country's **pollution**.

Land usage

European settlers and, later, returning World War I veterans spent years taming steep bush-covered hills only suitable for raising sheep. These **farms** were profitable when wool and lamb prices were high, but in recent years have become uneconomic, thus some areas are being allowed to revert to their natural state, through the **tenure review** process, opening them up to the public as parks and reserves. Far more often, marginal lands are planted with introduced **pines** and logged every 25 years, reducing them to barren fields of stumps. Meanwhile, the ever-growing need for housing, roads and associated infrastructure gobbles up productive farmland and threatens fragile wetland.

Pollution

In large parts of New Zealand you can inhale lungfuls of fresh air and gaze at crystal-clear lakes and rivers, but all is not idyllic. Due to poor public transport New Zealand's **car ownership** rates are some of the highest in the world. New Zealand also imports huge numbers of secondhand cars from Japan that would not be allowed off the boat in other countries, and there is no requirement for regular vehicle emission testing.

Mountain streams and alpine tarns look so clean and fresh you'll be tempted to drink straight from them. In most cases this is fine, but the water might also harbour **giardia**, an intestinal parasite that can easily ruin your holiday. It is best to treat all drinking water. Freshwater rivers have recently become prey to the **didymo** algae (*Didymoshenia geminata*); boaties, anglers and kayakers should thoroughly clean all their gear before moving to another river to prevent it spreading. Additionally, modern intensive **farming** techniques, particularly the use of fertilizers, have polluted many rivers and streams. On the bright side, **industrial pollution** is a relatively minor issue, but only because there is little manufacturing.

The search for power

With a population growing ever more power-hungry and a lack of major investment over the last thirty years, New Zealand's power supplies are inadequate. Green **hydro** and **geothermal power** account for only two-thirds of electricity supply, compared to eighty percent in the late twentieth century, and even these clean generation methods are contentious: hydro reservoirs have destroyed natural habitats, especially riverbanks where threatened birds live. More geothermal stations are planned but over-extraction detrimentally affects geysers and boiling mud pools.

Building coal power stations (and converting to oil and gas stations) could make New Zealand electricity self-sufficient for over a hundred years, but at a considerable cost to the environment. Clean emission technologies are strenuously debated. **Wind energy** meets resistance from those complaining of noise and visual pollution, and installed capacity is very low. For decades no one dared suggest New Zealand should invest in **nuclear power**, but the power pinch and the need to follow Kyoto commitments is eroding long-held resistance.

The good news is that, despite government vacillation and the paramount interests of big business, an ever-increasing number of New Zealanders are working to preserve the country's unique environment.

Film and music

n the wake of the *Lord of the Rings* films, shot in New Zealand, the Kiwi film industry enjoyed one of its intermittent revivals, previously most notable from 1988–1994 when *The Navigator*, *An Angel at my Table*, *The Piano*, *Once Were Warriors* and *Heavenly Creatures* all gained international recognition. Yet, while the directors involved went on to eminence, the renaissance faded like a closing shot. As with most small countries, New Zealand lacks the resources, infrastructure and finances to sustain a large-scale film industry on a permanent basis. More often, the country is used as a relatively inexpensive backdrop for American TV series and for movies that need big outdoors scenes, such as *The Chronicles of Narnia*. As a result the local film industry is known mainly for technical backup – Weta Studios (see box, p.429) do technical design work and special effects for films all over the world – and provide extras. One of the notable exceptions is the one-man New Zealand film saviour, Peter Jackson. As with the *LOTR* trilogy, he has brought the *Hobbit* movie series to New Zealand; the first kicked off in 2011 and will be released in 2012. Whether Jackson can repeat the miracle of the *LOTR* films and kick-start another "golden age of Kiwi cinema" with less source material remains to be seen, but it's probably not wise to bet against him.

★ **An Angel at my Table** *Jane Campion, 1990*. Winner of the Special Jury prize at the Venice Film Festival. One of the most inspiring films New Zealand has produced, based on the brilliant autobiographies of Janet Frame (see p.819).

Bad Blood *Mike Newell, 1981*. A New Zealand/British collaboration set in New Zealand in World War II that relates the true story of Stan Graham, a Hokitika man who breaks the law by refusing to hand in his rifle. The ensuing events give rise to a discussion of the Kiwi spirit.

★ **Bad Taste** *Peter Jackson, 1988*. Winner of the Special Jury prize at the Paris Film Festival. Aliens visit earth to pick up flesh for an inter-galactic fast-food chain and have a wild old time.

Black Sheep *Jonathan King, 2006*. Multi-award winner at film festivals all over the globe, *Black Sheep* tells the story of sheep-phobic Harry, who returns to the family sheep farm where he discovers his brother has been playing with the sheep, genetically, and has inadvertently created man-eating weresheep.

★ **Came a Hot Friday** *Ian Mune, 1984*. The best comedy to come out of New Zealand, based on the novel by Ronald High Morrieson (see p.820), concentrating on two incompetent confidence tricksters whose luck runs out in a sleepy country town.

Crush *Alison Maclean, 1992*. Offbeat, angst-ridden psychological drama set around Rotorua, where the boiling mud and gushing geysers underline the tensions and sexual chaos that arise when an American femme fatale enters the lives of a New Zealand family.

Desperate Remedies *Peter Wells and Stewart Main, 1993*. Winner of the Certain Regard Award at Cannes, this visually stimulating movie comments wryly on the melodramatic intrigues and desires of a group of Victorians on the edge of Britain's empire.

Eagle Versus Shark *Taika Waititi, 2007*. A low-key, well-realized love story starring Jemaine "Flight of the Conchords" Clement, with similar quirky humour.

Fifty Ways of Saying Fabulous *Stewart Main, 2005*. Clever adaptation of the book of the same name (see p.819) that grabs the spirit of the original and rings out lots of laughs as well as poignancy.

★ **Forgotten Silver** *Peter Jackson, 2000*. Jackson, at his tongue-in-cheek best, constructs a fake documentary about a Kiwi movie pioneer, who invents film, sound, colour and the biblical epic, from flax, in the bush on the West Coast.

Goodbye Pork Pie *Geoff Murphy, 1980*. New Zealand's favourite comedy/road movie following the adventures of two young men in a yellow mini, the cops they infuriate, and the mixed bag of characters they encounter.

★ **Heavenly Creatures** *Peter Jackson, 1994*. Winner of the Silver Lion at Venice and an Oscar nominee. This account of the horrific Parker/Hulme matricide in the 1950s follows the increasingly self-obsessed life of two adolescent girls. An evocative and explosive film that brings all Jackson's subversive humour to bear on the strait-laced real world and the girls' fantastic imaginary one. Kate Winslet's film debut.

In My Father's Den *Brad McGann, 2004*. Depicts an emotional rough ride for an exhausted war journalist (Matthew Macfadyen) who returns home and becomes involved in an unexpected and engrossing journey of discovery that descends into murder mystery. From a novel by Maurice Gee (see p.819).

Insatiable Moon *Rosemary Riddell, 2010*. Winner at the Moondance International Film Festival, this deeply moving and totally engaging film was shot mainly round Ponsonby. It addresses issues of social evolution and progress, from the point of view of Arthur, street person and self-proclaimed Son of God. The community tries to close the care-in-the-community home in which Arthur lives and he becomes the catalyst of miraculous and magical events.

★ **The Navigator** *Vincent Ward, 1988*. A well-received competitor at Cannes, this atmospheric and stylistically inventive venture employs all Ward's favourite themes and characters, including the innocent visionary, in this case a boy who leads five men through time from a fourteenth-century Cumbrian village to New Zealand in the twentieth century in a quest to save their homes.

Once Were Warriors *Lee Tamahori, 1994*. A surging fly-on-the-wall-style comment on the economically challenged Maori situation in modern south Auckland, bringing to mind the British kitchen-sink dramas of the 1950s and 1960s. More a study of class than a full-blown racial statement, it revels in ordinary drudgery and despair, with a warts-and-all story about human weakness and strength of spirit against a background of urban decay. Based on a novel by Alan Duff (see p.819).

Operation 8 *Errol Wright and Abi King-Jones, 2011*. Theatrical documentary based around the real events of October 2007, when government agencies used the 2002 Terrorism Suppression Act as justification for arresting a number of Maori activists and its repercussions on wider society.

The Orator *Tusi Tamaese, 2011*. New Zealand-financed Samoan-language film, selected for the Sundance Film Festival and winner of the Venice Horizons Award, dealing with the unconventional life of a farmer and his efforts to protect his plantation and family.

Out of the Blue *Robert Sarkies, 2006*. Based on the true events of the Aramouna Massacre, in which thirteen people lost their lives to a local unemployed gun collector. A dark tale, concentrating on the heroism of the out-gunned seaside-town police and inhabitants.

Patu *Merata Mita, 1983*. A powerful documentar recording the year of opposition to the 1981 Springbo rugby tour of New Zealand, which goes some way t showing the extraordinary passions ignited.

★ **The Piano** *Jane Campion, 1993*. With Holly Hunter Harvey Keitel, Sam Neill and Anna Paquin. This moody winner of the Cannes Palme d'Or (and three Oscars made Campion bankable in Hollywood. Its mixture o grand scenes and personal trauma knowingly synthesize paperback romance, erotica and Victorian melodrama – and includes Keitel's stab at the worst Scottish accent o all time.

Predicament *Jason Stutter, 2010*. Based on the gold that comes from Ronald Hugh Morrieson's pen (see p.820), this is a slow-burn gothic, comedy thriller that relishes in its slick black content.

River Queen *Vincent Ward, 2005*. Production problems on the Whanganui River saw Ward depart before the project was finished, but what's left is a beautifully shot, over-simplified and uneven film worth a look just for the locations.

★ **Scarfies** *Robert Sarkies, 2000*. A darkly funny story about students taking over a deserted house in Dunedin only to discover a massive dope crop in the basement. Things get progressively more unpleasant when the dope grower returns.

Sleeping Dogs *Roger Donaldson, 1977*. Perhaps the birth of the real New Zealand film industry, based on C.K. Stead's book *Smith's Dream*. Sam Neill plays a paranoid anti-hero hunted by repressive state forces. A slick thriller, which rushes to a violent conclusion.

Two Little Boys *Robert Sarkies, 2012*. Selected for the Berlin Film Festival, a typical Sarkies-style, black comedy that becomes ever blacker as two former friends, a hot meat pie and ginger cat lead to the premature death of a Scandinavian footballer.

The Ugly *Scott Reynold, 1996*. Shown at the 1997 Cannes Film Festival, and winner of rave reviews in the US, this edgy comment on incarceration, reform and mistrust revolves around a serial killer who has been locked away and wants to convince the world he is cured.

Utu *Geoff Murphy, 1983*. One of the official selections at Cannes, this portrays a Maori warrior in the late 1800s who sets out to revenge himself on the conquerors of New Zealand, in the form of a Pakeha farmer. A tense, well-acted representation of modern and historic issues.

Vigil *Vincent Ward, 1984*. A Cannes competitor, this dark, rain-soaked story portrays a young girl's sexual awakening and her negative reaction to a stranger who is trying to seduce her mother.

We're Here to Help *Jonothan Cullinane, 2007*. Inspiring film based on a true story about a man victimized by the Revenue Department who fought back and won.

CONTEMPORARY KIWI MUSIC

The country's musical traditions stretch back to the chants and instruments used by the earliest Maori arrivals (see p.785), and have been a defining part of the nation's culture ever since. These days Tiki Tane, once of Salmonella Dub, is pursuing a successful solo career using these Maori chants and cultural instruments to create a modern Maori sound, which is in turn being picked up and publicized because it is attractive to tourists.

Known for breaking new ground, the country has produced formative artists such as **Neil and Tim Finn**, first with the success of Split Enz, and later with Crowded House, as well as successful solo careers. Today, Neil's son, Liam Finn, is one of New Zealand's most talented singer-songwriters and multi-instrumentalists.

The new millennium saw an explosion of Kiwi roots, reggae, dub and electronica with Pacifica influences, which continues to be fundamental to minorities as a mode of expression, with artists such as Katchafire, Trinity Roots, Salmonella Dub, the Black Seeds and Fat Freddy's Drop among the greatest success stories.

More recently, there's a growing resurgence of hard-edge rock – from established names like the Mint Chicks, to the high-energy live shows of emerging Queenstown-based three-piece The Flaming Drivers.

During 2011, the primary trend in the Kiwi mainstream was electropop (Zowie, JGeek and the Geeks, Ruby Frost, and Kids of 88) and hip-hop artists (Ladi6, Ria, and Kidz in Space). Sitting somewhat uneasily alongside these are Gin Wigmore, a gutsy female vocalist imaginatively mixing Lady Gaga and Amy Winehouse, Midnight Youth, a modern straight-six rock band with early New York alternative roots, and The Naked and the Famous, an indie pop band in the mould of MGMT.

Perhaps the artist who truly provides the "soundtrack of the nation" is **Dave Dobbyn**. Best known outside the country for the catchy *Slice of Heaven*, recorded with the band Herbs (often considered New Zealand's unofficial national anthem), Dobbyn also formed the bands Th'Dudes and DD Smash and has had an enduring solo career. Several of his songs appear on *The Great New Zealand Songbook* (Sony; 2009), a double CD – "Last Century" and "This Century" – that showcases a diverse cross section of Kiwi artists. Unofficially, the most popular Kiwi anthem, which shows up at most special occasions, is the catchy *Why Does Love Do This To Me* by The Exponents.

Catching a **gig** is one of the best ways to tap into the country's music scene – the website ⓦ amplifier.co.nz lists upcoming shows, has downloads and sells CDs.

Whakataratara Paneke *Don C. Selwyn, 2001*. The Maori *Merchant of Venice*, with English subtitles, an ambitious home-grown film that brings much local acting talent to the screen in an involved, if overly long, epic.

★ **The World's Fastest Indian** *Roger Donaldson, 2005*.

Feel-good movie about old codger Burt Munro, who in real life proved you don't have to be young to achieve your dreams – though being barmy helps. Anthony Hopkins in the lead role is marvellous and even does a passable Invercargill accent.

Books

Kiwis publish extensively, including a disproportionate amount of glossy picture books, wildlife guides and things with "Middle Earth" in the title. Modern authors, inheritors of an increasingly confident tradition, regularly produce excellent novels, poems and factual material.

HISTORY, SOCIETY AND POLITICS

Carol Archie and Hineani Melbourne (eds) *Maori Sovereignty: The Maori Perspective*; and its companion volume *Maori Sovereignty: The Pakeha Perspective*. Everyone from grass-roots activists to statesmen gets a voice in these two volumes, one airing the widely divergent Maori visions of sovereignty, the other covering equally disparate Pakeha views. They assume a good understanding of Maori structures and recent New Zealand history but are highly instructive nonetheless.

Mark Beehre *Men Alone – Men Together*. Photographer and oral historian Mark Beehre documents the diverse lives of 45 gay men, recounting key events in their lives and those in New Zealand's social history before, during and after homosexual law reform.

James Belich *The New Zealand Wars*. Well-researched, in-depth study re-examining the Victorian and Maori interpretations of the colonial wars. A book for committed historians. *Paradise Reforged* is a history of New Zealanders from 1880 to 2000, concentrating on their relationship with the outside world.

Alistair Campbell *Maori Legends*. A brief, accessible retelling of selected stories with some evocative illustrations.

R.D. Crosby *The Musket Wars*. Account of the massive nineteenth-century upsurge in inter-*iwi* conflict, exacerbated by the introduction of the musket, which led to the death of 23 percent of the Maori population, a proportion greater even than that suffered by Russia in World War II.

Alan Duff *Out of the Mist and Steam*. A vivid memoir of the *Once Were Warriors* author's life that falls short of autobiography, but gives the reader a good idea of the basis of inspiration for his novels.

A.K. Grant *Corridors of Paua*. A light-hearted look at the turbulent and fraught political history of the country from 1984 to the introduction of MMP in 1996.

Mark Inglis *Legs on Everest*. In 1982 Mount Cook Search and Rescue mountaineer Inglis became stuck in an ice cave for 14 days, losing both legs below the knees to frostbite. In 2006, on artificial limbs, he was the first double amputee to climb to the summit of Mount Everest. An inspirational read.

Hamish Keith *The Big Picture: A History of New Zealand Art from 1642*. A fascinating and rewarding tome for anybody interested in the progression from early Maori art through European influence to today's fusion of styles.

★ **Michael King** *The Penguin History of New Zealand*. Published in 2003, this is a highly readable general history of New Zealand, from Maori oral history to uneasy Maori–Pakeha relations and the Maori renaissance. *Death of Rainbow Warrior* is a brilliant account of the farcical, and ultimately tragic, efforts of the French secret service to sabotage Greenpeace's campaign against French nuclear testing.

★ **Claudia Orange** *The Story of the Treaty*. A concise illustrated exploration of the history and myths behind what many believe to be the most important document in New Zealand history, the Treaty of Waitangi.

Margaret Orbell *A Concise Encyclopaedia of Maori Myth and Legend*. A comprehensive rundown on many tales and their backgrounds that rewards perseverance, though a little dry.

Jock Phillips *A Man's Country? The Image of the Pakeha Male*. Classic treatise on mateship and the Kiwi bloke, an exploration of formative pioneering years, rugby, wartime camaraderie and the family-man ideal.

Anne Salmond *Amiria: The Life Story of Maori Women*. Reprinted classic describing the traditional values passed on to the author, set against a background of tribal history and contemporary race relations.

D.C. Starzecka (ed) *Maori Art and Culture*. A kind of Maori culture primer, with concise and interesting coverage of Maori history, culture, social structure, carving and weaving.

K. Taylor and P. Moloney *On the Left: Essays on Socialism in New Zealand*. Comprehensive collection of political essays spanning over a century that shows why New Zealand society has such a strong egalitarian spine.

Chris Trotter *No Left Turn*. Wonderful episodic history of New Zealand that convincingly argues that the country has been continuously shaped by "greed, bigotry and right-wing politics".

Dorothy Urlich Cloher *Hongi Hika*. Compelling biography dealing with the foremost Maori leader at the time of the first contact between Maori and the Europeans, and his subsequent participation in the Musket Wars.

FICTION

Graeme Aitken *Fifty Ways of Saying Fabulous*. Extremely funny book about burgeoning homosexuality in a young farm boy, who lives in a world where he is expected to clean up muck and play rugby.

Eric Beardsley *Blackball 08*. Entertaining and fairly accurate historical novel set in the West Coast coal-mining town of Blackball during New Zealand's longest labour dispute.

★ **Graham Billing** *Forbush and the Penguins*. Described as the first serious novel to come out of Antarctica, this is a compelling description of one man's lonely vigil over a colony of penguins.

Samuel Butler *Erewhon*. Initially set in the Canterbury high country (where Butler ran a sheep station), but increasingly devoted to a satirical critique of mid-Victorian Britain.

Nigel Cox *Tarzan Presley*. Amusing reworking of the Tarzan myth where the hero grows up in New Zealand and then becomes the king of rock'n'roll – nothing if not ambitious.

★ **Ian Cross** *The God Boy*. Widely considered to be New Zealand's equivalent to *The Catcher in the Rye*, about a young boy trapped between two parents who hate each other and the violent consequences.

★ **Barry Crump** *A Good Keen Man; Hang on a Minute Mate; Bastards I Have Met; Forty Yarns, The Adventures of Sam Cash and a Song*. Just a few of the many New Zealand bushman books by the Kiwi equivalent of Banjo Paterson, who writes with humour, tenderness and style about the male-dominated world of hunting, shooting, fishing, drinking, and telling stories. Worth reading for a picture of a now-past New Zealand lifestyle.

Alan Duff *Once Were Warriors*. Shocking and violent social-realist book set in 1970s south Auckland and adapted in the 1990s for Lee Tamahori's film of the same name. Well intentioned and passionate.

Laurence Fearnley *The Hut Builder*. Mannered fiction concerning the life of a Kiwi poet, whose work never makes an appearance, and who happens to climb Mt Cook with Edmund Hillary.

★ **Janet Frame** *An Angel at My Table*. Though one of New Zealand's most accomplished novelists, Frame is perhaps best known for this three-volume autobiography, dramatized in Jane Campion's film, which with wit and a self-effacing honesty gives a poignant insight into both the author and her environment. Her superb novels and short stories use humour alongside highly disturbing combinations of events and characters to overthrow readers' preconceptions. For starters, try *Faces in the Water*, *Scented Gardens for the Blind*, *Towards Another Summer* and *Owls Do Cry*.

Maurice Gee *Crime Story; Going West; Prowlers; The Plumb Trilogy*. Novels from an underrated but highly talented writer. Despite the misleadingly light titles, Gee's focus is social realism, taking an unflinching, powerful look at motivation and unravelling relationships.

★ **Patricia Grace** *Potiki*. Poignant, poetic and exquisitely written tale of a Maori community redefining itself while its land is threatened by coastal development. *Baby No Eyes* is a magical weaving of real events with stories of family history told from four points of view. *Dogside Story*, shortlisted for the 2001 Booker Prize, is a wonderful story about the power of the land and the strength of *whanau* at the turn of the millennium. *Tu* is an astonishing novel about the Maori Battalion fighting in Italy in World War II, drawn from the experiences of the author's father and other relatives.

Peter Hawes *Leapfrog with Unicorns* and *Tasman's Lay*. Two from an unsung hero, cult figure and probably only member of the absurdist movement in New Zealand, who writes with great energy, wit and surprising discipline about almost anything that takes his fancy. Hawes has also written the not-to-be-missed *Inca Girls Aren't Easy*, a series of joyous, sad and slippery tales, under the name W.P. Hearst. A brilliant late addition to Hawes' eccentric canon, *Royce, Royce the People's Choice*, is a sort of *Old Man and the Sea* mixed with *Moby Dick*.

★ **Keri Hulme** *The Bone People*. The winner of the 1985 Booker Prize, and an extraordinary first novel, set along the wild beaches of the South Island's West Coast. Mysticism, myth and earthy reality are transformed into a haunting tale peopled with richly drawn characters.

★ **Witi Ihimaera** *Bulibasha – King of the Gypsies*. The best introduction to one of the country's finest Maori authors. A rollicking good read, energetically exploring the life of a rebellious teenager in 1950s rural New Zealand – it's an intense look at adolescence, cultural choices, family ties and the abuse of power, culminating in a masterful twist. Look out also for *The Matriarch* and *The Uncle Story*, *Whale Rider* (adapted into a highly successful film) and *Star Dancer* by the same author.

Lloyd Jones *Mister Pip*. Intriguing 2007 Booker-shortlisted novel dealing with an unreported war on a remote South Pacific island where the schoolchildren's futures are entwined with a boy called Pip and a man named Dickens. Jones' 2009 collection of short stories, *The Man In The Shed*, showcases his sharp observations about contemporary NZ life.

Shonagh Koea *The Grandiflora Tree*. A savagely witty yet deeply moving study of the conventions of widowhood, with a peculiar love story thrown in. First novel from a journalist and short-story writer renowned for her astringent humour.

★ **Katherine Mansfield** *The Collected Stories of Katherine Mansfield*. All 73 short stories sit alongside fifteen unfinished fragments in this 780-page tome of concise, penetrating examinations of human behaviour in apparently trivial situations, often transmitting a painfully pessimistic view of the world – startlingly modern considering when they were written in the early twentieth-century..

Craig Marriner Stonedogs. Frenetic, feral, culturally fraught tale of gang-controlled drug running between Rotorua, Auckland and Northland, portraying "a New Zealand the tourists and executives had better pray they never stumble upon".

★ **Ngaio Marsh** Opening Night; Artists in Crime; Vintage Murder. Just a selection from the doyenne of New Zealand crime fiction, who since 1934 has been airing her Anglophile sensibilities and killing off innumerable individuals in the name of entertainment, before solving the crimes with Inspector Allen. Perfect mindless reading matter for planes, trains and buses.

Owen Marshall Drybread. Sparingly written novel set between Christchurch and Central Otago that examines love and loss through its two protagonists: a mother returning to New Zealand to flee a court order from the US and an emotionally scarred local journalist pursuing her story.

★ **Ronald Hugh Morrieson** Came a Hot Friday. Superb account of the idiosyncrasies of country folk and the two smart spielers who enter their lives, in a visceral gothic comedy thriller focusing on crime and sex in a small town. Also worth checking out are The Scarecrow, Predicament and Pallet on the Floor, all of which reveal Morrieson to have been the outstanding genius of this very New Zealand take on the genre.

Frank Sargeson The Stories of Frank Sargeson. Though not well known outside New Zealand, Sargeson is a giant of Kiwi literature. His writing, from the 1930s to the 1980s, is incisive and sharply observed, with dialogue true to the metre of New Zealand speech. This work brings together some of his finest short stories. Once is Enough, More than Enough and Never Enough! make up the complete autobiography of a man sometimes even more colourful than his characters; Michael King wrote a fine biography, Frank Sargeson: A Life.

★ **Maurice Shadbolt** Strangers and Journeys. On publication in 1972 this became a defining novel in New Zealand's literary ascendancy and its sense of nationhood. A tale of two families, with finely wrought characters, whose lives interweave through three generations – very New Zealand, very human and not overly epic. Later works, which consolidated Shadbolt's reputation, include Monday's Warriors, Season of the Jew and The House of Strife.

C.K. Stead The Singing Whakapapa. Highly regarded author of many books and critical essays who is little known outside New Zealand and Australia. This powerful novel focuses on an early missionary and a dissatisfied modern descendant searching for meaning in his own life. All Visitors Ashore is a masterpiece based around the harbourfront strike of 1951 and slyly alluding to Stead's literary contemporaries, while Mansfield is an evocative fictional musing about New Zealand's most famous short-story writer.

★ **Damien Wilkins** The Miserables. One of the best novels to come out of New Zealand, shorn of much of the colonial baggage of many writers and surprisingly mature for a first novel, it sharply evokes middle-class New Zealand life from the 1960s to the 1980s through finely wrought characters.

ANTHOLOGIES

Warwick Brown 100 New Zealand Artists. Companion to the Picador Book of Contemporary New Zealand Fiction, but also allows room for sculptors, printmakers, photographers and graphic artists.

James Burns (ed) Novels and Novelists 1861–1979, a Bibliography. A sweeping and comprehensive introduction to the history of the New Zealand novel and the authors who made it a powerful art form.

Bill Manhire (ed) 100 New Zealand Poems. Manageable selection that provides an excellent introduction to the poetry of the nation and the characters who penned the rhymes and verses.

★ **Owen Marshall** (selected by) Essential New Zealand Short Stories. A representative collection of fascinating tales by some of New Zealand's best-known and finest authors, including Frame, Ihimera, Mansfield, Shadbolt, Stead and Gee.

★ **Ian Wedde and Harvey McQueen** (eds) The Penguin Book of New Zealand Verse. A comprehensive collection of verse from the earliest European settlers to contemporary poets, and an excellent introduction to Kiwi poetry; highlights are works by James K. Baxter, Janet Frame, C.K. Stead, Sam Hunt, Keri Hulme, Hirini Melbourne and Apirana Taylor.

REFERENCE AND SPECIALIST GUIDES

Angie Errigo Rough Guide to The Lord of the Rings. An essential companion for background on the whole J.R.R. Tolkien phenomenon with exhaustive detail about the man, the books, the films, fan websites and even the books' influence on 1970s prog rock.

Rosemary George The Wines of New Zealand. Entertaining and informative look at New Zealand's most important wine regions, the history, the people and the product.

John Kent North Island Trout Fishing Guide and South Island Trout Fishing Guide. Laden with information on access, seasons and fishing style, and illustrated with maps of the more important rivers.

FLORA, FAUNA AND THE ENVIRONMENT

J.H. Brathwaite *Native Birds of New Zealand*. Brilliant colour photographs and lots of information pinpointing thirty rare birds that, with a little effort and some patience, you can observe while travelling around.

Garth Cartwright *Sweet As: Journeys in a New Zealand Summer*. Brickbats and bouquets are liberally handed out (often about different aspects of the same place) as the London-based music journalist visits his boyhood haunts and the wider Kiwi landscape. Art, music, politics and fish and chips are the main themes.

★ **Andrew Crowe** *Which Native Tree?* Great little book, ideal for identifying New Zealand's common native trees – though not tree ferns – with diagrams of tree shape, photos of leaves and fruit and an idea of geographic extent.

Julian Bateman *Guide to Wild New Zealand*. Fabulous collection of all the flora and fauna you are ever likely to encounter in an easy-to-manage package – the perfect field guide for experts and amateurs alike.

Susanne & John Hill *Richard Henry of Resolution Island*. Comprehensive and very readable account of a man widely regarded as New Zealand's first conservationist. The book also serves as a potted history of this underpopulated area of Fiordland, peopled by many of the key explorers.

★ **Geoff Moon** *The Reed Field Guide to New Zealand Birds*. Excellent colour-reference book, with ample detail for species identification: *The Reed Field Guide to New Zealand Wildlife*, by the same author, is also stuffed with colour photos.

Rod Morris & Hal Smith *Wild South: Saving New Zealand's Endangered Birds*. A fascinating companion volume to a 1980s TV series following a band of dedicated individuals trying to preserve a dozen of New Zealand's wonderfully exotic bird species, including the kiwi, kakapo, takahe and kea.

Neville Peat *Manapouri Saved*. Full and heartening coverage of one of New Zealand's earliest environmental battles when, in the 1960s, a petition signed by ten percent of the country succeeded in persuading the government to cancel its hydroelectric plans for Lake Manapouri.

Kerry-Jayne Wilson *Flight of the Huia*. Focusing on Jurassic frogs and bizarre creatures such as the Alpine parrot, this book studies faunal change in New Zealand and current conservation issues.

TRAMPING

Pearl Hewson *New Zealand's Great Walks*. Hewson is a no-nonsense DOC officer working out of the Wellington office and what she doesn't know about the Great Walks isn't worth knowing. This is a practical, concise guide that concentrates her experiences into a useful aid to trampers. *Moir's Guide*. Probably the most comprehensive guide to tramping in the South Island, divided into two volumes: North, covering hikes between Lake Ohau and Lake Wakatipu; and South, which concentrates on walks around the southern lakes and fiords including the Kepler Track, plus the less popular Dusky and George Sound tracks.

CYCLING AND ADVENTURE SPORTS

Mike Bhana *New Zealand Surfing Guide*. Pragmatic handbook to the prime surf spots around the New Zealand coast, with details on access, transport, the best wind and tide conditions and expected swells.

★ **Graham Charles** *New Zealand Whitewater: 125 Great Kayaking Runs*. A comprehensive and entertaining guide to New Zealand's most important kayaking rivers with maps and details on access, supplemented by quick reference panels with grades, timings, and handy tips like which rapids not to even think about running.

Bruce Ringer *New Zealand by Bike*. The definitive Kiwi cycle-touring guide, with fourteen regional tours (with many side trips) that can be knitted together into a greater whole. Plenty of maps and altitude profile diagrams.

Nigel Rushton *Pedallers' Paradise*. Separate lightweight North Island and South Island volumes covering recommended routes.

Marty Sharp *A Guide to the Ski Areas of New Zealand*. Exactly what you'd expect, with full descriptions of the fields complete with tow plans and information on access, local towns and ski rental.

Paul Simon and Jonathan Kennett *Classic New Zealand Mountain Bike Rides*. All you need to know about off-road biking in New Zealand, with details of over four hundred rides. Simon Kennett runs the ⓦ mountainbike .co.nz site.

Language

English and *te reo Maori*, the Maori language, share joint status as New Zealand's official languages, but on a day-to-day basis all you'll need is English, or its colourful Kiwi variant. All Maori speak English fluently, often slipping in numerous Maori terms that in time become part of everyday Kiwi parlance. Mainstream TV and radio coverage of any event that has significance to Maori is likely to be littered with words totally alien to foreigners, but well understood by Anglophone Kiwis. It is initially confusing, but with the aid of our glossary (see p.825) you'll soon find yourself using Maori terms all the time.

A basic knowledge of Maori pronunciation will make you more comprehensible and some understanding of the roots of place names can be helpful. You'll need to become something of an expert to appreciate much of the wonderful oral history, and stories told through *waiata* (songs), but learning a few key terms will enhance any Maori cultural events you may attend.

To many Brits and North Americans, **Kiwi English** is barely distinguishable from its trans-Tasman cousin, "Strine", sharing much of the same lexicon of slang terms, but with a softer accent. Australians have no trouble distinguishing the two accents, repeatedly highlighting the vowel shift which turns "bat" into "bet", makes "yes" sound like "yis" and causes "fish" to come out as "fush". There is very little regional variation; only residents of Otago and Southland – the southern quarter of the South Island – distinguish themselves with a rolled "r", courtesy of their predominantly Scottish forebears. Throughout the land, Kiwis add an upward inflection to statements, making them sound like questions; most are not, and to highlight those that are, some add the interrogative "eh?" to the end of the sentence, a trait most evident in the North Island, especially among Maori.

Maori

For the 50–100,000 native speakers and additional 100,000 who speak it as a second tongue, **Maori** is very much a living language. It is gaining strength all the time as both Maori and Pakeha increasingly appreciate the cultural value of *te reo*, a language central to *Maoritanga* and forming the basis of a huge body of magnificent songs, chants and legends, lent a poetic quality by its hypnotic and lilting rhythms.

Maori is a member of the Polynesian group of languages and shares both grammar and vocabulary with those spoken throughout most of the South Pacific. Similarities are so pronounced that Tupaia, a Tahitian crew member on Captain Cook's first Pacific voyage in 1769, was able to communicate freely with the Aotearoa Maori they encountered. The Treaty of Waitangi was written in both English and Maori, but *te reo* soon began to lose ground to the point where, by the late nineteenth century, its use was proscribed in schools. Maori parents keen for their offspring to do well in the Pakeha world frequently promoted the use of English, and Maori declined further, exacerbated by the mid-twentieth-century migration to the cities. The language reached its nadir in the 1970s when perhaps only ten percent of Maori spoke their language fluently. The tide began to turn towards the end of the decade with the inception of *kohanga reo* **pre-schools** (literally "language nests") where **Maoritanga** is taught and activities are conducted in Maori. Originally a Maori initiative, it has now crossed over and progressive Pakeha parents are increasingly introducing their kids to biculturalism at an early age.

Fortunate *kohanga reo* graduates can progress to the small number of state-funded Maori-language primary schools known as *kura kaupapa*. For decades, Maori has been taught as an option in secondary schools, and there are now state-funded tertiary institutions operated by Maori, offering graduate programmes in Maori studies.

The success of these programmes has bred a young generation of Maori-speakers frequently far more fluent than their parents who, determined to recover their heritage, are attending Maori evening classes. Legal parity means that Maori is now finding its way into officialdom too, with government departments all adopting Maori names and many government and council documents being printed in both languages. Maori-language **radio stations** are now commonplace in the northern half of the North Island where the majority of Maori live, but the real boost came in 2004 with the launching of **Maori Television**. Substantially government funded, it still has relatively low ratings but is well worth tuning into for a very different take on what's going on. Partly in English, partly in Maori and occasionally a synthesis of the two, there's a wonderful cross-fertilization of styles. You can expect everything from movies and sitcoms to discussion panels on Maori issues and lifestyle programmes such as *Kai Time on the Road* (a cooking and Maori food show), and an animated show for pre-schoolers.

In your day-to-day dealings you won't need **to speak Maori**, though both native speakers and Pakeha may well greet you with *kia ora* ("hi, hello"), or less commonly *haere mai* ("welcome"). On ceremonial occasions, such as *marae* visits, you'll hear the more formal greeting *tena koe* (said to one person) or *tena koutou katoa* (to a group).

Maori words used in place names are listed below, while those in common use are listed in the general glossary (see p.825). If you are interested in learning a little more, the best handy reference is Patricia Turoa's *The Collins Maori Phrase Book*, which has helpful notes on pronunciation, handy phrases and a useful Maori–English and English–Maori vocabulary.

MAORI PLACE NAMES

The following is a list of some of the most common words and elements you will see in **town and place names** throughout New Zealand.

Ao	Cloud	**Pae**	Ridge
Ara	Road or path	**Papa**	Flat, earth, floor
Awa	River or valley	**Patere**	Chants
Hau	Wind	**Puke**	Hill
Ika	Fish	**Puna**	Spring
Iti	Small	**Raki**	North
Kai	Food, or eat	**Rangi**	Sky
Kainga	Home, village	**Roa**	Long, high
Kare	Rippling	**Roto**	Lake
Kino	Bad	**Rua**	Hole, cave, pit, two
Ma	White, clear	**Runga**	Top
Manga	Stream	**Tahu**	Light
Manu	Bird	**Tai**	Sea
Mata	Headland	**Tane**	Man
Maunga	Mountain	**Tapu**	Sacred
Mihi	Speeches	**Tara**	Peak
Moana	Sea, lake	**Te**	The
Motu	Island or anything isolated	**Tomo**	Cave
Muri	End	**Wai**	Water
Nui	Big	**Waka**	Canoe
O	The place of	**Whanga**	Bay, body of water
One	Sand, beach	**Whenua**	Land or country
Pa	Fortified settlement		

Pronunciation

Pakeha – and consequently most visitors – may still have a distorted impression of Maori pronunciation, which is usually mutated into an anglicized form. Until the 1970s there was little attempt to get it right, but with the rise in Maori consciousness since the 1980s, coupled with a sense of political correctness, many Pakeha now make some attempt at Maori pronunciation. As a visitor you will probably get away with just about anything, but by sticking to a few simple rules and keeping your ears open, apparently unfathomable place names will soon trip off your tongue.

Maori was solely a spoken language before the arrival of British and French missionaries in the early nineteenth century, who transcribed it using only fifteen letters of the Roman alphabet. The eight **consonants**, h, **k**, **m**, **n**, **p**, r, t and **w**, are pronounced much as they are in English. The five **vowels** come in long and short forms; the long form is sometimes signified in print by a macron – a flat bar above the letter – but usually it is simply a case of learning by experience which sound to use. When two vowels appear together they are both pronounced, though substantially run together. For example, "Maori" should be written with a macron on the "a" and be pronounced with the first two vowels separate, turning the commonly used but incorrect "Mow-ree" into something more like "Maao-ri".

Here are a few **pronunciation** pointers to help you get it right:

- Long compound words can be split into syllables which all end in a vowel. Waikaremoana comes out as Wai-ka-re-mo-ana. Scanning our list of place-name elements should help a great deal.
- All syllables are stressed evenly, so it is not **Wai**-ka-re-mo-ana or Wai-ka-re-**mo**-ana but a flat Wai-ka-re-mo-ana.
- Maori words don't take an "s" to form a plural, so you'll find many plural nouns in this book – kiwi, tui, kauri, Maori – in what appears to be a singular form; about the only exception is Kiwis (as people), a Maori word wholly adopted into English.
- **Ng** is pronounced much as in "sing".
- **Wh** sounds either like an aspirated "f" as in "off", or like the "wh" in "why", depending on who is saying what and in which part of the country.

Glossary

ANZAC Australian and New Zealand Army Corps; every town in New Zealand has a memorial to ANZAC casualties from both world wars.

Aotearoa Maori for New Zealand, the land of the long white cloud.

Ariki Supreme chief of an *iwi*.

Bach (pronounced "batch") Holiday home, originally a bachelor pad at work camps and now something of a Kiwi institution that can be anything from shack to palatial waterside residence.

Back-blocks Remote areas.

Bludger Someone who doesn't pull their weight or pay their way, a sponger.

Bro Brother, term of endearment widely used by Maori.

Captain Cooker Wild pig, probably descended from pigs released in the Marlborough Sounds on Cook's first voyage.

Chilly bin Insulated cool box for carrying picnic supplies.

Choice Fantastic.

Chook Chicken.

Chunder Vomit.

Coaster (Ex-) resident of the West Coast of the South Island.

Cocky Farmer, comes in "Cow" and "Sheep" variants.

Crib South Island name for a *bach*.

Cuz or **Cuzzy** Short for cousin, see "bro".

Dag Wag or entertaining character.

Dairy Corner shop selling just about everything, open seven days and sometimes 24 hours.

Dob in Reporting one's friends and neighbours to the police; there is currently a dobber's charter encouraging drivers to report one another for dangerous driving.

DOC Department of Conservation. Operators of the national parks, conservation policy, track administration and much more.

Docket Receipt.

Domain Grassy reserve, open to the public.

EFTPOS Card-based debit system found in shops, bars and restaurants.

Feijoa Fleshy, tomato-sized fruit with melon-like flesh and a tangy, perfumed flavour.

Footie Rugby, usually union rather than league, never soccer.

Freezing works Slaughterhouse.

Godzone New Zealand, short for "God's own country".

Good as (gold) First rate, excellent.

Greasies Takeaway food, especially fish and chips.

Greenstone A type of nephrite jade known in Maori as *pounamu*.

Haka Maori dance performed in threatening fashion before All Blacks rugby games.

Handle Large glass of beer.

Hangi Maori feast cooked in an earth oven (see box, p.41).

Hapu Maori sub-tribal unit. Several make up an *iwi*.

Harakeke Flax.

Hard case See "dag".

Hogget The meat from a year-old sheep. Older and more tasty (though less succulent) than lamb, but not as tough as mutton.

Hollywood A faked or exaggerated sporting injury used to gain advantage.

Hongi Maori greeting, performed by pressing noses together.

Hoon Lout, yob or delinquent.

Hori Offensive word for a Maori.

Hot dog A battered sausage on a stick, dipped in tomato ketchup. What the rest of the world knows as a hot dog is known here as an American hot dog.

Hui Maori gathering or conference.

Iwi Largest of Maori tribal groupings.

Jafa Just Another Fucking Aucklander. Semi-derogatory term now (over)used as a noun. "He's a bloody Jafa".

Jandals Ubiquitous Kiwi footwear, thongs or flip-flops.

Jug Litre of beer.

Kiwifruit In New Zealand they are always called kiwifruit, never "kiwis". Golden-fleshed kiwifruit are also available, and less acidic than their green counterparts.

Lucked in In luck. What "Lucked out" means elsewhere in the world.

Lucked out Out of luck. The meaning completely reversed on its way across the Pacific.

Kai Maori word for food, used in general parlance.

Kaimoana Seafood.

Kainga Village.

Karanga Call for visitors to come forward on a *marae*.

Kaumatua Maori elders, old people.

Kawa-Marae Etiquette or protocol on a *marae*.

Kete Traditional basket made of plaited harakeke.

Kiore Polynesian rat.

kiwi The national bird and mascot of NZ, always set lower case.

Kiwi An alternative label for a New Zealander.

Koha Donation.

Kohanga Reo Pre-school Maori language immersion (literally "language nest").

Kuia Female Maori elder.

Kumara Sweet potato.

Kuri Polynesian dog, now extinct.

Lay-by Practice of putting a deposit on goods until they can be fully paid for.

Mana Maori term indicating status, esteem, prestige or authority, and in wide use among all Kiwis.

Manaia Stylized bird or lizard forms used extensively in Maori carving.

Manuhiri Guest or visitor, particularly to a *marae*.

Maoritanga Maori culture and custom, the Maori way of doing things.

Marae Place for conducting ceremonies in front of a meeting house – literally "courtyard". Also a general term for a settlement centred on the meeting house.

Mauri Life force or life principle.

Mere War club, usually of greenstone.

Metalled Graded road surface of loose stones found all over rural New Zealand.

MMP Mixed Member Proportional representation – New Zealand's electoral system.

Moko Old form of tattooing on body and face that has seen a resurgence among Maori.

Muttonbird Gull-sized sooty shearwater that was a major component of the pre-European Maori diet and tastes like oily and slightly fishy mutton – hence the name.

Ngati Tribal prefix meaning "the descendants (or people) of". Also Ngai and Ati.

OE Overseas experience, usually a year spent abroad by Kiwis in their early twenties.

Pa Fortified village of yore, now usually an abandoned terraced hillside.

Paddock Field.

Pakeha A non-Maori, usually white and not usually expressed with derogatory intent. Literally "foreign" though it can also be translated as "flea" or "pest". It may also be a corruption of *pakepakeha*, which are mythical human-like beings with fair skins.

Pashing Kissing or snogging.

Patu Short fighting club.

Paua The muscular foot of the abalone, often minced and served as a fritter, while the wonderful iridescent shell is used for jewellery and decoration.

Pavlova Meringue dessert with a fruit and cream topping.

Pike out To chicken out or give up.

Piss Beer.

Pissed Drunk.

Podocarp Family of pine, native to New Zealand including rimu, kahikatea, matai, miro, totara etc.

Pohutukawa Gnarled native tree found around the coast of the upper North Island. Blooms bright red in mid-December and is sometimes known as New Zealand's Christmas Tree.

Poms Folk from Britain; not necessarily offensive.

Pounamu New Zealand greenstone, a unique type of jade.

Powhiri Traditional welcome onto a *marae*.

Puku Maori for stomach, often used as a term of endearment for someone amply endowed.

Puha Maori term for "sow thistle", a leafy plant traditionally gathered by Maori and eaten like spinach.

Rangatira General term for a Maori chief.

Rapt Well-pleased.

Rattle your dags Hurry up.

Root Vulgar term for sex.

Rooted To be very tired or beyond repair, as in "she's rooted, mate" – your car is irreparable.

Rough as guts Uncouth, roughly made or operating badly, as in "she's running rough as guts, mate".

Sealed road Bitumen-surfaced road.

Section Block of land usually surrounding a house.

She'll be right Everything will work out fine.

Shout To buy a round of drinks or generally to treat folk.

Skull To knock back beer quickly.

Smoko Tea break.

Snarler, snag Sausage.

Squiz A look, as in "Give us a squiz".

Stoked Very pleased.

Sweet Cool.

Taiaha Long-handled club.

Tall poppy Someone who excels. "Cutting down tall poppies" is to bring overachievers back to earth – every Kiwi's perceived duty.

Tamarillo Slightly bitter, deep-red fruit, often known as a tree tomato.

Tane Man.

Tangata whenua The people of the land, local or original inhabitants.

Tangi Mourning or funeral.

Taniwha Fearsome water spirit of Maori legend.

Taonga Treasures, prized possessions.

Tapu Forbidden or taboo. Frequently refers to sacred land.

Te reo Maori Maori language.

Tikanga Maori customs, ethics and etiquette – the Maori way of doing things.

Tiki Maori pendant depicting a distorted human figure.

Tiki tour Guided tour.

Togs Swimming costume.

Tohunga Maori priests, experts in *Maoritanga*.

True Left On the left facing downstream.

True Right On the right when facing downstream.

Tukutuku Knotted latticework panels decorating the inside of a meeting house.

Tupuna Ancestors; of great spiritual importance to Maori.

Ute Car-sized pick-up truck, short for "utility".

Varsity University.

Vegemite or **Marmite** dark, savoury yeast-extract spreads. There's always debate between those that love Vegemite (Australian) and those that prefer Kiwi Marmite – sweeter and more appealing than its British equivalent – and of course those that loathe all the above.

Wahine Woman.

Waiata Maori action songs.

Wairua Spirit.

Waka Maori canoe.

Waratah Stake, a term used to describe snow poles on tramps.

Wero Challenge before entering a *marae*.

Whakapapa Family tree or genealogical relationship.

Whanau Extended family group.

Whare Maori for a house.

Whare runanga Meeting house.

Whare whakairo Carved house.

Wop-wops Remote areas.

Small print and index

829 Small print

830 About the authors

832 Index

844 Map symbols

A ROUGH GUIDE TO ROUGH GUIDES

Published in 1982, the first Rough Guide – to Greece – was a student scheme that became a publishing phenomenon. Mark Ellingham, a recent graduate in English from Bristol University, had been travelling in Greece the previous summer and couldn't find the right guidebook. With a small group of friends he wrote his own guide, combining a highly contemporary, journalistic style with a thoroughly practical approach to travellers' needs.

The immediate success of the book spawned a series that rapidly covered dozens of destinations. And, in addition to impecunious backpackers, Rough Guides soon acquired a much broader readership that relished the guides' wit and inquisitiveness as much as their enthusiastic, critical approach and value-for-money ethos.

These days, Rough Guides include recommendations from budget to luxury and cover more than 200 destinations around the globe, as well as producing an ever-growing range of eBooks and apps.

Visit **roughguides.com** to see our latest publications.

Rough Guide credits

Editor: Harry Wilson
Layout: Nikhil Agarwal
Cartography: Deshpal Dabas
Picture editors: Mark Thomas, Michelle Bhatia & Rhiannon Furbear
Proofreader: Jan McCann
Managing editors: Keith Drew & Kathryn Lane
Assistant editor: Jalpreen Kaur Chhatwal
Production: Gemma Sharpe
Cover design: Mark Thomas & Nikhil Agarwal
Photographer: Paul Whitfield

Editorial assistant: Eleanor Aldridge
Senior pre-press designer: Dan May
Design director: Scott Stickland
Travel publisher: Joanna Kirby
Digital travel publisher: Peter Buckley
Reference director: Andrew Lockett
Operations coordinator: Becky Doyle
Publishing director (Travel): Clare Currie
Commercial manager: Gino Magnotta
Managing director: John Duhigg

Publishing information

This eighth edition published September 2012 by
Rough Guides Ltd,
80 Strand, London WC2R 0RL
11, Community Centre, Panchsheel Park,
New Delhi 110017, India
Distributed by the Penguin Group
Penguin Books Ltd,
80 Strand, London WC2R 0RL
Penguin Group (USA)
375 Hudson Street, NY 10014, USA
Penguin Group (Australia)
250 Camberwell Road, Camberwell,
Victoria 3124, Australia
Penguin Group (NZ)
67 Apollo Drive, Mairangi Bay, Auckland 1310,
New Zealand
Penguin Group (South Africa)
Block D, Rosebank Office Park, 181 Jan Smuts Avenue,
Parktown North, Gauteng, South Africa 2193
Rough Guides is represented in Canada by Tourmaline
Editions Inc. 662 King Street West, Suite 304, Toronto,
Ontario M5V 1M7
Printed in Singapore by Toppan Security Printing Pte. Ltd.

© Laura Harper, Catherine Le Nevez, Tony Mudd &
Paul Whitfield 2012
Maps © Rough Guides
No part of this book may be reproduced in any form
without permission from the publisher except for the
quotation of brief passages in reviews.
848pp includes index
A catalogue record for this book is available from the
British Library
ISBN: 978-1-40539-000-2

MIX
Paper from
responsible sources
FSC™ C018179

Help us update

We've gone to a lot of effort to ensure that the eighth edition of **The Rough Guide to New Zealand** is accurate and up-to-date. However, things change – places get "discovered", opening hours are notoriously fickle, restaurants and rooms raise prices or lower standards. If you feel we've got it wrong or left something out, we'd like to know, and if you can remember the address, the price, the hours, the phone number, so much the better.

Please send your comments with the subject line "**Rough Guide New Zealand Update**" to ✉ mail@uk. roughguides.com. We'll credit all contributions and send a copy of the next edition (or any other Rough Guide if you prefer) for the very best emails.

Find more travel information, connect with fellow travellers and book your trip on 🌐 roughguides.com

ABOUT THE AUTHORS

Catherine Le Nevez first travelled around New Zealand on childhood holidays, and she's been returning at every opportunity since, completing her Doctorate of Creative Arts in Writing, Masters of Professional Writing and post-grad qualifications in Editing and Publishing along the way, and authoring/co-authoring dozens of guidebooks worldwide, in addition to newspaper and magazine articles. Wanderlust aside, New Zealand remains one of her favourite destinations on earth.

Tony Mudd has been an author on the *Rough Guide to New Zealand* since the first edition; he also writes and takes photographs for newspapers and magazines and designs web pages and mobile phone apps. In his spare time he writes fiction and poetry and paddles the waterways of Britain in a canoe he built with his wife.

Paul Whitfield spent his formative years studying and working in New Zealand and after some time living in Britain co-authored the original edition of the *Rough Guide to New Zealand*. Since then he has moved back to his adopted home and spends his time updating several Rough Guides and doing photography commissions around the world. Until recently he also went kayaking, rock climbing and mountain biking though the birth of his daughter has put a temporary (?) hold on that.

Acknowledgements

Catherine Le Nevez: Thanks first and foremost to Julian, and to all the locals, fellow travellers and tourism professionals who provided insights and assistance along the way. Huge gratitude goes out once again to Tony Lyons and everyone at the aptly named Ace Rental Cars (and *The Great New Zealand Songbook* for providing the soundtrack); my "Kiwi bro" Carsten for the snow storm warning, insider tips and great times; and to Paulie – as well as Lloyd for the memorable welcome to the *iwi* in Rotorua, and everyone at the Kiwi home-from-Kiwi home Freedom Pub in Paris. At Rough Guides, cheers to editor Harry Wilson, and to my co-authors Paul and Tony. As ever, *merci encore* to my family.

Tony Mudd: Thanks to all the operators I visited, people I stayed with, those that provided invaluable help along the way and the dedicated staff of the NZ i-Sites, particularly Cheryl at Destination Northland and Ania at Positively Wellington. Special mention must be made of the hospitality of Gerry and Sally at The Great Ponsonby, Graeme and Jan in Bay Cottages, Kaikoura (thanks for all the fish!), the YHA team who always provide aid and a bed when necessary, Tony Lyons of Ace Rentals, and Maia for

help with the music section. Much gratitude goes to the editor, as I fell ill and he has taken up the burden. Most of all I'd like to thank Alison my wife for tireless encouragement, enthusiasm, love and taking world-class photographs – I would not be able to do it without her. Thanks to other Rough Guides staff who have contributed, and to my fellow authors. Finally a big thank you to all the friends and accomplices who make life fun.

Paul Whitfield: I'd like to thank everyone I met on research trips throughout the land, especially those who suggested great restaurants to check out, waxed lyrical about hotels, hostels and shared experiences. Special thanks go out to the helpful and knowledgeable staff of i-SITEs and visitor centres across the land, particularly Trudi in Te Anau. Cheers too to friends who have sussed out top places and passed on their impressions, especially Phil & Wendy in Arrowtown for their invaluable guidance over balmy dinners and good Central Otago wine on the back deck. Lastly, huge gratitude is due to Marion for helping with the restaurant sampling (not such a chore), and hanging in there through my long absences while she was pregnant.

Readers' letters

Thanks to all the readers who have taken the time to write in with comments and suggestions (and apologies if we've inadvertently omitted or misspelt anyone's name):

Johanna Adolfsson, Sarah and Graham Bell, Joy and Paul Biggin, S R Blench, Geoff Chadwick, Paul Compton, Fergus Day, Allan and Trish Duncan, Anne-Katrin Fein, Annelie Fitzgerald, Griet Gevers, Peter Gilbert, Christopher Green, Lena Grempel, Brooke Hargreaves, Mike Hart, Peter Hoare,

K Hotham, Brian King, Alfred Jacobsen, Richard Johnson, Daniel Kolobaric, Larry Klein, Sarah Lyle, Ross Middleton, David Oliver, Charles Pochin, Harry and Sally Sargent, Chris Scaife, Mandy Taylor, Ian Towle, Frits Tuijt, Andrew Wagstaff, D Walker, Peter and Sandra Whitlock

Photo credits

All photos © Rough Guides except the following:
(Key: t-top; c-centre; b-bottom; l-left; r-right)

p.1 4Corners: Massimo Ripani
p.2 4Corners: Massimo Ripani
p.4 Getty Images: David Clapp
p.5 Getty Images: Picturegarden
p.9 Alamy: Aurora Photos (c); Graham Warman (b)
p.10 Corbis: Bill Ross
p.11 Alamy: nobleIMAGES
p.12 Getty Images: Colin Monteath
p.14 Getty Images: Ed Freeman
p.15 Alamy: Ignacio Palacios (t); Getty Images: Bill Hatcher (b)
p.16 Alamy: Andrew Bain (c); Getty Images: Gerard Soury (t); Darryl Torckler (b)
p.17 Alamy: David Wall (t)
p.18 Alamy: Greg Balfour Evans (cr); Peter Szekely (b); Getty Images: ML Harris (cl)
p.19 Alamy: LOOK Die Bildagentur der Fotografen (b); Getty Images: age Fotostock (t)
p.20 Alamy: Greg Balfour Evans (t); Chris McLennan (b); Getty Images: Colin Monteath (c)
p.21 Alamy: Rolf Hicker Photography (bl)
p.22 Alamy: Andrew Court (b); David Wall (t)
p.23 Alamy: Ben Lewis (br); Henk Meijer (bl); Getty Images: John Hay
p.24 4Corners: Riccardo Spila
p.26 Getty Images: John Lamb
p.68 Getty Images: Scott E Barbour
p.71 Alamy: David Wall
p.91 Getty Images: Lasting Images (b); Andrew Watson (t)
p.133 Alamy: David Hancock
p.141 Alamy: Vincent Lowe
p.159 Alamy: Louise Heusinkveld (t)
p.200 Getty Images: Nick Green
p.203 Alamy: Chris McLennan
p.223 Alamy: ian woolcock

p.243 Alamy: Mark Boulton (b); Chris McLennan (t)
p.263 Alamy: David Wall
p.282 Alamy: Russell Kord (t)
p.283 Alamy: Ernie Janes (b)
p.329 Alamy: Darren Newbery (t); David Wall (b)
p.368 Getty Images: Danita Delimont
p.371 Getty Images: Travel Ink
p.392 Getty Images: Lasting Images (b)
p.393 Getty Images: Ken Schafer (t)
p.406 Alamy: Terry Whittaker
p.413 Alamy: Greg Balfour Evans
p.419 Getty Images: Travel Ink (b)
p.435 Alamy: Jon Arnold Images Ltd
p.487 Alamy: David Wall
p.509 Alamy: David Wall
p.543 Alamy: Paul Street
p.551 Alamy: David Wall
p.584 Alamy: Ian Dagnall
p.587 Alamy: David Wall
p.634 Alamy: ScotStock
p.637 Getty Images: Bo Tornvig Olsen
p.653 Alamy: Chris McLennan (b)
p.719 Getty Images: David Clapp (b)
p.747 Alamy: David Wall
p.751 Getty Images: Jason Hosking
p.767 Alamy: Chris McLennan
p.784 Alamy: Tips Images

Front cover Maori carved pillar © Jenny & Tony Enderby: Getty Images
Back cover Lake Pukaki © Getty Images: Panoramic Images
Aoraki/Mount Cook © Avalon/Alamy
Rafting, Shotover River © Rough Guides/Paul Whitfield

Index

Maps are marked in grey

4WD tours 699, 717
42 Traverse 303
309 Road..332

A

A.H. Reed Memorial Kauri
   Park...154
Abbey Caves..................................154
Abel Tasman Coast Track........475
Abel Tasman Drive 482
Abel Tasman Inland Track.......478
Abel Tasman National Park...20,
   21, 473–480
Abel Tasman National
   Park.................................... 474
accommodation........................... 36
aerobatics......................................698
Agrodome.....................................271
Agroventures 271
Ahipara..185
Ahuriri..389
airlines.. 29
Akaroa...................506, 529–534
Akaroa 530
albatrosses 503, 607, 813
Alexandra 740
Alley, Rewi....................................557
Altura Park....................................220
America's Cup 77, 94
amoebic meningitis.................... 63
Anakiwa...455
Anatoki River..............................481
Anaura Bay...................................366
Ancient Kauri Kingdom...........187
Anderson Park Art Gallery......622
Angelus Hut Loop 491
Angus, Rita 80
Aniwaniwa Falls 382
Aoraki/Mount Cook..... 574–580
Aoraki/Mount Cook
   Village.................................. 575
Aoraki/Mount Cook,
   around 577
Aoraki/Mount Cook National
   Park............................. 574–580
Aoraki/Mount Cook National
   Park, walks..............................576
Aramoana......................................602
Arataki Visitor Centre 112
Aratiatia Rapids...........................292
Arrowtown............708–713, 719
Arrowtown 708

Art Deco Napier 23, 371, 387
Arthur's Pass National
   Park............................. 560–563
Arthur's Pass Village.................560
Arthur's Pass Village.......... 561
Arthurs Point...............................707
Arts Factory, the.........................146
Ashhurst..252
Astrolabe Reef 344
astronomy........ 90, 232, 423, 503,
   572, 573, 579, 756
Atene...246
Athfield, Ian 252, 396, 415, 431
AUCKLAND.......................68–137
Auckland and around.......... 72
Greater Auckland................ 74
Central Auckland 76
Parnell and Newmarket 83
Ponsonby and Herne Bay.... 86
Devonport 89
Mount Eden, Epsom and
   Remuera 90
Acacia Cottage 92
accommodation................... 98–102
airport... 93
Albert Park.................................. 80
Aotea Centre............................. 78
Aotea Square............................. 78
Auckland Art Gallery 79
Auckland Botanic Garden............ 93
Auckland Cathedral 83
Auckland Museum 81
Auckland Zoo............................. 87
Bastion Point 85
bridge climb 94
Britomart Precinct 78
bungy jumping........................... 94
bus station.................................. 95
buses 95, 96
car buying.................................. 97
car rental.................................... 97
cinema......................................110
Civic Theatre 78, 109
Coast to Coast walkway 81
comedy.....................................109
concerts....................................109
Cornwall Park 91, 92
cruises... 94
cycling... 95
Devonport.................................. 88
DOC office.................................. 97
dolphin watching 94
Domain, the................................ 80
downtown................................... 77
drinking....................................107
driving.................................95, 97
eating..............................102–107
Eden Garden.............................. 84
Eden Park................................... 87

entertainment.............................107
Ewelme Cottage......................... 84
Fernz Fernery............................. 82
ferries.. 96
Ferry Building............................. 75
festivals.....................................109
Fort Street................................... 78
Freeman's Bay............................. 86
gay and lesbian Auckland 107
Herne Bay 87
High Street 78
Highwic....................................... 84
history.. 73
Holy Trinity Cathedral................ 83
Huia Lodge 92
i-SITE.. 97
Karangahape Road...................... 80
kayaking..................................... 94
Kelly Tarlton's............................. 85
Kinder House 84
Kingsland 87
Kohimarama 85
Maungakiekie.............................. 90
Maungawhau 90
Mission Bay................................ 85
Monte Cecilia Park..................... 92
MOTAT....................................... 81
Mount Eden 68, 90
Mount Victoria 89
Navy Museum............................. 88
Newmarket................................. 83
nightlife....................................107
North Head 71
North Head Historic Reserve........ 89
North Shore................................ 88
North Shore City Coastal Walk...... 81
One Tree Hill 91, 92
One Tree Hill Domain 90
Otara Market.............................. 93
Pah Homestead 92
parking.. 97
Parnell 83
planetarium................................ 92
Ponsonby.................................... 86
Princes Wharf.............................. 77
sailing.. 94
St Heliers 85
St Mary's..................................... 83
SkyJump...................................... 79
Skytower..................................... 78
Skywalk....................................... 79
Stardome Observatory 92
Symonds Street Cemetery............ 80
Takapuna 88
Tamaki Drive............................... 84
theatre......................................109
trains....................................95, 96
transport passes.......................... 96
Viaduct Harbour......................... 77
Victoria Park Market................... 86
visitor centre.............................. 97
volcanoes.................................... 75

Voyager: New Zealand Maritime
    Museum...................................75
Vulcan Lane...................................78
    walks..81
Wallace Arts Centre......................93
    waterfront, the..........................75
Western Springs............................86
whale watching.............................94
Wintergardens..............................82
Wynyard Quarter..........................77
Aupori Peninsula.......................186
aurora australis...........................626
Awanui..187

B

B&Bs..38
backpacker buses.........................30
backpackers..................................38
Balclutha....................................610
ballooning.................515, 565, 698
banks...65
Banks, Joseph...................395, 525
Banks Peninsula..........526–535
Banks Peninsula.................526
Banks Peninsula Track..............528
Bannockburn...............................738
Barry's Bay..................................529
Barrytown...................................657
Baxter, James K...........................245
Bay of Islands..............162–178
Bay of Islands, Whangaroa
    Harbour & Doubtless
    Bay....................................163
Bay of Islands Vintage
    Railway................................160
Bay of Plenty................343–360
Baylys Beach...............................198
Bealey Spur.................................559
Beehive, The................................423
beer...44
bellbird..............................256, 810
Bendigo.......................................738
Benmore Dam.............................581
Bethell's Beach............................115
Bethlehem..........................348, 351
Beyer, Georgina..............................8
biculturalism...............................799
bicycle touring..............................35
biking.............................see cycling
bio-security...................................62
Birding's Flat...............................528
Black Rocks.................................169
Blackball......................................643
Blenheim......................493–498
Blenheim.............................493
Blue Baths, the............................268
blue duck........295, 566, 651, 755,
    810, 812

Blue Lake............................277, 278
Bluff..624
Bluff Hill.....................................388
Bob's Cove..................................705
bone carving... 57, 186, 193, 337,
    365, 461, 664
Bone People, The...............667, 819
Boundary Stream Scenic
    Reserve................................380
Box Canyon cave.........................651
Brick Bay Sculpture Trail..........144
Bridal Veil Falls...........................214
Bridge to Nowhere.....242–244
Broken River ski-field 557
Brooklands Park..........................228
Bruce Bay....................................676
Brunner, Thomas....488, 639, 643,
    648, 652, 677
Brunner Industrial Site..............643
Buck, Peter..................................793
Buller Gorge................................639
Buller River.................................639
Bulls..249
bungy jumping... 23, 53, 94, 271,
    288, 308, 555, 693, 694, 714
Buried Village..............................279
Busby, James............164, 166, 788
buses...29
Bushy Park..................................238
Butler, John.................................174

C

Cable Bay....................................181
Cambridge...................................210
Campbell, John Logan..................90
campervan rental...........................33
camping...39
camping, freedom..........................40
campsites.......................................39
Cannibal Bay...............................612
canoeing.................53, 118, 244
Canterbury Association.............511
canyoning.................53, 114, 323,
    697, 732
Cape Brett...................................169
Cape Brett Track.........................161
Cape Egmont...............................236
Cape Farewell.............................486
Cape Foulwind............................644
Cape Kidnappers.............393, 394
Cape Kidnappers and Hawke's
    Bay wine country............394
Cape Palliser................................408
Cape Reinga.................................189
Cape Reinga Coastal
    Walkway..............................189
Cape Reinga tours.......................189

Cape Rodney–Okakari Marine
    Reserve................................145
Cape Runaway.............................363
Caples Track................................722
car buying.....................................34
car rental......................................33
Cardrona.....................................729
Cardrona ski-field.......................727
Cardrona Valley..........................729
Carey's Bay..................................587
Carterton....................................404
carving..802
Cascade Saddle Route..............731
Castle Hill Conservation
    Area............................548, 558
Castle Rock..................................332
Castlepoint..................................404
Cathedral Caves (Catlins).........616
Cathedral Cove..................310, 334
Catlins Coast..........18, 509–618
Catlins Coast......................611
Catlins Top Track........................615
Catlins tours................................610
Cavalli Islands............................179
Cave Stream Scenic Reserve....558
caving........................221, 654, 660
Cecil Peak...................................682
Central Otago..............682–747
Central Otago.....................686
chamois.......................................807
Charleston...................................654
Charming Creek Walk.................649
Chasm, the..................................765
children...57
Chinaman's Bluff.........................724
CHRISTCHURCH..........508–525
Christchurch and south to
    Otago..................................510
Central Christchurch....512–513
Greater Christchurch...518–519
    accommodation...................521–523
    Air Force Museum...................517
    airport.......................................520
    Antigua Boat Sheds.................515
    Botanic Gardens.......................514
    bus station................................520
    Canterbury Museum................514
    Cave Rock.................................519
    Christchurch Art Gallery...........514
    Christchurch Gondola...............518
    city transport............................520
    cycling......................................521
    Deans Bush..............................516
    Deans Cottage.........................516
    drinking....................................523
    driving......................................521
    eating.......................................523
    Hagley Park..............................514
    history.......................................511
    information...............................521
    International Antarctic Centre....516
    Mona Vale.................................516
    Nurses' Memorial Chapel............515

Orana Wildlife Park.........517
parking.........521
Riccarton Bush.........516
Riccarton House.........516
River Avon.........515
shopping.........524
Sumner.........519
Taylor's Mistake.........520
train station.........520
TranzAlpine train.........517
Willowbank Wildlife Reserve.........517
Christchurch earthquakes.........511
Claris.........131
Clark, Helen.........797
Clay Cliffs Scenic Reserve.........582
Clifden.........778
Clifden Caves.........778
Clifton.........395
climate.........59
Clyde.........739
Coast to Coast race.........661
coffee.........45
Colac Bay.........782
Collingwood.........484
Colville.........330
Conical Hill.........720
conservation organisations.........806
consulates.........61
Cook, James (Captain).........129, 162, 191, 312, 333, 366, 372, 386, 394, 408, 414, 453, 486, 525, 626, 639, 646, 753, 777, 786, 787, 808
Cook Strait.........412
Cooks Beach.........334
Cooks Cove Walkway.........366
Coopers Beach.........181
Coromandel.........327–330
Coromandel, Bay of Plenty and East Cape.........314–315
Coromandel Peninsula.........319–343
Coromandel Peninsula.........320
Coromandel Walkway.........331
Coronet Peak ski-field.........700
costs.........59
Cosy Nook.........782
Coudrey House Museum.........118
Craigieburn Forest Park.........559
Craigieburn Valley ski-field.........557
Craters of the Moon.........291
Crazy Paving cave.........651
credit cards.........65
crime.........60
Croesus Track.........644
Cromwell.........737
Crossroads.........131
Crown Range Road.........729
cruises.........170, 269, 289, 337, 454, 527, 572, 578, 770, 777
Curio Bay.........617
customs regulations.........62
cycle trail, NZ.........35
cycling.........35, 213, 463, 515, 733, 743
cycling tours.........52

D
D'Urville Island.........457
dam dropping.........237
dangers.........63
Dannevirke.........401
Dansey's Pass.........745
Dargaville.........197
dates.........66
Dawson Falls.........233
de Surville, Jean Francois Marie.........786
debit cards.........65
Denniston.........648
Department of Conservation.........48, 67
Desert Road, the.........307
Devil's Boots.........485
dialling codes.........66
Diamond Harbour.........527
Diamond Lake.........729
disabilities, travellers with.........67
discrimination.........61
Divide, the.........762
diving.........see scuba diving
DOC.........48, 67
DOC campsites.........40
DOC huts.........50
dolphin watching and swimming.........94, 170, 348, 356, 454, 502, 532
dolphins.........777, 813
Doubtful Sound.........748, 776–778
drinking.........44
driving.........32
Driving Creek Railway.........327, 328
drugs.........61
du Fresne, Marion.........162
DUNEDIN.........588–600
Dunedin.........590
Dunedin to Stewart Island.........588
accommodation.........596
airport.........595
Baldwin Street.........594
buses.........596
Cadbury World.........593
Chinese Gardens.........592
cinema.........599
city tours.........595
city transport.........596
clubs.........599
drinking.........598
Dunedin Botanic Garden.........594
Dunedin Public Art Gallery.........591
Dunedin Railway Station.........592
eating.........597
festivals.........600
First Church of Otago.........591
history.........589
Hocken Library.........592
hot pools.........595
information.........596
Municipal Chambers.........591
NZ Sports Hall of Fame.........592
Octagon, the.........591
Olveston.........593
Otago Museum.........593
Otago Settlers museum.........592
Regent Theatre.........591
rugby.........599
St Clair Beach.........594
St Clair Hot Salt Water Pool.........595
St Kilda Beach.........595
St Paul's Cathedral.........591
shopping.........600
Signal Hill.........594
Speight's Brewery Tour.........593
theatre.........599
Tomahawk Beach.........595
train station.........595
University of Otago.........594
Dusky Sound.........778
Dusky Track.........779
duty free.........62

E
earthquakes.........63, 511, 798, 806
East Cape.........22, 360–367
East Cape Lighthouse.........364
East Egmont.........233
Eastwoodhill Arboretum.........377
Edoras.........568
Edwin Fox.........448
eels.........8, 812
EFTPOS.........65
Eglinton Valley.........762
Egmont National Park.........232–235
Egmont Village.........232
electricity.........61
Elvis Presley Museum.........237
email.........64
embassies.........61
emergency calls.........61
etiquette.........57

F
falcon, NZ.........811, 812
fantail.........810
Farewell Spit.........18, 486
Farewell Spit tours.........486
farmers' markets.........43
farmstays.........38
Featherston.........405

ferrets....................................807
ferries.....................................36
festivals.............46, 392, 498, 600
film............................13, 815–817
Fiordland.......................748–783
Fiordland............................752
fishing.................54, 134, 158,
    170, 181, 269, 289, 348, 359,
    533, 678, 733
Flagstaff Hill...........................173
Fletcher Bay...........................330
Fletcher House.......................606
Flight of the Conchords...............8
flights..............................27–29
flightseeing.......53, 171, 278, 289,
    572, 579, 673, 698, 732, 756
Flock Hill...............................558
flying, microlight....................470
flying, stunt...........................470
Fomison, Tony..........................80
food.......................................41
football (soccer)......................56
Forgotten World Highway........239
Fort Stony Batter....................126
Fort Taiaroa...........................608
Foveaux Strait........................626
Fox Glacier...................673–676
Fox Glacier...........................674
Foxton...................................254
Foxton Beach.........................254
Frame, Janet...........................542
Franz Josef Glacier.......670–673
Franz Josef Glacier..............670
freedom camping.....................40
French Pass............................456
fruit picking....................174, 343

G

Gabriel's Gully Historic
    Reserve..............................741
gannets............115, 393, 395, 813
Gate Pa, battle of....................344
gay and lesbian New Zealand...62
Gemstone Bay........................335
geothermal power...................814
Geraldine...............................569
Gertrude Saddle......................763
getting around.........................29
geysers...............11, 270, 280, 317
giardia..............................63, 814
Gibbston...............................713
Gillespie Pass tramp................680
Gillespies Beach.....................675
Gisborne........................372–377
Gisborne...............................373
glacier hiking..........637, 672, 675
glaciers..........................18, 669

Glade Wharf...........................773
Glenfalloch Woodland
    Garden..............................605
Glenfern Sanctuary.................131
Glenorchy......................715–718
Glenorchy and the major
    tramps.............................716
gliding..................................583
glossary.........................825–827
glowworm kayaking.................348
glowworms....147, 219, 348, 654,
    675, 755, 778
Goat Island Marine Reserve...145
gold mining.....................689, 737
Golden Bay...................480–489
Golden Shears.........................404
Goldfields Mining Centre.......737
Goldfields Railway..................342
Goldie, Charles.................79, 152
Gore......................................618
Government Gardens..............267
Govett-Brewster Art Gallery....228
GPS..65
Granity..................................649
Great Barrier Island.....129–136
Great Barrier Island..........130
Great Fleet.............................785
Great Walks.............................49
green issues...........................814
Green Lake.............................278
greenstone......658, 659, 664, 803
Greenstone Track...................722
Grey, George....................144, 790
Grey, Zane.............................162
Grey River..............................642
Greymouth.....................657–662
Greymouth...........................658
Greytown...............................405
Grove Scenic Reserve.............482
GST.......................................60
Gunns Camp...........................763

H

Haast....................................677
Haast Beach...........................678
Haast Pass.............................679
Haast River............................679
Hahei....................................334
haka.....................................805
Halfmoon Bay.........................626
Hamilton.......................205–208
Hamilton, central...............206
Hamilton Gardens...................205
Hamurana Springs Recreation
    Reserve..............................277
hang-gliding...........462, 470, 698
hangi.......................23, 41, 275

Hanmer Forest Park................555
Hanmer Springs...........553–556
Hanmer Springs..................554
Harihari.................................667
Haruru Falls...........................167
Harvey, Les..............................84
Harwoods Hole.......................480
Hastings........................397–400
Hastings...............................398
Hau Hau, the..........................357
Hauraki Gulf..........................120
Hauraki Plains...............314–319
Havelock................................455
Havelock North......................398
Hawera..................................236
Hawke's Bay.......................372
Hawke's Bay wine country.....395
Hawke's Bay wine
    country............................394
Hawks Crag............................640
Hayes Engineering Works.......744
hazards...................................63
health....................................62
Heaphy, Charles.....488, 639, 648,
    652, 656
Heaphy Track.........................488
Heavenly Creatures.................816
Hector's dolphins................532,
    616–618
Heke, Hone....153, 156, 160, 169,
    172, 173, 174, 790
Helensville..............................116
heli-biking.............................699
heli-hiking.....................673, 675
heli-skiing.......................579, 727
Hell's Gate.............................278
herons..................................667
Hibiscus Coast, the..................116
Hicks Bay...............................363
hihi..............................see stitchbird
Hika, Hongi....169, 175, 266, 267,
    278, 280, 787, 788
hiking.....5, 48, see also tramping
hiking tours............................52
Hikurangi..............................160
Hillary, Sir Edmund...113, 576, 592
Hillary Trail, the.....................113
Hinemoa................................268
Hiroa, Te Rangi.......................793
Hiruharama.............................245
history...........................785–798
Hobbit, The.............13, 684, 715
Hobbit, The locations.............209
Hobbiton...............................209
Hobson, William.........76, 80, 164,
    166, 169, 529, 790
hoiho....................................607
Hokianga ferry.......................193
Hokianga Harbour.................19,
    190–194

Hokitika 662–666
Hokitika 663
Hokitika Gorge 666
Hole in the Rock........................169
holiday parks................................39
holidays..46
Hollyford Track...........................764
Hollyford Valley 763
Holyoake, Keith 795
Homer Tunnel 763
homestays.....................................38
Honeycomb Hill caves 651
Hongi's Track 278
horseriding 54, 114, 146,
  185, 213, 289, 309, 331, 337,
  365, 462, 488, 533, 555, 558,
  568, 572, 579, 656, 700, 717,
  733, 756
horse trekking 54
horseback tours 52
hostels 38
hot pools 11, 178, 317, 350,
  378, 553, 556, 670
hot springs........................ 116, 118,
  120, 134, 209, 215, 285, 286,
  295, 333, 336, 570, 677
Hot Water Beach 336
hotels 37
Hotere, Ralph 80, 600, 619
Houhora.......................................188
Huapai 111
Huka Falls 263, 290
Humboldt Falls 763
Hump Ridge Track.....................780
Hump Ridge Track 781
Hundertwasser, Friedrich 160
Hundertwasser toilets 160
Hunua Falls 119
Hunua Ranges, the 119
Hurworth cottage 229
Hutt Valley..................................430
hydroelectricity 775, 814

i-SITEs...66
ice-climbing 672
Ida Valley....................................743
Inangahua Junction 640
information...................................66
Inland Pack Track 655
insurance......................................64
internet 64
Invercargill 620–624
Invercargill 621
Iti, Tame......................................800
Iwikau Village.............................298

J

Jack's Blowhole 614
Jackson Bay 678
Jerusalem 245
jetboating............ 15, 53, 244, 269,
  281, 289, 359, 555, 558, 565,
  678, 696, 717, 733, 756, 779

K

kahikatea 810, 811
Kahurangi National Park........488
Kai Iwi Lakes 196
Kaiaraara kauri dam.................132
Kaiaua 120
Kaikohe 178
Kaikoura 499–505
Kaikoura 500
Kaikoura Coast Track 501
Kaikoura Peninsula
  Walkway..................................501
Kaikoura Wilderness Walks.....501
Kaitaia 184
Kaitake Range............................232
Kaiteriteri 469, 474
Kaiti Hill.....................................373
Kaitoke Hot Springs.................134
Kaituna River.............................272
kaka 256, 380, 626, 810
Kaka Point 612
kakapo...810
kakariki 810
kaki .... see stilt, black
Kaki/Black Stilt visitor hide 580
Kapiti Coast.................. 255–259
Kapiti Island..............................256
Karaka Bay..................................132
Karamea 649–652
Karamea and the Oparara
  Basin 651
Karangahake Gorge..................316
Karangahape Road 80
karearea .... see falcon, NZ
Karekare.....................................113
Karikari Peninsula, the 182
Karori Sanctuary 425
Katikati 343
Kauaeranga Valley.....................325
kauri 161, 195, 197, 332, 808
Kauri Forests, the......................194
kauri gum 185, 197
kauri museum.............................199
Kawakawa 160
Kawarau Bungy Centre............714
Kawau Island 144
Kawerau River............................737

Kawhia..215
kayak fishing 94
kayaking 53, 94, 118, 127, 134,
  145, 171, 181, 244, 289, 337,
  348, 454, 462, 476, 492, 503,
  532, 578, 629, 630, 656, 668,
  673, 717, 733, 756, 770, 777
kayaking tours 52
kea................................... 9, 560
Kekerengu Point 498
Kenepuru Road 455
Kepler Track 759
Kepler Track......................... 759
kereru...810
Kerikeri 174–178
Kerikeri 175
Kerikeri Basin Reserve..............176
Kerikeri Mission House............174
Kerosene Creek 9, 280
Key, John.....................................798
Key Summit 721
King Country, the 216
King Movement, the 216, 791
Kingston Flyer............................707
kitesurfing...................................213
kiwi 380, 653, 809
Kiwi North 153
kiwi spotting 196, 629, 668, 671
Knight's Point............................677
Kohaihai 652
Kohukohu...................................191
kokako 136, 810
korimako......................see bellbird
Koriniti..245
Kororareka...................................169
Kororipo Pa 175
Korowai/Torlesse Tussocklands
  Park...558
kotuku 667
kowhai...808
Kuaotunu....................................332
Kumeu 111
Kupe...143, 166, 181, 191, 414, 801
Kura Tawhiti 548, 558

L

Lady Bowen Falls 768
Lady Knox Geyser.......................280
Lake Brunner...............................643
Lake Dunstan..............................737
Lake Ellesmere...........................528
Lake Ferry....................................408
Lake Grassmere..........................498
Lake Gunn...................................763
Lake Hauroko..............................779
Lake Ianthe..................................667
Lake Kaniere................................666

Lake Mackenzie............................720
Lake Manapouri.........................774
Lake Marian.................................763
Lake Matheson............................675
Lake Ohau....................................582
Lake Okareka Walkway...........277
Lake Paringa...............................677
Lake Pukaki......................... 1, 574
Lake Rotoiti..............278, 445, 489
Lake Rotoroa 265, 490
Lake Tarawera 279
Lake Taupo..................................285
Lake Tekapo................................570
Lake Waikareiti..........................382
Lake Waikaremoana.... 381–384
Lake Waikaremoana 381
Lake Waikaremoana Track......381
Lake Wakatipu...........................682
Lake Wanaka..............................727
Lake Wilkie.................................616
Lang's Beach...............................147
Lange, David 179, 796
Langford's Store.........................485
language 822–827
Larnach Castle............................605
Lawrence.....................................741
Lawson, Robert A. 591, 601,
606, 594
Le Bons Bay...............................534
Leigh..145
Levin...255
Lewis Pass..................................556
Lindauer, Gottfried............79, 152
Lion, the Witch and the Wardrobe,
The... 13
Lion Rock............................91, 114
Little Paradise Gardens............705
Little River................................528
living in NZ..................................58
lodges...38
Lord of the Rings 13
Lord of the Rings locations 209,
293, 466, 684, 715
Lord of the Rings tours..............698
Lost Gypsy Gallery 615
Lost Spring, the.........................333
Lye, Len 228, 422
Lyell Walkway............................640
Lyttelton 526–528

M

Macetown 710
Macetown Circuit tramp...........711
MacKay Falls...................771, 773
Macraes Gold Mine....................747
Mahia Beach...............................379
Mahia Peninsula.........................379

Mahinapua Walkway................666
mail..64
Maitai Bay..................................182
Makarora.....................................679
Makarora and the Gillespie
Pass Tramp 679
Manapouri 774–776
Manapouri Underground Power
Station 775
Manawatu Gorge........................252
Mangamuka Bridge.................191
Mangapohue Natural
Bridge..................................222
Mangapurua Track 245
Mangapurua Valley...................240
Mangatainoka............................402
Mangaweka.................................309
Mangawhai..................................146
Mangawhai Heads 146
Mangonui....................................180
mangroves 192
Maniototo, The............. 742–747
Mansfield, Katherine 425
Manu Bay....................................213
manuka..812
Maori
Maori arrival.............................785
Maori arts and crafts............802–805
Maori concerts...........................275
Maori cuisine..............................42
Maori customs..........................801
Maori dance................................805
Maori language...................8, 822
Maori legend..............................800
Maori music................................805
Maori Party.................................798
Maori rock art............................537
Maori, the....................................10
Maori tours................................503
Maoritanga................................799–805
maps..65
Mapua..468
marae..802
Maraehako Bay.........................362
Marahau......................................475
Mare's Leg Cove 335
markets 43, 86, 93, 125, 144,
146, 155, 212, 251, 274, 347,
376, 380, 396, 400, 436, 460,
516, 527, 541, 545, 598, 703
Marlborough, Nelson and
Kaikoura 446
Marlborough Sounds 447–458
Marlborough Sounds ...448–449
Marlborough Wine Country
.... 492–498
Marlborough Wine
Country 495
Marlborough wineries..............494
Marokopa Falls 222
Marsden, Samuel............. 164, 787
Martin's Bay...............................764

Martinborough 405–408
Martinborough 406
Maruia Springs 556
Mason Bay...................................629
Masterton....................................403
matai...810
Matai Falls..................................614
Matakaea Scenic Reserve.......547
Matakana.....................................144
Matakana Coast 143
Matakohe.....................................199
Matamata.....................................209
Matapouri.....................................158
Matauri Bay................................179
Matukituki Valley......................730
Maui....................................414, 778
Maunga Taranaki 200, 224
Mavora Lakes............................695
Mavora Walkway......................722
Mayor Island..............................344
McCahon, Colin 80
McKenzie, James.......................570
McKinnon, Quentin 753, 757,
771, 773
Mckinnon Pass..........................773
McLaren Falls 351
McLean Falls..............................616
McLeod Bay 156
media..45
Medlands Beach 131
Mercury Bay...............................333
Methven 564–566
Methven 564
Middlemarch................... 601, 747
Milford Road................ 761–765
Milford Sound 14, 765–771
Milford Track.........12, 771–774
Milford Track 772
Miranda Hot Springs...............120
Miranda Seabird Coast............119
Miranda Shorebird Centre 120
miro...810
Mirror Lakes..............................762
Mitchells Gully Gold Mine......652
Mitre Peak..................................768
Moana...643
mobile phones 66
Moeraki.......................................547
Moeraki Boulders 17, 546
Mohua Park...............................614
Mokau...224
Mokoia Island............................269
Molesworth Station..................499
money...65
Monkey Island...........................782
Monro Beach..............................677
morepork....................................811
Morere...378
Moria Gate Arch............... 652, 653
Morrieson, Ronald Hugh 236

Morris & James Pottery & Tileworks.....................145
mosquitoes...............................63
motels.....................................37
motorbiking..............................35
motorhome rental......................33
Motoua Gardens.....................248
Motu River.............................359
Motuara Island........................453
Motuarohia.............................169
Motueka.................. 468–472
Motutapu Island..............121–123
Mount Aspiring National Park.................................730
Mount Bruce...........................402
Mount Cheeseman ski-field....557
Mount Cook................. 574–580
Aoraki/Mount Cook Village..................... 575
Aoraki/Mount Cook, around 577
Mount Dobson ski-field..........572
Mount Egmont................200, 224
Mount Fyffe............................501
Mount Hikurangi.....................365
Mount Hutt ski-field...............564
Mount Iron.............................729
Mount John............................572
Mount Karioi...........................212
Mount Lyford.........................505
Mount Manaia.........................157
Mount Maunganui 343–352
Mount Maunganui 349
Mount Maungaruawahine.....340
Mount Moehau........................321
Mount Ngauruhoe...................293
Mount Ngongotaha.................270
Mount Paku............................339
Mount Parihaka......................153
Mount Pihanga.......................293
Mount Ruapehu.......................293
Mount Somers.........................566
Mount Somers Track................567
Mount Tongariro.....................293
mountain biking...............55, 135, 278, 281, 288, 303, 453, 481, 555, 699, 717, 740, 745
mountaineering........53, 578, 732
Moutoa Island.........................245
mud pools................................11
Muldoon, Robert.....................795
Munro, Burt............................621
Murchison...............................491
Muriwai.................................115
Murupara...............................281
Museum of New Zealand........18, 418, 419
music.....................................817
mustelids...............................807
muttonbirds...................626, 813

N

Napier 385–392
Napier 385
Napier–Taupo Road.................292
Naseby..................................745
Nash, Walter...........................795
National Aquarium of New Zealand.............................388
National Park..........................303
Nelson........................... 458–466
Nelson........................... 459
Nelson, around 467
Nelson Lakes National Park........................... 489–491
Nelson Market........................460
netball.....................................56
Nevis Valley............................738
New Plymouth 226–232
New Plymouth 227
New Zealand Wars...................791
newspapers.............................46
Nga Haerenga cycle trail 35
Ngakawau...............................649
Ngarua Caves.........................480
Ngaruawahia...........................209
Ngata, Apirana........................792
Ngawha Springs......................178
Ngawi....................................409
nikau palm.............................808
Ninety Mile Beach............17, 186
Ninety Mile Beach tours.........189
Norsewood..............................401
North Egmont.........................232
North Island 6
North Island, central.......... 264
North West Circuit..................631
Northern Gateway Toll Road................................116
Northland.................... 138–199
Northland........................ 142
nuclear power.........................914
nudists..................................471
Nugget Point..........................612

O

Oakura..................................235
Oakura (Northland).................161
Oamaru...................... 539–546
Oamaru........................... 540
Oban.....................................626
Oban............................... 628
Ocean Beach...........................212
Ohakune...................... 305–307
Ohau Point.............................498
Ohau ski-field.........................572

Ohau Stream Walk...................498
Ohinemutu.............................269
Ohiwa Harbour.......................355
Ohope...................................355
Okains Bay.............................534
Okarito.................................667
Okere Falls Scenic Reserve....277, 278
Old Stone Store......................174
Omaio...................................361
Omakau..................................742
Omapere................................192
Omarama................................582
Once Were Warriors 90, 796, 816, 818
Onepoto Bay...........................363
Oneroa..................................124
Oneroa............................ 125
Onetangi...............................126
Oparara Arch..........................652
Oparara Basin, the..................651
opening hours..........................65
Opepe Historic Reserve..........292
Ophir....................................742
Opononi.................................192
Opotiki........................... 357–360
Opoutere................................339
Opua ferry.............................167
Opunake................................236
Orakei Korako.........................281
Oreti Beach............................623
Orewa...................................116
Orokonui Ecosanctuary..........602
Ostend...................................125
Otago, Central 682–747
Otago, Central.................... 686
Otago Central Rail Trail....16, 743
Otago Peninsula 603–609
Otago Peninsula 604
Otaki....................................255
Otorohanga............................217
Owaka...................................612
Oxenbridge Tunnel.................707
oysters, Bluff.........................626

P

Paekakariki............................257
Paeroa..................................315
Paihia........................... 164–169
Paihia and Waitangi 165
Paihia–Russell ferry...............167
pakihi....................................636
Pakiri....................................146
Palm Beach............................126
Palmerston.............................547
Palmerston North........ 251–254
Pancake Rocks................634, 656

Pania of the Reef......................386
Papakorito Falls.......................382
Papamoa Beach.......................352
**Paparoa National
  Park............................652–657**
Papatowai................................615
Papatuanuku............................800
Paradise...................................715
Paradise Valley Springs............271
paragliding 53, 462, 693, 698,
  732
Parakai Springs.........................116
parakeets.......................... 117, 256
Paraparaumu............................256
parasailing..................... 171, 698
Parengarenga Harbour............188
Paringa River...........................677
Paritutu Rock...........................229
Parry Kauri Park.......................154
Pataua North...........................157
Pataua South...........................157
Patea.......................................238
Paterson Inlet..........................626
Peel Forest...............................568
Pelorus Bridge Scenic
  Reserve..................................455
Pelorus Sound 455
penguins.................. 23, 137, 516,
  532, 542, 544, 547, 606, 607,
  677, 777, 813
phonecards................................66
phones 65
Piano, The 113, 816
Picton............................447–453
Picton....................................450
Piha...................................91, 113
Pillar Point Lighthouse 486
Pilots Beach.............................608
Pink and White Terraces..........279
Pinnacles, the..........................325
Pipiriki............................. 242, 245
Piripiri Caves...........................222
piwakawaka...................see fantail
Pohara....................................482
pohutukawa.............................808
Pohutukawa Coast....................326
Point Elizabeth 657
Point Elizabeth Track...............660
police......................................61
pollution.................................814
Polynesian Spa 268
Pomare, Maui 792
Pompallier...............................170
ponga......................................810
Poor Knights Islands.........19, 157
Porpoise Bay............................617
Port Chalmers...............600–604
Port Charles.............................331
Port Craig................................780
Port Fitzroy..............................131

Port Jackson 330
Port Nicholson.........................412
Porter's Pass............................558
Porters ski-field.......................557
Portobello 606
Penguin Place 606
post..64
Pouakai Circuit.........................232
Pouakai Range..........................232
pounamu............658, 659, 664, 803
Poverty Bay..............................372
**Poverty Bay, Hawke's Bay and
  the Wairarapa 372**
power supply 61
prejudice..................................61
pronunciation..........................824
public holidays 42, 46
Puhoi......................................118
Puhoi Bohemian Museum......119
Pukaha Mount Bruce National
  Wildlife Centre.....................402
Pukeiti....................................229
pukeko....................................811
Pukekura.................................667
Pukekura Park.........................228
Pukenui 188
Pukerangi................................601
Puketi Kauri Forest..................178
Punakaiki................................656
**Punakaiki and the Inland
  Pack Track......................... 654**
punting 509, 511, 515
Puponga..................................486
Purakaunui Falls......................614
Putangirua Pinnacles 408

Q

quad biking 462, 756
Quail Island.............................527
Queen Charlotte Drive 454
**Queen Charlotte Sound ....
  453–455**
Queen Charlotte Track... 453, 456
**QUEENSTOWN.................8, 682,
  689–705**
Queenstown, central 688
Queenstown, around 706
  4WD tours...........................699
  accommodation....................700–702
  aerobatics............................698
  airport.................................695
  ballooning............................698
  Bob's Peak...........................693
  bungy jumping................693, 694
  buses...................................695
  canyoning............................697
  drinking...............................704
  eating..................................703
  Eichardt's Hotel....................690

  entertainment......................704
  flightseeing..........................698
  gondola...............................693
  hang-gliding.........................698
  heli-biking............................699
  horseriding...........................700
  information...........................695
  jetboating.............................696
  kayaking...............................697
  Kiwi Birdlife Park...................692
  Lake Wakatipu......................694
  lakefront, the........................690
  Lord of the Rings tours 698
  Maori concert.......................704
  mountain biking....................699
  nightlife...............................704
  paragliding.....................693, 698
  parasailing............................698
  parking................................695
  rafting..................................696
  river surfing..........................697
  rock climbing........................699
  shopping..............................704
  skiing...................................700
  skydiving..............................698
  sledging...............................697
  swinging.........................693, 697
  tours....................................699
  transport..............................695
  TSS Earnslaw...................694, 719
  via ferrata............................699
  walks around Queenstown 692
  Walter Peak High Country Farm... 694
  whitewater rafting.................696
  wine tours............................699

R

racism 61
radio 46
rafting 52, 272, 308, 359, 492,
  515, 568, 659, 696, 733
Raglan......................20, 212–215
Rai Valley................................456
Rainbow Falls...........................176
Rainbow Springs Kiwi Wildlife
  Park....................................270
Rainbow Warrior, the........51, 171,
  179–181, 188, 197, 818
rainfall......................................60
Rakaia.....................................535
Rakaia Gorge...........................563
Rakiura National Park..............626
Rakiura Track...........................630
Rameka Track...........................481
Ranana....................................245
Ranfurly..................................746
Rangiatea Church....................255
Ranginui..................................800
Rangiputa................................182
Rangitaiki River 272, 355
Rangitata River 568

Rangitikei River 308
Rangitoto Island 121–123
Rangitoto and Motutapu
  islands 121
Rapahoe..................................657
Rapaura Watergardens............326
Rarawa...................................188
Raspberry Creek.......................730
rata.......................................810
Raurimu Spiral.........................238
Rawene..................................191
Rawhiti...................................161
Rawhiti Cave...........................482
RE:START Christchurch 20
Reefton..................................640
Rees-Dart Track 724
Reeves, William Pember.........792
Remarkables, the........................8
Remarkables ski-field..............700
Rere Falls................................378
Rere rockslide..........................378
restaurants 42
Rewa's Village..........................176
rifleman..................................812
rimu.......................................810
Rimutaka Forest Park 431
Rimutaka Rail Trail...................405
Ripiro Beach 198
river surfing.............................697
Riverton..................................782
Roaring Bay.............................612
Rob Roy Valley walk.................731
Roberton Island 169
robin......................................811
rock climbing 462, 558, 699,
  732
Ross 666
Rotoroa Island 129
Rotorua...................... 265–275
Rotorua, around 277
Rotorua, central 266
Roundhill ski-field 572
Routeburn Shelter....................720
Routeburn Track.................22, 718
Roxburgh................................741
Roy's Peak...............................729
Royal albatross 608
Ruakokore Church...........313, 362
Ruakuri Bushwalk.....................220
Ruapehu Crater Rim hike........298
Ruapekapeka Pa 160
Ruatahuna..............................381
Ruatoria..................................364
rugby...............................55, 599
rugby museum.........................252
Rugby World Cup 55, 87, 599
ruru .... see morepork
Russell......................169–174, 787
Russell....................................172
Rutherford, Ernest....................458

S

saddleback........................ 137, 811
sailing...................51, 94, 170, 289,
  462, 476
Samuel Marsden Memorial
  Church 180
sand yachting 114
sandboarding 188
sandflies...........................63, 753
Sandfly Point...........................773
Sarjeant Gallery.......................248
Savage, Michael Joseph...85, 794
scenic flights 675
scuba diving 19, 51,
  134, 145, 158, 171, 181, 257,
  337, 356, 388, 503, 533, 770
sea lions.................................618
seafood.....................................9
seal colony.............................646
seal swimming 356, 476
seals.......................532, 777, 813
seasons 59, 66
Seddon, Richard......................792
self-catering............................ 43
Shag Point...............................547
Shakespear Regional Park......117
Shakespeare Lookout 333
shark encounters.....................374
sharks..................................... 63
sheep 4
Sheppard, Kate........................424
Ship Cove...............................453
Ship Creek...............................677
Shipley, Jenny 797
shopping................................. 57
Shotover River.........................707
Siberia Experience...................680
silver fern................................810
Sinbad Gully............................768
six o'clock swill........................793
ski-fields.................................233
skiing.........54, 298, 505, 553, 557,
  564, 572, 579, 700, 727
Skippers Road..........................707
Skippers township 707
skydiving 53, 288, 470, 503,
  565, 673, 675, 698, 732
sledging..................................697
Slope Point..............................617
smoking.................................. 57
Smugglers Cove.......................157
snakes..................................8, 63
snorkelling 51, 145, 158
Snow Farm ski-field 727
snowboarding 54
soccer..................................... 56
South Coast Track....................780
South Coast Track 781

South Island 7
South Island, central 552
southern lights 626
Southern Scenic Route (east) ...609
Southern Scenic Route
  (west) 778–783
Southland Museum and Art
  Gallery 620
Spa at QE, the 269
specialist tours........................ 52
spiders.................................8, 63
Spirits Bay...............................188
Split Apple Rock.............. 469, 475
sports..................................... 55
Springbok Tour........................796
Springfield..............................557
St Arnaud................................490
St Bathans 744
St Clair....................................594
St Kilda...................................595
star gazing 373, 503, 572, 579,
  756
Staveley..................................566
Stewart Island 626–633
Stewart Island: the
  northeast......................... 627
stilt, black 810
Stingray Bay............................335
Stirling Falls............................768
Stirling Point...........................625
stitchbird 137, 811
Stonehenge Aotearoa 405
Stony Batter Historic
  Reserve................................126
Stony Bay................................330
Stratford.................................235
student discounts 60
Sugar Loaf Islands Marine
  Protected Area.....................229
Sumner...................................519
sunburn.................................. 63
Surf Highway...........................235
surfing 20, 51, 114, 181, 203,
  213, 235, 236, 348, 374, 515
Sutherland, Donald........ 753, 766,
  768, 771, 773
Sutherland Falls............... 771, 773
swimming................................ 51
swimming, safety..................... 63
swimming with seals 502
swinging....................53, 693, 697
Sydney, Grahame 744

T

tahr..807
Tahunanui Beach.....................461
Taiaroa Head 607

Taieri Gorge Railway.........15, 584, 601, 747
Taihape............................308
Taipa................................181
Tairua..........................2, 339
takahe................137, 256, 755
Takaka.......................... 481–484
Takaka Hill.....................480
Tane Mahuta...................196
tank driving....................515
Tapeka Point Historic Reserve..........................173
Tapu...........................326, 801
Taranaki 224–238
Taranaki Peninsula 225
Taranaki Around the Mountain Circuit...........................234
Taranaki summit route 232
Tararua Forest Park 403
Tasman, Abel..........414, 459, 473, 667, 786
tattooing..................................803
Taumarunui 238
Taupo 282–290
Taupo, central 284
Taupo, around.................... 291
Taupo Bay..............................180
Tauranga 343–352
Tauranga and Mount Maunganui, around........ 351
Tauranga, central............... 345
Tauranga Bay..............................646
Tawharanui Regional Park.....145
taxes..60
Taylor's Mistake.........................520
Te Anau......................... 753–758
Te Anau............................ 754
Te Anau Downs 762
Te Araroa, East Cape................363
Te Araroa hike...........................48
Te Aroha..................................317
Te Awamutu............................211
Te Hana 146
Te Henga 115
Te Horo Stock Tunnel 224
Te Kaha..................................361
Te Kao 188
Te Kooti 267, 283, 353, 383
Te Kopua...............................212
Te Kuiti..................................222
Te Mata Peak..........................399
Te Matua Ngahere..................196
Te Miko..................................656
Te Ngae 3D Maze.....................276
Te Paki Stream 188
Te Papa 18, 418, 419
Te Puia 270
Te Puia Hot Springs..................215
Te Puke................................352
Te Rauparaha 256, 460, 787

Te Urewera National Park 380–384
Te Waikoropupu Springs.........481
Te Waimate Mission House....178
Te Wairoa 279
tea 45
Tekapo 570
temperature 60
Temple Basin ski-field 557
Temuka...................................536
Thames 321–325
Thames 323
Thatcher, Frederick ..84, 228, 424
The Divide 721
Three Kings Islands...............189
tieke.................... see saddleback
Tikitiki 364
Timaru.......................... 536–539
Timaru 536
time zones....................................66
tipping.......................................57
Tirau.......................................210
Tiritiri Matangi 136
Titirangi 111
Tokaanu Thermal Pools 295
Tokatoka Peak...........................199
Tokerau Beach 182
Tokomaru Bay.........................365
Tolaga Bay...............................366
toll road..................................116
Tonga Island Marine Reserve..............................473
Tongariro Alpine Crossing....... 23, 300
Tongariro Around the Mountain track.....................................302
Tongariro National Park 292–308
Tongariro National Park.... 294
Tongariro National Trout Centre 295
Tongariro Northern Circuit 301
Tongariro Power Scheme 297
totara..810
Totara Estate...........................546
Totara North 180
Totaranui...473, 475, 477, 479, 482
Tourism New Zealand...............66
trains 31, 160
tramping...............................5, 48
tramping equipment 50
tramping safety.........................51
tramping tours 52
tramps
  Abel Tasman Coast Track.............475
  Abel Tasman Inland Track.............478
  Angelus Hut Loop.......................491
  Avalanche Peak Track....................562
  Banks Peninsula Track 528
  Bealey Spur 559
  Ben Lomond Summit Track............692

  Ben Lomond–Moonlight Track ...692
  Cape Brett Track 161
  Cape Reinga Coastal Walkway 189
  Caples Track 722
  Cascade Saddle...............................731
  Casey Saddle to Binser Saddle....562
  Cass-Lagoon Saddle Track...........559
  Catlins Top Track............................615
  Croesus Track................................644
  Gillespie Pass tramp....................680
  Great Barrier Island tracks...........134
  Greenstone Track 722
  Heaphy Track 488
  Hillary Trail....................................113
  Hollyford Track................................764
  Hump Ridge Track 780
  Inland Pack Track............................655
  Kaikoura Coast Track......................501
  Kaikoura Wilderness Walk..............501
  Kauaeranga Valley walks...............325
  Kepler Track....................................759
  Lake Waikaremoana Track 381
  Lyndon Saddle 559
  Macetown Circuit............................711
  Mangapurua Track..........................245
  Milford Track..................................771
  Mingha–Deception 562
  Mount Hikurangi...........................365
  Mount Karioi Track 212
  Mount Somers Track.......................567
  Mueller Hut route 577
  North West Circuit...........................631
  Pouakai Circuit...............................232
  Powell–Jumbo Tramp......................403
  Queen Charlotte Track 453, 456
  Rakiura Track..................................630
  Rangitoto Summit walk.................122
  Rees–Dart Track...............................724
  Routeburn Track...............................718
  Ruapehu Crater Rim hike.............298
  South Coast Track............................780
  Tapapakurua Falls Track................304
  Taranaki Around the Mountain Circuit 234
  Taranaki summit route.....................232
  Te Araroa..48
  Tongariro Alpine Crossing.............300
  Tongariro Northern Circuit.............301
  Tongariro Round the Mountain track...302
  Travers-Sabine Circuit 491
  Welcome Flat Hot Springs.............677
  Whirinaki Track 281
  Whitecliffs Walkway.......................224
  Wilkin and Young valleys circuit ...680
transsexual...................................8
TranzAlpine train 517
travel agents..............................28
travel passes...............................32
Travers-Sabine Circuit 491
Treaty of Waitangi.....166, 788, 789
Treble Cone ski-field.................727
tree ferns.........................15, 810
trekking..........48, see also tramps
Trounson Kauri Park 196
trout...............................618, 812

Tryphena..131
Tuai...381
Tuatapere.....................................779
tuatara..................................621, 811
Tuhua...344
tui......................................256, 811
Tui Community............................482
Tunnel Beach walk......................605
Tupare..229
Turanganui a Kiwa.......................372
Turangi.............................. 294–296
Turoa ski-field..............................298
Tutanekai......................................268
Tutea's Falls.................................272
Tutira..380
Tutukaka.......................................157
TV...45
Twizel...580

U

Ulva Island...................................628
Upper Moutere..............................468
Urquharts Bay..............................157
Urupukapuka Island.....................169

V

vaccinations...................................62
vegetarian food.............................42
vehicle buying................................34
vehicle rental.................................33
via ferrata....................................699
Victoria Battery............................316
visas...61
visitor centres................................66
Volcanic Plateau..........................262
voluntary work...............................59

W

Wai-O-Tapu...............21, 280, 283
Waiatoto River..............................678
Waiau Falls...................................332
Waihau Bay..................................362
Waiheke Island............ 123–129
Waiheke Island...................... 124
Waihi..341
Waihi Beach..................................342
Waikanae......................................255
Waikawa..616
Waikino...316
Waimakariri Gorge.......................557
Waimangu.....................................280

Waimate North.............................178
Waimea Inlet.................................466
Waingaro Hot Springs..................209
Wainui Beach................................366
Wainui Falls..................................482
Waioeka Gorge..............................360
Waioeka River...............................360
Waiohine Gorge.............................405
Waiouru...307
Waipapa Point..............................618
Waipara...505
Waipiro Bay...................................364
Waipoua Kauri Forest..... 141, 196
Waipu..147
Waipu Caves…..............................147
Waipu Cove...................................147
Waipunga Falls.............................292
Wairakei Terraces.........................291
Wairarapa, The............. 401–409
Wairarapa, The.................... 372
Wairaurahiri River........................779
Wairere Boulders..........................192
Wairoa..379
Wairoa River.........................272, 351
Waitakere Ranges.........................112
Waitaki Hydro Scheme..................581
Waitangi.......................................164
Waitangi, Treaty of......................166
Waitangi Treaty Grounds........164
Waitangi Treaty House............165
Waitangiroto Nature
  Reserve.....................................667
Waitiki Landing............................188
Waitomo...................... 217–222
Waitomo Caves.................... 218
Waitomo Walkway.........................220
Waiuta..642
Waiwera..118
Wakefield, Edward Gibbon....789
Wallace Gallery.............................209
Walter Peak...................................682
Walter Peak High Country
  Farm..694
Walters, Gordon.............................80
Wanaka...................... 725–736
Wanaka.................................. 726
Wanaka walks...............................729
Wanganui.................... 246–251
Wanganui.............................. 247
Warkworth....................................143
Warkworth and Districts
  Museum.....................................144
Washpen Falls...............................563
Waterfall Creek.............................729
Waterworks, the...........................332
weather...59
weka...................................256, 811
Welcome Flat Hot Springs............677
WELLINGTON............8, 412–441
Central Wellington..... 416–417

Wellington.................. 426–427
Wellington and around..... 414
  accommodation..........................434
  airport......................................431
  Archives New Zealand................424
  Beehive, The..............................423
  Botanic Gardens.........................422
  Brooklyn Hill.............................425
  Bucket Fountain.........................421
  buses.................................432, 433
  Cable Car..................................423
  Cable Car Museum......................423
  Carter Observatory.....................423
  cathedrals.................................424
  Central library..........................415
  cinema......................................440
  City Gallery Wellington..............415
  city tours..................................415
  City-to-Sea Bridge.....................418
  Civic Square..............................415
  clubs..439
  Colonial Cottage Museum...........421
  concerts....................................440
  Cook Strait crossing...................431
  Courtenay Place.........................421
  Cuba Street...............................421
  cycling......................................432
  DOC office.................................434
  Dowse Art Museum....................431
  drinking....................................438
  driving......................................433
  eating.......................................436
  ferry terminals..........................431
  festivals....................................441
  Frank Kitts Park................419, 422
  gay and lesbian Wellington........438
  Hikitia......................................418
  history......................................414
  Karori Sanctuary........................425
  Katherine Mansfield Birthplace....424
  kayaking....................................432
  kiteboarding..............................432
  Lambton Quay............................422
  Matiu Island..............................430
  Miramar Peninsula......................429
  Mount Victoria...........................421
  mountain biking.........................432
  Museum of New Zealand....418, 419
  Museum of Wellington City
    and Sea...................................422
  National Library of
    New Zealand.............................424
  New Zealand Film Archive...........421
  Oriental Parade..........................420
  Otari-Wilton's Bush....................429
  parking.....................................433
  Parliament Buildings..................423
  Parliamentary District...............423
  Petone Settlers Museum.............430
  Queens Wharf............................421
  scuba diving..............................432
  shopping...................................441
  Somes Island.............................430
  taxis...433
  Te Papa.............................418, 419
  Te Raukura................................418
  theatre.....................................440
  Thorndon...................................424

trains...............................432, 433
transport passes............................433
visitor centre............................434
Waitangi Park 420
walks.......................................428
Water Whirler 422
"Wellywood"..........................429
Weta Cave...............................429
windsurfing.............................432
Zealandia................................425
Wenderholm Regional Park...118
Wentworth Falls.........................340
West Coast, the 634–681
West Coast, the 638
West Coast beaches.................112
Western North Island 204
Westport...................... 644–648
Westport............................ 645
weta.............................811, 812
wetlands.................................811
Whakahoro 242
Whakapapa.............................297
Whakapapa ski-field.................298
Whakarewarewa Forest............278
Whakarewarewa State Forest
    Park.......................................277
Whakarewarewa Thermal
    Reserve....................................270
Whakarewarewa Thermal
    Village......................................270
Whakatane................... 352–357
Whakatane 353
Whale Bay (Northland)............158
Whale Bay (Waikato) 213
Whale Island...........................356
Whale Rider 366
whale watching............16, 94, 502
Whalers Base.................................629
whales.......................................812
Whanarua Bay...........................362
Whangamata..............................340
Whangamomona 239

Whangamumu Track................161
Whanganui National
    Park............................ 240–246
Whanganui National
    Park.................................... 241
Whanganui River 20
Whanganui River Road............244
Whanganui River Road mail
    run..246
Whanganui River trips..............242
Whangaparaoa Peninsula 116
Whangaparapara.......................131
Whangapoua 332
Whangara...................................366
Whangarei................... 151–156
Whangarei........................... 152
Whangarei Falls.........................153
Whangarei Heads 156
Whangaroa 180
Whangaroa Harbour 180
Whangaruru North Head Scenic
    Reserve..................................161
Whararariki Beach......................486
Whataroa 667
Whatipu 113
Whenuakite 333
whio......................... see blue duck
Whirinaki Forest Park 281
Whirinaki Track........................281
white herons 667
White Island............... 16, 328, 356
whitebait..................................636
Whitecliffs Walkway.................224
whiteheads 256
whitewater rafting 696
Whitianga.................... 333–339
Whitianga........................... 334
Whitianga, around............. 335
Whittaker's Music Museum....125
wi-fi..64
Wildfood Festival......................665

wildlife, rare and
    endangered...........................810
wildlife tours 52
Wilkin and Young valleys
    circuit 680
Wilmot Pass 778
wind energy 814
Wind Wand 228
windsurfing 51
wine................................... 21, 44
wine tours 496, 699
wineries...................112, 126, 128,
    144, 377, 395, 408, 468, 472,
    713, 727, 738
WOMAD...231
women travellers......................67
women's suffrage 792
Woodlyn Park............................220
Woollaston, Toss 460
work............58, 174, 343, 399, 468
working visas 58
World of WearableArt 441, 462
wrybill..812
WWOOF 58

Y

yachting..56
yellow-eyed penguins 607
YHAs..38

Z

Zealandia............................21, 425
Zealong 207
zorbing...271

Map symbols

The symbols below are used on maps throughout the book

✉	Post office	♜	Castle	〰	Spring	🔆	Lighthouse
ⓘ	Tourist office	♟	Museum	🌾	Viewpoint	●-●	Cable car
⊞	Hospital	∴	Ruins	⌒	Cave	⚱ ◧	Church
T	Toilets	Ⓧ	Campsite	rnh lʊlɔd	Gorge	▬	Building
P	Parking	🏠	Hut	▲	Peak	⬭	Stadium
⛽	Fuel station	🏌	Golf course	⋀⋀	Mountain range	⬚	Park/forest
🕐	Telephone	🍷	Winery	✈	International airport	☐	Beach
♦	Point of interest	🎿	Ski area	✕	Domestic airport	⊞	Cemetery
@	Internet access	🏊	Swimming pool	★	Bus stop	▨	Glacier
⚘	Gardens	🏄	Surf/beach	🚤	Boat		
⋈	Bridge	💦	Waterfall	⚓	Boat stop		

Listings key

■ Accommodation
● Restaurant/café
■ Bar/pub/club
● Shop

ROUGH GUIDES

SO NOW WE'VE TOLD YOU
HOW TO MAKE THE MOST
OF YOUR TIME, WE WANT
YOU TO STAY SAFE AND
COVERED WITH OUR
FAVOURITE TRAVEL INSURER

WorldNomads.com
keep travelling safely

GET AN ONLINE QUOTE
roughguides.com/insurance

RECOMMENDED BY
ROUGH GUIDES

MAKE THE MOST OF YOUR TIME ON EARTH™

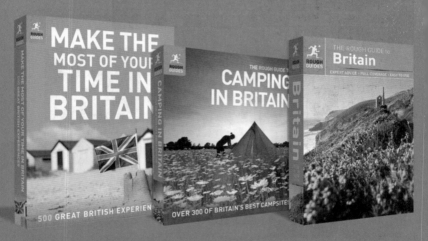